The Teachings of Modern Christianity
on Law, Politics, and Human Nature

{ VOLUME 1 }

The Teachings of Modern Christianity

❖ ON LAW, POLITICS, AND HUMAN NATURE ❖

{ VOLUME 1 }

EDITED BY

John Witte Jr. and Frank S. Alexander

COLUMBIA UNIVERSITY PRESS   NEW YORK

Columbia University Press
Publishers Since 1893
New York, Chichester, West Sussex
Copyright © 2006 Columbia University Press
All rights Reserved

Library of Congress Cataloging-in-Publication Data

The teachings of modern Christianity on law, politics,
and human nature / edified by John Witte, Jr. and Frank S. Alexander
p.cm.
Includes bibliographical references and index.
ISBN 0–231–13718–4 (set)—ISBN 0–231–13358–8 (v. 1 : cloth : alk. paper)—
ISBN 0–231–50831–X (v. 1 : electronic)
1. Christian sociology. 2. Man (Christian theology). 3. Christianity and politics.
4. Christianity and law. I. Witte, John, 1959– II. Alexander, Frank S., 1952–
BT738.T33 2006
261.8—dc22   2006045492

Columbia University Press books are printed on permanent and durable acid-free paper

Printed in the United States of America

c 10 9 8 7 6 5 4 3 2 1

Contents

II. The Protestant Tradition

III. The Orthodox Tradition

IV. Afterwords

Foreword

THE LEDGERS ARE found in the defendant's apartment. They record sales and cash receipts and show what is still owing. Who kept them cannot be established. An expert testifies that they are the kind of ledgers kept by drug dealers. Are these anonymous annotations admissible evidence to show the business carried on in the apartment?

The shipyard thinks the boiler bolts look like new and need no replacement, although the bolts are three years old and the owner's manual says they should be replaced every two years. The shipyard does not mention the manual to the ship's captain, who has his own copy of it. The bolts are not replaced. The boiler bursts, severely damaging the ship. By contract, the shipyard is liable only for gross negligence. Is not mentioning the manual's recommendation to the captain a matter of gross negligence?

An alcoholic young man from Chicago believes he can smuggle marijuana from Canada into Montana. He has no knowledge of the terrain. He is caught at once with seventy-eight pounds of the drug. He has no criminal record. The judge classifies his conduct as "aberrant" and on that basis sentences him to home confinement rather than to prison. The law defines "aberrant" as conduct "temporary in duration and not requiring significant planning," carried out by one whose life is "otherwise law abiding." Must an appellate court reverse the judge's finding of aberrant and compel a prison sentence?

These cases, drawn from the day's work, are representative of the kinds of cases with which American judges deal. It is not immediately obvious how any of them can be decided by looking at the teachings of modern Christianity about human nature. In the first case, the answer depends on whether evidence as to a place unfairly prejudices the person living in the place: Is it the man being tried, or his apartment? In the second, the question is whether the shipyard has a duty to tell the captain what he could find out for himself: Does the shipyard's superior knowledge about repairs give it greater responsibility? In the third, the court has to decide what "temporary," "significant" and "law abiding" should be interpreted to mean in relation to a finding of "aberrant" that will spare the defendant a prison term and perhaps provide more opportunity for rehabilitation. How much should the appellate judges defer to the judgment of the sentencing judge, who has actually seen the defendant and heard the case in all its detail? How much should the appellate judges depend on dictionary definitions of the key words in the statute?

You could read all that is written in this volume without finding how these cases should be judged in conformity with law. Law, it is almost at once apparent, is a term that is used differently, but analogously, in a variety of contexts. Its prime use for modern persons denotes the rules of conduct established by the constitution, statutes, administrative rulings, and court judgments of a particular civil society. For some Christian churches, there are a similar set of rules established by church authority for conduct within the church or involving its members. Beyond these human creations, theologians have recognized divine law, that is, ordinances for human conduct claiming a divine origin, and natural law, that is, dynamisms and purposes inscribed by the Creator in human beings that cannot be violated with impunity. Still further, there are the laws of nature, described now normally in tentative terms, that are treated as governing the entire observable world.

Only law in the first sense, the law of our society, will provide answers for the questions arising in the quotidian quota of cases. But when human nature is invoked, it is often in the belief that it has relevance, however remote, to the very specific perplexities and paradoxes of civil law. That belief has made relevant to our law the teachings of Christianity.

Israel accepted its laws as coming from God, and the founders of the Massachusetts Bay Colony thought that the Bible would provide a model for their commonwealth. Even these optimists tried only a judicious selection of the available legislation, and they could not stick literally to their paradigm. Other bodies of Christians have not thought that a law code could be derived bodily from the Bible. What Christians have done in the way of lawmaking has usually been a combination of ideas with explicit biblical roots, developed theological propositions, customs and conventions inherited from ancestors, newly devised solutions for new problems, and varied efforts to discern what God intended human beings to be and to do if they were to be happy in this life and in their destiny transcending this life. In this mix, the Hebrew teaching that God created the human being in the image of God and the Hebrew injunction, repeated by Jesus, to love your neighbor as yourself offered central insights into the relation that should hold between human nature and the law of communities of persons.

Christians recognize God as the creator of the universe and as the creator of their communities, at the same admitting the paradox that these creations are imperfect. They are imperfect because an element of the human condition is freedom to shape oneself and one's community. Demonstrably, this freedom is often used to produce human unhappiness. Yet Christians cannot believe that God has created them to be unhappy or to construct communities that produce unhappiness.

God and human persons are ultimate realities in Christian teaching. The civil community and the ecclesiastical community are realities, too; but they are not ultimate. They will pass out of existence. Human persons have a destiny transcending both communities, yet they are embedded in them. Law must deal with them in their embeddedness yet respect their orientation and trajectory to a good beyond any community. A tension exists as law organizes, channels, and teaches each community of persons destined for purposes beyond the community.

A society's system of law is not, from a Christian perspective, a set of rules to be carried out in the way a computer might carry out instructions. The legal system, according to Christian teachings, is made by human beings for the benefit of the human community. The participants—litigants, lawyers, legislators, judges, as well as those benefited or protected by the law—are interacting with each other and are to treat each other with justice and charity. The law is not an impersonal machine, a Moloch requiring human sacrifices. It is sometimes painful for those against whom it is enforced. It is never to be enforced without consideration of the human persons affected.

Three phenomena have modified attempts to bring Christian teaching to bear on ordinary law. The first appears to be inherent in the enterprise. Law must consist in rules. Rules are general. Persons are unique. No rule is exactly fitted to a person. Yet the only subjects of rules are persons. Willy-nilly, persons must be brought within rules for law to work. Law consequently has a masking effect, changing individuals into A and B, plaintiff and defendant, appellant and appellee. From a Christian perspective, tension exists between the person and the mask.

The second phenomenon is persistent but, to a degree, conquerable. A large part of law consists in customs and conventions that Christian lawmakers inherited and did not at once reject. To take a tragic example, the Christian Roman emperors inherited a society in which slavery was a major institution. The emperors did not demolish it. By nature, it was acknowledged, human beings are free. But as a result of sin, slavery exists.

Although the connection between sin and the human beings who were enslaved was never made clear, Christian moralists did not challenge the institution. Even Thomas Aquinas accepted slavery as "an addition" that was
not unnatural and foreign to human dignity. This easy accommodation to
inherited ways made possible the enormous European expansion of slavery
when Europeans began to populate what they called the New World and
needed Africans to perform their work in it.

Only by trial and error—by very big error—did Christians discover that
the enslavement of some human beings by other human beings is violative
of human nature and incompatible with gospel. The lesson in this evolution of morals needs to be emphasized and absorbed by modern Christians. Christian revelation was given once and for all in Jesus Christ. But
experience, considered in the light of revelation, was needed to make plain
that slavery was an institution that Christians were forbidden to accept.
The idea that all moral norms or all that human nature requires was conveyed when the gospel was first preached cannot survive before this and
other lessons of history.

The third phenomenon playing a part in Christian reflections on law and
human nature is that Christian theologians, beginning with St. Paul, have
not looked at human nature as it was originally created. They have looked
at human nature affected, more or less, by Adam and Eve's fall, and human
nature as perfected by grace. From one perspective, human nature is impaired; from the other, it is redeemed and made capable of more than what
was ungraced. Theological propositions on original sin and on the relation
of grace to free will have regularly restricted or enlarged Christian thought
on how law should respond to human nature.

With these qualifications, it is evident that Christian insights and reflection have created and can create a framework, set up a perspective, and enable analyses that have profound impact on the law of particular societies.
In the end, who brought about the abolition of slavery as a legal institution
except committed Christians such as Thomas Clarkson, Theodore Parker,
and William Wilberforce? Who are now most active in working for the
abolition of the death penalty in the United States? And even the quota of
quotidian questions may respond to an approach focused on persons and
attempting to discern what justice and charity require.

The present volume attacks this great subject from a variety of perspectives. It is wonderfully diverse in the origins of the authors considered,
from Vladimir Nikolai Lossky of Russia to Gustavo Gutiérrez of Peru, as
well as in the width of materials explored, from papal pronouncements
to mystic meditations such as those of Vladimir Soloviev. These diverse
perspectives are placed in relation to each other, related by their connec-

tion to God and sustained by friendship with God. How else can truth be sought ecumenically than by proceeding as God's friends and so as friends of one another?

Teaching is not only considered in formal presentations such as the liberating metaphysics of Jacques Maritain, but it is also conveyed by example in the lives of Susan B. Anthony, Dorothy Day, and Martin Luther King Jr. Did Jesus teach by word or by example? By both, as does modern Christianity. Which is more powerful? For many, his example is decisive, as with these modern Christians. In a teaching where God and persons count, who speaks more strongly than by example?

—John T. Noonan Jr.

Foreword

ARGUMENTS ABOUT WHETHER *law* in the Western nations has foundations in Christian teaching are frequent and intense in our time. For example, the teachings of the Ten Commandments, scriptural law shared by Jews and Christians alike, were brought to "premodern," colonial, America largely by Christians from European nations where they long had decisive influence. That influence is called into question in societies called secular and pluralistic, and defenders of the tradition try to counter them.

Arguments about whether *politics* in Europe or America should be influencing and be influenced by Christian teaching keep armies of professors, lawyers, politicians, and advocates of "church-state separation" or "faith-based interaction" busy as they divide communities.

Arguments about whether *societies* can endure if they have no strong rooting in a particular religious tradition and whether Western societies can prosper if few in them are responsible to the Christian impulses that for centuries animated them, run through debates about personal morality, popular and high culture, the nurture of children, education, and other zones of life about which millions care.

And arguments about whether Christian teaching on *human nature* takes this or that character, inclining individuals and societies toward good or evil or toward all the mixtures of the two, preoccupy theologians and ethicists and have a bearing on intimate zones of life, including counseling, therapies, and personal conduct.

It is one thing to argue the general case that Christian teaching does or should inform these four areas of human life. It is another to shift from the "whether" question about applying the teaching to the "what" and "why" and "how" questions.

This book is one of the most ambitious attempts yet made to recognize some of the main elements of significant traditions within Christianity as they relate to law, politics, society, and human nature, and to hear voices of responsible scholars expounding them. There is every likelihood that if information from these chapters attracts a reasonably wide readership, at least those who have confronted them will be able to bring knowledge, perspective, civility, regard for the other, and some patience—without an accompanying loss of passion over what really matters—to the debates and conversation.

In his book *The Vindication of Tradition* (1984), Jaroslav Pelikan, who wrote the masterpiece five-volume work *The Christian Tradition*, tells of a comment by the choreographer Jerome Robbins at the time he was to prepare dances for the Broadway play *Fiddler on the Roof.* Told that the tradition of Hasidic Judaism to which this play referred was dead or dying, Robbins said that if he was to treat it at all, he had to know what the tradition *was.* This massive volume deals with the "was" of the Christian teaching and tradition, which is very much alive but, of course, is constantly changing.

Similarly, the British historian D. W. Brogan told of an incident in which visitors came upon a tarred-and-feathered refugee as he ran away from the up-in-arms citizenry of a small town. Asked what had led him to this terrible treatment, he declared that an argument had arisen about the Monroe Doctrine and his attitude toward it. As I recall it, he said that he believed in the Monroe Doctrine, he lived by the Monroe Doctrine, he would die for the Monroe Doctrine; he just did not know what was in it. Many "doctrines" in which Christians and others in the "Christian" world believe and by which they claim to live—forget about the "dying" business at the moment—get clear and fair treatment on these pages.

I have emphasized four of the words in this book's title. Three others deserve emphasis, too. The first of these, *modern*, is decisive. While the Christian tradition, like most others, is conservative and while its adherents and advocates have long memories, the authors in this book bear responsibility only for the modern. Attempts to define the modern, if seriously made, would soon demand a book the length of the present one. In the most simple sense, "modern" here means that the authors do not and do not have to take up the first eighteen centuries of Christianity. But the modern comes in a far more complex package: it refers to a set of freedoms that are partly of Christian derivation but were sometimes resisted by Christian leaders. These freedoms allowed people to make choices, both against the tradition that had dominated, or for one or another of the subgroup expressions of it (Roman Catholic, Protestant, Eastern Orthodox, and the variations among them). "Subgroup expressions" signals a major feature of modernity: choice. It also reminds us that modernity meant a severing of old ties between a faith and a soil, as they had existed in "Christendom." Modernity implies uprooting, the chopping of old unities into new varieties, and more. The editors and authors, being moderns, had to choose which figures should represent these three subtraditions.

Christian refers to the heritage of those loyal to Jesus Christ, those who belong to or deal with the community, the church, devoted to his name, and to the culture that grew up around him and that community.

This is not a history of the ways Christians and their colleagues administered law, ventured in politics, shaped society, or tampered with human nature, though they had influence on all of these practical outcomes. Instead, the authors restrict themselves to accounting for and appraising the *teachings* themselves. These chapters are rich with description and exposition of these teachings, which became and become the raw material for what societies influenced by Christians regularly fabricate.

Three other terms deserve and demand emphasis, for they refer to the three main parts of the book.

The Roman Catholic tradition is embodied by one billion of the world's 1.8 billion Christians. Centuries ago, editors of a book like this would have drawn directly on canon law, official theology, and episcopal pronouncements. In the modern world, the custodians of the teachings with which scholars reckon are sometimes hierarchs—three popes make it into the collection—but others are often private citizens, clerical and lay, who win credentials among the faithful and those who deal with them.

The Protestant tradition is vastly more complex, since it lacks a single highest authority such as Catholicism recognizes in the papacy; there is no single formal magisterium, teaching office and contents of teaching. Here the editors really turn to the "postmodern" outlook, since there has to be a kind of eclectic principle at work. While names like Karl Barth, Dietrich Bonhoeffer, Reinhold Niebuhr, and Martin Luther King Jr. are familiar in these contexts, others are less so. Susan Anthony certainly "belongs" for her influence on women's roles; Abraham Kuyper will be a discovery to people who live far beyond the "Kuyperian circle" (and they might soon choose to enter it); William Stringfellow was an astonishingly gifted lay theologian and advocate who deserves more hearing than he has recently been getting; John Howard Yoder represents the voice of Christian nonviolence. Together, they make up a great company, but not a magisterium.

The Orthodox tradition, we can guess, will be less familiar to most readers in "the West," but the five figures—two of them admittedly new to me—demonstrate vitalities in a tradition often dismissed from a distance as being fossilized and static. The modern Orthodox, we do well to remember, have been on the frontier of Islam in the Ottoman Empire days and under the hammer and sickle in the years of Soviet Communism. What voices from that tradition have to say speaks far beyond that Eastern horizon.

What the authors have in common with their subjects is an awareness that the surrounding cultures do not grant them favors for their being Christian. Indeed, in many cases agents of those cultures hold religious believers in general and Christians in particular in contempt. Or, perhaps worse, they serenely ignore the Christian voices. The world around them is now described as secular, which can mean that people make their laws, engage in politics, form societies, and conceive of human nature the same way whether or not God exists. That same world, however, sees religions survive and evolve. A century from now chapters in a book like this will no doubt reckon with the way the Christian majority has "moved South," to the poor world of southern Africa, South America, and South Asia. They will make fresh contributions to the Christian tradition in what I like to call a "religio-secular" age. Almost certainly, as they do so, they will be drawing on the writings of figures like those who make their appearance in this book, which I warmly commend to readers.

—*Martin E. Marty*

Acknowledgments

THIS VOLUME AND its companion are products of a three-year project of the Law and Religion Program at Emory University. Our project is part of a broader effort of The Pew Charitable Trusts and the University of Notre Dame to stimulate and support new scholarship on the place of Christianity in various fields of academic specialty. Armed with a major grant from The Pew Charitable Trusts, Notre Dame Provost Nathan O. Hatch and his colleagues have assembled ten groups of scholars in such fields as law, philosophy, literature, and economics, who have an interest in the scholarly place of Christianity in their particular discipline. Each of these ten groups of specialists has been asked to address the general theme of "Christianity and the Nature of the Person" from the perspective of its particular discipline. Each group has been asked to produce a major new study that speaks to this theme in a manner that is edifying both to scholars in other fields and to peers of all faiths in its own field.

We have been privileged to lead the team on law. We wish to thank the immensely talented group of contributors to this volume, with whom we have deliberated our project mandate and divided the work. From among this group, we give special thanks to Kent Greenawalt for his sage advice on the structure of these volumes; Russell Hittinger, Patrick Brennan, and Angela Carmella for helping us shape the Catholic materials; Milner Ball, Timothy Jackson, and Nicholas Wolterstorff for helping us shape the Protestant materials, and Mark Noll for writing the section introduction after the fact; and Vigen Guroian, Paul Valliere, and Mikhail Kulakov for helping us shape the Orthodox materials. We also wish to thank other scholars who offered us advice and criticism at the early stages of this project: James Billington, Librarian of Congress; Wolfgang Huber, Bishop of Berlin-Brandenburg; Judge Michael McConnell; and Kathy Caveny, John Erickson, Jon Gunnemann, Emily Hartigan, Jaroslav Pelikan, Jefferson

Powell, Steven Smith, Steven Tipton, Robert Tuttle, Johan van der Vyver, Joseph Vining, and Paul Zahl.

On behalf of our colleagues in the Law and Religion Program, we express our deep gratitude to our friends at The Pew Charitable Trusts for their generous support of this project, particularly Pew's president, Rebecca Rimel, and program officers Luis Lugo, Susan Billington Harper, and Diane Winston. We also express our gratitude to our friends at the University of Notre Dame, particularly Nathan Hatch, Kurt Berends, and Linda Bergling.

We wish to thank Craig Dykstra and his colleagues at the Lilly Endowment in Indianapolis for their generous grant in support of John Witte's project on "Law, Religion, and the Protestant Tradition," which has provided him with release time to work on this and other book projects.

We wish to recognize and thank several of our colleagues in the Law and Religion Program for their exceptional work on the administration of this project and the production of these two volumes. We are particularly grateful to Linda King for masterminding the administration of this project, for coordinating the three conferences that it occasioned, and for working so expertly and assiduously on the production of these manuscripts. We express our gratitude to Anita Mann, Amy Wheeler, Eliza Ellison, and Janice Wiggins for sharing so generously of their administrative expertise, and William J. Haines and Kelly Parker for their impeccable library services.

We owe a special word of thanks to Gina Weiser, a graduate of the Candler School of Theology and a Spruill Fellow in the Center for the Interdisciplinary Study of Religion at Emory University in the 2003–2004 academic year. She set an enviable standard of dedication, precision, and acuity in her editorial critique and review of this entire manuscript. This volume has been much improved by her expert labors. We also wish to thank the members of the editorial team that Gina Weiser assembled—Katie Davis, Rouslan Elistratov, Laurie Ann Fallon, Heather Good, Rebekah LeMon, Kevin O'Brien, Michelle Roberts, and Sarah Toering—for their careful review of various chapters in this volume and its companion.

We would like to thank Wendy Lochner and her colleagues at Columbia University Press for taking on these volumes and working so efficiently and effectively to ensure their timely production. We appreciate as well the very helpful criticisms and suggestions of the three anonymous outside reviewers of an earlier version of this manuscript.

Finally, we dedicate this volume to the students of the Law and Religion Program at Emory University, past, present, and future.

Introduction

THE CONTEXT

The better the society, the less law there will be. In Heaven there will be no law, and the lion will lie down with the lamb. . . . In Hell there will be nothing but law, and due process will be meticulously observed.

SO REMARKED THE eminent legal scholar Grant Gilmore in closing his 1974 lecture series at Yale Law School, later published as *The Ages of American Law*. Gilmore crafted this catchy couplet to capture the pessimistic view of law, politics, and society made popular by the American jurist and Supreme Court Justice Oliver Wendell Holmes Jr. (1841–1935). Contrary to the conventional portrait of Holmes as the sage and sartorial "Yankee from Olympus,"[1] Gilmore saw him as a "harsh and cruel" man, chastened and charred by the savagery of the American Civil War and by the gluttony of the Industrial Revolution. These experiences, Gilmore argued, had made Holmes "a bitter and lifelong pessimist who saw in the course of human life nothing but a continuing struggle in which the rich and powerful impose their will on the poor and the weak."[2] The cruel excesses of the Bolshevik Revolution, World War I, and the Great Depression in the first third of the twentieth century only confirmed Holmes in his pessimism that human life was "without values."[3]

This bleak view of human nature shaped Holmes's bleak view of law, politics, and society. Holmes regarded law principally as a barrier against human depravity—a means to check the proverbial "bad man" against his worst instincts and to make him pay dearly if he yielded to temptation.[4] Holmes also regarded law as a buffer against human suffering—a means to protect the vulnerable against the worst exploitation by corporations, churches, and Congress. For Holmes, there was no higher law in heaven to guide the law below. There was no path of legal virtue up which a man should go. For Holmes, the "path of the law" cut a horizontal line between heaven and hell, between human sanctity and depravity. Law served to keep society and its members from sliding into the abyss of hell. But it could do nothing to guide its members in their ascent to heaven.

Holmes was the "high priest" of a new "age of faith" in American law, Gilmore wrote with intended irony, that replaced an earlier era dominated by the church and the clergy.[5] The confession of this new age of faith was that America was a land "ruled by laws, not by men." Its catechism was the new case law method of the law school classroom. Its canon was the new concordance of legal codes, amply augmented by New Deal legislation. Its church was the common law court where the rituals of judicial formalism and due process would yield legal truth. Its church council was the Supreme Court, which now issued opinions with as much dogmatic confidence as the divines of Nicea, Augsburg, and Trent.

This new age of faith in American law was in part the product of a new faith in the positivist theory of knowledge that swept over America in the later nineteenth and twentieth centuries, eclipsing earlier theories of knowledge that gave religion and the church a more prominent place. In law, the turn to positivism proceeded in two stages. The first stage was scientific. Inspired by the successes of the early modern scientific revolution—from Copernicus to Newton—eighteenth-century European and nineteenth-century American jurists set out to create a method of law that was every bit as scientific and rigorous as that of the new mathematics and the new physics. This scientific movement in law was not merely an exercise in professional rivalry. It was an earnest attempt to show that law had an autonomous place in the cadre of positive sciences, that it could not and should not be subsumed by theology, politics, philosophy, or economics. In testimony to this claim, jurists in this period poured forth a staggering number of new legal codes, new constitutions, new legal encyclopedias, dictionaries, textbooks, and other legal syntheses that still grace, and bow, the shelves of our law libraries.[6]

The second stage of the positivist turn in law was philosophical. A new movement—known variously as legal positivism, legal formalism, and analytical jurisprudence—sought to reduce the subject matter of law to its most essential core. If physics could be reduced to "matter in motion" and biology to "survival of the fittest," then surely law and legal study could be reduced to a core subject as well. The formula was produced in the mid-nineteenth century, most famously by John Austin in England and Christopher Columbus Langdell in America: Law is simply the concrete rules and procedures posited by the sovereign and enforced by the courts.

Many other institutions and practices might be normative and important for social coherence and political concordance. But they are not law. They are the subjects of theology, ethics, economics, politics, psychology, sociology, anthropology, and other humane disciplines. They stand beyond the province of jurisprudence properly determined.[7]

This positivist theory of law, which swept over American universities from the 1890s onward, rendered legal study increasingly narrow and insular. Law was simply the sovereign's rules. Legal study was simply the analysis of the rules that were posited and their application in particular cases. Why these rules were posited, whether their positing was for good or ill, how these rules affected society, politics, or morality were not relevant questions for legal study. By the early twentieth century, it was rather common to read in legal textbooks that law is an autonomous science, that its doctrines, language, and methods are self-sufficient, that its study is self-contained.[8] It was rather common to think that law has the engines of change within itself; that, through its own design and dynamic, law marches teleologically through time "from trespass to case to negligence, from contract to quasi-contract to implied warranty."[9]

Holmes was an early champion of this positivist theory of law and legal development. He rebuked more traditional views with a series of famous aphorisms that are still often quoted today. Against those who insisted that the legal tradition was more than simply a product of pragmatic evolution, he wrote, "The life of the law is not logic but experience."[10] Against those who appealed to a higher natural law to guide the positive law of the state, Holmes cracked, "There is no such brooding omnipresence in the sky."[11] Against those who argued for a more principled jurisprudence, Holmes retorted, "General principles do not decide concrete cases."[12] Against those who insisted that law needed basic moral premises to be cogent, Holmes mused, "I should be glad if we could get rid of the whole moral phraseology which I think has tended to distort the law. In fact even in the domain of morals I think that it would be a gain, at least for the educated, to get rid of the word and notion [of] Sin."[13]

Despite its new prominence in the early twentieth century, American legal positivism was not without its ample detractors. Already in the 1920s and 1930s, sociologists of law argued that the nature and purpose of law and politics cannot be understood without reference to the spirit of a people and their times—of a *Volksgeist und Zeitgeist*, as their German counterparts put it. The legal realist movement of the 1930s and 1940s used the new insights of psychology and anthropology to cast doubt on the immutability and ineluctability of judicial reasoning. The revived natural law movement of the 1940s and 1950s saw in the horrors of Hitler's Holocaust and Stalin's gulags the perils of constructing a legal system without transcendent checks and balances. The international human rights movement of the 1950s and 1960s pressed the law to address more directly the sources and sanctions of civil, political, social, cultural, and economic rights. Marxist, feminist, and neo-Kantian movements in the 1960s and 1970s used linguistic and structural critiques to expose the fallacies and false equalities of legal and political doctrines. Watergate and other political scandals in the 1970s and 1980s highlighted the need for a more comprehensive understanding of legal ethics and political accountability.

By the early 1970s, the confluence of these and other movements had exposed the limitations of a positivist definition of law standing alone. Leading jurists of the day—Lon Fuller, Jerome Hall, Karl Llewellyn, Harold Berman, and others—were pressing for a broader understanding and definition of law.[14] Of course, they said in concurrence with legal positivists, law consists of rules—the black letter rules of contracts, torts, property, corporations, and sundry other familiar subjects. Of course, law draws to itself a distinctive legal science, an "artificial reason," as Sir Edward Coke once put it.[15] But law is much more than the rules of the state and how we apply and analyze them. Law is also the social activity by which certain norms are formulated by legitimate authorities and actualized by persons subject to those authorities. The process of legal formulation involves legislating, adjudicating, administering, and other conduct by legitimate officials. The process of legal actualization involves obeying, negotiating, litigating, and other conduct by legal subjects. Law is a set of rules, plus the social and political processes of formulating, enforcing, and responding to those rules.[16] Numerous other institutions, besides the state, are involved in this legal functionality. The rules, customs, and processes of churches, colleges, corporations, clubs, charities, and other nonstate associations are just as much a part of a society's legal system as those of the state. Numerous other norms, besides legal rules, are involved in the legal process. Order and obedience, authority and liberty are exercised out of a complex blend of concerns and conditions—class, gender, persuasion, piety, charisma, clemency, courage, moderation, temperance, force, faith, and more.

Legal positivism could not, by itself, come to terms with law understood in this broader sense. In the last third of the twentieth century, American jurists thus began to (re)turn with increasing alacrity to the methods and insights of other disciplines to enhance their formulations. This was the birthing process of the modern movement of interdisciplinary legal study. The movement was born to enhance the province and purview of legal study, to refigure the roots and routes of legal analysis, to render more holistic and realistic our appreciation of law in community, in context, in concert with politics, social sciences, and other disciplines.[17] In the 1970s, a number of interdisciplinary approaches began to enter the mainstream of American legal education—combining legal study with the study of philosophy, economics, medicine, politics, and sociology. In the 1980s and 1990s, new interdisciplinary legal approaches were born in rapid succession—the study of law coupled with the study of anthropology, literature, environmental science, urban studies, women's studies, gay-lesbian studies, and African American studies. And, importantly for our purposes, in these last two decades, the study of law was also recombined with the study of religion, including Christianity.

THE CONTENT

In this context, it is no surprise that, until recently, modern Western Christian teachings on law, politics, and society have been largely lost on the academy.[18] To be sure, the valuable contributions of a few Christian lights of the twentieth century—Reinhold Niebuhr, Jacques Maritain, and Martin Luther King Jr. especially—have long been closely studied. And, to be sure, medieval and early modern Christian influences on the Western legal tradition were recognized. But the prevailing assumption of most scholars has been that, for good or ill, the historical contributions of Christianity to our understanding of law, politics, and society were gradually eclipsed in the modern period. Outside of specialty discussions of natural law and church-state relations, it has been widely assumed, modern Christianity has had little constructive or original to say.

The premise of this volume and its companion volume of readings is that modern Christianity did have a great deal to say about law, politics, and society, and that its teachings can still have a salutary influence today, in the West and well beyond. To be sure, many quarters of modern Christianity did become theologically anemic, ethically compromised, and jurisprudentially barren. But in each generation, we submit, strong schools of Christian legal, political, and social teaching remained, each grounded in a rich and nuanced Christian theology—particularly a theology of human nature or, more technically, a theological anthropology. Not surprisingly, given the prominence of legal positivism, most of the best such teaching emerged outside of the legal profession—in seminaries and church councils, among philosophers and ethicists, on soapboxes and in prison cells, in intellectual isolation if not outright exile. But by word, by deed, and by declaration, modern Christians addressed the cardinal issues of law, politics, and society, drawing on a rich theology of human nature.

These two volumes sample these teachings and map their insights for the most pressing issues of our day. Such issues include topics that are familiar to scholars of law, politics, and society whatever their persuasion:

the nature and purpose of law and authority, the mandate and limits of rule and obedience, the rights and duties of officials and subjects, the care and nurture of the needy and innocent, the rights and wrongs of war and violence, the separation and cooperation of church and state, the sources and sanctions of legal reasoning, among others. Such issues also include questions that are more specifically Christian in accent but no less important for our understanding of law, politics, and society: Are persons fundamentally good or evil? Is human dignity essentially rational or relational? Is law inherently coercive or liberating? Is law a stairway to heaven or a fence against hell? Did government predate or postdate the fall into sin? Should authorities only proscribe vices or also prescribe virtues? Is the state a divine or a popular sovereign? Are social institutions fundamentally hierarchical or egalitarian in internal structure and external relations? Are they rooted in creation or custom, covenant or contract? What is justice, and what must a Christian do in its absence?

These volumes address the lives, writing, and thought of twenty leading modern Catholic, Protestant, and Orthodox Christians who addressed just these types of questions. Gathered for analysis herein are modern theologians, philosophers, ethicists, jurists, statesmen, and churchmen who spoke to many issues of law, politics, and society on the strength of their theological anthropology—or spoke to one or two issues with particular acuity and originality. This volume provides a set of freshly commissioned analytical essays on these twenty Christian figures. The companion volume is an anthology of illustrative primary writings by each of these same figures. Twin forewords and twin afterwords to this volume, prepared by four scholarly giants in the field of law and religion today, offer inspiration, instruction, and illustration on how this material can be fruitfully used by the twenty-first-century reader.

First, these volumes focus on *modern* Christian teachings on law, politics, society, and human nature. *Modern, modernism,* and *modernity* are highly contested labels these days—not least within Christian churches, where the terms have often been associated with dangerous liberal tendencies. We are using the term *modern* nontechnically. We are focused principally on twentieth-century Christianity, reaching back into the later nineteenth century to understand movements that culminated in the twentieth century and affected Christianity. The time in question includes the Reconstruction era after the American Civil War, the later Industrial Revolution, the Bolshevik Revolution and the emergence of socialism, two world wars, the Holocaust and the Stalinist purges, the modern human rights revolution, the Great Depression and the rise of the Western welfare state, the technological revolution and the emergence of globalization, among other movements. These modern moments and movements had monumental, and sometimes devastating, effects on modern Christianity.

To be sure, many of these twentieth-century movements were continuous with earlier movements that are often also described as "modern." Among these are the great revolutions of the West: the Glorious Revolution of England (1689), the American Revolution (1776), and the French Revolutions of 1789 and 1848. Important also was the scientific revolution in the seventeenth and eighteenth centuries and the later rise of what Max Weber called technical rationality and the bureaucratization of the state and society. Most important of all was the eighteenth- and nineteenth-century Enlightenment in Europe and North America, with its new secular theology of individualism, rationalism, and nationalism that often challenged core Christian beliefs. The individual was no longer viewed primarily as a sinner seeking salvation in the life hereafter. To Enlightenment exponents, every individual was created equal in virtue and dignity, vested with inherent rights of life, liberty, and property, and capable of choosing his or her own means and measures of happiness. Reason was no longer the handmaiden of revelation, rational disputation no longer subordinate to homiletic declaration. The rational process, conducted privately by each person, and collectively in the open marketplace of ideas, was considered a sufficient source of private morality and public law. The nation-state was no longer identified with a national church or a divinely blessed covenant people; it was to be glorified in its own right. Its constitutions and laws were sacred texts reflecting the morals and mores of the collective national culture. Its officials were secular priests, representing the sovereignty and will of the people.

The introductory chapters to the Catholic, Protestant, and Orthodox sections of the volume address some of these earlier phases of the modern age, but not all of them, and not in a depth that will satisfy specialists. It would take a set of volumes considerably heftier than these to take full account of these earlier modern movements and their impact on Christian teachings on law, politics, and society. It is the later modern period that is less known, and it is that period with which these volumes are principally occupied.

Second, we have deliberately used the term *teachings*, rather than theories, theologies, or other formal labels, to describe what modern Christianity has offered to law, politics, and society. In part, this is to underscore that the call to "teach" is what all Christians, despite their vast denominational differences, have in common. Christ's last words to his disciples, after all, were, "Go ye, therefore, and make disciples of all nations . . . *teaching* them to observe all that I have commanded you."[19] In part this is to recognize that "social teachings," "political teachings," "moral teachings" and "legal teachings" have become terms of art in current scholarship. Particularly in the Catholic and Protestant worlds, "social teaching" has now become shorthand for a fantastic range of speculation on issues of law, politics, society, and morality.[20] And, in part, we use the term *teachings* to underscore that modern Christians have contributed to our understanding of law, politics, and society both by word and by deed, by books and by speeches, by brilliant writings and by sacrificial acts. It would be foolish to dismiss the novel teachings of Susan Anthony and Dorothy Day just because they had thin résumés. It would be equally foolish not to draw lessons from the martyrdom of Mother Maria, Dietrich Bonhoeffer, or Martin Luther King Jr. just because they left their papers in disarray.

Third, we have divided these twenty figures into Catholic, Protestant, and Orthodox Christian groups, even while recognizing that some of these figures were more ecumenically minded than others. We have included an introduction to each of these three traditions to contextualize and connect the studies of the individual figures that are included. We have arranged the chapters on these figures more or less chronologically for each tradition, assigning varying word limits to the chapters and selections for each figure in accordance with their relative importance for the themes of these volumes.

Fourth, with respect to the Catholic tradition, we have blended episcopal and lay voices from both sides of the Atlantic. Leo XIII, John XXIII, and John Paul II offered the most original and enduring contributions among modern popes, though Pope Pius XII was important as well. Leo XIII led the revival and reconstruction of the thought of the thirteenth-century sage Thomas Aquinas. He applied this "neo-Thomism," as it was called, to the formulation of several of the Catholic Church's core "social teachings," not least a theory of social institutions that would later ripen into subsidiarity doctrine, and a theory of labor that would later form the backbone of the church's stand for social, cultural, and economic rights. John XXIII was the architect of the Second Vatican Council (1962–65) with its transforming vision of religious liberty, human dignity, and democracy and with its deliberate agenda to modernize the Catholic Church's political platforms and social teachings. John Paul II, who faced the ravages of both Nazi occupation and the Communist takeover of his native Poland, was a fierce champion of democratization and human rights in the first years of his pontificate, as well as an active sponsor of rapprochement among Catholics, Protestants, and Jews and of revitalization of the church's canon law. In recent years, he has become an equally fierce critic of the growing secularization of society, liberalization of theology, and exploitation of human nature. These latter concerns have led its leadership to new (and sometimes controversial) interpretations of the Catholic Church's earlier "social teachings."

The French philosopher Jacques Maritain and the American theologian John Courtney Murray were among the most original and influential of the many European and American Catholic writers in the mid-twentieth century. Maritain combined neo-Thomism and French existentialism into an intricate new theory of natural law, natural rights, human dignity, equality, and fraternity, which inspired the Universal Declaration of Human Rights (1948). Murray combined neo-Thomism and American democratic theory into a powerful new argument for natural law, human dignity, religious liberty, church-state relations, and social organization. Both theories were initially controversial. Murray was censored for a time by the church; Maritain was blistered by his reviewers. But these two figures, and the many scholars whom they influenced, laid much of the foundation for the Second Vatican Council's declaration on human dignity and religious freedom, and the church's emerging global advocacy of human rights and democratization.

Both American political activist Dorothy Day and Latin American liberation theologian Gustavo Gutiérrez represent important new strains of social and political critique and activism within modern Catholicism. Day defied state and church authorities alike in her relentless crusade to protect the rights of workers and the poor, and to protest warfare, grounding her work in a robust theology of personalism. Gutiérrez combined some of the teachings of Vatican II and Marxism into a searing critique of global capitalism and its devastating impact on the poor and on the underdeveloped world. Both Day and Gutiérrez adduced scripture above all to press for a preferential option for the poor, the needy, and the vulnerable. While both these figures have been controversial, and both drew episcopal censure, they have helped to illustrate, if not inspire, many new forms of social and political activism among Catholics worldwide.

Fifth, the Protestant tradition, with its hundreds of independent denominations who share only the Bible as their common authority, does not lend itself to easy illustration. We present Abraham Kuyper and Karl Barth as two strong and independent voices who addressed, and sometimes defined, many of the main themes of law, politics, society, and human nature that have occupied many modern Protestants. Kuyper, though not so well known today, was something of the Leo XIII of his day. Kuyper called for a return to the cardinal teachings of the sixteenth-century Protestant Reformation, and he developed a comprehensive Reformed theory of human nature and human knowledge. He also developed an important new "sphere sovereignty" theory of liberty, democracy, and social institutions, which would become a Protestant analog, if not answer, to Catholic subsidiarity theory.

If Kuyper was the Leo of modern Protestantism, Barth was its Maritain. This brilliant Swiss theologian produced the most comprehensive Protestant dogmatic system of the twentieth century, centered on the Bible and on Christ. Many theories of law, politics, and society were embedded in his massive writings, not least Barth's famous critique of theories of natural law and natural rights, the source of a strong anti-naturalist and anti-rights tendency among many later Protestants. Most memorable of all was Barth's leadership in crafting the Barmen Declaration of 1934, which denounced the emerging laws and policies of Adolf Hitler and the German Nazi Party.

German theologian Dietrich Bonhoeffer knew firsthand about Nazi belligerence, for he was killed in a concentration camp for conspiring to assassinate Hitler. Bonhoeffer's decision to join this conspiracy had required a complex rethinking of his own Lutheran tradition of political ethics and Christian discipleship, and of the proper relations of the church and its members to a world that had abandoned reason and religion in pursuit of tribalism and totalitarianism. Bonhoeffer's American contemporary Reinhold Niebuhr saw some of these same lusts for power and self-interest in modern states and corporations alike. Building on the classic Protestant doctrine of total depravity, Niebuhr developed an applied theology of Christian realism that prized democratic government, but with strong checks and balances; that protected human rights but informed by moral duties; and that championed racial equality and economic justice.

We have included Susan B. Anthony, a freethinking Quaker, as an early exemplar of an important tendency of modern American Protestants to counsel both legal disobedience and legal reform at once on selected issues. Today, these Protestant political preoccupations include abortion, same-sex marriage, and religion in public schools. For Anthony, the cardinal issue was women's rights. Using basic biblical texts as her guide, Anthony worked relentlessly to affect many legal reforms in Congress and the states, not least passage of the Nineteenth Amendment to the Constitution, the world's first modern constitutional guarantee of a woman's right to vote.

Both Martin Luther King Jr. and William Stringfellow later led comparable movements for racial and economic justice, although they both grounded their advocacy more deeply in traditional biblical warrants and allied themselves more closely with the church. King was "America's Amos" who used pulpit, pamphlet, and political platform alike to lead America to greater racial justice, including passage of the Civil Rights Act of 1964.

When he faced political opposition and repression, King also developed a novel theology of nonviolent resistance to authority. William Stringfellow spent much of his career representing the interests of the poor and needy in Harlem as well as those who protested America's war policy, appearing in several sensational cases. He grounded his work in a novel Protestant theory of law and gospel. The Mennonite theologian John Howard Yoder likewise pressed for social and economic justice and democratic virtues, on the strength of a classic Anabaptist biblicism and pacifism coupled with a new appreciation for natural law, human rights, and democratization.

Sixth, we have thought it imperative to give ample time and space in the volumes to the Eastern Orthodox tradition. Many leading Orthodox lights dealt with fundamental questions of law, politics, society, and human nature with novel insight, often giving a distinct reading and rendering of the biblical, apostolic, and patristic sources. Moreover, the Orthodox Church has immense spiritual resources and experiences whose implications are only now beginning to be seen. These spiritual resources lie, in part, in Orthodox worship—the passion of the liturgy, the pathos of the icons, the power of spiritual silence. They lie, in part, in Orthodox church life—the distinct balancing between hierarchy and congregationalism through autocephaly, between uniform worship and liturgical freedom through alternative vernacular rites, between community and individuality through a trinitarian communalism, centered on the parish, on the extended family, on the wise grandmother, the *babushka*. And these spiritual resources lie, in part, in the massive martyrdom of millions of Orthodox faithful in the last century—whether suffered by Russian Orthodox under the Communist Party, by Greek and Armenian Orthodox under Turkish and Iranian radicals, by Middle Eastern Copts at the hands of religious extremists, or by North African Orthodox under all manner of fascist autocrats.[21]

These deep spiritual resources of the Orthodox Church have no exact parallels in modern Catholicism and Protestantism, and most of their implications for law, politics, and society have still to be drawn out. It would be wise to hear what an ancient church, newly charred and chastened by decades of oppression and martyrdom, considers essential to the regime of human rights. It would be enlightening to watch how ancient Orthodox communities, still largely centered on the parish and the family, will reconstruct Christian theories of society. It would be instructive to listen how a tradition, that still celebrates spiritual silence as its highest virtue, might recast the meaning of freedom of speech and expression. And it would be illuminating to feel how a people that has long cherished and celebrated the role of the woman—the wizened babushka of the home, the faithful remnant in the parish pews, the living icon of the Assumption of the Mother of God—might elaborate the meaning of gender equality.

To illustrate the potential of some of these Orthodox resources, and the rich theological anthropologies that Orthodoxy has already produced, we have selected three key Russian Orthodox scholars—Soloviev, Berdyaev, and Lossky. Each of these figures interacted with several Western Christian thinkers. Each challenged the (increasingly compromised) Russian Orthodox authorities of their day, even while channeling the best theology and jurisprudence of the Russian Orthodox tradition into fundamentally new directions. Vladimir Soloviev, a philosopher, was the first modern Russian to work out an intricate Orthodox philosophy of law that grounded law and political order in morality, and that anchored morality directly in a Christian theology of salvation. Soloviev also challenged the traditional Orthodox theology of theocracy, which tied church, state, and nation into an organic whole and laid some of the foundations for a new theory of social pluralism. Nicholas Berdyaev, a theologian, worked out a complex new theology of human nature anchored in an ethic of creation, redemption, and law. He also crafted an original theory of human dignity and salvation that he tied to the Orthodox doctrine of theosis. Vladimir Lossky, a philosopher, drew from several earlier church fathers and mystics a brilliant new theory of human dignity, freedom, and discipline anchored in the Orthodox doctrine of the Trinity. He also challenged the politically compromised church and its socially anemic members to reclaim both their freedoms and their duties to discharge divinely appointed tasks. The Romanian theologian Dumitru Stăniloae drew from some of these same church fathers and mystics a comparable theory of the meaning of human freedom and sinfulness and the symphony of natural and supernatural sources of law and authority. Unlike Lossky, Stăniloae supported Romanian ethnic nationalism and had little say to about the political compromises of the Romanian Orthodox Church during the period of Communism.

We have also included a chapter on the Russian nun and social reformer Mother Maria Skobtsova, whose thought and example evoke images of both Dorothy Day and Dietrich Bonhoeffer. Maria, who was exiled in Paris, worked tirelessly in the hostels feeding the poor and needy, even while developing a rich theology of incarnational living and sacramental care, and a harsh critique of some of the reclusive tendencies of many monastics. Her work during the Nazi occupation of Paris brought her to the attention of the Gestapo, which condemned her to death in a concentration camp.

The biographies of some of these twenty figures are as edifying as their writings, and the chapters that follow spend time recounting them. Fifteen of these figures served, at least for a time, as university professors of theology, philosophy, ethics, history, or law. Ten served in traditional church offices: three as popes (Leo XIII, John XXIII, and John Paul II), five as pastors (Gutiérrez, Barth, Bonhoeffer, Niebuhr, and King), two as monastics (Maria and Murray). Two served in political office—Kuyper as the prime minister of the Netherlands, Maritain as France's ambassador to the Vatican. One served as a lawyer (Stringfellow). One was active as a political advisor (Niebuhr). Eight were stirred to radical social or political activism (Gutiérrez, Day, Barth, Bonhoeffer, Niebuhr, King, Stringfellow, and Maria). Four were censured by church authorities (Anthony, Day, Murray, and Gutiérrez). Three were exiled from their homeland (Berdyaev, Lossky, and Maria). Two were removed from their professorships (Bonhoeffer and Stăniloae). Nine were indicted or imprisoned by state authorities (Anthony, Day, Bonhoeffer, King, Stringfellow, Soloviev, Berdyaev, Maria, and Stăniloae). One faced brutal and lengthy political imprisonment (Stăniloae). Two were murdered in concentration camps (Bonhoeffer and Maria). One fell to an assassin's bullet (King).

The diversity of these biographies underscores an important criterion of selection that we have used in assembling these two volumes. The twenty figures included herein are intended to be points on a large canvas, not entries on an exhaustive roll of modern Christian teachers of law, society, and politics. We present them as illustrations of different venues, vectors, and visions of what a Christian understanding of law, politics, and society entails. Some of these figures were lone voices. Others attracted huge throngs of allies and disciples, many of whom make no appearance in these pages. Moreover, we have not included figures who are still alive and well today—including several authors in this volume—whose work will likely shape Christian teachings on law, politics, and society in the twenty-first century.

Many readers will thus look in vain in these volumes for some of their favorite authors. Missing from this collection are some of our favorites who did or do speak to some issues of law, politics, and society with a distinctly Christian understanding of human nature. These include Hans Urs von Balthasar, John Finnis, Joseph Fuchs, Mary Ann Glendon, Germain Grisez, Etienne Gilson, Bernard Longeran, Karl Rahner, Heinrich Rommen, Thomas Schaeffer, and Yves Simon, among Catholics; Emil Brunner, Herman Dooyeweerd, Johannes Heckel, Carl Henry, Karl Holl, Wolfgang Huber, Richard Niebuhr, Oliver O'Donovan, Wolfhart Pannenburg, Paul Ramsey, Walter Rauschenbusch, and Rudolph Sohm, among Protestants; John Erickson, Pavel Florensky, Georges Florovsky, John Meyendorff, and Christoph Yannoros, among Orthodox. Every reader will have a list of favorites beyond those included in these pages. The greatest compliment that could be made to this book is that it stimulates the production of many other and better studies of the scores of other modern Christian thinkers who deserve analysis.

THE CHALLENGE

This last point invites a few final reflections on some of the main challenges that remain—beyond the formidable task of filling in the vast canvas of modern Christian teachings on law, politics, society, and human nature.

One challenge is to trace the roots of these modern Christian teachings into the earlier modern period of the seventeenth through early nineteenth centuries. Scholars have written a great deal about patristic, scholastic, early Protestant, and post-Tridentine Catholic contributions to law, politics, and society. But many of the best accounts of the history of Christian legal, political, and social thought stop in 1625. That was the year that the father of international law, Hugo Grotius, uttered the impious hypothesis that law, politics, and society would continue even if "we should concede that which cannot be conceded without the utmost wickedness, that there is no God, or that the affairs of men are of no concern to him."[22] While many subsequent writers conceded Grotius's hypothesis, and embarked on the great secular projects of the Enlightenment, many great Christian writers did not. They have been forgotten to all but specialists. Their thinking on law, politics, and society needs to be retrieved, restudied, and reconstructed for our day.

A second challenge is to make these modern Christian teachings on law, politics, and society more concrete. In centuries past, the Catholic, Protestant, and Orthodox traditions alike produced massive codes of canon law and church discipline that covered many areas of private and public life. They instituted sophisticated tribunals for the equitable enforcement of these laws. They produced massive works of political theology and theological jurisprudence, with ample handholds in catechisms, creeds, and confessional books to guide the faithful. Some of that sophisticated legal and political work continues in parts of the Christian church today. Modern Christian ethicists still take up some of the old questions. Some Christian jurists have contributed to the current discussion of human rights, family law, and church-state relations. But the legal structure and sophistication of the modern Christian church as a whole is a pale shadow of what went on before. It needs to be restored lest the church lose its capacity for Christian self-rule and its members lose their capacity to serve as responsible Christian "prophets, priests, and kings."

A third challenge is for modern Catholic, Protestant, and Orthodox Christians to develop a rigorous ecumenical understanding of law, politics, and society. This is a daunting task. It is only in the past three decades, with the collapse of Communism and the rise of globalization, that these three ancient warring sects of Christianity have begun to come together and have begun to understand each other. It will take many generations to work out the great theological disputes over the nature of the Trinity or the doctrine of justification by faith. But there is more confluence than conflict in Catholic, Protestant, and Orthodox understandings of law, politics, and society, especially if they are viewed in long and responsible historical perspective. Scholars from these three great Christian traditions need to come together to work out a comprehensive new ecumenical "concordance of discordant canons" that draws out the best of these traditions, that is earnest about its ecumenism, and that is honest about the greatest points of tension. Few studies would do more both to spur the great project of Christian ecumenism and to drive modern churches to get their legal houses in order.

A final, and perhaps the greatest, challenge of all will be to join the principally Western Christian story of law, politics, and society told in these volumes with comparable stories that are told in the rest of the Christian world. Over the past two centuries, Christianity has become very much a world religion, claiming nearly two billion souls. Strong new capitals of Christianity now stand in the south and the east—in Latin America and sub Saharan Africa, in Eastern Europe and the Russian theater, in Korea, China, the Indian subcontinent, and beyond. In some of these new zones of Christianity, the Western Christian classics, including the work of some of the figures in this volume, are still being read and studied. But rich new indigenous forms and norms of law, politics, and society are also emerging, premised on very different Christian understandings of theology and anthropology. It would take a special form of cultural arrogance for Western and non-Western Christians to refuse to learn from each other.

NOTES

1. Catherine Drinker Bowen, *Yankee from Olympus: Justice Holmes and His Family* (Boston: Little, Brown, 1944).
2. Grant Gilmore, *Ages of American Law* (New Haven, Conn.: Yale University Press, 1977), 48–56, 110, 147 n. 12.
3. Albert W. Alschuler, *Life Without Values: The Life, Work and Legacy of Justice Holmes* (Chicago: University of Chicago Press, 2000).
4. Oliver Wendell Holmes Jr., *Collected Legal Papers* (New York: Harcourt, Brace and Howe, 1920), 170.
5. Gilmore, *Ages of American Law*, 41–67.
6. I. Bernard Cohen, *Revolution in Science* (Cambridge, Mass.: Harvard University Press, 1985); Donald R. Kelly, *The Human Measure: Social Thought in the Western Legal Tradition* (Cambridge, Mass.: Harvard University Press, 1990).

7. See especially John Austin, *The Province of Jurisprudence Determined, Being the First of a Series of Lectures on Jurisprudence, or, The Philosophy of Positive Law*, 2d ed., 3 vols. (London: John Murray, 1861–63); Christopher Columbus Langdell, *A Selection of Cases on the Law of Contracts*, 2d ed. (Boston: Little, Brown, 1879), preface; Langdell, "Harvard Celebration Speeches," *Law Quarterly Review* 3 (1887): 123.

8. See, e.g., John Wigmore, "Nova Methodus Discendae Docendaeque Jurisprudentiae," *Harvard Law Review* 30 (1917): 812; Holmes, *Collected Legal Papers*, 139, 231; Robert Stevens, *Law School: Legal Education in America from the 1850s to 1980s* (Chapel Hill: University of North Carolina Press, 1983).

9. Barbara Shapiro, "Law and Science in Seventeenth-Century England," *Stanford Law Review* 21 (1969): 724, 728.

10. Oliver Wendell Holmes Jr., *The Common Law* (Boston: Little, Brown and Company, 1881), 1.

11. S. Pac. Co. v. Jensen, 244 U.S. 205, 222 (1917) (Holmes, J. dissenting); see also Michael H. Hoffheimer, *Justice Holmes and the Natural Law* (New York: Garland, 1992).

12. Lochner v. New York, 198 U.S. 45, 76 (1905)

13. Letter to Sir Frederick Pollock (May 30, 1927) in *Holmes-Pollock Letters: The Correspondence of Mr. Justice Holmes and Sir Frederick Pollock, 1874–1932*, ed. Mark DeWolfe Howe, 2 vols. (Cambridge, Mass.: Harvard University Press 1941), 2:200.

14. See especially Karl Llewellyn, *Jurisprudence* (Chicago: University of Chicago Press, 1962); Lon L. Fuller, *The Morality of Law*, rev. ed. (New Haven, Conn.: Yale University Press, 1964); Jerome Hall, *Studies in Jurisprudence and Criminal Theory* (New York: Oceana Publishers, 1958); Hall, *Foundations of Jurisprudence* (Indianapolis: Bobbs-Merrill, 1973); Harold J. Berman, *The Interaction of Law and Religion* (Nashville, Tenn.: Abingdon Press, 1974).

15. Anthony Lewis, "Sir Edward Coke (1552–1633): His Theory of 'Artificial Reason' as a Context for Modern Basic Legal Theory," *Law Quarterly Review* 84 (1968): 330.

16. See Harold J. Berman, *Law and Revolution: The Formation of the Western Legal Tradition* (Cambridge, Mass.: Harvard University Press, 1983), 4–5; Jerome Hall, *Comparative Law and Social Theory* (Baton Rouge: Louisiana State University Press, 1963), 78–82.

17. See, e.g., Richard A. Posner, "The Present Situation in Legal Scholarship," *Yale Law Journal* 90 (1981): 1113; Robert C. Clark, "The Interdisciplinary Study of Legal Evolution," *Yale Law Journal* 90 (1981): 1238; Symposium, "American Legal Scholarship: Directions and Dilemmas," *Journal of Legal Education* 33 (1983): 403.

18. For a notable recent exception, see Michael W. McConnell, Robert F. Cochran Jr., and Angela C. Carmella, eds., *Christian Perspectives on Legal Thought* (New Haven, Conn.: Yale University Press, 2000), with essays by twenty-eight distinguished American law professors, several of whom appear in this volume as well.

19. Matthew 28:20.

20. See, e.g., Ernst Troeltsch, *The Social Teachings of the Christian Churches*, trans. Olive Wyon, 2 vols. (Chicago: University of Chicago Press, 1981), and review of later literature in John Witte Jr., *Law and Protestantism: The Legal Teachings of the Lutheran Reformation* (New York: Cambridge University Press, 2002).

21. See James H. Billington, "Orthodox Christianity and the Russian Transformation," in *Proselytism and Orthodoxy in Russia: The New War for Souls*, ed. John Witte Jr. and Michael Bourdeaux (Maryknoll, N.Y.: Orbis Books, 1999), 51; Billington, "The Case for Orthodoxy," *The New Republic* (May 30, 1994), 24.

22. Hugo Grotius, *De Iure Belli ac Pacis* (1625), Prolegomena, 11, discussed in Oliver O'Donovan and Joan Lockwood O'Donovan, *From Irenaeus to Grotius: Christian Political Thought, 100–1625* (Grand Rapids, Mich.: Eerdmans, 1999); Brian Tierney, *The Idea of Natural Rights: Studies on Natural Rights, Natural Law, and Church Law, 1150–1625* (Atlanta: Scholars Press, 1997).

{ PART I }

The Roman Catholic Tradition

[CHAPTER 1]

Introduction to Modern Catholicism

RUSSELL HITTINGER

In his opening allocution to the Second Vatican Council on October 11, 1963, Pope John XXIII urged the bishops to heed what may be learned from history, "the teacher of life."[1] He recalled, for example, that previous councils were "often held to the accompaniment of the most serious difficulties and sufferings because of the undue interference of civil authorities." The more senior bishops assembled in 1962 could remember that at the papal conclave of 1903, the emperor of Austria effectively exercised the so-called *ius exclusivae*, the right of vetoing a papal candidate. The pope reminded the council that whatever the problems and challenges of the contemporary world, it is not true that in former times "everything was a full triumph for the Christian idea and life and for proper religious liberty."

All of the Catholic thinkers and writers in this volume were born and came of age prior to the Second Vatican Council and lived through different phases of the problematic history recalled by Pope John. Gioacchino Pecci, the future Pope Leo XIII, was the oldest of these Catholic "titans." He was born in 1810, as Napoleon's armies were reconstituting the political geography of Europe. The youngest is Karol Józef Wojtyla, who would become Pope John Paul II in 1978, exactly a century after Leo's election. Born in 1920, just two years after the end of World War I had swept away the last ruling families of Christendom (Hohenzollerns, Wittelsbachs, Romanovs, and Habsburgs), Wojtyla would live to see the political map drastically change yet again in 1939, 1945, and 1989. Remarkably, Pecci and Wojtyla's respective lives encompass nearly two centuries of lived experience, covering almost the entirety of what we would consider the "modern" situation of Catholicism.

These Catholic thinkers are notable for the contribution to the development of Catholic legal, political, and social thought and doctrine—"social teachings," as they are conventionally called, which have been one of the signal achievements of the church since the nineteenth century. This body of thought was not just the doctrinal work of popes and councils, but also the labor of scholars and activists, both clerical and lay. The Catholic mind was formed in a context of struggle with modern ideas and institutions. This conflict was often muddled, chaotic, and sometimes violent, but as so often happens in the history of ideas, it likewise provided the soil for creative advances in the areas of philosophy, theology, and jurisprudence. The problem of the state was the crucible in which the Catholic mind was sharpened. Its importance can be gauged by the fact that when John Paul II was elected pope in 1978, his thirteen predecessors had written some three hundred encyclicals, about half of which were devoted to problems relating to the nature, the ideologies, and the policies of the state.

Political society, of course, was not merely the preoccupation of Catholic thinkers, for the greatest, most sustained, and most troubling work of modernity is the state. If we ask a modern person who or what is sovereign, he or she would not say, "reason," "the individual," or "science," but instead, without hesitation, "the state." The states formed in the wake of the Napoleonic wars at the turn of the nineteenth century were the engines of science and military technology, colonialism, education, and law. Catholics certainly were not unique in having to reckon with the phenomenon of the state. In other respects, however, the Catholic Church had a different and more troubled relationship to the state. The church's enormous size and international scope, its public law and authority, its educational institutions, and, above all, its refusal to reconfigure itself into national churches, made conflict and rivalry with the modern state almost inevitable. State monopoly over law and, increasingly, education made canon law and the educational system of the church appear to be an *imperium in imperio*. Religious congregations and orders, with their vast properties, their ancient exemptions from taxation, and their legal privileges drawn from the solicitude of the Roman See and its concordats with temporal sovereigns, offended the new spirit of citizenship.

The rivalry, however, was never anything quite so simple as what is implied by the conventional rubric "church and state." Also at stake was the constitution of society as a spiritual and cultural order that has its own distinct forms of authority and modes of liberty. By the late nineteenth century, it was well understood that society is not a garment that can be divided between civil and ecclesiastical powers. Modern liberalism was also shaped by concern for the liberty of civil society. How to protect and enhance the relationship between three spheres—church, state, and society—is the kernel of what would come to be called "the social question," one that would test the speculative and practical wisdom of Catholicism.

Our survey of Catholic legal, political, and social thought begins with the crisis of the nineteenth century. The demise of Catholic political Christendom after the revolutions of 1848 was the matrix for the problems that defined Catholic social thought, even to our own time. We then look at the magisterial effort of Pope Leo XIII to craft a new approach to the issues of church, state, and society. Of particular importance was his *ressourcement* of scholastic Thomism. The so-called Leonine revival of Thomism not only left a deep imprint upon systematic theology and seminary education but also had far-reaching effects upon the way Catholics thought about legal, social, and political issues. Jacques Maritain, John Courtney Murray, and Karol Wojtyla (the future John Paul II) are products of this Leonine revival. Undoubtedly, they appropriated the thought of St. Thomas in different ways, but the similarities are also quite evident. The case for human rights grounded in natural law, the development of the principle of subsidiarity, and the argument for the integrity and quasi-autonomy of civil prudence are the work of a refurbished Thomism. If Pope John XXIII had good reason in 1962 to celebrate a normalization of relationships between the Catholic Church and temporal authorities, the work of the council certainly did not tie together every loose end. Therefore, we shall need to consider some of the tensions that have arisen within Catholic legal, political, and social thought since the council. Liberation theologians have questioned whether the synthesis of scholastic anthropology and liberal constitutionalism adequately diagnoses the problems of the developing world, and whether it gives proper scope to the prophetic social and political message of the gospel. Within the world of the economically developed Western democracies, that same synthesis of Catholic thought and liberal constitutionalism has become problematical, particularly along the axis of "life" issues concerning human dignity and natural law.

THE NINETEENTH-CENTURY CRISIS

After the revolutions of 1848, the Spanish diplomat and political theorist Juan Donoso Cortés asserted, "We cannot know what is religiously affirmed about God without also knowing what is politically affirmed or denied about government."[2] No Catholic could have disagreed with the proposition. Yet, on all sides, the best minds could arrive only at a negative consensus. Within the Catholic Church there was a broad and deep consensus that the church is not *in* the state. For their part, statesmen in the capitals and courts of Europe could agree that the state is not *in* the church. But it was far less clear how to formulate affirmative propositions about the relations between religious, political, and social authorities. Beginning with Leo XIII, Catholic theologians, philosophers, and jurists began to supply those missing propositions.

Their work, however, required an understanding of what had become dysfunctional in Catholic political Christendom. Such an understanding was not easily reached, among other reasons, because the political situation from which the church had to extricate itself was not simply the result of revolutionaries and new secular regimes overtly hostile to the church. It was also the handiwork of the church that clung for centuries to the altar-throne order. In *The Things That Are Not Caesar's* (1927), Jacques Maritain insisted that "it was five hundred years ago that we began to die."[3] The problem began in the politico-ecclesiastical soil of a decadent papacy, weakened first by the great schism (1378–1417), and then by the turmoil of the Protestant Reformation (1517). To avoid schism, to create a political climate friendly to the church's reforms in the Council of Trent (1545–1563), and to facilitate the burgeoning Catholic mission in the New World, the papacy conceded patronal privileges to monarchs. These privileges became a crucial juridical ground for building modern states, and would have a remarkably long-lived career. They survived not only the revolutions of the eighteenth and nineteenth centuries but also the formation of totalitarian states of the twentieth.

Since the sixth century, the temporal estate of the church had depended upon lay patronage. Prominent laypeople donated properties to the church and thus acquired certain rights and responsibilities over those properties and their clerical occupants. The cluster of rights and privileges was called the *ius patronatus*, from the word *patronus*, the father of a trust. Most important was the *ius praesentandi*, the right to nominate or present the clerical candidate. By the ninth century, patrons asserted the right to receive feudal homage from their clerical vassals, in exchange for which the layman vested the bishop, priest, or abbot in his temporality, his ecclesiastical property. This infeudation of the church led to the investiture crisis of the eleventh century. Pope Gregory VII (1015–85) and his successors tried to forbid clerics and religious from giving homage, lest the ecclesiastical office be confused with the fief of a vassal. On the model of the monastery of Cluny, whose monastic charter included immunity from lay control, medieval popes built a church within a church, consisting of religious houses and eventually religious orders, which enjoyed exemptions not only from lay control but also from the authority of local ordinaries. The Gregorian quest for a church independent of royal and lay supervision, autonomous in its own law, and answerable only to Rome was somewhat successful with respect to religious orders; but in its quotidian life, the church was not very effectively extracted from the tangle of patronal rights.

In the modern period, this patchwork of patronal rights came into the hands of royal families intent upon creating sovereign states. This new form of Catholic Christendom began in Spain.[4] As Ferdinand and Isabella completed the final stage of the *reconquista*, the 1486 Bull of Granada conferred on them, "as a reward of their crusade," the right to nominate all major prelacies as well as to hold in trust tithes and endowments in support of religion in Granada.[5] An entire province of the church thus became a benefice of the crown. When the conquest was complete and the New World was discovered in 1492, Pope Alexander VI issued the bull *Inter caetera* (1493), conceding to the monarchs title to the lands discovered and still to be discovered in the Indies. The grant included the power on the monarchs to license clerics who wished to sail to the Indies. In effect, the monarchs became transatlantic apostolic vicars. In 1508, Pope Julius II's bull *Universalis ecclesiae* conceded a universal patronage over the church in America. After the Anjou-Bourbon house acceded to the Spanish throne in 1700, it won from Pope Benedict XIV in 1753 the patronal right throughout all of Spain. Thus came into existence what was called the *Patronato Real Universal*. Rome had never before conceded, nor had any Catholic prince before received, such a package of delegated authority. The key point, however, is that Madrid did not regard the authority as delegated, but rather interpreted Roman concessions as recognition of authority inherent in state sovereignty.

The development of the modern Gallican church in France paralleled the situation in the Spanish dominions. In 1516 Pope Leo X made a remarkable concession to the king of France, granting Francis I a universal right of nomination to French bishoprics and abbacies.[6] Capitular elections were abolished, and the entire Gallican episcopacy, including some 800 abbeys and 280 priories, became the benefice of the king. Louis XIV astutely used the potentially schismatic Gallican Articles (1682) as a negotiating chip for another deal. Promising in 1690 not to enact the articles into law, Louis won from Pope Innocent XII regalian rights over four southern provinces theretofore exempt from the 1516 concordat. By vowing not to assert in legal theory what he was now entitled to do in practice, Louis XIV completed his hegemony over the church in France. The offices and temporal estates of the church were in effect national property distributed by the king. They flowed from Versailles to a nobility no longer organically tied to (or even present to) the land, the diocese, the monastery; indeed, bishops were consecrated in the royal chapel at Versailles rather than in their own dioceses. When the Estates General met in early summer 1789, every one of the 118 bishops and 18 archbishops was a noble on the state's dole. The architects of the French Revolution of 1789 did not invent, but rather inherited, the principle that the church, as a visible and temporal society, was the property of the state.

This form of Catholic political Christendom proved quite sturdy, lasting for nearly three hundred years. The church recognized the de facto reality of modern, state-making regimes, while demanding that they remain de jure within the fold of Catholicism. Except in the Papal States, Belgium, and in a handful of Protestant countries (such as the United States), virtually every baptized Catholic in the world lived under a regalist regime at the time of the French Revolution. Impressively, its basic features managed to survive the first wave of revolutions in Europe and in Latin America. In Republican France, royal patronage was swiftly translated into terms of popular sovereignty. The church in all of its temporalities was the property of the state, and all her bishops and clergy were its civil servants. In the former Spanish dominions, the Patronato Real became the Patronato Nacional. Venezuela, for example, would go through twenty-six constitutions without abandoning its law of patronage.

At first reluctantly, but then abruptly, Rome began to separate itself from political Christendom in the decade before the First Vatican Council (1870). Its initial reluctance was due to the Congress of Vienna (1815), where Austria, Russia, Great Britain, and Prussia attempted to arrest the revolutions. Partisans of Catholic order were to be satisfied with the liberation of Pope Pius VII from French captivity, the restoration of the Papal States in Italy and the Bourbon monarchy in France. Thus began the secular and ecclesiastical policy of legitimism. The tangled and tattered relationship between Catholicism and the states was to be solved by obedience to properly constituted authority. No encyclical better exhibits the principles and the failure of Legitimism than Pope Gregory XVI's *Cum primum* (1832). The issue at hand was the 1830–32 Polish uprising against Tsar Nicholas I. A regalist par excellence, Nicholas governed his dominions according to the slogan, "Orthodoxy, Autocracy, and Nationality." As part of the political settlement of the Congress of Vienna, Russia won the right of governing the former Kingdom of Poland, comprising the Duchy of Warsaw, bordered on the north and west by Prussian provinces and on the south by the eastern province of Galicia. The uprising was met with brutal Russian repression, begun in Warsaw on November 29, 1830. The constitution was suspended, the universities were closed, and both Roman and Uniate churches were subjected to severe restrictions.

Gregory told the Polish bishops in *Cum primum* that he had no greater hope but that their provinces would be "restored to peace and the rule of legitimate authority." Reminding the bishops of the scriptural warrants for obedience to temporal authority, Gregory wrote:

> "Let everyone," says the Apostle, "be subject to higher authorities, for there exists no authority except from God, and those who exist have been appointed

by God. Therefore he who resists the authority resists the ordination of God (Rom. 13.1–2).... Similarly St. Peter (1 Pet. 2:13) teaches all the faithful: "Be subject to every human creature for God's sake, whether to the king as supreme, or to the governors sent through him ... for (he says) such is the will of God, that by doing good you would silence the ignorance of foolish men." By observing these admonitions the first Christians, even during the persecutions, deserved well of the Roman emperors themselves and of the security of the state.[7]

The Polish bishops were surely puzzled, not to say appalled, by the suggestion that an eight-hundred-year-old church, with a tradition of fierce loyalty to Roman ecclesiastical authority, should abandon its self-government to a schismatic tsar on the model of the obedience owed by early Christians to the Roman emperors.

Undoubtedly, *Cum primum* represented the lowest point of the era of legitimism. However, it had the unintended effect of moving Catholic opinion in favor of a radical reckoning with the dysfunctional remnants of political Christendom. The doyen of the movement was Joseph de Maistre, whose *Du Pape* (1919) stands to nineteenth-century Catholic political theology as Rousseau's *Social Contract* stood to the eighteenth-century ideal of civic republicanism. Though he wrote for the broad project of the Restoration, his work would have nearly the opposite effect, for it was de Maistre who insisted that Gregory VII's work be completed in modern times. He remorselessly criticized the ecclesiology of national churches, taunting Gallicans to change the creed to read, "I believe in divided and independent Churches." He insisted that "nothing is accomplished" without overthrowing the "magic castle" of regalism (see chapter 2, this volume); he accused kings and princes of a "great rebellion."[8] For de Maistre, Pope Gregory VII, who declared the freedom of the church, was "the genius," the man without whom "all was lost, humanly speaking."[9]

It was a most unlikely proposition to declare Gregory VII's policies of the eleventh century to be the model for the church's relations to the restored crowns of 1815. But Maistre struck a nerve in the Catholic imagination by characterizing the French Revolution as a judgment on the nations, specifically a rod of chastisement for the captivity of Catholic political culture to regalism. De Maistre died in 1821, spurned by Pope Pius VII and the Roman Curia, but predicating a great future for what he called "my greatest work." As the political-ecclesiastical controversy stumbled into one dead-end after another, and as the ideas of *Du Pape* were filtered through many different minds, a new generation became convinced that the state cannot co-govern the church.

Catholic opinion was divided on the question of whether the political and social instability of Europe was due chiefly to an excess of liberty or to an excess of authority. Catholic "liberals" such as Lamennais, Montalembert, and Lacordaire, took the position that the main problem was an excess of authority. The new states were neither Christian nor secular, but exploited the alliance of throne and altar to repress the church and society. Liberals urged that the church put is moral authority behind liberty. Catholic "conservatives," such as Louis de Bonald, Joseph de Maistre, and Donoso Cortés, emphasized the pole of authority. The mediation of this dispute would have to await the magisterial encyclicals of Leo XIII and the formation of Catholic social doctrine in subsequent decades. In the middle of the nineteenth century, however, liberals and conservatives could agree on one point. The *ius patronatus*, in every one of its guises, had to be uprooted and the church restored to the Gregorian ideal of liberty. Almost every major Catholic thinker of the era wrote a treatise or pamphlet on the recovery of the Gregorian reform.[10]

This drumbeat of opinion could have only one practical conclusion—some kind of separation of church and state. How this could be accomplished was not clear. Rome was hemmed in by concordats that allowed the states to set and effect ecclesiastical policies. With the exception of Belgium, whose 1832 constitution forbade any use by the government of patronal rights, the former Catholic powers were not interested in relinquishing their titles to supervise religion. Unlike the American constitution, which was unfettered by any history of patronal rights and in any case did not use "separation" as a juridical term of art, separation in the European context was consistent with state authority over ecclesiastical properties, seminaries, and courts. Popes had condemned the principle for that very reason. In his famous speeches at the Malines Congress in August 1863, the Catholic liberal Charles de Montalembert pointed out that separation "can very well be combined with terrible oppression."[11]

The breakthrough did not occur in the serene atmosphere of theory or in the chambers of diplomats, but in Pope Pius IX's rather impulsive decision to issue the *Syllabus of Errors* (1864). Frustrated by the unraveling of the Restoration and by the loss of his dominions in Italy, save the city of Rome itself, Pius published a list of eighty erroneous propositions. The eightieth condemned proposition read: "The Roman Pontiff can, and ought to, reconcile himself, and come to terms with progress, liberalism and modern civilization." Public reaction to the *Syllabus* was a furious as the document itself. Though newspapers had fun mocking the pope's quixotic dismissal of modern civilization, political officials understood that something more serious was afoot. For the document contained several other propositions that, if acted upon, would amount to separation initiated from the side of the church. They carefully noted that seven propositions (§§28–30, 41, 49–51) denied that patronal rights inhere in state sovereignty, that four propositions (§§45–48) denied state monopoly in matters of education, and that four other propositions (§§29–30, 52–53) baldly reasserted the Gregorian position on the legal and economic autonomy of religious orders.

Their anxieties were confirmed four years later when Rome declined to invite nominally Catholic nations to send ambassadors (*oratores*) to the First Vatican Council. This broke with a conciliar custom dating not only to the Council of Trent (1545–63), but also to the Council of Nicea (325). Presiding at Nicea, the Emperor Constantine told the assembled bishops: "You, on the one hand, are certainly the bishops inside the Church. I, on the other, might then be the 'bishop' appointed by God of those outside."[12] So, too, in the West, the Catholic sovereign was a kind of *episcopus externus*. The secretary of state, Cardinal Antonelli, refused to extend the invitation on the ground that there could be no principle of selection between "good" and "bad" Catholic sovereigns. Privately, Antonelli said that "exclusively Catholic Governments had virtually ceased to exist."[13]

In France, Émile Ollivier declared in the Chamber of Deputies that the pope had in effect introduced the separation of church and state: "Yes, this is a new fact, a new deed indeed that the disseverance between the laical society and the religious society is put into effect by the pope's own hand."[14] The ever-mischievous Ultramontane editor of *L'Univers*, Louis Veuillot, gleefully agreed—princes are now "outside the Church." Moreover, rumor had it that the Jesuits intended to use the First Vatican Council as the occasion to doctrinalize the *Syllabus*. It was in this light that Ollivier would make bold to judge that once deprived of these instruments, the state can be said to be separated from the church. Shrewdly, he went on to say, "Undoubtedly, Gentlemen, I know that Rome earnestly wishes to separate itself from the State, but She does not want the State to separate itself from Her."[15] Count Daru, the French foreign minister, sent a memorandum to Cardinal Antonelli, anxiously pointing out that "all this is nothing else than the consecration of the supreme authority of the Church over society."[16]

Perhaps unwittingly, Count Daru had stated the issue with unusual clarity. Can we imagine a church autonomous in its own sphere, capable of acting upon and through its own members—and thus indirectly upon the wider society—without being an agent of the state (the older confessional model) or requiring the mediation of the state (the newer regalist model)? Such a solution would mean, on the side of the church, deep revision of the idea that the state has a juridical-political power of *cura religionis*, care of religion. In an 1892 allocution, Leo XIII told his curial cardinals that the church's temporal mission would center upon "faith embodied in the conscience of peoples rather than restoration of medieval institutions."[17] The much-disputed medieval doctrine of "indirect" ecclesiastical or papal power to suspend acts of states, much less to depose temporal authorities, was abandoned in favor of an "indirect" authority exercised through the teaching of faith and morals. On the part of the states, the solution would require not only jettisoning the idea that the modern state is a *sanctum* in the medieval sense of the term; it also pointed to the need for what the famous Catholic social theorist and politician Luigi Sturzo (1871–1959) termed a "rhythm of social duality."[18] Society is neither a creature of the state nor the church. It is not a "depersonalized whole" capacitated to act only through the superstructure of ecclesiastical or civil administration.[19]

The politico-ecclesiastical crisis of the nineteenth century became a lodestone for Catholic social doctrine, the lesson that oriented the work of the next generation of thinkers. Giaocchino Pecci, of course, was a bishop at the council. After becoming Pope Leo XIII in 1878, he would devote his magisterium to understanding the triadic relationship between church, state, and society. Angelo Roncalli, the future Pope John XXIII (1881), Jacques Maritain (1882), Dorothy Day (1897), and John Courtney Murray (1904) were all born in the wake of the crisis. As we saw, John XXIII opened the Second Vatican Council with an admonition to the bishops to recall the lessons on that era. Maritain's first important work in social and political philosophy, *The Things That Are Not Caesar's*, emphasized the Gregorian ideal of church liberty ("Canossa will always remain the consolation of free minds") and examined the new situation of "indirect power" in terms of the moral and prophetic voice of the church acting through society.[20]

No one studied the nineteenth-century crisis more carefully than John Courtney Murray, who invoked its lessons at a crucial stage in the debate over religious liberty at the Second Vatican Council. Bishop de Smedt, the *relator* of the group of bishops charged with formulating a position on the matter, invited Murray to present a summary of the issues disputed up to that point in the discussion. In the summer of 1964, he circulated a brief that was later published under the title "The Problem of Religious Freedom" (1964, 1993). Tracing the crisis through the *Syllabus of Errors* and the letters of Leo XIII, Murray showed why the church-state controversy was irresolvable on monistic grounds, namely the subordination of society to a single, undifferentiated citizenship superintended by the omnicompetent state. The crisis called for a recovery of "the Gregorian state of the question of public care of religion," as well as a new discernment of the "'growing end' of the tradition."[21]

THE LEONINE SYNTHESIS

Murray's notion of a "growing end" presupposed, of course, a tradition. Pope Pius XI (1922–39) was the first pope to speak of social doctrine as a unified body of teachings that develop by way of clarity and application. He thought of himself as inheriting a "doctrine" (*doctrina*) "handed on" (*tradita*) from the time of Leo XIII. Significantly, he contended that the tradition is communicated not only in the magisterial work of the papal office, but also in the ordinary work of bishops and priests, in the research and writings of lay scholars, as well as in the policies of non-Catholic statesmen.[22] Although it is doubtful that Leo deliberately launched a new doctrinal specialty per se, it cannot be doubted that his work gave a certain cachet to the idea. Indeed, the period from 1878 to 1939 could be called the era of Leonine synthesis. It reached its creative high-water mark in the 1930s between the two world wars, but its effects were consolidated at the Second Vatican Council (1962–65).

The expression "Leonine synthesis" is appropriate for two reasons. First, Leo had to reconcile Pius XI's *Quanta cura* (1864), and its appended *Syllabus of Errors*, with *Dei Filius* (1870), the dogmatic constitution of the Catholic faith adopted at the First Vatican Council. Whereas the *Syllabus* had pungently condemned errors of the Enlightenment, *Dei Filius* affirmed the integrity of reason and its harmony with the propositions of divine revelation to which faith assents. The council affirmed that God, "lord of sciences," is the same God who reveals sacred "mysteries." There is a "twofold order of knowledge," the council maintained, "distinct not only as regards its source, but also as regards its object."[23] The church does not seek to hinder the advancement of knowledge in the sciences and arts to which natural reason can attain. Leo's many teaching letters represent an extended commentary on the problems listed in the *Syllabus*, but always through the optic of *Dei Filius*, distinguishing the negative and affirmative propositions, and pointing to the different modes of knowledge and wisdoms that apply to a disputed issue.

Second, we can speak of a Leonine synthesis in terms of his ambitious and relentless effort to revive Thomism, for which his encyclical *Aeterni Patris* (1879) is the *magna charta*. His interest in St. Thomas began at the ripe old age of ten, during his training at Viterbo, and continued at the Roman College, where, at the age of fourteen, he became the student assistant of the Jesuit neo-Thomist Luigi Taparelli. In time, he would meet Taparelli's neo-Thomist colleagues Matteo Liberatore and Joseph Kleutgen, who would work on the drafts of *Dei Filius* and *Aeterni Patris*. As bishop of Perugia, Pecci recruited a Thomistic faculty for his Accademia di S. Tommaso, which was an incubator for what became known as the Leonine revival. Once he became pope, Leo swiftly moved to place Thomists into key positions in the curia and in the Roman colleges.

There were practical reasons for Leo's bid to install Thomism as the preferred method for Catholic education. The suppression of the Society of Jesus in 1773 had destroyed an international system of education that was broadly scholastic in orientation. The Napoleonic ideal of the state as teacher (*l'État enseignant*) brought what remained of Catholic schools to the brink of extinction in Europe and South America. Bismarck's *Kulturkampf* was ignited by the issue of church schools. With the more centralized and independent situation of Catholicism after Vatican I, Leo saw the chance to rebuild education, beginning with seminaries. Moreover, the institutions would need a curriculum. Although *Dei Filius* had a scholastic ambience, it did not attempt to settle questions of which particular philosophical schools or theological methods ought to be adopted. For example, *Dei Filius* asserted that the existence of God "can be known with certainty from the consideration of created things"; yet, as Gerald McCool has pointed out, the document did not "specify any definite argument through which the existence and nature of God could be established," nor did it affirm "that purely natural knowledge of God had ever been achieved in fact."[24] Leo seized upon the opportunity to institutionalize Thomism, the only method, in his estimation, capable of protecting positive revelation against modern historicism and naturalism without, at the same time, evacuating the claims of natural reason. Thomism would clarify and unify the internal deposit of faith and doctrine, maintain proper analogies to the discoveries of natural reason and the sciences, and would provide apologetics needed to defend the credibility of Catholicism. In his first encyclical, he made his intentions clear: We must "endeavor that not only a suitable and solid method of education may flourish but above all that this education be wholly in harmony with the Catholic faith in its literature and system of training, and chiefly in philosophy, upon which the direction of other sciences in great measure depends."[25]

The institutional and systematic thrust of Leo's program would leave a deep imprint upon the Catholic mind, both clerical and lay, until the 1960s, when Thomistic scholasticism gradually lost its institutional monopoly in the seminaries and universities. The Catholic mind in the 1960s began to gravitate more toward the social sciences than philosophy, and toward personalism rather than the ontology of an Aristotelian natural science. In the area of social thought, however, neo-Thomism both preceded and outlasted Leo's broader institutional aims. In *Aeterni Patris*, he pointedly recommended the teachings of St. Thomas Aquinas for the "true meaning of liberty" and for the "divine origin of all authority."[26] On these topics, the timeless air of the thirteenth-century scholastic system would not suffice without interpretive bridgework. Middle axioms needed to be devised in order to make a thirteenth-century scholasticism speak to the new social situation. Thomas, after all, had no conception of a modern state or an industrialized economy. Nor in Thomas could there be found a ready-made doctrine of subsidiarity, justiciable natural rights, social justice, political parties, or a lay-based democracy.

The interpretive bridgework began among Leo's Jesuit teachers and colleagues. It is not at all surprising that the intellectual work in the social and political area started with Jesuits. The Jesuits had been expelled first from the Catholic courts in 1759–68 and had been restored only in 1814. They could not fail to be acutely conscious of the political riptides of modern Europe. Pope Pius IX fled the revolution in Rome in 1848, taking refuge in the Kingdom of Naples. There, in exile with the pope, Jesuits began publication of *Civiltà Cattolica* on April 6, 1850. The journal became a venue for Taparelli and Liberatore to mount an aggressive and polemical case for Thomism as the only adequate method for meeting the challenges of the era. Some of their contributions were systematic in nature, covering issues of anthropology, epistemology, and metaphysics. The more controversial pieces, however, dealt with social issues: the nature of the common good, the respective jurisdictions of church and state, the nature and scope of law, and the origin of human authority. No one had seen such a dialectical and polemical Thomism since the sixteenth century, when Baroque-era scholastics in Spain and Portugal—Robert Bellarmine, Francisco de Vitoria, Bartolomé de Las Casas, Francisco Suarez, and Luis de Molina—used Thomas to counter the claims of absolute monarchs. The Jesuit *ressourcement* of sixteenth-century Thomistic political theory was pressed now against Rousseavians and physiocrats who laid the philosophical foundations for laicist republicanism.[27] Interestingly, in 1854 the Jesuit editors and writers of *Civiltà Cattolica* were expelled from the Kingdom of Naples for daring to assert that the natural law left the institutional form of polities somewhat indeterminate—a position that appeared dangerously subversive in an era of revolution.

At mid-century, neo-Thomists began to chart a middle course between the absolutist claims of monarchy and the absolutist claims of popular sovereignty. Above all, Leo and his neo-Thomist mentors and colleagues were interested in the problem of unity and plurality. In their view, the chief problem of the modern project was not the political "form" of republican or popular government. Thomists had always recognized that a human polity is amenable to plural, legitimate forms, and that such forms can either evolve by custom or change by acts of deliberate constitutional prudence. Thomas himself argued for the prudence of a mixed regime of monarchical, aristocratic, and popular elements, which he believed was embodied in the ancient Jewish state.[28] The problem, rather, lay in what the Jesuit neo-Thomists discerned to be a distinctively modern premise, namely, that unity is achieved only extrinsically by contracts, by the serendipitous outcomes of a market, or, more ominously, by the external application of law as the superior force of the state. Thomists argued that pluralities stem from intrinsic unities, beginning with human nature itself, and including matrimony, family, church, and body politic. The question was not whether there is social pluralism with distinctive modes of authority and freedom, but whether there is an ontological landscape internal to social forms. By nature and supernature, are there norms anterior to, and higher than, the laws imposed by civil law and contract? Indeed, from the nineteenth century to the present day, Catholic social thought has orbited around this issue. The great question of post-1789 Catholicism was whether the modern crisis is to be ameliorated by more or by less public freedom. Neo-Thomists reformulated this problem. It was first necessary, they argued, to understand the anthropological and social grounds of liberty and obligation.

These themes are evident in the great papal letters of Leo XIII, particularly *Rerum novarum* (1891), where Leo distinguished between the rights of obligations of individuals, families, voluntary associations, civil government, and Christian charity. But his work was not a finished product. He had relatively little to say about either the theory or practice of democratic government, and, until the end of his life, remained frustrated by the problem of (Catholic) political parties.[29] While his economic theory represented a huge advance in comparison with the thought of his predecessors, it was not well developed in any descriptive or scientific sense. Moreover, while Leo brilliantly delineated the triad of church, state, and society, defending the liberties of church and society vis-à-vis the state, he did not follow through the implications for a fuller doctrine of religious liberty. Nonetheless, Leo imparted to the Catholic world an important precedent. On issues of revealed theology proper, the deposit of faith and tradition would be organized scholastically; but, regarding the "changeable ocean of human affairs," which is to say, "in regard to purely human societies," Leo permitted, even encouraged, new applications of traditional principles.[30] As Thomas had said, the natural law can change by addition, as human prudence discovers new applications beneficial to human life.[31] Leo took inspiration from Luigi Taparelli, who coined the term "social justice," advanced the first philosophically rigorous account of "subsidiarity," and began the work of integrating natural rights with the older doctrine of natural law. Though inspired by the thought of Thomas, little of this could count as a seamless representation of Thomas's own doctrines.

SCHOLASTIC RENDITION OF A "NEW" CHRISTENDOM

The Leonine project came to fruition in the period framed by the two world wars. Indeed, it was during this time that most of the thinkers in this volume received their ecclesiastical and intellectual formation. It took a quarter of a century for the Leonine project to percolate in the institutions, producing such lay scholars such as Jacques Maritain, Yves Simon, and Heinrich Rommen, and priest scholars as Heinrich Pesch, Luigi Sturzo, and John Courtney Murray. However, two other things helped to propel the flowering of Catholic social, legal, and political thought after World War I. The first was the election to the papacy of Abrogio Damiano Achille Ratti (1922), who took the name Pope Pius XI. As a young cleric, Ratti had been trained by Leo's Thomistic colleagues in Rome. Ratti was especially influenced by the writings of Luigi Taparelli, whose work on social justice, subsidiarity, and natural rights was funneled into the Pian encyclicals of the 1920s and 1930s. Indeed, Pius explicitly recommended Taparellian neo-Thomism in the encyclical *Divini illius* (1929).[32] If anything, he was more insistent than Leo that Thomas's social, legal, and political thought be interpreted and adapted to the modern situation. In *Studiorum ducem* (1923), he went so far as to claim that the second part of Aquinas's *Summa Theologiae* "contains the foundations of a genuine 'League of Nations.'"[33]

Second, in the wake of World War I, it was imperative that legal, political, and social thought be deepened and sharpened because of the emergence of a new kind of regime. While Thomism had been revised in the baroque era to respond to the absolute monarchies, and revised once again with regard to the *étatisme* of laicist republican governments, Pius's pontificate witnessed the rise of totalitarian regimes in Russia and Germany. In the space of fourteen days in March 1937, Pius issued encyclicals against fascism in Germany, communism in the Soviet Union, and atheistic liberalism in Mexico.[34]

Totalitarianism prompted Catholic thinkers to support democratic government, to call for domestic and international authorities to be bound by justiciable natural or human rights, and more generally to develop what can be called a bottom-up model of legal, political, and social thought.[35] In one sense, the bottom-up motif captures a negative moment in Catholic thought. However the Vatican might treat diplomatically with this or that government, Catholic opinion after World War I was adamantly antistatist. We should not be surprised that the Catholic social reformer Dorothy Day converted to Catholicism at this time, and began her active ministries not only on behalf of the poor and needy, but often in opposition to the powers that be in the state, society, and economy. And beyond the Catholic communion, disillusionment with the claims of state sovereignty was evident, for example, in T. S. Eliot's *Murder in the Cathedral* (1935), a morality play in which the absence of a cathartic moment of a repentant state is notable. The bottom-up perspective acquired another meaning, one supplied by Jacques Maritain. In *Integral Humanism* (1936), Maritain spoke of a "New

Christendom" in which society is transformed by a church politically *in diaspora*. The church would be the leaven from below.

Jacques Maritain (1882–1973), the grandchild on his mother's side of Jules Favre, statesman and partisan of the Third Republic, was born in a family with impeccable republican credentials. It was all the more dramatic, then, that he converted to Catholicism and was baptized one year after the regime enacted the anticlerical separationist law of 1905. He soon found his way into the neo-Thomist movement spawned by *Aeterni Patris*. In 1919, he and his wife helped to organize Thomistic "circles" in Paris and Versailles. Although his first interests lay in philosophy of science, metaphysics, and epistemology, Maritain was thrown into legal, social, and political thought during the Action Française crisis. Founded in 1899 by Charles Maurras, Action Française rallied two seemingly opposite strands of French politics: the older monarchists and the new hypernationalists of a more secular bent. Himself an agnostic, indeed a disciple of Auguste Comte, Maurras distinguished the legal nation (*pays légal*) and the real nation (*pays réel*). The merely "legal" nation, he contended, harbored Freemasons, Jews, Protestants, and revolutionaries who thwart national destiny. This movement for an "integral nationalism" initially held some appeal for Catholics, if for no other reason than that it provided relief from the brutal anticlerical laws and seizure of church property by the Third Republic in France. Even Maritain, the son of Protestant and a republican, not to mention the husband of a Russian Jew, flirted with the Maurrassian position.

Having so recently battled monarchical and republican forms of regalism, ecclesiastical authorities in Rome and in France were clear-sighted about the nature of Maurras's ideology. The Congregation of the Index condemned some of Maurras's writings in 1914. In a consistorial allocution of December 20, 1926, Pope Pius XI forbade Catholics to belong "to a school which puts the interests of political parties above religion and causes the latter to serve the former." Excommunications followed in 1927. The Roman condemnations brought Maritain out of his slumbers. Over the next decade he wrote *Things That Are Not Caesar's* (1927), *Freedom in the Modern World* (1933), and his masterwork, *Integral Humanism* (1936), the title of which suggested his effort to counter the integral nationalism of Maurras.

In the foreword to *Integral Humanism*, Maritain noted that while he took inspiration from the perennial philosophy of Aristotle and Thomas, he would make no "claim to engage St. Thomas himself in debates in which the majority of the problems present themselves in a new manner."[36] Citing as evidence Mussolini's boast in 1926, "everything in the State, nothing against the State, nothing outside the State,"[37] Maritain contended that political Christendom is dead and that any practical program guided by nostalgia for a sanctified political authority would only fuel new despotisms and totalitarianisms. In its place, he advanced the idea of a "new humanism" and a "new Christendom." Not by the imposition of political power, but rather, by the sanctification of ordinary life through the leaven of the gospel, the church should aim to reform society from below. The new Christendom should be personalist, pluralist, and peregrinal.[38] The human person is constituted in the borderland of ends that are distinct but never entirely separated. On one hand, the person possesses a natural dignity with its corresponding perfections, liberties, and duties; on the other hand, through the spiritual powers of intellect and will, and decisively by grace, the person is called to a transcendent order. The state, he argued, fulfills its duty to God by a "minimal unity" that facilitates the development of the human person and his extraterritorial rights and privileges.[39] In the waning years of his life, as he looked back upon the development of Catholic thinking in the twentieth century, Maritain said that the project depended on discerning "the great reversal." "It is no longer the human which takes charge of defending the divine," he explained, "but the divine which offers itself to defend the human."[40]

Maritain's lay-oriented personalism, his scathing critique of modern notions of state sovereignty and nationalism, his interest in plural social entities enjoying liberties and authority distinct from the state, and, above all, his defense of natural rights, which he called the "proper achievement" of the eighteenth century,[41] not only anticipated but also increasingly began to influence the course of Catholic doctrine. Pope Pius XI not only gave papal cachet to the principle of subsidiarity, but also began to construct lists of human rights that must be honored across jurisdictions. Interestingly, Pius noted approvingly the effort of the U.S. Supreme Court to protect "prior rights" in the sphere of religion, family law, and education.[42] It was, of course, after World War II that the international community began in earnest to adopt lists, charters, and declarations of human rights, but this process was well under way in Catholic thought two decades earlier as a way to reckon with totalitarian regimes.[43] The ever-increasing prominence of the rights paradigm is one example, along with the principle of subsidiarity, of what we have called the bottom-up perspective. Catholics are to participate in the polity not merely by obeying properly constituted authority, but also by claiming their rights according to natural law. Writing to the Mexican church, Pius gave a cautious approval to the tactic of civil resistance to unjust laws, describing the duty (*munus*) of Catholic Action as "the preparation of Catholics to make just use of their rights, and to defend them with all legitimate means according as the common good requires."[44]

DEMOCRACY AND RIGHTS

In Catholic thought, rights theory developed more quickly than democratic theory. This was due, in part, to Pope Leo XIII, who admitted the principle that the forms of government are changeable, but stoutly defended
the rights of nonstate associations. Leo feared that democracy's current
"philological and philosophical significations" implied something more
than popular government—namely, a kind of anarchical contest of political parties devolving into class warfare. He worried that "Christian democracy" would drag episcopal authority and ecclesiastical institutions into a
strife that was merely "political" in the pejorative sense of the term.[45] To
make matters more difficult, since 1868, popes had maintained the policy
of *non-expedit* (literally "it is not opportune") regarding Catholic participation in the Italian regime. Leo himself had reaffirmed the ban in 1895.
It was not lifted until 1919, at which time was founded the nondenominational Partito Popolare Italiano inspired by Luigi Sturzo. Clarity about the
issue of democracy was also retarded by Roman reliance upon concordats
with governments, especially during the pontificate of Pius XI. The practical reason governing the proliferation of concordats was the abrupt change
of political geography after World War I, whereupon dozens of concordats
had lost their force and had to be renegotiated state-by-state.[46] Insofar as
concordats protected church liberties from the top down, they usually had
the effect of dampening Catholic action through political parties.

Two things changed the situation. First, since the death of Pope Leo
XIII, neo-Thomists aggressively investigated and propounded a natural
law ground of democracy. Some of the work had already been done by
sixteenth-century Thomists under the rubric of the "translation theory" of
authority. According to the translation theory, political authority is implicitly vested in the body politic, which, by custom or constitutional decree,
translates what is held in common to specific offices and persons. Not as to
its origin but rather as to its original mode of possession, political authority is democratic in nature, becoming in form a monarchical, aristocratic,
democratic, or mixed regime. There are only hints of such a doctrine in
Thomas, but the idea had strong credentials among modern scholastics.
It was easy to mistake the scholastic theory of an aboriginal democracy of
the body politic for modern theories that proposed that authority is a human construct either erected or dissolved by consent. For this reason, Pope
Leo and his Jesuit colleagues kept the translation account at arm's length,
neither ruling it in nor ruling it out. By the death of Pius XI in 1939, however, the translation theory had triumphed within most of the schools and
eddies of neo-Thomism. The most elegant account of the theory is to be

found in Yves Simon's *Philosophy of Democratic Government* (1951), where it is called the "transmission theory."[47] Pius XI certainly did nothing to discourage the proliferation of the theory. In 1930 and 1931 he made Robert Bellarmine a saint and a doctor of church. Bellarmine's *De Laicis* III.6 was widely cited as a scholastic proof-text for the translation account.[48]

As Leo XIII himself had pointed out, it is difficult to give a fixed meaning to the word "democracy," or to say precisely what the word "democratic" adds to the notions of republican or popular government, or to distinguish between majority rule as merely procedural or an absolute condition of a polity. Even its most ardent scholastic proponents understood that the translation theory did not imply the necessity of democracy as a concrete, historical form of government, for the theory was developed to place a limit on monarchy rather than to support a democratic regime per se. The word "democracy" is used but once in all of the letters of Pope John XXIII, and then only with qualification. Surprisingly, variations on the word "democracy" do not appear in any of the documents of the Second Vatican Council. All of this is difficult for Americans to understand because we equate the regime of limited government, natural rights, social liberties, and subsidiarity with democracy. Such was not evident to the broader Catholic world, for which democracy could imply (as it did for classical liberals) something antithetical to the bottom-up model of authority and liberty.

By the time of World War II, the question was not the bottom-up model, consisting of justiciable human rights, constitutionally limited government, and the liberties of nongovernmental societies. Rather, the question was whether democracy should be accredited (even contingently) as a more desirable form of government. A month after the invasion of Poland, Pope Pius XII rehearsed all of these principles, and declared that the state is a kind of instrument (*quasi instrumentum*), rather than an end, facilitating the "natural perfection of man."[49] In his Christmas message of 1942, he insisted that the purpose of a juridical order "is not to dominate but to serve, to help the development and increase of society's vitality in the rich multiplicity of its ends." In particular, he mentioned the need to protect "fundamental personal rights," including "one's corporeal, intellectual and moral life and especially the right to religious formation and education [and] the right to worship God in private and public life."[50] As John Courtney Murray pointed out a decade later, the constitutional issue of religious liberty was virtually settled not only with respect to the explicit statements of Pius XII, but in view of the "juridical" nature of the state. The juridical state coordinates and facilitates rather than exemplifies the perfections and actions of society. Not being an end in itself, the state cannot be sacralized nor directly assigned juridical care of religious institutions.[51] Involving as it does a very sharp distinction between the state and the body politic, the instrumental state is markedly different from the ancient conception of the *civitas* in which the offices of polity (for example, the Roman *cursus honorum*) express the very fabric of the social order. It is different, too, from the classical modern notion of the sovereign state, for which the offices of state are the organs of the body politic rather than mere instruments of an order that might have ontological grounding in their absence. In twentieth-century Catholic thought, one detects a steady deterioration of any ontological density to the state. Catholic thought increasingly tended to favor social order grounded in natural law and the transpolitical order represented by international organizations. Perhaps for this reason, a certain notion of political democracy would become more attractive.

In his Christmas address of 1944, sometimes translated as "True and False Democracy," Pope Pius XII took up the role of democracy in the postwar reordering of the world. He began on a practical note. Given the disaster and carnage of World War II, people have "awakened from a long torpor," and "rightly adopt in relation to the state an attitude that questions, criticizes, and distrusts."[52] A democratic form of government, he conceded, appears "as a postulate of nature imposed by reason itself."[53] But what is democracy? In the broad sense of term, it can be realized in monarchies as well as republics. Whatever the particular institutional form, democracy is indispensable insofar as it vests "efficient guarantees in the people itself." This is a defensive notion of democracy, one that emphasizes that the people are capacitated to put brakes on "unchecked and unlimited" state power.[54] Pius attempted to integrate two things that, until that time, were usually discussed as opposites.

On one hand, government requires a certain inorganic, even mechanical element of "checks"—an instrumental language, which Maritain insisted desubstantiates the apparatus of the state. The state is not itself a *societas perfecta* in the classical sense of term, but a "rational and juridical machine" that assists the perfections consisting in the very sociality of the body politic.[55] On this view, the state is not a thing or a substance, much less a large person imparting a soul to otherwise unorganized matter. Hence, we find three different notions of democracy, none of which is particularly strong in the institutional sense of the term: (1) democracy as a proto-institutional notion of political authority vested in the entire people; (2) democracy as a political regime containing popular elements; and (3) democracy in the defensive sense of popular checks upon government.

Society, on the other hand, is not a mere instrument. It consists of plural and intrinsic forms, not "masses" to be aggregated. Here, then, we find a distinctively modern conception of external "juridical" order distinct from, and subordinate to, a richer social ontology. This might help us to understand why the principle of subsidiarity, which has figured ever more prominently in Catholic thought since the 1930s, is not adequately represented as a question of scale (lowest possible level), and even less of devolution. Devolution, of course, implies that the state possesses powers that are recirculated to "lower" organs from the top down. At the level of public policy, subsidiarity sometimes is invoked on cost-benefit grounds to suggest that private agents and groups can accomplish public ends more efficiently. This, however, is not the principle of subsidiarity. Rather, subsidiarity presupposes that there are plural authorities and agents having their "proper" (not necessarily, lowest) duties and rights with regard to the common good. Pius XII noted that "every social activity is for its nature subsidiarity; it must serve as a support to the members of the social body and never destroy or absorb them."[56] As we said, the idea came from Taparelli, who used the term *ipotattico*, taken from the Greek *hypotaxis*, meaning the rules governing the order of clauses within a sentence. Rendered in Latin as *sub sedeo*, subsidiarity evokes the concept of auxiliary troops in the Roman legion which "sat below," ready and duty-bound to render service. Hence, it describes the right (*dritto ipotattico*) of social groups, each enjoying its own proper mode of action. While sometimes identified with the word *subsidium* (help, assistance), the point of subsidiarity is a normative structure of plural social forms, not a trickling down of power or aid.[57] To be sure, subsidiarity is often described and deployed in a defensive sense—as to what the state may *not* do or try to accomplish. But the principle is not so much a theory about state institutions, or about checks and balances, as it is an account of the pluralism in society. Once we distinguish subsidiarity from the similar but misleading notions of distribution, devolution, and aid, it is easier to grasp why it was introduced as an aspect of social justice. For Pius XII, social justice is that kind of order that ensues when each person is capacitated to "exercise his social *munus*," to contribute to the common good according to his proper office and role.[58] This may or may not require the giving of aid, the correction of a deficiency, or the removal of barriers to the performance of social duties, but what it always entails is respect for a pluriform social order.

Pope John XXIII's famous encyclical *Pacem in terris* (1963), issued at the outset of the Second Vatican Council, is a compendium of twentieth-century Catholic social, legal, and political thought. The "laws which govern man's relation with the State," he began, are not the same "as those which regulate the blind, elemental forces of the universe."[59] The natural moral law sets certain nonnegotiable norms for domestic and international political order. Of capital importance is the creation of a public order

based on three pillars. The first is that "a clear and precisely worded charter of fundamental human rights be formulated and incorporated into the
State's general constitution." This can be called the antityrannical pillar, for
the state is meant to serve human dignity, not the citizen the state. Second,
constitutions must clearly delineate the offices, competencies, and scope of
state authority, including a separation of powers. This is the antidespotic
pillar, insuring checks on any unilateral projection of state power. Third,
the state must respect the social diversity of functions. This represents the
antimonist or subsidiarity principle. The principal role of the state is to
"recognize, respect, coordinate, safeguard and promote citizens' rights and
duties."[60]

Together, the three pillars reflect what Maritain called the "instrumental" and Murray called the "juridical" nature of the state. The proposition
that the state is a facilitator rather than the substance of the common good
would be evident three years later in the Second Vatican Council's pastoral constitution, *Gaudium et spes* (1965). "The political community exists, consequently, for the sake of the common good, in which it finds its
full justification and significance, and the source of its inherent legitimacy.
Indeed, the common good embraces the sum of those conditions of the
social life whereby men, families and associations more adequately and
readily may attain their own perfection."[61]

Pacem in terris is striking for its lengthy and detailed enumeration of
rights (§§11–27). In the 1960s, international human rights covenants began to distinguish civil and political rights on one hand and social, economic, and cultural rights on the other.[62] Pope John's encyclical, issued
three years before the 1966 United Nations covenants on point, ranges
over both categories. Some represent inalienable rights (right to life, right
to pursue truth), others represent entitlements congruent with human dignity (health care, disability insurance), while still others represent political
rights (access to the political process, juridical security). It is important to
understand that this was not some sudden outbreak of rights talk. Of the
twenty-five discrete rights mentioned in the encyclical, all but three are
drawn from the teaching letters of previous popes.

But the bishops gathered at the Second Vatican Council noted that the
pope gave a rather prominent venue, near the beginning of the list, to the
right "to worship God in accordance with the right dictates of his own
conscience."[63] Put in just this way, it betokened nothing especially novel,
for such a moral right, carefully qualified, had already been enshrined in
papal letters. However, when put in the context of the rest of the encyclical,
particularly the three pillars of public order, it took on the complexion of
a civil or constitutional right that ought to be part of the positive law. This
really did represent what Murray termed the "growing end" of a tradition.

When *Pacem in terris* was issued, neither the original nor the revised schema of the council provided for an independent document on religious liberty. In hindsight, it seems truly remarkable that the topic was buried as a subsection ("freedom of cult") in an early draft of a document on ecumenism. There it remained when Pope John XXIII died in June 1963. It was not until the next year, after some three hundred and eighty amendments, that a draft was presented as a potentially independent document, and only in the fall of 1965 did it emerge a document that resembled what became known as *Dignitatis humanae*. There was nothing simple or smooth in the legislative history of *Dignitatis*; almost every sentence of its drafts was picked over until its final adoption on December 7, 1965. Some bishops objected that it confused civil toleration with a natural right. However, the great majority of bishops supported the declaration,[64] not only because of the recent papal statement in *Pacem in terris*, but also because they agreed with Murray's appeal to the "growing end" of the tradition. In the sixth and final schema Bishop de Smedt allowed a motion to insert the phrase, "in treating this religious freedom the synod intends to develop the teachings of more recent popes," in order to make clear that the council did not intend to recount and contextualize the entirety of the church's history on the issue but rather to track the trajectory of teachings from Pope Leo XIII onward.[65] Yet, even supporters of the document were divided over such details as the canonical and diplomatic implications for concordats, as well as the more substantive question of whether its emphasis ought to be biblical, philosophical, historical, or constitutional.[66]

Dignitatis is divided into two parts. The first part, "Religious Liberty Generally Considered" (§§2–8), elaborates the proposition that "the right to religious freedom has its foundation not in the subjective disposition of the person, but in his very nature" (§2).[67] The dignity of man as a knower, inclined and duty-bound to pursue, to know, and to abide by the truth establishes the ground for a right that has both personal and public aspects. Appealing to St. Thomas's discussion of divine authority over the *actus interior*, the interior act of human judgment and conscience, *Dignitatis* maintains that "no merely human power can either command or prohibit acts of this kind."[68] Coercion of conscience, then, violates human dignity *and* divine right: "Injury therefore is done to the human person and to the very order established by God for human life, if the free exercise of religion is denied in society, provided just public order is observed." The truly groundbreaking argument, however, did not concern the idea of rightful immunity from coercion of interior acts, for this issue was never in serious dispute. *Dignitatis* also contends that the right includes civil protection of external and corporate acts of religion, including not only worship (§3) but also teaching, writing, and forming religious societies for charitable, social, and cultural purposes (§4). The external dimension of the right can be limited in accord with "limits set by due public order." In this regard, Bishop Karol Wojtyla made a crucial intervention, proposing that when the state limits liberty it do so only "in conformity with the objective moral order" (§7). This was intended to prevent "public order" from being an excuse to criminalize otherwise innocent religious acts, or severely to limit such acts because they incidentally conflict with mere public policy. Yet, *Dignitatis* goes even further in providing that so long as government refrains from directing religious activity, it must "recognize and promote the religious life of its citizens" (§3). The proactive stance, of course, touches upon the historically controversial issue of religious schools (§5), but the principal point is that religious liberty should take its place within the entire galaxy of human rights—marriage, education, life, and health—as goods to be fostered and to be protected according to the citizens' equality before the law (§6).

The second part of *Dignitatis Humanae* considers "religious freedom in the light of revelation" (§§9–15), informed by the church's understanding of her own liberty. "In human society and in the face of government the Church claims freedom for herself in her character as a spiritual authority" (§13). The church's liberty is derived both from Christ (*principium fundamentale*), directly from divine mandate, and from her character as a society among men. Hence, the document speaks of a *concordia* but not a conflation of the two titles to freedom. In the civil sphere, Catholics enjoy no more (nor fewer) rights than any other citizens.[69] As citizens of the church, in their "pilgrimage through the twists and turn of human history," Catholics are under the obligation to preach the gospel as taught by the apostles and espoused by the church (§12). Society is not to be Christianized by the imposition of state law, but from below, by teaching and sanctifying. This principle was highlighted in the conciliar document, *Gaudium et spes*, where the laity's role is "to impress the divine law on the affairs of the earthly city."[70] Sacralization of society and culture is the business of society, not of the state. As for its indirect bearing upon the political order, the council emphasized the role of the laity rather than the clergy. In the Revised Code of Canon Law (1983), clergy are strictly forbidden to assume public offices "which entail a participation in the exercise of civil power."[71]

POSTCONCILIAR THEMES AND TENSIONS

At the conclusion of the ninth session of the Second Vatican Council in December 1965, three important documents were sent to Pope Paul VI for his signature: the declaration *Dignitatis humanae* on religious liberty, the decree *Ad Gentes* on missionary activity, and the pastoral constitution *Gaudium et spes*. As a triptych, these documents summarized, clarified, deepened, and extended more than a century of Catholic social, legal, and political thought and doctrine. Pope Paul VI was a disciple of Jacques Maritain, whom he wished to make a cardinal, and he certainly understood that the triptych of documents reflected Maritain's understanding of a "New Christendom," personalist, pluralist, and peregrinal in nature. Moreover, although *Dignitatis* became the occasion for a spirited and sometimes acrimonious debate, as a whole, the conciliar documents were produced in a remarkable atmosphere of unanimity. The new spirit of *aggiornamento* also gave impetus to studies and applications of the social sciences; theology was to be marked by a more biblical, historical, and practical sensibility. Social thought promised to outlast, if not improve upon the scholastic methods which shaped the revival initiated in the last century before by Pope Leo XIII.

Even so, certain tensions and loose ends in the council's work were soon evident. One problem was the enormity of the tasks of social justice, which dwarfed in scale and complexity the problems addressed by Leo XIII in *Rerum novarum* (1891) and by Pius XI in *Quadragesimo anno* (1934). The uneven pace of social, economic, and political development in different regions of the world made it difficult to access, and to make prudential recommendations for whether and where top-down and bottom-up models of authority ought to be emphasized. Particularly in the developing world of Africa, Asia, and South America, social and political turbulence as well as economic depravity made doubtful the conditions for realizing the three pillars of order spelled out in John XXIII's *Pacem in terris* (justiciable human rights, the juridical and limited state, and subsidiarity). These pillars of order represent a long and hard-won set of lessons drawn from European and North American experience. It was there, of course, that the modern state, economies, sciences, technologies, revolutions, and ideologies were not only created but also reconsidered in searching ways after the two world wars. Naturally, Catholic understanding of *this* "modernity" would be easier than crafting a social theory adequate to the contingencies of the non-Western and the developing world. Like their secular counterparts, conservative and progressive Catholic theorists often debate the weight which ought to attach to political, juridical, and economic rights such as those delineated in Pope John Paul II's *Centesimus annus* (1991) versus the cultural and developmental rights spelled out in an encyclical like *Sollicitudo rei socialis* (1987). This kind of debate, however, usually misses the most salient point, which is that the church's own history provided the occasion to work out, by trial and error, a nuanced account of the political and juridical track, while the social theory for the developing world would have to be a work in progress. Given the rapid expansion of Catholicism in Africa and Asia, it is reasonable to expect that in the future more of Catholic social thought and doctrine will be shaped by the problems and crises in that part of the world.

At the time of the election of Pope John Paul II in 1978, problems began to appear not in the Third World but in the West—interestingly, along the perimeter of issues that otherwise represented some of the Second Vatican Council's greatest accomplishments. These included clarification of the triadic relationship of church, state, and society, the appropriation of the principled understanding of the juridical state, the principled argument for religious liberty, the cross-fertilization of Catholic anthropology with the argument for universal human rights based on human dignity, and evangelization from below, indirectly shaping society without resort to a traditional Constantinian armature.

A few months after his election, John Paul II went to the Conference of Latin American Bishops at Puebla, Mexico. Latin America could hardly be regarded as a backwater of the Catholic intellectual world. It was for the Latin American situation that Spanish and Portuguese Thomists had made their first "modern" arguments about natural rights during the sixteenth century. In many ways relevant to the history of social, legal, and political thought and doctrine, Latin America paralleled the European experience—in the problem of state establishments and patronal rights that so bedeviled modern Catholicism, in the revolutions and process of state formation during the nineteenth century, and in the proliferation during the twentieth-century of right-wing and left-wing ideologies. From the time of Pope Leo XIII onward, several encyclicals were devoted to problems in that region, especially in Mexico. Although Latin America did not suffer the devastation of the two world wars or (aside from a few exceptions) the grip of totalitarian regimes, it did share many of the crises that formed the problematic context for Catholic social thought in Europe.

From one point of view, the Second Vatican Council provided an impetus in some ways tailor-made for the Latin American thinkers: the bottom-up model of evangelization and social change (for the Latin thinkers, "the view from below"), the emphasis on lay action and on the solidarity of the body politic rather than the apparatus of the state, and the decided preference for a pastoral and biblically informed language rather than a more abstract scholasticism all favored something like a liberation theology. Indeed, Pope John Paul II and the liberationists shared a commitment to a biblical and eschatological mode of discourse. Why, then, did Latin American liberation theology cause such controversy?

In part, and indeed in very serious part, the problem was theological and ecclesiological. Liberation theologians, even the more moderate such as Gustavo Gutiérrez (see chapter 6), engaged a scriptural exegesis strongly tinctured with Marxian themes of social conflict, class analysis, and a "preferential option for the poor" that was exclusionary in nature— exclusionary, that is, not only with regard to the scope of justice and the common good in the civil sphere, but also with regard to the meaning of ecclesial solidarity and the eschatological kingdom inaugurated by Christ. Though the "base communities" (*comunidades eclesiais de base*) emerged before the Second Vatican Council, and, indeed, before any controversy over liberation theology had broken out, by the late 1960s some of these communities seemed a strange and, in Rome's view, alarming amalgam of political, ecclesial, and revolutionary praxis. Rome eventually conceded, with qualifications, the importance of the base communities and the principle of a "preferential option for the poor." Some liberation theologians, Gutiérrez in particular, moderated their rhetoric about class warfare and violence and clarified their scriptural exegesis. Putting to one side the politics of Roman disciplinary authority, which so preoccupies and intrigues American observers, there are aspects of the Latin challenge that are likely to outlast the controversy of the 1970s and 1980s. At the nub of the issue is their suspicion of, and in the early phase of the movement, a rejection of the so-called distinction of planes. This called into question the sinews and arteries of the scholastic-informed social theory that was nearly two centuries in the making.

For Gutiérrez and other Latin thinkers, the distinction of planes usually meant, in the first place, the sharp distinction between sacred and secular, and correlatively between grace and nature. One may doubt that, on Thomistic grounds, sacred-and-secular accurately represent grace-and-nature. For nature is created and thus cannot exactly correspond to what moderns mean by "secular," that is, a sphere emptied of any theological referents. Moreover, the desacralized state never meant for neo-Thomists a desacralized human nature stripped of the dignities of creaturehood. The Catholic natural rights tradition, including the right declared in *Dignitatis humanae*, depended upon Thomas's definition of natural law as the creature's participation in the eternal law. This constituted the metaphysical ground for inalienable rights. Nevertheless, it is true that gratuity of grace, in distinction to the order of creation, is a signature position of Thomism.

As we have seen, neo-Thomists introduced analogous distinctions for the purpose of social, legal, and political thought. Most important is the distinction between the state, civil society, and the church. While the triadic relationship is subject to certain contingent variations, it is grounded in anthropological, moral, and theological principles. Maritain's "New Christendom" envisaged a fixity of spheres allowing a distinction between a "civic person" and a baptized member of a "kingly people"—each overlapping in a social sphere irreducible to either state of ecclesiastical government.[72] In essence, this is John Courtney Murray's position; and, insofar as it entered into social doctrine via papal letters and conciliar decrees, it was more than a mere social theory.

But there is one other distinction that perhaps comes closer to the discontent of the Latin American liberationist theologians. In grafting Thomistic principles to modern constitutionalism, the neo-Thomists brought in tow a distinctly liberal commitment to distinguishing law and politics. The purpose of the rule of law is not the grand task of doing justice (in general); its more specific purpose is to police the political. On this view, it is crucial to protect the boundary between law and ordinary politics. This purpose is institutionally embodied in the division of state powers, a point underscored by John XXIII, who insisted that it is "in keeping with human nature" to distinguish precisely the judicial from the executive and legislative functions.[73] In *Centesimus annus* (1991), John Paul II equated the "rule of law" with such a division of "powers."[74] Both popes discuss it in terms of checking political actions detrimental to rights. On the other hand, a strict distinction between law and politics is also embodied in the habits of the political and legal culture. In a liberal polity, one must think not only of the justice to be done but also the kinds of justice that can be accomplished in view of the rule of law. Latin American liberation theologians challenged this admittedly narrow conception of how the political and juridical orders stand to the problem of justice. Especially in the context of chronic poverty and despotic regimes, they called for a broader conception of a politics of emancipatory praxis. The rule of law too easily freezes the injustices embedded in the social, political, and economic spheres. Rather than constitute a defensive measure against the wiles of the state, the rule of law insures that political power cannot reach social injustice.

Their challenge was not merely a dispute with Maritain. It ran against the deeper historical grain of Catholic social, legal, and political thought. As we discussed earlier, Catholicism in Europe stumbled out of the nineteenth century with a visceral reaction against nationalism, modern notions of state sovereignty, and puppet churches. By the middle of the twentieth century, there existed a broad and deep consensus that the church should avoid what may be called "regime politics." This is why Catholic social theorists and the Second Vatican Council itself moved so decisively in favor of a liberal model of limited government and human rights—a kind of all-purpose regime the essentials of which need not be debated.

The two world wars and the shadow of totalitarianism had sobered both the church and the democracies, making plausible a convergence of perspective, based on the pillars surveyed and recommended by John XXIII. Considering their respective strengths, Catholic thought was ahead of the curve of the ontology of human rights and subsidiarity, while the secular democracies bore the heritage of a practical, constitutional wisdom. The more thoughtful Catholic thinkers were not in doubt that this entailed a weakening and diffusion of political passion; but this was the price to be paid for curbing *l'intégrisme* of the right and the left. The political order would not be the site of a sudden and profound conversion of culture. Writing "in homage to the people of France" in 1944, Maritain urged a cessation of the regime politics that for two centuries had been the national sport of France. There will be "no recovery of Paradise by revolution," he said, but rather a slow progress by "the carrying over of the structures of conscience and the structures of human life to better states."[75] A deep politicization of church-state relations, which meant a more radical understanding of church and politics as facets of an emergent and visible "kingdom," is just what European and North American Catholicism attempted to defuse. Even if the liberationists had made no disputable claims in scriptural exegesis or ecclesiology, their hermeneutic of suspicion regarding the rule of law would have triggered problems not only with Rome, but also with the broader consensus of Catholic social thought in the West. For reasons that we shall now consider, it is likely that at least part of their critique will resurface in the future evolution of Catholic social thought.

If the Latin American liberation theologians were intent upon a less abstract conception of politics and justice, the Northern Atlantic states moved in the opposite direction, toward an increasingly more restrictive understanding of what can count as "public reason." It is not quite right to think of the problem as a liberal versus neoliberal dispute over the size of government and the degree of state involvement in the economic sector, for Catholic social, legal, and political thought and the actual practices and policies of Western democracies admit of considerable variation on these issues. It consists rather in the tension between the dignitarian concept of human rights and the rule of law, the first and second pillars of order proposed by John XXIII in *Pacem in terris*. Catholic thinkers assumed that the first is organically related to the second. The rule of law is supposed to protect inalienable human rights from the transgressions of society and of the state. However, Catholic thought did not reckon seriously enough with the possibility that the rule of law could also mean state neutrality on the ontological grounds of rights, that the state is not entitled to adopt what John Paul II calls a "correct anthropology." Nor did it anticipate the more radical and perplexing position that immunity from a "correct anthropology" is itself a justiciable natural right.

From the outset, the pillars of justiciable natural rights and the rule of law stood in some tension. Rendering justiciable the ever-increasing lists of human rights will necessarily test the jurisprudential institutions of relatively healthy polities. Moreover, architects of the postwar human rights declarations and covenants, such as the 1948 Universal Declaration of Human Rights, diligently circumvented the question of how the rights are to be grounded. The philosopher-diplomat Charles Malik, a Lebanese Catholic who had something more than an amateur's knowledge of Catholic social thought, guided drafts of the Universal Declaration through the shoals of philosophical disagreements. In order to reach a "practical agreement among men who are theoretically opposed to one another,"[76] Maritain vigorously defended the rationale of this tactic. "A genuine democracy," he wrote, "cannot impose on its citizens or demand from them, as a condition for their belonging to the city, any philosophic or any religious creed."[77] For Maritain—and, generally, for the Catholic tradition—neither a contingent dissensus about philosophical groundings nor the principle prohibiting imposition of dogmas ruled out a fairly substantial practical agreement about human dignity and about those rights virtually convertible with the idea of dignity. Interestingly, Maritain considered the right to life a relatively unproblematic inalienable right.[78] Twenty-five years later, this position seemed to be upended, particularly, but not only, by the adoption of abortion rights.

In *Evangelium vitae* (1995), Pope John Paul II tells the story as one of "betrayal," a word used six times in the document. The constitutional democracies refused to live up to their end of the bargain. The modern idea of the juridical state never promised that the state can be an agent that sanctifies men or perfects the entirety of their moral virtue. It did, however, promise (it was their "boast," he adds) to protect fundamental human rights, especially life. Speaking ominously of a "conspiracy" against human rights, he accuses states of having reversed "the long historical process leading to the discovery of human rights."[79] States are poisoning the "culture of rights," even violating the "principles of their own constitutions."[80] The pope was especially baffled by the fact that abortion and euthanasia should become legal not only by the inadvertence or timidity of legislatures, but also by recognition of such acts as human rights.[81] John Paul II cited Acts 5:29 ("we must obey God rather than men") no fewer than eight times to drive home this point. He has also made striking use of Exodus 1:17. Recounting the story of the Egyptian midwives who defied Pharaoh because, as the scripture notes, "they feared God," the pope urged resistance to the temporal powers' usurpation of God's authority over life and death.[82] The language is reminiscent of papal letters during the church-state crisis of the nineteenth century.

It would be an exaggeration to suggest that Catholic social, legal, and political doctrine and the Western democracies are divided on every issue of importance. Regarding the death penalty, limits on justifiable war, and a mixed economy that includes economic entitlements, there is little difference of opinion between Catholic social doctrine and Western democracies (the United States notwithstanding). Even so, there is a serious difference of perspective with respect to the nature and scope of public reason. In *Centesimus annus*, Pope John Paul II observed, "Authentic democracy is possible only in a State ruled by law, and on the basis of a correct conception of the human person."[83] It might be argued that, for historically contingent reasons, polities do not have consensus about the anthropological groundings, and in any event the correction of that deficiency will have to be achieved, as Maritain and Murray put it, indirectly, through evangelization and education of society itself. This is not an entirely satisfying answer, for as John Paul goes on to note in *Centesimus*, those who are "convinced that they know the truth and firmly adhere to it are considered unreliable from a democratic point of view."[84] If, indeed, the state is required in principle to exclude moral and anthropological truths from politics, if even a convergence of opinion achieved in the social sphere is denied access to law on the ground that the state may not, in a way consistent with the principle of equality, endorse any particular moral anthropology, then the scaffolding of Catholic social thought slowly erected since the nineteenth century is *practically* thrown into question. Here, then, is a mirrored reversal of the challenge posed by the liberation thinkers, who complained that the liberal-democratic model is far too restrictive for purposes of social justice.

Such are some of the important tensions and themes of Catholic social, legal, and social thought since the Second Vatican Council. Above all, they call to our attention a continuity of problems stretching back to the pontificate of Leo XIII. The church-state issue; the nature and scope of the social contract; the ontological structure of social forms; the kind of justice achievable in the civil community; and the relative weighting of philosophical, historical, and theological methods for formulating social and moral theory, are all questions that have undergone historical permutation yet retained a distinctly familiar structure. Jacques Maritain contended that every epoch of Catholicism has its own "historic sky." The continuity of problems suggests that the "modern" period has not been eclipsed, but continues to test the mettle of the Catholic mind in troubling and interesting ways.

NOTES

1. *Gaudet Mater* (October 11, 1962), *Sacrosanctum Oecumenicum Concilium Vatican II, Constitutiones, Decreta, Declarationes* (Vatican City: Libreria Editrice Vaticana, 1993), 858.

2. Letter to Cardinal Fornari, "Errors of Our Times" (June 19, 1852), in Juan Donoso Cortés, *Selected Works*, trans. and ed. Jeffrey P. Johnson (Westport, Conn.: Greenwood Press, 2000), 110.

3. Jacques Maritain, *The Things That Are Not Caesar's*, trans. J. F. Scanlan (London: Sheed & Ward, 1930), 74.

4. For the legal structure and history the *Patronato Real*, one can rely on studies by W. Eugene Shiels, *King and Church: The Rise and Fall of the Patronato Real* (Chicago: Loyola University Press, 1961), containing important legal instruments in the original languages and English translation, and J. Lloyd Mecham, *Church and State in Latin America: A History of Politico-Ecclesiastical Relations* (Chapel Hill: University of North Carolina Press, 1966).

5. *Orthodoxe fidei* (November 13, 1486); original in Shiels, *King and Church*, 277–282.

6. Concordat of Bologna (1516), in *Church and State Through the Centuries: A Collection of Historic Documents with Commentaries*, trans. and ed. Sidney Z. Ehler and John B. Morrall (Westminster, Md.: Newman Press, 1954), 134–144.

7. *Cum primum* (June 9, 1832), §1, 3, in *Acta Gregorii Papae XVI*, ed. Antonius Bernasconi (Rome: S. C. de Propaganda Fide, 1901–1904), 1:143–144. Hereinafter and for similar collections, citations are to the section (§) where applicable, *Acta* volume, and page.

8. Joseph de Maistre, *The Pope*, translation of the 1819 edition of *Du Pape* by Aeneas M. Dawson (London: C. Dolman, 1850), III.4, 277.

9. Id., II.12 at 199, III.2 at 255.

10. Notable works in this genre include Félicité Robert de Lamennais's notes on the history of the Gregorian reform, *Tradition de l'église sur l'institution des évêques* (1814); Dom Guéranger, *Affaire de la Légende De Saint Grégoire VII*, in *Institutions liturgiques*, vol. II, chap. XXI (1841); Henri Lacordaire, *Éloge Funèbre de Daniel O'Connell* (February 10, 1848); John Henry Newman, *Present Position of Catholics in England* (1851); Wilhelm Emmanuel von Ketteler, *Freedom, Authority, and the Church* (1862), XXV; Donoso Cortés, "Errors of Our Times"; and Antonio Rosmini, *Delle cinque piaghe della Santa Chiesa* (1832, 1848), a scholarly but passionate compendium of arguments against the *ius patronatus*.

11. Charles de Montalembert, Malines Address (August 20, 1863), in J. F. Maclear, *Church and State in the Modern Age: A Documentary History* (New York: Oxford University Press, 1995), 162.

12. Eusebius's *Vita* 3.12.3, 4.24.

13. Lord Odo Russell to Earl of C. (March 7, 1870), in *The Roman Question, Extracts from the Despatches of Odo Russell from Rome, 1858–1870*, ed. Noel Blakiston (London: Chapman and Hall, 1962), 404.

14. Speech in Chamber of Deputies on July 10, 1868, in Émile Ollivier, *L'Église et l'État au Concile du Vatican*, 3d ed. (Paris: Garnier Frères, 1877), 1:400.

15. Ibid.

16. Ministre des Affaires Etranges à M le marquis de Banneville (February 20, 1870), appendix II in Ollivier, *L'Église et l'État*, 1:551–556.

17. *Onorare le ceneri* (March 1, 1892), *Acta* XII, 384–386.

18. Luigi Stuzo, *Church and State* (New York: Longmans, Green, 1939), 563.

19. Ibid., 385.

20. Maritain, *The Things That Are Not Caesar's*, 16.

21. John Courtney Murray, "The Problem of Religious Freedom," in *Religious Liberty: Catholic Struggles with Pluralism*, ed. J. Leon Hooper, S.J. (Louisville, Ky.: Westminster John Knox Press, 1993), 165, 188.

22. Pius XI, *Quadragesimo anno* (May 15, 1931) §§18–21, *Acta Apostolicae Sedis: Commentarium officiale* (Vatican City: Typis Polyglottis Vaticanis, 1909–) (hereafter AAS) 23, 182–184. On the emergence of the term *doctrina*, see Mary Elsbernd, "Papal Statements on Rights: A Historical Contextual Study of Encyclical Teaching From Pius VI–Pius XI (1791–1939)" (Ph.D. diss., Catholic University of Louvain, 1985), 587 n. 1.

23. *Dei Filius* (April 24, 1870), chap. IV, in *Decrees of the Ecumenical Councils*, ed. Norman P. Tanner (Washington, D.C.: Georgetown University Press, 1990).

24. *Dei Filius*, chap. 2; Gerald A. McCool, S.J., *Catholic Theology in the Nineteenth Century* (New York: Seabury, 1977), 219.

25. *Inscrutabile Dei* (April 21, 1878) §13, *Acta Leonis* 1:53–54.

26. *Aeterni Patris* (August 4, 1879) §29, *Acta Leonis* 1:280.

27. Walter T. Odell, "The Political Theory of Civiltà Cattolica From 1850 to 1870" (Ph.D. diss., Georgetown University, 1969).

28. *Summa theologiae* I–II, 105.1.

29. See his letter *Graves de communi* (January 18, 1901), on Christian democracy. Leo worried that Catholic associations would become politicized in the fashion of socialist parties.

30. *Au Milieu* (February 16, 1892), §17, *Acta Leonis* 12:31.

31. *Summa theologiae* I–II, 94.5.

32. On the issue of subsidiarity and education, he recommends Taparelli's *Saggio teoretico di Diritto Naturale* (*A Theoretical Treatise on Natural Right, Based on Fact*) (1840–43), "a work never sufficiently praised and recommended to university students," *Divini illius* (December 31, 1929), AAS 22:65.

33. *Studiorum ducem* (June 29, 1923), §20, AAS 15:319.

34. *Mit brennender Sorge* (March 14, 1937), *Divine Redemptoris* (March 19, 1937), and *Firmissimam constantiam* (March 28, 1937).

35. The phrase "from below upwards" was used by Pius XII in the 1945 "Allocution to the Sacred Roman Rota," AAS 37:256–262, originally to affirm the protodemocratic nature of the body politic according to translation theory (see chapter 3, this volume). Maritain was struck by how it summarized his own work and added it to his 1968 revision of his book *Integral Humanism* (see the following note), n. 10 at 251.

36. Jacques Maritain, *Integral Humanism, Freedom in the Modern World, and A Letter on Independence*, ed. Otto Bird, in *The Collected Works of Jacques Maritain* (Notre Dame, Ind.: University of Notre Dame Press, 1996), 11:150–151.

37. Ibid., 331.

38. Ibid., 237–239.

39. Ibid., 261–266.

40. Jacques Maritain, *Peasant of the Garonne: An Old Man Questions Himself About the Present Time*, trans. Michael Cuddihy and Elizabeth Hughes (Toronto: Macmillan, 1969), 12.

41. Jacques Maritain, *Man and the State* (Washington, D.C.: Catholic University of America Press, 1998), 94.

42. *Divini illius Magistri* §37, citing *Pierce v. Society of Sisters* (1925), 268 U.S., at 534–535.

43. See, e.g., *Divini Redemptoris* (1937), §27; AAS 29:78–79. On the emergence of lists of such rights in papal letters, see Elsbernd, "Papal Statements," 617–622.

44. Originally issued in Spanish, *Nos es muy conocida*, but in the Roman typical edition, *Firmissimam constantiam* (March 28, 1937), §28; AAS 29:196–197. Pius begins to describe rights also in terms of *munera*, perhaps best translated "gifts of service." The word *munus* highlights the inherently social nature of an office, role, or obligation in which rights are grounded. For a survey of relation between rights and *munera* in modern Catholic thought, see Russell Hittinger, "Social Roles and Ruling Virtues," *Annales theologici* 16 (2002): 385–408.

45. *Graves de communi* (1901), *Acta Leonis* 21:3–20.

46. Thomas P. Neill, "The Concordats of Pope Pius XI: Their Role in Adapting Church Relationship to the State" (Ph.D. diss., University of Notre Dame, 1939).

47. Yves R. Simon, *Philosophy of Democratic Government* (Chicago: University of Chicago Press, 1951), chap. 3.

48. This is so, although Bellarmine frequently stressed the historical and theological importance of monarchy, which is not ruled out by translation theory. Among American Catholics, the idea of a democratic Bellarmine reached mythic proportions with the publication of Gaillard Hunt's "Cardinal Bellarmine and the Virginia Bill of Rights," *Catholic Historical Review* (October 1917): 276–289. The legend that the Virginia Bill of Rights relied on Bellarmine was debunked by David S. Schaff, "The Bellarmine-Jefferson Legend and the Declaration of Independence," *Papers of the American Society of Church History* 8 (1928): 239–276. On the other hand, there can be no doubt that American Catholics were ahead of the Europeans in using various neo-Thomisms in support of democratic government. See, e.g., Archbishop John Ireland's "The Catholic Church and Civil Society," delivered at the Third Plenary Council of Baltimore (November 10, 1884), in J. Ireland, *The Church and Modern Society: Lectures and Addresses* (Chicago: D. H. McBride, 1896). Anticipating the work of John Courtney Murray, Ireland weaves together Thomas, Bellarmine, and the recent letters of Leo XIII to establish that scholastic theory provides a superior philosophical foundation for democratic institutions.

49. *Summi Pontificatus* (October 20, 1939) §59, AAS 31:433. The notion of an "instrumental" state was popularized several years later by Jacques Maritain in *Man and the State*, 13.

50. *Con sempre nuova* (December 24, 1942), AAS 35:19. The inalienable right of religious consciences was presented by Pius XI, invariably in response to totalitarian regimes: *Mit brennender Sorge*, §31, AAS 29:160; *Non abbiamo bisogno* (June 29, 1931), §§40–41, AAS 23:301–302; *Firmissimam constantiam* (1937), §26, AAS 29:196. Neither of the Pian statements suggested an all-purpose right of conscience, but rather religious conscience.

51. John Courtney Murray, "The Declaration on Religious Freedom: A Moment in Its Legislative History," in *Religious Liberty: An End and a Beginning* (New York: Macmillan, 1966), 13.

52. *Benignitas et humanitas* (December 24, 1944), AAS 37:11–12.

53. Ibid., 13.

54. Ibid., 17.

55. Maritain, *Man and the State*, 19.

56. *La elevatezza e la nobilità* (February 20, 1946), AAS 38:144.

57. The history and philosophy of subsidiarity are covered with unusual clarity by Thomas C. Behr, "Luigi Taparelli D'Azeglio, S.J. (1793–1862) and the Development of Scholastic Natural-Law Thought as a Science of Society and Politics," *Journal of Markets & Morality* 6 (Spring 2003): 99–115.

58. *Divini redemptoris* (March 19, 1937), §51, AAS 29:92.

59. *Pacem in terris* (April 11, 1963), §6, AAS 55:258.

60. Ibid., §§75–77, AAS 55:278ff.

61. *Gaudium et spes* (December 7, 1965), §74.

62. U.N. International Covenant on Civil and Political Rights and U.N. International Covenant on Economic, Social and Cultural Rights, both adopted in 1966.

63. *Pacem in terris*, §14, AAS 55:260, quoting Leo XIII's *Libertas praetantissimum*, *Acta* 8 (June 20, 1888), 237ff.

64. *Declaratio*, which differs from a *constitutio* and a *decretum*. Constitutions and decrees have binding force upon the whole church. A declaration, on the other hand, is reserved for matters and persons who are not under the public law of the church. Hence, the document on non-Christian religions (*Nostra aetate*, 1965) is called a *declaratio*.

65. The discussion of development on November 19, 1965, is contained in *Acta Synodalia Sacrosancti Concilii Oecumenici Vaticani Secundi* IV, part VI, Congregatio Generalis CLXIV (Vatican City: Typis Polyglottis Vaticanis, 1978). The phrase on "recent popes" is in *Dignitatis humanae*, §1, and the trail of citations to the popes is at §2, n. 2. For Murray's argument, see *Religious Liberty*, 167–174.

66. Jérôme Hamer, "Historique du texte de la Déclaration," *La liberté religieuse*, *Unam Sanctam*, ed. J. Hamer and Y. Congar (Paris: Éditions du Cerf, 1967), 60:53–110. A table of votes on schemata at each stage is at pages 106–108.

67. *Gaudium et spes*, §16, where conscience is said to be a *sacrarium*, a holy place: "For man has in his heart a law inscribed by God. His dignity lies in observing

this law, and by it he will be judged. His conscience is man's most secret core, and his sanctuary. There he is alone with God [*in quo solus est cum Deo*] whose voice echoes in his depths."

68. DH §3 n. 3, citing *Summa theologiae* I–II, q. 91, a. 1.

69. DH has almost nothing to say about "establishment" in the American sense of the term. It rules out, of course, any species of regalism and of the *cuius regio* doctrine, which marked establishment in the Catholic countries into the nineteenth century. DH §1 states that the document concerns religious liberty, and "therefore leaves untouched traditional Catholic doctrine on the moral duty of men and societies toward the true religion and toward the one Church of Christ." In §6 we find a passing reference to "circumstances where one religion is given "special civil recognition" (presumably, concordatory countries), which adds that "the rights of other citizens and religious communities should be "recognized and made effective in practice." On the silence of *DH* regarding establishment and disestablishment, see Russell Hittinger, "Dignitatis Humanae, Religious Liberty, and Ecclesiastical Self-Government," in *The First Grace* (Wilmington, Del.: ISI Books, 2003), 215–241.

70. *Gaudium et spes*, §43, and the parallel text at *Lumen gentium* §31.

71. *Codex Iuris Canonici* (1983), can. 285, §3.

72. Jacques Maritain, *Christianity and Democracy* (New York: Arno, 1980), 31, 46.

73. *Pacem in terris*, §68, AAS 55:276.

74. *Centesimus annus* (May 1, 1991), §44, AAS 83:848. He attributes this idea to Leo XIII, but in papal letters it surfaces for the first time in John XXIII's *Pacem in terris*. The premise that a division of powers is the rule of law, of course, was asserted in article 16 of the Declaration of the Rights of Man and Citizen (August 26, 1789).

75. Ibid., 30.

76. Jacques Maritain, *Man and the State*, 76.

77. Ibid., 110.

78. Ibid., 101.

79. *Evangelium vitae* (March 25, 1995), §12, AAS 87:414; §18, 420.

80. Ibid., §4, 405.

81. Ibid.

82. Ibid., §73, 486.

83. *Centesimus annus* (1991), §46, AAS 83:850.

84. Ibid.

[CHAPTER 2]

Pope Leo XIII (1810–1903)

RUSSELL HITTINGER

Having barely survived surgery for the removal of a diseased cyst, the ninety-year-old Leo XIII welcomed 350,000 pilgrims to Rome for the Jubilee of 1900. Measured against the past century, the event was a success by virtue of the fact that it took place at all. The jubilees of 1800 and 1850 had been cancelled because the popes were either kidnapped or in exile. Pius IX refused to call a jubilee in 1875 to protest the capture of Rome by the armies of the House of Savoy.

With this history in mind, Pope Leo wrote two encyclicals to put the troubled century into perspective. In *Tametsi futura*, he characterized his pontificate as "difficult and anxious."[1] What "experience constantly shows," he contemplated, is that "all our life on earth is the truthful and exact image of a pilgrimage."[2] In *Annum sacrum*, Leo dedicated the human race to the Sacred Heart of Jesus:

> When the Church, in the days immediately succeeding her institution, was oppressed beneath the yoke of the Caesars, a young Emperor saw in the heavens a cross, which became at once the happy omen and cause of the glorious victory that soon followed. And now, today, behold another blessed and heavenly token is offered to our sight—the most Sacred Heart of Jesus, with a cross rising from it and shining forth with dazzling splendor amidst flames of love. In that Sacred Heart all our hopes should be placed, and from it the salvation of men is to be confidently besought.[3]

Coming just a few years before the tattered monarchies of Europe committed cultural and military suicide in the trenches of World War I, Leo's admonition was prescient. Catholics should prepare themselves for a suffering king rather than a Constantine.

Leo's life bestrode one of the most traumatic centuries in the history of the papacy and the Catholic Church. At the time of Leo's birth in 1810, the French were holding Pope Pius VII, the second pope in less than a decade that they had kidnapped. One of Leo's earliest memories was the triumphant return of Pius to Rome after the fall of Napoleon. Though Leo was a man of aristocratic bearing, one who maintained the ambience of an old-world court inside the Vatican, modern gadgets such as telephones, recording devices, and elevators intrigued him. When he died in 1903, he was buried in the Lateran next to Innocent III, the very epitome of the medieval papal monarchy. Yet Leo spent the last decade of his pontificate trying to reconcile French Catholics to republican government. Before we study his teachings, we need to consider the situation of Catholic Christianity in his own time and place.

ECCLESIASTICAL CAREER

Gioacchino Vincenzo Pecci was born on March 2, 1810, at Carpineto in the Latium region, which lies along the ancient road connecting Rome and Naples. For a millennium, this area was part of the Papal States. The Congress of Vienna (1815) restored Latium, then under the sway of Napoleon, to papal governance. Pecci spent most of his adult life as a cleric helping to govern these states, even though he would never be able to do so as pope. Indeed, he would be the first pope since the eighth century not to inherit the papal temporalities in Italy.

Pecci attended the Jesuit college in Viterbo (1818) and then the Roman College (1824). His family background in minor nobility qualified him for admission to the Accademia dei Nobili Ecclesiastici (1832), where he pursued the career track of a Roman lawyer and diplomat. Pecci's training at the Accademia was typical for young men who sought careers in the *prelature*—a quasi-lay bureaucracy governing the Papal States. The prelates were entitled to wear violet-colored ecclesiastical dress and to be called *monsignori*. Some prelates, like Cardinal Rampolla, secretary of state under Pius IX, rose to the top of the papal bureaucracy without ever receiving major orders. Others, like Pecci, went on to become priests and bishops.

Although the Papal States constituted the oldest standing temporal monarchy in Europe, their administration at this time was comically incompetent. Having no steady policy of taxation or military conscription, the Papal States could not develop into a modern polity capable of competing with the great state-making regimes north of the Alps. After 1815 the papacy depended upon Austrian or French armies for military protection. In their waning years, the Papal States' only claim to fame was having more opera houses than any country in Europe and possessing the last crop of castrati singers.

Ordained a priest in 1837, Pecci spent forty years as an administrator, diplomat, priest, and bishop in the papal dominions. He fought brigands, established banks and cooperatives for farmers, built hospitals and schools, and supervised the construction of roads. In January 1843, Pope Gregory XVI made Pecci nuncio to Brussels, where he was able to see firsthand the Industrial Revolution in northern Europe. Consecrated archbishop of Perugia in 1846, he spent the next thirty-two years as a reformer in Umbria, notably in the field of education. In 1872 he established the Accademia di S. Tommaso. Appointing his brother Giuseppe Pecci and the Dominican Tommaso Zigliara to the faculty, Bishop Pecci hoped to build a Scholastic curriculum of studies. Although there were faint stirrings of Thomism in Italy at this time, it enjoyed only a marginalized position in the Roman schools. The revival of Catholic intellectual life along Thomistic lines was the great passion of Pecci's life—an unusual passion for a pastor and administrator. Immediately after becoming pope, he elevated his brother and Zigliara to the College of Cardinals to spearhead an international reform of Catholic education on the model of St. Thomas Aquinas.

Pecci was made a cardinal in 1853. The laicist Piedmontese government tested his mettle by occupying Perugia in 1859. Pecci protested the government's suppression of religious orders, absorption of marriage and education by state law, confiscation of church property, and induction of the clergy into the army. Cardinal Pecci managed to stay out of jail even while keeping his diocese intact. As the Papal States crumbled between 1860 and 1870, he remained the loyal servant of Pope Pius IX. Pecci supported, and had a minor role in formulating, the *Syllabus errorum* (1864). On matters political, he was a diplomat and pragmatist, but he rarely conceded ground that he thought rightfully belonged to the church. Heads of state would soon learn that Pecci was the wiliest pope in centuries.

In 1877 Pius IX called Pecci to Rome, where he was made Cardinal Camerlengo. When Pius died on February 7, 1878, Pecci had the duty of conducting the ceremony that attested the pope's death. The cardinal carried out this task not by applying the silver hammer to the deceased pope's forehead, but rather by putting a veil over Pius's face and lifting it three times with the query, "Giovanni, Giovanni, Giovanni?"[4] For once, the voluble pope had no retort. Pecci was not the front-runner on the list of *papabili* at the conclave of 1878; that dubious position went to Cardinal Bilio, one of the chief architects of the controversial *Syllabus errorum* (1864). But France, Austria, Spain, and Portugal still laid claim to the so-called *ius exclusivae* (the right of vetoing a papal candidate), and they indicated that Bilio was not satisfactory. Indeed, such were the political pressures on the conclave that Cardinal Manning urged the cardinals to retire to Malta under the protection of the British governor. They resolved to stay at the Vatican, where, on the third vote, Pecci was elected on February 30, 1878.

When asked what name he would take, he replied, "That of Leo XIII, out of the deference and gratitude I have always had for Leo XII and the veneration of Saint Leo I which I have had since my youth."[5] Pope Leo I (Leo Magnus) was one of only two popes to be recognized as a Doctor of the Church, and the first pope to be buried in St. Peter's. Perhaps Pecci was inspired by the magnificent marble relief by Alessandro Algardi in St. Peter's, a work that depicted Leo I confronting Attila the Hun outside Rome in 452, for Pecci made a point of mentioning this event in his first encyclical.[6] Leo would take as his pontifical coat of arms the heraldic depiction of a pine tree, two fleurs-de-lis, and a comet, the latter interpreted by his contemporaries as a confirmation of the so-called prophesy of Malachy that this pope would be *lumen in coelo*, a light in the heavens.[7]

A PASSION FOR TEACHING

No one expected the sixty-eight-year-old pope to preside over the 1900 Jubilee. He was an interim pope, elected to solve the dispute between the church and the Italian state. As it turned out, he never resolved this problem. Popes for another fifty years, in protest against the loss of papal dominions, would call themselves a "prisoner in the Vatican." Nor did anyone anticipate that Pecci, who had never written a scholarly treatise, would have the energy and composure to write some 110 encyclicals and other teaching letters—by far the most prodigious output of teaching on the part of any modern pope.[8] Within twelve months of his election, Leo had already issued four teaching letters.

Leo's letters reveal a relentless drive to diagnose historical contingencies in the light of first principles. Leo did not invent the genre of encyclical letters, nor was he the first pope to make encyclical letters an ordinary means of communication with the universal Church. His predecessor, Pius IX, wrote sixty-six letters during his turbulent pontificate. Leo so perfected the teaching letter that it became a new pedagogical art, best described as applied doctrine. At the same time, his letters effect in the reader a speculative insight that is deeper and more synthetic than that produced by mere policy statements on issues of the day. In this respect, Leo was a public intellectual who took full advantage of the greatest bully pulpit in the world. His achievement is all the more remarkable in that he did not begin writing these letters until he was almost seventy years old. All of his successors have tried, with varying degrees of success, to reduplicate the Leonine art of teaching.

Why did Leo XIII write so many letters? For one thing, the technology of the modern media made it possible for a papal letter to be read in every capital of Europe within hours of its publication. William George Ward (1812–82), the papalist editor of the *Dublin Review,* famously said, "I should like a new papal Bull every morning with my *Times* and breakfast."[9] Leo understood Europe's newfound and seemingly boundless appetite for the newspaper, and he used modern media to transform the arcane papal "bull" into the modern encyclical, which aimed at conveying teaching and information more than rendering legal verdicts.

The most important reason Leo made such extensive use of letters is that by 1878 the Catholic Church had lost (or was in the process of losing) its privileged political status in the Catholic nations of Europe and South America. With the death of Catholic political Christendom, it became impractical to rely upon local political and ecclesiastical elites to maintain the international character of the church. At the eclipse of the papacy's temporal rule in Italy and the altar-throne alliance in Europe, Leo rediscovered its teaching function.

The gradual, and sometimes violent, dissolution of Catholic political Christendom after 1789 left unresolved problems of a practical and theological nature. Since the early sixteenth century, Catholic sovereigns had acquired ecclesiastical privileges to govern the many facets of the church in their dominions. Originally, Rome conceded these privileges to reward crusades against Islam, to consolidate the Catholic response to the Reformation, and to facilitate missions in the New World. During the era of absolutism, monarchs and their courts in Versailles, Madrid, and Vienna insisted that royal governance of the church was an inherent right of sovereignty. The revolutions of the late eighteenth and nineteenth centuries, however, did not end the situation of national churches. In France, the royal ecclesiastical prerogatives were swiftly translated into the terms of popular sovereignty. The church in all its temporalities was property of the state, and her bishops and clergy its civil servants. In the former Spanish dominions, the royal Patronato Real became the Patronato Nacional, and Venezuela's first twenty-six constitutions retained its law of state patronage. As late as 1870, the Holy See nominated bishops in only five countries, four of them predominately Protestant.

This juridical and political remnant of Christendom perplexed Leo's nineteenth-century predecessors. After the Congress of Vienna, popes adopted the policy of legitimism, supporting nominally Catholic sovereigns as agents of law and order against the tides of revolution. The revolutions of 1848 demonstrated the obsolescence of this system. Pecci's generation detested state superintendence of the church, with the attendant ministers

of cults, confiscation of ecclesiastical property, and monopoly on education. Leo himself called such superintendence *regalismo*, or regalism, a
polemical term for the doctrine that the *res sacra in temporalibus* (sacred
reality insofar as it is temporal) rightfully belongs to the authority of the
civil sovereign.[10]

When the sixty-year-old Pecci attended Vatican Council I in December
1869, churchmen and statesmen understood that the church would have to
extricate itself from captivity to national churches. The bishops debated a
draft of a conciliar document *De Ecclesia Christi*, containing five chapters
and twenty-one canons on church and state.[11] If adopted, these chapters
and canons could mean nothing other than the end of church-state relations as they had existed in the Catholic world. There was talk in European
capitals of military intervention to stop the Council. As it turned out, the
bishops could not agree on the kind of overarching theory needed to take
a decisive position on these chapters and canons. Instead, at the Fourth
Session, on July 18, 1870, the Council approved the Dogmatic Constitution
Pastor aeternus. Politically, the definition of papal infallibility was less explosive than the sentence on jurisdiction: "Wherefore we teach and declare
that, by divine ordinance, the Roman church possesses a pre-eminence of
ordinary power over every other church, and that this jurisdictional power
of the Roman pontiff is both episcopal and immediate."[12] The local church
is not *in* the state but in the universal Church. There would be no more
national churches. Thus the bishops had, in effect, endorsed the result of
extricating the church from the states, but they did so indirectly, through
the device of papal jurisdictional authority.

The main problem facing Pope Leo was that the Council had put the nail
in the coffin of political Christendom but had provided no canon law to
legally organize the changes (the Code of Canon Law would not exist until
1917), no solution to the fractured diplomatic relations with governments,
and, most important, no picture of what ought to be the normal configuration of church, state, and society. It would be too strong to say that Leo had
to invent a new social and political theology from scratch; however, he did
have to pick up the pieces of the church's post-1789 experience and to put
together a synoptic view of where Catholicism stood in this new political
and social world. What we now call Catholic social teaching emerged in
this crisis.

A TWOFOLD PEDAGOGY

Throughout his letters, Leo used a twofold pedagogy to situate the human agent who participates in divine providence both through the natu-

ral law and through the law of the Gospel. In *Rerum novarum* (1891),[13] for example, he said that the state is "rightly apprehended" according to "right reason congruent with nature" and in light of the "dictates of divine wisdom."[14] The distinctions related to this double pedagogy—reason and faith, general and particular providence, nature and grace—represent two ways that the human knower participates in God's ordering wisdom. For Leo, however, the "natural" does not constitute a zone in which persons or things exist apart from divine providence. It does not track what we usually mean by the "secular." In the nineteenth century, this point was not easily made, for modern philosophy and science laid claim to a "secular" sphere unfettered from the traditional biblical understanding of authority flowing from either the order of creation or that of redemption. Catholic thinkers, wary of discourse about nature, general providence, and reason, preferred instead to emphasize the perspective of particular providence, scripture, and ecclesiastical history and law. This was the discourse of the older Christendom.

The animus against philosophy arose in reaction to the Enlightenment's critique of particular providence as the abode of superstition and priest-craft. Philosophy meant deism, the doctrine that the natural order is created but not governed by God. In the letter *Christianae reipublicae* (1766), we find Pope Clement XIII castigating philosophers who teach that God is "lazy and indolent."[15] Pius VI, in his first encyclical, criticized philosophy for teaching that particular providence is a "conspiracy against the innate liberty of man."[16] When the Revolution erupted in France, he lamented that the Eldest Daughter of the Church had "commended itself into the counsel of philosophers."[17] The philosophers seek to replace "old, customary, and legitimate constitutions" with novelties based upon abstractions.[18] The most dangerous abstraction is the scenario of a state of nature, espoused in different ways by Spinoza, Kant, and, above all, Rousseau, who said that the state of nature entitles us to consider human nature as "if it had been left to itself."[19] Against this perspective, Pius VI appealed to Genesis 2:17. Placing humanity in the "paradise of delectation," God constituted human liberty under a law.[20] There is no such thing, he concluded, as a human nature or a human condition bereft of a moral (natural) law. Every pope since Clement XIII (1758–69) had issued letters warning about the "virus" and "sects" of philosophy.

Catholic thinkers of the modern period eschewed talk about natural law lest it suggest a human condition untutored by faith and the discipline of the church. The great Jacques-Bénigne Bossuet, for example, as preceptor and tutor of the dauphin, impressed upon the prince that God's rule should never be understood in the way taught by Deists. "Thus he acted since the beginning of the world. At that time he was the sole king of men, and governed them visibly."[21] In *Mirari vos* (1832), Gregory XVI warned that philosophers make much of natural law in order to cast doubt upon particular providence.[22] Such doubt undermines the claims and titles of the particular ecclesiastical and civil institutions inherited from Christendom, which is to say, from the order of particular providence. The sacral order had to be defended against what the Spanish diplomat Donoso Cortés called "the iron age of philosophical civilization."[23] Perhaps the most influential Catholic writer for Leo's generation was Joseph de Maistre, the doyen of political conservatism, who asserted that "human reason, or what is ignorantly called philosophy" is an "essentially disruptive force."[24] Even a prominent Catholic liberal like Félicité Robert de Lamennais could write that "religion is found near the cradle of all peoples, as philosophy is found near their tomb."[25] Pius IX sometimes referred to natural law, but usually as a defensive measure against hostile state policies.[26] That he would even have to make recourse to natural law and natural rights indicates the much-weakened status of the customary sentiments and instruments by which temporal and ecclesiastical authorities negotiated their differences.

At the risk of oversimplifying, the case against philosophy was twofold. First, philosophy is abstraction that cannot reach, in any useful way, what God teaches through nature and general providence. The "law of history" is the matrix for the teachings of nature, for history discloses concrete relations between humanity, society, and God. Thus the French Catholic conservative Louis de Bonald contended that what is "written on the heart" is not the reliable index for "the natural"; rather, the "way of perfection" is shown in the actual evolution of institutions and societies.[27] Philosophers' quest for the primitive, either in nature or in the human mind, never locates something truly original. It locates fundaments that are figments, such as the asocial person and the social contract.[28] Knowledge does not arise from innate ideas, much less by words privately entertained, but by one mind teaching another through speech. Since no one teaches himself or herself to speak, we must admit that knowledge arose from an original speech act, that of God tutoring Adam.[29] In the order of epistemology, socially constituted knowledge was to be the conservative alternative to Cartesian reason (*cogito*). In matters political, it countered the Rousseauvian general will (*volunté généralité*), namely the idea that social relations are rightly constituted only by the fiat of human choice.

While Leo certainly agreed with the polemical thrust of this thought, he refused to consign philosophy to the status of a modern "sect." In an 1892 allocution, Leo explained that the Catholic project should aim at the "conscience of the people" rather than the "restoration of medieval institutions."[30] The church must enter the marketplace of ideas. He thought that Thomism was useful for something more than propping up historically obsolete institutions. His Jesuit preceptors at Viterbo and Rome had taught the young Pecci that the traditionalists had gone too far in demoting the natural law, the role of human intellection, and philosophy.[31] An adequate Catholic response to philosophers was overdue.

Quoting Matthew 28:19–20, "go and teach all nations," Leo laid out his new agenda in *Aeterni Patris*: "But the natural helps with which the grace of the divine wisdom, strongly and sweetly disposing all things, has supplied the human race are neither to be despised nor neglected, chief among which is evidently the right use of philosophy. For not in vain did God set the light of reason in the human mind; and so far is the super-added light of faith from extinguishing or lessening the power of the intelligence that it completes it rather, and by adding to its strength renders it capable of greater things."[32] "We hold that every word of wisdom," he continued, "every useful thing by whomsoever discovered or planned, ought to be received with a willing and grateful mind."[33] In another document he proclaimed, "The best parent and guardian of liberty amongst men is truth."[34] We misunderstand Leo if we think that he meant that philosophy should overshadow theology; rather, philosophy, like the gold of Egypt, is appropriated by theology and pressed into the service of the true God.[35] The church should reclaim its role as the "refuge of the liberal arts," a *domus sapientiae*, a "house of wisdom."[36] Both metaphors are interesting. The natural sources of human intellection, if rightly used, lead to natural theology, which considers the relationship between secondary causes and the unrestricted divine cause. So long as it is not shortchanged, philosophy is also permeable to the higher wisdom of revelation—hence the twofold pedagogy of creation and revelation. In either register, the intellect does not offer a blind submission to custom, nor indeed to any human authority:

> By obeying Christ with his intellect man by no means acts in a servile manner, but in complete accordance with his reason and his natural dignity. For by his will he yields, not to the authority of any man, but to that of God, the author of his being, and the first principle to Whom he is subject by the very law of his nature. He does not suffer himself to be forced by the theories of any human teacher, but by the eternal and unchangeable truth. Hence he attains at one and the same time the natural good of the intellect and his own liberty. For the truth which proceeds from the teaching of Christ clearly demonstrates the real nature and value of every being; and man, being endowed with this knowledge, if he but obey the truth as perceived, will make all things subject to himself, not himself to them; his appetites to his reason, not his reason to his appetites.[37]

Leo looked to St. Thomas to supply the method for this twofold pedagogy. Thomas "pushed his philosophic inquiry into the reasons and principles of things," but, more important, he developed the analogies between "things naturally known" and the theological "mysteries."[38] Leo believed that Thomism is uniquely suitable for affirming the dignity of the human intellect with respect to its natural resources even while showing how human knowledge is open-textured with respect to revelation. It need not be a "sect." Above all, Leo recommended the teachings of St. Thomas to illuminate the "true meaning of liberty" and the "divine origin of all authority."[39] In the early modern period, Thomists like Francisco Suarez, Robert Bellarmine, and Francisco de Vitoria proved especially agile in the field of legal and political philosophy. Two decades before Leo's election, Jesuits at the *Civiltà Cattolica* had begun to press Thomism into the service of political and legal philosophy. After World War I, during the pontificate of Pius XI, this would be called "social doctrine."

LAW IN DIVINE PROVIDENCE

The theme of law is paramount to Leo's understanding of how human persons and their works stand within God's ordering wisdom. In 1500, there were about five hundred independent political entities in Europe; when Leo wrote his magisterial encyclicals, there were twenty-five. The nation-states that emerged after the Napoleonic Wars had a prodigious capacity for lawmaking as the tool of civil order and uniformity. As state law became more expansive, and as customary law gave way to positive laws, the relation of law to a prior moral, anthropological, and theological order became an issue of the first importance. Who has authority to make law? Are there plural sources of law? What belongs inside or outside the positive law of the state?

Leo followed Thomas's well-known definition of law as a binding precept of reason, promulgated by a competent authority for the common good.[40] This definition can be regarded from two standpoints: from the perspective of the legislator, which is to say, a mind formulating, promulgating, and moving other persons to a common good through a precept of reason; and from the perspective of one subject to law, a mind receiving and acting according to a precept.[41] In the first, we attend to the measuring mind, in the latter to the mind being measured. From either standpoint, Leo argued, law presupposes natural liberty rooted in the intellect:

> It is with moral liberty, whether in individuals or in communities, that We proceed at once to deal. But, first of all, it will be well to speak briefly of natural liberty; for, though it is distinct and separate from moral liberty, natural

freedom is the fountainhead from which liberty of whatsoever kind flows. The unanimous consent and judgment of men ... recognizes this natural liberty in those only who are endowed with intelligence or reason; and it is by his use of this that man is rightly regarded as responsible for his actions. For, while other animate creatures follow their senses, seeking good and avoiding evil only by instinct, man has reason to guide him in each and every act of his life. Reason sees that whatever things that are held to be good upon earth may exist or may not, and discerning that none of them are of necessity for us, it leaves the will free to choose what it pleases. But man can judge of this contingency, as We say, only because he has a soul that is simple, spiritual, and intellectual—a soul, therefore, which is not produced by matter, and does not depend on matter for its existence.[42]

Leo did not say that natural liberty is a law, but a condition of lawmaking and law-abiding action. In its proper sense, law is a binding directive (*vis directiva*), not force (*vis coactiva*). Law imposes not physical but moral necessity, and this condition requires the intellect to grasp both an intelligible good and a term of action by which the good is to be pursued.[43] It is a mistake, therefore, to conceive of human law as an artifact that mimics physical necessities, or the so-called laws of nature investigated by the physical sciences.

Leo also wanted to head off another idea, closely related to the physicalist understanding of the laws of nature: namely, that human liberty consists chiefly in spontaneous instinct and will. For Leo, the intellect is able not only to apprehend particular goods, but also to judge their contingent nature and disposition. No created good is so absolutely good that the very act of knowing it short-circuits liberty. For example, knowing that nutrition is good does not impose a necessity that one take to eating food right there and then. The will freely inclines to different things by virtue of the intellect's various conceptions of the good.[44] Liberty is thus rooted in the intellect in a twofold manner: first, in the intelligible good that makes possible action rather than mere instinct, and second, in the intellect's ability to estimate the good in a variety of dispositions. Together, these elements constitute conditions for law being something more than a projection of force that cancels out human liberty:

> In man's free will, therefore, or in the moral necessity of our voluntary acts being in accordance with reason, lies the very root of the necessity of law. Nothing more foolish can be uttered or conceived than the notion that, because man is free by nature, he is therefore exempt from law. Were this the case, it would follow that to become free we must be deprived of reason; whereas the truth is that we are bound to submit to law precisely because we are free by our very nature.[45]

This passage mentions no particular philosophers. It is clear, however, that Leo was arguing against the view, famously advocated by Thomas Hobbes, that the human being is an appetitive mechanism whose instincts are reconditioned or redirected by threat of sanction. Liberty obtains wherever the natural instincts remain unbounded by law. Law and liberty are harmonized, but only at the price of putting both law and liberty within the genus of force and physical necessity; reason itself remains the slave of the passions. Leo argued, to the contrary, that legal motion is not reducible to executive force. The intellect is the term by which a legal authority, first by formulating a plan of action (*ordinatio*) and then by commanding (*imperio*), moves other minds to act; but command is essentially the work of the intellect.[46] Thomas thus contended that the maxim "The will of the prince has the force of law" can make sense only on the supposition that what is promulgated has the *ratio* of justice, which is to say a term of obligation.[47] In modern times the maxim had been revived for purposes of popular sovereignty. Human law is legitimated by an aggregation of wills or preferences that the machinery of state law must represent and then enforce. Leo thought that this conception was a seedbed of despotism—not because of democratic or republican forms of government in and of themselves, but because, according to this philosophy, law does not transcend the artifice of force.

For Leo, natural law is not Rousseau's "voice of nature" (*la voix de la nature*), which speaks to human beings in a state of nature prior to a rule of law. Leo deployed a rather conventional Thomistic understanding of natural law, but he never strayed far from the problem posed by modern social-contract theorists. Does natural law imply a state of nature in which legal predicates are absent because there is no jurisdiction, no legislator? Or does natural law imply that human beings, however they are contingently situated vis-à-vis a particular civil regime, are already under a law? In the first view, natural law is not a "law" except in a metaphorical sense of the term. Law makes its first appearance in an agreement among human agents to provide positive law. Government might arise from the needs and promptings of nature, but not from an antecedent order of obligation. So put, this position thwarts appeal to a normative order of creation. As we said, Catholic traditionalists had countered the state of nature hypothesis in a Burkean fashion by arguing that history discloses no such human condition bereft of social order, and therefore of the predicates of authority. Leo thought that the church needed an alternative model of natural law that affirms the original jurisdiction of divine providence.

In *Aeterni Patris*, Leo referred to "divine wisdom, strongly and sweetly disposing all things." This image is taken from Wisdom 8:1, where God is said to order creatures "sweetly" (*suaviter*).[48] It was one of Thomas's favorite scriptural texts for creaturely participation in divine governance. "He disposes all things sweetly, because to all things He gives forms and powers inclining them to that which He Himself moves them, so that they tend toward it not by force, but as if it were by their own free accord."[49] For Thomas, the signature effect of divine governance is a multitude of things moving toward the good by inclination, by the exercising of their own natures rather than by force. Every creaturely inclination is an impression from divine wisdom.[50] The human person, however, is the recipient of instilled or impressed law (*lex indita*). The instinctual acts of irrational creatures are directed by God inasmuch as such acts belong to the species, but human actions are directed inasmuch as they belong to the individual: the human being is directed "in his personal actions, and this is what we call law."[51] The natural law is law because God communicates the necessity of obligation; it is called natural because the law is instilled or indicted in us "so as to be known naturally [*naturaliter*]."[52] For Thomas, all human judgment is set within an already existing cosmological, not positivist legal order; natural order arises from a creative act that instills or engrafts rather than imposes the measures of action.[53] In the human soul, the habit of *synderesis* holds the "first precept of law" (*primum praeceptum legis*): "The good is to be done and pursued and evil resisted."[54] By the impression of created light, God induces the creature to share in the rules and measures of the eternal law.[55] The radical implications of Thomas's teaching should be evident: Every created intelligence has a competence not only to make judgments, but also to make judgments according to a real law—indeed, a law that is the form and pattern of all other laws. The legal order of things thus does not begin with an acquired virtue, possessed by a few; nor does it begin with the offices and statutes of human positive law. God speaks the law, at least in its rudiments, to each intelligent creature. "The right ends of human life are fixed," Thomas explained, and therefore there is a "naturally right judgment about such ends."[56] Thomas grouped these ends under the triad of *to be*, *to live*, and *to know*—effects of God that are desirable and lovable to all.[57] Thomas also called the new law of grace *lex indita*. By infused grace rather than any written or imposed directive, the soul is inclined to acts of faith, hope, and charity, and thereby to act in accord with the common good of a heavenly polity.[58] The concept of *lex indita* has three important implications. First, in different ways, both the natural law and the new law instill (infuse) terms of action in which the creature partakes personally. Just as the natural law is said to be "written on the heart," so too is the new law "poured out in the hearts" of the faithful. Second, instilled law not only makes known things to be done (*quid sit faciendum*) but also assists the doing (*adiuvans ad implendum*). *Lex indita* does not cancel natural liberty, for human persons are induced through the exercise of their own nature to know and direct themselves freely to goods to which they are inclined by nature or by divine grace. Third, for Leo, as for Thomas, instilled law is a mark of the sacred. *Lex indita* implies creation and recreation and therefore stands outside the orbit of human prudence and legal artifact. We can imitate but not make an instilled law. Human legal authorities cannot pretend to begin from scratch by imposing laws on a supposedly morally motionless human nature.

In his letters, Leo frequently circled back to the theme that human moral and legal judgments, indeed human liberty, depend upon an antecedent divine law:

> All prescriptions of human reason can have force of law only inasmuch as they are the voice and the interpreters of some higher power on which our reason and liberty necessarily depend. For, since the force of law consists in the imposing of obligations and the granting of rights, authority is the one and only foundation of all law—the power, that is, of fixing duties and defining rights, as also of assigning the necessary sanctions of reward and chastisement to each and all of its commands. But all this, clearly, cannot be found in man, if, as his own supreme legislator, he is to be the [supreme] rule of his own actions. It follows, therefore, that the law of nature is the same thing as the eternal law, implanted in rational creatures, and inclining them to their right action and end; and can be nothing else but the eternal reason of God, the Creator and Ruler of all the world. To this rule of action and restraint of evil God has vouchsafed to give special and most suitable aids for strengthening and ordering the human will. The first and most excellent of these is the power of His divine grace, whereby the mind can be enlightened and the will wholesomely invigorated and moved to the constant pursuit of moral good, so that the use of our inborn liberty becomes at once less difficult and less dangerous. Not that the divine assistance hinders in any way the free movement of our will; just the contrary, for grace works inwardly in man and in harmony with his natural inclinations, since it flows from the very Creator of his mind and will, by whom all things are moved in conformity with their nature.[59]

"Laws come before men live together in society," Leo wrote, "and have their origin in the natural, and consequently in the eternal law." The precepts of the natural law, contained materially in the human law, have not merely the force of human law but "possess that higher and more august sanction which belongs to the law of nature and the eternal law." "It is within this very genus of law," he concluded, "that the civil legislator exercises his *munus* [gift of service]."[60] It is not that human law merely replicates in written form the natural law. Even when a legislator devises new laws on the pattern of the natural law, this exercise of *ius facere* is always located "within the perimeter" (*in iusto genere*) of higher law. Rousseau contended that the social order is a "sacred right" (*un droit sacré*) because there can be no other higher law.[61] Leo, however, contended that this assertion offers a misplaced *sanctum* that cannot but do violence against the consciences of citizens who live already under the natural law and, as baptized, under the law of grace.

In this fashion, Leo attempted to provide an adequate interpretation of Romans 13:1 ("Let every person be subject to the governing authorities. For there is no authority except from God, and those that exist are constituted by God"). With respect to natural liberty, he granted the truth of what seemed like a radical premise, that "no man has in himself or of himself the power of constraining the free will of others by fetters of authority."[62] Though it had unimpeachable credentials in earlier Catholic thought, this idea was later obscured by Catholic traditionalists, who thought that it sailed too close to the shores of Rousseau and Enlightenment notions of equality. Leo, on the other hand, contended that from the premise of natural equality we should not conclude that humanity is naturally lawless, or that a social contract constructs a collective title to authority; rather, the idea of natural equality indicates that human authority to bind, sanction, and, if need be, coerce participates in divine authority. God alone "can commit power to a man over his fellow men."[63] Human command dislocated from the scheme of participation in higher law leads, inexorably, to law being "the servitude of man to man."[64] Leo argued that only Christ, the God-human, has *imperium* over other human beings by natural right.[65] Romans 13:1's teaching that "We must obey God rather than men" must therefore be interpreted also in light of Acts 5:29, because "where the power to command is wanting, or where a law is enacted contrary to reason, or to the eternal law, or to some ordinance of God, obedience is unlawful, lest, while obeying man, we become disobedient to God."[66] From 1791 to 1875, during which time popes issued more than fifty letters, they did not cite Acts 5:29 even once.[67] Instead, the popes continually cited Romans 13:1 ("Let every person be subject to the governing authorities") and 1 Peter 2:13 ("Be subject for the Lord's sake to every human institution"). Beginning with Leo, Acts 5:29 became a frequently quoted scripture in papal social teaching. Indeed, John Paul II cited it no less than eight times in *Evangelium vitae* (1995).

On the social contract, Leo sided with the conservative mainstream of Catholic thought, from Bossuet to the present. Leo's criticism of the social contract must be understood in tandem with his estimation of natural liberty and equality. At issue was not the institutional distribution of authority (constitutional allocation of powers), at least not in the civil sphere. Leo rather treated the social contract as a theory about the *origin* of authority. From the premise that humanity is naturally lawless, no mere aggregation of wills, however formal the fiat, can explain the emergence of authority to bind—force, yes, but not obligation. Nor can the social contract follow from the opposite premise that each individual is *sui iuris*, a self-constituting law, for this does not explain how that which properly belongs to an individual can be exercised by another. Such a formulation can explain a system of permission-giving but not true authority:

> Those who believe civil society to have risen from the free consent of men, looking for the origin of its authority from the same source, say that each individual has given up something of his right, and that voluntarily every person has put himself into the power of the one man in whose person the whole of those rights has been centered. But it is a great error not to see, what is manifest, that men, as they are not a nomad race, have been created, without their own free will, for a natural community of life. It is plain, moreover, that the pact which they allege is openly a falsehood and a fiction, and that it has no authority to confer on political power such great force, dignity, and firmness as the safety of the State and the common good of the citizens require. Then only will the government have all those ornaments and guarantees, when it is understood to emanate from God as its august and most sacred source.[68]

Leo here is paraphrasing an argument made by the Bishop of Mainz, Wilhelm Emmanuel von Ketteler, whose social and political sermons deeply influenced Leo's mind, particularly on the labor problem. Von Ketteler argued that the general will is the "fiction" that aggregations of force can create society and a true principle of authority.[69] A state erected on this doctrine is entitled to enforce rather than govern the will of the majority; Leo argued that the "doctrine of the supremacy of the greater number, and that all right and all duty reside in the majority" cannot (on its own terms) transcend force.[70]

In sum, Leo's pedagogy of natural law is a doctrine of participated authority as Thomas defined it: "Now among all others the rational creature is subject to divine providence in the most excellent way, insofar as it partakes of a share of providence by being provident both for itself and for others.... This participation of the eternal law in the rational creature is called the natural law." In answer to the objection that it is unnecessary to have two laws, one eternal, the other natural, Thomas responded that "this argument would hold if the natural law were something diverse from the eternal law, whereas it is nothing but a participation thereof."[71] The human intellect is "provident both for itself and for others" because humanity is first measured by a higher law. In recent papal literature this concept is called "participated theonomy."[72] Humanity, Leo said, is a "king by participation" in divine rule. Human beings rule both by obedience to the natural law and by obedience to Christ who fulfills and elevates the natural law.[73]

STRUCTURED PLURALISM

Leo developed the idea of participated authority for purposes similar to those of Abraham Kuyper, who propounded the idea of "sphere sovereignty" (see chapter 10). Leo and Kuyper were contemporaries. Like Leo, Kuyper insisted that authority does not arise originally through a social contract or the state. "*Higher authority,*" he writes, "is of necessity involved" if we are to make sense of plural spheres of society that have real authority and are not reducible one to the other: "In a Calvinistic sense we understand hereby, that the family, the business, science, art and so forth are all social spheres, which do not owe their existence to the state, and which do not derive the law of their life from the superiority of the state, but obey a high authority within their own bosom."[74] Kuyper and his disciples spoke of higher law rather than natural law. Here, we make no effort to effect a superficial reconciliation of "sphere sovereignty" and "participated authority" except to say that both use a theonomic principle to account for a structured pluralism of authority.

For Leo, authority to command is distributed in such a way that, "through the medium of men," plural agents might imitate God's ruling wisdom by bringing about perfection in themselves and others.[75] All human ruling is *ad imaginem dei*, unto the image of God.[76] Authority to render judgments according to a law does not belong to the civil power alone. "There is," he wrote, "a difference between the political prudence that relates to the general good and that which concerns the good of individuals. This latter is shown forth in the case of private persons who obey the prompting of right reason in the direction of their own conduct; while the former is the characteristic of those who are set over others, and chiefly of rulers of the State, whose duty it is to exercise a preeminent power of command."[77] Judgment and command can be distinguished according to three modes of prudence, each suggesting the ground of a jurisdictional boundary. Individual prudence takes the antecedent (natural) law and renders it efficacious in one's own actions. Such prudence proceeds from the rules and measures of law, rooted in intellect's native capacity to render judgment according to the natural law, and is perfected in self-governance rather than in issuing commands to others. Domestic prudence delivers ordering judgments for a family (but by extension to other societies as well, such as corporations or monasteries). This type of prudence, too, proceeds from law, but its end term is a command that moves others. Thomas calls these commands "ordinances or statutes," but they lack the *ratio* of civil law.[78] When one commands one's children to go to bed, one has not issued a curfew. The kind of prudence that proceeds from law to law is regnative prudence (*prudentia regnativa*). Such prudence is essentially legislative prudence, the capacity to make and impose laws (*leges ponere*).[79] The chief act of a political authority (*principatus regalis*) is to direct a multitude by law to a political end. What makes this ordering judgment unique is that it remains totally within the genus of law. Having received the (natural or revealed) law, the human intellect makes more law. For Leo, there are two centers of legislative prudence, the state (*civitas*) and the church (*ecclesia*).

In his letters, Leo repeatedly used the phrase *iura et officia*, rights and duties, with respect to individuals and the various orders of society.[80] There are four main orders, each with its own competence to render judgment: the family, voluntary private associations (which we call civil society), the church, and the state or *civitas*. The distinction and overlap between these orders was a subject of considerable debate, and none more than marriage and the family, for this institution touches upon all of the others. The married person is at once a citizen, a member of the church, and, often as not, a member of voluntary societies. Most important for Leo, the material and formal aspects of matrimony have an immediate propinquity to divine providence, both by creation and by sacrament; there is no more evident example of *lex indita* than the society "established for reciprocal affection and for the interchange of duties."[81] Marriage, being "sacred by its own power, in its own nature, and of itself," does not belong to the "*imperio* of civil rulers."[82] No human power—the state, society, the spouses themselves—has authority over marriage as such. Marriage can have different customs, but, unlike political authority, it is not amenable to a prudential introduction of plural forms. The sacrament can introduce a new form, but not by way of derogating from the natural principle.

Regarding marriage, Leo deployed his typical twofold pedagogy. The rights and duties of marriage proceed from the natural order instituted by God (*Deo et natura*) and from Christ's institution of the sacrament (*de sacramentis*).[83] The ordering judgments of domestic prudence include, as a native right, education of children as well as the right to establish free schools.[84] Moreover, the legitimate sphere of domestic judgment embraces the right to possess and order property and the right to form associations.

Leo drew out these implications in his most famous encyclical, *Rerum novarum* (1891). The immediate purpose of *Rerum novarum* was public policy, specifically the question of just wages for laborers and their right to form associations. In no letter do we find Leo writing so ambidextrously with respect to policy and theory. We leave the policy issues to one side in order to see what the encyclical teaches about structured pluralism.[85] As usual, Leo treated property and associations in light of divine providence giving rise to different kinds of human prudence.

Arguments for a natural right of possessing and using private property can be summarized under three anthropological points.[86] First, the human person is an intelligent animal, and hence providential for himself or herself. What is most characteristic of human intelligence is not having but ordering. For this reason, property cannot be possessed in a way that befits human beings if it is merely for "temporary and momentary" use.[87] Second, the ordering wisdom requires the agent to possess something "as his very own," for one cannot dispose and give what one does not have. Moreover, the fruit of the agent's labor bears "the impress of his own personality."[88] Third, because the family is a "true society, governed by an authority peculiar to itself," the father must have a native competence and right to acquire property and to order it according to the needs of the household.[89] Thus Leo concludes: "Provided, therefore, the limits which are prescribed by the very purposes for which it exists be not transgressed ... the domestic household is antecedent, as well in idea as in fact, to the gathering of men into a community, [and] the family must necessarily have rights and duties which are prior to those of the community, and founded more immediately in nature."[90] Property befits human beings chiefly because of the dignity of intelligent labor and the capacity to make ordering judgments. The "sacred law of nature," in this regard, is not mere preservation, but provident action that freely fulfills duties and social offices.[91] "This great labor question," Leo wrote, "cannot be solved save by assuming as a principle that private ownership is a *ius sanctum*. The law, therefore, should favor ownership, and its policy should be to induce as many as possible of the people to become owners."[92] Although Leo certainly emphasized more than Thomas the right of possession, the overarching argument is possession as a condition of being able to intelligently order and dispose resources for the good of others.[93] The other main issue of *Rerum novarum* is the right of voluntary associations. The following passage deserves to be quoted in full because it is so important for the development of papal social doctrine:

> These lesser societies and the larger society differ in many respects, because their immediate purpose and aim are different. Civil society exists for the

common good, and hence is concerned with the interests of all in general, albeit with individual interests also in their due place and degree. It is therefore called a public society, because by its agency, as St. Thomas of Aquinas says, "Men establish relations in common with one another in the setting up of a commonwealth." But societies which are formed in the bosom of the commonwealth are styled private, and rightly so, since their immediate purpose is the private advantage of the associates. "Now, a private society," says St. Thomas again, "is one which is formed for the purpose of carrying out private objects; as when two or three enter into partnership with the view of trading in common." Private societies, then, although they exist within the body politic, and are severally part of the commonwealth, cannot nevertheless be absolutely, and as such, prohibited by public authority. For, to enter into a "society" of this kind is the natural right of man; and the State has for its office to protect natural rights, not to destroy them; and, if it forbid its citizens to form associations, it contradicts the very principle of its own existence, for both they and it exist in virtue of the like principle, namely, the natural tendency of man to dwell in society.[94]

By "societies of this kind," Leo referred to a wide range of associations, such as labor associations, confraternities, schools, and religious orders that, "by sanction of the law of nature," have legal personality and thus "rights as corporate bodies."[95] They are called "private" in the sense that their nature, purposes, and rights are not constituted by the state. The legal world of private law (*lex privata*) developed from contracts, associations, charters, endowments—and, in the case of religious orders, of course, constitutions under the public law of the church. What puts private societies into a distinct category from marriage is the fact that their forms are amenable to human prudence. Whereas through birth one can enter a family, a political community, and a church, membership in voluntary associations depends upon choice.

Interestingly, Thomas's tract on the life of voluntary poverty, which comes down to us under the title *Contra impugnantes,* shaped Leo's discussion of the right of association. The tract helps us to understand how Leo adapted medieval notions to contemporary situations.

Thomas Aquinas argued that every society is a friendship involving "communications." The word *communicatio* means making something common, one rational agent participating in the life of another.[96] The multiplicity of vocations and avocations are grounded "primarily in Divine Providence, and, secondarily, in natural causes whereby certain men are disposed to the performance of certain functions in preference to others."[97] At issue was laity and religious partaking in a common work of teaching and learning. Thomas contended that "an association of study is a society, established with the object of teaching and of learning; and as not only lay-men, but also religious, may lawfully teach and learn, there can be no doubt that, both these classes are able to unite in one society."[98] Competence to perform the common activity rather than one's status should be the mea-sure of voluntary societies. To insist that "religious and laymen ought not, mutually, to communicate their gift of knowledge" is contrary to the scrip-tures, specifically to 1 Corinthians 12:21: "The eye cannot say to the hand: I need not thy help."[99] The contemplative is not less graced in preaching what he or she receives from God; nor is the teacher less learned when he or she communicates knowledge to the student; nor is anyone less "free" by virtue of imparting a gift to another. Thomas here quoted Augustine's *De doctrina christiana*: "Everything that is not lessened by being imparted, is not, if it be possessed without being communicated, possessed as it ought to be possessed."[100]

But what about authority? Is it not depleted if multiplied? Thomas an-swered that the free "communications" of a private society are lawful be-cause they proceed from friendship. No human authority can ban friend-ship, so long as it is for a blameless purpose. Private voluntary societies exhibit authority, but the kind of authority that ensues upon meeting stan-dards inherent to the activities. Such societies are therefore not in compe-tition with civil and ecclesiastical legislators.

Leo's use of this literature calls our attention to two points of capital importance. First, he did not depict civil society in its negative function of counterbalancing the state. That idea comes from Montesquieu, who held that liberty is found only in moderate governments, where "power must check power by the arrangement of things."[101] We notice that Leo did not use the term "intermediate" societies, which suggests not a plurality of inherently valuable social forms but a merely instrumental good, a "buf-fer" between the individual and the state. Second, his analysis emphasized that these are "real societies" that embody the principle of friendship. The question is not whether they are cost-effective, or whether indeed private action is more efficient than the state. No natural right could depend upon such a contingency. The strong claim for these societies is that they bring about mutual perfection by free activity, with the emphasis upon the activ-ity more than the product. Leo insisted that "the State should watch over these societies of citizens banded together in accordance with their rights, but it should not thrust itself into their peculiar concerns and their orga-nization, for things move and live by the spirit inspiring them, and may be killed by the rough grasp of a hand from without."[102] This assertion is the germinal form of the principle of subsidiarity developed by Pius XI.

The situation of the Catholic Church is a more complicated subject. The post-1870 church, we said, had rejected the ecclesiological and canonical grounds for civil rulers exercising the role of *episcopus externus*. Unbendingly opposed to every trace of *regalismo*, Leo was intent upon drawing a sharp line between the church and the governments. Considered solely in terms of ecclesiology, this goal was the easiest part of the puzzle, for there was no significant dispute within Catholicism that the church is directly instituted by Christ with a visible hierarchy and a public law. The First Vatican Council had decisively eliminated the historic option of de facto or de jure national churches. Ongoing persecutions and legal harassment usually clarified rather than obscured the situation. Nor was the bilateral relation of church and state especially difficult to formulate in the abstract. Leo refurbished the ancient two power (*duo sunt*) doctrine of Pope Gelasius: "So there are twin powers," Leo wrote, "both subordinate to the eternal law of nature, and each working for its own ends in matters concerning its own order and domain." Divine providence decrees (1) that these twinned powers operate each in its own order (*in suo ordine*), and (2) that concord (*concordia*) ought to mark their relationship.[103]

The more difficult issue was the triadic relation of church, state, and society. One way to eliminate the tension would be to think of the church as a private, voluntary society. Under the rubric of "separation," some states attempted to fashion a solution along this line. In the first act of separation in Latin America, Colombia (1853) confiscated church property and transferred it to laity in the parishes. This action was but a prelude to the infamous French laws (1902–5), which transferred church property to cultural associations administered by the laity. Leo wrote repeatedly against such policies and argued not only that they violate Catholic ecclesiology and discipline, but also that these policies implicitly assert that what exists outside the state ceases to be a true society.[104] John Courtney Murray would call this social form the monistic "society-state"—that is, what is truly social is, or belongs to, the state, all else having the status of individuals temporarily in concert for merely private purposes.[105] Leo saw clearly enough that this solution doomed the church *and* the principle of voluntary societies.

As the separationist movement gained steam in France, Leo warned that separation is "indifferent to the interests of Christian society, that is to say, of the Church," and has as its aim putting French Catholics "outside of the common law itself [*le droit commun*]."[106] Similarly, with respect to the purported "neutral" marriage laws in Italy, he wrote: "What judgment is to be formed of a Catholic state which throws overboard the sacred principles and the wise enactments of the Christian law on matrimony, and sets about the wretched job of creating a marital morality all its own, purely human in character, under forms and guarantees that are merely legal; and then with all its power goes on forcibly to impose this morality on the consciences of its subjects, substituting it for the religious and sacramental morality."[107]

In these passages, Leo was not recommending a state establishment of religion; he rather complained that the state, by refusing to recognize the habits, customs, and conscience of the people, imposes its own morality upon society.[108] In effect, the church is separated from society.[109]

Leo returned time and again to the liberty of the church,[110] particularly with respect to its sanctifying and teaching missions.[111] In *Quod Apostolici*, he appealed to the governments: "Let them restore that Church to the condition and liberty in which she may exert her healing force for the benefit of all society."[112] The church's role is to communicate the wisdom of Christ, and, through sacramental action, to impart a supernatural "form" to society.[113] Society needs more than a morality drawn from the natural law, not only because of the deformation of sin, but also because it is a part of human dignity to be open to a supernatural life, without which "it is impossible to please God (Heb. 11:6)."[114] The civil power receives from God no power to sanctify; power to govern souls "excludes altogether the civil authority." The church "alone in divine matters" exercises a doctrinal magisterium.[115] There are thus two powers, the proximate end of one being "the temporal and worldly good of the human race," the other religious, "whose office it is to lead mankind to that true, heavenly, and everlasting happiness for which we are created."[116] Yet this distinction is not an entirely tidy boundary. With respect to society, the church is superior to the state not only in the "mixed matters" like marriage and education, but also more generally in the church's having a superior title to imprint itself upon society. In *Immortale*, Leo asserted, "Whatever, therefore in things human is of a sacred character, whatever belongs either of its own nature or by reason of the end to which it is referred, to the salvation of souls, or to the worship of God, is subject to the power and judgment of the Church."[117]

For practical purposes, Leo was happy enough to abide an accommodation where church and state enjoy a kind of equal access to society. On more than one occasion, he warmly noted that the church thrives in the United States, where the two powers do not "trespass on the rights of the other," and where each can be about its business without "barren quarrels." "The Church," he added, "claims liberty before all else."[118] It is a mistake, however, to think that Leo regarded negative liberty as a perfectly satisfactory situation. He wrote to the American bishops that the church ought to have the "favor of the laws."[119] In *Immortale*, he insisted that the civil power should "not in any way hinder" but also "in every manner to render as easy as may be the possession of that highest and unchangeable good for which all should seek."[120]

Did Leo believe in the "establishment" of religion? He certainly did not abjure a union of church and the civil commonwealth "as between soul and body."[121] But, with respect to what we mean by establishment, the answer is (a complicated) no. First, he spent his ecclesiastical career trying to protect the church from the strange "establishments" that survived the revolutions. If he sometimes yearned for the *status quo ante*, it was for the twelfth and not the eighteenth century, and even then he accented the social form rather than the political details.[122] Second, Leo was an antiseparationist. In his world, antiseparationism did not mean a state church. It meant a rather rich and proactive *concordia* in which each power recognizes the other's theological title to rule. Leo did not think that civil authorities ought to be epistemically blind about their place in the order of providence. The state's incompetence to teach doctrine does not entail its incompetence to be taught and to learn; moreover, the concord should include *adiumenta*, assistance, especially on mixed matters such as marriage and education.

Leo's position on the "form" of government departed markedly from that of his predecessors. While "God has always willed that there should be a ruling authority [*principatus*], and they who are invested with it should reflect the divine power and providence in some measure," it is not "necessarily bound up with any particular form of government."[123] Here he suggested two conditions that must inform prudential creation or alteration of political forms. The first is that God has always decreed that human beings come under a visible ruling authority. He dismissed a hypothetical state of nature, the scenario allowing human beings either to invent or to render absent political authority. Second, the word *principatus* signifies a real, active ruling power having authority to bind and loose in a political community. It is not, therefore, merely a power giving executive force to collective decisions. When Leo spoke critically of a "novel conception of law [*ius*]," he referred not to new constitutions but to the idea that there can be law that facilitates liberty but has no authority to bind.[124] The conception, he believes, is "simply a road leading straight to tyranny."[125] The first institutional limit on government is that it be a real government.

The political common good and the principle of the *principatus* are mutually entailed. A mere steering mechanism suggests no political community. It is true, of course, that the civil authority is limited by the presence of other social forms—the church, family, voluntary associations—each having a different mode of authority. While these entities indicate social goods to be coordinated, they cannot of themselves establish the civil *principatus*. For this reason, we will not find in Leo's thought the notion of an instrumental state, an idea that in fact will emerge (with important qualifications) in Catholic social thought during World War II.[126]

When Leo wrote about the *civitas* "rightly apprehended," his thoughts were never far from the situation in France. This was a nation that suffered a dozen changes of power in Leo's lifetime, that squabbled constantly over the "forms" of government, and that had a pronounced sense of the sacrality of political power. In a letter addressed to all French Catholics, he wrote that while the church must cross the "changeable ocean of human affairs," it has no legitimate prudence over its "essential constitution," received directly from Christ; but, "in regard to purely human societies, it is an oft-repeated historical fact that time, that great transformer of all things here below, operates great changes in their political institutions."[127] Regarding the temporal regime, it falls legitimately to the human intelligence to make prudential judgments of a constitutional nature—the distribution of authority according to the pattern of one, few, many, or indeed a mixed regime. Leo often made the point that it is not "of itself wrong to prefer a democratic form of government,"[128] that there are "plural forms" of legitimate regime,[129] and that it is not the prudence of the church "to decide which is the best amongst many diverse forms of government and the civil institutions."[130] Indeed, he even allowed that human prudence extends to the judgment of whether to change a regime midstream, if necessary, to remedy a great evil.[131] All of these assertions are qualified by the proviso that "the respect due to religion and the observance of good morals be upheld."[132]

Did Leo abandon interest in the classical question of what form of government makes the best regime? In one sense, yes. His practical imperative was to extract the church from the "regime politics" tearing nations apart in the Catholic world. To the French, he wrote:

> By giving one's self up to abstractions, one could at length conclude which is the best of these forms, considered in themselves; and in all truth it may be affirmed that each of them is good, provided it lead straight to its end—that is to say, to the common good for which social authority is constituted; and finally, it may be added that, from a relative point of view, such and such a form of government may be preferable because of being better adapted to the character and customs of such or such a nation. In this order of speculative ideas, Catholics, like all other citizens, are free to prefer one form of government to another precisely because no one of these social forms is, in itself, opposed to the principles of sound reason nor to the maxims of Christian doctrine.[133]

Above all, however, he was interested in the best society, where he thought the mission of the church is best directed. Important as the issue of political "forms" might be for jurisprudence, Leo thought it was a distraction from the problems of his era. In these senses, his teaching represents not only a post-Christendom but also a postclassical moment for the Catholic mind. His position was well accepted in the United States, where Catholics had a connatural understanding of how to align political prudence under general providence or "higher law."[134] In France, however, Leo's policy of *ralliement*, rallying Catholics to the Third Republic, fell flat. As he lay on his deathbed, the regime politics of the Dreyfus Affair (1898–1900), which originally targeted a Jewish officer accused of spying for Germany, spilled over into anticlerical laws.

One aspect of the question of political "forms" cannot be passed over in silence because it is so important to Leo's teaching as well as to the subsequent development of Catholic political theory. This is the question of the relation of the "form" and the "power." Leo recognized that the people can establish a form of government, if this be understood as "designating the ruler," but not if it be understood as conferring the very "authority of ruling."[135]

Human beings are free to designate the form (*designatur principes*), which is to say the distribution of offices and holders of office. Human beings are not free to confer the authority (*non conferuntur iura principatus*) by which a multitude is bound by laws and legitimate commands. The immediate background of this distinction is modern contract theories of the origin of political authority. We have seen that Leo held that no human being has a natural right to bind another, for this power is divine, and can only be participated. We have also seen that Catholic conservatives, such as Joseph de Maistre, hold that "human will counts for nothing in the establishing of government."[136] The remote background, however, concerns the arguments of Baroque-era Thomists such as Robert Bellarmine, Francisco Suarez, Tommaso Cajetan, and others. They argued that when the people communicate a new form of government, they do more than merely designate a ruler. To be sure, all authority comes from God, and therefore no human can create the *principatus*; yet Thomists of this time contended that by natural law God vests political authority in the entire people. Any additional specification of the protopopulist form entails what was called a "translation" from the people to the king or the parliament. Mere designation of the office does not settle how political authority is translated whole and complete to the new form. If it is not so translated, whoever holds the office does not possess true authority. Thus emerged a scholastic dispute between "designation" and "translation" theories, both claiming pedigree in the texts of Thomas Aquinas.[137]

The translation theory achieved its full elaboration during the struggle against the absolute monarchs, while the designation theory came into vogue during the nineteenth-century struggles against the extreme democrats.[138] Leo and his advisors appeared to side with the designation theory, among other reasons to head off the idea that the church's own constitution requires a translation from the people. But it is hard to say absolutely, because Leo never addressed the dispute *ex professo*.[139] In fact, it has never been settled by the papal magisterium.[140] The reader may wonder what difference it makes whether a God-given *principatus* is designated or translated by the people. The translation account is a much more powerful ground for the norm of democracy; if the eternal law vests political authority in the people, the specific democratic form of a regime corresponds to the prototype, and, furthermore, it would seem that a principle of consent is crucial for it to be otherwise. Within a generation of Leo's death, Thomists recovered the translation theory and deployed it against totalitarian regimes.[141] We may doubt that Leo subscribed to the translation theory, just as we may doubt that this axiomatic principle of neo-Thomism is very clearly rooted in Thomas's own work. Yet Leo certainly triggered the issue by opening up three lines of thought. Against the conservatives, he allowed human prudence to invent regimes. Against the Enlightenment, he denied a merely anthropocentric ground for the *principatus*. And finally, he denied that any human being has a natural right to bind another. We should not be surprised that the tension would be resolved in favor of a divine blessing on popular sovereignty.

THE LEONINE LEGACY

Leo's immediate successor, Pius X (1903–14), directed his energies to internal matters of the church. While he took some important practical steps in the relationship between church and state during the French separationist crisis (1905) and undertook a reform of canon law that took into account the post-1870 changes in the church's law, Pius was content to leave the Leonine teachings untouched. So untouched, indeed, that he did not once refer to Leo's favorite theme of eternal law.[142] The pope most responsible for developing the Leonine tradition was Pius XI (1922–39), who cited Leo more than one hundred times in his encyclicals. Ordained a priest in the first full year of Leo's pontificate, and eventually taking three doctorates, Ambrogio Achille Ratti studied under Leo's Thomist colleagues. Like Leo, Ratti looked to Thomas for the twofold pedagogy of "the natural and the supernatural order."[143] When Ratti was elected pope in 1922, he faced a world ruined by World War I; in a few years' time, he faced virulent totalitarian regimes and the onset of the Great Depression. In the midst of these crises, Pius XI reworked the Leonine legacy and rendered to social doctrine a sophisticated and supple body of thought. He was the first pontiff to speak of social teachings as a single body of "social doctrine." On his watch emerged the now familiar concepts of "social justice" and "subsidiarity." Though Pius regarded himself as reaching the "true and exact mind of Leo," most scholars would judge *Quadragesimo anno* (1931) a significant improvement over Leo's *Rerum novarum* in that the later document made clearer the relationship between possession and use of property.[144]

The Leonine understanding of the double pedagogy, the motif in Wisdom 8:1 of God's law "sweetly" moving creatures, the native authority of the family, the intrinsic value of social forms, and the dignity of the human soul radiate through papal letters of the twentieth century. Pius XII's inaugural letter, *Summi pontificatus* (1939), published at the beginning of World War II, was a compendium of Leonine arguments. Yet, in his famous Christmas address of 1944, Pius recommended democracy and thus went well beyond Leo's philosophical rumination on the legitimacy of plural forms of regimes.[145]

The documents of the Second Vatican Council (1962–65) quote Leo more than forty times, and his letters were pivotal in the protracted debate over the Declaration on Religious Liberty, *Dignitatis humanae* (1965). John Courtney Murray's crucial summary of the debate for the drafting committee in 1964 called Leo's letters a *ressourcement* of the program of Gregory VII on the liberty of the church.[146] That argument, Murray contended, posed no impediment to affirming religious freedom as a civil liberty. John Paul II's *Centesimus annus* (1991), celebrating the centenary of *Rerum novarum*, offered some new and very strong lines of reinterpretation in relation to the situation of peoples at the end of the Cold War. The encyclical *Veritatis splendor* (1993), on the other hand, presented a classic Leonine understanding of how human practical reason is situated in the order of divine providence.

Perhaps the most important development given to Leo's thought concerns the order of special providence. We began this essay with *Annum sacrum*, Leo's Jubilee encyclical on christological kingship. We saw Leo teaching the pilgrims that the divine sign would not be a new Constantine but the Sacred Heart of Jesus. In *Ubi arcano* (1922), Pius XI dedicated his pontificate to the *Regnum Christi*. In a series of encyclicals on Leo's *Annum sacrum*—*Quas primas* (1925), *Miserentissimus Redemptor* (1928), *Rappresentanti in terra* (1929), *Caritate Christi* (1932), and *Divini Redemptoris* (1937)—Pius began to explicate the analogies between Christ's kingly office and *munera* of baptized Christians. Although scholars rightly pay attention to the theme of natural law in papal social thought, Catholic political theology has tilted quietly but persistently toward the christological principle in which the notion of "participation" has much richer content. The Second Vatican Council's constitution on the church, *Lumen gentium* (1964), gave special importance to participated kingship according to Christ's threefold office of priest, prophet, and king. John Paul II contended that the reinvigorated christological center is a truly "novel" element of the council, and when he promulgated the 1983 *Code of Canon Law*, he remarked: "In the wake of the Second Vatican Council, at the beginning of my pastoral ministry, my aim was to emphasize forcefully the priestly, prophetic and kingly dignity of the entire People of God."[147] This Christ-centered understanding of the *principatus* (ruling power) indicates how the Leonine project of scouting and marking the sacred perimeter[148] continues apace, now with more emphasis on the laity. Leo's chief legacy is to have prompted the papal magisterium to think, and to think at levels deeper than diplomacy and public policy.

NOTES

1. *Tametsi futura* (November 1, 1900), §2, in *Leonis XIII Pontificis Maximi Acta*, 23 vols. (Rome: Ex Typographia Vaticana, 1881–1905), 20:295. Hereinafter, citations are to the section (§) where applicable, *Acta* volume, and page. Subsequent citations of particular documents include section and page.

2. Ibid., §6, 300.

3. *Annum sacrum* (May 25, 1899), §12, *Acta* 19:78–79.

4. Francis A. Burkle-Young, *Papal Elections in the Age of Transition, 1878–1922* (Lanham, Md.: Lexington Books, 2000), 44.

5. Ibid., 67.

6. *Inscrutabili Dei* (1878), §10, *Acta* 1:50.

7. Jacques Martin, *Heraldry in the Vatican* (Gerrards Cross, England: Van Duren, 1987), 197.

8. Only the *litterae encyclicae* and the *epistolae encyclicae* are encyclicals in the strict sense of the term. I use the expression "encyclicals and other teaching letters" to cover more inclusively other species of papal documents containing ordinary magisterial teaching. My enumeration of all species of teaching letters follows the *Enchiridion delle Encicliche*, 8 vols. (Bologna: Edizioni Edhoniane Bologne, 1994–98).

9. Wilfrid Ward, *William George Ward and the Catholic Revival* (London: Macmillan, 1893), 14.

10. *Praeclara gratulationis* (June 20, 1894), *Acta* 14:207. See John Courtney Murray's commentary on this letter, "Leo XIII: Separation of Church and State," *Theological Studies* 14 (1953): 145–214.

11. Ioannes Dominicus Mansi, ed., *Sacrorum Conciliorum Nova et Amplissima Collectio*, vol. 51 (Arnhem and Leipzig, 1926). *Primum Schema Constitutionis de Ecclesia Christi*, chaps. X–XV, 543–551; canons I–XXI, 551–553.

12. *Pastor aeternus* (July 18, 1870), chap. III, in *Decrees of the Ecumenical Councils*, ed. Norman P. Tanner, 2 vols. (Washington, D.C.: Georgetown University Press, 1990), 2:813ff.

13. *Rerum novarum* (May 15, 1891), §32, *Acta* 11:120.

14. The First Vatican Council affirmed a twofold order of cognition, faith, and reason, each with its own "distinct source and object." But this order does not constitute a dualism of truth, "since it is the same God who reveals the myster-

ies and infuses faith, and who has endowed the human mind with the light of reason" (*Dei Filius* [24 April 1870], chap. IV, in Tanner, *Decrees*, 2:808).

15. *Christianae reipublicae* (November 25, 1766), Bullarium Romanum, Cont. (Rome: Camera Apostolica, 1835–58), 3:226.

16. *Inscrutabile* (December 25, 1775), Bullarium Romanum, Cont., 3, no. 5: 178ff.

17. *Communicamus vobiscum* (9 March 1790), in *Collection générale des brefs et instructions de notre très-saint père le pape Pie VI, relatifs a la Rèvolution Françoise*, ed. M. N. S. Guillon, 2 vols. (Paris: Chez Le Clere, 1798), 1:8.

18. *Adeo nota* (April 23, 1791), in Guillon, *Collection générale*, 2:72.

19. Jean-Jacques Rousseau, preface to "Discourse on the Origin and Foundations of Inequality Among Men," in *Discourse on the Origins of Inequality (Second Discourse), Polemics, and Political Economy*, ed. Roger D. Masters and Christopher Kelly, in *The Collected Writings of Rousseau*, 6 vols. (Hanover, N.H.: University Press of New England, 1992), 3:15.

20. *Quod aliquantum* (March 10, 1791), in Guillon, *Collection générale*, 1:124–126.

21. Jacques-Benigne Bossuet, *Politics Drawn from the Very Words of Holy Scripture*, trans. and ed. Patrick Riley (Cambridge: Cambridge University Press, 1990), II.1, prop. 2, 40.

22. *Mirari vos* (August 15, 1832). Antonius Bernasconi, ed., *Acta Gregorii Papae XVI*, 4 vols. (Rome: S. C. de Propaganda Fide, 1901–1904), 1:171.

23. Donoso Cortés to Montalembert (June 4, 1849), in Juan Donoso Cortés, *Selected Works*, trans. and ed. Jeffrey P. Johnson (Westport, Conn.: Greenwood, 2000), 63.

24. Joseph de Maistre, *Considerations on France*, trans. and ed. Richard A. Lebrun (Cambridge: Cambridge University Press, 1994), 41.

25. Félicité Robert de Lamennais, *Essai sur l'indifférence* (1820), in *Oeuvres complètes de F. de La Mennais*, 12 vols. (Paris: P. Daubrée et Cailleux, 1836–1837), 1:21.

26. Communism is "opposed to the very natural law," *Qui pluribus* (November 9, 1846), §16, in *Pii IX Pontificis Maximi Acta*, part 1, 7 vols. (Rome: Ex Typographia Bonarum Artium, 1854–1878), 1:13; against socialism, he refers to "immutable" and "natural" principles (*Nostis et nobiscum* [December 8, 1849], §20, in *Pii IX Acta*, part 1, 1:211); and he appeals to natural rights (*Syllabus errorum* [December 8, 1864], §§26, 30, 33, 56, 67, in *Pii IX Acta*, part 1, 3:701–717).

27. Louis de Bonald, *On Divorce*, trans. and ed. Nicholas Davidson (New Brunswick, N.J.: Transaction, 1992), 73.

28. De Maistre, *Considerations*, 49.

29. An early use of this argument is found in Pius VI's *Quod aliquantum* (1791), in Guillon, *Collection générale*, 1:126. A more ambitious use of the argument can be found in Bonald, *On Divorce*, 48ff. On romantic conservatism in Catholic thought, see Ward, *George Ward and the Catholic Revival*, 95–100, and Heinrich A. Rommen, *The State in Catholic Thought: A Treatise in Political Philosophy* (St. Louis, Mo.: B. Herder, 1950), 238.

30. *Onorare le ceneri* (March 1, 1892), *Acta* 12:384ff.

31. Luigi Taparelli, whose work on natural law very much influenced Leo XIII, broke with the traditionalists on just these points. See Robert Jacquin, *Taparelli* (Paris: P. Lethielleux, 1943), 244.

32. *Aeterni Patris* (August 4, 1879), §2, *Acta* 1:257ff.

33. Ibid., §31, 282.

34. *Immortale Dei* (November 1, 1885), §40, *Acta* 5:144.

35. *Aeterni Patris*, §4, 259ff.

36. *Inscrutabile Dei* (April 21, 1878), §10, 50.

37. *Tametsi futura*, §9, 307.

38. *Aeterni Patris*, §18, 273.

39. Ibid., §29, 280.

40. Thomas Aquinas, *Sancti Thomae de Aquino Summa theologiae* (Rome: Editiones Paulinae, 1962), I–II, 90.1–4.

41. Ibid., 91.1, ad 3.

42. *Libertas* (June 20, 1888), §3, *Acta* 8:214.

43. Thomas does not include coercion and punishment in the definition of law; however, it is essential to coercion and punishment that they be acts of law (*Summa theologiae* I–II, 92.2).

44. Here, Leo draws from Thomas's distinction of the necessity imposed by the "contact of its action with the object on which it is acting" and the necessity of "obligation" arising from knowledge of a precept. *De Veritate*, 17, 3. St. Thomas Aquinas, *Quaestiones Disputatate*, vol. 1, ed. Raymundo Siazzi, O.P. (Turin: Casa Marietti, 1949).

45. Leo paraphrases Thomas, who says, "The root of liberty is the will as to its subject, but as to its cause it is reason" (*Summa theologiae* I–II, 17.1, ad 2).

46. *Libertas*, §7, 218.

47. *Summa theologiae* I–II, 17.1.

48. Ibid., I–II, 90.1, ad 3.

49. *Aeterni Patris*, §2, *Acta* 1:258; Vatican I: *Dei Filius*, chap. 2, Tanner, *Decrees*, 1:806.

50. *De caritate*, 1, in *Quaestiones Disputatae*, vol. 2. For other uses of Wisdom 8:1: (on creation) *S. Thomae Aquinatis doctoris angelici Liber de Veritate Catholicae Fidei contra errores Infidelium seu "Summa contra Gentiles"* (Turin: Casa Marietti, 1937), III.97; (on the virtue of charity) *Summa theologiae* II–II, 23.2; (on divine justice) *De potentia*, II.6. S. Thomas Aquinas, *Quaestiones Diputatate*, vol. 2, ed. P. Bazzi, M. Calcaterra, T. S. Centi, E. Odetto, and P. M. Pession (Turin: Casa Marietti, 1949).

51. *Summa theologiae* I, 103.8.

52. *Summa contra Gentiles* III.114.

53. *Summa theologiae* I–II, 90.4, ad 1.

54. Ibid., I–II, 91.1.

55. See Matthew Cuddeback, "Light and Form in St. Thomas Aquinas's Metaphysics of the Knower" (Ph.D. diss., Catholic University of America, 1998).

56. *Summa theologiae* II–II, 47.15.

57. Ibid., II–II, 34.1. The triadic structure of first precepts in I–II, 94.2, follows this pattern.

58. Ibid., I–II, 106.1.

59. *Libertas*, §8, 219.

60. Ibid., §9, 220.

61. Jean-Jacques Rousseau, *The Social Contract and Other Later Political Writings*, ed. and trans. Victor Gourevitch (Cambridge: Cambridge University Press, 1997), I.1, 41.

62. *Diuturnum illud* (June 29, 1881), §11, *Acta* 2:274.

63. *Sapientiae Christianae* (January 10, 1890), §8, *Acta* 10:15.

64. *Immortale Dei*, §18, 130.

65. *Annum sacrum* (May 25, 1899), §§5–6, 74ff. This refers to Thomas's discussion of the judicial powers of Christ in *Summa theologiae* II–II, 67.2, ad 2.

66. *Libertas*, §13, 223. See also *Quod Apostolici muneris* (December 28, 1878), §7, *Acta* 1:177; *Diuturnum*, §15, 277 (where it is used in connection to Rom. 13:1 and Matt. 22:21 on the things that are Caesar's); *Sapientiae Christianae*, §7, 15 (on the duty of citizens not to be treasonous to God); *Immortale Dei*, §12, 126 (on the liberty of the church, but also in light of Rom. 13:1 at §3); *Officio sanctissimo* (December 22, 1887), §9, *Acta* 7:233 (on Catholic resistance to the Bavarian *Kulturkampf*).

67. After all hope of altar-throne alliance was dashed, Pius IX used Acts 5:29 to trace the boundary of Matt. 22:21 regarding the things not owed to Caesar (*Quod Quod Nunquam* [February 5, 1875], §10, in *Pii IX Acta*, part 1, 7:10ff).

68. *Diuturnum*, §12, 275ff.

69. Wilhelm Emmanuel von Ketteler, "The Labor Problem and Christianity" (1871), in *The Social Teachings of Wilhelm Emmanuel von Ketteler*, trans. Rupert J. Ederer (Washington, D.C.: University Press of America, 1981), 363ff. For his argument that the natural dignity of the human soul under the eternal law requires a structured pluralism of authority, see "Freedom, Authority and the Church" (1862), in *Social Teachings*, 155ff.

70. *Libertas*, §15, 224ff. See also *Quod Apostolici*, §2, 173, and *Immortale*, §24, 133ff.

71. *Summa theologiae* I–II, 91.2, ad 1.

72. See John Paul II, *Veritatis splendor* (August 6, 1993), §41, in *Acta Apostolicae Sedis: Commentarium officiale* (hereinafter AAS) (Rome: Typis Polyglottis Vaticanis, 1909–), 85:1166: "Others speak, and rightly so, of 'theonomy,' or 'participated theonomy,' since man's free obedience to God's law effectively implies that human reason and human will participate in God's wisdom and providence."

73. *Tametsi futura*, §7, 303.

74. Abraham Kuyper, *Lectures on Calvinism* (Grand Rapids, Mich.: Eerdmans, 1961), 91, 90. Emphasis in original.

75. *Immortale*, §18, 130.

76. *Quod Apostolici*, §6, 176.

77. *Sapientiae Christianae*, §36, 34.

78. *Summa theologiae* I–II, 90.3, ad 3.

79. Ibid., II–II, 50.1, ad 3.

80. Some forty times, according to the word count by Mary Elsbernd in "Papal Statements on Rights: A Historical Contextual Study of Encyclical Teaching from Pius VI–Pius XI (1791–1939)" (Ph.D. diss., Catholic University of Louvain, 1985), 282 n. 1.

81. *Arcanum divinae* (February 10, 1880), §14, *Acta* 2:19.

82. Ibid., §19, 23.

83. Ibid., §32, 19.

84. By the natural duty and participated authority of the parents, as well as by virtue of their religious obligation. *Officio sanctissimo*, §11, 235. A good summary of Leo's thought on the school question is provided by Elsbernd, "Papal Statements," 305–309.

85. For an account of the policy issues, see Lillian Parker Wallace, *Leo XIII and the Rise of Socialism* (Durham, N.C.: Duke University Press, 1966).

86. The complications and finer texture of Leo's arguments are well considered by Matthew Habiger, *Papal Teaching on Private Property, 1891–1981* (Lanham, Md.: University Press of America, 1990).

87. *Rerum novarum*, §6, 101.

88. Ibid., §5, 99; §9, 103.

89. Ibid., §13, 105.

90. Ibid., 106.

91. Ibid., 105.

92. Ibid., §46, 131.

93. Some scholars point out that Leo seems to differ markedly from Thomas on the use/possession distinction. See Habiger, *Papal Teaching*, 15–24; and Elsbernd, "Papal Statements," 312–325. The most provocative essay on the issue is Ernest L. Fortin's "'Sacred and Inviolable': *Rerum Novarum* and Natural Rights," *Theological Studies* 53 (June 1992): 203–233.

94. *Rerum novarum*, §51, 134–135.

95. Ibid., §53, 137. On liberty of religious associations, see *Pastoralis vigilantiae* (June 25, 1891), *Acta* 11:27ff.

96. St. Thomas Aquinas, *Contra impugnantes Dei Cultum et Religionem* (Rome: Ad Sanctae Sabinae, 1970).

97. Ibid., I.5.

98. Ibid., I.3.

99. Ibid.

100. Ibid., I.4. citing Augustine, *De doctrina christiana*, I.1.

101. Charles Montesquieu, *The Spirit of the Laws*, trans. and ed. Anne M. Cohler, Basia Carolyn Miller, and Harold Samuel Stone (Cambridge: Cambridge University Press, 1989), 11.4, 155.

102. *Rerum novarum*, §55, 138.

103. *Nobilissima Gallorum* (February 8, 1884), §4, *Acta* 4:15ff.

104. *Immortale*, §27, 135; *Iampridem* (January 6, 1886), §6, *Acta* 6:7; *Libertas*, §§39–40, 242ff.; *Inimica vis* (December 8, 1892), *Acta* 12:325–330. See his warning to Americans not to confuse "the Church, which is a divine society, and all other social human organizations which depend simply on the free will and choice of men" (*Testem benevolentiae* [January 22, 1899], *Acta* 19:9).

105. Murray, "Leo XIII: Separation," 173. This is first of four essays on Leo, including also "Leo XIII on Church and State: The General Structure of the Controversy," *Theological Studies* 14 (1953): 1–30; "Leo XIII: Two Concepts of Government," *Theological Studies* 14 (1953): 551–567; and "Leo XIII: Two Concepts of Government: II. Government and the Order of Culture," *Theological Studies* 15 (1954): 1–33. Murray's essays are a towering achievement. They are tinged, however, with his polemic against Roman curialists and European thinkers on the church-state issue. A plodding but more careful evaluation of Leo's thought and precedent for Catholic social teaching on church and state is the six-part study by Basile Valuet, *La liberté religieuse et la tradition Catholique: Un cas de développement doctrinal homogène dans le magistère authentique*, 2d rev. ed., 3 vols. (Le Barroux: Abbaye Sainte-Madeleine, 1998).

106. *Au milieu* (February 16, 1892), §29, *Acta* 12:39.

107. *Ci siamo* (June 1, 1879), *Acta* 1:240.

108. See Murray, "Leo XIII: Separation," 160, 176.

109. Using a typology that goes back to Leo's time, Roman canonists distinguished *La separazione pura*, in which all churches are treated as private societies and equally protected by law; *La separazione ostile alla chiesa*, in which the state seeks to deny to the church the right to guide the moral life of her subjects as citizens; and *La separazione parziale*, which concedes to the church some rights proper to a moral person in public law. See Ludovicus Bender, *Chiesa e stato* (Rome: Editrice A. V. E., 1945).

110. Murray finds the phrase *libertas ecclesiae* or its cognates used in more than sixty Leonine documents. John Courtney Murray, "The Problem of State Religion," *Theological Studies* 12 (1951): 156 n. 3.

111. According to the threefold *munera Christi*—priest, prophet, and king. Leo had much to say about Christ's ruling powers, and by participation, those of the church.

112. *Quod apostolici*, §10, 181.

113. *Diuturnum*, §18, 279 (on the form); *Licet multa* (1881), §3, *Acta* 2:323 (penetrating all orders of the *civitas*); *Graves de communi* (January 18, 1901), *Acta* 21:6ff. (the form impressed by God).

114. *Tametsi futura*, §11, 310.

115. *Sapientiae christianae*, §27, 28; *Arcanum divinae*, §19, 23.

116. *Noblissima*, §4, 15ff.

117. *Immortale*, §14, 128.

118. In an interview given to French journalists, published in *Petit Journal* (February 7, 1892), quoted in Eduardo Soderini, *Leo XIII, Italy and France*, trans. Barbara Barclay Carter (London: Burns, Oates & Washbourne, 1935), 219.

119. "For the Church amongst you, unopposed by the Constitution and government of your nation, fettered by no hostile legislation, protected against violence by the common laws and the impartiality of the tribunals, is free to live and act without hindrance" (*Longinqua oceani* [January 6, 1895], §6, *Acta* 15:7).

120. *Immortale*, §6, 122ff.

121. *Libertas*, §18, 228.

122. "There was once a time when *civitates* were governed by the philosophy of the Gospel. Then it was that the power and divine virtue of Christian wisdom had diffused itself throughout the laws, institutions, and morals of the people, permeating all ranks and relations of civil society" (*Immortale*, §21, 132).

123. *Immortale*, §4, 121.

124. *Libertas*, §2, 119.

125. Ibid., §16, 225.

126. The first pope to use this language was Pius XII, who spoke of the state as having the role of coordinating action, *quasi-instrumentum*, toward the common good (*Summi pontificatus* [October 20, 1939], §59; AAS, 31:433). See also John XXIII, *Pacem in terris* (April 11, 1963), §68, *Acta Synodalia Sacrosancti Concilii Oecumenici Vaticani Secundi, Congregatio Generalis CLXIV* (Vatican City: Typis Polyglottis Vaticanis, 1978), 55:276. Jacques Maritain developed the concept extensively in *Man and the State* (Chicago: University of Chicago Press, 1951), 1–27.

127. *Au milieu*, §17, 31.

128. *Libertas*, §44, 245.

129. *Immortale*, §36, 141.

130. *Sapientiae christianae*, §28, 28.

131. *Libertas*, §43, 245.

132. *Sapientiae christianae*, §28, 28.

133. *Au milieu*, §14, 28–29.

134. See Bishop John Ireland's sermon "The Catholic Church and Civil Society," given at the Third Plenary Council of Baltimore (1884), in John Ireland, *The Church and Modern Society: Lectures and Addresses*, 2 vols. (Chicago: D. H. McBride, 1896), 1:27–65.

135. *Diuturnum*, §§5–6, 271ff.

136. Joseph de Maistre, *Du Pape* (Geneva: Droz, 1966), II.1, 130.

137. And on slender textual reeds. Cardinal Cajetan (1480–1547), in his commentary on *Summa theologiae* II–II, 50.1, ad 3, introduced the notion of the people translating authority to a king (*potestatem in eum transtulerunt*), and then went on to speculate about a primordial election. Cajetan's commentary was included in the 1895 Leonine edition of the *Opera S. Thomae*. Undoubtedly, Thomas thought that authority is the predicate of a political community, but this is about all that can be concluded from the texts.

138. The history of the debate is considered most judiciously by Jeremiah Newman, *Studies in Political Morality* (Dublin: Scepter, 1962). For the thought of Leo's mentors, such as Taparelli, who clearly rejected the translation theory, see Jacquin, *Taparelli*, appendix K, 259–265.

139. In *Au milieu*, Leo says in light of Rom. 13:1 that "all the novelty is limited to the political form of civil power or to its mode of transmission; it in no way affects the power considered in itself" (§18, 32). This remark can be interpreted either way. At the time, Cardinal Billot explained that Leo denied what has "ways been denied with unanimous consent by Catholic theologians," namely, that the people create the *principatus*. For Billot's response, see Alfred Rahilly, "The Sovereignty of the People," *Studies* (Dublin) X (1921): 39–56, 277–287. At 280 Rahilly cites Cardinal Billot: "What is denied is what has always been denied with unanimous consent by Catholic theologians." Rahilly lists some 139 scholastic thinkers who held the translation theory. The roll call is assessed somewhat more carefully by Gabriel Bowe, *The Origin of Political Authority: An Essay in Catholic Political Philosophy* (Dublin: Clonmore & Reynolds, 1955).

140. But see Pius XII's address to the Roman Rota (October 2, 1945): "We bear in mind the favorite thesis of democracy—a doctrine which great Christian thinkers have proclaimed in all ages—namely, that the original subject of civil power derived from God is the people (not the 'masses')" (AAS 37:258ff.).

141. Rommen, *The State in Catholic Thought*, 380–470; Maritain, *Man and the State*; and Yves R. Simon, *Philosophy of Democratic Government* (Chicago: University of Chicago Press, 1951), who called it "transmission theory."

142. Here, relying on the word count by Elsbernd, "Papal Statements," 406.

143. *Studiorum ducem* (June 29, 1923), §20, AAS 15:319.

144. *Quadragesimo anno* (May 15, 1931), §44, AAS 23:191.

145. "The democratic form of government appears to many as a postulate of nature imposed upon reason itself." *Benignitas et humanitas* (1944), AAS 37:13.

146. Written and mimeographed for distribution at the council in the fall of 1964, and published under the title "The Problem of Religious Freedom," in John Courtney Murray, *Religious Liberty: Catholic Struggles with Pluralism*, ed. J. Leon Hooper (Louisville, Ky.: Westminster John Knox Press, 1993), 127–197.

147. On the *ratio novitatis*, see the apostolic constitution *Sacrae disciplinae* (January 25, 1983); AAS 75, part 2: xii; for the pledge to devote his pastoral ministry to the idea, see *Christifideles laici* (December 20, 1988), §14, AAS 81:410ff.

148. The term *périmètre sacré* is from de Maistre's *Du pape*, where it refers to the orbit in which papal authority must prevail.

{ CHAPTER 3 }

Jacques Maritain (1882–1973)

PATRICK MCKINLEY BRENNAN

According to a commonplace expression, which is a very profound one, man must become what he is. In the moral order, he must win, by himself, his freedom and his personality.
—JACQUES MARITAIN, *SCHOLASTICISM AND POLITICS*

Of the twenty figures selected for study in this volume, only one appears in the most comprehensive textbook of Anglo-American jurisprudence. The singleton is Jacques Maritain (1882–1973), and included in *Lloyd's Introduction to Jurisprudence* are excerpts from one of Maritain's leading books in political philosophy, *Man and the State.*[1] Absent from *Lloyd's*, however, is any analysis of the inclusions from Maritain. This omission of analysis, a deviation from the textbook's usual practice, perhaps suggests something of the meaning of Jacques Maritain to mainstream English-language jurisprudence. Maritain's work is acknowledged in the wide world of legal philosophy, but not comprehended. Jacques Maritain was a philosopher; indeed, to philosophize, he believed, was his vocation. But Jacques Maritain philosophized, inveterately, in a once-regnant dialect that many today hear but cannot—or will not—understand, let alone defend. It was Maritain's passionate vocation as a philosopher to know, develop, and apply the thought of St. Thomas Aquinas, that thirteenth-century member of the Dominican order to whom Pope Leo XIII in 1879 recalled the attention of his faithful. But though Maritain applied his Thomism to the times, to the engines and aspirations of "analytic philosophy" of law, his contribution has seemed largely irrelevant.[2]

It is not only mainstream philosophers of law who have trouble embracing Maritain. To numerous contemporary Catholics, even those who find in Maritain great jurisprudential treasures, the man is an enigma. Some find in Maritain an authentic Thomist. Others warm to him for going beyond Thomist principles and conclusions. Still others find Maritain's expansions of Aquinas's mind completely foreign.

What is particularly noteworthy about the incomprehension of Maritain is not just that Maritain spoke the dialect of a philosophy that Catholics and others have regarded as perennial or lasting. Paradoxically, there are those who blame Maritain for contributing to the end to the eighty-year revival of Thomism to which he himself was one of the outstanding contributors. Those holding this latter view—who would convict Maritain of ushering in an era of polyvocal Catholic moral discourse anathema to a true Thomist—point to Maritain's influential role in the thinking and teaching of the Second Vatican Council (1962–65). Consulted both in preparation for and during the council's sessions,[3] Maritain was the lone layperson singled out by Pope Paul VI for honor at the council's end. Promptly upon the completion of Vatican II, however, Maritain published a book, *The Peasant of the Garonne: An Old Man Questions Himself About the Present Time*, decrying dangerous social and intellectual movements apparently spawned by the council.

But if in the old man's book there erupts reaction to unintended consequences of what the pope had called *aggiornamento* (updating), Maritain, even as an octogenarian, was still no reactionary. *The Peasant of the Garonne* began with Maritain's celebration of the council's clarification, even its amplification, of doctrines touching deeply the meaning of human life in the world. Referring to the council's work, Maritain wrote: "It is a joy to think that the true idea of freedom—of that freedom to which man aspires in his profoundest self, and which is one of the privileges of the spirit—is henceforth recognized and given a place of honor among the great germinal ideas of Christian wisdom; and likewise the true idea of the human person, and of his dignity and his rights."[4] These ideas enjoyed, in addition to their truth, the support of Maritain's philosophizing. During the half-century preceding the Second Vatican Council, Jacques Maritain had been making the Christian philosopher's case for ideas that, within his own lifetime, became Catholic doctrine on humankind and the state. Ideas that were not easily traceable to Aquinas—"liberal" ideas of liberty, equality, and fraternity, associated with modernity and even the French Revolution—were celebrated and expanded by the Second Vatican Council. In the council's declarations and decrees on social and political matters, one hears resounding echoes of Maritain's teachings on humankind and the state.

Maritain was not in the first instance a philosopher of politics or law. Social and political thoughts issued from Maritain's pen as products of his dedicated quest to understand the whole of reality, created and redeemed.

The challenge for any student of Jacques Maritain, even the one interested above all in his jurisprudence, is to comprehend the whole of the man's mind. Maritain's mind traveled forcefully but fluently among the subjects of philosophy, biology, art, poetry, theology, mystical theology, moral philosophy, political philosophy, and jurisprudence—indeed, the whole of the Western tradition of learning, and a considerable amount of Eastern learning as well. There is no trace of the dilettante or souvenir-collecting tourist in Maritain, however. There was force to his march, for Maritain the philosopher was after nothing short of truth. Yet his march was not forced, but smooth, natural, even supernatural. As James Schall, an insightful student of Maritain, observes, "What is most striking about [Maritain] ... is his capacity to indicate how one thing leads to everything else."[5]

Everything in Maritain's thought eventually led to the instance of *being*. Maritain's jurisprudence was, in its essentials, the expansion of a *philosophy of being* that delights in the unity and overflowing generosity of the being that is God's creation. Maritain's jurisprudential corpus pulses with hope for the free unfolding of the human person into communities of friendship, justice, and love wherein art, beauty, music, and mutual sacrifice are the ordinary incidents of a life springing from recognition of the dignity and correlative rights of every person rooted in his or her nature and transcendent destiny. "Maritain ever remains," as Schall comments, "a philosopher of *all that is*, of God and nature, of logic and metaphysics, of mathematics and art, and, yes, of man and the state."[6]

BIOGRAPHY

In his more than ninety years, Jacques Maritain wrote some ninety books and hundreds of articles and smaller pieces. He spoke out against Nazism, fascism, and racism. He worked to bring democracy not only to Europe but also to Central and South America. He taught at Princeton and lectured at many of the world's great universities. He served as France's ambassador to the Holy See, and in humility he declined to receive from Pope Paul VI a cardinal's red hat and the attendant honor of standing as a prince of the church he loved dearly and served devotedly. Until 1960, when his wife Raissa died, Jacques did all his work in deep collaboration with her; he referred to her as *"dimidium animae,"* half my soul. After Raissa's death, Jacques lived with the Little Brothers of Jesus in near reclusion near Toulouse, France, and eventually made vows as one of the brethren.

The extraordinary life of Jacques Maritain began in Paris in 1882. His father was Catholic; his mother, Genevieve Favre (the daughter of Jules Favre, a founder of the Third Republic) was Protestant. His father and mother divorced when Jacques was a youth, and he was baptized in the French Reformed Church and received religious instruction from the liberal Protestant theologian Jean Reville. During his youth, however, Maritain considered himself an unbeliever. From 1899 to 1906, he studied at the Sorbonne. Of this experience he wrote in 1941, "The scientist and phenomenist philosophy of my teachers at the Sorbonne at last made me despair of reason."[7] It was early in this barren period that Maritain met the seventeen-year-old Russian Jewish immigrant Raissa Oumansoff, whom he would marry in 1904. From the beginning Jacques and Raissa were united by a desire to search together untiringly for the truth. At one point the husband and wife contemplated suicide should their quest for truth not succeed. Raissa and Jacques Maritain's life together was structured, in important respects, according to a monastic ideal of prayer and work in the tradition of St. Benedict of Nursia.[8] One does well to remember, as one encounters the sometimes strident and always passionate Jacques Maritain, that he was a convert, " '[a] man God has turned inside out like a glove.' "[9]

Three figures stood out in the Maritains' pilgrimage to the Catholic faith. The first was the great and charismatic philosopher Henri Bergson. For the Maritains, Bergson was "the first to answer our deep desire for metaphysical truth—he liberated in us the sense of the absolute."[10] For this emancipation both Maritains remained forever and profoundly grateful to Bergson. The two other crucial influences in the early period were their friends Leon Bloy and Charles Peguy. Bloy taught that for the Christian there is just one sadness: not to be a saint. Arrested by Bloy's uncompromising commitment to the call to sainthood, the Maritains began a tutorship in Catholicism under Bloy and received the sacrament of baptism in 1906. Raissa wrote that as a result "an immense peace descended" upon them. "There were no more questions ... there was only the infinite answer of God."[11]

Not long after this conversion came another. In 1910, Maritain recorded in his *Notebooks*, "Finally! Thanks to Raissa, I begin to read the *Summa Theologiae* [of Thomas Aquinas]. As it was for her, it is a deliverance, an inundation of light. The intellect finds its home."[12] But perhaps it is a mistake to characterize this experience as a second conversion, for it was Maritain's sense that he was a Thomist even before he read St. Thomas, and that when he came upon the *Summa*, "its luminous flood was to find no opposing obstacles in me."[13] Even more dramatic, perhaps, and explanatory of so much that was to follow was Jacques Maritain's declaration: "Woe is me if I do not thomisticize."[14] The Thomistic revival called for by Pope Leo XIII in 1879 was well under way by the time Maritain discovered his vocation to "thomisticize." One of Maritain's particular contributions was to direct his work on Aquinas beyond the largely clerical audiences targeted by many of the first efforts.[15] Amid a revival of interest in Thomas that was often called "neo-Thomist," Maritain adamantly insisted that he was a Thomist plain and simple.[16] But it must be said at once, that if Maritain was a Thomist, he was one who, without blinking, could cheerfully use "traditional Thomistic categories to argue to a conclusion that would have horrified Saint Thomas."[17]

From 1906 to 1908 the Maritains were in Germany, where Jacques studied biology at the University of Heidelberg. In 1912, following several years of editing and other independent intellectual work, Maritain accepted the offer of the chair of philosophy at the Institut Catholique of Paris. In 1914, he published his first book, *Bergsonian Philosophy*; this scathing critique of his mentor's account of the mind's grasp of being promptly earned the young Maritain a reputation as a controversialist. Many other works followed, most notably *Art and Scholasticism* (1920), *The Degrees of Knowledge* (1932), and *A Preface to Metaphysics* (1934). These early speculative works revealed the young Maritain heeding Pope Leo XIII's call to take Thomas as the privileged starting point for meeting the challenges of the day. *The Degrees of Knowledge*, subtitled *Distinguish in Order to Unite*, is regarded by many as Maritain's masterwork, and is without doubt one of the greatest contributions to Thomism in the twentieth century. Ralph McInerny, one of Maritain's leading students, writes of that book that "better than any other single work of Maritain, [it] displays the comprehensiveness and range of his interests. Its author takes his inspiration from Thomas Aquinas, reargues his basic positions in the light of the problems posed for them in the twentieth century, and ends by writing a profoundly original work."[18]

By working out the distinctions and unity among the philosophy of nature, experimental science, metaphysics, and mystical theology—in light of the underlying unity and distinctions of *being* knowable by human intelligence—Maritain affirmed the *unity* of faith and reason. This unity and its consequences are a hallmark of all Maritain's work. A truly "Christian philosophy," such as Maritain sought and expounded, "while pursuing a method that is not theological but purely and strictly philosophical ... will produce 'a conception of nature and reason open to the supernatural,' confirmed by data natural of themselves, and not repugnant to data supernatural of themselves contained in the deposit of Revelation."[19] When Maritain distinguished modes of human knowing, it was in order to call attention to the need for *wisdom*, both natural and supernatural. Jacques Maritain understood it to be his vocation, in sum, to work out a distinctly Christian and properly Thomist philosophy for the twentieth century, making way for wisdom to enter.

The Maritains first turned their search for truth in political matters in the mid-1920s. In the years leading up to 1926, Jacques had been connected to Action Française, the traditionalist and monarchist movement led by Charles Maurras and supported by many conservative Catholics. In that year Pope Pius XI condemned the movement, a most unsettling turn of events for Maritain, who had believed that Action Française "was devoted to preserving traditional values and restoring order and justice."[20] Grasping at last the fundamentally secularist scope of the movement, which was content to use the church to its own ends, Maritain broke with the movement. Then, at the pope's request, he wrote his first book of political philosophy, *The Primacy of the Spiritual* (1927), a forecast of much that would follow.

When Hitler came to power and then war loomed, "the circumstances of the time and their own zeal for justice obliged the Maritains to set aside some of their cherished projects in philosophy to devote more and more of their thought to social and political questions."[21] By 1936, when Jacques published his charter work in political philosophy, *Integral Humanism*, he and Raissa had spent a decade involved in movements of many kinds, resisting totalitarianism both of the left and of the right.[22] But even if Jacques operated in the thick of politics, he adhered to no party and declared, "to remain [a] philosopher and act as [a] philosopher, one must maintain everywhere the liberty of philosophy and in particular to affirm ceaselessly the independence of the philosopher from whatever political parties there are."[23]

Maritain's *Scholasticism and Politics*, the product of lectures given at the University of Chicago in 1938, appeared in 1940. The book contains some of Maritain's most trenchant treatments of the practical topics that would dominate all his philosophizing on political topics. Here Maritain made abundantly clear that to discern humankind's proper place in the world, the Christian philosopher must respect the truth about humankind revealed in Christ and in the Christian tradition. Maritain's audience was not always so convinced. After the fall of France in 1940, while the Maritains were traveling in the United States, Maritain's friends at the University of Chicago tried to arrange for him a visiting appointment in the Department of Philosophy. Historian John T. McGreevy reports the result: "The department chairman refused to pursue the matter. 'Professor Maritain's reputation in this part of the world,' he explained, 'is largely that of an apologist or propagandist for Catholic doctrine.' "[24]

The Maritains were forced to live in exile in the United States until 1945. Then, from 1945 to 1948, Jacques was in Rome, serving at General de Gaulle's request as France's ambassador to the Vatican. Pope Pius XII apparently took inspiration from Maritain's philosophical work, as did the young Monsignor Giovanni Battista Montini, the future Pope Paul VI, who in time would consider Maritain his "master."[25] A monumental moment in Maritain's ambassadorial service occurred in Mexico City, in November 1947, when as head of the French delegation and president of the UNESCO General Conference, he spoke powerfully on "The Possibilities of Cooperation in a Divided World"—a moment to "[s]peak to the whole world, as it were."[26] Ambassadorial duties kept Maritain busy, but he continued to write and during this period published two works of great significance to his jurisprudence, *Essence and the Existent* (1947) and *The Person and the Common Good* (1946).

His work in Rome completed, Maritain accepted an appointment in philosophy at Princeton University in 1948, at the age of sixty-five. He taught for five years, retiring in 1953. He remained in the United States until Raissa's death in 1960. In those dozen years Maritain published fifteen books. These included, most notably, *Creative Intuition in Art and Poetry* (1953), *An Introduction to the Basic Problems of Moral Philosophy* (1951), and *Moral Philosophy* (1960). They also included *Man and the State* (1951), arguably his leading work in political philosophy. This last work was based on his Walgreen Lectures of 1949, delivered at the University of Chicago. Maritain continued to publish until his death in 1973. Even then, he was awaiting the proofs of a new book.

Although Maritain continued to be the philosopher, which to the end he insisted was his vocation, two complementary facets of the man and his life should be noted. First, relationships of all kinds, including deep friendships, were an integral part of this philosopher's life. Maritain had many friends and formed friendships of all kinds, often products of intense spiritual or intellectual encounters. In Paris, Maritain interacted, for example, with Vladimir Lossky and Nicholas Berdyaev. In America, Maritain was good friends with Saul Alinsky, the secular Jew who delighted in cooperating with Catholic clergy to create community organizations. In his last visit to the United States in 1966, Jacques traveled to a hermitage near the Trappist-Cistercian Abbey of Gethsemani in Kentucky to spend time with his friend Thomas Merton, monk and antiwar protester. Maritain was a philosopher in the world, rooted in real fraternal relationships.

Second, Maritain's life ended where he and Raissa began: in a passionate unwavering pursuit of the whole truth,[27] a truth sometimes found only on one's knees. The discovery, contemplation, and dissemination of the whole truth about humankind in unfolding Christian history: these are the sources and springs of Jacques Maritain's jurisprudence.

The path ahead begins with Maritain's existential starting points; it proceeds from there to his account of human freedom and the natural law that is its guide; and from there it turns to his correlative but controversial account of natural human rights. With those foundations in place, it becomes possible to trace the outlines of the development of Maritain's account of humankind in the state. The central components of Maritain's jurisprudence proper are considered, including the distinction between the individual and the person, civil society and the state, positive law and authority, the common good, equality and democracy and humankind's rights before the state, and, finally, grace's operation in the world of civil society and the state. Maritain "makes demands on the modern reader that he will not often encounter" elsewhere.[28] At the same time, Maritain offers to the persevering reader an understanding of the world, and humankind's transcendent place in it, that can open new horizons and, in doing so, generate fresh hope for life under law.

ESSENCE AND EXISTENCE, NATURAL LAW AND NATURAL RIGHTS

Maritain's writings about political matters teem with references to his writings in other areas, particularly his works on the philosophy of being. These references are not merely decorative; they carry freight. Maritain's political philosophy is *philosophy*; his views on politics depend on his philosophy of being and of human nature. Accordingly, the place to begin to understand Maritain's political philosophy is at the heart of his philosophy, an existentialism that he found already adumbrated in Aquinas. The purpose of Maritain's jurisprudence was to unleash being in the act of essentially, but fully, human existence.

What this means will begin to become clear by looking at the familiar contrast between essence and existence. The most enduring insight of Aristotle, taken up and developed by Thomas Aquinas, was that every constituent of the natural world is what it is by virtue of its essence. The essence of a thing is the intelligible form or unifying principle that constitutes the thing. This is what distinguishes a thing from every other sort of thing that is. It is one thing to be constituted as a horse, quite another to be constituted as a human being. Contrary to the "nominalist" tradition that denied that in the givens of the world are essences that would and should guide their development, the Thomistic tradition insisted upon the reality of essences. These essences are the stable but dynamic structures that determine—or, in the face of human freedom, *ask* to determine—what is in, or what will come into, being.

Maritain stood squarely in the Thomistic philosophical tradition that affirmed the *reality* of essences. He maintained as ardently as any Thomist that the world has naturally been given essences, discernible organizing principles or purposes.[29] But Maritain insisted that to focus obsessively on essences is to miss the *decisive* point. Essences were important, yes, but *existence* was even more so. Whether something exists, or fails to exist, makes all the difference! Against a mere "philosophy of essences," a "thumbing through a picture-book," Maritain called for "the philosophy of existence and of existential realism, the confrontation of the act of existing by an intelligence determined never to disown itself."[30] Reacting against the increasingly static and geometricized rationalisms that had crept into the interpretation of Aquinas through the centuries, Maritain affirmed essences. But this affirmation was only an overture, first, to the intelligibility of being and the correlative power of the human intellect to penetrate being, including human being, and second, to the primacy of the dispositive *act of existence.*

As to the first point, Maritain held that the human mind can be in *intuitive* contact with that which exists. The following remarkable passage summarized Maritain's assessment of this cognitive act and of what, by way of that act, reaches human understanding:

> [This intuition] is a perception direct and immediate.... It is a very simple sight, superior to any discursive reasoning or demonstration, because it is the source of demonstration. It is a sight whose content and implications no words of human speech can exhaust or adequately express and in which in a moment of decisive emotion, as it were, of spiritual conflagration, the soul is in contact, a living, penetrating and illuminating contact, with a reality which it touches and which takes hold of it.... It is being more than anything else which produces such an intuition."[31]

That the human mind can grasp all this, directly and immediately (without a mediating act of "judgment"), is a point bitterly disputed among Thomists.[32] This important dispute cannot detain us here. Maritain's position required a high level of confidence in the human person's capacity to know the real, so long as the intellectual work is done. As Maritain put it: "One is a Thomist because one has repudiated every attempt to find philosophical truth in any system fabricated by an individual ... and because one wants to seek out what is true—for oneself, indeed, and by one's own reason—by allowing oneself to be taught by the whole range of human thought, in order not to neglect anything of that which is."[33] Knowledge enters thanks to "docility to the real."[34]

As to the second point, for Maritain the primacy of the act of existence meant moving beyond a petrified notion of the real—that "picture-book" of essences to be thumbed through," as he had called it—and, "with that great zeal for being which animates Thomist thought,"[35] "understanding ... all things in the light and the generosity of being."[36] As Maritain prefaced the *Degrees of Knowledge*: "No treasuring up of experiences, none of the advantages, none of the graces of thought's advancing age can possibly replace the youth, the virginity of observation, the intuitive upsurge of intellect, as yet unwearied, towards the delicious novelty of the real."[37] The human mind is offered the freedom—indeed, the exigence—to try to keep up with the dynamism of all created being. From nothingness God brought forth not static stuffs but, rather, potencies bursting with being. Maritain identified the existential dynamism of being in these terms:

> Things are not only what they are. They ceaselessly pass beyond themselves, and give more than they have, because from all sides they are permeated by the activating influx of the Prime Cause. They are better and worse than themselves, because *being superabounds*, and because nothingness attracts what comes from nothingness. Thus it is that they communicate with each other in an infinity of fashions and through an infinity of actions and contacts, sympathies and ruptures.[38]

All this takes on its full import in light of a related Thomistic doctrine, much mined by Maritain, that of the transcendental passions or properties of all being. According to many philosophies, what is simply *is*. For Thomists, however, being not only is; being enjoys unity, truth, beauty, and *goodness*. Maritain never equivocated on this point: "Every thing is good to the extent that it is, that it has *esse* [being]. Being and the good are convertible notions."[39] That which is, is good. Creation is the going forth of being from God, and it abounds according to God's universal governance,[40] the Eternal Law. Except where angels and persons are concerned, this is the simple and glorious end to the story. And it is all very *good*.

The human person, however, holds the potential to be a free contributor to "the expansion and generosity of being."[41] All that is, all being—existence and essence—is good. So, inasmuch as a person *is*, he or she is good. But further, "in casting a good action into the universe, a free agent increases the being of the universe."[42] Being, as such, is superabounding and good. When it comes to the human being, his glory is his created *freedom* to contribute to being's increase, what Maritain referred to as the "freedom of expansion."[43] This celebration of human freedom rankles in the ears of some traditional Thomists and others. For, while Maritain's insistence that humankind's conquest of freedom consists in freedom's being conformed to truth was quite traditional,[44] his boasts about the glory of human freedom were not.

But with the glory of freedom comes the risk of evil. Human beings cause evil exactly when they exercise their freedom to block the unfolding of being and its goodness. Evil, specifically moral evil, enters—or, more precisely, good fails to continue to enter and abound—upon the related occurrence of both a nonevent and an event. The nonevent is the person's failure to advert to, or to consider, "the rule" that would shape and guide one's action so that one's being might continue, and continue to expand. This is a purely negative moment, what Maritain calls a "nihilating."[45] This nonevent, this free refusal to attend to "the rule" of human conduct, is but the first stage in the two-stage process that eventuates in moral evil. Evil is, exactly, the lack of what is *due*, of what *ought* to be; but humanity is not obligated to know the rule about what is due, or ought to be. "What is required of the soul," according to Maritain, "is not that it should always look to the rule or have the ruler constantly in hand, but that it should *produce its act* while looking at the rule."[46] Moral evil results when, in the second moment, the person acts in accordance with that negation, acts without being informed by the rule that *ought* to measure his conduct and would thereby allow being to grow and increase. A mere nihilation becomes a privation by the person's allowing the divine initiative to go forward without benefit of the rule that should direct it.

Gazing upon the havoc and harm wrought in the first half of the twentieth century, Maritain had no doubt that moral evil abounds. Why does God allow creatures to use their "power of nihilating to develop all forms of degradation and corruption of being" and to "flounder in the mire"? Because "God plays fair," said Maritain.[47] Women and men work great harm to themselves and their fellow travelers; they work moral evil, and in doing so, they sin. But God "did not invent moral evil and sin.... Those were born solely of nihilation by human liberty. They came forth from that abyss. God permits them as a creation of our power to make the thing which is nothing."[48]

Even granting the philosophical fairness of God's permitting his creatures to bear the wages of nihilating, still the human story seems remarkably bleak and destined too much to failure. "Fortunately, there is also the order of grace," Maritain continued. "Without infringing the laws of divine fair play," grace introduces "into the most secret recesses of the plot factors which transfigure it."[49] This was a theological, indeed a Catholic theological, perspective. But it was also philosophical perspective. As we have seen, Maritain insisted upon a unified perspective, one that respects difference while perceiving deeper unity: "If [Thomas's] spirit and his doctrine tend to create unity in man it is always by virtue of the same secret—which is to understand all things in the light and the generosity of being."[50] Maritain was so committed to creation's unity in a graced nature that he averred that God "would not have created nature if He had not destined it for grace."[51] We must therefore elaborate Maritain's economy of grace, but not without first saying much more about the natural essences it perfects. For in Maritain's marvelous line, "Existence is the place of the realization of essences."[52]

NATURAL LAW: ONTOLOGICAL AND GNOSEOLOGICAL

What is the essence or nature of human beings, the expansion of which they must not block? What is the "rule" that the acting person is obligated to consider? For Maritain, the short answer is the natural law.

Maritain's account of the natural law in its ontological element, that is, of what the natural law *is*, begins with one of his best-known remarks, a sentence that captures the mood of the man: "Since I have not time here to discuss nonsense (we can always find very intelligent philosophers, not to quote Mr. Bertrand Russell, to defend it most brilliantly) I am taking it for granted that we admit that there is a human nature, and that this human nature is the same in all men."[53] Maritain, as we have seen, affirmed that every thing in the natural order has a nature, an essence. This thing's "normality of functioning," said Maritain, is the natural law in its ontological element. "Any kind of thing existing in nature, a plant, a dog, a horse, has its own natural law, that is, the *normality of its functioning*, the proper way in which, by reason of its specific structure and specific ends, it '*should*' achieve its fullness of being either in its growth or in its behavior."[54]

The case of the human person is similar to that of every other thing existing in nature, but dispositive in the respect already developed; "since man is [a being] endowed with intelligence and determines his own ends, it is up to him to put himself in tune with the ends necessarily demanded by his nature."[55] While in the case of everything that is not the rational person the natural law works automatically, in the case of the human person there is nothing automatic about natural law. It falls to the freedom of human beings to decide whether to become what they are, whether to seek to fulfill the natural law. But why, one might ask, is a human's essence something he or she is *obligated* to realize? Why, in other words, is it a *law*? The reason the essence of human beings is to them (natural) *law* is that natural law or human essence is a participation in the Eternal Law, the divine mind disposing all creation to its end. As Maritain explained, in terms that St. Thomas would have no difficulty affirming: "It is essential to law to be an order of *reason*; and natural law, or the normality of functioning of human nature known by knowledge through inclination, is *law*, binding in conscience, only because nature and the inclinations of nature manifest an order of reason—that is of *Divine Reason*. Natural law is law only because it is a participation in Eternal Law."[56]

The reference to "knowledge by inclination" invites Maritain's account of the natural law in what he called its "gnoseological"[57] element, that is, how the natural law is *known*. Some regard Maritain's account of how natural law is known as among his most impressive philosophical contributions; others dismiss it contemptuously.[58] The human capacity for connatural knowledge was a topic to which Maritain turned time and again, for it is this mode of knowing by which, according to Maritain, the poet knows the poetical, the musician knows the musical, the mystic knows the mystical, and, yes, the human person knows how to be human. This is knowledge "which is implicit and preconscious and which advances, not by the mode of reason or concepts, but by the mode of inclination,"[59] but not of just any inclination.

Maritain distinguished two kinds of human inclinations. First, there are the inclinations that come from instincts rooted in humankind's animal nature. Second, there are inclinations of another sort, those "issuing from *reason* or from the *rational nature* of man."[60] Here Maritain must speak for himself:

> These inclinations *presuppose* the instinctive inclinations—for example, the animal instinct to procreate for the survival of the species—let us say more generally that they presuppose the tendencies impressed in the ontological structure of the human being. But they also presuppose that these tendencies and instinctive inclinations have been grasped and transferred into the dynamism of the intellect's field of apprehension and the sphere of human nature where it is most typically itself, that is, as endowed and imbued with reason. They are a specifically new recasting, a transmutation or recreation of these tendencies and instinctive inclinations which originates in the intellect or reason as the "form" of man's interior universe.... Here are inclinations which are properly *human*, even if they concern the animal realm. Nature has passed through the lake of Intellect (functioning unconsciously). The element which fixes these inclinations is not an ontological or instinctive structure, a "building code," but rather the object of an (unformulated) view of the intellect, let us say certain essential ends perceived or anticipated in a non-conceptual or preconscious way.[61]

Philosophical and conceptual knowledge of the natural law is possible and even desirable; Maritain did not put the moral philosopher out of a job. But Maritain did insist that before the philosopher goes to work, the common person, as a human being, knows how to live as a human being, how to realize his or her existential potential. Maritain wrote that "in its ontological aspect, natural law is an *ideal order* relating to human actions," but this, "the rule" of human conduct, is discoverable exactly in the being that is the human person himself or herself. Natural law is "the ideal formula of development of a given being ... a *divide* between the suitable and the unsuitable, the proper and the improper, which depends on human nature or essence and the unchangeable necessities rooted in it."[62] The solutions to life's ever-unique situations are not written inside human beings to be read; the natural law is unwritten law. Even what is written down in the name of natural law, no matter who writes it, is not itself the natural law. The natural law is humankind's essence, and is knowable only through the person's asking "questions of that essence."[63]

> Men know [the natural law] with greater or less difficulty, and in different degrees, running the risk of error here as elsewhere.... Natural law is the ensemble of things to do and not to do which follow therefrom in *necessary* fashion, and *from the simple fact that man is man*, nothing else being taken into account. That every sort of error and deviation is possible in the determination of these things merely proves that our sight is weak and that innumerable accidents can corrupt our judgment.... All this proves nothing against natural law, any more than a mistake in addition proves anything against arithmetic.[64]

One way to summarize Maritain's natural law theory is to say that what the human person is to do is to live *according to reason*.[65] But this common locution obscures Maritain's insistence that human beings must use their practical reasoning capacity to discover the natural law; that law, not human reason, is the true and proper measure of human living, for as a participation in the Eternal Law it is truly law.[66] Moreover, rationalism per se was alien to Maritain's ethics, rooted as it was not in abstract propositions but instead in a dynamic creation governed by the Eternal Law. The following text, from one of Maritain's mature and most careful treatments of the topic, indicates the full force of his antirationalist commitment:

> The genuine concept of Natural Law is the concept of a law which is natural not only insofar as it expresses the normality of functioning of human nature, but also insofar as it is *naturally known*, that is, known through inclination or through connaturality, not through conceptual knowledge and by way of reasoning.... My contention is that the judgments in which Natural Law is made manifest to practical Reason do not proceed from any conceptual, discursive, rational exercise of reason; they proceed from that *connaturality or congeniality* through which what is consonant with the essential inclinations of human nature is grasped by the intellect as good; what is dissonant, as bad.... Be it immediately added ... that man being an historical animal, these essential inclinations of human nature either developed or were released in the course

of time: as a result, man's knowledge of Natural Law progressively developed, and continues to develop.[67]

Working out their natural law in history, human beings need the intellectual virtue that is prudence. This habit of the mind, itself the product of connatural knowledge, allows persons to judge in particular cases what is to be done, and then to will to do it.[68] The possibility of historical growth in our basic knowledge of the natural law, a consequence of our connatural knowledge thereof, is one of the distinctive and controversial notes of Maritain's account of natural law.

Among those who praised Maritain's notion of connatural knowledge was the influential Protestant philosopher and moral theologian Paul Ramsey. Ramsey found particularly congenial Maritain's notion that our knowledge of natural law has its source in individual personal discernment rather than in the rationalistic, deductive method characteristic of many other Catholic accounts of the natural law. For Ramsey, this was a point of rapprochement between Protestant and Roman Catholic ethics and theology.[69] Ramsey did criticize Maritain for failing to break from the rationalist, deductive model in his *The Rights of Man and Natural Law*. But Ramsey praised Maritain's later works in which he progressively abandoned this model and gave nearly full scope to his doctrine of connatural knowledge of the natural law.[70]

NATURAL RIGHTS AND HUMAN EQUALITY

In a chapter of *Man and the State* titled "The Rights of Man," Maritain began: "I need not apologize for having dwelt so long on the subject of natural law. How could we understand human rights if we had not a sufficiently adequate notion of natural law? The same natural law which lays down our most fundamental duties, and by virtue of which every law is binding, is the very law which assigns to us our fundamental rights."[71]

Maritain's defense of human rights is famous, as is his involvement in UNESCO's drafting of the Universal Declaration of Human Rights (1948). Modern analytic philosophers, however, who are generally unimpressed with Maritain, make no exception when it comes to his theoretical elaboration of human rights.[72] Likewise, some Thomists and conservative political philosophers see the alliance between Thomist natural law and "human rights" to be altogether wrong, un-Thomist, even dangerous. The French Thomist jurisprude Michel Villey, for example, vigorously denied that Thomist thought has any connection to or resources for a theory of human rights. Leo Strauss, the influential advocate of natural law, disavowed any connection between authentic natural law and natural rights.[73] And the estimable Alasdair MacIntyre, regarded Maritain's account of natural rights to be "an uncharacteristic lapse.[74] To be sure, much of what is said today in the name of "rights" is inimical to the Thomist tradition. But the question is what Maritain was up to in the name of natural rights, and, further, what sense it might make to contemporary minds.

Maritain's central claim was straightforward. If human beings are obligated under natural law to do (or forbear to do) X, they should have a natural right to do (or forbear to do) X. "If man is morally bound to the things which are necessary to the fulfillment of his destiny, obviously, then, he has the right to fulfill his destiny; and if he has the right to fulfill his destiny he has the right to the things necessary for this purpose."[75] This is very different from theories of natural rights that would assign human beings "rights" based simply on the subjective desire for, or some deontological privileging of, negative liberty. For Maritain, "the true philosophy of the rights of the human person is ... based upon the idea of natural law. The same natural law which lays down our most fundamental duties, and by virtue of which every law is binding, is the very law which assigns to us our fundamental rights."[76] Thus natural right is, for Maritain, what is due a person because of who he or she is.

We will come shortly to what Maritain had to say about the translation of natural rights into civic rights. But first, let us note what Maritain claimed in the name of natural law and natural rights.

First, there is human dignity, of which Maritain wrote: "The dignity of the human person? The expression means nothing if it does not signify that by virtue of natural law, the human person has the right to be respected, is the subject of rights, possesses rights."[77] Maritain consistently maintained that the discovery and widening affirmation of *natural* human rights were abetted by the gradual spread of the biblical message that the human person is made in God's image and likeness. Gradually in history these evangelical facts were better appreciated.

> The consciousness of [the human person's] dignity little by little won over the sphere of the natural order itself.... The transcendence of the person, which appears most manifest in the perspectives of faith and redemption ... first asserts itself in the philosophical perspectives and relates first and foremost to the order of nature. That is, moreover, in complete accord with Christian theology which teaches that grace perfects nature and does not destroy it.[78]

Second, the first of the natural rights that Maritain imputed to the human person is the correlate of what Maritain took to be the most basic human duty under the natural law, that is, to seek the truth and follow one's informed conscience. This correlation led Maritain to a robust commitment to freedom of conscience and a sharp limitation on the state's power to attempt to alter a person's conscience.[79]

Third, among Catholic, indeed among Christian, thinkers, Maritain advanced what is perhaps the richest and clearest theory of the natural equality among human beings. Maritain was moderately egalitarian in his politics. But, in his philosophy, he affirmed that humans are, as they stand, importantly equal.[80] While there may have been intimations of a theory of natural human equality in Aquinas, there was nothing of the depth and clarity of Maritain's articulation of an existing human equality.[81] As we will see, it is a doctrine that bore fruit in Maritain's jurisprudence and political theory.

PERSON AND COMMON GOOD, LAW AND GRACE

Maritain wrote his leading works on politics and law under the press of various amalgams of war, racism, and totalitarianism. Responding to a crisis threatening to annihilate humankind, Maritain was without patience for those who "seem to think that to put our hands to the real, to this concrete universe of human things and human relations where sin exists and circulates, is in itself to contract sin, as if sin were contracted from without, not from within."[82] He may indeed have been more optimistic than his critics think he had reason to be, but Jacques Maritain was not naive. He knew the forms that evil takes, but still he was undeterred in his hope for humanity's realizing the conditions of the possibility of persons' flourishing. Maritain fashioned a theory of "man and the state" that insisted (1) that "one can respect justice and have brains at the same time, and manage to be strong,"[83] and (2) that to "[t]o rise above [the] fatalities [suffered by modern civilizations] we need an awakening of liberty and of its creative forces, we need the energies of spiritual and social resurrection of which man does not become capable by the grace of the State or any party pedagogy, but by a love which fixes the center of his life infinitely above the world and temporal history."[84] That love comes from the gift the theologians and the Catholic philosopher call grace.

THE INDIVIDUAL AND THE PERSON

Maritain knew that in a world grown accustomed to justifying—or merely allowing—political regimes without regard to human nature, sorting out humankind's true political calling would demand uncommon subtlety. Discussing the *human person* and *society*, which Maritain regarded as the fundamental subject of all social and political philosophy, requires "an exercise of metaphysical insight to which the contemporary mind is hardly accustomed."[85] The key distinction, which Maritain discerned in Aquinas, is between the individual and the person, or between individuality and personhood. This distinction arises from the fact that "the human being is caught between two poles: a material pole, which, in reality, does not concern the true person but rather the shadow of personality or what, in the strict sense, is called *individuality*, and a spiritual pole, which concerns true *personality*."[86] To every human being there are "two metaphysical aspects ... each with their own ontological physiognomy."[87] This is not to say, as Maritain was quick to emphasize (lest one slip into a Cartesian dualism according to which the human soul is one complete being and the body another equally complete being) that the human being is the intersection of two independent realities. "There is not in me," Maritain writes, "one reality, called my individual, and another reality, called my person. One and the same reality is, in a certain sense an individual, and, in another sense, a person."[88]

By the human being's individuality Maritain meant, following Aquinas, the material side of humankind. But here "matter" is not the "concept used in physics."[89] It instead designates a "kind of non-being," a "pure potentiality," "a simple power of receptivity and of substantial mutability, an avidity for being."[90] This pure potentiality becomes something, whether animate or inanimate, through the determination received in its form or essence; in the case of human beings, we call that form or essence *soul*. According to Maritain: "Man, in so far as he is a material individuality, has but a precarious unity, which wishes only to slip back into multiplicity; for matter as such tends to decompose itself."[91] The ensouled individual is a person; ensoulment endues an individual with personality. Maritain took focused aim at those who taught that humankind is no more than a material self, "a single dot in the immense network of forces and influences, cosmic, ethnic, historic, whose laws we obey."[92] The human *person* Maritain knows is not just a specified location in the unremitting cosmic flux; the human person bursts forth as the incarnation of freedom for contributing to being's increase. As mere individuals, "we are subject to the determinism of the physical world." But "each man is also a person and, in so far as he is a person, he is not subject to the stars and atoms; for he subsists entirely with the very subsistence of his spiritual soul, and the latter is in him a principle of creative unity, of independence and of freedom."[93] Against every form of creeping materialism Maritain posed a fact that was obvious and surpassing to him—that the human being in not mere body, but is also personality.

Though Maritain found the fact of personality obvious, he was still eager to insist that compared to individuality, "*personality* is an even deeper mystery, whose profound significance it is still more difficult to discover."[94] Personality is as deep as it gets. The Christian God is triune, one God in

three persons, and human beings, God's image and likeness, enjoy personality as well. "God is spirit, and the person proceeds from Him, having as
its principle of life a spiritual soul, a spirit capable of knowing and loving,
and of being elevated by grace to participate in the very life of God, so as to
finally love Him and know Him even as He knows and loves Himself."[95] The
human person's participation in the life of God has political consequences
that Maritain was eager to announce.

SOVEREIGNTY, THE COMMON GOOD, AND OPEN POLITICS

Out of compassion for the *persons* who before history's eyes suffered under
political regimes that purported to absolutize their own power to the neglect of God's sovereignty, Maritain debunked the notion of sovereignty as
it appears in modern political theory. But, full of hope for the human person's proper expansion and flourishing, Maritain sought to put politics on
a footing that acknowledged God as the only true sovereign. The realism of
this subordination of humanity to God allows the people (of God) to be the
source of the political power that derives its legitimacy from its conforming to human nature, to natural law and natural right. While Maritain certainly meant "to limit the state,"[96] he also, in a qualified but very important
sense, meant to enlarge it as well. Against modern absolutisms, Maritain
denied the sovereignty of the state. Against medieval political theory that
regarded the state as merely the temporal instrument of the spiritual order,
however, Maritain insisted that the temporal order is its own "intermediate
or infravalent end."[97]

A profitable way to approach Maritain's new understanding of the state
is to focus on his distinction between community and society. Both terms
refer to "ethico-social and truly human"[98] realities, for they are not purely
biological but instead involve the use of reason. Community, however, is
based on a brute fact a fact recognized by and responded to, but not the
product of, reason. Community results from, say, people's being born in
Hyde Park. Society, by contrast, is born not of such a given fact, but of
purpose. As Maritain wrote, the "*community* is a product of instinct and
heredity in given circumstances and historical frameworks; the *society* is a
product of reason and moral strength (what the Ancients called 'virtue')."[99]
Maritain explained: "In the *community*, social pressure derives from coercion imposing patterns of conduct on man and comes into play in a deterministic mode. In *society*, social pressure derives from law or rational
regulations, or from an idea of the common aim; it calls forth personal
conscience and liberty, which must obey the law freely."[100]

From the distinction between society and community, Maritain turned
to the term *nation* and sought to situate it with respect to the division be-

tween society and community. Though the word "nation" is derived from the Latin verb *nasci*, meaning to be born, the nation is "not something biological like the Race," Maritain insisted. "It is something ethico-social: a human community based on the fact of birth and lineage, yet with all the moral connotations of those terms."[101] The nation still does not rise to the level of society, however, for the nation is not a work of reason. The nation "does not appeal to the freedom and responsibility of personal conscience, it instills in human persons a second nature."[102] And, as modern history has witnessed with alarming frequency, the claims the nation makes on persons can tread upon human dignity and usurp human freedoms. Indeed, the modern nation has become "an earthly divinity whose absolute selfishness is sacred."[103]

To the modern nation thus understood, Maritain counterposed his notions of the body politic and the state, both of which pertain to the order of society inasmuch as they are works of reason. The body politic or political society "is the most perfect of temporal societies." It "has flesh and blood, instincts, passions, reflexes, unconscious psychological structures and dynamism—all of these subjected, if necessary by legal coercion, to the command of an Idea and rational decisions. Justice is a primary condition for the existence of the body politic."[104] The body politic is vivified and preserved by "the accumulated energy and historical continuity of that national community it has itself caused to exist,"[105] by the "empirical, practical wisdom, much deeper and denser and much nearer the hidden complex dynamism of human life than any artificial construction of reason."[106]

The state is that part of the body politic whose purpose is to work for the whole political society. Its concern is "the maintenance of law, the promotion of the common welfare and public order, and the administration of public affairs."[107] The state "is a set of institutions combined into a topmost machine."[108] But again, the state is not to be divinized. The lesson is clear, and is encapsulated in perhaps the most famous line associated with Maritain: "Man is by no means for the State. The state is for man."[109] What authority the state enjoys it possesses "only by virtue and to the extent of the requirements of the common good."[110]

What Maritain means by the common good is not the collection or a summation of private goods; neither is it the good of a whole such that the goods of the components are sacrificed to the good of the whole. "The end of the state is the common good," wrote Maritain, "which is not only a collection of advantages and utilities, but also rectitude of life, an end good in itself, which the old philosophers called *bonum honestum*, the intrinsically worthy good.... It is only on this condition, of being in accordance with justice and with moral good, that the common good is what it is: the good of a people, the good of a city, and not the 'good' of an association of gangsters or of murderers."[111] The common good is a thing that is ethically good. And this common good includes as an essential element the greatest possible development of human persons—those persons who form the multitude, united in order to constitute a community according to relations of justice.[112] The common good is the shared life of a political community of free persons living oriented toward justice, friendship, and the transcendent.

The earthly common good is no longer to be taken as a mere means in relation to eternal life, but instead as a genuine, if subordinate, end in itself. Civil society, and with it the state, takes its distinct but subordinate place from humanity's nature as both natural and at the same time spiritual. As a person, the human being enjoys a "destination to the absolute. . . . As regards the things *that are not Caesar's*—it is to the perfect achievement of the person and of its supra-temporal aspirations, that society itself and its common good are subordinated, as to the end *of another* order, which transcends them."[113]

Maritain identified a modern but not absolutist role for political society and with it the state. He cited the teachings of Pope Leo XIII:

> The end of political society is not to lead the human person to his spiritual perfection and to his full freedom of autonomy. . . . Nevertheless, political society is essentially destined, by reason of the earthly end which specifies it, to the development of those environmental conditions which will so raise men in general to a level of material, intellectual, and moral life in accord with the good and peace of the whole, that each person will be positively aided in the progressive conquest of his full life as a person and of his spiritual freedom.[114]

Political society has been given its own end, and from it the state is to take its marching orders. Maritain understood the state and its purpose to be "instrumentalist" in the sense that "the apparatus of public law is an instrument serving the rights and liberties of various societies, which, together, form a whole that cannot be equated with the state."[115] But although the common good is society's ultimate end, even society is limited insofar as the person has an end in another, surpassing order. Maritain articulated this belief in *The Person and the Common Good*: "The common good of civil life is not closed within itself, for, of its very nature, it is intended to favor the higher ends of the human person. The human person's vocation to goods which transcend it is embodied in the essence of the common good."[116] Hence political society must be, with the state's help, open at the top.

The idea of a state that is open at the top but is neither sacral nor the principle of humankind's solidarity, though largely advanced in the writings of Leo XIII, was not roundly accepted in the Catholic thought of the 1940s. The rise of totalitarian despotisms in the twentieth century, however, shifted the tides of concern. With additional support from the papal magisterium, "Maritain's generation" won "the argument about the nature of the state."[117] By 1965, the Second Vatican Council proclaimed:

> Culture must be subordinated to the integral development of the human person, to the good of the community and of the whole of mankind.... The scope of public authority extends, not to determining the proper nature of cultural forms, but to building up the environment and the provision of assistance favorable to the development of culture.... The political community, then, exists for the common good: this is its full justification and meaning and the source of its specific and basic right to exist. The common good embraces the sum total of all those conditions of social life which enable individuals, families, and organizations to achieve complete and efficacious fulfillment.[118]

As for the stance of the current papal magisterium on the nature of the state and civil society, it can be said that "today, one can discern the stamp of [Maritain's] mind on the encyclicals of John Paul II, who, if anything, expounds the instrumentalist conception of the state more aggressively than did Maritain himself."[119]

LAW AND AUTHORITY, JUSTICE AND FRATERNITY

Maritain defined the state as that part of the body politic whose aim is to secure the common good, including persons' achieving their normality of functioning, for the body politic. And the state, in order to aid the realization of the natural law and its correlative natural rights, creates laws and gives them effect. Such "positive" laws—that is, laws *posited* by the rightful authority—have as their purpose and measure conformity with the natural law and rights of persons living together, constituted as political society. Positive law, thus understood, exercises a weighty office in human affairs.

Maritain never wrote a freestanding treatise on law. Like Aquinas, Maritain came to law in general, and to positive law in particular, as but a part—though a critical part—of humanity's realizing its potential. Maritain did give answers to the classic legal chestnuts about, say, whether an unjust positive law is truly law, and to these we shall come. But we shall come to them, as Maritain did, from the context of identifying the terms and conditions of human beings' using their connatural reason to realize their essence. Maritain believed that "it is essential to law to be an order of *reason*."[120]

There is an order that it is the office of reason, as practical reason, to make: it is, to be exact, the order of human acts and operations which ... defines the field of ethics. Continuing and collaborating with the divine action, reason has at every moment to fashion in conformity with the Eternal order the contingent and perpetually renewed order of the works of time.... In this way to the natural law reason adds the determinations of positive law; in this way are established organs of civil society which is indeed prescribed by nature and necessarily presupposes certain laws of nature but which is the work of reason and of virtue and has in Justice "the mystical basis of its authority."[121]

What this passage reveals in short compass is that Maritain's understanding of law has the support of—indeed, springs from—his existential starting points, with which we began. The divine action initiates and sustains a creative process in which every human person's collaborative contribution is to exercise his or her freedom to allow natural law to unfold as time and place both allow and require.[122] Referring to the ethics that must inform politics and law, Maritain declared:

In actual fact, the principles of morality are neither theorems nor idols, but the supreme rules of a concrete activity which aims at a work to be done in such-and-such circumstances, with the help of more proximate rules and with the help, finally, of the rules *never traced in advance* of the virtue of prudence, which apply the ethical precepts to the particular cases in the climate of a concretely upright will. They do not seek to devour human life, but to build it up.[123]

For Maritain, positive law is *law* exactly inasmuch as it comports with human practical reason. For this did not prevent him from distinguishing natural law from positive law. It is a function of Maritain's realism that he saw clearly and insisted forcefully upon the need for *authority* and its exercise in human living, and one of positive law's characteristics is that it issues from an authority. By authority, Maritain meant "the *right* to direct and to command, to be listened to or obeyed by others."[124] Unlike power, which is force others are merely obliged to obey,[125] authority imports obligation. It does so, moreover, not as a mere remedy for disorder but as a necessary condition of human beings' exercising their freedom to realize their normality of functioning using the sort of practical reason they have. Human practical reason does not necessarily lead to one course of conduct, nor are its requirements demonstrable. Authority is necessary to determine, through the application of prudence, the specific terms of human living, and to shape that living through law.

As with the authority from which it issues, positive law is necessary to create order; rightful authority's successful creation of order, however, does not by itself render a putative law a genuine law. As Maritain put it: "There is order in hell."[126] For a putative law to have authority—to obligate the consciences of men and women who should be realizing their essence—it must be in accord with natural law as it works itself out through prudence. On the classical question of the status of an unjust law mandated by the state and purporting to be law, Maritain sided with Augustine, who had observed, famously, that an unjust law is considered to be no law at all. In Maritain's words: "An unjust law is not a law. This follows ... from the fact that the positive law obliges by virtue of the Natural Law which is a participation in the Eternal Law. It is inconceivable that an unjust law should oblige by virtue of the Natural Law, by virtue of regulations which go back to the Eternal Law and which are in us a participation in that Law."[127] *True* positive law is, rather, "a prolongation or an extension of natural law, passing into objective zones which can less and less be sufficiently determined by the essential inclinations of human nature."[128] As such, true positive law obligates in conscience.[129]

Unlike Maritain, some Thomists are uncomfortable affirming the proposition that an unjust law is not a law (*lex iniusta non est lex*). To be sure, there is a fair casuistry to be worked out about the unjust law's being law in some partial or nonfocal sense.[130] But if Maritain was ready to affirm this principle, one recalls that he knew of totalitarian regimes that were devastatingly good at making "laws" that were very bad for human beings. In Maritain's view: "It is *essential* to a philosophy such as that of Saint Thomas to regard an unjust law as not obligatory. It is the counterpart of this truth that the just law binds in conscience because it binds by virtue of the Natural Law. If we forget the one, we forget the other."[131]

We can imagine that Maritain, when confronted with a concrete case, might have concluded that citizens can be obligated in conscience to obey positive laws that are unjust in small ways. But his basic and fundamental commitment to law's being the working out of the existential conditions of human persons' realizing their essence renders legal formalism inapt and inept. There is, in Maritain's estimation, "a dynamism which impels the unwritten law to flower forth in human law, and to render the latter ever more perfect and just in the very field of its contingent determinations. It is in accordance with this dynamism that the rights of the human person take political and social form in the community."[132] Maritain could thus make quick work of any question as to what must happen when positive rules of decision are lacking: "A recourse to the principles of Natural Law is unavoidable [*sic*], thus creating a precedent and new judicial rules. That is what happened, in a remarkable manner, with the epoch-making Nazi war crimes trial in Nuremberg."[133] All this is both possible and necessary because, on Maritain's account, law is not only, or even primarily, what has been posited by those in authority. Law is, in the first place, the Eternal Law, to which all other forms and phases of law are related analogically.[134]

LAWS AND RIGHTS, EQUALITY AND DEMOCRACY

When the human person avoids the temptation to block being's increase, natural law tends to flower into positive law. This was the existential core of Maritain's jurisprudence proper. Maritain observed that "every kind of law, from the spontaneous, unformulated group regulations to customary law and to law in the full sense of the term, contributes to the vital order of political society."[135] And, until men and women learn to live according to love, law is necessary to human living. Maritain, no idolater of human law, affirmed this unflinchingly: "If the person has a chance of being treated as a person in social life ... it is first of all due to the development of law and legal institutions."[136] But even so, Maritain insisted that law's function is to liberate persons for a life beyond law. "The function of law is to constrain the *protervi*, the perverse and the hardened, to a behavior of which they are not of themselves capable, and also to educate men so that in the end they may cease to be under the law—since they themselves will voluntarily and freely do what the law enjoins, a condition reached only by the wise."[137] And this free expansion of being depends, as Maritain never tired of reminding us, on the entry and operation of love: "True political emancipation depends on the Christian ferment deposited in the world, and presupposes finally, as its most profound stimulus, evangelical love exalting the things of earthly civilization in their own order."[138]

As for criminal law, not surprisingly Maritain affirmed that law's proper aim is to lead people to virtue, or at least to the avoidance of the larger vices.[139] When the criminal law imposes punishment on wrongdoers, moreover, the legitimating point of that imposition is to restore the wrongdoers to their proper place, to situate them back where they should be. If a person accepts his or her punishment as just, that person is cured and is existentially reordered; if a person does not accept the punishment as just, still a basic restoration of the balance of good and evil will have occurred in the objective order.[140]

The logic of Maritain's avowal that the state exists for the realization of human potential led him to insist:

> The State has the right to punish me if, my conscience being blind, I follow my conscience and commit an act in itself criminal or unlawful. [But] in like circumstances the State has not the authority to make me reform the judgment of my conscience, any more than it has the power of imposing upon intellects

its own judgment of good and evil, or of legislating on divine matters, or of imposing any religious faith whatsoever.[141]

Maritain was unstinting in his assertion that the first natural right

is that of the human person to make its way towards its eternal destiny along the path which its conscience has recognized as the path indicated by God. *With respect to God and truth*, one has not the right to choose according to his own whim any path whatsoever, he must choose the true path, in so far as it is in his power to know it. But *with respect to the State, to the temporal community and to the temporal power*, he is free to choose his religious path at his own risk, his freedom of conscience is a natural, inviolable right.[142]

The distinction that Maritain emphasized merits recapitulation. No one enjoys a *right* to "liberty of conscience" or "religious liberty" in the presence of God. In the face of the state, however, the human person's conscience stands as an *absolute barrier*—even if, as Maritain observed, someone's supposed religious path should lead him or her so far as to commit acts violating the natural law or threatening the state's security, such that the state is justified in interdicting the acts and punishing the person.[143] Thus, this right to freedom of conscience, along with all basic human rights, though it is inalienable, is subject to just limitation as to its exercise.[144]

Maritain's understanding of the natural rights that belong to a person because of who the person is led him to postulate a rich panoply of rights he believed the state should recognize for the person as citizen. In his early political writings Maritain expressed misgivings about "democracy," for he associated it with what he calls an anthropocentric humanism, the humanism that "believes that man himself is the center of man, and therefore of all things."[145] But in the period from the mid-1930s to the mid-1940s, Maritain came to appreciate that his "integral humanism" favored democracy properly understood. The right of self-governance belongs to the people (collectively) because the duty and right to realize existential freedom belongs to each person.[146] In *Man and the State*, Maritain argued that the "right of the people to govern themselves proceeds from Natural Law: consequently, the very exercise of their right is subject to Natural Law. If Natural Law is sufficiently valid to give this basic right to the people, it is valid also to impose its unwritten precepts on the exercise of this same right."[147] And in *Christianity and Democracy*, Maritain elaborated "the essential characteristics of the democratic philosophy of man and society" in these terms: "The inalienable rights of the person, equality, political rights of the people whose consent is implied by any political regime and whose rulers rule as vicars of the people, absolute primacy of the relations of justice and law at the base of society, and an ideal not of war, prestige, or power, but of the amelioration and emancipation of human life—the ideal of fraternity."[148]

Maritain's early affirmations of democracy were cautious, but his eventual embrace of democracy was passionate and complete.[149] Nothing short of Christianity's teaching the dignity and equality of persons locates the power of authoritative governance in the people, as Maritain argued at length in his *Christianity and Democracy.*

To the right to self-government and its correlatives, Maritain added the right to "freedom of investigation and discussion"—a locution meant to improve on the phrase "freedom of speech and expression." "Freedom of investigation and discussion," meant that the state should avoid regulating through "censorship and police methods."[150]

Maritain also insisted upon the citizen's right to three forms of equality: equality in the state, equality before the law, and equal access to public employment and the professions without regard to race or social standing.[151] And finally, to these rights of the citizen Maritain added a list of the rights of the working person. Recognition of these is the result of "consciousness of the dignity of work and of the worker, of the dignity of the human person in the worker as such."[152] Although capitalism was something of a dirty word for the young Maritain, in time he came to believe that capitalism can (and in the United States eminently did) serve the interests and expansion of the human person.[153] In *Reflections on America*, written in 1958, Maritain looked back approvingly on his earlier *Integral Humanism* and commented that it "appears to me now as a book which had, so to speak, an affinity with the American climate by anticipation."[154] And certainly one of the elements of American culture that to Maritain's mind provided a proper limit on the American enthusiasm for capitalism was the American people's passion (earlier observed by Tocqueville) for equality. While Maritain's affirmation of the equality in dignity among human beings led him to insist on every person's being treated properly across the board, he also saw such dignity as liberating him and the society he envisioned from homogenizing the differences and inequalities among people who are essentially equal.

> Every man is a man in his very essence, but no man is man in essence, that is, exhausts in himself all the riches of the various perfections of which humankind is capable. In this sense all the diversity of perfections and virtues distributed through the generations of men in space and time is but a varied participation in the common and inexhaustible potentialities of man.[155]

It is the office of positive law, as we have seen, to give effect to the natural law and its correlative natural rights, as prudence prescribes. But if, as

Maritain liked to say, genuine positive law is just the flowering of natural law, midway between natural law and positive law is the *ius gentium*, or what traditionally is referred to as the law of nations. This body of law, the stuff upon which modern "international law" is built, often proves to be troubling for legal minds schooled in positivism and the expectation that law is only (or eminently) what is posited in written form by a legislator. Even Maritain found the *ius gentium* "difficult to define"[156] and changed his mind as to its nature between his early treatment of it in *The Rights of Man and Natural Law* (1944) and *Man and the State* (1951). In the former book, Maritain described the *ius gentium* as the principles that follow from the natural law "*supposing* certain conditions of fact, as for instance the state of civil society or the relationships between peoples."[157] In the latter work, the *ius gentium* emerged as the basic principles of morality as known "not through inclination but through the *conceptual exercise of reason*, or through rational knowledge."[158] Maritain summarized his mature view, and his reasons for adopting it, in these terms:

> It is necessary to insist on the manner in which the law in question is known. The law of nations is known, not through inclination, but through the conceptual exercise of reason. This is the specific difference distinguishing the law of nations from the Natural Law. The Natural Law is known through inclination, the law of nations is known through the conceptual exercise of the human reason (considered not in such and such an individual, but in common civilized humanity). In this sense it pertains to the positive law: since wherever human reason intervenes as author, we are in the general domain of the positive law. In this case, the human reason does not intervene as the author of the *existence of the law* (which is the case with positive law in the strict sense), but it does intervene as the author of the *knowledge of the law*.[159]

This development of Maritain's view on the nature and status of the *ius gentium*, as Paul Ramsey noted, reflects Maritain's giving ever-fuller effect to his view that what involves "the intervention of conceptual reason" is already beyond the natural law, which is known connaturally and not through concepts.[160]

Development of and reliance on the *ius gentium* would be particularly instrumental in the creation of a world polity, mention of which is necessary to round out the picture of what Maritain was up to in his work on law and politics. The idea of world government perhaps seems quixotic today, but Jacques Maritain took the idea seriously. He thought hard about it as something not only consistent with but also, perhaps, required by his understanding of what the common good for humanity is.[161] But however things go for world government, things have gone very well for Maritain's ideas about human rights as a civilizing and uniting force across the world, a point of practical convergence among peoples divided at the level of theory.[162]

GRACE AND THE GOSPEL IN WORLD HISTORY

One might expect an innovator such as Maritain to push against the sacral synthesis of the medieval political ideal with something like "the body belongs to the state, the soul to God."[163] But a marvel of Maritain's jurisprudence is that it went forward with something much more subtle, something springing from what John Noonan has called Maritain's "ontological preamble."[164] This ontology—Maritain's existentialism, which is more foundation than preamble—led him to hope for a "new Christendom," "a Christian secular conception and not a Christian sacral conception of the temporal."[165] Neither assuming nor aiming for sameness of creed as its unifying principle, the new Christendom would anticipate a pluralist body politic, "an organic heterogeneity in the very structure of civil society, whether it is a question, for example, of certain economic structures or of certain juridical and institutional structures."[166] This heterogeneity would call for the ample application of the principle of subsidiarity. For Maritain, subsidiarity meant allowing the various societies that make up political society the greatest autonomy possible consistent with the good of the body politic as a whole. The pluralism of the people and of the societies within civil society would properly lead, moreover, to the legislator's taking "into account the existential conditions of this people and the condition of the moral ideal, the more or less defective, yet a *de facto* existing ideal, of the various spiritual families or lineages which make up this people."[167] Maritain's position was an advance over law's role in the laicized or liberal state, for "law will regain in this pluralist body politic its moral function, its function as *pedagogue of freedom*."[168] The result, Maritain wrote in 1936, is that "it is toward the perfection of natural law and Christian law that the pluriform juridic[al] structure of the body politic would be *oriented*, even at those stages of it which would be the most imperfect and the farthest removed from the Christian ethical ideal.... In this way the city or body politic would be vitally Christian and the non-Christian spiritual families within it would enjoy a just liberty."[169] But, over a decade later in *Man and the State* (1951), Maritain rejected the state's establishing or privileging one religion and thus went even further in the direction of pluralism. "The fact of inserting into the body politic a particular or partial common good, the temporal common good of the faithful of one religion (even though it were the true religion), and of claiming for them, accordingly, a privileged juridical position in the body politic, would be inserting into the latter a divisive principle and, to that extent, interfering with the temporal common good."[170]

Maritain's ideal body politic would do justice, and justice is that moral virtue by which we render to each what is due to him or her. But justice is only part of the picture. Maritain, in deep concert with the classical political tradition that linked friendship and justice, marked the place of friendship in securing the conditions of justice and flourishing civic life. Maritain acknowledged, in a beautiful and profound study, the higher forms of friendship.[171] But for him, fraternity or civic friendship was at the once the aim of the state and body politic *and* the necessary condition for the instantiation of law and justice. As Maritain explained:

> If the person has the opportunity of being treated as a person in social life, and if the unpleasant works which this life imposes can be made easy and happy and even exalting, it is first of all due to the development of law and to institutions of law. But it is also and indispensably due to the development of civic friendship, with the confidence and mutual devotion this implies on the part of those who carry it out. For the true city of human rights, fraternity is not a privilege of nature which flows from the natural goodness of man and which the State need only proclaim. It is the end of a slow and difficult conquest which demands virtue and sacrifice and a perpetual victory of man over himself. In this sense, we can say that the heroic ideal towards which true political emancipation tends is the inauguration of a fraternal city.[172]

Maritain did congratulate humanity on having at last reached, thanks to the gospel's taking root in the unfolding of history, a deep appreciation of the rights of human beings, the dignity of the person, and the civic ideal of fraternity. But, in what can sometimes seem to be a non sequitur, he admonished that "as regards an effective realization or refraction of the Gospel in the socio-temporal sphere, we are still truly in a prehistoric age."[173] There is much to be done; and for it come to pass in impressive proportions, individuals will need to choose one by one to bring to the world "the gifts of grace and of charity."[174] But the message is clear: The charity that is gift, if it be accepted, can transform the world. Maritain's belief was that "by virtue of the Charity which is its essential source and principle, Christian spirituality overflows into things outside; it diffuses its own excellence. It acts upon the world, on culture, on the temporal and political order of human life."[175] In reality, as Maritain assessed it, things are going better for the world than for the women and men who populate it:

> Because of the weakness of our species, evil is more frequent than good among men; and in the growth of history, it grows and deepens at the same time as the good mingled with it: these statistical laws concern the comportment of men. Social structures, on the other hand, institutions, laws and cus-

toms, economic and political organizations are human things, they are not men; insofar precisely as they are things and not men, they can be purified of certain miseries of human life; and like many of the works of man they issue from man and they are better than man, in their own order and under a certain relationship. They can be measured by justice and fraternal love, whereas the acts of men are on the whole rarely measured by that measure; they can be more just than the men who employ them and apply them. But they remain *things*, and by that very fact realities of a degree essentially inferior to that of *persons* whose communications and life they serve to regulate.[176]

Maritain's position on the human person in the world brought grace to bear on nature in a way that reversed the effects of the philosophy of nature that Aquinas (and with him Maritain) took from Aristotle. Purely Aristotelian theories did not distinguish the *goodness* of human beings from their worldly success and happiness; the Greek term is *eudaimonia*, and literally means having a good god watching over one. Maritain fiercely rejected a cosmic elitism fueled by luck.[177] In opposition to a philosophy of human life that identifies consummate achievement with what only a fortunate few can achieve, Maritain proposed universal opportunity—not for temporal happiness, but for goodness, for good will, indeed for sanctity: "The great novelty introduced by Christianity is this appeal to all, to free men and slaves, to the ignorant and the cultivated, adolescents and old men, a call to a perfection which no effort of nature can attain but which is given by grace and consists in love, and from which therefore no one is excluded except by his own refusal."[178] All are called to goodness and holiness, and this thanks to grace.

For Maritain, no adequate account of humankind in the state can proceed without adverting to how nature is already graced by what comes from beyond itself. Moral philosophy must be "subalternated" to theology, as he put it.[179] "Moral philosophy adequately considered" respects the data of revelation and the "true principles of [the] science" of theology.[180] It thereby can discern the place in practical affairs not just of naturally acquired virtues such as prudence, but also of the virtues, including prudence, infused by divine grace.[181] Furthermore, moral philosophy adequately considered respects the fact that God wishes all people to be saved and to act aright, and that when human beings sin and soil themselves, when they fail to instantiate the gospel in their lives and relations in the body politic, the source of the evil is not God but themselves.[182] "Without love and charity," Maritain wrote, "man turns the best in him into an evil that is yet greater. When one has understood this, he no longer puts his hope on earth in anything less than that good will of which the gospel speaks."[183] But even the person who knows nothing of Christ and the Good News performs "the first act of freedom"—by which the person begins that *freedom of expansion* that is his glory. This "is a moral act par excellence, and, at least implicitly, a religious act, since it can only be realized rightly if it is realized in divine charity."[184]

THE LEGACY OF THE PHILOSOPHER OF ALL THAT IS

Many of Maritain's big ideas have been assimilated in geographically diverse Catholic circles and on all levels of the church. The church in Latin America, in particular, has been much inspired by him. Maritain had an intellectual hand in the creation of Christian Democratic parties and, indirectly, of the liberation movements that followed them. Maritain's argument for the desacralization of the state carried the day in the Second Vatican Council, and Maritain's defense of liberty of conscience and religion was given expression, with the considerable help of the American Jesuit John Courtney Murray, in the Second Vatican Council's Declaration on Religious Liberty, *Dignitatis humanae* (1965). When the Catholic Church belatedly embraced the ideal of religious liberty as its own heritage and gift, it employed Maritain's approach.[185]

A sector of Catholic traditionalism bitterly opposed this development of Catholic doctrine. But, as traditionalists, the members of this group were bound to accede to, indeed to affirm, the teachings of an authentic ecumenical council of the Catholic Church. By now there is little resistance to the magisterially announced implications of Maritain's philosophy of humankind and the state, rooted in the human person's existential amplitude.

When Maritain first began to explore the existential depths and destiny of the human person, Catholic moral teaching tended to talk in terms of the individual, with reference to his nature and ends. Maritain was the most influential among those Catholics who shifted the terms and targets of inquiry from individual to person, thereby installing "personalism" as the Catholic touchstone for applying scripture and tradition to today's world.[186] The magisterium of John Paul II has been tireless in its development and applications of personalism, of a rather different sort from Maritain's and yet still leading in relevant respects to similar jurisprudential consequences. Not all personalisms are created equal. What Maritain and, for example, Martin Luther King Jr. took to be the significance of personhood for human living and statecraft is not identical. But Maritain knew that a focus on the person, like the dialect of human rights that grows out of such an emphasis, can provide a point of practical agreement for philosophers, theologians, and activists otherwise quite diverse in their thinking.

The revival of Thomism initiated by Pope Leo XIII has been succeeded and surpassed by the teachings of the Second Vatican Council on humanity in the world, which owe much to the work of the new Thomists, and perhaps above all to Jacques Maritain. In the realm of law and politics, we now take for granted many of the conclusions Maritain reached with bold originality. Ironically, the success of Maritain's conclusions has led to his own eclipse. It might be, as Paul Sigmund suggests, that Maritain will still be read a hundred years from now, but this more because of the role he had in changing the way the world thinks about democracy and human rights than because of "the intrinsic content of his arguments."[187] Indeed, as to Maritain's persuasiveness with respect to matters of law and politics, Jacques Maritain gets mixed marks even from those who are broadly sympathetic to the tradition(s) of natural law and natural rights. While he was never at a loss for words, at foundational jurisprudential moments, some readers find Maritain more assertive than persuasive. Ralph McInerny, Maritain's admiring intellectual biographer, has observed an occasional maladroitness in Maritain's way of interacting and engaging.[188] James Schall provides the complementary observation that Maritain knew his philosophizing cut against the grain all the way down, and that Maritain therefore asked, in genuine humility, that people give honest ear to his very different message.[189] Everything on which Maritain wrote was controversial. His application of a revised but inevitably embattled Thomism, as a self-described "man of the left," could hardly avoid frequent fireworks.

Whatever the various judgments on the specific successes or failures of Maritain's work on humankind and the state, there remains the antecedent issue that we flagged at the outset. In a legal-philosophical climate in which orthodoxy insists that "We are world-makers through language,"[190] even the best attempt to pursue a genuine philosophy of being and the jurisprudence *it* calls forth will meet incomprehension, resistance, even principled hostility. Philosopher Michael White was on the trail of this anesthesia of human aspiration when he observed of the regnant jurisprudential doctrines of political liberalism and positivism that they would "stop history—by the rules."[191] Rather than stop with language, rules, positive law and civil authority, or other human artifice, Jacques Maritain insisted on going all the way to *being*, including the being that is God. And he did so not atemporally, but realistically and in light of how beings are working themselves out in time and history.[192] Any alternative course of action, as a contemporary Thomist concludes with Maritain's help, "is a sterile cop-out, and cannot for long satisfy the innate, unrestricted desire of the human mind to know all being—all that there is to know about all that there is. As the great modern Thomist, Jacques Maritain, has put it beautifully, 'There is a nuptial relationship between mind and reality' that longs to be consummated."[193] It was to that surpassing work that Maritain was called as a philosopher, "a philosopher of all that is, of God and nature, of logic and metaphysics, of mathematics and art, and, yes, of man and the state."[194]

NOTES

1. M. D. A. Freeman, *Lloyd's Introduction to Jurisprudence*, 6th ed. (London: Sweet & Maxwell, 1994), 145–147.

2. See Anthony J. Lisska, *Aquinas's Theory of Natural Law: An Analytic Reconstruction* (Oxford: Clarendon Press, 1997), 30.

3. Philippe Chenaux, "Paul VI et Maritain," in *Jacques Maritain et ses contemporains*, ed. B. Hubert and Y. Floucat (Paris: Desclée, 1991), 323–342.

4. Jacques Maritain, *Peasant of the Garonne: An Old Man Questions Himself About the Present Time*, trans. Michael Cuddihy and Elizabeth Hughes (New York: Holt, Rinehart and Winston, 1968), 2.

5. James V. Schall, *Jacques Maritain: The Philosopher in Society* (Lanham, Md.: Rowman & Littlefield, 1998), 223.

6. Ibid., 225.

7. Jacques Maritain, "Confession of Faith," in *The Social and Political Philosophy of Jacques Maritain*, ed. Joseph W. Evans and Leo R. Ward (New York: Charles Scribner's Sons, 1955), 331.

8. Ralph McInerny, *The Very Rich Hours of Jacques Maritain: A Spiritual Life* (Notre Dame, Ind.: University of Notre Dame Press, 2003), 91. After Raissa's death it became known through her *Journal*, published by Jacques, that early in marriage the couple vowed to live together like brother and sister.

9. Donald Gallagher and Idella Gallagher, *The Achievement of Jacques and Raissa Maritain: A Bibliography, 1906–1961* (New York: Doubleday, 1962), 12.

10. Maritain, "Confession of Faith," 331.

11. Raissa Maritain, *We Have Been Friends Together and Adventures in Grace*, trans. J. Kernan (New York: Doubleday, 1941), 178.

12. Jacques Maritain, *Notebooks*, trans. Joseph W. Evans (Albany, N.Y.: Magi Books, 1984), 65.

13. Jacques Maritain, *Bergsonian Philosophy and Thomism*, trans. Mabelle L. Andison (New York: Philosophical Library, 1955), 16–17.

14. "*Vae mihi si non thomistavero*," in Maritain, "Confession of Faith," 331.

15. Gallagher and Gallagher, *The Achievement of Jacques and Raissa Maritain*, 9.

16. Jacques Maritain, *Existence and the Existent*, trans. Lewis Galantière and Gerald B. Phelan (New York: Pantheon Books, 1948), 1. It is somewhat ironic, then, that Maritain reached his Thomism not by going to the mind of Thomas by way exclusively of the texts of Thomas, as did that other great contributor to the Thomist revival Etienne Gilson, but rather with the aid of the great sixteenth- and seventeenth-century commentators (Cardinal Cajetan, the Dominican friar John of St. Thomas, and the anonymous Carmelites of Salamanca, the *Salamanticenses*).

17. Paul E. Sigmund, "Maritain on Politics," in *Understanding Maritain: Philosopher and Friend*, ed. Deal Hudson and Matthew Mancini (Macon, Ga.: Mercer University Press, 1987), 161.

18. Jacques Maritain, *The Degrees of Knowledge*, trans. Gerald B. Phelan, in *The Collected Works of Jacques Maritain*, 20 vols. (Notre Dame, Ind.: University of Notre Dame Press, 1995), 7:xx.

19. Ibid., 328.

20. Gallagher and Gallagher, *The Achievement of Jacques and Raissa Maritain*, 18. For a compendious account of the fascinating business of Maritain's association and then break with Action Française, the latter nothing short of a crisis in his life, see Bernard E. Doering, *Jacques Maritain and the French Catholic Intellectuals* (Notre Dame, Ind.: University of Notre Dame Press, 1983), 6–59.

21. Gallagher and Gallagher, *The Achievement of Jacques and Raissa Maritain*, 18.

22. See Doering, *Maritain and the French Catholic Intellectuals*, 60–84.

23. Jacques Maritain, "A Letter on Independence," in *Integral Humanism, Freedom in the Modern World, and A Letter on Independence*, ed. Otto Bird, trans. Otto Bird, Joseph Evans, and Richard O'Sullivan, *Collected Works* 11:122.

24. John T. McGreevy, *Catholicism and American Freedom: A History* (New York: Norton, 1993), 203.

25. Doering, *Maritain and the French Catholic Intellectuals*, 208. As a young priest Montini had translated Maritain's *Three Reformers*.

26. Gallagher and Gallagher, *The Achievement of Jacques and Raissa Maritain*, 23.

27. Ibid., 217–41.

28. Schall, *Jacques Maritain*, xii.

29. See Jacques Maritain, *An Introduction to Philosophy*, trans. E. I. Watkin (New York: Sheed & Ward, 1947), 189–260.

30. Maritain, *Existence and the Existent*, 2.

31. Jacques Maritain, *A Preface to Metaphysics* (New York: Sheed & Ward, 1948), 50–51.

32. A compendious treatment of this important question, which separates Maritain from such Transcendental Thomists as Karl Rahner, Bernard Lonergan, and Joseph Maréchal, can be found in Gerald A. McCool, *From Unity to Pluralism: The Internal Evolution of Thomism* (New York: Fordham University Press, 1989), 114–132, especially 117–121. A fuller treatment is Georges Van Riet, *L'Épistémologie Thomiste: Recherches sur le problème de la connaissance dans l'école thomiste contemporaine* (Louvain: Institut Supérieur de Philosophie, 1946), 349–376. On the general neo-Thomist project (including Maritain's place in it) with respect to epistemology, see Fergus Kerr, *After Aquinas: Versions of Thomism* (Oxford: Blackwell, 2002), 17–34.

33. Maritain, *The Degrees of Knowledge*, xiv.

34. Ibid., xiv.

35. Maritain, *Existence and the Existent*, 142.

36. Ibid., 143.

37. Maritain, *The Degrees of Knowledge*, xiv.

38. Jacques Maritain, *Creative Intuition in Art and Poetry* (Princeton, N.J.: Princeton University Press, 1953), 127. For the Thomist and specifically neo-Thomist background on questions of the "philosophy of being," as it is called, see Kerr, *After Aquinas*, 73–96.

39. Jacques Maritain, *An Introduction to the Basic Problems of Moral Philosophy*, trans. Cornelia N. Borgerhoff (Albany, N.Y.: Magi Books, 1990), 32–33. The text continues immediately: "They are not synonymous, for there is a distinction between the objects of thought, but they are convertible because there is no real distinction between the realities known; there is only a distinction of reason which is based on reality" (33).

40. Maritain, *Introduction to Basic Problems*, 66–68.

41. Ibid., 79.

42. Ibid., 80.

43. Maritain, "Confession of Faith," 336.

44. Jacques Maritain, "The Conquest of Freedom," in *The Social and Political Philosophy of Jacques Maritain*, 17.

45. Jacques Maritain, *St. Thomas and the Problem of Evil* (Milwaukee: Marquette University Press, 1942), 34–35.

46. Ibid., 26–27.

47. Maritain, *Existence and the Existent*, 120–121.

48. Ibid., 120.

49. Ibid., 121.

50. Ibid., 143 (footnote omitted).

51. Maritain, *St. Thomas*, 13.

52. Maritain, *Integral Humanism*, 290.

53. Jacques Maritain, *Man and the State* (Chicago: University of Chicago Press, 1951), 85.

54. Ibid., 87.

55. Ibid., 86.

56. Ibid., 96.

57. A not-quite-neologism with, in this context, a meaning close to that of epistemic.

58. Gerald McCool, for example, observes that "In *Art and Scholasticism* and in *Creative Intuition in Art and Poetry* Maritain extended St. Thomas' metaphysics of connaturality from the moral sphere in which St. Thomas had employed it to the entire realm of aesthetic knowledge. This is one of Maritain's most original contributions to Neo-Scholastic philosophy and perhaps his greatest and most lasting one." McCool, *From Unity to Pluralism*, 129. John Finnis, on the other hand, praising Yves Simon's account of the place of *authority* in human living concludes, "Discount, however, his theory (taken from Maritain) of 'affective knowledge'"; Finnis, *Natural Law and Natural Rights* (Oxford: Clarendon Press, 1980), 255. Anthony Lisska, as enamored of "analytic philosophy" as Finnis is, comments that "Maritain appeals almost to metaphor while attempting to explicate connaturality"—as if such an assertion itself amounted to argument against Maritain. Lisska, *Aquinas's Theory of Natural Law*, 28.

59. Maritain, *Introduction to Basic Problems*, 53.

60. Ibid., 54.

61. Ibid.

62. Maritain, *Man and the State*, 88.

63. Ibid.

64. Jacques Maritain, *The Rights of Man and Natural Law*, trans. Doris C. Anson (New York: Gordian Press, 1971), 62–63.

65. See Schall, *Jacques Maritain*, 81–86.

66. Jacques Maritain, "Natural Law and Moral Law," in *Moral Principles of Action: Man's Ethical Imperative*, ed. Ruth Anshen (New York: Harper, 1952), 67.

67. Jacques Maritain, *The Range of Reason* (New York: Charles Scribner's Sons, 1952), 26–27.

68. Jacques Maritain, *Introduction to Philosophy*, 201–202.

69. Paul Ramsey, *Nine Modern Moralists* (Englewood Cliffs, N.J.: Prentice-Hall, 1962), 209–232.

70. Ramsey, *Nine Modern Moralists*, 217–223.

71. Maritain, *Man and the State*, 95.

72. Lisska, *Natural Law*, 228.

73. Brian Tierney, *The Idea of Natural Rights* (Atlanta: Scholars Press, 1997), 13–42. See also Jean Porter, *Natural and Divine Law: Reclaiming the Tradition for Christian Ethics* (Grand Rapids, Mich.: Eerdmans, 1999), 268–277.

74. Alasdair MacIntyre, *Three Rival Versions of Moral Inquiry* (Notre Dame, Ind.: University of Notre Dame Press, 1990), 76.

75. Maritain, *Rights of Man*, 65.

76. Ibid., 66.

77. Ibid., 65.

78. Ibid., 73–74.

79. Ibid., 81–82.

80. Jacques Maritain, "Human Equality," in *Redeeming the Time*, trans. Harry Lorin Binsse (London: Geoffrey Bles: Centenary Press, 1946), 15–16.

81. See also John E. Coons and Patrick M. Brennan, *By Nature Equal: The Anatomy of a Western Insight* (Princeton, N.J.: Princeton University Press, 1999), 33–37, 145–214; Patrick McKinley Brennan, "Arguing for Human Equality," *Journal of Law and Religion* 18 (2003): 101.

82. Coons and Brennan, *By Nature Equal*, 309.

83. Maritain, *Man and the State*, 57. See Schall, *Jacques Maritain*, 1–19.

84. Jacques Maritain, *Scholasticism and Politics*, ed. Mortimer J. Adler (London: Geoffrey Bles, 1940), 18.

85. Jacques Maritain, *The Person and the Common Good* (Notre Dame, Ind.: University of Notre Dame Press), 11.

86. Ibid., 33.

87. Maritain, *Scholasticism and Politics*, 52.

88. Maritain, *The Person and the Common Good*, 43.

89. Maritain, *Scholasticism and Politics*, 48. In what follows I draw explicitly on Maritain's early (1938) treatment of these issues in *Scholasticism and Politics*. His later (1946) extensive treatment of these same issues, in chapter 3 of *The Person and the Common Good*, is substantially and in most particulars the

same. (Maritain does, in the later book, alter or clarify his stance on the issue of the primacy of the common good.)

90. Maritain, *Scholasticism and Politics*, 48.

91. Ibid., 49.

92. Ibid.

93. Ibid., 50.

94. Ibid.

95. Ibid., 52.

96. Schall, *Jacques Maritain*, 73.

97. Maritain, *Integral Humanism*, 264.

98. Maritain, *Man and the State*, 2.

99. Ibid., 3–4.

100. Ibid., 4.

101. Ibid., 5.

102. Ibid., 6.

103. Ibid., 7.

104. Ibid., 10.

105. Ibid.

106. Ibid., 11.

107. Ibid., 12.

108. Ibid.

109. Ibid., 13.

110. Ibid.

111. Maritain, *Scholasticism and Politics*, 56.

112. Ibid.

113. Ibid., 58.

114. Maritain, *Integral Humanism*, 237, 264.

115. Russell Hittinger, "Reasons for a Civil Society," in *Reassessing the Liberal State: Reading Maritain's "Man and the State,"* ed. Timothy Fuller and John P. Hittinger (Washington, D.C.: American Maritain Association, 2001), 11–12.

116. Maritain, *The Person and the Common Good*, 64. On the primacy of the common good in Maritain's philosophy, and on where Maritain might be situated in the communitarian-liberal debate that postdates him, see Michelle Watkins and Ralph McInerny, "Jacques Maritain and the Rapprochement of Liberalism and Communitarianism," in *Catholicism, Liberalism, & Communitarianism*, ed. K. Grasso, G. Bradley, and R. Hunt (Lanham: Rowman & Littlefield, 1995), 151–172, and Mary M. Keys, "Personal Dignity and the Common Good: A Twentieth Century Thomistic Dialogue," ibid., 173–195.

117. Hittinger, "Reasons for a Civil Society," 23.

118. *Gaudium et spes*, in *Vatican Council II: The Conciliar and Post Conciliar Documents*, ed. Austin Flannery (Boston: St. Paul Editions, 1975), 59, 74.

119. Hittinger, "Reasons for a Civil Society," 13. The future John Paul II, Karol Wojtyla, was first exposed to Maritain's ideas during his student days in Poland in the 1930s. George Weigel, *Witness to Hope: The Biography of Pope John Paul II* (New York: Harper Collins, 1999), 139.

120. Maritain, *Man and the State*, 96.
121. Jacques Maritain, *Freedom in the Modern World*, in *Works*, 11:43.
122. Maritain, *Man and the State*, 97.
123. Maritain, *Integral Humanism*, 289.
124. Maritain, *Man and the State*, 126.
125. Ibid. 126–128.
126. Maritain, *Freedom in the Modern World*, 42.
127. Maritain, "Natural Law and Moral Law," 76.
128. Maritain, *Man and the State*, 99.
129. See Maritain, "Natural Law and Moral Law," 76.
130. See Finnis, *Natural Law*, 363–366. Maritain elaborates the analogical nature of law in "Natural Law and Moral Law," 62, 65–69.
131. Maritain, "Natural Law and Moral Law," 76 (emphasis added).
132. Maritain, *Man and the State*, 100.
133. Ibid., 95 n. 12.
134. Maritain, "Natural Law and Moral Law," 68.
135. Maritain, *Man and the State*, 11.
136. Maritain, "The Conquest of Freedom," 21.
137. Maritain, *Integral Humanism*, 268.
138. Maritain, "The Conquest of Freedom," 22.
139. Maritain, *Man and the State*, 167–168; *Integral Humanism*, 257–258.
140. Maritain, *Introduction to Basic Problems*, 206–208; *Man and the State*, 183–197; *Integral Humanism*, 291–292.
141. Maritain, *The Rights of Man and Natural Law*, 77–78.
142. Ibid., 81–82.
143. Ibid., 82 n. 1.
144. Maritain, *Man and the State*, 101–103.
145. Maritain, *Integral Humanism*, 169.
146. Maritain, *The Rights of Man and Natural Law*, 87.
147. Maritain, *Man and the State*, 48.
148. Jacques Maritain, *Christianity and Democracy*, trans. Doris C. Anson (New York: Charles Scribner's Sons, 1944), 68.
149. See McGreevy, *Catholicism and American Freedom*, 200.
150. Maritain, *The Rights of Man and Natural Law*, 89, 90.
151. Ibid., 88.
152. Ibid., 93.
153. See Michael Novak, *The Spirit of Democratic Capitalism* (London: IEA Health and Welfare Unit, 1991), 328–329.
154. Maritain, *Reflections on America*, 175.
155. Maritain, "Human Equality," 18.
156. Maritain, *Man and the State*, 98.
157. Maritain, *The Rights of Man and Natural Law*, 70.
158. Maritain, *Man and the State*, 98.
159. Maritain, "Natural Law and Moral Law," 72–73.
160. Ramsey, *Nine Modern Moralists*, 219.

161. See Schall, *Jacques Maritain*, 201–218.

162. Jacques Maritain, introduction to the UNESCO compendium *Human Rights: Comments and Interpretations* (New York: Columbia University Press, 1949), 11.

163. John T. Noonan Jr., *The Lustre of Our Country: The American Experience of Religious Freedom* (Berkeley: University of California Press, 1998), 336.

164. Ibid.

165. Maritain, *Integral Humanism*, 255.

166. Ibid., 256.

167. Ibid., 257.

168. Ibid., 268.

169. Ibid., 258.

170. Maritain, *Man and the State*, 176. See Sigmund, "Maritain on Politics," 161.

171. See, e.g., Maritain, *Notebooks*, 219–257.

172. Jacques Maritain, "The Conquest of Freedom," 21–22.

173. Maritain, *Integral Humanism*, 305.

174. Ibid., 259.

175. Maritain, *Freedom in the Modern World*, 59.

176. Maritain, *Integral Humanism*, 222 n. 9.

177. Jacques Maritain, *Moral Philosophy: An Historical and Critical Survey of the Great Systems* (New York: Charles Scribner's Sons, 1964), 48–49.

178. Ibid., 85.

179. Jacques Maritain, *Science and Wisdom* (New York: Charles Scribner's Sons, 1940), 200.

180. Ibid.

181. Ibid., 210–220.

182. Maritain, *Introduction to Basic Problems*, 196.

183. Maritain, "Confession of Faith," 343.

184. Maritain, *An Introduction to the Basic Problems of Moral Philosophy*, 141.

185. See Noonan, *The Lustre of Our Country*, 350.

186. On the emergence of personalism from the new focus on "the human person," see generally John Mahoney, *The Making of Moral Theology: A Study of the Roman Catholic Tradition* (Oxford: Oxford University Press, 1987).

187. Sigmund, "Maritain on Politics," 153.

188. McInerny, *The Very Rich Hours of Jacques Maritain*, 46.

189. Schall, *Jacques Maritain*, xii, xviii–xx.

190. W. Norris Clarke, *The One and the Many: A Contemporary Thomistic Metaphysics* (Notre Dame, Ind.: University of Notre Dame Press, 2001), 39.

191. Michael J. White, *Partisan or Neutral: The Futility of Public Political Theory* (Lanham, Md.: Rowman & Littlefield, 1997), 81–121.

192. Maritain, *Integral Humanism*, 233–234; see also Jacques Maritain, *On the Philosophy of History* (New York: Charles Scribner's Sons, 1957).

193. Clarke, *The One and the Many*, 39.

194. Schall, *Jacques Maritain*, 225

[CHAPTER 4]

John Courtney Murray, S.J. (1904–1967)

ANGELA C. CARMELLA

In *Dignitatis Humanae* (1965), the Declaration on Religious Freedom, the Second Vatican Council rejected earlier papal teaching and affirmed religious freedom as a human and civil right. One cannot understand the declaration's embrace of religious freedom and the intense doctrinal development it signaled without knowing the life and thought of one of its primary architects, John Courtney Murray, S.J. Equipped with a brilliant command of church history and theology, and profoundly influenced by the First Amendment, Murray had long argued that religious freedom, not religious establishment, represented the church's authentic doctrine.

In addition to being known as a theologian, Murray is also known as a public philosopher whose work "was incomparably the most important instance of liberal Catholic Americanism in the post–World War II era."[1] His best-known work, *We Hold These Truths*, describes the deep affinities between Catholic social thought and American political principles. By Murray's account, American liberalism is not associated with individualism, the privatization of religion, and the secularization of society; rather, it is rooted in medieval Christian political and legal traditions and respects the dignity and freedom essential to the flourishing of the human person. In this role, Murray's major contribution was to help a predominantly Protestant America better understand and accept Catholics as citizens and as political leaders.

"THE ETERNAL RETURN OF NATURAL LAW"

Murray's education with the Jesuits came at a time when Catholic learning was steeped in a neo-Thomist revival, thanks to the efforts of Pope Leo XIII decades before. Born into an Irish-Scottish family in New York City and educated at Boston College, Woodstock College in Maryland, and the

Gregorian University in Rome, Murray was, for most of his professional life, a professor at Woodstock College, teaching the theology of grace and the Trinity.[2] He became most widely known, however, for his work in public philosophy, politics, and law. As editor of the Jesuit journal *Theological Studies*, as advisor to church officials and public officials alike, and as a frequent contributor to journals with broad appeal to an educated public, Murray engaged in dialogue on numerous topics, such as religious freedom and pluralism, Catholic education, international relations and war, racial justice, free speech and censorship, contraception, and the tradition of reason or "natural law." In this way Murray adapted to a pluralistic context the traditional Thomist methodology of Christian intellectual encounter with the world grounded in an openness to the world and to all things human.

Murray's writing relied heavily on the Thomist notion of natural law, "written on the hearts" of all people, knowable by reason and without the aid of revelation. Natural law thinking acknowledges the capacity of human reason to recognize the principle that one should do good and avoid evil, and then to give content to that principle through reasoning. According to Murray, the human person is intelligent and reality is intelligible; people can grasp reality and can derive from it a set of moral obligations. People are "natural lawyers" all the time: when they work out their common life together according to reason, when they consider conduct unjust despite its formal legality, and when they equate morality with right reason. Importantly, for Murray, as for Aquinas, natural law was not a remote and abstract set of ideas, but was instead grounded in sociohistorical life, which gave it a dynamic quality.

Murray's natural law was the Catholic natural law of the Thomist tradition, complete with a natural theology (the God of reason) and a theological anthropology (the human person as participant in God's eternal reason). It helped him to engage the wider society and the framework of political liberalism because natural law "give[s] a philosophical account of the moral experience of humanity and ... lay[s] down a charter of essential humanism. It does not show the individual the way to sainthood, but only to manhood. It does not promise to transform society into the City of God on earth, but only to prescribe, for the purposes of law and social custom, that minimum of morality which must be observed by the members of a society, if the social environment is to be human and habitable."[3] Thus, while rooted in a Catholic worldview, his public philosophy emphasized the language of reason, the language that all can understand. This language—not the language of faith or revelation—made possible deliberative, civil conversation among Catholics, Protestants, Jews, and secularists, citizens "locked in argument."

Murray claimed the philosophical superiority of this tradition and noted the "eternal return of natural law."[4] For him, only through the discourse of reason could civility be sustained. Further, civil conversation was critical to the emergence of the public consensus, "an ensemble of substantive truths … whereby the people acquires its identity as a people."[5] This consensus was not defined as majority opinion. It was the domain of the "wise and honest," those who act as stewards of truth and justice, who "have a 'care,' but who are not 'interested parties,'"[6] and in this sense could very well represent minority opinion.

This posture of intellectual engagement with America and appreciation for the American experiment in freedom and pluralism did not characterize the Catholic Church in the middle of the twentieth century. In its nineteenth-century reaction to anti-Catholic, ideological liberalism on the European continent, the church had condemned liberalism, democracy, freedom of conscience, freedom of speech, and other civil liberties. Its antimodernist (and, by extension, anti-American) position created enormous difficulties for American Catholics. The very ideals America was based upon were considered evils. Moreover, pluralism was condemned because it departed from the ideal of religious unity. Catholics in America were even urged to avoid interfaith cooperation on social issues, because it might lead to "indifferentism"—the belief that all religions are equally true.[7]

For Murray, however, the natural law tradition answered these concerns. That tradition suggested, as his own experiences on a variety of postwar social justice issues had confirmed, that interreligious cooperation need not lead to indifferentism, in that theological agreement was not necessary for agreement on ethical and political goals. More fundamentally, Murray considered natural law to be the critical element linking Catholicism to basic American ideals. Murray saw in the work of the founders the embodiment and exposition of natural law, particularly as America was "organized in an era when the tradition of natural law and natural rights was still vigorous."[8] Although Catholics had little to do with the actual American founding, the founders had inherited not just Enlightenment rationalism but also a strong classical civic republicanism (with its heavy emphasis on virtue) and a medieval political and legal legacy (with its tradition of reason) as well.[9]

Murray emphasized those structural and substantive principles of American government that were outgrowths of medieval political institutions. That medieval legacy found its way into the American Declaration of Independence (in which God is the source of rights and sovereign over nations), the Bill of Rights (in which rights are found to inhere in the human person, "antecedent to his status of citizen"), the constitutional structure of government, and concepts such as the consent of the governed, the rule of law, and the state as political (and not theological) sovereign. Murray argued to the vigorously anti-American culture of the church that America was Catholic to its roots—just as he argued to the vigorously anti-Catholic American culture that Catholics were just as closely related to the "American proposition" as the Protestant majority that claimed the proposition as its own.

The church's condemnation of church-state separation was particularly problematic for American Catholics, because it fostered suspicions concerning their citizenship and the goals of their political activity. But Murray was convinced that the freedom the church experienced in America had made it more vibrant and had allowed Catholics a deeper religious life when compared with other societies in which the church was legally "established" but had little spiritual or moral influence within the population. For him, the American experiment was proof that religious freedom could produce an environment of respect for religion, in contrast to the harsh and hostile treatment toward religion found in the antireligious "religious freedom" of Continental liberalism.

Murray spent years crafting a theological argument that much of what was antimodern and antiliberal in the church's teaching was actually a historically conditioned response to particular ideological liberal movements, and that religious freedom represented the authentic doctrinal position. But in 1955 his superiors prohibited him from writing on church-state matters. In obedience to the silencing, Murray focused on public philosophy for nearly a decade. Although under suspicion within the Catholic Church, Murray won broad approval in the public arena. He appeared on the cover of *Time* in 1960 and advised John F. Kennedy's campaign on the Houston address, in which Kennedy assured the nation that the pope would not control the White House.

MURRAY ON THE PERSON, LAW, SOCIETY, AND THE STATE

THE PERSON

Murray was keenly aware that a new human consciousness had begun to emerge among people in civil community—a consciousness of the dignity and freedom of the human person and the necessary realization of that dignity and freedom in political and juridical terms, a reality later affirmed by Pope John XXIII in *Pacem in terris*. Murray insisted that the recognition of a new consciousness in the human person did not depart from natural law and move toward relativism—though some of his critics thought it did.[10] Nor did it in any way imply a malleable human nature that changed with historical-material conditions. Murray argued that natural law becomes clearer through the unfolding of different historical circumstances over time:

> The fundamental structure of man's nature is, of course, permanent and unchanging; correlatively constant are the elementary human experiences. Every man, simply because he is a man, has to "meet" himself, others, and God. In these relationships he must avoid the evil and do the good that come home to him as evidently evil or good.... History does not alter the basic structure of human nature, nor affect the substance of the elementary human experiences, nor open before man wholly new destinies. Therefore history cannot alter the natural law.... But history, as any history book shows, does change what I have called the human reality. It evokes situations that never happened before.... The nature of man is an historical nature.... In this sense, the nature of man changes in history, for better or for worse; at the same time that the fundamental structure of human nature, and the essential destinies of the human person, remain untouched and intact.[11]

And what is the fundamental structure of human nature? Murray, drawing on Aquinas and on the more recent popes (Leo XIII, Pius XII and John XXIII), restated the tradition: the human person is social and rational, possesses dignity, and needs freedom. The human person is social by nature, in Pius XII's words, "the subject, the foundation, and the end of social life."[12] This meant for Murray that political theories that focus on the individual, apart from social context, could never be complete. The human person is always a person-in-society, embedded in numerous kinds of communities of formation and common interest. And those communities, like the family, must have the necessary autonomy to fulfill the functions proper to them.

The human person is also rational, and is capable of using reason for proper ends; that is, the natural law tradition allows the capacity of human reason to recognize the principle that one should do good and avoid evil, and then to give content to that principle through reasoning. As a matter of human nature, the person "is intelligent; ... reality is intelligible; and that reality, as grasped by intelligence, imposes on the will the obligation that it will be obeyed in its demands for action or abstention."[13] To use our intellect to follow natural law fulfills our humanity.

And where is Jesus in natural law? While natural law is common to all of humanity, the "Gospel invitation" lies beyond the ethical obligations of natural law.[14] Consistent with the Thomist tradition in which grace perfects and does not eradicate nature, Murray believed that the choice to follow

Jesus left one's human nature intact. The rules of the moral life still apply. "The law of nature, which prescribes humanity, still exists at the interior of the Gospel invitation, which summons to perfection.... The Christian call is to transcend nature, notably to transcend ... the faculty of reason. But it is not a call to escape from nature."[15]

In addition to a social and rational nature, the human person is endowed with profound dignity. The Incarnation, in which Jesus is fully God and fully human, "teaches man his proper dignity."[16] The person (as Thomas Aquinas had said) "now dares to think worthily" of himself or herself.[17] Made in the image of God, the human person is "sacred, inviolable, gifted with the divine prerogative of freedom and charged with all the responsibilities of that gift."[18] Murray tied human dignity to the fact that we are responsible for ourselves and the world, given our social nature; and we are capable of assuming that responsibility only because of our rational nature. Finally, the inherent sociality, rationality, and dignity of the person create a demand for responsible freedom, for a "free society," because the nature and destination of the human person can be fully realized only in conditions of freedom.

Against this background of Catholic anthropological thought, Murray detailed the four premises of natural law, which formed the basis of the argument that all can grasp the sociality, rationality, dignity and freedom of the human person: (1) a realist epistemology, (2) a metaphysic of nature, (3) a natural theology, and (4) a morality. These four premises give rise to a picture of human nature, a nature that finds freedom through reason. Human nature finds freedom in both rights and duties, in the self and in relation to others. As Murray explained,

> Natural law supposes a realist epistemology, that asserts the real to be the measure of knowledge, and also asserts the possibility of intelligence reaching the real, i.e., the nature of things—in the case, the nature of man as a unitary and constant concept beneath all individual differences. Secondly, it supposes a metaphysic of nature, especially the idea that nature is a teleological concept,... that there is a natural inclination in man to become what in nature and destination he is—to achieve the fullness of his own being. Thirdly, it supposes a natural theology, asserting that there is a God, Who is eternal Reason, *Nous*, at the summit of the order of being, Who is the author of all nature, and Who wills that the order of nature be fulfilled in all its purposes, as these are inherent in the natures found in the order. Finally, it supposes a morality, especially the principle that for man, a rational being, the order of nature is not an order of necessity, to be fulfilled blindly, but an order of reason and therefore of freedom.[19]

THE PERSON IN THE MORAL ORDER AND LEGAL ORDER

Murray employed the overarching "legal" framework of the Thomist-Leonine tradition, which sets divine law on one side and human law on the other. Divine law, or the moral order, comprises law both natural and revealed and "is to make man good as man," conformed "to the intentions of nature and to the higher intentions of Christ." In contrast, human law, or the legal order, has a more limited purpose: "to make a society good as a society, to create an order of social rectitude that is the necessary condition of man's pursuit of his goodness as man. What human law formally and proximately envisages is not man as man but man *as citizen.*"[20] Because these orders come together within the human person, they must be in harmony, but they are not coextensive. For the Thomist, the purpose of human law is a modest one, only "to assure those minimal conditions of actualized morality within society which are necessary for the coexistence and cooperation of the citizens 'toward the common good of justice and peace.'"[21] This affirms considerable freedom for the human person, recognizing that the state cannot require of its citizens all that God and nature require. Thus, the Thomist tradition never permits the direct translation of a moral norm into the terms of human law. Human law making is only legitimate when it meets the intermediate norms of prudence.

Human law is, in St. Thomas's definition, "the discipline that is coercive through fear of penalty." Law is indeed a form of moral discipline, directed to a moral end, which is civic virtue. But law is also a social discipline, directed to the common good of the body politic, which is primarily "the unity which is called peace," in St. Thomas's phrase. More specifically, law is a coercive discipline, whose specific mode of action is "through force and fear."[22]

Because of the social and coercive aspects of law, actual legal decisions must be based upon two prudential concerns: the "juristic norm—the general and particular exigencies of the common good, the needs and the advantages of the community," and the "political norm, the norm of wisdom in the use of force." Thus, prudence requires that a law be "necessary or useful for the common good in the given circumstances. The morality of a law is not an immediate guarantee of its necessity or utility."[23] So one moves from the moral order of revealed and natural law to the legal order of human law by way of prudential reasoning and judgment, assessing the needs of the common good in particular historical circumstances. Natural law is the skeleton law "to which flesh and blood must be added by that heart of the political process, the rational activity of man, aided by experience and by high professional competence."[24]

Murray's work emphasized, almost exclusively, the external, coercive aspect of human law and the notion that "men can be coerced only into a minimal amount of moral action."[25] He paid little attention to didactic and theological "uses" of law (as those are developed in the Reformation tradition, for instance). While he did note a "public educative" value to the law when it is "ahead" of public consensus as in the area of racial equality, he was particularly pessimistic that law can play any role in "reforming" sexual or personal behavior, where he thought law has no educative value whatsoever.[26] Murray was particularly critical of a strain of American Protestant thought that had influenced legislation on a host of topics, such as the prohibition of contraception and alcohol. In these cases, he argued that lawmakers, influenced by the belief that what is moral should be legislated, had failed to engage in the proper assessment of the prudential norms of jurisprudence and political wisdom.[27]

THE PERSON IN SOCIETY AND IN RELATION TO THE STATE

Murray wrote extensively on two distinct but related spheres—society and the state and its laws. As a matter of their nature, society and the state are distinct, with the state contained within society and charged with performing a well-defined set of duties; further, society and the state are secular, in possession of their own dynamisms, their own rules governed by reason. Society and the state are "natural institutions with their relatively autonomous ends or purposes." Their purposes are public, and "therefore strictly limited." They relate solely to the temporal order, "and even within this order they are not coextensive with the ends of the human person as such."[28] Their secularity is not to be misunderstood as atheistic or nontheistic. Murray was quite clear that society and the state are under God's sovereignty. In fact, although society is properly secular, Murray believed secular society must have a "spiritual substance that underlies the order of law, the order of public morality and all other orders and processes within society."[29] While the state should acknowledge God's sovereignty, the state itself is never to be sacralized.

Given the social nature of the person, and the notion that the human person is the subject, foundation, and end of the entire social life, a "personalist" conception of society emerges.[30] In this understanding of society, Murray placed a heavy emphasis on the principle of subsidiarity, in which society comprises multiple institutions such as the family, religious communities, professional and occupational organizations, voluntary associations, and cultural groups. These nongovernmental groups function autonomously and freely, without undue interference from the state, and all are charged with the pursuit and promotion of the common good. The social preconditions are thereby set that allow the human person "to become what in nature and destination he is—to achieve the fullness of his own being."[31] This especially means the recognition of human dignity in conditions of freedom. In fact, the state-society distinction and emphasis on subsidiarity led both Murray and contemporary Catholic philosopher Jacques Maritain to affirm "religious liberty and constitutional democracy and opposition ... to all forms of totalitarianism and state absolutism."[32]

The state, in contrast, has the more circumscribed role within society to maintain public order through law as it directs and coordinates the common good. Murray's limited, nonsacral state was predominantly a response to the horrific experiences of twentieth-century totalitarianism and World War II, but his response came in the form of a retrieval of threads from tradition, ancient and more recent, that could be woven in a distinctly modern way. Specifically, he drew upon the writings of fifth-century Pope Gelasius on the two authorities, spiritual and temporal (that is, church and state); of eleventh-century Pope Gregory VII on the freedom of the church; of thirteenth-century Dominican John of Paris on the independence and nonderivative nature of the state; and of the modern popes, Leo XIII and Pius XII, on the political and constitutional nature of the state. Pope Pius XII, also responding to the horrors of totalitarianism, had articulated the limited "juridical" state in light of the personalist conception of society—a state focused primarily on "the protection and promotion of the rights of man and the facilitation of the performance of man's native duties."[33]

Because the state acts primarily through coercive law, the nature of the state's purpose and function mirrors the limited nature of the purpose and function of law. The state must respect the existence and autonomy of society's many institutions and may not assume their functions. Thus, Murray, drawing on Pope Leo XIII, noted that

> government, strictly speaking, creates nothing, that its function is to order, not to create. Perhaps more exactly, its function is to create the conditions of order under which original vitalities and forces, present in society, may have full scope to create the values by which society lives. Perhaps still more exactly, the only value which government *per se* is called upon to create is the value of order. But the value of order resides primarily in the fact that it furnishes [opportunities] for the exercise of ... freedoms."[34]

The state's purposes are "justice, freedom, security, the general welfare, and civil unity or peace," in short, ensuring those rights (and enforcing the duties) of persons and their communities and helping to establish the necessary preconditions for achieving the fullness of our own being.[35]

Murray's work highlighted some important divisions in Christian social and political thought, such as those between Thomists like Murray and Augustinians like Reinhold Niebuhr, who criticized Murray's confidence in human reason and lack of emphasis on sin. For Murray, state power was not necessarily or inevitably connected to sin. The state's self-interest was natural, but this interest was harnessed by law and its guide, reason. Furthermore, the state's use of force could be proper, to uphold public order. But, for Niebuhr, human nature was permeated by sin and by a consequent tendency to abuse power. He considered any use of power an evil, even if a lesser evil, and thus always insisted on balancing power against power.[36]

Murray also contrasted the secular, autonomous, reason-based society and state with the notion that society and state must be "Christianized," as proposed in some Protestant circles. These efforts attempted to "bring the organized action of politics and the practical art of statecraft directly under the control of the Christian values that govern personal and familial life." They insisted on transferring Christian values directly into social life (as though the moral obligations of the individual were those of the society and the state), and placed the eradication of sin within the domain of human law. For Murray, such a view of society and the state failed to recognize that their purposes "are not coextensive with the wider and higher range of obligations that rest upon the human person (not to speak of the Christian)."[37] He noted that Christianity "profoundly altered the structure of politics by introducing the revolutionary idea of the two communities, two orders of law and two authorities. But it did not change the nature of politics, law and government, which still remain rational processes. To the quality of these processes Christian faith and grace contribute only indirectly, by their inner effect upon man himself, which is in part the correction and clarification of the processes of reason."[38]

With this general theory of the autonomous, secular, and reason-based society and state, one can see why Murray was comfortable with many presuppositions of American liberalism. Murray, like political theorist John Rawls, recognized "the independence of law and politics from certain religious arguments" and believed that "political and legal discourse and decision making should be conducted according to norms accessible to all citizens, i.e., according to 'natural law' or 'public reason.'"[39] Like Rawls, Murray saw "the importance of consensus amidst pluralism.... Christians ... could find common ground [with others in areas of social reconstruction and justice] without appeals to religious truth, and without compromise of religious truth."[40]

But Murray rejected the liberal notion that the competing "comprehensive doctrines" or visions of the good—particularly religious ones—held deeply by different groups within society were private or equal. He always held that the Catholic faith was the true faith, and that it could contribute publicly (through natural law discourse) and through its religious mission. In this way, he primarily lauded liberal structures—such as limited government, checks and balances, federalism, and constitutional rights—because those structures respect the freedom proper to the dignity of the human person. These structures involve no metaphysical assertions, imply nothing about truth of religion or morality, and do not mean that each person can make his or her own moral or religious truth. Nor do they connote an ideal of a "neutral state" in which each individual adopts and pursues his/her own vision of the good.[41]

Further, Murray rejected the emphasis on the individual that often appeared at the heart of much of liberalism, because of the Catholic emphasis on the social nature of the person. He was a particularly harsh critic of seventeenth-century English philosopher John Locke, the dominant Enlightenment political theorist. In contrast to the inherent sociality of the human person, Murray claimed that

> individualism, this atomistic social outlook, is the predominant characteristic of Locke's system. His law of nature is solely a law of individual nature, conceived after the abstract fashion of the rationalist.... Locke's individualism completely deprives society of any organic character.... In Locke's theory all forms of sociality are purely contractual.... Finally, the individualism of Locke's law of nature results in a complete evacuation of the notion of the "rights" of man.[42]

Although his reading of Locke is contestable,[43] Murray crafted his society and state argument over against such a liberal vision.

THE PUBLIC ORDER FUNCTION OF THE STATE AND ITS LAWS

In Murray's thought, the lawmaking authority of the state is circumscribed not only by the prudential norms of the Thomist, but also by the state's defined function, which Murray referred to as its "public order" role. He wrote:

> The public order is that limited segment of the common good which is committed to the state to be protected and maintained by the coercive force that is available to the state—the force of law and of administrative or police action. The public order thus comprises a threefold good—the political good, which is the public peace; the moral good, which is proper custody of public morality as determined by minimal and generally accepted standards; and the juridical good, which is harmony among citizens in the exercise of their civil rights.[44]

Because the state is only part of society, its public order function involves only part of the common good; thus, the law promulgated by the state for public order cannot claim to define the whole of the society's common good. Human law can restrict human freedom only when public order—public peace, public morality, and civil rights—is at stake, and then only when it is prudent to do so. In fact, Murray thought that much of social life and public policy could be directed through civil conversation and public consensus, and by the proper functioning of nonstate groups within society, with no need for legal intervention.

Yet despite what seems to be a minimal role for the state and its laws, the scope of public order is closely related to society's common good and can therefore be quite broad. The state's concern for society's political, moral, and juridical "goods" necessarily involves the state in a host of areas of social life in order to accomplish its ordering role, to ensure that the social fabric does not unravel, and to enforce rights and duties substantively. Even when the state respects subsidiarity, it is still charged with the coordination and direction of efforts to promote the common good—which is no small task. And in the face of increasing "socialization"—the term Pope John XXIII used to describe the growing interdependence of social groups—the state may have to assume partial or full regulatory (or even substantive) responsibility for many of these efforts. Further, it appears that "human law" for Murray was broadly conceived to include all kinds of legal relationships, and certainly was not limited to legislation. But Murray maintained the clear requirement that all human law had to be justified as a political, moral, or juridical good and meet the intermediate prudential norms.

Murray's thinking about the state's role in ensuring public peace and civil rights, the political and juridical goods, is closely related to his understanding of a new awareness of human freedom and dignity and of the right to religious freedom. It is best expressed in his working thesis—"as much freedom as possible, as much coercion as necessary."[45] The state ensures peace, which, for Aquinas, is "the work of justice [and] highest political end,"[46] and enforces civil rights in order to promote the necessary preconditions for human development. Murray also wrote a fair amount about "moral good," the public morality prong of the public order function. Laws relating to morality should involve only public (never private) morality, which would be the case "when a practice seriously undermines the foundations of society or gravely damages the moral life of the community as such, in such wise that legal prohibition becomes necessary to safeguard the social order as such."[47] The determination of what is public morality is a matter for public consensus, which is why a vigorous civil conversation,

based upon reasoned discourse, is vital to the life of the community. Without "a reasonable correspondence between the moral standards generally
recognized by the conscience of the community and the legal statutes concerning public morality," Murray wrote, the "laws will be unenforceable
and ineffective and they will be resented as undue restrictions on civil or
personal freedom."[48]

And even if public morality can be said to be involved, law should be
the tool of choice only if it meets the prudential norms that Aquinas established.[49] Will the law be obeyed? Is it enforceable? Could the law give
rise to harmful effects in other areas of society? Is coercive law the proper
means for eliminating this social problem? What has experience taught us
in this area? What does prudent reflection tell us? Murray believed that
"the greater the social evil, the less effective against it is the instrument
of coercive law."[50] But his dislike for a legal solution certainly did not license immoral behavior. Under the subsidiarity model of society, families,
churches, schools, and the like are charged with imparting moral direction
and other human goods.[51] The obligations of the moral order still bind the
person; the legal order is simply not always appropriate to enforce those
obligations.

Murray applied this analysis when he counseled the Catholic Church in
Massachusetts to support legislation decriminalizing contraception. His
reasoning was that contraception was a private matter, not one of public
morality. Additionally, on grounds of prudence, such laws are publicly divisive and attempt to coerce a moral standard that is not shared by the wider
community. (The fact that many other religious groups of his day did not
ban contraception carried weight in this determination.) Further, to make
contraception legal certainly did not make it moral. It simply recognized
that the topic did not fall within the state's public order role. He advised
the church to exhort Catholics to "lift the standards of public morality in
all its dimensions, not by appealing to law and police action, but by the
integrity of their Christian lives. This, to set the birth-control issue in its
proper perspective."[52]

Was there room for dissent from a law legitimately promulgated pursu-
ant to a state's public order function? For Catholic natural law, all civil law
stands under the judgment of the moral order, but Murray wrote little on
actual instances of dissent. As a member of the Presidential Commission
on Selective Service in the mid-1960s, Murray was a supporter of broad
conscientious objector status in war, desiring to expand the exemption status to include not only pacifists but also those who objected to a particular unjust war (as might arise under Catholic just war tradition). But even
here, Murray was a careful conservative. He thought those making the se-

lective conscientious objection bore the burden of proof. The "State too has its conscience which informs its laws and decisions." The conscientious objector "still stands within the community and is subject to its judgment as already declared."[53]

MURRAY AND RELIGIOUS FREEDOM AS A HUMAN FREEDOM

Murray's vision of religious freedom was a natural outgrowth of his understanding of the person, society, and the state and the limitations of its law. For Murray, religious freedom was a demand of human dignity and an exigence of a nonsacral state, and consisted of immunity from both coercion and restraint.[54] No one could be coerced to believe or practice a faith, nor could anyone be restrained from religious belief or practice in the absence of a threat to public order. Because Murray was vigorously opposed to any effort to privatize religion, his vision of "religious freedom" broadly encompassed freedom of conscience, freedom of religious association, and ecclesial freedom (in the sense of internal autonomy), as well as personal and corporate freedom of religious expression in worship, witness, teaching, and practice. The state was "competent to do only one thing in respect of religion, that is, to recognize, guarantee, protect, and promote the religious freedom of the people. This is the full extent of [its] competence." While the state has this limited role, "the care of religion, in so far as religion is an integral element of the common good of society, devolves upon those institutions whose purposes are religious—the church and the churches, and various voluntary associations for religious purposes."[55]

In Murray's thought, religious freedom can be restricted only when religious conduct seriously violates the public order. To ensure that the application of this general principle is never arbitrary, he added a fourfold requirement: "that the violation of the public order be really serious; that legal or police intervention be really necessary; that regard be had for the privileged character of religious freedom, which is not simply to be equated with other civil rights; [and] that the rule of jurisprudence of the free society be strictly observed, scil., as much freedom as possible, as much coercion as necessary."[56] With respect to restrictions to enforce public morality, Murray was careful to distinguish between the illegitimate state "care" of religious truth (and consequent suppression of other religions) and its legitimate enforcement of minimal standards when prudent.

Murray's vision of religious freedom and of the nonsacral nature of the state was also shaped—quite decisively, in fact—by his understanding of the religion clauses of the First Amendment, which prohibit any law "respecting an establishment of religion or prohibiting the free exercise thereof." He wrote that the clauses "may claim the honor of having first clearly formulated the principle and established the institution" of religious freedom.[57]

Murray understood the religion clauses within the uniquely American tradition of vibrant religious pluralism, untarnished by the absolutist "separation of church and state" and privatized religion of continental liberalism, or laicism. Thus, in contrast to this ideological religious "liberty" of Europe, Murray identified two distinguishing features of the religion clauses. First, their purpose was primarily the protection of the free exercise of religion, with "non-establishment" (i.e., separation) concerns held subordinate to and in service to this freedom. His reading of the historical record supported this primacy of religious freedom, and it found a clear framers' intent: no constraints on freedom of conscience and religious exercise; political equality regardless of religious affiliation; and no privileged national religion.[58]

Second, the religion clauses are articles of peace, not articles of faith. By this he meant that they "have no religious content. They answer none of the eternal human questions with regard to the nature of truth and freedom or the manner in which the spiritual order of man's life is to be organized or not organized."[59] For him the clauses do not embody, as some Protestant interpreters had assumed, the theological assertion that religion can only be a voluntary, private matter, and that all churches are equal. Because of the nonsacral nature of the state, he vigorously opposed any interpretation of the clauses that would imply "ultimate beliefs, certain specifically sectarian tenets with regard to the nature of religion, religious truth, the church, faith, conscience, divine revelation, human freedom."[60] Thus, Catholics could still believe their church to be the "true" church, knowing that the state had not taken a position on that belief. As articles of peace, the religion clauses are "only a law, not a dogma ... not invested with the sanctity that attaches to dogma, but only with the rationality that attaches to law."[61]

Murray often wrote that religious people and institutions require only one thing of the state: freedom from interference, a negative immunity. His vision of broad protections for religious freedom, with its framework set by civil law, complemented his vision of a religiously vibrant society. All citizens and groups could participate actively in public affairs, cooperate on temporal matters of common concern, and help shape the public consensus—of course, through civil conversation, using the language of reason, not of revelation. This process also applied to attempts to elevate standards of public morality. But failing that, Catholics and any other "minority group" holding standards different from those of the general public were free to set those standards for their own members; they could not demand that others be required to follow those standards. One can see here the influence of the medieval writings of John of Paris, who had developed a theory of "indirect influence" by the church on the state. In Murray's revival of the theory, it was not for the church to "teach the prince his politics," but rather to "affect the temporal order through the person who is both citizen and Christian" whose conscience has been formed by the church.[62] Thus, for America, Murray envisioned a pluralistic society, with active religious communities contributing to the dialogue and winning by superiority of argument rather than through privileged legal position.

But Murray admitted that affirmative state assistance was sometimes necessary to ensure religious freedom. For instance, he argued for aid to Catholic schools, finding its denial a grave violation of the parental right to educate children. Murray believed that religious schools should be treated in parity with public and nonreligious private schools because they were, primarily, schools. Because the state had assumed responsibility for education (in opposition to the principle of subsidiarity) and had committed its resources to support it, principles of distributive justice required that benefits provided to "education" should be distributed equitably, so that "a proportionately just measure of public support should be available to such schools as serve the public cause of popular education."[63] He did not see this as the illegitimate care of religion but rather as the legitimate protection of religious freedom.

MURRAY'S ROLE IN THE DEVELOPMENT OF THE CHURCH'S DOCTRINE ON CHURCH AND STATE

Murray's ideas about religious freedom certainly did not comport with what was considered at the time to be the church's teaching on church-state relations. The "thesis-hypothesis" distinction provided that the ideal situation (the "thesis") was one of legal establishment of the Catholic Church and legal intolerance of other faiths. In this view, the Catholic faith, as the truth, "has an exclusive divine right to be the public religion of men and societies"[64] and thus the right to legal privilege; "error" (i.e., any non-Catholic faith) has no rights, and thus should be eradicated from public existence. The "thesis" was to be pursued wherever Catholics had sufficient political power to realize it; but where circumstances made this impossible, or where Catholics were in a minority, then the "hypothesis" came into play. In that case, Catholics should defend their right to free exercise, but general religious liberty for all was to be tolerated only on the grounds of expediency and as a necessary evil.

Murray had nothing but contempt for this position for many reasons, not the least of which was that it regarded the dictatorship of Spain to be the ideal Catholic state, while considering the constitutional democracy of the United States an evil to be tolerated. Murray refused to accept "the assumption that whenever and wherever the population is Catholic the public advantage is inevitably served by legal establishment and legal intolerance [and that] Catholic unity ... is the highest social good."[65] He thought that the thesis-hypothesis distinction wholly misrepresented church tradition and the Western Christian political legacy, and he wrote sarcastically: "It is true that you may not find in these [Catholic] countries a Catholic people that intelligently and actively professes its public faith *animo et moribus*.... You certainly will fail to find the fulfillment of the Western Christian ideal of political life and government, which is certainly not dictatorship. No matter. You do find establishment and intolerance, and therefore you find the ideal Catholic state."[66]

For Murray this position was a violation of the basic distinction between the order of morals and the order of law, wherein a theological truth is not supposed to be translated directly into coercive law unless public order and the norms of prudence so demand. More fundamentally, he considered the spiritual goals of religious unity and promotion of religious truth to fall outside the scope of the state's public order role. Further, the contemporary situation of mid-twentieth-century life had seen the emergence of a new human consciousness of the dignity and freedom of the person. The church had to face this new consciousness. The person in civil society had become aware of his or her adulthood: the church could not continue to treat him or her as a child. "The truth of human dignity is as old as Christianity, and in a sense, even older. The new thing today, and the thing that matters for the argument, is the newly common human consciousness of this truth.... Man demands civil liberties that he may lead in society a life worthy of a man. And this demand for freedom from coercion is made with special force in what concerns religion."[67]

THE LEONINE REINTERPRETATION

With his passion for religious freedom, Murray became committed to establishing an intellectual foundation for the abandonment of the thesis-hypothesis distinction. To do this, Murray engaged the tradition broadly, pruning away those elements that had obscured doctrines on freedom and the limited nature of the state. For a time Murray paid particular attention to the late-nineteenth-century writings of Pope Leo XIII, because they constituted both an enormous obstacle to and a source for the task of doctrinal retrieval and renewal. Leo XIII was known for his scathing critique of modern liberalism, for the unequivocal rejection of civil liberties and the "separation of church and state," and for a conception of a paternalistic Catholic state that "cared for" the "one true faith" in political and legal terms. To overcome these positions, Murray characterized them as polemical and therefore of limited doctrinal value, crafted in response to the historical situation of anti-Catholic Continental laicism and a church population of uneducated masses. After isolating and diminishing the force of these positions, Murray emphasized two traditional Christian political themes also found in Leo XIII's work: the freedom of the church and the concept of a limited state. He later connected these arguments to teachings of Pope Pius XII on the nature of the state. Thus, in a series of articles in *Theological Studies* in the early to mid-1950s, Murray reinterpreted Leo's (and Pius's) writings to demonstrate that the "thesis-hypothesis" position did not represent the church's authentic doctrine.

Murray's task when reading Leo XIII's texts was "to know what in them is history, and what is still the doctrine."[68] This was no "change" in doctrine, as Murray characterized it, but a "development" of doctrine.[69] The revelation was given, but understanding evolves over time. For Murray, doctrinal development was a plain fact, universal and ancient. All traditions, religious and political, must grow. "It only remains to know what the dynamism of growth is, what directions the progress in the tradition should take, and what new forms the development should show forth."[70] And growth can be seen throughout the life of the church, a "change of perspective that is brought about by the asking of either a new question, or of an old question in a new mode of statement or with a new note of urgency."[71] The "new question" posed at mid-century was presented by the new human consciousness of the dignity and freedom of the human person and necessary realization of that dignity and freedom in political and juridical terms.

The growth of the tradition depended upon the act of pruning away those principles developed primarily in response to the particularities of history, to enable the full flowering of those principles that assert themselves over time in continuity with the past. Murray regarded much of Leo XIII's antimodern writing as history, not as doctrine. Leo XIII's rejection of the "separation of church and state" was the rejection of Jacobin separationism, of "totalitarian democracy," as Murray called it, under which the state was "juridically omnipotent and omnicompetent," autonomous reason was supreme, and religion was merely a "private matter" with no public or social presence or purpose.[72] The result of this ideology was the sacralization of the state, the collapse of society into the state, and the "forcible evacuation of European society's traditional Christian content,"[73]

creating, in Murray's terms, a juridical and social "monism." Further, Leo
XIII's call for a paternalistic state in union with the church and vested with
broad cultural and religious responsibilities was an attempt to protect the
church and its uneducated membership from these efforts to eradicate the
church and Christianity from public life.

Having established the urgency of the historical situation in nineteenth-
century Europe and the polemical nature of Leo XIII's response to it, Murray focused on those elements of Leo's writings that could serve as resources
for doctrinal development on religious freedom and a limited state. Murray
cast Leo XIII as the chief expositor of Pope Gelasius's thesis of the "two societies" and their proper relationship. Leo XIII had preserved the "two leading principles of Christian social organization"—first, a clear distinction
between the two societies, spiritual and temporal, and their powers and
laws; second, the primacy and freedom of the spiritual.[74] He had further
developed the Gelasian thesis by adding a third principle of his own: the
need for an orderly relationship, or harmony, between these two societies
because the same person "is both citizen and Christian."[75] Leo XIII placed
particular emphasis on the freedom of the church. It must be free to have its
own "legislative, judicial, administrative, and disciplinary authority" and its
people must have the civil freedom to follow God's will without obstacles.[76]
Furthermore, because religious truth benefits the common good of society,
"the Church must be free to make society religious."[77]

Murray coupled Leo XIII's emphasis on the church's freedom with Leo's
other conception of the state, which is not the paternal caretaker of the
church but a political entity of limited authority. Leo XIII had noted repeatedly in his criticism of Continental laicism that the scope of the state
and its laws was necessarily limited by the law of Christ and the necessary
freedom of the church. By emphasizing this notion of limitation, and by
minimizing the significance of Leo XIII's paternalistic state as history and
not doctrine, Murray borrowed the "political" state that Leo XIII developed
in the socioeconomic context and argued by analogy that such a state was
plausible in the religious context, too: "The essential action of government,
here as in the case of the socioeconomic order, is ... in favor of freedom.
The essential duty of government is not directly toward religion in society,
even though religion [is] integral to the common good."[78] Thus, turning the
common understanding of Leo XIII's ideal Catholic state on its head, Murray made the exaggerated claim that "if one wished to sum up Leo XIII's
political concept of government ... one might well use the phrase, 'as much
freedom as possible, as much government as necessary.'"[79]

Murray's goal was not only to uncover the roots of religious freedom and
the limited temporal state within the tradition, but also to place before the
church the experience of America as a model of religious freedom in con-

trast to that of Europe. The American experiment, he had always believed, had its roots in the ancient Christian political traditions and "has remained substantially untouched by the two radical vices which ruined the medieval heritage on the Continent—absolutism and the sacralization of politics."[80] America had shown that monism and Jacobin separationism were not the inevitable outcomes of political liberalism and constitutional democracy. The American government was limited to temporal matters, and its "separation of church and state" represented the traditional Christian understanding of the two spheres of activity, temporal and spiritual, with the limitations on the state ensuring a freedom for religion, not a hostile freedom from it. State and society remained distinct, with primacy given to the society, wherein the "spiritual" was located. Religious groups, including the Catholic Church, were free to "make society religious." And the individual had the freedom to search for the highest good. Murray made his "articles of peace" argument here not as a public philosopher but as a theologian, praising the First Amendment, which

> has no religious overtones whatever; that is, it does not imply any ultimate vision of the nature of man and society.... Its purpose is not to separate religion from society, but only from the order of law. It implies no denial of the sovereignty of God over both society and state, no negation of the social necessity and value of religion, no assertion that the affairs of society and state are to be conducted in disregard of the natural or divine law, or even of ecclesiastical laws.... It confines law and government to secular purposes (which are understood to include the moral purposes of freedom, justice, peace, and general welfare).... It simply [restricts] the legal activity of the state.[81]

In 1955 Murray was officially rebuked for attempting to publish an article that concluded first, that neither Leo XIII nor Pius XII called for the legal establishment of the Catholic Church (although varying degrees of cooperation between church and state could exist on matters of mixed jurisdiction), and second, that legal intolerance of "error" could not withstand Pius XII's recent emphasis on unity and peace as the highest political good and on the political purposes of human law, which Murray claimed had marked "a certain progress within the tradition."[82] American theologians enraged by this position brought pressure to bear on Rome, which in turn called upon Murray's Jesuit superiors to prohibit him from publishing this article and any other on the church-state topic.[83]

DIGNITATIS HUMANAE: THE DECLARATION ON RELIGIOUS FREEDOM

Despite the ire that his work evoked among certain of his colleagues, Murray's main ideas on religious freedom soon gained the attention, and in large part approval, of the church as a whole. Twentieth-century popes, most notably Pius XII and John XXIII, had come to accept democracy and the constitutional state in the face of the terrible experience of totalitarian governments. And by the time of the Second Vatican Council (1962–65), John XXIII had added to the traditional vocabulary of truth, justice, and charity, "the missing fourth term, freedom."[84] In fact, the right to religious freedom was part of the enumeration of the rights and duties of the human person in John's 1963 encyclical *Pacem in terris*. But the mention of such a right left much open for the bishops of the world to debate at the later sessions of the Second Vatican Council, when the issue was addressed.

It was clear that some statement on church-state relations would come out of the council (American bishops were particularly insistent upon this), but it was the subject of intense controversy.[85] Some bishops continued to support the thesis-hypothesis distinction. Among those supporting a right to religious freedom, there were deep divisions on the proper grounding of the right. Still subject to official rebuke, Murray did not participate in the Vatican sessions that produced the first two drafts of the text of the statements on religious freedom. These drafts, influenced by French-speaking theologians, considered religious freedom primarily an ethical and theological concept and grounded the right in human conscience.

Murray argued instead for grounding the right in the objective dignity of the human person and the consequent need for clear limits on state power. After eight years of rebuke, he finally had the opportunity to advance this reasoning at the third session of the council in 1963 when he participated as a *peritus* (expert). Together with Pietro Pavan (the lead drafter of *Pacem in terris*) he produced the third draft for consideration by the bishops. Rejecting the prior ethical/theological approach, the Murray-Pavan draft located the source of the right to religious freedom in the inherent dignity of the person, and addressed religious freedom primarily as an issue of the legal and political order.

After repeated delays, intrigue, and continued redrafting (some of it without Murray's involvement), *Dignitatis Humanae*, the Declaration on Religious Freedom, was passed in 1965 at the urging of Pope Paul VI (John's successor), by a vote of 2,308 to 70.[86] The final text declared a right to religious freedom for persons, families, communities, and religious bodies when engaged in worship, education, observance, practice, witness, and institutional governance. The text retained Murray's foundation in human dignity and his political-juridical emphasis on the role of the state in protecting the right. The declaration squarely rejected the thesis-hypothesis position. The text continued to affirm that the Catholic Church is the one, true faith, and that all have a moral obligation to seek and follow the truth.

But it was radically new to consider religious freedom consistent with, rather than contrary to, this affirmation.

The declaration, the only conciliar document addressed to the world, contained a preamble and two chapters, the first articulating the right to religious freedom based upon reason and the second based upon revelation. The preamble acknowledges the fact that a "sense of the dignity of the human person has been impressing itself more and more deeply on the consciousness of contemporary man," and that the resulting desires for human freedom and limits to governmental power are "greatly in accord with truth and justice." The text makes explicit that the council "intends to develop the doctrine of recent Popes on the inviolable rights of the human person and on the constitutional order of society." The council "searches into the sacred tradition and doctrine of the Church—the treasury out of which the Church continually brings forth new things that are in harmony with the things that are old."[87]

Papal recognition of the new awareness of human dignity had come in the writings of Pius XII and John XXIII, paving the way for the use of this historically conscious methodology in the declaration.[88] Murray had attributed the outrage among fellow theologians at his Leonine reinterpretation to his attempt to "develop doctrine" and to identify the "growing edge of tradition." This, he thought, had been more threatening than his attempt to convince the church to recognize religious freedom as a legitimate human freedom. In fact, Murray considered doctrinal development the issue that underlay all issues for the modern church, and especially those taken up at the Second Vatican Council. The declaration, he wrote, "frankly recognizes that progress has taken place in the understanding of an ancient truth, in itself and in its implications for social and civil life."[89]

Chapter 1 of the Declaration on Religious Freedom describes the content of the right as entailing a double immunity of no-coercion, no-restraint: no one can be forced to act in a manner contrary to his or her beliefs, and no one can be restrained from acting in accordance with his or her beliefs. Murray noted that the no-coercion position had always been part of church teaching. The no-restraint position was the "new thing."[90] It squarely rejected the restraint of error (i.e., non-Catholic practice) which had been called for by the "thesis" position. Thus, the "double standard" of freedom for Catholics but not others had ended.[91] With respect to the ideal of legal establishment, the text never states that the church must or should be the established religion of the state. It does acknowledge, however, that as a matter of historical circumstance "special legal recognition" may exist in some places. But even where such historical circumstances exist, the text provides that "it is at the same time imperative that the right of all citizens and religious bodies to religious freedom should be recognized and made effective in practice" (Sec. 6). Thus, Murray noted that religious freedom is doctrinal, while the specific level of church-state interaction or cooperation is variable, and "a matter of historical circumstance, not of theological doctrine."[92] This structure was present in Murray's earlier work, and is in fact analogous to Murray's interpretation of the First Amendment: the free exercise provision was the primary right, while the nonestablishment provision (referring to particular church-state relations) was merely instrumental—subordinate to, and in service of, religious freedom.

The declaration places the foundation of the right to religious freedom "in the very dignity of the human person, as this dignity is known through the revealed Word of God and by reason itself.... It is in accordance with their dignity as persons—that is, being endowed with reason and free will and therefore privileged to bear personal responsibility—that all men should be at once impelled by nature and also bound by a moral obligation to seek the truth, especially religious truth" (Sec. 2). But the declaration recognizes that this truth-seeking cannot be done unless there is immunity from coercion and restraint. As a consequence, the text states, "the right to this immunity continues to exist even in those who do not live up to their obligation of seeking the truth and adhering to it" (Sec. 2). Thus, the "erring" believer is still protected, because the right is grounded in the objective dignity of the person and the consequent restrictions on government power, and not in the subjective conscience of the person. In this way, the church continues to claim that it professes the true faith while at the same time calling for the political and juridical conditions of freedom for the pursuit of truth (which conditions must obtain even in the case of the pursuit of error).

The declaration's protection of the nonbeliever was not an affirmation of a right to believe what is false or to do what is evil, but rather the affirmation of freedom from coercion in matters religious. In fact, Murray urged that the Declaration on Religious Freedom be read as he had read the First Amendment, as articles of peace, not articles of faith.

> The unbeliever or atheist makes with equal right this claim to immunity from coercion in religious matters. It is further to be noted that, in assigning a negative content to the right to religious freedom (that is, in making it formally a "freedom from" and not a "freedom for"), the Declaration is in harmony with the sense of the First Amendment to the American Constitution. In guaranteeing the free exercise of religion, the First Amendment guarantees to the American citizen immunity from all coercion in matters religious. Neither the Declaration nor the American Constitution affirms that a man has a right to believe what is false or to do what is wrong. This would be moral nonsense. Neither error nor evil can be the object of a right, only what is true and good.

It is, however, true and good that a man should enjoy freedom from coercion in matters religious.[93]

Murray's imprint is clear throughout the declaration, particularly in the statements on religious education and on the participation in civil conversation, and most notably in the discussion of the role of the state and society. But he did not succeed in having the declaration articulate the role of the state in wholly negative terms or to adopt the position that the state is incompetent in all matters religious. In addition to its concession to existing Catholic privilege (so long as religious freedom is granted non-Catholics), the declaration provides that the state's task is to help create conditions favorable to the fostering of religious life, and further, that "government ... ought indeed to take account of the religious life of the people and show it favor, since the function of government is to make provision for the common welfare. However, it would clearly transgress the limits set to its power were it to presume to direct or inhibit acts that are religious" (Sec. 3). This language has an accent quite different from most of the rest of the text, where religious freedom entails a negative right, a double-immunity from coercion and restraint. But Murray explained that the language was an attempt to prevent the declaration from appearing skeptical, hostile, or indifferent toward religion and to "affirm the traditional doctrine that religion is a social good." For him, government "'favor' of religion" and "'conditions favorable to religious life'" meant favor of religious freedom and conditions favorable to religious freedom. "[The state] must somehow stand in the service of religion, as an indispensable element of the common temporal good. This duty of service is discharged by service rendered to the freedom of religion in society. It is religion itself, not government, which has the function of making society religious. The conditions favorable to the fulfillment of this function are conditions of freedom."[94]

Chapter 2 of the Declaration on Religious Freedom declares that the doctrine of religious freedom has roots in divine revelation. The inclusion of this section appears to run contrary to Murray's commitment to public discourse in the language of reason and not in the language of faith. But the chapter is most interesting because it contains the contours of Murray's 1950s reinterpretation of Leo XIII on the freedom of the church, "the fundamental principle in what concerns the relations between the Church and governments and the whole civil order." In the text the church claims for itself a divine right to freedom, as it should "enjoy that full measure of freedom which her care for the salvation of men requires.... This independence [resulting from civil religious freedom] is precisely what the authorities of the Church claim in society. At the same time, the Christian faithful, in common with all other men, possess the civil right not to be hindered in leading their lives in accordance with their conscience. Therefore, a harmony exists between the freedom of the Church and the religious freedom which is ... the right of all men" (Sec. 13). The church makes no claim to privilege, but only to freedom.

In looking back at the Second Vatican Council, one author recalled that "the contest between liberalism and Catholicism was most dramatically fought" over the text of the Declaration on Religious Freedom. Because the declaration maintained the singular truth of the Catholic Church and the importance of religion to the society, it "[made] no concessions to doctrinaire liberalism." But its rejection of the ideal confessional state and adoption of a constitutionally guaranteed right to religious freedom for all persons and all religious groups was an acceptance of political liberalism.[95] The declaration is thus considered the uniquely American contribution to the council. Murray rightly predicted that it would open "the way toward new confidence in ecumenical relationships, and a new straightforwardness in relationships between the Church and the world."[96] But he expressed the greatest enthusiasm for its implications for the theological meaning of Christian freedom. Unfortunately, he died before having the chance to enjoy this conversation.

THE CONTINUING CONVERSATION

Murray's work continues to generate interest and debate. Numerous scholars in a wide array of disciplines attempt to apply his framework and insights to the issues of our time, by working out the "balance between continuity and change, retrieval and renewal" proper to the task of appropriating Murray's work.[97] Now that the church-state issue has been addressed, a new issue—of church and society—has become the primary focus of the Murray scholars. "The central issue of confrontation between Catholicism and liberalism [has] returned under the form of a church-*society* debate about the place of religious principles and the public role of the church in the formation of a public consensus on the values and rights that constitute the substance of human society."[98]

This task of church-society discourse is particularly challenging because many of the social assumptions Murray made for the postwar era are simply no longer applicable.[99] And Murray is often accused of forging too close an alliance with liberal individualism, owing to his emphasis on the limited nature of the state and freedom of the person.[100] In light of these difficulties, many Murray scholars have rejected his exclusive reliance on the language of reason in public discourse and have advocated the inclusion of the language of faith owing to its "social power."[101] Still others have attempted to articulate more carefully the relationship between Murray and liberalism,[102] or to defend his use of natural law philosophy.[103]

Yet, despite the critical scrutiny given Murray's thought, as well as the diversity among those who claim to be faithful appropriators of his work, his legacy remains profound. The focus is no longer a church-state question, but a church-society question: what is the "spiritual substance [of society] that underlies the order of law, the order of public morality and all other orders and processes within society"?[104] And this is precisely where Murray wanted the discourse: in the civil society, the location of both the spiritual realm and the temporal common good. In the civil society—and *not* in the state. He would be pleased to know that he was a major contributor to this paradigmatic shift.

NOTES

1. Philip Gleason, "American Catholics and Liberalism, 1789–1960," in *Catholicism and Liberalism: Contributions to American Public Philosophy*, ed. Bruce Douglass and David Hollenbach (Cambridge: Cambridge University Press, 1994), 65.
2. For biographical information, see Donald E. Pelotte, *John Courtney Murray: Theologian in Conflict* (New York: Paulist Press, 1976).
3. John Courtney Murray, S.J., *We Hold These Truths: Catholic Reflections on the American Proposition* (New York: Sheed & Ward, 1960), 297. See, generally, J. Bryan Hehir, "The Perennial Need for Philosophical Discourse," in David Hollenbach, ed., "Theology and Philosophy in Public: A Symposium on John Courtney Murray's Unfinished Agenda," *Theological Studies* 40 (1979): 710–713.
4. Murray, *We Hold These Truths*, 295.
5. Ibid., 9.
6. Ibid., 122–123.
7. Leslie Griffin, "Good Catholics Should Be Rawlsian Liberals," *Southern California Interdisciplinary Law Journal* 5 (Summer 1997): 325–328.
8. Murray, *We Hold These Truths*, 30.
9. John A. Coleman, S.J., "A Possible Role for Biblical Religion in Public Life," in Hollenbach, "Theology and Philosophy," 702–703.
10. For discussion of Lonergan's influence on Murray, see J. Leon Hooper, S.J., *The Ethics of Discourse: The Social Philosophy of John Courtney Murray* (Washington, D.C.: Georgetown University Press, 1986), 124–125.
11. Murray, *We Hold These Truths*, 112–113.
12. Pope Pius XII, radio message (December 24, 1944), quoted in John Courtney Murray. S.J., "The Problem of Religious Freedom," in *Religious Liberty: Catholic Struggles with Pluralism*, ed J. Leon Hooper, S.J. (Louisville, Ky.: Westminster John Knox Press, 1993), 166.
13. Murray, *We Hold These Truths*, 109.
14. Ibid., 297.

15. Ibid., 298.
16. John Courtney Murray, S.J., "The Construction of a Christian Culture," in *Bridging the Sacred and the Secular: Selected Writings of John Courtney Murray, S.J.*, ed. J. Leon Hooper, S.J. (Washington, D.C.: Georgetown University Press, 1994), 107.
17. Ibid., 106.
18. Ibid., 105.
19. Murray, *We Hold These Truths*, 327–328.
20. John Courtney Murray, S.J., "Leo XIII and Pius XII: Government and the Order of Religion," in Hooper, *Religious Liberty,* 58 (emphasis added).
21. Ibid., 58.
22. Ibid., 50.
23. Ibid., 66–67, 73.
24. Murray, *We Hold These Truths*, 335.
25. Ibid., 166.
26. John Courtney Murray, S.J., "Memo to Cardinal Cushing on Contraception Legislation," in Hooper, *Bridging the Secular and Sacred*, 83.
27. Murray, *We Hold These Truths*, 156–158.
28. Ibid., 286.
29. John Courtney Murray, S.J., "The Return to Tribalism," in Hooper, *Bridging the Sacred and Secular*, 151.
30. John Courtney Murray, S.J., "The Issue of Church and State at Vatican Council II," in Hooper, *Religious Liberty*, 205–206.
31. Murray, *We Hold These Truths*, 328.
32. David Hollenbach, "Afterword: A Community of Freedom," in Douglass and Hollenbach, *Catholicism and Liberalism*, 326.
33. Murray, "The Issue of Church and State," 205.
34. Murray, "Government and the Order of Religion," 78.
35. Murray, *We Hold These Truths*, 286.
36. See, generally, J. Bryan Hehir, "Murray on Foreign Policy and International Relations: A Concentrated Contribution," in *John Courtney Murray and the Growth of Tradition*, ed. J. Leon Hooper, S.J., and Todd David Whitmore, 218–240 (Kansas City, Mo.: Sheed & Ward, 1996).
37. Murray, *We Hold These Truths*, 286.
38. Ibid., 289.
39. Griffin, "Good Catholics," 297–298.
40. Ibid., 328.
41. Robert P. Hunt, "Moral Orthodoxy and the Procedural Republic," in *John Courtney Murray and the American Civil Conversation*, ed. Robert P. Hunt and Kenneth L. Grasso, 262–267 (Grand Rapids, Mich.: Eerdmans, 1992). This essay argues that such a state would simply be the modern version of the nineteenth-century continental liberalism Murray so vigorously opposed.
42. Murray, *We Hold These Truths*, 306–307.
43. See generally, Ruth W. Grant, *John Locke's Liberalism* (Chicago: University of Chicago Press, 1987).

44. John Courtney Murray, S.J., "This Matter of Religious Freedom," *America* 112 (January 9, 1965): 40.

45. Murray, "The Problem of Religious Freedom," in Hooper, *Religious Liberty*, 154.

46. Murray, "Government and the Order of Religion," 93.

47. John Courtney Murray, S.J., "Memo to Cardinal Cushing on Contraception Legislation," in Hooper, *Bridging the Secular and Sacred*, 82.

48. Ibid., 83.

49. Murray, *We Hold These Truths*, 166–167.

50. Ibid., 167.

51. Ibid., 166.

52. Murray, "Memo to Cushing," 86.

53. John Courtney Murray, S.J., "Selective Conscientious Objection," in Hooper, *Bridging the Sacred and Secular*, 95.

54. See, generally, John Courtney Murray, S.J., "The Problem of Religious Freedom" in Hooper, *Religious Liberty*, 127–197.

55. Ibid., 152.

56. Ibid., 153–154.

57. John Courtney Murray, S.J., Annotations to "Declaration on Religious Freedom," in *The Documents of Vatican II*, ed. Walter M. Abbott, S.J. (New York: America Press, 1966), 688–689 n. 24.

58. John Courtney Murray, S.J., "Law or Prepossessions?" in *Essays in Constitutional Law*, ed. Robert G. McCloskey, 342–345 (New York: Knopf, 1957). Murray criticized early Supreme Court establishment clause decisions, which appeared to him to adopt a Jacobin hostility toward religion so contrary to this intent and to historical and contemporary practice. Ibid., 325, 331.

59. Murray, *We Hold These Truths*, 49.

60. Ibid., 48. Here Murray was referring to Protestant thought that considered democracy and religious freedom to reflect anti-authoritarian church structure and religious individualism, associated with the Free Church tradition, early American deism and rationalism, and thought influenced by the Great Awakening. Ibid., 49–50.

61. Ibid., 49.

62. Charles E. Curran, "The Role of the Laity in the Thought of John Courtney Murray," in Hooper and Whitmore, *Growth of Tradition*, 252.

63. Murray, *We Hold These Truths*, 146.

64. Murray, "Government and the Order of Religion," 97.

65. Ibid., 99.

66. Ibid., 100.

67. Murray, "This Matter," 41.

68. John Courtney Murray, S.J., "The Church and Totalitarian Democracy," *Theological Studies* 13 (1952): 560.

69. Murray, "Government and the Order of Religion," 102–103.

70. John Courtney Murray, S.J., "On the Future of Humanistic Education," in Hooper, *Bridging the Secular and Sacred*, 164–165.

71. Ibid., 165.

72. See, generally, Murray, "Totalitarian Democracy," and "Leo XIII on Church and State: The General Structure of the Controversy," *Theological Studies* 14 (1953): 1–30.

73. Murray, "Totalitarian Democracy," 555.

74. Ibid., 556.

75. Ibid., 556, 559.

76. Murray, "Government and the Order of Religion," 70.

77. John Courtney Murray, S.J., "Leo XIII: Two Concepts of Government," *Theological Studies* 14 (1953): 562.

78. Ibid., 564.

79. Ibid., 559.

80. John Courtney Murray, S.J., "Leo XIII: Separation of Church and State," *Theological Studies* 14 (1953): 151.

81. Ibid., 152–153.

82. Murray, "Government and the Order of Religion," 102.

83. See generally Pelotte, *John Courtney Murray*, 7–73. The suppressed article is now available as Murray, "Government and the Order of Religion," 49–125.

84. Murray, "Annotations to Declaration," 687 n. 21.

85. For general discussion of the history of the Declaration, see Pelotte, *John Courtney Murray*; and Herminio Rico, S.J., *John Paul II and the Legacy of Dignitatis Humanae* (Washington, D.C.: Georgetown University Press, 2002).

86. "Declaration on Religious Freedom: On the Right of the Person and of Communities to Social and Civil Freedom in Matters Religious" in Abbott, *Documents of Vatican II*, 675–696.

87. Ibid., 675–677.

88. This differed from the "classical consciousness" underlying most of the Church's teachings, in which truth is Platonic and objective, existing apart from anyone holding it, so that truth can have no historical dimension. The historical consciousness also considers truth to be objective, but sees truth as possessed by human persons in particular historical circumstances. Classicism therefore focuses heavily on certainty and authority (even infallibility), whereas a methodology conscious of historicity allows one to develop doctrine over various historical contexts. John Courtney Murray, S.J., "Toledo Talk," in Hooper, *Bridging the Sacred and Secular*, 335–336.

89. Murray, "This Matter," 41.

90. Murray, "Annotations to Declaration," 678 n. 5.

91. Murray, "Religious Freedom," in Abbott, *Documents of Vatican II*, 672–674.

92. Murray, "Annotations to Declaration," 685 n. 17.

93. Ibid., 678 n. 5.

94. Murray, "The Issue of Church and State," 216–217.

95. Joseph A. Komonchak, "Vatican II and the Encounter Between Catholicism and Liberalism," in Douglass and Hollenbach, *Catholicism and Liberalism*, 76, 84–85.

96. Murray, "Religious Freedom," 673. See also John Courtney Murray, S.J., ed., *Religious Liberty: An End and a Beginning* (New York: Macmillan, 1966).

97. Todd David Whitmore, "The Growing End: John Courtney Murray and the Shape of Murray Studies," in Hooper and Whitmore, *Growth of Tradition*, v, xv.

98. Rico, *Legacy of Dignitatis Humanae*, 12.

99. Cf. Mary C. Segers, "Murray, American Pluralism, and the Abortion Controversy," in Hunt and Grasso, *American Civil Conversation*, 228, with Todd David Whitmore, "What Would John Courtney Murray Say? On Abortion and Euthanasia," *Commonweal* 121 (October 7, 1994): 16–22.

100. Coleman, "Possible Role," 705. Some of Murray's critics have suggested that his dialogue with liberalism forced him to adopt, unwittingly, liberalism's terms, which included a liberal theory of religion. Some have argued that the negative definition of religious freedom, together with his "articles of peace" interpretation, disposes society toward religious indifference and a naked public square and invites privatization of religion and a pluralism based upon relativism (and not upon natural law)—precisely those things that Murray himself rejected. See David L. Schindler, "Religious Freedom, Truth, and American Liberalism: Another Look at John Courtney Murray," *Communio* 21 (Winter 1994): 696, 709–713; Gerard V. Bradley, "Beyond Murray's Articles of Peace and Faith," in Hunt and Grasso, *American Civil Conversation*, 181.

101. Hollenbach, "Unfinished Agenda," 701.

102. Griffin, "Good Catholics," 297; Frederick Lawrence, "John Courtney Murray and the Ambiguities of Liberalism," in Hooper and Whitmore, *Growth of Tradition*, 41.

103. Hehir, "Perennial Need for Philosophical Discourse," 710; Joseph A. Komonchak, "John Courtney Murray and the Redemption of History: Natural Law and Theology" in Hooper and Whitmore, *Growth of Tradition*, 60, 81.

104. Murray, "Return to Tribalism," 151.

CHAPTER 5

Pope John XXIII (1881–1963)

LESLIE GRIFFIN

Pope John XXIII's view of human nature was very optimistic, and this optimism translated specifically into a positive perspective on the modern world. The legacy of his papacy (1958–63) was the *aggiornamento* (updating) of Roman Catholicism through a critical acceptance of modernity, which his predecessors had regarded with much suspicion. Pope John's three major accomplishments—the convocation of the Second Vatican Council (1962–65) and the promulgation of the encyclical letters *Mater et magistra* (1961) and *Pacem in terris* (1963)—reflected his unflagging confidence that human beings could build ecclesial, economic, social, and political institutions that promoted unity, truth, justice, charity, peace, and freedom.

Unlike other figures in this volume, Pope John did not propose a systematic theory of human nature. Instead, in sharp contrast to his papal predecessors and successors, he embraced the modern world and led the Catholic Church into dialogue with it. Readers should not underestimate the difficulty or originality of this accomplishment. When Angelo Roncalli took the papal throne in 1958, many church leaders longed to restore the Catholic Church to its prior primacy as the established religion of every empire or state. They opposed the liberal reforms that the Enlightenment had brought to Europe, including freedom of speech, freedom of religion, and democratic government. In other words, in 1958, much of the church's bureaucracy was antimodern.

John's three significant achievements demonstrate that he successfully placed the church in, not against, the modern world. The council, which gathered the world's Catholic bishops in Rome, prompted reform *ad intra* and *ad extra*, within the church and in the church's relationships with non-Catholics. It "ended the Constantinian era of the Church and [began] a new historical period."[1] *Mater et magistra* adopted contemporary economic theory. It advocated an expanded role for the state to protect human welfare and expressed a new "optimism about capitalism" within Catholicism.[2] With *Pacem in terris*, which was issued in response to the Cuban Missile Crisis, the Catholic Church became an unequivocal articulator and defender of human rights as well as a proponent of world government. *Pacem in terris* was also the first official Catholic document to recognize that religious freedom is a fundamental right of *every* human being.

The resurgence of religious fundamentalism at the twentieth century's end provides some context for comprehending the achievement of Pope John XXIII. Fundamentalism opposes modernity and seeks to reconstruct a golden past.[3] Although fundamentalists prefer the past to the modern, their ideal is usually a "selective" history of the past, adopted in support of an antimodern ideology.[4] In contrast, Pope John persuaded the Catholic Church to join him in an embrace of the modern world and to reexamine the church's traditional teaching in light of the "signs of the times." Thus, on the classic Christian subject of nature and grace, his papacy represents the perspective that the world is a good place where humans may discern the will of God.

Finally, on the subject of human nature, the pope's personal legacy matched his professional achievement. Indeed, the former was largely responsible for the latter. His exuberant yet simple pastoral style impressed numerous observers worldwide and won him the affection of the world. As Rabbi Abraham Joshua Heschel describes him: "Pope John was a great miracle. Contrary to all expectations, a Roman pontiff all of a sudden captured the heart of everybody, Christian and non-Christian. How that happened, we don't know. It didn't happen through any philosophy. It happened through the sheer humanity and love of one human being."[5]

The nickname John acquired in life matched his own positive assessment of the nature of the human person; he was Good Pope John. Yet, as one observer notes, his goodness was not a "gift of nature" but was "the fruit in him of a long and hard-won struggle" to be good.[6] Hence he was a fitting modern exemplar of the centuries-old tradition that he led, for an enduring Catholic belief has been that God endows human beings with a nature that is capable of discerning the goodness of God's law and choosing to obey it. In the Second Vatican Council, in *Mater et magistra*, and in *Pacem in terris*, John urged humans to do just that, and thus to build a lasting order of justice, truth, love, freedom, and peace.

BIOGRAPHY

The future Pope John XXIII, Angelo Roncalli, was born on November 25, 1881, the fourth of thirteen children in a family of sharecroppers, in Sotto il Monte, Italy, during the pontificate of Pope Leo XIII. Roncalli left home to attend the Bergamo Seminary in 1893, when he was almost twelve years old. Thanks to a scholarship, in 1900 he began studies at the Pontifical Seminary in Rome, studies that were interrupted by a call to military service as a private in the Italian army from 1901 to 1902. After this unhappy period of "Babylonian Captivity,"[7] he returned to the Roman seminary and was ordained a priest in August 1904.

In 1905, Pope Pius X appointed Roncalli as secretary to the new bishop of Bergamo, Giacomo Radini-Tedeschi. Radini-Tedeschi had been a leader of Opera dei Congressi, which organized Catholic lay groups for social action. These groups worked to implement the principles of Pope Leo XIII's encyclical letter about social justice, *Rerum novarum*. Roncalli revered the progressive bishop, who remained a focus of Vatican suspicion even after his "banishment to Bergamo."[8] Roncalli served as the bishop's secretary from 1905 to 1914 and later wrote a biography of Radini-Tedeschi.

In Bergamo, Roncalli also taught history, a subject of lifelong interest. On visits to Milan he gained access to the thirty-nine volumes recording St. Charles Borromeo's (1538–84) visitation of the Bergamo diocese, to which he brought the reforms of the Council of Trent. Borromeo consumed Roncalli's attention and energy in ensuing years. He edited five volumes of the saint's work, which came out in 1936, 1937, 1938, 1946, and 1957.[9] Roncalli's papal coronation took place on St. Charles's feast day, November 4, 1958.

Both Pope Pius X and Radini-Tedeschi died in August 1914, as World War I began. Once again, Roncalli was called to military service from May 1915 until December 1918, as an army medic and chaplain. At war's end, he returned to Bergamo as a spiritual counselor to students. In 1921, Pope Benedict XV recalled Roncalli to Rome to direct the Congregation for the Propagation of the Faith, which coordinated the church's missionary activity throughout the world.

Roncalli remained in Rome until Pope Pius XI (a former librarian from Milan, where Roncalli had discovered the Borromeo archives) sent him to Bulgaria in 1924, perhaps because Angelo had been too supportive of Christian political parties and too critical of Mussolini, with whom Pius achieved a concordat in 1929.[10] Roncalli was apostolic visitor and apostolic delegate to Bulgaria from 1925 to 1935. In 1935 he went to Istanbul (in Christian history, Constantinople), where he served as apostolic delegate to Turkey and Greece until December 1944. These years as "ecumenical apprentice"[11] provided tremendous exposure not only to the concerns of Orthodox Christians in Bulgaria and Greece, but to Muslims in Turkey who were in the process of transforming Turkey into a "thoroughly secular" state; in Turkey, for example, Roncalli wore secular clothes after religious garb was outlawed.[12]

From his location in Istanbul, "the crossroads of information" during World War II,[13] Roncalli learned early of the plight of Jews in Nazi Germany. He used his diplomatic privileges to help Jews escape by sending to Hungary and Romania Vatican immigration certificates that allowed admission to Palestine. Historians disagree whether or not it is "legend"[14] or "myth"[15] that Roncalli also issued baptismal certificates to Jews so that this Christian status could save their lives. The most recent biography of the pope concludes that the forms were not baptismal certificates but "Vatican visas, which announced that the individual named was under the protection of the Holy See—and which Angelo certainly issued to fleeing Jews in large quantities."[16] Roncalli himself referred to 24,000 Jews whose lives he had saved with the help of the German ambassador to Turkey.[17]

After Charles de Gaulle refused to work with the papal nuncio and French bishops who had collaborated with the Vichy regime, Roncalli was hurriedly sent to Paris in December 1944. He served as papal nuncio to France from 1944 to 1953. He was the Vatican's first permanent observer at UNESCO (the United Nations Educational, Scientific, and Cultural Organization), and he addressed its sixth and seventh general assemblies in 1951 and 1952. In January 1953, Pope Pius XII appointed Roncalli the Cardinal and Patriarch of Venice, where he served until his election to the papacy in October 1958.

By the time Pope Pius XII died in 1958, he had been pope since 1939 and, before that, Vatican secretary of state since 1930. The aging pontiff was austere, aristocratic, and aloof. The end of every long pontificate brings complaints of stagnation in the Vatican and recommendations for a fresh and brief new papacy. So it was in October 1958, when fifty-one cardinal-electors gathered in Rome to choose Pius's successor. Their ranks were thin because Pius had appointed cardinals only twice during his long pontificate. Most notably absent from the conclave was Giovanni Battista Montini, whom Roncalli had known well since the 1920s and who shared some of Roncalli's progressive opinions. Many Vatican observers had selected the intellectual Montini as Pius's likely successor when Montini worked at the Secretariat of State. Pius, however, had sent Montini to Milan as archbishop in 1954 without giving him the cardinal's hat. Montini had support at the conclave, especially among the French cardinals, and Roncalli may have voted for him;[18] nonetheless, the custom was that the pope was chosen from the cardinals, and he was at this conclave as well.

Although Roncalli's election is often described as a complete surprise, the Roman odds makers favored him as the conclave started,[19] and he was on almost everyone's list of *papabile*.[20] Victory was never certain, but he knew before the conclave began that he had a good chance of election. After his many years of service, he was well known to the large voting blocs of eighteen Italian and six French bishops. Even at the age of seventy-six, Roncalli was still younger than twenty-four of the electors and yet, unlike the younger men, was old enough to be a transitional pope only.[21]

The conclave was held on October 25–28, 1958. After eleven ballots, white smoke issued from St. Peter's after Roncalli received thirty-eight votes, three more than the required thirty-five (two-thirds plus one). He took the name of John, the name of his father, his parish, the Baptist, the Beloved Disciple, one antipope, and twenty-two popes, "almost all of [whom] led short lives as pontiffs."[22] In his first radio broadcast to the world, Pope John announced "the two major themes that would mark his pontificate: *unity* in the life of the Church and *peace* in the secular order.... He quoted Jesus' prayer 'that all may be one' (John 17:11); it became the linking thread of his pontificate."[23]

On that feast day of St. Charles in 1958, in his papal coronation address, Pope John asserted "vigorously and sincerely" that he intended to be a pastor. As he stated, "All other human gifts and accomplishments—learning, practical experience, diplomatic finesse—can broaden and enrich pastoral work, but they cannot replace it."[24] His promise was promptly kept. In contrast to his predecessor, who had remained a prisoner in the Vatican, John soon visited Roman prisons, hospitals, and parishes. He insisted that the pope was the bishop of Rome.[25] "The Romans called him 'John-outside-the-Walls.'"[26]

CALLING THE ECUMENICAL COUNCIL: *AGGIORNAMENTO*

On January 25, 1959, three months after Roncalli's election, this student of the Council of Trent announced an ecumenical council of Catholic bishops to a gathering of cardinals in Rome. In this context, ecumenical means general, not local or Roman, that is, including the bishops throughout the world who are in communion with Rome. Vatican II would be the first ecumenical council in the Roman Church since 1870, when the Franco-Prussian War and the invasion of Rome by the Italian army disrupted the First Vatican Council, which defined the doctrine of papal infallibility. Since the loss of the Papal States to the Italian army, the popes had remained "prisoners in the Vatican" and critics of the Italian state. Although both Pope Pius XI and Pope Pius XII had commissioned plans for a council,[27] some Catholics believed that, by defining infallibility, the First Vatican Council had rendered further councils unnecessary.

Although the pope stated that the "decision to hold an ecumenical council came to me in the first instance in a sudden flash of inspiration,"[28] there is evidence that the new pope had thought about the council in the days immediately after his election and that by November 28, 1958, he had made the definite decision to convoke it.[29] Sudden or not, the decision was his alone. "It was a free and independent decision such as perhaps was never made before in the history of ecumenical or general Councils."[30]

Unlike Vatican I and the proposed councils of Pius XI and Pius XII, the purpose of John's council was not to define or condemn the errors of the modern world. The celebrated metaphor was that John's council would bring fresh air into the fortress of the Vatican. When asked about the objectives of the council, Pope John, according to the report, "stood up, walked over to the window, opened it, and said, 'What do we intend to do? We intend to let in a little fresh air.'"[31] That famous story may be apocryphal; John's personal secretary, Don Loris Capovilla, insisted that the pope disliked drafts.[32] In any event, John's fresh ideas were that his council would be pastoral, not doctrinal, and that the "separated" Christian brethren would be invited to observe the event.

The Second Vatican Council began in October 1962. Between January 1959 and October 1962 the Catholic Church underwent extensive preparations for it. Eleven commissions and three secretariats were formed to study possible topics for discussion. Members of the Roman Curia (the church's bureaucracy), whose agenda was to reaffirm church tradition and avoid change, led the commissions. They drafted documents with the expectation that the council fathers would automatically approve them when the bishops arrived in Rome. The Curia's focus on these texts, which included extensive definitions of church teaching, appeared to contradict John's intention that the council be pastoral rather than doctrinal.[33]

Curial critics of the council were worried, among other things, about Catholic truth and unity. In 1962, the church taught that Catholicism was the one true religion. The twentieth-century popes had opposed Catholic participation in the growing Christian ecumenical movement (which sought unity among all Christians, Protestant, Catholic, and Orthodox) because they feared religious "indifferentism."[34] Indifferentism is the belief that all religions are equal, or, in other words, indifference to the truth that Catholicism is the only true religion. Many bishops believed that any ecumenism, even interfaith gatherings that promoted social reform, fostered indifferentism. For such Catholics, Christian unity could occur only when the erroneous Christians returned to the truth of Rome.

Ecumenism—here meaning the unity of Christians and cooperation among the world's religions—was a topic dear to the pope's heart. It had been his life's work in Bulgaria, Turkey, Greece, and France. It now guided his actions in Rome. For example, early in his papacy he had removed the offensive "adjective *perfidus* in the exhortation *Oremus et pro perfidis Iu-daeis* [let us pray also for the unbelieving Jews] and also the expression *perfidia Iudaica*" from the Good Friday prayer for the Jews because of the connotations of "perfidious."[35] He received the archbishop of Canterbury in Rome in December 1960 and sent greetings and envoys to Ecumenical Patriarch Athenagoras I of Istanbul and Patriarch Alexis of Moscow. Although Catholics had boycotted World Council of Churches meetings since the 1920s out of the fear that they encouraged religious indifferentism, Pope John sent the first Catholic representatives to the World Council of Churches Assembly in November 1961.[36]

In this context, two of Pope John's most important decisions in conciliar preparation were the creation of the Secretariat for Christian Unity in November 1960 and the appointment of Jesuit Cardinal Augustin Bea of Germany to lead it. The secretariat focused on unity with Protestant Christians. Protestant leaders insisted that ecumenism required Catholic recognition of a universal right to religious freedom and requested conciliar discussion of that topic. They understandably rejected the idea that Christian unity could occur only when Protestants recognized the truth of Rome.

John asked Cardinal Bea to draft a text for the council about the Catholic Church and the Jewish people. He also protected the secretariat against the more conservative commissions, which challenged the secretariat's right to compose council documents and refused to include ecumenical perspectives in their own drafts.[37] For example, when the Theological Commission ignored the subject of ecumenism in its schema on the nature of the church, Bea prepared his own draft. Unlike the commission's product, Bea's text included the important subject of religious freedom. Roman Catholicism had identified religious freedom as a right belonging only to Catholics, because (Catholic) truth has rights but "error has no rights."[38] John backed the secretariat when the Theological Commission tried to retain control over the subject by later including the traditional teaching in its own schema on the nature of the church.[39] Throughout the preconciliar and conciliar period, Bea "was supported by the unshaken trust of the pope" and reported directly to him.[40]

After three years of planning, John welcomed the world's bishops to Rome on October 11, 1962, with an opening address that he had written himself.[41] His words reflected his optimism about history, human nature, and the modern world and decried the prophets of doom and gloom who ignored God's role in history.[42] The words expressed John's confidence that the church could be both modern and true to the gospel. Although the pope acknowledged that prior popes and councils had condemned errors, he preferred "to use the medicine of mercy rather than of severity."[43] It was not clear that the bishops shared the pope's optimism; "the opening ceremony had disclosed the Constantinian face of the Church of Rome,"[44] and, as French theologian Yves Congar wrote, "Leaving the Constantinian era has never been its program."[45] Yet Pope John's address had set the agenda: it would be a council of acceptance of the modern era.

Cardinal Bea, because of his and the pope's commitment to ecumenism, had invited numerous non-Catholic observers to the council. Fifty-four non-Catholics were present at the first session, including forty-six official observers (representatives of other denominations who were invited by Bea) and eight guests of the pope. "They were not passive spectators at the conciliar event but had a positive influence on the definitive text of various conciliar documents."[46] Two Russian Orthodox Christians from Moscow were among the dramatic last-minute arrivals whose presence was noteworthy.

Commentators on John's papacy have debated whether he was liberal or traditional, a revolutionary or a reformer.[47] Although he had asked for renewal in the church, his piety and theology were very traditional. Although he had announced the council, he let the Curia set the agenda for it through the commissions. To some observers, his actions in defending the council while refusing to restrict the Curia "remain mysterious."[48] Did the pope agree with the commissions' conservatives, or did he shrewdly realize that their own schemata would defeat them? The answer remains unclear. In any event, after the opening address, John left the bishops to their work. He watched the proceedings on closed-circuit television and intervened only a few times to keep the Second Vatican Council on track. Those interventions, however, supported the fathers who wanted revisions of the curial drafts. For example, on the second day of the council, John approved a delay in voting for members of the commissions; the changed timing allowed more noncurial members to participate. He also elevated the Secretariat for Christian Unity to the status of a commission when its authority was challenged.

At the first session, the fathers discussed the liturgy, the sources of revelation, communications media, Christian unity, and the church, but did not promulgate any declarations.[49] The biggest controversy arose about the sources of revelation. In retrospect, the major accomplishment of the first session was the realization that the curialists did not hold a majority of the votes.[50] When the first session ended in December 1962, a second session was scheduled for September 8, 1963. Thanks to Pope John's interventions, the commissions' texts would be revised during the intervening nine months; the council would continue.

John knew that he was dying when he addressed the closing of the council's first session on December 8, 1962. The optimistic pontiff did not share others' assessment that the council had been unproductive or a failure. In his closing address, he argued that the "slow" timing was "necessary" for the fathers to meet and understand one another. Disagreements were also "healthy" and "necessary."[51] The pope, who knew he would not be there, reminded the bishops that if they finished their work by December 1963, they would be "properly celebrating the four hundredth anniversary of the closing of the Council of Trent."[52]

Pope John died of cancer on June 3, 1963, before the council reconvened. Montini, the first cardinal named by Pope John and his anticipated successor, became Pope Paul VI. He led the council through three more sessions and sixteen promulgated documents to its conclusion in December 1965. At a mass celebrated by Pope Paul at the second session of the council on October 28, 1963, the anniversary of John's election, Belgian Cardinal Suenens eulogized Pope John by observing the "harmony ... that existed between his life and his teaching" and concluded that "in him there was no dualism": "If one had to express it all in one word, it seems to me that one could say that John XXIII was a man *surprisingly natural and at the same time supernatural*. Nature and grace produced in him a living unity filled with charm and surprises. Everything about him sprang from a single source. In a completely natural way he was supernatural. He was natural with such a supernatural spirit that no one detected a distinction between the two."[53]

While the commissions were drafting documents for the council and the council fathers were debating reform, John commissioned the two major encyclicals that form another part of his legacy: *Mater et magistra* (May 1961) and *Pacem in terris* (April 1963). Their optimistic voice about modernity marked a new emphasis in the tradition of Catholic social thought. "Both letters have in common a tremendous confidence in man and an optimism grounded in simple faith in Divine Providence."[54]

MATER ET MAGISTRA: SOCIALIZATION AND DEVELOPMENT

Pope John wrote eight encyclical letters during his pontificate. The first was *Ad petri cathedram*, issued on June 29, 1959, on the subject of truth, unity, and peace. Upon his election to the papacy, Pope John had announced that peace and unity would be "the two major themes that would mark his pontificate."[55] *Ad petri cathedram* taught that unity and peace must be rooted in the truth. The encyclical demonstrated the pope's commitment to traditional Catholic natural law jurisprudence. In that account of human nature, God has created an objective moral order. Humans may understand this order by employing their reason to seek the truth. Without a foundation in God's truth, the encyclical concluded, society would crumble and peace and unity would be unattainable.

Pope John's blueprint for a just society, rooted in God's truth and the moral order, was enunciated in the encyclical *Mater et magistra*. The letter was issued in 1961 to commemorate the seventieth anniversary of Pope Leo XIII's encyclical letter *Rerum novarum*, which had inaugurated modern Catholic social thought in 1891, primarily through its defense of workers' rights against the state. We have seen that *Rerum novarum* inspired bishops like Bergamo's Radini-Tedeschi to support lay Catholic groups that sought social justice. John's encyclical *Mater et magistra* reaffirmed the economic rights of workers and placed a new emphasis upon the state's responsibility to protect those rights. This highlighting of the state's obligation to protect workers, which is summarized in the word "socialization," was the encyclical's primary contribution to international discussions of development and human rights. Conservative opposition to John's expanded state was encapsulated in William Buckley's memorable rejoinder "*Mater, si. Magistra, no.*"[56] Although the encyclical bears the date May 15, 1961 (the anniversary of *Rerum novarum*), it was published on July 15, 1961. Pietro Pavan, a priest and professor of social economy at the Lateran University in Rome, was the top consultant on the encyclical. (Pavan was also the author of *Pacem in terris.*) *Mater et magistra* reflected the "mysterious" style that John had displayed in his preparation for the council, in that it was "at one and the same time traditional and daring."[57] While it announced its continuity with Leo XIII, Pius XI, and Pius XII, it also offered a "newness"[58] and "novelty"[59] of perspective.

This "novelty" was evident in the encyclical's style and method as well as in its content. Contemporaries almost uniformly praised its clear and straightforward writing style, its "linguistic simplicity"[60] and its "direct, familiar tone."[61] That tone reflected the encyclical's "positive and constructive"[62] content as well as the perennial optimism of the man who commissioned the letter. "Pope John, in short, in the optimism of his encyclicals, was *sui generis.*"[63] Matching John's approach to the council, *Mater et magistra* displayed the pope's active embrace of the social and economic circumstances of modernity and his resolve that humans achieve social justice.

Mater et magistra's attitude toward the world was not marked by "nostalgia,"[64] nor was it "romantic"[65] or "doctrinaire"[66] as earlier encyclicals had been. In contrast to John's predecessors' pronouncements, with their lists of deductive principles by which the modern world should be evaluated, *Mater et magistra* "approved the use of the inductive method in elaborating the social doctrine of the Church."[67] Such a method identified the church's responsibility, not to condemn, but to learn from the events of the modern world and to craft a modern witness to the gospel. The inductive approach was best summarized in the encyclical's novel admonition to "look, judge, act": "There are three stages which should normally be followed in the reduction of social principles into practice. First, one reviews the concrete situation; secondly, one forms a judgment on it in the light of these same principles; thirdly, one decides what in the circumstances can and should be done to implement these principles. These are the three stages that are usually expressed in the three terms: look, judge, act."[68]

The Jesuit scholar Jean-Yves Calvez, whose book on papal social teaching was sent to press right after the death of Pius XII, soon wrote a second book, this one on *Mater et magistra*, because its perspective was so different. As Calvez explains: "The effect on the readers was one comparable to that produced on travelers who pass into a different climate."[69] Some critics noticed problems with the new attempt to relate to the modern world, however. Reinhold Niebuhr, for example, noted "how blandly oblivious this clerical document is of its own indebtedness to the moral achievements of modern civilization."[70] Although Niebuhr's remark was accurate, it ignored the ecclesial context of a pope seeking to persuade antimodernist Catholics to change.

In content, the encyclical's two most important contributions were the subjects of socialization and development. "Socialization," which appears in section number 59, was the most noteworthy and controversial concept in the encyclical. In one English translation, section 59 states: "Certainly one of the principal characteristics which seem to be typical of our age is an *increase in social relationships*" (that is, socialization).[71] The difficulty was that the original drafts were in Italian and Latin; French, German, and English translations quickly followed. Commentators vigorously disputed what the original words meant and how they should be translated.

The debate was so spirited because of the church's long-standing opposition to socialism. Indeed, Pope Pius XII had condemned "all-embracing socialization."[72] John's predecessors had been stalwart opponents of Marxism, communism, and any form of socialism. In France and Italy, for example, they not only forbade Catholic citizens to vote for communists or socialists but also instructed Catholic politicians not to collaborate with the communists in any way. Such orders obstructed the efforts of Christian Democratic leaders like Aldo Moro to undertake the "opening to the left" that might have assured the Christians' election through coalitions with the socialists.[73] Pope John steered clear of any specific advice about the

contested political situation in Italy. Instead, in *Mater et magistra* he offered a social program that every state must follow.

Pope John was not the first pope to commemorate *Rerum novarum*. In
1931 Pope Pius XI had celebrated the fortieth anniversary of *Rerum novarum* with the encyclical *Quadragesimo anno*. In the 1930s, the church
had obvious reasons to criticize that notorious opponent of individual
freedom, the totalitarian state. Pius's encyclicals advocated "corporatism"
or "corporativism," namely the development of guildlike intermediate economic or vocational associations that could protect workers' interests and
keep the state from accumulating too much power.[74] Subsidiarity—the
idea that social problems should be handled by the smallest, most local
organizations that could manage them—emerged as a defining principle
of Catholic social thought. Subsidiarity, workers' guilds, and local organizations were means of limiting the range of the totalitarian state. Like
Leo XIII, Pius XI also emphasized an individual right to private property
against the collectivist state.

It was within this context—of the church's fear of a totalitarian or socialist state that crushed individual freedoms—that *Mater et magistra's*
recognition of "socialization" was controversial. Despite all the avowals of
continuity with Leo and the two Piuses, John "stood the argument [about
human freedom] on its head" by expecting the state to promote and protect individual freedom.[75] *Mater et magistra* "does not merely make more
specific the teaching of Pius XI, it develops it out of recognition by giving
to the State functions which Pius would never have dreamed of giving it
and by recognizing personal claims of the individual upon the community
which would not have occurred to him.... *With* Mater et Magistra *we are,
in fact, brought right into the world of the Welfare State.*"[76]

Of course the conservatives said, "Magistra, no!" The transitional pope
advocated the welfare state and argued that the state must protect human
freedom by ensuring that the needs of its citizens are met. Moreover, the
encyclical's support for modern trade unions was inconsistent with the old
ideal of corporate guilds.[77] Nonetheless, the encyclical's acceptance of modernity and the welfare state was not all bad news to proponents of democratic capitalism. "On the record, [Pope John] embraced the essence of the
liberal institutions of human rights and of economic development far more
closely than any of his predecessors."[78]

Donal Dorr offers a useful explanation of the encyclical's traditional yet
daring perspective. The earlier popes' praiseworthy support of subsidiarity,
private property, local entrepreneurs, and guilds could be used to justify a
capitalism of unbounded free enterprise and a state that did not provide the
services needed by the poor.[79] Often Catholic social teaching was invoked

to oppose the very rights that it protected. To counter such a perspective, *Mater et magistra* taught that, in an era whose dominant feature was socialization (that is, an increase in social relationships or interdependence), the state was required to do much more. The state could promote individual freedom by providing for education, health care, housing, and other human rights, especially for the poorest and neediest members of society.

Given the Catholic Church's long condemnation of communism, *Mater et magistra*'s "virtually complete silence" on that subject was surprising; many observers criticized the silence as an unwarranted and unwise *apertura a sinistra*.[80] Nor were the communists satisfied with the encyclical, as it offered some defense of capitalism and the liberal state.[81] Still others have read the letter as "not so much an opening to the left as a decisive move away from the right" of corporatism and unbridled capitalism.[82]

These criticisms from all sides are not surprising; Catholic social thought has often sought to criticize both capitalism and communism and to carve out an independent voice offering a third way for society. Pope John desired to foster dialogue among opponents rather than to condemn their views. Although he engaged all sides in the debate, his fundamental philosophy was at odds with both camps. From his perspective, human beings are social by nature, not autonomous liberals. The well-being of human beings depends, not only upon the protection of individual rights, but upon the establishment of the common good, which, in the interdependent 1960s, could be accomplished only by the actions of the state.

In *Mater et magistra*, John replaced his predecessors' preoccupation with communism and its ills with a new international focus on the developing world. *Mater et magistra* was "the first encyclical to address the issues of international relations and economic development."[83] The encyclical recognized the worldwide dimensions of social justice and called for a world community and world authority to address the problems of the poor. Respect for human nature requires justice among the nations, not merely a government's commitment to justice for its citizens.

Finally, *Mater et magistra*'s recommendations for social justice were rooted in the pope's theological vision. The pastoral pope, who throughout *Mater et magistra* focused the world's attention on the needs of the poor, insisted that "the solution to the 'social question' is found in religion and 'return' to God's moral law."[84] Human nature is both spiritual and temporal and is ordered by God's law. Pope John believed that any social arrangement that ignored the order of human nature, both spiritual and temporal, would fail. As one of the earliest commentaries on *Mater et magistra* explains: "Those who misjudge the nature of man can hardly hope to evolve a perfect theory of society. It is bad enough to fail to see the whole man, but it is far worse to exclude the most important part of our nature, namely, the spiritual."[85] The protection of workers' economic rights promotes their spiritual well-being. As Pietro Pavan phrases it, human beings "must be inspired to live their work as a means of achieving spiritual enrichment and perfection."[86]

Inductive arguments are concerned with particulars, with the world and human nature as they are. Look, judge, act. Hence *Mater et magistra*, with its new inductive style, was full of practical suggestions, including a lengthy section, reflecting the pope's upbringing in rural Italy, on the needs of agriculture. In 1965, E. E. Y. Hales accurately predicted that "later generations will lose interest in many of the practical suggestions that loom large in the Johannine encyclicals,"[87] adding, "since they were pastoral rather than dogmatic there was no particular reason why they should have any important surviving influence after Roncalli's death."[88]

Forty years later, the particulars of *Mater et magistra* are not very relevant to current social questions; nonetheless, its contemporaneous impact demonstrated the importance of the pope's advice to "look, judge, act" in the world that God has created. The encyclical shattered the idea (popular with many Catholics after *Quadragesimo anno*) that the church is wedded to one corporativist economic system. *Mater et magistra* demonstrated that a natural law theory can respond to modern circumstances rather than romanticize the institutions of the past. The door (or window?) was opened for both liberal and conservative Catholics to develop economic plans that promoted social justice. While Michael Novak praises the encyclical's movement "from the classic emphasis on distributive justice to what might be called 'productive justice,'"[89] Donal Dorr hails its "move towards the left ... on social and economic matters."[90]

Mater et magistra was the initial statement of the pope's new approach to social questions. A more systematic statement of the pope's vision of social justice appeared in his last encyclical, *Pacem in terris*.

PACEM IN TERRIS: ALL MEN OF GOOD WILL

In the fall of 1962, the first session of Vatican II was almost suspended because of the Cuban Missile Crisis, the worst confrontation between the Soviet Union and the United States during the Cold War. President John F. Kennedy had seen pictures of Soviet missiles in Cuba on October 16 and announced a naval blockade on October 22.[91] Pope John had enjoyed some positive exchanges with Premier Nikita Khrushchev in the fall of 1961, when the Soviet leader had praised the pope's work for peace and the pope had sent him cordial greetings.[92] We have seen that the pope refused to denounce the communists in *Mater et magistra*. The arrival of the Russian Orthodox observers at the Second Vatican Council on October 12 had also suggested a thaw in church-communist relations.

On October 23, President Kennedy contacted Norman Cousins, who had written about the papacy's capacity to resolve conflicts and who was attending a meeting of Soviet and American scientists in Maryland. After negotiations between Khrushchev and the Vatican by intermediaries, including Cousins and Father Felix Morlion, the pope was encouraged to make a public statement on peace. Both *Pravda* and the *New York Times* carried accounts of the pope's October 25 plea for "'all rulers not to remain deaf to the cry of mankind'" for peace.[93] Khrushchev later told Cousins that history would remember John's contribution to world peace.[94]

At the council, the fathers initially wondered if they should suspend the session so that the bishops could return home before the cataclysm. After the crisis was over, the Ukrainian bishops demanded to know why Russian Orthodox observers should attend the council while the Catholic Metropolitan of the Ukraine, Josef Slipyi, was imprisoned.[95] The pope and his aides secured Slipyi's release in February 1963. Then, in March, Pope John welcomed Khrushchev's daughter and son-in-law to the Vatican. In the same month he received the Balzan Peace Prize for his work on behalf of world peace.[96]

John's personal secretary "dates the origin of *Pacem in terris* to October 25, 1962, when Pope John was working on his message" to Khrushchev and Kennedy.[97] In November, Pietro Pavan was again called in to put the pope's ideas into the encyclical format. John told Pavan that there should be no attributions of "ill will" in the encyclical, because he wanted to foster a genuine dialogue for peace.[98] Time was of the essence; John had learned in September that he was dying. Pavan's draft was ready by January 7, 1963. Pavan reported that the pope "was very happy with the work. When [Pavan] gave him the complete text, he read it. Then [they] prayed together and [the pope] cried."[99] The pope announced the release of *Pacem in terris* on March 31, 1963; its official publication date was Holy Thursday, April 11, 1963.

Pacem in terris was the first papal encyclical addressed to "all men of good will" rather than to fellow Catholics, and the first papal encyclical published in full in the *New York Times*.[100] The encyclical's vision of world peace rooted in human dignity appealed to many non-Catholics throughout the world, especially those frightened by the confrontation of the superpowers. *Pacem in terris* was more systematic and comprehensive than John's first seven encyclicals and appeared to complete the arguments of *Mater et magistra*. Many readers found its prose even more simple and engaging than the new language of *Mater et magistra*. The accessible style was consistent with the document's substantive claim that the Roman Catholic Church must read "the signs of the times"[101] in light of the gospel rather than condemn the modern world.

According to Jesuit theologian John Courtney Murray, "the word 'order' " provided the encyclical's "basic theme."[102] That theme was proclaimed in the encyclical's opening sentence: "Peace on Earth—which man throughout the ages has so longed for and sought after—can never be established, never guaranteed, except by the diligent observance of the *divinely established order*."[103] Once again, the pope espoused a traditional Catholic natural law vision of a human nature that is part of the order of God's creation. Individuals must make their moral choices in accordance with that order; world politics and law must conform to it as well. Father John Murray (not John Courtney Murray) explains that "the order in the last resort is the order belonging to God's plan for human nature and for proper human relationships. In Nature there reigns an astonishing order—a delicate and complicated and highly diversified pattern. It is *part of man's dignity* that possessed of mind he can observe and appreciate this pattern."[104]

According to *Pacem in terris*, human dignity is part of the natural order and the source of human rights and duties. The pope's letter proclaimed the fundamental dignity of the human person—every human person—and identified the rights and duties that such dignity entails. More than in the earlier proclamations of his papacy, the pope emphasized that unity and peace (the goals of his pontificate) depend upon the *universal* quality of human nature. The encyclical's four major sections reflected the preoccupation with the proper order of human relationships. Those parts analyzed the relationships between human beings, between individuals and the public authorities within a state, between states, and between states and individuals and the world community.

Although *Pacem in terris* presented many traditional aspects of Catholic thought about the nature of the human person, in fact, "within the traditional framework of natural law and Catholic political philosophy a seismic shift [had] begun."[105] The "seismic shift" was the letter's adaptation of secular natural rights theory to Catholic thought. The new natural law was most evident in three subjects of the encyclical: human rights, freedom (especially religious freedom), and democracy.

First, human rights. *Pacem in terris* gave "the most complete and systematic list of these human rights in the modern Catholic tradition."[106] The list of rights was extensive and comprehensive, including both the political and civil rights favored by the liberal tradition (such as freedom of association, life, and bodily integrity) and the social and economic rights supported by Marxists (such as the right to food, clothing, shelter, and health care). If nations are to live in peace, *all* these rights must be protected.

This generous acknowledgment of rights marked a development from earlier papal teaching. Until *Pacem in terris*, the Catholic natural law tradition had distinguished itself from the natural rights tradition, which was the product of the Enlightenment. Catholicism had emphasized the social nature of the human person and the need for individuals and the government to cooperate for the common good. In contrast, the natural rights proponents focused on the freedom of the individual. Indeed, in 1864 the pope of the First Vatican Council, Pius IX, had condemned many liberal rights in the *Syllabus of Errors*. "The significance of *Pacem in Terris* lies in the fact that, for the first time, Roman Catholicism [had] co-opted the modern theory of 'natural rights' as an extension of its natural law theory."[107]

Yet the encyclical retained a voice that was different from liberalism and socialism and that offered a "distinctively Catholic moral and political framework.... Among the 'Catholic' features of the human rights theory are: (1) the correlation of rights and duties; (2) an attitude of cooperation (and adjustment) in the implementation of rights; and (3) the assimilation of rights to the common good."[108] *Pacem in terris*'s extensive list of rights was immediately succeeded by the duties that correspond to those rights.

Second, freedom. Consistent with earlier encyclicals, *Mater et magistra* advocated a society of justice, truth, and love. In *Pacem in terris*, there was "one fascinating development" in the pope's thought;[109] Pope John added freedom to the list. Henceforth society must be ordered according to justice, truth, love, *and* freedom. John Courtney Murray wrote, "The summation of the Pope's thought is in the sentence which asserts that all order, if it is to be qualified as reasonable and human, must be 'founded on truth, built according to justice, vivified and integrated by charity, and put into practice in freedom.'"[110] This recognition of freedom was evidence of yet another "rapprochement with the Enlightenment and political liberalism."[111]

Within the framework of *Pacem in terris*'s new emphasis on rights and freedom, the encyclical's most original contribution to Catholic thought was its acknowledgment of a right of religious freedom for every human person. In the words of the encyclical: "Also among man's rights is that of being able to worship God in accordance with the right dictates of his own conscience, and to profess his religion both in private and in public."[112] This was the first time that an official Roman Catholic document had recognized a human right to religious freedom.

Recall that in the discussions about Christian unity and the Second Vatican Council, many members of the Curia were concerned to safeguard the truth of the Catholic faith. The church taught that Catholicism was the one true religion. The curialists believed that Christian unity could occur only if the erroneous Protestants returned to the truth of Rome. The political implications of that stance were quite severe. The church taught that Catholicism should be the established religion of every state and that erroneous religions should not have rights to public worship. The old slogan was "error has no rights." After the announcement that Vatican II would be convened, the World Council of Churches and other churches urged the church to address ecumenism and religious freedom as central topics of the council. "Error has no rights" did not provide a firm foundation for ecumenism. *Pacem in terris*'s announcement of a human right to religious freedom was a significant contribution to the ecumenical movement.

Third, democracy. The encyclical also defended a limited, constitutional state that would protect human rights but not interfere with human liberties. Before World War II, the church's skepticism about the Enlightenment had included much uncertainty about the merits of democracy. Pope Pius XII, however, in his Christmas addresses during the war, had praised democracy and citizens' participation in government. Nonetheless, democracy was not preferred. The church taught that different forms of government were appropriate in different cultures and different historical circumstances; members of a nation could decide the proper form of government.

John's support for democracy over other forms of government was more evident. "The preference clearly expressed in *Pacem in Terris* for democracy was, in fact, something new in papal political teaching";[113] indeed, "if not a new departure, at least a new emphasis."[114] Although *Pacem in terris* acknowledges that local circumstances influence the structure of government, the encyclical concludes that "it is in keeping with *human nature* for the State to be given a form which embodies a threefold division of public office [i.e., legislative, judicial and executive] properly corresponding to the three main functions of public authority."[115] *Pacem in terris* also offered the first papal endorsement of the "modern conception of the written constitution."[116]

Democracy did not always appeal to the curialists in Italy. Several weeks after *Pacem in terris* appeared, the Italian Communist Party picked up a million new votes in the April 30 Italian election. Curial officials blamed the pope's meeting with Khrushchev's family and the new encyclical; "an evening paper in Milan changed its title to *Falcem in Terris* ('The Sickle on Earth')."[117]

As with *Mater et magistra*, however, analysts have disagreed about the encyclical's political and social implications. John Langan concludes that *Pacem in terris* "provided a basis for the transformation of Catholicism from an ally and ward of traditionalist regimes to a critic of repression by both reactionary and revolutionary regimes."[118] Drew Christiansen's assessment is even stronger; he states that "a case may be made that [*Pacem in terris*] was among the most influential encyclicals in the corpus of modern social teaching," rivaling *Rerum novarum* and *Gaudium et spes*.[119] Christiansen attributes the growth of church-based human rights and justice and peace commissions throughout the world, including in South Africa, East Timor, El Salvador, Poland, and the Philippines, to the "revolution unleashed" by *Pacem in terris*; "however naïve the encyclical might seem to arm-chair theorists and practitioners of *realpolitik*, John XXIII had found an Archimedean point from which to lift the world to a new kind of political order: one founded in the dignity and rights of the human person."[120]

The twentieth century's preeminent practitioner of Christian realpolitik, the theologian Reinhold Niebuhr, objected: "This idealism is a little too easy."[121] To critics, *Pacem in terris*, like *Mater et magistra* and the Second Vatican Council, possessed the flaws associated with the pope's optimism about the possibilities of building a just and peaceful world. The critics doubted that human nature could achieve "justice, truth, love and freedom" and questioned "the utopia of Pope John."[122]

THE CHURCH IN THE MODERN WORLD

When Apostolic Delegate Angelo Roncalli left Bulgaria in 1934 for Turkey, he told the Bulgarians, "No one knows the ways of the future. Wherever I may go in the world, if anyone ... should pass before my door, at night, and in dire need, he will find a lamp lit in my window. Knock! Knock! *I shall not ask you whether you are a Catholic or not*."[123] As pope, John lighted that lamp of welcome in the windows of Vatican City. In October 1962, he welcomed 2,778 fathers from five continents and 136 nations and of ninety-three nationalities, to Rome for the Second Vatican Council. "Vatican II was the first council where all the races were represented."[124] John's vision of the unity of Christians and the reconciliation of Christians with non-Christians inspired and sustained the council's preparation and first session, as well as the conclave that selected a successor who pledged to complete the council's work. The vision survived John in the council's later sessions and in the sixteen documents that were promulgated by the council and Pope Paul after John's death. Vatican II is his legacy.

According to Philippe Levillain, the council's new ecclesiology "was the axis around which the [four] dialogues of Vatican II were organized: on ecumenism (dialogue with non-Catholic Christians); on the non-Christian religions; on the Church and the world; and on religious freedom."[125] The influence of Pope John was evident in all four dialogues, in the new ecclesiology, and in the council's documents expounding those themes, namely the Decree on Ecumenism, the Declaration on the Relationship of the Church to Non-Christian Religions, the Declaration on Religious Freedom, the Dogmatic Constitution on the Church, and the Pastoral Constitution on the Church in the Modern World.

Angelo Roncalli had learned the lessons of ecumenism from his years in Bulgaria, Greece, and Turkey. In his first address as Pope John, he had pledged his papacy to the pursuit of Christian unity. He created the Secretariat for Christian Unity and appointed the persistent Cardinal Bea to direct it. His support enabled Bea to withstand opposition from the curialists who thought that erroneous Christians must seek unity with Rome on Rome's terms. The pope and the cardinal invited the numerous non-Catholic observers and guests to the Roman Catholic Council, thus transforming an ecumenical Catholic council into a council of broader ecumenical significance.

Pope John asked Cardinal Bea to prepare a text that would address the church's relationship with the Jews. When he realized that the Theological Commission would not offer an adequate ecumenical text, Bea and the Secretariat for Christian Unity prepared an initial text on ecumenism. The first three chapters of this Schema on Ecumenism considered unity among Christians. Chapter 4 concerned the church's relationship with the Jews. Chapter 5 addressed the subject of religious freedom. Versions of the secretariat's initial draft were eventually promulgated as three separate conciliar documents: the Decree on Ecumenism (*Unitatis redintegratio*), the Declaration on the Relationship of the Church to Non-Christian Religions (*Nostra aetate*) and the Declaration on Religious Freedom (*Dignitatis humanae*). Hence Cardinal Bea's Secretariat, created and sustained by Good Pope John, initiated the three important ecumenical dialogues of Vatican II: ecumenism with Christians, ecumenism with the world's religions, and religious freedom.

The fathers passed *Unitatis redintegratio* at the third session of the council; it was promulgated on November 21, 1964. With its proclamation that the "restoration of unity among all Christians is one of the principal concerns of the Second Vatican Council,"[126] the decree marked "the full entry of the Roman Catholic Church into the ecumenical movement."[127]

Nostra aetate originated "in the unique personality of Pope John XXIII,"[128] who had asked Cardinal Bea in September 1960 to write a document that would heal the church's relationship with the Jews. Council consideration of Jewish-Christian relations was delayed because of complaints that the document expressed political support for Israel. Because of these political concerns, the declaration was not passed until the fourth session of the council, on October 28, 1965, and was amended to include the world's religions. In the declaration, "a Council for the first time in history [acknowledged] the search for the absolute by other men and by whole races and peoples, and [honored] the truth and holiness in other religions as the work of the one living God."[129] Judaism received more extended treatment than the other religions; the declaration condemned anti-Semitism and discrimination against Jews. It also concluded that the Jewish people must not be blamed for the death of Jesus.

At the council, religious freedom was the "most controversial" subject, "largely because it raised with sharp emphasis the issue that lay continually below the surface of all the conciliar debates—the issue of *development of doctrine.*"[130] Accordingly, the Declaration on Religious Freedom, *Dignitatis humanae*, was the last document promulgated at the Second Vatican Council, on December 7, 1965.

The secretariat's drafts provided the first conciliar defense of religious freedom, which was not debated at the council's first session. *Pacem in terris* was published between the first and second sessions of the council, before the issues of church and state and ecumenism were discussed on the council floor. *Pacem in terris* was thus the first official Catholic document to recognize that the right of religious freedom inheres in human nature, that is, belongs to every human person, not to Catholics only. This "transitional text ... moved the Roman Catholic discussion beyond the teaching of Pius XII, yet it did not attempt the more comprehensive argument of *Dignitatis Humanae.*"[131] Although *Pacem in terris* identified the right of religious freedom, it did not explain how a church that had opposed religious freedom for non-Catholics could suddenly support it. That task was left to the *periti* (experts) John Courtney Murray and Pavan, and to the council fathers. Pope Pius XII had silenced Murray in the 1950s for his writings on church and state.

If Murray was right that the "development of doctrine" was the "sticking-point" for passage of the Declaration on Religious Freedom,[132] then it was Pope John XXIII who provided the most decisive argument for its enactment. As a papal encyclical, *Pacem in terris* provided the best precedent for those fathers who worried about drafting a conciliar document that was faithful to the church's prior teachings on religious freedom. John had told Cardinal Gabriel-Marie Garrone that the pope's "task was that of launching this big and heavy ship. 'Another,' he said sadly and prophetically, 'will have the task of taking it out to sea.'"[133] Although Murray and the American bishops have received the most credit for *Dignitatis humanae*, it was Pope John, by calling the council, creating the Secretariat for Christian Unity, and defending Cardinal Bea, who launched the ship of religious freedom that the Americans brought to shore.

Finally, on the subject of ecclesiology, Pope John had adopted Cardinal Suenens's suggestion that the Second Vatican Council must proceed *ad intra* and *ad extra*, that is, reflecting both on its own nature and on its relationship to the modern world. The council did so in its two constitutions on the church, the dogmatic constitution (*Lumen gentium*) and the pastoral constitution (*Gaudium et spes*).[134] *Lumen gentium*, which passed on November 21, 1964, during the third session, described a church in which both laity and hierarchy are important. Together they form the "People of God"[135] and the "pilgrim church."[136] John's influence and the method of his encyclicals *Mater et magistra* and *Pacem in terris* were evident in *Gaudium et spes*, the Pastoral Constitution on the Church in the Modern World, which was passed in December 1965 during the fourth session of the council. *Gaudium et spes* followed the method of *Pacem in terris* in identifying the church's "duty of scrutinizing the *signs of the times* and of interpreting them in light of the Gospel."[137] Consistent with John's plans for the council and his encyclicals, *Gaudium et spes* was a "pastoral," not a "dogmatic," constitution. In other words, it "did not define or decree immutable dogma,"[138] but sought to express the relation of the church to the world and modern mankind."[139] The church, too, would look, judge, and act. Since Vatican II, "the attempt to scrutinize the signs of the time has provoked an unprecedented inquiry into the methodology of Catholic social action, particularly at the intersection of faith and history, ethics and politics."[140]

"THE QUESTION MARK"

In a tribute to the late pope, John Courtney Murray wrote that John "raised some questions himself—notably the great, sprawling, ecumenical question—to which he returned no definitive answers. He encouraged the raising of other questions, both old and new, both theological and pastoral—and even political. The symbol of him might well be the question mark—surely a unique symbol for a Pope."[141] John's holiness and goodness were not often questioned. He has been hailed as the "pope of the century"[142] and the "most beloved pope in all of history."[143] On September 3, 2000, Pope John Paul II beatified him. Good Pope John is now Blessed Pope John, one step away from becoming Good Saint John.

Yet "John was [also] the Pope who—started something *new*."[144] "He had truly been a pope of transition, in the stronger sense of the word, for he had ended the Constantinian era of the Church and begun a *new* historical period."[145] Murray, who had helped Pope John to launch the church's new era by drafting the Declaration on Religious Freedom, eulogized the pope who understood that the church's mission was to "bring salvation to men in the moment when they need salvation, *which is always today*."[146]

John's critics did not want a church that followed the mores and fashions of the day. "Maybe the story of Cardinal Siri sums up everything. On the day after Pope John's death he said, 'It will take us 50 years to remedy the disasters of this man's pontificate.'"[147] Although Siri later moderated this opinion, the comment encapsulates the ongoing debate within Roman Catholicism as to whether the innovations of Vatican II were a disaster or a success for the church. Pope John set the agenda for the church's next fifty years. The primary commitment of John's immediate successor, Paul VI, was to complete the work of the council. To their joint successor, Pope John Paul II, fell the task of discerning the appropriate scope of the council's teachings and of implementing its reforms.

In contrast to Pope John, however, Pope John Paul is pessimistic about human nature and a severe critic of modernity. John Paul has recognized that the truth claims of Catholicism may be undermined by ecumenism, religious freedom, and democracy. Murray, who was silenced by Pope Pius XII for his writings on church and state, writes, "After John XXIII ... it is not possible abruptly to impose silence on any of the parties to the talk in the Church concerning old things and new."[148] Nonetheless, John Paul has silenced theologians who disagree with his interpretations of church teaching and proposed a deductive social and moral teaching. Hence Pope John's "great, sprawling, ecumenical question"—namely, how the church can be faithful to its traditions *ad intra* and ecumenical *ad extra*—remains open.

John's papacy raised anew, as his Second Vatican Council put it, "the perennial questions which men ask about this present life and the life to come, and about the relationship of one to the other"[149]—in other words, questions about nature and grace, which together "produced in [Pope John] a living unity filled with charm and surprises."[150]

NOTES

1. Giuseppe Alberigo, "John XXIII," in *The Papacy: An Encyclopedia*, ed. Philippe Levillain, 3 vols. (New York: Routledge, 2002), 2:856.

2. Donal Dorr, "Pope John XXIII—A New Direction?" in *Readings in Moral Theology, No. 5: Official Catholic Social Teaching*, ed. Charles E. Curran and Richard A. McCormick (New York: Paulist Press, 1986), 82.

3. Martin Marty and Scott Appleby, eds., *Fundamentalisms Observed* (Chicago: University of Chicago Press, 1991), vii–ix.

4. Ibid., ix.

5. Abraham Joshua Heschel, "Choose Life!" in *Moral Grandeur and Spiritual Audacity: Essays* (New York: Farrar, Straus & Giroux, 1996), 254.

6. Carlo Falconi, *Pope John and the Ecumenical Council*, trans. Muriel Grindrod (Cleveland: World Publishing, 1964), 30.

7. John XXIII, *Journal of a Soul*, trans. Dorothy White (New York: McGraw-Hill, 1980), 331.

8. Peter Hebblethwaite, *John XXIII: Pope of the Century* (London: Continuum, 2000), 25.

9. Ibid., 30; Thomas Cahill, *Pope John XXIII* (New York: Viking, 2002), 101.

10. Hebblethwaite, *John XXIII*, 54.

11. Paul Johnson, *Pope John XXIII* (Boston: Little, Brown, 1974), 45.

12. Hebblethwaite, *John XXIII*, 71.

13. Ibid., 91.

14. Cahill, *Pope John XXIII*, 137.

15. Hebblethwaite, *John XXIII*, 94. See also Peter Hoffman, "Roncalli in the Second World War: Peace Initiatives, the Greek Famine and the Persecution of the Jews," *Journal of Ecclesiastical History* 40 (1989): 90.

16. Cahill, *Pope John XXIII*, 137.

17. Ibid.; Hebblethwaite, *John XXIII*, 95.

18. Ibid., 127; Richard P. McBrien, *Lives of the Popes: The Pontiffs from St. Peter to John Paul II* (San Francisco: HarperCollins, 1997), 370.

19. Johnson, *Pope John XXIII*, 110.

20. Hebblethwaite, *John XXIII*, 135.

21. Ibid.

22. John XXIII, *The Encyclicals and Other Messages of John XXIII* (Washington, D.C.: TPS Press, 1964), 9.

23. Hebblethwaite, *John XXIII*, 148.

24. John XXIII, *Encyclicals and Other Messages*, 17.

25. McBrien, *Lives of the Popes*, 371.

26. Eric John, ed., *The Popes* (New York: Hawthorne, 1964), 47.

27. Hebblethwaite, *John XXIII*, 158.

28. John XXIII, *Encyclicals and Other Messages*, 381.

29. Hebblethwaite, *John XXIII*, 157.

30. Giuseppe Alberigo, "The Announcement of the Council: From the Security of the Fortress to the Lure of the Quest," in *History of Vatican II*, ed. Joseph A. Komonchak (Maryknoll, N.Y.: Orbis Books, 1996–2000), 1:13.

31. Norman Cousins, "Pope John and His Open Window," *Saturday Review* 46 (January 19, 1963), 20.

32. Hebblethwaite, *John XXIII*, 155.

33. Joseph A. Komonchak, "The Struggle for the Council During the Preparation of Vatican II (1960–1962)," in *History of Vatican II*, 1:350–356.

34. Thomas T. Love, *John Courtney Murray: Contemporary Church-State Theory* (New York: Doubleday, 1965), 34.

35. John M. Oesterreicher, "Declaration on the Relationship of the Church to Non-Christian Religions," in *Commentary on the Documents of Vatican II*, ed. Herbert Vorgrimler (New York: Herder & Herder, 1967–69), 3:4.

36. McBrien, *Lives of the Popes*, 374.

37. Komonchak, "The Struggle for the Council," 287.

38. Love, *John Courtney Murray*, 94.

39. Ibid.; Andrea Riccardi, "The Tumultuous Opening Days of the Council," in Komonchak, *History of Vatican II*, 2:44–47.

40. Giuseppe Alberigo, "Conclusion: Preparing for What Kind of Council?" in Komonchak, *History of Vatican II*, 1:505.

41. Alberigo, "John XXIII," 855.

42. John XXIII, "The Opening Address to the Second Vatican Council," in *The Teachings of the Second Vatican Council: Complete Texts of the Constitutions, Decrees, and Declarations*, ed. Gregory Baum (Westminster, Md.: Newman Press, 1966), 4.

43. Ibid., 8.

44. Riccardi, "Tumultuous Opening Days," 19.

45. Yves Congar, *Journal of Y.M.-J. Congar* (December 11, 1962), typescript 71, quoted in Andrea Riccardi, "The Tumultuous Opening Days of the Council," 2:19.

46. Hilari Raguer, "An Initial Profile of the Assembly," in Komonchak, *History of Vatican II*, 2:178.

47. E. E. Y. Hales, *Pope John and His Revolution* (London: Eyre & Spottiswoode, 1965); Xavier Rynne, *Vatican Council II* (Maryknoll, N.Y.: Orbis Books, 1999), 123, 138; Giancarlo Zizola, *The Utopia of Pope John XXIII*, trans. Helen Barolini, 2d ed. (Maryknoll, N.Y.: Orbis Books, 1978).

48. Komonchak, "The Struggle for the Council," 355.

49. Rynne, *Vatican Council II*, 56–123.

50. Ibid., 91.

51. Ibid., 122.

52. Ibid.

53. Leo Josef Cardinal Suenens, sermon given on October 28, 1963, quoted in Michael Novak, *The Open Church: Vatican II, Act II* (New York: Macmillan, 1964), 20 (emphasis added).

54. John F. Cronin, *Christianity and Social Progress: A Commentary on Mater et Magistra* (Baltimore: Helicon, 1965), 1.

55. Hebblethwaite, *John XXIII*, 148.

56. "For the Record," *National Review* 11 (August 12, 1961), 77.

57. J.-B. Desrosiers, "'Mater et magistra,'" *Monde nouveau* 23 (September 23, 1961), 1, quoted in Donald R. Campion, "Mater et Magistra and its Commentators," *Theological Studies* 24 (1963): 7.

58. Dorr, "Pope John XXIII—A New Direction?" 95.

59. Jean-Yves Calvez, *The Social Thought of John XXIII: Mater et Magistra*, trans. George J. M. McKenzie (Chicago: Henry Regnery, 1964), xi.

60. Donald R. Campion, "Mater et Magistra and Its Commentators," *Theological Studies* 24 (1963): 5.

61. Marcel Laloire, "L'Encyclique 'Mater et magistra,'" *Revue nouvelle* 34 (September 1961): 203, quoted in Campion, "Mater et Magistra and Its Commentators," 3.

62. Richard Arès, "Présentation et vue d'ensemble," *Relations* 21 (September 1961): 230, quoted in Campion, "Mater et Magistra and Its Commentators," 3.

63. Hales, *Pope John and His Revolution*, 39.

64. Jules de Meij, "'Mater et magistra,'" *Streven* 15 (December 1961): 216, quoted in Campion, "Mater et Magistra and Its Commentators," 4.

65. Osvald Nell-Breuning, "'Mater et magistra,'" *Stimmen der Zeit* 87 (November 1961), 116, quoted in Campion, "Mater et Magistra and Its Commentators," 4.

66. "Réactions à l'encyclique 'Mater et magistra': Voix polonaises," *Informations catholiques internationals* 152 (September 15, 1961): 25, quoted in Campion, "Mater et Magistra and Its Commentators," 4.

67. Alberigo, "John XXIII," 856.

68. *Mater et magistra*, §236.

69. Calvez, *Social Thought of John XXIII*, x.

70. Reinhold Niebuhr, "The Eternal Church and the Modern World," *The Christian Century* 78 (September 20, 1961): 1105.

71. *Mater et magistra*, §59.

72. Pius XII, Radio Broadcast to the Katholikentag of Vienna, September 14, 1952, quoted by Marvin L. Krier Mich, "*Mater et Magistra*," in *Catholic Social Thought*, ed. Kenneth Himes (Washington, D.C.: Georgetown University Press, forthcoming).

73. Hebblethwaite, *John XXIII*, 183.

74. Cronin, *Christianity and Social Progress*, 11.

75. Mich, "*Mater et Magistra*."

76. Hales, *Pope John and His Revolution*, 45 (emphasis added).

77. Mich, "*Mater et Magistra*."

78. Michael Novak, *Freedom with Justice: Catholic Social Thought and Liberal Institutions* (San Francisco: Harper & Row, 1984), 133.

79. Dorr, "Pope John XXIII—A New Direction?" 96–98.

80. Campion, "Mater et Magistra and Its Commentators," 32.

81. Ibid., 35–37.

82. Dorr, "Pope John XXIII—A New Direction?" 103.

83. Mich, "*Mater et Magistra*."

84. Ibid.

85. Cronin, *Christianity and Social Progress*, 161.

86. Pietro Pavan, "The Place of Mater et Magistra in Papal Social Teaching," *Christus Rex* 16 (December 1962): 242.

87. Hales, *Pope John and His Revolution*, 91.

88. Ibid., 93.

89. Novak, *Freedom with Justice*, 128.

90. Dorr, "Pope John XXIII—A New Direction?" 103.

91. Gerald P. Fogarty, "The Council Gets Underway," in Komonchak, *History of Vatican II*, 2:94.

92. Ibid., 97.

93. Cousins, "Pope John and His Open Window," 21; Hebblethwaite, *John XXIII*, 230.

94. Fogarty, "The Council Gets Underway," 102; Cahill, *Pope John XXIII*, 205.

95. Fogarty, "The Council Gets Underway," 101.

96. Ibid.

97. Hebblethwaite, *John XXIII*, 232.

98. Ibid., 243.

99. Pietro Pavan, "Pacem in Terris Twenty Years Later," *Vida Nueva* 12 (June 1983): 52.

100. Arnaldo Cortesi, "Peace Encyclical Addressed to All," *New York Times*, April 10, 1963; "Text of Pope John's Encyclical 'Pacem in Terris,' Calling for a World Community," *New York Times*, April 11, 1963.

101. *Pacem in terris*, §§126–129.

102. John Courtney Murray, "Things Old and New in 'Pacem in Terris,'" *America* 108 (April 27, 1963): 612.

103. *Pacem in terris*, §1 (emphasis added).

104. John Murray, "The Peace That Comes of Order: Reflections Upon the Encyclical 'Pacem in Terris,'" *Studies* 52 (Autumn 1963): 295.

105. Drew Christiansen, "*Pacem in terris*: A Commentary," in Himes, *Catholic Social Thought* (forthcoming).

106. David Hollenbach, *Claims in Conflict: Retrieving and Renewing the Catholic Human Rights Tradition* (New York: Paulist Press, 1979), 66.

107. Reinhold Niebuhr, "*Pacem in Terris*: Two Views," *Christianity and Crisis* 23 (May 13, 1963): 81.

108. Christiansen, "*Pacem in terris*: A Commentary."

109. Charles E. Curran, "The Changing Anthropological Bases of Catholic Social Ethics," in Curran and McCormick, *Readings in Moral Theology*, 195.

110. Murray, "Things Old and New," 613.

111. Christiansen, "*Pacem in terris*: A Commentary."

112. *Pacem in terris*, §14.

113. Hales, *Pope John and His Revolution*, 54.

114. Ibid., 56.

115. *Pacem in terris*, §68.

116. Murray, "Things Old and New," 612.

117. Hebblethwaite, *John XXIII*, 253.

118. John Langan, "Human Rights in Roman Catholicism," in Curran and McCormick, *Readings in Moral Theology*, 110.

119. Christiansen, "*Pacem in terris*: A Commentary."

120. Ibid.

121. Niebuhr, "*Pacem in Terris*: Two Views," 83.

122. Zizola, *Utopia of Pope John XXIII*.

123. Ernesto Balducci, *John: The Transitional Pope*, trans. Dorothy White (New York: McGraw-Hill, 1964), 2 (emphasis added).

124. Philippe Levillain, "Vatican II (Ecumenical Council of)," in *The Papacy: An Encyclopedia*, 3:1575.

125. Ibid., 3:1585.

126. *Unitatis redintegratio*, §1.

127. Walter Abbott, "Ecumenism," in *The Documents of Vatican II*, ed. Walter Abbott (New York: Guild Press, 1966), 339.

128. Vincent A. Yzermans, ed., *American Participation in the Second Vatican Council* (New York: Sheed & Ward, 1967), 569.

129. Oesterreicher, "Declaration on the Relationship," 1.

130. John Courtney Murray, "Religious Freedom," in Abbott, *Documents of Vatican II*, 673.

131. J. Bryan Hehir, "*Dignitatis Humanae* in the Pontificate of John Paul II," in *Religious Liberty: Paul VI and Dignitatis Humanae*, ed. John T. Ford (Brescia: Istituto Paolo VI, 1995), 170.

132. Murray, "Religious Freedom," 673.

133. Hebblethwaite, *John XXIII*, 229.

134. Levillain, "Vatican II," 1584.

135. *Lumen gentium*, chap. 2.

136. Ibid., chap. 7.

137. *Gaudium et spes*, §4 (emphasis added).

138. Abbott, *Documents of Vatican II*, 199 n. 1.

139. Ibid., 199 n. 2.

140. Dennis P. McCann, "Signs of the Times," in *The New Dictionary of Catholic Social Thought*, ed. Judith A. Dwyer (Collegeville, Minn.: Liturgical Press, 1994), 882.

141. John Courtney Murray, "Good Pope John: A Theologian's Tribute," *America* 108 (June 15, 1963): 855.

142. See the subtitle of Hebblethwaite, *John XXIII: Pope of the Century*.

143. McBrien, *Lives of the Popes*, 369.

144. Murray, "Good Pope John," 854 (emphasis added).

145. Alberigo, "John XXIII," 856 (emphasis added).

146. Murray, "Good Pope John," 854 (emphasis added).

147. Pavan, "Pacem in Terris," 52.

148. Murray, "Good Pope John," 855.

149. *Gaudium et spes*, §4.

150. Cardinal Suenens, sermon given on October 28, 1963.

[CHAPTER 6]

Gustavo Gutiérrez (b. 1928)

PAUL E. SIGMUND

Is liberation theology, which emerged in the midst of the Cold War, still relevant in the post–Cold War era? And is a discussion of Gustavo Gutiérrez, the leading architect of liberation theology, relevant in a volume devoted to modern Christian teachings on law, politics, and human nature?

The answer, on both counts, is yes. The approach of liberation theology to society and politics, and to the relation of the Bible to the contemporary world, has made a distinctive contribution to the teachings of modern Christianity. And liberation theology is still a relevant topic of study—despite the failure of the socialist systems that liberationists initially espoused as alternatives to capitalism, and despite the discrediting of the economic theory of dependency that formed an important component of its thinking. The rediscovery by Gustavo Gutiérrez and other liberation theologians of the special position of the poor in salvation history, their attempt to link the message of the Bible to contemporary social and economic problems, and their insistence that Christians have a duty to change "sinful structures" and to promote genuine liberation from all forms of oppression, all remain valid and valuable insights.

Initially, Gutiérrez and his liberationist followers described the legal and political system of capitalism as sinful and called for its replacement by socialism, which would end capitalist exploitation and oppression. Today, liberationists no longer believe that a socialist revolution will resolve the problems of the poor. But they continue to criticize the negative aspects of capitalist development, including, most recently, the effects on the poor of globalization and international economic relations and the international legal structures that support them. As far as human nature is concerned, Gutiérrez and the other liberation theologians initially hoped for a transformation of human relations as a result of a change in socioeconomic structures from capitalism to socialism. More recently, however, they have focused on a more biblically based awareness of the effects of sin on human behavior, especially that of the rich and powerful. Liberation theologians are still suspicious of the abstract and ideological character of much of the natural law tradition that has played a central part in Roman Catholic political and social thought. But they now give more emphasis to the links between Christianity and political freedom and are more appreciative of the positive role of constitutional democracy.

BIOGRAPHICAL AND INTELLECTUAL CONTEXT

Gustavo Gutiérrez is a Peruvian mestizo—that is, of mixed European and American Indian origin. He was born in Lima on June 8, 1928. He studied medicine and philosophy at universities in Lima and joined the priesthood of the archdiocese. As part of his training, he was sent to Europe to study philosophy and psychology at the Catholic University of Louvain, where he received a master's degree in 1955 for a thesis on Sigmund Freud. He continued his studies in theology at the Catholic University of Lyons in France but did not complete his doctorate; the university awarded him a doctoral degree in 1985, accepting a number of his books and articles in place of the dissertation.[1] In 1959–60 he also studied in Rome for a semester before returning to Lima to teach at the Catholic University.

In 1960 Gutiérrez became chaplain to the National Union of Catholic Students in Lima. During his studies in Louvain and Lyons, he had become acquainted with efforts to develop religious sociology and to encourage dialogue between Christianity and Marxism, but his real radicalization took place after his return to Peru. Living in a poor sector of Lima, he was confronted directly by the problems of underdevelopment and poverty. It was a time of increasing revolutionary fervor, influenced by Castro's adoption of Marxism in Cuba and the efforts of the Kennedy administration's Alliance for Progress to answer the challenge that Castro posed. Guerrilla movements emerged in Peru and in most parts of Latin America, and a wave of military coups swept the continent. In Brazil in the early 1960s, Catholics on the left, influenced by Paulo Freire's ideas of *concientizaçao* (consciousness-raising), organized Christian Base Communities among the poor to discuss the application of the Bible to their problems. The students and professors in the Latin American universities felt that radical measures were needed to combat poverty and underdevelopment in Latin America. Father Camilo Torres, a fellow student of Gutiérrez's at Louvain and a member of an elite Colombian family, returned from Europe to become chaplain to the students at the National University of Colombia. He organized a national reform movement, and, when that did not succeed, he joined a Marxist guerrilla group and was killed in a skirmish with the Colombian military in 1966.

Meanwhile, in Europe, the Second Vatican Council, meeting from 1962 to 1965, supported the involvement of the church in the modern world and endorsed ecumenical dialogue with other religions—and even with atheists. In 1967 Pope Paul VI published an encyclical, *Populorum Progressio*,[2] that attacked "the international imperialism of money"[3] and decried "situations whose injustice cries to heaven [when] whole populations destitute of necessities live in a state of dependence … [in which] recourse to violence, as a means to right these wrongs to human dignity, is a grave temptation."[4] However, the pope also criticized revolutionary solutions except in cases of "manifest, long-standing tyranny which would do great damage to fundamental personal rights."[5] The pope's reference to "dependence" seemed to give religious legitimization to the theory of *dependencia*, recently developed in Chile (by, among others, the future president of Brazil, Fernando Enrique Cardoso), which blamed Latin American underdevelopment on its dependent relationship with world capitalism.

In his discussions with other radicalized priests in ONIS, the National Organization for Social Research, which he had helped to found, as well as at theological encounters in several countries, Gutiérrez began to think and write about the relation of the church to poverty and revolution in Latin America. He first used the expression "theology of liberation" at an ONIS meeting in July 1968 in Chimbote, Peru, where he presented his criticisms of the inadequacies of the reformist development model and his arguments for the involvement of the church in radical structural change in Latin America. In September 1968 he attended the meeting of the Latin American Bishops Conference (CELAM) in Medellín, Colombia.[6] Its final documents spoke of a "deafening cry" of the people "asking their pastors for a liberation that reaches them from nowhere else"[7] and urged the church to give effective "preference to the poorest and most needy sectors."[8] The Conference's *Document on Justice* referred to *concientización* and called for the establishment of basic communities.[9] Its *Document on Peace,* of which Gutiérrez was reportedly the principal author, denounced the "sinful situation"[10] in many Latin American countries and their "dependence on a center of economic power, around which they gravitate."[11] In its most controversial paragraph, the document described the Latin American situation "in many instances" as one of "institutionalized violence" demanding "profoundly renovating transformations." The authors added, "We should not be surprised therefore that the 'temptation to violence' is surfacing in Latin America."[12] The Medellín conference thus incorporated and gave ecclesiastical endorsement to key phrases and concepts of liberation theology shortly after their initial formulation by Gutiérrez.

Gutiérrez gave a revised version of the Chimbote paper in Montevideo and at a conference in Switzerland in 1969. In 1970 it became available to the English-speaking world when the paper was published, under the title "Notes for a Theology of Liberation," in the Jesuit journal *Theological Studies*. In 1971 Gutiérrez published *Teologia de la Liberación*, the classic expression of liberation theology, the English translation of which, *A Theology of Liberation*, was published by Orbis Books in 1973.[13] The English version went through twelve printings, and a revised edition was published in 1988. Other Latin American theologians and religious writers in other parts of the world identified themselves with Gutiérrez's theological approach, and his book began to be studied in seminaries and universities around the world.

A RADICAL ALTERNATIVE

Why did a book by a hitherto unknown Peruvian priest receive such a response? Part of its success came from its timing. At a time of increasing dissatisfaction with the response of the developed nations—especially the United States—to the challenge of underdevelopment, liberation theology focused on the need for Christians to respond to the problem of poverty in what was later called "the Third World." It argued for a religiously based radicalism that offered an alternative to the reformism advocated by Christian Democratic and social democratic parties, as well as to the military dictatorships in Latin America that had taken power in the name of rapid development and anticommunism. That alternative was not described in detail, but it was clearly inspired by the socialist tradition, both in its criticisms of capitalism and as a source of an alternative model of development.

It would be a misunderstanding of Gutiérrez's approach, however, to see it simply as an argument for socialism. He argued, first, for a link between theology and lived experience (he used the Hegelian and Marxist term *praxis*), especially that of the poor, and defined liberation theology as "critical reflection on Christian praxis in the light of the Word."[14] Gutiérrez criticized the abstract character of the prevailing Thomist-influenced theology of Catholic seminaries and universities as remote from the problems of the modern world and as not sufficiently biblically based. He declared that God's word, as expressed in the Bible, is best understood by direct application to the day-to-day life of the poor. Through that process, he believed, it will be clear that the political and economic institutions in Latin America are oppressive and exploitative and that the church is obliged to commit itself to liberation, understood as radical institutional change. Both incremental reforms, such as those proposed by the church-influenced Christian Democratic parties of Latin America, and distinctions between the natural and supernatural "planes" of human experience, as argued by the French Catholic philosopher Jacques Maritain, are to be rejected. Neither approach, in Gutiérrez's views, was in keeping with the revolutionary and "integral" character of the Christian message.

It was not difficult for Gutiérrez to quote the Bible (which he began to do in the second half of the book) in support of the special responsibility of Christians to the poor. Isaiah 61 states that God's mission is one of liberation of the oppressed; and in Luke 4, Jesus begins his public life by reading this passage in the synagogue of Nazareth and announcing that he is the fulfillment of Isaiah's prophecy. In addition, the version of the Beatitudes in the Sermon on the Mount given in Luke 6 says, "Blessed are the poor," rather than the more familiar phrase of Matthew 5, "Blessed are the poor in spirit." Christ criticized the rich and powerful and compared the rich man's chances of salvation with the possibility of a camel passing through the eye of a needle (Luke 18:25). There are many similar passages—Gutiérrez's book has more than three hundred biblical quotations or citations—in both the Old Testament and the New Testament.

DEPENDENCY AND MARXISM

Gutiérrez, however, went beyond the claim that Christians should have special concern for the poor to the assertion that the church must reject the dominant political and economic system of "dependent capitalism." In support of his argument, he had to make another innovative claim for his method of doing theology—that it should make use of social science in the application of biblical understandings to contemporary life. He focused on the recently developed theory of *dependencia* to explain Latin American poverty and underdevelopment. He argued that Latin America is kept poor and underdeveloped because of its dependence on and exploitation by the developed countries. Gutiérrez linked dependency theory, as many of its proponents did, to Marxist-influenced ideas of class conflict. Dependence, he said, must be understood "within the framework of the worldwide class struggle.... There can be authentic development for Latin America only if there is liberation from the domination exercised by the great capitalist countries, and especially by the most powerful, the United States of America."[15] Later in the book, in a section that was omitted in the 1988 revised edition, Gutiérrez argued that the recognition of the class struggle implies "a will to abolish its causes ... to build a socialist society, more just, free, and human, and not a society of superficial and false reconciliation and equality." "To deny the fact of class struggle," he continued, "is really to put oneself on the side of the dominant sectors.... To love all men does not mean avoiding confrontations; it does not mean preserving a fictitious harmony. Universal love is that which in solidarity with the oppressed seeks also to liberate the oppressors from their own power, from their ambition, and from their selfishness."[16]

The linkage of dependence theory to the class struggle and the replacement of capitalism by socialism gave Gutiérrez's theory a more distinctly Marxist flavor at the outset than in later reformulations. Yet Gutiérrez's theory differed in important respects from classical Marxism. Gutiérrez, of course, rejected Marx's atheism. The class struggle for him is between oppressors and oppressed rather than the proletariat and bourgeoisie, and revolutionary violence is not the only solution. Yet Gutiérrez's theory retained Marx's emphasis on the centrality of economic causation, as well as his belief that socialism will end exploitation by eliminating the class struggle. A Latin American writing in the 1960s could have easily identified the social sciences with dependency theory and Marxism, since the few social science courses available in Latin American universities, mainly sociology or radical economics, were dominated by Marxist or dependency approaches.

Gutiérrez did not explicitly discuss the role of law in dependent capitalism, but his initial formulation of liberation theology, with its sharp dichotomy between oppressor and oppressed and its conflictive view of human society, would have been likely to consider law as yet another expression of class domination. Class domination would not exist, however, under socialism. The change from "the capitalistic mode of production to the socialistic mode" involves moving to "one oriented towards a society in which man can begin to live freely and humanly. He will have controlled nature, created the conditions for a socialized production of wealth, done away with private acquisition of excessive wealth, and established socialism."[17]

Rights, too, have a class basis. For Gutiérrez, group rights—in particular, the right of the poor to be freed from oppression—trump individual rights, especially the right to property. He left vague the details of the socialism that he advocated, such as the nature of a socialist legal system and the relation of individual and group rights. He rejected the writings of Jacques Maritain, the principal proponent of a religiously based theory of human rights, because of the association of Maritain's work with Christian Democratic "reformism" and "developmentalism." At the very time when the spread of military dictatorships in Latin America made the defense of the rights of the person most necessary, the dialectical and experiential approach of liberation theology, as well as its suspicion of abstract theory as ideological in character, made it difficult for liberation theology to develop a theory of human rights. A more explicit rejection of the human rights tradition was the claim by the Uruguayan liberation theologian Juan Luis Segundo that "what are called 'human rights' are certain freedoms particularly useful to the middle classes."[18]

A similar overemphasis on class analysis characterizes Gutiérrez's concept of human nature. The opening sentence of A Theology of Liberation speaks of "men and women committed to the process of liberation."[19] But the emphasis of the book on the economic impediments to liberation under capitalism rather than on cultural factors such as, for example, Latin American *machismo* seemed to imply that, as in the case of Marx's description of the classless society, the principal obstacle to social harmony is the class struggle.

Gutiérrez did not deny the effects of the continuing reality of sin. In the second chapter of A Theology of Liberation, he enumerated three approaches to liberation—the liberation of oppressed people and social classes, freedom as an historical process leading to "the creation of a new man and a qualitatively different society," and liberation from sin, which is "the ultimate root ... of all injustice and oppression."[20] He insisted, however, that all three are interdependent and did not discuss the ways in which man's sinfulness might reassert itself in the new society. Later in the book Gutiérrez claimed that socialism "represents the most fruitful and far-reaching approach," although it could take different forms, including the "indigenous socialism" advocated by the Peruvian writer José Carlos Mariátegui. Socialism, Gutiérrez said, will produce a "qualitatively different society" and "the building up of a *new man*," "free of all servitude," as described in the writings of Che Guevara.[21]

Similar statements appeared in Gutiérrez's other writings. In an essay in The Power of the Poor in History, which was published in Spanish in 1979 but originally written in 1973, he wrote: "Only by overcoming a society divided into classes, only by installing a political power at the service of the great popular majorities, only by eliminating the private appropriation of the wealth created by human toil, can we build the foundation of a more just society."[22] The Power of the Poor was published in English in 1983. In 1986, in a book critical of liberation theology, Michael Novak took this passage as representative of liberation theology's Marxist orientation, although later in the book he admitted that Gutiérrez had become "less Marxist" in more recent years.[23] In 1988, ten years after it was written, another sentence from *The Power of the Poor*—"God loves the poor with a special love because they are poor and not necessarily because they are good"[24]—was attacked by another critic of liberation theology as contrary to the teachings of the Bible.[25]

There are further instances of Marxist influence in the 1970s. In 1975, Gutiérrez replied to Canadian theologian Gregory Baum's criticisms that he seemed to think that Marxism was the only valid form of social analysis: "The marginated nonpersons have a way of understanding history and their social situation (social sciences, Marxist analysis, socialist path) that begins to be illuminative for the thinking through of faith in our day.... We must recognize our enemies in history; we must live our faith in this different commitment." In 1977 he wrote, "The popular movement is also the locus of encounter of the social sciences and Marxist analysis with theology.... The project of crafting a new and different society includes the creation of new human persons as well, who must be progressively liberated from whatever enslaves them."[26]

DIFFERENCES FROM MARXISM

To focus simply on the Marxist aspects of Gutiérrez's earlier writings, as Michael Novak and others were to do, is to miss important elements of his theory. One of them is his belief in the importance of the view from below, of the lived experience of the poor and its relation to revelation, the Word of God, as contained in the Bible. Gutiérrez and other liberation theologians saw the Basic Ecclesial Community structure that emerged in Brazil in the early 1960s as the appropriate place for the type of reflection endorsed by liberation theology. There were estimates—probably exaggerated—that as many as 100,000 Christian Base Communities were organized in Brazil, and, with the encouragement of committed priests and nuns, similar groups developed in Chile, Colombia, Peru, and Central America. Those in Brazil provided leadership training for the poor, some of whom became active in national politics during and after the transition to democracy in the 1980s. (One of the members of the base communities became a cabinet minister in the Brazilian government in 2003.) In a few cases there were conflicts with the church hierarchy, but, at a time of increasing competition with Evangelical and Pentecostal groups, the base communities provided group support and reinforced religious commitment for workers, peasants, and shantytown dwellers in many countries in Latin America.

A second point against those who see liberation theology as a kind of Christianized Marxism is the important role of the Bible and spiritual reflection in liberation theology. In 1974 Gutiérrez coedited a book entitled

Mystical and Political Dimensions of the Christian Faith and contributed a deeply spiritual article to it. His more recent publications became more biblical in their approach and their content. He never substituted political for religious commitment, as some of his followers were to do, and since his primary concern was with the poor, not revolution, he was aware of the danger of transforming religion into revolutionary ideology. In 1973, for example, he did not participate in the Christians for Socialism meeting in Santiago, organized by supporters of Chile's socialist government. (The final document of the meeting did not contain a single reference to the Bible or the social teaching of the church, but quoted Che Guevara and called for a "strategic alliance between Marxists and Christians" as well as a "revolutionary praxis of the proletariat" and "the takeover of power by the exploited masses."[27])

By the mid-1970s, liberation theology had become a worldwide movement, but in the process the salience of Marxist analysis declined as feminist liberation movements and black liberation theology gave more emphasis to sexism and racism than to capitalism as sources of oppression. In the case of Latin America, liberation theologians recognized that male domination and discrimination against blacks and Indians were obstacles to liberation that were principally cultural rather than economic in origin.

The mid-1970s were also a time when guerrilla movements and military coups produced a political polarization that increased the appeal of calls for radical change, especially when those calls drew on the Christian tradition. Leftist governments in Chile, Argentina, Bolivia, and Peru were overthrown, and guerrilla groups and those suspected of supporting them were hunted down and exterminated, while in Uruguay and Brazil military governments imprisoned, tortured, and murdered those accused of leftist tendencies. In 1979, however, the prospects for the left improved. An alliance of Marxists and Christians in the Sandinista movement defeated Nicaragua's dictator, Anastasio Somoza, and in El Salvador and Guatemala, guerrilla movements involving Christians and Marxists were becoming increasingly successful.

THE VATICAN STATEMENTS

The new political relevance of liberation theology aroused the interest of the Vatican, where it already had strong critics. In May 1979 the newly elected pope, John Paul II, flew to Mexico to attend the Conference of Latin American Bishops at Puebla, where the battle lines for and against liberation theology had already been drawn. Gutiérrez had not been invited to be a theological advisor (*peritus*) as he had been at the Medellín Conference in 1968. However, the liberation theologians met near the building where the bishops were assembled and kept in close communication with those inside who sympathized with their views. At a press conference on his plane, the pope had signaled his attitude by distinguishing between true liberation theology and the false politicization of theology, and concluding his remarks, "Theology of liberation, but which one?"[28] At the Puebla meeting he delivered a speech denouncing attempts to link Jesus to the class struggle and to establish a parallel church of the poor. However, he also argued for a "Christian conception of liberation" that recognizes the need for a more just and equitable distribution of goods both nationally and internationally, and he criticized the "ever increasing wealth of the rich at the expense of the ever increasing poverty of the poor." The Final Document of the Puebla Conference had something for everybody. It condemned the politicization of theology and the "popular church" but endorsed Christian Base Communities and committed the Latin American church to "the preferential option for the poor"—a major element in the program of the liberation theologians.

As liberation theology played an increasing role in justifying Marxist-Christian cooperation in Nicaragua and Christian involvement with the guerrilla movements in El Salvador and Guatemala, the Vatican weighed in again in 1974 and 1976. First came the *Instruction on Certain Aspects of "Liberation Theology,"* issued by the Congregation for the Doctrine of the Faith. The document, while recognizing that there were many varieties of liberation theology, warned against "concepts uncritically borrowed from Marxist ideology" and declared that Marxism's commitment to the class struggle, its denial of human rights, and its "partisan conception of the truth" are incompatible with Christian doctrine.[29]

The Instruction also promised a further document on the subject. When it was published in April 1986, the *Instruction on Christian Freedom and Liberation* committed the universal church to a "love of preference for the poor"—thus avoiding the partisan tones of the "preferential option." It also endorsed the Christian Base Communities—provided they were in communion with the local and universal church. The 1986 instruction denounced those who propagated the myth of revolution and warned that a "purely earthly plan of salvation" can lead to "new forms of slavery." The more positive tone of the second Instruction was reinforced a week later in a message from the pope to the Brazilian bishops that endorsed a "correct and necessary theology of liberation … in full fidelity to church doctrine, attentive to the preferential but not excluding or exclusive love for the poor."[30]

Gutiérrez greeted the second instruction with relief and hailed it as the beginning of a new positive period in the relations of Latin America (by which he meant Latin American liberation theologians) and Europe (by which he meant the Vatican). He cited the two instructions, especially that of 1986, many times in chapter 3 of his book *The Truth Shall Make You Free*. In this chapter, Gutiérrez said that the second instruction's criticisms of modern individualism needed to be deepened by drawing on the "faith experience of the poor" in Latin America. And he continued to emphasize the need for a "radical change of the socio-economic order" in Latin America. But Gutiérrez also insisted that this new society must include personal liberty, which he described as "a necessary condition for any authentic political liberation."[31] Later in the chapter he listed the two requirements of human society as justice and liberty and, in a discussion of property, he wrote, "Many think that a healthy balance between private ownership, social ownership, and state ownership would be a good way of meeting and promoting these two requirements."[32] In a 1986 article, published in Peru, he also condemned the "terrorist violence" of the Peruvian Shining Path guerrilla group by concluding: "It is necessary to defend democratic life, however imperfect and fragile, which makes it possible to propose and discuss alternative formulas for the construction of a different kind of society."[33]

GUTIÉRREZ'S DEFENSE

Gutiérrez originally wrote the second chapter of *The Truth Shall Make You Free*, entitled "Theology and the Social Sciences" in connection with an investigation of his orthodoxy by the bishops' conference in Peru in 1984. The chapter amounted to a point-by-point refutation of the charge that liberation theology is a form of Christian Marxism. Insisting that Marxist tools of analysis continue to be utilized in contemporary social science, Gutiérrez argued that dependence theory, which was a major source of the social science he used in *A Theology of Liberation*, can be differentiated from classical Marxism and that it seemed, at the time, to be the best explanation of Latin American reality. He rejected what he called the exclusivity (that is, the reductionism) and the atheism of Marxism, and he argued against the direct derivation of specific party programs from theology.

The most decisive break with his earlier writings came in the book's explicit rejection of Marx's reduction of all social conflict to the class struggle. Gutiérrez observed that discrimination based on race, culture, and gender is also an important source of oppression. He rejected economic determinism as completely alien to liberation theology and argued that his lengthy discussion of the class struggle in his original 1971 book was an effort to explore the tensions between commitment to the poor and the universality of Christian love. Yet he continued to insist that there are some issues on which neutrality is impossible for a Christian. He cited the Nazi dictatorship as an example and argued that "the Latin American experience of wretchedness and oppression" may be a similar case.

Marxist themes were also absent from two other books written by Gutiérrez and published in Spanish and English in the mid-1980s. *We Drink from Our Own Wells: The Spiritual Journey of a People*, published in English in 1984, is "an extended meditation on the spirituality of liberation." At the beginning, Gutiérrez stated that since the first days of the theology of liberation, the question of spirituality (specifically the following of Jesus) has been of deep concern. But he admitted in a footnote that, despite his intention to develop the theme more fully, "only now has it been possible for me to do so."[34] He cited biblical descriptions of "the way" practiced by early Christians to argue that "'walking according to the Spirit' is an activity undertaken within a community, a people on the move" and that Christ is our way both to the Father and to each other. Thus a spiritual approach must be a collective adventure.[35]

In 1986 Gutiérrez published *On Job: God-Talk and the Suffering of the Innocent,* an extended meditation on the Book of Job that sought to explain the love of God in situations in which the innocent suffer and to understand Job's experience of moving from a comfortable life to sharing the suffering of the poor. In the introduction to the book, Gutiérrez insisted that theology is an activity that must be preceded by silent contemplation and practice. The book has more than four hundred references to the Bible, and no references to Marxism or dependency theory.

THE REVISED EDITION

In 1988, after twelve printings of the 1973 edition, a revised English translation of *A Theology of Liberation* was published.[36] Gutiérrez wrote a new introduction in which he again emphasized the theological importance of the oppression of racial and cultural minorities and of women. Yet despite his criticism of what he called "the simplistic position we were perhaps in danger of initially adopting in analyzing the situation of poverty," he continued to speak of the structural causes of poverty—in particular, the economic and political relations of the wealthy and powerful nations to the poorer and weaker countries. In support of his position, he quoted from recent encyclicals of Pope John Paul II.

The revised edition included a number of responses to the criticisms of Gutiérrez's earlier writings. The new introduction explained that the preferential option for the poor "denies all exclusiveness and seeks rather to call attention to those who are the first—though not the only ones—with whom

we should be in solidarity."[37] The introduction also quoted at length from
the 1986 letter of Pope John Paul II to the Brazilian bishops in which the
pope endorsed liberation theology. A significant change in the new version
was the replacement of the section in the 1973 edition headed "Christian
Brotherhood and Class Struggle" by a more general discussion of "Faith
and Social Conflict." Gutiérrez excised his earlier references to the class
struggle and instead quoted at length from the discussion of "The Conflict
Between Labor and Capital in the Present History" in Pope John Paul II's
1988 encyclical on work, *Laborem Exercens*, in order to argue that that the
universality of Christian love does not permit the Christian to remain neutral in the face of poverty. Gutiérrez omitted a footnote in the 1973 edition
from the French philosopher Louis Althusser that called for Christians to
join the ranks of the proletariat. He also shortened a lengthy passage from
Marx that called for the dictatorship of the proletariat and the establishment of the classless society, and followed the abbreviated quotation with
the statement that "the determinist approach based on economic factors
is completely alien to the kind of social analysis that supplies a framework
for the theology of liberation." Gutiérrez then added a new footnote that
quoted from his earlier statement that the central issue for Christians is
not the class struggle but how Christians are to live their faith, hope, and
love in the face of the conflicts analyzed by the social sciences.[38]

Many factors influenced the shift in Gutiérrez's position. He was after all
a priest and not a politician, and more comfortable with discussions of the
Bible than of Marx. Latin America was beginning to open up to democracy. In Gutiérrez's native Peru, now under an elected civilian government, a
brutal Marxist insurgency, Shining Path, slaughtered innocent peasants in
the name of the revolution. With its members suffering torture, disappear-
ances, and murder by military dictatorships, the Latin American left had
begun to rethink the notion that bourgeois constitutional democracy was
nothing more than a facade for capitalist exploitation. Russian repression in
Poland and Afghanistan, as well as increasing evidence that Castro's Cuba
was able to survive only with substantial infusions of Soviet military and
economic aid, led to doubts about the feasibility of the socialist alternative.
The Sandinista government in Nicaragua seemed for a while to represent a
positive example for the liberationists, but even that country began to betray evidence of government corruption and popular dissatisfaction. The
Final Document of the Latin American Theologians, presented at a meeting of Third World theologians in December 1986, gave more attention
than heretofore to the importance of democracy and described "forging a
new democracy with the participation of the majorities" as a first challenge
for liberation theologians. The new document noted that there was a new

positive evaluation of democracy on the part of the popular sectors "as a space in which they can carry out various popular projects."[39]

NEW THEMES IN THE 1990S

In May 1991 Pope John Paul II published *Centesimus annus,* an encyclical on the occasion of the hundredth anniversary of Pope Leo XIII's *Rerum novarum,* the founding document of modern Catholic social thought. Commenting on the recent collapse of the Soviet Union and of the economic system that it represented, the pope asked whether this meant that the capitalist system was the only alternative for countries in the developing world. His reply, recognizing the "fundamental and positive role" of business, private property, and what he preferred to call "the free economy," was taken by the *Wall Street Journal* and other observers in the West to constitute a significant departure from the criticisms of capitalism in earlier papal writings. In the next sentence, however, the pope added that the free enterprise system should be set within a "juridical framework" that puts it at the service of ethical and religious values and of "human freedom in its totality."[40] Gutiérrez's comments on the encyclical did not even mention the pope's endorsement of the market system but rather argued that the pope had recognized "the necessary social dimension of freedom." Gutiérrez also quoted with approval the pope's reference in the same section to the danger of the "spread of a radical capitalist ideology" that refuses even to consider the realities of the marginalization and exploitation of the poor.[41]

Gutiérrez himself had embarked on a new project, a study of the writings of Bartolomé de Las Casas, the sixteenth-century Spanish bishop who defended the rights of the Indians against their Spanish conquerors. He published his study in Spanish in 1992 to coincide with the five hundredth anniversary of the arrival of Columbus in the New World. It was translated into English in 1993 as *Las Casas: In Search of the Poor of Jesus Christ.*[42] The book develops at length Las Casas's ideas about religious freedom, the equality of the Indians, and their right to govern themselves. In addition, it draws comparisons between the oppression of the Indians in the sixteenth century and in present-day Peru.

In the 1990s Gutiérrez continued to discuss current international and national economic relations from the point of view of their impact on the poor. Following the meeting of the Latin American bishops in Santo Domingo in 1992, he commented on their final declaration and endorsed their criticisms of Latin American democracy as more formal than real, as well as their assertion that poverty and injustice were in themselves violations of basic human rights. He joined the bishops' criticism of neoliberalism—a doctrine that, among other things, espouses laissez-faire economics—as a cause of the increasing poverty of the masses in Latin American cities and of the crushing burden of debt owed by less developed countries.[43]

In a 1992 seminar in Lima, Gutiérrez delivered a paper on "Liberation and Development" that marked a further movement away from dependency theory. While stating that the theory had been an important tool of social analysis "in the early years of theological reflection in Latin America," Gutiérrez admitted that he was now aware of its shortcomings, notably its overemphasis on the external causes of development. Changes in the international realities of globalization and transnational capitalism as well as improved Latin American understandings of those realities, he concluded, have rendered dependency theory an ineffective tool of social analysis.

GUTIÉRREZ'S LEGACY: LIBERATION THEOLOGY TODAY

By the 1990s Gutiérrez was well known at American universities. He lectured regularly in summer programs at Boston College and was a visiting professor at Brown University and at the Princeton Theological Seminary. He received honorary degrees from Harvard University, Southern Methodist University, Holy Cross College, and the University of Toronto. His writings were collected into an anthology,[44] and his spirituality and mysticism were analyzed and compared with that of Simone Weil.[45] In the year 2000, after the appointment of a conservative archbishop over the diocese of Lima, Gutiérrez joined the Dominican order, to which Bishop Las Casas had belonged, and became a professor of theology at the University of Notre Dame.

The distancing of Gutiérrez's thought from Marxism and dependency theory has not meant that liberation theology has abandoned its radical criticism of the rich and powerful. In the late 1980s it inspired Father Jean-Bertrand Aristide to lead the poor against the military dictatorship in Haiti. The influence of liberation theology also led Bishop Samuel Ruíz to support the 1994 Indian uprising in Chiapas, Mexico. In Brazil, the church-supported Organization of the Landless (Sim Terra) has continued to press for land reform, and the base communities have provided leadership training to future political activists. Internationally, the legal and economic system is still dominated by the wealthy countries, although in at least one case, the Jubilee Movement, a religiously inspired worldwide group favoring the cancellation of Third World debt, has persuaded the lending agencies and countries to grant limited debt relief to the poorest countries.

Moving away from class analysis, Gutiérrez's later writings in particular emphasize the central position of God's love for all, especially for the poor, as the inspiration for the struggle against oppression. Again, however, what the liberation theologian Juan Luis Segundo has called the "hermeneutic of suspicion" is likely to characterize the attitude of liberation theology to reforms from above, preferring a solution to oppression that comes from below.

Those reforms are now less likely to take place through revolution, and liberation theology no longer proposes socialism as the solution to poverty. Gutiérrez's more recent writings are more explicitly spiritual, but they still criticize the injustices of contemporary economic and political structures, particularly in their effects on the poor. He still makes radical criticisms of the status quo and of national and international economic inequality. His teachings and writings continue to remind Christians that a central element of the message of the Bible is its criticism of the rich and its love for the poor. His books are still read, and his teachings heard, even if their political impact is not as direct as it has been in the past. He has not changed the world, but he has changed our way of thinking about the Christian message.

NOTES

1. The dissertation defense appears as chapter 1 of Gustavo Gutiérrez, *The Truth Shall Make You Free: Confrontations* (Maryknoll, N.Y.: Orbis Books, 1990).
2. The papal and conciliar documents quoted in this article are available in David J. O'Brien and Thomas A. Shannon, eds., *Catholic Social Thought: The Documentary Heritage* (Maryknoll, N.Y.: Orbis Books, 1992).
3. *Populorum Progressio* (1967), §26, 246.
4. Ibid., §30, 247.
5. Ibid., §31, 247.
6. The major documents of the Medellín conference, including those quoted here, are published in Alfred T. Hennelly, ed., *Liberation Theology: A Documentary History* (Maryknoll, N.Y.: Orbis Books, 1990), 89–119.
7. *Document on the Poverty of the Church*, §2, 114.
8. Ibid., §9, 116.
9. *Document on Justice*, §20, 104.
10. *Document on Peace*, §1, 106.
11. Ibid., §8, 107.
12. Ibid., §16, 110.
13. Gustavo Gutiérrez, *A Theology of Liberation: History, Politics, and Salvation*, ed. and trans. Sister Caridad Inda and John Eagleson (Maryknoll, N.Y.: Orbis Books, 1973).
14. Ibid., 13.
15. Ibid., 87–88.
16. Ibid., 274–275.
17. Ibid., 30.
18. Quoted in Paul E. Sigmund, *Liberation Theology at the Crossroads: Democracy or Revolution?* (New York: Oxford University Press, 1990), 232.

19. Gutiérrez, *A Theology of Liberation*, ix.

20. Ibid., 36–37.

21. Ibid., 90–91.

22. Gustavo Gutiérrez, *The Power of the Poor in History: Selected Writings*, trans. Robert R. Barr (New York: Orbis Books, 1983), 46.

23. Michael Novak, *Will It Liberate? Questions About Liberation Theology* (New York: Paulist Press, 1986), 167, 265.

24. Gutiérrez, *Power of the Poor*, 116.

25. James Burtchaell, "How Authentically Christian Is Liberation Theology?" *Review of Politics* 59 (Spring 1988): 264–281. Gutiérrez argues in reply (personal interview, December 13, 2002) that he does not believe in what theologians call "the hermeneutical privilege of the poor," but only that they offer an important perspective in understanding the application of the gospel to the contemporary world.

26. Quoted in Sigmund, *Liberation Theology*, 86–67.

27. Translated in Sigmund, *Liberation Theology*, 46–47.

28. *New York Times*, January 30, 1979.

29. Quoted in Sigmund, *Liberation Theology*, 161.

30. Quotations are taken from the analysis of the two documents in Sigmund, *Liberation Theology*, 167–169.

31. Gutiérrez, *The Truth Shall Make You Free*, 113, 132, 135.

32. Ibid., 137.

33. Translated in Sigmund, *Liberation Theology*, 171.

34. Gustavo Gutiérrez, *We Drink from Our Own Wells: The Spiritual Journey of a People*, trans. Mathew J. O'Connell (Maryknoll, N.Y.: Orbis Books, 1984), 1, 138.

35. Ibid., 89.

36. Gustavo Gutiérrez, *A Theology of Liberation: History, Politics, and Salvation*, trans. Sister Caridad Inda and John Eagleson, rev. ed. (Maryknoll, N.Y.: Orbis Books, 1988).

37. Ibid., xxv.

38. Ibid., 249.

39. Quoted in Sigmund, *Liberation Theology*, 175.

40. *Centesimus annus* (1991), §42, 471.

41. Translated from Gustavo Gutiérrez et al., *De la Rerum novarum a la Centesimus annus* (Lima: Universidad del Pacifico, 1992), 24–25.

42. Gustavo Gutiérrez, *Las Casas: In Search of the Poor of Jesus Christ*, trans. Robert R. Barr (Maryknoll, N.Y.: Orbis Books, 1993).

43. Gustavo Gutiérrez, *The Density of the Present: Selected Writings* (Maryknoll, N.Y.: Orbis Books, 1999).

44. James B. Nickoloff, ed., *Gustavo Gutiérrez: Essential Writings* (Minneapolis: Fortress Press, 1996).

45. Alexander Nava, *The Mystical and Prophetic Thought of Simone Weil and Gustavo Gutiérrez* (Albany: State University of New York Press, 2001).

[CHAPTER 7]

Dorothy Day (1897–1980)

DAVID GREGORY

Dorothy Day, perhaps the most important Catholic in the history of the church in the United States, lived out a call to "divine obedience"—that is, civil disobedience—throughout her life. She put into practice the adage that if one truly gives to God what belongs to God, not much should remain to give to Caesar.[1] She was a champion for peace and a deep critic of materialism. An enthusiast of the great Russian novelists, she believed that the world would be saved by beauty.[2]

Day was an anarchist and member of the Wobblies, the International Workers of the World.[3] She never joined the Communist Party, but her principles and her activism grew from the social, the communal, and the personal and always emphasized the dignity of the individual person. Like St. Francis of Assisi, she endeavored to see Christ in every person.[4] In her late twenties, Day became a Catholic. She was radical in her social action and orthodox in her theology. She appreciated the moral lessons of great literature, which supplemented her groundwork of daily prayer, scripture reading, and the Holy Sacrifice of the Mass.[5]

In light of these facets of Day's life, her relationship to law, politics, and society carries much that is both interesting and problematic. Dorothy Day fervently practiced the two great biblical commandments, love of God and love of neighbor.[6] She believed, however, that much of the secular law in the materialist and militarist economy of the United States is unjust and, indeed, contradicts the law of God written in the human heart. Day was a zealous devotee of God's law, but she had little use for anything that impeded the Law of Love.

Day first achieved fame as a journalist. In 1933, while living in New York in the depths of the Great Depression, she cofounded the *Catholic Worker* newspaper as a deliberate alternative to the *Daily Worker* newspaper of the Communist Party.[7] She concurrently initiated the Catholic Worker movement, which opened "houses of hospitality" throughout the United States, Canada, and Europe. These sites were established to provide shelter for the homeless population and special care for the psychologically disabled.

Dorothy Day's personal life of special solidarity with the poor inspired many, including Trappist monk Thomas Merton; Cesar Chavez, president of the United Farm Workers Union; Robert Coles, the Harvard University medical professor; and the single most famous "alumnus" of the *Catholic Worker* movement to date, the socialist Michael Harrington,[8] whose classic book *The Other America* served as inspiration for President Lyndon Johnson's "War on Poverty."[9]

Throughout her life, Dorothy Day's primary witness took place through living out the precepts of the Gospel of St. Matthew, practicing corporal works of mercy for the poor and the homeless, standing in solidarity with workers, and, perhaps most important, working unfailingly for peace. When necessary, she practiced civil disobedience and, in the spirit of St. Paul, went to jail. Her theology applied directly to her actions. Although Day was an engaging thinker and wrote prolifically—her corpus includes essays and articles in the *Catholic Worker* newspaper, an autobiography, and other books of essays and reflections—she was not an abstract theoretician or academic theologian. Her theology grew from her involvement with the daily Mass, the sacraments, and the scriptures, and not from esoteric speculations.

These broad themes manifested themselves in her life of activism for peace, her opposition to war and materialism, her solidarity with workers, and her personalist emphasis on the dignity of the human being.

BIOGRAPHY

The life of Dorothy May Day began on November 8, 1897, in Bath Beach, Brooklyn, New York, and ended eighty-three years later on November 29, 1980. Day's early years were anything but those of a model Catholic. Like St. Augustine, she spent much of her youth indulging in the offerings of the material world.[10] She was a hedonist who engaged in love affairs with many men, had an abortion, attempted suicide, experienced two failed marriages, and became the unmarried mother of a daughter.[11]

Day's family of origin was not easy to be part of. Day and her family usually lived in poverty, primarily because of the inability of her father, John I. Day, to find regular work, a situation that forced the family to relocate a number of times.[12] John Day's only true loves were the racetrack and alcohol, and he uprooted his family constantly in order to search for a permanent position writing about horses and horseracing.[13] Dorothy Day and her father were never close, and only later in their lives were they able to treat each other with civility.[14] In contrast, Day, especially during her early adulthood, was very close to her mother, Grace Satterlee Day. Dorothy Day later pointed out that her mother, though deprived of many material items, enjoyed the little things in life. Neither Day's mother, an Episcopalian, nor her father, a Congregationalist, attended church services or took any steps to bring religion into their children's lives. Day and her siblings were not baptized as infants. Though she was eventually baptized and confirmed in the Episcopal Church, Dorothy Day's connection with Christianity proved to be weak during her teenage years.[15]

In the fall of 1914, Day matriculated into the University of Illinois at Urbana,[16] where her grades befit a student without distinction. Her entrance into college marked the beginning of a period of further distancing from spirituality, and yet her college years became a time of enlightenment about social concerns. She was stirred by injustice, which she believed to be the true human concern, and she looked to Marxism to provide answers for the problems presented by injustice.[17]

When Day left the University of Illinois in June 1916, she was a different person from the impressionable, naive, and relatively apathetic young woman who had entered college two years before. She had developed a passion for a relatively new and radical movement, socialism, and completely ignored or dismissed two very traditional institutions, namely religion and formal education.[18] The nineteen-year-old Day headed to New York City. She received her first opportunity as a journalist with the socialist paper *The Call*, a sister paper to *The Masses*. Perhaps Day's first article offered an omen of future events, for in it she chronicled her attempt to live for a month on five dollars per week.[19]

When the United States entered World War I, Day began appearing at Columbia University student war protests.[20] She resigned from *The Call*, began working for *The Masses*, and in the summer of 1917 took up residence in Greenwich Village. From 1917 to 1924, most of Day's friends and associates either lived in or were intellectually or culturally connected with Greenwich Village, which had become the wellspring of a new vision of life in America, divorced from any established moral order. The most prominent of these associates was the playwright Eugene O'Neill. In 1918, Day began working for *The Liberator*, which succeeded *The Masses* and became the American voice of the Russian Revolution. Day also enrolled in a nurse's training course in response to her need to do something for her fellow human beings. Day later said of this period of her life, "Though I felt the strong, irresistible attraction to good ... there was also ... a deliberate choosing of evil."[21]

It was during this time that she met and became infatuated with Lionel Moise. But Moise soon ended their brief romance, and the breakup threw Day into a massive depression that resulted in a suicide attempt. Thereafter, she and Moise had romantic interludes, and Day became pregnant in 1919. When Moise refused to marry her, she decided to terminate the pregnancy.[22]

In 1920, only months after her tragic romance with Moise ended, Day "married a man on the rebound."[23] Her short-lived marriage to Barkeley Tobey was a disaster.[24] In the summer of 1921, Day left him and traveled to Chicago in an unsuccessful attempt to win Moise back. While there, she became a member of the International Workers of the World (the "Wobblies"),[25] and was jailed, for the first time, in a Red Scare–era raid on the Wobbly rooming house where she had sought hospitality.[26] Her presence, along with Mae Craemer, another jilted lover of Moise, gave the police the opportunity to raid the house on the pretense of arresting them for prostitution.[27] The confluence of her realization that no Edenic future with Moise was possible and her firsthand experience of the state's punishment of dissenters reawakened her commitment to radicalism. Flush with royalties from the publication of her first book, *The Eleventh Virgin* (1924), she left Chicago for New Orleans, where she did investigative reporting for the *Item* on the city's libertine dancehalls.

Upon her return to New York City in early April 1924, Day reunited with some old friends, who subsequently introduced her to Forster Batterham. A year later, the two were joined in a common-law marriage.[28] The aloof and inarticulate Forster, an English anarchist and biologist, embodied none of the ideals that Day admired. During the winter of 1925, she spent much of her time socializing and indulging with her many friends. She bought a fishing shack on the shore of Staten Island, where the seclusion offered by this more rustic existence allowed her to focus upon her personal idea of God's handiwork, namely nature. It was at this time that Day began to pray informally.[29]

In the beginning of June 1926, Day discovered that she was again pregnant. Batterham found the prospects of fatherhood and family life extremely unattractive; he deeply resented the pregnancy as well as Day's newfound faith in religion.[30] The birth of Tamar Theresa Day in March 1927 simultaneously enhanced Day's working-class consciousness and brought her closer to the church. Day's determination to have Tamar baptized finalized her own commitment to established religion, and her choice of Catholicism reflected her desire to combine her passion for helping the less fortunate with her faith.[31] Years later, in recounting the resolve she had begun to feel after Tamar's baptism, she stated, "I had become convinced that I would become a Catholic."[32] For Day, the Roman Catholic Church was the church of the working poor, and as a marked contrast to her earlier experience with the more patrician elements of the Episcopal Church, it provided her with a vehicle to help those in need.[33] When the August 1927 execution of Sacco and Vanzetti induced in Forster a catatonic state, the rift between them was complete and Day left him the following December.[34]

Day later attributed her introduction to Peter Maurin, on December 9, 1932, to direct providential intervention.[35] George Shuster, the editor of *Commonweal* magazine, a publication by liberal lay Catholics, had suggested that Day and Maurin meet. Maurin was one of twenty-two children of a strong family of Catholic peasants from southern France. He received his education from the Christian Brothers before his emigration to Canada; two years later, now in his forties, Maurin emigrated illegally to the United States, where he held a series of itinerant jobs.[36] He deeply believed in both the dignity of the worker and the dignity of labor;[37] most importantly, Maurin believed in the practice of personalism.[38] He took seriously Jesus' statement that in loving one's neighbor one fulfills the second of the two greatest commandments, and Maurin felt that love of neighbor could best be achieved by the renewal of the Christian community.[39] He became Day's tutor in applied Catholic theology and in the hard, daily practice of personalism. With Maurin's entrance into her life, Day began the task that would be the primary focus of her life: the creation and direction of the Catholic Worker movement.

During the 1960s and 1970s, the natural consequences of age, combined with depression due to the deaths of so many of her early friends, began to limit Day's practice of advocacy; her physical condition particularly made it difficult for her to continue her work. Her last major action of political resistance and solidarity took place in August 1973, when she traveled to California to join Cesar Chavez's United Farm Workers' protest.[40] There she was arrested during a peaceful march on behalf of workers' rights. After this protest, she returned to her Third Street apartment in the New York City Catholic Worker House, where she remained until her death, following a long illness, in 1980.

THE FOUNDING OF THE CATHOLIC WORKER

In 1932, Peter Maurin proposed the institution of a manifold action program via the establishment of roundtable discussions, the creation of farming communes, the opening of houses of hospitality, and the promulgation of a newspaper.[41] The Catholic Worker movement was one of the first post-Reformation Roman Catholic social initiatives to support revolutionary gospel applications throughout the social order.[42] Day became

Maurin's collaborator and the instrument for the realization of his Catholic social vision.

From its inception, the Catholic Worker featured Friday evenings of reflection, during which a speaker on a particular theme—labor rights, peace activism, economic justice, or the like—led an open discussion and conversation among all of the attendees. The Catholic Worker Maryhouse in New York City has observed these Friday evenings of reflection, September through May, since 1934. The meetings are still open to the entire community and to the public at large, and, of course, are free of charge.

Through the houses of hospitality, Maurin hoped to combat the growing passive, fatalist belief that the state has to assume the social work that God wants each person to perform.[43] Day immediately adopted his plan, and her Fifteenth Street apartment served as the first Catholic Worker house of hospitality. One of the key purposes behind the establishment of the houses lay in training the unemployed, and the houses of hospitality soon attracted many young men and women who were eager to volunteer their time and energy for the benefit of the poor. Day later wrote of Maurin's philosophy about the houses:

> Every house should have a Christ's room.... It is no use turning people away to an agency, to the city or the state or the Catholic Charities. It is you yourself who must perform the works of mercy. Often you can only give the price of a meal, or a bed on the Bowery. Often you can only hope that it will be spent for that. Often you can literally take off a garment if it only be a scarf and warm some shivering brother. But personally, at a personal sacrifice.[44]

The houses of hospitality distributed food to the hungry, provided beds for the homeless, and served as "newspaper offices, volunteer centers, soup kitchens, boarding houses, schools [and] places of worship."[45] Today, there are more than 130 Catholic Worker houses worldwide, scattered across twenty-nine states and five countries. Day felt that the church should follow the example of the hospitality houses and fill the empty rooms in rectories, seminaries, and monasteries with the poor; or, at the least, each parish should have a hospice for the poor.[46]

The first edition of the *Catholic Worker* newspaper was published on May 1, 1933. The fifty-four-year-old Peter Maurin served as the tangible "rock" upon which the newspaper was founded.[47] While Maurin provided the theoretical framework for the paper, Day participated in all the practical tasks: fundraising, circulation, and reporting. Maurin ultimately became the elder statesman of the *Catholic Worker* and contributed "Easy Essays" to its pages. He and his theories supplied the catalysts that motivated Dorothy Day to find meaning and purpose in her life; Day, in turn, absorbed Maurin's ideas and, through her writing, communicated them in more tempered fashion to the rest of the population.[48]

Dorothy Day's column, "Day By Day," was in some ways the centerpiece of the *Catholic Worker* newspaper. It contained straightforward monthly essays presenting her personal views on issues that appealed to the common person. Day's greatest articles focused upon topics directly relevant to the general work force; she developed a large working class readership by reporting on strikes, union discussions, and other labor issues. But Day and her fellow journalists at the *Catholic Worker* did not merely "report" the news—they were often on the scene to support and participate in pickets or work stoppages. In this way, Day saw the *Catholic Worker* as fulfilling its role as a major supporter of both the labor movement and Christian ideals.

The growth of the *Catholic Worker* from the 2,500 copies distributed on May 1, 1933, to its peak of 185,000 copies sold in December 1940 was truly dramatic. Today, the paper continues to sell for a penny a copy. The *Catholic Worker* still delivers approximately 91,000 copies of each of its seven annual issues, produced in its New York offices on the lower East Side of Manhattan.[49]

DIVINE OBEDIENCE, CIVIL DISOBEDIENCE, AND PACIFISM

Dorothy Day embraced pacifism even before her conversion to Catholicism. During her tenures at *The Call* and *The Masses*, Day vigorously protested World War I.[50] She believed that the imperialist competitive system of international capitalism had caused the war. When the United States entered the fray in 1917, Day and her co-workers at *The Masses* were subjected to intense governmental scrutiny; then in July 1917, the federal government, including the Department of Justice, the United States Attorney, and the Postal Inspection Service charged the publication with violating the Espionage Act, a piece of legislation that permitted the postmaster general to direct postal workers to withhold unsealed materials that advocated treason, insurrection, or forcible resistance to law.[51] The governmental histrionics effectively closed *The Masses* down and thus robbed Day and her antiwar associates of a voice.[52]

Given the discriminatory and oft-cited charge that Catholics were un-American because of their exclusive allegiance to the pope, Day, as a Catholic pacifist, faced even greater scrutiny by the government. Her religious faith only served to strengthen her antiwar views. During her time as a secular radical, Day had become disenchanted with the Left's inability to make a real difference. But, after her conversion to Catholicism, she felt her faith provided her with renewed determination.[53] She incorporated her religious faith into her pacifist stance and believed that Jesus' command to love one's neighbor requires the practice of nonviolence. Accordingly, she argued, "We are still pacifists. Our manifesto is the Sermon on the Mount, which means that we will try to be peacemakers. Speaking for many of our conscientious objectors, we will not participate in armed warfare or in making munitions, or by buying government bonds to prosecute the war, or in urging others to these efforts."[54] To Day, nonviolence was as integral to church doctrine as the dogma of the Immaculate Conception or the infallibility of the pope.

WAR AND PACIFISM

Day often faced conflicting loyalties to social radicals and to the Catholic hierarchy, respectively. At the outset of the Spanish Civil War, Day took a neutral stance and in doing so enraged many of her former socialist and radical acquaintances, who supported the anti-Franco forces.[55] Yet she also drew the ire of the church, which supported Franco's Spanish fascists because of the antireligious philosophy of the Republican forces, dominated by the Communist Party. Day responded to the left wing by saying: "And now the Communist is teaching that only by the use of force, only by killing our enemies, not by loving them and giving ourselves up to death, giving ourselves up to the Cross, will we conquer."[56] To her critics in the church she remarked, "The Catholic Church cannot be destroyed in Spain or in Mexico ... we do not believe that force of arms can save it."[57] To Day, the question was about pacifism, not fascism, communism, or capitalism.

From 1939 to 1941,[58] Day condemned President Roosevelt's veiled preparation for war. She argued: "Instead of gearing ourselves in this country for a gigantic production of death-dealing bombers and men trained to kill, we should be producing food, medical supplies, ambulances, doctors and nurses for the works of mercy, to heal and rebuild a shattered world."[59] The attack on Pearl Harbor, however, galvanized American support for the war effort. Many within the Catholic Church argued that the American entrance into World War II was justified. Even hundreds of Day's own Catholic Workers, believing that the invasion required a military response, now ignored her call for pacifism.[60]

Day maintained that an invasion did not justify a violent response. Arguing that pacifism does not mean appeasement, she contended that one should use spiritual weapons like prayer, reception of the sacraments, and other forms of nonviolent resistance to ward off invaders.[61] She found it hypocritical that the white establishment in the United States used foreign aggression as an excuse to wage war but expected pacifism from oppressed minorities within the country. Citing this double standard, Day wrote:

> Last month a Negro in Missouri was shot and dragged by a mob through the streets behind a car. His wounded body was then soaked in kerosene. The mob of white Americans then set fire to it, and when the poor anguished victim had died, the body was left lying in the street until a city garbage cart trucked it away. Are the Negroes supposed to "Remember Pearl Harbor" and take to arms to avenge this cruel wrong? No, the Negroes, the workers in general, are expected to be "pacifist" in the face of this aggression.[62]

Still, the majority viewed her position as unfathomable, and the Catholic Worker movement paid a price. The *Catholic Worker* newspaper lost more than 100,000 readers during the war years, and by 1946, only eleven houses of hospitality continued to operate.[63] Nevertheless, Day, refusing to tone down her rhetoric, persevered in her insistence upon pacifism. As the nation celebrated imminent victory following the bombings of Hiroshima and Nagasaki, she mocked President Truman:

> Mr. Truman was jubilant. President Truman. True man; what a strange name, come to think of it. We refer to Jesus Christ as true God and true Man. Truman is a true man of his time in that he was jubilant. He was not a son of God, brother of Christ, brother of the Japanese, jubilating as he did. He went from table to table on the cruiser which was bringing him home from the Big Three conference, telling the great news; "jubilant" the newspapers said. Jubilate Deo. We have killed 318,000 Japanese.
>
> That is, we hope we have killed them, the Associated Press, on page one, column one of the Herald Tribune, says. The effect is hoped for, not known. It is to be hoped they are vaporized, our Japanese brothers—scattered, men, women and babies, to the four winds, over the seven seas. Perhaps we will breathe their dust into our nostrils, feel them in the fog of New York on our faces, feel them in the rain on the hills of Easton.
>
> Jubilate Deo. President Truman was jubilant. We have created. We have created destruction. We have created a new element, called Pluto. Nature had nothing to do with it.[64]

She argued that God had already pronounced judgment on America's decision to drop the bomb and wrote in the *Catholic Worker*, "James and John (John the beloved) wished to call down fire from heaven on their enemies, Jesus said: 'You know not of what spirit you are. The Son of Man came not to destroy souls but to save.'"[65]

Despite Day's unwavering commitment to pacifism during the war, the revelation of the Nazi death camps did give her pause. Upon learning of the Holocaust, she wondered aloud: "If I had known all this ... would I have maintained my pacifism?" But, she added, "all the violence didn't save the Jews."[66]

Following World War II, Day protested the growing military complex with which the United States government responded to the increasing tension of the Cold War. The government initiated a number of civil defense drills, which simulated a nuclear attack on New York City and required citizens to seek shelter for the duration of the drill. In order to highlight the futility of seeking refuge during a nuclear attack, Day and other Catholic Workers, led by Ammon Hennacy, refused to take shelter and sat in park benches as the air raid sirens wailed.[67] Not only did Day hope that her civil disobedience would reveal the drills as a farce, but she also saw it as an opportunity to perform penance for her sin as a citizen of the country that had first developed and used the atomic bomb.[68] The protests served as an adequate penance in her view, but Day did not enjoy her martyrdom status, nor did she revel in her participation in these protests. Describing them, she wrote:

> God knows, it is a suffering. I don't think any of us, not even Ammon Hennacy, enjoys these demonstrations, this "going to the man in the street." It is so much easier to sit behind a typewriter, to sit in an office or a meeting house and talk about these actions and these ideas. There is a tenseness in the atmosphere, both among those who are engaged in civil disobedience, and those who are officers of the law and forced into the duty of arresting us.[69]

Day served some jail time as a result of the protests, but she continued to engage in civil disobedience. On May 3, 1960, more than a thousand protesters, drawn from the *Catholic Worker*, the War Resisters League, the Fellowship Reconciliation, and other pacifist groups, led a peace rally in New York.[70] Embarrassed, the government ceased the drills shortly thereafter.

Day detested the nuclear arms race. Her worst nightmare came agonizingly close to becoming a reality when, in early October 1962, President Kennedy learned of a Soviet nuclear buildup in Cuba. The president ordered a naval blockade of Cuba to force the removal of the missiles, a confrontation with the Soviet Union that brought the world near to "the abyss of destruction."[71] In response, Day visited Cuba in order to give a human face to the Cuban people.[72] In her article detailing the trip, she wrote of meeting devout Catholic families who feared an impending invasion, much as American families feared a nuclear strike.[73] Day hoped to bridge the gap between Americans and Cubans, in spite of their governments. She condemned both nations for their continued militarization and proclaimed, "I hate the arms buildup in Cuba as I hate it in my own country";

however, she continued to strive to create an understanding in the United States that "the Cubans are our next door brothers, and knowing them, [we] will love them."[74]

THE SECOND VATICAN COUNCIL

The increasing Cold War militarization coincided with the convocation of the Second Vatican Council. The twenty-first ecumenical council of the church convened in four autumnal sessions from 1962 to 1965. Day was one of fifty "Mothers for Peace," a group of international peace advocates, who traveled to Rome in 1963 to support and thank Pope John XXIII for his encyclical *Pacem in terris*.[75] In the encyclical, the pope asked that stockpiles of weapons be reduced and nuclear weapons banned. As pleased as Day was by these words from the Holy Father, she still longed for a "more radical condemnation of the instruments of modern warfare."[76] In one of his last appearances, John XXIII blessed Day and her fellow pilgrims and thanked them for their efforts.

In September 1965, Day returned to Rome for the last session of the Second Vatican Council. She wanted to ensure that the council included in its pastoral constitution a condemnation of nuclear war and support for conscientious objection. She faced opposition from certain factions within the church hierarchy on both accounts. Some bishops argued that without a nuclear arsenal the world could not face down Communism, which threatened the church. Day mocked such circular logic and asserted, "To establish a balance of terror, and so keeping the world at peace was long ago condemned by Benedict XV, who spoke of 'the fallacy of an armed peace.'"[77] The idea of conscientious objection concerned many church leaders because they believed that such an action caused one to choose church over state. In response, Day was quick to quote St. Peter, who said, "We must obey God, not men."[78]

In order to "overcome the spirit of violence in the world," Day took part with other women in a ten-day fast during the final session of the Second Vatican Council. The women's efforts were recognized during a council session by Bishop Boillon of Verdun, France. On her return home in October, even before the council had produced a constitution, Day already deemed the trip a success and wrote: "Everyone said our visits and our fast and vigil (we each kept an hour before the Blessed Sacrament each day besides daily Mass) did much good."[79] Her optimism was vindicated when the council promulgated *Gaudium et spes*. This central document condemned the "indiscriminate destruction of cities," declared conscientious objection a valid option, and questioned the billions of dollars being spent on the arms race while millions starved and suffered. Most satisfying to Day was the constitution's condemnation of nuclear war.

VIETNAM WAR

Unfortunately, Vatican II had little effect on the seemingly inexorable escalation of violence in Vietnam. Day was not blinded by the euphoria over the Second Vatican Council's pronouncements on peace; she understood that though the clergy could speak out, wars would go on.[80] Not surprisingly, Day gave little credence to the Defense Department's domino theory, which claimed that Southeast Asia provided a necessary plug to stop the flow of communist aggression. As Day saw it, the conflict in Vietnam was not about freedom or Christianity, but instead stemmed from the inexorable materialist and imperialist compulsion to add to "our possessions."[81] As usual, Day viewed events on a broader scale, and she reiterated that communists and imperialists, South and North Vietnamese, are all children of God.

Catholic Workers were among the first to use public demonstrations and sit-ins to protest the U.S. government's actions in Vietnam.[82] The protest movement benefited from the fact that the war in Vietnam did not have as broad a base of support as had American involvement in World War II.[83] The Catholic Workers organization, no longer the pariah that it had been in its earlier antiwar campaigns, now had considerable cachet with the next generation of protesters. Day, detailing for the *Catholic Worker* a 1967 protest she attended in Central Park, commented on the gaining momentum of the antiwar movement:

> Christ is our Peace! On April 15th I could not help but think of that poem of Francis Thompson's about meeting Christ at Charing Cross. I felt that the hundreds of thousands of people who assembled in the Sheep Meadow at Central Park, New York City, coming from all points east of the Mississippi, and from St. Louis (not to speak of other cities further west) were meeting him too, in each other, on this great peace march. It was the greatest mass meeting and march in American history and clearly demonstrated to the American people as a whole the unpopularity of the war in Vietnam and the longing of the people for peace. On the same day there was a similar demonstration in San Francisco, the largest ever held in that city.[84]

As the war escalated, however, antiwar advocates began to use more drastic methods to protest the conflict. In 1965, Catholic Worker Richard Laporte immolated himself in front of the United Nations headquarters in

New York.[85] Day was utterly horrified, and she worried that there would be copycats. LaPorte's action was followed by less severe acts of civil disobedience by the Berrigan brothers. Priests Daniel and Philip Berrigan, who were good friends of the Catholic Worker movement, poured blood on and burned draft registration files in Catonsville, Maryland; the act was the first of its kind and encouraged other protesters to partake in similar actions.[86] Although Day understood the frustration of the protesters, she grew concerned that acts of violence or the destruction of property could leave the movement spiritually vulnerable. She always supported the Berrigans by expressing her love and offering her prayers, but she refused to condone vandalism. Day reminded her readers that those involved in the Catholic Worker movement had suffered destruction of property by vandals, and she cited the Golden Rule in urging antiwar protesters not to resort to such means.[87]

The Catholic Worker movement gained a number of converts through its antiwar stance during the turbulent Vietnam period. Day had weathered the storm of negative public reaction to her advocacy of pacifism during the World War II era. Vilified in the 1940s, she was now celebrated.

THE POLITICAL AND SOCIAL THEORY OF DOROTHY DAY

Day never proclaimed a grand masterwork or a sophisticated intellectual agenda. Her political theory can be best understood through its manifestations in her applied journalism and social activism, framed by her Catholic faith and her commitment to social justice and the performance of the corporal works of mercy. Day described this amalgamation of Catholic doctrine and a strong social conscience as she explained one of the primary purposes of the hospitality houses:

> To reach the masses through the spiritual and the corporal works of mercy. Of course, getting Catholic literature around is performing quite a few of those tasks. It is enlightening the ignorant and counseling the doubtful, comforting the afflicted, and you might even say that walking on a picket line is doing these things, too, as well as rebuking the sinner. But when we talk of the works of mercy, we usually think of feeding the hungry, clothing the naked, and sheltering the homeless.[88]

Day was an applied pragmatist, not an abstract theoretician. Most important, she practiced what she preached.

The key operatives in Dorothy Day's political and social theory were the philosophy of personalism, which stresses the centrality of the individual,[89] and the social organizing principle of subsidiarity, which emphasizes the local community (with its constituent components) as the primary locus for political organization.[90] Personalism lies at the center of Catholic social teachings and holds that human beings are created in the likeness of God and are endowed by God with a soul, an intellect, and a rational free will.[91] As the creatures of God, made in God's image and possessing these innate spiritual attributes, humans can neither be regarded merely as a means to a goal nor reified as objects; rather, every human being deserves to be treated as a subject in and of himself or herself.

According to the philosophy of personalism, individuals realize their potential when they utilize their unique talents in their work.[92] In line with this assertion, personalism affirms two basic human needs: the material need and the need for dignified work. In order for a social order to function properly, it must address these necessities.[93] Dorothy Day and the Catholic Worker movement sought to facilitate this goal by direct application of the philosophy of personalism in the *Catholic Worker* newspaper, houses of hospitality, and job training schools.[94]

Personalism is closely related to the principle of subsidiarity.[95] Subsidiarity maintains that local, community-centered organizations are the most efficacious, conducive, and responsive associations in existence for the fulfillment of social needs.[96] Thus, political and social activity should be reduced to the most immediate and local context possible.[97] Subsidiarity has political roots many centuries old and is powerfully situated in Catholic social theory. This principle was integral to the first modern papal encyclical on the rights of workers, Leo XIII's *Rerum novarum* (1891).[98]

At its core, the principle of subsidiarity champions both responsible self-determination and social cooperation. Subsidiarity emphasizes individual free will and the primacy of the human being. It recognizes that "the state should intervene and provide help (*subsidium*) for only that portion of need that the private sector is unable to provision by itself."[99] This dynamic places effective decision-making control in the hands of each individual and reaffirms basic democratic principles. The weakening significance of the workplace and the neighborhood leads to greater dependence on the state for provision and consequently to the compromising of personal freedom. But Day believed that individual efforts to perform "corporal works of mercy" were preferable to dependence on the government. She wrote:

> As for perpetuating the social order, we consider the spiritual and corporal works of mercy and the following of Christ to be the best revolutionary technique and a means of changing the social order rather than perpetuating it. Did not the thousands of monasteries, with their hospitality change the social pattern of their day? They did not wait for a paternal state to step in nor did they stand by to see destitution precipitate bloody revolt.[100]

Because local social groups provide the best forum for the kind of self-determination envisioned in subsidiarity theory, the privatization of provision does not imply radical individualism. The practice of subsidiarity thus transforms the attainment of human needs from an exclusively individual concern to one of concern for the entire society, without rendering individuals helplessly dependent on the (national) government. Consonant with this vision, Dorothy Day and her colleagues refused to pay any federal income taxes and thus protested the war economy and materialism of our late capitalist political economy, but the Catholic Workers believed in and paid local taxes as good members of the local community.

Personalism and subsidiarity both focus on the dignity of the individual person.[101] While personalism stresses individual activism, subsidiarity calls for as many decisions as possible to be decided on the smallest possible level, though this level may not necessarily be that of the individual. Personalism seems to reject any form of communalism and materialism; the personalist philosophy understands individual spiritual vision as the means to reshape the community. Subsidiarity, on the other hand, requires some variety of mid-level organization, whether in the form of a public association, union, fraternal club, or daily human interaction, as the means of developing our individual abilities to directly control our lives and world.[102]

Personalism and subsidiarity comprise two adjacent limbs on the tree representing the activities and message of Dorothy Day. Their intentional renewal and nurturing of public relationships of mutual respect and accountability across the divisions of a pluralistic, atomized society make Day's theory, practice, and Catholic social teaching extraordinarily relevant today.

THE CENTRALITY OF LABOR

The dignity of meaningful work, especially through the mediating device of the organized labor union, is a very important unifying thread between the individual and the responsible community. Dignified work contributes significantly to fundamental human dignity, and the absence of such work can significantly retard progress toward the establishment of human dignity. Dorothy Day and the members of the Catholic Worker movement consistently emphasized the dignity and the importance of work while encouraging the solidarity of labor with the unemployed and the ever-present poor. Day's writing on these subjects was eloquent, and her personal commitment to and solidarity with workers was magnificent.

In her autobiography, *The Long Loneliness*, Day recounted how her awareness of labor issues had first emerged during her college years. The stories of Eugene Debs, the "Haymarket martyrs," the women who led the first strike against the exploitation of women and children in the New England cotton mills—these both inspired Day and made her aware of how much work remained to be done to institute fair labor practices.[103] Religion played no role in Day's awakening labor consciousness, and her growing desire to help workers manifested itself outside of the contours of the Catholic Church and Catholic social teaching. In her autobiography, she summarized the nonreligious social influences on her early thought and described Catholicism as a sort of alien enclave that had little to do with her.[104] In her words:

> I wavered between my allegiance to socialism, syndicalism (the I.W.W.'s) and anarchism. When I read Tolstoi, I was an anarchist. Ferrer with his schools, Kropotkin with his farming communes, the I.W.W.'s with their solidarity, their unions, these all appealed to me.... I do not remember any antireligious articles in the Call.... I was surprised to find many quotations from Rerum Novarum of Pope Leo XIII and a very fair exposition of the Church's social teachings. I paid no attention to it at the time. Catholics were a world apart, a people within a people, making little impression on the tremendous non-Catholic population of the country.[105]

Upon Day's conversion, she found herself increasingly isolated from the radical community, and she did not make inroads into the society of this "people within a people" until after an important epiphany she experienced as a writer for *Commonweal*.[106]

In 1932, Day wrote a piece regarding a Washington, D.C., convention of protesting tenant farmers. In it, she described the poverty of the demonstrators, the willingness of the participants to share food, and the camaraderie that blossomed between the farmers, the poor, and the unemployed. In reflecting on this protest years later, Day related the shame and remorse she had experienced over her abstraction, her absence of solidarity, and her detachment from workers: "How little, how puny my work had been since becoming a Catholic, I thought. How self-centered, how ingrown, how lacking in sense of community! My summer of quiet reading and prayer, my self-absorption seemed sinful as I watched my brothers in their struggle, not for themselves but for others. How our dear Lord must love them, I kept thinking to myself. They were His friends, His comrades, and who knows how close to His heart in their attempt to work for justice."[107] In this galvanizing epiphany, Day's labor and social consciousness fused with her Catholic faith and was rejuvenated in a transforming way. After she finished her article about the protest, she went to Mass on the Feast of the Immaculate Conception; there she prayed, "with tears and with anguish, that some way would open up for me to use what talents I possessed for my fellow workers, for the poor."[108]

The first issue of the *Catholic Worker* newspaper, printed on May 1, 1933, gave Day the opportunity she desired. The *Catholic Worker* embodied solidarity, and while the paper spoke directly to workers of all classes, its first consideration was the poor.[109]

LABOR THEORY

Dorothy Day's statements on labor reveal a rich, complex, and sophisticated mind; they also reveal her deep, personal, and lifelong commitment to workers as human beings. Day's theory of labor is best articulated in her articles appearing in the *Catholic Worker*, and her essays and columns from 1933 until the immediate post–World War II period of the late 1940s, particularly reflect her concern that theory be merged with praxis. Day set forth perhaps the greatest synthesis of her labor theory in an essay entitled "The Catholic Worker and Labor," published in the June 1939 issue of the *Catholic Worker*. She asserted that the very basis of fighting for the rights of workers lies in their dignity as individuals created in the image of God:

> We are not only urging the necessity for organization to all workers ... but [are] also stressing over and over again the dignity of labor, the dignity of the person—a creature composed of body and soul made in the image and likeness of God, and a Temple of the Holy Ghost. It is on these grounds that we fight the speed-up system in the factory, it is on these grounds that we work toward de-proletarianizing the worker, working toward a share in the ownership and responsibility.... We pointed out again and again that the issue is not just one of wages and hours, but of ownership and of the dignity of man.

Throughout the article, she emphasized the example of Christ as well as the teaching of the church in its great social and labor encyclicals of 1891 and 1931.

From its inception, the *Catholic Worker* focused upon the catholic nature of work. Remarking on the view of her cofounder, Peter Maurin, Day noted, "In Peter's vision, work is a gift. Given for the common good—and the reason why one works is to share gifts and talents, in common with others, to help create a better kind of society."[110] Day and the *Catholic Worker*, by emphasizing "catholicity" in both the religious and universal sense of that word, sought the unity of workers. In direct, working class language, the newspaper promulgated Catholic social teaching, with its thoroughly integrative and truly universal language about social justice.

Day and the *Catholic Worker* unsparingly repudiated the influences of atheistic communism within labor and thoroughly condemned the materialism of the capitalist ownership elites. Indeed, established organized labor itself was not exempt from Day's censure, and she condemned the unions' inattention to the poor and the unorganized in trades like mining and textile manufacturing. She blamed this "aristocracy of labor" for the organizing success of radical trade unions, which benefited from the bias the poor workers felt against the established unions.[111]

The immediate post–World War II era saw an increasing sophistication on the part of society in its awareness of the corrosive effects of industrial production on the human psyche. The *Catholic Worker* took note of such trends but made no attempt to commercialize the newspaper, which continued to be sold for a penny. Day refused to idealize or romanticize her theory of labor beyond the hard lessons of the Christian gospel. In fact, she took great pains to expose the false romanticism, fostered by a lost concept of work, which upper-middle-class intellectuals often attached to organized labor. She wrote in the *Catholic Worker*, "I wish to fling down the challenge at once, that what is the great disaster is that priests and laity alike have lost the concept of work, they have lost a philosophy of labor as Peter Maurin has always said. They have lost the concept of work, and those who do not know what work in the factory is, have romanticized both it and the workers."[112] With statements such as these, Day shattered romanticism; she urged realism and professed that, in reforming reality, one can envision and perhaps even achieve ideals.

Day's emphasis on the human dignity of workers, along with her refusal to romanticize the situation of labor, informed her interpretation of the movement toward mass production. According to Day, mass production deemphasizes the role of the individual and compels workers to submit themselves to a dehumanizing process of "'work without end,' which chains workers to machines and especially to the authority of those who own and control them—capital and its managerial retainers." This was the reality of the industrial assembly-line era, and the *Catholic Worker* warned its readers against the great sin of "submitting oneself to a process." Such submission diminishes a human being to a mere extension of a machine, to an unthinking, but efficient, hand. Day argued that this dehumanization posed the real threat of mass industrialization, and she spoke out against a growing false consciousness:

> In the great clean shining factories, with good lights and air and the most sanitary conditions, an eight-hour day, five-day week, with the worker chained to the belt, to the machine, there is no opportunity for sinning as the outsider thinks of sin. No, it is far more subtle than that, it is submitting oneself to a process which degrades, dehumanizes. To be an efficient factory worker, one must become a hand, and the more efficient one is, the less one thinks. Take typewriting, for instance, as an example ... or driving a car, or a sewing machine. These machines may be considered good tools, an extension of the hand of man. We are not chained to them as to a belt, but even so, we all know

that as soon as one starts to think of what one is doing, we slip and make mistakes. One is not supposed to think. To think is dangerous at a machine. One is liable to lose a finger or a hand, and then go on the scrap heap and spend the rest of one's life fighting for compensation for one's own carelessness, as the factory owners say, for not using the safety devices invented and so plentiful.... And here is the dangerous part, it is not so much the loss of the hand or the arm, but the loss of one's soul. When one gives one's self up to one's work, when one ceases to think and becomes a machine himself, the devil enters in. We cannot lose ourselves in our work without grave danger.[113]

Day believed that the mechanization of industry also leads easily to an indifference to artisanship on the part of the laborer. Running throughout her *Catholic Worker* essays was an ongoing call for each individual worker to take pride and care in the work given him or her by God.[114] These continuing themes resonated powerfully with the newspaper's annual mission statement, which noted that, as the purpose of work moves from human need to capitalist greed, workers are trapped in producing disposable goods for the consumer society and without work that contributes to human welfare.[115]

Dorothy Day saw her lessons as enduring ones. In an analysis eerily prescient of the high-technology computer age, she concluded her September 1946 article on labor by stating, "Cities have fallen in the past and they will fall again. Perhaps that will be the judgment of God on the machine which has turned man into a hand, a part of a machine. He who lives by the sword will fall by the sword and he who lives by the machine will fall by the machine."[116]

From her lifetime of solidarity with workers and the poor, Day wrote of the absolute imperative of the fusion of labor theory and labor practice: "Going around and seeing such sights is not enough.... One must live with them, share with them their suffering too."[117] Day's unequivocal and courageous personal commitment to walk the picket lines with striking workers and to be a member of the labor community in a real and dramatic way gives her understanding of labor genuine meaning. This submersion of self into the world of those whom one seeks to understand and help was essential to Day, who remarked, "Going to the people is the purest and best act in Christian tradition and revolutionary tradition and is the beginning of world brotherhood."[118]

DAY'S LABOR ACTIVISM

Throughout the volatile period of labor organizing that accompanied the Great Depression of the 1930s, Dorothy Day constantly supplemented her journalistic efforts in the *Catholic Worker* by physically joining workers at job sites and on picket lines. In 1934, Day and other employees of the *Catholic Worker* picketed the Ohrbach Department Store in Manhattan, the journalists standing side by side with the store's own striking employees.[119] Day later recalled:

> There was mass picketing every Saturday afternoon during the Ohrbach strike, and every Saturday the police drove up with patrol wagons and loaded the pickets into them with their banners and took them to jail. When we entered the dispute with our slogans drawn from the writings of the popes regarding the condition of labor, the police around Union Square were taken aback and did not know what to do. It was as though they were arresting the Holy Father himself, one of them said, were they to load our pickets and their signs into their patrol wagons. The police contented themselves with giving us all injunctions. One seminarian who stood on the side lines and cheered was given an injunction too, which he cherished as a souvenir.[120]

Day and the *Catholic Worker* provided housing and food to strikers during the formation of the National Maritime Workers Union in May 1936.[121] Then in February 1937,[122] with the support of the Archbishop of Detroit, Day traveled to Flint, Michigan, to cover a sit-down strike being staged in a number of General Motors factories.[123] For more than two decades, beginning in 1937, the *Catholic Worker* was the intellectual home for the Association of Catholic Trade Unionists; at its zenith, the Association maintained fourteen chapters and one hundred labor schools, most of which were concentrated in New York and Detroit.[124]

Perhaps Day's most direct advocacy on behalf of labor came in her challenge to Cardinal Francis Spellman, Archbishop of New York. In 1949, the unionized gravediggers of Calvary Cemetery went on strike against their employer, the trustees of St. Patrick Cathedral and, principally, Cardinal Spellman. The strike continued for over a month until it was crushed by the cardinal, who personally ordered the union-breaking and who led his seminarians into the cemetery as replacement workers. Cardinal Spellman stated that his resistance to the strike was "the most important thing I have done in my ten years in New York."[125] He proclaimed that the union's strike was "communist-inspired" and that he was "happy to be a strike breaker."[126]

Dorothy Day and the *Catholic Worker* bore profound and direct witness to the Cardinal's egregious repudiation of Catholic social teaching on the rights of workers. Day and the movement publicly supported the gravediggers' union, even when other unions would offer only clandestine assistance.[127] She said later that if the trustees truly could not pay what the strikers asked, the church board could have shown the books to the workers and thus avoided the strike altogether; instead, the cardinal chose to use "so overwhelming a show of force against a handful of poor working men."[128] In response to the archbishop's actions, Day wrote a very eloquent letter to Cardinal Spellman on March 4, 1949:

> I am deeply grieved to see the reports ... of your leading Dunwoodie seminarians [sic] into Calvary cemetery, past picket lines, to "break the strike".... Of course you know that a group of our associates at the Catholic Worker office in New York, have been helping [sic] the strikers, both in providing food for their families, and in picketing.... I am writing to you, because this strike, though small, is a terribly significant one in a way. Instead of people being able to say of us "see how they love one another," and "behold, how good and how pleasant it is for brethren to dwell together in unity" now "we have become a reproach to our neighbors, an object of derision and mockery to those about us." It is not just the issue of wages and hours as I can see from the conversations which our workers have had with the men. It is a question of their dignity as men, their dignity as workers, and the right to have a union of their own, and a right to talk over their grievances. It is no use going into the wages, or the offers that you have made for a higher wage (but the same work week). A wage such as the Holy Fathers have talked of which would enable the workers to raise and educate their families of six, seven and eight children, a wage which would enable them to buy homes, to save for such ownership, to put by for the education of the children—certainly the wage which they have in these days of high price prices [sic] and exhorbitant [sic] rents, is not the wage for which they are working. Regardless of what the board of trustees can afford to pay, the wage is small compared to the wealth of the men represented on the board of trustees. The way the workers live is in contrast to the way of living of the board of trustees.... Regardless of rich and poor, the class antagonisms which exist between the well-to-do, those who live on Park Avenue and Madison Avenue and those who dig the graves in the cemetery—regardless of these contrasts, which are most assuredly there, the issue is always one of the dignity of the workers. It is a world issue.[129]

The 1949 cemetery workers' strike clearly highlights Dorothy Day's perspective on the authority of the church, as well as the attempt of Day and the Catholic Workers to engage in responsible dialogue with the church hierarchy. In spite of, or perhaps because of, the confrontation over the rights of workers, Day continued to respect the cardinal's office.[130] But the relationship between Day, committed lay Catholic, and Cardinal Spellman, the most powerful leader among the American Catholic hierarchy, was both very simple and very complex. Day was theologically and liturgically traditional, while radical in her social justice activism. She once stated,

"When it comes to labor and politics ... I am inclined to be sympathetic to the left, but when it comes to the Catholic Church, then I am far to the right." Years after the strike, Dorothy Day discussed at some length her relationship with church authority in general, and with the cardinal in particular:

> I didn't ever see myself as posing a challenge to church authority. I was a Catholic then, and I am one now, and I hope and pray I die one. I have not wanted to challenge the Church, not on any of its doctrinal positions.... Well, that brings us back to the Cardinal.... I have my own way of disagreeing with him. Anyway the point is that he is our chief priest and confessor; he is our spiritual leader—of all of us who live here in New York. But he is not our ruler. He is not someone whose every word all Catholics must heed, whose every deed we must copy.... The Catholic Church is authoritarian in a way; it won't budge on what it believes it has been put here to protect and defend and uphold. The Church has never told its flock that they have no rights of their own, that they ought to have no beliefs or loyalties other than those of the Pope or one of his cardinals. No one in the Church can tell me what to think about social and political and economic questions without getting a tough speech back; please leave me alone and tend your own acreage; I'll take care of mine.[131]

Because Day believed that everyone in the church is called by God to consider the actions of the church and their consequences, she called the leadership of her archdiocese to account for its actions in breaking the strike in 1949. In doing so, she offered a model of how to communicate within the church and how to call to witness the church's professed commitments to social justice.

Even near the end of her life, Day continued her commitment of physical presence with organizing workers. Her last major effort came in August 1973, when she went to California to join Cesar Chavez's United Farm Workers in demonstration. Because of her support of Chavez and the Mexican itinerant workers, she, along with a thousand or so others, was arrested and briefly jailed. Speaking of her jailhouse accommodations, Day characteristically remarked, "If it weren't a prison, it would be a nice place to rest."[132]

Day recognized that the struggle for workers' dignity must be perpetual and incessant. In a 1939 article in the *Catholic Worker*, she detailed the sacrifices she and other must be willing to endure in supporting the rights of workers:

> Is this asking a tremendous sacrifice? We know it is. And yet, it is necessary sometimes for workers to make overwhelming sacrifices. You have made them in order that your right to organize, to strike, to picket, to get a fair share

of the profits of industry be recognized. Hundreds of workers have suffered imprisonment, injury and death, at the hands of those very people who make war, in order that they and their work might be accorded the dignity that belongs to them. You do not think their sacrifices were in vain. You honor and revere the memory of labor's martyrs. Sacrifice has been labor's lot; it still is. Sacrifice is always the lot of the noble, and only sacrifice can keep noble what sacrifice has ennobled.[133]

Despite the endless and often grueling nature of the struggle, however, Day also believed that it made a difference for the lives of workers. Progress may come slowly, she said, but "in the long view the efforts of the workers have achieved much."[134] Throughout her half-century of direct personal commitment to workers and of participation in labor strikes and picket lines, Dorothy Day had as her ultimate goal the recognition of the dignity of all persons, including workers; her emphasis lay on peace and conciliation and on the imperatives of charity, decency, and kindness to all.

DAY'S VIEWS ON UNIONS

By taking up residence with the unemployed, Day observed the stark and "pitiable" contrast between organized workers, who gained inner strength and dignity from their work and their unions, and unorganized workers.[135] Throughout the years of her advocacy, therefore, she gave a considerable amount of attention to the organized labor union. According to Day, the labor union offers the greatest tool available, in the midst of a system of fallible alternatives and mediating social structures, to the working individual. The organization of labor into unions is not an end in itself, however, but rather a means toward the achievement of human dignity, the central theme of the papal encyclicals on the rights of workers. In her February 1936 *Catholic Worker* column, Day emphatically stated:

> The Catholic Worker does not believe that unions, as they exist today in the United States, are an ideal solution for the social problem, or for any part of it. We do believe that they are the only efficient weapon which workers have to defend their rights as individuals and Christians against a system which makes the Christ-life practically impossible for large numbers of workers. We believe that Catholic workers must use unions in their efforts to heed the exhortations of the Popes to "de-proletarianize" the workers. (For we too are working toward a classless society, one in which all may become owners, instead of none as the Marxian would have it, or only the ruthless few as capitalism decrees.)

In this measure unions are a form of propaganda for more constructive measures toward a truly Catholic social order. As Pius XI has said in speaking of the work of Catholic unions and of Catholics in unions: "Thus they prepare the way for a Christian renewal of the whole social life."[136]

Wherever possible, Dorothy Day urged Catholic employees to strengthen their Catholic solidarity by seeking one another out, both within the union structure and outside of it in the non-unionized workplace. This ideal of solidarity applied to workers outside of the United States as well. The *Catholic Worker* saw Catholicism as the first and foremost affiliation of its readers; therefore, they were to embrace the paper's goal of bringing "Catholic social principles [internationally] to the workers in industry."[137] In this way, the *Catholic Worker* also focused on the international human rights dimension of unionization; a September 1937 page-one article proclaimed: "The *Catholic Worker* is not a local paper."[138]

Day believed that unions must be autonomous and independent, with each individual constituent member contributing to the collective common good. She particularly emphasized the critical importance of a collective consciousness, the "sacrifice of individual freedom for the common good."[139] Union organizing leads to advantages for all workers, but Day understood that individual workers would be required to assume personal risks. She felt that each individual Catholic worker has the responsibility of becoming familiar with the church's teaching on labor and of using this knowledge for the common benefit of all laborers. The *Catholic Worker* thus elevated one's right to organize to the level of duty. Citing Pope Leo XIII's great 1891 Letter on Labor, *Rerum novarum*, the paper told its readers "to organize into unions so that they could achieve better wages and hours of labor, better working conditions, and the right to be recognized as men, creatures of body and soul, temples of the Holy Ghost."[140]

Day and the *Catholic Worker* viewed the enhancement of human dignity as the ultimate and imperative end to be achieved by labor's collective organization. The labor union should offer more than a means of organizing the workplace and benefiting those who return to the job site each day; it has the additional imperative of seeking broader social justice.[141] In fact, Day told her readership that once workers achieve unionization and its improved lifestyle in their town, they must look beyond their own world and help other towns reach a more ideal labor situation.[142]

Day acknowledged that this broad-based approach required the support of nationalized labor organizations, and she drew parallels between the wider labor community and the universal Church. One of the central facets of Catholicism is its understanding that each individual believer belongs to a larger unifying body, the Mystical Body of Christ. Day powerfully invoked this Communion of Saints and applied it to the solidarity of workers on a national scale. Immediately after urging the national organization of labor, she proclaimed:

As Catholics you certainly ought to realize the necessity to work as a body. You are all members of the Mystical Body of Christ and St. Paul's saying was that when one member suffers, the health of the whole body is lowered. If some of you, in other words, are satisfied with your wages and hours, you have no right to sit back and be comfortable while great masses of workers are suffering under deplorable conditions—poor wages that are not sufficient to maintain a family and keep them in decent health, let alone afford them education and other needs. As long as the great mass of workers have to live in unsanitary, unheated tenements, no one has a right to his comfort while his brother is in misery.[143]

The *Catholic Worker* continually emphasized the example of Christ as the worker who acts in solidarity with and as liaison to the poor.[144] As love of neighbor is the prerequisite for loving God and fulfilling the commandments,[145] Christ the worker, in his love for his neighbor workers, set the example that all should emulate. Since no individual worker can alone achieve improved conditions, workers must band together in solidarity, even as Christ stood in solidarity with all those who labor. To refuse to work collectively would be to deny "Christ and His poor."[146]

CONCLUSION

In 1997, John Cardinal O'Connor officially began the process of the canonization of Dorothy Day. Although the Archbishop of New York drew a great deal of criticism over this decision, there is good reason to consider her a modern-day saint. Day was not only a powerful force in reshaping the way in which Catholic social teaching is understood in America, but she was also someone who led by example. Her legacy is not solely ideological, however, for she had a significant material effect on the world.

Day's material influence involves the creation of a major periodical dedicated to spreading the message of Catholic social teaching, *The Catholic Worker*, which is still published today. Additionally, the movement continues to operate houses of hospitality that directly perform the corporeal works of mercy.

Day's Catholic Workers have also inspired other groups to take up the banner of Catholic social teaching and support societal change leading to greater dignity in the workplace. Her influence continues today in Catholic organizations such as Plowshares and Pax Christi, contemporary social justice movements that oppose the use of nuclear weapons and promote peace through nonviolent civil disobedience.

Her adoption and implementation of Peter Maurin's thinking have had a profound effect on the current ideological tenor of Christianity in our

American society, particularly in relation to its ministry to the poor. Even the compassionate conservatism elucidated by the Bush administration has made use of the concept of subsidiarity in its advocacy of "faith-based initiatives." Likewise, the fusion of personalism and subsidiarity in Day's thought provides a roadmap for contemporary Christians to eliminate the divisions of our pluralistic, atomized society, thereby fostering public relationships of mutual respect and accountability. It is this stress on the commonalty of our humanity, especially before God, that is perhaps the most important of Day's lessons for our time.

But the power of Dorothy Day's message is amplified beyond that of a learned philosopher and persuasive writer. She was a leader by example, and it was her willingness to practice what she preached that separates her from the theologians, turning mere words into living, breathing doctrine. Day made her own life a model for her belief in Catholic social teaching, denying her own needs and wants in order to offer whatever hospitality she could to those who needed it more.

NOTES

1. Jesus concedes that citizens should "render unto Caesar the things which are Caesar's," but he adds that citizens must also give "unto God what is God's" (Matt. 22:21 RSV).
2. William D. Miller, *Dorothy Day: A Biography* (New York: Harper & Row, 1982), 36.
3. Ibid., 147; Dorothy Day, *The Long Loneliness: An Autobiography* (New York: Harper & Row, 1959), 52.
4. Mel Piehl, *Breaking Bread: Catholic Worker and the Origins of Catholic Radicalism in America* (Philadelphia: Temple University Press, 1982), 63.
5. Miller, *Dorothy Day*, 192–201.
6. Matthew 22:40.
7. Miller, *Dorothy Day*, 254.
8. Rosalie Riegle Troester, ed., *Voices from Catholic Worker* (Philadelphia: Temple University Press, 1993), 120–133.
9. Ibid., 120.
10. Piehl, *Breaking Bread*, 8.
11. Robert Coles, *Dorothy Day: A Radical Devotion* (New York: Addison-Wesley, 1987), 3–9; Troester, *Voices*, 79.
12. Day, *The Long Loneliness*, 48.
13. Miller, *Dorothy Day*, 5, 9, 14.
14. Day, *The Long Loneliness*, 24.
15. Miller, *Dorothy Day*, 5–6, 21.
16. Ibid., 31–35.
17. Jim O'Grady, *Dorothy Day: With Love for the Poor* (New York: Ward Hill Press, 1993), 35–39.

18. Miller, *Dorothy Day*, 55–57, 77.

19. Ibid., 71.

20. Quoted by ibid., 123.

21. Miller, *Dorothy Day*, 140; Troester, *Voices*, 95.

22. Miller, *Dorothy Day*, 143.

23. Troester, *Voices*, 95.

24. Miller, *Dorothy Day*, 150.

25. Ibid., 152.

26. Ibid., 152–153.

27. Ibid., 166.

28. Ibid., 170–171; William D. Miller, *A Harsh and Dreadful Love: Dorothy Day and Catholic Worker Movement* (New York: Liveright, 1973), 55.

29. Miller, *Dorothy Day*, 180.

30. Bridgid O'Shea Merriman, *Searching for Christ: the Spirituality of Dorothy Day* (Notre Dame, Ind.: University of Notre Dame Press, 1994), 20–21.

31. Miller, *Dorothy Day*, 192.

32. Merriman, *Searching*, 20–21.

33. Miller, *Dorothy Day*, 195.

34. Ibid., 228; Jim Forest, "A Biography of Dorothy Day," *The Encyclopedia of American Catholic History* (Collegeville, Minn.: Liturgical Press, 1997).

35. Arthur Sheehan, *Peter Maurin: Gay Believer* (Garden City, N.Y.: Hanover House, 1959), 88.

36. Miller, *Dorothy Day*, 243.

37. Ibid., 244.

38. Ibid., 244–247.

39. Ibid., 500.

40. Ibid., 252.

41. Piehl, *Breaking Bread*, 95.

42. Miller, *Dorothy Day*, 259.

43. Quoted by ibid., 259.

44. Quoted by Piehl, *Breaking Bread*, 96.

45. Miller, *A Harsh and Dreadful Love*, 106.

46. Piehl, *Breaking Bread*, 3.

47. Ibid., 63–69.

48. Tom Cornell, "A Brief Introduction to Catholic Worker Movement," http://www.catholicworker.com.

49. Miller, *Dorothy Day*, 71.

50. Espionage Act, chap. 30, tit. I, 40 Stat. 217 (1917).

51. Bob Guilis, "The Masses: Where Are They When We Need Them?" *Greenwich Village Gazette*, 28 September 2002.

52. Mark and Louise Zwick, "Dorothy Day, Prophet of Pacifism for the Catholic Church," *Houston Catholic Worker*, September–October 1997.

53. Dorothy Day, "Our Country Passes from Undeclared War to Declared War; We Continue Our Christian Pacifist Stand," *Catholic Worker*, January 1942.

54. Rosalie G. Riegle, "Mystery and Myth: Dorothy Day, Catholic Worker, and the Peace Movement," *Fellowship Magazine*, November–December 1997.

55. Dorothy Day, "The Use of Force," *Catholic Worker*, November 1936.

56. Ibid.

57. Michael Sherry, *In the Shadow of War: The United States Since the 1930s* (New Haven, Conn.: Yale University Press, 1995), 36–44. President Roosevelt intensified his rhetoric and began to mobilize the military for, as he saw it, the "business of carrying out a war without declaring a war." Ibid., 36.

58. Day, "Our Country Passes," 4.

59. Miller, *Dorothy Day*, 344–345.

60. Dorothy Day, "Works of Mercy Oppose Violence in Labor's War," *Catholic Worker*, April 1941.

61. Dorothy Day, "Why Do Members of Christ Tear At One Another," *Catholic Worker*, February 1942.

62. Miller, *Dorothy Day*, 344, 376.

63. Dorothy Day, "We Go On Record the CW Response to Hiroshima," *Catholic Worker*, September 1945.

64. Ibid.

65. Riegle, "Mystery and Myth," 3.

66. Miller, *Dorothy Day*, 437–438; Forest, "A Biography of Dorothy Day."

67. Dorothy Day, "On Pilgrimage," *Catholic Worker*, July–August 1957.

68. Dorothy Day, "C.W. Editors Arrested in Air Raid Drill," *Catholic Worker*, July–August 1956.

69. Piehl, *Breaking Bread*, 214–215

70. Sherry, *In the Shadow*, 246.

71. Riegle, "Mystery and Myth," 3.

72. Dorothy Day, "On Pilgrimage in Cuba: Part III," *Catholic Worker*, November 1962.

73. Dorothy Day, "More About Cuba," *Catholic Worker*, February 1963.

74. Dorothy Day, "On Pilgrimage," *Catholic Worker*, June 1963.

75. Ibid., 6.

76. Ibid., 1–2.

77. Ibid., 2 (quoting Acts 5:29).

78. Ibid., 8.

79. Dorothy Day, "On Pilgrimage," *Catholic Worker*, December 1965.

80. Dorothy Day, "Theophane Venard and Ho Chi Minh," *Catholic Worker*, May 1954.

81. Charles Catfield, "Dorothy Day, Catholic Worker, and American Pacifism," *Fellowship Magazine*, November–December 1997.

82. Piehl, *Breaking Bread*, 214–215.

83. Dorothy Day, "Spring Mobilization," *Catholic Worker*, May 1967.

84. Cornell, "Catholic Worker Pacifism."

85. Catfield, "Dorothy Day," 4.

86. Dorothy Day, "Dan Berrigan In Rochester," *Catholic Worker*, December 1970.

87. Dorothy Day, "Letter To Our Readers at the Beginning of Our Fifteenth Year," *Catholic Worker*, May 1947.

88. Edward J. O'Boyle, "Homo Socio-Economicus: Foundational to Social Economics and the Social Economy," *Review of Society and Economy* 52 (1994): 292.

89. Miller, *Dorothy Day*, 244–245.

90. Miller, *A Harsh and Dreadful Love*, 6.

91. O'Boyle, "Homo Socio-Economicus," 299–300.

92. Ibid., 299.

93. Piehl, *Breaking Bread*, 168–180.

94. Thomas C. Kohler, "Lessons from the Social Charter: State, Corporation, and the Meaning of Subsidiarity," *University of Toronto Law Journal* 43 (1993): 614–621.

95. Ibid., 620.

96. O'Boyle, "Homo Socio-Economicus," 295 n. 5. See further George A. Bermann, "Taking Subsidiarity Seriously: Federalism in the European Community and the United States," *Columbia Law Review* 94 (1994): 331; Deborah Z. Cass, "The Word That Saves Maastricht? The Principle of Subsidiarity and the Division of Powers Within the European Community," *Common Market Law Journal* 29 (1992): 1107; W. Gary Vause, "The Subsidiarity Principle in European Union Law: American Federalism Compared," *Case Western Reserve Journal of International Law* 27 (1995): 61.

97. Kohler, "Lessons," 304.

98. O'Boyle, "Homo Socio-Economicus," 295.

99. Dorothy Day, "Catholic Worker Ideas on Hospitality," *Catholic Worker*, May 1940.

100. Thomas C. Kohler, "Individualism and Communitarianism at Work," *Brigham Young University Law Review* (1993): 727.

101. Thomas C. Kohler, "The Overlooked Middle," *Chicago-Kent Law Review* 69 (1993): 230.

102. Day, *The Long Loneliness*, 44–45.

103. Ibid., 60–61.

104. Ibid., 160–161.

105. Miller, *Dorothy Day*, 225–226.

106. Day, *The Long Loneliness*, 160–161.

107. Ibid., 161–162.

108. Ibid., 199–200. Day described the solidarity of Catholic Worker as follows: "Catholic Worker, as the name implied, was directed to the worker, but we used the word in its broadest sense, meaning those who worked with hand or brain, those who did physical, mental or spiritual work. But we thought primarily of the poor, the dispossessed, the exploited." Ibid.

109. Troester, *Voices*, 104.

110. Ibid., 104–105. Dorothy notes the existence of graft in organized labor. Dorothy Day, "The Dignity of Labor," *Catholic Worker*, November 1934.

111. Dorothy Day, "The Church and Work," *Catholic Worker*, September 1946.

112. Ibid.

113. Day, "The Dignity of Labor," 4.

114. Troester, *Voices*, 577–578.

115. Day, "The Church and Work," 1.

116. Day, *The Long Loneliness,* 210–211.

117. Ibid.

118. Ibid., 201.

119. Ibid., 241.

120. Ibid., 203.

121. Troester, *Voices*, 12.

122. Day, *The Long Loneliness*, 213; Piehl, *Breaking Bread*, 78. See Sidney Fine, *Sit-down: The General Motors Strike of 1936–1937* (Ann Arbor: University of Michigan Press, 1969).

123. Troester, *Voices*, 13.

124. Miller, *Dorothy Day*, 404.

125. Ibid.

126. John Cooney, *The American Pope: The Life and Times of Francis Cardinal Spellman* (New York: Times Books, 1984).

127. Miller, *Dorothy Day*, 405.

128. Dorothy Day to Francis Cardinal Spellman, Archbishop of New York (March 4, 1949), copy on file with author, courtesy of the Marquette University Library Catholic Worker Archives.

129. Miller, *Dorothy Day*, 405.

130. Rosalie Riegle, *Dorothy Day: Portraits by Those Who Knew Her* (Maryknoll, N.Y.: Orbis Books, 2003), 94.

131. Quoted by Miller, *Dorothy Day*, 500.

132. Dorothy Day, "To the Workers," *Catholic Worker*, October 1939.

133. Day, *The Long Loneliness*, 212.

134. Ibid., 210–212.

135. Dorothy Day, "Catholics in Unions," *Catholic Worker*, February 1936.

136. Dorothy Day, "Join The Union! Natural And Supernatural Duty," *Catholic Worker*, September 1937.

137. Ibid.

138. Day, "Catholics in Unions," 7.

139. Dorothy Day, "Catholic Worker and Labor," *Catholic Worker*, June 1939.

140. Day, "Join The Union," 1.

141. Day, "Catholic Worker and Labor," 1.

142. Ibid., 2.

143. Solidarity with, liaisons to, and preferential options for the poor have long been essential elements of Catholic social teaching. Jesus Christ is the source of these teachings, through his life and many parables on themes of wealth and poverty. For example, the Sermon on the Mount tells us, "Blessed are the poor in spirit, for theirs is the kingdom of heaven," (Matt. 5:3 RSV) and later Christ says, "It is easier for a camel to go through the eye of a needle, than for a rich man to enter the kingdom of God" (Matt. 19:24 RSV). See also the stories of the blessed widow giving her last coins to the Temple (Mark 12:41–44) and of Christ driving the moneychangers from the Temple (Matt. 21:12).

144. Day, "Join the Union," 2.

145. Ibid.

{ CHAPTER 8 }

Pope John Paul II (1920–2005)

ROBERT P. GEORGE AND GERARD V. BRADLEY

"The sheer drama of Karol Wojtyla's life would defy the imagination of the most fanciful screenwriter,"[1] writes his admiring biographer George Weigel about the man who would become Pope John Paul II. Born just months after Poland regained its independence, Wojtyla came of age—as student, actor, athlete, seminarian, and manual laborer—during the Nazi occupation. As a young priest he studied in Rome, earned two doctoral degrees, and served twenty years as a professor of ethics. Pope Pius XII made Wojtyla an auxiliary bishop in 1957. As Archbishop of Krakow, he actively participated in all the sessions of the Second Vatican Council (1962–65), making significant interventions during discussions of *Dignitatis humanae* and *Gaudium et spes*—the documents on religious liberty and the church in the modern world.[2]

When Cardinal Wojtyla was consecrated as Pope John Paul II in 1978, he became the first non-Italian pontiff in centuries. He has also become the most traveled and the most prolific writer of all the popes. John Paul II promulgated a new Code of Canon Law in 1983, issued a much-debated constitution on Catholic universities, *Ex corde Ecclesiae*, in 1990, and promulgated a universal Catechism of the Catholic Church in 1997, the first since the Catechism of the Council of Trent (1566).

As part of his unblinking engagement with modern secularism, and in the face of widespread dissent by some theologians and others, John Paul II initiated an unprecedented systematic investigation of the foundations of Catholic moral theology. *Veritatis splendor,* the 1993 encyclical on moral theology, is the main fruit of this effort so far, an effort to bring forth an integral Christian humanism.

John Paul II is surely among the twentieth century's most significant persons, a world historical figure of the first rank. He played a critical role in the collapse of the Soviet empire in Eastern Europe. He shaped the Catholic Church for the new millennium.

A BRIEF BIOGRAPHY

On May 18, 1920, Karol Józef Wojtyla was born in Wadowice, a small city fifty kilometers from Krakow in southern Poland.[3] He was the second of two sons born to Karol Wojtyla and Emilia Kaczorowska.[4] His father was a tailor by trade, and he served as an administrative officer of the Austro-Hungarian army. He retired from the Polish army in 1927 on a pension with the rank of captain.[5] Wojtyla's mother died of kidney and heart disease in 1929, while he was in the third grade.[6]

In the fall of 1930, Wojtyla entered Marcin Wadowita, an all-boys state secondary school in Wadowice. There he achieved top grades in a classical curriculum: Latin, Greek, history, and mathematics, as well as Polish language and literature. In 1932 his eldest brother Edmund, a medical doctor, died after contracting scarlet fever from a patient. Wojtyla was struck harder, it seems, by his brother's unexpected death than by his mother's passing. However, he drew special solace and strength from his brother's example of self-sacrifice.[7]

After graduating from Marcin Wadowita in 1938, Wojtyla spent his summer fulfilling his national service with a road construction crew.[8] That fall he began his undergraduate studies at Krakow's Jagiellonian University and participated in experimental theater and poetry recitations.[9] In 1939, the Nazi occupation forces closed the university. A work card was required of every able-bodied male between fourteen and sixty who wished to remain in Krakow, and those without such a card were sent to a concentration camp or summarily executed. To forestall deportation and imprisonment, Wojtyla found work as a restaurant store messenger. In 1940, he began working as a manual laborer for the Solvay chemical company, a position he would hold for nearly four years.[10] During the same year, Wojtyla met Jan Tyranowski, a man of profound Carmelite spirituality. Tyranowski introduced him to the writings of John of the Cross and Theresa of Avila, both spiritual masters in the tradition of Catholic mysticism.[11]

On February 18, 1941, Wojtyla's father died. The future pope would later say that he had never felt so alone.[12] Recalling that his father was a man of constant prayer, he said, "We never spoke about a vocation to the priesthood, but his example was in a way my first seminary, a kind of domestic seminary."[13]

Wojtyla entered the clandestine seminary of Krakow, run by Cardinal Adam Stefan Sapieha. At the same time he was a founder of the "Rhapsodic Theatre," also clandestine.[14] In 1945, Wojtyla wrote his first play, *Our*

God's Brother, about Adam Chmielowski, an important figure in modern Polish cultural and religious life. Chmielowski joined the 1863 uprising against Russian rule and, wounded, suffered an amputated left leg. After the uprising was suppressed, Chmielowski became an accomplished artist.[15] Growing in his affection for the poor and homeless, Chmielowski made vows before Cardinal Dunajewski and founded the Albertine Brothers and Sisters.[16] The play's central tension concerns a vocational struggle, the discernment of God's will for one's own life. In this case the struggle was about a young man's strain to justify his comfortable artist's life, while wrestling with a call to poverty and service.[17]

Wojtyla continued his studies for the priesthood at the major seminary of Krakow, which reopened just after the war. He studied theology at the Jagiellonian University as well, until his priestly ordination on November 1, 1946.[18] Immediately after ordination he attended the Angelicum University in Rome.

In July 1947, Wojtyla earned a licentiate in theology. In June 1948, he defended his thesis and earned a doctorate.[19] Father Reginald Garrigou-Lagrange, O.P., a traditionalist in philosophy and dogmatic theology, directed Wojtyla's thesis, *The Problems of Faith in the Works of St. John of the Cross*.[20] In it the future pope addressed the proper balance "between knowledge that is granted to man in the act of faith and the limits of cognitive penetration accorded the finite, created mind before the inexhaustible light of God." He relied upon St. John's "deeply mystical sense of humanity," which attributed an incomprehensibility to the human person "normally predicated of God himself." Wojtyla identified this human mystery as the "dwelling place of freedom and personal dignity."[21]

During 1949 Wojtyla wrote his first two published articles. One was "Mission de France," a look at the worker-priest movement as a pastoral response to postwar French Catholicism. The second was "Apostle," about his friend and mentor in the life of prayer, Jan Tyranowski.[22] His poem "Matka" (Mother) was published in 1950.

In 1951 Eugeniusz Baziak, Archbishop of Lvov, asked Wojtyla to complete his qualifying exams for a university position. Wojtyla defended his thesis on *The Evaluation of the Possibility of Founding a Catholic Ethic on the Ethical System of Max Scheler*[23] two years later, at Lublin Catholic University. The thesis combined "the metaphysical realism of Aristotle and Thomas Aquinas [with] the sensitivity to human experience [exhibited in] Scheler's phenomenology."[24] Scheler failed to come to grips, Wojtyla argued, with how moral choices actually shape a person. To Scheler, morality was suspended somewhere "outside" the human universe. Wojtyla, on the other hand, argued that the moral act was a real act with real consequences.[25]

Wojtyla accepted a professorship from Lublin Catholic University in 1954 to teach moral theology and social ethics in the Faculty of Theology and in the major seminary of Krakow.[26] Two years later he was appointed to the Chair of Ethics. Two years after that, on July 4, 1958, he became Auxiliary Bishop of Krakow.[27]

In 1960, Wojtyla published his first book, *Love and Responsibility*. In it he argued that although biology, psychology, and sociology provided useful insights into the relations between the sexes, a full understanding required study of the human person as a whole and, thus, demanded reflection in the realms of philosophy, metaphysics, and theology. Over against a utilitarian view of the sexual partner as an object for use or means for the release of sexual tension, Wojtyla viewed marriage as a profound and mysterious "interpersonal relationship, in which the well-being and self-realization of each partner are of overriding importance to the other."[28]

Wojtyla continued his exploration of marriage in the play *The Jeweler's Shop*, published in December 1960. The play told the story of three marriages, and "gently insist[ed] that love and fidelity [can never] be reduced to emotions," which had to be purified, "transforming them, over time, into the more solid reality of self-giving love."[29]

On January 13, 1964, Pope Paul VI named Wojtyla Archbishop of Krakow. In 1966, he was further named President of the Episcopal Commission for the Apostolate of the Laity. Pope Paul VI made him a cardinal on June 26, 1967.[30]

Wojtyla published his magnum opus, *The Acting Person*, in 1969. Of it, the critic Thomas Guarino writes, "The work examines familiar philosophical themes: the nature of experience, the possibility of authentic intersubjective relations, the constitution of consciousness, the synergy between receptivity and activity, and the essence of intentionality." The book, Guarino adds, is "a phenomenological examination of how man dynamically enacts his freedom and intelligence in concrete experience. Wojtyla [wanted the reader] to understand that ... human action reveals the person as the dwelling place of dignity, transcendence, and spirituality."[31]

On October 16, 1978, shortly after the death of his predecessor and namesake, Cardinal Karol Wojtyla was elected the 264th pope and took the name John Paul II. In 1994, following many years of activism and ministry, he published *Crossing the Threshold of Hope*. In this book, John Paul II spoke forthrightly about the existence of God, salvation, ecumenism, and hope. He addressed the dignity of humankind as well as the problems of pain, suffering, and evil. The book, an expression of his beliefs, feelings, and hopes for the world, discusses the major issues facing humankind at the close of the twentieth century.[32]

In 1996, the pope's concise autobiography, *Gift and Mystery: On the Fiftieth Anniversary of My Priestly Ordination,* was published. In it, John Paul II takes the reader from his youth all the way to his years as pope. In a moving description of the Nazi occupation of Poland and the conditions endured under the Soviet-backed Communist government, John Paul II barely mentioned the role he played in the downfall of Communism in Poland. Rather, he "express[ed] his conviction that the battle for human dignity [had] hardly [been] won. Consumerism threaten[ed] to undermine [human dignity] in a way Communism never could. He assert[ed] that the answer to the corrosive philosophies of the modern world lies in priests fulfilling their ministry. His plea to his brother priests: celebrate the Eucharist with faith, hear confessions, be with young people, encourage married couples and above all, pray."[33]

PHILOSOPHER AND WRITER

Karol Wojtyla was an accomplished philosopher whose published work was influenced not only by the church's perennial teachings and by Thomism, but also by twentieth-century European philosophical thought. He was most famously influenced by the phenomenological school, mainly the works of the German philosophers Edmund Husserl and Max Scheler. Nevertheless, we advert to these influences only as a proper understanding of the papal texts requires.[34]

Why do we limit our exposition to papal writings and a few conciliar documents? As interesting a philosopher as Wojtyla was neither Wojtyla's work nor his phenomenology would have commanded space in this volume. It is instead the authoritative character of the pope's extensive teachings that justifies this chapter. Besides, when a man becomes pope, he takes over the teaching office and the accumulated writings of his predecessors. His task, therefore, is to preserve and enhance (in appropriate ways) the deposit of faith and to apply it as pope to contemporary conditions. Though there are some analogues to this combination of authorial constraint and creativity—the limited license appropriate to a judge in common-law jurisdictions comes to mind—the relationship between a pope's published teachings and Catholic faith and tradition is unique. Suffice it to say that there is a powerful yet marvelously productive set of constraints upon our subject, unlike those shaping the reflections of any other writer. Implied by one's ascension to the papacy, then, is a certain farewell to writing and thought of a nonpastoral sort, and to more speculative intellectual work of all sorts—including, in the case of a scholar pope, one's own.

The texts on which we rely in this chapter are mainly the encyclical letters *Laborem exercens, Sollicitudo rei socialis, Centesimus annus, Veritatis splendor*, and *Evangelium vitae*, and the 1994 *Letter to Families*.[35] We also rely on three documents of the Congregation for the Doctrine of the Faith: *Instruction on Certain Aspects of the "Theology of Liberation"* (1984), *Instruction on Christian Freedom and Liberation* (1986), and *Dominus Iesus: On the Unicity and Salvific Universality of Jesus Christ and the Church* (2000).[36] We consider a few other published statements of the pope, including an address to the United Nations.[37] We rely on the 1997 Catechism of the Catholic Church[38] for authoritative statements of the faith, where necessary, to fill in the thought and teaching of John Paul II.

We also rely upon the pronouncements of the Second Vatican Council. John Paul II was surely a man of the council. He stated, "Vatican II has always been, and especially during these years of my Pontificate, the constant reference point of my every pastoral action, in the conscious commitment to implement its directives concretely and faithfully."[39] And in *Tertio millennio adveniente*, he wrote: "the best preparation for the new millennium ... can only be expressed in a renewed commitment to apply, as faithfully as possible, the teachings of Vatican II to the life of every individual and of the whole Church."[40] Our investigation confirms these self-descriptions. We therefore also rely on certain documents of Vatican II—notably, *Gaudium et spes*[41] and *Dignitatis humanae*.[42] In these Wojtyla was especially interested, and to them he most significantly contributed.

The papal texts upon which we rely are not theological treatises or philosophical tracts. They possess a summary quality, as do most authoritative papal writings, due to their didactic purpose. This is especially the case with the Catechism, and with *Evangelium vitae*. Papal teaching documents often exhibit the style of a compilation or encyclopedia, and almost invariably strive to retain all plausible appearances of continuity with past teaching. These two features combine to give the texts an elliptical, even incomplete quality. The scholarly commentator is therefore obliged to build upon the texts to bring forth from them a coherent, fuller treatment of the matters addressed therein. We attempt to provide such a treatment of selected topics in John Paul II's writings, always striving to remain true to the mind of the author.

Looking at papal writings, one soon notices the habit of popes, obviously rooted in more than inclination, to preserve continuity—and the appearance of it—with the tradition. "Tradition" here is distinguishable from the faith. Tradition is more than the faith itself; it includes all the authoritative teaching of prior popes, as well as the writing of distinguished expositors of the faith, especially doctors of the church.[43]

The most useful comparison may again be to the legal world: one thinks of the way a Supreme Court opinion, even one that is strikingly innovative, strives for the appearance of continuity with past Court decisions. The analogy fails to illustrate a key difference. These days at least, the binding quality of a court decision is not thought to depend upon its fidelity to what has come before. Papal teaching on faith and morals, on the other hand, is ineffective where it contradicts a proposition previously established as true. Because there is often considerable uncertainty, even among faithful commentators, as to whether a prior authoritative teaching is certainly true, the contours of this boundary are often controversial. Put differently, interpretations of papal writings—that is, accounts of what they mean— will differ according to what the interpreter believes to be previously established as true, and sometimes according to the interpreter's understanding of the tradition, more widely considered.

We do not seek to align what John Paul II said with prior papal teaching and tradition, to reconcile his assertions with extant authoritative pronouncements. Two areas in which such work is most needed are the death penalty and the traditional doctrine, affirmed but not explained by the council fathers in *Dignitatis humanae*, of the moral duty of human beings and societies toward the true religion and the true Church of Christ. We do not doubt that in these places (and elsewhere) the church has taught new things. We are sure that John Paul II understood that the church broke new ground, too. To say that teaching is "new" is not to say, or imply, that it contradicts any previous teaching.

VICAR OF CHRIST

A sound understanding of John Paul II's writings on human nature and law depends upon understanding his unique competence as supreme pastor of all the world's Catholics, as Vicar of Christ on earth, as Peter.

In the words of the Second Vatican Council's *Decree on the Apostolate of the Laity*, "the Church was founded for the purpose of spreading the Kingdom of Christ throughout the earth for the glory of God the Father, to enable all men to share in His saving redemption, and that through them the whole world might enter into a relationship with Christ."[44] The mission of the church is "to proclaim and to spread among all peoples the Kingdom of Christ and of God and to be, on earth, the initial budding forth of that kingdom."[45] The church is missionary by its very nature: "She cannot do other than proclaim the Gospel, that is, the fullness of the truth which God has enabled us to know about himself" through Jesus Christ.[46]

All activity of all the church's members toward its evangelistic end is called "apostolate." The laity possesses a distinct apostolate, as do bishops, including (in a special way) the Bishop of Rome, the pope. Bishops are "pastors of souls."[47] In union with the pope, they carry on until the end of time the work of Christ, "the eternal pastor."[48] Theirs is the task of spiritual superintendence. The measure of their success is, fundamentally, the salvation of souls.

The source and measure of John Paul II's teaching on law and human nature is Jesus Christ. "One can and must say that Jesus Christ has a significance and a value for the human race and its history, which are unique and singular, proper to him alone, exclusive, universal, and absolute.... The Lord is the goal of human history, the focal point of the desires of history and of civilization, the center of mankind, the joy of all hearts, and the fulfillment of all aspirations.... [Jesus is] the Alpha and the Omega, the first and the last, the beginning and the end (Rev. 22:13)."[49] "Jesus Christ is the new beginning of everything.... Christ is thus the fulfillment of the yearning of all the world's religions and, as such, he is their sole and definitive completion."[50] "Man's true identity is only fully revealed to him through faith, and it is precisely from faith that the church's social teaching begins. While drawing upon all the contributions made by the sciences and philosophy, her social teaching is aimed at helping man on the path of salvation."[51] In other words, the church's "social" teaching is, at bottom, the gospel itself, the good news: "God and his mystery of salvation in Christ to every human being."[52]

To know humanity, John Paul II argued, one must know God. To know God one must know Jesus. The human person is the "visible image of the invisible God."[53] John Paul II asserted, too, that "the decisive answer to every one of man's questions, his religious and moral questions in particular, is given by Jesus Christ, or rather is Jesus Christ himself."[54] The notion of humanity as *imago Dei* is the still center, the hub, of all matters pertaining to law and human nature—social, political, moral, and spiritual. The notion is made possible, intelligible, only by Jesus Christ.

TWO QUESTIONS ABOUT PAPAL TEACHINGS

How is it possible for John Paul II—or any pope—to teach *creatively* about temporal things? Upon what basis does this pastor of souls and guardian of revealed truth write *authoritatively* about the things of this world?

CREATIVITY

Papal teaching about temporal things involves several stages or steps: identification of true norms, articulation of them to and for modern humanity, and application of them to specified contemporary threats to humanity, to human dignity and eternal salvation. Identifying these threats is mostly what is meant by the phrase, often said by John Paul II to be his task, seeking "the signs of the times."

Creativity is most important when the pope seeks to discern the "signs of the times." Since these "signs" have principally to do with acts and threats of a moral and spiritual nature, they do not consist of reports (such as experts or journalists might compile) about human disasters and needs. No pope possesses a special competence regarding facts of that sort. They do nevertheless form the substratum upon which the pope can mount an analysis of what people should do, and must not do. More commonly, the "signs" appear differently to secular experts than they do to the pope, even where they agree about certain basic facts. Everyone might agree, for example, on the present population of India, and on what it is likely to be in 2050. Everyone might also agree on the facts of current income distribution in, say, Guatemala. But what, exactly, constitutes the problem of "poverty" in the latter, and whether there is "overpopulation" in the former, are matters upon which the pope and the United Nations population officials might disagree.

These divergences do not owe to different tastes, preferences, or circumstances. They arise, John Paul II repeatedly warned, from different conceptions of the person and his or her flourishing. Social science is not a value-free undertaking; social diagnostics is, rather, John Paul II wrote, "the accurate formulation of the results of a careful reflection on the complex realities of human existence, in society and in the international order, in the light of faith and of the Church's tradition."[55]

New things can stimulate fresh insights into the meaning of received doctrine and, in that sense, bring forth new (hitherto implicit, unarticulated) teachings. Perhaps Vatican II's development of doctrine on religious liberty best illustrates this creativity. A new norm, conferring a certain immunity from coercion upon non-Catholics in matters of religious expression, there emerged from sustained reflection, in the light of experience, upon the inviolable freedom of the act of faith.[56]

Finally, perennial truths may find new expression. The best compact statement of this possibility is from *Veritatis splendor*: "Certainly there is a need to seek out and to discover the most adequate formulation for universal and permanent moral norms in the light of different cultural contexts.... The norms expressing that truth remain valid in their substance, but must be specified and determined ... in the light of historical circumstances by the Church's Magisterium."[57]

TEMPORAL AUTHORITY

John Paul II recognized that temporal things are "penultimate." Because he was the universal pastor, temporal concerns were not the heart of his apostolate. But neither John Paul II nor his teaching was "otherworldly." His teachings on moral, social, and political matters are not ethereal, vague, or desultory. On social and political matters, those teachings are indeed limited. But where John Paul II intervened, he did so precisely because he perceived a threat—in social or political proposals and ideologies—to the salvation of souls. His method was to identify the anthropological, metaphysical, and ethical presuppositions of a particular proposal, practice, or institution; their implications for the moral and spiritual welfare of persons; and the morality of actions required of persons in order to maintain the system or activity under review, and to evaluate them all according to their implications for persons' salvation. "The social doctrine of the Church does not propose any particular system; but in the light of other fundamental principles, she makes it possible at once to see to what extent existing systems conform or do not conform to the demands of human dignity."[58]

John Paul II's method leaves on the table a range of political and social options eligible for choice. "Eligibility" means that the option is consistent with human beings' eternal welfare; it is not contrary or a danger to the faith. "Eligibility" does not imply or entail the equivalence, all things considered, of options, one with another. Some admissible options, we may well suppose, are vastly superior (even in the pope's judgment) to others, considered just as solutions to legal, political, or social problems. But John Paul II's competence was limited to gauging their merit according to enduring standards. Selecting from among the eligible possibilities was beyond his competence as pope.

How might one best describe this limited competence of pastors? They are called to state clearly "the principles concerning the purpose of creation and the use of temporal things and must offer the moral and spiritual aids by which the temporal order may be renewed in Christ."[59] Pastors (just as such) lack the competence, however, in technical, sociological, and other specialized fields of knowledge to choose effectively and reliably the option best suited to serve the common good. In any event, these choices, and the communication, coordination, and cooperation with believers and nonbelievers alike required to execute them, are for the laity to make.

John Paul II often reiterated the thought, here expressed in *Centesimus annus*:

The Church has no models to present; models that are real and truly effective can arise only within the framework of different historical situations, through the efforts of all those who responsibly confront concrete problems in all their social, economic, political and cultural aspects, as these interact with one another.... The Church ... is not entitled to express preferences for this or that institutional or constitutional solution. Her contribution to the political order is precisely her vision of the dignity of the person revealed in all its fullness in the mystery of the Incarnate Word.[60]

How or why does the pope teach authoritatively on temporal matters? The question can be fully answered only by asking what "temporal," more exactly, denotes. The Second Vatican Council fathers identified the constituent elements of the temporal order as "the good things of life and the prosperity of the family, culture, economic matters, the arts and professions, the laws of the political community, international relations."[61] They possess value as instruments or material of salvation; they "aid in the attainment of man's ultimate goal."[62] But they also possess their own intrinsic value. "This value has been established in them by God. ... 'God saw that all He had made was very good' (Gen 1:31)."[63]

The basic goods of this world are terminal points in the practical reasoning of choosing, acting persons. They anchor human choices, and human choices last forever, unless repented, in which case the choice to repent lasts eternally. And choices are forever decisive: "The Church teaches the way which man must follow in this world in order to enter the kingdom of God. Her teaching therefore extends to the whole moral order, and notably to the justice which must regulate human relations."[64] "Not everyone who cries, 'Lord, Lord,' will enter the kingdom of heaven, but those who do the Father's will by taking a strong grip on the work at hand."[65]

The writ of moral truth runs all the way to the statehouse and to the barracks, and all the way to St. Peter's. As stated in *Veritatis splendor*: "When it is a matter of the moral norms prohibiting intrinsic evil, there are no privileges or exceptions for anyone. It makes no difference whether one is the master of the world or the 'poorest of the poor' on the face of the earth. Before the demands of morality we are all absolutely equal."[66] The encyclical continues by saying: "The negative [moral] precepts of the natural law are universally valid. They oblige each and every individual, always and in every circumstance."[67]

In *Evangelium vitae*, John Paul II explained, "Each individual in fact has moral responsibility for the acts which he personally performs; no one can be exempted from this responsibility, and on the basis of it everyone will be judged by God himself."[68] John Paul II recounted the "infamies" that "poison human society" —slavery, prostitution, murder, abortion, genocide, and more. The fathers at the Second Vatican Council said that these things "do more harm to those who practice them than to those who suffer from the injury."[69]

The council's statements about last things shaped John Paul II's response, as he described it in *Veritatis splendor*, to the Second Vatican Council fathers' call "for a renewal of moral theology, so that its teaching would display the lofty vocation which the faithful have received in Christ, the only response fully capable of satisfying the desire of the human heart."[70] The council depicted heaven as the fulfillment of a morally upright Christian life, "a dwelling place and a new earth where justice will abide, and whose blessedness will answer and surpass all the longings for peace which spring up in the human heart."[71] "The kingdom of God, being in the world without being of the world, throws light on the order of human society, while the power of grace penetrates that order [and] gives it life."[72]

Vatican II called for a renewal of moral theology, effectively for an integral Christian humanism. The fathers there taught that "the norm of human activity is this: that in accord with the divine plan and will, it harmonize[s] with the genuine good of the human race, and it allow men as individuals and as members of society to pursue their total vocation and fulfill it."[73] In *Veritatis splendor*, John Paul II explained the young man's question—"What good must I do to have eternal life?"—as "not so much about rules to be followed, but about the full meaning of life."[74] The negative prohibitions in the Decalogue, moreover, are meant not simply to stifle or suppress; they "are meant to safeguard the good of the person, the image of God, by protecting his goods."[75]

FREEDOM YESTERDAY, TODAY, AND TOMORROW

Karol Wojtyla attended all three sessions of the Second Vatican Council. Rocco Buttiglione, John Paul II's commentator and collaborator, explains that Wojtyla believed Vatican II's "greatest achievement" "was its acknowledgment of freedom of conscience as a natural right of the person. He was concerned, however, that this freedom, [if] exercised improperly," could lead to relativism. Wojtyla also worried about a "misunderstanding of philosophical pluralism within Catholicism. While the Council ... endorsed dialogue with a variety of contemporary philosophies, Wojtyla claimed that if certain living elements of classical philosophy did not survive, there [would be] little chance of maintaining the link with traditional affirmations of the faith."[76] John Paul II's writings on politics, society, and human nature are a sustained, deep, fruitful meditation on natural religiosity, in relation to Catholic faith—a supernatural gift that is a *free* response to revelation in Jesus—in relation to the objective demands of moral truth.

The requirements of authentic religious freedom are a fount of the pope's legal, social, and political teachings. Those teachings flow, in part, from what it takes—on the part of each person, acting for himself or herself, and of societies to help others—to shape up to be open to, and then to receive, Catholic faith. His teachings are often warnings of the hindrances that persons and societies throw up instead.

The pope held that a person fully knows himself or herself only in and through faith, as a disciple of Jesus Christ, called to build the Kingdom and thus to achieve salvation by, first, adhering to the objective moral law and, second, discerning and faithfully carrying out his or her unique vocation. This destiny transcends earthly things, and requires that person be free. "In constantly reaffirming the transcendent dignity of the person, the Church's method is always that of respect for freedom."[77]

Why *free*? Because God, through Jesus, calls human beings to a response of faith, by which they freely entrust themselves to the God revealed by Jesus. Faith is also free assent of the individual to the truths God has revealed.[78] Faith is thus friendship with Jesus, and it is accepting certain propositions as true. Neither of these two components of Catholic faith is effective save where the individual acts freely. No one can profess faith for another.

This is theological faith. The pope contrasted it sharply with "religious belief": "That sum of experience and thought that constitutes the human treasury of wisdom and religious aspiration, which man in his search for truth has conceived and acted upon in his relationship to God and the Absolute."[79] Religious belief is experience in search of absolute truth, "lacking assent to God who reveals himself."[80]

This searching, too, must be free. "Each individual has a right to be respected in his own journey in search of the truth," John Paul II wrote, though there is a prior "grave" moral obligation to search for the truth and to adhere to it once known.[81] "In Christ," however, "religion is no longer a 'blind search for God' but the response of faith to God who reveals himself … a response made possible by that one Man" by which, and in whom, "all creation responds to God."[82]

The picture presented by John Paul II was that of natural humanity, reaching up to God, seeking the truth about God and God's will for us. This human reaching is limited in its fulfillment to the truths and rewards of natural religion. Natural religion includes the truths that there is a greater than human source of meaning and value; that this source is somehow responsible for the existence of contingent beings and matter; and that human beings are therefore dependent, in an important way, upon this source for their well-being, even for their existence.

John Paul II believed that humanity naturally wants God, or wants to want God, and will seek God if not deterred or prevented by disorder. Human beings are spiritually native fliers; they are hardwired to soar after things hidden beyond the skies.

Evangelization seeks to fulfill and perfect this natural urge by the light of revelation in Jesus. "Those who obey the promptings of the Spirit of truth are already on their way to salvation. But the Church, to whom this truth has been entrusted, must go out to meet their desire, so as to bring them the truth."[83]

Culture is the religious question writ large. "At the heart of every culture lies the attitude man takes to the greatest mystery: the mystery of God. Different cultures are basically different ways of facing the question of the meaning of personal existence."[84] John Paul II referred to this as the essential "subjectivity" of culture. He defined culture as "the specific mode of a truly human existence to which one gains access through the development of one's intellectual capacities, moral virtues, abilities to relate with other human beings, and talents for creating things which are useful and beautiful."[85]

In *Veritatis splendor*, the pope wrote that "it is not difficult to discover at the bottom of these situations [of injustice] causes which are properly 'cultural,' linked to particular ways of looking at man, society and the world. Indeed, at the heart of the issue of culture we find the moral sense, which is in turn rooted and fulfilled in the religious sense."[86] And culture, too, must be free: "It is not within the competence of public authorities to determine culture. Their function is to promote and protect the cultural life of everyone, including that of minorities."[87]

At the heart of John Paul II's "church-state" doctrine is, then, freedom. He adheres to the council's teaching: "It is only right ... that at all times and in all places, the Church should have true freedom to preach the faith, to teach her social doctrine, to exercise her role freely among men, and also to pass moral judgment in those matters which regard public order when the fundamental rights of a person or the salvation of souls require it."[88] In a neglected section of the council's decree concerning bishops, we read that, to promote the church's freedom and for the welfare of the faithful, "no more rights or privileges of election, nomination, presentation, or designation for the office of bishop may be granted to civil authorities."[89]

Freedom is not identical with separation, isolation, or mutual abstention—and, in that sense, "autonomy." The council fathers stated clearly that public authority is to "promote" the religious life of the people. And public authority is surely on notice to refrain from programs, policies, and practices—including ideological training—that hinder the human capacity to search for and freely embrace religious truth, or that frustrate that search more directly.

PERSONAL VOCATION

John Paul II mined the Second Vatican Council's development of the concept of personal vocation. Understanding personal vocation is essential to understanding John Paul II's teachings on law, politics, society, and human nature.

Vocation means, most simply, calling. As a protocol matter, during the centuries before the council, vocation almost always referred to the religious life. Laypersons, it surely seemed, had no vocation. Married life was sometimes said to be a calling, but rarely a vocation; "vocation," in reference to the family, meant the possibility that one of the children might become a priest, brother, or nun.

But Catholic faith teaches, and has always taught, that we and everything we do are envisioned by God from before time; that we are all called to be God's adopted children; that we all may be saved. The faith has always taught that nothing happens save according to God's will, at least by God's permission; everything we do is encompassed by God's Providence. The implication of these truths must be that each of us is somehow involved, in all that we do, in carrying out the work initiated by Jesus Christ, the work of sanctifying the world. Recent Catholic Church teaching is that there is such an organizing principle of the life of each Christian; it is called a "personal vocation."

What is a "personal vocation"? Christians have a common calling to lives of faith, hope, and charity. All are required to observe the moral law. The Ten Commandments are not variables according to our vocation; they are universally binding. These common obligations are, one might say, the foundational elements, the infrastructure, of one's Christian life. They are parts of one's vocation, one might also say, but they are not distinguishing features. These indispensable common features are not strictly pertinent to the concept of personal vocation. Personal vocation involves an individualized plan of life. Beyond the common obligations of Christians, we must choose from among alternatives, often many, that are equally consistent with the moral law and theological virtues. What is God's will for me? Which option has my name written on it?

The concept of personal vocation presupposes justification by grace through faith. But justification transforms a person—God's gracious work makes one a new "creature," a new "human being," a member of Christ's gloriously risen body. Living now in Christ, one has one's own part or function to perform, just as each bodily organ has its own work to do. But being a member of Christ does not make one do one's part automatically. Persons still are free human beings; they contribute to the building up of the one body by cooperating with Jesus in completing God's overall plan. Each one has a unique life of good works, planned by God beforehand, to "walk in." This unique life of good works is not always easy or pleasant: as Jesus' disciple, a person must take up his or her cross each day and follow Christ.

There is a simulacrum of personal vocation abroad in today's culture. This counterfeit would have one ask oneself: What do I really want out of life? What is my dream? It is a matter of identifying one's objectives or goals, as guidance counselors might phrase it, of setting one's priorities, and persevering despite obstacles with an optimistic expectation of success. Personal vocation refers to putting oneself entirely at the service of God, and of others, after clearheaded, protracted discernment. It is not, like the counterfeit, a thing of imaginative fancy, of emulating the well-known, or of pursuing enlightened self-interest.

In sum, personal vocation is God's plan for using, with our cooperation, God's special gifts to us in serving others, and thereby building up the heavenly *communio*.

SUBJECTIVISM AND SOCIAL ENGINEERING

The central aim of John Paul II's teaching on temporal matters may thus be described as liberation, but this liberation "involves all the processes which aim at securing and guaranteeing the conditions needed for the exercise of an *authentic* human freedom."[90] We would add, to display fully the pope's intentions, the word "effective" before "exercise." Freedom is threatened principally in two ways, one internal, the other external. They correspond to the two types of disorder which impedes humankind's native drive toward God and, beyond that, to Catholic faith.

INTERNAL DISORDER

Let us start with internal disorder. The best summary statement of this part of the truth about freedom is from the Congregation for the Doctrine of the Faith: "Freedom is not the liberty to do anything whatsoever. It is the freedom to do good, and in this alone happiness is to be found."[91] It is "interior mastery of one's own acts and self-determination," and as such "immediately entails a relationship with the ethical order."[92] "Man becomes free to the extent that he comes to a knowledge of the truth and to the extent that this truth—and not any other forces—guide his will.... Freedom attains its full development only by accepting the truth. In a world without truth, freedom loses its foundation and man is exposed to the violence of passion and to manipulation, both open and hidden."[93]

The all-too-common conception of freedom that the pope criticized is self-sufficiency, autonomy, the individual as master of an array of techniques to get what he or she wants—in short, moral subjectivism. The antonyms of this popular notion are heteronomy (dependence upon the will of another), impotence, and powerlessness. Much of the encyclical *Veritatis splendor* is concerned to reconnect freedom to law, to reason, to the givenness of moral truth. The pope there and elsewhere movingly described the "servitude" and "slavery" to which persons consign themselves by hankering after an illusory emancipation from reality and the moral law. Persons would become like God: they would create good and evil, and fancy themselves masters, if not of millions, at least entirely of themselves.

But the person who would emancipate himself or herself by bursting the bounds of reality, including the truth about humanity's temporal good and supernatural destiny, ends up in shackles. Such people succeed, not in liberating themselves, but in putting on the brand of a new master. These emancipated persons seem foolishly to believe that they are free of the delusion of wishful thinking. They manage instead to become slaves to their own passions, to their own appetites.

EXTERNAL DISORDER

External disorder results from technical innovations characteristic of our era; modernity makes new forms of slavery possible. People are in danger as never before of being spiritually kidnapped by principalities and powers, ideologies and systems, by huge projects governed by imperatives of various sorts. John Paul II said: "The individual today is often suffocated between two poles represented by the state and the marketplace. At times it seems as though he exists only as a producer and consumer of goods, or as an object of State administration."[94]

The pope criticized collectivism and bureaucratization—political or otherwise—because they strip persons of initiative and, almost always, constitute organized exploitation and manipulation. At the same time, he said that markets are dangerously prone to exploitation and manipulation. Buyers are lured into purchases that do them no genuine good; wealth may be used unfairly to reinforce socioeconomic injustices.

Socialism, John Paul II wrote in *Centesimus annus*, considers a person as a cog in the big human machine, "a molecule within the social organism.... Socialism, likewise, maintains that the good of the individual can be realized without reference to his free choice, to the unique and exclusive responsibility which he exercises in the face of good or evil."[95] Socialism's errors are therefore anthropological in nature. Being anthropological, they are moral and, ultimately, theological.

"Structures of sin" stand at the confluence of internal and external disorder. By this term John Paul II did not mean to excuse modern humanity's moral failings by attributing them, at least partially, to objective conditions beyond our control. "Structures of sin" are "always linked to the concrete acts of individuals who introduce these structures, consolidate them and make them difficult to remove."[96] The pope explicitly distinguished his usage from sociological usages. Sociologists typically deploy the language of structure to alleviate human moral responsibility (as if structures were beyond human agency), but also from nonmoral human dereliction—"shortsightedness," "mistaken political calculations," "imprudent economic decisions."[97]

According to the Congregation for the Doctrine of the Faith, structures are institutions and practices that people find or create to organize political, economic, or social life. "Being necessary in themselves, they often tend to become fixed and fossilized as mechanisms relatively independent of human will.... However, they always depend on the responsibility of man, who can alter them, and not upon an alleged determinism of history."[98]

Structures of sin are, in truth, human sins, accumulated, now turned around and threatening persons. "The manner in which the individual exercises his freedom is conditioned in innumerable ways. While these certainly have an influence on freedom, they do not determine it; they make the exercise of freedom more difficult or less difficult, but they cannot destroy it."[99] "God calls man to freedom. In each person there lives a desire to be free. And yet this desire almost always tends toward slavery and oppression."[100]

SOLIDARITY, SUBSIDIARITY, AND WORK

Morally upright social relations are characterized by "solidarity." Solidarity is "not a vague feeling of compassion or shallow distress at the misfortunes of so many people, both near and far. On the contrary, it is a firm and persevering determination to commit oneself to the common good; that is to say, to the good of all and of each individual because we are all really responsible for all."[101]

Subsidiarity protects individuals and communities against overweening larger powers. The Congregation for the Doctrine of the Faith states, "Neither the state nor any society must ever substitute itself for the initiative and responsibility of individuals and of intermediate communities at the level on which they can function, nor must they take away the room necessary for their freedom."[102] One deficiency in the notion is its partly formal quality. Nothing in the statement of systematic preference tells you on what level different communities function adequately.

Through work, a person "makes part of the earth his own, precisely the part which he has acquired through work; this is the origin of [private] property."[103] "Private property or some ownership of external goods affords each person the scope for personal and family autonomy."[104] Private property thus is required by the principle of subsidiarity; the state must give persons and their families the room necessary to acquire a proper autonomy.

The right of economic initiative is often suppressed, though it is a right important to and for individuals as well as for the common good.[105] "It would appear that, on the level of individual nations and of international relations, the free market is the most efficient instrument for utilizing resources and effectively responding to needs."[106]

But "this is true only for those needs which are 'solvent,' insofar as they are endowed with purchasing power, and for those resources which are 'marketable,' insofar as they are capable of obtaining a satisfactory price."[107] Many human needs, however, have no place in the market. Yet it is precisely these needs that constitute a morally compelling reason for effective action to alleviate distress, wherever one has the opportunity and the means to do so, subject to one's other moral responsibilities, of a similarly grave nature, concerning one's goods. "It is a strict duty of justice and truth not to allow fundamental human needs to remain unsatisfied."[108]

This moral duty is supported by the church's unswerving commitment to the notion that all the goods of the earth, including those called into being by the hand of human beings, are destined for all. "God ... gave the earth to the whole human race for the sustenance of all its members, without excluding or favoring anyone. This is the foundation of the universal destination of the earth's goods."[109] Even the most advanced synthetic foods or gadgets arise from material of some kind, created and held in being by God the Creator. Human beings contribute their own talents of similar origins and always subject to a mortgage held by humankind.

SECULARISM

"In seeking the deepest roots" of the contemporary crisis, "we cannot restrict ourselves to [this] perverse idea of freedom.... We have to go to the heart of the tragedy being experienced by modern man: the eclipse of the sense of God and of man, typical of a social and cultural climate dominated by secularism."[110] Secularism produces, "with its ubiquitous tentacles," these ill effects: a loss of human dignity and life; "the systematic violation of the moral law"; a "practical materialism, which breeds individualism, utilitarianism and hedonism"; a culture of "having" and "doing," rather than of "being"; a depersonalized and distorted, manipulative sexuality.[111]

Secularism produces a culture of death. "It is at the heart of the moral conscience that the eclipse of the sense of God and of man, with all its various and deadly consequences for life, is taking place"; an "extremely serious and mortal danger: that of confusion between good and evil, precisely in relation to the fundamental right to life."[112]

We understand the pope's assertion to be that the "eclipse" is the immediate effect, if not a corollary, of "secularism": the condition of human affairs where God is practically absent, presumed to be either nonexistent or uninvolved with human affairs. At least as John Paul II used the term, "secularism" is a possible description of societies or human collectives of some sort; individuals are believers, atheists, agnostics. It is important to note, too, that everyone in a secularized society, including fervent believers, is affected by God's practical absence. Even "Christian communities [are] themselves [put] to the test," the pope wrote.[113]

The pope seemingly said that the eclipse and secularism are conceptually distinct from and temporally prior to negative effects such as subjectivism, social engineering, and ideology. But these latter phenomena are not entirely derivative conditions; they do not surface in consciousness and choice only after secularism has persons in its grasp. Subjectivism and social engineering—the will to power over one self and over others—are perennial temptations. A well-ordered culture helps persons resist their allure. In a secularized culture, the pope suggested, these temptations wear down and overcome many, if not most, people.

How does secularism work its devastating consequences? As we understand John Paul II: where God is eclipsed, the Creator is occluded, and human beings lose their sense of creatureliness. This sense, where intact and healthy, provides persons with the psychological, intellectual, and spiritual humility necessary, or, highly conducive, to accepting limits, law, givens—in short, dependence upon God for all that one is and all that one has. Where this theistic psychology is broken, human beings can scarcely avoid considering themselves a colossus.[114]

While nowhere to our knowledge did John Paul II identify his target as a distinctly post-Christian secularism, we think that is exactly what he did describe. Wherever Christianity entered a culture, it sought to supplant all the other false gods; neither nature nor the heavens nor fate retained spiritual authority in the wake of the gospel. The First Commandment requires no less. Wherever Christianity succeeded in its efforts, there could be just two possible sources of meaning and value for human beings: God—who commanded human beings to have no other gods and to smash graven images and idols—and humankind. Where secularism achieves cultural and political hegemony, then, there remain only human beings to supply their own meaning and value.

IDEOLOGY AND LIBERATION THEOLOGY

"Too often culture is debased by ideology, and education is turned into an instrument at the service of political and economic power."[115] John Paul II's objection to ideology is, at first glance, a simple reductionist criticism. Ideologies err by building a totalistic worldview upon fragmentary truths. The part is made paradigmatic for the whole. Since this improper substitution is characteristic of ideology, ideologies as such are harmful. There are elements of truth in them, but they serve us poorly by obscuring or distorting the rest of the truth.

Marxist collectivism and liberal capitalism are ideologies. The former denies human individuality and moral freedom; the latter is all too prone to lead humanity into a consumerist or profit mentality (or both), in which having eclipses being. Neither is fit for human consumption.

A second glance at John Paul II's usage and criticism of ideology suggests a different and bolder criticism. John Paul II referred to "very different visions of man and his freedom and social role" that form the basis of liberal capitalism and Marxist collectivism.[116] His criticism now seems to be that their visions are simply false. Only a correct view of the person—and nothing else—will do. "The guiding principle of … all of the Church's social doctrine is a correct view of the human person."[117]

The difference in the criticisms is that the first implies that ideologues do not have, in truth, a complete vision of humanity. They have bits of one, and unwisely overstate or inflate the value of the bits. The second objection holds that ideologues do have a total vision of humanity. But the vision is false.

On a third, and final, glance we think the pope is mounting an extraordinarily sophisticated criticism, one that creatively synthesizes both criticisms we just described. We think this method of evaluating social scientific analyses is not only sound, but portable, very important, and vastly underappreciated.

The pope seems to have said this: Ideologies are a species of viewpoint within social science. All social scientific theories (accounts, paradigms) depend crucially upon concept formation, hypotheses, definitions, and other mental constructs for their explanatory power. These tools of the trade, we take the pope to be insisting, are as sharp or as blunt as the validity of the theorist's overall conception of humanity. A false view of human nature can only produce, even in the hands of the most intelligent theorist, crude and misleading explanatory tools that will dim rather than enlighten our understanding of the social phenomenon under study.

We find some confirmation of our interpretation in *Sollicitudo rei socialis*:

> The Church's social doctrine is not a "third way" between liberal capitalism and Marxist collectivism nor even a possible alternative to other solutions less radically opposed to one another: Rather, it constitutes a category of its own. Nor is it an ideology, but rather the accurate formulation of the results of a careful reflection on the complex realities of human existence, in society and in the international order, in the light of faith and of the Church's tradition. Its main aim is to interpret these realities, determining their conformity with or divergence from the lines of the Gospel teaching on man and his vocation, a vocation which is at once earthly and transcendent; its aim is thus to guide Christian behavior. It therefore belongs to the field, not of ideology, but of theology and particularly of moral theology.[118]

We find further confirmation of the concerns for ideology in the Vatican's published critiques of liberation theology. These are, however, surely not a condemnation, for the Congregation for the Doctrine of the Faith takes over from liberation theology much of the liberationists' indictment of injustice in Central and South America. Nor does the critique condemn concrete courses of action, save those that everywhere and always violate the moral law.[119] In accord with the moral law, the Congregation for the Doctrine of the Faith does not rule out armed rebellion as a last means of overthrowing obdurate injustice.

The target of the Congregation's objections is rather a mentality, a worldview, an ideology that contains "serious deviations" and "risks of deviation, damaging to the faith and to Christian living, that are brought about by certain forms of liberation theology which use, in an insufficiently critical manner, concepts borrowed from various currents of Marxist thought."[120] The Congregation for the Doctrine of the Faith then warns against several distinct propositions or fundamental tenets, more theoretical than practical, as "not compatible with the Christian conception of humanity and society." Among these are: atheism; "class struggle" (a Marxian concept not synonymous with "severe social conflict"); the theory of class struggle as the fundamental law of history; and a perversion of the Christian term, "the Church of the poor," limiting it to a solely material meaning.[121] The document dismisses the "classless society" as a "myth," and cautions that revolutionary promises (of various sorts) promise more than can be delivered.[122] Often, revolutionary struggle worsens the condition of those it proclaims to serve. At the heart of the critique, swinging free from the Latin American context, is the analysis of social scientific constructs, including ideologies, which we call the pope's third avenue of criticism.

POLITICAL COMMUNITY AND PUBLIC AUTHORITY

John Paul II embraced the Second Vatican Council's teaching that the purpose of political society is to help persons to achieve their perfection. John Paul II found in the teaching of Pope Leo XIII much the same doctrine as that held by the Second Vatican Council fathers. Leo, he said, "frequently insist[ed] on necessary limits to the State's intervention and on its instrumental character."[123]

The legitimate moral aim of political community, and the principle of all its activity, is the common good: "the sum total of social conditions which allow people, either as groups or as individuals, to reach their fulfillment more fully and more easily."[124] So long as the public authority works for the common good, various political and social arrangements are morally acceptable. As the pope asserted in his address to the United Nations in 1995, "There is no single model for organizing the politics and economics of human freedom; different cultures and different historical experiences give rise to different institutional forms of public life in a free and responsible society."[125]

The political community is an expression of humankind's natural sociability. In our time it is a ubiquitous, indispensable aid to the realization of the human personality. The polity is nevertheless subordinate, instrumental:

> Men, families and the various groups which make up the civil community are aware that they cannot achieve a truly human life by their own unaided efforts. They see the need for a wider community, within which each one makes his specific contribution every day toward an ever broader realization of the common good.[126]

> Hence, the purpose of the political community is to enable (men, families and associations ... attain their own perfection.[127]

The political community supplements, in other words, the efforts of men and nonpolitical associations to flourish. The polity flourishes—achieves its distinctive perfection or common good—precisely as persons and their associations achieve their good. In this way, the polity is secondary, subsidiary, instrumental, not basic. Stated perhaps most succinctly in the Catechism, largely taken from *Gaudium et spes*: "The common good is always oriented towards the progress of persons: 'The order of things must be subordinate to the order of persons, and not the other way around.' "[128]

The moral authority of those exercising public authority is firmly established. The Catechism provides, we think, the sound interpretation of the classic text on the moral legitimacy of political authority, Romans 13. The Catechism states: "Human society can be neither well-ordered nor prosperous unless it has some people invested with legitimate authority to preserve its institutions and to devote themselves as far as is necessary to work and care for the good of all." This "authority" is that quality whereby persons or institutions make laws and expect obedience from others.[129]

The need for authority arises from an obvious moral need for coordination and direction whenever human beings act for common purposes: "If the political community is not to be torn apart while everyone follows his own opinion, there must be an authority to direct the energies of all citizens toward the common good, not in a mechanical or despotic fashion, but by acting above all as a moral force which appeals to each one's freedom and sense of responsibility."[130]

Public authority is "founded on human nature and hence belongs to the order designed by God."[131] It is rooted in facts of human condition and arises to deal with the problem of coordinated action that any society of diverse persons faces, even where those persons all possess good will. Public authority directs the activities of free and responsible persons, who are morally obliged, however, to obey legitimate authority: those acting for the common good, within the limits of morality, and "according to the juridical order legitimately established or due to be established."[132]

Gaudium et spes continues:

> But where citizens are oppressed by a public authority overstepping its competence, they should not protest against those things which are objectively required for the common good; but it is legitimate for them to defend their own rights and the rights of their fellow citizens against the abuse of this authority, while keeping within those limits drawn by the natural law and the Gospels.[133]

LAW, MORALS, AND THE FAMILY

The tradition stretching back through Aquinas never held that civil law could or should reproduce morality as such, that it could and should enforce all moral obligations. *Evangelium vitae* states that "the purpose of civil law is different and more limited in scope than that of the moral law."[134] Whether those entrusted with legislative authority for the common good should pass this or that law depends (even if the action prohibited by the law is truly immoral) upon a host of contingent prudential considerations.

Society has a compelling interest in marriage and stable family life. This does not mean that there are no moral limits to the means that governments may employ to protect the institution of marriage. It does mean, however, that governments must decline to treat all sexual relationships as legally equal, or confer the status of marriage on nonmarital relationships. Marriage "is constituted by the covenant whereby 'a man and a woman establish between themselves a partnership of their whole life'.... Only such a union can be recognized and ratified as a 'marriage' in society." No other relationship may be so recognized, lest there be a "serious threat to the future of the family and of society itself."[135]

The family originates in marital communion, a community of persons that is "the first human 'society'."[136] The political community should recognize it as primordial, pre-political, foundational—"in a way entirely its own, a sovereign society."[137] The family requires recognition by society of its status as a subject. "Subject" is scarcely a univocal term in John Paul II's thought, but it means at least that a subject is due appropriate treatment by others, including the state, as an expression of human beings' deepest nature, as an irreducible aspect of their well-being.

We see throughout the pope's many encomiums to marriage a recurring image, that of an antidote to the subjectivism and manipulation rampant in modern society. The family and especially the marital union itself are occasions for selfless giving, for making oneself a "gift" to the other, for genuine interpersonal communion, for two-in-one-flesh unity. Family is a refuge from the selfishness of the ambient culture, an exemplar of truly human living, a training ground for saints.

A NEW FEMINISM

The closing remarks of the Second Vatican Council act as a suitable precursor to the new feminism proclaimed by John Paul II:

> The hour is coming, in fact has come, when the vocation of women is being acknowledged in its fullness, the hour in which women acquire in the world an influence ... never hitherto achieved. That is why, at this moment when the human race is undergoing so deep a transformation, women imbued with the spirit of the Gospel can do so much to aid humanity in not falling.[138]

In *Redemptoris mater* (1987), John Paul II laid groundwork for his theology of women by teaching on the priority of the "Marian Church" over the "Petrine Church." The discipleship represented by the Blessed Mother preceded and, indeed, made possible the authority of the church exhibited by Peter and his successors. Because Marian Church discipleship precedes Petrine Church hierarchy, a fundamental baptismal equality exists between men and women that is prior to any distinction of functions between the two. It is Mary who "sheds light on womanhood as such by the very fact that God, in the sublime event of the Incarnation of his Son, entrusted himself to the ministry, the free and active ministry of a woman."[139]

The philosophical and theological foundation of John Paul II's feminism is furthered in his 1988 apostolic letter, *Mulieris dignitatem*. From the beginning, the pope teaches, there was an inherent equality between male and female. Just as the human person was created in the likeness of God as male and female, Christ redeemed humanity as male and female. Relations between the two have been distorted over time; this distortion has included domination of women by men that denied the equal dignity of women. Liberation from this domination is achieved by woman's embrace of her distinct vocation, her "personal originality." John Paul II stressed that "women must not appropriate to themselves male characteristics contrary to their own feminine 'originality.'"[140] God has inscribed in human nature a unity and equality-in-diversity between the sexes—"masculinization" only serves to deform and strip woman of her essential richness.

The "originality" of woman is dramatically manifested in motherhood. Christ came as savior through the motherhood of a woman, thus originating a covenantal relationship. The pope wrote that "every time that *motherhood* is repeated in human history, it is always *related to the Covenant* which God established with the human race through the motherhood of the Mother of God."[141] Because God entrusts humanity to women in a special way, a distinct "genius" belongs to the woman, a moral force that "strengthens their vocation" and "which can ensure sensitivity for human beings in every circumstance."[142]

Addressing married women, John Paul II discussed St. Paul's highly debated instruction that wives should be subject to their husbands and husbands must love their wives (Eph. 5:22–23). To "be subject" refers to a "'mutual subjection ... out of reverence for Christ'" and not a unilateral subjection.[143] Further, it is this mutual subjection to Christ that gives rise to the exercising of authority within marriage.[144]

Adopting the language of the women's movement, John Paul II called for a "new feminism" in 1995. He wrote that "women occupy a place, in thought and action, which is unique and decisive" in transforming culture so that it supports life.[145]

THE DEATH PENALTY AND WARFARE

In *Veritatis splendor*, the pope powerfully reaffirmed the absolutely-without-exception character of the basic negative moral norms, such as those in the Decalogue. Even "the master of the world" is bound by the demands of morality, just as and by the same measure as the "poorest of the poor."[146] Affairs of state count for nothing against these inviolable guarantees of human integrity. The pope also asserted the centrality of these norms to any decent social order. These negative moral norms form the backbone of any coherent account of inalienable human rights, including the right not to be intentionally killed, the right not to be lied to by public officials, and the right to be free of treatment as a subhuman thing or piece of property. The latter is the moral basis for prohibition on slavery, as well as the foundation for evaluating various reproductive technologies whereby a human person is at least initially brought into existence with the status of a manufactured thing.

In *Veritatis splendor*, John Paul II stated, "These norms in fact represent the unshakable foundation and solid guarantee of a just and peaceful human coexistence."[147] In *Evangelium vitae*, the pope said that the equality of all innocent lives is "the basis of all authentic social relationships which, to be truly such, can only be founded on truth and justice, recognizing and protecting every man and woman as a person and not as an object to be used."[148]

John Paul II's most striking reliance upon the notion of inviolable rights, grounded in universal duties expressed as moral norms without exception, was his position on capital punishment. Underlying the emerging papal teaching on this important issue is the "source of all other rights," "the right to life."[149] This right is the obverse of the commandment "You shall not kill" which, the pope taught in *Evangelium vitae*, "is at the basis of all life together in society."[150]

How, then, are these teachings consistent with the moral licitness of capital punishment, which has been taught by the church for centuries? Is the pope rejecting entirely the received teaching? Is his teaching ambiguous or uncertain?

One way of reconciliation would be to say that the criminal forfeits the right to life by his or her bad actions. The criminal, one might say, descends to the moral status of a beast. This possibility of reconciliation is now foreclosed by church teaching: "Not even a murderer loses his personal dignity, and God himself pledges to guarantee this."[151]

Another possibility is to hold that the state shares a divine prerogative to take the lives of those who attack the common good by committing capital crimes. If so, one might say that capital punishment involves no intentional killing—that the executioner's intention is simply to carry out God's judgment. But to hold this view, one would have to hold that God might intend to kill (as perhaps in the case of Abraham and Isaac, and elsewhere in the Old Testament) and that public authority is delegated divine authority (on one common interpretation of Romans 13:1).

The pope in *Evangelium vitae* denied both of these propositions. He said that God "preferred the correction rather than the death of a sinner."[152] Whatever might have been the case in the Old Testament, with Jesus and the New Covenant it is clearly revealed that God never intends anyone's death. "Life is always a good,"[153] and the pope meant to judge public authority by its adherence to the commandment not to kill. We are invited to test anyone's claim to be doing God's will by this prescription. Once we figure out what acts the Commandment excludes, we will know whatever there is of importance to know about God's delegation of authority.

Did the pope mean to say in *Evangelium vitae* that no one at all may be intentionally killed? There is considerable textual warrant (the use of "innocent") for supposing that it is not indicated. The norm articulated in this document usually includes the term "innocent": "the direct and voluntary killing of an innocent human being is always gravely immoral"; "no one can … claim for himself the right to destroy directly an innocent human being"; the "absolute inviolability of innocent human life."[154] But the usage of "innocent" is not consistent, and the meaning of individual statements of the norm (whatever exactly it is) is unclear. The pope defined euthanasia ("in the strict sense"), for instance, as an action or omission which "of itself and by intention causes death." Euthanasia violates God's law, he continued, because it is the "deliberate and morally unacceptable killing of a human person."[155] "Deliberate" probably denotes "freely chosen." If so, euthanasia is the freely chosen, morally unacceptable killing of a human person insofar as it intends death, by whatever means. "Innocent," so often used in statements of the norm, is nowhere used regarding euthanasia. Abortion is, the pope declared, "the deliberate killing of an innocent human being."[156] Innocent means here, though, that the unborn are in no sense "aggressors" against their mothers, as some proponents of legal abortion have suggested they are.[157]

There is considerable textual evidence that the pope did indeed mean to say that capital punishment is subject to the (adverse) judgment of a norm against all intentional killing whatsoever. John Paul II introduced his discussion of capital punishment in *Evangelium vitae* by conceding that in some circumstances ordinary persons may use deadly force. This is the question, he asserted, of "legitimate defense," which the text (and, more, the footnote in *Evangelium vitae* to the Catechism), makes clear is to the morally licit use of lethal force, not to intentional killing.[158] The pope's citation includes the statement of St. Thomas that an "act of self-defense can have a double effect: the preservation of one's own life; and the killing of the aggressor…. The one is intended, the other is not."[159] The portion of the Catechism to which the pope referred continues:

> Someone who defends his life is not guilty of murder even if he is forced to
> deal his aggressor a lethal blow: "If a man in self-defense uses more than nec-
> essary violence, it will be unlawful: whereas if he repels force with modera-

tion, his defense will be lawful.... Nor is it necessary for salvation that a man
omit the act of moderate self-defense to avoid killing the other man, since one
is bound to take more care of one's own life than of another's."[160]

Evangelium vitae cites this for the textual proposition that "the fatal outcome is attributable to the aggressor whose action brought it about," even if
the aggressor is morally irresponsible due to "lack of the use of reason."[161]

Both *Evangelium vitae* and the Catechism treat private defense of "persons" and of the family as belonging to the same moral species as defense
of "societies" and "state." Public authority's use of force, in other words,
seems to be assimilated to the one set of actions that would disable aggressors without intending to kill. In any case, public authority is the
referent of the pope's statement: "This is the context in which to place the
problem of the death penalty"—"render[ing] the aggressor incapable of
causing harm."[162] Precisely on the question of when capital punishment
is permitted, the pope said: (1) only "in cases of absolute necessity: in
other words, when it would not be possible otherwise to defend society";
and (2) " 'If bloodless means are sufficient to defend human lives against
an aggressor and to protect public order and the safety of persons, public authority must limit itself to such means.' "[163] The pope referred to a
"growing public opposition to the death penalty, even when such a penalty is seen as a kind of 'legitimate defense' on the part of society. Modern
society in fact has the means of effectively suppressing crime by rendering criminals harmless without definitively denying them the chance to
reform."[164] "Legitimate defense" of society, the whole context of this passage makes clear, refers to neutralizing those already apprehended, and
it excludes the notion of killing harmless (effectively subdued) prisoners
to threaten or cower the population at large. The pope's settled conviction was that, because of "improvements in the organization of the penal
system," cases in which death is needed "are very rare, if not practically non-existent."[165] If the pope had in mind the deterrence justification
for imposing death, he could not say this at all, much less say it without adverting to the legitimate diversity of views on the subject. In
other words, whether capital punishment "deters" in modern society is
debatable. The pope did not seem to think the question to which the
answer is "rare" is one permitting much disagreement. Thus, the pope
was not talking about deterrence when he used the phrase "protect society."

Now let us consider the decision to wage war. In what we believe to
be another manifestation of the emerging teaching we have described, the
Catechism—in line with the teaching of Pope Pius XII and contrary to the
views of Augustine and Aquinas—holds that legitimate defense is the sole

legitimate reason for engaging in war: "governments cannot be denied the right of lawful self-defense, once all peace efforts have failed."[166] Those with responsibility for the common good are enjoined by the Catechism to apply the traditional elements of just war teaching as "strict conditions for legitimate defense by military force."[167] These provisions omit—pointedly and no doubt deliberately—the traditional authority by which nations might urge war for purposes of punishment or revenge.

The Catechism makes explicit one implication of the teachings about killing, even as we have interpreted them: no one is bound by natural law or by baptism to be a pacifist. Pacifism—the renunciation of violence and bloodshed—is a legitimate option for private persons, a proper vocation for those who are called by Jesus to bear witness to, and build up, the Kingdom in that way. Pacifists "bear witness to evangelical charity" and "to the gravity of the physical and moral risks of recourse to violence, with all its destruction and death."[168]

No one who has chosen to accept responsibility for the protection of others, especially including public authority, may rightly decline to use necessary force, where called for by the facts, and by the vocational responsibilities of that particular station in life.

CONCLUSIONS

One surely does not have to confess (as Catholics do) that the pope is Peter's successor to understand John Paul II's views on law, human nature, and society. One does need to understood the office fully, however, to grasp those views. For the relevant contributions of John Paul II are *precisely* those of a man who understood himself to be, first and foremost, a bishop, the Bishop of Rome, the supreme pastor of the Catholic Church. John Paul II spoke not, as another scholar would, according to his own theories and interpretations, earning his place in this volume by the daring or uniqueness of his writings. John Paul II spoke instead as custodian of the deposit of faith, straining to hand it on intact to his successor, and to the church of tomorrow.

John Paul's legacy includes the lasting effects of his administration of the church, not least the opportunity over his twenty-five-year pontificate to appoint a majority of the world's Catholic bishops. His legacy includes a share of responsibility for the demise of communism as a political force, and all else that future historians will count important enough to list in their chronicles of our time. His legacy includes, too, several distinctive intellectual contributions to Christianity's confrontation with our postindustrial, secular society.

Among those contributions, three are paramount. One is John Paul's sensitive and, we think, successful and sound response to liberation theology. Though he rejected many aspects of that theology as incompatible with Catholic faith, John Paul made none the less urgent the universal call to solidarity with the world's poor. And he made clear his wariness of corporate capitalism. The foundation of his adverse judgment upon liberation theology was not economic efficiency (about which John Paul said almost nothing), but the implications and entailments for the *faith* of hewing to Marxist analytical categories and prescriptions.

The second area was John Paul's response to secularism. He labored in the heat of the day to persuade his contemporaries that denying a transcendent source of meaning and value does not lead to freedom and happiness—for the one or for the many. He argued (brilliantly, in our view) that denial leads instead to new forms of enslavement, despair, turmoil—for the one and for the many. It is too soon to say that his analysis of secularism and its effects has failed to attract the support it deserves. But it is not too soon to say that it has not clearly done so.

The leading effects of secularism constitute the final area of paramount interest. Those perils are the dangers to human rights and flourishing posed by the market and democracy, where they subsist in a secularized culture. Each of these institutions is, formally, a matter of counting sheer preferences, and of deciding to act according to the greater number of them. The precondition of a humane market economy, and of a just democracy, according to John Paul is a culture of objective morality. Such a culture stands between these mechanisms and a willful (that is, exploitative) majoritarianism. Such a culture, John Paul argued, can only be effectively secured by a theism—a widespread, stable commitment to a greater-than-human source of meaning and value.

NOTES

1. George Weigel, *Witness to Hope: The Biography of Pope John Paul II* (New York: HarperCollins, 2001), 2.
2. Ibid., 2–6.
3. Holy See Press Office, "His Holiness John Paul II: Short Biography," http://www.vatican.va/news_services/press/documentazione/documents/santopadre_biografie/giovanni_paolo_ii_biografia_breve_en.html.
4. Weigel, *Witness to Hope*, 27. Emilia also gave birth to a daughter some years after her first son, Edmund, but the infant girl apparently only lived for a few weeks (ibid.).
5. Ibid., 28.
6. Ibid., 29.

7. Ibid., 32.

8. Ibid., 39 (citing Boniecki, *Kalendarium*, "School Years"). John Paul II recalled spending most of his time peeling potatoes.

9. Ibid., 40.

10. Ibid., 55. The half-hour walk to the Solvay limestone quarry required Karol to smear petroleum jelly over his face to keep his skin from freezing during the subzero winter.

11. Holy See Press Office, "His Holiness John Paul II: Biography, Pre-Pontificate," http://www.vatican.va/news_services/press/documentazione/documents/santopadre _biografie/giovanni_paolo_ii_biografia_prepontificato_en.html.

12. Weigel, *Witness to Hope*, 68.

13. Ibid., 31, quoting John Paul II, *Gift and Mystery* (New York: Doubleday, 1999), 20.

14. Holy See Press Office, "His Holiness John Paul II: A Short Biography."

15. Weigel, *Witness to Hope*, 112–113.

16. Ibid., 113.

17. The play was finally performed in Cracow in 1980 (ibid., 114).

18. Holy See Press Office, "His Holiness John Paul II: A Short Biography."

19. Weigel, *Witness to Hope*, 87. Because the Angelicum required the dissertation to be published before the degree could actually be conferred, Wojtyla did not receive a doctoral degree from the Angelicum. At that time, he could not pay for the printing. Instead, Wojtyla resubmitted the dissertation to the Faculty of Theology of the Jagiellonian University, which conferred to him a doctorate in Theology (ibid.).

20. Ibid., 85.

21. Thomas Guarino, "Review of *Karol Wojtyla: The Thought of the Man Who Became John Paul II* by Rocco Buttigione," *First Things* 82 (April 1998): 39.

22. Weigel, *Witness to Hope*, 110–111. See also Holy See Press Office, "His Holiness John Paul II: Biography, Pre-Pontificate," *Tu Es Petrus*.

23. Wojtyla's dissertation was later published by the Academy of Sciences of the Catholic University of Lublin in 1960 (ibid.).

24. Weigel, *Witness to Hope*, 128.

25. Ibid., 129.

26. Holy See Press Office, "His Holiness John Paul II: A Short Biography."

27. Holy See Press Office, "His Holiness John Paul II: Biography, Pre-Pontificate."

28. Kenneth Briggs, jacket comment on Pope John Paul II, *Love and Responsibility*, trans. H. T. Willetts (New York: Farrar, Straus & Giroux, 1981).

29. Weigel, *Witness to Hope*, 116.

30. Holy See Press Office, "His Holiness John Paul II: A Short Biography."

31. Guarino, "Review," 40.

32. John Paul II, *Crossing the Threshold of Hope* (New York: Knopf, 1994).

33. Books by and About John Paul II," LucidCafe Website, http://www.lucidcafe.com/library/96may/johnpaul.html.

34. Readers of the preceding brief biography will detect echoes in the account of John Paul II's thought that we provide in this chapter. The echoes may grow

louder according to the reader's familiarity with Wojtyla's entire oeuvre. Re-
verberating emphases include John Paul II's diagnosis of the spiritual ailments
of modern human beings, their most perplexing questions, and the greatest
threats to humankind's temporal flourishing and eternal salvation. The Polish
bishop's brief against mere "toleration" of non-Catholic religious expression,
advanced at Vatican II, adumbrates John Paul II's defense of human freedom to
search for the truth as the apex of development. His dramatic writings as well
as *Love and Responsibility* are all detectable in the pope's moving descriptions
of married life as spousal gift giving, and of the child as a gift that supervenes
upon the marital act of the spouses.

35. *Laborem exercens* (1981), http://www.vatican.va/holy_father/john_paul_ii/
encyclicals/documents/hf_jp-ii_enc_14091981_laborem-exercens_en.html; *Sollicitudo rei socialis* (1987) (Washington, D.C.: United States Catholic Conference);
Centesimus annus (1991), Vatican translation (Boston: Pauline Books & Media, 2000); *Veritatis splendor* (1993), http://www.vatican.va/holy_father/john_
paul_ii/encyclicals/documents/hf_jp-ii_enc_06081993_veritatis-splendor
_en.html; *Evangelium vitae* (1995), Vatican translation (Boston: Pauline Books
& Media, 1995); *Letter to Families from Pope John Paul II* (1994), http://www.
vatican.va/holy_father/john_paul_ii/letters/documents/hf_jp-ii_let_02021994_
families_en.html.

36. See *Dominus Iesus: On the Unicity and Salvific Universality of Jesus Christ
and the Church* (Vatican City: Libreria Editrice Vaticana, 2000); *Instruction
on Certain Aspects of the "Theology of Liberation"* (August 6, 1984) (Washington, D.C.: United States Catholic Conference, 1984); *Instruction on Christian
Freedom and Liberation* (March 22, 1986) (Washington, D.C.: United States
Catholic Conference, 1986).

37. *Address of His Holiness Pope John Paul II to the Fiftieth General Assembly
of the United Nations Organization* (October 5, 1995), http://www.vatican.
va/holy_father/john_paul_ii/speeches/1995/october/documents/hf_jp-ii_spe_
05101995_address-to-uno_en.html.

38. Catechism of the Catholic Church, http://www.vatican.va/archive/ccc_css/
archive/catechism/ccc_toc.htm.

39. *Fidei depositum* (1992), §1, http://www.vatican.va/holy_father/john_paul_ii/
apost_constitutions/documents/hf_jp-ii_apc_19921011_fidei-depositum_
en.html.

40. *Tertio millennio adveniente* (1994), §20, http://www.vatican.va/holy_father/
john_paul_ii/apost_letters/documents/hf_jp-ii_apl_10111994_tertio-millennio-
adveniente_en.html.

41. *Gaudium et spes* (1965), http://www.vatican.va/archive/hist_councils/ii_vatican
_council/documents/vat-ii_cons_19651207_gaudium-et-spes_en.html.

42. *Dignitatis humanae* (1965), http://www.vatican.va/archive/hist_councils/ii_
vatican_council/documents/vat-ii_decl_19651207_dignitatis-humanae_en.html.

43. A "doctor" of the Catholic Church is a canonized saint whose writings, or "doctrine," are declared by competent authority to be particularly illuminating of the
faith. Aquinas, Augustine, Jerome, Ambrose, and Teresa of Avila are among the
best-known doctors.

44. *Apostolicam actuositatem* (1965), §2, http://www.vatican.va/archive/hist_ councils/ii_vatican_council/documents/vat-ii_decree_19651118_apostolicam-actuositatem_en.html.

45. *Lumen gentium* (1964), §5, http://www.vatican.va/archive/hist_councils/ii_ vatican_council/documents/vat-ii_const_19641121_lumen-gentium_en.html.

46. *Dominus Iesus*, §5, quoting *Redemptoris missio* (1990), §5.

47. *Christus Dominus* (1965), §2, http://www.vatican.va/archive/hist_councils/ ii_vatican_council/documents/vat-ii_decree_19651028_christus-dominus_ en.html.

48. Ibid.

49. *Dominus Iesus*, §15.

50. *Tertio millennio adveniente*, §6.

51. *Centesimus annus*, §55.

52. Ibid.

53. Ibid., §44.

54. *Veritatis splendor*, §2.

55. *Sollicitudo rei socialis*, §41.

56. We do not suggest—in fact, we deny—that *Dignitatis humanae* contradicts any proposition previously taught by the church as surely true. Many authors have taken the measure of *Dignitatis humanae* and its continuity with the tradition. We highly recommend one treatment: Brian W. Harrison, *Religious Liberty and Contraception* (Melbourne: University of Melbourne Press, 1988).

57. *Veritatis splendor*, §53, quoting St. Vincent of Lerins, *Commonitorium Primum*, c. 23: *Patrologia Latina*, §§50, 668.

58. *Instruction on Christian Freedom*, §74.

59. *Apostolicam actuositatem*, §7.

60. *Centesimus annus*, §§43–47.

61. *Apostolicam actuositatem*, §7.

62. Ibid.

63. Ibid.

64. *Instruction on Christian Freedom*, §63.

65. *Gaudium et spes*, §93 (paraphrasing Matt. 21:7).

66. *Veritatis splendor*, §96.

67. Ibid., §52. And all the way to St. Peter's. John Paul II has put these words into practice. He publicly forgave the man who attempted to assassinate him in 1981, and who succeeded in gravely wounding him. He endured considerable criticism from within the church for his comments, which sounded to some like a confession of error, for the church's treatment of Galileo. Most important, he publicly acknowledged the church's sins against the Jews. On one occasion, after his welcome into Rome's synagogue by the city's Chief Rabbi Elio Toaff, he acknowledged sins of complicity even by his papal predecessors in anti-Jewish campaigns. John Paul II declared that the church condemned anti-Semitism "'by anyone'; I repeat, 'by anyone'" ("From Pope John Paul II's discourse during his visit to the Rome Synagogue on 13 April 1986," http://www.vatican.va/jubilee _2000/magazine/documents/ju_mag_01111997_p-42x_en.html). John Paul II was the first pope ever to visit the synagogue, in 1986.

He unambiguously condemned the Holocaust as a horrible evil, stating that there is, and never has been, a theological justification for hostility against Jews. On his historic visit to Israel in March 2000, he publicly stated that the Catholic Church is "deeply saddened by the hatred, acts of persecution and displays of anti-Semitism directed against Jews by Christians at any time and in any place" ("Pope's Address at Yad Vashem," http://news.bbc.co.uk/1/hi/world/middle_east/688059.stm). The Vatican's Commission on Religious Relations with the Jews, working at the pope's instruction, published in 1998 the Vatican's first official statement on the Holocaust. *We Remember: A Reflection on the Shoah* (statement by the Commission by the Religious Relations with the Jews) described it as an "unspeakable tragedy" before which "no one can remain indifferent" (§1, http://www.vatican.va/roman_curia/pontifical_councils/chrstuni/documents/rc_pc_chrstuni_doc_16031998_shoah_en.html). The document also contained a lengthy footnote defending Pope Pius XII's actions during the war (ibid., n. 16), a position for which some continue to criticize the church and John Paul II.

68. *Evangelium vitae*, §74.
69. Ibid., §3.
70. *Veritatis splendor*, §7.
71. *Gaudium et spes*, §39.
72. *Centesimus annus*, §25.
73. *Gaudium et spes*, §35.
74. *Veritatis splendor*, §7.
75. Ibid., §13.
76. Guarino, "Review," 41.
77. *Centesimus annus*, §46.
78. *Dominus Iesus*, §7.
79. Ibid.
80. Ibid.
81. *Veritatis splendor*, §34.
82. *Tertio millennio adveniente*, §6.
83. *Dominus Iesus*, §22.
84. *Centesimus annus*, §24.
85. *Instruction on Christian Freedom*, §92.
86. *Veritatis splendor*, §98.
87. *Instruction on Christian Freedom*, §93.
88. *Gaudium et spes*, §76; see also *Dignitatis humanae*, §13.
89. *Christus Dominus*, §20. Many suppose that the received teaching, absent circumstances preventing it, required *some sort* of Catholic establishment of religion, defined not with regard to any particular privilege, but rather as recognition by the state—or at least the political community in some audible way—of the truth of Catholicism. We do not take a position on the content of the traditional doctrine. But, supposing it to be as we just described it, we do not think John Paul II said anything squarely contradictory of it. That said, we do observe

that the tendency and tenor of his thought seem unsympathetic to it. John Paul II did not say a word in favor of "establishment" and favored what could be called a "low church" view of the state's competence. He never (as far as we have found) approvingly referred to traditional statements of establishmentarian sentiments.

John Paul II surely held the following propositions: the Catholic faith is true; persons acting both individually and socially are bound to act according to the truth, the whole truth, no matter how they come to know it, by reason or faith or both; the state is obliged to grant the Catholic Church full freedom to perform its divine mission. The state must respect and safeguard the religious freedom of all citizens—Catholic and non-Catholic alike.

90. *Instruction on Christian Freedom*, §31.
91. Ibid., §26.
92. Ibid., §27.
93. *Centesimus annus*, §46.
94. Ibid., §49.
95. Ibid., §13.
96. *Sollicitudo rei socialis*, §36.
97. Ibid.
98. *Instruction on Christian Freedom*, §74.
99. *Centesimus annus*, §25.
100. *Instruction on Christian Freedom*, §37.
101. *Sollicitudo rei socialis*, §38.
102. *Instruction on Christian Freedom*, §73.
103. *Centesimus annus*, §31. A prominent theme of John Paul II's social teaching was the sanctification of everyday life, especially including work. How is it to be organized in a humane way? Is it anything more than drudgery, manipulation, exploitation? Because human beings *need* certain materials for their survival, work is necessary. Work is also the means by which the vast majority of people are able to support their families.

But work is much more than a necessary evil. God has commanded humanity to subdue all the earth, "to govern the world with justice and holiness" (*Laborem exercens*, §25). By working human beings make things, advance in their knowledge of subhuman creation, and achieve a certain likeness to God. It is thus a proper expression of the power of human beings, their individuality, their intelligence. Work, even in Joseph's carpenter shop, and much more so in the modern business firm, requires close cooperation and partnership among many diverse persons, and so constitutes a community of persons, specified by its distinctive purpose or common good.

Work has great theological significance. In work human beings imitate Jesus Christ, a human craftsman, a carpenter like his foster father. Human beings "can justly consider that by their labor they are unfolding the Creator's work, consulting the advantages of their brothers and sisters, and contributing by their personal industry to the realization in history of the divine plan" (ibid.).

The sweat and suffering so often characteristic of work are an "*announcement of death:* 'In the sweat of your face you shall eat bread till you return to the ground, for out of it you were taken'" (ibid., §27, quoting Gen. 3:19).

104. *Gaudium et spes*, §71 (quoted in *Centesimus annus*, §30).

105. *Sollicitudo rei socialis*, §15.

106. *Centesimus annus*, §34.

107. Ibid.

108. Ibid.

109. Ibid., §31.

110. *Evangelium vitae*, §21.

111. Ibid., §§21–23.

112. Ibid., §24.

113. Ibid., §21.

114. See ibid., §§21–23.

115. *Instruction on Christian Freedom*, §93.

116. *Sollicitudo rei socialis*, §20.

117. *Centesimus annus*, §11.

118. *Sollicitudo rei socialis*, §41.

119. We put aside important cautions that do not state a norm clearly enough to rule out particular proposals for action. Examples include strictures against "blind violence" and "class hatred."

120. *Instruction on Certain Aspects*, introduction.

121. Ibid., §§7.8–9.9.

122. Ibid., §11.11.

123. *Centesimus annus*, §11.

124. *Catechism*, §1906, paraphrasing *Gaudium et spes*, §26.

125. *Address to United Nations*, §3.

126. *Gaudium et spes*, §74.

127. Ibid.

128. *Catechism*, §1912, quoting *Gaudium et spes*, §26.

129. *Catechism*, §1897, quoting *Pacem in terris*, §46.

130. *Gaudium et spes*, §74.

131. Ibid.

132. Ibid.

133. Ibid.

134. *Evangelium vitae*, §71.

135. *Letter to Families*, §17.

136. Ibid., §7.

137. Ibid., §17.

138. *Mulieris dignitatem* (1988), §1, citing Second Vatican Council Closing Address by Pope Paul VI, 8 December 1965, http://www.vatican.va/holy_father/john_paul_ii/apost_letters/documents/hf_jp-ii_apl_15081988_mulieris-dignitatem_en.html.

139. *Redemptoris Mater* (1987), §46, http://www.vatican.va/holy_father/john_paul_ii/encyclicals/documents/hf_jp-ii_enc_25031987_redemptoris-mater_en.html.

140. *Mulieris dignitatem*, §10.

141. Ibid., §19.

142. Ibid., §30.

143. *Mulieris dignitatem*, §24, citing Eph. 5:21.

144. Weigel, *Witness to Hope*, 580, citing his conversation with John Paul II in October 1998.

145. *Evangelium vitae*, §99.

146. *Veritatis splendor*, §96.

147. Ibid.

148. *Evangelium vitae*, §57.

149. Ibid., §72.

150. Ibid., §53.

151. Ibid., §9.

152. Ibid.

153. Ibid.

154. Ibid., §§53, 57.

155. Ibid., §65.

156. Ibid., §62.

157. Ibid., §58.

158. Ibid., §55.

159. *Catechism*, §2263, quoting St. Thomas Aquinas, *Summa Theologiae* II–II, 64, 7.

160. Ibid., §2264, quoting ibid.

161. *Evangelium vitae*, §55.

162. See ibid., §§55–56; *Catechism*, §2263.

163. *Evangelium vitae*, §56.

164. Ibid., §27.

165. Ibid., §56.

166. *Catechism*, §2308, quoting *Gaudium et spes*, §79.

167. Ibid., §2309.

168. Ibid., §2306.

PART II

The Protestant Tradition

[CHAPTER 9]

Introduction to Modern Protestantism

MARK A. NOLL

It is always precarious to attempt a history of Protestants because there are so many different kinds of them, they exist in so many different places, and (at least for the purposes of this book) they have approached questions of law, politics, and society in so many different ways.[1] Today, for example, a satisfactory general account of Protestantism would have to treat long-standing differences that have divided Protestants from each other: Lutheran from the Reformed, Anglicans and Episcopalians from Mennonites, Presbyterians from Baptists or Methodists, and still other ancestral groupings from each other. It should take into account broad liberal and conservative tendencies that now run as strongly within denominations as between them. In addition, it would need to include treatment of the many new Protestant churches, especially the Pentecostals, that have sprung up in such rich profusion since the start of the twentieth century. And, at the start of the twenty-first century, it should by rights deal with the spread of Protestant movements around the globe: Baptists and Anglicans are now present in more than 160 counties, Presbyterians and the Reformed in more than 140, Lutherans and Methodists in more than 100, and other, somewhat smaller bodies are almost as widely spread.[2]

Rapid and nearly unprecedented change in the shape of world Christianity over recent decades adds special complexity to the engagement of Protestants with the law, politics, and society. In the course of the twentieth century, Protestantism precipitously declined as a culture-shaping force in Europe and some traditional European dependencies (such as Canada, Australia, and New Zealand). In the United States, where there are more Protestants than in any other single country in the world, Protestantism has been fragmented and reshaped into forms and proportions looking very different in the early twenty-first century than they did in the early twentieth. And although it is difficult to adjust to new worldwide realities, it is simply the case that there are today many more active Protestants in Nigeria than in Great Britain, many more in Brazil than in Germany, more in the Congo than in Denmark and Finland combined, about three times as many in Indonesia as in the Netherlands, more each in India and the Philippines than in any European country except perhaps Germany, nearly twice as many in each of Tanzania, Uganda, Kenya, or South Korea than in Canada—and these comparisons do not include China, where a tremendous number (though only imperfectly counted) of Protestants or Protestant-like Christians have emerged in just the last three decades.[3] Providing a succinct historical introduction as a context for specific consideration of the eight Protestant thinkers treated in this section of the book is not, in other words, a simple task.

That task, however, does become somewhat more manageable if attention remains fixed on Europe and North America where these particular thinkers lived. Even if less than half of the world's affiliated Protestants now dwell in these two parts of the world (down from over 90 percent in 1900), the story of Protestants in these former heartlands still possesses a certain coherence because of a continuous history stretching back to the Reformation of the sixteenth century. Despite massive demographic shifts, much of worldwide Protestantism still looks to Western Europe and North America as the crucial educational centers. In only a few years it will almost certainly not be possible to treat Western Europe and North America as the Protestant keys for intellectual and theological endeavor. Rather, the sort of political-religious connections explored recently by Paul Freston for Evangelical groups outside of Western Europe and North America will almost certainly be moving to center stage.[4] Yet for the purposes of this book, a focus limited to the main Protestant movements of the West not only provides a useful introduction to treatment of important figures from the late nineteenth and twentieth centuries, but also offers an important (historical) story in itself.

STATUS QUO ANTE: PROTESTANTISM IN 1900

At the end of the nineteenth century, world Protestantism was still most easily and obviously identified with the churches of the magisterial Reformation.[5] In the German empire and in Scandinavia, Lutheran territorial churches enjoyed state support and exercised proprietary oversight over national religious life. In uneasy coexistence with the Catholic Church, they also attempted, though with diminishing success, to maintain their hereditary oversight of intellectual and social aspects of public life. A roughly similar situation obtained in Great Britain, where Anglicans in England

and Presbyterians in Scotland were trying to exercise the same sort of state-sanctioned authority. Reformed, or Calvinist, churches enjoyed a similar establishmentarian status in the Netherlands and several Swiss cantons. In parts of France, Hungary, and Germany, Reformed churches enjoyed state recognition and some state support as, in effect, the second-string established churches after the Catholics or the Lutherans. Throughout Europe relatively small minorities of Free Church or dissenting Protestants were tolerated to one degree or another. Nonconformists—Independents, Wesleyans, and Baptists—were most vigorous in England and Wales (as were Presbyterians in the north of Ireland), where for more than a century they had exerted a significant influence on British economic, educational, and political history. Pockets of Mennonites and other Anabaptists descended from sixteenth-century movements lived quietly in the Netherlands, southern Germany, Switzerland, and amid the German diaspora in Eastern Europe, but faithfulness to pacifist teaching had mostly meant their withdrawal from European public life.

All of the established or quasi-established Protestant churches had been weakened in different ways by events and circumstances of the nineteenth century. Early in that century the Prussian monarch had forced most Lutheran and Reformed churches in his territory to merge into an Evangelical Union, which subsequently manifested less self-directing energy than had the original churches. Strong theological partisanship between pietistic-leaning and modern-leaning or scientific-leaning factions weakened the remaining Lutheran state churches, even as similar partisan differences divided Anglicans into high church (often Anglo-Catholic), low church (often Evangelical), and broad church (often liberal) factions. Schism among Dutch Reformed and Scottish Presbyterians testified to the feisty vigor of the splintering factions but also to a general drift among the Reformed and Presbyterian traditions in general. While Evangelical or Pietist movements had breathed new life into some dissenting churches and led to the creation of entirely new free (or nonestablished) churches, those revival movements, which also touched the established churches, were not able to overcome the increasing disengagement of working-class populations from church life. Yet well into the twentieth century, and in some cases until today, European Protestantism was most easily identified with the territorial state churches descended from the Protestant Reformation. Together they constituted a Protestant Christendom aspiring to the same establishmentarian place that European Christendom had exercised for over a millennium and that remained even more vigorous in some Catholic sections of Europe.

In North America the situation by 1900 was substantially different. Canada remained somewhat closer to European patterns, but the democratic character of the United States had affected religion as much as politics, economics, and society. Most obviously, there were no established churches. To be sure, older denominations with Old World roots still exercised some of the proprietary and civilizing functions of the European state churches. For lack of a better term, they can be called the formalist denominations. Thus, Episcopalians (or Anglicans in Canada), Congregationalists, and Presbyterians, who had enjoyed considerable prestige as established or quasi-established churches in the colonial period, continued to be major sponsors of seminaries, colleges, and social programs; they continued as well to enjoy the patronage of well-placed business and political leaders. These denominations were joined in their comprehensive cultural interests by the Lutheran churches of Pennsylvania, the Upper Midwest, and the Canadian prairies that from mid-century had been greatly strengthened by immigration from Germany and Scandinavia. Yet in the United States, these churches, which most closely resembled European established churches in their self-conception and social duties, were vastly outnumbered by what might be termed the antiformalist denominations. In 1890, against roughly 5,000 Episcopal, 5,000 Congregational, 8,500 Lutheran, and 25,000 Presbyterian churches, there were in the United States more than 40,000 Baptist churches, more than 50,000 Methodist churches, and probably another 50,000 or so churches representing an incredibly broad diversity of smaller, often sectarian denominations.[6] Moreover, a substantial portion of the churchgoing population was made up of African Americans (mostly Baptist and Methodist) whose churches shared considerable Christian doctrine with the white churches, but who were products of an oppressive social history unlike anything ever experienced in the entire history of Protestantism.[7] None of the churches had enjoyed establishmentarian status or privileges since early in the history of the American republic. In comparative terms, the United States benefited from an unusual combination: vigorous church life and a nearly complete freedom of religion (though never experienced fully by African Americans, Catholics in some predominately Protestant regions, and members of minority Christian and non-Christian groups in many parts of the country).

What Alexis de Tocqueville identified in the 1830s in his landmark book *Democracy in America* still characterized religion in the United States: "America is ... the place in the world where the Christian religion has most preserved genuine powers over souls; and nothing shows better how useful and natural to man it is in our day, since the country in which it exercises the greatest empire is at the same time the most enlightened and most free."[8]

To be sure, American Protestants had not enjoyed an easy progress through the nineteenth century. The American Civil War (1861–65) witnessed a significant failing in theology as Bible-believing Northerners and Bible-believing Southerners found no means except war to resolve their differences over what the scriptures mandated concerning slavery.[9] The postwar adjustment to rapid industrialization and urbanization was just as disquieting, since Protestants who had mastered social and political life in rural and small-town America seemed overmastered by the realities of large-scale manufacturing, mass-market commerce, and the new media of popular culture.[10] In the face of heavy immigration by Roman Catholics, Jews, and nonbelievers, American Protestants wavered between following the universalistic claims of democratic freedom and asserting a hereditary right to act as arbiters of the public sphere. Growing deference to self-directed scientific inquiry in universities organized for largely secular purposes was also threatening what had been, in effect, a Protestant hegemony in American higher education.[11]

Still, at the end of the nineteenth century there were no organized movements of thought, voluntary organization, or civil influence that rivaled the importance of Protestant institutions in American life. The Roman Catholic population, though having become the largest of any specific Christian tradition, was more taken up with constructing its own churches, schools, and community organizations than with contending for dominance in public. The nation's most respected educational and eleemosynary institutions remained Protestant in some general sense. And there was also a strong Protestant position in publishing and the mass media. Protestants were not supported by governmental funding, as was still often the case in Europe, but precisely for that reason they probably exercised a broader cultural influence than did Protestants on the other side of the Atlantic.

In Canada, outside of French and Catholic Quebec, Protestants were, if anything, in an even stronger position than in the United States.[12] The older proprietary churches, especially Anglican, Presbyterian, Methodist, and (in the Maritime Provinces) Baptist, were the most important institutions of any kind for providing education, direction for public organizations, and standards for public morality. Protestant churchgoers probably made up a higher percentage of the population in English Canada than in any other Western nation.

At the end of the nineteenth century, Protestants in North America joined their European counterparts in struggling to adjust to the exigencies of mass industrialization and mass consumer culture. Relationships with Roman Catholics remained strained in most regions. Yet Protestants were still shaping culture, and they still provided a potent vocabulary for talking about law, politics, and society. The rapid survey that follows of geopolitical history, as well as of church history and theology, reveals a rising tide of intellectual, social, and economic challenges in the twentieth century. Yet it also shows that, amid many reverses and renovations of inherited positions, Protestants of several kinds were able to contribute significantly to critical discussions about the functioning of human beings in society.

PROTESTANT GEOPOLITICS

In the course of the twentieth century, Protestant geopolitics experienced dramatic change. To put matters in starkly simplistic terms: European Christendom, including the Protestant part of Christendom, imploded. American Protestantism developed from a regional into an international force. And worldwide Protestant leadership had no sooner passed from Europe to America than the entire character of Protestantism began to be transformed by the realities of globalization.

The implosion of European Protestantism over the course of the twentieth century, and with accelerating speed in the century's last half, awaits a satisfactory general history. For the change from a situation where one-quarter to one-half, or more, of the people in Protestant regions regularly attended church to one where substantially less than one-tenth of Protestant populations now do so, there must perforce be multiple, subtle explanations. Even casual observers, however, can sense that the seventy-five years of hot and cold war that stretched from 1914 (the outbreak of World War I) to 1989 (the beginning of the end of state communism) took a grievous toll on the churches. The unprecedented destruction of World War I, the chaos of politics, economies, and ideologies that followed through much of the next two decades, the even greater death and destruction of World War II, the division of Europe into West and East that followed hard on the heels of the defeat of Nazism, the sudden collapse of Marxist regimes and the tangled course of reconstruction that has followed this collapse—all overpowered the efforts of churches to manage, or even fathom, events. Cataclysmic warfare, the brutal displacement of populations, genocide aimed at the entire Jewish people, and manifest failures of much-trumpeted ideologies do not necessarily create conditions inimical to Christian faith. The rise of Pietism after the Thirty Years' War of the seventeenth century and, much more recently, the emergence of vigorous Christian movements in China after the surpassing destruction of Mao Zedong show the capacity of Protestant or Protestant-like forms of Christianity to advance amid great social disorder.[13] Yet in twentieth-century Europe, recession rather than advance has characterized the Protestant churches.

It is impossible to say to what extent this recession was owing directly to the wars, armed camps, and preoccupation with military security of this most bellicose European century, or whether it can be accounted for more by the exhaustion of doctrinal, liturgical, and intellectual traditions, by the success of capitalist and Marxist varieties of materialism in displacing religious loyalties, or by preoccupation with entertainment or self-fulfillment borne along by a wave of enticing mass media. It was certainly not the case that European Protestants were struck dumb by the scourges of war or class conflict. In the crises of World War II alone it is possible to find many examples of vigorous Protestant conviction: The Barmen Declaration of 1934 spoke courageously against the promotion of a "German Christianity" adapting itself to Hitlerism. Dietrich Bonhoeffer found resources in classical Christian teaching for actions of great ecclesiastical, and then great political courage. The Anglican bishop, George Bell, displayed a similar courage in chastising the Allies for indiscriminate fire bombing of German cities. The French pastor André Trocmé drew on the traditions of his historic Reformed faith to nerve his rescue of Jewish children. And Helmut Thielicke from his pulpit in a bombed-out Hamburg knew how to proclaim a message of gospel hope given shape by a revived theology of the Reformation.[14] Even when moving forward several more decades into a Europe that had become much more systemically secular, it is remarkable that the public demonstrations of 1989 leading to regime change in both East Germany and Romania began in churches (Lutheran and Hungarian Reformed, respectively) where at least some residue of Protestant teaching remained alive. In the face of Europe's vicious tribal wars and its determined flight from forms of Christian faith that had guided its life through centuries, Protestant Christianity did not simply wither away. But, objectively considered, it was much reduced in both reach and influence.

In North America, Protestant communions seemed to have adjusted better to modern culture and society. Canada, to be sure, experienced a history that eventually conformed to a European pattern.[15] Into the 1960s, church attendance and other marks of religious practice remained considerably higher than in the United States. But after that time religious observance declined to levels that, while remaining above the European average, fell considerably below the American. In the years immediately after World War II, Canadians were leaders at the United Nations and other international gatherings in defending references to God and religious belief as critical for international peace.[16] And when the British Parliament repatriated the Canadian Constitution in 1982, an action that acknowledged full Canadian control over every aspect of Canadian government, that constitution began with an assertion that "Canada is founded upon principles that recognize the supremacy of God and the rule of law."[17] Despite these indications of hereditary religious conviction, Canada since the 1960s has secularized faster and more comprehensively than its national neighbor to the south.

To be sure, the twentieth-century history of Protestantism in the United States has been anything but tranquil. Yet through a whole series of reversals, unanticipated innovations, and incursions of modernity, adherence to Protestant churches has remained strong. In the last half-century the once dominant mainline churches (Methodist, Presbyterian, Lutheran, Episcopal, and Congregational), while maintaining large and relatively well-funded denominations, have yielded public space to a multitude of more Evangelical, fundamentalist, Pentecostal, sectarian, Holiness, and independent churches. Careful empirical research suggests that mainline Protestants now make up about 15 percent of the total population, with 26 percent adhering to mostly Caucasian Evangelical or conservative Protestant churches, 9 percent to African American churches, 20 percent to the Catholic Church, 10 percent to other religious groups, and 20 percent functionally unattached.[18] For many years the Southern Baptist Convention, which since 1979 has moved decisively in a more conservative direction, has been the largest Protestant denomination in the country, and one of the largest in the world.[19] A few more details on recent American history are presented below, but from a global perspective it is important to make this point: as American society throughout the twentieth century became more affluent, more modern, and more diverse, it has not followed the European pattern in experiencing a decline in church adherence. Instead, American religion, with sectarian and theologically conservative Protestants in the lead, has adjusted to modern circumstances. The result may be a thinner form of Christianity than present in the strongly Protestant sections of the country a century ago, since it now must compete with many more alternative activities and worldviews. It is also a Christianity that tacitly accepts the fact that education, mass media, the courts, and most governments now take less guidance from the churches than ever before in American history. But by comparison with Europe, there are more people who actively practice Protestant faiths, the vitality of Protestant churches and voluntary organizations is greater, and the influence of Protestants in public life is much more extensive.

The shift of worldwide influence from Europe to America, which arises as a consequence of contrasting national histories during the twentieth century, can be indicated by examining the ranks of overseas missionary personnel.[20] Of course, much else goes into the exertion of religious influence around the world than just missionary endeavor; in all of recorded history, imperialistic expansion through military or commercial means has regularly paved the way for an expansion of the imperialists' religion as well. But missionary statistics offer one concrete means of charting the direction of global Christian influence.

In 1903 roughly one-fourth of all Protestant missionaries serving outside their home countries were American. Britain's missionary force was probably twice that of the American. By 1972, the proportions were reversed: almost two-thirds of all Protestant missionaries serving overseas were American, and the number of American missionaries was more than five times the number of British missionaries. Significantly, as the American proportion of the worldwide Protestant missionary force increased, so also did the Evangelical proportion rise among American missionaries. Early in the century, mainline denominations contributed the overwhelming majority of all American missionaries; by 1950 the division was about half and half; by the end of the century Evangelical denominations and independent agencies sponsored about 90 percent of the American overseas personnel.

Just as important as the rise of the United States as a missionary-sending country, however, has been the more recent proliferation of missionary-sending nations. Even though the total number of American Protestant missionaries has remained relatively steady since the early 1970s, when the United States contributed about two-thirds of all the Protestants missionaries in the world, by 2001 the United States now sponsored slightly less than half. New Protestant missionaries are as likely to come from Brazil, South Korea, the Philippines, Nigeria, or India as from the United States. Overseas mission work, in other words, has been globalized in the same way that Christianity itself has been globalized. While major missionary-sending bodies like the Southern Baptist Convention, the Churches of Christ, and the Assemblies of God still draw most of their volunteers from the United States, the interdenominational and independent agencies are now much more likely to recruit from outside the United States. Thus, in 2001 less than 10 percent of Campus Crusade for Christ's more than 15,000 international workers were American, less than 20 percent of Youth with a Mission's nearly 12,000 workers, and less than 40 percent of the more than 7,000 missionaries with the Wycliffe Bible Translators.

Statistics for missionary service, as with all other statistics, must be handled cautiously. But the suggested patterns are clear. As Europe has declined as a global Protestant presence, the United States has grown, but now Western Protestantism as a whole is beginning to recede as a worldwide force due to the rapid expansion of Protestant churches in other parts of the globe.

The globalization of Christianity, including Protestant Christianity, is now being recognized as one of the great events of the twentieth century. It is reflected in many striking phenomena. The availability of the Christian scriptures in non-Western languages has burgeoned over the course of the century.[21] In China, where during the Great Proletarian Cultural Revolution of 1966–76 every one of the vast nation's churches was shuttered, the dramatic emergence of Christian groups over the last three decades has been little short of astounding, and that emergence has owed very little to direct Western influence. Indigenous forms of Pentecostal and loosely Protestant faith, which are linked lightly to Western Christianity, if at all, now spread rapidly in many parts of Africa, Latin America, and Oceania.[22]

These sudden changes have dramatically altered the shape of worldwide Protestantism. Yet they make Western Protestant reflection on law, politics, and society more, rather than less, important. Christian civilization, Christian learning, and formal Christian theology—in contrast to numbers of Christian adherents—still remain concentrated in the Western world. Protestants from all over the globe still look to the West for educational guidance. What Western Protestants think about the place of humans in society may have an even greater influence throughout the world than was imaginable when Christians dwelt primarily in the West. Protestants in other parts of the world will never simply accept Western reasoning wholesale, but the deliberations probed in this section of the book are now available to much wider potential audiences than when they were first spoken or published. Karl Barth wrote with Germany, Switzerland, Europe, or the West in view, but he is being read today in Sao Paolo, Manila, and Seoul. John Howard Yoder produced his theology of Christian pacifism as an argument against the assumptions of Western Christendom, but he has the potential now to influence believers in Sudan, Nigeria, India, Indonesia, and other places where violence intrudes into daily life. Recent Protestant reflections on the state of human culture and law in the West have taken place against the backdrop of immense change in the configuration of the world. Because the growth of Christian adherence always brings with it a concern for Christian ethics, Christian political action, and Christian civilization, what Western figures have said on these matters now assumes worldwide significance.

CHURCH HISTORY

The church history, more narrowly conceived, of Europe and North America has always provided an important frame for Protestant reflection on law, politics, and society. What figures as disparate as Susan B. Anthony and Abraham Kuyper at the end of the nineteenth century or Martin Luther King Jr., William Stringfellow, and John Howard Yoder in the last part of the twentieth century wrote about the great issues of human destiny was always affected by the local and national faith communities where their firsthand experiences lay. Those experiences, in turn, were always connected to main developments in the broader ecclesiastical world. A sketch of some of those developments illuminates more of the terrain in which significant Protestant thinking took place on issues of law, politics, and society. In a tumultuous flood of events, people, organizations, and relationships, it is useful to think of Protestant church history in the recent past as experiencing an era of ecumenicity, an era of Catholic engagement, an era of women, an era of the Holy Spirit, and an era of dechristianization.

ECUMENICITY

The World Missionary Conference that was held at Edinburgh in June 1910 represented a landmark in Protestant ecumenical history.[23] Although earlier organizations like the Evangelical Alliance and earlier mission conferences (London 1888, New York 1900) had drawn participants from both Europe and North America, Edinburgh exceeded earlier efforts both in the number of its participants and the extent of its goals. About 1,200 delegates attended the conference, with the great majority from Britain and North America, but also substantial representation from the European continent. (Edinburgh spoke much of Christianity in the non-Western world, but it was the last such major Protestant gathering without substantial non-Western participation.) The conference organizers and those who addressed the gathering expressed the hope that the kind of Christian cooperation that marked many mission fields would catch fire in Protestant homelands as well. Besides the theme of Christian unity, the conference also directed major attention to other matters that would loom large in succeeding decades, including the relationship of churches to governments and the encounter between Christianity and non-Christian religions.

In retrospect, it is evident that the Edinburgh conference represented the high tide of Western missionary expansion. Soon the traumas of World War I would combine with vigorous Christian growth in the non-Western world to end the Western dominance of world Christianity. Yet the positive experience of the conference had a wide-ranging effect on Protestant ecumenicity. Discussions and personal connections begun at Edinburgh carried on and eventually led to the founding of the International Missionary Council (1921) and then less directly to two other significant organizations. The Universal Christian Conference on Life and Work convened for the first time at Stockholm in 1925, and the World Conference on Faith and Order held its inaugural meeting at Lausanne in 1927. The first of these explored ways in which Protestant churches might cooperate on practical social questions, the second pursued consideration of doctrine and practice more directly. These two bodies were the principal motivators leading in 1948 to the creation of the World Council of Churches. Its programs and international meetings went on to provide unprecedented opportunities for dialogue and cooperation among Protestants connected to the older, more traditional denominations, and eventually also to non-Western Protestants linked to these same denominations.

Within the various Western nations, parallel movements drew together increasing numbers for fellowship, discussion, and united action. The ecumenical process went furthest in Canada, where in 1925 a United Church was constructed by the merger of the country's Methodist, Congregational, and a majority of its Presbyterian churches.[24] In its early years the United Church of Canada combined Evangelical and Social Gospel emphases; subsequently it became a champion of liberal theology and liberal social policy. In the United States the National Council of Churches of Christ was founded in 1950 as a successor to a Federal Council of Churches that had been launched early in the century. Through its social services arm, the Church World Service, the National Council has promoted development projects in many parts of the world. At home it was the primary sponsor of the Revised Standard Version, a major updating of the King James Bible that has enjoyed great currency in mainline churches. Most of the European countries have also developed cooperative church councils similar in constituency and programs to the American National Council.

Evangelicals, Fundamentalists, Pentecostals, Anabaptists, conservative Lutherans, and most Holiness denominations did not join the National Council or the World Council, but rather sought partners for fellowship and practical action in bodies like the National Association of Evangelicals (1942) or in agencies, like the Mennonite Central Committee, defined by denominational traditions. To use terms popularized by Ernst Troeltsch at the end of the nineteenth century, "sectarian" bodies have been more reluctant than "churchly" bodies to join broad ecumenical coalitions. But the sectarians have excelled in informal fellowship. As an example, the Lausanne Conference on World Evangelization of 1974, which was sponsored by the Billy Graham Evangelistic Association, drew 2,700 delegates from more countries and more denominations than any other international Protestant meeting ever held to that time. The worldwide travels of Billy Graham, as also similar journeys by the Pentecostal evangelist Oral Roberts and the Anglican Bible expositor John R. W. Stott, have functioned as powerful devices for creating broad networks of conservative Protestant believers.[25]

In whatever shape—formal and conciliar or informal and ad hoc— Protestantism became thoroughly ecumenical over the course of the twentieth century. That process has meant that, although Christian thinkers may speak out of their own distinctive traditions, their voices are increasingly heard by audiences far from home.

CATHOLIC ENGAGEMENT

During the last four decades of the twentieth century, a special ecumenism of a hitherto unthinkable sort exerted a growing influence on world Protestantism. This ecumenism concerned the Roman Catholic Church. Since the Reformation of the sixteenth century, Protestants with only a few exceptions had defined themselves over against the Catholics. Well into the twentieth century, the historical antagonism between these two streams of Western Christianity influenced much formal church life and thought in both Europe and North America. This situation began to change as a direct result of the Second Vatican Council (1962–65), which Pope John XXIII convened in order to breathe new life into worldwide Catholicism. The council's treatment of non-Catholic Christians (as well as of non-Christian religions in general) was much gentler than in previous Catholic dispensations, and this visible softening led on to a series of official dialogues initiated by the Vatican. These dialogues were, however, only the most visible public signs of many Catholic–Protestant connections, ranging from shared neighborhood Bible studies to high-level theological exchange.

The high point of discussions sparked by Vatican II was the announcement by the Vatican and the Lutheran World Federation in October 1997 that a substantial measure of official agreement had been reached on the doctrine of justification by faith. This crux of the Protestant Reformation had historically been one of the great sticking points with the Catholic Church. Now, however, the joint committee declared that Catholics and Lutherans could agree on two essentials: God redeemed humans freely and only by his grace; redeemed humans properly responded to the reception of God's grace by doing good works. Not all Protestants and not all Catholics were convinced that this joint declaration overcame as much contentious history as its promoters suggested. But by comparison with only a few decades earlier, the degree of agreement (however interpreted) was astounding.

For Protestant deliberations on law, politics, and society, the increasing pace of Protestant–Catholic dialogue is unusually important. Catholic traditions of natural law reasoning, which were developed with particular ability by Thomas Aquinas in the thirteenth century and by modern neo-Thomists in the twentieth century, are now more easily exploited by Protestants. Protestants also look more self-consciously to landmark Catholic statements on society and political responsibility, like Pope Leo XIII's *Re-*

rum Novarum of 1891 and some of the encyclicals of Pope John Paul II, to find constructive assistance for their own deliberations. Breakthroughs in Catholic–Protestant ecumenism have probably done as much for Protestant reflection on social-political matters as any other significant development of the recent past.

WOMEN

The twentieth century also witnessed a much more comprehensive participation by women in the public life of Protestant churches than was possible during earlier centuries. Women have contributed a majority of members in almost all Christian communions in all times and places, but only in the last period of Western history have women become recognized public leaders. Even before Susan B. Anthony brought resources from her Quaker experience to bear on questions of suffrage and women's rights, women in other sectarian traditions, especially Wesleyan and Holiness churches, had begun to take a more active part in preaching, evangelizing, and organizing church programs. Missionary service enjoyed a long history as a viable platform for such work.[26] The Pentecostal movements that spread so rapidly in the early twentieth century likewise led to further participation by women who felt called by the Holy Spirit to take on public tasks.

Before too many years had passed in the twentieth century, female voices were gaining public recognition as important promoters of Christian faith and practice. As examples, in England the lay Anglican Dorothy L. Sayers (1893–1957) exploited her fame as a writer of detective novels to produce several notable Christian dramas, introduce Dante to wide audiences, and publish articulate expositions of classically Christian orthodoxy. In America, the Methodist deacon Georgia Harkness (1891–1979) became a key participant in early meetings of Life and Work and the World Council of Churches, while her older contemporary, the Baptist scholar, Helen Barrett Montgomery (1861–1934), was a notable promoter of missions as well as an accomplished translator of scripture.[27]

After mid-century, the traditional mainline denominations joined a range of Wesleyan, Holiness, and Pentecostal denominations in beginning to ordain women for the office of pastor.[28] This departure from traditional practice worried, and continues to worry, some confessional and conservative Protestants, and it provided the occasion for a noteworthy exchange between Georgia Harkness and Karl Barth at the first meeting of the World Council of Churches in 1948. But by the end of the century broader public participation by women in church activities throughout the Protestant world had become an accepted fact of religious life.

For thinking about law, politics, and society, the fuller participation of Protestant women has produced overt and subtle effects. Overtly, the range of issues now routinely canvassed has broadened considerably. Books like Jean Bethke Elshtain's *Women and War* (1987) were not unknown in earlier generations, but they became much more common as women began to study and teach in all of the theological institutions and when women were more routinely included as full participants in ecclesiastical councils. More subtly, the public agency of Protestant women has assured that questions of family, procreation, gender, domestic economy, and health care—that is, the range of issues related to practical Christian life in the world— receive attention from more angles and with broader resources of scriptural exegesis and life experience than was the case when men monopolized the public life of the churches.

HOLY SPIRIT

The rise of Pentecostalism and, then later, of charismatic movements has also worked broad and deep changes in Protestant life over the last century.[29] Formally recognized Pentecostalism is usually traced to the revival at Azusa Street in Los Angeles that began in 1906, and particularly to the manifestation there of the sign gift of speaking in tongues. But themes stressing the Holy Spirit, the immediate touch of God for healing or wisdom, and the possibilities for higher levels of consecration had influenced many Christian movements throughout the nineteenth century and earlier.

Pentecostalism remained a curiosity for several decades, with flamboyant, but appealing, preachers like Aimee Semple McPherson and her Angelus Temple in Los Angeles presenting to the public a dramatic picture of healing, spectacle, and media savvy.[30] Soon, however, the development of strong denominations like the mostly black Church of God in Christ and the mostly white Assemblies of God, along with effective mission work at home and abroad, transformed Pentecostal currents into major tributaries of modern Christianity. Pentecostal emphases caught on also in Eastern, Southern, and Western Europe, though never to the same degree as in North America. When, after World War II, Pentecostal and Pentecostal-like churches began to proliferate in the non-Western world, the movement was transformed into a genuinely global force.

In recent decades charismatic impulses within older Protestant denominations, as well as the Catholic Church, have transformed the face of much Christian worship. These impulses owe much to Pentecostalism with their stress on immediate apprehension of the Holy Spirit and a style of worship marked by exuberance, spontaneity, subjective song lyrics, and the exploitation of pop, folk, and soft rock music. Even churches that have not embraced Pentecostal or charismatic principles as such now often reflect in public worship a line of influence that began at Azusa Street.

Pentecostals have not as yet contributed a great deal to reflections on legal, political, or social issues. Yet Protestants who have taken such matters seriously sometimes function as tutors, especially to second and third generation Pentecostals, both in the West and the rest of the world, who want to add meaningful public service to personal and small-group renewal. Since charismatic themes have not loomed large in historic Protestant consideration of law and human nature, the rise of Pentecostalism may point toward an important intellectual challenge. When added to historic Protestant reflections on the work of God the Father and Christ the Son, Pentecostal emphasis on the person and work of the Holy Spirit may push Protestant reflections to a more fully Trinitarian stance on public issues, as well as for more narrowly theological concerns. That, at least, is the potential for systematic social reflection opened up by the dramatic rise of Pentecostal Christianity.

DECHRISTIANIZATION

A final feature of Protestant church history since the late nineteenth century has been the retreat of Protestantism from some parts of Europe and North America where the Protestant churches had once been a dominant cultural presence.[31] It is sobering to realize that the vigorous Protestant constituencies that nourished the thought of, for example, Abraham Kuyper in the Netherlands, Karl Barth in Switzerland, Dietrich Bonhoeffer in Germany, and Reinhold Niebuhr among the elite educational stratum of the American East Coast have all declined precipitously since those landmark thinkers did their work. The Dutch Reformed, Swiss Reformed, German Lutheran, and mainline American Protestant churches that provided the first audiences for these intellectual giants are by no means exhausted, but the commanding position they once enjoyed, and from which prescient observers surveyed the whole of Christendom, have been much reduced.

Dechristianization could come with a rush, as when the Nazis strong-armed German churches to exchange traditional Christianity for a semi-pagan Hitlerism. Much more typically it has arisen from the incremental advance of material, therapeutic, commercial, or entertainment concerns at the expense of historic Christian commitments. In whatever form it has appeared, in most of Protestant Europe and Protestant Canada and in significant sectors of American society, dechristianization poses challenges for the use of Christian thinking, as it does to every other aspect of the Christian religion.

Given this situation, there could be a temptation to treat the proposals of the authors surveyed in this part of the book as voices from an unrecoverable past, as perhaps relevant to their worlds where Christian memories, if not always Christian practice, were firmly embedded in a broad expanse of culture, but now mostly irrelevant since the Christian cultures in and to which they spoke are rapidly passing away. This logic can, however, be met with a counterlogic. If Christian reflections on law, politics, and society were part of a social order in which a certain measure of general Christian vitality could be taken for granted, or at least remembered, then serious attention to that Christian reflection may now be more relevant rather than less. If what has been lost, or is being lost, represented a fully formed Christian civilization in which wellsprings of personal piety watered rivers of vigorous Christian tradition flowing to seas of Christian culture, then critical attention to the proper functioning of Christian cultures may offer a way to recommend personal piety and vigorous Christian tradition, as well as the broader reconsideration of Christian culture that presupposed a measure of spiritual health among persons and in churches. Dechristianization, in other words, may offer students of legal, political, and social principles an unexpected opportunity for evangelism alongside more ordinary tasks of cultural analysis.

The foregoing brief commentary on ecumenism, engagement with Roman Catholics, women, Pentecostals, and dechristianization by no means constitutes an adequate general history of modern Protestantism. What such snapshots do make possible, however, is a sense of the shifting backgrounds against which notable Protestant thinkers and actors did their work.

THEOLOGY

The story of Protestant theology since the end of the nineteenth century lacks the defining plot lines found among the Orthodox and the Catholics. Orthodoxy and Catholicism both feature much theological pluralism. In the Orthodox case, this pluralism comes from different responses to a similar question—how to preserve the practices of traditional faith and the norms of traditional worship midst the tumults of revolution, war, and immigration. In the Catholic case, it comes from differing reactions to a single series of events—what were the effects of neo-Thomist dominance and what happened after neo-Thomism was unsettled in the wake of the Second Vatican Council?

Protestant theology, by contrast, has had a nearly chaotic recent history. A pessimist might suggest that Protestant theology has simply collapsed into a series of "modernisms" defined as Christian glossing for convictions rooted substantially in some other contemporary absolutism. Modernisms on the radical left have included Christianized versions of Marxism, extreme feminism, or nature mysticism; on the more moderate left of inevitable progress and divine-right self-fulfillment; and on the right of American messianism, cantankerous antigovernmentalism, and prophetic apocalypticism. In all cases the "modernism" emerges when Christian reasoning from scripture and broad Christian tradition gives way to reasoning based on some certainty of the contemporary age. Of such "modernisms" there have been no shortage among Protestant groups, large and small, whether in Europe or North America, whether early or late. Adding sting to the pessimist's indictment is the observation that publishers regularly sell many more books promoting these modernist viewpoints than they do in marketing more sober and traditional theological efforts.

A pessimist might likewise want to make the case that the most important events in Protestant theological history since the late nineteenth century have been contentious standoffs testifying to the sterility of Protestant reasoning as a whole. Proof of this assessment would begin with attention to the persistent division between liberals and conservatives, which took one shape in Abraham Kuyper's Netherlands, with strife between confessionalists like Kuyper who rejected the sovereignty of Enlightenment reason and liberals who championed it. That division took another shape in the split between American fundamentalists who insisted on an inerrant Bible interpreted by the canons of static Baconian science versus liberals who insisted on a mythological Bible interpreted by the canons of organic Darwinian science. This indictment could go on to document implacable Protestant struggles on a range of issues related to gender, sexuality, and the family: the use of contraceptives, the ordination of women, the access to abortion, and the right to same sex marriage—all issues on which Protestants have opposed Protestants with determined conviction based on contradictory interpretations of scripture, church tradition, and personal religious experience. Spectacular individual disagreements—with the most spectacular coming in the 1930s with Barth's denial and Emil Brunner's defense of the usefulness of natural revelation for distinctly Christian purposes—could also be multiplied as an indication of the inability of Protestants to promote cohesive and compelling theology.

If this indictment were all that could be said about recent Protestant theology, it would be devastating for commentary on issues of law, politics, and society, since such commentary would be thoroughly compromised by the fragmented incoherence of theological foundations.

In fact, however, much more can be said than that Protestants have regularly battled each other over many conflicted issues and in many venues. A more comprehensive view reveals, not necessarily theological coherence, balance, or completeness, but rather vitality of several sorts and visible in many parts of the Protestant world. The compelling Protestant theologians of the recent past have not spoken with one voice, for differences among Protestant traditions and local differences in working out Protestant practices prevent such cohesion, not to speak of the absence of any universally recognized pope or patriarch who could persuade all Protestants to reason together.

Notwithstanding manifest Protestant diversity, a common approach can be identified for those Protestants who have made the type of enduring theological contribution that provides stable grounding for legal, social, and political analysis. That is, for most of the Protestant figures examined in the chapters that follow, it is possible to discern similar processes at work. These figures were, first, serious about the riches found in scripture. To be sure, their uses of the Bible differed considerably among themselves—from Reinhold Niebuhr's evocation of biblical symbols and Karl Barth's Christocentric hermeneutic to Martin Luther King Jr's tropes of liberation and William Stringfellow's call for radical biblical justice. But all of them were serious Protestant thinkers, only because they were first serious students of the Bible. They were also solidly informed by Christian tradition. Several, including Barth and Dietrich Bonhoeffer, mastered significant aspects of patristic and medieval theology, as well as materials since the Reformation. But all—for instance, Kuyper as a Dutch Calvinist, John Howard Yoder as a committed Anabaptist, King as a beneficiary of African American experiential religion—were given major impetus by a specific tradition of weighty theology. They were, third, also unusually thoughtful about the usefulness of reason and experience to complement their study of scripture and appropriation of tradition, and unlike many of their contemporaries they worked carefully to mold scripture, tradition, reason, and experience into a coherent whole. Barth was the great exemplar in this balancing act, although all of the figures were both broad in their search for theological resources and discriminating in how they put them to use. Finally, they were creative in assessing their contemporary circumstances in light of divine revelation. Kuyper, in his educational and journalistic exposure to conditions in the Netherlands, Barth in his involvement with church politics that led to the Barmen Declaration, Niebuhr through his participation in many debates over public policy, Bonhoeffer in the crises of the Nazi era, King in addressing the realities of civil discrimination, Stringfellow in his demand for justice to the poor and needy in the streets, Yoder as a theologian of peace at the height of the Cold War—all were thinkers deeply immersed in their own times, yet never simply a product of those times. In fact, their ability to do consequential theology depended on securing a standpoint grounded in religious resources from which to address the pressing issues of the day.

Susan B. Anthony presents an exception to this pattern, though String-fellow emulates her somewhat, since she said what she wanted to say in opposition to what she perceived as the manifest errors of scripture, the ineffectiveness of traditional theological reasoning, and the relative unimportance of systematic thought. Anthony's experience-driven and action-oriented achievements, however, did open a way for other women who in the wake of Anthony's generation of feminist pioneers were able to appropriate for their own purposes the standard repertory of theological procedures that were so powerfully at work among the other notables profiled below.

Kuyper, Barth, Niebuhr, Bonhoeffer, Stringfellow, King, and Yoder were able to offer telling theological reflections about problems in society in large part because of their broader theological achievements. Kuyper skillfully blended elements from traditional Dutch Calvinism and from the populist piety he experienced as a young minister to forge a vision of Reformed faith and life that continues to win eager readers to this day. Barth became the century's most widely read academic theologian because of an even greater skill at enlivening central themes of continental Reformed tradition with his own energetic study of scripture and his own mastery of European philosophical debate. Niebuhr was less interested in the traditional *loci* of theology as such, but the dialectics with which he interpreted events (humanity as sinner and saint, subject to history and shaper of history, egotistical but able to live for others) were effective because they were rooted in classical Christian categories. The trauma of events pushed Bonhoeffer far beyond the standard categories of his inherited Lutheranism, but his theology forged in crisis continues to inspire many throughout the world, again, at least in part because it was so profoundly Lutheran. King took black preaching into the streets and by so doing altered it to suit his purposes, but the worldwide impact of that preaching is unimaginable apart from the rock of African American tradition from which it was hewn. Yoder engaged in the sort of broad-ranging ecumenical dialogue that was quite foreign to his Mennonite heritage, but it was the innovative grasp of that heritage that made Yoder's ecumenical contribution so powerful. In a word, the Protestant figures described in this book testify decisively to the ongoing vigor of Protestant theology.

If this were a comprehensive history of recent Protestantism, the signs of vitality could be multiplied. The Anglican world, despite reverses in its English homeland and a large measure of controversy over what modern Anglicanism should mean, continued to produce theologians distinguished by their immersion in Christian tradition, their sensitivity to scripture, and their responsiveness to the challenges of the hour. Archbishop William Temple (1881–1943), who combined philosophical interests with ecumenical and social advocacy, and Oliver O'Donovan (b. 1945), who has looked to the resurrection of Christ as the key to enduring ethical integrity, are only two of the many who have extended the strength of Anglican reasoning to the present.[32] Theological vitality of a very different sort arose in the twentieth century from the proclamation of nondenominational classical Christian orthodoxy, or "mere Christianity." The Oxford and Cambridge don, C. S. Lewis (1898–1963), was the great exemplar of this kind of exposition, but there were many other imitators in several other communions.[33] A recovery of measured theology from the ranks of former fundamentalists was also notable development of the recent past. Led by the American educator and editor, Carl F. H. Henry (b. 1913), a growing number of those who had once despised formal learning have made increasingly significant contributions to the recovery of theology.[34] Similar quickening has marked the ranks of some mainline bodies, with the narrative theology of Hans Frei (1922–88) and George Lindbeck (b. 1923) among the most notable examples.[35] Thinkers out of France, Switzerland, and especially Germany made an especially notable contribution to the recovery of moral and theological balance amid the devastations of a traumatic century. Such ones include Oscar Cullmann (1902–99), with discerning biblical reflection on the "powers" in their ancient and contemporary manifestation;[36] Emil Brunner (1889–1966), with special attention to God's concern for all of life;[37] Jürgen Moltmann (b. 1926), with concern for how hope in evil days may grow from the central biblical narrative;[38] and Wolfhart Pannenberg (b. 1928), with wide-ranging arguments for the pertinence of the biblical narrative for modern science, modern historical understanding, and much else.[39]

Protestant theology has passed through many difficulties in the recent past; it is all but impossible to overstate the amount of theological negligence or the degree of theological irresponsibility manifest among Protestants since the end of the nineteenth century. But along with much dross has appeared as well much depth. That theological depth, which is represented so well by the figures in this Protestant section of the volume, has meant that when Christian thinkers turned to questions of law and human nature, they had something to say.

REFLECTIONS ON LAW, POLITICS, AND SOCIETY

The main legal, political, and social subjects of interest to significant Protestant thinkers are well explored in the chapters that follow. Reflecting the multivalent character of Protestantism itself, these subjects range widely. If they do not focus as comprehensively on issues of community or social solidarity as Catholic thinkers have done, they nonetheless offer a great deal on a wide array of critically important subjects.

The positive regard for the state, as an institution created by God and intended by God for the flourishing of all people, was a strong theme in Abraham Kuyper's groundbreaking practical labor, as well as in what he wrote. Yet Kuyper's picture of "sphere sovereignty" also provided for significant checks on the power of any state that would overstep the boundaries that were also set by God. The result was a vision of political responsibility that has encouraged many, especially Reformed Christians, in many parts of the world, to contend for a properly functioning state within God-ordained limits as a distinctly Christian good. Dietrich Bonhoeffer's reasoning about the Christian's obligation to the state took a very different course, but ended with similarly profound insights about the potential (for good and for ill) of the state.

Karl Barth and Reinhold Niebuhr are among the most important twentieth-century voices to make arguments of similar force respecting the virtues of democracy and the rule of law. Neither was blithely optimistic about the workings of a democratic polity, for they regarded democratic structures as just as susceptible to ordinary failings as any other human institution. Yet, with unusual clarity, Barth and Niebuhr were able to highlight the important advantages of democracy as, among possible political systems, preserving important elements of what God had provided for the flourishing of human society. Barth's commitment to democracy and his wariness of political abuse from unchecked power fed directly into his lifelong commitment to socialism. Niebuhr was eventually weaned from earlier socialist convictions, but never from a commitment to democracy as a gift from God.

The power of God-ordained action to reform degenerate or evil social structures may be the most widely shared product of Protestant thinking during recent decades. In this sense, at least some Protestants have retained a proclivity for the type of witness that originally brought the Protestant churches into existence. Susan B. Anthony thought that she could find in purified Christian tradition, as well as more general experience rightly apprehended, an engine for reducing the evils of patriarchy and offering liberation for women. Kuyper felt that living Calvinism, rightly understood, could rectify injustices of Dutch education and society. The basis of Niebuhr's realism was the use of Christian resources, rightly interpreted, to encourage a measured, incremental, but determined push for justice. Stringfellow took the basic biblical themes of the incarnation, crucifixion, and resurrection, and classic Protestant doctrines of worship, vocation, and law-gospel directly into his efforts to reform the laws of the state, particularly on subjects of war, poverty, and social justice. Yoder thought he possessed in wisdom from the marginalized communities of the Anabaptists exactly the tonic that the violence-ravaged world needed as an alternative to tearing itself apart. Supremely, King knew how to combine basic Christian principles with the professed ideals of the United States in order to stimulate a long-overdue attention to civil rights, first for African Americans but soon by extension for many others in the world as well. Much Protestant effort has always gone into protecting the status quo of rights, privileges, and property of Protestants themselves. But at their most attractive, Protestant insights have also provided a great impetus for altruistic reform.

The Protestant appeal for reform draws attention to one major Protestant figure who is not profiled in this book. Walter Rauschenbusch (1861–1918) was a German American who served for eleven years as a pastor during an age of uncontrolled industrialization in one of the most squalid sections of New York City.[40] That experience drove him to rethink the theology he had been taught in the United States and Germany, to study the scriptures afresh, and to cultivate contacts with others who worried about the degradation left behind by runaway laissez-faire industrial capitalism. The result was a landmark book from 1907, *Christianity and the Social Crisis*, as well as a number of other significant publications in the years that followed. Drawing inspiration from the biblical concept of the Kingdom of God, Rauschenbusch appealed for progressive, democratic reform guided by the spirit of Christ. The start of World War I sobered Rauschenbusch and led him to place greater stress on the reality of sin and the need for an active divine presence in the world. But in both early and later periods of his life, Rauschenbusch's understanding of the "Social Gospel" represented a powerful Protestant response to the rapidly changing conditions of urban modernity. The significance of his work is indicated by the fact that it has inspired many later thinkers and reformers, including Reinhold Niebuhr and Martin Luther King Jr.

The theological resources that these Protestant thinkers brought to their tasks were drawn from the standard array of classical Christian tradition, but with a few particular emphases. As explained in greater detail in the chapter by Davison Douglas below, Niebuhr found in Augustine's depictions of sin and human nature a subtle, complex, and conflicted understanding of humanity that matched the subtle, complex, and conflicted circumstances of modern society. Barth and Bonhoeffer in their different ways were, if anything, more fundamentally shaped by the assertions of the Chalcedonian definition about Jesus as fully God and fully human in one perfectly integrated person. Yoder made equal capital from the Anabaptist conviction that the New Testament presented the church as an alternative community standing over against the world in judgment and love.

The use of such theological resources for social and political analysis was never harmonious. Barth and Yoder, for example, were much less sanguine about the prospect of finding universal natural law in scripture and general human experience than was, for example, Kuyper with his considerable confidence in what God had generously bestowed on all peoples by "common grace." Yet those with patience to examine such differences over how best to use the resources of Christian tradition receive the greatest heuristic benefit from studying these thinkers with care.

At the start of the twenty-first century, religion is more obviously alive as a public force—in the West, as well as the rest of the world—than it has even been in living memory. International politics is once again fixated on conflicts involving Christians, Muslims, and Jews. The European Union, itself to all appearances the product of strictly secular developments, has paused to deliberate at some length on whether to include mention of God in its new constitution. In several European countries authorities are shaken by the sudden appearance of large Christian congregations made up of Caribbean and African believers. In more European countries, there is even more consternation resulting from the rising tide of Muslim citizens and immigrants. In the United States, controversy swirls around the display of the Ten Commandments in public space, the phrase "under God" in the Pledge of Allegiance, and the use of governmental funding for social services operated by religious organizations. In Canada, federal proposals to legitimate same-sex marriage on the same basis as male-female marriage have elicited the kind of religiously inspired tumult that Canadians have long prided themselves as avoiding.

In the midst of such unusual attention to religion and public life the great need for both religious communities and the public at large is for solidly grounded argument that might be as persuasive in its claims as it is humane in its purposes. The chapters that follow offer by no means the only sources for such argument. But their accounts of serious Protestant wrestling with momentous issues concerning persons, societies, law, and politics deserve to be taken seriously indeed. Among many other things, they are a timely Protestant gift from the past to the present.

NOTES

1. A good general survey from an earlier generation is Martin E. Marty, *Protestantism: Its Churches and Cultures, Rituals and Doctrines, Yesterday and Today* (New York: Holt, Rinehart and Winston, 1972).

2. David Barrett et al., *World Christian Encyclopedia*, 2d ed., 2 vols. (New York: Oxford University Press, 2001), 1:16.

3. Ibid., 836–837.

4. Paul Freston, *Evangelicals and Politics in Asia, Africa and Latin America* (New York: Cambridge University Press, 2001).

5. Outstanding overviews are found in Hugh McLeod, ed., *European Religion in the Age of Great Cities, 1830–1930* (London: Routledge, 1995), and *Secularization in Western Europe, 1848–1914* (New York: St. Martin's, 2000).

6. Edwin Scott Gaustad and Philip L. Barlow, *New Historical Atlas of Religion in America* (New York: Oxford University Press, 2001), 401.

7. For the continuing effects of this singular situation, see Michael O. Emerson and Christian Smith, *Divided by Race: Evangelical Religion and the Problem of Race in America* (New York: Oxford University Press, 2000).

8. Alexis de Tocqueville, *Democracy in America*, ed. Harvey Claflin Mansfield and Delba Winthrop (Chicago: University of Chicago Press, 2000), 278.

9. See Mark A. Noll, *America's God, from Jonathan Edwards to Abraham Lincoln* (New York: Oxford University Press, 2002), 367–437.

10. See Henry F. May, *Protestant Churches and Industrial America* (New York: Harper, 1949); Paul Carter, *The Spiritual Crisis of the Gilded Age* (DeKalb: Northern Illinois University Press, 1971).

11. A solid survey is Robert Handy, *Undermined Establishment: Church-State Relations in America, 1880–1920* (Princeton, N.J.: Princeton University Press, 1991).

12. Outstanding are John Webster Grant, *A Profusion of Spires: Religion in Nineteenth-Century Ontario* (Toronto: University of Toronto Press, 1988), and *The Church in the Canadian Era*, 2d ed. (Burlington, Ontario: Welch, 1988).

13. Daniel H. Bays, "Chinese Protestant Christianity Today," *China Quarterly* 174 (June 2003): 489–504.

14. See R. C. D. Jasper, *George Bell, Bishop of Chichester* (New York: Oxford University Press, 1967); Philip Paul Hallie, *Lest Innocent Blood Be Shed: The Story of the Village of Le Chambon, and How Goodness Happened There* (New York: Harper & Row, 1979); and Helmut Thielicke, *Notes from a Wayfarer: The Autobiography of Helmut Thielicke* (New York: Paragon House, 1995).

15. Expert guidance is provided in a series of books by Reginald W. Bibby, including *Fragmented Gods: The Poverty and Potential of Religion in Canada* (Toronto: Irwin, 1987) and *Restless Gods: The Renaissance of Religion in Canada* (Toronto: Stoddard, 2002).

16. George Egerton, "Entering the Age of Human Rights: Religion, Politics, and Canadian Liberalism, 1945–1950," paper delivered at the Anglo-American Conference of Historians, University of London, 2000.

17. "The Constitution Act, 1982," in *Canada and the New Constitution*, ed. S. M. Beck and I. Bernier, 2 vols. (Montreal: Institute for Research on Public Policy, 1982), 2:253.

18. A summary may be found in Mark A. Noll, *The Old Religion in a New World: The History of North American Christianity* (Grand Rapids, Mich.: Eerdmans,

2002), 288–290, which draws heavily on the work of political scientists John Green, James Guth, Lyman Kellstedt, and Corwin Smidt.

19. On the leaders who engineered the conservative change, see Barry Hankins, *Uneasy in Babylon: Southern Baptist Conservatives and American Culture* (Tuscaloosa: University of Alabama Press, 2002).

20. The following comparisons are drawn from information provided in Harlan P. Beach and Charles H. Fahs, *World Missionary Atlas* (New York: Institute of Social and Religious Research, 1925), 76; Joel A. Carpenter, "Appendix: The Evangelical Missionary Force in the 1930s," in *Earthen Vessels: American Evangelicals and Foreign Missions, 1880–1980*, ed. Joel A. Carpenter and Wilbert R. Shenk (Grand Rapids, Mich.: Eerdmans, 1990), 335–342; Edward R. Dayton, ed., *Mission Handbook 1973* (Monrovia, Calif.: MARC, 1973); A. Scott Moreau, "Putting the Survey in Perspective," in *Mission Handbook 2001–2003*, ed. John A. Siewert and Dotsey Wellner, 18th ed. (Wheaton, Ill.: EMIS, 2001), 33–79; and Patrick Johnstone and Jason Mandryk, *Operation World* (Carlisle, England: Paternoster, 2001).

21. Lamin Sanneh, *Translating the Message* (Maryknoll, N.Y.: Orbis Books, 1989).

22. For implications, see Andrew Walls, *The Missionary Movement in Christian History* (Maryknoll, N.Y.: Orbis Books, 1996); Walls, *The Cross-Cultural Process in Christian History* (Maryknoll, N.Y.: Orbis Books, 2002); and David Martin, *Pentecostalism: The World Their Parish* (Oxford: Blackwell, 2002).

23. For orientation, see Brian Stanley, "Twentieth-Century World Christianity: A Perspective from the History of Missions," in *Christianity Reborn: The Global Expansion of Evangelicalism in the Twentieth Century*, ed. Donald M. Lewis, (Grand Rapids, Mich.: Eerdmans, 1998), 52–83.

24. An outstanding study is N. Keith Clifford, *The Resistance to Church Union in Canada, 1904–1939* (Vancouver: University of British Columbia Press, 1985).

25. Works stressing these worldwide connections include David Edwin Harrell, *Oral Roberts: An American Life* (Bloomington: Indiana University Press, 1985); Billy Graham, *Just As I Am: The Autobiography of Billy Graham* (San Francisco: HarperCollins, 1997); and Timothy Dudley-Smith, *John Stott*, 2 vols. (Leicester, England: Inter-Varsity Press, 1999–2001).

26. Dana Robert, *American Women in Mission* (Macon, Ga.: Mercer University Press, 1996).

27. Barbara Reynolds, *Dorothy L. Sayers: Her Life and Soul* (New York: St. Martin's, 1993); Georgia Harkness, *Grace Abounding* (Nashville, Tenn.: Abingdon Press, 1969); H. B. Montgomery, *Helen Barrett Montgomery: From Campus to World Citizenship* (New York: Revell, 1940).

28. Mark Chaves, *Ordaining Women: Culture and Conflict in Religious Organizations* (Cambridge, Mass.: Harvard University Press, 1997).

29. Grant Wacker, *Heaven Below: Early Pentecostals and American Culture* (Cambridge, Mass.: Harvard University Press, 2001); Vinson Synan, *The Century of the Holy Spirit* (Nashville, Tenn.: Thomas Nelson, 2001).

30. Edith Blumhofer, *Aimee Semple McPherson: Everybody's Sister* (Grand Rapids, Mich.: Eerdmans, 1993).

31. Hugh McLeod, *Religion and the People of Western Europe, 1789–1989*, 2d ed. (New York: Oxford University Press, 1997); Grace Davie, *Religion in Britain Since 1945: Believing Without Belonging* (Oxford: Blackwell, 1994).

32. See, e.g., William Temple, *Nature, Man and God* (London: Macmillan, 1934); Oliver O'Donovan, *Resurrection and Moral Order* (Grand Rapids, Mich.: Eerdmans, 1986).

33. C. S. Lewis, *Mere Christianity: The Case for Christianity, Christian Behavior, and Beyond Personality* (New York: Macmillan, 1952).

34. Carl F. H. Henry, *Confessions of a Theologian: An Autobiography* (Waco, Tex.: Word, 1986).

35. Hans W. Frei, *The Eclipse of Biblical Narrative* (New Haven, Conn.: Yale University Press, 1974); George A. Lindbeck, *The Nature of Doctrine* (Philadelphia: Westminster, 1984).

36. Oscar Cullmann, *Christ and Time* (London: SCM, 1951).

37. Emil Brunner, *Christianity and Civilisation* (London: Nisbet, 1948).

38. Jürgen Moltmann, *Theology of Hope: On the Ground and the Implications of a Christian Theology*, trans. James W. Leitch (New York: Harper & Row, 1967); Moltmann, *The Crucified God: The Cross as the Foundation and Criticism of Christian Theology*, trans. R. A. Wilson and John Bowden (New York: Harper & Row, 1974).

39. Wolfhart Pannenberg, *Systematic Theology*, trans. Geoffrey W. Bromiley, 3 vols. (Grand Rapids, Mich.: Eerdmans, 1991–98).

40. See Paul M. Minus, *Walter Rauschenbusch, American Reformer* (New York: Macmillan, 1988); and Robert T. Handy, ed., *The Social Gospel in America, 1870–1920* (New York: Oxford University Press, 1966).

[CHAPTER 10]

Abraham Kuyper (1837–1920)

NICHOLAS WOLTERSTORFF

Abraham Kuyper was born in Maassluis, near Rotterdam, in 1837 to a Dutch Reformed minister and a former schoolteacher; he died at The Hague in 1920. He was an astonishing polymath and an organizational genius. He was originally an ordained minister in the Dutch Reformed Church; in 1892, he became one of the founders of a new denomination, the Gereformeerde Kerken in Nederland. He was the founder of a nationwide society to promote the formation and funding of Calvinist day schools (1878), the founder of the Free University of Amsterdam (1880), a professor of theology in the Free University for some twenty years (1880–1901), and rector of the university on several occasions. He was the chief editor for almost fifty years of the daily newspaper *De Standaard* and of its weekly supplement, *De Heraut*. He was the founder (1879) and acknowledged leader until his death of the first mass political party in the Netherlands, the Anti-Revolutionary Party. He twice served as a member of the Dutch Parliament and was prime minister of the Netherlands from 1901 to 1905. In addition to all this he was, throughout his adult life, a writer of devotional literature, of theological treatises, of social and cultural analyses, and of an astonishing number of "tracts for the occasion," as well as being an extraordinarily gifted and busy platform speaker and lecturer.

He was a polymath, but by no means a dilettante. In all that he did, diverse though it was, Kuyper was a religious leader, albeit of an unusual sort. In the course of his theological studies at the University of Leiden (1855–63), Kuyper studied the classics of the Reformed (Calvinist) tradition and wrote a dissertation on Calvin and the Polish reformer John à Lasco. Simultaneously, he became enamored with the theological modernism of some of his professors. That got him into trouble during his first pastorate, in the small country village of Beesd in the southern part of the Netherlands. A number of devout parishioners refused to attend services because his modernism offended their orthodox Calvinist theological convictions. Rather than simply ignore these "malcontents," Kuyper called on them and listened to their complaints. He was fascinated. Here "was more than mere routine. Here was conviction. Here the topics of conversation went beyond the nice weather and who happened to be ill and who had dismissed his workman. Here was interest in spiritual matters." The eventual effect was that Kuyper was jolted out of his theological modernism and moved to embrace the same Calvinist tradition that inspired his orthodox parishioners.[1]

His embrace was an embrace with a difference, however. Here already, at the beginning of his career, was manifested what would become an endemic habit of mind—the habit, namely, of digging beneath the surface of whatever religious, social, cultural, or intellectual development he was dealing with to discover its fundamental principles. Thus, he committed himself not to the particular form of theologically conservative Calvinism that he found among his critics in Beesd, but to the "essence" of the Calvinist tradition, to the "Reformed ground-principles," as he would later call them.

At this point, Kuyper made an imaginative and fateful move. Though doctrine, piety, and familiarity with the Bible seem to have been prominent in the minds of his discontented parishioners in Beesd, the young Kuyper concluded that the essence of the authentic Calvinist tradition was not so much a body of theological doctrine as a certain *Weltanschauung*, a world-and-life view—in Dutch, a *wereldbeschouwing*. Calvinism is a world-and-life view in competition with other such views. Throughout his career Kuyper would be opposed by theological conservatives who disputed this worldview-construal of the Calvinist tradition.[2]

In 1867, when Kuyper left his pastorate in Beesd, his religious identity was firmly formed and would not change to any significant degree thereafter. Already upon arriving in Beesd, he said: "I longed with all my soul for a sanctified Church wherein my soul and those of my loved ones can enjoy the quiet refreshment of peace, far from all confusion, under its firm, lasting, and authoritative guidance."[3] His experience with the "malcontents" in Beesd gave form to this longing; it was for the orthodox Calvinist tradition and understanding of the church that he now labored. He embraced with all his heart what he understood to be the world-and-life view of historic Calvinism. He sang its praises whenever the occasion arose and attributed all manner of good things to its influence, and he committed himself passionately to its revivification in the Netherlands.

He soon came to believe that this *Weltanschauung* remained alive in a good many of the laypeople of the Reformed churches in the Netherlands—the "small people," *kleine luyden*, as he called them.[4] Or, if it was not actually alive, Kuyper believed that it could be stirred to life. He also soon came to believe, however, that in all sorts of ways those with power in church and state made it difficult if not impossible for these traditionally Calvinist lay-people to live out their Calvinist world-and-life view in the modern world. They were inhibited and oppressed. It was these convictions that gave specific form to Kuyper's religious leadership.

Because it has become a shopworn phrase, one hesitates to call the movement Kuyper initiated and led a "liberation movement." Yet, undeniably, that is what it was.[5] It was a movement to secure for these Calvinist laypeople the social, political, and ecclesiastical space necessary for the free exercise of their religion. Given Kuyper's understanding of the character of their religion—not just theological convictions but a "comprehensive perspective," to use John Rawls's phrase—what was required was not just the relatively narrow space necessary for freedom of conscience and worship, but the much broader space necessary for them to live out their world-and-life view.[6] Hence it was that Kuyper's religious leadership required action on such a dizzying variety of fronts.

Not just action was required, but theory—descriptive and normative analysis. Kuyper did not regard the infringement by the power elite of church and state on the religious free exercise of the traditionally Calvinist laypeople of the Netherlands as a matter of mere happenstance. Nor did he regard it as the consequence merely of ill will on the part of the elite, although he both discerned, and by his often aggressive polemics and determined organizational activities provoked, a great deal of it. He thought the oppression was ultimately the consequence of mistaken understandings of society, religion, and religion's place in society. If his liberation program was to succeed, he had to develop a critique of those mistaken understandings and to articulate alternatives.[7]

It was for this reason that he developed his theories of sphere sovereignty and of the pluralist society, which we will examine to discover his theological account of human nature and the legal theories that, he argued, were not his own invention but simply the articulation of strands of thought deep in the Calvinist world-and-life view.

It was not in the serenity of the scholar's study that Kuyper developed the analyses that we shall be considering, but in the hurly-burly of leading a liberation movement. An implication is that Kuyper's articulation of his views rather often fails to measure up to the standards of development and rigor of the present-day academy. Kuyper was an intuitive genius given to a passionate and flowery baroque sort of rhetoric; he had neither time nor inclination for careful, rigorous, detailed, methodical articulation. Nor indeed was that what the occasion called for. So when interpreting him, one often has to look around and past the details of exposition so as to discern what he was getting at, rather than engaging in close exegesis.

The sociopolitical vision that Kuyper developed has proven to be the most influential appropriation and elaboration of the sociopolitical dimension of the Calvinist tradition in the past two centuries. Kuyper's closest competitor for such influence is probably Karl Barth, but Barth's influence has mainly been among academics. Partly because Kuyper was not just a theorist but an activist who tried to implement his theories, partly because he wrote regularly in the popular press and spoke regularly in the public arena, partly because he offered concrete analyses of modern society and its dynamics, and partly because his views often have obvious and direct implications for social and political action, Kuyper's influence has proven far more widespread than Barth's. It has gripped the imagination of readers of many sorts in many different places on the globe.

HISTORICAL CONTEXT AND CAREER

Already, in my attempt to describe what sort of religious leader Kuyper was, some of the details of his life and circumstances have come to light. But more must be said on both counts if we are fully to understand his thought.

The French Revolution represented for Kuyper—and for many others, of course—a watershed in European history.[8] Kuyper's horror at the Revolution constituted an ever-present background to his thought. Though the name of the political party that he founded, the Anti-Revolutionary Party, was no doubt meant to express opposition to revolution in general, for him and his followers the paradigmatic example of the sort of revolution to which they were opposed was the French Revolution.

The French Revolution represented at least four great evils for Kuyper. First and foremost, it represented aggressive atheism. Kuyper believed with all his heart that we must expect something like the French Revolution to happen when political power falls into the hands of militant atheists, hostile to religion, who believe that there is no transcendent source of authority by which our actions are to be measured. Second, it represented rampant individualism. Instead of seeing individuals as inescapably members of social formations that in good measure determine their identity and provide the conditions for their flourishing, the revolutionaries tended to see society as composed of individuals whose equal freedom to act as they see fit is of paramount importance. In this view, social formations are created by compact among sovereign individuals for utilitarian considerations. Third, the French Revolution represented the destruction of civil society; the totalitarian regime of the state replaced society's multiple, dispersed loci of authority and claimed that all authority belongs ultimately to the state. Lastly, it represented for Kuyper the triumph of abstract reason. Rather than honor the organic unfolding of society, the leaders of the French Revolution reasoned their way to what they thought would be a better social order and then set about implementing their plans.

The abstract/organic contrast captures the last of these four aspects of what, in Kuyper's view, went wrong with the French Revolution. In fact, one regularly finds him using the contrast to characterize each of the last three aspects. A descriptive and normative understanding of society as organic in its structure and functioning will recognize that individuals are at least as much shaped by social formations as such formations are formed by them, and that that is how it must be. Such an understanding will recognize that a healthy social order requires a thick and rich civil society whose diverse loci of authority are not derived from the state but instead require the state's protection; and it will be suspicious of all rational centralized planning, especially of centralized planning that does not take due account of the actualities of how a society has developed. The great evil of the French Revolution, apart from its aggressive atheism, was that it thought abstractly rather than organically about society, thus failing to recognize society as the organic entity that it is and refusing to allow it to be the organic entity that it should be.[9]

It has often been charged that Kuyper's own reform program was itself highly rational and ideological. Though adamantly opposed to revolution, nonetheless Kuyper himself, so it is said, rode roughshod over the traditional Dutch way of doing things in favor of a rationally determined better way. It is true that Kuyper did not share the social conservatism characteristic of many Romantics; Kuyper was not a Dutch Edmund Burke. Nonetheless, Kuyper would have insisted that he was not promoting some rational plan for Dutch society. Rather, convinced as he was that the organic development of life in the Netherlands, especially the religious life of the *kleine luyden* of whom he was the leader, was stifled and inhibited by rules and laws laid down without the consent of the people by the elite of state and church, he, Kuyper, was struggling for the elimination of those inhibiting rules and laws. Kuyper had the better of this argument.

Kuyper's liberation movement took several directions. By the beginning of the nineteenth century, the glorious days of the Dutch Republic of the seventeenth century were but a distant memory. Poverty was widespread. And though Napoleon was gone, replaced for the first time in the history of the Lowlands by a king (William I, r. 1813–40), whatever hopes there might have been of restored political glory were dashed by the loss in 1830 of what became Belgium. Religious unrest was widespread. In 1816, William reorganized the governance of the Dutch Reformed Church (Nederlandse Hervormde Kerk) so as to bring church affairs under the direct regulation of the state. This action by itself created unrest. When the state later imposed new liturgical regulations while at the same time doing nothing to halt the spread of theological liberalism in pulpits and theological faculties, the unrest increased until there was a rupture (*Afscheiding*) in 1834, and a separate free church was formed.

Under the leadership of Johan R. Thorbecke, a constitution was put in place in 1848 whereby the government became a constitutional monarchy, sovereignty being divided between the monarch and a newly formed parliament, divided into one chamber representing the provinces and another directly elected by the people. The Constitution evoked protests from some conservatives, but nothing like those that arose when Thorbecke succeeded in severely limiting the scope of the franchise by the device of imposing a tax on voters, and when, in April 1853, he proposed allowing the reintroduction of the Catholic hierarchy into the Netherlands. The Protestant populace exploded in protest against this last move—ineffective protest, as it turned out, since the archbishop did return to Utrecht.

The decade of the 1860s, when Kuyper concluded his university training and entered the pastorate, was, on the account of some historians, "the most decisive of modern Dutch history."[10] In his edition of Kuyper's selected writings, James Bratt observes,

Politically, "the half-way solutions, the policy of adaptation, evasion, and delay practised by the 'higher classes,' the blurring of issues by the moderates, these were no longer acceptable." Internationally, colonial questions regarding the Netherlands Indies spelled trouble at a distance; the unification of Germany and Italy raised threats nearby. Industrialization would finally begin at the end of the decade and with it a rapid process of differentiation that multiplied the number of interest groups and voluntary associations in society. Custom and local hierarchy broke down as the orbit of life and mode of control, inviting new grids to replace them.... In 1867 regulations for church elections were altered so that consistories (congregational boards) would no longer be self-perpetuating but subject to congregational vote. In 1868 the long-standing parliamentary coalition between Liberals and Catholics broke up, the latter's gratitude for 1853 no longer compensating for the former's secular agenda. In 1869 the first Radical-Liberal was elected to the Second Chamber and the Conservative caucus entered its years of dissolution. If things were pliable in church and state, the reduction of statutory and economic restrictions on voluntary associations and the popular press supplied new tools for the right sculptor.[11]

Kuyper correctly discerned that the new church law represented an opportunity to break the control of the ecclesiastical elite. He began his public career with an 1867 pamphlet urging laypeople to use the new law to get
orthodox Calvinists elected to church office. That same year he left Beesd
for a pastorate in Utrecht. Here he spoke and wrote forcefully in favor of
retaining the traditional creeds of the Dutch Reformed Church, thereby
stirring up the opposition of a number of leading theologians and ministers. He also entered the fray concerning the school system by arguing that
state schooling could not possibly be neutral and that, accordingly, Christians should have the freedom to establish confessionally based schools
independent of the state system. He was severely disappointed by the fact
that, though he saw himself as fighting for Calvinist orthodoxy, the conservative clergy in Utrecht refused to support him. Thus when a call came in
1870 to a pastorate in Amsterdam, he accepted.

His farewell sermon in Utrecht was a blast against a pattern of thought
he called "killing conservatism." Authentic Christianity cannot "refrain
from raging against a false conservatism which seeks to dam up the stream
of life, swears by the status quo, and resists the surgery needed to save the
sick."[12] The conservatives want to repristinate, but "*repristination* is an undertaking that is self-condemned."[13] If you wish to honor your forebears, as
you should, "first seek to have for yourself the life your fathers had and then
hold fast what you have. Then articulate that life in your own language as
they did in theirs. Struggle as they did to pump that life into the arteries of
the life of our church and society."[14] "It is our calling to hold fast what we
have in Christ *in our own time*, not in theirs, and so it is from our own time
that we must take the material with which to prepare that form today."[15]

A year after arriving in Amsterdam, Kuyper, in order to advance the
cause that he now saw lying before him, became chief editor of the weekly
religious periodical *De Heraut*. The next year, in 1871, he founded and became chief editor of the daily newspaper *De Standaard*. (*De Heraut* soon
became a weekly supplement of *De Standaard*.) In these papers he published hundreds of articles on a wide variety of religious, social, political,
cultural, and educational issues.

In 1874 he presented himself as a candidate in a by-election for the lower
house of Parliament and was elected by a comfortable majority. As required
by law, he resigned from clerical orders. By no means did he see that resig-
nation as meaning that he was choosing no longer to be a religious leader;
rather, he would now be giving that leadership from a different location.

He used his first full parliamentary address to pick up the school cause
that he had joined in Utrecht. He argued that though it was the responsibility of the federal government to set general standards for lower school

education, that education itself should not be a function of the state but of independent boards and societies, and that all parents should have the right to send their children to schools where the education offered was in accord with their own worldview. The speech stirred up a vigorous defense of the state monopoly in education, to which Kuyper replied with charges of "state absolutism" and "liberalistic despotism." In 1877 he resigned his seat in Parliament to concentrate on his editorship of *De Standaard*, which he had interrupted for about a year on account of a nervous breakdown.

In 1878 the school question broke out once again when the prime minister (from the Liberal caucus) introduced a bill that required a wide range of educational reforms and stipulated that whereas the federal government would pay for the cost of these reforms in the state schools, independent schools would have to pay for the cost on their own. In the interim between the time that Parliament passed the bill and the king (Willem III) was to sign it, Kuyper, along with Catholic leaders, organized a huge petition-signing campaign urging the king to reject the bill; altogether some 469,000 signatures were collected (at a time when only 122,000 people enjoyed the franchise). The petition was presented to the king in August 1878. The king had made it clear that Kuyper would not be welcome in the delegation; two weeks later the king signed the bill.

In January 1879, building on the enthusiasm evoked by the petition-signing campaign, Kuyper and his followers established a national organization to promote the formation and funding of independent Christian schools; and in April of that same year, they established the Anti-Revolutionary Party, which, as mentioned earlier, was the first mass political party in the Netherlands. Previously there had been little more than caucuses and factions.

Action was simultaneously taking place on the front of university education. In 1876 Parliament had passed a bill, at the instigation of a conservative member of Parliament, reaffirming the principle of educational freedom stipulated in the 1848 Constitution and making it somewhat easier for nonstate institutions of higher education to be formed. Kuyper seized the opportunity offered. In 1878 he was instrumental in establishing the Society for Higher Education on the Basis of Reformed Principles. In June 1879 the Society elected directors and a board of trustees; in September they appointed Kuyper and F. L. Rutgers to chairs in theology; and in October 1880 the Free University of Amsterdam officially opened with a ceremony in the venerable New Church in Amsterdam. Kuyper, as the new university's first Rector Magnificus, gave as his inaugural address the now-famous "Sovereignty Within Its Own Sphere" ("Souvereiniteit in Eigen Kring").

Kuyper retained his positions as leader of the Anti-Revolutionary Party and chief editor of *De Standaard* and *De Heraut* while serving as professor of theology. In his position as party leader, he argued vigorously that the ARP should cooperate in Parliament with the Catholic caucus, a position that many of his followers found hard to swallow given their long-standing antipapalism. Nonetheless, Kuyper's position became official ARP policy at its convention in 1887; and in the general election of 1888, the Anti-Revolutionary Party and the Catholics together won a majority of seats in Parliament, enabling them to form a coalition cabinet. A bill on primary education was shortly introduced and passed, making possible for the first time the partial subsidy of nonstate schools, whether religiously oriented or not. (In 1917 full subsidy was finally granted, thereby laying to rest "the school question" that had so long agitated Dutch politics.)

Two other aspects of Kuyper's political thought and action should be mentioned before we conclude this background and biographical sketch. As might be expected, Kuyper was vigorously in favor of extending the franchise beyond those few well-to-do males who, on Thorbeke's proposal, could afford to vote. Kuyper's struggle to break the power of the political and ecclesiastical elites and to liberate and empower the Reformed little people (*kleine luyden*) to live out their Calvinistic worldview in the various spheres (*kringen*) of society naturally required that they be allowed to choose their own political leaders. It was Kuyper's view that the same should be the case for the other members of Dutch society—Catholics, Lutherans, secular socialists, libertarians, whomever. As we shall see in some detail later, it was an important plank in Kuyper's Calvinistic-Christian view of society that Christians are not to have special political privileges; for example, religious qualifications are not to be attached to the franchise.

On the other hand, Kuyper was also opposed to a one person, one vote extension of the franchise; that smacked to him of the individualism born of the Enlightenment and come to maturity in the calamity of the French Revolution. The proper unit of the franchise is not the individual person but the household. If there is a male head of the household, then that person should cast the vote; if the head of the household is a woman—a widow, say—then she would cast the vote. When in 1893 a Liberal member of Parliament introduced a bill proposing universal male suffrage, Kuyper, against strong opposition within his own party, came out in favor of the bill on the ground that it came relatively close to the Anti-Revolutionary ideal of universal household suffrage.

A second aspect of Kuyper's struggle to liberate and empower the little people was his concern over the impoverishment of the working class in the late-nineteenth-century Netherlands. At the First Christian Social Congress in the Netherlands, held in November 1891, Kuyper gave a speech titled "The Social Question and the Christian Religion."[16] Whole paragraphs read as if they had been written by a late-twentieth-century liberation theologian. This, for example: "When rich and poor stand opposed to each other, [Jesus] never takes His place with the wealthier, but always stands with the poorer. He is born in a stable; and while foxes have holes and birds have nests, the Son of Man has nowhere to lay His head.... Both the Christ and also just as much His apostles after Him as the prophets before Him, invariably took sides *against* those who were powerful and living in luxury, and *for* the suffering and oppressed."[17] And this:

> God has not willed that one should drudge hard and yet have *no bread* for himself and for his family. And still less has God willed that any man with hands to work and a will to work should suffer hunger or be reduced to the beggar's staff just *because* there is no work. If we have "food and clothing" then it is true the holy apostle demands that we should be therewith content. But it neither can nor may ever be excused in us that, while our Father in heaven wills with divine kindness that an abundance of food comes forth from the ground, through *our* guilt this rich bounty should be divided so *unequally* that while one is surfeited with bread, another goes with empty stomach to his pallet, and sometimes must even go without a pallet.[18]

Kuyper attributed the social misery that he was witnessing in the Netherlands, of which poverty was but the most tragic manifestation, to a laissez-faire political system arising from the Enlightenment coupled with an economic system motivated by profit-seeking. The result was a class struggle. Kuyper's analysis becomes strikingly similar to Marx's:

> On the side of the *bourgeoisie*, there was experience and insight, ability and association, available money and available influence. On the other side was the rural population and the working class, bereft of all means of help, and forced to accept any condition, no matter how unjust, through the constant necessity for food. Even without prophetic gifts, the result of this struggle could readily be foreseen. It could not end otherwise than in the absorption of all calculable value by the larger and smaller capitalists, leaving for the lower strata of society only as much as appeared strictly necessary to maintain these instruments for nourishing capital—for in this system, that is all the workers are held to be.[19]

Only if we once again see society not as a heap of souls on a piece of ground but as a God-willed community, a living human organism, can there be a cure for the misery of poverty. And that, says Kuyper, is "the socialist path." He adds, "I do not shrink from the word," provided one not identify socialism with the program of the Social Democrats.[20] A program, though, is indeed necessary—a program of social reform. Piety and charity are not sufficient, for it is a *social* question we are dealing with, not a devotional or philanthropic question.

> This one thing is necessary if a social question is to exist for you: that you realize the *untenability* of the present situation, and that you realize this untenability to be one not of incidental causes, but one involving the very *basis* of our social association. For one who does *not* acknowledge this and who thinks that the evil can be exorcised through an increase in piety, through friendlier treatment or kindlier charity, there exists possibly a religious question and possibly a philanthropic question, but not a *social* question. This does not exist for you until you exercise an *architectonic* critique of human society itself and hence desire and think possible a different arrangement of the social structure.[21]

The years from 1880 to 1900 were Kuyper's most productive as a thinker and writer. He delivered four rectoral addresses (1881, 1888, 1892, and 1899) in addition to his initial "Sovereignty Within Its Own Sphere," and composed a three-volume theological treatise with the title, quaint to our present-day ears, *Encyclopedia of Sacred Theology*. He published a large number of pamphlets on a wide variety of topics, most of them the texts of lectures or speeches that he had given or a collection of newspaper articles that he had written on some topic. In 1907 a five-volume treatise on systematic theology appeared, derived from notes made by students of his lectures. He published large, multivolume books on the Holy Spirit, on the Heidelberg Catechism, on the doctrine of common grace, and on the Reformed liturgy, all of these being assembled from his weekly columns in *De Heraut*, as was a multivolume book of meditations. The capstone of his career as social, political, and cultural theorist was the six Stone Lectures that he gave at Princeton Theological Seminary in 1898 under the title *Calvinism*; here he put it all together. It is these lectures on Calvinism that will be most useful to us in our analysis of his views on human nature and the law, along with some passages from his *Encyclopedia of Sacred Theology*[22] and the excellent selection of shorter writings assembled by James Bratt on the centennial of Kuyper's Stone Lectures in *Abraham Kuyper: A Centennial Reader*.

HUMAN NATURE AND THEORETICAL KNOWLEDGE

Dutch society in the latter half of the nineteenth century and the early decades of the twentieth had become religiously pluralistic. Kuyper thought that any attempt to get rid of that pluralism by force would be not only futile but also a violation of the right to liberty of conscience; there could be no going back to the religious unanimity of earlier days. Furthermore, Kuyper believed that the right of his followers for which he was fighting, the right to exercise their religious worldview in church, society, and polity, was the right of all other Dutch citizens as well. Accordingly, as with John Locke in the late seventeenth century and John Rawls in the late twentieth, one of the fundamental questions around which Kuyper's thought about law and the state revolved was this: how can people of diverse worldviews, religious and otherwise, live together in peace and justice within the same polity?

Unlike Locke and Rawls, Kuyper's answer to this question did not involve trying to find some body of principles that as a totality is ample for settling at least the basic political issues that confront us, and that individually are such that we can fairly ask everybody to appeal to them when debating and deciding basic political issues. Kuyper broke at this point with classic liberal theory. Let it be said that the sort of society Kuyper was arguing and struggling for was a liberal democratic society. He was in favor of all the basic rights definitive of such a society—freedom of speech, freedom of assembly, the right to choose one's representatives, and so forth. Indeed, when it came to such issues as the scope of the franchise, Kuyper was more democratic in his thinking than were most of his opponents. His disagreement was not with liberal democratic society but with classic liberal theory.

I remarked that, as with Locke and Rawls, Kuyper's thought about law and the state was in good measure shaped by the question of how people of diverse worldviews can live together in peace and justice within the same polity. What is distinctive of Kuyper is that this particular angle of approach to law and the state was set within the context of reflections on social practices and institutions generally; and that always the same question guided his reflections. No matter what shared social institution or practice he was discussing—the state, the university, schooling in general, whatever—each time we find him asking how, given our religious diversity, we can work together in peace and justice within those common practices and institutions. We would miss the full import of Kuyper's reflections on law and the state if we did not set them within this larger context. That then will be our project for the next several sections.

It was in good measure Kuyper's anthropology that led him to take a different tack from Locke and Rawls; and what was especially decisive here was his view concerning the workings of human thought and the nature of religion. Kuyper's most careful reflections on these matters are to be found in his discussions of how a person's practice of theoretical learning is shaped by his or her worldview.[23] So, let us look at what he has to say on that matter, keeping in mind that his views were the same concerning the bearing of a person's worldview on his or her social or political thought. The essential point is that a person's religious or nonreligious worldview is not something added on to other convictions; a person's worldview pervades and comprehends his or her thought in general.

Theoretical learning, Kuyper insisted, is not something done individually by this person here and individually by that person there; it is a shared social practice into which individuals are inducted and within which they participate. "The subject of science cannot be this man or that," he says.[24] If you insist on specifying a subject for it, it is best to say that its subject is "man*kind* at large, or, if you please, *the* human consciousness."[25]

The goal of this social practice is, of course, to engage reality in such a way that the theoretical disciplines, the *wetenschapen*, are built up. The main point Kuyper wanted to make about this engagement was that a particular person's participation in theoretical learning does not and cannot consist simply of allowing episodes of outer or inner experience to activate one's innate belief-forming faculties of perception and introspection. It is true, of course, that at the bottom of the whole enterprise there has to be the activation of these faculties; reality has to act on us. But that, Kuyper insisted, is not sufficient for the construction of theoretical learning.

Kuyper emphasized that in the theoretical disciplines, our goal is not just to collect individual facts but also to arrive at an account of their interconnections. Accordingly, since "science means that our human consciousness shall take up into itself what exists as an organic whole, it goes without saying that she makes no progress whatever by the simple presentation of the elements; and that she can achieve her purpose only when, in addition to a fairly complete presentation of the *elements*, she also comes to a fairly complete study of their *relations*."[26] For the most part, however, these interconnections are not part of what is "given" us. Accordingly, when we move beyond elementary reporting, counting, weighing, measuring, and the like to developing an account of interconnections, we must ourselves make a contribution to the engagement.

Theorizing emerges from engagement with an organically interconnected reality by a complex body of thought developed so as to capture those interconnections. Our faculties of perception and introspection only put us in touch with, as it were, the periphery of that organically interconnected reality. In its totality, theoretical learning is not so much report as construction. At the point where theoretical learning goes beyond the "given" to constructing a comprehensive account of interconnections, it unavoidably incorporates a subjective element: "That a science should be free from the influence of the subjective factor is inconceivable."[27]

This thesis is true, as Kuyper saw it, for the natural sciences; it is even truer for the human sciences, where human consciousness is itself a component of the subject matter. Kuyper concluded a discussion of empiricism in the human sciences with a brief and dismissive comment: "Your own subjective-psychical life is ever shown to be your starting-point [in the human sciences], and empiricism leaves you in the lurch. This is most forcibly illustrated by Philosophy in the narrower sense, which, just because it tries logically to interpret, if not the cosmos itself, at least the image received of it by us, ever bears a strongly subjective character, and with its [leaders], least of all, is able to escape this individual stamp."[28] With the downfall of empiricism over the past thirty or forty years, the perspective that Kuyper expressed has become widely accepted; Kuyper was making the point more than a hundred years ago.

The entrance into the academy in recent years of forthrightly particularized perspectival learning, in the form of feminist perspectives, African American perspectives, and the like, has made Kuyper's next point similarly familiar:

> The subjective character which is inseparable from all spiritual science, in itself would have nothing objectionable in it, if ... the subjectivity of A would merely be a variation of the subjectivity in B. In virtue of the organic affinity between the two, their subjectivity would not be mutually antagonistic, and the sense of one would harmoniously support and confirm the sense of the other. ... But, alas, such is not the case in the domain of science. It is all too often evident, that in this domain the natural harmony of subjective expression is hopelessly broken; and for the feeding of scepticism this want of harmony has no equal. By an investigation of self and of the cosmos you have obtained a well-founded scientific conviction, but when you state it, it meets with no response from those who, in their way, have investigated with equally painstaking efforts; and not only is the unity of science broken, but you are shaken in the assurance of your conviction. For when you spoke your conviction, you did not mean simply to give expression to the insight of your own *ego*, but to the universal human insight; which, indeed, it ought to be, if it were wholly accurate. But of necessity we must accept this hard reality, and in every theory of knowledge which is not to deceive itself, the fact of sin must henceforth claim a more serious consideration.[29]

"The fact of sin." The fact that when we move beyond the elementary recording of data to offer an account of the connections and significance of it all, we regularly get into near-intractable disagreements with each other, is, so Kuyper said, on account of sin. I think he was in error on that point. Better if he had said "fallenness," or, to use his own word, "disturbance." For though some of our near-intractable disagreements are the manifestation or consequence of culpable action or inaction on the part of one or the other of us, not all are, nor did Kuyper think they are. I doubt that all are due even to our fallenness; some are due to our finitude. I readily concede to Kuyper, however, that many of them are due to sin or fallenness.

So fundamental is the phenomenon of disagreement that is resistant to resolution within our social practice of theoretical learning, Kuyper said, that it would not be an exaggeration to say that "the entire interpretation of science, applied to the cosmos as it presents itself to us now, and is studied by the subject 'man' as he now exists, is in an absolute sense governed by the question whether or no[t] a disturbance has been brought about by sin either in the object or in the subject of science."[30] That is to say: in accounting for this phenomenon of near-intractable disagreements within our shared social practice of theoretical learning, can we avoid acknowledging the presence of a "disturbance ... brought about by sin"? Kuyper's answer was that we cannot. To put flesh on the bones of this theological claim, he then embarked on an extensive discussion of the ways in which our fallenness affects our work in the academy;[31] he structured his discussion by developing a typology and then offering examples of the various types. The whole discussion is extraordinarily insightful and suggestive. So as to give the flavor of it, let me cite three of the types, along with a few examples of each.

One source of near-intractable theoretical disagreement "is the influence of the sin-disorganized *relationships of life*—an influence which makes itself especially felt with the pedagogic and the social sciences."[32] For example: "He who has had his bringing-up in the midst of want and neglect will entertain entirely different views of jural relationships and social regulations from him who from his youth has been bathed in prosperity. Thus, also, your view of civil rights would be altogether different, if you had grown up under a despotism, than if you had spent the years of early manhood under the excesses of anarchism."[33]

Another source of near-intractable disagreement is our distorted and parochial "personal interests." For example: "An Englishman will look upon the history of the Dutch naval battles with the British fleet very differently from a Netherlandish historian; not because each purposely desires to falsify the truth, but because both are unconsciously governed by national interests.... A Roman Catholic has an entirely different idea of the history of the Reformation from a Protestant's, not because he purposely violates the truth, but simply because without his knowing it his church interests lead him away from the right path."[34]

And third, our dislikes and hatreds are often at the root of our disagreements, as are our conflicting loves. Where "love, the sympathy of existence," is active,

> you understand much better and more accurately than where this sympathy is wanting. A friend of children understands the child and the child life. A lover of animals understands the life of the animal. In order to study nature in its material operations, you must love her.... Sin is the opposite of love.... Our mind feels itself isolated; the object lies outside of it, and the bond of love is wanting by which to enter into and learn to understand it.... What once existed organically, exists now consequently as foreign to each other, and this *estrangement* from the object of our knowledge is the greatest obstacle in the way to our knowledge of it.[35]

Kuyper clearly found these three types of disturbance in human existence crucially important for understanding our near-intractable disagreements in theoretical learning; however, for him none of them has anywhere near the importance of our diverse worldviews, be they religious or not, in accounting for those disagreements. Of course it was this, all along, that he wanted to get to.

In *Principles of Sacred Theology*, Kuyper's argument took a somewhat unexpected turn at this point, one more explicitly biblical and theological. He did not just argue that many if not most of us operate with what amounts to a worldview, and that there is a distinctly Christian worldview, or perhaps *range* of worldviews. Instead, without actually referring to Augustine, Kuyper rung a change on Augustine's doctrine of the two cities, the city of God and the city of the world, created by two loves, love of God and love of what is other than God. Kuyper appealed to St. Paul's teaching that the Christian is one who has been born again of the Spirit; and then he argued that this second birth inevitably "exercises ... an influence upon his *consciousness*"—that is, upon his or her way of thinking.[36] In agreement with Augustine, Kuyper argued that there is a change in the object of love deeper than this change in thinking: at the spiritual center of the Christian's existence is the sense and reality of living before the face of God in love and adoration. Nonetheless, Kuyper was adamant in his opposition to all purely spiritualistic or moralistic understandings of Christian existence. Speaking of "a religion," but clearly meaning Christianity, and writing in exuberantly Romantic language, he said:

> A religion confined to feeling or will is ... unthinkable to the Calvinist. The sacred anointing of the priest of creation must reach down to his beard and to the hem of his garment. His whole being, including all his abilities and powers, must be pervaded by the *sensus divinitatis*, and how then could he

exclude his rational consciousness,—the *logos* which is in him,—the light of thought which comes from God Himself to irradiate him? To possess his God for the underground world of his feelings, and in the outworks of the exertion of his will, but not in his inner self, in the very centre of his consciousness, and his thought; ... all of this [is] the very denying of the Eternal Logos."[37]

A question that ineluctably comes to mind at this point is whether we must just resign ourselves to the perpetuation in the academy of disagreements rooted in the sort of phenomena to which Kuyper has called attention, and in particular, to those rooted in distinct religious or nonreligious worldviews. The same question, of course, is faced by each of that considerable number of thinkers who nowadays join with Kuyper in defending a particularist perspectival account of theoretical learning. The problem is more acute in Kuyper's case, however, since his defense of particularist perspectivalism seems to have plunged his overall account of learning into internal contradiction.

I began this part of our discussion by citing Kuyper's point that theoretical learning is a shared human social practice. Rather than something that we each do individually, theoretical learning is larger than any of us, something within which we participate; what is required for participation is merely competence, not any particular religion, philosophy, social orientation, or whatever. I then presented Kuyper's claim that the particular mode of engagement with the world that constitutes theoretical learning is necessarily a blend of subjectivity with receptivity—or to use Kantian language, of spontaneity with receptivity. And from there I moved on to present Kuyper's way of accounting for the fact that the contribution of subjectivity, rather than being shared by all alike, is riddled with near-intractable disagreements. But does not this last point conflict with the first? In what way is theoretical learning still a shared human practice if the subjective contribution, rather than being shared, is broken into fragments?

The true genius of Kuyper's position lies in his answer to this question—a question often put to him in his own lifetime. Those who expound and defend a particularist perspectival view of learning today often combine that view, tacitly or explicitly, with a doctrine of incommensurability: learning shaped by one perspective is incommensurable with learning shaped by another. In Kuyper's own day, the "Lockean" picture of the academy, as we may call the opposing viewpoint, was much more common: when engaging in the practice of theoretical learning, we are to put in cold storage all that we have come to believe from our life in the everyday and make use only of our generically human belief-forming faculties. Kuyper steered a path between these two positions. De facto what we find in theoretical learning is a plurality of particularistic perspectives; but we are not to rest content with this fractured actuality. The actuality is a science of this type of person and a science of that type of person; but our goal is a shared science, humanity's science. Bodies of learning shaped by different world-views are not incommensurable on account of being so shaped.

Throughout this section I have spoken not of intractable, but of "near-intractable," disagreements, not of disagreements impossible of resolution but of disagreements "resistant" to resolution. It is true that the ideal will never be reached; we pursue it nonetheless. Not, however, by the Lockean strategy of trying to shed all one's particularities upon entering the academy so as to function as a generic human being; that is impossible. We engage in learning as who we are, with whatever our particularities; and then, as part of that engagement, we engage each other in dialogue, each trying to show the other where he or she has gone wrong and listening to the other as he or she tries to show where we have gone wrong. Engaged pluralism, one might call it.

Kuyper put it this way in one passage: "In the domain of the sciences,... experience shows that, after much resistance and trial, the man of stronger and purer thought prevails at length over the men of weaker and less pure thought, convinces them, and compels them to think as he thinks, or at least to yield to the result of his thinking. Many convictions are now the common property of the universal human consciousness, which once were only entertained by individual thinkers."[38]

A fascinating feature of the passage is the almost inadvertent recognition of the role of power in the academy. But let that pass, so as to take note of the caveat that Kuyper immediately added. Yes, it often happens that the other person convinces me of my error; and sometimes, even though I am not convinced, I am silenced. But while not minimizing the point, we must also not exaggerate it; the ideal of consensus, and certainly the ideal of rationally achieved consensus, remains beyond our grasp. One of the reasons for this elusiveness, apart from those already highlighted, is that all too often what drives the scientist is not just the aim, focused on the objects, of discovering them in their relationships, but the aim, focused on his or her colleagues, of squelching their views and advancing his or her own. Once again we touch on sin and fallenness; had there been no "disturbance," there would have been no such prideful defensiveness. It is because of sin that

> where two scientific men arrive at directly opposite results, each will see the truth in his own result, and falsehood in the result of his opponent, and both will deem it their duty to fight in the defence of what seems to them the truth, and to struggle against what seems to them the lie. If this concerns a mere point of detail, it has no further results; but if this antithesis assumes a more

universal and radical character, school will form itself against school, system against system, world-view against world-view, and two entirely different and mutually exclusive representations of the object, each in organic relation, will come at length to dominate whole series of subjects. From both sides it is said: "Truth is with us, and falsehood with you." And the notion that science can settle this dispute is of course entirely vain, for we speak of two all-embracing representations of the object, both of which have been obtained as the result of very serious scientific study.[39]

The "unity of science is gone. The one [person] cannot be forced [by argument] to accept what the other holds as truth, and what according to his view he has found to be truth."[40] And to suppose that there is some sort of "absolute science" available to us human beings that would settle such issues "is nothing but a criminal self-deception."[41] "There is no ... objective certainty to compel universal homage, which can bring about a unity of settled result."[42] Sometimes dialogue is fundamentally inadequate for achieving agreement; what is needed is conversion of one sort or another.

POLITICS, LAW, AND CHURCH

All these points have their exact parallels in Kuyper's reflections on politics. A corollary of Augustine's distinction between the *civitas dei* and the *civitas terrena* is that just as the institutional church is the polity of the *civitas dei*, so the state is the polity of the *civitas terrena*. The citizens of these two polities are intermingled in this present age, so much so that a member of the *civitas dei* may occupy a position in the state, and a (hypocritical) member of the *civitas terrena* may occupy a position in the institutional church; nonetheless, so Augustine held, each of these two fellowships has its own polity, its own governance.

Earlier, in our discussion of theorizing, I mentioned an important way in which Kuyper was Augustinian in his thinking. Indispensable to understanding his thought about law, however, is the realization that he broke decisively with Augustine in his understanding of the state. When it comes to the church, Kuyper distinguished between the church as organism and the church as institution; the distinction, in all but its fine-mesh details, is the same as Augustine's between the City of God, on the one hand, and its institutional governance, on the other.[43] But for Kuyper, the state is not the governing institution of the *civitas terrena*; the *civitas terrena* has no governing institution peculiar to itself. The state is the governing institution of all of us together, Christian and non-Christian, members of the *civitas dei* and members of the *civitas terrena*. Kuyper's way of thinking of the state is analogous at this point to his way of thinking of the practice of theoretical learning; just as academic learning is a social practice of humankind generally, not just of Christians or non-Christians, so too the state is the governing institution of all the human beings who live in a certain area, Christian and non-Christian alike. Christians are not resident aliens vis-à-vis the government of Holland or the United States; they do not carry green cards. They are citizens; they carry passports. Christians have dual citizenship. They are all, in the modern world, citizens of some state and also citizens of the institutional church. In Kuyper's own words, "It is one and the same *I* who is a citizen of the country and a member of the church."[44]

What, then, is to be the basis of politics in the modern world, given that the citizenry of every state is religiously diverse? More specifically, what is to be the basis of politics in a liberal democracy? On what basis are we, the citizens, to debate political issues and make political decisions? For of course weighing and measuring, counting and polling, are no more adequate for settling political issues than for settling theoretical issues. Our convictions about political issues are shaped by all those same "subjective" factors that Kuyper highlighted when he was talking about theorizing—in particular, by our diverse world-and-life views, be they religious or otherwise.

Kuyper was not presented with John Rawls's proposal, a variant of the classic liberal theorists' attempt to find a neutral basis for politics. Rawls proposed that we obtain a neutral basis—a social foundation acceptable to all the comprehensive perspectives represented in the society—by articulating the core idea of a liberal democratic society into principles of justice.[45] There can be no doubt what Kuyper's response to this proposal would have been. We must expect that our diverse comprehensive perspectives will yield both different views as to the acceptability of this proposal and different articulations of the idea of a liberal democratic society. Neutrality is as much a will-o'-the-wisp in politics as in the academy.

There is a vigorous debate currently taking place on these matters between "inclusionists" and "exclusionists." The inclusionists hold that the ethos of a citizen of a liberal democratic society allows a citizen to use his or her particular comprehensive perspective, religious or otherwise, to debate and decide political issues. The exclusionists disagree. Though citizens may offer and use such reasons if they wish, the decisive considerations must always be drawn from shared "public reason." Religious reasons are never to be anything more than dispensable add-ons. One knows where Kuyper would come down: firmly on the side of the inclusionists. Kuyper's own decisive reasons for the political positions he adopted were usually explicitly biblical and theological; reasons drawn from "public reason" were for him the dispensable add-ons.

No exclusionist proposes making it illegal to give decisive weight to religious reasons in political debate and decision. Persuade people that it is against the ethos of a citizen of a liberal democracy; but do not make it illegal. Accordingly, this aspect of Kuyper's views on how people of diverse worldviews are to live together within a single liberal democratic state, though exceedingly important as part of the whole picture and influential in many quarters, does not speak directly to the issue of legal structure. Quite the contrary for another aspect.

Every religious community has some sort of institutional basis for its religious life. The most obvious of such bases are those institutions whose purpose is (or includes) the conduct of communal worship. Only slightly less obvious are the educational and journalistic institutions that many religious communities establish: Catholic and Muslim day schools, Presbyterian and Jewish weeklies, and so forth. Of course, religious communities differ from each other a great deal with respect to the scope and diversity of such institutional bases. Presbyterians in the United States, unlike Catholics and Lutherans, have seldom established Presbyterian day schools; they have established Presbyterian colleges. Quakers, unlike Catholics, have rarely if ever established Quaker hospitals; they have established Quaker relief organizations. One of the reasons Kuyper stirred up so much enthusiasm among some, and so much hostility among others, was that he not only saw the need for new and strengthened institutional bases for religious communities, but he also set about forming those institutions for his followers: a political party, a university, a denomination, day schools, a labor union, daily newspapers, weekly journals—the list goes on and on. University professors are easily ignored. But a religiously based political party, labor union, broadcasting organization, newspaper, university: these are in your face!

Because the lives of religious communities have these institutional bases, the existence of a diversity of comprehensive perspectives within the citizenry of a single liberal democratic state confronts us with a new issue. We have already considered the question of the basis upon which political issues are to be debated and decided; but the institutional bases of religion confront us with the following issue as well: how is the state to be related to the religiously oriented institutions present within society? In the United States this issue is often discussed under the rubric of church and state. But if one means by "church" the institutional church—what Kuyper called "the church as institute"—then the question is obviously much broader than the question of how the state is to be related to the various ecclesiastical institutions present in society. It includes, for example, what the Dutch called "the school question"—a question which, as we saw earlier, agitated

Dutch politics for a good many decades and in which Kuyper participated passionately.[46]

Beginning during World War II and until recently, the United States Supreme Court has quite consistently interpreted the First Amendment to the Constitution as mandating a no-support/neutrality policy on the part of the federal and state governments. That is to say, the Court has interpreted the First Amendment as mandating that the primary purpose of a piece of legislation shall never be to give financial support to some religiously oriented institution, and conversely, that the institutions the government does operate or support shall be neutral in their orientation vis-à-vis each and all of the religions present in American society. It is clear from Kuyper's answer to "the school question" that his position was not one of no-support/neutrality, but instead that the government should follow what might be called an impartiality policy: In its operation and support of institutions, the government is to treat the religious and irreligious present in society impartially. For example, if the government decides to fund *any* schools, it should impartially fund *all* schools regardless of their orientation, religious or otherwise, provided only that they meet certain formal educational requirements.

Kuyper's argument was twofold. He thought that there could not be such a thing as a religiously neutral program of day school education, for a reason that will now be familiar to the reader: day school education necessarily goes beyond the weighing and measuring, the counting and recording, that we can all pretty much agree on. Like theorizing and politics, day school education is shaped by our diverse "subjectivities," and by our diverse worldviews in particular. Second, given this fact about education, it is a violation of both equity and the right to free exercise of one's religion if the state funds schools of one orientation and not those of another. On this latter point, perhaps it is worth reminding the reader that, in Kuyper's understanding, a religion, whatever else it may be, incorporates a certain *Weltanschauung*. That worldview will come to expression in how the community that embraces the particular religion worships. But the worldview will also come to expression in how it wants its children to be educated, in what it thinks the policy of the state should be on such matters as welfare, abortion, and international law, in what it thinks about art and business, and so forth. The right to free exercise of one's religion is thus far more comprehensive than the right to worship freely.

It need scarcely be said that a legal structure determined by an impartiality policy on the part of the government will be considerably different from a legal structure determined by a no-support/neutrality policy. It is a matter of debate as to which is more equitable; but the legal structure of a society can be of either sort in a liberal democracy. It would be implausible to hold that the Netherlands, on account of having a legal structure shaped in good measure by the impartiality policy, is not a liberal democracy. It would likewise be implausible to hold that the United States, on account of having a legal structure shaped in good measure by the no-support/neutrality policy, is not a liberal democracy.

COMMON GRACE AND HUMAN PROGRESS

Kuyper is particularly famous for his doctrine of common grace. It is common practice among theologians to debate whether the doctrine of creation plays an adequate role in this or that theologian's thought—or whether, perhaps, it plays an inflated role. The doctrine plays an exceedingly important role in Kuyper's thought, though often it functions as ancillary to his doctrine of common grace.

A persistent theme in Kuyper is opposition to all versions of Christianity that give priority to the salvation of individual souls. The error of people who embrace such constructions of Christianity lies, he says, in that they "focus on *their own salvation* instead of on the *glory of God*."[47] What Kuyper had in mind by this reference to the glory of God is eloquently conveyed in a passage from his argument concerning the image of God. Kuyper is here arguing that the image referred to in Genesis must be understood socially rather than individualistically; only humankind as a whole can adequately image God, and then only in the culmination of its historical development. With his rhetorical powers in full flower, Kuyper wrote:

> The social side of man's creation in God's image has nothing to do with salvation nor in any way with each person's state before God. This social element tells us only that in creating human beings in his likeness God deposited an infinite number of nuclei for high human development in our nature and that these nuclei cannot develop except *through the social bond between people*. From this viewpoint the highly ramified development of humanity acquires a significance of its own, an independent goal, a reason for being aside from the issue of salvation. If it has pleased God to mirror the richness of his image in the social multiplicity and fullness of our human race, and if he himself has deposited the nuclei of that development in human nature, *then* the brilliance of his image *has to* appear. Then that richness *may not* remain concealed, those nuclei *may not* dry up and wither, and humanity will *have* to remain on earth for as long as it takes to unfold as fully and richly as necessary those nuclei of human potential. Then will have occurred that full development of humanity in which all the glory of God's image can mirror itself.[48]

Kuyper does not dispute that the "salvation of souls" also bespeaks God's glory; but the truly grand work of God with respect to human beings, that for the sake of which God created humankind and guides its history, is the full development of the potentials "deposited" in our species. "A finished world will glorify God as Builder and supreme Craftsman. What Paradise was in bud will then be in full bloom."[49]

And what of sin? Sin disturbs and disrupts this grand march of humankind toward fulfillment. But God responds to sin with a grace, a favor, a generosity that can be thought of as re-creative. This re-creative grace takes two forms. It takes the form of "a *temporal restraining* grace, which holds back and blocks the effect of sin" so that humankind's full flowering, for which God created us, is not frustrated; and it takes the form of "a *saving grace*, which in the end abolishes sin and completely undoes its consequences."[50] The latter is particular in scope; only some are destined for God's New Creation. This is Kuyper's orthodox Calvinist doctrine of election. The former is universal in scope; that mode of divine generosity whereby God restrains the effects of sin is dispensed to all humankind. This is common grace. "To every rational creature, grace is the air he breathes."[51]

God's common grace is to be seen at work in the inward life of humankind wherever "civic virtue, a sense of domesticity, natural love, the practice of human virtue, the improvement of the public conscience, integrity, mutual loyalty among people, and a feeling for piety leaven life." It is to be seen at work in the outward existence of humankind "when human power over nature increases, when invention upon invention enriches life, when international communication is improved, the arts flourish, the sciences increase our understanding, the conveniences and joys of life multiply, all expressions of life become more vital and radiant, forms become more refined, and the general image of life becomes more winsome."[52]

This doctrine of common grace proved to be, in Kuyper's hand, an extraordinarily rich mine for argumentation. In particular, it provided him with an argument for action by Christians in political, social, and cultural affairs, against all those forms of Christianity that concentrate on the salvation of souls and their own "dear, devout fellowships."[53] Since there is "*grace* operating outside the church," since "there is *grace* even where it does not lead to eternal salvation," we are "duty-bound to honor [this] operation of divine grace in human civic life by which the curse of sin, and sin itself, is restrained even though the link with salvation is lacking."[54] To focus all one's attention on the church is to deny, tacitly or explicitly, the existence of grace outside the church.[55] Kuyper thought that those on the opposite end of the spectrum from the sectarians, those who promote a national church of which all citizens are members, likewise operate with the assumption that "all that lies outside and cannot be absorbed in the church remains bereft of grace and so helplessly in bondage to the curse."[56] Rather than distinguish common from special grace and affirming the existence of both, proponents of a national church absorb the special into the common, blending church into civil society; thereby they deprive the church of any distinct voice within society and culture.

The church, if it remains true to itself, recognizing and living by special grace in distinction from common grace and not becoming merely the place where the nation expresses its religiosity, has something distinct to say—that is, something distinct to say about society and culture. The "lamp of the Christian religion" burns within the walls of the church as institute. But the light of that lamp "shines out through its windows to areas far beyond, illumining all the sectors and associations that appear across the wide range of human life and activity. Justice, law, the home and family, business, vocation, public opinion and literature, art and science, and so much more are all illuminated by that light, and that illumination will be stronger and more penetrating as the lamp of the gospel is allowed to shine more brightly and clearly in the church institute."[57]

The goal of Christian social and cultural action is not to confessionalize society. "What we want," Kuyper insisted, "is a strong confessional church but *not* a confessional civil society *nor* a confessional state," adding that the "secularization of state and society is one of the most basic ideas of Calvinism."[58] "The Christian character of society ... cannot be secured by the baptism of the whole citizenry but is to be found in the influence that the church of Christ exerts upon the whole organization of national life. By its influence on the state and civil society the church of Christ aims only at a *moral triumph,* not at the imposition of confessional bonds nor at the exercise of authoritarian control."[59]

Terms such as "a Christian nation," "a Christian country," "a Christian society," "Christian art," and the like, do not mean that such a nation consists mainly of regenerate Christian persons or that such a society has already been transposed into the kingdom of heaven.... No, it means that in such a country special grace in the church and among believers exerted so strong a formative influence on common grace that common grace thereby attained its highest development. The adjective "Christian" therefore says nothing about the spiritual state of the inhabitants of such a country but only witnesses to the fact that public opinion, the general mind-set, the ruling ideas, the moral norms, the laws and customs there clearly betoken the influence of the Christian faith. Though this is attributable to special grace, it is manifested on the terrain of common grace, i.e., in ordinary civil life. This influence leads to the abolition of slavery in the laws and life of a country, to the improved position of women, to the maintenance of public virtue, respect for the Sabbath, compassion for the poor, consistent regard for the ideal over the material, and—even in manners—the elevation of all that is human from its sunken state to a higher standpoint.[60]

It will now be clearer than it was before why Kuyper was opposed to conservatism. Orthodoxy, yes; conservatism in church and society, no. "The tendency in devout circles to oppose ... progress and perpetual development of human life" is "misguided.... Those who are in Christ must not oppose such development and progress, must not even distance themselves from it. Their calling ... is rather to be in the vanguard.... The ongoing development of humanity is *contained in the plan of God*. It follows that the history of our race resulting from this development is not from Satan nor from man *but from God* and that all those who reject and fail to appreciate this development deny the work of God in history. Scripture speaks of the 'consummation of the ages.' "[61]

SPHERE SOVEREIGNTY AND ORGANIC DEVELOPMENT

The main topic that remains to be considered, so as to have the structure of Kuyper's reflections on law fully before us, is his doctrine of sphere sovereignty. It was for this doctrine, along with that of common grace, that Kuyper became most famous. The doctrine, at its core, is a normative understanding of civil society and its relation to the state. This normative understanding is, once again, a striking departure from classic liberal theory while remaining, nonetheless, a defense of the liberal democratic society.

The doctrine of sphere sovereignty sits at the intersection of a number of different lines of thought in Kuyper. Let us begin by picking up where we have just left off. When regarded in its totality, the story of humankind on earth is not the story of the same old things happening over and over again but the story of progress. And the story of progress is the story of the progressive actualization, by human beings, of "the powers, which, by virtue of the ordinances of creation, are innate in nature itself." Theoretical learning is "the application to the cosmos of the powers of investigation and thought created within us." Art is "the natural productivity of the potencies of our imagination."[62] And so forth. The picture one gets from Kuyper is that of human existence, seen in its totality, filled with teeming life. Over and over he employs his organic metaphor at this point. The "expressions of life" in theoretical learning, art, business, and so forth, "all together ... form the life of creation, in accord with the ordinances of creation, and therefore are *organically* developed."[63] "The development is spontaneous, just as that of the stem and the branches of a plant."[64]

A crucial point about Kuyper's understanding of this organic development is that, as it progresses, distinct social spheres of activity emerge. Kuyper does not give theoretical articulation to this concept of a sphere; he does not, for example, give criteria for the identity and diversity of spheres. For this omission he has been much criticized. One of Kuyper's followers in the twentieth century, the Dutch philosopher Herman Dooyeweerd, tried to repair what he saw as Kuyper's deficiency on this point.[65]

But Kuyper's concept of a sphere was not a technical one; had it been that, he would indeed have owed us a careful explanation. It was a concept borrowed by Kuyper from ordinary language. You and I, more than a century later, still employ the concept. Consider, for example, the following passage in Kuyper: "Just as we speak of a 'moral world,' a 'scientific world,' a 'business world,' the 'world of art,' so we can more properly speak of a 'sphere' of morality, of the family, of social life, each with its own *domain*."[66] You and I still speak familiarly of "the art world," "the business world," "the world of politics"; in so doing, we are employing the same concept of a sphere, a *kring*, that Kuyper employed. Let it be added that this was also the concept employed by Max Weber when he developed his theory of differentiation as the hallmark of a modernized society: a modernized society is one in which human activity is differentiated into distinct social spheres. Weber goes somewhat beyond Kuyper in claiming that what differentiates one sphere from another is that a different ultimate value is pursued: the governing value in the art world is different from the governing value in the business world. But if one reads just a bit between the lines, I think it is clear that Kuyper assumes this without ever quite saying it.[67]

Should Kuyper be faulted for not having developed a theoretical ontological articulation of this ordinary concept of a social sphere? That would have been a worthwhile contribution to theory. But his failure to do so does not represent a fatal gap in his social thought, any more than Weber's failure to do so represents a fatal gap in his thought, or the failure, say, of writers on philosophy of art to do so when speaking of "the art world" represents a fatal gap in their thought.

A second crucial point that Kuyper makes about the organic development of human life on earth is that authority, dominion, sovereignty—he uses the words interchangeably—naturally and spontaneously emerge in the course of this development. This "organic social authority"[68] comes in two significantly different forms. One such form is that of "personal sovereignty," or "the sovereignty of genius." Kuyper's thought is that in any field (sphere, sector, world), certain individuals come to have a dominating formative impact on how that field develops. Take, for example, the "dominion of men like Aristotle and Plato, Lombard and Thomas, Luther and Calvin, Kant and Darwin." The "dominion" of each of these figures extends "over a field of ages. Genius is a *sovereign* power; it forms schools; it lays hold on the spirits of men, with irresistible might; and it exercises an immeasurable influence on the whole condition of human life. This sovereignty of genius is a gift of God."[69]

Though this sovereignty of genius is important for Kuyper, its importance is overshadowed by that of the other kind of sovereignty that spontaneously emerges from the organic development of life. Social institutions and their authority structures emerge—authority in this case being the right to issue directives to others that place those others under the (prima facie) obligation to obey. Life could not flourish, and many if not most modes of life could not even exist, without the emergence of institutional bases for such life along with their authority structures. And when the life of humankind is differentiated into distinct spheres, institutions and authority structures specific to those spheres emerge. Theoretical learning could scarcely exist, and certainly could not flourish, without such institutional bases as universities, colleges, research institutes, and the like, each with its head or governing body.

Kuyper placed governmental authority within this grand picture of directive authority as pervading our human existence. Governmental authority is but one species of a vast genus. We will misunderstand both its nature and its proper scope if we do not place our thinking about it within that context.

What, then, is sphere sovereignty? Two ideas come together here. One is the idea that authority structures always have a limited scope: they have the right to issue directives only to certain people and only on certain matters; God alone has the right to issue directives to all human beings on all matters. Second, and rather obviously, for an authority structure, to be sovereign within its own sphere is to have the right to issue directives on matters that fall within that sphere (sector, world). "The University exercises scientific dominion; the Academy of fine arts is possessed of art-power; the guild exercised a technical dominion; the trades-union rules over labour; and each of these spheres or corporations is conscious of the power of exclusive independent judgment and authoritative action, within its proper sphere of operation."[70]

Of course, the fact that a certain authority structure has the right to issue directives within its sphere does not imply that it has the right to issue directives for the totality of life within that sphere; the president of Yale has no right to issue directives to the students and staff of Harvard University.

Thus Kuyper says that "the social life of cities and villages forms a sphere of existence, which arises from the very necessities of life, and which therefore must be autonomous;"[71] and thus he mentions the "lower magistrates" in France of Calvin's time as an example of a distinct sphere. Obviously, he was here using "sphere" in a somewhat different sense from how he customarily used it.

Now for the crucial questions: What grounds the right of authority structures to issue directives within their spheres? And what determines the rightness or wrongness of their directives—assuming that those directives can be right or wrong?

Start with the former: Kuyper was almost fierce in his insistence that no human being (or institution) just comes with the right to issue authoritative directives to another. All authority to issue directives to one's fellow human beings is grounded, ultimately, in God's authority to issue directives to human beings.[72] What Kuyper says in the context of his discussion of governmental authority is clearly meant to apply to authority in general: "Authority over men cannot arise from men.... When God says to me, 'obey,' then I humbly bow my head, without compromising in the least my personal dignity, as a man. For in like proportion as you degrade yourself, by bowing low to a child of man, whose breath is in his nostrils; so, on the other hand do you raise yourself, if you submit to the authority of the Lord of heaven and earth."[73]

Human authority, in all its forms, is in one way or another to be understood, at bottom, as divinely delegated authority. God, our "supreme Sovereign," "delegates his authority to human beings, so that on earth one never directly encounters God Himself in visible things but always sees his sovereign authority exercised in *human* office."[74] What this implies, naturally, is that the criterion for right and wrong directives is God's will for life in that sphere, at that time and place; right directives are those that conform to God's "ordinances," wrong directives, those that do not conform. All humanity "must exist for [God's] glory and consequently after his ordinances, in order that in their well-being, when they walk after His ordinances, His divine wisdom may shine forth."[75]

The epistemological question now rears its head: how do we know God's ordinances? Which is to say: how do we know what will promote the proper development and authentic flourishing of humankind? Kuyper's answer was always twofold. On one hand, humankind is created with the capacity to discover the answer to this question; and though sin threatened to undo this capacity, the doctrine of common grace implies that it was only impaired, not destroyed. On the other hand, the light of the gospel illuminates what promotes our authentic flourishing; hence the imperative for Christians to be active in social and cultural matters.

To say that the gospel illuminates God's will for our social and cultural development is not to say that authority structures within the various spheres of life are to take instructions from the church. What Kuyper says concerning government applies to all: "The government has to judge and to decide independently. Not as an appendix to the Church, nor as its pupil. The sphere of State stands itself under the majesty of the Lord. In that sphere therefore an independent responsibility is to be maintained. The sphere of the State is not profane. But both Church and State must, each in their own sphere, obey God and serve His honor. And to that end in either sphere *God's Word* must rule, but in the sphere of the State only through the conscience of the persons invested with authority."[76]

THE MECHANICAL SOVEREIGNTY OF THE STATE

The question that remains for our discussion to be complete is how the directive authority of the state is to be related to all the other authority structures present within society. Before we get to that, though, a word must be said about the nature of governmental authority.

Kuyper wanted us to see directive authority as pervading our social existence, and he presented governmental authority as one species of the genus. He nonetheless held that the authority of the state is a very distinct species. To highlight one aspect of what makes it distinct, Kuyper often called its authority mechanical as distinct from organic: "The sovereignty of God, in its descent upon men, separates itself into two spheres. On the one hand the mechanical sphere of *State-authority*, and on the other hand the organic sphere of the authority of the *Social circles*. [In both spheres] the inherent authority is sovereign, that is to say, it has above itself nothing but God."[77]

What does he mean in calling the authority of the state "mechanical"? Well, the actualization of humankind's in-created potentials gives rise not only to institutional bases for theoretical learning, economic activity, and the like, along with their authority structures, but also to states, or more generally, governments. The "impulse to form states arises from man's social nature," says Kuyper, adding that this thought "was expressed already by Aristotle when he called man a ['political animal']."[78] In that respect, the state is as much an organic development as universities, the academy of fine arts, and so forth.

In this fallen world of ours, however, the dominant task of the state has become to restrain sin. As such, the state is a primary instrument of God's common grace.[79] Kuyper speculates that had there been no sin, political life "would have evolved itself, after a patriarchal fashion, from the life of the family."[80] There would have been no magistrates, no police, no army. In fact, however, every state is a "means of compelling order and of guaranteeing a safe course of life." As such, it is "mechanical," "always something unnatural," "something against which the deeper aspirations of our nature rebel."[81] *God has instituted the magistrates, by reason of sin*"; they "rule mechanically, and do not harmonize with our nature."[82]

Not only is the magistrates' relation to human development "mechanical" in this way rather than "organic," but the magistrates are also themselves fallen. They are constantly seeking to expand their authority beyond its proper scope in one direction, and allowing it to be unduly restricted or influenced in another. Hence there is always a duality in the Christian attitude toward the state. On one hand, we "gratefully ... receive, from the hand of God, the institution of the State with its magistrates, as a means of preservation, now indeed indispensable." On the other hand, "we must ever watch against the danger, which lurks, for our personal liberty, in the power of the State."[83]

So much for the nature of state authority and how it differs from other modes of directive authority; now for how state authority ought to be related to those other authority structures. The overarching point is that authority structures ought to have authority only within their own spheres. In particular, the authority structures of civil society and of family life ought not to be divisions of state or church; all attempts at state and church aggrandizement must be vigorously resisted. The authority structures within a given sector of society are directly responsible to God for their exercise of authority, not indirectly responsible through the mediation of state or church—nor indeed, of any other authority structure outside their own sphere. "The family, the business, science, art and so forth are all social spheres, which do not owe their existence to the State, and which do not derive the law of their life from the superiority of the state, but obey a high authority within their own bosom; an authority which rules, by the grace of God, just as the sovereignty of the State does.... These different developments of social life *have nothing above themselves but God*." Kuyper added: "As you feel at once, this is the deeply interesting question of our *civil liberties*."[84] A large component in Kuyper's lifelong opposition to the French Revolution was that he saw in it the attempt by the state to get as much directive authority into its own hands as possible. "The State may never become an octopus, which stifles the whole of life."[85]

This understanding of the role of the state, so far, is negative. What is the positive role of the state? Strictly speaking, there is no sphere within society of which the state is sovereign; in that way, too, it is unlike other authority structures. It is, as it were, "the *sphere of spheres*, which encircles the whole extent of human life."[86] So what then is its role?

"Neither the life of science nor of art, nor of agriculture, nor of industry, nor of commerce, nor of navigation, nor of the family, nor of human relationship may be coerced to suit itself to the grace of government." Government "must occupy its own place, on its own root, among all the other trees of the forest, and thus it has to honour and maintain every form of life, which grows independently, in its own sacred autonomy."[87] What that amounts to, Kuyper suggested, is a "threefold right and duty" on the part of the state: "1. Whenever different spheres clash, to compel mutual regard for the boundary-lines of each; 2. To defend individuals and the weak ones, in those spheres, against the abuse of power of the rest; and 3. To coerce all together to bear *personal* and *financial* burdens for the maintenance of the natural unity of the State."[88]

So far, and no farther. "A people ... which abandons to State Supremacy the right of the family, or a University which abandons to it the rights of science, is just as guilty before God, as a nation which lays its hands upon the rights of the magistrates. And thus the struggle for liberty is not only declared permissible, but is made a duty for each individual in his own sphere."[89] The best protection against state aggrandizement is a vital civil society and a vigorous defense thereof.

Kuyper's words about the importance of a vital civil society for the defense of freedom have proved prescient of developments in the twentieth century. Ultimately "it depends on the life-spheres themselves whether they will flourish in freedom or groan under State coercion. With moral tensile strength they cannot be pushed in, they will not permit themselves to be cramped. But servility, once it's become shackled, has lost even the right to complain."[90]

And, last, what is the overarching goal of the state in its interventions? Justice and the common good: "The highest duty of the government remains therefore unchangeably that of *justice*, and in the second place it has to care for the people as a unit, partly *at home*, in order that its unity may grow ever deeper and may not be disturbed, and partly *abroad*, lest the national existence suffer harm."[91]

The entire picture is compellingly summarized in the following lengthy but vivid passage from that address on sphere sovereignty that Kuyper gave at the founding of the Free University:

The cogwheels of all these spheres engage each other, and precisely through that interaction emerges the rich, multifaceted multiformity of human life. Hence also rises the danger that one sphere in life may encroach on its neighbor like a sticky wheel that shears off one cog after another until the whole operation is disrupted. Hence also the raison d'être for the special sphere of authority that emerged in the State. It must provide for sound mutual interaction among the various spheres, insofar as they are externally manifest, and keep them within just limits. Furthermore, since personal life can be suppressed by the group in which one lives, the state must protect the individual from the tyranny of his own circle. This Sovereign, as Scripture tersely puts it, "gives stability to the land by justice" [Prov. 29:4], for *without* justice it destroys itself and falls. Thus the sovereignty of the State, as the power that protects the individual and defines the mutual relationships among the visible spheres, rises high *above* them by its right to command and compel. But *within* these spheres that does not obtain. There another authority rules, an authority that descends directly from God apart from the State. This authority the State does not *confer* but *acknowledges*. Even in defining laws for the mutual relationships among the spheres, the State may not set its own will as the standard but is *bound* by the choice of a Higher will, as expressed in the nature and purpose of these spheres. The State must see that the wheels operate as intended. Not to suppress life nor to shackle freedom but to make possible the free movement of life in and for every sphere: does not this ideal beckon every nobler head of state?[92]

CONCLUSIONS AND LEGACY

Abraham Kuyper's theological reflections on law, politics, society, and human nature are now before us. What remains is only to highlight a few points in conclusion. Several times I have remarked that while Kuyper defended a liberal democratic polity,[93] he departed in significant ways from classic liberal theory. Two points of difference especially stand out. First, Kuyper defended what I have called an impartiality policy of the state with respect to the religiously (and antireligiously) oriented institutions in society, rather than a no-support/neutrality policy. Second, in his rights-based defense against the aggrandizement of the state, Kuyper combined a defense of the rights of individuals with an even more emphatic and articulate defense of the rights of social institutions. It is evident that these differences will yield a quite different legal structure for liberal democracy from that favored by such classic liberals as John Locke and John Rawls. Some of the differences jump out; others require the sort of detailed analysis and speculation characteristic of legal theorists to be brought to light. And no doubt others will turn up only when jurists are confronted with cases that no one had anticipated.

As to Kuyper's view of the ontology and epistemology of law: right law is law that conforms to God's will for the development of humankind. When such law emerges, that emergence should be seen as "a jewel coming down to us from God himself" rather than the product of "a functionally developing organ of nature."[94] And though our in-created capacity to discern right law has been damaged by sin, by virtue of common grace it has by no means been destroyed. Accordingly, when considering issues of law, all of us together, each from our own worldview, are to reflect on what it is that serves justice and human flourishing; for it is justice and flourishing that God desires for humankind. On the other hand, Holy Scripture provides a special source of light on justice and the common good; it is the calling of those who recognize that light to cast it on the public debate rather than keeping it hidden within the institutional church.

What of Kuyper's legacy? From its small beginnings in 1880, the Free University of Amsterdam has expanded until today it is one of the major comprehensive universities within the Dutch university system. Not only its size but also its religious orientation would make it unrecognizable to Kuyper. Though it announces itself as a Protestant Christian university, and though it (along with the Catholic University of Nijmegen) has the status within Dutch educational law of being a confessional university, what it is to be a Protestant Christian confessional university is for it today a topic of perennial discussion rather than of settled conviction. For decades now it has declined to affirm Kuyper's goal of a university whose education and research are based on Reformed principles. And the legacy of Kuyper's Anti-Revolutionary Party, which no longer exists, has been dispersed into a number of different confessionally oriented parties, the largest of which currently is the Christian Democratic Appeal, a union of Calvinist and Catholic parties. What remains striking to an American is the degree to which there remain Dutch social and political institutions organized along confessional lines, this, in good measure, being Kuyper's legacy. What would strike Kuyper himself is how little distinctive institutional expression there remains of his own beloved version of the Calvinist tradition. My examples of this change-within-continuity have been the university and the party that Kuyper founded; the same point could be made for his institution-founding efforts in lower school education, in journalism, and so forth.

In the first sixty or so years of the twentieth century, a substantial number of Dutch people inspired by Kuyper's vision emigrated to the United States and Canada, where their institution-building impulses have gone mainly, though not exclusively, into the formation of educational institutions, both a system of elementary and secondary schools (Christian Schools International, headquartered in Grand Rapids, Michigan), and a number of institutions of higher education, the oldest and largest of which is Calvin College, also in Grand Rapids. There can be no doubt that Kuyper's religious and intellectual legacy is reflected more faithfully in these American and Canadian educational institutions than it is in the educational institutions that Kuyper founded in the Netherlands.

A sizable number of thinkers, especially in the Netherlands and North America, have employed Kuyper's idea of sphere sovereignty, and his alternative theory of the liberal democratic society that I sketched out above, in writing on political and legal affairs. Of these, the one who articulated Kuyper's political and legal thought most elaborately is Herman Dooyeweerd (1894–1977), longtime professor of jurisprudence at the Free University of Amsterdam. Dooyeweerd developed an ontology of the state, a topic that seems to have been of no interest to Kuyper himself, gave theoretical articulation to Kuyper's concept of a sphere, and discussed in far more detail than Kuyper ever did the proper goals and limits of state activity. Dooyeweerd's major work, already referred to, was *The New Critique of Theoretical Thought*; his major legal work was a multivolume *Encyclopedia of Legal Science*. A good deal of Kuyper's influence on legal and political thought has been transmitted through Dooyeweerd. John Witte Jr., one of the editors of this anthology, is a prominent example of a jurist who uses some of Kuyper's and Dooyeweerd's teachings on law, politics, and society.

It has to be said, however, that though Kuyper's legacy in political and legal thought has been substantial, both in Dooyeweerdian and non-Dooyeweerdian forms, it has not entered the mainstream of discussion in North America. Perhaps that will change as thinkers cast about for alternatives to the increasingly discredited Lockean-Rawlsian account of liberal democracy.

NOTES

1. Kuyper himself tells the story in *Confidentially*, excerpted in *Abraham Kuyper: A Centennial Reader*, ed. James D. Bratt (Grand Rapids, Mich.: Eerdmans, 1998), 46–61. The quotation here is found at page 55. "Of course I did my best," adds Kuyper, "to maintain my ministerial honor but despite myself I felt more inclined to listen than to speak during these encounters." Ibid., 56.

2. More than thirty years later, introducing the third of his Stone Lectures, on Calvinism and politics, Kuyper would say that in the lecture he would be combating "the unhistorical suggestion, that Calvinism represents an exclusively ecclesiastical and dogmatic movement." Abraham Kuyper, *Calvinism: Six Lectures Delivered in the Theological Seminary at Princeton* (New York: Revell, 1899), 98.

3. Kuyper, *Confidentially*, 55.

4. Kuyper writes that in the "malcontents" of Beesd he found, in addition to piety, Bible knowledge, and orthodox Calvinist doctrine, "a well-ordered worldview, be it of the old Reformed type." Ibid.

5. It is striking, for example, how often the word "free" and its linguistic variants occur already in the final sermon of Kuyper's pastorate in Utrecht. See "Conservatism and Orthodoxy: False and True Preservation," in *Abraham Kuyper: A Centennial Reader*, 66–85.

6. While struggling against the power elite of church and state for this multifaceted freedom, Kuyper also never ceased to remind his followers of the comprehensive character of true religion. Here is just one of very many passages: "The Christian spirit is not an oil that floats on the surface of the water but a caustic fluid that has to permeate every drop of your stream of life.... Almost all of us have families; we are all members of a society and the sons and daughters of a nation. Those connections too are indispensable and must be bound to the reality of the eternal to keep that eternal life. Christ does not tolerate our living a double life: our lives must be one, controlled by one principle, wherever it may express itself. Life forms in all its rich ramifications one high and holy temple in which the fragrance of the eternal must rise" Kuyper, "Conservatism and Orthodoxy," 82–83.

7. "A confessing Christian who lives amid this world cannot be satisfied with a profession of faith but, like anyone, needs a firm understanding of the world in which he lives. Without the guidance of Christian scholarship, he cannot help but absorb the conclusions of unbelievers. Doing so, he will live with a world-and-life view that does not fit but comes into conflict with his confession on any number of points. His thinking will divide into two." Abraham Kuyper, *Common Grace in Scholarship and Art*, in *Abraham Kuyper: A Centennial Reader*, 474.

8. Kuyper calls 1789 "the birth year of modern life" in *Uniformity: The Curse of Modern Life*, in *Abraham Kuyper: A Centennial Reader*, 24.

9. The *locus classicus* for Kuyper's celebration of organic life as opposed to the rationally planned is his *Uniformity: The Curse of Modern Life*. It is, in fact, the most witty and eloquent attack on the pressures toward uniformity of the modern world that I know of. Here is a sample: Everything must "become uniform, level, flat, homogeneous, monotonous. No longer should each baby drink warm milk from the breast of its own mother; we should have some tepid mixture prepared for all babies collectively." Ibid, 32.

10. E. H. Kossman, *The Low Countries, 1780–1940* (Oxford: Clarendon Press, 1978), 283.

11. James D. Bratt, "Abraham Kuyper: His Work and Work," in *Abraham Kuyper: A Centennial Reader*, 9–10.

12. Kuyper, "Conservatism and Orthodoxy," 71.

13. Ibid., 73. In this chapter, all emphases within quotes are from the original.

14. Ibid., 74.

15. Ibid., 82.

16. Two years earlier, Kuyper published a series of articles on the issue in *De Standaard*; these were collected in a pamphlet called *Manual Labor*. See *Abraham Kuyper: A Centennial Reader*, 231–254.

17. Abraham Kuyper, *Christianity and the Class Struggle*, trans. Dirk Jellema (Grand Rapids, Mich.: Piet Hein Press, 1950), 27–28, 50.

18. Ibid., 48–49.

19. Ibid., 35–36.

20. Ibid., 40.

21. Ibid.

22. Abraham Kuyper, *Encyclopedia of Sacred Theology: Its Principles*, trans. J. Hendrick De Vries (New York: Charles Scribner's Sons, 1898).

23. "Theoretical learning" is the translation that I prefer for the Dutch *wetenschap*, cognate with the German *Wissenschaft*. Both the Dutch and German words are often translated as "science"; they are so translated in passages that I will be quoting. But our English word "science" has come to have a considerably narrower scope of application than the Dutch and German words. Philosophy is one of the *wetenschapen*, one of the *Wissenschaften*. Nobody would think to call it a *science*!

24. Kuyper, *Principles of Sacred Theology*, 63. *Principles of Sacred Theology* is made of up translated selections from Kuyper's three-volume *Encyclopedia of Theology*.

25. Ibid.

26. Ibid., 75.

27. Ibid., 169. Elsewhere Kuyper writes, "I readily grant that if our *natural sciences* strictly limited themselves to weighing and measuring, the wedge of principle would not be at the door. But who would do that? What natural scientist operates without a hypothesis? Does not everyone who practices science as a *man* and not as a *measuring stick* view things through a subjective lens and always fill in the unseen part of the circle according to subjective opinion?" *Abraham Kuyper: A Centennial Reader*, 487–488.

28. Kuyper, *Principles of Sacred Theology*, 103–104.

29. Ibid., 106–107.

30. Ibid., 92.

31. Ibid., 106–114.

32. Ibid., 109.

33. Ibid.

34. Ibid., 110.

35. Ibid., 111.

36. Ibid., 152. Here is the central passage: the Christian religion "speaks of a regeneration (*palingenesis*), of a 'being begotten anew' (*anagenesis*), followed by an enlightening (*photismos*), which changes man in his very being; and that indeed by a change or transformation which is effected by a supernatural cause.... This 'regeneration' breaks humanity in two, and repeals the unity of the human consciousness. If this fact of 'being begotten anew,' coming in from without, establishes a radical change in *the being* of man, be it only potentially, and if this change exercises at the same time an influence upon his *consciousness*, then as far as it has or has not undergone this transformation, there is an abyss in the universal human consciousness across which no bridge can be laid." Ibid.

37. Kuyper, *Calvinism*, 62.

38. Kuyper, *Principles of Sacred Theology*, 151.

39. Ibid., 117–118.

40. Ibid., 119.

41. Ibid., 118.

42. Ibid., 116.

43. For Kuyper's elaboration of the distinction, see *Abraham Kuyper: A Centennial Reader*, 187–188.

44. Ibid., 185.

45. See John Rawls, *Political Liberalism* (New York: Columbia University Press, 1993).

46. It is worth noting that "the school question" is also now agitating American politics and litigation and has done so for a long time, though never with the intensity of its agitation of Dutch politics late in the nineteenth century and early in the twentieth.

47. Ibid., 169.

48. Ibid., 178.

49. Ibid., 181.

50. Ibid., 168.

51. Ibid., 167

52. Ibid., 181. Common grace "opens a history, unlocks an enormous space of time, triggers a vast and long-lasting stream of events, in a word, precipitates a series of successive centuries. If that series of centuries is not directed toward an endless, unvarying repetition of the same things, then over the course of those centuries there has to be constant change, modification, transformation in human life. Though it pass through periods of deepening darkness, this change has to ignite ever more light, consistently enrich human life, and so bear the character of perpetual development from less to more, a progressively fuller unfolding of life." Ibid., 174.

53. The quoted phrase can be found at ibid., 192. Speaking to the sectarian Christian who denies common grace, Kuyper says, "You run the danger of isolating Christ for your soul and you view life in and for the world as something that exists *alongside* your Christian religion, not controlled by it. Then the word 'Christian' seems appropriate to you only when it concerns certain matters of faith or things directly connected with the faith—your church, your school, missions and the like—but all the remaining spheres of life fall for you *outside the Christ*. In the world you conduct yourselves as others do; that is less holy, almost unholy, territory that must somehow take care of itself.... [You] concentrated all sanctity in the human soul and dug a deep chasm between this inward-looking spirituality and life all around. Then scholarship becomes unholy; the development of art, trade, and business becomes unholy, unholy also the functions of government; in short, all that is not directly spiritual and aimed at the soul. This way of thinking results in your living in two distinct circles of thought: in the very circumscribed circle of your soul's salvation on the one hand, and in the spacious, life-encompassing sphere of the world on the other. Your Christ is at home in the former but not in the latter." Ibid., 172.

54. Ibid., 193.

55. The "doctrine of common grace proceeds directly from the Sovereignty of the Lord which is ever the root conviction of all Reformed thinking. If God is sovereign, then his Lordship *must* remain over *all* life and cannot be closed up within church walls or Christian circles. The extra-Christian world has not been given over to Satan or to fallen humanity or to chance. God's Sovereignty is great and all-ruling also in unbaptized realms, and therefore neither Christ's work in the world nor that of God's child can be pulled back out of life. If his God works in the world, then there he must put his hand to the plow so that there too the Name of the Lord is glorified." Abraham Kuyper, "Voorwoord," in *De Gemeene Gratie*, 3 vols. (Amsterdam: Höveker & Wormser, 1902–4), quoted in *Abraham Kuyper: A Centennial Reader*, 166.

56. Kuyper, *Common Grace*, 192.

57. Ibid., 194.

58. Ibid., 197.

59. Ibid.

60. Ibid., 198–199.

61. Ibid., 175.

62. Kuyper, *Calvinism*, 118.

63. Ibid.

64. Ibid., 117.

65. Dooyeweerd's major work is *A New Critique of Theoretical Thought*, 4 vols., trans. D. H. Freeman and W. S. Young (Philadelphia: Presbyterian and Reformed Publishing Co., 1953–58).

66. Kuyper, "Sphere Sovereignty," 467.

67. A good access to Weber's thought on these matters is the collection of his writings translated and edited by H. H. Gerth and C. Wright Mills, *From Max Weber: Essays in Sociology* (New York: Oxford University Press, 1977).

68. Kuyper, *Calvinism*, 121.

69. Ibid., 122.

70. Ibid., 123.

71. Ibid.

72. Thus Kuyper opposes both the theory of popular sovereignty and the theory of state-sovereignty, which holds that states possess sovereignty inherently. See ibid., 108–113.

73. Ibid., 104. "No one on earth can claim authority over his fellow-men, unless it be laid upon him '*by the grace of God*'; and therefore, the ultimate duty of obedience, is imposed upon us not by man, but by God Himself." Ibid., 106. "God only—and never any creature—is possessed of sovereign rights, in the destiny of nations, because God alone created them, maintains them by His Almighty power, and rules them, by His ordinances.... Man never possesses power over his fellow-man, in any other way than by an authority which descends upon him from the majesty of God." Ibid., 108.

74. Kuyper, "Sphere Sovereignty," 466.

75. Kuyper, *Calvinism*, 103.

76. Ibid., 134–135. "Every magistrate is in duty bound to investigate the rights of God, both in the natural life and in His Word. Not to subject himself to the decision of any church, but in order that he himself may catch the light which he needs for the knowledge of the Divine will." Ibid., 133–134.

77. Ibid., 121.

78. Ibid., 100.

79. "The magistrate is an instrument of 'common grace', to thwart all license and outrage and to shield the good against the evil.... He is instituted by God as *His Servant*, in order that he may preserve the glorious work of God, in the creation of humanity, from total destruction." Ibid., 104–105.

80. Ibid., 101.

81. Ibid.

82. Ibid., 102. "It is ... of the highest importance sharply to keep in mind the difference in grade between the *organic* life of society and the *mechanical* character of the government. Whatever among men originates directly from creation, is possessed of all the data for its development, in human nature as such.... The development is spontaneous, just as that of the stem and the branches of a plant." Ibid., 116–117. The state, as we know it in this fallen world, is for the most part not "a natural head, which organically grew from the body of the people, but a *mechanical* head, which from without has been placed upon the trunk of the nation. A mere remedy therefore, for a wrong condition supervening. A stick placed beside the plant to hold it up, since without it, by reason of its inherent weakness, it would fall to the ground." Ibid., 119.

83. Ibid., 102–103.

84. Ibid., 116.

85. Ibid., 124.

86. Kuyper, "Sphere Sovereignty," 472.

87. Kuyper, *Calvinism*, 124.

88. Ibid., 124–125.

89. Ibid., 127.

90. Kuyper, "Sphere Sovereignty," 473.

91. Kuyper, *Calvinism*, 120.

92. Kuyper, "Sphere Sovereignty," 467–468.

93. My attention here has focused entirely on the *liberal* aspect of the polity that Kuyper defends, not the *democratic*; but in fact a good deal, for example, of the Stone Lectures devoted to Calvinism and politics is a defense of democracy. See Kuyper, *Calvinism*, chap. 3.

94. Kuyper, "Sphere Sovereignty," 487.

[CHAPTER 11]

Susan B. Anthony (1820–1906)

MARY D. PELLAUER

A century after her death, Susan B. Anthony is the most familiar name of the American women's suffrage movement. Beyond her name, however, we are less well aware of what she believed and did. Anthony's religious position, which had few parallels in her time and has few even in ours, is especially unfamiliar. Yet Anthony's themes resonate, especially with those who have learned from liberation theology.

Unlike other figures analyzed in this volume, Anthony was not a professional theologian; indeed, theological education opened up for women only during the decades of her struggle. An activist's religious perspective is perhaps inevitably different from that of seminary professors, church people, or clergy. But it may be no less instructive; indeed, it may be more so. Religious disputes were routine in the suffragist movement. St. Paul's exhortations to women to "be silent in the churches" (1 Cor. 14:34–35), for instance, had to be countered, whether by suffragists or by women in the antislavery movement. Since earlier women, such as Lucretia Mott and the Grimke sisters, had pioneered in answering such claims, Anthony took it for granted that she could be a public activist against slavery and for women's rights.

A BIOGRAPHICAL SKETCH

Susan B. Anthony was born in 1820 and brought up by an unconventional Quaker family in upstate New York.[1] Her parents belonged to the abolition and suffrage causes before she did. They attended the first women's rights convention and signed its Declaration of Sentiments. The Anthony family encouraged, supported, and often financed their daughter Susan's work throughout her life. For fifteen years, Anthony earned her living as a schoolteacher, leaving that career only for full-time devotion to struggling for justice, initially in the temperance movement and then for antislavery and women's rights.

At a temperance convention in 1853, Anthony met Elizabeth Cady Stanton, the daughter of a judge, who had been heartbroken in her youth when told that girls could not become lawyers. She was steeped in the American democratic tradition and adept at explicating legal precedents. Her husband, Henry Stanton, was a lawyer active in a less radical wing of the antislavery struggle than the one that held Anthony's allegiance. Stanton and Anthony became lifelong friends and collaborators, often working together to write speeches that one of them would deliver. Both agreed that they complemented each other's strengths.

The two women wrote and campaigned together often, especially after Stanton's children were older. They collaborated, developed tactics and strategy, comforted, and provoked each other. After Stanton's death, decades after the two women began working together, Anthony was asked what period of their lives she had enjoyed the most. She replied:

> The days when the struggle was the hardest and the fight the thickest; when the whole world was against us and we had to stand the closer to each other; when I would go to her home and help with the children and the housekeeping through the day and then we would sit up far into the night preparing our ammunition and getting ready to move on the enemy. The years since the rewards began to come have brought no enjoyment like that.[2]

In 1854, Anthony began her career as a full-time activist by systematizing a New York organization to work for women's property and custody rights. During the late 1850s, she was the general agent for the New York State Anti-Slavery Society, and, along with many speakers whose campaigns she scheduled and assisted, met her trials by mob. To Anthony, the parallels between the struggles against slavery and for women's rights were vivid. In these antislavery days she absorbed principles such as "no union with slave-holders," "no compromise," "of two evils, choose neither," "do right and leave the consequences to God," and "resistance to tyranny is obedience to God." Grassroots defiance of the Fugitive Slave Law was especially important and formative for her. In later years, she often prefaced a comment with, "I was on the old Garrison platform."[3]

After the Civil War ended in 1865, the women's rights movement split, painfully, into two wings. One group argued that "this is the Negro's hour," and therefore advocated that women should lay aside their claims so as not to detract from measures for the newly emancipated. This group became the nucleus of the Boston wing, the American Woman Suffrage Association (AWSA). A second group argued variously that all the disfranchised should stand together, or sometimes, more disastrously, that the most educated should be enfranchised first. This group became the National Woman Suffrage Association (NWSA), and it was led by Stanton and Anthony. It was more fiery and confrontational than AWSA, and focused on national rather than on state-by-state action. NWSA's conventions often featured resolutions against patriarchal religion, many of them from Stanton's pen. These resolutions claimed, for instance, that women's suffering stems from religion, whether Christianity or any other. At AWSA meetings, in contrast, with many clergy in attendance, the members voted that Christianity had done more for women's status than any other single force. The split in the woman suffrage moment was not healed until 1890, when the NWSA and the AWSA became the NAWSA, an event largely attributable to Anthony's work with younger women in the Boston group.

In the late 1860s, Anthony published the stormy paper *The Revolution*, with its slogan, "men, their rights and nothing more; women, their rights and nothing less." Stanton and Parker Pillsbury, a controversial "come-outer" from the antislavery ranks, wrote most of the copy for the paper. *The Revolution* did not hesitate to take sides on Victorian scandals, thus causing outrage among its readers and others. The paper's eventual failure committed Anthony to six years' work to repay its $10,000 debt.

In addition to her publishing work, Anthony attempted to create a working-women's association, a move that sparked friction with male unionists. She also took to the lecture circuit and tramped the country from end to end as she agitated for women's rights from a variety of angles. She spoke, for instance, on "the true woman," "homes of single women," "bread and the ballot," and "social purity." Her diary for 1871 sums up the year's efforts: "6 months of constant travel, full 8,000 miles, 108 lectures. The year's full work 13,000 miles travel, 170 meetings."[4]

The next year, 1872, was another turning point for women's rights activists. Several people had argued that the Reconstruction amendments to the Constitution, passed in the aftermath of the Civil War, already enfranchised women. Women turned out around the country to test this proposition by casting their ballots, and Anthony was one of the voters. She was the only one indicted and brought to trial for it, however, placing her in a long line of American activists who hoped the judicial system would solve the issues of their particular movements. Anthony's impassioned extempore response to this behavior is a fine example of the kind of political rhetoric that was dear to her heart.

For the next thirty years, Anthony dedicated herself to convincing the Congress to pass a constitutional amendment enfranchising women.

The amendment became so identified with her that through its successive numerical designations (from XVI to XX), it was called "the Anthony Amendment."

In her sixties, Anthony—still very active in political work—turned her attention also to chronicling the movement of which she was a part. In the 1880s, Stanton and Anthony realized that no one else would write the history that they and their friends had made. The two women passed hundreds of hours with old letters and documents from women's rights conventions all over the country and by 1886 produced three large volumes (nine hundred or so pages each) of *The History of Woman Suffrage*. Anthony hated this time of enforced inactivity. "I love to make history but hate to write it," she commented in a letter to a friend.[5]

During the 1890s, while Anthony remained a prime mover in the NAWSA, Stanton was often in Europe or moving residence from the home of one child to that of another. Stanton had grown increasingly convinced that religion was at the heart of women's degradation. Gathering a group of like-minded women (several of them theologically trained), she set about writing vehement commentaries on the biblical texts related to women. The *Woman's Bible* was published in time for the NAWSA convention of 1896 to vote to dissociate itself from the project. The vote was a stinging rebuke to Stanton, a pioneer of the movement. Anthony publicly defended Stanton's freedom to express her religious beliefs as part of the suffragist platform, but she privately expressed her disagreements with Stanton's religious views. As Stanton put it, "like husband and wife, each has the feeling that we must have no differences in public."[6]

Anthony spent fifty-odd years of her life agitating for reform, enticing others to join her, and doing the tedious "common work" of reform movements. She engaged speakers, laid out their itineraries in statewide or national campaigns, and arranged publicity for them while herself giving innumerable lectures, frequently to hostile crowds. She recruited a whole generation of younger women to join the struggle. She was interminably busy at fundraising. She went door-to-door with petitions. She arranged and gave testimony to congressional committees, both state and national. She buttonholed congressmen and more than one American president. And she demanded a suffrage plank on the platforms of political parties of all sorts. Ever unmarried despite a series of reported proposals, she was castigated, mocked, stereotyped, and lied about by the press. Everywhere, Anthony was the object of personal comments that Stanton's maternal status and respectable appearance did not provoke.

A contemporary gives a rare glimpse of the two women during the Kansas campaign of 1867:

Of course it is nothing new to say that Mrs. Stanton was the object of honor and admiration everywhere. Miss Anthony looked after her interests and comfort in the most cheerful and kindly manner, occasionally complaining good naturedly of Mrs. Stanton's carelessness in leaving various articles of her wearing apparel scattered over the State, and of the trouble she had in recovering a gold watch which Mrs. Stanton had left hanging on the bed post in a little hotel in Southern Kansas. I remember one evening of the Convention in Lawrence when the hall was crowded with an eager and expectant audience. Miss Anthony was there early, looking after everything, seats, lights, ushers, doorkeepers, etc. Presently, Gov. Robinson came to her and said, "Where's Mrs. Stanton? It's time to commence." "She's at Mrs. ——'s waiting for some of you men to go for her with a carriage," was the reply. The hint was quickly acted upon and Mrs. Stanton, fresh, smiling and unfatigued, was presented to the audience.[7]

As the two women grew older, these patterns did not change much. An annual convention drew near, and Stanton claimed she was not going, that it was too much. A week before it opened, Anthony arrived at Stanton's home, started her writing the major address, packed her bags, and detrained with Stanton in tow and complaining all the while. Perhaps Stanton truly was growing weary. While she had grown used to accolades, her religious critiques brought her waves of outraged virulent criticism. Many AWSA members hated her and agreed to make her president of the new NAWSA only on the condition that she take a ship for Europe right after the first meeting. Anthony's star, on the other hand, shone ever more brightly as she aged, becoming "Aunt Susan" to hundreds of suffragists. In 1892 she was voted president for life of the NAWSA, venerated by all and sundry, until, at her death, she was hailed as a veritable incarnation of the Great Mother.

Anthony did not believe she was a good public speaker. "I know nothing and have known nothing of oratory or rhetoric,"[8] she said. She called Stanton her "sentencemaker" and "penartist."[9] Stanton recalled their collaboration as follows: "In writing we did better work together than either could alone. While she is slow and analytical in composition, I am rapid and synthetic. I am the better writer, she the better critic. She supplied the facts and statistics, I the philosophy and rhetoric, and together we have made arguments that have stood unshaken by the storms of thirty long years: arguments that no man has answered. Our speeches may be considered the united product of our two brains."[10]

This statement is probably true for most of the speeches the two women gave, especially about enfranchisement. Where religion was involved, however, Stanton overstates the case. Of Presbyterian origin,

Stanton went through a Finneyite revival at school and was traumatized by depictions of original sin and hellfire. Her religious journey was to be tempestuous on the road to the *Woman's Bible*, one of the few projects not shared by her beloved Susan. Anthony, on the other hand, had been raised a Quaker. While she had quarrels with some of the Friends' doctrines, controversies around biblical issues left her unperturbed. To Anthony, "all those theological questions had been discussed and settled by the Quakers long ago."[11]

In larger terms, Stanton advocated "a more rational religion," one that emphasized women's right to think (the same right that Luther, Calvin, and John Knox had had), the sacredness of democratic principles (only sometimes conceded by her to be Christian principles, too),[12] and especially the "great immutable laws" that rule life both morally and physically.[13] She gave her allegiance to the God of Justice, Mercy, and Truth. Anthony, too, may have believed some or all of this; she did mention the great immutable laws on more than one occasion.

Both Anthony and Stanton rejected original sin and the need for a uniquely redeeming savior figure. Both believed that human nature is basically good and that real strides of progress can be made. Both certainly believed that democratic principles are sacred. But Anthony's emphases, as we shall see, were biblical and prophetic in character. According to Anthony, believers are especially commanded "to break every yoke and let the oppressed go free" (Isa. 58:6 RSV), "to love your neighbor as yourself" (Matt. 22:39 RSV), and to feed the hungry and clothe the naked in the awareness that as one performs these deeds for the least among us, one does them for Jesus himself (Matt. 25:31–46). Though Anthony called God "Father" or "All-Father," which strikes today's feminist ears badly, her God was a God who loved freedom and helped to bring it about.

WOMEN'S SERVITUDE: SEX-SLAVERY

Women's subjection to men was, for Anthony, the greatest injustice that women suffered. Sometimes she called this powerlessness, sometimes dependency, especially since married women did not control their earnings or property in this era. Her most pungent expression, however, was that the subjection of women was "sex-slavery." She drew explicit parallels between women's subject and black slavery in the South. Since the Fifteenth Amendment outlawed disenfranchisement for "previous conditions of servitude," she enumerated the ways in which women's condition constituted a comparable servitude suffered by American slaves that needed to be outlawed.

Married women, Anthony argued, were in a condition of servitude because they did not have rights to custody and control of their persons or earnings or the right to sue. But more, "by all the great fundamental principles of our free government," *all* women were in servitude:

> Women are taxed without representation, governed without their consent, tried, convicted, and punished without a jury of their peers. And is all this tyranny any less humiliating and degrading to women under our democratic-republican government today than it was to men under their aristocratic, monarchical government one hundred years ago?[14]

She quoted Benjamin Franklin: "They who have no voice or vote in the electing of representatives do not enjoy liberty, but are absolutely enslaved to those who have votes and their representatives." And she quoted Tom Paine: To take away the right to vote "is to reduce a man to a state of slavery."

Anthony construed justice for women accordingly. If the injustice against women is servitude, then its remedy must be freedom. Women must be free to cast their own ballots. But more than that, they must be free to act for themselves, in their own cause, the cause of women's rights. "She who would be free, herself must strike the blow," Anthony insisted.[15] Too many women, however, lived a "hot-house existence," far from the struggles of the world and of politics, protected from reality. Working women needed the ballot to protect themselves against employers and so to raise their earning power. Less tangibly but no less important, women did not respect themselves or believe in themselves enough; they lacked allegiance to themselves first. The consciences of women were asleep. Just as antislavery workers had used fiery language to wake the conscience of the nation, so "agitation" was needed to wake up the women.

The Fugitive Slave Law, and its enforcement by the Supreme Court in the infamous Dred Scott case, had awakened abolitionists against the laws of slavery in the 1850s. A comparable awakening was needed to combat the laws of women's servitude. Anthony drew the parallel explicitly in this 1870 letter to a group in England:

> All are lulled into the strictest propriety of expression, according to the gospel of St. Republican [the Republican Party]. And unless that saint shall enact some new and more blasphemous law against woman, which shall wake our confiding sisterhood into a sense of their befoolment, you will neither see nor hear a word from suffrage society or paper which will be in the slightest out of line with the plan and policy of the dominant party. Nothing less atrocious to woman than was the Fugitive Slave Law to the Negro, can possibly sting the women of this country into a knowledge of their real subserviency, and out

of their sickening sycophancy to the republican politicians associated with them.

So while I do not pray for anybody or any party to commit outrages, still I do pray, and that earnestly and constantly, for some terrific shock to startle the women of this nation into a self-respect that will compel them to see the abject degradation of their present position; which will force them to break their yoke of bondage, and give them faith in themselves; which will make them proclaim their allegiance to woman first; which will enable them to see that man can no more feel, speak or act for woman than could the old slave-holder for his slave. The fact is, women are in chains and their servitude is all the more debasing because they do not realize it. O, to compel them to see and feel, and to give them the courage and conscience to speak and act for their own freedom, though they face the scorn and contempt of all the world for doing it.[16]

Much later, at the turn of the twentieth century, Anthony sometimes still said that "agitation is the word."[17] When the country was considering adding new territories without including women among the voters, she was furious with the younger generation's refusal to protest: "I really believe I shall explode if some of you young women don't wake up and raise your voice in protest.... I wonder if when I am under the sod—or cremated and floating in the air—I shall have to stir you and others up. How can you not be all on fire?"[18]

Drawing on Jesus' adage, "By their fruits, you will know them" (Matt. 7:16), Anthony's brand of practical religion put reformist action over the content of any particular doctrine or belief. Merely believing that the Bible was inspired by God meant nothing if people did not act upon their beliefs. Indeed, mere beliefs were only so much ineffective "creed and dogma" to Anthony. They were the nonessentials —what she sometimes called the "mint, anise and cumin" instead of "the weightier matters of the law, justice and mercy and faith" (Matt. 23:23). Indeed, her low opinion of "creed and dogma" or odd religious views was thoroughly connected to her this-worldly commitments.

> The truth is, I can no more see through Theosophy than I can through Christian Science, Spiritualism, Calvinism, or any other of the theories, so I shall have to go on knocking away to remove the obstructions in the road of us mortals while in these bodies and on this planet; and leave Madam Besant and you all who have entered into the higher sphere, to revel in things unknown to me.... I will join you at Mrs. Miller's Saturday, and we'll chat over men, women and conditions—not theories, theosophies and theologies, they are all Greek to me.[19]

It is easy to see how such a position might be understood to be irreligious or secular. But to Anthony it was not. She copied a quote into the back of a diary: "Many are called impious, not for having a worse, but a *different* religion from their neighbors, and many atheistical, not for denying God but for thinking somewhat peculiarly of him."[20] Writing to another spiritualist, declining an invitation to visit, she said she would have enjoyed the chance "to chat over the world of work for our good cause. Of the before and after I know absolutely nothing, and have very little desire and less time to question or study. I know this seems very material to you, and *yet to me it is wholly spiritual*, for it is giving time and study rather to making things better in the between which is really all that we can influence; but perhaps when I can no longer enter into active practical work, I may lapse into speculations."[21]

In the earliest years of her activist career, she often spoke of "right action" in New Testament terms. "The plain practical principles of Jesus" included "love thy neighbor as thyself" (Matt. 22:39), the condemnation of mere lip service (Mark 7:6), and the denunciations of hypocrisy evident in the "Woe" speeches of Jesus (Matt. 23:13–36). For Anthony, the work of righteousness was "feeding the hungry, clothing the naked, visiting the sick and in prison (Matt. 25:31–46), undoing the bonds of the slave and letting the oppressed go free (Isa. 58:6)." From the abolitionists, too, she learned the moral worth of sympathy for the suffering, as many of them quoted the New Testament: "Remember those in bonds as though bound with them" (Heb. 13:3).[22] In later years she spoke more of "the energetic doing of noble deeds," but the point was always the same: "Idle wishes, vain repinings, loud-sounding declamations never can bring freedom to any human soul."[23]

Nor was mere prayer any more effective. In one of her earliest temperance speeches, Anthony said: "If we would have God answer our prayers, they must be accompanied by corresponding action."[24] When good church people told her that they were praying for the cause, she asked them pithily to pray "by action"[25] or to "pray with your ballots."[26] As she often put it, "I pray every single second of my life; not on my knees, but with my work. My prayer is to lift woman to equality with man. Work and worship are one with me. I can not imagine a God of the universe made happy by my getting down on my knees and calling him 'great.' "[27]

She had learned this lesson from the antislavery movement. She told, with relish, a story from Frederick Douglass. When he was a slave, Douglass said, he had often prayed for freedom, but God answered only when he prayed with his heels—that is, when he ran away.

IGNORING ALL LAW

Frederick Douglass's escape from slavery was not an unusual example to Anthony, for the antislavery struggle was her highest ethical model. "I can but acknowledge to myself that Antislavery has made me richer and braver in spirit and that it is the school of schools for the true and full development of the nobler elements of life."[28] By 1857 Anthony had enough experience and confidence to begin making her antislavery speeches only from notes, rather than reading a full text. This excerpt is typical of the antislavery material in some of the primary texts:

> Everybody is anti-slavery, ministers and brethren. There are sympathy, talk, prayers and resolutions in ecclesiastical and political assemblies. Emerson says, "Good thoughts are no better than good dreams, unless they be executed"; so anti-slavery prayers, resolutions and speeches avail nothing without action. . . . Our mission is to deepen sympathy and convert it into right action; to show that the men and women of the North are slave-holders, those of the South slave-owners. The guilt rests on the North equally with the South, therefore our work is to rouse the sleeping consciences of the North. . . . We preach revolution; the politicians reform. We say, disobey every unjust law; the politician says obey them, and meanwhile labor constitutionally for repeal. [29]

Action over mere words, agitation to rouse the conscience, and the rule of ethics over the law: these were central themes in the course of Anthony's public career and central to her religious views.

In late 1860 came an unexpected test. Anthony was approached by a woman fleeing her prominent husband with her daughter. After hearing the tale, she agreed to help, and shepherded them to New York City the next day, searching for some friend to shelter them. During the following spring, while on the lecture platform, Anthony was harassed by the husband's agents, who threatened her with arrest for abducting his child. (Custody of the children, as well as all the earnings and property of the wife, was vested in the husband at this time.) Letters and telegrams from her allies poured in, warning of the terrible consequences sure to befall the movements she loved if she did not relent. Anthony was most pained by the remonstrances of Wendell Phillips and William Lloyd Garrison: "Only to think that in this great trial I should be hounded by the two men whom I adore and reverence above all others." She wrote to Garrison:

> I can not give you a satisfactory statement on paper, but I feel the strongest assurance that all I have done is wholly right. Had I turned my back upon her

I should have scorned myself. In all those hours of aid and sympathy for that outraged woman, I remembered only that I was a human being. That I should stop to ask myself if my act would injure the reputation of any movement never crossed my mind, nor will I now allow such a fear to stifle my sympathies or tempt me to expose her to the cruel, inhuman treatment of her own household. Trust me that as I ignore all law to help the slave, so will I ignore it all to protect an enslaved woman.[30]

Later that spring, Anthony and Garrison were together at a convention in Albany. Garrison argued that Anthony was entirely in the wrong, for she was breaking the law. Anthony defended herself, pointing by analogy to the need to break the Fugitive Slave Law:

He said, "Don't you know the law of Massachusetts gives the father the entire guardianship and control of the children?" "Yes, I know it," she replied, "and does not the law of the United States give the slaveholder the ownership of the slave? And don't you break it every time you help a slave to Canada?" "Yes, I do." "Well, the law which gives the father the sole ownership of the children is just as wicked and I'll break it just as quickly. You would die before you would deliver a slave to his master, and I will die before I will give up that child to its father."[31]

Anthony did find some support among her family and friends. Her friend Lydia Mott had been present when the fugitive wife appealed to Anthony. And her father had supported her: "Legally, you are wrong, but morally you are right, and I will stand by you," he said.[32] Being morally right was always most important to Anthony, the standard by which all else was judged.

Judging what was morally right was, for Anthony, the work of conscience. If conscience discerned a difference between "man-made laws" and the "higher law," there was no question but that one was justified in breaking the "man-made laws," come what will. In quite typical Quaker fashion, Anthony believed that God was to be found "now as of old in the 'still, small voice'" of conscience. This was the only access to "truth, that will never err, however hard its promptings may be sometimes."[33] These references to conscience almost always included this latter point, that conscience might lead one against the opinions of many. So Anthony exhorted the Women's Loyal League in 1863:

And now, women of the North, I ask you to rise up with earnest, honest purpose, and go forward in the way of right, fearlessly, as an independent human being, responsible to God alone for the discharge of every duty, for the faithful use of every gift the good Father has given you. Forget conventionalisms;

forget what the world will say, whether you are in your place or out of your place; think *your* best thoughts, speak your best words, do your best works, looking to your own conscience for approval.[34]

She counseled another suffragist that her power lay in speaking "the absolute truth, not in echoing the popular cry of the multitude. And so long as you look within for guidance in the spirit and letter of your utterances, you are safe. To speak as will please the people is always failure."[35]

Courage was necessary to bear the scorn that most likely would come from following one's conscience against the will of others. "Do right and trust the consequences to God" was an abolitionist slogan. It helped Anthony through many dark days when her agitation brought criticism.

> Cautious, careful people, always casting about to preserve their reputation and social standing, never can bring about a reform. Those who are really in earnest must be willing to be anything or nothing in the world's estimation, and publicly and privately, in season and out, avow their sympathy with despised and persecuted ideas and their advocates, and bear the consequences.[36]

Anthony had grown used to being mobbed in the late 1850s. In the tempestuous winter of 1861–62 she and a party of antislavery speakers were "mobbed and broken up in every city from Buffalo to Albany."[37] Later in the 1860s she would receive hisses from audiences when she mentioned women in sex scandals of the period. Newspapers did not hesitate to caricature her. Her policy was simply to persevere, ignoring such criticism.

Anthony not only ignored criticism, but she also ignored the law when it ran afoul of conscience. When "man-made laws" violate God's laws and perpetrate injustice, Anthony insisted, they must be disobeyed. Anthony's fullest indictment of unjust laws came during her trial in 1872 for illegally casting a vote. Convinced by a group of suffragists to try to change the male-only voting laws by judicial review, Anthony and a group of friends and family members (and several dozen women elsewhere around the country) had gone to the polls in November. "Well, I have been & gone & done it!! Positively voted the Republican ticket—straight—this a.m. at 7 o'clock & swore my vote in at that."[38] She was arrested and indicted. After her indictment, she stumped the local county to convince potential jurors of a woman's right to vote. When the venue of the trial was moved, she blanketed that county for a month as well.

The trial itself was a sham. Though her counsel ably rehearsed the arguments at great length, after closing arguments, the judge directed the verdict. He pulled from his pocket the written text of his conclusion, and directed the jury to find Anthony guilty and then simply dismissed them.

Before pronouncing his sentence, the judge asked Anthony if she had anything to say for herself. Extemporaneously, she denounced the whole trial. When the judge protested that she had been tried according to established forms of law, she shot back:

> Yes, your honor, but by forms of law all made by men, interpreted by men, administered by men, in favor of men, and against women; and hence, your honor's directed verdict of guilty, against a United States citizen for the exercise of "that citizen's right to vote," simply because that citizen was a woman and not a man. But, yesterday, the same man-made forms of law declared it a crime punishable with $1,000 fine and six months' imprisonment, for you, or me, or any of us, to give a cup of cold water, a crust of bread, or a night's shelter to a panting fugitive as he was tracking his way to Canada. And every man or woman in whose veins course a drop of human sympathy violated that wicked law, reckless of consequences, and was justified in so doing. As then the slaves who got their freedom must take it over, or under, or through the unjust forms of law, precisely so now must women, to get their right to a voice in this government, take it; and I have taken mine, and mean to take it at every possible opportunity.[39]

Indeed, she said, she had been trying to educate women to do what she had done, "rebel against your man-made, unjust, unconstitutional forms of law, that tax, fine, imprison and hang women, while they deny them the right of representation in the Government."[40] She promised to continue to urge women to the "practical recognition" of the revolutionary maxim: "Resistance to tyranny is obedience to God."

The judge levied a fine as well as a prison sentence. She refused to pay the fine; the judge refused to imprison her until she did, thereby closing off an avenue for publicity and protest by her allies as well as foreclosing an appeal to a higher court. The cases against the other women were dropped; eventually, the officials who had been convicted of receiving their illegal ballots were given a presidential pardon.

If defying the law did not work, Anthony concluded, changing the law might be better. If women could not "take" their rights to vote under the Reconstruction amendments, there was only one way left to get women the right to vote—by another constitutional amendment. Amending the Constitution had helped former slaves; it could help women as well.

THE ANTHONY AMENDMENT

Working to change the law was not new to Anthony. Stanton and Anthony had campaigned in New York State for the Married Women's Property Act and for more liberal divorce laws. They had stumped Kansas in 1868 when its proposed state constitution sought to enfranchise both women and black men. They lost, the first of many state-by-state campaigns they were to lose over the coming decades.

What was new in this effort of legal reform was Anthony's single-minded focus on crafting and ratifying a constitutional amendment that guaranteed women the right to vote. It was "Anthony's first major departure from her twenty-five-year-long organizing strategy," says one of her biographers.[41] Typical was her 1875 comment to one of the women penning anticlerical resolutions to the NWSA, Matilda Joslyn Gage:

> I want it to be on the one & *sole point of women disfranchised*—separate & alone—and not mixed up with—or one of 19 *other points of protest*—each all of the 19 good & proper perchance.... However good and needed, we must keep our claim first and most important overshadowing every other. Mrs. Stanton answered me that she agrees with me—just women & her disfranchised—leaving the other 19 demands of the *Old Liberty* to wait our emancipation.[42]

When Stanton grew increasingly convinced that religion was at the root of women's subjection, Anthony refused to let her muddy the issues during a California campaign: "I shall no more thrust into the discussions the question of the Bible than the manufacture of wine. What I want is for the men to vote 'yes' on the suffrage amendment, and I don't ask whether they make wine on the ranches of California or Christ made it at the wedding feast."[43]

As this comment implied, though herself an old temperance fan and a firm supporter of the Women's Christian Temperance Union, Anthony tried to keep the WCTU away from suffragist campaigns, knowing full well that suffragists needed the votes of many men who were not "dry." She used her considerable influence to keep NAWSA regulars from endorsing any particular political party—a policy that continued into the League of Women Voters (NAWSA's heir) after 1920.

Today historians tend to regard this focus on the constitutional amendment as "narrowing the suffrage platform,"[44] but Anthony believed that the "one and sole point" of women disfranchised was not a small matter. The ballot was the "open sesame to equal rights."[45] It would place women and men on an equal footing in all dimensions of life. Indeed, for Anthony, it was virtually the cause of all causes: "The cause of nine-tenths of all the misfortunes which come to women, and to men also, lies in the subjection of women, and therefore the important thing is to lay the axe at the root."[46] Anthony put this point in a variety of pithy ways: "Men who fail to be just to their own mothers cannot be expected to be just to each other.[47] "It is idle for us to expect that the men who rob women (of their rights) will not rob each other as individuals, corporations and Governments."[48]

The more traditional work of women in charitable and benevolent institutions, which Anthony sometimes called mere "man-appointed missions," was bound to be ineffective. For this was work "without knowledge."

> It is aimed at the effects, not the cause; it is plucking the spoiled fruit; it is lopping off the poisonous branches of the deadly upas tree, which but makes the root more vigorous in sending out new shoots in every direction.... The tap-root of our social upas lies deep down at the very foundation of society. It is woman's dependence. It is woman's subjection. Hence the first and only efficient work must be to emancipate woman from her enslavement.[49]

"Any and every reform work is sure to lead women to the ballot-box," Anthony believed. Without the vote, nothing women could do would be effective. "Suffrage was the key to unlock every door."[50] "It has always been clear to me that woman suffrage is the one great principle underlying all reforms. With the ballot in her hand woman becomes a vital force—declaring her will for herself, instead of praying and beseeching men to declare it for her."[51]

Anthony again adverted to the metaphor of the Fugitive Slave Law, this time not to press people to defy the unjust man-made laws, but to illustrate going to the root of the evils around them:

> Ordinary benevolence will ever minister to individual suffering—even the Hard-Shell Democratic Fugitive Slave Law man in the olden time would hide the fleeing bondman from the chase of his master, and give him $10 to pass him on to Canada. But ... this Woman Suffrage movement goes to the root of the evil—demands the ballot—the right, the power, in woman's hands to help herself.[52]

These instrumentalist arguments, however, usually paled for Anthony beside the one most fundamental claim for women's right to vote: that it was just. "To prevail with the rank and file of voters, you must appeal to their sense of justice," she insisted.[53]

After Stanton's death in 1902, Anthony was asked to reflect on the changes they had seen and accomplished. After sketching a history of the suffrage cause up to the present, she noted that women's "enlarged opportunities in every direction" have almost regenerated the roles of women.

> The capability they have shown in the realm of higher education, their achievements in the business world, their capacity for organization, their executive power, have been a revelation.... In no department of the world's activities are the higher qualities so painfully lacking as in politics.... Does not logic also justify the opinion that, as they have been admitted into every other channel, the political gateways must inevitably be opened?[54]

Despite the five decades of struggle she had been through, she was still hopeful:

> The common remark that "all has been gained for women except the suffrage" is by no means true. In not one of the several departments above named do women possess perfect equality of rights, but in each so much has been granted as to make it logically sure that the rest will eventually follow.... The future contains more than hope—it shines in the clear light of certainty.[55]

Perhaps these many changes in American society, which she had witnessed, are why these last years brought something of a qualification to her claims about justice—not that suffrage for women would not be just, but that it was only a small bit of justice: "Such a little simple thing we have been asking for a quarter of a century. For over forty years, longer than the children of Israel wandered through the wilderness, we have been begging and praying and pleading for this act of justice."[56]

According to Anna Howard Shaw, one of her closest intimates, Anthony had a similar perception in the last few days of her life: "She never complained, but once when the consciousness of approaching death seemed strongly to impress itself upon her, she said, holding up her hand and measuring a little space on one finger, 'Just think of it, I have been striving for over sixty years for a little bit of justice no bigger than that, and yet I must die without obtaining it. Oh, it seems so cruel.'"[57]

These comments perhaps resonate more deeply with us a century later than Anthony's notion that lack of women's suffrage lay at the root of all social ills. Today, we know only too well that enfranchisement has not solved all the problems of women's emancipation. The sense that the vote is a piece of justice, yes, but only the size of the tip of one's finger, speaks to us more than it could have to Anthony. We now see that the right to vote was a necessary but not a sufficient condition for justice for women. It remains unclear whether Anthony believed it to be both necessary *and* sufficient.

Unlike Anthony, Stanton maintained to the end of her career that the subjection of women called for a complete overhaul of four different elements of society—the family, society (including education), the state, and the church. As women's rights advocates, prompted by Anthony, focused more strenuously upon the vote, Stanton became more firmly convinced that religion was the most powerful strand of women's debasement, and more vehement in her condemnations.

Unlike Stanton, Anthony had among her protégées ordained women like Anna Howard Shaw. Anthony knew that more clergymen were endorsing the cause, and put the case to Stanton:

I cannot help but feel that in this you are talking down to the most ignorant masses, whereas your rule always has been to speak to the highest, knowing there would be a few who would comprehend and would in turn give of their best to those on the next lower round of the ladder. The cultivated men and women of today are above the need of your book. Even the liberalized orthodox ministers are coming to our aid and their conventions are passing resolutions in favor of woman's equality, and I feel that these men and women who are just born into the kingdom of liberty can better reach the minds of their followers than can any of us out-and-out radicals. But while I do not consider it my duty to tear to tatters the lingering skeletons of the old superstitions and bigotries, yet I rejoice to see them crumbling on every side.[58]

Anthony chided her old friend Stanton for "singling out the church and declaring it to be especially slow in accepting the doctrine of equality to women. I tried to make her see that it had advanced as rapidly as the other departments but I did not succeed, and it is right that she should express her own ideas, not mine."[59]

Stanton wrote many of her critiques of male-dominated religion for the *Index*, the magazine of the Free Religious Association, a left-wing group of Unitarians, whose circulation was tiny. After she and Anthony had finished their history of the women's suffrage movement, Stanton was determined to have a go at the Bible and to publish her conclusions as a book to reach a wider audience. Stanton tried to get Anthony to be part of the project; Anthony refused, arguing that this would confuse her "one and sole" point with another: "No—I don't want my name on that Bible Committee—You fight that battle—and leave me to fight the secular—the political fellows.... I simply don't want the enemy to be diverted from my practical ballot fight—to that of scoring me for belief one way or the other about the Bible."[60]

Anthony disagreed with her old friend, however, not only for political reasons, but because in principle she thought Stanton's antireligious approach to be wrongheaded:

You say, "women must be emancipated from their superstitions before enfranchisement will be of any benefit," and I say just the reverse, that women must be enfranchised before they can be emancipated from their superstitions. Women would be no more superstitious today than men, if they had been men's political and business equals and gone outside the four walls of home and the other four of the church and come in contact with and discussed men and measures on the plane of this mundane sphere, instead of living in the air with Jesus and the angels. So you will have to keep pegging away, saying "Get rid of religious bigotry and then get political rights"; while I shall keep pegging away, saying, "Get political rights first and religious bigotry will melt like dew before the morning sun"; and each will continue still to believe in and defend the other.[61]

Volume 1 of Stanton's *Woman's Bible* was published in 1896, just before that year's convention of the NAWSA. A resolution on the subject came before that body: "This association is non-sectarian, being composed of persons of all shades of religious opinion, and has no official connection with the so-called 'Woman's Bible' or any theological publication."[62]

Anthony left the chair in order to speak against this resolution at some length. Her arguments were deeply influenced by William Lloyd Garrison's policies of free speech and agitation in the antislavery struggle. She opened by claiming that "the one distinct feature of our association has been the right of individual opinion for every member."[63] There had often been contention "on account of religious theories," but they had not made resolutions about them. "To pass this one is to set back the hands on the dial of reform... . What you should say to outsiders is that a Christian has neither more nor less rights in our association than an atheist. When our platform becomes too narrow for people of all creeds and no creeds, I myself cannot stand upon it."[64]

The policy of agitation of the old antislavery radicals was "that as public opinion was educated, they must take even more advanced positions," as one historian put it.[65] So Anthony reminded them of old examples: When Stanton had first demanded the right to vote, at Seneca Falls in 1848, some had thought she had damaged the cause. When, in 1860, Stanton made a case for divorce on the grounds of drunkenness, other friends believed she had killed the cause. Who could tell if these Bible commentaries might not prove a great help to women's emancipation in the future? It would be "narrow and illiberal" of the delegates to vote for this resolution. And the movement needed to "inspire in women a broad and catholic spirit," since suffragists were claiming that women would be a power for better government. Indeed, "ten women educated into the practice of liberal principles would be a stronger force than 10,000 organized on a platform of intolerance and bigotry."[66]

But the woman suffrage movement was no longer radical. It was respectable. The motion passed 53–41.

ANTHONY'S RELIGIOUS ACTIVISM

On public platforms, Anthony's policy of free speech meant that she was careful to be noncommittal about religious opinions stated by others. One time, however, she was drawn away from this discrete stance to offer a sort of "amen" to a speaker. The 1888 International Council of Women included a session on religion. After lengthy and very diverse speeches, a woman named Ednah Cheney said, "This has seemed to me to be a most religious meeting all through the week.... It has been a holy week to those who are not wont to think that religion depends on times and seasons, but on consecration to right purposes and great philanthropic and human enterprises."[67]

As chair, Anthony could only hint at her agreement. (Perhaps she also wanted to say "amen" because Cheney called them away from "the subtleties of metaphysics and theology" and back "into works.") She reminded the audience of Lucretia Mott's slogan, "Truth for Authority, not Authority for Truth," and drew their attention to a poem in a pamphlet on sale near the door:

> Thou, from on high, perceivest it were better
> All men and women should be on earth be free;
> Laws that enslave and tyrannies that enfetter
> Snap and evanish at the touch of thee.[68]

To Anthony, it was liberation from the slavery of the laws and any other kinds of bondage that was the heart of her religious view. That had been occurring, as Cheney said, "all through the week."

Away from the public platform, however, Anthony sometimes stated the focus of her faith more fully though simply. Our duty, she said, is to "make things better in the between," to put things right, or to do what we can here, because that is all we can really influence. For Anthony, the task was to follow the "plain practical principles of Jesus," the Golden Rule to "do unto others, as you would have done unto you" (Matt. 7:12). Sometimes it might be even more simply, "to help" in the way that people helped fugitive slaves to achieve their freedom. It was the consistent practice of one's beliefs, and not merely their repetition in words, that proved one's faith. Anthony did not write a treatise about any of this. She lived it.

The simple clarity of her thought was echoed in her language. If you disagreed with her, you knew it at once. There was no jargon, no highly technical language, no obfuscation, no circumlocution. She and Stanton both abhorred the circumlocution encouraged in ladies. You knew were you stood with Anthony; there were no hidden agendas.

Sympathy for others was what Anthony aimed for in her audiences—pity, sometimes, or indignation even, but perhaps more classically the "feeling-together-with" of the word's roots. "Empathy" is perhaps a more precise term: Imagine that you are a slave, or one of your loved ones. Put yourself in the other's shoes. "Make the slave's case our own," was the title of one of Anthony's antislavery speeches. "Remember those in bonds as though bound with them" (Heb. 13:3) was an old antislavery Bible verse that taught this same lesson. As Anthony said: "We are knit together for weal or woe." Her point, however, was not merely to feel with those who were oppressed; it was to deepen the sympathy, yes, and then "convert it to action," as she said in her first temperance speech.

Anthony's earliest speech in support of women's suffrage claimed that a religion that ruled one's life every day except Election Day "was not worthy of possession." It was clear to her that faith was to move into the ballot box. Her later slogans, "prayer by action" or "pray with your ballots," were developments in this line. Her analysis of the social injustices she faced led her toward the causes, not merely the symptoms, of the problems she saw in the lives of women. Simply to put bandages over the wounds was "inefficient," indeed "unphilosophical." Enfranchising women aimed to change the system, to be a radical work. Anthony did not have adequate theological or sociological language to conceptualize this, in comparison to the extended languages we now have at our disposal. But her religious activism was no less effective, or cogent.

Anthony liked to quote Isaiah 58:6: "to break the yoke and let the oppressed go free."[69] For her this was a call to religious activism. Once, when she was in the company of a famous spiritualist, she "could not conceal her disapproval" of the woman's otherworldliness. Anthony asked her, "Why don't you make that aura of yours do its gallivanting in this world, looking up the needs of the oppressed, and investigating the causes of present wrongs? Then you could reveal to us workers just what we should do to put things right, and we could be about it."[70]

Anthony's version of religious activism was a liberation theology without Marxism, born out of America's struggles against slavery and for women's rights. It was extremely difficult for her contemporaries, and even for many of her successors, to recognize this dimension of her religious life.[71] I believe this misunderstanding came because there was no religious tradition there to receive her insights. Her tradition flowered only in the last half of the twentieth century, when the civil rights struggle and the women's liberation movement gave birth to black theology and feminist theology. Black theologians have remained oriented toward tangible changes in the social order. Some feminist theologians have aimed at subtler changes, like images of God or versions of sin that do not betray androcentric bias; others have chosen political engagement. I cannot imagine that Anthony would care much for the word "praxis" so typical today in liberation theology, since she was too plainspoken for what can become a technical locution. But the notion of "praxis" is consistent with her emphasis on practical righteousness. I believe she would have rejoiced to hear that "resistance is the holy ground wherein divine presence is known and experienced."[72] She would have appreciated the insights of the German theologian Dorothee Soelle that "God has no other hands than ours,"[73] or "God's action without us is a misunderstanding."[74]

Since so few people know of Anthony's activist faith, it is hard to trace its influence on anyone in particular. Her impulses to disobedience for the sake of conscience have entered the broad stream of anti-authoritarianism in left-wing and liberal religion. (When she met Queen Victoria, Anthony shook her hand instead of curtseying, which stunned her compatriots as much as it did the English.) It is important to recognize how strange and unique this aspect of the American religious heritage may appear to others. When Soelle arrived at Union Theological Seminary in the 1970s to teach, she was startled:

> I did not know that there were people who burned their draft cards with napalm and blocked trains that would transport weapons to Vietnam. To hear this, to meet people who almost casually tell me that they spent time in jail because of some religious and political activities made me more aware of the alternative (to obedience) than before. It made me fall in love with this non-obedient tradition in the United States. It gave me hope, it renewed my trust in the better parts of the religious tradition.[75]

That Anthony's name might be unknown in this tradition would not have bothered her, I think. On birthdays in her later years, she always seemed surprised that people were gathering to honor her. She tried to send the honors back, rehearsing the history of the suffragist movement whenever she could, starting a session of the annual conventions with the "pioneers" recounting what they did. Just as Garrison had said, "where there is a sin, there must be a sinner," she was always naming the names of those who had helped the movement. Her biographer became annoyed at this:

> And then the contest over the *names* that should be mentioned. In vain the writer begged, expostulated and protested that the book would be swamped with them. "It is all the return I can offer for the friendship, the hospitality, the loyalty of those who have made it possible for me to do my work all these years," was the unvarying reply, and not one could be smuggled out from under that watchful eye.[76]

In Anthony's view, it was the followers, as much as the leaders, who made the women's rights movement possible. "The life-long privates in the war for equal rights" were the ones who "enable us at the front to stand strong and steady."[77]

NOTES

1. See generally Ida Husted Harper, *The Life and Work of Susan B. Anthony*, 3 vols. (Indianapolis: Hollenbeck Press, 1898–1908), and further sources listed in Mary D. Pellauer, *Toward a Tradition of Feminist Theology: The Religious Social Thought of Elizabeth Cady Stanton, Susan B. Anthony, and Anna Howard Shaw* (Brooklyn, N.Y.: Carlson, 1991).

2. Harper, *Life and Work*, 2:596.

3. The best brief introduction to Garrison and his conflicts is Aileen S. Kraditor, *Means and Ends in American Abolitionism: Garrison and His Critics on Strategy and Tactics, 1834–1850* (New York: Vintage Books, 1970), esp. chap. 3, "The Woman Question," and chap. 4, "Religion and the Good Society."

4. Susan B. Anthony, *Diary* (December 30–31, 1871) (unpublished ms. in Susan B. Anthony Papers, Library of Congress).

5. Harper, *Life and Work*, 2:913.

6. Elizabeth Cady Stanton et al., eds., *The History of Woman Suffrage*, 6 vols. (New York: Arno Press, 1969), 1:459.

7. Ibid., 2:254.

8. Harper, *Life and Work*, 1:507.

9. Ibid., 1:187.

10. Stanton et al., *History of Woman Suffrage*, 1:459.

11. Harper, *Life and Work*, 2:648.

12. Stanton et al., *History of Woman Suffrage*, 2:644.

13. For more on Stanton's religious perspective, see Pellauer, *Toward a Tradition of Feminist Theology*, chaps. 2–3.

14. Stanton et al., *History of Woman Suffrage*, 2:644.

15. Susan B. Anthony, "Working Man's National Congress," *The Revolution* (September 17, 1868).

16. Harper, *Life and Work*, 1:366.

17. Ibid., 2:972.

18. Alma Lutz, *Susan B. Anthony: Rebel, Crusader, Humanitarian* (Boston: Beacon Press, 1959), 283.

19. Harper, *Life and Work*, 2:918.

20. Anthony, *Diary*, 1853–55.

21. Harper, *Life and Work*, 2:899 (emphasis added).

22. Ibid., 1:389.

23. Ibid., 169.

24. Anthony, Speech on Temperance, 1852, Folder 22, Schlesinger Library, Anthony Family Collection, 21–22.

25. Harper, *Life and Work*, 2:709.

26. Ibid., 1:457.

27. Ibid., 2:289.

28. Lutz, *Susan B. Anthony*, 62.

29. Harper, *Life and Work*, 1:153.

30. Ibid., 203–204.

31. Ibid., 204.

32. Kathleen Barry, *Susan B. Anthony: A Biography* (New York: New York University Press, 1988), 144.

33. Harper, *Life and Work*, 1:215.

34. Stanton et al., *History of Woman Suffrage*, 2:58.

35. Katherine Anthony, *Susan B. Anthony: Her Personal History and Her Era* (Garden City, N.Y.: Doubleday, 1954), 182.

36. Harper, *Life and Work*, 1:158.

37. Ibid., 1:208.

38. Quoted in Barry, *Susan B. Anthony*, 249.

39. Stanton et al., *History of Woman Suffrage*, 2:688.

40. Ibid., 2:689.

41. Barry, *Susan B. Anthony*, 265.

42. Ibid., 264.

43. Harper, *Life and Work*, 2:857.

44. See, e.g., Aileen Kraditor, *The Ideas of the Woman Suffrage Movement 1890–1920* (Garden City, N.Y.: Doubleday, 1971).

45. Harper, *Life and Work*, 1:385.

46. Ibid., 2:920.

47. Ibid., 3:1386–1387.

48. Ibid., 1199–1200.

49. Ibid., 2:1011.

50. Susan B. Anthony, "Working Women's Association," *The Revolution* (September 9, 1869).

51. Harper, *Life and Work*, 2:898.

52. Anthony, "Woman's Suffrage Meeting."

53. Harper, *Life and Work*, 2:923.

54. Ibid., 3:1265–1266.

55. Ibid., 1266.

56. Stanton et al., *History of Woman Suffrage*, 4:223.

57. Harper, *Life and Work*, 3:1420.

58. Ibid., 2:856–857.

59. Ibid., 847.

60. Kraditor, *The Ideas of the Woman Suffrage Movement*, 66.

61. Harper, *Life and Work*, 2:857.

62. Stanton et al., *History of Woman Suffrage*, 4:263.

63. Ibid.

64. Ibid., 4:264.

65. Aileen S. Kraditor, *Means and Ends in American Abolitionism: Garrison and His Critics on Strategy and Tactics, 1834–1850* (New York: Vintage Books, 1967), 30.

66. Stanton et al., *History of Woman Suffrage*, 4:264.

67. *Report of the International Council of Women* (Washington, D.C.: National Woman Suffrage Association, 1888), 421.

68. Ibid, 422.

69. Harper, *Life and Work*, 2:708.

70. Anna Howard Shaw with Elizabeth Jordan, *The Story of a Pioneer* (New York: Harper, 1915), 214.

71. Even in our time, Anthony is sometimes called "secular." A recent biographer has misunderstood her as a transcendentalist owing to her occasional appreciation of nature. See Barry, *Susan B. Anthony*, 242, 293.

72. Wendy Farley, *Tragic Vision and Divine Compassion* (Louisville, Ky.: Westminster John Knox Press, 1990), 127.

73. Dorothee Soelle, *Suffering* (Philadelphia: Fortress Press, 1975), 149.

74. Dorothee Soelle, *Thinking About God: An Introduction to Theology* (Philadelphia: Trinity Press International, 1990), 85.

75. Dorothee Soelle, *Beyond Mere Obedience* (New York: Pilgrim Press, 1982), xxi.

76. Harper, *Life and Work*, 3:1116.

77. Ibid., 3:1201.

{ CHAPTER 12 }

Karl Barth (1886–1968)

GEORGE HUNSINGER

Pope Pius XII once described Karl Barth, the Swiss Reformed professor and pastor, as "the most important theologian since Thomas Aquinas."[1] Barth's enormous contribution to theology, church, and culture will take generations to assimilate and assess. As the principal author of the Barmen Declaration of 1934, he was the intellectual leader of the German "Confessing Church," the Protestant congregations that resisted Adolf Hitler. Among Barth's many books, sermons, and essays, the great, multivolume *Church Dogmatics*—a closely reasoned, eloquently stated argument in nearly ten thousand pages—stands out as his crowning achievement. Of this work Thomas F. Torrance has written, "Most people regard Volume IV as the high point of the *Church Dogmatics*.... [It] surely constitutes the most powerful work on the doctrine of atoning reconciliation ever written."[2]

Barth's ecumenical importance has been widely recognized. "We have in Barth," writes Hans Urs von Balthasar, "two crucial features: the most thorough and penetrating display of the Protestant view and the closest rapprochement with the Catholic." According to von Balthasar's assessment of Barth, "in him Protestantism has found *for the first time* its most completely consistent representative."[3] During the last decade of his life, Barth was increasingly hopeful about the "astonishing renewal" in the Catholic Church initiated by the Second Vatican Council (1962–65).[4] "I often sense in Catholicism," he once said, "a stronger Christian life than in the Protestant churches."[5] After reading Hans Küng's book *Justification* (1957), the thesis of which is that the teachings of Barth and Catholicism are compatible, Barth stated: "It occurs to me as something worth pondering that it could suddenly take place that the first will be last and the last first, that suddenly from Rome the doctrine of justification by faith alone will be proclaimed more purely than in most Protestant churches."[6]

Karl Barth was born in Basel, Switzerland, on May 10, 1886. Inspired by his father, a professor of New Testament at Bern, Barth resolved to study theology. He matriculated at the University of Bern and studied Reformed theology as well as the thought of the philosopher Immanuel Kant and theologian Friedrich Schleiermacher, who left a deep impression on him. He also studied at the University of Berlin with the great church historian Adolf von Harnack and at the University of Marburg with the neo-Kantian theologian Wilhelm Hermann. After his ordination in Geneva, he took a pastorate in Safenwil, Switzerland.

It was during this first pastorate that Barth came to an acute rethinking of his theology, as well as his views of law, politics, and society. As his biographer James B. Torrance puts it, "On the one hand, when World War I broke out, he was deeply disturbed by the 'Manifesto of the Intellectuals,' 'the black day,' as he called it, when ninety-three scholars and artists, including his own teachers Harnack and Hermann, supported the war policy of Kaiser Wilhelm II, which seemed to him to call into question his colleagues' understanding of the Bible, history, and dogmatics. Was this where the synthesis of (German) culture and religion was leading the Christian church? On the other hand, in his industrial parish, he became acutely aware of the issues of social justice, poor wages, factory legislation, and true union affairs."[7]

Never having studied for a doctorate, Barth did more than anyone to revitalize theology in the twentieth century. His massive *Church Dogmatics* remained unfinished—like the cathedral in Strasbourg, he once quipped, with its missing tower. Thoroughly modern, he rejected modernism in theology. Deeply traditional, he left no stone of tradition unturned. Without deterring easy classifications from critics, he has defied easy classification. Not since Luther and Calvin has there been a Protestant theologian so prodigious in written output and so active in worldly affairs, both ecclesiastical and political. Though Barth was reputed for sharp polemic, his infectious childlike joy, his self-deprecating humor, his love of Mozart, and his profound understanding of Holy Scripture have endeared him to many whose lives he has immeasurably enriched.

Dietrich Bonhoeffer once suggested that in Barth we find the same *hilaritas* that we do in Mozart. The good cheer that knows how to incorporate all that is negative within itself without losing its basic gladness was surely one of Barth's most appealing characteristics. It was a *hilaritas* that was informed by *gravitas* but never succumbed to it. For all his greatness, or perhaps just because of it, Barth did not take himself too seriously. Along with *hilaritas* and *gravitas*, an element of *humilitas* pervaded his work. Barth had no higher aspiration than to place his intellect in the service of

God's grace. Grace inspires the cheerfulness, gravity, and humility he saw as proper to the theologian's task.

THEOLOGY AND POLITICS

Late in life, Barth captured the thrust of his political views in a single line. In a letter of 1967 to Eberhard Bethge, he wrote of "the outlook which I presupposed without so many words and emphasized merely in passing, namely ethics, co-humanity (*Mitmenschlichkeit*), a servant Church, discipleship, Socialism, movements for peace—and throughout all these, politics."[8] Political matters, while never minor for Barth, were constantly overshadowed, as he admitted, by his chief concern, which was "to give a new interpretation of the Reformation."[9] Nevertheless, Barth's political writings make up a significant portion of his corpus. It is only because his dogmatic output looms so large that his political output seems diminutive by comparison.

Whereas Barth's work in theology was detailed and sustained, his political essays were more or less ad hoc. He always saw an integral connection between the two, with theology holding the center while politics was assigned to the periphery. He believed that they could not possibly be separated, especially when it came to grave social evils. "It is not enough," he once remarked, "only to say, 'Jesus is risen,' but then to remain silent about the Vietnam War."[10] Ethics without doctrine is nothing, he believed, but doctrine without ethics is worse than nothing. He therefore reconceived ethics as internal to the dogmatic task. In modern Protestant theology, he felt, neither the left nor the right could adequately set forth the gospel. Neither knew how to uphold doctrinal substance simultaneously with contemporary, political relevance. The left wanted relevance without substance even as the right wanted substance without relevance—the very impasse Barth discerned in the nineteenth century. "These two extremes," he stated, "are for me a thing of the past. On both sides one must go forward instead of always moving backwards."[11]

In politics as well as in theology, we might say that Barth understood himself as a "postliberal" theologian. That is, he understood himself as breaking with the thought forms of modern academic theology as well as with "economic liberalism" (modern capitalism). He usually associated the beginning of his break with theological liberalism with his turn to the left. In about 1916, during his Safenwil pastorate, he became a Swiss religious socialist. Because of his trade-union activities on behalf of the workers in his village, he was known as the Red Pastor. Looking back on that period, he once said in an interview, "I decided for theology, because I felt I needed to find a better basis for my social action."[12]

Barth's political views can be surveyed under three broad headings: church and state, democratic socialism, and international peace. Since these themes are not easy to disentangle, their separation cannot always be neat. Moreover, in a manner that could be exasperating for his critics, to say nothing of his supporters, Barth would sometimes seem to operate more intuitively in arriving at political decisions than on the basis of explicit argumentation. What he regarded as the flexibility and freedom necessary to being a Christian, others have dismissed as arbitrary. While that charge would not be impossible, it could be made to stick only after careful consideration (not always evident in his critics). It is generally true, however, that Barth's political views manifested a double aspect. A fixed side, for Barth, was always made to coexist with an open-ended side. While he wanted the fixed side to allow for stability while avoiding the pitfalls of legalism, he wanted the open-ended side to permit a fresh response to new actualities, under the sovereign leading of God.

CHURCH AND STATE

Church-state relations reached a crisis for Barth during the rise of Hitler and the Third Reich. A stance had to be taken in the 1934 Barmen Declaration[13]—one strong enough to be meaningful, yet broad enough to gain as much support from the churches as possible. The Barmen Declaration, with Barth as its principal author, served as the manifesto of the German confessing church, which resisted Hitler.

The positive thesis of Barmen Article I was this: "Jesus Christ, as he is attested for us in Holy Scripture, is the one Word of God which we have to hear and which we have to trust and obey in life and in death."[14] This thesis means that in matters of faith and practice, Jesus Christ, as attested by scripture, is both necessary and sufficient. His is the only voice that the church may trust in life and in death, and the only one that it must obey. No other person or principle can carry this authority, for no other is the Word of God.

Each positive thesis in Barmen was followed by a negative one. For Article I, the negative thesis can be paraphrased as saying that nothing apart from or alongside the authentic, scriptural voice of Jesus Christ can properly become a source of authority for the church in its own proclamation and teaching. Here Barmen famously rejected natural theology, and this rejection has implications for the question of natural law, to be discussed later. But two points about Barmen and natural theology may be noted here.

First, the Barmen Declaration rejected natural theology primarily in the form of culture-religion. The "natural" is essentially understood as something that is culturally mediated and historically conditioned. No nonmediated "nature" is accessible as such. This point pertains to how Barmen understood the centrality of Jesus Christ. Since Christ is seen as the Lord, his centrality cannot be separated from his exclusive sovereignty (in line with the First Commandment, "You shall have no other gods beside me" [Ex. 20:2; Deut. 5:7]). Where Jesus Christ "no longer speaks the first and last word, but only at best an additional word," wrote Barth, an "assimilated and domesticated theology" will be the inevitable result.[15] Even in forms that may seem benign and congenial, natural theology in its independence of revelation is always a rival claimant. Here is the place to remember, Barth urged, that the church cannot serve two masters; it will either hate the one and love the other, or be devoted to the one and despise the other (Matt. 6:24). Either Christ relativizes natural theology, or natural theology relativizes Christ.

When relativized by natural theology, Jesus Christ no longer functions as the one Lord who is necessary, sufficient, and supreme. While some forms of relativization are more blatant than others, the more subtle and sophisticated forms can serve to pave the way for versions that are cruder and even barbaric. The Christ of natural theology is always, for Barth, the relativized Christ of culture. The trajectory of natural theology leads, in effect, from the Christ who is not supreme, to the Christ who is not suffi-cient, and finally to the Christ who is not necessary. Culture-religion, rela-tivization, and domestication or assimilation indicate that the Lordship of Christ is no longer acknowledged or understood. By rejecting all indepen-dent or second authorities, Barmen reaffirmed the unabridged Lordship of Jesus Christ against the modern inroads of cultural (and in Germany, finally Nazi) self-assertion in the church.

Second, it is important to realize that Barmen's rejection of natural the-ology was broadly cognitive in force. It did not imply that nothing good, beautiful, true, or worthwhile can be found outside of scripture and the church. "God may speak to us," wrote Barth, "through Russian commu-nism or a flute concerto, a blossoming shrub or a dead dog. We shall do well to listen to Him if He really does so."[16] No such source can serve as an authority or norm for the church's preaching, however, for it has no inde-pendent revelatory or epistemic status. Only by criteria derived from the gospel can it be determined whether God might be speaking through those other sources or not. The question of natural theology, for Barth, is thus a question about the justification of belief.

The political implications of Barmen's first article were spelled out, in various ways, by the rest of the Declaration. Only a sketch can be given here. Article II, which asserted that no area of life falls outside the lord-ship of Christ, implies that faith cannot be disconnected from politics or from political judgments. Article III, which saw the church as exclusively the possession of Jesus Christ, carried the reverse implication that faith may not be reduced or made subordinate to political programs and pursuits. In other words, whereas Article II implied that faith and politics cannot be separated, Article III implied that they must not be blurred or confused. Article IV rejected the imposition on the church of an alien polity and thus suggested a measure of autonomy and nonconformity in the church's relation to the world. Article V then interpreted the traditional two-kingdoms doctrine in a Christ-centered way, so that the church's order of loyalties is clear and only conditional loyalty to the state is permitted. Finally, Article VI, which rejected any "arbitrarily chosen desires, purposes and plans,"[17] while affirming service to the message of the gospel, implied that all political activity engaged in by the church assumes the status of a witness to grace. Of these themes, two are perhaps especially important: Barmen's interpretation of the two-kingdoms doctrine and the proposal that faith and politics are related by a pattern of order, unity, and distinction.

It can be argued that in the history of the church, two competing views of governmental authority have contended with one another. One view, dominant in German Protestant theology right down to the confessing church (as well as elsewhere), understood scripture to teach that the state, because it was instituted by God, can command unconditional authority within its own sphere of competence. The secular authority is a bulwark against anarchy. No matter how repressive, it is to be resisted only if it seeks to meddle in ecclesiastical beliefs and affairs. This view is associated (perhaps more rightly than wrongly) with Augustine and Luther.

The alternate view agreed about the state's limited sphere of competence, as well as about the legitimacy of resistance if the state oversteps its boundaries relative to the church. Unlike the first view, however, this second view believed that scripture does not teach a requirement of unconditional obedience to the secular authority, no matter how repressive it might be (as long as it respects ecclesiastical boundaries). Instead, this view understood scripture to mean that the state, because it was instituted by God, has obligations to fulfill, such as rewarding good and punishing evil. If these obligations are violated so as to establish a pattern of serious malfeasance, the state forfeits its legitimacy as well as its divine mandate. This view is associated, in turn, with Aquinas and Calvin.

A salient difference between the two views is clear. The one held that to obey the state, even the radically unjust state, is to render obedience to God. The other held that times may come when obedience to God requires political disobedience and resistance to the state.

The fifth article of the Barmen Declaration, though circumspect, was so formulated as to remain open to the second view. It is a novel version of that view to the extent that the question of obligation(s) is stated, implicitly, in terms of a graduated schedule of loyalties culminating in the church's loyalty to Jesus Christ. The state is seen as divinely appointed to the task of "providing for justice and peace,"[18] and to this end it is allotted the means of coercion. The justice and peace that the state can provide will never be more than rough, however, since we live in "the as yet unredeemed world."[19] Nevertheless, if the state should grievously violate its defining purpose, then Article V implied that the church must then obey "the power of the Word of God by which God upholds all things."[20] As 1 Peter 2:17, cited at the beginning of Barmen V, suggests, although the emperor is certainly to be honored, God alone is to be feared. While the wording of Article V was not quite the open appeal for resistance that Barth would later issue in his own name, it seemed to be as close as he could come at that time for the confessing church.

During the Nazi period, especially after 1935, Barth constantly appealed to these ideas to encourage the confessing church to resistance. For, as was clear to him, the National Socialist state was increasingly implicated (to use a later terminology) in crimes against humanity and peace. Neither Article V nor Barmen as a whole was free from ambiguity, however. They did not rule out the possibility that the Barmen Declaration could be read as compatible with the very deep-seated view that requires unconditional obedience to the secular authority, no matter what. Although Barmen V set forth the state's basic obligations, it did not indicate what the church should do if they are breached. Resistance was at best a possible implication of Barmen V; although not ruled out, neither was it clearly ruled in. Barmen established a graduated schedule of loyalties, but it remained silent about what to do in cases where they come into conflict.

Barth lamented that the confessing church too often took the path of "inner immigration" rather than outward resistance. In 1943 he wrote about the Protestant churches in Europe for the American journal *Foreign Affairs*.[21] He believed that the churches in Holland, Norway, and Britain stood in contrast with the confessing church in Germany. The former were politically progressive yet theologically lacking, because while they opposed Nazism, they failed to attack culture-bound theology. The German situation was much the reverse. Theological assimilation was opposed, yet resistance to Nazism was lacking. The confessing church displayed "a kind of schizophrenia" in adopting "totally divergent yardsticks ... for the inner and the external life."[22] The disconnection of faith and politics that Barmen rejects was overruled by the traditional two-kingdoms doctrine.

Barth often illustrated the inseparability he saw between faith and politics with the metaphor of a circle comprised of a center and a periphery.

"No matter how far [the confessing church] may have progressed in other directions," he wrote, "they will have to learn from the other churches that there are a Christian center and a Christian periphery, that the Christian substance and its political application are indeed two different things, but that there is only one truth and one righteousness—and no [one] can serve two masters."[23] The center of the circle is the gospel, while political decision constitutes the periphery. Together they form an organic whole within which the two remain distinct.

The pattern of order, unity, and distinction became the hallmark of how Barth saw the relationship between faith and politics. His view of the gospel's epistemic status could be described as "nonfoundationalist." The gospel does not rest on anything other than itself, or, to put it another way, on anything other than the miracle and mystery of divine grace. Because faith in the gospel takes precedence, with politics as a secondary and dependent application, their ordering is asymmetrical. Within that asymmetry, however, the two form a unity-in-distinction. Faith and politics, the center and the periphery, are related, in effect, by the Chalcedonian pattern. They exist "without separation or division," on one hand, yet "without confusion or change," on the other. In the church, as Barth saw it, politics is a function of the gospel, but the gospel is essentially independent of politics. Politics is not central, the gospel is not peripheral, but neither can be had without the other.[24]

Between the late 1930s and the 1940s, Barth wrote several seminal essays in which he explored these matters further.[25] In particular he expanded the metaphor of a circle, with its center and periphery, so that it now included the idea of concentric circles. If we place Christ at the center, he proposed, we could then think of two concentric circles, the inner one representing the church ("the Christian community"), and the outer one the state ("the civil community"). Although a more complex pattern results from unity-in-distinction, certain aspects remain the same. By setting up the relations in this way, Barth avoided setting church and state over against one another in a fundamental opposition or dichotomy. On the contrary, each exists in its own way under the one lordship of Christ.

The overall conception that Barth proposed with his image of concentric circles can be summarized in thesis form. Christ, church, and state (center, inner circle, and outer circle) are related in these essays as follows:[26]

1 The state belongs to the redeemed creation. It involves more than the need for order under the destabilized conditions of the fall.

1.1 The state is a part of the created order (*status integritatis*), because like all of creation, it exists in its own way as a theater for the glory of God.

1.1.1 As a part of the creation, the state finds its origin and limit in God.

1.1.2 Because of its origin and limit in God, the state's tendency to deify itself, under the conditions of the fall, is illegitimate. It must not be taken seriously, but inwardly and outwardly opposed.

1.2 The state belongs to the redeemed order of creation, moreover, because all power on heaven and on earth has been given to the risen Lord, Jesus Christ.

1.2.1 Because all power (not just some) has been given to the Lord Jesus Christ, the state finds its positive goals and limits with reference to the kingdom of God.

1.2.2 Since its goals and their limits are set by its relation to God's kingdom, the state must beware not only of attempting too much, but also of attempting too little.

1.2.3 Utopian schemes, for example, would mean attempting too much while merely preventing anarchy would, in general, mean attempting too little.

1.2.4 The state has the positive task, divinely appointed, not only of preventing the worst, but also of promoting the common good, so far as possible, by securing justice, freedom, and peace.

1.2.5 The means of coercion at the state's disposal are meant to be used for the sake of justice, freedom, and peace. As far as possible, these coercive means should be subject to constitutional checks and balances and democratic controls.

2 The church is that part of creation whose special task is to bear witness to redemption.

2.1 Since the church, like the state, is a part of the good creation, its relationship to the state cannot be essentially negative.

2.1.1 Because the church's relation to the state is essentially positive, the church can never place itself in fundamental opposition to the state, no matter how corrupt, nor can it withdraw from participating in the responsibilities of the state, even when they may include the use of coercion.

2.2 Since the church knows, unlike the state, that the creation has been redeemed, the church knows the state's origins, limits, and goals better than the state does itself.

2.2.1 Knowing these origins, limits, and goals, the church has a special responsibility to work and pray that the state might conform to them.

3 The tasks of the state are, so to speak, strictly horizontal; the tasks of the church are both vertical and horizontal. The state exists for the humanization of creation; the church exists for the Christianization of human beings.

3.1 The state's tasks are horizontal because they concern relations among human beings, which pertain to the material creation.

3.1.1 The state exists for the sake of humanizing creation, because at the secular level the grace of creation involves making and keeping human life human.

3.1.2 Insofar as the state humanizes the creation as redeemed by Jesus Christ, it anticipates the kingdom of God.

3.2 The church's tasks are both vertical and horizontal because they concern the relationships of God for human beings and human beings for God, and therefore of human beings for one another.

3.2.1 The church exists for the sake of Christianizing human beings, because at the spiritual level the grace of redemption involves their conversion from themselves to Christ.

3.2.2 By Christianizing human beings as redeemed by Jesus Christ, the church anticipates the kingdom of God.

3.3 Therefore, both church and state anticipate the kingdom of God and the redemption of creation, but they do so in fundamentally different ways. Members of the church are obligated to participate in the tasks of the state, but only by working towards humanization, while members of the state (of the civil community) are obligated to participate in the tasks of the church, but only by becoming Christians.

4 The state cannot become a church, and the church cannot become a state.

4.1 The state cannot become a church, because the horizontal tasks allotted to it are relative, provisional, and external.

4.1.1 Since its tasks are horizontal, the state can have no direct concern with the relationship of God to human beings or of human beings to God.

4.1.2 Because the state's aims are relative, they can never usher in the kingdom of God or be of ultimate importance. Most importantly, they can never be made absolute. However, because they are provisional, they can and must point to God's kingdom, at least parabolically. Finally, because they are merely external, they can never make an ultimate claim on the inner, spiritual life of citizens of the state.

4.2 The church cannot become a state, because its vertical and horizontal tasks, while relative and provisional, are not only external, but also, so to speak, internal or spiritual. As such the church does not use means of coercion—and if it does, it enters into self-contradiction.

4.2.1 Since its tasks are vertical as well as horizontal, the church is properly concerned with the relationship of God to human beings and of human beings to God, as well as of human beings to one another, including their political relationships.

4.2.2 Since the church's tasks, like those of the state, are both relative and provisional, they cannot usher in God's kingdom; but they can and must point to it parabolically. Yet because the church's tasks, unlike those of the state, are internal or spiritual as well as external, they make an ultimate claim on both the inner and outer lives of its members.

4.3 Since the state cannot become a church, it has no right to establish a civil religion; and since the church cannot become a state, it has no right to establish "Christian" political organizations, such as labor unions or political parties.

4.4 Neither church nor state will exist in the kingdom of God, but God will be all in all.

5 The state needs the church, and the church needs the state.

5.1 The church needs the state to establish the orderly preconditions for the church's proclamation and witness, and the state needs the church to remind the state of its divinely appointed origins, limits, and goals.

5.2 Therefore, the state best serves the church by remaining the state, and the church best serves the state by remaining the church.

These theses reflect Barth's distinctive understanding of creation from the standpoint of redemption. This standpoint allowed Barth to establish a strong relationship between the tasks of the state and the kingdom of God. At the same time, it allowed for an essentially positive relationship between the tasks of the church and those of the state, which, though distinct, are nonetheless complementary.

If we consider these theses in light of the Barmen Declaration, we can see that they elaborate Barth's ideas along the lines Barmen sets forth. The same basic pattern of order, unity, and distinction is evident in each case. After Barmen, Barth refined and developed, but did not fundamentally change, his viewpoint. The image of concentric circles—perhaps the root metaphor of all Barth's thinking about church and society—was used to explain how, since Christ is the center, the church is then the first circle out, followed next by the larger society. The two concentric circles are each governed in distinctive ways by that single center, which establishes their unity-in-distinction. The inner circle of the church can even function, at best, as a role model for a properly ordered human society. The power of a good example, Barth believed, would do more to influence the surrounding world than would any political action in which the church might engage. Moreover, a church that is disordered within—by racism, for example, or social inequality, or chauvinism—can scarcely expect to be taken seriously if it undertakes political advocacy in the civil society for justice, freedom, and peace.

In society, Barth maintained, the church should stand for social values consistent with the gospel. The church should stand for placing the needs of concrete human beings over abstract causes, for the rule of law and constitutionality in government, for giving priority to those who are socially

and economically vulnerable, for freedom of conscience and political judgment, for the political responsibility of all adult citizens regardless of race,
creed, sex, or class, for the separation of powers (legislative, executive, judicial), for freedom of speech, for political power in the form of service, for
the larger social good over narrow, parochial interests, and for making war
and political violence legitimate only as a last resort. Barth's attempt to derive and support these positions with analogies drawn from the gospel was,
as is generally recognized, only partially successful, at best. Nevertheless, it
has not always been noticed that Barth explicitly presented his analogies as
being suggestive rather than definitive. While his argumentation by analogy seems deficient, perhaps the task of evangelical social ethics after Barth
would be not to reject his analogical procedure wholesale (as some have
done), but rather to find better analogies where necessary, and to present
them less impressionistically, and more carefully and extensively.

RESISTANCE TO TYRANNY

If we look back from these summary theses on church and state to Barth's
earlier social ideas, some interesting developments stand out. Among
them, the right to resist tyranny calls for special comment. This right was
explicit in Barth's 1928–29 "Theses on Church and State," which he formulated in his course lectures on *Ethics* (published only posthumously in
1978).[27] Barth maintained that because the secular authority rests on force,
persons faced with tyranny or oppression cannot rule out, as a last resort,
"violent revolution on the part of the rest of the citizens."[28] Nothing even
close to this idea was inserted into the Barmen Declaration, presumably
not because of Barth, but because he perceived that in 1934 the German
church was simply not ready for it. In his circular letters and other communications with the confessing church throughout the Nazi period, Barth
repeatedly had to contend with the prevailing fear that greater resistance
would be unpatriotic.

In his 1937–38 Gifford Lectures, published as *The Knowledge of God and
the Service of God*, Barth took up the question of political resistance in
more detail. Perhaps one reason he chose to comment on "The Scots Confession" of 1560 as the basis for his lectures was that it allowed him to address this very theme.[29] The Confession itself states that it is the Christian's
duty to "repress tyranny" and "defend the oppressed." John Knox and his
friends provided "unambiguous commentary," Barth observed, with "their
words and deeds."[30]

Sometimes, Barth acknowledged, the abuse of political power must be
endured. Under certain conditions, however, according to the Scots Con-

fession, "there may be a *resistance* to the political power, which is not merely allowed but enjoined by God."[31] The Scots Confession drew a very clear distinction between lawful and unlawful authority. It spoke concretely on the basis of what the secular authority in question wills and does. Barth explained: "Does the political power—this king or that magistrate—do what it is its business to do? Does it abide by God's commandments? Does it remain within the bounds of justice and within the bounds of its task? Does it therefore, by showing this attitude, possess legitimate 'authoritie'? That is the question. Is it not one which can and must be raised constantly in connection with every political power? This question is certainly asked by God."[32]

The secular authority ceases to be legitimate when it violates the freedom it ought to safeguard and destroys justice and peace. Barth commented: "Just because there is no alteration in the Divine appointment of the political order, it is now manifestly true that 'God Himself does ... judge even the judges themselves' and that the sword they wield is turned against themselves."[33] Therefore, Barth concluded, there are times when endurance is not enough, and when even passive resistance must be left behind. "It could well be," he stated, "that we had to do with a Government of liars, murderers, and incendiaries, with a Government which wished to usurp the place of God, to fetter the conscience, to suppress the church and become itself the Church of Antichrist."[34] In such cases "active resistance as such cannot and may not be excluded."[35]

It is worth noting that Barth's argument here, as elsewhere, was based solely on scripture—and on the Scots Confession that interpreted it. Barth did not move to scriptural interpretation only after having engaged in more general considerations, such as those based on "natural law." On the contrary, as was characteristic of him, he moved only from the particular to the general. Here the particularity of scripture and its witness to divine revelation were taken as sufficient (as well as necessary).

When Barth discussed resistance to tyranny, he also addressed the theme of desacralization. Whether political power is being exercised legitimately does not depend, Barth noted dryly, on whether rulers profess to be Christians: "When this is the case, one can rejoice at it for their sakes, and perhaps for the sake of the church also. But that in itself does not make clear the significance of the political order as service of God."[36] The service that the state owes to God "does not become clear by rulers professing the Christian faith and indeed being known as men who personally are sincerely pious."[37] Piety, of course, can be used to obscure injustice. Similarly, the secularism of a non-Christian ruler can make clear—and sometimes "clearer in fact than where the State seems to have a very Christian appearance"[38]—that living up to the state's divinely appointed obligations is independent of the religiosity (or lack thereof) of those who hold political office.

Earlier in his career, Barth had made much the same point with respect to political resistance. In the first edition of his commentary on Romans (1919), he wrote, "That Christians have nothing to do with monarchy, capitalism, militarism, patriotism, free-thinking, is so self-evident that I do not even need to mention it."[39] He then went on to exhort "desacralization" as a basic Christian duty: "Thou shalt starve the state of religion. Thou shalt deny it the elevation, the seriousness, and significance of the divine. Thou shalt not have your heart in your politics. Your souls are and remain alien to the ideals of the state."[40] Barth then enjoined this attitude on those engaged in active resistance: Let there be "strike, general strike, and street fighting, if need be, but no religious justification or glorification of it ... military service as soldier or officer, if need be, but on *no* condition as military chaplain ... social democratic but not religious socialist!"[41] Over the years Barth's political views continued to develop and became more nuanced, but the desacralizing, deflationary imperative remained a constant, as he saw it, in how the church should relate the gospel to the state.

DEMOCRATIC SOCIALISM

Parliamentary democracy, Barth believed, does not work very well without economic democracy. Economic liberalism (or capitalism) is a system that inevitably concentrates wealth and power into the hands of a small minority. By contrast, economic democracy (or democratic socialism) is a system that promises to distribute political power more equitably precisely by eliminating extreme inequalities and concentrations of wealth. Without economic democracy, parliamentary democracy is hobbled. Concentrated power in the hands of the few means that parliamentary means are twisted for elitist ends. Necessities are denied to the many while luxuries are delivered to the few. Antisocial phenomena such as huge armaments industries, imperialist adventures abroad, and nationalist diversions at home are less often the exception than the rule. Capitalism goes hand in hand with the thwarting of democratic change and with large quotients of social misery. Throughout his life Barth favored "practical," nonauthoritarian socialism, essentially because he believed in democracy.

Unlike some of his adherents, Barth was always a "public intellectual" embroiled in political controversy, a situation that persisted until the end of his life. When friends gathered for the celebration of his eightieth birthday, he reminded them of his origins:

The reader of the *Church Dogmatics* certainly needs to know that I come from religious socialism. And I originally pursued something other than "church dogmatics"—namely, lectures on bringing factories to justice and on trade union problems—and I also became a member of the Swiss Socialist Party. And when I took part in these activities, it somehow hung together with a particular discovery—namely, that the children of this world are often wiser than the children of light.[42]

Elsewhere he reminisced further about his early pastorate: "The socialists were among the most avid listeners to my sermons, not because I preached socialism, but because they knew I was the same man who was also attempting to help them."[43]

A milestone in Barth's view of theology and socialism was his 1911 essay "Jesus Christ and the Movement for Social Justice." It was a talk he presented to the Safenwil workers during his early pastorate. Although both his theology and his socialism would change significantly as time went on, elements of continuity would remain.

Barth criticized his socialist listeners for their tactics, but not for their goals. "I have said that Jesus wanted what you want, that he wanted to help those who are least, that he wanted to establish the kingdom of God upon this earth, that he wanted to abolish self-seeking property, that he wanted to make persons into comrades. Your concerns are in line with the concerns of Jesus. *Real* socialism is real Christianity in our time."[44] Socialism fights against the capitalist system, he explained to a critic, "because the net profits which become part of the private wealth of the entrepreneur are by no means equivalent to his contribution to the common production."[45] Underlying this social analysis was a modern liberal christology. It values Jesus less for his once-for-all saving work than for the power of his saving influence: "The best and greatest thing that I can bring to you as a pastor will always be Jesus Christ and a portion of the powers which have gone out from his person into history and life."[46]

The later Barth would no longer flatly identify Jesus with a human project as he did in Safenwil; "Jesus *is* the movement for social justice," he told the workers, "and the movement for social justice *is* Jesus in the present."[47] He would distinguish more thoughtfully between two different plights: that of the victim and that of the sinner. Sin by definition is a plight, he came more clearly to see, that sinners cannot overcome by their own efforts. They need a Savior who bears their judgment for them and bears it away even as they also need one who can confer upon them the righteousness they completely lack, and so make them capable of eternal life in communion with God. Not only is the terrible plight of sin beyond human remedy, but it is also universal in scope, because no human being is excluded from it. The significance of the Savior is correspondingly universal in scope. Barth broke with the liberal view of Jesus (that saw him essentially as a source of empowerment) when he realized that Jesus is unique in kind—a unique person who came to do a unique work. Barth then embraced more fully the ecumenical faith that no one else other than Jesus would ever be God incarnate, that no one else would die for the sins of the world, and that no one else would ever be in himself or herself the mediator of righteousness and life.

For the later Barth, the plight of the sinner does not abolish the plight of the victim; but it does relocate the victim within a larger soteriological scheme. While the sinner's plight is beyond human remedy, universal in scope, and a matter of hostility and estrangement toward God, the victim's plight is essentially different. It is not beyond all human remedy, not universal in scope (since if there are victims, there are also perpetrators and bystanders), and the hostility and estrangement at stake exists primarily among human beings. Being a victim of injustice is a social disorder rooted in the deeper disorder of sin toward God; however, the God who became incarnate in order to deal with our deepest need is by no means indifferent to our lesser needs. Since God's very being is mercy, Barth argued, God takes all our distress into God's heart, participating in it by sympathy and doing what is necessary to remove it.[48] God makes the suffering of the world God's own, and abolishes it in God's own self for the good of all. Although a hierarchy of needs exists, with sin at its very root, God's compassion reaches out to every level of our misery and guilt.

The Old Testament constantly bears witness, the later Barth observed, to God's vindication of the right of all those who are vulnerable and downtrodden: the oppressed, the poor, the widows, the orphans, and the aliens in the land. "God always stands on this and only on this side, always against the exalted and for the lowly, always against those who already have rights and for those from whom they are robbed and taken away."[49] In this divine care for the downtrodden, Christians will discern a parable of how God has acted toward themselves in their plight as sinners: "There follows from this character of faith a political attitude, decisively determined by the fact that man is made responsible to all those who are poor and wretched in his eyes, that he is summoned on his part to espouse the cause of those who suffer wrong. Why? Because in them it is manifested to him what he himself is in the sight of God."[50] By any other political attitude, stated Barth, we reject the very mercy we receive from God. On these grounds, Barth concluded that the "Church must stand for social justice in the political sphere."[51] Standing for social justice is at once an end in itself and yet also an act of witness to something beyond itself.

The church is witness of the fact that the Son of Man came to seek and to save the lost. And this implies—casting all false impartiality aside—that the church must concentrate first on the lower and lowest levels of human society. The poor, the socially and economically weak and threatened, will always be the object of the church's primary and particular concern, and it will always insist on the state's special responsibility for these weaker members of society.[52]

The church must remain vigilant, for example, that "equality before the law" does not become a smokescreen behind which the weak are exploited by the strong, the poor by the rich, the dependent by the independent, the employees by the employers. To Barth this concern meant that the church must stand on the political left. That was the fixed side that then allowed, in practice, for a measure of open-endedness: "And in choosing between the various socialistic possibilities (social-liberalism? co-operativism? syndicalism? free trade? moderate or radical Marxism?), it will always choose the movement from which it can expect the greatest measure of social justice (leaving all other considerations to one side)."[53]

Barth's argument was thus constructed from a sequence of analogies derived from the gospel. First, he established a hierarchy of needs in which the deepest misery, that of sin, stands in analogy to social misery, which, though lesser by comparison, is not trivial. The church's response to social misery, in turn, must reflect God's compassionate response to human sin as known and attested by the church. Compassion in its political form will be discerned in movements that give priority to the neediest sectors of society. For Barth, this compassion meant some form of democratic socialism—that socialism which is as wholly committed to the freedoms of parliamentary democracy and civil liberties as it is to the struggle implicit in economic democracy against the abuses that always accrue from vast concentrations of wealth and power in the hands of the privileged few. While Barth's argument was not exhaustive and left a fuller case to be made, prima facie, it seems fair to say that it was not implausible.

The high point in Barth's espousal of democratic socialism came in *Church Dogmatics*, when he discussed the ethics of work in modern society. Among the standards that Barth established for assessing work, three are especially noteworthy: the criteria of objectivity, worthy aims, and sociality. The first concerns a wholehearted engagement in the practices necessary for achieving excellence in one's field of endeavor; the second, the worthwhileness of the ends being pursued; and the third, "the humanity of human work," that is, the degree to which it promotes humane coexistence and social cooperation.[54] It was the second and third criteria, above all, that Barth brought to bear against capitalism. Work as it is now organized in Western capitalist society, he suggested, conforms poorly to the criteria of worthy aims and humane sociality.

Capitalism, Barth believed, exacerbates some of the worst propensities of human nature. It fosters a revolution of empty and inordinate desires. It promotes "lust for a superabundance," "lust for possessions," and "lust for an artificially extended area of power over [human beings] and things."[55] It generates enormous disparities in wealth and power, thus concentrating life-and-death decisions "in the hands of the relatively few, who pull all the strings ... in a way wholly outside the control of the vast majority."[56] A system that heightens self-seeking, debases culture, and, not least, obscures its own injustices, it is "almost unequivocally demonic."[57] In these and other ways, it violates the dignity of work. Work that possesses human dignity, Barth observes, would look very different:

> What are we to think of all the work which is thought worthwhile, and which is therefore done by those involved, only because they can definitely count on the stupidity and superficiality, the vanity and bad taste, the errors and vices of numerous other people? What are we to think of all the work to which people are drawn only because there are others who are prepared to ruin themselves either physically or morally? What are we to think of the work which flourishes in one place only because [human beings] elsewhere are afflicted with unemployment and therefore with want? What are we to think, as we must ask in relation to the problem of war, of direct or indirect participation in the work of an armaments factory, the achievements of which in so-called peace have often proved to be one of the most potent causes of war? Finally, what are we to think of work which, while it is intrinsically neither useful nor harmful, presents so unworthy an aspect just because it is directed neither to good nor evil, nor indeed to [human beings] at all, but past them to a purely illusory yet dynamic and in its conjunction of the two, almost unequivocally demonic process which consists in the amassing and multiplying of possessions expressed in financial calculations (or miscalculations), i.e., the "capital" which in the hands of the relatively few, who pull all the strings, may equally well, in a way wholly outside the control of the vast majority and therefore quite arbitrarily or accidentally, be a source of salvation or perdition for whole nations or generations?[58]

The Christian community, Barth urged, must not allow itself to "participate in the great self-deception" of capitalism.[59] It must not regard its supposed benefits, necessity, or even legitimacy as something that conforms to what is commanded by God. It must not accept the proposition, for example, that although the wealth under capitalism is inequitably distributed, each person's income reflects how hard or how valuably that person has worked. For "the only choice which employees often have is between starvation and doing work which either does not benefit the cause of [humanity], is detrimental to it, or is completely alien, being performed in the service of a sinister and heartless and perpetually ambiguous idol"—namely, mammon in the guise of "capital."[60] Because capitalism forces people to work for "meaningless ends and therefore dishonestly," Barth wondered whether it was not almost inevitable that communism would triumph over it. "Is it not almost inevitable," he asked, "that the Marxist tyranny should finally overwhelm us, with its new and very different injustices and calamities, to teach us *mores*, true ethics, in this respect?"[61] If we substitute the term "Islamist" for the term "Marxist" in this quotation, Barth's concerns might not seem irrelevant today.

The command of God, Barth wrote, "is self-evidently and in all circumstances a call for countermovements on behalf of humanity and against its denial in any form, and therefore a call for the championing of the weak against every kind of encroachment on the part of the strong."[62] Since the Christian community has been slow to recognize what God's command means in a capitalist society, Barth felt that it was scarcely in a position to point the finger at injustices elsewhere. Instead, he urged the Christian community to concentrate on "the disorder in the decisive form still current in the West, to remember and to assert the command of God in the face of this form, and to keep to the 'Left' in opposition to its champions, i.e., to confess that it [the Christian community] is fundamentally on the side of the victims of this disorder and to espouse their cause."[63]

INTERNATIONAL PEACE

It should not be forgotten that Barth first became a theologian in opposition to a "preemptive" war. More precisely, he felt compelled to reexamine everything he had learned from his revered teachers because of his fierce opposition to what he called their "war theology"—a theology that turned the gospel to sacralize a war of aggression.

> And then the First World War broke out and brought something which for me was almost even worse than the violation of Belgian neutrality—the horrible manifesto of the ninety-three German intellectuals who identified themselves before all the world with the war policy of Kaiser Wilhelm II and Chancellor Bethmann-Hollweg. And to my dismay, among the signatories I discovered the names of almost all my German teachers (with the honorable exception of Martin Rade). An entire world of theological exegesis, ethics, dogmatics, and preaching, which up to that point I had accepted as basically credible, was thereby shaken to the foundations, and with it everything which flowed at that time from the pens of the German theologians.[64]

Not long afterward, in a step that would lead to the rebirth of twentieth-century theology, Barth sat down under an apple tree and "began, with all the tools at my disposal, to apply myself to the Epistle to the Romans."[65]

After the outbreak of the war, things did not go smoothly for Barth even with his teacher Martin Rade, a man of pacifist leanings. Barth had once served as an assistant editor at *Die Christliche Welt*, where Rade was the longtime editor. Barth responded to Rade's first three wartime issues with a letter of protest and told him that the journal had ceased to be Christian and had simply gone over to the world. While Barth could see only a debased power struggle and a racist bid for superiority, Rade had been investing the war with a halo of piety. From a Christian standpoint, "the only possibility at the present moment," wrote Barth, "would be unconditional protest against war as such and against the human failures that brought it about."[66] If no other form of protest were possible, even silence would be better than what Rade had been putting out, because even silence would be a form of protest. But Rade was permitting Christians to support the war with a good conscience. "How are people to make progress," asked Barth, "if now, in this terrible explosion of human guilt, their actions are rewarded with the consolation of a good conscience? At the present moment, unless one prefers to keep wholly silent, can anything be said other than 'Repent'?"[67] Barth's own 1914 sermons bristled with protests against "war theology."[68]

If we consider his whole career, Barth's stance on the problem of war is not easy to characterize. He seems to have hovered somewhere between what might be called "relative pacifism" and "chastened nonpacifism." Yet in some sense he never wavered from his early Safenwil convictions: "War is always terrible, and we know that we must find a way even for our own country to extricate itself from its entanglements in militarism and armaments. Let us not be deceived by the pagan wisdom that 'whoever wants peace must prepare for war.' On the contrary, whoever wants peace must prepare for peace."[69] Or again, "God however is love and his kingdom is not of this world. God has nothing to do with violence. Love wants to dismantle injustice, to renounce the advantages of status or property.... There are two orders that we need to keep straight so that we don't confuse them: the one that arises from self-seeking and leads to violence; the other that aims to be based on God's love.... Where violence reigns, there is simply no just peace and no lasting blessing to be expected—not in the family, not in business, not in our country."[70] The gospel, according to Barth, established a self-evident presumption against war.

A presumption, however, was not, to Barth's mind, an absolute proscription. Here, too, the fixed side requires dialectical balance by an open-ended side. What God might require of us in any particular situation has to remain open. The burden of proof is always heavily on Christians who think they can participate in war, or in preparations for war, with a good conscience. Nevertheless, borderline situations cannot be ruled out in advance. Barth did not ask the abstract question: Is war intrinsically right or wrong? Nor did he ask the casuistic question: Under what general circumstances is war right or wrong? He always asked the situational question: Is this particular war actually demanded of us, in spite of everything, by God?

The upshot of Barth's complex, dialectical stance seemed to be a kind of informed intuitionism. One responds to the contingencies of the moment on the basis of discernment formed by a conscientious immersion in the ethos of the Christian community. One listens, in light of the gospel, for what God is commanding here and now through the language of the facts. One then acts on one's own responsibility (though not without consultation with others) in fear and trembling. On this basis, during World War II, Barth could give the Czech soldiers who defended their homeland a good conscience while denying it to the Germans who invaded it. He could stand for peace in 1914 and call for war in 1939. He could endorse Swiss armed neutrality against the Germans, even donning the uniform himself, but then oppose nuclear armament in Europe after the war.

We might say that Barth was a "just-war pacifist," except that his relation to the just-war tradition was idiosyncratic. He strongly upheld the *ius ad bellum* principles of last resort (into which he subsumed the principle of right intention) and acting only in self-defense. Yet he argued that war should sometimes be fought even without a reasonable chance of success, and he presupposed the principle of legitimate authority. Even more strangely, he said next to nothing about *ius in bello* principles such as noncombatant immunity and proportionality, perhaps because he took them for granted (though even that would be odd, given the brutality of twentieth-century warfare).[71]

Nevertheless, what Barth wrote about war in the *Church Dogmatics* not only reflected his peculiar dialectics of responsible, situational discernment, but also moved much closer to the pacifism of his early career than to the chastened nonpacifism of his anti-Nazi period. "It is not exaggerating," writes John Howard Yoder, "to say that in the pages devoted to the question of war Barth offers a criticism of the belligerent tradition of official Christianity which is unprecedented and unparalleled from the pen of the occupant of any official European chair of theology."[72] Barth wrote, for example, "Does not war demand that almost everything God has forbidden be done on a broad front? ... Can it and should it nevertheless be defended and ventured? ... [Almost] all affirmative answers to this [latter] question are wrong if they do not start with the assumption that the inflexible negative of pacifism has almost infinite arguments in its favor and is almost overpoweringly strong."[73] The mass slaughter of modern war, Barth averred, is difficult to distinguish from mass murder.[74] Peace is therefore "the real emergency,"[75] and no peace can be made secure without real social justice. As long as "interest-bearing capital" reigns supreme, the mechanism for war is already set going. It must be replaced, for the sake of peace, by democracy and social democracy in its stead.[76]

Barth's final word on the subject in the *Church Dogmatics* reflected his generally anti-ideological and situational outlook:

> The direction of Jesus must have embedded itself particularly deeply in the disciples.... They were neither to fear force nor to exercise it.... What the disciples are enjoined is that they should love their enemies (Matt. 5:44). This destroys the whole friend-foe relationship, for when we love our enemy he ceases to be our enemy. It thus abolishes the whole exercise of force, which presupposes this relationship, and has no meaning apart from it.... There is a concrete and incontestable direction which has to be carried out exactly as it is given. According to the sense [*Sinn*] of the New Testament we cannot be pacifists in principle, only in practice. But we have to consider very closely whether, if we are called to discipleship, we can avoid being practical pacifists, or fail to be so.[77]

Like the orientation Barth discerned in scripture toward justice for the oppressed, his presumption in favor of pacifism was patterned on the prior activity of God. Nonviolence is the pattern manifested in Christ's passion as it led him to the cross. It is therefore the pattern to which Christian obedience is called to conform.

BARTH AND NATURAL LAW

If the term "ethics" is taken to mean a system of ideal values purporting to be applicable to the conduct of men everywhere and in all times, then the discussion of it has no place in this book. To me there are no such things as abstract and universally applicable rules of ethics.... In large part, of course, what most of us would regard as ethically commendable values and virtues are culturally and sometimes religiously conditioned—culturally, even by those who are scarcely conscious of their own cultural inheritance; and religiously, even by those who would scoff at the mere suggestion that religion had anything to do with their reactions.

—GEORGE F. KENNAN, *AROUND THE CRAGGED HILL* (1993)

George F. Kennan's words are not far, in spirit, from Barth's doubts about "natural law." Much like Kennan, Barth rejected the idea of an unmediated and unconditioned moral law to which human beings have universal access, even in their fallen state. What is regarded as "natural law" is always at bottom a cultural construct. From the standpoint of Christian ethics, it can offer no reliable basis for knowing what is right, nor can it offer any firm and clear basis for making ethical decisions. Natural law theory posits an autonomous ground of ethical reflection completely separate from divine revelation. Christian ethics cannot build on this basis, Barth argued, because no such basis exists on which to build.

Like Calvin, Barth believed that God is present to us *in continuo actu.* God is not an aloof deity, passively waiting for us to discover God and the moral law. If Barth had a "moral ontology," it might best be described as "an ontology of active relations." The God whose being is in action is constantly present to us as the Lord at every moment of our lives. When we know this God by faith through the witness of the church, we enter into active fellowship with God. The Lord God does not leave us to our own devices, but rather reconfigures us into moral agents and slays us daily to make us alive, through word and sacrament, through scriptural meditation and prayer, through all that bears down upon us, all that we undergo and undertake, so that what God wills for us and commands of us emerges concretely in the texture of our lives. "For in every moment and act of human activity the point at issue is a concrete and specific human choice and decision, in which the inner intention and external action are not to be separated from each other, but make up a whole."[78] The context of decision is established by an ongoing encounter with the command of God: "And this whole of human activity is undoubtedly confronted every time by a command of God which is also concrete and specific."[79]

What would a principled imagination that was shaped by Barth's moral ontology look like? It seems that narratives are better than "cases" for conveying a thick sense of what Barth meant when he spoke of concrete existential encounters with the command of God. While he restricted himself primarily to biblical narratives, other more modern examples might also facilitate an appreciation of his argument. The following can at least be mentioned: *Lest Innocent Blood Be Shed* by Philip Hallie (Christian decision making in action); *Jane Eyre* by Charlotte Bronte (a classic not always recognized as a theological novel); *The Lost Child* by Marietta Jaeger (a true and excruciating story of sanctification); *Adam Bede* by George Eliot (Dinah's speech to Hetty); *The Hiding Place* by Corrie ten Boom (more Christian decision making); and *The Warden* by Anthony Trollope (Christian decency confronts moral ambiguity). At the risk of being cryptic, each

of these narratives contains theological content that is arguably susceptible, in various ways, to a more or less Barthian ethical interpretation.

Apart from the possible difficulty of imagining how Barth's moral ontology might apply to our lives, another difficulty also commonly arises.
In trying to grasp what Barth's rejection of "natural law" implies, it is not
always appreciated that Barth actually gave back with one hand much
of what he took away with the other. Although no way exists from natural law to the revelation of God's command in Christ, he argued, a way
does exist from this revelation to "natural law." Barth did not think about
"natural law" from the general standpoint that "grace does not destroy but
takes up and perfects nature."[80] On the contrary, he thought that grace
relates itself to nature according to a very different pattern: the death-and-
resurrection pattern of *Aufhebung*. Barth did not argue that the good required of a person cannot be known in any sense outside the church; he
argued that it cannot be known in any sense "without grace."[81] Grace is
operative incognito and, so to speak, in irregular ways outside the walls of
the church (*extra muros ecclesiae*). What natural law theory would ascribe
to nature, Barth critically relocated in a context of grace.[82]

Apart from an explicit reliance on grace, Barth argued, moral perceptions are always profoundly ambiguous. Taken as a whole, they lack a proper center in Christ, and therefore in one sense are completely inadequate.
Nevertheless, not every perception within the whole will be equally dubious, and elements of validity will coexist with much that is incompatible
with the gospel. Insofar as elements of validity are present, they are to be
ascribed to the secret workings of grace. What those elements may be cannot be determined apart from the gospel—in other words, not by the light
of unaided reason. But, even outside the church, human incapacity is constantly being overruled by the sovereignty of grace, and faith will properly
be on the alert for signs of the occurrence of that overruling. Because of
grace, it may even be that the children of this world are often wiser than
the children of light; but that is no reason to set up "nature" as a source of
moral knowledge that exists independently of and alongside grace. On the
contrary, "natural" perceptions of moral law, as culturally conditioned and
historically mediated, and sometimes even influenced by the gospel itself,
must always be negated and reconstituted on the higher plane of grace
(*Aufhebung*) if they are to be properly appreciated and assessed. The Christian community cannot base its political responsibility on natural law, nor
can it appeal to natural law as an unproblematic given in its proposals to
the civil community. But the Christian community can appeal to whatever
seems valid in the cultural moral perceptions of the time, and make arguments in and for the civil community on that basis. And the Christian

community can remain alert to "the power which God has to make good come of evil, as He is in fact always doing in the political order."[83] This is the light in which to set Barth's conclusion: "The tasks and problems which the Christian community is called to share, in fulfillment of its political responsibility, are 'natural,' secular, profane tasks and problems. But the norm by which it should be guided is anything but natural: it is the only norm which it can believe in and accept as a spiritual norm, and is derived from the clear law of its own faith, not from the obscure workings of a system outside itself; it is from knowledge of this norm that it will make its decisions in the political sphere."[84]

CONCLUSIONS

If we are asked to identify Barth's main disciples and schools of thought that have emerged around the legal and political topics that he addressed, then perhaps the following outlines can be sketched.

Within a few years after Barth's death in 1968, a division started to appear among his followers on matters of faith and politics. Not unlike what had happened after Hegel, "right-wing" and "left-wing" Barthians emerged on the theological scene. In the first group, probably the most prominent representative was Eberhard Jüngel of Tübingen. Jüngel, who had grown up under Communism in East Germany, argued for an essentially apolitical and nonsocialist Barth. He contended that Barth's political views were not essential to his theology. In later years Jüngel also endorsed a "mission to the Jews"—something Barth always insisted was a terrible mistake.

Meanwhile, a non-Barthian group emerged in Munich advancing the line that Barth's theology had been essentially antidemocratic and that it had contributed to the rise of fascism. Arguably, however, this interpretation was little more than special pleading on the part of regrouped liberals who were still smarting under Barth's criticism of modern academic theology. Among the representatives of this tendency were Trutz Rendtdorff and Falk Wagner.

"Left-wing" Barthianism first came to prominence with Friedrich Wilhelm Marquardt's *Theologie und Sozialismus*.[85] A student of Helmut Gollwitzer's, Marquardt generated much controversy but failed fully to persuade because of the reductionist way in which he seemed to turn Barth's theology into a mere instrument of his political commitments. Gollwitzer, whom Barth had wanted as his successor, and who was rejected because of his radical politics, remained more judicious than Marquardt. Although he was probably the quintessential "left-wing" Barthian, Gollwitzer did not like to think of himself in that way. He was simply a Barthian, and like most European Barthians, he took strong progressive stands for justice and peace, not only in theology but also in practice.

Other Barthians distinguished themselves in the post-Holocaust era with a concern for Jewish-Christian relations. Marquardt and Gollwitzer were prominent also on this front, and they received the honor of special commendations from Jewish organizations. Eberhard Busch, Barth's great biographer, produced a massive volume on Barth's active solidarity with the Jews during the Nazi reign of terror. Perhaps even more significantly, Berthold Klappert took up the direction that Barth had laid down, developing it in creative ways that have yet to be appreciated in English-language circles.

Barth's stance toward the Jews has been subjected to admirably incisive analysis, both critical and sympathetic, by the American Jewish theologian Michael Wyschogrod. Katherine Sonderegger of Virginia Theological Seminary has also been an important American voice in this discussion. Less well known, though at once exemplary and profound, is Ulrich Simon's *A Theology of Auschwitz*,[86] written by a Barth-influenced theologian who lost close family members, including his father, in the Nazi death camps.

An anthology I edited, *Karl Barth and Radical Politics*, mediated the Marquardt thesis into American discussion. Until that time, American perceptions of Barth's political views were dominated by the interpretations of Reinhold Niebuhr and Will Herberg, who had portrayed Barth as politically irrelevant. Although the anthology seems to have had its greatest impact in South Africa and South Korea (where Reformed churches found themselves in revolutionary situations), it did change the American reception of Barth on this question.

Most recently, Barth's way of combining traditional faith with progressive politics has received a powerful boost from Jeffrey Stout, who argues that Barth shows us how to avoid the "sectarianism" of a Hauerwas and the "authoritarianism" of a Milbank, through a strong confessionalist stance that respects democratic pluralism while working passionately for justice, freedom, and peace.[87]

NOTES

1. James B. Torrance, "Barth, Karl," in *The Encyclopedia of Religion*, ed. Mircea Eliade, 16 vols. (New York: Macmillan, 1987), 2:68.

2. Thomas F. Torrance, "My Interaction with Karl Barth," in *How Karl Barth Changed My Mind*, ed. Donald K. McKim (Grand Rapids, Mich.: Eerdmans, 1986), 61–62.

3. Hans Urs von Balthasar, *The Theology of Karl Barth: Exposition and Interpretation*, trans. Edward T. Oakes (San Francisco: Ignatius Press, 1992), 22–23.

4. Karl Barth, *Gespräche 1964–1968*, ed. Eberhard Busch (Zürich: Theologischer Verlag, 1997), 324.
5. Ibid., 199.
6. Ibid., 100.
7. Torrance, "Barth," 69. See also Eberhard Busch, *Karl Barth: His Life from Letters and Autobiographical Texts*, trans. John Bowden (Philadelphia: Fortress Press, 1976).
8. Karl Barth, *Fragments Grave and Gay*, ed. Martin Rumscheidt, trans. Eric Mosbacher (London: Collins, 1971), 120–121.
9. Ibid., 120.
10. Barth, *Gespräche*, 408.
11. Ibid., 213.
12. Quoted from manuscript notes of an interview between Karl Barth and Margareta Deschner, April 26, 1956, in John Deschner, "Karl Barth as Political Activist," *Union Seminary Quarterly Review* 28 (1972): 56.
13. "The Theological Declaration of Barmen," in Arthur C. Cochrane, *Reformed Confessions of the 16th Century* (Philadelphia: Westminster Press, 1966), 334–336.
14. Ibid., 334.
15. Karl Barth, *Church Dogmatics*, 4 vols. (Edinburgh: T & T Clark, 1936–61), 2:163.
16. Ibid., 1:60.
17. "Theological Declaration of Barmen," 336.
18. Ibid.
19. Ibid., 335.
20. Ibid., 336.
21. Karl Barth, "The Protestant Churches in Europe," *Foreign Affairs* 21 (1943): 260–275.
22. Karl Barth, *The Church and the War*, trans. Antonia H. Froendt (New York: Macmillan, 1944), 12.
23. Ibid.
24. An earlier version of this analysis of Barmen appeared in George Hunsinger, "Barth, Barmen and the Confessing Church Today," *Katallagete* 9, no. 2 (1985): 14–27.
25. Karl Barth, *Community, State and Church: Three Essays* (Garden City, N.Y.: Doubleday, 1960). The essays are "Gospel and Law," "Church and State," and "The Christian Community and the Civil Community."
26. An earlier version of these theses appeared in George Hunsinger, "Karl Barth and Radical Politics: Some Further Considerations," *Studies in Religion/Sciences Religieuses* 7, no. 1 (1978): 167–191.
27. Karl Barth, *Ethics*, ed. Dietrich Braun, trans. Geoffrey W. Bromiley (New York: Seabury, 1981), 517–521.
28. Ibid., 520.
29. Karl Barth, *The Knowledge of God and the Service of God* (New York: Charles Scribner's Sons, 1939).

30. Ibid., 229.

31. Ibid.

32. Ibid., 224.

33. Ibid., 225.

34. Ibid., 230.

35. Ibid., 231.

36. Ibid., 223.

37. Ibid.

38. Ibid., 224.

39. Karl Barth, *Der Römerbrief* (Bern: G. A. Bäschlin, 1919), 381.

40. Ibid., 388.

41. Ibid., 390.

42. Barth, *Gespräche*, 401.

43. Ibid., 506.

44. Karl Barth, "Jesus Christ and the Movement for Social Justice," in *Karl Barth and Radical Politics*, ed. and trans. George Hunsinger (Philadelphia: Westminster Press, 1976), 36.

45. Ibid., 44.

46. Ibid., 19.

47. Ibid.

48. Barth, *Church Dogmatics*, 2:369.

49. Ibid., 386 (translation revised).

50. Ibid., 387.

51. Barth, *Community, State and Church*, 173.

52. Ibid.

53. Ibid.

54. Barth, *Church Dogmatics*, 3:535.

55. Ibid., 538.

56. Ibid., 532.

57. Ibid., 531.

58. Ibid., 531–532.

59. Ibid., 541.

60. Ibid., 532.

61. Ibid.

62. Ibid., 544.

63. Ibid.

64. Karl Barth, "Concluding Unscientific Postscript on Schleiermacher," in *The Theology of Schleiermacher* (Grand Rapids, Mich.: Eerdmans, 1982), 263–264.

65. Ibid., 264.

66. Karl Barth, "Letter to Martin Rade," in *Neue Wege: Blätter für religiöse Arbeit* 8 (1914): 430, quoted in Walter Bense, "The Pacifism of Karl Barth: Some Questions for John H. Yoder," in *The American Society of Christian Ethics, 1977, Selected Papers*, ed. Max L. Stackhouse (Waterloo, Ontario: Council on the Study of Religion, 1977), 63.

67. Barth, "Letter to Martin Rade," 431, quoted in Bense, "Pacifism," 63.

68. Karl Barth, *Predigten 1914*, ed. Ursula and Jochen Fähler (Zürich: Theologischer Verlag, 1974).

69. Karl Barth, *Konfirmandenunterricht, 1909–1921*, ed. Jürgen Fangmeier (Zürich: Theologischer Verlag, 1987), 174.

70. Ibid., 179–180.

71. But see Barth, *Church Dogmatics*, 3:453.

72. John Howard Yoder, *The Pacifism of Karl Barth* (Washington, D.C.: Church Peace Mission, 1964), 16.

73. Barth, *Church Dogmatics*, 3:454–455.

74. Ibid., 456.

75. Ibid., 459.

76. Ibid.

77. Barth, *Church Dogmatics*, 4:549–550.

78. Ibid., 8.

79. Ibid.

80. Ibid., 2:529.

81. Ibid., 530.

82. On this whole question, see Friedrich Lohmann, "Barths Stellung zum Naturrecht," in *Zwischen Naturrecht und Partikularismus: Grundlegung christlicher Ethik mit Blick auf die Debatte um eine universale Begründbarkeit der Menschenrechte* (Berlin: de Gruyter, 2002), 74–80.

83. Barth, "The Christian Community and the Civil Community," 165.

84. Ibid.

85. Friedrich Wilhelm Marquardt, *Theologie und Sozialismus* (Munich: Christian Kaiser Verlag, 1972, rev. 1985).

86. Ulrich Simon, *A Theology of Auschwitz* (Richmond, Va.: John Knox Press, 1979).

87. Jeffrey Stout, *Democracy and Tradition* (Princeton, N.J.: Princeton University Press, 2003).

[CHAPTER 13]

Dietrich Bonhoeffer (1906–1945)

MILNER BALL

In an exceptional act in an exceptional time, Dietrich Bonhoeffer, a German Lutheran theologian and pastor, joined the conspiracy against Adolf Hitler. The Nazis imprisoned and then executed him shortly before the end of World War II.

During his final months, he developed a daring theological interpretation of his life that his closest friend and biographer, Eberhard Bethge, describes as "the relinquishment of a special Christian life and as the acceptance ... of an incognito existence." With this theology, he achieved a breakthrough that reveals "the future normality: 'being for others' as sharing in the suffering of Jesus." His life and work lose their exceptional character and become, as Bethge says, "an example of being Christian today."[1]

A statue of Bonhoeffer is one of ten in Westminster Abbey honoring Christian martyrs of the twentieth century. But the greater living tribute lies in the challenging influence of his example beyond Europe, in places as far flung as America, Latin America, South Africa, and Korea—especially among the embattled and those led by Christ to make responsible use of power on their behalf.

Such influence has been unexpected. It could scarcely have been foreseen from the experimental, incomplete nature of Bonhoeffer's late theology and the need to piece it together from the tantalizing fragments that survived the war and his imprisonment. Nor could it have been predicted from his prior life. He was one of eight children of a privileged German family. He was an accomplished pianist, an elegant dancer, and a theologian with the promise of a brilliant career in the academy. He appeared to be far removed from the suffering of outcasts and the dark politics of military conspiracy when he entered upon his academic career in Berlin in 1931 just after a first visit to the United States. Two events intervened to change the person and the career: Bonhoeffer became a practicing believer who would no longer be merely a theologian, and Germany sank into the furious pathology of the nation-state.

Bonhoeffer was no stranger to war. Although he was too young to fight in World War I—he was born in 1906—he lost a brother in that conflict and lived with the deprivations that followed it. Even so, he could not know from that experience what the next war would bring. As he began to teach and to serve as a pastor, Germany moved toward combat and the Holocaust, and the church in Germany moved toward turmoil and division.

He would soon play a leading role in and be much influenced by the church struggle, the difficult fight for the faithfulness and integrity of the Protestant church in Germany during the Third Reich. A clear line was drawn between the majority German Christians and the minority Confessing Church when the latter adopted the Barmen Declaration in 1934, a decisive confession of faith drafted by Karl Barth. Over against the German Christians and their commitment to Hitler, the Barmen Declaration centrally affirmed that Jesus Christ "is the one Word of God whom we are to hear, whom we are to trust and obey" and that there are no "areas of our life in which we belong not to Jesus Christ but another lord."[2]

The Barmen Declaration was adopted in May 1934. The previous year had been critical for the German Evangelical Church, a federal union of twenty-eight Protestant regional churches of the Lutheran and Reformed traditions. Adolf Hitler took control of the German government in January 1933. In April of that year, anti-Semitism became official German policy with the passage of the Aryan Clause excluding Jews from civil service. Because the German Evangelical Church was a state church, its pastors, including some of Jewish descent, were considered civil servants. Church elections were held in July, and, by an overwhelming majority, German Christians assumed positions of power. A synod held in Prussia that September became known as the Brown Synod because many of the delegates appeared in brown Nazi uniforms.

These developments did not go unchallenged. A Young Reformation movement sprung up in various informal theological circles around the country, including one of Bonhoeffer's to which he delivered a controversial but prescient paper arguing that the Jewish Question was critical for the church. He and others then drafted the Bethel Confession, which was so watered down in the process of circulation and adoption that he refused to sign the final version. But shortly afterward, in response to the Brown Synod, Bonhoeffer and pastor Martin Niemöller wrote a protest to the Aryan Clause that, surprisingly, drew the signatures of two thousand pastors and gave birth to the Pastors' Emergency League. The League soon elected for its leadership a Council of Brethren that would persevere to the end of the Nazi period.

Bonhoeffer assumed pastorates in London in October 1933 and did not take part in the following year's Barmen Synod, which produced the Barmen Declaration and the formation of the Confessing Church. However, throughout his time in London, Bonhoeffer kept in close contact with the Confessing Church through correspondence, telephone calls, and visits home. His London congregations aligned themselves with the Confessing Church, and he represented that body's cause in ecumenical circles, an activity that led to his important friendship with the Anglican bishop of Chichester, George K. A. Bell.

In Germany, insistence on Aryan purity and adherence to the party line increasingly would be accompanied by regulations and intimidation and by the arrest and eventually the torture and murder of resisters. Already in 1934, nonconforming seminaries were forced to close, and the Confessing Church set about establishing its own, illegal preachers' seminaries. Bonhoeffer returned from London in 1935 to become the founding director of one of these seminaries, which eventually settled out of the way in Finkenwalde, in what was then northern Germany and is now Poland. It attracted an initial class of twenty-three students and an assistant director, Wilhelm Rott.

As Bonhoeffer developed it, Finkenwalde had the Bible at the center of its learning and living, and it featured monastic intensity, a common life, service, meditation, debate, and evangelism. Bonhoeffer was thoroughly devoted to his responsibilities and to his students. He wrote his book *Discipleship* during his years there, and his subsequent *Life Together* has the Finkenwalde discipline as its subject. The Gestapo closed the Finkenwalde seminary in 1937. Bonhoeffer carried on the work as best he could by various means in one remote place after another until the police again closed it down, and he was again forced to move. When war and persecution took over, Bonhoeffer visited, wrote, and supported his former students as long as he was able, even after military conscription became the rule and his students were sent to the front (80 of the 150 alumni would die in action).

Persecution from the outside, erosion from the inside, nationalism, war fever, and the war exacted a heavy toll on the Confessing Church and its will to resist. Already in 1938 many Confessing pastors took an oath of faith in and obedience to Hitler. Eberhard Bethge, a Finkenwalde alumnus, said it was during this year that "Bonhoeffer began to distance himself from the rearguard actions of the Confessing Church's defeated remnants."[3] War broke out shortly after he returned from a hasty second trip to the United States in 1939.

Bonhoeffer had undertaken that trip to the United States to lecture and teach for a year. After a few agonizing weeks, however, he cut the visit short and returned home. He wrote a letter of explanation to Reinhold Niebuhr, who had sponsored the visit together with Paul Lehmann, Bonhoeffer's best American friend:

> I have come to the conclusion that I have made a mistake in coming to America. I must live through this difficult period of our national history with the Christian people of Germany. I will have no right to participate in the reconstruction of Christian life in Germany after the war if I do not share the trials of this time with my people.... Christians in Germany will face the terrible alternative of either willing the defeat of their nation in order that Christian civilization may survive, or willing the victory of their nation and thereby destroying our civilization. I know which of these alternatives I must choose; but I cannot make that choice in security.... [4]

Back in Germany in 1939, Bonhoeffer soon found himself led into relationships that were well beyond the limits of anything he had been prepared for by his community and the Lutheran tradition. He joined the active conspiracy against Hitler and became a double agent in the employ of the Abwehr, the Nazi military's counterintelligence agency. The use of his ecumenical, international church connections became part of his contribution to the resistance and, at the same time, served as cover in explaining his travels to Nazi authorities.

"The year 1932 had placed Bonhoeffer in a world where things were comparatively clear-cut, where it was a matter of confessing and denying," Eberhard Bethge observed. "In 1939 he entered the difficult world of assessing what was expedient—of success and failure, tactics and camouflage."[5] Then he arrived at the "last stage: active conspiracy. For members of the Lutheran tradition this was the most difficult, since their tradition allowed for nothing of this kind. In this final stage the church offered no protection and no prior justification for something that fell outside all normal contingencies."[6]

In an affirmation of hope for the future, Bonhoeffer became engaged to Maria von Wedemeyer in January 1943. In April of that year he was arrested and jailed. He would not be released. The extent of his involvement in the conspiracy came to light after an attempt to assassinate Hitler failed on July 20, 1944.[7] Bonhoeffer was convicted of treason. On Hitler's orders he was hanged on April 9, 1945. The nation-state's butchering apparatus that had slaughtered so many people ground on through the chaos of the last days of World War II destroying many more, including not only Dietrich but also another of his brothers and two brothers-in-law. Hitler killed himself on April 30, 1945, and Germany surrendered on May 7.

Bonhoeffer did not arrive readily at his conspiratorial action or its accompanying theology. His first theological heritage was that of the typical, nineteenth-century liberal theology of the German Lutheran tradition, represented by Adolf von Harnack and Reinhold Seeberg, his teachers at Berlin University, where he had transferred after a year of study at the University of Tübingen. He soon found his thinking reoriented by Swiss theologian Karl Barth. Bonhoeffer read Barth long before he met him, a delay in personal contact that he sorely regretted. Although he was deeply indebted to Barth, and Barth praised Bonhoeffer's work, these two great Protestant theologians had their differences. In a letter from prison, Bonhoeffer made the stinging, undeserved remark that Barth's theology was "a positivism of revelation."[8]

Bonhoeffer also learned from American theologians. His initial trip to America in 1930–31 brought him to Union Theological Seminary in New York. There he studied with Reinhold Niebuhr and met Paul Lehmann. Bonhoeffer detected in Niebuhr "a lack of foundational strength in Christology," but he certainly took to heart the admonition Niebuhr wrote on one of Bonhoeffer's papers: "Obedience to God's will may be a religious experience but is not an ethical one until it issues in actions that can be socially valued."[9] Lehmann, too, gave him a thorough grounding in the political theology that figured in Bonhoeffer's own later turn to politics. Lehmann[10] and the lawyer William Stringfellow are good American representatives of those essential commitments and qualities that they had in common with Bonhoeffer. (Stringfellow had no direct connection with him.)

While he was a student in New York, Bonhoeffer was a regular participant at the Abyssinian Baptist Church, whose minister was Adam Clayton Powell. That experience gave him a deep, abiding appreciation of the black church and of the struggle of African Americans against racist oppression.

The postwar American reception of Bonhoeffer's theology was like that elsewhere. His letters and papers from prison were first published in German in the winter of 1951–52 and were greeted with surprise. A few studies of them became available in English beginning in the late 1950s. The 1960s brought some enthusiastic misinterpretation, like that of William Hamilton, who claimed that Bonhoeffer was the "father of the God-is-Dead theology."[11] Bishop John A. T. Robinson's 1963 book *Honest to God* dramatically popularized Bonhoeffer's work,[12] and Harvey Cox's widely read *The Secular City* (1965) was a theologically sound response to and development of Bonhoeffer's insights in the American context.[13]

The subject of most attention has been Bonhoeffer's post-1939 life and writings, the pieces that compose his never-completed *Ethics* and the *Letters and Papers from Prison*. Two earlier works, *Discipleship* (1937) and *Life*

Together (1938), have proven equally important both for their independent contributions and for the revealing counterweight they provide to the later material.[14] His doctoral thesis, *The Communion of Saints* (1927), and the dissertation (*Habilitationschrift*) required for professorships, *Act and Being* (1931), are necessary to a thorough understanding of Bonhoeffer, and they made major contributions to theology.[15]

Eberhard Bethge was first Bonhoeffer's student, then his friend and colleague, and last his correspondent. His *Dietrich Bonhoeffer* is a remarkable achievement in its own right and is indispensable to an understanding of the life and work of its subject.

Bonhoeffer's thinking and acting have less to teach about legal theory or law and politics in the abstract than they do about using the power of law and politics, about God's use of this power and ours. Readers of Bonhoeffer's writings must be prepared both for the fragmentary, incomplete quality of the later material and for what appears to be its indulgence in contradiction. Enough does remain of his late work to provide a reliable path into the abiding challenge of his thinking, and its unfinished exploration of new territory may be taken as an invitation to carry the journey forward in our own way in our own generation. The seeming contradictions are in fact the dialectics—the simultaneous "yes" and "no"—made necessary by his venture in theology. Bonhoeffer spoke of a religionless Christianity in a world come of age, a secret discipline that enables public action, God's power as powerlessness in the world, the worldliness of believers, Christ as reality embracing all things human, and God's commandment as freeing. Bonhoeffer was developing a language for the future, and, as we have entered further into that future, it is likely that our capacity for dialectics and our need of them have increased. For us, too, there is cause both to embrace the contemporary world's vast, humanizing capacities and to reject its dehumanizing tendency.

Whatever the changes and developments that took place in Bonhoeffer's thinking and living, and however incomplete, fragmentary, or novel his later writing may be, Christ was perennially at the center. Bonhoeffer concluded his academic life with a series of lectures at the University of Berlin in the turbulent summer of 1933, not long after Hitler had become chancellor and a series of actions against Jews followed. The lectures were devoted to an exploration of christology. Although Christ was presently hidden and humiliated, Bonhoeffer declared, Christ "is the center of human existence, the center of history, and ... the center of nature.... The human who I am, Jesus has also been. Of him only is it valid to say that nothing human was alien to him. Of him, we say: 'This is God for us.'"[16] Kelly and Nelson observe that in these lectures Bonhoeffer's "life and his theology appeared to converge.... Christ in all the robustness of the prophetic Sermon on the Mount now stood at the very center of Bonhoeffer's vocation as a minister."[17]

CRITIQUE OF RELIGION

Bonhoeffer was familiar with Ludwig Feuerbach's critique of religion and his questions about the veracity of religion's assertions and about its concurrence with real life, questions that the liberal theology of the nineteenth century had not answered.[18] It was not Feuerbach, however, but Karl Barth whose work chiefly animated Bonhoeffer's approach. Barth's *The Word of God and the Word of Man* and his commentary on the epistle to the Romans introduced theological critique to the twentieth century. Barth said that religion is "a misfortune which takes fatal hold upon some men, and is by them passed on to others.... It is the misfortune ... which laid upon Calvin's face that look which he bore at the end of his life."[19] In Barth's estimation, religion is humans' constricting, fruitless effort to justify themselves before a capricious picture of a highest being of their own imagining.[20]

Bonhoeffer agreed and believed that bringing in "against religion the God of Jesus Christ ... remains [Barth's] greatest service."[21] But Bonhoeffer also judged that Barth's thinking about religionless Christianity was incomplete. Thus, late in his short life, Bonhoeffer undertook his own, more daring exploration of the subject. As it turned out, his thinking, too, would be incomplete. He had no chance, for example, to spell out exactly what he meant by "religion." And, as Eberhard Bethge warned, although Bonhoeffer "certainly went beyond Barth ... he had not sufficiently considered how disturbing all this was."[22] Certainly when Bonhoeffer first became popular in America, and when little was known about the full scope of his work, the available experimental material was vulnerable to superficial interpretation.

Readers today are far less likely to be disturbed by Bonhoeffer's views on religion than they are to be initially puzzled and then challenged by his distinction between the biblical faith and religion. For Bonhoeffer, the priority and centrality of Christ lead to worldliness. A late letter from prison stated his central concern: "What is bothering me incessantly is the question what Christianity really is, or who Christ really is, for us today.... We are moving towards a completely religionless time."[23] The issue for Bonhoeffer is not Christ's absence but how to discern, state, and be faithful to Christ's presence in an increasingly secular world whose secularity is to be justly celebrated.

Bonhoeffer opposed the diversionary power of religion. Jesus calls a person, he believed, "not to a new religion, but to life."[24] Religion directs people away from life, away from reality. It directs us to a God beyond the boundaries of human experience and away from the God at work in the world. As human knowledge and strength push the boundaries further out, the God of religion becomes more and more distant. Religion then struggles to preserve itself. It must save a domain for its God. To contend with God's increasing distance, it summons God from outside human boundaries as a *deus ex machina*. It summons God "either for the apparent solution of insoluble problems, or as a strength in human weakness."[25] But this approach requires selling people the idea that they have the problems for which this God is the solution. It addresses and exploits peoples' weakness rather than speaking to their strength, and it makes God dependent on our needs and limits.

The companion strategy is to attempt to secure an inner domain for God in the individual's private sphere.[26] This move assumes both that individuals "can be addressed as sinners only after their weaknesses and meannesses have been spied out" and that their "essential nature consists of their inmost and most intimate background" rather than their public lives and relationships, as though "Goethe and Napoleon [were] sinners because they weren't faithful husbands."[27] This strategy, too, is demeaning and divisive. It emphasizes the sins of weakness when it is the sins of strength that matter, and, contrary to the biblical witness that takes people as wholes, it divides the inner life from the outer life and privileges the former. It tries to save space for God in personal, secret places.

Bonhoeffer thought that Christianity was perhaps the truest form of religion. He therefore tried to imagine what the consequences would be if religion proved to be a historically conditioned, transient phenomenon and not, as Barth thought, a continuing characteristic of believers. What would it mean if humans, Christians especially, were to become religionless? Bonhoeffer did not ask what a secular world would be like without Christ; he asked who Christ is in such a secular world.

This question precipitated others: "If our final judgment must be that the western form of Christianity, too, was only a preliminary stage to a complete absence of religion, what kind of situation emerges for us, for the church? How can Christ become the Lord of the religionless as well?" "What is a religionless Christianity?" "How do we speak of God—without religion?" "In what way are we 'religionless-secular' Christians?" In this latter case, "Christ is no longer an object of religion, but something quite different, really the Lord of the world. But what does that mean? What is the place of worship and prayer in religionless situation?"[28]

Bonhoeffer only started to answer these questions. As he put it:

> I ... want to start from the premise that God shouldn't be smuggled into some last secret place, but that we should frankly recognize that the world, and people, have come of age, that we shouldn't run people down in their worldli-

ness, but confront them with God at their strongest point, that we should give up all of our clerical tricks, and not regard psychotherapy and existentialist philosophy as God's pioneers.... The Word of God is far removed from this revolt of mistrust.... On the contrary, it reigns.[29]

THE WORLD COME OF AGE

Bonhoeffer saw signs that the world was in process of becoming religion-less, of outgrowing its ward-guardian relationship with the God of religion. He described what he saw variously as a "world come of age," a "world that has come of age," and a "world coming of age."[30] Bonhoeffer seems to have been developing a realistic, theological language and way of thinking about the relation of God to the world. He thought it possible that doing away with a religious, "false conception of God, opens up a way of seeing the God of the Bible."[31] He thought that a world come of age would perhaps be closer to God exactly because it is "more godless."[32] In a 1944 message from prison, he indicated that, in a godless world, people "will once more be called so to utter the word of God that the world will be changed and renewed by it. It will be a new language, perhaps quite nonreligious, but liberating and redeeming—as was Jesus' language; it will shock people and yet overcome them by its power."[33]

Bonhoeffer intended nothing shallow by his talk of religionlessness, nothing like the "banal this-worldliness of the enlightened, the busy, the comfortable or the lascivious." Instead, he intended "the profound this-worldliness characterized by discipline and the constant knowledge of death and resurrection."[34] Living in the belly of Nazi Germany did not al-low him the luxury of dreaming that a world come of age would be a ro-mantic idyll. This was to be a religionless world, not a sinless one. It was to be a world in which mature people accept responsibility. Bethge helpfully points out that Bonhoeffer had been using the term "autonomy" until it was replaced in his writing by the notion of "coming of age" and that this change of terms indicated his engagement with Kant's proposal that "the Enlightenment is the emergence of humanity from self-imposed immatu-rity. Immaturity is the incapacity to use one's own intelligence without the guidance of another person."[35] In a world come of age, humanity develops its own resources for taking responsibility. Christ has freed us for politics, for science, and for the liberal arts.[36]

In Bonhoeffer's thinking, this was a profound theological issue. The secularization of the world requires that we live in it without the working hypothesis of God, "that we have to live in the world *etsi deus non daretur.* And this is just what we do recognize—before God! God compels us to recognize it. So our coming of age leads us to a true recognition of our situation before God. God would have us know that we must live as people who manage their lives without him."[37]

The church is thereby placed in a radically different role. Instead of addressing us in our weakness, which the religious message exploits, she confronts us in our strength and responsibility and encourages and nurtures them. The church can no longer, as Bethge puts it, "demonize worldliness, instead of helping human beings realize their true humanity."[38] And the church can no longer be a religious sanctuary to which people flee from the world. The church and the Christian, like Jesus, must enter the world fully and responsibly.

But, also like Jesus, the Christian's commitment to the world must have no share in triumphalism. Humans' realization of their true humanity, their taking responsibility, is given expression in the crucifixion. Because Christ is the person for others, his is the form that will mark us and our acting. Religiosity makes us look in our distress "to the power of God in the world: God is the *deus ex machina*. The Bible directs humans to God's powerlessness and suffering; only the suffering God can help."[39]

Because God is in the midst of the world in the form of the crucified Jesus, our relation to God is not a religious, falsely transcendent relation to a highest, most powerful, supreme being. Instead "our relation to God is a new life in 'existence for others,' through participation in the being of Jesus. The transcendental is not infinite and unattainable tasks, but the neighbor who is within reach in any given situation."[40] And our relation to our neighbors is correspondingly liberated from any need to trick or dominate them.

THE ARCANE DISCIPLINE

For persons to be set free for others, to become secular or worldly in this way, did not mean that they must abandon the worship that was critical to their understanding, action, and identity. To the contrary, their thinking and life must exhibit the ongoing interaction between discipleship and secularity.

Bonhoeffer had begun to reach this understanding already early in his life. His friends detected a change in him after his 1930–31 stay in the United States. He was in process of becoming a fully committed believer and not merely a theologian. He adopted a daily discipline of prayer, meditation, and reflective study of the Bible that he maintained for the rest of his life. (In 1942 he expressed amazement that, in the complexities of his theological and conspiratorial work, he could live for days without reading the Bible. He also found that reopening its pages was always accompanied by fresh wonder.)[41]

He came to speak of the *arcanum* of the Christian, the "arcane" or "secret discipline." The term originally referred to the early church's practice of admitting only baptized members to the celebration of the sacrament of the Lord's Supper. Such withdrawal of the community into a secret place appears to be the very kind of separation and retreat from the world that Bonhoeffer criticized as a fault of religion. There is no simple way to resolve the contradiction.

Prayer, worship, and the Bible nourished his exploration of worldliness and nonreligious Christianity. He maintained an incognito existence in the resistance movement in full solidarity with the other conspirators and at the same time practiced the arcane discipline of the Christian. His life was a performance of what he meant by the arcane and the worldly and their interdependence.

In Bonhoeffer's view, the church is not to be the world. It is to maintain its independent identity. The Confessing Church in Germany was, after all, *confessional*. It had a creed and made its confession of faith in the Barmen Declaration. It broke with other German Christians because the latter abandoned their creedal identity and surrendered to the world. The hard core of specific, theological, creedal commitment had been a focus of Bonhoeffer's from the start. He thought that the liberal theology of his German teachers wrongly allowed the world to set the church's agenda. And one of his concerns about the church in America was its self-conception as primarily denominational rather than as a church, as constituted not so much by creed as by culture, liturgy, community life, and organization.[42] In Germany, the creedal commitment of the Confessing Church required it to resist and strengthened it to do so.

Bonhoeffer did not think that religionlessness required abandonment of such distinguishing, creedal commitment. When the church is led into worldliness in a world come of age and is given a new language for addressing that world, it will still be identified as the church. Until then, the church maintains the traditional discipline in the traditional terms within the *arcanum* and is silent about it outside.

One function of the silence outside is what Bethge refers to as protection of "the world ... from violation by religion."[43] Bonhoeffer's experience in prison provides an example of the point. In the midst of a bombing raid a fellow prisoner lay on the floor, exclaiming, "O God, O God!" Bonhoeffer offered no religious comfort: "All I did was to look at my watch and say, 'It won't last more than ten minutes now.' ... I felt that it was wrong to force religion down his throat just then."[44]

Silence outside the *arcanum* also serves to cultivate solidarity with others. In the confusion in Germany as the war was ending, prisoners were haphazardly shuffled from one sometimes makeshift prison to another. Bonhoeffer was thrown together with a Russian, Kokorin, the nephew of the Communist leader Molotov. The day before Bonhoeffer would be executed was the Sunday after Easter. A fellow prisoner asked that he conduct worship. Reportedly he was reluctant to do so. Kokorin was an atheist, and as Bethge reports, Bonhoeffer "didn't want to ambush him with a worship service."[45] But at the request of other prisoners and with Kokorin's approval, he led the service.

In the meantime, awaiting an adequate language for addressing a world come of age, the traditional arcane discipline will continue to nourish believers in a way that "cannot be propagated or demonstrated externally."[46] This is a further and critical reason for silence outside the *arcanum*: the preservation of the integrity of the biblical story and the identity of the church. The mysteries of the faith must be defended against cheap and misleading public distribution.

The danger here is that protective secrecy creates exclusiveness and privilege. The hope is that the action of the discipline itself does not tolerate them: "In the *arcanum*," Bethge points out, "Christ takes everyone who really encounters him by the shoulder, turning them around to face their fellow human beings and the world."[47] Preservation of the mysteries paradoxically dismantles barriers. "In other words," he says, "the 'ultimate' is praised with the initiates gathered together, so that in the 'penultimate' stage there can be a share in godlessness. Christ prays a cultic psalm and dies a profane death."[48]

The interplay of "arcane discipline" and "worldliness" presented in Bonhoeffer's writings was climactically enacted in the last two days of his life. On Sunday, he led the worship that included an atheist. On Monday, he prayed before he was profanely hanged. His final recorded words, a message sent to a friend through a fellow prisoner: "This is the end—for me the beginning of life."[49]

ACTION

Bonhoeffer said that confession of faith is not to be confused with professing a religion. He thought the latter turned confession into propagandistic ammunition against the godless. Confession belongs in the *arcanum*. Outside of that context, the "primary confession of the Christian before the world is the deed which interprets itself.... The deed alone is our confession of faith before the world."[50] If neighbors are hungry, feed them. Neither evangelistic propaganda nor explanation accompanies the deed. To turn an act into a religious pitch, "running after people, proselytizing, every attempt to accomplish something in another person by our own power is vain and dangerous."[51]

It would certainly have been futile and dangerous for Bonhoeffer to attempt to explain his conspiracy against Hitler, or even to disclose his involvement in it to anyone other than a fellow conspirator. He could only act in the circumstance without interpreting the deed. Although in this "'inner exile' where he could no longer justify his actions before his church and fellow pastors,"[52] Bonhoeffer could nonetheless offer his fellow conspirators an encouraging, supportive interpretation of their actions. He did so in the form of an essay, "After Ten Years," done as a Christmas gift for them in 1942.[53]

When action requires the use of power, then "power enters the service of responsibility."[54] Bethge observes that, after the failure of a first coup attempt against Hitler, it became clear to the pacifist Bonhoeffer that "any opposition serious about stopping Hitler had to ensure that it held the instruments of power; only this could restrain him."[55] The necessary power was that of the army, and a military plot would be necessary to deploy it.

This was an extreme situation requiring extreme measures, but Bonhoeffer had no interest in a heroic ethics. He made it clear that action and the use of various forms of power belong to ordinary people in ordinary times. Wherever one person meets another, he said, "there arises genuine responsibility."[56] All the regular, diverse encounters that take place in our callings as parents, citizens, and laborers are occasions for responsible use of power.

God is fully and particularly in the world and engaged in its events. Hearing the call of Christ within our callings and acting in response to it in any given situation begins sensibly with an assessment of the facts, "a serious weighing up of the vocational duty which is directly given, of the dangers of interference in the responsibility of others, and finally the totality of the question which is involved."[57] This factual analysis is to be distinguished from the continuous hand-wringing of moralists who "assume that a person must continuously be doing something decisive, fulfilling some higher purpose."[58] It is instead "to recognize the significant in the factual."[59]

Bonhoeffer's unfinished essay on telling the truth, written during a period when he was under intense prison interrogation, is a good example of what factual assessment of a situation amounts to. "The more complex the actual situations of a person, the more responsible and more difficult will be the task of 'telling the truth,'" he wrote. "Telling the truth is, therefore, something which must be learnt."[60] It is no simple matter. Another example is Bonhoeffer's change of approach to the details of resistance. Early on, he had urged pastors and others to demonstrate their opposition publicly. But, as more members of the opposition were discharged from their positions, there was greater need for "people of character" to "remain at the controls at all costs and not let themselves be pushed out. That meant that things which had been issues of character now became mere bagatelles—greeting with the Hitler salute, for instance. Even if it meant giving up a 'clean slate,' they had to try to get into key positions. The use of camouflage became a moral duty."[61]

The process of weighing and judging the facts in a situation might well bar some courses of action and open others. It is a necessary start but will seldom yield a determinative answer of what to do—what to say to speak the truth, whether to give the Hitler salute, and the like. Rules, regulations, and principles provide no answer, and there is no guidebook. Nor is conscience a guide. Bonhoeffer discovered that "people whose only support is their conscience can never realize that a bad conscience may be stronger and more wholesome than a deluded one."[62] The use of camouflage as a moral duty is a recipe for a bad if healthy conscience.

After assessing the facts and possibilities of a given situation, Bonhoeffer said, "I shall be guided in the one direction or the other by a free responsibility towards the call of Jesus Christ."[63] The "I shall be guided" engages the whole person and the full range of apperception, intuition, and sensibility. It is not mysterious to people nourished by the arcane discipline. It is a function of the interaction of responsibility and freedom: the responsibility that is "the freedom of humans ... given only in the obligation to God and our neighbor."[64] Even conscience is set free; it is free "to enter into the guilt of another person for the other person's sake."[65]

Assessment of facts and the guidance that comes with it lack mystery, but they do not lack ambiguity. Ambiguity remains because our decisions are not made for us. Our binding to God and our neighbor really does free us to take responsibility. Given ambiguity, we nonetheless take action. "Responsible action is a free venture; it is not justified by any law; it is performed without any claim to a valid self-justification, and therefore also without any claim to an ultimate valid knowledge of good and evil."[66] Succumbing to the temptation to know good and evil was the originating sin. Because we have been freed to act for others in response to the call of Christ and because we are free to accept responsibility where ambiguity accompanies the need for action, we are also free to accept guilt.

Free responsibility "depends on a God who demands responsible action in a bold venture of faith, and who promises forgiveness and consolation to the person who becomes a sinner in that venture."[67] So we seek forgiveness in place of self-justification. And although forgiveness is not cheaply given, it is freely given, thus making public action possible. As Jean Bethke Elshtain puts it: One "acts in full knowledge of guilt. One knows one cannot expiate the wrong one has committed. But one embraces forgiveness—what Hannah Arendt calls Christianity's greatest contribution to politics."[68]

Our relation to God is not religious. It is "a new life in 'existence for others,' through participation in the being of Jesus."[69] We are not to apply Christ's teachings directly to the world, and we are certainly not to apply "Christian principles." Rather, nurtured by the arcane discipline, we take freely responsible action when we are "drawn in into the form of Jesus Christ ... when the form of Jesus Christ itself works upon us in such a manner that it molds our form in its own likeness."[70]

No deus ex machina appeared in Hitler's Germany. Bonhoeffer had to act. He did not shrink from using power and taking responsibility for it. He assumed the guilt of conspiracy and died a profane death. No deus ex machina appeared, but God was there, in the thick of the action.

> The God who lets us live in the world without the working hypothesis of God is the God before whom we stand continually. Before God and with God we live without God. God lets himself be pushed out of the world on to the cross. He is weak and powerless in the world, and that is precisely the way, the only way, in which he is with us and helps us.[71]

THE NATURAL

Imprisonment sharpened Bonhoeffer's appreciation of the natural world. In a letter to his parents he recorded the intense pleasure he took from permitted walks in the prison yard with its nesting tomtits, anthill, and bees. But he also told them that the prisoner "may react too strongly to anything sentimental that affects him personally," and he should take "a cold shower of common sense and humor, to avoid losing his sense of proportion." He added, "I believe it is just here that Christianity, rightly understood, can help particularly."[72]

His unsentimental appreciation of the natural arose out of an understanding of nature as penultimate, the thing before the last, the preparation for the coming of Christ. "With respect to its origin," he wrote, the natural world "is called creation." "With respect to its goal it is called the 'kingdom of God.'"[73] By deriving his understanding of nature from the priority of Christ, Bonhoeffer joined Barth in recovering the category of the natural from a stern Protestant theology that had made nature the antithesis of grace. In Bonhoeffer's view, the natural is opposed to the unnatural and not to grace. It enjoys a positive relation to grace. Bonhoeffer also joined Barth in opposing the Roman Catholic regard for nature based on an analogy of being between the natural world and God. He believed that respect for nature is grounded in christology: "The natural is that which, after the Fall, is directed toward the coming of Christ."[74]

Because it is penultimate, nature cannot rule us in any of its forms, including that of natural law. But, because it is penultimate, nature is an end as well as a means and is to be cherished rather than exploited. As "the outer covering of the ultimate," nature has its own time and place supplied by Christ the ultimate.[75]

Nature prepares the way for the coming of the kingdom of God, and since that kingdom is always near at hand, natural life is an expectant political one. It is lived in a nexus of responsibility for others: "To provide the hungry person with bread is to prepare the way for the coming of grace."[76] Bonhoeffer was very careful in his expression of the obligations the natural entails. He said that "natural life must be lived within the framework of certain definite rights and certain definite duties." The order in his formula is critical. It constitutes a rejection of the order proposed by Kant who spoke first of duties and only later of rights. Bonhoeffer insisted on the biblical witness in which what is given to life comes first. What is demanded comes after. "God gives before he demands."[77]

REALITY

The worldly life, the arcane life, the responsibly active life, the natural life—these are all ways of talking about the human life that life in Christ is.[78] "To be Christian does not mean to be religious in a particular way, to make something of oneself ... on the basis of some method or other, but to be human—not a type of human, but the human that Christ creates in us."[79] The human so created is authentically human. This is who we truly are and who we are meant to be. In this way, "the irreconcilable conflict between what is and what should be is reconciled in Christ, that is to say, in the ultimate reality."[80]

Bonhoeffer cautioned that in order to think about reality and the really human, it "is necessary to free oneself from the way of thinking which sets out from human problems and which asks for solutions on this basis." We must abandon the religious way of thinking that allows the penultimate to set the agenda for the ultimate and restrict discussion to what we think our needs to be. "The way of Jesus Christ, and therefore the way to all Christian thinking, leads not from the world to God but from God to the world."[81] We begin with the reality of God. And since the reality of God "has become manifest in Christ in the reality of the world," we cannot partake of one apart from the other anymore than we can divide the divinity of Christ from his humanity.[82] There is not a godly sphere separate from a worldly sphere. There is the one reality of Christ.

What we know of God, we know from Jesus. He is the reality of God in the world.

Jesus is also the reality of the human in the world. "Theologically expressed, human beings only know who they are from the perspective of God."[83] In Jesus we see the human from the perspective of God. We see who we authentically are. And to be conformed with him, Bonhoeffer says, "that is to be a real person."[84]

The human reality of Christ in the world is always social.[85] Christ takes form in the church. "So the Church is not a religious community of worshipers of Christ but is Christ himself who has taken form among people."[86] One can never become a new person, one conformed with Christ, as a solitary individual. One becomes a member of the body of Christ. "The new person is not the individual believer who has been justified and sanctified, but the Church, the Body of Christ, Christ himself."[87] The church, Bonhoeffer concludes, is "nothing but a section of humanity in which Christ has really taken form."[88] As the form of Christ, the church cannot separate itself from the world. It summons "the world into the fellowship of this body of Christ, to which in truth [the world] already belongs." Its sole difference from the world is the fact that it affirms in faith "God's acceptance of [all humanity] which is the property of the whole world."[89]

THE COMMANDMENT OF GOD

In his 1937 book *Discipleship*, Bonhoeffer said that following Jesus liberates people "from the hard yoke of their own laws" and allows them to submit "to the kindly yoke of Jesus Christ"—but only by single-mindedly following his command to absolute discipleship.[90] Grace is costly because it requires submission to Christ; it is grace because the burden is light.[91] Paul Lehmann detected a certain scorn of the world, an ultra-Lutheranism, just below the surface of this book.[92]

In a 1944 letter to Eberhard Bethge, Bonhoeffer said he could now see that *Discipleship* had marked the end of a long period during which he had sought to "acquire faith by trying to live a holy life" and that he had subsequently learned how it is "only by living completely in this world that one learns to have faith."[93] He said he could see dangers in the book even though he still stood by it.

Lehmann suggested that the difference between *Discipleship* and the later, unfinished writings was Bonhoeffer's steady preoccupation with "the dialectic between faith and worldliness." He proposed that Bonhoeffer had increasingly moved from "response to the Lordship of Christ in the church to response to the Lordship of Christ in and over the world."[94] In Bonhoeffer's late work, the command of God together with what he called "mandates" become references for Christ's worldly lordship and the worldliness of his disciples.

This movement is reflected in Bonhoeffer's reflections on the church's uses of the law.[95] In the Lutheran tradition, there are three uses of this law in Christian preaching: (1) believers' accomplishment of external works; (2) their recognition of their opposition to the law and their just condemnation; and (3) "as a rule of conduct for converts and as a punishment for the flesh."[96] The first use of the law, Bonhoeffer said, demonstrates that the church "does not leave the world to its own devices."[97] It is directed to secular institutions rather than to Christians in secular institutions, and "is not concerned with the christianizing of the secular institutions or with subordinating them to the Church, that is to say, with abolishing their relative autonomy; it is concerned rather with their true worldliness or 'naturalness' in obedience to God's word."[98]

The commandment of God is not a negation of the world but an affirmation of Christ's dominion in and over it. Besides forbidding and commanding, God's law joins the gospel in freeing us for action in the world. It is different "from all human laws in that it commands freedom"; it frees the person to live in the world as a person before God—as a person rather than "as a taker of ethical decisions or as a student of ethics."[99] We need not play Hercules at the crossroads, always striving to make the right decision, for the commandment frees us from the anxiety of decision making.[100] It sets us free by binding us.

Marriage is an example of Bonhoeffer's point.[101] With the binding of one person to another in marriage, understood as an institution mandated by God, "there comes an inner freedom ... of life and action." The divine prohibition of adultery removes that subject as a preoccupying issue, and in the process the command becomes the liberating "permission to live in marriage in freedom and certainty."[102]

Psalm 119 is an artfully wrought, long poem on the law. Bonhoeffer had hoped to write on it but was able to complete meditations on only some of its verses, including verse 19: "I am a sojourner on earth; hide not thy commandments from me!" A comment he makes in response to this poem captures his understanding of God's commandment as freeing us for worldly life:

> The earth that nourishes me has a right to my work and my strength. It is not fitting that I should despise the earth on which I have my life; I owe it faithfulness and gratitude. I must not dream away my earthly life with thoughts of

heaven and thereby evade my lot—that I must be a sojourner and a stranger—and with it God's call into the world of strangers. There is a very godless homesickness for the other world, and it will certainly not produce any homecoming. I am to be a sojourner, with everything that entails. I should not close my heart indifferently to earth's problems, sorrows and joys; and I am to wait patiently for the redemption of the divine promise—really wait, and not rob myself of it in advance by wishing and dreaming.[103]

MANDATES

God's commandment is "clear, definite and concrete to the last detail," Bonhoeffer said, and it comes to us in one form as "mandates."[104] There are principally four mandates understood from the Bible and history to be the will of God: family, labor, government, and church.[105] They allow us to live in the world with security and quietude in the regular flow of daily life without necessarily being always aware of the commandment.

The bearers of the mandates are deputies of God, and we owe them the duty of obedience.[106] Nevertheless, in fulfilling our mandated duties, we are to remember that it is not the duties themselves or the bearer of the mandate but Christ who calls us. And Christ's call "is never a sanctioning of worldly institutions as such; its 'yes' to them always includes at the same time an extremely emphatic 'no,' an extremely sharp protest against the world."[107] Accordingly, where a particular instance of labor, marriage, government or church "persistently and arbitrarily violates the assigned task, then the divine mandate lapses" in that instance.[108]

THE MANDATE OF GOVERNMENT

According to Bonhoeffer, the concept of the state is pagan in origin, and the New Testament replaces it with the concept of "government." The latter implies no particular form of state. Government, he says, is "the power which creates and maintains order," and is the "divinely ordained authority to exercise worldly dominion by divine right. Government is deputyship for God on earth."[109]

Bonhoeffer thereby abandoned traditional stances of both Roman Catholic and Reformation theology. Roman Catholic theology viewed the state as derived from creation and human nature. The Reformation tradition thought it to originate in response to sin. Bonhoeffer held that "the true basis of government is ... Jesus Christ Himself"—Christ, rather than natural law.[110]

Although government "cannot itself produce or engender life" and "is not creative," it is preservative.[111] Government serves Christ's dominion on earth "in maintaining by the power of the sword an outward justice in which life is preserved and is thus held open for Christ." For Christ's sake, government is to be obeyed, and the "demand for obedience is unconditional and qualitatively total."[112]

Obedience for Christ's sake is required quite apart from the way any particular form of government comes into being. Government is an institution of God no matter if the human path to governmental office "repeatedly passes through guilt, no matter if almost every crown is stained with guilt (cf. Shakespeare's histories)."[113] And the citizen-believer enjoys no luxury of ethical isolation from a share in the guilt. "There is no glory in standing amid the ruins of one's native town in the consciousness that at least one has not oneself incurred any guilt."[114]

This is a very strong argument for involved obedience in the ordinary circumstances of life, but Bonhoeffer qualified it. The obligation to obey is not binding if government forfeits its claim by openly denying its commission and compelling offense against the divine commandment.[115] Should that happen, disobedience must be considered. Bonhoeffer was very careful to say that disobedience is "a venture undertaken on one's own responsibility."[116] No higher or greater claim can be made for it. His participation in the conspiracy against Hitler became the interpretive demonstration of what he meant the venture of disobedience to be.

THE MANDATE OF CHURCH

The church fulfills its divine mandate when she proclaims the lordship of Christ. Because this proclamation enables the Word to be realized in the world, the church acts as deputy for the world and exists for its sake.[117] Its announcement that its Lord is also the lord of the world carries with it no authority to claim that secular institutions are to be subservient to the church and no authority to attempt to Christianize the state or its ministers. Its commissioned message is the message of the world's liberation and not of its subordination to the church. "The purpose and aim of the dominion of Christ is not to make the worldly order godly or to subordinate it to the Church but to set it free for true worldliness."[118] The office of the church is to free the world to be the world.

CHURCH AND STATE

Just as the mandate of government implies no particular form of the state, it also implies no single form of church-state relations. Whatever the form, Bonhoeffer argued, always essential to it is the church's responsibility to proclaim the dominion of Jesus Christ over the state as well as the church. Its aim in doing so "is not that government should pursue a Christian policy ... but that it should be true government" in obedience to Christ.[119] Bonhoeffer clearly did not think in terms of two, separate realms for church and state.

The emancipation of the state to be the state takes place in its encounter with the proclamation and life of the church. The state, therefore, serves its own best interest when it supports this encounter by making room for the church. Bonhoeffer's notion of "making room" for the church should not be misread. In his visits to America he had heard much talk of religious freedom, where "freedom" meant "the possibility of unhindered activity given by the world to the church." Bonhoeffer was critical of such talk. He understood the freedom of the church not as the possibility but as the power of the gospel to make "room for itself on earth." This freedom "is not the gift of the world to the church, but the freedom of the Word of God itself to gain a hearing." Bonhoeffer thought that the American churches' praise of freedom can stem from a pact with the world "in which the true freedom of the Word of God is surrendered."[120] If the state makes room for the church, any gift it bestows is a gift to itself: the possibility of its own liberation in encounter with the proclamation of the Word. Bonhoeffer had in mind a coexistence of church and state characterized by mutual limitation and tension.[121]

The church should continually remind the state of government's divine commission and draw attention to its shortcomings when it is derelict. Although no particular form of state is necessary, Bonhoeffer did think that there are some types relatively better than others in fulfilling government's commission. A state is relatively better when it makes the divine origin of government evident. It is relatively better when it sustains its power by doing justice, specifically by protecting the rights of family and labor and by protecting the proclamation of the gospel. And it is relatively better when it attaches itself to its subjects by just action and truthful speech.[122] These characteristics of the better state could be read as possible general subjects of the church's exhortation to the state.

The church does not fulfill its responsibility of proclamation to the state by offering "dogmatically correct delivery" or "general ethical principles." "What is needed is concrete instruction in the concrete situation."[123] There is no Christian solution for the world's problems, and instruction cannot be based on some rational or natural law knowledge that the church shares with the world.[124] Rather, instruction "follows solely from the preaching of Christ." Then "by the authority of the word of God," the church will necessarily declare wrong such things as "economic attitudes or forms ... which obviously obstruct belief in Jesus Christ." Additionally, "not by the authority of God but merely on the authority of the responsible advice of Christian specialists and experts, she will be able to make her contribution towards the establishment of a new order."[125]

If government abandons its commission, it acts on its own without divine mandate, and the church's responsibility may take different shape. Bonhoeffer had to confront the subject in April 1933, when the German government adopted the Aryan Clause excluding Jews from civil service and cultural life, including church office for those who had converted to Christianity. He wrote *The Church and the Jewish Question* for a church group assembled to take action.[126] In this tract, Bonhoeffer proposed that the church is compelled to question the state about the legitimacy of its action when it provides either too much or too little law and order. It provides "too little" law and order, "if any group of subjects [is] deprived of their rights, too much where the state [intervenes] in the character of the church and its proclamation, e.g. in the forced exclusion of baptized Jews from ... Christian congregations." In the latter case, the church must reject the encroachment because of the church's "better knowledge of the state and the limitations of its action." Such confrontation of the state is the first possibility for church action. The church can also then aid the victims as part of its "unconditional obligation to the victims of any ordering society, even if they do not belong to the Christian community." And, finally, it can not only "bandage the victims under the wheel, but ... put a spoke in the wheel itself."[127]

Bonhoeffer was the first pastor to identify Nazi treatment of Jews as critical and central, and his proposal was remarkable in its time and place. That the church should "put a spoke in the wheel" of the state was a singular statement for a Lutheran to make to Lutherans.

SOLIDARITY WITH THE OPPRESSED: BONHOEFFER'S LEGACY

Geffrey Kelly and Burton Nelson, the editors of *A Testament to Freedom*, a highly acclaimed presentation of selected Bonhoeffer writings, chose as the title for their introduction "Solidarity with the Oppressed" because they believed that it states the animating heart of his conspiratorial life and late theology.[128] Bonhoeffer had written, perhaps to his fellow conspirators, "We have for once learnt to see the great events of world history from below, from the perspective of the outcast, the suspects, the maltreated, the powerless, the oppressed, the reviled—in short, from the perspective of those who suffer." He added that justice must be done "from a higher satisfaction, whose foundation is beyond any talk of 'from below' or 'from above.'"[129]

Paul Lehmann suggested that this perspective accounts for the shift in Bonhoeffer's expression of his central question. In a letter of June 30, 1944, two months after he asked "who Christ really is for us today," Bonhoeffer wrote, "Let me just summarize briefly what I am concerned about—how to claim for Jesus Christ a world that has come of age."[130] Lehmann proposed that the difference in formulation was "a sign of Bonhoeffer's own move from the implicit to the explicit in the obedience of faith, from the perspective of the powerful upon the story to the story from the perspective of those who suffer."[131] Bonhoeffer had now learned to see events from the perspective of the outcast because he had been cast out. His solidarity with the oppressed is his response to the question about how to claim for Jesus Christ a world come of age.

Bonhoeffer's proposal that the church—and not just the individual Christian—must "put a spoke in the wheel" of a state bent on oppressing Jews was unique. Nonetheless, it was still burdened with statements indicating that Bonhoeffer was not yet free of the anti-Semitism of his culture and his religious tradition. "We were against Hitler's church policy," Bethge repentantly said years after the war, "but at the same time we were anti-Semites."[132] Bethge had grown in self-critical understanding, and it is likely that Bonhoeffer, too, would have done so or had done so in fact. By the time he was writing his *Ethics*, he had come to see that "an expulsion of the Jews from the West must necessarily bring with it the expulsion of Christ. For Jesus Christ was a Jew."[133] And he declared that the church was "guilty of the deaths of the weakest and most defenseless brothers and sisters of Christ."[134]

The German treatment of Jews was central and critical for Bonhoeffer's thinking in later life. But Bonhoeffer had likely already learned something of the meaning of "solidarity with the oppressed" earlier during his time in New York, where he witnessed the American treatment of African Americans. The Abyssinian Baptist Church in New York, where he was a regular participant, would have given him early instruction on this theme. Josiah Young wagers "that Bonhoeffer's ongoing commitment to obey Christ concretely ... was related to the 'visible emotion' of the black worship that he experienced."[135] Bonhoeffer's thought and life would later make a return gift, for young African American ministers, "desperate to understand the racial injustice that surrounded them ... looked to Bonhoeffer for theological insight."[136] It was the ministers of The Sanctified Church, the Soul Saving Station, who introduced Young to Bonhoeffer's work.[137] They found in Bonhoeffer's witness a strengthening "denunciation of the racism that threatens to sabotage the possibilities for life together."[138]

The fruits of Bonhoeffer's solidarity with the oppressed and his theological interpretation of it have also nourished liberation theology. "Most of us, South of the Rio Grande, experience an overwhelming, incomprehensible nightmare," Otto Maduro writes. "This may be why, of all the modern, liberal Christian theologians, Dietrich Bonhoeffer is the closest to our hearts."[139] Clarke Chapman explains that liberation theologians particularly welcome Bonhoeffer's "vision of ultimate reality, a vision that undermines oppression."[140] But he adds that the reception has not been uncritical, and he offers the example of Gustavo Gutierrez's criticism that economic and social analysis are missing from Bonhoeffer's theology. When Bonhoeffer "speaks of a world come of age he never refers to the underside of this world."[141]

The Seventh International Bonhoeffer Congress was held in 1996 in Cape Town, South Africa. Bonhoeffer has been the subject of academic study in South Africa, but also and more significantly, John de Gruchy reports, participants in the struggle for justice and liberation "discovered fragments of his theology which have helped them remain faithful and hopeful."[142] De Gruchy says that Bonhoeffer has been a particular challenge to members of the white elite and has helped liberate them to be of some use in seeking solidarity with the victims and enemies of apartheid.[143]

Chung Hyun Kyung, a theologian from South Korea, invited to address the Bonhoeffer Congress in South Africa, said she had "stopped reading dead white European men's theologies and memoirs" after completing her doctorate but reacquainted herself with Bonhoeffer in preparation for the Congress.[144] She had been introduced to his life and thought by her participation in the persecuted Korean Christian Student movement, for which Bonhoeffer was the "major theological mentor."[145] The Western orientation of his theology led Koreans to lose interest in him, she said, but young pastors returned to Bonhoeffer in the late 1980s in their search for identity during the period of Korea's rapid secularization.

Kyung tested Bonhoeffer's designation of Jesus as the exemplary "man for others." She found that it did not work as "women for others" because of its oppressive patriarchal overtones: Women are already compelled to be for others and now need to be for themselves first.[146] For similar reasons she questioned Bonhoeffer's emphasis on suffering and death. She thought it ill suited for Asian women: "We ask not what we can die for, because our children's lives are dependent on us. We ask rather what we can live for?"[147] The present need "is to find the way to invigorate Life in our midst."[148]

Chung Hyun Kyung's presentation was cast as an imagined letter to Bonhoeffer. One can imagine a reply in which Bonhoeffer eagerly encourages further correspondence and questioning. He begins by repeating a statement he had made earlier in another context: "I [too] should like to speak of God ... not in weakness but in strength; and therefore not in death and guilt but in human life and goodness."[149] Women have rights, he says, and a rightful need to embrace themselves even as God embraces them.

And he asks about discoveries for ways to invigorate Life that she and other Asian women have made. His question springs from a keenly felt hope.

For years, Bonhoeffer sought to travel to Asia. Not long after he took up a pastorate in London in 1933, he wrote his brother Karl-Friedrich that, since he was "becoming more convinced each day that Christianity is approaching its end in the West—at least in its previous form and its previous interpretation—I should like to go to the Far East."[150] To Barth's great puzzlement, Bonhoeffer laid plans for a trip to India, where he would stay with Gandhi. He wanted to learn from Asian spirituality and political action. He would not be shopping for religions. Nor would he abandon or dilute the arcane discipline. He suspected he would be led to possibilities for the arcane discipline's new forms and new interpretation. He would celebrate God's love of all things human.

It was not to be. As Bethge put it, Bonhoeffer had "presented the path of liberation of the [W]estern spirit, law, philosophy, and secular life."[151] He would be denied firsthand exposure to the path of liberation of Eastern spirituality, thought, and political action presented by people like Gandhi and, now, Chung Hyun Kyung.

NOTES

1. Eberhard Bethge, *Dietrich Bonhoeffer: A Biography*, ed. Victoria Barnett (Minneapolis: Fortress, 2000), 886.

2. John Leith, ed., *Creeds of the Churches* (Garden City, N.Y.: Anchor Books, 1963), 520.

3. Bethge, *Dietrich Bonhoeffer*, 607.

4. Dietrich Bonhoeffer, *A Testament to Freedom: The Essential Writings of Dietrich Bonhoeffer*, ed. Geffrey B. Kelly and F. Burton Nelson (San Francisco: HarperCollins, 1990), 504.

5. Bethge, *Dietrich Bonhoeffer*, 678.

6. Ibid., 792.

7. Other members of Bonhoeffer's family were also involved. Bonhoeffer's assignments included such tasks as passing on information to Allied sources and seeking information on possible peace terms and aims. The lasting merit of his participation may lie in what Bethge says is his "effective witness" from inside the conspiracy as "a Christian theologian of the resistance." Ibid., 796; see also ibid., 626–702.

8. Dietrich Bonhoeffer, *Letters and Papers from Prison*, ed. Eberhard Bethge, trans. Reginald Fuller (New York: Simon & Schuster, 1997), 328. Stanley Hauerwas says that Bonhoeffer's offhand remark betrays the deep continuity between the two theologians. Hauerwas, *With the Grain of the Universe* (Grand Rapids, Mich.: Brazos Press, 2001), 190 n. 37.

9. Quoted in the introduction to Bonhoeffer, *A Testament to Freedom*, 10.

10. Paul Lehmann, *Ethics in a Christian Context* (New York: Harper & Row, 1963), *The Transformation of Politics* (New York: Harper & Row, 1975), and *The Decalogue and a Human Future* (Grand Rapids, Mich.: Eerdmans, 1995).

11. William Hamilton, "A Secular Theology for a World Come of Age," *Theology Today* 18 (1962): 440; quoted in Ralf Wüstenberg, "Bonhoeffer's Christianity: Dietrich Bonhoeffer's Tegel Theology," in *Bonhoeffer for a New Day*, ed. John W. de Gruchy (Grand Rapids, Mich.: Eerdmans, 1996), 58.

12. John A. T. Robinson, *Honest to God* (London: SCM, 1963).

13. Harvey Cox, *The Secular City* (New York: Macmillan, 1965).

14. Dietrich Bonhoeffer, *Discipleship*, trans. Martin Kaske and Ilse Tödt, *Dietrich Bonhoeffer Works* (Minneapolis: Fortress Press, 1996), vol. 6; Dietrich Bonhoeffer, *Life Together*, trans. John Doberstein (New York: Harper & Row, 1954).

15. Dietrich Bonhoeffer, *The Communion of Saints*, trans. Ronald Gregor Smith et al. (New York: Harper & Row, 1963); and *Act and Being*, trans. Bernard Noble (New York: Harper & Row, 1962). All of his works have been assembled and published in German in the seventeen volumes of the *Dietrich Bonhoeffer Werke*, now being translated into English as *Dietrich Bonhoeffer Works*. The International Bonhoeffer Society maintains a web site at http://www.dbonhoeffer. org that provides information about Bonhoeffer studies, as well as the society's activities.

16. Bonhoeffer, *A Testament to Freedom*, 127.

17. Ibid., 118.

18. Ralf Wüstenberg, *A Theology of Life* (Grand Rapids, Mich.: Eerdmans, 1998), 51.

19. Karl Barth, *The Epistle to the Romans*, trans. Edwyn C. Hoskyns, 3d ed. (London: Oxford University Press, 1953), 258–259.

20. Karl Barth, *Church Dogmatics*, 4 vols. (Edinburgh: T & T Clark, 1936–61), 1:280–361.

21. Bonhoeffer, *Letters and Papers*, 328.

22. Bethge, *Dietrich Bonhoeffer*, 872.

23. Bonhoeffer, *Letters and Papers*, 279.

24. Ibid., 362.

25. Ibid., 281–282.

26. Ibid., 341.

27. Ibid., 345.

28. Ibid., 280–281.

29. Ibid., 346.

30. Bonhoeffer's thinking about autonomy and maturity—a world come of age— drew upon Wilhelm Dilthey's philosophy of life. See generally Wüstenberg, *A Theology of Life*.

31. Bonhoeffer, *Letters and Papers*, 361–362.

32. Ibid., 362.

33. Ibid., 300.

34. Ibid., 369.

35. Quoted in Bethge, *Dietrich Bonhoeffer*, 867.

36. W. H. Auden expresses it this way:

> Because in Him the Flesh is united to the Word without magical transforma-
> tion, Imagination is redeemed from promiscuous fornication with her own
> images....
> Because in Him all passions find a logical In-Order-That, by Him is the per-
> petual recurrence of Art assured....
> Because in Him the Word is united to the Flesh without loss of perfection,
> Reason is redeemed from incestuous fixation on her own logic....
> Because in Him abstraction finds a passionate For-The-Sake-Of, by Him is
> the continuous development of Science assured.

    W. H. Auden, "For the Time Being," in *The Collected Poetry of W. H. Auden* (New York: Random House, 1945), 405.

37. Bonhoeffer, *Letters and Papers*, 360.

38. Bethge, *Dietrich Bonhoeffer*, 869.

39. Bonhoeffer, *Letters and Papers*, 361.

40. Bonhoeffer, *A Testament to Freedom*, 536.

41. Bethge, *Dietrich Bonhoeffer*, 721 722.

42. Dietrich Bonhoeffer, *No Rusty Swords*, ed. Edwin H. Robertson, trans. Edwin H. Robertson and John Bowden (London: Collins, 1965), 100–101.

43. Bethge, *Dietrich Bonhoeffer*, 882–883.

44. Bonhoeffer, *Letters and Papers*, 199.

45. Bethge, *Dietrich Bonhoeffer*, 926.

46. Ibid., 882.

47. Ibid., 883.

48. Ibid., 884.

49. Quoted ibid., 927. The message was sent through the English officer Payne Best to Bonhoeffer's friend in England, the Bishop of Chichester. Ibid., 927, 1022 n. 54.

50. Bonhoeffer, *A Testament to Freedom*, 91. See also the formulation, "our be-ing Christian today will be limited to two things: prayer and righteous action among people." Bonhoeffer, *Letters and Papers*, 300.

51. Bonhoeffer, *Discipleship*, 172.

52. Bonhoeffer, *A Testament to Freedom*, 506.

53. Bonhoeffer, *Letters and Papers*, 1–17.

54. Dietrich Bonhoeffer, *Ethik*, in *Dietrich Bonhoeffer Werke*, 6:244.

55. Bethge, *Dietrich Bonhoeffer*, 627.

56. Dietrich Bonhoeffer, *Ethics*, trans. Neville Horton Smith (New York: Simon & Schuster, 1995), 247.

57. Ibid., 245.

58. Ibid., 260.

59. Ibid., 71.

60. Ibid., 359.
61. Bethge, *Dietrich Bonhoeffer*, 628.
62. Bonhoeffer, *Letters and Papers*, 4.
63. Bonhoeffer, *Ethics*, 254.
64. Ibid., 244.
65. Ibid., 240.
66. Ibid., 245.
67. Bonhoeffer, *Letters and Papers*, 6.
68. Jean Bethke Elshtain, "Freedom and Responsibility in a World Come of Age," in *Theology and the Practice of Responsibility: Essays on Dietrich Bonhoeffer*, ed. Wayne Whitson Floyd, Jr. and Charles Marsh (Valley Forge, Pa.: Trinity Press International, 1994), 277. There was a Bonhoeffer-like quality to William Stringfellow's practice of law. He found that any practice of law is an engagement in politics, power, and violence and that religion had nothing positive to do with such things. He was totally reliant on the grace of God that freed him for an exuberant practice of law. See chapter 16, this volume.
69. Bonhoeffer, *Letters and Papers*, 210.
70. Bonhoeffer, *Ethics*, 81–82.
71. Bonhoeffer, *Letters and Papers*, 360.
72. Ibid., 71.
73. Bonhoeffer, *Ethics*, 191.
74. Ibid., 143. In his lectures on christology, Bonhoeffer had explained: "In the sacrament of the Church, the old enslaved creature is set free to its new freedom. As the center of human existence and of history, Christ was the fulfillment of the unfulfilled law, i.e., their reconciliation. But nature is creation under the curse—not guilt, for it lacks freedom. Thus nature finds in Christ as its center, not reconciliation, but redemption. Once again, this redemption, which happens in Christ, is not evident, nor can it be proved, but it is proclaimed. The word of preaching is that enslaved nature is redeemed in hope. A sign of this is given in the sacraments, where elements of the old creation are become elements of the new. In the sacraments they are set free from their dumbness and proclaim directly to the believer the new creative Word of God. They no longer need the explanation of man. Enslaved nature does not speak the Word of God to us directly. But the sacraments do. In the sacrament, Christ is the mediator between nature and God and stands for all creatures before God." Bonhoeffer, *A Testament to Freedom*, 127.
75. Bonhoeffer, *Ethics*, 131.
76. Ibid., 136.
77. Ibid., 150.
78. In prison, Bonhoeffer undertook a systematic reading of Wilhelm Dilthey, from whom he had drawn his thinking about a world come of age. Bonhoeffer's emphasis on "life" is a further reflection of his dependence on Dilthey. As opposed to metaphysics and abstraction, Dilthey's "point of departure is always human life as it is actually lived in a particular epoch." Wüstenberg, *A Theology of Life*, 104. Bonhoeffer had read William James during his time at Union Seminary in

New York, and James, too, was an important influence in his thinking about life as well as his thinking about religionlessness. Ibid., 96. Bonhoeffer arrived at his own nonreligious, theological interpretation of "life": Authentically human life is life in Christ in being for others.

79. Bonhoeffer, *Letters and Papers*, 361.

80. Bonhoeffer, *Ethics*, 192–193.

81. Ibid., 351.

82. Ibid., 195.

83. Dietrich Bonhoeffer, *Who Is Christ for Us?* ed. and trans. Craig Nessan and Renate Wind (Minneapolis: Fortress Press, 2002), 34.

84. Bonhoeffer, *Ethics*, 82.

85. See Clifford Green, *Dietrich Bonhoeffer: A Theology of Sociality* (Grand Rapids, Mich.: Eerdmans, 1999).

86. Bonhoeffer, *Ethics*, 84.

87. Bethge, *Dietrich Bonhoeffer*, 455.

88. Bonhoeffer, *Ethics*, 85.

89. Ibid., 203.

90. Bonhoeffer, *Discipleship*, 39.

91. Ibid., 45.

92. Paul Lehmann, "Faith and Worldliness in Bonhoeffer's Thought," in *Bonhoeffer in a World Come of Age*, ed. Peter Vorkink (Philadelphia: Fortress Press, 1968), 37.

93. Bonhoeffer, *Letters and Papers*, 369.

94. Lehmann, "Faith and Worldliness," 38.

95. In August 1942, Bonhoeffer presented a study of the subject to a group of the Confessing Church appointed to prepare a declaration on the Commandment "Thou shalt not kill." Bethge, *Dietrich Bonhoeffer*, 709. The subject of Bonhoeffer's paper was the first use of the law, which, he said, concerns the Church's responsibility for the world. In the preaching of the law, the congregation will be reminded of the universality of its mission to the world. Otherwise "it would become a mere religious association." Bonhoeffer, *Ethics*, 311. After Bonhoeffer's imprisonment, the Confessing Church adopted a statement on the Fifth Commandment that denounced the "elimination" of Jews and called for reading a message on a day of repentance that included the statement: "Woe to us and our nation if it is held to be justified to kill people because they belong to another race." Quoted in Bethge, *Dietrich Bonhoeffer*, 709.

96. Bonhoeffer, *Ethics*, 301.

97. Ibid., 321.

98. Ibid.

99. Ibid., 277.

100. Ibid., 279, 276.

101. Ibid., 272.

102. Ibid., 276.

103. Quoted in Bethge, *Dietrich Bonhoeffer*, 620. For his Psalm 114 meditations, see Dietrich Bonhoeffer, *Meditations on the Word*, ed. and trans. David M. Gracie (Cambridge, Mass.: Cowley, 1986).

104. Bonhoeffer, *Ethics*, 273. He opposed that term to the traditional Lutheran terms "orders of creation" and "orders of preservation," which were subject to appropriation by Nazi ideology.

105. Ibid., 272–274.

106. Ibid., 282.

107. Ibid., 251.

108. Ibid., 205.

109. Ibid., 327.

110. Ibid., 332. Bonhoeffer argued that natural law "can furnish equally cogent arguments in favor of the state which is founded on force and the state which is founded on justice, for the nation-state and for imperialism, for democracy and for dictatorship. A solid basis is afforded only by the biblical derivation of government from Jesus Christ. Whether and to what extent a new natural law can be established on this foundation is a theological question which still remains open." Ibid., 334. The state will take actions that are not Christian but that do not exclude Christ if the second table of the Decalogue as a criterion has become known from the preaching of the Church. In pagan governments, there is "a providential congruity between the contents of the second table and the inherent law of historical life itself. Failure to observe the second table destroys the very life which government is charged with preserving.... Does this mean that the state is after all based on natural law? No; for in fact it is a matter here only of the government which does not understand itself but which now is providentially enabled to acquire the same knowledge, of crucial significance for its task, as is disclosed to the government which does understand itself in the true sense in Jesus Christ. One might, therefore, say that in this case natural law has its foundation in Jesus Christ." Ibid., 336.

111. Ibid., 339.

112. Ibid., 337.

113. Ibid., 334.

114. Ibid., 335.

115. Ibid., 337–338.

116. Ibid., 338.

117. Ibid., 208, 295–296.

118. Ibid., 324.

119. Ibid., 342.

120. Bonhoeffer, *No Rusty Swords*, 104.

121. Bonhoeffer, *A Testament to Freedom*, 97.

122. Bonhoeffer, *Ethics*, 347–348.

123. Ibid., 349.

124. Ibid., 353.

125. Ibid., 355–356.

126. Reprinted in Bonhoeffer, *No Rusty Swords*, 221–229.

127. Ibid., 224–225.

128. Introduction to Bonhoeffer, *A Testament to Freedom*, 5.

129. Bonhoeffer, *Letters and Papers*, 17.

130. Ibid., 342.

131. Paul Lehmann, "The Indian Situation as a Question of Accountability," *Church & Society* 75, no. 3 (1985): 66.

132. Quoted in Dagmar Herzog, "Theology of Betrayal," *Tikkun* 16, no. 3 (2001): 70.

133. Bonhoeffer, *Ethics*, 90–91.

134. Bonhoeffer, *A Testament to Freedom*, 373. On the issue of Bonhoeffer and Jews, see Robert Ericksen and Susannah Heschel, eds., *Betrayal: German Churches and the Holocaust* (Minneapolis: Augsburg Fortress, 1999); Eberhard Bethge, "Dietrich Bonhoeffer and the Jews," in *Ethical Responsibility: Bonhoeffer's Legacy to the Churches*, ed. John Godsey and Geffrey Kelly (Lewiston, N.Y.: Edwin Mellen Press, 1981), 43; Geffrey B. Kelly, "Bonhoeffer and the Jews: Implications for Jewish-Christian Reconciliation," in *Reflections on Bonhoeffer: Essays in Honor of F. Burton Nelson*, ed. Geffrey B. Kelly and C. John Weborg, 133–166 (Chicago: Covenant Publications, 1999).

135. Josiah Ulysses Young III, *No Difference in the Fare: Dietrich Bonhoeffer and the Problem of Racism* (Grand Rapids, Mich.: Eerdmans, 1998), 8.

136. Ibid., 6.

137. Ibid., 1.

138. Ibid., 14.

139. Otto A. Maduro, "The Modern Nightmare: A Latin American Christian Indictment," in *Theology and the Practice of Responsibility: Essays on Dietrich Bonhoeffer*, ed. Wayne Whitson Floyd Jr. and Charles Marsh (Valley Forge, Pa: Trinity Press International, 1994), 81. Geffrey B. Kelly draws a comparison between Bonhoeffer and Archbishop Romero, "defender of the poor of El Salvador," in "Bonhoeffer and Romero: Prophets of Justice for the Oppressed," in *Theology and the Practice of Responsibility*, 85.

140. G. Clarke Chapman, "Bonhoeffer, Liberation Theology, and the 1990s," in Kelly and Weborg, *Reflections on Bonhoeffer*, 301.

141. Gustavo Gutiérrez, *The Truth Shall Make You Free: Confrontations* (Maryknoll, N.Y.: Orbis, 1990), 24.

142. John W. de Gruchy, "Bonhoeffer, Apartheid and Beyond: The Reception of Bonhoeffer in South Africa," in de Gruchy, *Bonhoeffer for a New Day*, 354.

143. Ibid., 355, 359.

144. Chung Hyun Kyung, "Dear Dietrich Bonhoeffer: A Letter," in de Gruchy, *Bonhoeffer for a New Day*, 11.

145. Ibid., 10.

146. Ibid., 15.

147. Ibid., 17.

148. Ibid., 18.

149. Bonhoeffer, *Letters and Papers*, 282.

150. Quoted in Bethge, *Dietrich Bonhoeffer*, 406.

151. Ibid., 869.

[CHAPTER 14]

Reinhold Niebuhr (1892–1971)

DAVISON M. DOUGLAS

Reinhold Niebuhr was the twentieth century's most influential American theologian and, after Martin Luther King Jr., the most prominent American preacher. Extraordinarily prolific—he wrote twenty-one books and more than 2,600 articles[1]—Niebuhr interpreted the theological significance of contemporary national and world events for a broad and diverse audience. Niebuhr was also a highly influential political theorist, particularly in the field of international relations. In 1962, the distinguished political theorist Hans Morgenthau called Niebuhr "the greatest living political philosopher of America, perhaps the only creative political philosopher since Calhoun."[2]

Niebuhr articulated a "Christian realist" perspective in which he challenged many of the secular and religious orthodoxies of his day by emphasizing the depths of human sinfulness. Possessed of a passion for social justice characteristic of the biblical prophets, Niebuhr urged the creation of political structures that might contribute to a more just society; at the same time, he realized the profound difficulty of achieving such a society in light of the realities of human nature. Niebuhr directed his incisive critiques at both the church and the secular world. He sought to bring "the judgment of Christ to bear as rigorously on the household of faith as upon the secular and pagan world, even as the prophets of Israel were as severe in mediating the divine judgment upon Israel as upon Babylon."[3] In the process, Niebuhr caused many modern secular thinkers to take more seriously the claims of Christianity. As one Niebuhr scholar puts it, Niebuhr "attempted to overcome, and to a remarkable degree has succeeded in overcoming, the estrangement of the modern mind from the insights and content of the Christian faith."[4]

BIOGRAPHY

Born in 1892, Niebuhr grew up in Missouri and Illinois, the son of a minister of the German Evangelical Synod of North America, a church in the tradition of the Union Church of Prussia with both Lutheran and Reformed roots. Niebuhr was educated for three years at Elmhurst College, near Chicago, and then at Eden Theological Seminary, near St. Louis, both institutions operated by the German Evangelical Synod. Upon graduation from Eden at the age of twenty, Niebuhr was ordained a minister in his denomination, but he promptly left for two years' additional training at Yale Divinity School. Upon receiving his B.D. and M.A. degrees from Yale, Niebuhr began a parish ministry in 1915 at Bethel Evangelical Church in Detroit, where he remained until 1928.

Niebuhr's years in the parish would be formative in his thinking. Niebuhr witnessed at close hand the racism that oppressed southern blacks who had migrated to Detroit during and after World War I, as well as the poor treatment of workers in the city's automobile industry. Niebuhr spoke publicly against the Ku Klux Klan and its influence in Detroit politics, and he chaired an interracial committee to investigate racial conflicts in the city. A sharp critic of Henry Ford, Niebuhr helped lead a campaign against the industrialist's labor policies and published a series of articles in which he documented the harsh conditions of the assembly line in Ford's automobile factories. Aspiring to build a labor party in the United States modeled on the British Labour party, Niebuhr would later comment that his experience with Ford made him a socialist.[5] While in Detroit, Niebuhr also embraced pacifism and served for a time as national chairman of the Fellowship of Reconciliation.

During these years in his Detroit parish, Niebuhr obtained a national reputation as a compelling speaker and thoughtful writer, a renown fueled in part by his service as a writer for the liberal Protestant publication *The Christian Century*. In 1928, Niebuhr accepted a position as associate professor of applied Christianity at Union Theological Seminary in New York City, where he would remain until his retirement in 1960. But Niebuhr's immersion into the academy did not stem his interest in the political struggles of the day. When Niebuhr moved to New York City, he became actively involved in politics, joining the Socialist Party, editing its journal *World Tomorrow*, and helping to found the Fellowship of Socialist Christians. Writing in 1930, Niebuhr claimed that the concentration of economic power in private industry in modern society had become the source of great injustice "because the private ownership of the productive processes and the increased centralization of the resultant power in the hands of a few, make inevitably for irresponsibility."[6] Niebuhr ran unsuccessfully for the New York state senate in 1930 and for the United States Congress in 1932 as a candidate of the Socialist Party.

Over the course of the 1930s, however, Niebuhr became disenchanted with both socialist politics and pacifism. In significant measure, Niebuhr's shift in viewpoint owed to the rise and abuses of authoritarian states in Europe—in particular, Stalinism in the Soviet Union and Nazism in Germany. In addition to leaving the Socialist Party, Niebuhr resigned in 1940 from the editorial board of *The Christian Century* because of its advocacy of a policy of neutrality in the face of Nazi Germany's aggressive expansionism. Niebuhr founded another journal instead, *Christianity and Crisis*, which articulated his "Christian realist" theology, grounded in the reality of human sinfulness and the need to develop political and legal institutions to corral the manifestations of that sinfulness.

Niebuhr actively urged American entry into World War II. As chair of the Union for Democratic Action, founded in 1941, Niebuhr vigorously supported the Lend-Lease program to assist Great Britain as well as American participation in the war. During the war, Niebuhr was one of the few prominent Americans who spoke publicly of the plight of European Jews and who urged a more generous immigration policy to relieve their suffering.

After World War II, Niebuhr joined a number of other former socialists to form the Americans for Democratic Action, committed to both the continuation of New Deal domestic programs and a strong anticommunist foreign policy. Before the war, Niebuhr, like many socialists, had viewed the New Deal as an ill-fated attempt to reform capitalism; in time, he embraced it as a pragmatic effort to deal with the devastating consequences of the Depression. Niebuhr became an important figure in the postwar democratic left; he served as advisor to Secretary of State George Marshall and helped to define what would be described as the "vital center" of American politics. Indeed, during the postwar era, Niebuhr exercised considerable influence over the development of American foreign and domestic policy. Niebuhr's "political realism" helped to justify America's postwar domestic and international commitments, even though Niebuhr ultimately found all "political and social constructs wanting when measured against the yardstick of divine justice."[7]

In addition to his political engagements, Niebuhr was a remarkably productive writer throughout his life. In several of his books, Niebuhr combined his theological reflections with his political insights. During the early 1930s, Niebuhr attempted to synthesize certain aspects of Marxism and Christianity. By the late 1930s, Niebuhr had concluded that such a synthesis was "neither possible nor desirable ... and [instead] worked out the design for a Christian realism, grounded equally in the Augustinianism of the Reformation and his own hard-won political wisdom."[8] Although Niebuhr's early writings were more social criticism than theological reflection, many of his subsequent works were more explicitly theological. In this regard, Niebuhr was influenced by both Paul Tillich, the great German theologian who joined the Union Seminary faculty in 1933, and his brother, H. Richard Niebuhr, a Christian ethicist at Yale Divinity School.

During the late 1930s and early 1940s, Niebuhr wrote his most systematic theological compilation, the two-volume *The Nature and Destiny of Man*, which Niebuhr presented in 1939 as the Gifford Lectures in Edinburgh. The publication of these lectures established Niebuhr as a major Christian thinker and cultural critic. But throughout his life, Niebuhr resisted describing himself as a theologian: "I cannot and do not claim to be a theologian. I have taught Christian Social Ethics for a quarter of a century and have also dealt in the ancillary field of 'apologetics.' ... I have never been very competent in the nice points of theology; and I must confess that I have not been sufficiently interested heretofore to acquire the competence."[9] Rather than consider the finer points of Christian theology, such as the doctrine of God or of Christ, Niebuhr addressed most of his attention to the meaning of contemporary events in light of his Christian understandings. As one Niebuhr scholar noted: "Probably more than any other U.S. theologian, Niebuhr moved with utter ease between the language of Zion and that of regnant secular culture."[10] Niebuhr's production was slowed by a series of strokes that beset him beginning in 1952, but he remained an active writer until his death in 1971.

Niebuhr, throughout his life, offered a "Christian realist" critique of twentieth-century utopian movements such as socialism, pacifism, communism, and statist liberalism. He powerfully influenced those interested in pursuing social justice, while at the same time urging recognition of the limits of such efforts. Niebuhr continually counseled reformers to have a healthy skepticism about their work, to retain "the firm resolve that inherited dogmas and generalizations will not be accepted, no matter how revered or venerable, if they do not contribute to the establishment of justice in a given situation."[11] One of the striking ironies of Niebuhr and his work is the broad array of later thinkers who claim him as their intellectual antecedent—from conservatives drawn to his emphasis on the depths of human sinfulness and the corruption of authoritarian government, to liberals drawn to his unbridled passion for social justice. Niebuhr's influence extended far beyond those with religious sensibilities. Arthur Schlesinger

Jr. noted of Niebuhr that he articulated the great themes of Christianity "with such irresistible relevance to contemporary experience that even those who have no decisive faith in the supernatural find their own reading of experience and history given new and significant dimensions."[12]

THEOLOGICAL AND INTELLECTUAL CONTEXT OF NIEBUHR'S WRITINGS

Niebuhr, appropriate to his task of teaching applied Christianity at Union Theological Seminary, was deeply influenced by the contemporary intellectual and political currents of his day. His writings reflect an effort to articulate a Christian theology in the context of contemporary social realities. Hence, one cannot fully understand Niebuhr's writings without exploring the theological and intellectual context in which he wrote.

Niebuhr began his parish ministry during the Progressive Era, a time of great optimism among religious and secular liberals about the possibility of social reform. Religious liberals of the early twentieth century championed the ability of humanity to be "redeemed" and sought to establish a "kingdom of God" on earth, marked by justice for all groups. Writing from a variety of Protestant traditions, these religious liberals "were confident that a new age of social Christianity was about to begin, transforming the raw realities of life in industrial cities and ushering in an era of international peace by the application of Christian love."[13] For example, Walter Rauschenbusch, the leading proponent of the Christian Social Gospel movement, claimed that "for the first time in religious history we have the possibility of so directing religious energy by scientific knowledge that a comprehensive and continuous reconstruction of social life in the name of God is within the bounds of human possibility."[14] Other religious liberals extended this optimism to class and race relations. Presbyterian theologian William Adams Brown wrote in 1930, "In relations between races; in strife between capital and labor; in our attitude toward the weaker and more dependent members of society ... we are developing a social conscience and situations which would have been accepted a generation ago as a matter of course are felt as an intolerable scandal."[15]

Secular liberals shared the optimism of their religious counterparts about the capacity for human progress and expressed confidence in the capacity of science and education to lead to greater progress and to mitigate human suffering. John Dewey, for example, believed that social injustice had "its main roots in ignorance—which must itself gradually yield before the extension of enlightenment through education and before the power of moral suasion."[16] These secular liberals, Dewey included, developed a theory of history that emphasized an upward trajectory of human moral development.

Niebuhr rejected this optimistic conception of the development of human history and held that liberal optimism toward moral progress was profoundly misplaced. "We have interpreted world history as a gradual ascent to the Kingdom of God which waits for final triumph only upon the willingness of Christians to 'take Christ seriously,'" Niebuhr wrote in 1940. "There is nothing in Christ's own teachings ... to justify this interpretation of world history."[17] Influenced by the racial and labor strife he witnessed initially during his years in Detroit, Niebuhr expressed pessimism about the "moralistic utopianism of the liberal Church"[18] that in his view failed to grasp the dark realities of human nature. In particular, Niebuhr charged that liberal optimists located the cause of evil in certain social conditions that can be overcome, as opposed to certain inherent features of human nature that are much more difficult to control.[19] To Niebuhr, contrary to the religious and secular liberals of the 1920s and 1930s, the ultimate source of evil in human society is not lack of education or deficient social or economic arrangements, but is rather the self-interestedness of human nature. Niebuhr viewed self-interest, coercion, and the struggle for power as inevitable in human relations.

For the rest of his life, Niebuhr would challenge those political and social philosophies that lacked a due regard for the depths of human sinfulness. During the late 1930s and 1940s, he criticized the utopian enthusiasm of those who embraced Marxist solutions to economic problems, particularly when such solutions were accompanied by authoritarian government. Niebuhr was strongly influenced by the biblical tradition of the Hebrew prophets, who railed against injustice, and by the apostle Paul, who recognized the depths of human sinfulness. Moreover, both Augustine and the Protestant reformers who also emphasized the problem of human sin had a profound influence on the development of Niebuhr's thinking.

NIEBUHR'S THEOLOGY OF HUMAN NATURE

The starting point for Niebuhr's theology was clearly his understanding of human nature. Virtually all of his theological and political reflections were rooted in the problem of human self-interest and how it impedes the struggle to establish a society grounded in principles of love and justice. Niebuhr believed that the modern world did not fully grasp the realities of human nature and that many of the world's thorniest social and political problems were grounded in that failure.

Niebuhr's first major book, *Moral Man and Immoral Society*, published in 1932, "sent a series of shockwaves through America's liberal Protestant community."[20] Niebuhr targeted his book at "the moralists, both religious and secular, who imagine that the egoism of individuals is being progressively checked by the development of rationality or the growth of a religiously inspired goodwill and that nothing but the continuance of this process is necessary to establish social harmony between all the human societies and collectives."[21] Liberal reviewers suggested that Niebuhr's "emphasis on sin made him a traitor to progress."[22] Niebuhr, for his part, never retreated from his pessimistic assessment of human self-interest. Writing almost thirty years later, Niebuhr commented that he should have titled his book *The Not So Moral Man in His Less Moral Communities*.[23]

In *Moral Man and Immoral Society*, Niebuhr conceded that individuals, despite their sinful nature, may on occasion be capable of moral behavior in the sense that they are "capable, on occasion, of preferring the advantages of others to their own."[24] But this capacity for moral behavior is far less prevalent among social groups: "Human groups, classes, nations, and races are selfish, whatever may be the moral idealism of individual members within the groups."[25] Accusing liberalism of embracing a "romantic overestimate of human virtue and moral capacity," Niebuhr complained that "what is lacking among all these moralists, whether religious or rational, is an understanding of the brutal character of the behavior of all human collectives, and the power of self-interest and collective egoism in all inter-group relations."[26]

Niebuhr argued that although an individual may occasionally restrain his or her self-interested behavior, "every human group which benefits from a present order in society will use every ingenuity and artifice to maintain its privileges and to sanctify them in the name of public order; that political life is, in short, a thinly veiled barbarism."[27] Recognizing that Christianity articulates self-sacrifice as a central ethic, Niebuhr argued that this ideal "is achieved only rarely in individual life and is not achieved in group life at all. No nation, race, or class sacrifices itself. Human groups make a virtue of the assertion of self-interest and will probably do so until the end of history."[28]

Noting that secular and religious liberals believe that deep-seated self-interest can be controlled through either "the development of rationality or the growth of a religiously inspired goodwill,"[29] Niebuhr was emphatic that the tendency of groups toward self-interest is too great to overcome through education or moral instruction:

Social intelligence and moral goodwill ... may serve to mitigate the brutalities of social conflict, but they cannot abolish the conflict itself. That could be accomplished only if human groups, whether racial, national or economic, could achieve a degree of reason and sympathy which would permit them to see and to understand the interests of others as vividly as they understand their own, and a moral goodwill which would prompt them to affirm the rights of others as vigorously as they affirm their own. Given the inevitable limitations of human imagination and intelligence, this is an ideal which individuals may approximate but which is beyond the capacities of human societies....Thus, scientists "who dream of 'socializing' man and religious idealists who strive to increase the sense of moral responsibility ... are not conscious of the limitations in human nature which finally frustrate their efforts."[30]

While *Moral Man and Immoral Society* was primarily a social and political critique of liberal optimism, in *The Nature and Destiny of Man* Niebuhr developed a theological basis for his earlier social and political theories. Surveying classical, biblical, and modern views of human nature, Niebuhr concluded that modern thinkers were too optimistic about the essence of human nature:

> Modern man has an essentially easy conscience; and nothing gives the diverse and discordant notes of modern culture so much harmony as the unanimous opposition of modern man to Christian conceptions of the sinfulness of man. The idea that man is sinful at the very center of his personality ... is universally rejected.... If modern culture conceives man primarily in terms of the uniqueness of his rational faculties, it finds the root of his evil in his involvement in the natural impulses and natural necessities from which it hopes to free him by the increase of his rational faculties.[31]

By contrast, Niebuhr articulated an Augustinian notion of human sin that manifests itself as pride. Niebuhr identified three types of pride that humans exhibit as a means of dealing with the anxieties and insecurities of life: pride of power, pride of knowledge, and pride of virtue. Expanding on certain ideas about group behavior that he had introduced in *Moral Man and Immoral Society*, Niebuhr argued that this tendency toward pride is particularly nefarious when exhibited in groups: "Collective pride is thus man's last, and in some respects most pathetic, effort to deny the determinate and contingent character of his existence. The very essence of human sin is in it.... Collective egotism and group pride are a more pregnant source of injustice and conflict than purely individual pride."[32] Some feminist theologians would later criticize Niebuhr's emphasis on pride as the core human sin by arguing that pride "is a peculiarly male temptation" and is "an inadequate description of women."[33] Rather, argued one feminist critic of Niebuhr, the problem that a woman confronts is not the sin of pride but instead that "she insufficiently values herself."[34]

One manifestation of human pride is what Niebuhr termed the "will-to-power," a concept that he developed in his 1944 book, *The Children of Light and the Children of Darkness*. Niebuhr observed that humans, like animals, have a will-to-live, which is essentially a survival instinct. The problem for society, however, is that humans also have a will-to-power:

> The will-to-live is also spiritually transmuted into the will-to-power or into the desire for "power and glory." Man, being more than a natural creature, is not interested merely in physical survival but in prestige and social approval. Having the intelligence to anticipate the perils in which he stands in nature and history, he invariably seeks to gain security against these perils by enhancing his power, individually and collectively. Possessing a darkly unconscious sense of his insignificance in the total scheme of things, he seeks to compensate for his insignificance by pretensions of pride.[35]

Thus, conflicts between humans are not merely conflicts driven by the need to survive. The will-to-power places humans "fundamentally in conflict" with other humans:

> The conflicts between men are thus never simple conflicts between competing survival impulses. They are conflicts in which each man or group seeks to guard its power and prestige against the peril of competing expressions of power and pride. Since the very possession of power and prestige always involves some encroachment upon the prestige and power of others, this conflict is by its very nature a more stubborn and difficult one than the mere competition between various survival impulses in nature.[36]

Niebuhr identified the root of many of the problems that beset the twentieth century, particularly World War II, in this will-to-power: "If we survey any period of history, and not merely the present tragic era of world catastrophe, it becomes quite apparent that human ambitions, lusts and desires, are more inevitably inordinate ... [and] are of more tragic proportions" than previously understood.[37]

THE LAW OF LOVE

Against this will-to-power grounded in human self-interest is the "law of love," best articulated in the ethic "Thou shalt love thy neighbor as thyself."[38] Niebuhr wrote extensively about the "law of love," which he described as the ultimate norm for all human conduct.[39] "Love is really the law of life," Niebuhr wrote. "It is not some ultimate possibility which has nothing to do with human history."[40] Though difficult to obtain, the law of love must remain the normative goal for individuals and communities:

What is significant about the Christian ethic is precisely this: that it does not regard the historic as normative. Man may be, as Thomas Hobbes observed, a wolf to his fellowman. But this is not his essential nature. Let Christianity beware, particularly radical Protestantism, that it does not accept the habits of a sinful world as the norms of a Christian collective life. For the Christian only the law of love is normative.[41]

Niebuhr believed that this law of love, or "original justice," is part of the essential nature of humans. But Niebuhr conceded that humans, in their sinfulness, reject this law of love: "The freedom of man creates the possibility of actions which are contrary to and in defiance of the requirements of this essential nature."[42] Nevertheless, this essential nature has not been completely obliterated, because "sin neither destroys the structure by virtue of which man is man nor yet eliminates the sense of obligation toward the essential nature of man, which is the remnant of his perfection."[43] Niebuhr reasoned from experience that the "universal testimony of human experience is the most persuasive refutation of any theory of human depravity which denies that man has any knowledge of the good."[44] In fact, argued Niebuhr, "faith in Christ could find no lodging place in the human soul, were [the human soul] not uneasy about the contrast between its true and present state."[45] Thus, for Niebuhr, "sin is a corruption of man's true essence *but not its destruction*."[46] For Niebuhr, "against pessimistic theories of human nature which affirm the total depravity of man it is important to assert the continued presence in man of the *justitia originalis* [original justice], of the law of love."[47]

By the same token, Niebuhr emphasized the extraordinary difficulty of living the law of love and noted, "It is equally important, in refutation of modern secular and Christian forms of utopianism, to recognize that the fulfillment of the law of love is no simple possibility."[48] Reflecting the paradoxical style so typical of his writings, Niebuhr described the law of love as an "impossible possibility."[49] For Niebuhr, "the law of love stands on the edge of history and not in history ... [and] it represents an ultimate and not an immediate possibility."[50] Simply teaching the law of love is insufficient: "If we believe that the only reason men do not love each other perfectly is because the law of love has not been preached persuasively enough, we believe something to which experience does not conform."[51]

So, then, is true love of neighbor ever attainable? This question took Niebuhr directly into the heart of the concept of grace and the meaning of Christ's atoning death. As Niebuhr put the question: is the grace of Christ "primarily a power of righteousness which so heals the sinful heart that henceforth it is able to fulfill the law of love," or is it "primarily the assurance of divine mercy for a persistent sinfulness which man never over-comes completely"?[52] Niebuhr claimed that "the general answer of pre-Reformation Christianity was that the *justitia originalis*, the law of love, was not a possibility for natural man but that it could be realized by the redeemed man in whom 'grace' had healed the hurt of sin."[53] Niebuhr dis-agreed. Though he does suggest that grace is "the power of God in man" and "represents an accession of resources, which man does not have of himself, enabling him to become what he truly ought to be,"[54] Niebuhr ultimately concluded that humans will not completely overcome their sin-ful inclinations, even as they find the religious peace "of being accepted by God despite the continued sinfulness of the heart."[55] For Niebuhr, "this is the truth which the Reformation emphasized and which modern Protes-tant Christianity has almost completely forgotten."[56] Niebuhr elaborated on the Reformation perspective: "The Reformation took the fact of sin as a perennial category of historic existence more seriously [than pre-Reformation thinkers] and ... defined divine 'grace' not so much as a divine power in man which completes his incompletion but as a divine mercy toward man which brings his uneasy conscience to rest despite the con-tinued self-contradiction of human effort."[57] In reaching this conclusion, Niebuhr turned, as he often did, to the teachings of human experience:

> The sorry annals of Christian fanaticism, of unholy religious hatreds, of sin-ful ambitions hiding behind the cloak of religious sanctity, of political power impulses compounded with pretensions of devotion to God, offer the most irrefutable proof of the error in every Christian doctrine and every interpreta-tion of the Christian experience which claim that grace can remove the final contradiction between man and God.[58]

Niebuhr's consideration of the limits of the law of love in light of hu-man nature led him directly into a reconsideration of pacifism, which he embraced in his early adulthood but jettisoned as his understanding of the depths of human sinfulness became more profound. By the late 1930s, Niebuhr concluded that pacifism is unrealistic in light of the need to re-sist evil in the world: "The [pacifist] ethic of Jesus [is] finally and ultimate-ly normative, but [is] not immediately applicable to the task of securing justice in a sinful world.... In every political situation it is necessary to achieve justice by resisting pride and power."[59] The pacifists miss this point, argued Niebuhr, because they "do not know human nature well enough to be concerned about the contradictions between the law of love and the sin of man."[60] Rather, Niebuhr concluded, pacifists "assert that if only men loved one another, all the complex, and sometimes horrible, realities of the political order could be dispensed with. They do not see that their 'if' begs the most basic problem of human history. It is because men are sinners that justice can be achieved only by a certain degree of coercion on the one hand, and by resistance to coercion and tyranny on the other hand."[61]

Niebuhr also identified a certain naiveté in the church with respect to the possibility of living by the law of love: "The sum total of the liberal Church's effort to apply the law of love to politics without qualification is really a curious medley of hopes and regrets. The Church declares that men ought to live by the law of love and that nations as well as individuals ought to obey it.... These appeals to the moral will and this effort to support the moral will by desperate hopes are politically as unrealistic as they are religiously superficial."[62]

For Niebuhr, mere appeals to the "love thy neighbor" ethic of Jesus do not deal with the realities of human nature: "The ethic of Jesus does not deal at all with the immediate moral problem of every human life—the problem of arranging some kind of armistice between various contending factions and forces."[63] Or, put another way, "the gospel is something more than the law of love. The gospel deals with the fact that men violate the law of love."[64]

THE STATE: POSSIBILITIES FOR BOTH JUSTICE AND EVIL

Given the depths of human sinfulness that impede fulfillment of the law of love, how then should we organize our social and political institutions accordingly? As Niebuhr posed the issue, "The contradiction between the law of love and the sinfulness of man raises not only the ultimate religious problem how men are to have peace if they do not overcome the contradiction ... it also raises the immediate problem how men are to achieve a tolerable harmony of life with life, if human pride and selfishness prevent the realization of the law of love."[65] In addressing this dilemma, Niebuhr displayed his fundamental "realist" perspective on human nature. For Niebuhr, given the realities of the will-to-power and human failure to fulfill the law of love, justice demands that society use the coercive power of the state to resist tyranny and evil.

The problem, of course, is that those who utilize the power of the state to resist evil are subject to the same will-to-power that inflicts all humans. Accordingly, Niebuhr devoted considerable attention to the question of how to structure the power of the state so that it might resist evil without becoming evil itself. "Governments must coerce," Niebuhr conceded, but he also recognized that "there is an element of evil in this coercion. It is always in danger of serving the purposes of the coercing power rather than the general weal. We cannot fully trust the motives of any ruling class or power. That is why it is important to maintain democratic checks upon the centers of power."[66] Niebuhr's distrust of the potential of those in power to abuse their authority extended to all governments, both the authoritarian states of Germany and the Soviet Union as well as democratic ones. "To look at human communities from the perspective of the Kingdom of God is to know that there is a sinful element in all the expedients which the political order uses to establish justice. That is why even the seemingly most stable justice degenerates periodically into either tyranny or anarchy."[67]

As authoritarian governments gained power in Europe during the 1930s, leading to extraordinary human suffering during the 1940s, Niebuhr emerged as an articulate apologist for democratic government. "Man's capacity for justice makes democracy possible," Niebuhr famously wrote in *The Children of Light and the Children of Darkness* in 1944, "but man's inclination to injustice makes democracy necessary."[68] Niebuhr elaborated: "Democracy is a perennial necessity because justice will always require that the power of government be checked as democracy checks it; and because peace requires that social conflict be arbitrated by the non-violent technique of the democratic process."[69]

Beginning with the presupposition that "it is not possible to eliminate the sinful element in the political expedients,"[70] Niebuhr urged that society create checks and balances in its political structures that might control the natural human impetus toward self-aggrandizement: "Justice is basically dependent upon a balance of power. Whenever an individual or a group or a nation possesses undue power, and whenever this power is not checked by the possibility of criticizing and resisting it, it grows inordinate."[71] In Niebuhr's view, diffusion of power is necessary to prevent oppression: "It may be taken as axiomatic that great disproportions of power lead to injustice, whatever may be the efforts to mitigate it. Thus the concentration of economic power in modern technical society has made for injustice, while the diffusion of political power has made for justice."[72] Niebuhr was an enthusiastic proponent of the checks and balances in the American constitutional system. As he often commented, the framers of the Constitution were individuals who embraced the notion of original sin.[73]

Niebuhr viewed the world cataclysm of the early 1940s as due in part to the lack of an international body capable of controlling the aggressive actions of individual nation states: "One reason why the balances of power, which prevent injustice in international relations, periodically degenerate into overt anarchy is because no way has yet been found to establish an adequate organizing center, a stable international judicatory, for this balance of power."[74]

Some of Niebuhr's contemporaries, sharing his pessimistic view of human nature, urged the necessity of authoritarian government. Niebuhr disagreed: "A consistent pessimism in regard to man's rational capacity for justice invariably leads to absolutistic political theories; for they prompt the conviction that only preponderant power can coerce the various vitalities of a community into a working harmony."[75] But Niebuhr viewed the unchecked power characteristic of authoritarian government as particularly nefarious: "But the pessimism which prompts and justifies this policy is not consistent; for it is not applied, as it should be, to the ruler. If men are inclined to deal unjustly with their fellows, the possession of power aggravates this inclination. That is why irresponsible and uncontrolled power is the greatest source of injustice."[76]

One Niebuhr scholar has aptly described Niebuhr as a "pessimistic optimist." Humans can use "power creatively in the service of justice, and that is our glory. But we can also abuse power destructively in the service of self ... and that is our demonry."[77] Niebuhr urged that we become neither too pessimistic nor too optimistic about human nature. In his 1959 foreword to a new edition of *The Children of Light and the Children of Darkness*, Niebuhr wrote that a "free society prospers best in a cultural, religious and moral atmosphere which encourages neither a too pessimistic nor too optimistic view of human nature. Both moral sentimentality in politics and moral pessimism encourage totalitarian regimes, the one because it encourages the opinion that it is not necessary to check the power of government, and the second because it believes that only absolute political authority can restrain the anarchy, created by conflicting and competitive interests."[78]

In support of his embrace of democracy as the superior organizing imperative for human society, Niebuhr appealed to the prophetic tradition of Judaism and Christianity:

> Who can deny that the development of prophetic religion, which challenges rather than supports political majesty in the name of the majesty of God, helps to destroy priestly-military oligarchies and to create democratic societies? In this way, the prophetic elements in Christianity have contributed to the rise of modern democratic societies, just as conservative elements in the Christian tradition have strengthened the pretensions of oligarchies by their uncritical identification of political power with the divine authority.[79]

Niebuhr elaborated on the ways in which certain insights of the Christian faith support the dispersion of power in democratic government:

> The facts about human nature which make a monopoly of power dangerous and a balance of power desirable are best understood from the standpoint of the Christian faith.... It cannot be denied that Biblical faith is unique in

offering three insights into the human situation which are indispensable to democracy.

The first is that it assumes a source of authority from the standpoint of which the individual may defy the authorities of this world. ("We must obey God rather than man.") The second is an appreciation of the unique worth of the individual which makes it wrong to fit him into any political program as a mere instrument....

The third insight is the Biblical insistence that the same radical freedom which makes man creative also makes him potentially destructive and dangerous, that the dignity of man and the misery of man therefore have the same root.[80]

Niebuhr also commented about the relationship between the believer and the state. Niebuhr acknowledged that there are two biblical traditions that address this issue. According to one tradition, which draws from Paul's discussion in Romans 13 about the relationship of the Christian and the state, government "is an ordinance of God and its authority reflects the Divine Majesty," which suggests that the Christian must respect the state's authority. According to the other tradition, represented by the Old Testament prophets such as Amos (about whom Niebuhr said, "All theology really begins with Amos"[81]), "the 'rulers' and 'judges' of the nations are particularly subject to divine judgment and wrath because they oppress the poor and defy the divine majesty."[82] Niebuhr sought to reconcile the two traditions, recognizing the tension between them: Government "is a principle of order and its power prevents anarchy; but its power is not identical with divine power. ... It cannot achieve the perfect union of goodness and power which characterizes divine power. The pretension that its power is perfectly virtuous represents its false claim of majesty."[83] Niebuhr noted that "St. Paul's very 'undialectical' appreciation of government in Romans 13 has had a fateful influence in Christian thought, particularly in the Reformation."[84] In fact, Niebuhr argued that Luther's undue emphasis on respect for civil authorities had contributed to the tradition of German authoritarianism.[85]

NATURAL LAW

Niebuhr's reflections about the state and its role in securing justice in human society inevitably brought him into a consideration of whether there are "general principles of justice," or natural law, against which all positive law norms must be assessed. He observed the broad embrace of notions of natural law across cultures:

There are no living communities which do not do have some notions of justice, beyond their historic laws, by which they seek to gauge the justice of their legislative enactments. Such general principles are known as natural law in both Catholic and earlier liberal thought.... Every human society does have something like a natural-law concept; for it assumes that there are more immutable and purer principles of justice than those actually embodied in its obviously relative laws.[86]

Niebuhr, himself, identified the law of love as the "one fundamental principle"[87] against which all behavior is to be assessed and claims that the "ideal of love ... transcends all law."[88] How did Niebuhr know that love is the fundamental norm for human life? Niebuhr claimed that "all human life is informed with an inchoate sense of responsibility toward the ultimate law of life—the law of love."[89] Furthermore, humans in a "moment of self-transcendence" gain understanding of the fundamental nature of love.[90] He also noted that the New Testament regards love "as the final norm of human life."[91] Along with his assertion that the law of love is *the* fundamental principle, however, Niebuhr remained deeply skeptical of articulations of the specific content of natural law or particular applications of the law of love, particularly the self-confident articulations of the parameters of natural law in Catholic moral theology.

For Niebuhr, one of the central questions concerning natural law was who possesses the ultimate authority to give definition to such fundamental principles. Should they be subject to redefinition through the democratic process? Niebuhr commented, "Should [natural law principles] not stand above criticism or amendment? If they are themselves subjected to the democratic process and if they are made dependent upon the moods and vagaries of various communities and epochs, have we not sacrificed the final criterion of justice and order?"[92] He argued that it "is on this question that Catholic Christianity has its final difficulties with the presuppositions of a democratic society in the modern, liberal sense.... For Catholicism believes that the principles of natural law are fixed and immutable.... It believes that the freedom of a democratic society must stop short of calling these principles of natural law in question."[93]

Given the difficulties of human self-interest, Niebuhr questioned whether humans can accurately define the contours of the natural law. To those who think natural law principles could be fully articulated, Niebuhr replied that such persons fail "to appreciate the perennial corruptions of interest and passion which are introduced into any historical definition of even the most ideal and abstract moral principles."[94]

Niebuhr criticized both the Catholic Church and eighteenth-century Enlightenment thinkers' articulations of how we come to know and define the parameters of the natural law. Niebuhr contended that the Catholic Church "wrongly sought to preserve some realm of institutional religious authority which would protect the uncorrupted truths of the natural law."[95] As for Enlightenment thinkers, with their notions of "inalienable rights" and other natural law concepts, Niebuhr argued that they "erroneously hoped for a general diffusion of intelligence which would make the truths of the natural law universally acceptable."[96]

Niebuhr rejected both Catholic and Enlightenment assumptions about the ability of institutions or individuals to identify an immutable natural law. Evoking the thinking of later postmodernists, Niebuhr argued that natural law claims are invariably contextual: "There is no historical reality, whether it be church or government, whether it be the reason of wise men or specialists, which is not involved in the flux and relativity of human existence; which is not subject to error and sin, and which is not tempted to exaggerate its errors and sins when they are made immune to criticism."[97] The problem, as Niebuhr saw it, is that humans who articulate natural law principles are inevitably influenced by their own biases: "The question which must be raised [concerning natural law] is whether the reason by which standards of justice are established is really so pure that the standard does not contain an echo and an accent of the claims of the class or the culture, the nation or the hierarchy which presumes to define the standard."[98] Indeed, Niebuhr contended that it is not possible "to arrive at completely valid principles, free of every taint of special interest and historical passion.... The interests of a class, the viewpoint of a nation, the prejudices of an age and the illusions of a culture are consciously and unconsciously insinuated into the norms by which men regulate their common life. They are intended to give one group an advantage over another. Or if that is not their intention, it is at least the unvarying consequence."[99]

In fact, Niebuhr worried, if natural law principles become "fixed," they "will destroy some of the potentialities of a higher justice, which the mind of one generation is unable to anticipate in the life of subsequent eras."[100] Niebuhr agreed with Karl Marx about the contingent character of articulations of natural law principles:

> The Marxist cynicism in regard to the pretended moral purity of all laws and rules of justice is justified. Marxism is right, furthermore, in regarding them as primarily rationalizations of the interests of the dominant elements of a society. The requirements of "natural law" in the medieval period were obviously conceived in a feudal society; just as the supposed absolute and "self-evident" demands of eighteenth-century natural law were bourgeois in origin.
>
> The relative and contingent character of these ideals and rules of justice refutes the claim of their unconditioned character, made alike by Catholic, liberal and even Marxist social theorists.[101]

Niebuhr's skepticism about natural law can be illustrated by his consideration of natural law claims in the area of gender relations. Niebuhr noted that "Catholic natural law ... enjoins the supremacy of the husband over the wife."[102] Although Niebuhr conceded that both the Bible and the "natural fact that the woman bears the child" help create a differentiated role for women, he argued, "It is important to realize that no definition of the natural law between the sexes can be made without embodying something of the sin of male arrogance into the standard."[103] Niebuhr elaborated: "Any premature fixation of certain historical standards in regard to the family will inevitably tend to reinforce male arrogance.... The sinfulness of man ... makes it inevitable that a dominant class, group, and sex should seek to define a relationship, which guarantees its dominance, as permanently normative."[104] Niebuhr also persistently criticized Catholic prohibition of birth control, justified on the theory that it is "intrinsically against nature,"[105] as an example of an improper use of natural law.[106]

Yet despite Niebuhr's deep skepticism about the articulation of natural law principles, he did hold that there are certain ethical norms that are "permanent" applications of the fundamental law of love. In *The Nature and Destiny of Man*, Niebuhr claimed that "there are of course certain permanent norms, such as monogamy, which ... are maintained not purely by Scriptural authority but by the cumulative experience of the race."[107] Niebuhr then wrote tantalizingly, "About these universalities, amidst the relativities of standards, a word must be spoken presently."[108] He did not elaborate as to why ethical norms such as monogamy are "permanent," while others are culturally contextual.

Although Niebuhr criticized the Catholic Church on a variety of issues, including its position on natural law and its "tendency to be too sure of its truth,"[109] he grew to have a profound respect for many aspects of Catholicism, particularly its embrace of racial and economic justice. Niebuhr, for example, admired the Catholic Church's opposition to racial segregation in the American South during the 1950s. In 1961, he commented that it "has always been one of the virtues of Catholicism that it ... never doubted that political authority should exercise dominance over the economic sphere in the interest of justice."[110] Niebuhr had particularly high regard for Pope Leo XIII's encyclical *Rerum novarum* and Pope John XXIII's encyclical *Pacem in terris*, both of which reflected a deep commitment to social justice.[111]

RACIAL JUSTICE

Although racism was by no means the primary focus of Niebuhr's social ethics, he wrote extensively about the treatment of African Americans, a choice of subject influenced in part by his exposure to southern blacks who had migrated to Detroit during and after World War I as part of the Great Migration. Niebuhr's reflections on the problem of race in America offer a useful application of his theories about individual and group self-interest. "It is a gentle conceit of northern people that race prejudice is a vice peculiar to the south," Niebuhr wrote from his Detroit parish in 1927. "The tremendous migration of southern Negroes into the industrial centers of the north is rapidly dispelling this illusion."[112] In that same 1927 essay, Niebuhr called racial discrimination "one of the greatest challenges to the spirit of real Christianity. The whole validity of the Christian faith is in the balance as men try to solve the race problem. Either there is in Christ neither white nor black or the whole Christian faith becomes absurd."[113]

Niebuhr conceived of racial discrimination as a manifestation of group pride. He explained in a 1942 essay: "Racial prejudice, as every other form of group prejudice, is a concomitant of the collective life of man. Group pride is the sinful corruption of group consciousness. Contempt of another group is the pathetic form that respect for our own group frequently takes."[114] During the late 1950s, for example, Niebuhr wrote that southern white resistance to school desegregation "was caused by the ineradicable tendency of men to build integral communities upon the sense of ethnic kinship and to exclude from that kinship any race which diverges too obviously from type. In the white South, the Negro's primary offense is that he is black."[115] In commenting on the difficulties of securing civil rights legislation in the United States during the early 1960s, Niebuhr noted: "The effort ... to give Negroes the full and equal status of citizenship and of a common humanity was bound to prove more difficult than even the most realistic idealists imagined ... [because] Western man—in common with all men—remains an unregenerate tribalist."[116]

Niebuhr also believed that efforts to combat racial discrimination by relying solely on moral appeals would be of limited utility. Commenting on ongoing efforts at "interracial cooperation," Niebuhr concluded that these efforts "accomplish little more than spin a thin veil of moral idealism under which the white man does not really hide his determination to maintain the Negro in a subordinate position in our civilization."[117] Moral idealism alone, Niebuhr wrote in 1932, will never be sufficient to overcome the deeply entrenched self-interest of majority groups:

> It is hopeless for the Negro to expect complete emancipation from the menial social and economic position into which the white man has forced him, merely by trusting in the moral sense of the white race.... However large the number of individual white men who do and who will identify themselves completely with the Negro cause, the white race in America will not admit

the Negro to equal rights if it is not forced to do so. Upon that point one may speak with a dogmatism which all history justifies.[118]

Writing in 1942, Niebuhr concluded, "There are, in other words, no solutions for the race problem on any level if it is not realized that there is no absolute solution for this problem. There is no absolute solution in the sense that it is not possible to purge man completely of the sinful concomitant of group pride in his collective life."[119]

Throughout his life, Niebuhr retained his pessimism about the possibilities of meaningful racial reform. Writing in 1963 at the height of the civil rights movement, Niebuhr responded critically to the suggestion of Robert Kennedy that African Americans, like Irish Americans, would eventually overcome discrimination and enter the political mainstream: "But the analogy is not exact. The Irish merely affronted us by having a different religion and a different place of origin than the 'true' Americans. The Negroes affront us by diverging from the dominant type all too obviously. Their skin is black. And our celebrated reason is too errant to digest the difference."[120] While much of liberal America hailed the enactment of the Civil Rights Act of 1964 as a triumph of the American creed of equal treatment, Niebuhr remained decidedly pessimistic about the ability of law to corral human behavior. Writing four days after President Lyndon Johnson signed into law the 1964 civil rights legislation, Niebuhr dissented from the euphoria surrounding this landmark event. In an essay entitled "Man, the Unregenerate Tribalist," Niebuhr expressed pessimism that the new statute would transform race relations in the United States.[121] In another essay published the same day, Niebuhr commented: "It will be a crisis-filled decade and century before the nation has solved—or even taken the most rigorous steps toward the solution of—this 'American dilemma.' The dilemma is actually wider than our national life; it is the dilemma of validating the humanity of man despite the strong tribal impulses in his nature."[122]

Niebuhr's profound pessimism about human nature and the ability of white America to embrace African Americans earned him rebukes from many civil right proponents who accused him of being "too pessimistic about [the possibility of] radical social change."[123] Niebuhr, who had consistently urged racial reform in the United States since the 1920s, welcomed the civil rights legislation of the 1960s. His view of the profound human tendency toward self-interest, however, prevented him from sharing the enthusiasm of many racial liberals about the ultimate significance of those legislative gains.

What, then, in Niebuhr's view, should African Americans do in the face of persistent racial discrimination? Niebuhr argued, "The relations between groups must therefore always be predominantly political rather than ethical, that is, they will be determined by the proportion of power which each group possesses at least as much as by any rational and moral appraisal of the comparative needs and claims of each group."[124] As a result, "outsiders" such as blacks or workers must "develop both economic and political power to meet the combination of political and economic power which confronts him."[125] For example, Niebuhr recommended that African Americans use various cooperative arrangements such as economic boycotts to confront majority power—"boycotts against banks which discriminate against Negroes in granting credit, against stores which refuse to employ Negroes while serving Negro trade, and against public service corporations which practice racial discrimination."[126]

NIEBUHR'S IMPACT ON THE NEXT GENERATION

Niebuhr has had a significant impact on a broad range of thinkers—religious and secular—as well as political figures. Indeed, some of the most influential individuals of the second half of the twentieth century were profoundly shaped by Niebuhr. For example, Niebuhr's writings about human nature had a significant influence on Martin Luther King's understanding of the nature of social change. Writing in 1958, King observed of Niebuhr:

> Niebuhr's greatest contribution to contemporary theology is that he has refuted the false optimism characteristic of a great segment of Protestant liberalism.... [Niebuhr's] theology is a persistent reminder of the reality of sin on every level of man's existence. These elements in Niebuhr's thinking helped me to recognize the illusions of a superficial optimism concerning human nature and the dangers of a false idealism.[127]

Indeed, one King scholar has concluded that "the Christian realism of Reinhold Niebuhr ... was probably ... the greatest sobering influence upon King's optimistic anthropological assumptions."[128] Moreover, although King did not embrace Niebuhr's rejection of pacifism, Niebuhr's influence caused King to conclude that "too many [pacifists] had an unwarranted optimism concerning man." King also credited Niebuhr for "the fact that in spite of [my] strong leaning toward pacifism, [I] never joined a pacifist organization."[129]

Many national politicians of the second half of the twentieth century also asserted Niebuhr's influence on the development of their thinking. In 1966, Vice President Hubert Humphrey addressed Niebuhr's influence on the generation who "came out of the Great Depression":

We knew there were urgent demands of social justice that required direct action and idealism. At the same time, we learned that politics was complicated and many-sided, that life just wasn't that simple. Dr. Niebuhr was the man more than any other who put these two things together, and showed how they are both connected with religious faith. Yes, he helped us to see that politicians and theologians had a mutual interest in sin in the world.[130]

Other public figures for whom Niebuhr served as a primary intellectual mentor include McGeorge Bundy, George Kennan, and Arthur Schlesinger Jr.[131]

Niebuhr's influence on President Jimmy Carter was more personal. Early in his political career, Carter struggled with the question of whether a Christian could serve in politics. He read a collection of Niebuhr's writings, *Reinhold Niebuhr on Politics*, which became Carter's "political Bible."[132] Niebuhr's writings helped Carter to reconcile his Christian faith with his passion for politics and allowed Carter to see politics as a venue for bringing justice to the world. Carter's favorite quotation was one from Niebuhr: "The sad duty of politics is to establish justice in a sinful world."[133]

CONCLUSION

Niebuhr's "realist" perspective of human nature influenced all of his theological and political positions. Despite his apparent pessimism about the possibilities of fulfilling the "law of love," however, Niebuhr's passion for justice for the oppressed caused him to urge believers not to abandon hope:

A Christian pessimism which becomes a temptation to irresponsibility toward all those social tasks which constantly confront the life of men and nations … cannot speak redemptively to a world constantly threatened by anarchy and suffering from injustice. The Christian gospel which transcends all particular and contemporary social situations can be preached with power only by a Church which bears its share of the burdens of immediate situations in which men are involved, burdens of establishing peace, of achieving justice, and of perfecting justice in the spirit of love.[134]

By the same token, Niebuhr, always the realist, urged the church to recognize that "perfecting justice in the spirit of love" would never be fully achieved on this earth. Appropriately, Niebuhr's best-known single work is the "Serenity Prayer" made famous by Alcoholics Anonymous: "God give us the grace to accept with serenity the things that cannot be changed, courage to change the things that should be changed, and the wisdom to distinguish the one from the other."[135]

NOTES

1. Larry Rasmussen, introduction to *Reinhold Niebuhr: Theologian of Public Life*, ed. Larry Rasmussen (Minneapolis: Fortress Press, 1991), ix.

2. Hans J. Morgenthau, "The Influence of Reinhold Niebuhr in American Political Life and Thought," in *Reinhold Niebuhr: A Prophetic Voice in Our Time*, ed. Harold R. Landon (Greenwich, Conn.: Seabury, 1962), 109.

3. Quoted in Nathan A. Scott Jr., *Reinhold Niebuhr* (Minneapolis: University of Minnesota Press, 1963), 7.

4. Paul Lehmann, "The Christology of Reinhold Niebuhr," in *Reinhold Niebuhr: His Religious, Social, and Political Thought*, ed. Charles W. Kegley and Robert W. Bretall (New York: Macmillan, 1956), 2:253.

5. Dennis P. McCann, *Christian Realism and Liberation Theology: Practical Theologies in Creative Conflict* (Maryknoll, N.Y.: Orbis Books, 1981), 14.

6. Reinhold Niebuhr, *The Contribution of Religion to Social Work* (New York: Columbia University Press, 1932), 77.

7. Robert McAfee Brown, introduction to *The Essential Reinhold Niebuhr: Selected Essays and Addresses*, ed. Robert McAfee Brown (New Haven, Conn.: Yale University Press, 1986), xvi.

8. McCann, *Christian Realism*, 12.

9. Reinhold Niebuhr, "Intellectual Autobiography," in Kegley and Bretall, *Reinhold Niebuhr*, 2:3.

10. Rasmussen, "Introduction," 3.

11. Reinhold Niebuhr, "Theology and Political Thought in the Western World," in *Faith and Politics: A Commentary on Religious, Social and Political Thought in a Technological Age*, ed. Ronald H. Stone (New York: George Braziller, 1968), 55.

12. Quoted in Scott, *Reinhold Niebuhr*, 40–41.

13. Robin W. Lovin, *Reinhold Niebuhr and Christian Realism* (New York: Cambridge University Press, 1995), 5.

14. Walter Rauschenbusch, *Christianity and the Social Crisis* (Louisville, Ky.: Westminster John Knox Press, 1991), 209.

15. William Adams Brown, *Pathways to Certainty* (New York: Charles Scribner's Sons, 1930), 247.

16. Scott, *Reinhold Niebuhr*, 14.

17. Reinhold Niebuhr, *Christianity and Power Politics* (New York: Charles Scribner's Sons, 1940), 20.

18. Reinhold Niebuhr, *An Interpretation of Christian Ethics* (New York: Meridian Books, 1958), 155.

19. Lovin, *Reinhold Niebuhr and Christian Realism*, 6.

20. Daniel F. Rice, *Reinhold Niebuhr and John Dewey: An American Odyssey* (Albany: State University of New York Press, 1993), 17.

21. Reinhold Niebuhr, *Moral Man and Immoral Society* (New York: Charles Scribner's Sons, 1932), xii.

22. Taylor Branch, *Parting the Waters: America in the King Years, 1954–63* (New York: Simon & Schuster, 1989), 84.

23. Brown, "Introduction," xv.

24. Niebuhr, *Moral Man and Immoral Society*, xi.

25. Reinhold Niebuhr, "Moralists and Politics," *The Christian Century* 49 (July 6, 1932): 857.

26. Niebuhr, *Moral Man and Immoral Society*, xx.

27. Niebuhr, "Moralists and Politics," 857.

28. Ibid., 858.

29. Niebuhr, *Moral Man and Immoral Society*, xii.

30. Ibid., xxiii–xxiv.

31. Reinhold Niebuhr, *The Nature and Destiny of Man: A Christian Interpretation*, 2 vols. (New York: Charles Scribner's Sons, 1941–43), 1:23.

32. Ibid., 213.

33. Daphne Hampson, "Reinhold Niebuhr on Sin: A Critique," in *Reinhold Niebuhr and the Issues of Our Time*, ed. Richard Harries (London: Mowbray, 1986), 47. See also Judith Plaskow, *Sex, Sin, and Grace: Women's Experience and the Theologies of Reinhold Niebuhr and Paul Tillich* (Washington, D.C.: University Press of America, 1980).

34. Hampson, "Reinhold Niebuhr on Sin," 49.

35. Reinhold Niebuhr, *The Children of Light and the Children of Darkness: A Vindication of Democracy and a Critique of its Traditional Defense* (New York: Charles Scribner's Sons, 1960), 20.

36. Ibid.

37. Ibid., 22.

38. Niebuhr, *An Interpretation of Christian Ethics*, 101.

39. Brown, "Introduction," xvi.

40. Niebuhr, *Christianity and Power Politics*, 21–22.

41. Ibid., 215.

42. Niebuhr, *The Nature and Destiny of Man*, 1:269.

43. Ibid., 272.

44. Ibid., 266.

45. Ibid.

46. Ibid., 269 (emphasis added).

47. Ibid., 296.

48. Ibid.

49. Niebuhr, *An Interpretation of Christian Ethics*, 109.

50. Niebuhr, *The Nature and Destiny of Man*, 1:298.

51. Niebuhr, *Christianity and Power Politics*, 6.

52. Ibid., 18.

53. Niebuhr, *The Nature and Destiny of Man*, 1:299.

54. Ibid., 2:99.

55. Niebuhr, *Christianity and Power Politics*, 19.

56. Ibid.

57. Niebuhr, *The Nature and Destiny of Man*, 1:299.

58. Ibid., 2:122.

59. Niebuhr, *Christianity and Power Politics*, 9–10.

60. Ibid., 14.

61. Ibid.
62. Niebuhr, *An Interpretation of Christian Ethics*, 160–161.
63. Ibid., 45.
64. Niebuhr, *Christianity and Power Politics*, 18.
65. Ibid., 21.
66. Ibid., 14–15.
67. Ibid., 22.
68. Niebuhr, *The Children of Light and the Children of Darkness*, xiii.
69. Niebuhr, *Christianity and Power Politics*, 85.
70. Ibid., 22.
71. Ibid., 26.
72. Niebuhr, *The Nature and Destiny of Man*, 2:262.
73. Brown, "Introduction," xii.
74. Niebuhr, *Christianity and Power Politics*, 26.
75. Niebuhr, *The Children of Light and the Children of Darkness*, xii–xiii.
76. Ibid., xiii–xiv.
77. Brown, "Introduction," xi–xii.
78. Niebuhr, *The Children of Light and the Children of Darkness*, viii.
79. Niebuhr, *The Nature and Destiny of Man*, 2:264.
80. Reinhold Niebuhr, "Government and the Strategy of Democracy," in *Reinhold Niebuhr on Politics: His Political Philosophy and Its Application to Our Age as Expressed in His Writings*, ed. Harry R. Davis and Robert C. Good (New York: Charles Scribner's Sons, 1960), 187.
81. Quoted in Rasmussen, *Reinhold Niebuhr: Theologian of Public Life*, 269.
82. Niebuhr, *The Nature and Destiny of Man*, 2:269.
83. Ibid.
84. Ibid., 270.
85. Charles C. Brown, *Niebuhr and His Age: Reinhold Niebuhr's Prophetic Role in the Twentieth Century* (Philadelphia: Trinity Press International, 1992), 84–85.
86. Niebuhr, *The Children of Light and the Children of Darkness*, 67–68.
87. Paul Ramsey, "Love and Law," in Kegley and Breatall, *Reinhold Niebuhr*, 2:91.
88. Niebuhr, *An Interpretation of Christian Ethics*, 136.
89. Ibid., 105.
90. Niebuhr, *The Nature and Destiny of Man*, 1:277.
91. Reinhold Niebuhr, *Faith and History: A Comparison of Christian and Modern Views of History* (New York: Charles Scribner's Sons, 1949), 184.
92. Niebuhr, *The Children of Light and the Children of Darkness*, 68.
93. Ibid., 68–69.
94. Ibid., 70.
95. Ibid.
96. Ibid.
97. Ibid., 70–71.
98. Niebuhr, *Faith and History*, 186.
99. Niebuhr, *The Nature and Destiny of Man*, 2:256.

100. Niebuhr, *The Children of Light and the Children of Darkness*, 71.

101. Niebuhr, *The Nature and Destiny of Man*, 2:252–253.

102. Ibid., 1:281.

103. Ibid., 282.

104. Ibid.

105. Niebuhr, *Faith and History*, 181, quoting Pope Pius XI, *Encyclical on Christian Marriage in Our Day*, par. 55.

106. John C. Bennett, "Reinhold Niebuhr's Contribution to Christian Social Ethics," in *Reinhold Niebuhr: A Prophetic Voice in Our Time*, ed. Harold R. Landon (Greenwich, Conn.: Seabury, 1962), 74.

107. Niebuhr, *The Nature and Destiny of Man*, 1:282–283.

108. Ibid., 283.

109. Charles C. Brown, *Niebuhr and His Age*, 225.

110. Quoted in Richard Wightman Fox, *Reinhold Niebuhr: A Biography* (New York: Pantheon Books, 1985), 286.

111. Brown, *Niebuhr and His Age*, 225–226.

112. Reinhold Niebuhr, "Race Prejudice in the North," *The Christian Century* 44 (May 12, 1927): 583.

113. Ibid., 584.

114. Reinhold Niebuhr, "The Race Problem," *Christianity and Society* 7 (Summer 1942): 3.

115. Reinhold Niebuhr, "The States' Rights Crisis," *New Leader* 41 (September 29, 1958): 7.

116. Reinhold Niebuhr, "Man, the Unregenerate Tribalist," *Christianity and Crisis* 24 (July 6, 1964): 133.

117. Niebuhr, "Moralists and Politics," 857.

118. Niebuhr, *Moral Man and Immoral Society*, 252–253.

119. Niebuhr, "The Race Problem," 4.

120. Reinhold Niebuhr, "Revolution in an Open Society," *New Leader* 46 (May 27, 1963): 8.

121. Niebuhr, "Man, the Unregenerate Tribalist," 133.

122. Reinhold Niebuhr, "The Struggle for Justice," *New Leader* 47 (July 6, 1964): 11.

123. Ronald Preston, "Reinhold Niebuhr and the New Right," in Harries, *Reinhold Niebuhr and the Issues of Our Time*, 90.

124. Niebuhr, *Moral Man and Immoral Society*, xxiii.

125. Niebuhr, "Moralists and Politics," 858.

126. Niebuhr, *Moral Man and Immoral Society*, 254.

127. Martin Luther King Jr., *Stride Toward Freedom: The Montgomery Story* (New York: Harper & Brothers, 1958), 99.

128. Lewis V. Baldwin, *There is A Balm in Gilead: The Cultural Roots of Martin Luther King, Jr.* (Minneapolis: Fortress Press, 1991), 78.

129. King, *Stride Toward Freedom*, 99.

130. Quoted in Paul Merkley, *Reinhold Niebuhr: A Political Account* (Montreal: McGill-Queen's University Press, 1975), 205.

131. Merkley, *Reinhold Niebuhr*, vii.

132. William Lee Miller, *Yankee from Georgia: The Emergence of Jimmy Carter* (New York: Times Books, 1978), 214–215.

133. Leslie Griffin, "Jimmy Carter's Absolute Separation of Church and State," unpublished manuscript.

134. Niebuhr, "The Christian Church in a Secular Age," 216.

135. Quoted in Ronald H. Stone, *Professor Reinhold Niebuhr: A Mentor to the Twentieth Century* (Louisville, Ky.: Westminster John Knox Press, 1992), 140.

Pages 417–19 and 430–37 of this chapter were drawn in part from Davison M. Douglas, "Reinhold Niebuhr and Critical Race Theory," *Christian Perspectives on Legal Thought,* Michael W. McConnell, Robert F. Cochran, Jr., and Angela C. Carmella, eds. (New Haven: Yale University Press, 2001).

[CHAPTER 15]

Martin Luther King Jr. (1929–1968)

TIMOTHY P. JACKSON

Any person ... who shall be guilty of printing, publishing, or circulating print-
ed, typewritten or written matter urging or presenting for public acceptance
or general information, arguments or suggestions in favor of social equality
or of intermarriage between whites and negroes, shall be guilty of a misde-
meanor and subject to fine of [sic] not exceeding five hundred (500.00) dollars
or imprisonment not exceeding six (6) months or both.

—MISSISSIPPI "JIM CROW" LAW

It seemed as though I could hear the quiet assurance of an inner voice, say-
ing, "Stand up for righteousness, stand up for truth. God will be at your side
forever."

—MARTIN LUTHER KING JR.

Martin Luther King Jr. was neither an influential legal theorist nor a major systematic theologian. Rather, he was something much more necessary to his time, and arguably all times: a person of righteousness and faith
who stood up for his convictions in obedience to God and in service to
his neighbors. He was schooled in sociology and divinity, as well as skilled
in practical jurisprudence, and he wrote very insightfully of his creed and
causes. Yet King is included in this volume chiefly because he brought
about constructive social change, by both legal and extralegal means, and
because he inspired others to do the same. He embodied, above all, the
"uses" of the law and theology, rather than their innovation or scholarly
analysis. In short, he was a prophet rather than a pedant.

King courageously cross-fertilized Christian doctrines and democratic
principles in a way that is rare today. In an age in which preeminent theorists of both the Christian church and the liberal state often seem to lose
their way—by retreating into a narrow sectarianism on one hand and an

empty proceduralism on the other—King's example still has much to teach us about justice, law, and human nature. He refused to divorce the sacred (the God worshipped by Jews and Christians) and the secular (the legal realities of American democracy). As a Baptist clergyman, King considered it not merely permissible but actually obligatory to engage publicly controversial political and economic issues. He offered neither dogmatic self-congratulation to believers nor neutral self-interest to nonbelievers, and in the process, he lived out the meaning of the First Amendment. Indeed, it was precisely because he believed that the call to and capacity for justice is built into the nature of "all of God's children"[1] that King was the foremost American public intellectual of the second half of the twentieth century.

King's legacy turns, in large measure, on a concrete moral commitment and a more elusive personal talent: his lived dedication to the poor and oppressed, together with his capacity for holism and synthesis. In his life, work, and death we have a model of service to the marginalized and vulnerable—the scriptural "widow and orphan"—as well as a guide to balancing a range of human goods, public and private. We have, more specifically, a picture of how to relate American law and the Christian gospel. This prophet eventually averred that "we as a nation must undergo a radical revolution of values,"[2] and the dialectic he suggested between politics and scripture is necessarily incomplete. Indeed, he gave decisive priority to the gospel. But King knew that "all life is interrelated" and that "life at its best is a creative synthesis of opposites in fruitful harmony."[3] He knew that a good society could no more separate social justice from personal charity, for instance, than it could segregate its white and black citizens.[4] King's life and thought were not without flaws, of course,[5] and one may question, as I do, aspects of his optimism and personalism. His ongoing influence for the good is testified to, however, by the fact that both lawyers and theologians still read and discuss him in trying to comprehend civic virtue.

One more introductory point must be addressed before I turn to the body of my text. There is often a backlash today when Martin King is held up as a moral hero. The understandable fear is that King, since his assassination, has become the darling of white conservatives, that invoking King's name will call up images of patient suffering and a "color-blind" community that take the edge off radical calls for black pride, black self-defense, and black separatism. What of the countervailing messages of W. E. B. Du Bois and Marcus Garvey, of Elijah Muhammad and Malcolm X, of Huey P. Newton and Stokely Carmichael, of Louis Farrakhan and Elaine Brown? In focusing so much on King, the thesis runs, the impression may be given that resistant African American identity is monolithic; it might even seem that the struggle for civil rights and racial justice is a thing of the past. I hope to illustrate in this chapter, in contrast, the depth of King's critique of American law and culture, together with the height of his faith in the biblical God. His critique and the faith are still relevant today; in fact, in King's case (if not our own), the latter is indispensable to the former.

BIOGRAPHY

In dealing with a prophet, an exemplary public voice, there can be little understanding without some biography. In the case of Martin Luther King Jr., law and human nature are writ large in the story of a particular life, leaving us to comprehend and respond.

Martin Luther King Jr. was born on January 15, 1929, into an upper-middle-class home on Auburn Avenue in Atlanta, Georgia. His father was a Baptist preacher and active in the NAACP, while his mother was a homemaker and church organist. Young Martin, called "M.L.," was shaped by three basic factors: his family's emphasis on spiritual and cultural values, such as biblical literacy and piety, secular education, and social service; his family's social and financial standing in a comparatively prosperous (though largely segregated) black neighborhood; and the racism of the South, including the Jim Crow laws that enforced white supremacy and racial separatism. Growing up on "Sweet Auburn," just a few hundred yards up the road from Ebenezer Baptist Church, where his father was pastor, allowed King to see three worlds at once: a vibrant black church, a thriving black community, and an unjust wider society. This vantage point clearly influenced how he would eventually understand justice, law, and human nature. He was given a moral education and sense of self that allowed him both to perceive social problems and to address them without despair, to see the importance and power of human laws and to appreciate their limit and fallibility.

This education took time. "In his preschool years," Stephen B. Oates informs us, "M.L.'s closest playmate was a white boy whose father owned a store across the street from the King home."[6] When the two boys eventually entered separate schools, his friend's parents declared that Martin could no longer play with their son. This was King's first real experience of the race problem. "I was determined to hate every white person," King later wrote,[7] and his ire was further aggravated when, as a high school student, he and a teacher were forced to give up their seats to whites on a crowded bus. "It was the angriest I have ever been in my life," he subsequently observed.[8]

How did King avoid growing into a bitter and lawless young man? The maturing prophet did not initially endorse Christianity. Though his father was a Protestant minister, the younger King grew up doubting that religion could ever be "emotionally satisfying" or "intellectually respectable." Fundamentalist belief in particular seemed to have little relevance to the modern world, Oates informs us, including interracial relations.[9]

When King entered Morehouse College at age fifteen, however, several teachers began to revolutionize his worldview. George D. Kelsey helped him to see that Daddy King's fundamentalism was not the only form of Christianity, and thus Martin started to rethink his religious opinions. Benjamin Mays, the college president, also deeply affected King with his attack on "socially irrelevant patterns of escape" for the black church and his accent on liberation through knowledge and social engagement.[10] By 1946, the once-skeptical King felt called to the ministry, and in 1947 he was licensed to preach and became assistant to his father at Ebenezer Baptist Church. On February 25, 1948, King was ordained to the Baptist clergy. While still at Morehouse, he read Thoreau's "Civil Disobedience" and for the first time was exposed to the idea of nonviolent resistance: the power "of refusing to cooperate with an evil system."[11] In June 1948, King graduated from Morehouse College with a B.A. in sociology, and in September he entered Crozer Theological Seminary in Chester, Pennsylvania.

At Crozer, King became a disciple of Walter Rauschenbusch and the Christian activism of the Social Gospel movement. In Rauschenbusch, King found what Oates calls "a theological foundation for the social concerns he'd had since he was a boy," "a socially relevant faith" that could "deal with the whole man—his body and soul, his material and spiritual well-being."[12] King also read Marx and Lenin at this time, but he came to have three major objections to their thought. As he later recalled in *Stride Toward Freedom*, "First I rejected their materialistic interpretation of history.... Second, I strongly disagreed with communism's ethical relativism.... Third, I opposed communism's political totalitarianism."[13] King concluded that both communism and capitalism are partial truths, and he forever after insisted that no just reform movement could separate means from ends.[14] We are so embedded in our actions, he recognized, that to do evil that good might come is to pervert our selves as well as our societies.[15]

About this time, King heard a lecture by Mordecai W. Johnson, president of Howard University, on the life and teachings of Mahatma Gandhi. Johnson argued that the moral power of nonviolence (*ahimsa*) could improve race relations in the United States. King was impressed by the fact that Gandhi was not out to harm or humiliate the British but to redeem them through love.[16] After reading Marx and Nietzsche, King had "about despaired of the power of love in solving social problems."[17] But Gandhi's notion of *Satyagraha* (literally "truth-power") reconciled love and force and convinced King that it was the only moral and practical means for an oppressed people to struggle against social injustice. As King later noted:

Prior to reading Gandhi, I had about concluded that the ethics of Jesus were only effective in individual relationship. The "turn the other cheek" philosophy and the "love your enemies" philosophy were only valid, I felt, when individuals were in conflict with other individuals; when racial groups and nations were in conflict a more realistic approach seemed necessary. But after reading Gandhi, I saw how utterly mistaken I was.

Gandhi was probably the first person in history to lift the love ethic of Jesus above mere interaction between individuals to a powerful and effective social force on a large scale. Love for Gandhi was a potent instrument for social and collective transformation. It was in this Gandhian emphasis on love and non-violence that I discovered the method for social reform that I had been seeking for so many months.[18]

King always insisted that Christ provided the "spirit and motivation," and Gandhi the practical "method," of the civil rights movement.[19]

In June 1951, King graduated from Crozer with a bachelor of divinity degree; in June 1953, he married Coretta Scott in Marion, Alabama; and in June 1955, he received his doctorate in systematic theology from Boston University. Shortly after he embraced Gandhi at Crozer, King had to come to grips with Reinhold Niebuhr and his critique of Protestant liberalism's optimism about human nature and tendency toward a vapid pacifism. This King did at Boston University. For all of Niebuhr's insight, King concluded,

Many of his statements revealed that he interpreted pacifism as a sort of passive nonresistance to evil expressing naïve trust in the power of love. But this was a serious distortion. My study of Gandhi convinced me that true pacifism is not nonresistance to evil, but nonviolent resistance to evil.

I came to see that Niebuhr had overemphasized the corruption of human nature. His pessimism concerning human nature was not balanced by an optimism concerning divine nature. He was so involved in diagnosing man's sickness of sin that he overlooked the cure of grace.[20]

Part of what contributed to King's own optimism was his study at Boston University of personalist philosophy with Edgar S. Brightman and L. Harold DeWolf. "Personalism's insistence that only personality—finite and infinite—is ultimately real strengthened me in two convictions: it gave me metaphysical and philosophical grounding for the idea of a personal God, and it gave me a metaphysical basis for the dignity and worth of all human personality."[21]

In January 1954, King received an offer from Dexter Avenue Baptist Church in Montgomery, Alabama, to give a trial sermon. He preached on "The Three Dimensions of a Complete Life"—love of self, love of neighbor, and love of God—was offered the post, and began his full-time pastorate on Septem-

ber 1, 1954.[22] The Kings' first child, Yolanda Denise, was born in Montgomery on November 17, 1955. On December 1, Rosa Parks, a forty-two-year-old
Montgomery seamstress, refused to relinquish her bus seat to a white man
and was arrested. On December 5, local organizers (mostly black churchmen
and churchwomen) began a boycott of city buses to coincide with the trial
of Mrs. Parks. At a meeting of movement leaders that same day, King was
unanimously elected president of what had come to be called the Montgomery Improvement Association (MIA). On December 10, the Montgomery
Bus Company suspended service in black neighborhoods.

At biweekly meetings of the MIA, King related his philosophy of nonviolent love and redemptive suffering. Yet his call for Negro self-respect
and his appreciation of the vagaries of law and violence were also evident
from the beginning. In an early essay entitled "Our Struggle," written in
1956, King summarized several of his basic beliefs and objectives:

> The extreme tension in race relations in the South today is explained in part
> by the revolutionary change in the Negro's evaluation of himself and of his
> destiny and by his determination to struggle for justice. *We Negroes have re-
> placed self-pity with self-respect and self-depreciation with dignity.*[23]

> Although law is an important factor in bringing about social change, there are
> certain conditions in which the very effort to adhere to new legal decisions
> creates tension and provokes violence. We had hoped to see demonstrated a
> method that would enable us to continue our struggle while coping with the
> violence it aroused. Now we see the answer: face violence if necessary, but
> refuse to return violence. If we respect those who oppose us, they may achieve
> a new understanding of the human relations involved.[24]

> We do not wish to triumph over the white community. That would only result
> in transferring those now on the bottom to the top. But, if we can live up
> to nonviolence in thought and deed, there will emerge an interracial society
> based on freedom for all.[25]

The vision of an interracial society governed by the "liberal" values of
freedom and equality continued, in part, to define the balance of King's
career.

Even as King and others attempted to put a just vision into practice in
Montgomery, hate mail and crank calls flowed in. On January 26, 1956,
King was arrested on speeding charges—going 30 in a 25 mph zone—and
feared for his life when he was taken out of town to the jailhouse. In the
face of death threats and legal obstructionism, anxiety and frustration grew
among members of the MIA and in King's own soul. The day after his short
stay in jail, as King later recalled, things came to a head:

After a particularly strenuous day, I settled in bed at a late hour. My wife had already fallen asleep and I was about to doze off when the telephone rang. An angry voice said, "Listen, nigger, we've taken all we want from you. Before next week you'll be sorry you ever came to Montgomery." I hung up, but I could not sleep. It seemed that all of my fears had come on me at once. I had reached the saturation point.

I got out of bed and began to walk the floor. Finally, I went to the kitchen and heated a pot of coffee. I was ready to give up. I tried to think of a way to move out of the picture without appearing to be a coward. In this state of exhaustion, when my courage had almost gone, I determined to take my problem to God. My head in my hands, I bowed over the kitchen table and prayed aloud. The words I spoke to God that midnight are still vivid in my memory. "I am here taking a stand for what I believe is right. But now I am afraid. The people are looking to me for leadership, and if I stand before them without strength and courage, they too will falter. I am at the end of my powers. I have nothing left. I've come to the point where I can't face it alone."

At that moment I experienced the presence of the Divine as I had never before experienced him. It seemed as though I could hear the quiet assurance of an inner voice, saying, "Stand up for righteousness, stand up for truth. God will be at your side forever." Almost at once my fears began to pass from me. My uncertainty disappeared. I was ready to face anything. The outer situation remained the same, but God had given me inner calm.[26]

Thus unfolded the most memorable moment of King's life, one resonant with the legendary pronouncement of his sixteenth-century namesake[27] and one to which King returned again and again for inspiration.[28] Three nights later, an unknown assailant threw a bomb onto the porch of King's Montgomery home. Though Coretta, Yolanda, and a family friend were in the house, no one was injured. Three days after that, on February 2, a suit was filed in federal district court asking that Montgomery's travel segregation laws be declared unconstitutional. On June 4, the federal district court ruled that racial segregation on city bus lines was unconstitutional. On November 13, the Supreme Court affirmed the lower court, thus voiding Alabama's state and local segregation laws. And on December 21, 1956, a year and twenty days after Rosa Parks's protest, the Montgomery buses were integrated.

King's leadership of the MIA inaugurated a dozen years of crusading for social justice. Elected to the leadership of the Southern Christian Leadership Conference (SCLC) in Atlanta on January 10–11, 1957, he was assassinated on a balcony of the Lorraine Motel in Memphis on April 4, 1968. King and his associates were strikingly effective in bringing about legal reforms in America and often used federal courts to challenge state practices and regulations. But King also suffered many setbacks. It is notable that, in his 1956 "kitchen table epiphany," he was not promised legal successes or even personal safety. (He was murdered before reaching the age of forty, after all.) Instead, he was given a mandate to champion those things that undergird positive law—righteousness and truth—together with an assurance of the presence of God. The distinction between political efficacy and moral principles, between temporal goods and an eternal God, shaped much of King's subsequent thought and action.

LAW AND JUSTICE

Two of King's favorite biblical passages were "Be not conformed to this world, but be ye transformed by the renewing of your mind" (Rom. 12:2 KJV) and "Let judgment [justice] roll down as waters, and righteousness as a mighty stream" (Amos 5:24 KJV).[29] The ability to hold these two quotations together in a lived unity, faithful to both heaven and earth, defined King's genius. More concretely, he recognized and acted on both the limits to and the potency of human laws. On the side of law's limits, King was no moral constructivist or legal positivist, refusing to appeal to a higher authority than regnant social conventions.[30] In his famous "Letter from a Birmingham Jail" (1963), for example, he insisted that there are "two types of laws": just and unjust. With Augustine, he held that "an unjust law is no law at all," and with Thomas Aquinas, he affirmed that "an unjust law is a human law that is not rooted in eternal and natural law."[31] More politically, "an unjust law is a code inflicted upon a minority which that minority had no part in enacting or creating because they did not have the unhampered right to vote."[32] These distinctions permitted King to explain how he could advocate the breaking of certain legal statutes in the name of civil rights; civil disobedience is permitted, even required, in order to resist codified social wrongs, because there is "a higher moral law" with a prior claim on us.[33]

The logic of King's lawbreaking is notable. One might expect him to hold that, since an unjust law is not really a law, one might violate it at will and with impunity. There will be *practical* consequences, of course—one will likely be arrested and imprisoned, or worse—but *morally* one is unconstrained. One might even expect King to conclude that, in the face of a system of predominantly unjust laws, the entire system is null and void. These were not King's judgments, however. He argued that, rightly understood, civil disobedience must be properly motivated and should not be allowed to slip into anarchic disregard for law in general. As King wrote: "One who breaks an unjust law must do it *openly, lovingly* ... and with a willingness to accept the penalty. I submit that an individual who breaks a law that conscience tells him is unjust, and willingly accepts the penalty by staying in jail to arouse the conscience of the community over its injustice, is in reality expressing the very highest respect for law."[34]

Why accept a penalty for violating an immoral (non-) law? One reason, of course, is pragmatic; in undergoing punishment without retaliation, one is more likely to engage the scruples of the wider society and thus to encourage legal reform. But political utility is not the whole story. Requiring that civil disobedience be practiced in a particular way and that a penalty be accepted was King's way, I believe, of granting that even an unjust law remains a "law" in some sense. It is a fundamental Protestant conviction that, after the Fall, all human efforts and institutions are tainted by sin and that even an unjust law is the fruit of temporal powers ordained by God to restrain evil. For King, this means that, especially within a society that aspires to be democratic, the social processes by which laws are passed, as well as the political actors who interpret and enforce these laws, are due a measure of respect. This is the case even when the processes are in fact undemocratic, the actors personally corrupt, and the laws themselves horribly unfair. In spite of statements suggesting the contrary, even unjust laws retain some moral force for King. What he objected to was these laws' being given *undue* force or authority, their "lawness" alone being taken as a compelling reason for obedience.[35]

Especially troubling to King in the 1950s and 1960s was the appeal by "the white moderate" to "law and order," well-meaning but paternalistic advice to the American Negro to be "patient" and to "wait" for a more opportune moment for social protest. King saw this advice as "more devoted to 'order' than to justice," and he insisted that "law and order exist for the purpose of establishing justice, and ... when they fail to do this they become dangerously structured dams that block the flow of social progress."[36] As *Why We Can't Wait* makes clear, it was precisely because King had a sense of the patience of a personal God that he could be "impatient" with human injustice without becoming either cynical or despairing.[37] In learning over a cup of coffee how to wait for the righteous Lord, he also learned how *not* to wait for an unjust or indifferent humanity.

On the side of law's potency, King recognized the power of constitutional ideals and jurisprudential traditions. In "Letter from a Birmingham Jail," he called the nation back to "those great wells of democracy which were dug deep by the Founding Fathers in the formulation of the Constitution and the Declaration of Independence."[38] And in his "I Have a Dream" speech, he again makes a point of referring to "the architects of *our* republic" and "the promise that all men, yes, black men as well as white men, would be guaranteed the unalienable rights of life, liberty, and the pursuit of happiness."[39] He was well aware that the Constitution itself had left slavery intact—even as had the Bible. But he typically countered American history with more American history, in citing the Emancipation Proclamation and the Thirteenth, Fourteenth, and Fifteenth Amendments, for example.[40] That said, King was not an historicist; he had no interest in merely codifying the practices of a distant past. Rather, he availed himself of both natural law arguments and a version of what Ronald Dworkin has recently called "the moral reading of the Constitution."[41] In interpreting and appealing to the Constitution, that is, King sought to honor American ideals and principles, not simply to follow American practices and precedents.[42]

In 1957, King had vigorously condemned the Supreme Court's 1896 *Plessy v. Ferguson* decision, which endorsed a "separate but equal" understanding of race relations. "Through this decision," he wrote, "segregation gained legal and moral sanction. The end result of the Plessy doctrine was that it led to a strict enforcement of the 'separate,' with hardly the slightest attempt to abide by the 'equal.' So the Plessy doctrine ended up making for tragic inequalities and ungodly exploitation."[43] On the hundredth anniversary of the Emancipation Proclamation, which was issued in 1863, King lamented how little progress had been made in the true liberation of African-Americans over the past century.[44] But his critique of Plessy and his refusal to be satisfied with the paper equality promised by *Brown v. Board of Education* (1954) avoided the snare of looking *only* to legal remedies from Washington. Law was important, but so was education. As King, presumably thinking of the debates between Booker T. Washington and W. E. B. Du Bois over a generation earlier, put it, "We must continue to struggle through legalism and legislation. There are those who contend that integration can come only through education, for no other reason than that morals cannot be legislated. I choose, however, to be dialectical at this point. It is neither education nor legislation; it is both legislation and education.... The law cannot make a man love—religion and education must do that—but it can control his efforts to lynch."[45] In addition to pushing for legal redress and reform (for example, a voting rights act), then, King's discontent with the status quo took the form of petitions to individual conscience (in the Negro and in the nation at large) as well as calls for community resistance (direct but nonviolent protest). King's strength was always to wed theory and praxis, but he was emphatic that "nonviolence is no longer an option for intellectual analysis, it is an imperative for action."[46]

King knew how important state legislatures, Congress, federal courts, the Supreme Court, and finally the public could be in insuring civil rights for African Americans. He knew the power of laws and lawmakers to resist or reform other laws and lawmakers. He also knew the power of the executive branch to rein in or augment the other two branches of government, especially at the local level. King had a sound understanding of American political theory—majority rule subject to judicial review, constitutional checks and balances, and so forth. And he explicitly acknowledged that in demonstrating for the rights to adequate housing, adequate income, and adequate education, "we have left the realm of constitutional rights and we are entering the area of human rights."[47] But his signal contribution was to galvanize all these legal, political, and cultural mechanisms into proper practice, at least for a time and to some significant degree. Put most briefly, King helped induce the American system (morally and materially) to recognize and act on its highest principles, even as he inspired individuals (black and white) to be their best selves. His success was not complete, of course, but it was remarkable even so.

Again, King was not merely interested in conserving past historical practices or even in realizing stated yet unattained legal and ethical goals. King's Christian faith in an eternal and righteous God allowed him to relativize *all* temporal human systems and to question *each* temptable human heart. Like Socrates having glimpsed the Good above Athenian "democracy," King was able to challenge even the (erstwhile) highest principles of his country and the (putative) best selves of his interlocutors. Especially in the mid- to late 1960s, King vigorously denounced "the giant triplets of racism, materialism, and militarism."[48] He proclaimed the need for "a radical restructuring of the architecture of American society" and asserted that "a new set of values must be born."[49] He brought capitalism under particularly sharp criticism and called for an economy that is "more person-centered than property- and profit-centered."[50] This meant, among other things, "a guaranteed income," "a revitalized labor movement," and "a broader distribution of wealth."[51] King's prophetic gift to the American state was to challenge it to become what it was not and perhaps never wanted to be: a democracy without "compromise."[52] Similarly, King's prophetic gift to the American church was to call it to become much more than it had ever been: "the true Body of Christ."[53] Neither the democratic state nor the integrated church, as such, is the realized kingdom of Heaven,[54] but both can plausibly aspire to be part of what King, following Josiah Royce, called "the beloved community."[55]

Always the Baptist minister, King focused on spiritual ends as well as political means, and he was far from alone in his efforts.[56] Andrew Young and a cadre of lawyers were often King's point people in court, and King himself emphasized his dispensability in the context of the mass movement for racial justice; as David Garrow has observed, as early as Montgomery,

King and other leaders came to realize that "the people, and not simply their lawyers, could win their own freedom."[57] Yet the record, starting with the MIA bus boycott, is impressive. King and the SCLC had a significant hand in President Eisenhower's setting up the Civil Rights Commission and sending in the National Guard to integrate Arkansas public schools; in President Kennedy's federalizing the Alabama National Guard to integrate that state's schools and then delivering a televised speech to the nation in which he spoke out against segregation and racism; in Congress's passing and President Johnson's signing the Civil Rights Act of 1964, "to enforce the constitutional right to vote" and "to provide injunctive relief against discrimination in public accommodations"[58] and more.

King did not hesitate to use the language of "freedom and equality" and "citizenship rights," so dear to liberal democrats—indeed, he boldly declared that "the goal of America is freedom."[59] But neither did he flinch from a trumping emphasis on spiritual values such as faith, nonviolence, "soul force," and "the glory of the Lord."[60] To those who were tempted to accommodate Christianity too completely to temporal politics, King insisted that "the calling to be a son of the living God" is "beyond the calling of race or nation or creed."[61] "I just want to do God's will," he often declared.[62] Even his identity as civil rights activist or Vietnam War protester was second to "my commitment to the ministry of Jesus Christ."[63] To those who were tempted to withdraw from political and economic struggles as too messy or worldly, in contrast, he emphasized that faith without works is sterile. He advocated "nonviolent direct action" and "a practical pacifism" as obligations in the quest for social justice. Only in this way could one be true to both "the sacred heritage of our nation and the eternal will of God."[64]

LAW AND GOSPEL

In both Martin Luther and John Calvin, as well as in Thomas Aquinas, the word "law" can denote one or more of four things: (1) eternal law, which is the very Being of God, God's heart/mind as it is in itself; (2) divine law, which is the special revelation of God's requirements for humanity, as recorded, for example, in the Old Testament Decalogue; (3) natural law, the principles of moral order built by God into creation itself, including human reason and will; and (4) human law, the civil statutes of a particular political regime aimed at applying the natural law to concrete times, places, actions, and individuals.

Beyond the denotation of "law," there is the question of its connotation, its purpose or meaning.[65] According to Calvin, the three meanings or "uses" of the law are: (1) theological: "by exhibiting the righteousness of God—in other words, the righteousness which alone is acceptable to God—it admonishes every one of his own unrighteousness, certiorates, convicts, and finally condemns him;"[66] (2) civil: "by means of its fearful denunciations and the consequent dread of punishment, to curb those who, unless forced, have no regard for rectitude and justice;"[67] and (3) didactic: "enabling [believers] daily to learn with greater truth and certainty what that will of the Lord is which they aspire to follow, and to confirm them in this knowledge."[68] For his part, Luther spoke of only two "uses" of the law: (1) the civil use (*usus civilis*), in which political norms and mechanisms both restrain evil behaviors and encourage good ones; and (2) the theological use (*usus theologicus*), in which God employs the law as a hammer or fire to indict the conscience of the sinner.[69] All of these senses of the "law" were evident, more or less explicitly, in the life and work of Martin Luther King Jr.

As we have seen, King also distinguished between the positive statutes of a specific political body and the eternal law and natural law that the statutes are ideally to express or apply. He, too, thought that one of the functions of human law is to restrain evil actions, and he, too, held that divine law aims to prick the consciences of persons and thereby goad them to repentance and reform. Foundational to all these points about the law, however, was an additional commitment that he shared with Aquinas, Luther, Calvin, and ultimately Augustine: the priority of the Gospel of Jesus Christ. Because King believed that Christ embodies the very person of God, Immanuel here with us, King had confidence that God's mercy and forgiveness are even more basic or powerful than God's condemnation and punishment. In the cross of Christ, God gratuitously restored right relationship to a fallen world by taking its guilt and suffering onto Himself. Christ named personal sins and resisted social evils, but he did so without indulging in hatred or violence. Faith in Christ, in turn, allowed King to identify human injustices and to struggle against them, but also to trust in divine providence (not just in human law or power) to carry the day.

LAW AND POWER

Confidence in the gospel (good news) of God's love did not render King naive about social realities. He saw the importance of power in human relations, including those between the races. He frequently noted that oppressors do not give up their privileges voluntarily but must be forced to do so by "determined legal and nonviolent pressure" from the oppressed.[70] Moreover, he never confused legal statutes alone with real power. "Laws only declare rights," he observed; "they do not deliver them."[71] King never tired of highlighting the "tragic gulf between civil rights laws passed and civil rights laws implemented,"[72] a gulf that required African Americans in the North and South alike to continue to agitate for social equality. If the *goal* of America is freedom, its *history* was that of "the inexpressible cruelties of slavery."[73]

Eventually defining power as "the ability to achieve purpose ... the strength required to bring about social, political or economic changes,"[74] King emphasized that "power is not only desirable but necessary."[75] Even so, he insisted that law is not merely a matter of power but also of right. It is remarkable that in spite of centuries of slavery, lynchings, and Jim Crow,[76] King did not give up on law as one means of human advancement. It is even more remarkable that he insisted that law is wedded to a "new kind of power"—"power infused with love and justice."[77]

To the end of his life, King continued to believe in the project of marrying American law with biblical morality. Put less pointedly, he steadfastly refused to segregate positive law (acts actually on the books) from natural law (timeless dictates of a good conscience) and eternal law (the will of God). The latter two must ground and judge the first, and without this moral foundation, no one in the struggle for racial justice could hope for true victory. This cognizance of something beyond time and chance, something transcending skin color and factional interest, allowed King to be critical of both whites and blacks. He could indict white racists for their overt hatred and aggression, as well as white moderates for valuing peace and mere (positive) legality over justice. But he could also fault black leaders who were tempted to lapse into a hatred or irresponsibility of their own. King was able to appreciate "the marvelous new militancy"[78] that surged up among young black activists in the 1960s, and he saw a "broad and positive meaning" in Black Power as "a call to black people to amass the political and economic strength to achieve their legitimate goals."[79] He did not refrain, nevertheless, from also identifying "Black Power" as a slogan fraught with peril. To the extent that it suggested violent intimidation or cynical lawlessness, he believed it to be both counterproductive and wrong. "Power and morality must go together, implementing, fulfilling and ennobling each other."[80]

LAW AND NONVIOLENT RESISTANCE

Yet why, specifically, should nonviolence have been so key to King's social activism? Once one rejects passivity, complete nonresistance, and accepts the moral obligation to stand athwart injustice, and once one maintains that some positive laws are unjust and thus that civil disobedience may be legitimate, why insist on *nonviolent* resistance? Why not work against evil "by any means necessary," to echo Malcolm X's notorious phrase?[81] King's answer was that actions and intentions matter, as well as consequences.[82]

In addition to maintaining that some laws are improper ends, King held that violence is an improper means for several reasons. In *Stride Toward Freedom*, King's first book, he listed six basic points to help explain and justify the nonviolent resistance under way in Montgomery:

1. "Nonviolent resistance is not a method for cowards; it does resist."
2. "Nonviolence ... does not seek to defeat or humiliate the opponent, but to win his friendship and understanding."
3. "It is evil that the nonviolent resister seeks to defeat, not the persons victimized by evil."
4. "Nonviolent resistance is [characterized by] a willingness to accept suffering without retaliation, to accept blows from the opponent without striking back."
5. "Nonviolent resistance ... avoids not only external physical violence but also internal violence of spirit. The nonviolent resister not only refuses to shoot his opponent but he also refuses to hate him."
6. "Nonviolent resistance ... is based on the conviction that the universe is on the side of justice. Consequently, the believer in nonviolence has deep faith in the future. This faith is another reason why the nonviolent resister can accept suffering without retaliation. For he knows that in his struggle for justice he has cosmic companionship."[83]

Across the years, King's briefs for nonviolence appealed to traits of character, principles of justice, social utility, as well as theological convictions. The moral eclecticism of his views is quite clear in this oft-quoted passage: "[Violence] is impractical because it is a descending spiral ending in destruction for all. The old law of an eye for an eye leaves everybody blind [a consequentialist argument]. It is immoral because it seeks to humiliate the opponent rather than win his understanding; it seeks to annihilate rather than to convert [a deontological argument]. Violence is immoral because it thrives on hatred rather than love [an aretological argument]. It destroys community and makes brotherhood impossible."[84] As King summarized in his final book, *Where Do We Go from Here?*: "Beyond the pragmatic invalidity of violence is its inability to appeal to conscience."[85]

HUMAN NATURE/PERSONALITY AND AGAPIC LOVE

Having a conscience was, for King, central to being made in the image of God. And being made in God's image was, in turn, foundational to what he intermittently called "the nonviolent affirmation of the sacredness of all human life" and "respect [for] the dignity and worth of human personality."[86] In a powerful Christian universalism, King affirmed that "every man is somebody because he is a child of God.... Man is more than a tiny vagary of whirling electrons or a wisp of smoke from a limitless smoldering. Man is a child of God, made in His image, and therefore must be respected as such.... We are all one in Christ Jesus. And when we truly believe in the sacredness of human personality, we won't exploit people, we won't trample over people with the iron feet of oppression, we won't kill anybody."[87] The common integrity of the human personality is the lynchpin in much of King's comments on law. Or, rather, the creative kindness of the *divine* Personality is the *anti*-lynching pin. "Human worth lies in relatedness to God."[88] If all finite persons are equal before God, how then can they be treated as unequal before the state or the wider society? Because all human persons are loved by God, they have value and are capable of loving themselves and one another. Injustice is quite often due to willful blindness to the image of God in others, a point King could put in either Kantian or biblical terms. "The immorality of segregation," for instance, "is that it treats men as means rather than ends, and thereby reduces them to things rather than persons."[89] Conversely, "the highest good is love."[90] One of the most sublime lines that King ever wrote, in my estimation, is this: "Since the white man's personality is greatly distorted by segregation, and his soul is greatly scarred, he needs the love of the Negro."[91]

The New Testament Greek name for the love in question is *agape*, "the love of God operating in the human heart."[92] This graced capacity allows individuals to hold in balance justice and power by transcending yet comprehending both. *Agape* transcends justice in that it does not limit itself to economies of exchange, calculations of merit and demerit, or even the natural sympathies of friendship. (Think of the parable of the generous vineyard owner in Matthew 20:1–16.) Rather, *agape* entails "an all-embracing and unconditional love for all men."[93] *Agape* comprehends power in that it is active and bold rather than passive and timid. "Structures of evil do not crumble by passive waiting."[94] As King put it, "When I speak of love I am not speaking of some sentimental and weak response. I am speaking of that force which all of the great religions have seen as the supreme unifying principle of life."[95]

King unabashedly placed agapic love at the core of his political thought and social action and offered four defining theses about such love:

1. "*Agape* is disinterested love. It is a love in which the individual seeks not his own good, but the good of his neighbor (I Cor. 10:24). *Agape* does not begin by discriminating between worthy and unworthy people, or any qualities people possess. It begins by loving others *for their sakes*."
2. "[*Agape*] springs from the *need* of the other person—his need for belonging to the best in the human family. The Samaritan who helped the Jew

on the Jericho Road was 'good' because he responded to the human need that he was presented with. God's love is eternal and fails not because man needs his love."

3. "*Agape* is a willingness to sacrifice in the interest of mutuality. *Agape* is a willingness to go to any length to restore community.... The cross is the eternal expression of the length to which God will go in order to restore broken community. The resurrection is a symbol of God's triumph over all the forces that seek to block community."

4. "*Agape* means a recognition of the fact that all life is interrelated. All humanity is involved in a single process, and all men are brothers.... Whether we call it an unconscious process, an impersonal Brahman, or a Personal Being of matchless power and infinite love, there is a creative force in this universe that works to bring the disconnected aspects of reality into a harmonious whole."[96]

If *agape* comprehends yet transcends justice and power, it also embodies both law and Gospel. King suggested more than thirty-five years ago that, as a matter of *justice*, the United States government owes African Americans reparations for slavery.[97] And he was clear that *agape* never intentionally falls below the just requirements of the law, in all four senses. But King also knew that, in expanding sympathy and inspiring forgiveness, love rises above legalism to the prophetic. It is divine love, King would "re-mind" the world, that transforms and renews us (cf. Romans 12:2), by breaking us out of grasping self-interest (me vs. you) and invidious group elitism (us vs. them).

As understandable, historically, as was Marcus Garvey's call for black nationalism; as inspiring, intellectually, as was W. E. B. Du Bois's insistence that "the talented tenth" pursue a liberal education; as indispensable, legally, as was Thurgood Marshall's victory in *Brown v. Board*; as galvanizing, psychologically, as were Malcolm X's and Angela Davis's commitments to black manhood and womanhood; the most effective remedy, both politically and morally, for American racism and Jim Crow laws has been Martin King and Christlike love.

KING'S PROPHETIC OPTIMISM AND PERSONALISM

King's realism, what might be called his "holistic pessimism," enabled him to see that "injustice anywhere is a threat to justice everywhere."[98] As the preceding four quotes make clear, however, King's holistic optimism triumphed in his account of the harmonizing power of love. King was well aware that practitioners of *agape* would suffer at the hands of their unjust fellows, but he continued across the years to affirm "the faith that unearned suffering is redemptive."[99] He was not indiscriminate or masochistic in his call for suffering, any more than he was Machiavellian or cynical in his call for resistance. As he allowed in "Letter from a Birmingham Jail": "it is wrong to use immoral means to attain moral ends ... [but] it is just as wrong, or even more so, to use moral means to preserve immoral ends."[100] Yet even when moral means and ends seem to fail, he held that "right defeated is stronger than evil triumphant."[101]

Unquestionably, Jesus Christ was "an extremist for love,"[102] but does love always employ exclusively nonviolent means? I am not as sure as King that *agape* must eschew the use of lethal or injurious force under all circumstances. King consistently affirmed "the reality of evil" and "man's capacity for sin," and, at his best, he avoided both "superficial optimism" and "crippling pessimism."[103] Still, I am not as confident as he that "evil carries the seed of its own destruction."[104] In a fallen world, at any rate, I believe that protecting the innocent may move some Christians, properly, to take up the sword against evil, as in the American Civil War. Regrettably, the law sometimes needs the support of police forces, national guards, and armies, and love itself may enlist in these services.[105] One may doubt the consistency of King's protesting to President Eisenhower that Montgomery blacks were "without protection of law,"[106] when King himself was unwilling to endorse the necessary (moral) means to enforce the law.

Unquestionably, American blacks have for centuries been "drained of self-respect and a sense of 'somebodiness.'"[107] But is personality the highest good? I sometimes worry that King neglected the value of the *im*personal: the natural or animal world and those shared human needs and potentials that have nothing to do with freedom or self-conscious dignity.[108] Human nature is more than autonomous personality, as fetuses, babies, the retarded, and the senile demonstrate. Still, it is important to emphasize that, for King, the person is not some disembodied mind or self-sufficient will. King consistently took care to avoid "a completely otherworldly religion which makes a strange, unbiblical distinction between body and soul, between the sacred and the secular."[109] Moreover, for him, "other-preservation is the first law of life ... precisely because we cannot preserve self without being concerned about preserving other selves."[110]

I have suggested that part of what made Martin Luther King Jr. prophetic was his commitment to the will of God and the full range of human existence: bodies and souls, self and others, thought and action, church and state, the private and the public, means and ends, love and justice, time and eternity.[111] I have also suggested that his upbringing at the intersection of societies in tension—black and white, rich and poor—prepared him for his prophetic vocation of recognizing the marginalized and empathizing with the weak. Indeed, as an embodiment of the theological, civil, and didactic "uses" of the law, King himself indicted our consciences, helped restrain social evils, and educated the church concerning the will of God.

Secular liberals typically fear that admitting the prophet's "Thus saith the Lord" into public discourse will lead to intolerance: Christian optimism and personalism run amok into theocratic dogmatism and oppression.[112] This was a reasonable worry in the West during the sixteenth and seventeenth centuries, even as the dangers of fundamentalism remain a concern in the Near East today. But our chief domestic threat is currently from social fragmentation and the hegemony of possessive individualism, rather than from religious tyranny and the hegemony of the Protestant church. In King's case, Christian convictions led him to affirm freedom of conscience and the ubiquity of sin and error, as well as to champion racial equality, the right to vote, and so on. His righteous indignation at injustice was paired with a self-limiting humility. Rather than denying liberal values, then, he clarified and disciplined them.

Christian traditionalists often fear, in turn, that prophetic defenses of liberal democracy and human rights will erode true virtue and amount to a sellout of the ancient church to the modern state. They suspect, in Robert Kraynak's words, "that democracy is tyrannical in its ruthless leveling of higher and lower goods and of the hierarchies of the soul that are absolutely necessary for spiritual life."[113] Ever since Constantine, the argument goes, secular laws and loyalties have perverted the Christian gospel. On King's behalf, nevertheless, I must enter a plea of "not guilty." The epiphany at the kitchen table in Montgomery—hearing God over a cup of coffee and in the midst of a bus boycott—provides a graphic image of how the sacred and the profane, Christian faith and democratic politics, converged in King's life. By placing all of human existence under the governance of *agape*, he taught Christians to be in the world but not of it. King was under no illusions about the sins of U.S. culture—its history of slavery, its ongoing racial and economic exploitation—but he was still able to trust God and serve his neighbors in situ.

King's legacy partly consists in the civil rights acts he helped to pass into law, and a legal holiday now honors his memory. But perhaps his main contribution was to stir in Christians in America (and around the world) a political conscience. His example may still move us to ask: Even though religious fanaticism is dangerous, did not democracy itself spring, in part, from Christian teachings about God and humanity? Are we to forget the Puritans and the religious rationales behind so many of the state constitutions of the newly liberated colonies? If commitments to freedom, equality, and the rule of law seem to undermine biblical faith, hope, and love, are the latter virtues really being practiced?

There is more than one version of liberal democracy and its relation to law, society, and human nature, just as there is more than one version of Christian faith. Yet Martin Luther King Jr. was a peculiarly American prophet in being able to speak the broad languages of democracy and Christianity, simultaneously, without confusing the two. For all the preceding observations, even so, it is ultimately a mystery what makes someone prophetic.[114] Jurisprudes, religion professors, and the general population can only be grateful, both to God and to the individual, for the prophet's life and work. It is appropriate, therefore, that I give our American Amos the last word:

> Man-made laws assure justice, but a higher law produces love.... A vigorous enforcement of civil rights will bring an end to segregated public facilities, but it cannot bring an end to fears, prejudice, pride and irrationality, which are the barriers to a truly integrated society. These dark and demonic responses will be removed only as men are possessed by the invisible inner law which etches on their hearts the conviction that all men are brothers and that love is mankind's most potent weapon for personal and social transformation. True integration will be achieved by men who are willingly obedient to unenforceable obligations.[115]

NOTES

1. Martin Luther King Jr., "I Have a Dream" (1963), in *I Have a Dream: Writings and Speeches That Changed the World*, ed. James M. Washington (San Francisco: HarperCollins, 1992), 105.

2. Martin Luther King Jr., *The Trumpet of Conscience* (San Francisco: Harper & Row, 1967), 32.

3. Ibid., 69; Martin Luther King Jr., *Strength to Love* (Philadelphia: Fortress Press, 1963), 9.

4. Compare the appraisals of King by Stanley Hauerwas in *Wilderness Wanderings: Probing Twentieth-Century Theology and Philosophy* (Boulder, Colo.: Westview Press, 1997), 225–237, and by John Rawls in *Political Liberalism* (New York: Columbia University Press, 1993), 247 n. and 250.

5. With respect to the charges of plagiarism and marital infidelity, I can only say that in Dr. King, "we have this treasure in earthen vessels" (2 Cor. 4:7 KJV). For more, see the work of Clayborne Carson, senior editor of the King Papers Project and professor of history at Stanford University, including the introductions to *The Papers of Martin Luther King, Jr.*, 4 vols. (Berkeley: University of California Press, 1992–2000). See also Scott McCormack, "Carson: King Borrowed Ideas for Famous Speech," *The Stanford Daily*, March 6, 1991.

6. Stephen B. Oates, *Let the Trumpet Sound: The Life of Martin Luther King, Jr.* (New York: New American Library, 1982), 10. I am dependent on Oates for a

good deal of the biographical material that follows. I have also relied on the chronology provided in King, *I Have a Dream*, xxiii–xxx; and on David J. Garrow, *Bearing the Cross: Martin Luther King, Jr., and the Southern Christian Leadership Conference* (New York: Vintage Books, 1988).

7. Oates, *Let the Trumpet Sound*, 10.

8. Ibid., 16.

9. Ibid., 14; the phrases in quotations in this paragraph are King's, as quoted by Oates.

10. Ibid., 19; the phrase in quotations in this sentence is Mays's, as quoted by Oates.

11. Martin Luther King Jr., *Stride Toward Freedom* (New York: Harper & Row, 1958), 91.

12. Oates, *Let the Trumpet Sound*, 26.

13. King, *Stride Toward Freedom*, 92.

14. Ibid., 94–95.

15. See, e.g., King, *Strength to Love*, 98.

16. See Oates, *Let the Trumpet Sound*, 32.

17. King, *Stride Toward Freedom*, 95.

18. Ibid., 96–97.

19. Ibid., 85. For an engaging study of "the prior basis for Gandhi's appeal in the African-American community," one that explores the "pre-1950s traditions upon which King and others built," see Sudarshan Kapur, *Raising Up a Prophet: The African-American Encounter with Gandhi* (Boston: Beacon Press, 1992); quoted phrases from ibid., 3–4.

20. King, *Stride Toward Freedom*, 98, 100.

21. Ibid., 100.

22. Ibid., 16–23; see also Martin Luther King Jr., *The Words of Martin Luther King, Jr.*, ed. Coretta Scott King (New York: Newmarket Press, 1983), 64.

23. Martin Luther King Jr., "Our Struggle" (1956), in *I Have a Dream*, 5.

24. Ibid., 7.

25. Ibid., 13.

26. King, *Strength to Love*, 113.

27. Martin Luther is often quoted as concluding his remarks before the Imperial Diet of Worms with the words, "Here I stand, I can do no other. God help me. Amen." This may be an early redacted press report, however. Many scholars believe he actually said, "I cannot and I will not recant anything, for to go against conscience is neither right nor safe. God help me. Amen." See "Luther at the Imperial Diet of Worms (1521)," http://www.luther.de/en/worms.html.

28. For more on the historical context and aftermath of this night, see Garrow, *Bearing the Cross*, 56–60.

29. He quoted both of these lines often; see, e.g., King, *Strength to Love*, chaps. 2 and 10.

30. How precisely to define "legal positivism" is much disputed, as is its cogency as a theory of law. At one extreme, some construe positivism as making only the de-

scriptive, conceptual claim that, given a certain historical pedigree, something may be both a law and immoral. Having the status of law says little or nothing about whether the law should be obeyed, on this account. At the other extreme, some see positivism as defending the normative thesis that something's being a law is, in and of itself, a compelling (perhaps even the only) ground for obeying it. My use above of the phrase "legal positivist" presumes the latter, stronger definition. For careful discussions of positivism, especially its relation to competing views (such as natural law theory), see Robert P. George, ed., *The Autonomy of Law: Essays on Legal Positivism* (Oxford: Oxford University Press, 1996).

31. Martin Luther King Jr., "Letter from a Birmingham Jail" (1963), in *I Have a Dream*, 89.

32. Ibid., 90.

33. Ibid. As King puts it in *Stride Toward Freedom*, 212: "Noncooperation with evil is as much a moral obligation as is cooperation with good."

34. King, "Letter from a Birmingham Jail," 90.

35. Kent Greenawalt has offered an interesting critique of the view that an unjust law is not truly a law, as well as a sympathetic reading of chastened forms of legal positivism; see his "Too Thin and Too Rich: Distinguishing Features of Legal Positivism," in George, ed., *The Autonomy of Law*, 1–29. For Greenawalt, positivism involves both descriptive and normative theses. Nonetheless, its descriptive emphasis on the social origins of law makes it more plausible to an "outsider-observer" of the legal system than to an "insider-participant," who looks more tellingly to law's content and moral validity (20). King, for his part, often straddled these two perspectives. In giving more weight to moral validity, however, his accent is on the participant who must decide whether to obey an unjust law or to go to jail. King's personalism dictates that, in cases of conflict, individual conscience and decision must supersede group structures and traditions.

36. King, "Letter from a Birmingham Jail," 91.

37. Martin Luther King Jr., *Why We Can't Wait* (New York: Mentor Books, 1963).

38. King, "Letter from a Birmingham Jail," 100.

39. King, "I Have a Dream," 102 (italics mine).

40. King, *Why We Can't Wait*, 25.

41. Ronald Dworkin, *Freedom's Law: The Moral Reading of the American Constitution* (Cambridge, Mass.: Harvard University Press, 1996).

42. James E. Fleming discussed the distinction between "aspirational principles" and "historical practices" in constitutional interpretation in "Are We All Originalists Now? I Hope Not!" Lecture given at Princeton University, September 19, 2002.

43. Martin Luther King Jr., "Facing the Challenge of a New Age" (1957), in *I Have a Dream*, 17.

44. King, *Why We Can't Wait*, 23–25.

45. King, "Facing the Challenge of a New Age," 25.

46. King, *The Trumpet of Conscience*, 64. For a detailed examination of how King combined the "theoretical and experiential deconstruction/reconstruction" of

law and society, see Anthony E. Cook, "Beyond Critical Legal Studies: The Reconstructive Theology of Dr. Martin Luther King, Jr.," *Harvard Law Review* 103 (March 1990): 985–1044.

47. Martin Luther King Jr., "Nonviolence: The Only Road to Freedom" (1966), in *I Have a Dream*, 131.

48. Martin Luther King Jr., "A Time to Break Silence" (1967), in *I Have a Dream*, 148.

49. Martin Luther King Jr., *Where Do We Go from Here: Chaos or Community?* (Boston: Beacon Press, 1968), 133.

50. Ibid.

51. Ibid., 162, 142, and Martin Luther King Jr., "Where Do We Go from Here?" (1967), in *I Have a Dream*, 176.

52. King, *Why We Can't Wait*, 131.

53. King, *Strength to Love*, 141.

54. King warned against this mistaken identification in *Stride Toward Freedom*, 91.

55. Ibid., 220.

56. For a compelling narration of the larger context of King's activism, including his dependence on and disagreements with other civil rights leaders (among them Ralph Abernathy, Septima Clark, W. E. B. Du Bois, and Medgar Evers), see Taylor Branch, *Parting the Waters: America in the King Years, 1954–1963* (New York: Simon & Schuster, 1988).

57. Garrow, *Bearing the Cross*, 86.

58. *Civil Rights Act of 1964, U.S. Code*, vol. 42, title VII, beginning at section 2000e.

59. King, "Letter from a Birmingham Jail," 98.

60. See King, "I Have a Dream," 102–105.

61. King, "A Time to Break Silence," 140.

62. See, for instance, Martin Luther King Jr., "I See the Promised Land" (1968), in *I Have a Dream*, 203.

63. King, "A Time to Break Silence, 139.

64. King, "Letter from a Birmingham Jail," 98.

65. See Edward A. Dowey, "Law in Luther and Calvin," *Theology Today* 41, no. 2 (July 1984): 148.

66. John Calvin, *Institutes of the Christian Religion* (1536/1539), book 2, chap. 7, trans. Henry Beveridge, 2 vols. (Edinburgh: Calvin Translation Society, 1845), 1:304.

67. Ibid., 1:307.

68. Ibid., 1:309.

69. Martin Luther, "A Commentary on Saint Paul's Epistle to the Galatians" (1531), in *Martin Luther: Selections from His Writings*, ed. John Dillenberger (Garden City, N.Y.: Anchor Books, 1961), 139–145.

70. King, "Letter from a Birmingham Jail," 87.

71. King, *Where Do We Go From Here?* 158.

72. Ibid., 82.

73. King, "Letter from a Birmingham Jail," 98.

74. King, *Where Do We Go From Here?* 37.
75. Ibid.
76. Visitors entering the display area of the Martin Luther King, Jr., Center for Non-violent Social Change in Atlanta are confronted by a range of Jim Crow laws displayed on a large glass wall. The laws, from several southern states, date from the 1880s to the 1960s; for examples (such as this one from Mississippi: "The marriage of a white person with a negro or mulatto or person who shall have one-eighth or more of negro blood, shall be unlawful and void"), see http://www.nps.gov/malu/documents/jim_crow_laws.htm.
77. King, *Where Do We Go from Here?* 66.
78. King, "I Have a Dream," 103.
79. King, *Where Do We Go from Here?* 36.
80. Ibid., 59.
81. John Kelsay has noted in conversation that in some Islamic texts, the Arabic phrase commonly translated into English as "by any means necessary" is better read as "by the necessary (i.e., appropriate) means." I am not sure whether Malcolm X had this latter sense in mind, but, given his other early views, I doubt it.
82. At one point, Malcolm X considered "an integrationist like King" to be akin to a "house Negro" of pre–Civil War days, a slave who identified with "the master" and ultimately sold out to him. Minister Malcolm clearly had Reverend King in mind when he said in a 1963 interview, "I think that any black man who goes among so-called Negroes today who are being brutalized, spit upon in the worst fashion imaginable, and teaches those Negroes to turn the other cheek, to suffer peacefully, or love their enemy is a traitor to the Negro." Malcolm X, "The Old Negro and the New Negro," in *The End of White World Supremacy*, ed. Imam Benjamin Karim (New York: Arcade, 1971), 116. Malcolm met King face to face only once, in March 1964. After Malcolm's transforming trip to Mecca the following month, he tempered his remarks on the SCLC and its leadership.
83. King, *Stride Toward Freedom*, 102–103, 106. In his "Letter from a Birmingham Jail," written five years after the publication of *Stride*, King responded to various white clergy's deploring of the civil rights "demonstrations" underway in Birmingham by noting that "in any nonviolent campaign there are four basic steps: (1) collection of the facts to determine whether injustices are alive, (2) negotiation, (3) self-purification, and (4) direct action." He went on to assert, "We have gone through all of these steps in Birmingham," adding that the protests were thus appropriate (85).
84. King, *The Words of Martin Luther King, Jr.*, 73; see also King, *Stride Toward Freedom*, 213.
85. King, *Where Do We Go from Here?* 59.
86. King, *The Trumpet of Conscience*, 72, 77; see also King, *Where Do We Go from Here?* 180.
87. King, *The Trumpet of Conscience*, 72.
88. King, *Where Do We Go from Here?* 97.

89. Ibid.

90. King, *Strength to Love*, 145.

91. King, *Stride Toward Freedom*, 105.

92. Ibid., 104.

93. King, "A Time to Break Silence," 150; see also his *Where Do We Go from Here?* 190.

94. King, *Where Do We Go from Here?* 128.

95. King, "A Time to Break Silence," 150.

96. King, *Stride Toward Freedom*, 104–107. King's lines on Christian love are highly indebted to the writings of Anders Nygren and Paul Ramsey; see Garrow, *Bearing the Cross*, 112. Nicholas Wolterstorff has maintained, in discussion, that King's comments on *agape*, its appreciation of mutuality and of the worth and dignity of the individual, are actually more applicable to *eros*. To the extent that *eros* looks to the merit of the other and to what that merit can do for one's own interests, however, I believe that King is correct in distinguishing it from *agape*. As King defines *eros*, it is concerned with justice and giving admirable persons their due rather than with charity and service to needy strangers. *Agape* and *eros* are not necessarily opposed, but they are not identical either.

97. King, *Where Do We Go from Here?* 79, 109; see also King, *Why We Can't Wait*, 134–139.

98. King, "Letter from a Birmingham Jail," 85.

99. King, "I Have a Dream," 104; see also *Stride Toward Freedom*, 103.

100. King, "Letter from a Birmingham Jail," 99.

101. Ibid., 98.

102. Ibid., 94.

103. King, *Strength to Love*, 109, 130, and 83, respectively.

104. Ibid., 82.

105. See Timothy P. Jackson, *The Priority of Love: Christian Charity and Social Justice* (Princeton, N.J.: Princeton University Press, 2003), esp. chap. 3.

106. See Branch, *Parting the Waters*, 191.

107. King, "Letter from a Birmingham Jail," 93.

108. See Jackson, *The Priority of Love*, esp. chap. 5.

109. King, *Why We Can't Wait*, 90. This phrase from "Letter from a Birmingham Jail" is printed somewhat differently in the version of the letter in *I Have a Dream*, 96. I use the quoted version because its employment of the present tense better suits my purposes.

110. King, *Where Do We Go from Here?* 180.

111. For more on these themes, see King, *Stride Toward Freedom*, 36, 91.

112. Jeffrey Stout has pressed this point, in conversation; see also Richard Rorty, *Philosophy and Social Hope* (London: Penguin, 1999), chap. 11.

113. Robert Kraynak, "Statement of Author Prepared for Background for Discussion at American Maritain Association Meeting," October 2002, Princeton University. On Christianity and democracy, see also Stanley Hauerwas, *Wilderness Wanderings*; *Against the Nations: War and Survival in a Liberal Society* (Min-

neapolis: Winston Press, 1985); *In Good Company: The Church as Polis* (Notre Dame, Ind.: University of Notre Dame Press, 1995); and *With the Grain of the Universe: The Church's Witness and Natural Theology* (Grand Rapids, Mich.: Brazos Press, 2001).

114. King himself observed: "Not every minister can be a prophet, but some must be prepared for the ordeals of this high calling and be willing to suffer courageously for righteousness." King, *Stride Toward Freedom*, 210.

115. King, *Where Do We Go from Here?* 100–101.

[CHAPTER 16]

William Stringfellow (1928–1985)

FRANK S. ALEXANDER

William Stringfellow spoke to the world in which he lived. His actions and his words were set in a context of community and conflict, of power and pretension, of advocacy and authority, of opportunity and oppression. His words and his deeds, however, were not designed to confront or to condemn, but simply to understand that context biblically. In his own words, he sought "to understand America biblically ... not to construe the Bible Americanly."[1] With his intentionally awkward grammar, this graduate of Harvard Law School made poignant his passion for understanding not the gospel in light of our lives, but our lives in light of the gospel.

In a world coming of age in the aftermath of World War II and Hiroshima, Stringfellow himself came of age as he completed law school and went to work for an East Harlem Protestant parish in 1956. For the next three decades until his death in 1985, he sought to interpret the American experiences of the 1950s, the 1960s, and the 1970s in light of the incarnation, the crucifixion, and the resurrection. He was present in the poverty and racism of Harlem. His voice was raised in criticism of the McCarthy hearings. He was active in the civil rights movement. He was charged with harboring Daniel Berrigan, a fugitive during the antiwar movement. He represented the Episcopal priests charged with the illegal ordination of women. He served as a warden in the local government of his community. Though he happened to be a lawyer, an active Episcopalian, and certainly an advocate, he recoiled from the common label given to him of a prophet. Stringfellow's response to scripture was a sense of calling to his vocation as a Christian, no more and no less.

The author of sixteen books and more than one hundred essays,[2] Stringfellow wrote as one more concerned with communicating his message than with proving his sources. With the exception of his first extensive law review article,[3] Stringfellow rarely included footnotes, bibliographies, or references to other scholars. Quite self-consciously, his writings were polemic in nature, relying solely on scriptural references; they were never designed to be treatises or systematic treatments of theology and jurisprudence. Though he described himself as "theologically illiterate,"[4] he was quite familiar with a broad range of Roman Catholic, Orthodox, and Protestant theologians writing in the middle of the twentieth century. He simply chose, in his writings and in his speaking, to call upon the biblical story. The absence of formal scholarship is, however, anything but an indictment of the depth or purity of his message. Karl Barth, participating in a panel discussion with Stringfellow in 1962, exhorted the audience, "Listen to this man!"[5]

The theological foundations of Stringfellow's views, and the implications for his views of law and human nature, can be traced conceptually to the intellectual and philosophical context of the 1950s. In the aftermath of World War II, simultaneous and parallel struggles emerged in both theology and jurisprudence. In theology the struggle primarily took the form of articulating a common Christian message to a world community that now knew the horrors of Auschwitz and Hiroshima, of state-imposed terror and state-sponsored triumphs. In jurisprudence the struggle took the form of articulating not only a theory of law adequate to define law with precision both across cultures and within cultures, but also a conception of law that could condemn as lawless those statutes and decrees that violate fundamental norms. In theology the focus became that of the relationship of law and gospel; in jurisprudence it became the debates between positivism and natural law. Stringfellow was present in both of these struggles and proclaimed a clear position that left most theologians and most legal scholars uncomfortable. The biblical witness, from his perspective, leaves little room for doctrines of natural law, for theologies based upon a social gospel, or for a Christian jurisprudence. "Instead of proposition or principle, the biblical witness offers precedent and parable. The Bible does not propound guidelines but relates events; the biblical ethic does not construct syllogisms but tells stories; the gospel is not confined in verities but confesses the viability of the Word of God."[6]

Within a year of his graduation from law school and the beginning of his legal practice in East Harlem, Stringfellow became a key voice in conferences on law and Christianity. In two such conferences, in 1957 and in 1958, a wide range of theologians, practicing attorneys, judges, and professors gathered to explore the relationship of law and gospel, of theology and jurisprudence, of the religious and ethical obligations of attorneys.[7] In these conferences and in the published essays of the conferences, Stringfellow's voice rose against the dominant attempts to find common grounds for theology and law, as well as for recognition of a Christian ethic about law, if not a Christian jurisprudence. The great danger of all such attempts, according to Stringfellow, is the failure to acknowledge the radical tension between law and gospel and between law and grace as reflected in Romans 13:1–8. "When the Gospel is taken seriously, the decisive issue between theology and jurisprudence and the central vocational problem of a lawyer who is a Christian is the tension between grace and law."[8] For Stringfellow, any conflation of gospel and law diminishes the crucifixion, and thereby also the resurrection.

The struggle in legal theory and jurisprudence differed from the theological debates only (and crucially!) in being devoid of the gospel. The debates in the halls of the legal academy were those of H. L. A. Hart and Lon Fuller, of positivism and the connections between law and morality. Such debates arise from the same need—to see the connections between the normative and the descriptive, between law and those things that are the limits of the law. Such debates, according to Stringfellow, suffer from the same dangers of reduction to either radical relativism or of self-righteous authority. "The Gospel is opposed to the imagination of both positivists and natural lawyers. The tension between grace and law is absolute."[9]

As a Christian who happened to be a lawyer, Stringfellow's expression of the biblical witness included the institutions that sought to define the identity of the Christian and of the lawyer. Within his own Episcopal denomination he was initially appointed a representative of the church on formal commissions, though he was later removed because of his criticism of the ecclesiastical structure. He defended Bishop James Pike of California, whom, in 1966, the Episcopal House of Bishops charged with heresy for having questioned doctrine on original sin, the Trinity, and the infallibility of scripture, among other things.[10] Similarly, he defended the Episcopal priests who participated in the first ordination of women to the priesthood.[11] In both cases he challenged the church to recall its own vocation of life in worship and in advocacy. As a member of the legal profession, Stringfellow found that at times his advocacy as a Christian coincided with his advocacy as a lawyer; yet at other times he felt that the legal profession itself was a restraining and constraining principality. He was, as he put it, "haunted with the ironic impression that I may have to renounce being a lawyer the better to be an advocate."[12]

Three themes permeate Stringfellow's writings in a manner that allows his calling on the word of God for us today to blossom in a uniquely "Stringfellow" manner: the centrality of worship, the experience of vocation, and the presence of death.

WORSHIP, VOCATION, DEATH

At its core, Stringfellow's theology was confessional. The experience of worship is not just the purest but also the only acceptable form of our expression of the incarnation, the crucifixion, and the resurrection.[13] His reluctance to proceed down the paths toward philosophical ethics or systematic theology stemmed from his deep conviction that any humanly created formula is a broken distortion of the word of God. His view of worship thus was one far more expansive than ecclesiastical, far more demonstrative than doctrinaire, far more creative than conforming. Liturgy is a participatory event that is at once confessional, communal, and political.[14]

Worship is not some peculiar cultural practice, some esoteric folk activity, to which Christians resort out of sentiment or superstition, or even for inspiration or self-motivation. On the contrary,

> worship is the celebration of God's presence and action in the ordinary and everyday life of the world. Worship is not separated or essentially distinguishable from the rest of the Christian life. It is the normative form and expression of the Christian life; it is the integration of the whole of the Christian life into history.[15]

As worship is the experience of the word of God, the understanding of role and identity in response to the word of God is the concept of vocation. Vocation, as developed by Stringfellow, bears little correlation to work, career, or socially defined roles and expectations. It is simply the response to the antecedent grace of God. "Vocation has to do with recognizing life as a gift and honoring the gift in living."[16] For individuals, vocation is a sense of one's own story as revealed through the gospel,[17] and the gospel is what permits us not to become gods but indeed to become human. "In the Gospel, vocation means being a human being, now, and being neither more, nor less than a human being, now."[18] The concept of vocation, however, is not limited to the human; it applies to all of creation. All institutions, most particularly the church and the political authorities, are called to a vocation, and the ethical is understood as faithfulness to vocation.[19]

The third theme that permeates Stringfellow's writings is the theme of death. Stringfellow wrote of death in its conventional physical sense because he became aware of it wherever he lived and worked. He encountered death in his legal ministry in Harlem and saw death in the civil rights movement, in the Vietnam War, and in political assassinations. Stringfellow was only in his late thirties when he was told he was dying of a terminal illness,[20] and he later wrestled with his deep loss in the death of his companion, Anthony Towne.[21] Though he wrote of death personally and interpersonally in his later works, he had identified death as a powerful concept in his early writings.[22] Death is a characteristic of all of creation, a consequence of the Fall, and the experience of isolation from

God. The primacy of death in his writings was not a sense of despair or of melancholy; rather, it was a description of the power of the gospel and its proclamation of life in the midst of death. A depiction of death, for William Stringfellow, is an affirmation of the triumph of the resurrection over the crucifixion. The "essential and consistent task of Christians is to expose the transience of death's power in the world."[23] With his wonderful dry wit, Stringfellow explained that he had a passion for the circus precisely because the circus performer excels in mocking the power of death in our lives.[24]

DEATH UNTO THE LAW: LAW AND SIN

Though he said he read little theology, Stringfellow once admitted to his desire to read all of Augustine, Luther, Bonhoeffer, and Barth.[25] His own writings bore deep resemblance to the points of emphasis of each of these scholars, but nowhere was the connection stronger than on the nature of sin and death.

The story of the Fall into sin in Genesis 1–3 is the story of the alienation of all of creation from God. The incarnation stands as God's affirming presence, but the crucifixion stands as our rejection of the incarnation. The resurrection is God's gift to us despite our rejection. What happens in the Fall, and what is relived in the crucifixion, is our refusal to acknowledge and accept our own frailty, the hopelessness of our own insistence on being in control. Stringfellow had no patience for Pelagian or semi-Pelagian assertions of limited goodness or limited free will. He insisted, as did each of the scholars he sought to read, on our complete and total inability, in the absence of grace, to know or to do that which God asks of us. As was true of these earlier scholars, Stringfellow insisted on naming this nature *sin*: "It is the essence of human sin for man to boast of the power to discern what is good and what is evil, and thus to be like God."[26] Convinced that "most Americans are grossly naïve or remarkably misinformed about the Fall,"[27] he designed his writings to educate about the Fall in order that the gospel could become manifest:

> Sin is not essentially the mistaken, inadvertent, or deliberate choice of evil by men but the pride into which men fall in associating their own self-interest with the will of God. Sin is the denunciation of the freedom of God to judge men as it pleases Him to judge them. Sin is the displacement of God's will with one's own will. Sin is the radical confusion in men's lives as to whether God or man is morally sovereign in history.[28]

The Fall is pervasive; it is not limited to the nature of individuals or even social groups. "The Fall implicates the whole of creation, not human life alone and not human beings uniquely, and further, that each and every creature or created thing suffers fallenness in its own right."[29] The state, the government, and the church are all equally characterized by their fallen reality. Principalities and powers are simply institutions, and we tend to forget that they, too, possess a fallen nature.

With this heavy emphasis on the nature of the Fall, the nature and function of law could have become critical in the development of Stringfellow's writings. Perhaps because he was a practicing attorney, or more likely because of his own self-identification as a Christian who happened to be a lawyer, he chose to reject the possibility that law exists as more than the indicative declaration of reality. Law, as God's proclamation, is the word that all have sinned and fall short of the glory of God (Rom. 3:23): "For law, the proclamation of the Gospel means, in the first instance, the comprehension that law, though sometimes it can name sin, originates itself in sin and cannot overcome the power of sin."[30]

The moral reality of death follows from the doctrine of the Fall. "Death is not only the terminal experience; it is the imminent truth about every and any event in this world."[31] Death is not to be equated with evil, though the evil that lies within death is the refusal to acknowledge that death is not the only reality.

Stringfellow's strong emphasis on the Fall and the radical and pervasive nature of all of moral reality as sinful was precisely what enabled him to point to the resurrection as the complete word, and story, of God's sovereignty. His emphasis on death was overwhelmed by his emphasis on the completeness of the grace of God. "The grace of Jesus Christ in this life is that death fails."[32] Understanding the fallen nature of all of creation simply makes possible an understanding of the sovereignty of Jesus Christ over all of creation.

THE HEARING OF THE WORD: GOSPEL AND LAW

With his view of the Fall, Stringfellow was most uncomfortable with any interpretation, theory, or approach that would tend to blur the distinction between gospel and law. Three dangers flow from the failure to adhere to this difference: the impoverishment of the critique of law and of the state; the arrogance of the righteousness of the church; and the loss of justification by faith. To the extent that the gospel becomes merged with or even subordinate to law, the gospel no longer stands as a declaration of the fallen nature of law itself. Legal institutions and legal theories then become sources of their own lawless authority.[33] Correspondingly, a blurring of the distinction between law and gospel allows the institutions that proclaim the gospel to become righteous in their proclamations not just of the gospel but also of the law. In both the first and second dangers we forget that the crucifixion followed the incarnation. The third danger in the blurring of distinctions between law and gospel is the failure to recall that justification is by faith through grace. Fulfillment of the law can become a means to grace. This third danger is the failure to know that the resurrection followed the crucifixion. Such is simply not the gospel as Stringfellow understood it. "Faith is the success of God's quest for men, not the outcome of men's search for God."[34]

In preserving the tension between gospel and law, Stringfellow's theology bears close affinity to the theology not only of Augustine and Luther, but also of Karl Barth,[35] Jacques Ellul,[36] and Dietrich Bonhoeffer. Accused of being "Barthian" in his theology, Stringfellow responded that, in the most important sense, not even Karl Barth was "Barthian," for Barth refused to create a systematic theology or structure for the relationship of gospel and law.[37] Stringfellow insisted, as did Barth, that the work of theology is at its core a confessional act, "the marvel of the Word of God addressing men in ordinary history."[38] He was also clearly influenced in this context by Nicholas Berdyaev: "Christian faith is the revelation of grace, and Christian ethics is the ethics of redemption and not of law."[39]

The centrality of the gospel in Stringfellow's writings, as well as his views on the tension between gospel and law, also bear close relationship with the writings of Dietrich Bonhoeffer. The extent to which Stringfellow had access to Bonhoeffer's work is unknown, since Bonhoeffer's work was still being translated into and published in English early in Stringfellow's career. But it is clear that Stringfellow relied on Bonhoeffer. Stringfellow made explicit reference to what he termed "The Bonhoeffer Dilemma" in describing Bonhoeffer's struggle with the necessity of violence against a violent lawless authority,[40] and many points in Bonhoeffer's own writings are echoed in Stringfellow's works. Both Bonhoeffer and Stringfellow cautioned the church, in finding its role in the world, against the pitfalls of "cheap grace,"[41] and both followed Barth in speaking of the need to distinguish religion from the message of Jesus Christ.[42] As Stringfellow expressed it: "I am reminded, if sometimes ruefully, that the Gospel is no mere religion in *any* essential respect."[43]

If a tension between gospel and law is to be maintained, it is in order that we might hear the gospel unconstrained by our own attempts to judge it worthy. If the crucifixion is our response to the incarnation, the resurrection is God's response to the crucifixion. "The power to discern the presence of the Word of God in the world is the knowledge of the Resurrection."[44] The presence of the word of God, not a system of laws or set of principles, is what ultimately conquers the power of death in this world and makes life possible. "His power over death is effective, not just at the terminal point of a man's life, but throughout his life, during *this* life in *this* world right now … His resurrection means the possibility of living in this life, in the very midst of death's works, safe and free from death."[45]

CONFIDENCE PLACED AND MISPLACED: LAW, GRACE, KNOWLEDGE

When Christian theology is grounded in the Fall, in sin and death, and thus leaves the starkness of the resurrection as the proclamation of God's gift to us, the hearer of the word of God must come to a new understanding of knowledge itself. If the Fall is the story of the existential futility of the search for the knowledge of good and evil, and the crucifixion is the declaration of the utter impoverishment of our knowledge, the puzzle then becomes the nature of knowledge itself. The emphasis is on sin in order that the clarity of the gospel be known, and this emphasis is combined with an insistence on the tension between gospel and law in order that the fullness of the gospel not be undermined. This perspective forces the epistemological question of how we know the contents of law, of that which is asked of us. Well aware of the importance of this issue, both in theology and in jurisprudence, Stringfellow's response was that knowledge can flow, if at all, only from first understanding who and what we are. The epistemological question can be asked only after the ontological question is answered.

The starting point is the gift of faith, and the prayer in faith for faith.[46] The "double-minded" person (James 1:6–8) is one who insists on holding on to a claim of knowledge and of wisdom while being aware that the knowledge may not be perfect—resulting in instability and uncertainty. It is not possible to grasp the completeness of sin and at the same time claim knowledge of law. The attempt to create or to discern a theology of law will be inherently unsuccessful. "To contort the word of grace into the law of nature is to make the Gospel unintelligible, however neatly it resolves the query about the relations of theology and law."[47] The ontological premise is the confessional presence of faith, and the response is action, not ideology. "I look for style, not stereotype, for precedent, not model, for parable, not proposition, for analogue, not aphorism, for paradox, not syllogism, for signs, not statutes. The encounter with the biblical witness is empirical, as distinguished from scholastic, and it is confessional, rather than literalistic."[48]

As a consequence, Stringfellow was deeply suspicious of any attempt to develop a theory or system of theology and jurisprudence. Indeed, the very concept of Christian jurisprudence is not a viable endeavor. "The tension between law and grace is such that there is no Christian Jurisprudence.... To have no special Christian jurisprudence does not mean that Christians are indifferent, or wholly negativist, toward law. Rather their concern is primarily an issue of vocation, not of jurisprudence."[49] The natural law tradition, Stringfellow felt, runs the risk of a Pelagian comfort with the human capacity to know and to do what is good, tempered (but not vitiated) by the existence of sin.[50]

The biblical witness that Stringfellow understood as the vocation of a Christian was to resist creating a jurisprudence of daily life. He did not seek, nor did he offer, prescriptions for ethical actions, nor "some rules, some norms, some guidelines, some rubrics for a sacred discipline that, if pursued diligently, would establish the holiness of a person. I do not discern that such is the biblical style, as admirable as that may happen to be in the worldly sense."[51] In this approach Stringfellow again echoed the words of Dietrich Bonhoeffer: "Christ did not, like a moralist, love a theory of good, but He loved the real man. He was not, like a philosopher, interested in the 'universally valid' but rather in that which is of help to the real and concrete human being.... For indeed, it is not written that God became an idea, a principle, a program, a universally valid proposition or a law, but that God became man."[52]

The gospel story and the biblical style Stringfellow embraced was the response in one's actions to the gift of the word of God. We are more likely to be more faithful in our actions than in our theories. The word of God is present in all aspects of life, and there is no part of life in which the presence of Jesus Christ is not felt. The vocation of the Christian is the discernment of, the reliance upon, and the celebration of this presence.[53] "What the ordinary Christian is called to do is to open the Bible and listen to the Word."[54]

PRINCIPALITIES AND POWERS: LAW AND THE STATE

Principalities and powers are those aspects of fallen reality that demand attention, loyalty, service, commitment, and obedience all in contradiction to the word of God. The biblical witness is a call to resist the principalities and powers[55] or to seek to impart wisdom to them.[56] Principalities and powers are the state and the church, but are also "the institutions, systems, ideologies, and other political and social powers."[57] They are "legion in species, number, variety, and name (e.g., Luke 8:29–33; Galatians 4:3; Ephesians 1:21, 6:10–13; Colossians 1:15–16, 2:10–23)."[58] The existence of principalities and powers reveals each of the aspects of the gospel story emphasized repeatedly by Stringfellow. These principalities and powers are themselves part of fallen reality and cannot be the source of either truth or salvation. They lay claim to obedience in asserting righteousness and assert authority in searching for righteousness. They become a source of their own justification and are intolerant of those who seek to unmask their pretentiousness. "The fallenness of the nations and powers is conjunctive with the fallenness of humanity, but it is not dependent or derivative."[59] The difficulty lies not just with these principalities and powers, but also with our failure to realize how we have become subservient to them. "Human beings do not readily recognize their victim status in relation to the principalities."[60]

The most common principality, but certainly not the sole or even primary one, is the state. Charged with harboring Daniel Berrigan, a fugitive due to his protests against the war in Vietnam,[61] Stringfellow relished the opportunity to respond to the federal government agent's admonition that he should "obey the emperor" and be subject to the governing authorities (1 Pet. 2:17; Rom. 13:1). Having just completed the manuscript for *An Ethics for Christians and Other Aliens in a Strange Land*, Stringfellow responded to the agent's admonition by writing *Conscience and Obedience: The Politics of Romans 13 and Revelation 13 in Light of the Second Coming*. In this text, he addressed directly the dual words that are spoken to political authority. Political authority is instituted by God and is part of fallen reality. It is not one without the other. It is both.

Stringfellow offered two keys to a biblical view of the state as a principality. The first is that Romans 13 and Revelation 13 portray, respectively, conceptions of legitimate political authority and conceptions of illegitimate political authority, which Stringfellow further explained do not resolve the simultaneous characteristic of lawful or lawless political authority.[62] The second key is that these essential elements of legitimacy (or illegitimacy) and lawfulness (or unlawfulness) are to be understood as honoring the sovereign and calling the "emperor" to its own vocation.[63] To honor the sovereign means holding the sovereign accountable to its faithfulness to the word of God. "The relationship between the Christian and the state is never one of uncritical allegiance or obedience.... This means that the Christian is not only concerned with what the content and policy of the law is, but with how it is enacted and promulgated as law, how it achieves the status of law, how it is administered, when it is invoked, and against whom it is enforced, how it is adjudicated, and how it is changed and modified."[64]

The institution of the church is just as much a principality and power as is the state, and both exist as part of fallen reality. Stringfellow viewed the "Constantinian Arrangement" as a reversal of the apostolic relationship between the church and the political authority, and an arrangement that has cast a heavy burden on the church ever since. By virtue of accommodating privileges such as tax exemption, the church loses its vocation. "Thus the church becomes confined, for the most part, to the sanctuary, and is assigned to either political silence or to banal acquiescence."[65]

Just as vocation and witness are keys to understanding the state as a principality, the vocation of the church as a witness is central to its faithfulness to the word of God. The vocation of the church is to be an advocate and witness for all victims, and all victims of victims.

> Advocacy is how the church puts into practice its own experience of the victory of the word of God over the power of death, how the church lives in the efficacy of the resurrection amid the reign of death in this world, how the church expends its life in freedom from both intimidation and enthrallment of death or of any agencies of death, how the church honors the sovereignty of the word of God in history against the counterclaims of the ruling principalities. This advocacy, in its ecumenical scope as well as its actual specificity, constitutes the church's political task, but, simultaneously, exemplifies the church's worship of God, as intercession for anyone in need, and for the need of the whole of creation, which exposes and confounds the blasphemy of predatory political authority.[66]

THE POSSIBILITY OF HOPE: LAW AND JUSTICE

The pervasiveness of death and the fallen nature of all of creation is not a cause for despair. To the contrary, William Stringfellow claimed celebration in the midst of death because the gospel is the word of triumph over death. He wrote in order to share the word of the possibility of hope.[67] He was never disillusioned by human beings, because he was never enchanted by them. He was never let down by political institutions, because he never believed in their ultimate power. To the question of whether there is any American hope, he simply stated, "The categorical answer is no."[68] What he believed in was the simple power of the risen Lord. "In the face of death, live humanly. In the middle of chaos, celebrate the Word. Amidst babel, I repeat, speak the truth. Confront the noise and verbiage and falsehood of death with the truth and potency and efficacy of the Word of God."[69]

The possibility of hope lies in the gospel and is expressed in several forms. One form of expression of hope is the certainty of the gospel itself. The faith that is given by God "is the assurance of things hoped for, the conviction of things not seen" (Heb. 11:1 NASV). A witness of advocacy is possible and is powerful; Stringfellow offered the life and work of Dorothy

Day as an example of the biblical witness in the life of the church.[70] A biblical witness of advocacy, however, will never bring triumph in and of itself. While sharing a common political agenda with proponents of the "social gospel," Stringfellow distanced himself from their theology out of concern that it assumed too much on the part of human nature and social institutions. We cannot be assured that our actions will achieve justice in this world, in this time; we are assured that nothing in this world can interfere with the presence of the word of God. The biblical experience of hope is quite distinct from optimism about the world, for "optimism refers to the capabilities of principalities and human beings, while hope bespeaks the effort of the Word of God in common history."[71] The absence of optimism in human nature allows the presence of the fullness of the word of God.

From a biblical point of view, there is nothing whatever that the Supreme Court or any school board or any principalities or any persons—including the president of the United States—can say or do that can determine the character or action of the word of God in common history—and nothing, issuing from any such source, that can obviate, diminish, alter, modify, prejudice, detract from, or otherwise change the pervasive presence of the word of God in this world.[72]

A second expression of hope lies in the constant experience of worship. Worship is not an optional activity to be expressed on certain occasions; neither is it solely a collective activity. Worship is the primary mode of responding to the word of God. In the context of law, whether one understands law in terms of gospel or of advocacy as legal counsel for victims, worship can and does take place. "Worship is not peripheral, but decisive in the relationships of Christian faith and secular law."[73]

The hope made possible by the gospel is that we can become human. The vocation of the Christian, and the central ethical issue confronting every Christian, "concerns how to live, what to decide, how to act humanly in the midst of the Fall."[74] When we forget, or ignore, or diminish the gospel, we denigrate the very persons we are called to be, and called to be with. "Deception is more humiliating than rejection. Exploitation is more inhuman than exclusion. Indifference is more embittering than open hostility. Condescension is more provocative than hate."[75] By stark contrast, the gospel allows us not to become god, but to become human. "In the face of death, live humanly."[76] Dietrich Bonhoeffer articulated this same christological foundation of hope: "Man becomes man because God became man. But man does not become God. It is not he, therefore, who was or is able to accomplish his own transformation, but it is God who changes his form into the form of man, so that man may become, not indeed God, but, in the eyes of God, man."[77]

Hope is possible because death is not the final word. In its repudiation of death, the gospel makes life possible. "To be ethical is to live sacramentally.

To discern apocalyptic signs heightens the expectation of the eschatological events. In resistance persons live more humanly. *No* to death means *yes* to life."[78]

In a culture struggling to hold together and to hold up for all to see a vision of law that coincides with a vision of the gospel, William Stringfellow's life and work and voice stand as a proclamation of the futility of such a gesture. His life was one of service to those on the margins of power, indeed to the powerless in the face of oppression. His work was a vocation of responding to the word of God. His voice was a call to hear that word. Rare among theologians, scholars, and advocates of the late twentieth century is the centrality of the gospel in understanding the law. The legacy that Stringfellow has given is a constantly renewed understanding that law cannot be conflated with gospel, that death is not the final word, and that human nature can never be the source of its own justification.

NOTES

1. William Stringfellow, *An Ethic for Christians and Other Aliens in a Strange Land* (Waco, Tex.: Word Books, 1973), 13.

2. The most comprehensive bibliography of Stringfellow's writings has been prepared by Paul West; it is found in Bill Wylie Kellermann, ed., *A Keeper of the Word: Selected Writings of William Stringfellow* (Grand Rapids, Mich.: Eerdmans, 1994), 416–426.

3. William Stringfellow, "The Christian Lawyer as a Churchman," *Vanderbilt Law Review* 10 (1956–57): 939.

4. "People assume that I have read prodigiously in theology, whereas the truth is that I am practically a theological illiterate, so far as the works of the theologians are concerned. In my whole life I have, maybe, read two dozen theological books, Aquinas or Calvin or Tillich or the like.... The truth is I have, practically, just read the Bible." William Stringfellow, *A Second Birthday* (Garden City, N.Y.: Doubleday, 1970), 151.

5. Kellermann, *A Keeper of the Word*, 1.

6. William Stringfellow, *Conscience and Obedience: The Politics of Romans 13 and Revelation 13 in Light of the Second Coming* (Waco, Tex.: Word Books, 1977), 24.

7. The 1957 conference was sponsored by the Faculty Christian Fellowship and the United Student Christian Council, with essays prepared by Wilber Katz, Samuel Enoch Stumpf, William Ellis, and William Stringfellow. These essays were published as "A Symposium on Law and Christianity," *Vanderbilt Law Review* 10 (1957): 879–968. The second conference was held at the University of Chicago with papers prepared by James A. Pike, Albert Mollegen, Markus Barth, Harold J. Berman, Paul Lehmann, and Jacques Ellul. The essays from the second conference were published as "A Symposium on Law and Christianity," *Oklahoma Law Review* 12 (1959): 45–146.

8. Stringfellow, "The Christian Lawyer as a Churchman," 956.

9. Ibid., 962.

10. See William Stringfellow and Anthony Towne, *The Death and Life of Bishop Pike* (Garden City, N.Y.: Doubleday, 1976).

11. See William Stringfellow, "A Matter of Conscience," *The Witness* 62 (May 1979): 4–6.

12. William Stringfellow, *A Simplicity of Faith: My Experience in Mourning* (Nashville, Tenn.: Abingdon, 1982), 133.

13. "The approach to Romans 13 and Revelation 13 here is confessional, that is to say, a living contact betwixt the Word of God exposed in the biblical texts and the same Word of God active now in the situation of the common reader so that the encounter in Bible study becomes, in itself, an event characteristically biblical." Stringfellow, *Conscience and Obedience*, 13. See also William Stringfellow, *My People Is the Enemy: An Autobiographical Polemic* (New York: Holt, Rinehart and Winston, 1964), 96: "The characteristic approach to the Bible of the Christian is confessional."

14. William Stringfellow, *Dissenter in a Great Society: A Christian View of America in Crisis* (New York: Holt, Rinehart and Winston, 1966), 150–154.

15. William Stringfellow, *Instead of Death*, 2d ed. (New York: Seabury, 1976), 48.

16. Stringfellow, *A Second Birthday*, 95.

17. Stringfellow, *A Simplicity of Faith*, 21.

18. Stringfellow, *A Second Birthday*, 95.

19. See Stringfellow, *Conscience and Obedience*, chaps. 1 and 5. In one of the rare instances in which Stringfellow offered a citation to another scholar, he cited Dietrich Bonhoeffer's *Creation and Fall* (New York: Macmillan, 1959), as a text for the interpretation of vocation in light of the Fall. Stringfellow, *Conscience and Obedience*, 27.

20. See Stringfellow, *A Second Birthday*.

21. Stringfellow, *A Simplicity of Faith*, 15–23.

22. See Stringfellow, *Instead of Death*.

23. William Stringfellow, *Free in Obedience* (New York: Seabury, 1964), 44.

24. "The circus performer is the image of the eschatological person—emancipated from frailty and inhibition, exhilarant, militant, transcendent over death—neither confined nor conformed by the fear of death any more." Stringfellow, *A Simplicity of Faith*, 90.

25. Stringfellow, *A Second Birthday*, 151.

26. William Stringfellow, *A Private and Public Faith* (Grand Rapids, Mich.: Eerdmans, 1962), 25.

27. Stringfellow, *An Ethic for Christians*, 19.

28. Stringfellow, *Instead of Death*, 10.

29. Stringfellow, *Conscience and Obedience*, 64. "Biblically, all men and all principalities are guiltily implicated in the violence which pervades all relationships in the Fall." Stringfellow, *An Ethic for Christians*, 130.

30. Stringfellow, "The Christian Lawyer as a Churchman," 964.

31. Stringfellow, *Free in Obedience*, 68–69.

32. Stringfellow, *A Second Birthday*, 133.

33. Stringfellow, *Conscience and Obedience*, 37–48.

34. William Stringfellow, *Count It All Joy: Reflections on Faith, Doubt, and Temptation Seen Through the Letter of James* (Grand Rapids, Mich.: Eerdmans, 1967), 47.

35. Stringfellow had occasion to meet with Karl Barth during a conference at the University of Chicago in 1962. He described their close affinity in theology as more than "an intuitive thing," to which Barth replied, "How could it be otherwise? We read the same Bible, don't we?" Quoted in Stringfellow, *A Second Birthday*, 151–152. See also chapter 12, this volume.

36. Stringfellow spent time with Ellul shortly after the end of World War II. See Stringfellow, *An Ethic for Christians*, 117. Among the few works cited by Stringfellow is Jacques Ellul, *The Theological Foundation of the Law* (Garden City, N.Y.: Doubleday, 1960), which first appeared in English in 1960. On Stringfellow's view of the importance of Ellul's thinking, see William Stringfellow, "The American Importance of Jacques Ellul," *Katallagete* 2 (Spring 1970): 47–48, and William Stringfellow, "Kindred Mind and Brother," *Sojourners* (June 1977): 12.

37. Stringfellow, *Count It All Joy*, 58–59.

38. Ibid., 58.

39. Nicholas Berdyaev, *The Destiny of Man*, trans. Natalie Duddington (New York: Charles Scribner's Sons, 1937), 85–86, quoted in Stringfellow, "The Christian Lawyer as a Churchman," 957 n. 70. In this same note Stringfellow describes Karl Barth and Jacques Ellul as the only other scholars "who take seriously the extremity of the tension between grace and law."

40. Stringfellow, *An Ethic for Christians*, 131–133.

41. See Dietrich Bonhoeffer, *The Cost of Discipleship*, trans. R. H. Fuller (New York: Macmillan, 1963), 45–60, and Stringfellow, *Free in Obedience*, 107–116.

42. See Stringfellow, *A Private and Public Faith*, 14 ("The crisis is the real possibility that Protestantism has become mere religion"); Dietrich Bonhoeffer, *Letters and Papers from Prison*, ed. Eberhard Bethge (New York: Macmillan, 1972), 328. See also chapter 13, this volume.

43. Stringfellow, *A Private and Public Faith*, 14.

44. Ibid., 63.

45. Stringfellow, *Free in Obedience*, 72.

46. Stringfellow, *Count It All Joy*, 47–61.

47. William Stringfellow, "Christian Faith and the American Lawyer," *Federation News* (January–February 1957): 81.

48. Stringfellow, *Conscience and Obedience*, 11.

49. Stringfellow, "The Christian Lawyer as a Churchman," 964.

50. "Indeed, the natural lawyers invert the Biblical conception of sin in order to accommodate the intrinsic necessities of the natural law hypothesis. The natural lawyers treat too lightly the Gospel, for if sin is just moral deficiency then grace and natural law amount to the same thing, that is, the final corrective of moral deficiency, and men need not look for their salvation to Jesus Christ our Lord but may as well look to Sophocles." Stringfellow, "The Christian Lawyer as a Churchman," 958.

51. William Stringfellow, *The Politics of Spirituality* (Philadelphia: Westminster, 1984), 89.

52. Dietrich Bonhoeffer, *Ethics*, trans. Neville Horton Smith (New York: Macmillan, 1965), 85.

53. Colossians 3:17. See Stringfellow, *A Private and Public Faith*, 56.

54. Stringfellow, *Count It All Joy*, 16.

55. Romans 8:38; Ephesians 6:12; Colossians 2:15.

56. Ephesians 3:10; Colossians 1:16.

57. Stringfellow, *An Ethic for Christians*, 17. See also Stringfellow, *Free in Obedience*, 52: "What the Bible calls 'principalities and powers' are called in contemporary language 'ideologies,' 'institutions,' and 'images.'"

58. Stringfellow, *An Ethic for Christians*, 77.

59. Stringfellow, *Conscience and Obedience*, 30.

60. Stringfellow, *An Ethic for Christians*, 84.

61. See William Stringfellow and Anthony Towne, *Suspect Tenderness: The Ethics of the Berrigan Witness* (New York: Holt, Rinehart and Winston, 1971).

62. Stringfellow, *Conscience and Obedience*, 39, 43.

63. Ibid., 32, 46.

64. William Stringfellow, "Race, The Church, and the Law," *The Episcopalian* 127 (November 1962): 34.

65. Stringfellow, *Conscience and Obedience*, 103.

66. Ibid., 94–95.

67. "My sole intention in this book is to affirm a biblical hope which comprehends politics and which transcends politics." Stringfellow, *Conscience and Obedience*, 9.

68. Stringfellow, *An Ethic for Christians*, 155.

69. Ibid., 142–143.

70. Stringfellow, *Conscience and Obedience*, 96. See also chapter 7, this volume.

71. Stringfellow, *A Simplicity of Faith*, 95.

72. Stringfellow, *The Politics of Spirituality*, 59.

73. Stringfellow, "The Christian Lawyer as a Churchman," 939.

74. Stringfellow, *An Ethic for Christians*, 62–63.

75. Stringfellow, *My People Is the Enemy*, 105.

76. Stringfellow, *An Ethic for Christians*, 142.

77. Bonhoeffer, *Ethics*, 82.

78. Stringfellow, *An Ethic for Christians*, 156.

[CHAPTER 17]

John Howard Yoder (1927–1997)

DUNCAN B. FORRESTER

John Howard Yoder was born in 1927 and raised in an Amish Mennonite family, living in Wayne County, Ohio. He was nurtured as a Christian in Oak Grove Mennonite Church, where his father, a prominent leader, was declared to be "one of the most powerful, influential, and widely known bishops in the Amish Mennonite church during the last four decades of the nineteenth century."[1] Yoder was educated largely in Mennonite schools, but his education was in no way narrow or sectarian. After World War II, with other young American Mennonites, he helped with postwar reconstruction in Europe, played a part in the revival of the Mennonite cause in France, was active in ecumenical discussions, particularly of pacifism, and took a doctorate after studying with Karl Barth and others in Basel, Switzerland.

When Yoder returned from Europe to the United States, he was at the height of his powers, but he held down a variety of jobs, some administrative, some educational, many of them part-time. He taught at the Mennonite Biblical Seminary in Elkhart from 1960 to 1965, and from 1965 to 1973 he was at Goshen Biblical Seminary. All the while he was producing essays, articles, and lectures, although he published mainly with small Mennonite publishing houses and was not yet widely known outside Mennonite circles. The publication of *The Politics of Jesus* in 1972, however, caused something of a theological sensation and gave him a high profile as a constructive and critical theological thinker of the highest rank, one whose work had to be taken seriously by Christian theologians of all varieties. In 1977 Yoder became a full-time professor at the University of Notre Dame, an interesting sign of recognition, which provided him with a platform from which to address a wider audience and an opportunity for dialogue with Roman Catholic theological traditions. He became a respected dialogue partner with a number of legal scholars, perhaps most notably Thomas L. Shaffer, whose work he deeply influenced.[2] Yoder was now quickly and widely recognized as a fresh and distinctive theological voice, and he became well known partly through the work of his disciples, of whom Stanley Hauerwas (not always a totally reliable interpreter of Yoder) is the best known, and, of course, through his own teaching, publishing, and lecturing.[3]

Yoder's particular Christian heritage, which he embraced with great but not uncritical conviction throughout his life, was Mennonite. In brief, this meant that his thought had from the beginning four distinctive emphases. First, his theology was always biblical. He was not a fundamentalist, but he accepted the Bible as the ultimate authority in Christian discipleship and Christian theology, and his exegesis was often fresh, imaginative, and penetrating. Second, he believed in the gathered church, with the local worshipping congregation of believers as the primary manifestation of what it is to be a "church." This church has a structure of "discipline"—a way of dealing with offenses and failures that is directed toward reconciliation. Third, the church and individual Christians alike are expected to express, in their relations both within the community and outside of it, loving service or "servanthood." Finally, the peace witness is central for Yoder. Not only are believers expected to be peaceable themselves, but they should also seek peace in the wider society as a necessary expression of their faith.

From the beginning, the Mennonite Church offered Yoder no pietistic escape from the problems of the world or from rigorous academic debate. He was early regarded primarily as a Mennonite Church theologian, but, like Karl Barth, he was always a theologian who swam "against the stream" and maintained his own critical judgment. Yoder was in Europe at a crucial and challenging moment. Barthian theology and the broader movement much influenced by Barth and labeled "biblical theology" or "biblical realism" was at its peak. Yoder found much that was congenial in this new theological mood—and much to question. In particular, he was attracted by the distinctive blending of theological orthodoxy with social and political radicalism—and disturbed that Western theology was still so deeply "infected" with what he believed were Constantinian assumptions. He saw these assumptions as distorting the theological understanding and giving the church a false view of its nature and mandate.

KARL BARTH AND BIBLICAL THEOLOGY

Partly as a result of his involvements in Europe, Yoder quickly found himself deeply immersed in a new and vigorous theological movement in Europe and the United States. As a critical disciple, he saw Barth's theology, although deeply rooted in the tradition of the magisterial Reformation, as converging with the radical Reformation tradition as represented by the

Mennonites. This makes Barth's thought a useful point of comparison and contrast with Yoder's own. Both Barth and Yoder were deeply suspicious of liberal theology and uneasy about the heritage of the Enlightenment. Both took the Bible with profound seriousness, but they resisted fundamentalism as an attempt to reduce scripture to a system of absolute and infallible propositions. Both Barth and Yoder saw theology as necessarily *ecclesial*, rooted in the life of the church and the church's proclamation. And Barth, from the Reformed tradition, became increasingly suspicious of the intertwining of church and state, the Christianity and culture characteristic of the Constantinian settlement, of "Christendom." Indeed, in some ways, Barth's mature understanding of the church is congenial to the Mennonite belief in a "gathered church" that represents a sort of counterculture. Yoder agreed that, in a broad sense, Barth's early socialism was the harbinger of his "radical ecclesiology."[4] Both Barth and Yoder combined a fairly conservative theological orthodoxy with social and political radicalism. And although Barth was never a pacifist, his position on war and peace issues in the aftermath of World War II moved remarkably close to the traditional peace witness of the Mennonites.[5]

The initial impact of Yoder's theology was certainly helped by the fact that from the beginning of his career as a theologian he engaged constructively and sympathetically not only with Barth, whom he recognized as probably the most important Reformed theologian since the Reformation, but also with the debates in and about the post–World War II movement loosely labeled "biblical theology." Here Yoder recognized themes with which he had a great deal of sympathy. But he also represented a distinctive theological voice that was heard at an opportune moment, as many churches around the world reconciled themselves to minority status and as the foundations of Christendom (or what Yoder preferred to call Constantinianism) were rapidly eroded, particularly in Europe.

Barth and Yoder both sought to root their theology in the Bible, but they were innovative in their approach to biblical interpretation. Both believed that fundamentalism and most Protestant readings of scripture "subordinated the actual reading of scriptural texts to an *a priori* discussion of how the texts were so written and preserved as to be infallibly revelatory and how they should be so read as to coincide with an all-inclusive system of propositions."[6] The Bible must rather be seen as in tension with the cultural assumptions of this, and every, age. For both Barth and Yoder, the Bible is not primarily a law book or a collection of rules. Barth saw it as the indispensable aid or stimulus to hearing and responding to the specific commands of God to us here and now. Yoder tended to regard scripture, responsibly interpreted within the church, as a chosen vehicle through which God speaks to us today.

Much of Yoder's writing on ethics was unabashedly exegetical. He was himself a well-regarded biblical scholar. Richard B. Hays speaks of Yoder's *The Politics of Jesus* as "a path-breaking attempt to do Christian ethics in vigorous dialogue with biblical scholarship" and "an impressive foray by a theological ethicist into exegetical territory."[7] Yoder, according to Hays, argued for three central theses: that the Jesus of the New Testament eschews violence and coercion; that the example of Jesus is binding on the Christian community; and that discipleship is a political choice that necessarily has implications for the public realm. The church appears as the conscience, critic, and servant of human society, and the role of the state is presented in terms of the New Testament teaching on the "principalities and powers," which are intended to be servants of God that enable human beings to flourish in peaceableness. In fact, however, these principalities and powers often rebel and deny their divine mandate.[8] Long before liberation theology became fashionable, Yoder saw the Bible as a handbook of liberation, a liberating narrative.

Hays suggests that Yoder, like Barth, "eschews the hermeneutical strategy of extracting moral *principles* from Scripture ... [because] the exercise of applying principles to situations leaves too much room for straying away from the truth revealed in Jesus."[9] Jesus, for Yoder, "reveals the true nature and vocation of human beings" in all times and places.[10] He was too responsible an exegete to attempt to derive moral rules directly from the Bible. But he did give the Bible, and in particular the picture of Jesus and his teaching that emerges from the Gospels, an absolute normative status, and he was reluctant to see scripture as reflecting the assumptions of a very different age.

NATURE AND NATURAL LAW

Like Barth, but with his own emphases, Yoder was critical of the use of nature and natural law in ethical discourse.[11] But, unlike Barth, Yoder saw the discourse of natural law, or something very like it, as having a necessary place in the search for a common morality in pluralistic societies, as people strive together to resolve complex ethical issues in, say, the area of bioethics. Frequently, however, in his judgment, too much is claimed for natural law and "common morality." Yoder tended to see natural insights as reflecting the assumptions of the age and the culture rather than any universal reality. The Thomist and classical visions of nature, Yoder suggested, privilege things as they are. Such ways of understanding nature thus easily become oppressive, and they make virtually impossible a subversive ethics such as, Yoder believed, the gospel teaches. Furthermore, natural law thinking has an overly optimistic understanding of the ability of human reason to discern moral truth. Yoder, on the other hand, spoke freely of the fallenness and finiteness of human reason, limitations that make it often a confusing guide to moral truth.

There are, Yoder suggested, two broad approaches to the understanding of nature. In the first:

> Nature is the way things obviously are. The epistemology is simple, descriptive. Socially it is positivistic; the institutions of slavery, of patriarchy, of monarchy are obviously the way it is. Biologically it is also positivistic: contraception and artificial insemination interfere with the "natural" functioning of the body. Its first ethical impact is usually conservative, since the nation, the class structure, the marketplace, the repertory of roles or vocations is the way it is. The system will seem convincing as long as all parties have been educated under the same customs, so that they really think "everyone knows…" whatever they know, and as long as no skeptic draws attention to the is/ought equation.[12]

The second family of understandings of nature was more congenial to Yoder. It speaks of "things as they ought to be":

> The essence of things is different from the appearance, the "true nature'" as contrast with the empirical one, the "real me" as better than the me you see. This normative, non-empirical or 'ideal' nature can be rooted in an ideal past (Eden, the Founding Fathers) or in the command of God, or perhaps in the future toward which one holds that we are moving or should move.[13]

This second family is not rooted in the way things are, and therefore it is capable of being more critical, or even subversive, of existing realities. But the way ethical guidance is derived from such an understanding of nature is still complex and confusing. It is certainly not a simple deduction from examination of the world around us and its potentialities. Yet even after all necessary cautions and qualifications have been made, Yoder still believed that arguments from nature have a necessary place in moral discernment. Nonetheless, *Christian* ethics must never sacrifice the priority of the call and demand of Jesus, or forget that what Jesus demanded was and is *unreasonable* behavior.

"There is the need in public life [not only in politics] for a common denominator language in order to collaborate with relative strangers in running the world despite our abiding differences," Yoder acknowledged. But he was rather reluctant to spell out how this shared language is related to the gospel, whether it is separate and independent, and how, if at all, it relates to the call to discipleship. Yoder recognized the need for some common language of morals, but he argued that this common morality is limited and needs constantly to be challenged and enriched by insights from Christian discipleship. Christians need in discussion with non-Christians to decide what the right thing to do is. "In ethics," he wrote, "we have to act, and sometimes act together, by the nature of the issue. Scarce resources cannot be spent everywhere. Life will be taken or spared; we can't have it both ways."[14] In such situations we cannot simply appeal to the Bible, to Christian doctrine, or to a command of God without giving reasons. Yoder was deeply suspicious of claims that natural law on its own can provide an adequate "neutral" structure for such decision-making discussions.

Yoder then pushed the argument further:

> The function of the notion of "nature" in medieval Catholic thought was *not* the modern one of knowing how to talk with outsiders.... The appeal to "nature" was an instrument of *less* rather than *more* commonality with non-Christians.... The concern with "nature" then bespoke not a growing readiness to converse with others in non-Christian language, but rather a growing conviction that the way Christians see reality is the way it really is. But the way to affirm our respect for others is to respect their particularity and learn their languages, not to project in their absence a claim that we see the truth of things with an authority unvitiated by our particularity.[15]

Yoder was thus uneasy also about an ethical method that starts from the universal and expects the particular to conform. "The Biblical story and the Biblical world view," he argued, "widen out from the particular to take in the general, not the other way 'round."[16] And so it should be with moral reasoning. It should start not from principles with a claim to universality, nor from moral laws, but from specific cases, issues, and commands of God. Yoder would have found himself siding with Mahatma Gandhi against Immanuel Kant in that Gandhi implied a rejection of the Kantian stress on "universalizing one's maxim"; instead, Gandhi asserted that when one is facing an awkward moral choice, the thing to do is to recall the face of the poorest and weakest person one may have seen and ask if the step one contemplates is going to be of any use to that person.

"The reason I do not trust claims to 'natural insight,'" Yoder wrote, "is that the dominant moral views of any *known* world are oppressive, provincial, or (to say it theologically) 'fallen.'"[17] Yoder was less likely than Barth to argue that natural law introduces a different lord, at odds with the lordship of Christ. But both agreed that ethics for Christians, and in principle for all, is ultimately a matter of obedience to the command and call of the living God as made known in Jesus Christ, rather than the falling back on a set of rules, principles, or laws that claim universal validity.

Ethics, for Yoder, was thus primarily a matter of obedience to the command and example of Jesus in concrete situations in relation to specific issues and challenges. Nature and natural law too easily lend a spurious universality and absoluteness to the assumptions of the age. When Yoder spoke of nature and human nature, he usually stressed the need to transform nature, to challenge nature with grace, rather than speaking about some sort of complementarity between nature and grace or of "nature" as having some kind of inherent normative status.

GOSPEL AND LAW

Yoder was suspicious of the traditional distinction and relationship between law and gospel, particularly as Martin Luther and nineteenth-century Lutherans expounded it. In the Lutheran tradition, law and gospel operate on different, usually opposed, principles in separate spheres largely independent of one another. Yoder's position can be expounded as giving priority to the gospel over the law. In some ways echoing Barth's affirmation that dogmatics is ethics,[18] Yoder spoke of social ethics as gospel, or "The Kingdom as Social Ethics." The inner or true nature of law, he claimed, is the gospel. The law is essentially the command and call of the gracious God, which are themselves expressions of grace. The law is not independent of the gospel, or opposed to the gospel, or merely a preliminary to the gospel. Both law and gospel have at their heart the same gracious reality. And that means that grace, forgiveness, encouragement, and hope rather than limitation, threat, and despair are the core of the law. "Normal Christian moral discourse," he wrote, "should be about enablement more than prohibition; about law as a form of grace, not a polar alternative to it; about pardon more than duty."[19] Forgiveness and reconciliation are in fact an integral part of a Christian understanding of justice. Both criminal and social justice are directed toward the restoration of fellowship and the healing of relationships. Obedience to God's law is, Yoder suggested, a way of proclaiming the gospel.

For Yoder, the law is enriched and clarified by the gospel. Apart from the gospel, the law becomes destructive. A system of criminal law, for instance, that is not open to the possibility of forgiveness and reconciliation makes situations and people worse rather than better. Law and gospel do not operate in separate, insulated spheres. When Christians discuss legal matters or apply the law, they must not leave the gospel behind, for that would be to deny what is indeed the heart of the law.

CHURCH AND ETHICS

Disciples are never alone, Yoder insisted; they are always part of the church, which is the body of Christ. Most theology in the aftermath of

World War II was ecclesial and deeply rooted in the life of the church. But Yoder brought to the fore a rather different emphasis in his understanding of the church. The true church for him was the *free* gathered church, which regards minority status as a challenge and an opportunity rather than a disaster. Since Constantine, Yoder argued, the church and the world had been fused; now it was again possible to distinguish them and spell out the responsibilities of the church toward the world, which are essentially to proclaim and to exemplify the gospel rather than attempting to impose a law. As an evangelical theologian, Yoder saw scripture as it is interpreted within the community of faith—rather than the academy—as at the heart of discipleship and proclamation. What Barth called "the strange new world of the Bible" is always, Yoder believed, in tension with the cultural and political assumptions of every age. The church's language must always be culture-critical and politically constructive. Yoder presented his mature work as "a late ripening, in the field of ethics, of the same biblical realist revolution, in which precisely ecclesiology and eschatology come to have a new import for the substance of ethics."[20]

The church, according to Yoder, is an alternative community in which disciples and people of virtue—or rather of holiness—are formed. In Nancey Murphy's words, it is "a laboratory for imagining and practicing new forms of social life."[21] Yoder called the church "a hermeneutic community."[22] It is a creative minority in diaspora, rather than sheltering in a ghetto, and witnessing to and exemplifying the loving community that is to come. Yoder asserted very strongly "the paradigmatic role of the people of God in offering the world a vision of God's restoration of humanity, in Christ, in the faith community, and beyond."[23] This goal is accomplished through the various distinctive practices of the community—baptism, eucharist, discipline, and the like—that sustain the life of the community and are exemplary for the broader society.[24] Worship is, Yoder suggested, "the communal cultivation of an alternative construction of society and of history."[25]

Yoder emphatically did not regard the church as a fellowship of moral giants, or of those whose behavior and virtues are exemplary. Nor did he understand the church as being beyond error and sin. Christians, members of the church, are not Pharisees, trusting in their own righteousness, but rather forgiven sinners, people who know themselves to be offenders and rely on God's grace and the experience of forgiveness. For this reason, like most Reformed Christians, he regarded a structure of "discipline" as essential to the faithful being of the church, as a "mark" of the true church. Yoder used the typical Mennonite term for ecclesiastical discipline—"binding and loosing"—as a power and a task given to the Mennonite Church whereby members who fall into sin may be brought back to the true path and find reconciliation and forgiveness. Yoder himself in his last years was disciplined in this way, and after showing penitence he was forgiven by the community and restored to fellowship.

To grasp the implications of Yoder's ecclesiology, it is useful to bring him into conversation with his disciple and colleague, Stanley Hauerwas. Yoder sometimes came close to reiterating Stanley Hauerwas's rather triumphalistic slogan, "The Church does not have, but is, a social ethic."[26] For neither in works nor in grace are we alone, rather in fellowship. Yoder was more cautious than Hauerwas, and more sensitive to the dangers of ecclesiastical triumphalism, however. In Yoder's words, "The new peoplehood constituted by the grace to which the readers of these [apostolic] texts had responded is *by its very essence* a message to the surrounding world."[27] The message is grace, and the church is a testimony to the triumph of grace. This position is to be welcomed for its rejection of the false individualism of the pietist tradition and the Enlightenment. But there are problems when we ask what message in fact is being communicated to the world by the empirical, fallible, and often bitterly divided churches of this or any age.

"The church does not have, but is, a social ethic," an epigram worthy of Yoder himself, appears in many places in Hauerwas's writings.[28] It is a very attractive notion, suggesting that Christian ethics must be embodied in the life of a community, that ethics is not a possession of the church but the gift to the church that constitutes it. The church, for Hauerwas and for Yoder, is a social ethic insofar as it is a "faithful manifestation of the peaceable Kingdom in the world."[29] Its first task is to *be* the church, a community that "can clearly be distinguished from the world."[30] It is shaped by a story that is sharply different from the world's story. "Its most important social function is *to be itself*."[31] It is called to be a community of the cross, and an alternative to the hostilities and divisions to be found elsewhere.

This is all heady stuff, to which one is tempted to say that the church that we know provides an empirical refutation: *that* church is not very much like the church of which Hauerwas and Yoder speak. Paradoxically, the virtues that they see as central to the Christian community are often exemplified in costly ways far from the orbit of the church. And is it not true that the actual visible church to which we belong falls far short of living up to its calling? This truth simply underlines the fact that the church must be a community of forgiven sinners who have learned to live by grace rather than a fellowship of moral heroes and virtuous achievers.

In itself, the existence of the body is a moral statement, a demonstration and exemplification of the ethic that is integral to the gospel. The behavior of the community confirms or questions the truth of the gospel that its members proclaim. The congregation, the body, the church is thus a kind of hermeneutic of the gospel. The message and the ethics are inseparable from the life of the church.

Within the body, divisions of hostility, suspicion, and competition are pathological and can destroy its vitality and integrity. Yet the unity and harmony of the body does not remove particularity, plurality, and difference; indeed, the former enhances and enriches the latter and blends them into a common purpose. In Christ, the old animosities and separations, as exemplified in the classic division between Jew and Gentile, are overcome. God's purpose is to create a single new humanity—the unity of the church is simply a sign and foretaste of the broader unity of humankind, which is God's goal. The unity of the church is therefore not simply for its own sake, a matter, perhaps, of streamlining church structures. The New Testament teaches that the way the church is structured and operates is to be at the service of the gospel and to confirm that gospel. Eucharist, baptism, and discipline mean that "the church can be a foretaste of the peace for which the world was made."[32] The church points to and already expresses in a partial way the coming unity of humankind. For Yoder, the being of the church is therefore a vital expression of the gospel and of the law, as well as a demonstration of the truth of the gospel and the validity of the law.

CHRISTOLOGY AND DISCIPLESHIP

Yoder said little about human nature, but much about Jesus Christ and much about discipleship. His anthropology, like Barth's, is christological: *Ecce Homo*, in Christ, and only in Christ, is true humanity to be found. The moral character of God and true humanity are revealed in Jesus. "God," Yoder wrote, "broke through the borders of man's definition of what is human, and gave a new, formative definition in Jesus."[33] In principle, the call to discipleship is universal, available for all, and at its heart is a challenge of obedience to Jesus Christ rather than to some universal law or set of principles. Humans are sinners, called to be disciples, and the real test is whether we follow and whether we obey. But in Yoder's understanding, the sin of human beings does not have the central place that it possesses in the Augustinian tradition and in modern times, especially perhaps in the theology of Reinhold Niebuhr. Sin is a problem, a defect, an issue that has to be faced and responded to with repentance and forgiveness. But it is not part of the essence of humanity.

According to Yoder, discipleship involves deep engagement with the life of the world and grappling with the issues and challenges of the world; it is not withdrawal to a ghetto or an isolated church. Yoder was thus moved to engage with the traditional theology of vocation, whereby God is understood as calling people to salvation and discipleship, and to a "secular" vocation or vocations in which discipleship is manifested in a particular sphere of life. Yoder was, however, unhappy about the classical understanding of vocation as presented, for instance, by Martin Luther. This understanding of vocation seems to offer a source of ethical challenge and opportunity alternative to the gospel, another source of moral authority not dissimilar to natural law, two spheres in which we find different, and sometimes contradictory, moral guidance.

Yoder's caution here is well taken. Luther's understanding of vocation has often been understood as effectively relegating rigorous discipleship to the private realm. In public affairs, the disciple is expected to follow the accepted standards and responsibilities of the office, which are the same for disciples and for nonbelievers. We have here an autonomous and independent ethics that is in fact secular, although it is capable of receiving a theological interpretation. And the standard theological account both affirms the God-givenness of the worldly structure of vocations and provides a ready-made justification for disciples doing things in their vocations that appear to be in stark contrast to the ethic of Jesus. Luther did not hesitate to affirm that the politician, Christian or not, is obliged in seeming contradiction to both law and gospel to resort to force, coercion, and violence. He, characteristically, took the argument to the extreme: "For the hand that wields this sword and slays with it is then no more man's hand, but God's, and it is not man, but God, who hangs, tortures, beheads, slays and fights. All these are His works and His judgments."[34]

In reaction to this extreme line of reasoning, Yoder seemed reluctant to engage fully with the fact that disciples are judges, and physicians, and police officers, and stockbrokers, and fulfill their discipleship in large part through their various "worldly" vocations. It is not enough to suggest that Christians should express "servanthood" in their various spheres of responsibility. A viable and convincing Christian ethic must address head-on the dilemmas and problems such people face day by day.

"To affirm the normativeness of discipleship is simply classical," Yoder wrote.[35] The way of discipleship, following Jesus, not any theory of human nature, exemplifies the truly human. Such an affirmation means that Jesus' vulnerable love of the enemy and renunciation of dominion comes to the center of the picture, as against the classical virtues of prudence, temperance, justice, and so on. People are defined by their relationships to God and to their neighbors, near and far.

MORAL DISCERNMENT

In discipleship within the community of faith, something of the true humanity that was fully manifested in Christ may be glimpsed. The household of faith needs a structure of discipline for shaping and reshaping disciples and for guiding believers in a life of servanthood. Within the community of faith, gathered around the table and the scriptures, a process of communal ethical discernment takes place, which is inseparable from the striving for faithful discipleship. Discipleship is understood as more radical, free, and distinctive involvement in public life than the "responsible involvement" advocated by the "Christian realists" and indeed by the World Council of Churches at its Amsterdam Assembly.

Reflection on issues of identity, character, and virtue leads directly to a recognition that these concepts are socially shaped. We do not choose or fashion afresh for ourselves accounts of virtue, character, and identity; we have to draw on resources that have not been devised by us as we develop our characters, learn how to seek virtue, and refashion our identity. These things arise in communities that are stewards of a tradition, that constantly tell and retell a story, that nurture new generations. We situate ourselves, we decide who we are, and we establish guidelines for moral behavior by reference to the communities to which we belong and to the tradition we have inherited.

Any great community of shared faith, such as the Christian Church, has at its heart a canonical story that is constantly examined and reinterpreted, and that presents a rich mosaic of models of virtue and vice. Out of this process of retelling, of criticism, and of debate comes a tradition of disciplined reflection on the kinds of behavior which are praiseworthy or to be deplored. The community nurtures new generations by inducting them into the story and thus into the community. All communities of shared faith and commitment are concerned with the moral formation of their members. Most are also concerned with reformation, because human lives are so easily distorted.

When we speak about the church as a moral community, we do not mean simply that it is a forum for serious moral discourse—although the church ought to be that, contributing insights from its heritage to public debate and deciding how to witness to the truth of the gospel in the way it organizes its life. The church is also concerned with the moral formation and reformation of believers, so that they may live lives of virtue: "Let your light so shine before others that they may see your good works and give glory to your Father in heaven."[36] The church must attend to Christian values and how these may be best expressed in acts and in social structures, as well as to commands and principles that take a concrete form. And in many ways most important of all, the church offers a moral vision that enables discernment and a distinctive way of seeing. All of these elements are necessary if the church is to be a lively moral community.

The church that is holy is a communion of saints, of holy people. Saints are not people who have arrived at some plateau of moral achievement, but people on a journey together who have learned and are still learning to live by grace. Characteristically, Christian saints are regarded by others as good people but know themselves to be sinners constantly in need of forgiveness. The community shapes and sustains the individuals in their discipleship, and they in their turn are the agents and representatives of the church. The way a church is structured and operates expresses an ethic and is morally formative.

Yoder rarely spoke in terms of virtue ethics, but he agreed that ethics is not at its heart simply a matter of dealing with quandaries and ethical choices. It is about character, *habitus*, a way of life, an orientation of the whole person. He saw the ethical life as the life of discipleship, as responding to the call and command and example of Jesus Christ. Moral formation takes place in community through education, the discipline of binding and loosing, and the ongoing worship of the congregation.

Yoder was uncomfortable with the commonly affirmed position that there is an ugly ditch between the ethics of Jesus and that of the early church. It was important for Yoder to challenge this ethical duality, partly because it has been used to suggest that, since the early church found the "absolutist ethics" of Jesus impossible to apply, modern Christians are also permitted to compromise or even abandon the ethics of Jesus as a challenging possibility. As Søren Kierkegaard suggested, "Most people really believe that the Christian commandments (e.g., to love one's neighbor as oneself) are intentionally a little too severe—like putting the clock on half an hour to make sure of not being late in the morning."[37]

Yoder responded with a vigorous, but not fully convincing, counterattack to this view of Christian ethics as an impossible standard. The ugly ditch between the ethical thinking of Jesus and the compromises of the early church does not exist. In fact, the household tables (*Haustafeln*) of the epistles, which are often cited as ethical compromises with the standards of the contemporary context, express rather "the revolutionary innovation in the early Christian style of ethical thinking for which there is no explanation in borrowing from other contemporary cultural sources."[38] These household tables do not simply confirm the hierarchical structures of the broader society by instructing slaves to be obedient, wives to obey their husbands, and so on; rather, according to Yoder, "The *subordinate* person in the social order is *addressed as a moral agent*. He is called upon to take responsibility for the acceptance of his position in society as meaningful before God."[39] In other words, people who have no independent moral status in the culture and society are declared to have personal moral responsibility before God in a manner that is subtly corrosive of the hierarchical moral order in which they find themselves. Their position in society is not a matter of fate, to be passively accepted, but a destiny, and even a vocation, a context in which they may witness to the freedom of the gospel and the liberation they have received in Christ.[40]

ESCHATOLOGY AND ETHICS

Yoder resisted the liberal assumption that the language of eschatology and the apocalypse has had its day and is no longer relevant. He would have suggested, I feel, that in the world after September 11, 2001, we must perforce fall back on apocalyptic language, so laden with calls to action and to doxology, if we are to understand and engage as Christians with today's realities.[41] The language with which the Bible, particularly the New Testament, is peppered about principalities and powers, angels and demons, thrones and dominions, seemed, to many liberal exegetes, to be "obscure mythology" that should and must now be dispensed with. But when Christians had to struggle with the manifest evil of Nazism and the language of nature seemed inadequate, they turned to these themes in the Bible and found in them clues and guidance as to how to respond faithfully and well to Hitler's evil tyranny. This particular symbolic structure sprang back to life.[42] It seemed to provide meaning and guidance. It was a symbolic structure in which many people found they could live.

The apocalyptic, as it were, comes to life, is reborn, in times of crisis.[43] Characteristically, it arises among groups that despair about the conditions of the present world order and believe in its imminent destruction or overthrow.[44] The apocalyptic has three functions that are particularly relevant to our present discussion. First, the apocalyptic claims to reveal, unveil, make manifest the inner reality of what is actually happening in the world today. It is concerned to understand things as they are now, not simply to predict the future.[45] It seeks to discern what is happening in history, and what God is calling God's people to do. The powers of evil that have presented themselves as angels of light are unmasked, and believers are enabled to discern what is really happening. Second, the apocalyptic denies the finality and acceptability of the existing order of things. The pretensions of rulers and dominant authorities are cut down to size and relativized. The apocalyptic declares that the existing powers that be are not the final manifestation of God's purposes; their days are numbered. An alternative order in which the weak and the excluded will have an honored place is not only possible but is also promised, and it will break in and disrupt the existing order. And, third, the apocalyptic nourishes a confident hope not only that things *can* be different, but that they *will* be different, for if believers are faithful God will bring out of the present disorder a new era that will be characterized by peace and justice and the vindication of the oppressed.

In much apocalyptic literature, as in the book of Revelation, alongside a radical political critique there is much imagery of a holy war. In this war, martyrs are the real victors, despite appearances. The holy war may be a spiritual or a real conflict; God may take the initiative, or call on the saints to wage war on God's behalf. And "waging war" may simply be a metaphor for keeping the faith in times of persecution. But the Christian nature of an authentically Christian apocalyptic is represented, according to Yoder, by the centrality in the book of Revelation of the triumphant Lamb that has been slain and is praised by the faithful, singing a new song.[46]

There are, of course, specific problems associated with a lively apocalyptic worldview. In the first place, the dualism of Jerusalem and Babylon (or their equivalents in other systems of apocalyptic thought) presents as central to its radical political critique a polarization between absolute evil and absolute good, which is at the least a colossal simplification of any actual situation in the world. It can breed a very dangerous and unqualified self-righteousness. And these distortions can have a malign effect on political judgments—as can a relativism that hesitates to make a clear distinction between good and evil. A second major problem is that, although much apocalyptic thought encourages the saints to be patient until God brings their deliverance, other forms encourage the faithful to take things into their own hands, so that they understand themselves as saints combating and destroying unqualified evil in the name of God and at the direct command of God. This is not a conception that I find in the book of Revelation or as a significant element in Jewish and Christian apocalyptic generally.

More positively, apocalyptic thought holds out an open future and offers hope to the poor, the powerless, and the excluded. Its message to the powerful, the prosperous, and the complacent is one of judgment and a challenge to hear the uncomfortable word that the Spirit is saying to the churches. Apocalyptic language is language of people who feel themselves weak, marginalized, oppressed, and forgotten.[47] It is a language of hope for change, and it is language of judgment. It is language that motivates powerfully, for good or ill, and it is language that polarizes between Jerusalem and Babylon, the good and the evil, the saints and the wicked, in a quite Manichaean way. This kind of polarization is always, of course, a huge simplification at the very least. In the real world we have always to deal in subtle shades of gray rather than a contrast between black and white. But sometimes we need to highlight the awfulness of evil or the wonder of goodness. The temptation simply to dismiss it all as irrational and pathological should be resisted, as should the temptation of simply reversing the polarization of radical evil and radical good. We have to deal with it discerningly and sensitively, if we are to respond wisely.

Yoder's vindication of a Christian apocalyptic goes right to the heart of his theological/ethical project:

> To see history doxologically meant for John's addressees that their primordial role within the geopolitics of the *Pax Romana* was neither to usurp the throne of Nero or Vespasian, Domitian or Trajan, nor to pastor Caesar prophetically, but to persevere in celebrating the Lamb's lordship and in building the community shaped by that celebration. They were participating in God's rule over the cosmos, whatever else they were or were not allowed by the civil powers to do. That it was not given them to exercise those other more blatantly "powerful" roles—whether assassinating Trajan or becoming his chaplain—was not for them either a renunciation or a deprivation. They considered themselves to be participating in ruling the world primordially in the human practices of doxological celebration—perhaps in Ephesus?—of which John's vision of the Heavenly Throne Hall is the projection. Some would take John's vision to mean "if we keep the faith through these tough times, in a century or two the tides will turn and we can dominate the Empire then the way Domitian does today." Others would think it meant: "If we keep the faith, the world as we know it will very soon be brought to a catastrophic end, and a new nonhistorical state of things will be set up, with us on top." Some would favor this latter interpretation because they are themselves enthusiasts, believing themselves to be on the brink of the final saving catastrophe, as its beneficiaries. Others would ascribe that meaning to John's vision in order to discredit it, since, after all, that catastrophic victory did not happen.
>
> What then did the vision mean? "Neither of the above," we must respond. Each of those restatements is incompatible with the hymnic text.... Our strophe, the "new song" elicited by the work of the Lamb, describes the seer's present, the same age in which people of every tribe and tongue are being called into a new community. It is not about a future, either organic and therefore distant, or imminent and therefore catastrophic. It has to be taken as a statement about their own time, the late first or early second century, and about what they were then involved in doing.[48]

Or, again: "The point that apocalyptic makes is not only that people who wear crowns and who claim to foster justice by the sword are not as strong as they think.... It is that people who wear crosses are working with the grain of the universe ... by sharing the life of those who sing about the Resurrection of the slain Lamb."[49]

PEACE

The central, and nonnegotiable, ethical issue for Yoder and the peace churches, of course, was peace and nonviolence. This matter was for him an absolute beyond question. And in creating and sustaining peace the church has a central role. "The Church," he writes, "can be a foretaste of the peace for which the world was made. It is the function of minority communities to remember and to create utopian visions."[50]

There is at this point a problem that Yoder did not fully resolve. Accepting, as one must if one takes the New Testament seriously, that the ruling authorities receive their power from God and are "God's servants for your good,"[51] including in the use of the sword, it would appear clear that there is a place in God's ordering for the use of coercion and state-sanctioned violence in police action, in criminal law, and—in extreme cases—in war. One may accept that violence has no place in the life of disciples or in the church. But what happens when disciples are the rulers? Is it then legitimate for them to use the sword? And, following this line of argument, does Yoder not explicitly have to acknowledge a distinction between the sphere of the gospel, where violence has no place, and the sphere of law, where violence and coercion persist in a fallen world as the ultimate sanctions?

Barth combined a rejection of "principled pacifism" with a thoroughgoing critique of war and political violence and was a stout nuclear pacifist after World War II. But through his understanding of the *Grenzfall*, or "boundary situations," he left open a chink allowing Christians to take up arms in extreme situations, such as a threat to the independence of Switzerland! In relation to Nazism, Barth in 1940 issued a resounding, unambiguous call to arms. In his *Letter to Great Britain from Switzerland* he declared, "The obedience of the Christian to the clear will of God compels him to support this war."[52] During the Cold War period, Barth disagreed with those who saw close parallels between Nazism and Bolshevism and argued strongly in favor of nuclear disarmament.

Yoder was, in a way, far more consistent in his commitment to peaceableness in all circumstances than was Barth. Perhaps this unswerving commitment makes Yoder an ethical absolutist rather than a situationalist or one who believes that the specific command of the living God is not the same in every context and cannot be confidently predicted.

Yoder engaged with great penetration and cogency with traditional just war thinking and with the thought on war and peace of Karl Barth, Reinhold Niebuhr, and Paul Ramsey in particular.[53] Yoder was sympathetic with Barth's move to the very fringe of a pacifist commitment in the Cold

War period, and even with his reluctance to adopt "principled pacifism" of a sort that might limit the freedom of the God who commands. Yoder saw Niebuhr as failing to allow his "Christian realism" to be controlled entirely by the gospel. Like much just war thinking, Christian realism, Yoder felt, is too prudential and unwilling to give absolute priority to the challenge of Jesus' nonviolence.

For Yoder, our attitude to the enemy is the test of whether we really love our neighbor, and a willingness to refrain absolutely from violence seemed to be for him the central test of discipleship. His arguments are challenging and must be taken seriously. But once more it needs to be said that he did not really engage with the fact that in the post-Constantinian era disciples are still often responsible for others and must sometimes make decisions that are necessary rather than good, and that force them to fall back on the divine grace. Nor did Yoder totally convincingly show that nonviolence and peace must have the centrality in Christian ethics in a fallen world that he claimed. Yet he was, and looks set to continue to be, one of the most significant, radical, socially committed, and creative theologians of our time.

NOTES

1. Mark Thiessen Nation, "John H. Yoder, Ecumenical Neo-Anabaptist: A Biographical Sketch," in *The Wisdom of the Cross: Essays in Honor of John Howard Yoder*, ed. Stanley M. Hauerwas, Mark Thiessen Nation, Chris K. Huebner, and Harry J. Huebner (Grand Rapids, Mich.: Eerdmans, 1999), 3. Nation's essay provides a good brief biography of Yoder.

2. See the following works by Thomas L. Shaffer: "The Radical Reformation and the Jurisprudence of Forgiveness," in *Christian Perspectives on Legal Thought*, ed. Michael W. McConnell, Robert F. Cochran Jr., and Angela C. Carmella (New Haven, Conn.: Yale University Press, 2001), 321–339; *On Being a Christian and a Lawyer: Law for the Innocent* (Provo, Utah: Brigham Young University Press, 1981); "Maybe a Lawyer Can Be A Servant; If Not … ," *Texas Tech Law Review* 27 (1996): 1345–1357; "Faith Tends to Subvert Legal Order," *Fordham Law Review* 66 (1998): 1089–1099; and "Legal Ethics and Jurisprudence from Within Religious Congregations," *Notre Dame Law Review* 76 (2001): 961–992.

3. On Yoder's relation to Hauerwas and his other "disciples," see especially Arne Rasmusson, "Historicizing the Historicist: Ernst Troeltsch and Recent Mennonite Theology," in Hauerwas et al., *The Wisdom of the Cross*, 213–248, and Stanley Hauerwas, "Remembering John Howard Yoder," *First Things* 82 (April 1998): 15–16.

4. John Howard Yoder, "Karl Barth, Post Christendom Theologian," http://www.nd.edu/~theo/jhy/writings/philsystheo/barth.htm.

5. See John Howard Yoder, *The Pacifism of Karl Barth* (Scottsdale, Pa.: Herald Press, 1968), and *Karl Barth and the Problem of War* (Nashville, Tenn.: Abingdon, 1970).

6. Yoder, "Karl Barth, Post Christendom Theologian."

7. Richard B. Hays, *The Moral Vision of the New Testament: A Contemporary Introduction to New Testament Ethics* (Edinburgh: T & T Clark, 1997), 239, 246.

8. Yoder translated Hendrik Berkhof's seminal *Christ and the Powers* (Scottsdale, Pa.: Herald Press, 1962) and anticipated Walter Wink's work on "the Powers" by some thirty years. I discuss this matter in *Beliefs, Values, and Policies: Conviction Politics in a Secular Age* (Oxford: Clarendon Press, 1989), chap. 5.

9. Hays, *Moral Vision*, 249.

10. Ibid., 243.

11. See especially Yoder's unpublished paper, "Regarding Nature," http://www.nd.edu/~theo/jhy/writings/philsystheo/nature.htm. See also John Howard Yoder, *Christian Attitudes to War, Peace and Revolution: A Companion to Bainton* (Elkhart, Ind.: Peace Resource Center, 1983).

12. Yoder, "Regarding Nature."

13. Ibid.

14. Ibid.

15. John Howard Yoder, *The Priestly Kingdom: Social Ethics as Gospel* (Notre Dame, Ind.: University of Notre Dame Press, 1984), 42.

16. Yoder, "Regarding Nature."

17. Yoder, *The Priestly Kingdom*, 40.

18. Karl Barth, *Church Dogmatics*, 4 vols. (Edinburgh: T & T Clark, 1956–1975), 1:782ff.

19. John Howard Yoder, "'Patience' as Method in Moral Reasoning: Is an Ethic of Discipleship 'Absolute'?" in Hauerwas et al., *The Wisdom of the Cross*, 42.

20. John Howard Yoder, *The Politics of Jesus: Vicit Agnus Nostra* (Grand Rapids, Mich.: Eerdmans, 1972), 5–6.

21. Nancey Murphy, "John Howard Yoder's Systematic Defense of Christian Pacifism," in Hauerwas et al., *The Wisdom of the Cross*, 60.

22. Yoder, *The Priestly Kingdom*, 117.

23. Yoder, "Karl Barth, Post Christendom Theologian."

24. John Howard Yoder, "Sacrament as Social Process: Christ the Transformer of Culture," *Theology Today* 48 (1991): 33–44.

25. Yoder, *The Priestly Kingdom*, 43.

26. See, for example, Hauerwas, *The Peaceable Kingdom: A Primer in Christian Ethics* (London: SCM Press, 1983), 99.

27. John Howard Yoder, *For the Nations: Essays Public and Evangelical* (Grand Rapids, Mich.: Eerdmans, 1997), 41.

28. For a fuller discussion, see Duncan B. Forrester, "The Church and the Concentration Camp: Some Reflections on Moral Community," in *Faithfulness and Fortitude: In Conversation with the Theological Ethics of Stanley Hauerwas*, ed. Mark Thiessen Nation and Samuel Wells (Edinburgh: T & T Clark, 2000), 189–207.

29. Hauerwas, *The Peaceable Kingdom*, 99, quoted in Forrester, "The Church and the Concentration Camp," 205.

30. Stanley Hauerwas, *Christian Existence Today: Essays on Church, World, and Living in Between* (Durham, N.C.: Labyrinth Press, 1988), 101.

31. Stanley Hauerwas, *Vision and Virtue: Essays in Christian Ethical Reflection* (Notre Dame, Ind.: University of Notre Dame Press, 1981), 240.

32. Yoder, *The Priestly Kingdom*, 93–94.

33. Yoder, *Politics of Jesus*, 101.

34. Martin Luther, "Whether Soldiers, Too, Can Be Saved," trans. C. M. Jacobs, in *Works of Martin Luther*, 6 vols. (Philadelphia: Holman, 1915–1932), 5:36.

35. Yoder, *The Priestly Kingdom*, 8 (emphasis added).

36. Matthew 5:16 (NRSV).

37. Søren Kierkegaard, *The Journals of Søren Kierkegaard*, ed. and trans. Alexander Dru (London: Fontana, 1958), 142.

38. Yoder, *Politics of Jesus*, 174.

39. Ibid.

40. Ibid., 174–190.

41. See especially Yoder, *The Politics of Jesus*, chap. 12 ("The War of the Lamb") and "To Serve Our God and to Rule the World," *Annual of the Society for Christian Ethics* (1988): 3–14.

42. For a fuller discussion, see Forrester, *Beliefs, Values, and Policies*, 70–74.

43. H. H. Rowley, *The Relevance of Apocalyptic: A Study of Jewish and Christian Apocalypses from Daniel to the Revelation*, 2d ed. (London: Butterworth, 1947), 8.

44. Christopher Rowland, *The Open Heaven: A Study of Apocalyptic in Judaism and Early Christianity* (London: SPCK, 1982), 1–2.

45. Ibid., 2.

46. See Yoder, "To Serve Our God."

47. On this see especially the sociological literature on millenarianism, such as Norman Cohn, *The Pursuit of the Millennium: Revolutionary Millenarians and Mystical Anarchists of the Middle Ages* (London: Paladin, 1970).

48. Yoder, "To Serve Our God."

49. John Howard Yoder, "Armaments and Eschatology," quoted in Stanley Hauerwas, *With the Grain of the Universe* (London: SCM Press, 2002), 6.

50. Yoder, *The Priestly Kingdom*, 94.

51. Romans 13:4 (NRSV).

52. Karl Barth, *A Letter to Great Britain from Switzerland* (London: Sheldon, 1941), 9. On Barth on war, see especially Rowan Williams, "Barth, War and the State," in *Reckoning with Barth: Essays in Commemoration of the Centenary of Karl Barth's Birth*, ed. Nigel Biggar, 170–190 (London: Mowbray, 1988).

53. See Michael G. Cartwright, "Sorting the Wheat from the Tares: Reinterpreting Reinhold Niebuhr's *Interpretation of Christian Ethics*," in Hauerwas et al., *The Wisdom of the Cross*, 349–372; John Howard Yoder, *When War Is Unjust: Being Honest in Just-War Thinking*, 2d ed. (Maryknoll, N.Y.: Orbis Books, 1996); and Hauerwas, *Vision and Virtue*, 197–221.

{ PART III }

The Orthodox Tradition

[CHAPTER 18]

Introduction to the Modern Orthodox Tradition

PAUL VALLIERE

In her study of the Orthodox Church in the Byzantine Empire, Joan Hussey begins with a caveat: "In the present state of our knowledge a book on the Byzantine Church must necessarily be in the nature of an interim report since much pioneer work remains to be done."[1] The same must be said about the attempt to present the "teachings" of modern Orthodoxy concerning law, society, and politics. While the historical sources for the study of modern Orthodox social ethics stand closer to us in time than those on which Byzantinists must rely, our level of knowledge about the subject is not markedly higher.

There are at least two reasons for this. The first is the catastrophe of the Russian Revolution (1917), which ruined the largest, richest, and best-educated Orthodox church in the world. The destruction wrought by Communism in Russia and elsewhere made civilized discourse on church and society in the Orthodox East extremely difficult for most of the twentieth century. The second is misleading stereotypes of Orthodoxy. The perception of Orthodoxy in the West has been deeply affected by a Christian "orientalism" that alternates between a condescending, essentially imperialist view of Orthodoxy as a backward form of Christianity and a romantic view of it as preserving mystical values from which a putatively rationalistic Western Christianity has fallen away.[2] Both stereotypes, though opposed, promote the notion that Orthodox theology is not fundamentally concerned with law, society, and politics. In fact, Orthodoxy has been wrestling with issues of modern legal, political, and social order for almost three hundred years, and a large body of primary source material for the study of the subject is at hand, albeit underexplored.

Orthodoxy's meeting with modernity began in Russia during the reign of Peter the Great (1682–1725), and by the late eighteenth century this encounter was having a significant impact throughout the Orthodox world.

In the nineteenth century, as Russia emerged as one of the most dynamic cultural centers of world civilization and as smaller Orthodox nations won their independence from the Ottoman Empire, a broad modern-style discourse about church and society was cultivated through a number of channels: new educational institutions, arts and letters, secular and theological journalism, scholarship, politics, secular and ecclesiastical courts, and other venues. In short, there is a historical record—the annals of what might be called the Orthodox Enlightenment—against which to check our generalizations about the teachings of modern Orthodoxy on law, society, and politics. Because this record has been so little investigated, however, checking it is an arduous procedure. Hence the caveat about an "interim report."

In the following pages, the views of five modern Orthodox thinkers on issues of law, society, and politics are presented—Vladimir Soloviev, Nicholas Berdyaev, Vladimir Lossky, Mother Maria Skobtsova, and Dumitru Stăniloae. It cannot be stressed strongly enough that all five of these thinkers were *modern*; that is to say, they wrestled with the situation of Orthodoxy in the expansive global civilization produced by the scientific and political revolutions of the Enlightenment. As Orthodox thinkers, all five also drew on patristic sources, that is to say, the writings of the church fathers.[3] However, it is not always possible to make a neat distinction between patristic and modern elements in their thought. The patristic corpus is variegated. Interpreters find different elements of significance in it, depending on the issues they wish to pursue. There is no reason to suppose that all elements drawn from the patristic tradition by modern Orthodox thinkers will be consistent with each other. On the contrary, one should expect to find differences of opinion, tensions, even contradictions.

Modern historical scholarship on patristics is another variable. To their credit, modern Orthodox thinkers have always paid close attention to historical research on the ancient and medieval church. Some, such as Vladimir Lossky, were patristic or medieval scholars in their own right. Like all scholarly disciplines, however, patristics evolves. New facts are discovered, new hypotheses are introduced, old views are revised. As a result, the scholarly consensus keeps shifting. What is deemed patristic at one point in time might be viewed otherwise at a later time; and of course the later view, too, is susceptible to revision. This is a perfectly natural state of affairs, but it is often forgotten by theologians who accuse their predecessors of betraying the church fathers without taking into account what the scholarship of an earlier day had to say about those same fathers. In short, the patristic connection in modern Orthodox theology is itself a modern, not just a traditional, factor; it is a complicating, not just a clarifying, factor.

This point bears directly on the relations between the thinkers presented in this volume. Their collective labors span about a century—from Vladimir Soloviev's first book (*The Crisis of Western Philosophy*, 1874) to Dumitru Stăniloae's magnum opus (*Orthodox Dogmatic Theology*, 1978). The most important historical event affecting Orthodox theology in this period was the Russian Revolution of 1917 and its long, sad aftermath. The most significant theological shift occurred a bit later, however, with the rise of the neopatristic theology of Father Georges Florovsky and Vladimir Lossky. The key books signaling the neopatristic turn were Florovsky's *The Paths of Russian Theology*, published in Russian in 1937, and Lossky's *The Mystical Theology of the Eastern Church*, published in French in 1944.[4] Florovsky and Lossky sharply rejected the religious-philosophical approach to theology practiced by Soloviev and those whom he inspired, such as Nicholas Berdyaev, Sergei Bulgakov, Pavel Florensky, and Lev Karsavin. As Florovsky and Lossky saw it, Soloviev and his heirs were bad expositors of the mind of Orthodoxy because of the heavy dose of nineteenth-century German idealism and other modern tendencies in their thought. The antidote was to return to the church fathers, hence the name neopatristic. By the middle of the twentieth century, Florovsky and Lossky's approach had won the day, and it has dominated the Orthodox theological scene ever since. Its long life is due in no small measure to a brilliant second generation, such as Father John Meyendorff and Bishop Kallistos Ware, who quietly set aside the polemical spirit of the founders and developed the positive features of the neopatristic approach.

When reading the neopatristic theologians, however, one should not accept their initial assumption at face value—namely, that they returned to the church fathers while their rivals served other masters. To take this view is to ignore the fact that the fathers are not monolithic. Vladimir Soloviev was well versed in patristics as it was practiced in his time. Sergei Bulgakov was even better schooled, thanks to advances in the discipline that he followed carefully. The fact that neither Soloviev nor Bulgakov viewed the fathers in neopatristic terms does not mean that they failed to take the patristic heritage seriously, as their neopatristic critics subsequently alleged. It is true that Soloviev and Bulgakov were subject also to other intellectual and spiritual influences, but so were the neopatristic theologians. Neopatristic theology was not a unique or isolated phenomenon in modern theology. It was the Orthodox manifestation of the pan-European, pan-confessional rebellion against liberalism and modernism that reshaped the theological scene following World War I. It is no accident that Roman Catholic neo-Thomism, Protestant neo-orthodoxy, and Orthodox neopatristic theology bear similar names. The three streams had much in common, and mutual influences abounded. Secular influences, such as existentialism and cultural pessimism, also had an impact on all three.

An area of concern which neopatristic theology did not share with the other movements in twentieth-century theology is the one with which this volume is chiefly concerned, namely, law, society, and politics. Neo-Thomism, with which most modern Roman Catholic thinkers were connected in one way or another, is inconceivable without its legal, social, and political agenda. Protestant neo-orthodoxy, however we understand its original motivation, inspired the ethical and political genius of Dietrich Bonhoeffer. Its American counterpart produced Reinhold Niebuhr. The Orthodox neopatristic movement, by contrast, did not inspire much work on law, society, or politics.[5] Some would explain this apparent anomaly by observing that the construction of ethical systems reflects the West's "scholastic" approach to theology, that is, the interpretation and application of mysteries of faith by means of discursive reasoning. The procedure is supposedly alien to Orthodoxy, which prefers to set theology in a liturgical and mystical context. Orthodox theologians, so the argument goes, do not seek general principles but focus on personal experience.[6]

Whatever the merits of this explanation, it must be qualified in at least two respects. First, it is not true that Orthodox thinkers have always steered clear of systematic reflection on law, politics, and human nature. Many modern Orthodox thinkers, including (in this volume) Vladimir Soloviev and Nicholas Berdyaev, have engaged in just such a project. To assume that this separates them from "genuine" Orthodox theology is to grant the neopatristic case without investigating it. Presumably it is better to examine what Soloviev and Berdyaev actually had to say before passing judgment on them.

Second, one must not fail to connect the neopatristic movement with the peculiar circumstances produced by the devastation of the Orthodox world in the twentieth century. Neither neo-Thomism nor Protestant neo-orthodoxy developed in exile or in emigration. Both were products of a well-patronized theological establishment. Even the martyred Dietrich Bonhoeffer was no exception: he ended his career in the catacombs, but he certainly did not begin it there. Orthodox theologians, after the Russian Revolution in 1917, and again after World War II ended in 1945, found themselves in a completely different situation. Almost all of the social and institutional networks for the support of theology in the historic Orthodox lands lay in ruins. Orthodox theology was cultivated for the most part in small communities of émigrés and Western converts without access to a large natural audience. Except in Greece, Orthodox theologians worked in contexts where they had virtually no access to social or political power and bore no responsibility for its management. It is no wonder that they regarded theological reflection on law, society, and politics to be disconnected from reality—scholastic in the pejorative sense.

Neopatristic writers occasionally did concede that the legal, social, and political dimensions of human life can be theologized. Bishop Kallistos Ware, for example, pointed to the implications of trinitarian dogma for social philosophy:

> The doctrine of the Trinity is not merely a theme for abstract speculation by specialists; it has practical and indeed revolutionary consequences for our understanding of human personhood and society. The human person is made in the image of God, that is to say, of God the Trinity, and the doctrine of the Trinity affirms that God is not just a monad, the One loving himself, but a triad of divine persons loving each other. Formed in the trinitarian image, the human person is thus created for relationship, sharing, and reciprocity. Cut off from others, isolated, unloving and unloved, no one is a true person, but only a bare individual. Our human vocation is therefore to reproduce on earth at every level, in the church and in society, the movement of mutual love that exists from all eternity within God the Trinity. In the words of the Russian thinker Nikolai Feodorov (c. 1828–1903), "Our social program is the dogma of the Trinity."[7]

Clearly this is an insight that could inspire a major work on Christian law, society, and politics. Indeed, it has done so—in Leonardo Boff's *Trinity and Society*.[8] Yet one looks in vain for a neopatristic Orthodox contribution to match that of this Brazilian Catholic liberation theologian.[9] It is telling that the arresting summation of Bishop Kallistos's case—"our social program is the doctrine of the Trinity"—is taken from Fedorov, one of the Russian religious philosophers whom the first generation of neopatristic theologians excoriated as misguided modernists.

PHILOKALIA AND PHILOSOPHY

Two streams of thought have been especially important in shaping the discourse about human nature and human destiny in modern Orthodoxy. They may be called the *philokalic* and the *philosophic*. The first, issuing from a revival of contemplative monasticism, reenergized and popularized the patristic concept of *theosis* (deification). The second took shape in nineteenth-century Russian philosophy. Its guiding ideas were wholeness and *sobornost* (fellowship, togetherness, spiritual unity).

After declining in the seventeenth and eighteenth centuries, Orthodox contemplative monasticism began to revive in the later eighteenth century. The vehicle of the revival was an anthology of patristic and medieval mystical-ascetical texts known as the *Philokalia*. The pioneers in the dissemination of this material were the Greek monks Makarios of Corinth and Nikodemos of the Holy Mountain, whose *Philokalia* was published in Venice in 1782, and the Russian monk Paisy Velichkovsky, who directed a Slavonic edition at about the same time. In the nineteenth century, Russian and other vernacular translations began to be made.[10]

The spiritual practices associated with the *Philokalia* are usually called hesychasm, from the Greek word *hesychia*, meaning quietness. These practices include quiet sitting, contemplative prayer, and the Jesus Prayer. The last consists of the words "Lord Jesus Christ, Son of God, have mercy on me a sinner," repeated as a mantra in fulfillment of the Apostle Paul's counsel to "pray without ceasing" (1 Thess. 5:17). These practices were traditionally cultivated by a monastic elite. With the wider vernacular dissemination of philokalic literature in modern times, a certain democratization of hesychasm occurred as laypeople, including some intellectuals, began assimilating the material and applying it in new ways. The prestige of monks as confessors and spiritual directors, a relationship that could be conducted by correspondence as well as in person, also widened the appreciation for hesychasm. Dostoevsky's celebrated portrait of Russian monasticism in *The Brothers Karamazov* (1878–80), based on the author's pilgrimage to Optina Hermitage, a center of the hesychast revival in Russia, is an early example of this democratization.

The aspiration of hesychast piety is *theosis* (deification), an idea containing both an anthropological and an eschatological dimension. Anthropologically, theosis is related to Orthodoxy's traditionally strong affirmation of the enduring, substantial reality of the image of God in human beings. Unlike Catholic theology, which came to distinguish sharply between nature and grace, Orthodox theology prefers to see nature and grace as forever connected because created nature is always and everywhere dependent on the power of God.[11] Even in their fallen state, humans possess a divine beauty because their very being is irradiated by the energies (grace) of God. Human beings are potentially "gods." The realization of this potential is eschatological. In Orthodoxy, however, eschatological does not mean "far off." Orthodoxy inclines to a realized eschatology; that is to say, it proclaims the kingdom of God as something that can be seen and experienced *already*. Many features of Orthodox practice reinforce this view, such as the all-engulfing sacramentalism of the liturgy, the icons that mystically host the glorified beings who already live in the kingdom, and the veneration of the saints. Realized eschatology means that theosis has already begun and that its effects can be perceived and assimilated in a holy life.

The idiom of theosis sometimes strikes Western Christians as an invitation to idolatry. In fact, it is a Greek way of stating a truth about eternal life: since only God is eternal, all who are granted eternal life must in some way partake of the divine life. Eternalization implies deification. That there is a danger of idolatrous misunderstanding here has always been clear to Orthodox theologians, who guard against it by distinguishing between the "essence" and the "energies" of God. Not even the saints in glory partake of the essence of God; they are eternalized by the divine energies, God's gracious, indwelling, transfiguring presence in them. These energies are fully divine, however, not an intermediate, subdivine reality (which, if it existed, would indeed be the stuff of idolatry).

Theosis may also be understood as a way of speaking about sanctification, the being-made-holy of the redeemed. This interpretation makes the concept relatively easy for Roman Catholics to appreciate, since Roman Catholics, like Orthodox, have an optimistic view of the possibilities of growth in holiness, a view warranting the canonization and veneration of saints. Protestants have greater difficulty with the concept because of their ambivalence about sanctification as such. Protestantism sees the essence of the gospel as consisting in God's gracious, unprompted justification of the sinner. The issue of whether and to what extent justified sinners can achieve personal holiness has been a divisive issue for Protestants ever since the sixteenth-century Protestant Reformation. Martin Luther and many after him held that justified sinners are holy only by imputation: God in his mercy chooses to regard the justified as holy by imputing to them the holiness of Christ, which they themselves cannot approximate, much less achieve. Ulrich Zwingli and John Calvin believed that justified sinners are regenerated in a more concrete way, being empowered by God's grace to live a holier life than the unredeemed. Because the template of a righteous and holy life is found in the divine law revealed in scripture, these theologians sometimes referred to the cultivation of holiness as "the third use of the law."[12] While such a pointed appeal to law in the context of sanctification would strike Orthodox as strange and somehow unevangelical, one may nevertheless draw an analogy between the third use of the law and monasticism. The zealous pursuit of theosis in Orthodoxy has always been closely connected with the ascetical life. In modern times this connection has been loosened a bit by the democratization of piety mentioned above, but traditionally the pursuit of theosis was a project that belonged to contemplative monks. To the extent that monasticism involves a structured, closely regulated lifestyle constituting a kind of polity or "republic" of its own, its connection with theosis is in some ways comparable to the third use of the law.

The primary social and political legacy of hesychasm has been quietism, as the name suggests. In cases where the threshold of political advocacy was crossed, the results were usually conservative, ranging from conventional acceptance of the status quo to reactionary forms of expression. For more constructive approaches to Christian legal, social, and political thought, one must turn to philosophic Orthodoxy.

Modern Orthodox religious philosophy emerged in Russia in the second quarter of the nineteenth century. It began as an effort to make sense of Russia's anomalous status in Europe after the end of the Napoleonic wars. Militarily, Russia had become one of the arbiters of European destiny. Yet Russia was not European in the sense that its Western neighbors were. Russia's political tradition (autocracy), socioeconomic system (peasant communalism), and religious affiliation (Orthodoxy) set it apart from the West. In the 1820s and 1830s, Russian intellectuals began a debate about Russia's destiny that would last until the revolution. What was Russia called to be and to do in the modern world? The answers turned largely on the assessment of Russia's Eastern Christian heritage. Those who lamented Russia's affiliation with "miserable, despised Byzantium" (as Pyotr Yakovlevich Chaadaev put it) imagined a future in which Russia would be fully integrated into Western European civilization. They were called Westernizers. Those who preached loyalty to Russian tradition, opining that Orthodoxy held the solution to the problems of modernity, were called Slavophiles.

The most important thinkers of the first generation of Slavophiles were Ivan Kireevsky (1806–56) and Aleksei Khomiakov (1804–60).[13] Both were well acquainted with Western thought. They had studied in Germany and were indebted in particular to the German Romantic tradition, especially the philosophy of Friedrich W. J. Schelling. Like their Romantic mentors, the Slavophiles rejected the materialism, liberalism, and egoistic individualism of the Enlightenment. They believed that such trends, if left unchecked, would cause people to devour each other just as the leaders of French Revolution had devoured each other. The alternative to this evil prospect lay in rediscovering the wholeness of life, the reality of spiritual things, and the ethics of Christian love. Kireevsky elaborated a philosophy of "wholeness" embracing both reason and faith, with faith leading reason to the experience of God. Khomiakov elaborated a social philosophy based on Christian love, the socio-ethical counterpart to the wholeness cultivated by Kireevsky in the noetic sphere. His model for the good society was the loving communion of the church at prayer, a fellowship uniting each with all and all with God. The neologism *sobornost* was subsequently devised to express this vision in a resonant word.[14] Both Kireevsky and Khomiakov contrasted external or political freedom with inner or spiritual freedom: spiritual freedom opens people to fellowship with their neighbors and with God; liberal individualism isolates people and enslaves them to selfish passions.

The political legacy of the early Slavophiles was conservative without being reactionary. In fact, Slavophilism had reformist implications to the extent that its vision of what an ideal Orthodox society should look like was obviously at odds with the Russia that actually existed in their day. This dissonance did not escape the notice of the censors, who prevented the publication of most of Kireevsky and Khomiakov's writings during their lifetime. It would be wrong to cast the Slavophiles as dissidents, however. Their discontent did not impel them to political activism, which they distrusted. Nor did they look to law as a means of solving social and political problems. On the contrary, they viewed "juridicalism" as the quintessential expression of Western rationalism, the very opposite of *sobornost.* Slavophile antilegalism, inspired as much by Western Romantic philosophers as by evangelical conscience, contributed to what has been called "the tradition of the censure of law" in Russia.[15] The antilegalism of Aleksandr Solzhenitsyn is a more recent example of the same phenomenon.[16]

In the next generation the Slavophile tradition grew more complicated. The towering figure of Russian religious philosophy, Vladimir Soloviev (1853–1900), had one foot in the Slavophile tradition. His philosophy of "integral knowledge" picked up where Kireevsky's had left off, and his Christian social philosophy developed some of Khomiakov's insights. But Soloviev was also interested in the reconciliation of Orthodoxy with European liberalism, a project that led him far from the Slavophile path. Soloviev's philosophy inspired the flowering of interest in religion among Russian intellectuals at the turn of the twentieth century and contributed to the emergence of an indigenous Russian liberalism.[17]

Later Slavophiles became increasingly nationalistic. Slavophilism encouraged the development of Russian nationalism to the extent that it celebrated the differences between Russia and Europe. For Kireevsky and Khomiakov, the affirmation of difference was not an end in itself but a means of promoting the universal Christian faith, which according to them was better preserved in Orthodoxy than in Catholicism or Protestantism. For many nationalists, by contrast, difference was the end, and Orthodoxy was a means of promoting it.

The philokalic and philosophic streams of modern Orthodox thought were not completely isolated from each other. Beginning with Kireevsky, religious philosophers took an interest in philokalic sources. Conversely, the appropriation of philokalic values by artists and intellectuals always involved some sort of philosophical mediation. Dostoevsky's pilgrimage to

Optina Hermitage in the company of the philosopher Vladimir Soloviev is the perfect symbol of such mediation.

Scholarly studies of hesychasm in the twentieth century, of which John Meyendorff's *A Study of Gregory Palamas* (1959) was the most influential, furthered the democratization of hesychast spirituality and made an important contribution to neopatristic theology in particular.[18] The philosophical mediation of hesychasm, while much less prominent than historical-theological appropriations of the subject, also continues.[19]

CHURCH AND STATE IN THE ORTHODOX TRADITION

For a long time, Western scholars persisted in characterizing the system of church-state relations in the Christian East as "caesaropapism." The term denotes "the rigid control of matters spiritual and ecclesiastical by the temporal ruler."[20] Although the stereotype of a docile, politically apathetic Orthodox Church still flourishes in the popular imagination, scholars have for some time agreed that the concept of caesaropapism is flawed.[21] The most obvious problem is that it construes Orthodoxy in Western terms by assuming that the Orthodox Church has a "pope" of some kind, that is to say, a central executive authority. Since the Orthodox Church does not possess such an authority yet has been closely linked to the state for most of its history, the political ruler was seen as "pope." That the Christian church can avoid papalism without becoming Protestant was not considered.

Another problem with the concept of caesaropapism is that it does not fit the facts of the church-state relationship in the Christian East, especially in the Byzantine period for which it was invented. While the Byzantine emperors, beginning with Emperor Constantine in the fourth century, were active and sometimes aggressive participants in the affairs of the church, relations between secular rulers and Orthodox bishops were often stormy, with many leading churchmen suffering deposition, exile, or worse in the defense of dogmatic and canonical positions that they deemed non-negotiable. Almost all of the great heresies of the patristic period—Arian, Monophysite, Monothelite, Iconoclast—enjoyed extensive imperial patronage, yet none of them prevailed in the long run. Even Justinian in the sixth century, who came closer than any Byzantine emperor to mastering the church, failed to achieve his most crucial objective in ecclesiastical affairs, which was the reconciliation of Orthodoxy and monophysitism.[22] Justinian's interest in this issue was political and strategic. By his time monophysitism had become the majority view among the Christians of Syria and Egypt, and Justinian feared for the loyalty of these important Eastern provinces. The Islamic conquest a century later proved the emperor's fears to be well founded, and it is certainly legitimate to wonder whether a more moderate stance in the monophysite controversy might not have served the Orthodox Church better than the one it took. What is not legitimate is to characterize the Byzantine church as a passive tool in the hands of Justinian or any other caesar. On the issues it deemed crucial, the Orthodox Church followed its own lights.

The concept that Orthodox thinkers have traditionally used to describe the right relationship between church and state is "harmony" (Greek *symphonia*). The idea is that church and state are two parts of an ensemble whose conductor is Christ. The two entities are distinct, for without distinction there can be no harmony; but they complement and support each other in the larger whole, which is a godly Christian society. Justinian's epitome of the ideal in his sixth *Novella* is famous:

> There are two greatest gifts which God, in his love for man, has granted from on high: the priesthood and the imperial dignity. The first serves divine things, the second directs and administers human affairs; both, however, proceed from the same origin and adorn the life of mankind. Hence, nothing should be such a source of care to the emperors as the dignity of the priests, since it is for the welfare [of the empire] that they constantly implore God. For if the priesthood is in every way free from blame and possesses access to God, and if the emperors administer equitably and judiciously the state entrusted to their care, general harmony will result, and whatever is beneficial will be bestowed upon the human race.[23]

The most striking feature of this ideal is the positive, theocentric view of the state: the state, like the church, receives its mandate directly from God. It is not subordinate to the church any more than the church is subordinate to the state. Church and state do not occupy higher and lower points in a great chain of being. Each is divinely gifted with its own being and vocation. The gifts are distinct, but the sacred body politic is one. The powerful theological paradigm of the Incarnation underlies this conception. "In the thought of Justinian, the 'symphony' between 'divine things' and 'human affairs' was based upon the Incarnation, which united the divine and human natures, so that the person of Christ is the unique source of the two—the civil and ecclesiastical hierarchies."[24] In a word, the state is as "Christic" as the church, albeit in a different sphere.

Symphonia helps us appreciate many idioms of Orthodoxy. When Orthodox Christians honor certain rulers, such as Constantine the Great or Vladimir of Kiev, as "equals of the apostles" (*isapostoloi*), Western Christians tend to take offense. Secular rulers as apostles? Is this not caesaropapism? Viewed in terms of symphonia, however, the usage makes more sense. When Prince Vladimir of Kiev made the decision to invite missionaries from Byzantium to evangelize and baptize his people, he was accomplishing a divine mission, using the charisma of rulership bestowed upon him by God to cause the gospel to be preached in his heathen land. As the first of his princely line to exercise power in this way, Vladimir was "like" an apostle. His power was political and spiritual at the same time; his decision to invite the missionaries was a creative act, a fresh actualization of the spirit-guided charisma of right government. The "palladian" display of icons during sieges and military campaigns is another example of symphonia. When General Kutuzov and his army prayed before an icon of the Mother of God in the field at Borodino in 1812, they were engaging in a public as well as a personal act, affirming the divine source of the state as well as of the church.[25]

While appreciating the logic of symphonia, however, one must keep two facts in mind. First, symphonia was the ideal, not the reality, of church-state relations in the East. It was constantly proclaimed but seldom realized. Second, conditions for the realization of the ideal, at least in its original sense, have not existed in the Orthodox world for some time. Symphonia assumes the existence of a Christian empire or at least a Christian state. In fact, after the fall of the Byzantine Empire in 1453, most Orthodox Christians except for the Russians lived in Muslim states. After 1917 most Russians lived in an atheist state. Today, most Orthodox Christians live in secular states. Symphonia has become problematic in a way that cannot be mitigated by the banal observation that ideals always fall short in practice.

To the extent that symphonia persists as an ideal in the Orthodox world—and the extent to which it persists demands investigation—the reason is probably the majority status of the Orthodox community in the populations of most of the post-Ottoman and post-Soviet successor states. The locus of symphonia has simply shifted from ruler to society. This fits in with the general democratization of political charisma in modern times: traditionally the prince or emperor was the "earthly god," in modern times the state or society assumes the role. Because the majority of the population in historic Orthodox countries still identifies with Orthodoxy at least nominally, it is possible to dream of effecting symphonia on the social and cultural, if not the political, plane. The Orthodox Church's claims to special status in postcommunist states are a reflection of this mentality, the expression of an ingrained sense of religious establishment that has survived the political disestablishment of Orthodoxy.[26] In theological terms, of course, populist symphonia is suspect. Symphonia depends on charisma, and charisma is conferred on persons, not abstract entities. While it might be possible, given the logic of symphonia, to appreciate evaluations of Constantine or Vladimir of Kiev as "equal of the apostles," it is a stretch to extend the honor to a society or nation. The emotional appeal of such theologized populism is nevertheless considerable in modern Orthodoxy.

The political challenge for Orthodoxy in modern times is to find a resonant alternative to symphonia as traditionally conceived. The thinkers represented in this volume all wrestled with this challenge in one way or another. Of the five, Vladimir Soloviev took the most traditional approach in that he continued to think in terms of an organic Christian society in which the disparate elements of spiritual, social, and political life are harmoniously interconnected. As we shall see, Soloviev's way of conceiving symphonia was quite modern; nevertheless, he stood firmly in the historic tradition of Orthodox social and political thought. The fact that he still lived in an Orthodox empire had much to do with this.

The neosymphonic approach was also adopted by most of the Russian Orthodox religious philosophers inspired by Soloviev, including Sergei Bulgakov.[27] Nicholas Berdyaev was more radical, however. While inspired by Soloviev, Berdyaev was also a great admirer of nineteenth-century Westerners such as Friedrich Nietzsche, Søren Kierkegaard, and other fountainheads of the individualist and anarchist orientation that eventually came to be called existentialism. Berdyaev's "philosophy of freedom" left no room for organicism of any kind. Unlike many existentialists, however, Berdyaev remained loyal to the Solovievian tradition of social Christianity. Mother Maria Skobtsova, who was close to Bulgakov and Berdyaev, also promoted an Orthodox social gospel, and in the best possible way: by living it.

Neopatristic thinkers broke with symphonia in an even more radical way than Berdyaev: they stopped looking for an Orthodox legal, social, and political doctrine. They did not address issues of law, society, and politics in any of their major works. In part this was a reaction to their special social and political circumstances, which have already been noted. But there was another factor. Lossky, Florovsky, and other first-generation neopatristic thinkers embraced a rigorously mystical and apophatic view of theology that effectively discouraged the theological interpretation of legal, social, and political questions.[28] Mystical or apophatic theology is an effective means of contemplating the mystery of God as experienced in the depths of personal being. It is not a useful tool for fashioning a theory of the state, evaluating a system of positive law, forging an interpretation of history, or other tasks normally involved in the construction of a social and political ethic.

Not all theologians who contributed to the neopatristic movement were as radical as Florovsky and Lossky. Dumitru Stăniloae, for example, was shaped by the *Gândirea* circle in Romania between the world wars, a religious-philosophical movement strongly resembling Russian Slavophilism in its blending of Orthodoxy with national and cultural values. The effects can be detected in the more organic character of his theology.[29] In the Communist era, of course, the search for Orthodox legal, social, and political thought came to a halt in Romania as it did elsewhere. Only in recent years, with the emergence of free if struggling civil societies in the Christian East, has the search resumed, and it is too early to predict where it will lead. Orthodox nationalism, Christian socialism, neosymphonism, quietism, and some sort of accommodation between Orthodoxy and liberalism are all possible outcomes.

ORTHODOXY AND LAW

The fourth-century Constantinian settlement that regularized the status of the Christian church in the Roman Empire did not involve a legal revolution. On the contrary, the Roman legal system was a key element of the new arrangement. To be sure, the system was incorporated into symphonia. But the law did not depend on symphonia. One might even argue that it was the other way around, since symphonia necessarily involves an extra-ecclesiastical element: the imperial dignity as well as the priesthood, in Justinian's words. The Western medieval ideal of the supreme pontiff as the supreme lawgiver, or at least as the supreme arbiter of law in Christian society, was alien to Byzantium from the beginning. The emperor was the supreme lawgiver, a vocation conferred on him by God without priestly mediation and put into practice by his respect for the Roman legal tradition. When Eusebius of Caesarea, Constantine's apologist and the architect of symphonia, "developed the notion of a human viceroy dispensing Divine justice on earth in God's name,"[30] he was Christianizing the Roman imperial office. But the justice the emperor dispensed was defined first of all by Roman law. Over time Christian ethical teachings had an impact on the law, especially in the areas of marriage, sexuality, inheritance, the treatment of women and children, capital punishment, and of course religion. Although significant, however, the impact fell short of being revolutionary.[31] Some of the differences between Orthodox and Catholic ethical norms, such as the Orthodox Church's toleration of divorce, are traceable to the fact that for a thousand years the Orthodox Church had to accommodate itself to the preexisting Roman legal system. The Western church had a freer hand to legislate as it saw fit because of the fifth-century collapse of imperial authority in the West.

The Orthodox Church's legal competence widened in the twilight centuries of Byzantium (1204–1453), initiating a metamorphosis that was completed in the Ottoman period when the sultan recognized the Orthodox Church as the judicial authority over his Christian subjects. Roman law still figured in the system to the extent that bits and pieces of it had long been incorporated into the "nomocanons" which guided the Church in matters of civil and ecclesiastical law. Nomocanons were concise reference works assembled in the Byzantine period to facilitate the judicial tasks of bishops and the ecclesiastical dealings of imperial bureaucrats. The distinctive feature of the books was the conflation of ecclesiastical and imperial legislation. Imperial laws (*nomoi*) and church canons dealing with related issues appeared side by side, carrying equal weight and supposedly harmonizing with each other. The continued use of such instruments by the Orthodox Church during the Turkish period was a powerful statement of loyalty to the Byzantine heritage, but it did not and could not replicate the Byzantine legal order. In Byzantium, law was crafted by the imperial authority, not by the church; and the study of law flourished as an independent discipline with its own specialists and schools. All of this passed away with the collapse of the empire. The system patronized by the Turks may be called an ecclesiocracy. It left no room for an autonomous legal order.

The influence of Roman law in the Slavic lands converted to Orthodoxy during the Byzantine period is a complicated question.[32] Nomocanons were part of the cultural and ecclesiastical legacy transmitted to the converts. In Slavonic translation, these "pilot books" — *kormchie knigi*, as they were called—had an impact on the legislative monuments with which medieval Slavic princes occasionally adorned their "little Byzantiums."[33] But as has often been noted, the Byzantines were selective in what they shared with the "barbarians." They focused on religion rather than culture, on Christianization rather than Hellenization. The missionary strategy of evangelizing the Slavs in their own language rather than the imperial language reinforced this selectivity by withholding the tool that would have given the Slavs direct access to the Byzantine cultural tradition. Roman legal science was not transmitted to the Slavs any more than classical Greek poetry was. Even if it had been, the effects would have been minimized by the Mongol conquest of Russia and the Ottoman conquest of the South Slavs in the thirteenth and fourteenth centuries. By the time the Russians regained their independence and began building a great Orthodox empire in the north, Byzantium was no more. The Russians fashioned their polity from a variety of sources including nomocanons, Slavic customary law, and Mongol administrative practices. The state that emerged was emphatically Orthodox, and its ruler proudly claimed the Byzantine imperial titles of *tsar* (caesar) and autocrat. But Russian Byzantinism was one-sided: it replicated Roman autocracy without Roman law. The political reforms of Peter the Great did nothing to correct this deficiency.[34]

Orthodox canon law survived the fall of Byzantium, of course, and shaped personal life and civil society both in Muscovy and in the ecclesiocratic system of the Ottoman Empire.[35] But Orthodox canon law was a conservative discipline. It did not stimulate jurisprudence as the study of Roman Catholic canon law did in the West. The dynamism of Roman Catholic canon law depended on two conditions that did not exist in the East: a complex ("feudal") web of competing secular and ecclesiastical jurisdictions requiring regulation, and the existence of a supreme legislator in the church, namely the Pope of Rome, whose decrees were a constant source of new law ("reform") for the church. Like the Protestants of a later age, the Orthodox regarded the growth of law in the Western church as a hypertrophy, a violation of the spirit of the gospel. But Protestant and Orthodox criticisms of Roman legalism were differently motivated. The Protestants were interested in reforming the church, a concept for which they were ironically indebted to the authority structure against which they rebelled, namely, the reforming papacy of the Middle Ages. The Orthodox rejected papalism on grounds of tradition, a standard quite different from reform.

The traditional character of Orthodox canon law is reflected in the organization of the canonical collections and in the fact that one must speak of collections in the plural. The Orthodox Church does not possess a "Code of Canon Law."[36] It preserves a number of esteemed collections and commentaries, some medieval, some more recent. The drive to forge a "Concordance of Discordant Canons," as Gratian did around 1140 for medieval Catholicism, never caught on in Orthodoxy, probably because of the recognition that such an enterprise would end up making new laws, hence in some sense "reforming" the church. Orthodox canonists do not relish such a prospect, preferring to regard themselves as faithful transmitters of that which they have received from the ancients. The outlook is reflected in the tripartite organization of Orthodox canonical collections: apostolic canons come first, the canons of the ecumenical councils and other important synods stand next, and selected chapters from the writings of the church fathers round out the collection. Apostles, councils, and fathers—in that order—are treasured as prototypes of the unbroken practice of the church, not as raw material to be manipulated by legal rationality.

The strength of the Orthodox approach to canon law is the sense of limits brought to the subject by respect for tradition, in spiritual terms a kind of humility. Orthodoxy, like other forms of Christianity, has had its share of power-hungry prelates, but they have not found it easy to use canon law to justify their rapaciousness. The dictatorial legalism of the Roman papacy at its worst is absent from Orthodoxy. Unfortunately, another kind of legalism has not been absent: that which springs from an exaggerated and excessively literal dependence on the past, "the tendency to freeze history," as Meyendorff has characterized it.[37] One might call it paleocracy. Modern Orthodox theologians attempt to mitigate this type of legalism by distinguishing between tradition and traditions, that is to say, between the inalterable essentials of Orthodoxy and the many historically relative customs that not only can but in some circumstances must be changed in order to preserve the core values of tradition. The distinction is an important one, but it is not itself traditional, at least not in its strong form. An invention of modern theologians beginning with John Henry Newman, the distinction would have seemed strange to Orthodox churchmen of an earlier age. The history of Orthodoxy is full of conflicts over small points of practice that were deemed inalterable because they were traditional.

The most tragic case was the Russian Orthodox schism of the seventeenth century, when Old Believers separated from the Patriarchal church as a result of minute changes in prayer books and ritual practices. The defection probably commanded the loyalty, active or tacit, of the majority of Russian Orthodox Christians at the time. There are many other examples. A bitter dispute over the appropriate day (Saturday or Sunday) for memorial services for the departed embroiled the Greek church for many decades in the eighteenth century. In our day, Old Calendrists and New Calendrists battle each other in many Orthodox jurisdictions. If disputes of this kind were the work of an obscurantist fringe, as is sometimes thought, they could be ignored. In fact, they reflect the power of the paleocratic mentality in Orthodoxy. When Russian Orthodox Old Believers accepted torture and death rather than change (for example) the number of fingers they used to make the sign of the cross, they were not manifesting willful hearts as their detractors charged. They were abiding by a pattern which they honestly believed to be apostolic—and reasonably so, in that the apostles and saints were shown crossing themselves in just such a way on the icons that festooned their churches, images that were regarded as absolutely faithful copies of their prototypes.

The same attitude sometimes appears in learned theology. When one of the greatest Orthodox canonists of modern times, Nikodemos of the Holy Mountain (1749–1809), in his celebrated collection and commentary known as the *Pedalion* (The Pilot), emphatically defended the authenticity of all eighty-five Apostolic Canons against the Roman Catholic count of fifty—an old dispute—he was doing more than excoriating "Latin heretics." As he saw it, he was standing up for the actual practice of the apostles of Christ. That the Apostolic Canons is a fourth or fifth century composition, that the Roman count also dates from antiquity, and that even some Byzantine authorities doubted whether the Apostolic Canons issued from the hands of the apostles—these considerations were trumped by the force of a long-standing tradition. The eighty-five Apostolic Canons appeared in all Orthodox collections of canons since formal compendia began to be made in Byzantium in the ninth century. It was inconceivable to Nikodemos that the tradition of the church in this matter could be anything other than what it claimed to be, namely, apostolic.[38]

The Orthodox canonical tradition did not always lead the church to defend the status quo. In some historical contexts, appeal to the canons had reformist implications, especially where the Orthodox Church was forced by an oppressive political regime to violate its canonical structure. In these situations the appeal to restore canonical order was in effect a demand for political reform and greater latitude for civil society.

Orthodox resistance to the Petrine ecclesiastical settlement in the Russian Empire had this character. In his zeal to make Russia a European power, Peter the Great reconstructed the Muscovite polity along the lines of Western European absolutism. In the process he imposed a radically untraditional constitution on the Russian Orthodox Church.[39] The patriarchate of Moscow and the conciliar institutions of the church were suspended and replaced by a small synod of bishops chaired by a lay bureaucrat, or oberprocurator, responsible solely to the emperor. Every aspect of church life was brought under government supervision. Even the sanctity of confession was violated as priests were charged with certain police functions. The bishops of the Holy Synod were not at liberty to assemble without the permission of the oberprocurator. The episcopate as a whole never assembled, not once during the entire synodal period (1721–1917).

There was much dissatisfaction with this patently uncanonical system of church government among learned Russian Orthodox, although state censorship limited public expression of dissent. Unfortunately, no one ever found a way to change the system from within. The Great Reforms of the 1860s, which abolished serfdom, created a modern judicial system, put a system of local government in place, and reformed the army, ignored the church. A promising conciliar movement in 1905–1906 enjoyed widespread support but failed to convene a council because the tsar's government withheld permission.[40] The council did not assemble until 1917, after the imperial regime had fallen and the Bolsheviks were literally at the door. The Local Council of 1917 restored the patriarchate and cast off the other oppressive features of the synodal regime, but its resolutions soon became moot as the young Soviet regime set about forcibly dismantling the Orthodox Church.

Following World War II, when the Soviet government allowed the Orthodox Church to reconstitute itself within strict limits and under state supervision, the appeal to canonical order again emerged as a vehicle for dissent. Soviet laws on religion had suppressed almost all of the canonical structures that protect the autonomy of the church, such as conciliar government and the clerical presidency of parish councils. The criticism of this legislation was the point of the celebrated letters to the patriarch and the Soviet president by Fathers Eshliman and Yakunin in 1965, one of the opening salvos of the Soviet human rights movement.[41] Meanwhile the quiet but forceful example of Father Aleksandr Men, a Moscow priest with a gift for ministry to intellectuals, showed that a profound Orthodox ministry to society was possible (if rare) in spite of the suppression of canonical order by the Soviet regime.[42] Canonical order was restored by the *glasnost*-era Council of 1988, two years before Soviet legislation on religion was officially changed.

Of course, some disturbances of canonical order come from within the church. A contemporary example is the "canonical chaos" that obtains in the Orthodox diaspora.[43] Nothing is more basic to canonical order in Orthodoxy than the unity of the local church: one city, one bishop, one church. Yet nothing is more characteristic of the Orthodox diaspora than the maze of overlapping and competing ecclesiastical jurisdictions operating in the same space. In most places this antisystem is the result of the movement of populations in modern times. Relocated ethnic groups wish to maintain their ties with the mother church and introduce its hierarchy abroad. Understandable as these loyalties are, their effect has been to undercut the unity and mission of Orthodoxy. In America, for example, most non-Orthodox regard the various Orthodox bodies as completely different churches. The extent to which these bodies agree on doctrine, liturgy, and discipline is rarely appreciated. Divisions of a more serious kind, springing from internecine conflict, are also a problem. In Estonia, Ukraine, and elsewhere, bitter divisions and jurisdictional disputes bedevil the life of the church.

What makes these internal lapses of canonical order especially demoralizing is that the Orthodox Church today has the freedom to correct them but, so far, cannot seem to do so. Aside from vested interests, the problem is the absence of central authority. Interjurisdictional coordination is difficult in Orthodoxy because no one in particular is responsible for it. Not even the Ecumenical Patriarch (the Patriarch of Constantinople) has this authority; indeed, he is often one of the parties in need of coordination. The national and regional churches that constitute the Orthodox communion are "autocephalous," that is to say, administratively and judicially independent of each other. The unity of Orthodoxy is expressed through fidelity to a common tradition and in conciliar gatherings. When Orthodox bishops come into conflict with each other, only a council can restore order. In the case of conflicts between autocephalous churches, this means a worldwide or general council. But there is a problem here: for all its famed *sobornost*, the Orthodox Church has not actually held a worldwide council since the year 787—not exactly a recent precedent. In effect, worldwide Orthodoxy finds itself in the situation that the Roman Catholic Church would be in if, while professing the ideal of a papal monarchy, it lacked an actual papacy.

The gap between the theory and practice of *sobornost* is a manifestation of a general problem in the Orthodox canonical tradition, namely, the tendency to cherish mystically authenticated concepts without doing much to effectuate them. The distinguished Orthodox canonist John Erickson has written of the need "to rediscover the implications of communion for community, lest our much-vaunted [Orthodox] 'spirituality' and 'mystical theology' degenerate into dilettantish escapism."[44] His plea, delivered in 1982, is as relevant as ever today.

ORTHODOXY AND DEMOCRACY

The overarching challenge for Orthodox thought on law, politics, and society in the twenty-first century is to clarify the role the church should play in the construction of a democratic civil society. The church has a huge stake in the matter. No responsible party wishes to repeat the catastrophes of the Communist era, and most Orthodox leaders today recognize that a stable democratic order is the surest safeguard against doing so. The situation is nevertheless unprecedented. The large majority of Orthodox have little if any experience of democracy. Moreover, like other churches that relied on state establishment, the Orthodox Church has inherited a low degree of popular participation in its institutions and programs. In *The Russian Question at the End of the Twentieth Century*, Aleksandr Solzhenitsyn lamented "our ingrained and wretched Russian tradition: we refuse to learn how to organize *from below*, and are inclined to wait for instructions from a monarch, a leader, a spiritual or political authority."[45] This is not just a Russian question. It applies to state and church in most parts of the Orthodox world today.

The Orthodox thinkers treated in this volume offer various resources on the issue of Orthodoxy and democracy without providing anything like a blueprint of the solution. The latter is too much to expect, given the enormous changes that have taken place in the social and political circumstances of Orthodoxy in recent years. The gap between the world that our five Orthodox thinkers knew and the present situation of their faith tradition is greater than in the case of the Protestant or Roman Catholic figures treated in this volume. Of the five, the one who thought the most systematically about the role of Orthodoxy in civil society is the farthest removed from us in time: Vladimir Soloviev. The apparent irony is dispelled when one considers that Soloviev was the only one of the five who completely predated the Communist upheaval. A modern-style civil society was emerging in Russia in Soloviev's day, however unevenly, and his social and political philosophy contributed to it.

The other Orthodox thinkers presented here endured the political traumas of twentieth-century Europe in one way or another, including the lengthy political imprisonment suffered by Dumitru Stăniloae and martyrdom in a Nazi death camp in the case of Mother Maria Skobtsova. Yet there is a brighter side to the picture in that Berdyaev, Lossky, and Mother Maria also experienced democracy by virtue of their many years of residence in France. During their lifetimes, they did not have the opportunity to share their experience with those living on historically Orthodox soil, but their example has fresh relevance for their co-religionists who wrestle with the issue of Orthodoxy and democracy today.

There is evidence that contemporary Orthodox leaders recognize the need for greater attention to problems of law, society, and politics in the postcommunist environment. A good example is the detailed outline of Christian social teachings, "Bases of the Social Concept of the Russian Orthodox Church," that the episcopate of the Russian Orthodox Church (Moscow Patriarchate) adopted at a council in 2000.[46] The document contains specific teachings on topics as various as church-state relations, Orthodoxy and secular law, economic justice, criminal law, bioethics, environmental ethics, sexual ethics, religion and science, and international relations. The 125-page compendium represents a striking innovation in Orthodox practice, bearing greater resemblance to a papal encyclical or a report by a national Roman Catholic bishops' conference than to any traditional Orthodox form of expression. Some of the positions incorporated in it, such as the theological defense of civil disobedience in certain circumstances, are virtually unprecedented in Orthodox legal, social, and political thought.

The cultivation of *sobornost* also bears on the practice of Orthodoxy in a democracy. To be sure, a church council is not a democratic assembly. Yet it is an assembly, and the virtues and skills that sustain it are transferable. These include the practice of shared responsibility, an understanding of due process, techniques of discussion, debate, and decision making, and above all the experience of participating in decisions about matters that affect one's life. For this reason one may claim that conciliar practice and democracy, though not the same thing, can reinforce and enrich each other. This connection also works in the negative: oligarchy in the state and oligarchy in the church reinforce each other.

The issue of initiative and participation pertains to other sectors of Orthodox church life besides councils, such as liturgy and parish life. The great liturgies of the Christian East are the glory of Orthodoxy, but as currently practiced in most parts of the Orthodox world they discourage broad participation in worship. Liturgical reforms are needed to address this problem, but few churchmen are willing to touch the issue because of the explosive potential of Orthodox legalism. Priests who have experimented with new forms have been marginalized and sometimes vilified. Although fears that reform could land Orthodoxy in a state of liturgical confusion comparable to that of post–Vatican II Catholicism are by no means groundless, criticism of Western pathologies cannot compensate for absence of renewal in the East. As for the Orthodox parish, its renewal is closely connected with liturgical reform. There are other challenges as well, such as the need for a theology of the laity in Orthodoxy.[47]

Admittedly, one should not abuse the theme of Orthodoxy and democracy by implying that the primary vocation of the Orthodox Church is to build democracy. For the sake of its distinctive mission, the church must keep its distance from the powers of this world, including the democratic powers of this world. The distance is healthy not just for the church but for the democratic state because it keeps prophetically open the issue of how the Christian love-ethic relates to the ethics of democracy. This profound question has not yet been adequately clarified anywhere. Democracy is still a relatively new phenomenon in world history, and neither its grandeur nor its pitfalls have been sufficiently probed. The transcendent love which Orthodoxy serves—the "acosmic love" that so impressed Max Weber in the heroes of Dostoevsky and Tolstoy[48]—has not figured conspicuously in the ethics of democracy. Yet Orthodox Christians are clearly called to witness to this "more excellent way" (1 Cor. 12:31).

And witnesses there have been. Surely the most enduring legacy of twentieth-century Orthodoxy will be the veneration of the martyrs and confessors who suffered for their faith at the hands of the Communist state—a state, let it be remembered, that called itself "social-democratic." No discussion of justice, law, and society in modern Christianity can pass over this historical record in silence. A life-giving resource for the church, the blood of the new martyrs is a thundering stream of judgment on the powers of the modern world, including the democratic powers. It will not do to object that Communism was not "true" democracy. Of course it was not; but neither was it unconnected with modern democratic ideas. The ethicist will do better to follow Reinhold Niebuhr at this point and recognize the threat of the demonic in all social and political ideologies.

As the Orthodox churches that suffered under Communism investigate the historical record, a new martyrology is emerging. The process is most advanced in the Russian Orthodox Church. At the Council of 2000, no fewer than 1,149 new Russian saints were canonized, most of them martyrs of the Communist period. The number alone is an indication of how long it will take to assimilate the meaning of what happened to the Orthodox Church in the twentieth century.

The report of the investigative commission that recommended the canonizations to the Council of 2000 is a document without much rhetorical embellishment, and therein lies its eloquence.[49] The record speaks for itself. The "throng" (*sonm*) of the martyred embraces all canonical stations of the church: metropolitan bishops, archbishops, bishops, archimandrites, archpriests, hegumens, priests (the largest group), hieromonks, protodeacons, deacons, monks and nuns, novices, and laypersons. Presented by diocese and distinguished by canonical rank, the martyrs are listed alphabetically by their first name, a reminder of the ultimate significance of the individual person—and of personal responsibility—in the kingdom of God. Also included among the canonized are forty-six individuals who are "not yet revealed to the world by name, but known to God."

The council also resolved "to canonize as passion-bearers, in the throng of new martyrs and confessors of Russia, the Imperial Family: Emperor Nicholas II, Empress Aleksandra, the Tsarevich Aleksy, and the grand princesses Olga, Tatiana, Maria, and Anastasia." "Passion-bearers" (*strastoterptsy*) is a term traditionally applied to princes who manifested Christian virtues while suffering at the hands of their political enemies. But the princely connection was less important to the authors of the report than the national connection: "Through the sufferings of the Imperial Family in their captivity, borne with meekness, patience and humility, and in their martyr's death in Yekaterinburg on the night of July 4 (17), 1918, the light of the faith of Christ which overcomes evil was made manifest, just as it shone in the life and death of the millions of Orthodox Christians who endured persecution for Christ in the twentieth century."

In time, the annals of the new martyrs will become part of the sacred story of every diocese in Orthodoxy. Icons of the new saints have been prepared, and more will follow. The cloud of witnesses to a more excellent way will shine as a perpetual reminder of the glory of the kingdom of God and the limits of all earthly polities.

Yet the critique of democracy, important as it is, cannot be the first order of business in twenty-first century Orthodoxy. More important for the church's present welfare is the task of measuring up to the challenges facing it in a democratic society, including the need for a more positive understanding of law. In rising to this occasion, Orthodoxy will discover more about itself than it has known before and more about the gospel than it has known before. A new challenge is at hand. In the Communist era

Orthodox Christians died for their faith. In the world after Communism they must learn to live for it.

NOTES

1. J. M. Hussey, *The Orthodox Church in the Byzantine Empire* (Oxford: Clarendon Press, 1986), 1.

2. The insights of Edward Said's concept of "orientalism" have long been assimilated by scholars of Islam and non-Western religions. The concept is also relevant to the study of Orthodox Christianity, although this has rarely been recognized.

3. The branch of theology concerned with the writings of the "fathers" of the ancient and medieval church is usually called patristics. The fathers did not occupy any one station or office in the church. Some were bishops, some presbyters (priests), some monks, some scholars. Because they were male, the discipline devoted to studying their writings is accurately named. However, inasmuch as the role of women in the ancient church was enormous, albeit traditionally ignored, the pursuit of "matristics" is sure to grow in the coming years and provide a corrective to one-sided attention to the fathers.

   The major languages of patristic literature are Greek, Latin, and Syriac. The literature falls into three historical periods: the early period, when Christianity was a persecuted faith (first to early fourth centuries); the classical period, when Christianity became the established religion of the Roman Empire and codified its fundamental doctrines at the first ecumenical councils (fourth through sixth centuries); and the medieval period, when the Greek-speaking (Byzantine) East and the Latin-speaking West gradually uncoupled (seventh through fifteenth centuries). Before the twentieth century, Western patristic scholarship focused almost exclusively on the first two periods, ignoring Byzantine (but not medieval Latin) theology. Since the early twentieth century, Byzantine theology has received attention. Some of its greatest minds—Maximus the Confessor (ca. 580–662), Symeon the New Theologian (949–1022), and Gregory Palamas (1296–1359), among others—have begun to be appreciated beyond the boundaries of Orthodoxy and have also become much better known in the Orthodox world. In general it is fair to say that interest in the Greek and Syrian fathers of all three patristic periods is growing steadily. The early Byzantine theologians Gregory of Nazianzus (Gregory the Theologian, ca. 329–390), Basil of Caesarea (Basil the Great, 330–379), and Gregory of Nyssa (331/40–ca. 395)—called the Cappadocians after the name of their native province in Asia Minor—are especially prominent reference points in contemporary theological discussions.

   The standard handbook to patristic literature of the early and classical periods is Johannes Quasten, *Patrology*, 4 vols. (Westminster, Md.: Christian Classics, 1990). Another useful tool is *Dictionary of Early Christian Literature*, ed. Siegmar Döpp and Wilhelm Geerlings, trans. Matthew O'Connell (New York: Crossroad, 2000). For a survey of early patristic theology by a contemporary Orthodox scholar, see John Behr, *The Way to Nicaea: The Formation of Christian Theology*, vol. 1 (Crestwood, N.Y.: St. Vladimir's Seminary Press, 2001). A magnificent introduction to the world of the Cappadocians is provided by John McGuckin, *Saint Gregory of Nazianzus: An Intellectual Biography* (Crestwood, N.Y.: St. Vladimir's Seminary Press, 2001). The best introduction to Byzantine theology in English is John Meyendorff, *Byzantine Theology: Historical Trends and Doctrinal Themes* (New York: Fordham University Press, 1974). Good monographs also exist on individual theologians: for example, Aidan Nichols, *Byzantine Gospel: Maximus the Confessor in Modern Scholarship* (Edinburgh: T & T Clark, 1993); John Meyendorff, *A Study of Gregory Palamas*, trans. George Lawrence, 2d ed. (Crestwood, N.Y.: St. Vladimir's Seminary Press, 1974); and Hilarion Alfeyev, *St. Symeon the New Theologian and Orthodox Tradition* (Oxford: Oxford University Press, 2000).

Some of the most readable English-language editions of patristic writings are found in the Paulist Press series "Classics of Western Spirituality," which includes a fair sampling of Eastern Christian works. ("Western" in the series title refers collectively to Jewish, Christian, and Islamic traditions, not to Western as opposed to Eastern Christianity.) Standard collections of the fathers in English include two continuing series, "Ancient Christian Writers: The Works of the Fathers in Translation," now published by the Catholic University of America Press, and "The Fathers of the Church: A New Translation," now published by the Paulist Press. Still useful, although extremely antiquated, are two nineteenth-century collections: *The Ante-Nicene Fathers: Translations of the Fathers down to A.D. 325*, ed. Alexander Roberts and James Donaldson, 10 vols., and *A Select Library of the Nicene and Post-Nicene Fathers of the Christian Church*, ed. Philip Schaff and Henry Wace, 28 vols., repr. ed. (Grand Rapids, Mich.: Eerdmans, 1978–79).

4. Lossky's book had a considerable impact in the English-speaking world thanks to a relatively early translation: Vladimir Lossky, *The Mystical Theology of the Eastern Church* (Cambridge: James Clarke, 1957). Florovsky's long and difficult book was translated much later: Georges Florovsky, *The Ways of Russian Theology*, part 1, trans. Robert L. Nichols, *The Collected Works of Georges Florovsky*, vol. 5 (Belmont, Mass.: Nordland, 1979); part 2, *The Collected Works of George Florovsky*, vol. 6 (Vaduz, Liechtenstein: Büchervertriebsanstalt, 1987). The best introduction to Florovsky's thought is not *The Ways of Russian Theology* but the elegant, pithy essays on a wide variety of patristic topics in *The Collected Works of Georges Florovsky*, 14 vols. (Belmont, Mass.: Nordland, 1972–89).

5. The pioneering work in Orthodox ethics by Stanley Harakas, Vigen Guroian, and other American scholars is not primarily neopatristic in inspiration. It owes more to the sustained dialogue between creative Orthodox ethicists and the interconfessional discipline of Christian ethics as practiced in North America. The Greek theologian Christos Yannaras comes closer to being an ethicist of neopatristic inspiration. See his *The Freedom of Morality*, trans. Elizabeth Briere with a foreword by Bishop Kallistos of Diokleia (Crestwood, N.Y.: St. Vlad-

imir's Seminary Press, 1984). For a fine example of the American contribution, see Vigen Guroian, *Incarnate Love: Essays in Orthodox Ethics*, 2d ed. (Notre Dame, Ind.: University of Notre Dame Press, 2002).

6. "Actually, one can hardly find, in the entire religious literature of Byzantium, any systematic treatment of Christian ethics, or behavior, but rather innumerable examples of moral exegesis of Scripture, and ascetical treatises on prayer and spirituality. This implies that Byzantine ethics were eminently 'theological ethics.' The basic affirmation that *every* man, whether Christian or not, is created according to the image of God and therefore called to divine communion and 'deification,' was of course recognized, but no attempt was ever made to build 'secular' ethics for man 'in general.'" Meyendorff, *Byzantine Theology*, 226.

7. Kallistos Ware, "Eastern Christianity," *The Encyclopedia of Religion*, ed. Mircea Eliade (New York: Free Press, 1987), 4:571.

8. Leonardo Boff, *Trinity and Society*, trans. Paul Burns (Maryknoll, N.Y.: Orbis Books, 1988).

9. Michael Aksionov Meerson's *The Trinity of Love in Modern Russian Theology: The Love Paradigm and the Retrieval of Western Medieval Love Mysticism in Modern Russian Trinitarian Thought (from Solovyov to Bulgakov)* (Quincy, Ill.: Franciscan Press, 1998) is an important contribution to a widened trinitarianism in Orthodox theology. Although this book has ethical implications, it is not primarily an essay in ethics; neither can the author be called a neopatristic theologian.

10. Makarios and Nikodemos's work is available in English: *The Philokalia: The Complete Text, compiled by St Nikodimos of the Holy Mountain and St. Makarios of Corinth*, trans. G. E. H. Palmer, Philip Sherrard and Kallistos Ware, 3 vols. (London: Faber and Faber, 1979–84). Dumitru Stăniloae produced a twelve-volume Romanian *Philokalia* (1946–91). See chapter 23, this volume.

11. "The view of man prevailing in the Christian East is based upon the notion of 'participation' in God. Man has been created not as an autonomous or self-sufficient being; his very *nature* is truly itself only inasmuch as it exists 'in God' or 'in grace.' Grace, therefore, gives man his 'natural' development. This basic presupposition explains why the terms 'nature' and 'grace,' when used by Byzantine authors, have a meaning quite different from the Western usage; rather than being in direct opposition, the terms 'nature' and 'grace' express a dynamic, living, and necessary relationship between God and man, different by their *natures*, but in *communion* with each other through God's energy, or grace." Meyendorff, *Byzantine Theology*, 138.

12. The first two uses are the civil use of the law as a means of preserving public order and the theological use of the law as a means of convicting sinners of unrighteousness, thereby awakening in them a hunger for redemption.

13. The best introduction to Slavophilism is Andrzej Walicki, *The Slavophile Controversy: History of a Conservative Utopia in Nineteenth-Century Russian Thought*, trans. Hilda Andrews-Rusiecka (Notre Dame, Ind.: University of Notre Dame Press, 1989). The best collection of Slavophile writings in English is

On Spiritual Unity: A Slavophile Reader, trans. and ed. Boris Jakim and Robert Bird (Hudson, N.Y.: Lindisfarne Books, 1998).

14. *Sobornost* comes from the Slavic root meaning "gather." So, for example, the noun *sobor* means "church council" and also "cathedral" (where the people gather for liturgy). The adjective *sobornyi* translates "catholic" in the Nicene Creed: "one holy, catholic and apostolic Church." Community, fellowship, conciliarity, catholicity, cathedral-feeling—all these meanings resound in the term *sobornost*. In recent decades the word has begun an international career, appearing, for example, in *Webster's Third New International Dictionary* (1981).

15. Andrzej Walicki, *Legal Philosophies of Russian Liberalism* (Oxford: Clarendon Press, 1987), 9–104.

16. For a fine discussion, see Harold J. Berman, "The Weightier Matters of the Law: A Response to Solzhenitsyn," in *Faith and Order: The Reconciliation of Law and Religion* (Atlanta, Ga.: Scholars Press, 1993), 381–392.

17. On the liberalism of Soloviev and some of the thinkers inspired by him, see Walicki, *Legal Philosophies of Russian Liberalism*; and the classic Russian work of 1902, *Problems of Idealism: Essays in Russian Social Philosophy*, trans. and ed. Randall A. Poole (New Haven, Conn.: Yale University Press, 2003).

18. See note 3 above.

19. Sergei Horuzhy, a mathematical physicist, has elaborated a philosophy of "energetism" based, as he claims, on hesychasm. See Sergei Khoruzhii, *K fenomenologii askezy* (Moscow: Izdatel'stvo gumanitarnoi literatury, 1998) and *O starom i o novom* (St. Petersburg: Aleteiia, 2000). For a related essay in English see Sergei S. Horuzhy, "Neo-Patristic Synthesis and Russian Philosophy," *St. Vladimir's Theological Quarterly* 44 (2000): 309–328.

20. John W. Barker, *Justinian and the Later Roman Empire* (Madison: University of Wisconsin Press, 1966), 97.

21. The essential essay on the subject is Deno J. Geanakoplos, "Church and State in the Byzantine Empire: A Reconsideration of the Problem of Caesaropapism," in id., *Byzantine East and Latin West: Two Worlds of Christendom in Middle Ages and Renaissance, Studies in Ecclesiastical and Cultural History* (New York: Harper & Row, 1966), 55–83.

22. Monophysitism, literally "one-nature-ism," is the view that humanity and divinity were so integrally united in Christ that one may speak of "one incarnate nature of God the Word." The Orthodox doctrine, confirmed at the Council of Chalcedon in 451, is that, in Christ, two distinct natures (divine and human) were united without confusion or division in one Person. The Chalcedonians rejected monophysitism because they believed it compromised the humanity of Christ. The monophysites rejected Chalcedon because they believed it compromised the fullness of the incarnation. Orthodox, Roman Catholic, and Protestant churches are Chalcedonian. Coptic, Syrian, Armenian, and Ethiopian churches are non-Chalcedonian. The popularity of monophysitism in the Eastern provinces of the Byzantine Empire owed much to regional resentment against the political and cultural hegemonism of Constantinople.

23. Quoted by Meyendorff, *Byzantine Theology*, 213.

24. Ibid., 213–214. Meyendorff views this civil-political application of incarnational theology as misguided because it assumed "that the ideal humanity which was manifested, through the Incarnation, in the person of Jesus Christ could also find an adequate manifestation in the Roman Empire." But this is the assessment of a theologian reflecting on the fall of the two great Orthodox empires in world history, the Byzantine and the Russian. The vast majority of Orthodox Christians until quite recently shared Justinian's view that the Orthodox state was as much a divine institution as the Orthodox Church.

25. On the "palladian" qualities of icons, see Hussey, *The Orthodox Church in the Byzantine Empire*, 31–32; Judith Herrin, *The Formation of Christendom* (Princeton, N.J.: Princeton University Press, 1987), 307–308, 314–315; and Leo Tolstoy, *War and Peace*, book 3, chap. 2.

26. Orthodox appeals to the state to help resist proselytism by other Christian groups are a good example. See John Witte Jr. and Michael Bourdeaux, eds., *Proselytism and Orthodoxy in Russia: The New War for Souls* (Maryknoll, N.Y.: Orbis Books, 1999).

27. English-language discussion of Bulgakov's thought has flourished in recent years. See Judith Deutsch Kornblatt and Richard F. Gustafson, eds., *Russian Religious Thought* (Madison: University of Wisconsin Press, 1996), 135–192; Catherine Evtuhov, *The Cross and the Sickle: Sergei Bulgakov and the Fate of Russian Religious Philosophy* (Ithaca, N.Y.: Cornell University Press, 1997); Rowan Williams, ed., *Sergii Bulgakov: Towards a Russian Political Theology* (Edinburgh: T & T Clark, 1999); Paul Valliere, *Modern Russian Theology: Bukharev, Soloviev, Bulgakov* (Grand Rapids, Mich.: Eerdmans, 2000), 227–371; and the pioneering study by Philip Max Walters, "The Development of the Political and Religious Philosophy of Sergei Bulgakov, 1895–1922: A Struggle for Transcendence" (Ph.D. diss., London School of Economics and Political Science, 1978).

28. "Apophatic" comes from a Greek word meaning "negative." In theology it refers to discourse about the divine in terms of what God is not (e.g., God is not finite, not mortal, not human, not comprehensible, not reducible to the measure of this world or of any world, and so on), as opposed to positive or "kataphatic" statements about God (e.g., God is good, just, loving, wise, and so on). The aim of apophatic discourse is to induce the mind to confess the radical transcendence and mystery of God.

29. The contrast is developed by Silviu Eugen Rogobete, "Mystical Existentialism or Communitarian Participation? Vladimir Lossky and Dumitru Staniloae," in *Dumitru Staniloae: Tradition and Modernity in Theology*, ed. Lucian Turcescu (Iasi, Romania: Center for Romanian Studies, 2002), 167–206. On *Gândirea* (*Thought*, the name of a journal), see Keith Hitchins, "*Gândirea*: Nationalism in a Spiritual Guise," *Social Change in Romania, 1860–1940: A Debate on Development in a European Nation*, ed. Kenneth Jowitt (Berkeley: Institute of International Studies, University of California, 1978).

30. Herrin, *The Formation of Christendom*, 38.

31. Stephen Runciman, *Byzantine Civilization* (London: Edward Arnold, 1959), 75–76. For a concise presentation of Justinian's legislation, including its Christian elements, see Percy Neville Ure, *Justinian and his Age* (Harmondsworth, England: Penguin, 1951), 139–167.

32. For an introduction to the issues and the literature see Ia. N. Shchapov, *Vizantiiskoe i iuzhnoslavianskoe pravovoe nasledie na Rusi v XI–XIIIvv* (Moscow: Izdatel'stvo Nauka, 1978).

33. The phrase is from John Meyendorff, *Living Tradition: Orthodox Witness in the Contemporary World* (Crestwood, N.Y.: St. Vladimir's Seminary Press, 1978), 195.

34. "In Russia, unlike the West, no rising class of jurists, specially trained in rational law, had prepared the way for eighteenth-century absolutist rule and modernization. Therefore Russian absolutism adopted the ethos of rational legislation and the policy of the *état bien policé*, while preserving many features of a traditional patriarchal autocracy, and did not have to concern itself with an organized legal profession. The institution of the Bar only appeared in Russia with the judicial reforms of 1864." Walicki, *Legal Philosophies of Russian Liberalism*, 15. See also Marc Raeff, *The Well-Ordered Police State: Social and Institutional Change Through Law in the Germanies and Russia, 1600–1800* (London, 1983).

35. For an introduction to Orthodox canon law and some of its applications, see the essays by John H. Erickson, *The Challenge of Our Past: Studies in Orthodox Canon Law and Church History* (Crestwood, N.Y.: St. Vladimir's Seminary Press, 1991); and "*Oikonomia* in Byzantine Canon Law," in *Law, Church and Society: Essays in Honor of Stephan Kuttner*, ed. K. Pennington and R. Somerville (Philadelphia: University of Pennsylvania Press, 1977), 225–236.

36. A unitary "code" of canon law as opposed to a "corpus" of officially recognized sources is a recent development even in Roman Catholicism. The first *Codex iuris canonici* was promulgated in 1917. A new code was issued in 1983.

37. *Byzantine Theology*, 54, 225.

38. For an introduction to Nikodemos, see *Nicodemos of the Holy Mountain: A Handbook of Spiritual Counsel*, trans. Peter A. Chamberas (New York: Paulist Press, 1989); and the penetrating critique by John H. Erickson, "On the Cusp of Modernity: The Canonical Hermeneutic of St. Nikodemos the Haghiorite (1748–1809)," *St. Vladimir's Theological Quarterly* 42 (1998): 45–66. The *Pedalion* is available in a not altogether satisfactory English edition: *The Rudder*, trans. D. Cummings (Chicago: Orthodox Christian Educational Society, 1957).

39. The standard account in English is James Cracraft, *The Church Reform of Peter the Great* (Stanford, Calif.: Stanford University Press, 1971). See also *The Spiritual Regulation of Peter the Great*, trans. and ed. Alexander V. Muller (Seattle: University of Washington Press, 1972).

40. Many changes in the regulation of the church, some of them constructive, were made in the nineteenth century, but they cannot be said to add up to a reform of the synodal system, much less of the church itself. For a detailed account, see Gregory L. Freeze, *The Parish Clergy in Nineteenth Century Russia: Crisis, Re-*

form, Counter-Reform (Princeton, N.J.: Princeton University Press, 1983). The standard work on the conciliar movement of 1905–6 is James W. Cunningham, *A Vanquished Hope: The Movement for Church Renewal in Russia, 1905–1906* (Crestwood, N.Y.: St. Vladimir's Seminary Press, 1981).

41. For a complete English translation see "Documents: Appeals for Religious Freedom in Russia," *St. Vladimir's Seminary Quarterly* 10 (1966): 67–111. For a detailed discussion of Orthodox dissent during the Soviet period, see Jane Ellis, *The Russian Orthodox Church: A Contemporary History* (Bloomington: Indiana University Press, 1986), 285–454. See also Paul Valliere, "Russian Orthodoxy and Human Rights," in *Religious Diversity and Human Rights*, ed. Irene Bloom, J. Paul Martin, and Wayne L. Proudfoot (New York: Columbia University Press, 1996), 278–312.

42. For an introduction, see *Christianity for the Twenty-first Century: The Prophetic Writings of Alexander Men*, ed. Elizabeth Roberts and Ann Shukman (New York: Continuum, 1996).

43. The phrase is from John Meyendorff, *Living Tradition*, 105.

44. Erickson, *The Challenge of Our Past*, 20.

45. *The Russian Question at the End of the Twentieth Century*, trans. Yermolai Solzhenitsyn (New York: Farrar, Straus & Giroux, 1995), 98.

46. "Osnovy sotsial'noi kontseptsii russkoi pravoslavnoi tserkvi" (Bases of the Social Concept of the Russian Orthodox Church). The document, with English translation, can be found at the website of the Moscow Patriarchate, http://www.russian-orthodox-church.org.ru.

47. On this issue, see *Religion, State & Society* 27, no. 1 (March 1999), the record of a conference on "Reflection on the Laity: a Focus for Christian Dialogue Between East and West" sponsored by Keston College and the University of Leeds.

48. Max Weber, "Politics as a Vocation," in *From Max Weber: Essays in Sociology*, trans. H. H. Gerth and C. Wright Mills (New York: Oxford University Press, 1970–72), 126.

49. "Deianie iubileinogo osviashchennogo arkhiereiskogo sobora russkoi pravoslavnoi tserkvi o sobornom proslavlenii novomuchenikov i ispovednikov rossiiskikh XX veka." See also the report of the chair of the canonization commission, "Doklad mitropolita krutitskogo i kolomenskogo Iuvenaliia, predsedatelia sinodal'noi komissii po kanonizatsii sviatykh, na arkhiereiskom sobore," and the summary of the proceedings, "Proslavlenie sviatykh na iubileinom arkhiereiskom sobore." The documents can be found at the website of the Moscow Patriarchate, http://www.russian-orthodox-church.org.ru.

[CHAPTER 19]

Vladimir Soloviev (1853–1900)

PAUL VALLIERE

The systematic study of law, one of the central concerns of Western Christian civilization since the Middle Ages, has not enjoyed comparable centrality in the Christian East. The Byzantine legal tradition, described in the previous chapter, perished with the fall of the Byzantine Empire (1453). Since then, the catalyst for the development of legal thought in the Orthodox East has been contact with the West. The dynamic, often aggressive, projection of Western influence into the Orthodox world in modern times forced Eastern Christians to take an interest in Western civilization whether they wished to or not. Among the many subjects demanding attention, Western legalism—civil, political, and ecclesiastical—was particularly difficult for Orthodox people to appreciate because of the absence of analogous structures in their own living tradition.

Orthodox reflection on modern legalism began in Russia, not because the Russians were better prepared to think about law than the other Orthodox peoples, but because Russia was the first Orthodox country to attempt to remake itself into a state and society of the modern type. The reforms of Peter the Great and Catherine the Great in the eighteenth century stimulated profound reflection on the foundations of civil society. During the "Moscow Spring" of 1809–12, the statesman and jurist Mikhail Speransky—the son of an Orthodox village priest—convinced Tsar Alexander I to contemplate an extensive reform of the Russian Empire along legal lines. Napoleon's invasion in 1812 put an end to this project, but Russian legal science continued to develop. Speransky devoted the second half of his career to preparing the first systematic code of law in the history of Russia. The first edition of this massive work was published in 1832. Later in the century Timofei Granovsky (1813–55) and Boris Chicherin (1828–1903) laid the foundations of Russian legal philosophy. As part of the Great Reforms of the 1860s, a new judicial system was set up, jury trial was introduced, and a Russian bar was created. The rule of law appeared to have begun in Russia.

What had not begun was the reconciliation of the fledgling Russian legal tradition with the Orthodox Christian tradition, which commanded the religious loyalty of the large majority of the population of the Russian Empire. Aleksei Khomiakov (1804–60), Ivan Kireevsky (1806–56), and the other early Slavophiles who created modern Russian Orthodox religious philosophy viewed legal rationality as the quintessential manifestation of coldhearted, ultimately atheistic Western rationalism. Against it they preached an Orthodox Christian ethic of love and community. Later in the century the novelist Leo Tolstoy propounded a similar view along humanist rather than Orthodox lines. Unfortunately, Orthodox hierarchs and church theologians had little to say on the subject. The close, not to say confining, bonds that tied the Orthodox Church to the imperial state meant that church leaders had much less freedom to address the issues of the day than lay theologians. Many Russians were thus left with the impression that they had to choose between the Orthodox moral and spiritual tradition on one hand and modern legalism on the other, between Christian love and human rights. The most brilliant Orthodox jurists, such as Speransky, certainly did not view the case in such stark terms. But they were specialists. They did not deal directly with the religious and theological implications of their subject.

The breakthrough came with Vladimir Soloviev (1853–1900). Soloviev was the first modern Orthodox thinker who both regarded law in a positive light and set out to relate it to the grand themes of Orthodox theology. He applied himself to the project in a variety of venues for more than twenty years, assigning it a central place in his magnum opus, *The Justification of the Good* (1897). No other modern Orthodox thinker has yet matched his contribution to the discussion of law, society, and human nature from an Orthodox perspective.

SOLOVIEV'S LIFE AND WORK

Vladimir Sergeevich Soloviev was born in Moscow in 1853 to a prominent academic family.[1] His father, Sergei Mikhailovich, descended from a long line of Orthodox priests, and was a professor of history at Moscow University. His mother, Poliksena Vladimirovna, came from a military family of Polish and Ukrainian extraction.

Vladimir matriculated at Moscow University in 1869 after receiving an excellent classical education. Somewhat unexpectedly, he chose to study the natural sciences, although he eventually completed his degree in the faculty of history and philology. Soloviev's false start in the sciences is sometimes attributed to a youthful passion for philosophical materialism, the doctrine of choice for young intellectuals in Russia in the 1860s. But one should reckon also with a young man's need to put some distance between himself and his famous father. Sergei Soloviev (1820–79) was the most prominent Russian historian of his generation. His massive *History of Russia from Ancient Times* remains one of the most impressive monuments of Russian intellectual culture.[2] When Vladimir matriculated at Moscow University, Sergei was dean of the faculty of history and philology. In 1871 he became rector of the university.

Vladimir discovered where his genius lay thanks to the mentoring of Pamfil Danilovich Yurkevich (1827–74), a professor of philosophy. Yurkevich had been at Moscow University since 1861, but his roots lay in the Orthodox theological schools where he trained and taught for many years. Yurkevich is remembered for seminal essays in philosophical anthropology in which he criticized modern materialist conceptions of human nature from a biblical perspective emphasizing the wholeness and moral consciousness of human beings—what the Bible calls the "heart."[3]

After graduation in 1873 Soloviev elected to spend a postgraduate year at Moscow Theological Academy, one of four graduate schools of theology operated by the Russian Orthodox Church. This was an unusual step for an aspiring academic to take at the time and attests to Soloviev's unconventional personality as well as to his religious interests. In 1874 Soloviev returned to the university to defend his master's thesis and first book, *The Crisis of Western Philosophy*. The following year he began teaching at his alma mater but soon departed for a year's study in London. There he did research on mysticism and gnosticism in the British Museum and mixed with the local spiritualist community. The spiritualists left him cold, but in the museum he had a mystical vision of Divine Wisdom (Sophia). Sophia directed him to travel to Egypt, promising to reveal herself again there—which she did, although not until Soloviev nearly lost his life at the hands of hostile Bedouin on a walk in the desert near the pyramids.

In 1876 Soloviev resumed teaching at Moscow University only to resign before the end of the academic year and move to St. Petersburg. It was becoming obvious that Soloviev was a man who disliked established paths. Restless, impulsive, visionary, he gravitated to a peripatetic lifestyle. He would have made a fine bohemian were it not for his extraordinary work ethic. He finished his second book, *The Philosophical Principles of Whole Knowledge* in 1877, began *Lectures on Divine Humanity* in the same year, and defended his doctoral dissertation, which became *The Critique of Abstract Principles*, in 1880. The author of four books in six years was twenty-seven years old.[4]

SOLOVIEV'S SLAVOPHILISM

In Petersburg Soloviev lectured in both academic and popular venues, presenting himself as a young Slavophile. Slavophilism and its antagonist, Westernism, were vehicles of the culture wars of nineteenth-century Russia, the century-long debate over Russia's destiny in the modern world. The debate concerned the features of Russian civilization that distinguished it from the West: Orthodox Christianity, political autocracy, and a tradition of communalism in economic and social life. The Westernizers believed that Russia should set aside its traditional value system and integrate itself into modern European civilization. The Slavophiles affirmed Russian distinctiveness. Differences of opinion existed within as well as between the two points of view. In Westernism there was a split between evolutionists and revolutionists. In Slavophilism, the affirmation of Russian particularity at times inspired isolationism (Russia should keep away from the West), at other times militancy (Russia has a mission to the West). Soloviev was a missionary Slavophile, believing that Russia had a message the world needed to hear.

The message was the advent of a new, modern cultural synthesis combining the best values of the European Enlightenment with the deepest truths of Christianity. The idea had been advanced in Russia in the previous generation by Ivan Kireevsky, who in turn was indebted to German Romanticism, especially the philosophy of Schelling.[5] Kireevsky had studied in Berlin and Munich and carefully followed developments in European philosophy. Thanks to his Orthodox wife and the proximity of his estate to Optina Hermitage, he also paid close attention to the revival of monastic spirituality in Russia. His hope, stated in an essay "On the Possibility and Necessity of New Principles in Philosophy" (1854), was that "Orthodox enlightenment should master the whole intellectual development of the contemporary world, so that, having enriched itself with secular wisdom, Christian truth may the more fully and solemnly demonstrate its prevalence over the relative truths of human reason."[6]

Kireevsky's quest for wholeness of life through the synthesis of reason with religion was Soloviev's point of departure. In *The Crisis of Western Philosophy (Against the Positivists)* he argued that the analytic and materialistic approaches to philosophy were spiritual dead-ends showing the need for new principles in philosophy. In *The Philosophical Principles of Integral Knowledge* he stated the case for wholeness in more positive terms. In *The Critique of Abstract Principles* he masterfully recapitulated both his critique of Western philosophy and the case for wholeness, lending a militant spirit to his program by calling for its realization in a "free theocracy."

In *Lectures on Divine Humanity* Soloviev focused on the theological substance of his vision, what he called *bogochelovechestvo*. The term is translated into English as Godmanhood, divine humanity or humanity of God. The concept is a thematization of the Orthodox Christian doctrine of the incarnation. For Orthodox theology, God's becoming-human accomplishes not just the moral transformation of humanity (Christ "for" us) but also an ontological transformation (Christ "in" us). Thanks to God's assumption of human nature, human nature can be raised from glory to glory to the point of assimilation to divine nature, or *theosis* (deification). Theosis is an eschatological state, but the process is already underway and can be seen in the radiant lives of the saints. Soloviev gave this conceptuality a historical-prophetic application: the divine-human union in the incarnation points the way to the cultural synthesis of the future by offering the world a better moral and spiritual ideal than the "godless human individual" of modern Western civilization or the "inhuman God" of Islam. Orthodox Russia, poised between West and East, has the providential mission of proclaiming the good news of "divine humanity."[7]

One of the Petersburg intellectuals to whom Soloviev's prophetism appealed was the novelist Feodor Dostoevsky (1821–81). Although Dostoevsky was much older than Soloviev, the two men became friends, as evidenced by the fact that Dostoevsky invited Soloviev to accompany him on his pilgrimage to Optina Hermitage in 1878 following the death of the novelist's three year-old son Alyosha.[8] The excursion occupies a special place in Russian literary history because the community at Optina was the model for Dostoevsky's portrait of Russian monasticism in *The Brothers Karamazov* (1878–80). Not surprisingly, critics have looked for Soloviev's portrait as well, and indeed *The Brothers Karamazov* portrays a brilliant young philosopher in Ivan Karamazov.

While it would be a mistake to equate Soloviev and Ivan Karamazov—Soloviev's optimistic, believing personality bears no resemblance to Ivan's tortured soul—there is definitely a link between the two on the level of ideas. During the Karamazov family's visit to the monastery, Ivan becomes involved in a conversation about the scope of the jurisdiction of ecclesiastical courts, a subject on which he has published a controversial article. Ivan's thesis is that the modern secular state, because it has severed its connection with the church, cannot deal with crime and punishment in spiritual terms and so administers justice in a mechanical and utilitarian manner. Incapable of fostering repentance and amendment of life, the state can only repress the criminal. The criminal reacts by construing his relationship to society in equally utilitarian terms, at times even regarding his crime as a justifiable act of rebellion against an oppressive social order. If

Russia is to avoid this outcome, Ivan argues, the state must reaffirm and expand the role of the church in society and in the legal system in particular. "Ultramontanism!" exclaims Mr. Miusov, a Westernizer horrified by the theocratic implications of Ivan's logic. But the monks are stirred to enthusiasm: "It will be! It will be!"[9] As we shall see, in *The Critique of Abstract Principles* Soloviev advocated an ideal much like Ivan's, envisioning a theocracy of love inspired and sanctified by the church.

The reference to ultramontanism interjects a comparison between Orthodoxy and Roman Catholicism. The comparison is taken further by one of the monks, Father Paisy, who criticizes Roman Catholicism for making the church into a kind of state, whereas Orthodoxy envisions the transformation of the state by the spirit of the church. The indictment of Roman Catholicism for juridicalizing the gospel is also a theme in the most famous chapter of *The Brothers Karamazov*, "The Grand Inquisitor." Soloviev repeated the charge in his *Lectures on Divine Humanity*.[10] The contrast between the supposedly harsh, legalistic Western church and the loving, all-embracing Eastern church was a cherished stereotype in Slavophilism.

UNIVERSALISM AND ECUMENISM

Soloviev's theocratism underwent a significant change in the 1880s. The decade began with a crisis. On March 1, 1881, Tsar Alexander II was assassinated in Petersburg by populist revolutionaries. As Russians reeled in horror and confusion, Soloviev delivered a public lecture in which he called on the new tsar, Alexander III, to deal with his father's assassins in the spirit of Christian love by refusing to condemn them to death. The revolutionaries had acted as death-dealers, but a Christian monarch should not. Unfortunately for Soloviev, the tsar and his government were not impressed by this interpretation of theocracy and forced the young philosopher to resign from the university. The incident was important because it caused Soloviev to reassess his understanding of theocracy. He did not question the ideal, but he began to question some of the forms in which he had been preaching it, especially the facile association of Orthodox Christianity with the Russian way of life. He also began saying positive things about Western civilization, including Roman Catholicism. His Slavophile friends soon closed their journals to him.

Soloviev pressed his case for a more cosmopolitan understanding of theocracy by taking a critical look at how the Russian Orthodox community related to its non-Russian and non-Orthodox neighbors inside and outside the Russian Empire. In *The National Question in Russia*, a collection of essays written between 1883 and 1891, Soloviev criticized Russian national egoism and the oppression of ethnic and religious minorities.[11] He also stepped forward as a strong advocate of religious liberty, which in 1889 he called "the good which [Russia] needs first of all."[12] In "The Development of Dogma and the Question of Church Union" (1886) he examined Orthodoxy's relations with the Roman Catholic Church, arguing that there were no insuperable obstacles to reunion. The essay makes a passionate case for what would eventually be called ecumenism.

The ecumenical cause occupied much of Soloviev's time in the later 1880s. In 1886 he spent three months in Zagreb, Croatia, for discussions with two other nineteenth-century prophets of the idea, Bishop Josip Juraj Strossmayer of Bosnia and Canon Franko Racki of the South Slav Academy. In 1888 he lived most of the year in France in dialogue with Catholics and other Christians and arranged for the publication of *La Russie et l'Eglise universelle* (1889). Through Bishop Strossmayer, Soloviev's vision of a reunited Christendom was shared with Pope Leo XIII. "Bella idea," the pontiff reportedly replied, "ma fuor d'un miracolo è cosa impossibile"—a good idea, but without a miracle it's impossible.[13]

THE JEWS AND THE "CHRISTIAN QUESTION"

A new relationship between Christians and Jews also figured in Soloviev's theocratic program. Here the issue went beyond minority rights. To Soloviev, the Jews were exactly who they claimed to be: the chosen people, the theocratic people par excellence, "the axis of universal history."[14] He regarded the Hebrew Bible, with its detailed account of the collaboration of prophets, priests, and kings in the history of Israel, as the constitution of theocracy. When he designed *The History and Future of Theocracy*, a three-volume study of the theocratic idea in human history, he assigned the first volume to ancient Israel.[15] To enhance his competence in the subject matter he studied Hebrew with the help of Faivel B. Gets, a Jewish intellectual who became one of his closest friends. Gets also introduced Soloviev to the study of rabbinic texts.

Soloviev reflected on the meaning of Judaism in several essays including "The Jews and the Christian Question" (1884) and "The Talmud and Recent Polemics in Austria and Germany" (1886).[16] The point of "The Jews and the Christian Question" is adumbrated in the title. Breaking with the nearly universal assumption by nineteenth-century Christians that there was a Jewish Question in Europe, Soloviev argued that the so-called Jewish Question was in fact a Christian Question, that is to say, a question about how Christians treat the Jews:

> The Jews have always and everywhere regarded Christianity and behaved towards it in accordance with the precepts of their religion, in conformity with their faith and their law. The Jews have always treated us in the Jewish way; we

Christians, on the contrary, have not learned to this day to adopt a Christian attitude to the Jews. They have never transgressed their religious law in relation to us; we, on the other hand, have always broken the commandments of the Christian religion in relation to them.[17]

What Soloviev meant is that the Jews, whose law constitutes them as a people set apart by a special religio-historical vocation, have obeyed their law by preserving their identity apart from Christianity; while Christians, whose Lord calls them to an ethic of universal love, have repeatedly violated this ethic in their relations with Jews. Since the group in need of repentance and change of life is the Christians, not the Jews, one should speak of a Christian Question rather than a Jewish Question.

In his essay on the Talmud, Soloviev promoted a positive attitude toward Jewish law against anti-Semitic denigration of it. He pointed out that, while Christians tend to make a sharp distinction between Christianity and Judaism, most Christians have never even read, much less studied, the Jewish law. If they did so, they would discover that Jewish and Christian ethical teachings are basically the same. What Christianity has to offer is not a new ethic but the redemptive humanity of God in Christ. This is a truth that the Jews need to receive, but they should not be expected to receive it until Christians do a better job of showing how Christian doctrine can transform life. The enduring paganism of supposedly Christian societies and the sectarian divisions in the church itself present a sorry spectacle to law-abiding Jews. "As we see it," Soloviev imagined Jews saying to Christians, "truth cannot be abstract, it cannot be separated from practice. We are a people of law, and truth itself for us is not so much an intellectual idea as it is *a law of life.*... Your religious ideal expresses absolute holiness, but the law of your life remains the law of sin and injustice."[18]

Soloviev recognized that Christianity and Judaism have different historical vocations, but he did not regard this as justifying Christian hostility toward the Jews. Judaism and Christianity are still in process, and both are destined for consummation in the same kingdom of God. Penultimately, there is much that the two communities can do together. In "The Jews and the Christian Question," Soloviev envisioned a three-way collaboration between the Russian Orthodox, Polish Catholic, and Jewish communities of the Russian Empire as a way of realizing the theocratic ideal in Russia and showing the rest of Europe what the right relationship between prophet, priest, and king in a modern state might look like. The significance of the scheme stands out when one compares it with the Slavophile vision: Soloviev's theocracy had become a project for all Europe, all Christendom, all communities of biblical faith.

THE UNION OF OPPOSITES

The synthesis of Christian-theocratic and liberal-universalist values that Soloviev achieved in the 1880s set him apart from most of his contemporaries. The remaking of a Romantic Christian as a liberal universalist was not unknown in nineteenth-century spiritual culture, but the conversion usually involved the abandonment of dogmatic and theocratic beliefs for a more secularized faith. Soloviev, by contrast, was able to hold the entire spectrum of values together in a highly original synthesis, the union of opposites forcing him to push at the limits of ordinary language to name his vision. It was theo-philosophical, free-theocratic, mystical-historical. The term preferred by Soloviev was *bogochelovecheskii*, "divine-human," from *bogochelovechestvo*, Godmanhood, divine humanity, humanity of God. For all its difficulties in translation, this term is the most appropriate because it refers to the source of Soloviev's intellectual confidence—the incarnation. Soloviev preached a transcendent both/and. As he saw it, people do not have to choose between Orthodoxy and modernity, religion and science, tradition and change, Christian faith and religious universalism, gospel and law, not even between God and the world. Why are these false choices? How is such wholeness of life available to us? Because "the Word became flesh and lived among us, full of grace and truth, and we have seen his glory" (John 1:14). In Christ the humanity of God, all things in heaven and on earth are reconciled and destined for incorporation in the kingdom of God. Inspired by this faith, Soloviev pursued his vocation: to advance the work of reconciliation on earth and, if need be, to storm the heavens, to wrest saints, seers, mystics, even gnostics from their ethereal mansions and enlist them in the sacred cause.[19]

In the 1890s Soloviev pulled back from the activism of the previous decade to allow more time for writing projects in academic philosophy. His shift is often interpreted as evidence of disillusion with theocracy, but a positive factor was involved as well. In 1889 Nikolai Grot, professor of philosophy at Moscow University and president of the Moscow Psychological Society, founded Russia's first professional philosophical journal, *Questions of Philosophy and Psychology*. Soloviev was one of the original collaborators in this enterprise, which called him back to his primary vocation. During the 1890s he produced brilliant philosophical essays and monographs including *The Justification of the Good* (1897). This large work, which among other things contains Soloviev's mature philosophy of law, remains the most magisterial work of moral philosophy in the Russian tradition.

In 1899–1900 Soloviev composed his final work, *Three Dialogues on War, Progress and the End of World History, with a Brief Tale of the*

Anti-Christ. The last section is a literary apocalypse featuring a fight to the finish between the armies of an urbane, humanitarian Antichrist and a faithful remnant of ecumenical Christians and unassimilated Jews. The subject matter and proximity of the work to Soloviev's death—he died on July 31, 1900—have led many interpreters to suppose that Soloviev rejected activist-humanist Christianity at the end of his life and embraced radical apocalypticism. Recently, however, Judith Deutsch Kornblatt and others have shown that this view is open to serious question. It will not be adopted here.[20]

LAW AND THE THEOCRACY OF LOVE

Soloviev's first essay in the philosophy of law is embedded in the masterpiece of his early career, *The Critique of Abstract Principles* (chaps. 15–20). The social ideal advanced in *The Critique* is a symphonic wholeness in which "all constitute the end of each, and each the end of all."[21] As soon as the project of realizing this kingdom of ends begins, however, the partiality of human beings undermines the task. Even when they embrace the ideal of all for each and each for all, human beings find it difficult to do justice to both sides at once. Those who lean to "each" generate individualism; those who favor "all" generate some form of collectivism; and so the common project of building the good society is undermined. Instead of addressing living human beings in the actual world, ethicists deal with "the individual" and "society." But these are abstractions. In actuality no absolute individual exists; if he did, he would be a case of "empty personhood."[22] Conversely, no society exists except as composed of living individuals.

Soloviev's critique of abstractions was connected with his understanding of moral evil, or sin. As he saw it, the root of moral evil in humanity is the tendency to "exclusivity," that is to say, the temptation to substitute the part for the whole, to affirm oneself or one's dependents in isolation from the all-encompassing whole of things. "This abnormal attitude toward everything else—this exclusive self-assertion, or egoism, all-powerful in our practical life even though we deny it in theory, this opposition of the self to all other selves and the practical negation of other selves—constitutes the radical *evil* of our nature."[23]

The evil of exclusivity is overcome through renunciation. Renunciation does not mean self-annihilation, which is actually another sort of exclusivity, but the overcoming of partiality. The paradigm is given in Jesus, the incarnate Word who accomplishes "the double exploit of divine and human self-renunciation." Though very God, the Word lays aside his divine glory to become a human being; and as a human being Jesus does his father's will, not his own. The moral grandeur of the accomplishment is seen at the very beginning of Jesus' ministry in the temptation in the wilderness. Three times the prince of darkness invites the Messiah to self-assertion, but "Christ subordinates His human will to, and harmonizes it with, the divine will, deifying His humanity after the humanization of His Divinity."[24] Dostoevsky, too, was enchanted by the temptation story, making it the crux of Ivan Karamazov's parable of the Grand Inquisitor.

NEEDS, RIGHTS, AND LOVE OF THE WHOLE

Soloviev's critique of abstract principles began with the collectivist option, represented in his time by socialism. Soloviev was reasonably well acquainted with socialism. In his youth he had been deeply impressed by reading Saint-Simon and other early socialists, and he always evinced more sympathy for socialism than for capitalism.[25] In his estimation, socialists are right to reject plutocracy and demand an economic order embodying ethical norms. The error of socialism lies in supposing that a material or economic order by itself generates ethical norms, "that an unexampled economic set-up (some kind of fusion of capital and labor, the organization of industry by unions, etc.) is obligatory in and for itself, unconditionally normative and moral, that is, that this economic set-up as such already contains a moral principle and is the sole condition of social morality." This is a classic example of partiality: "the moral principle, the principle of the obligatory and the normative, is determined exclusively by one of the elements of the totality of human life—the economic element."[26]

Other elements, besides the material-economic, need to be accommodated in a social ethic. One of them is betrayed by the rhetoric of socialism itself. Socialists typically cloak the economic arrangements they preach in a moral discourse that reveals the transeconomic status of their ideal. Socialists call for a "just" economy and the "rights" of workers. But the concepts of justice and right cannot be derived from the material-economic process. Interests can be derived from it, but not rights. Rights derive from the freedom and rationality of human beings, features of human nature that are by definition spiritual. That such values should be realized in and through the economic order, that the latter should not be abandoned to anarchy while so-called spiritual people seek happiness in another world— these demands of socialism are quite valid. But that matter in motion and the interests generated by it are the source of freedom and rationality is a proposition Soloviev rejected. Far from being a derivative of the economic order, our consciousness of freedom and rationality points to something else: the juridical order.

A powerful personalism underlay Soloviev's appreciation for the reality of the juridical order:

> The concept of right first lends to a human being the status of *person*. Indeed, as long as I strive for material prosperity and pursue my personal interests, other people have no independent significance for me, they are merely things which I can use well or poorly [in pursuit of my interests]. But if I acknowledge that other people are not only useful to me but have rights in and for themselves, rights by virtue of which they determine my activity just as much as they are determined by it; if, when I encounter the right of another, I must say to myself, this far and no further—by this very fact I acknowledge in the other something unalterable and unconditional, something that cannot serve as the means of my material interest, and consequently something higher than this interest; the other becomes something sacred to me, that is, ceases to be a thing, becomes a person.[27]

The discovery of the juridical order represents a step forward on the path to realizing an ethical society, a kingdom of ends in which all respect the rightful claims of each, and each the rightful claims of all. But again, the task is more difficult in practice than in theory. The juridical order is no more immune than the economic order to the spell of abstract principles. In the case of law, the warring abstractions are an organic or genetic understanding of law—what Soloviev called the "abstract-historical concept of law"—and the idea of law as an external or mechanical social contract, the "abstract-utilitarian concept of law." He was referring to the split between historicist and rationalist philosophies of law, the former usually linked with Romantic conservatism, the latter with liberalism or revolution.

As always, the partisans of each abstraction tend to be right in what they affirm but wrong in what they suppress or deny. The historicists are right to insist that law does not spring full-grown and armed from the heads of political theorists but is historically embedded. Soloviev, whose debt to Slavophilism has been noted, accepted this point without difficulty. Aboriginally, all law is customary law in which "the principle of justice functions not as a principle that is theoretically grasped but as an immediate moral instinct or practical reason expressing itself in the form of symbols."[28] But historicists err when they suppose that the essence of law is satisfactorily accounted for by its historical origins. This is tantamount to replacing theory of law with history of law, which is to commit the logical error of "taking the origin or genesis of a thing in empirical reality to be the essence of that thing, confusing the historical order with the logical order, and losing the content of a thing in the process through which it is manifested."[29] Although historically conditioned, law possesses formal properties without which it would not be law, properties that are gradually clarified in the historical process itself by the emergence of concepts of personhood and freedom. Here is where the essence of law must be sought.

Still, there is a right way and a wrong way to seek this essence. The wrong way is to seize upon the formal personhood implicit in the concept of law and, isolating it from the historical process, to absolutize it. The sovereign individual who supposedly precedes history and enters into a contract with his fellows as a means of pursuing his ends is an abstraction. Historicists are right to reject it as purely hypothetical, a formula for utopianism. Soloviev sought a middle way between utopianism and Romantic conservatism in a formula acknowledging both the free-personal and the social aspects of law: "*Law is freedom conditioned by equality*," or "*the synthesis of freedom and equality*." [30]

The crafting of a definition of law provided Soloviev with an occasion to clarify his concept of natural law. Soloviev rejected the concept in the sense of an actual ordering of life preceding the rise of political associations in a supposed state of nature. To think of natural law in this way is "to take an intellectual abstraction for reality." But the concept is useful as an expression of the necessary formal properties which positive law must reflect, "to the extent that it is really law and not something else":

> The concepts of personhood, freedom, and equality constitute the essence of so-called natural law. The rational essence of law is distinguished from its historical manifestation, namely positive law. In this sense, natural law is that general algebraic formula into which history inserts the various real quantities of positive law; it exists in reality only as the general form of all positive legal relations, in them and through them. [31]

One of the prominent themes of *The Critique of Abstract Principles* is the essentially negative character of law. The idea is that law sets boundaries and establishes rules but does not prescribe moral content or ends. "For [law] there is no *normative* end, no normative will or intention. Heroic self-sacrifice and selfish calculation make no difference to law; it does not demand the former and does not forbid the latter. A lawful government, in its ordinances, does not and cannot demand that all *should assist* each, and each all; it demands only that no one *should do harm* to anyone else." [32] In *The Justification of the Good* (1897), written much later in his career, Soloviev changed his mind on this point, having come to see that law and morality, while by no means identical, are organically linked in ways that the unsubtle distinctions of *The Critique* failed to accommodate. The rather artificial disjunction of "negative" law from "positive" morality in *The Critique* is probably to be explained by Soloviev's youthful enthusiasm for

Schopenhauer, who made much of the distinction between the supposedly negative ethic of justice and the positive ethic of compassion.[33]

The motivation of Soloviev's negative theory of law seems to be moral and metaphysical rather than juridical, a pretext for an observation about the grandeur and misery of human beings as such. Law is grounded in metaphysical personhood (freedom and reason), the inalienable glory of the human being. But human beings have the capacity to misuse their personhood, "quite fully justifying Mephistopheles' observation in Goethe's *Faust*":

> Ein wenig besser würd' er leben
> Hätt'st Du ihm nicht den Schein des Himmelslichts gegeben;
> Er nennt's Vernunft und braucht's allein,
> Nur tierischer als jedes Tier zu sein.[34]

Thus personhood threatens to collapse into the abyss; the hoped-for kingdom of ends, into a barely domesticated anarchy of interests. This is surely a miserable outcome, unless of course one has overlooked the place where the truly worthy end of human life is to be found. "Unconditional form demands unconditional content. Beyond the legal order, the order of negative means, must stand a positive order defined by an absolute end."[35]

Soloviev was confident about the availability of an absolute end because he had already posited it. The absolute end is the whole of things, the symphonic unity that transcends abstractions, the Living One that gives life to all else.

Soloviev argued the case for the absolute end anthropologically, proceeding from the observable nature of human beings. The paradox of human beings is that they do not seem to be content with being themselves, that is to say, free, rational agents. They are drawn in two other directions as well: to the material world, which they love with a passion, and to the world of divine and demonic forces. "It is impossible to eliminate the fact that the human being appears to himself to be not just a human being but also and equally an animal and a god." The passions of the flesh and "the mystical attractions making [the human being] a divine or demonic being" profoundly complicate human life.[36] To deny these forces is to exchange actual human nature for the abstract model constructed by rationalism.

Mystical attractions are the various ways in which human beings are grasped by the desire to unite with all things, the yearning "to be *all*." In practical terms this can only mean attaching oneself somehow to the whole of things, since it is obvious that "the infinitely small unit" that is a human being cannot in fact be all. The desire to unite with the whole is the essence of what Soloviev calls the "religious principle." The contrast with the juridical order is clear: law demarcates, delimits, distinguishes, divides; religion connects, embraces, unites. Put another way, religion is about love—the loving union realized in "a mystical or religious community, that is to say, *the church*."[37] Loving union with the whole of things is the absolute end.

FREE THEOCRACY

The clarification of the religious principle of love, while revealing the end of life, complicates the actual business of living because of the tension between love and law. The tension would not be a problem if these values could be confined to separate spheres. But this is not possible. The religious and juridical principles are both moral principles; they pertain to "one and the same sphere, namely the sphere of practical, moral or social life." Soloviev regarded attempts to reconcile the two principles through compartmentalization as flawed. For example, he denied "that I could *actually* show Christian love to a neighbor whom, in my capacity as a judge, I send to the gallows." Love and law demand acknowledgment from the same person at the same time in the same society. An "inner, harmonious relation or synthesis" of the two must be established. But how? Soloviev's answer was, through a "free theocracy."[38]

To avoid misunderstanding Soloviev's proposal, it is crucial to underscore the attributive "free." Admittedly, readers who are put off by the term "theocracy" in the first place will regard "free theocracy" as an oxymoron. But Soloviev was quite serious about the idea, taking pains to distinguish it from what he called "false theocracy" or "abstract clericalism." False theocracy results from the absolutization of the religious principle, that is to say, from developing the religious element in human life in isolation from the others and so making it into an abstract principle. This is what happens in traditional theocracies where religious forces dominate all others and dictate to society. The antidote to this pathology is freedom: freedom of conscience first of all, and more generally the freedom to exercise rationality in all sectors of life. Soloviev's conceptuality here parallels his view of the right relationship between the juridical order and economic interest: economic initiative should not be abolished or suppressed by the law, even though law is the higher good. Similarly, the religious principle transcends the juridical, both metaphysically (it expresses the whole of things) and practically (love transcends law). But it must not abolish the juridical order. The juridical order is to be affirmed and incorporated into the free-theocratic synthesis. As Soloviev saw it, a theocracy that violates the free-rational rule of law vitiates not only law but also religion itself and the God it claims to serve. In false theocracy God is reduced to "thunder and lightning which extinguish completely the still small voice of reason and conscience."[39] But reason and conscience, and the material world itself, are God-given. A free theocracy must embrace them fully.

In his criticism of traditional theocracy, Soloviev clearly sought to distance himself from the religious and political conservatives of his day. Yet he also distanced himself from the doctrinaire liberals. Nineteenth-century European liberals, if they did not wish to expel religion from society altogether, usually embraced the formula of "a free church in a free state" to express the proper relationship between the juridical and religious principles. Soloviev rejected this formula. He accepted the need to distinguish between church and state, but not the isolation of the church from the state, which he believed the formula implied. He agreed that in a clericalist theocracy there is not enough space between church and state. But in a secularist liberal state there is not enough interaction. Soloviev believed that a sharp separation between the juridical and religious spheres is unrealistic, for in actual life, religion and law interact in all sorts of concrete ways. They *should* interact, for without a dynamic relationship, no synthesis of elements can be achieved. Of course, the synthesis must be realized in such a way as to affirm the ultimacy of the religious principle in the hierarchy of values. Otherwise the more inclusive principle is subordinated to the less. Soloviev preached theocracy, not nomocracy.

Soloviev knew that many modern legal and political thinkers rejected a value hierarchy grounded in religion, viewing "the state as the highest and final form of human society and the universal kingdom of law as the apogee of human history."[40] This statist ultimate would be valid only if human beings were free-rational creatures and nothing more. But they are more. A human being is *"a being comprising in himself* (in the absolute order) *a divine idea*, that is to say, *the whole of things* or unconditional fullness of being, *and realizing* this idea (in the natural order) *by means of rational freedom in material nature."*[41] Creatures with such an all-embracing nature need more than the state to order their affairs and give them peace; they need a church that embraces the whole of life from its material surface to its divine ground. Beyond a just society, they need a loving community; beyond their fellow human beings, fellowship with God; beyond the kingdom of ends, the kingdom of God.

Historical imagination is required to appreciate what Soloviev's theocracy meant in his time and how it might be relevant to the twenty-first century world. Soloviev actually lived in a kind of theocracy, for in the nineteenth-century, Russia was still an Orthodox Christian empire. Only secularized elites and the religious minorities questioned the arrangement. Most Russians along with their rulers regarded themselves as trustees of Orthodoxy (to them, true Christianity). Placing Soloviev's free theocracy against this background, one can see that his project was to a considerable extent a critical enterprise. Soloviev challenged his compatriots to measure the existing theocracy against the ideal concept. So, for example, Soloviev argued that freedom of conscience was an essential requirement in a true theocracy; yet there was no freedom of conscience in the Russian Empire in his lifetime. He argued that the free exercise of reason and the healthy pursuit of material interests without ascetical interference were consistent with a true theocracy, but these prescriptions hardly described the conditions of intellectual and social life in tsarist Russia. An essentially prophetic idea, Soloviev's *free* theocracy challenged the status quo.

At the same time, by preaching free *theocracy*, Soloviev made it clear that he did not finally agree with the secularist critics of Russia. The need for an establishment of religious values at the heart of society seemed clear to him; and that this establishment should be sealed by a Christian monarchy was agreeable to him as well. His celebrated appeal to Alexander III to spare the regicides of 1881 assumed the existence of a Christian monarch. Soloviev did not wish to abolish the office but to reinvigorate it. Although he became more critical of the tsarist state later in his career, Soloviev never embraced republicanism or "post-Constantinian" Christianity, nor for that matter did many of his heirs in the next generation. In the essay on Leo XIII in this volume, Russell Hittinger traces the elimination of national churches and "political Christendom" in nineteenth-century Catholicism leading to the view that the church is not in the state, nor the state in the church.[42] No such process was at work in nineteenth-century Orthodoxy, and even the catastrophes of the twentieth century have not completely dislodged the idea of a national church. Soloviev presents a good example of the ideal of national or Constantinian Christianity in action.

Besides his Constantinianism, Soloviev's theocratism was a response to the idea of the kingdom of God in the gospel. By recognizing the centrality of the kingdom in the Christian message, Soloviev was ahead of his time. The majority of Christian theologians and ethicists in the nineteenth century were tone-deaf to the theocratic theme in the gospel. For them, Jesus preached an inner, spiritual kingdom that was to be sharply distinguished from the supposedly crude, nationalist theocracy of the Jews. Soloviev rejected this one-sided spiritualizing of the gospel along with its anti-Semitic implications. In this he anticipated Albert Schweitzer and others who rediscovered the Jewish apocalyptic roots of Christianity at the turn of the century. He also anticipated twentieth-century theologians such as Reinhold Niebuhr, Martin Luther King, and John Howard Yoder, who demonstrated the political seriousness of the gospel.[43]

Soloviev's theocratism also expressed his vision of a universal love ethic as the practical essence of Christianity. Soloviev did not believe that a love ethic could be grounded in either the natural-economic or the rational-

550 ◆ PAUL VALLIERE

juridical order of things. In the natural order, love occurs as an instinct or passion, but there is no way to build an ethic of *universal* love ("the inner, essential solidarity of all things") on this foundation. Love as an instinct is too random; its range of application is too narrow. One naturally loves family, friends, close neighbors—but "all and each?" A love ethic cannot be grounded in the rational-juridical order of things, either. Here human beings are recognized as free rational agents; but there is no love, not even in the form of instinct or passion. The rational order of things is just that: rational, intellectual. Human beings are not appreciated as "living people but only as abstract juridical persons" by virtue of the characteristics they share with all other human beings. It cannot be otherwise. The grandeur of the rational-juridical order lies precisely in its generality and impersonality, its applicability to all human beings regardless of their preferences, passions, loves, or hates. Proclaiming love as the constitutive principle of the rational order of things would be the philosophical equivalent of a judge or jury deciding cases on the basis of their personal feelings for the individuals involved.[44]

The true ground of love lies in the mystical or divine order of things. To function as a moral principle as distinguished from an accidental passion, love must be "at one and the same time *a living personal force and a universal law.*" But this is nothing less than a description of God, the absolute ground of being. Love in the natural world is a force but not a universal law, and its personal status is moot. In the rational order of things there is universal law but no love, indeed no actual living beings. God is both love and law. This is a unity transcending reason, which is why Soloviev describes it as "mystical," or, in the social-political context, "theocratic." An ethic of universal love is an ethic of absolute relatedness or connectedness. One loves and serves one's fellow human beings as ends in themselves when one recognizes them as ends in God, acknowledging them as beings with the "power to become children of God" (John 1:12), beings whose destiny is theosis.[45]

The concept of theonomy, a terminological cousin of theocracy, might shed light on what Soloviev has in mind. The term came into currency in English-speaking theology thanks to Paul Tillich, whose thought resembles Soloviev's in a number of ways. Tillich's project in ethics and social philosophy was to transcend the antagonism between heteronomy (Soloviev's false theocracy) and autonomy (Soloviev's rational-juridical order) in an ethic of theonomy (Soloviev's theocracy of love). A theonomous ethic retains the virtues of heteronomy and autonomy (reverence and freedom) while shedding the defects (authoritarianism and selfishness) and leading us through love to the divine ground of being. Theonomy may be a better name for Soloviev's ideal than theocracy, which suggests a vicariate of some kind.[46]

JUSTICE AS THE FRAMEWORK OF LOVE

What is the impact of an ethic of universal love on law? In the history of religion and ethics, preachers of universal love have often been suspicious of law, even contemptuous of it. In Russia, Leo Tolstoy preached a Christian ethic that rejected the legal system and the state as such. Soloviev saw the matter differently. True, love stands above law in Soloviev's hierarchy of values. But unlike thinkers for whom hierarchy is a pretext for forgetting about everything below the apex, Soloviev recognized that the point of a hierarchy is to do justice to all its components. The ideal of universal love springs from the ecstatic connectedness of human beings to the divine ground of being, but this love cannot be actualized by human beings as it is in the divine ground. That would be possible only if human beings had already achieved theosis; but in fact they are unfinished creatures. Therefore universal love, although inspired from above ("mystically"), must be sought in and through engagement with the economic and juridical spheres.

Soloviev's point can be seen in his interpretation of the biblical account of the creation of human beings. In Genesis 1–2 human beings are said to be created "from the dust of the earth," "in [God's] image," and "according to [God's] likeness." Soloviev insisted that all three points are essential to a proper understanding of human nature. As dust of the earth, human beings are weak and imperfect, separated from God. As bearers of the image of God, they are endowed with the idea of perfection, a vision of the goodness and beauty which they lack. As shaped by the "likeness" of God, human beings are filled with the desire to conform themselves to the divine image, to be assimilated to the divine beauty. Three moments of moral experience follow from these determinations: confession of imperfection, contemplation of perfection, and the process of actually becoming perfect.[47] All three moments are important. A corresponding relatedness exists between the economic, juridical, and religious spheres.

In the case of love and law, Soloviev formulated the right relationship as: *"justice is the necessary framework of love."* [48] That is to say, love without respect for law will be defective, cut loose from its moorings in the ontological hierarchy and doomed to distortion through sentimentalization, self-deception, demonic obsession, or other pathologies. For example, one's love is defective if one loves a person without respecting that person's rights. That is how slave owners and serf owners "loved" their servants. A human being is a free, rational creature; and a free, rational creature, as juridical theory makes plain, is a creature endowed with inalienable rights. To violate these rights, or not to perceive them in the first place, amounts to treating a human being as something other than a human being. No appeal to "love" can rectify this original wrong. Justice is the indispensable framework of human relations.

LAW AND THE GOOD

Soloviev's most developed philosophy of law is found in his magnum opus, *The Justification of the Good* (1897), and in *Law and Morality*, a collection of essays that came out the same year.[49] In both works Soloviev treated philosophy of law as a branch of moral philosophy. The task of moral philosophy is "the justification of the Good." But what is the Good? And what does it mean to justify it?

By the Good, Soloviev meant the source of all value, that which lends meaning to the whole of life, the Good as distinguished from goods. All human beings recognize certain goods; but a list of goods does not address the issue of goodness as such. Goods, viewed analytically, are partial; they do not embrace the whole of life. The moral philosopher is looking for that which ties the partial goods together. To put it in Tillichian language, the moral philosopher seeks the ultimate concern of human beings as moral agents.

Many moral philosophers would reject this line of inquiry because it assumes that only an overarching Good can satisfy the human moral quest. What warrants this assumption? Soloviev believed it is warranted by the nature and destiny of human beings:

> "Know ye not that we shall judge angels?" [1 Cor. 6:3] St. Paul writes to the faithful. And if even the heavenly things are subject to our judgment, this is still more true of all earthly things. Man is in principle or in his destination an *unconditional* inner form of the good as an unconditional content; all else is conditioned and relative.[50]

Here Soloviev stepped forward in the mantle of theocratic prophecy and Orthodox mysticism to relate the justification of the Good not just to the partial, unfinished world of the present, but also to the consummated kingdom of God. Human beings are conditioned by nature and history but open to eternity, destined for theosis. They bear the unconditional form of the unconditional Good.

The unconditional Good as Soloviev envisioned it bears three characteristics, all of which have ethical relevance:

> The good as such is not conditioned by anything, but itself conditions all things, and is realized through all things. In so far as the good is not condi-

tioned by anything, it is *pure*; in so far as it conditions all things, it is *all-embracing*; and in so far as it is realized through all things, it is *all-powerful*.[51]

Without a standard of purity, human beings cannot make the clear distinction between good and evil that is the essence of moral choice. Without the all-inclusiveness of the Good, morality breaks up into mutually contradictory demands. "Finally, if the good had no power, if it could not in the end triumph over everything, including 'the last enemy death' [1 Cor. 15:26]—life would be in vain."[52] Such is the Good, which the moral philosopher seeks to know. Most people call it God.

If the Good is God, what did Soloviev mean by justification? Did he presume to justify God? His preface to the second edition of *The Justification of the Good* sheds light on the question:

> The object of this book is *to show the good as truth and righteousness*, that is, as the only right and consistent way of life in all things and to the end, for all who decide to follow it. I mean the Good *as such*; it alone justifies itself and justifies our confidence in it. And it is not for nothing that before the open grave, when all else has obviously failed, we call to this essential Good and say, "Blessed art Thou, O Lord, for Thou has taught [me] Thy justification" [Ps. 119:12].[53]

Soloviev was not proposing to justify the ways of God to man. The Good justifies *itself*. Human beings are justified by standing in a relationship to the Good, for which Soloviev finds the paradigm at the utter limit of human life where human weakness cannot be denied, but where the deceased nevertheless "speaks" from the dust through the mouth of the priest to bless God in the words of the great Psalm of the Law. The Slavonic version of Psalms 119:12 pertains to the title of Soloviev's book: "teach me thy justification" (*nauchi mia opravdaniem Tvoim*; Hebr. "thy statutes"), that is, teach me to see and acknowledge you rather than miss you, to see you as the Good. This is the Orthodox contemplative version of what Protestants call justification by faith. Human beings do not justify the Good by doing it. If that were true, the Good would depend on human beings, whereas the opposite is the case.

A word of clarification is required here, however. One should not suppose that appreciating the Good *in itself* means regarding the Good *by itself*, that is to say, construing it in isolation from the world. It is possible to think about the Good in this way, but the consequence of such thinking is to reduce the Good to an abstract principle. Because human life is embodied and historical, seeing the Good means seeing it in and through the world, seeing the Good in all things and all things in the Good. This is not easy to do precisely because of the embodied character of human life with its pressures and distractions. But prayer, religious instruction, and moral philosophy can help.

The connectedness of the Good to the world, that is, the fullness and wholeness (*vseedinstvo*) of the Good, is the primary focus of *The Justification of the Good*. The themes of purity and power receive less attention. Soloviev believed that the purity of the Good received unsurpassed treatment in Kant's moral philosophy. Soloviev did not try to better the German master on this point. But Kant did not investigate how the Good enters into the immense process of life. His moral vision, while beautiful in formal terms, lacked actuality and suffered from formalism. Soloviev proposed to focus on the actualization of the Good through the "complete and exhaustive moral norms for all the fundamental practical relations of individual and collective life."[54]

The Justification of the Good, in its very title, shows how far Soloviev stood from anything resembling a divine command theory of ethics. The idea that morality means doing what God commands raises the question that Socrates and Euthyphro debated more than two millennia ago: is something good because God commands it, or does God command it because it is good? For Soloviev, the very form of the question is wrong because it dissociates in principle what is never dissociated in actuality, namely, God and the Good. God and the Good are the same ultimate reality and are differentiated only perspectivally depending on the aspect of the whole of things under consideration in a given context. In a work of moral philosophy, the Good is the appropriate term. Hence Socrates was right to argue against Euthyphro that God commands only the good and, in the *Republic*, to argue that God is good. However, this must not be taken to mean that the Good is something other than God, since the Good as Plato and Soloviev described it—the unconditionally pure, full, ever-living source of all value—is obviously divine. To posit God apart from the Good or the Good apart form God is to create abstract principles, to generate the anticosmic ideologies of godless humanism (autonomy) and goodless religion (heteronomy). Both fail to do justice to the presence of God/Good in the actual grace-filled world.

The Russian word for grace, *blagodat'*, is helpful on this point. The term is a compound of *blago* ("good") and *dat'* ("give"); hence, the good that is given, or good gift. Western and especially Protestant theories of grace emphasize the act of giving as opposed to the gift. The Russian term suggests a more balanced view: grace is the free act of giving but also that which is given, namely the Good.[55] In adopting this view, Soloviev affirmed the traditional understanding of grace in the Orthodox tradition. The anticosmic dualism of nature and grace so common in Western theology is foreign to Orthodoxy, ancient and modern.

An oblique illustration of the difference between East and West on this point is found in Leslie Griffin's essay on Pope John XXIII included in this volume. Griffin cites Cardinal Suenens's attempt to express what was special about Angelo Roncalli:

> If one had to express it all in one word, it seems to me that one could say that John XXIII was a man surprisingly natural and at the same time supernatural. Nature and grace produced in him a living unity filled with charm and surprises. Everything about him sprang from a single source. In a completely natural way he was supernatural. He was natural with such a supernatural spirit that no one detected a distinction between the two.[56]

From an Orthodox point of view the only problem here is that the cardinal treats as an exception what should be seen as the rule, that is, as the norm of creation and sanctification alike. "A living unity [of nature and grace] filled with charm and surprises" is a good description of what the whole cosmos looked like in the beginning, still looks like in the lives of the saints and will look like in a more wonderful way in the realized kingdom of God.

THE PRIMARY DATA OF MORALITY

The Justification of the Good is a massive work, but its design is economical. Soloviev divided his subject into three parts: the Good in human nature, the Good from God, and the Good in the course of history. That is to say, one may see the Good in humanity, in divinity and in the divine-human process.

In this book Soloviev approached the discussion of human nature in a rather unexpected way. Rather than capturing his subject in a formal definition as he did in *The Critique of Abstract Principles*, or through a metaphysical doctrine of freedom, or a theological affirmation of the image of God, Soloviev undertook a quasi-empirical investigation of what he called "the primary data of morality."[57] By these he meant universally observable facts of human behavior that betoken moral consciousness and serve as the foundation for the higher moral principles. The three primary data are shame, compassion, and reverence. Shame, which expresses itself first of all in sexual modesty, is the evidence that human beings regard themselves as beings transcending material nature. The moral principle that arises from shame is asceticism (discipline, self-control). Compassion for suffering companions shows that human beings are other-regarding creatures cognizant of the neighbor's right to exist. The moral principle here is justice. Reverence, appearing first in the awe that children feel toward their parents, shows that human beings seek an object of worship. From reverence comes piety, or the religious principle. Taken together, the three principles define the right relationship to the whole of life: to nature through asceticism; to human beings through justice; to God through worship.

Soloviev used this scheme once before, in *The Spiritual Foundations of Life* (1882–84), where he described spirituality as consisting of prayer, sacrifice or almsgiving, and fasting.[58] The order is reversed, but the terms are the same: reverence, compassion, and shame.

In *The Spiritual Foundations of Life* Soloviev's purpose was edification, not systematic philosophy. In *The Justification of the Good*, however, Soloviev took as his task to show that the "primary data" are universal and logically bound to the principles he derived from them. This was not easy to do, as critics were quick to point out. In a long and extremely negative review of *The Justification of the Good*, the distinguished political and legal philosopher Boris Chicherin argued that Soloviev's treatment of the supposedly primary data of morality was arbitrary.[59] Take the case of shame. Soloviev believed that the modesty human beings feel about sexuality betokens an awareness of their transcendence over material nature, hence the beginnings of asceticism. Even if we grant that feelings of modesty toward sex are universal—a proposition that field anthropologists would have to evaluate—Chicherin pointed out that other reasons besides asceticism could be adduced to explain it. Far from implying transcendence *over* material nature, sexual restraint might be a biological adaptation to protect health and further the enjoyment *of* material nature. Chicherin also rejected the notion that shame as a moral phenomenon implies asceticism. Human beings often feel shame because of a deficit of passions or possessions: shame over weakness, poverty, sexual inadequacy, and so on. Chicherin accused Soloviev of making an unwarranted leap from behavioral fact (if it *is* a fact) to moral principle. The same problem attended Soloviev's move from natural compassion to justice and right, and his attempt to ground belief in God in a feeling of awe rather than in reason. Chicherin believed that Soloviev had been seduced by "the empiricist school now holding sway" in European intellectual culture. For Chicherin, what is needed in moral philosophy is not just facts—a "shaky foundation" for systematic thought—but first principles, or metaphysics.[60]

It is not difficult to appreciate Chicherin's criticism of Soloviev's account of primordial human nature. That Soloviev discovered three "primary data" of morality—not two, or four, or more—is obviously related to his abstract outline: morality in relation to that which is below human beings (material nature), on a par (fellow humans), and above them (God). The outline is elegant but can scarcely be said to emerge from an investigation of facts. The facts have been selected to fit the outline. Still, it is worth asking why

Soloviev began his most comprehensive work of moral philosophy in this way.[61] Chicherin's explanation—that Soloviev was seduced by empiricism—is implausible. The thinker who inspired the passionate interest in God, freedom, and immortality in the Russian religious-philosophical renaissance of the next generation was not blind to the metaphysics of morals.

One way of accounting for Soloviev's treatment of human nature in *The Justification of the Good* is to see it as an experiment in embodied or applied metaphysics, a rudimentary phenomenology. One must remember that Soloviev's aim in *The Justification of the Good* was not to make the theoretical case for God, freedom, and immortality but to show how God, freedom, and immortality enter into actual human experience. It is appropriate, then, that the author began his book not with first principles but with first phenomena; and in point of fact *The Justification of the Good* is one of the most concrete works in the Solovievian corpus. A wide range of social issues, including nationalism, crime and punishment, war, and economic justice, is discussed.

LAW AND COLLECTIVE EVIL

Given that the issues treated in *The Justification of the Good* have to do mainly with public order, it is not surprising that Soloviev also devoted a good deal of attention to law. Soloviev's interest in "collective evil" (*sobiratel'noe zlo*) reinforced his attention to the subject: if collective evil demands attention, so presumably does the collective norm-setting designed to combat it.[62] The fact that Soloviev recognized collective evil as a matter demanding attention in its own right is significant in itself. Many nineteenth-century Christian moralists regarded social morality as an extension of individual morality. Soloviev rejected such "abstract subjectivism."[63]

Soloviev identified three quintessential manifestations of collective evil in society: the immoral relations between nations, between society and the criminal, and between social classes. The first evil manifested itself in nationalism; the second, in vengeful and punitive judicial practices such as capital punishment; the third, in economic injustice, the coexistence of luxury and squalor. A separate chapter of *The Justification of the Good* was devoted to each of these problems.[64]

On the national question Soloviev tried to steer a middle course between nationalism and cosmopolitanism (the latter based on "the abstract *man in general* of the philosophers and jurists"). The evangelical commandment to love one's neighbor as oneself transcends national boundaries and rules out national egoism. However, the actual neighbor is never an abstract being but is always embedded in a specific tribe, people, or nation. Therefore the evangelical commandment must also be taken to mean: "Love all other nations as your own." While the Christian is not called to be a "human being in general" (*obshchechelovek*), he is called to be a "pan-human" or "universal man" (*vsechelovek*). Soloviev preached a pluralist, historically concrete internationalism.[65]

A full discussion of internationalism and international law is not found in *The Justification of the Good*, although Soloviev dealt with these subjects by implication in his late essays on war. A chapter on war forms part of *The Justification of the Good*,[66] and his last book, *Three Dialogues on War, Progress and the End of World History, with a Brief Tale of the Anti-Christ* (1899–1900), offered a fuller discussion of the same theme.[67] In both essays, Soloviev aimed to challenge Tolstoyan pacifism, then at the height of its popularity in Russia. Soloviev's argument was simple and sobering: that Christian love requires us to protect the defenseless when it is in our power to do so, by force if necessary. Or more colorfully: after the murder of Abel by Cain, "justly fearing lest the same thing should happen to Seth and other peaceful men, the guardian angels of humanity mixed clay with copper and iron and created the soldier and the policeman."[68] In *Three Dialogues* Soloviev used a recent historical example: the ethnic cleansing of Armenia by Turkish and Kurdish irregulars during the Russo-Turkish War of 1877–78, a wound reopened by the Armenian Massacres of 1895. As a nineteenth-century progressivist, Soloviev believed strongly in "the approaching end of [all] wars," but he also believed that "it would be irrational ... to think and to act as though that approaching end had already come."[69]

Soloviev's views on war were not always well received by the liberal Christian circles that were his natural audience. The reservations expressed by the reviewer of *The Justification of the Good* in the official journal of the Moscow Theological Academy, *The Theological Herald*, are a case in point. The reviewer recognized that in *Justification of the Good* Soloviev was attempting to make the case for the "relative good" against absolutists of various types, but he felt that the clarity of the evangelical love ethic was sometimes obscured rather than illuminated by Soloviev's moderation. The critic was prepared to acknowledge that war had brought certain benefits to civilization; however,

> this does not prevent us from feeling greater sympathy for those moralists who actively summon us to cast off this inhuman means of civilization than for those who try to sooth our conscience by pointing out that the individual soldier does not harbor evil intentions toward any particular human being, "especially with the present method of fighting by means of guns and cannons against an enemy who is too far off to be *seen.*" We agree with Mr. Soloviev

that one cannot survive without the "relative good." But a moralist should be as careful as possible with his "justification" because, having set foot on this slippery slope, it is easy to go too far.[70]

In his treatment of criminal justice Soloviev again attempted to steer a middle course between Tolstoyan Christianity, which rejected criminal law, and its opposite, the traditional view of justice as vengeance or retribution. Both extremes fail to see the essential hallmark of justice, which is not force or retribution but "right." In a system of criminal justice there are three rights to be reckoned with: the right of the injured party to defense and compensation; the right of society to security; and the right of the criminal "to correction and reformation."[71] The first two rights are universally accepted. The third is controversial, for it entails rejecting judicial practices that assail the humanity of the criminal. These include not just bloody and cruel acts of vengeance but also any type of punishment that treats the offender simply as a means to an end. This is why Soloviev rejected capital punishment. The traditional justification of the practice in terms of vengeance or retribution clearly violates the principle of right, which is the basis of justice. The modern argument for the death penalty as a deterrent is equally bad in his opinion because it reduces a human being to the status of a means only and so undermines the common good:

> The common good is *common* only because it contains in itself the good of all individual persons without exception—otherwise it would be only the good of the majority.... But from the concept of the *common* good [it] follows with logical necessity that, while limiting particular interests and aspirations precisely as common (by common boundaries), it in no way can abolish even one bearer of personal freedom, or subject of rights, taking from him life and the very possibility of free action. The common good, according to its very idea, should be the good *of this man too.*[72]

The penal system should instruct and correct the offender, not destroy him. Since correction implies the possibility of repentance and amendment of life, Soloviev also rejected mandatory life imprisonment.

In *Law and Morality*, Soloviev offered a biblical argument against capital punishment that is worth pausing over as a good example of his hermeneutics as well as of his position on the judicial issue. Soloviev regarded the Bible as the book that brought humanity out of the realm of "savage religion and religious savagery" to a kingdom of mercy and universal reconciliation. As far as capital punishment is concerned, Soloviev identified three crucial moments in biblical history: the punishment of Cain, which is reserved to God alone (Gen. 4:15); the institution of retributive justice after the Flood, an accommodation continued in the Mosaic Law; and a "return to the norm" in the prophets of Israel and in the gospel, both of which proclaim that God, and God alone, will repay sinners, and will repay them according to the principle, "I desire mercy, and not sacrifice" (Matt. 9:13 and 12:7; cf. Hosea 6:6). Soloviev was convinced that a person who considers the biblical evidence as a whole rather than seizing on bits and pieces of text will conclude that capital punishment violates the divine norm:

> The Bible is a complex spiritual organism which developed over a thousand years. It is completely free of external monotony and unilinearity but amazing in its internal unity and in the harmony of the whole. To snatch out arbitrarily from this whole only intermediate parts without a beginning and an end is an insincere and frivolous business; and to rely on the *Bible in general* in favor of the death penalty—attests either to a hopeless incomprehension or a boundless insolence. Those who, like Joseph de Maistre, draw together the concept of the death penalty with the concept of a sin offering, forget that a sin offering has already been brought for all by Christ, that it has abolished all other blood sacrifices, and itself continues only in the bloodless Eucharist—an amazing lapse in consciousness on the part of persons who confess the Christian faith. Indeed, to permit any kind of sin offerings still—means to deny that which was accomplished by Christ, which means—to betray Christianity.[73]

ECONOMIC JUSTICE

Soloviev dealt with the issue of economic justice as he dealt with criminal justice: by seeking a middle way transcending one-sided approaches, in this case a way between capitalism and socialism. Once again Soloviev evinced no sympathy for unregulated market capitalism. The dislocations of early capitalism were everywhere to be seen in the big cities of Russia in the 1890s. A justification of the Good that validated plutocracy, pauperism, and other economic pathologies by invoking the "laws" of economics would be as great a travesty as pietistic theodicies that present cosmic and historical catastrophes as evidence of God's plan for the world. Even if capitalists could demonstrate beyond a reasonable doubt that the prosperity of the many was the certain outcome of the suffering of the few, their system would still be wrong for the same reason that capital punishment is wrong: it reduces some human beings to the status of a means only. The common good is "the good of all and each and not of the majority only."[74]

Applying this criterion to economic relations generally, Soloviev formulated the most celebrated concept in *The Justification of the Good*: the right of human beings to a "dignified" or "worthy" existence.[75] Human beings should live decently. An economy that makes degradation a condition of survival is immoral, and collective action should be taken to change it. "The duty of society is to recognize and to secure to each of its members the *right* to enjoy unmolested *worthy* human existence both for himself and his family."[76] "To recognize and to *secure*": Soloviev's emphasis on securing decent economic circumstances for all clearly implied the need for social and economic legislation, law being the arrangement that guarantees a certain outcome as opposed to merely recommending it.

Because of his interest in economic legislation, Soloviev has been called a "new liberal" to distinguish him from classical liberals like Chicherin.[77] The term also distinguishes Soloviev from the socialists of his day. While there is much in his criticism of capitalism that approximates socialism, Soloviev never accepted the economic determinism of socialism. He rejected its radical egalitarianism as well. "It is one thing to strive for an impossible and unnecessary equalization of property, and another, while preserving the advantages of larger property to those who have it, to recognize the right of everyone to the necessary means of worthy human existence."[78] Not equality but dignity should be the aim of economic legislation. Soloviev was an early advocate of what came to be called the democratic welfare state.[79]

Soloviev's concept of the right to a dignified existence resulted from the synthesis of his idea of law with the patristic concept of human nature as capable of theosis. Soloviev invoked the concept in the chapter on economic justice in *The Justification of the Good*:

> The absolute value of man is based, as we know, upon the *possibility* inherent in his reason and his will of infinitely approaching perfection or, according to the patristic expression, the possibility of becoming divine (*theosis*). This possibility does not pass into actuality completely and immediately, for if it did man would be already equal to God—which is not the case. The inner potentiality *becomes* more and more actual, and can only do so under definite real conditions.[80]

To appreciate the appeal to theosis here, one must keep two things in mind. First, before the revival of contemplative monasticism in nineteenth-century Russia and the labors of twentieth-century patristics scholars, the concept of theosis was in deep eclipse, even in Orthodox theology. Soloviev was one of the first modern thinkers to recognize the distinctiveness and vast implications of the idea. Second, it is highly unusual to come across the patristic concept of theosis, or any other patristic concept for that matter, in a discussion of economic justice. The paragraph quoted above comes from a passage where Soloviev discussed social statistics that show a correlation between income level and life expectancy in modern society. By interjecting the concept of theosis into this discussion, Soloviev drew on patristic piety to protest dehumanizing social conditions and so managed to connect the *summum bonum* of contemplative monks with the travails of the working class in Paris and Petersburg. Soloviev had the natural-born philosopher's ability to make connections between things that seem to most people to lie worlds apart. One can begin to appreciate why it was Soloviev and not someone else who inspired the Russian religio-philosophical renaissance of the early twentieth century. Soloviev showed that it was possible to overcome extremes, to reconcile opposites: Gospel and law, church and world, contemplation and social action, Orthodoxy and humanism, God and human beings. Soloviev loved the Good—*all* of it.[81]

Another unusual feature of Soloviev's discussion of economic issues is a fledgling environmentalist ethic. The right to a dignified existence involves the right of human beings to use nature for human ends. However, Soloviev did not regard this right as validating the unlimited exploitation of nature, nor did he regard the relationship between human beings and nature as unilateral. The right relationship between human beings and nature is neither submission nor exploitation but "looking after [nature] for one's own and its [own] sake."[82] The phraseology (*ukhazhivanie za [prirodoi] dlia sebia i dlia nee*) suggests a relationship of mutuality and intimacy. Soloviev even extended the concept of "right" to the material world, as when he wrote that "matter has a right to be spiritualized by man," suggesting a prophetic vision of nature as destined for more than it has yet become. This vision underlies Soloviev's assertion that "without loving nature for its own sake one cannot organize material life in a moral way."[83] This was an unusual claim to make in a discussion of economic justice in late-nineteenth-century Europe. Not just capitalists but even most socialists at the time assumed that nature existed solely to be exploited by human beings. Soloviev anticipated environmentalism, and more. As a recent Russian commentator observed, Soloviev's vision of the spiritualization of nature is "a cause in comparison with which the objectives of contemporary ecology seem rather modest."[84] Soloviev's environmentalism was inspired by the Pauline vision of the whole creation being destined to share in "the glorious liberty of the children of God" (Rom. 8:21).

LAW, MORALITY, AND THE CHURCH

Soloviev's view of the relation between law and morality in *The Justification of the Good* advanced beyond his position in *The Critique of Abstract Principles*. In the *Critique* Soloviev emphasized the gap between law and morality by contrasting the formal character of law with the substantive values of morality. He had little to say about how law and morality should interact concretely, even though his theocratic ideal demanded such interaction. In *The Justification of the Good* he saw a substantive relationship between law and morality, defining law as the "compulsory demand for the realization of a definite minimum of good, or for a social order which excludes certain manifestations of evil."[85] This definition rules out the view of law as a framework that can accommodate any end; law is now seen as comprising normative ends, albeit minimally conceived.[86] As we have seen, *The Justification of the Good* presented a remarkably concrete exposition of some of the moral ends that a legal order can promote in various spheres of life.

A tension between law and morality endures in the notions of a "minimum" of good and "[only] certain manifestations" of evil, restrictions which morality in its purest form would reject. Moral demands are unlimited, never finished, and effected voluntarily. "Be perfect, therefore, as your heavenly Father is perfect" (Matt. 5:48) is the standard.[87] Legal demands, by contrast, are limited, realizable, and compulsory.[88] Laws must be precise and doable; and they must actually effect, by force if necessary, the minimal good that is their raison d'être. If these characteristics are lacking, one is dealing with something other than law, or with defective laws.

The tension between law and morality need not lead to a divorce, however. Soloviev construed the evangelical call to perfection in such a way as to allow relative ethical goods including law to be affirmed:

> The *absolute* moral principle, the *demand*, namely, or the *commandment* to be perfect as our Father in heaven is perfect, or to realize in ourselves the image and likeness of God, already contains in its very nature the recognition of the *relative* element in morality. For it is clear that the demand for perfection can only be addressed to a being who is imperfect; urging him to *become* like the higher being, the commandment presupposes the lower stages and the relative degrees of advance.[89]

As a relative good, law pertains to imperfect beings. Yet as his words show, Soloviev viewed imperfection optimistically: the imperfect beings are *advancing*, heeding an upward call, participating in a process of transformation extending from here to eternity. This faith helped Soloviev to achieve his nuanced appreciation of law in *The Justification of the Good*, vindicating law as an ethical "minimum" without severing its connection to the moral and spiritual maximum.

The church has an indispensable role to play in the "moral organization of humanity as a whole," as the last chapter of *The Justification of the Good* is entitled. The church "indicates the general direction of the goodwill of mankind and the final purpose of its historical activity." Without the church and the kingdom to which it bears witness, the end of life would be opaque; history would lack a moral compass. For this reason "the state recognizes the supreme spiritual authority of the universal Church" in the moral ordering of life as Soloviev imagined it. However, this does not mean that the church may use state power to advance its mission. "The Church must have no power of compulsion, and the power of compulsion exercised by the state must have nothing to do with the domain of religion."[90] The reason for these restrictions is that piety resembles morality rather than law: it is unlimited, unfinished, and voluntarily effected. And of course the object of piety must never be construed as a "minimum." God is unlimited, unfathomable, and free, and so are the demands of piety. Soloviev's long-standing advocacy of freedom of religion in the Russian Empire also underlay his position here.

Whether Soloviev ever envisioned the formal separation of church and state is debatable. Most interpreters have emphasized the contrast between his earlier works and *The Justification of the Good*, construing the former as vehicles of theocratic utopianism, the latter as evidence of the "dissolution of theocratic views."[91] Yet the status of theocracy in Soloviev's later works has not been adequately clarified. The issue is what Soloviev meant in practical terms when he wrote that "the state recognizes the supreme spiritual authority of the universal Church." Walicki claims that, for the later Soloviev, "free theocracy was, so to speak, stripped of its millenarian features and reduced to something like a Kantian 'regulative idea' in ethics."[92] But this seems to understate the case in order to make Soloviev more acceptable to a secularist audience. In the closing pages of *The Justification of the Good* Soloviev still wrote of a "Christian state" whose "progressive task" is "to prepare humanity and the whole earth for the Kingdom of God."[93] He still entrusted the moral organization of humanity to the "harmonious cooperation" of prophet, priest, and king.[94] Is this language merely ornamentation for a proto-secular ideal? In a perverse way Boris Chicherin may have been closer to the truth when he criticized the author of *The Justification of the Good* for taking positions "which Torquemada could adopt."[95] It was an unfair comparison, of course, and would have been unfair even if Chicherin were discussing Soloviev's earlier works. Soloviev never preached clericalism, far less the Inquisition, but always a "free" theocracy. Still, Chicherin saw something that Soloviev's cultured admirers tend to minimize or to miss: for all its modernism and moderation, *The Justification of the Good* remains the work of a mystic, a prophet, and a Christian theocrat.[96]

An arresting example of the impact of Soloviev's strong Christian faith on his view of the legal order is found in his observations on Plato's *Laws* in a late essay.[97] The case is all the more poignant because of the similarity between Plato's *Laws* and Soloviev's *Justification of the Good*. Both are essays of applied ethics in which an aging philosopher attempts "to reconcile [his] ideal with practicality, combining minimalism in the former sphere with maximalism in the latter."[98] Soloviev gave a sobering account of the path that led the Plato of the *Laws*, like so many thinkers after him, to absolutize the legal and political order. Smitten as a young man by the goodness, truth, and beauty revealed in Socrates, Plato became increasingly frustrated by his inability to realize these values in the world of flesh and blood, leading him first, in the *Republic*, to accommodate such dubious means of social order as slavery, war, and tyranny, and finally, in the *Laws*, to advocate the death penalty for "any man who rejects or upsets the authority of the ancestral laws, both relative to the gods and relative to the public order.... Thus the greatest disciple of Socrates, who had been called to independent philosophical creativity by his indignation at the *legal* murder of his teacher, toward the end totally rests on the point of view of Anytos and Melitos, who had obtained the death sentence for Socrates precisely because of his liberal attitude to the established religious-civil order." Why did this happen? It happened, Soloviev believed, because Plato attempted "the *reform* of societal relations" without believing in "the *regeneration* of human nature"; and he did not believe in the regeneration of human nature because he did not know "the One who has the power of resurrection to eternal life." Plato knew Socrates, but not Christ, the "authentic, substantive *God-Man*." The Russian Plato would not make the same mistake. As an Orthodox Christian, he knew the Resurrected One.[99]

SOLOVIEV'S LEGACY

In the conclusion to his monograph on Soloviev's philosophy of law, Hans Helmut Gäntzel offers a generalization that few would dispute: that "the defining characteristic of the whole of Soloviev's philosophy is the unity of faith, science and life." What this means for jurisprudence is "the ultimate grounding of law in morality and, through morality, in the Christian idea of salvation."[100] Soloviev did not construe these connections in such a way as to deny the important analytical and methodological distinctions separating law, morality, and Christian faith; but he rejected all viewpoints, secular or religious, that would absolutize those distinctions. Reality for Soloviev was an ever-flowing stream issuing in the eschatological kingdom of God.

The impact of Soloviev's theo-philosophical vision on Russian intellectual culture in the next generation, usually called the Silver Age (1900–17), was enormous. Within two years of his death, Russian neoidealism issued its manifesto.[101] The young ex-Marxists Sergei Bulgakov and Nicholas Berdyaev began recreating themselves as religious philosophers, soon to be joined by others. The most important work of collective self-criticism in the history of the Russian intelligentsia, *Vekhi* (1909), struck Solovievian chords in essay after essay.[102] Even anti-Solovievian thinkers, such as Lev Shestov, could not escape his influence. Nor was Soloviev's impact limited to philosophers. The Vladimir Soloviev Religious-Philosophical Society that existed in Moscow from 1905 to 1918 numbered prominent cultural figures from many fields among its members or participants, including the poets Aleksandr Blok and Andrei Belyi, the literary critic Viacheslav Ivanov, the painter Mikhail Nesterov, and the composer Aleksandr Scriabin.[103] No Russian philosopher had ever attracted such wide attention.

Of course it was possible to take an interest in Soloviev without paying attention to his philosophy of law. It was easier to appreciate Soloviev's literary criticism, political commentary, and Sophia poems than to plough through the 550 pages of *The Justification of the Good*. Writing in a commemorative volume six months after Soloviev's death, Pavel Novgorodtsev made an observation that applies to Soloviev's readership at all times including our own: "The person who knows Soloviev mainly in terms of his mystical speculations and yearnings will surely be surprised to learn that he was a brilliant and outstanding spokesman for the philosophy of law. It is difficult to see at first just how something as concrete and practical as the idea of law found a place among his reveries and prophecies."[104]

There were important exceptions, however, including Novgorodtsev himself, who was already emerging as one of Russia's leading philosophers of law. Moreover, apart from Soloviev, a new legal consciousness was emerging in Russia at the beginning of the twentieth century. The inauguration of a quasi-constitutional order in 1905–6 strengthened this development, as did the formation of the Constitutional Democratic Party ("Kadets"), which directly or indirectly enjoyed the allegiance of many of Russia's neoidealists and religious philosophers. A little-known fact about Russia's early twentieth-century religious thinkers is that many of them had received academic training in law. Sergei Bulgakov, Evgeny Trubetskoi, Lev Shestov, Ivan Ilyin, and Boris Vysheslavtsev were all graduates of law faculties, while others had studied law at some point in their education. Several of the religious philosophers worked professionally in law and contributed monographs in the field. Even when they chose other paths, however, evidence of a well-formed legal consciousness can usually be found in their work. Most early twentieth-century Russian religious philosophers were comfortable with the view of Orthodoxy as part of a modern legal-constitutional order, a view pioneered by Soloviev.

Among professional church theologians the attitude toward Soloviev ran the gamut from traditionalist censure to deep admiration. Interestingly, the first monograph on Soloviev's philosophy came not from the pen of one of his heirs in the intelligentsia but from a teacher in a provincial Orthodox theological seminary, Aleksandr Nikolsky (1866–1915). Nikolsky, whose graduate degree was from the Moscow Theological Academy, exemplified the high level of philosophical and theological culture that had been achieved in the Russian Orthodox Church by the beginning of the twentieth century. The title of his book, *The Russian Origen of the Nineteenth Century, Vl. S. Soloviev*, presents Soloviev as a mixed blessing for the church, much like the Alexandrian genius of the third century. Soloviev in this account was admirable in his sincere Christian faith and determination to grapple with the eternal questions of human existence in the light of the gospel, but deserved criticism for "approaching the examination and investigation of the Divine mysteries with less humility and less faith in Scripture than one might have expected from a believing Christian, and with greater confidence in the power of abstract reason than one should allow on the basis of the strictly logical demands of philosophy."[105]

Unfortunately, this balanced view of Soloviev is not as widely held in the Orthodox world today as it was in Nikolsky's time. Following a brief renaissance of Solovievian theology during the 1920s and 1930s, thanks to the influence of Sergei Bulgakov, church theologians began to lose interest in him. The neopatristic school of Georges Florovsky and Vladimir Lossky, which has dominated Orthodox theology since the 1940s, judges Soloviev harshly, as do contemporary neotraditionalist theologians. One of the by-products of the marginalization of the Solovievian legacy is the absence of work on philosophy of law by Orthodox theologians.

In Russian intellectual culture generally, on the other hand, interest in Soloviev remains significant. During the Soviet period, of course, Soloviev was a nonperson, neither published nor publicly discussed. Of course, philosophy of law as an independent discipline was not practiced, either. With the recovery of the Solovievian corpus during the *glasnost* reforms of the 1980s, Soloviev assumed a place of distinction in what is sometimes called the "Russian religio-moral philosophy of law."[106] The claim implicit in this phrase was advanced long ago by Pavel Novgorodtsev in an essay in which he argued that modern Russian philosophy of law inclines to "the establishment of a [close] bond between law and morality" and "the subordination of culture and the state to religion and Church."[107] The fact that

Novgorodtsev's characterization continues to have some currency in Russian legal philosophy today is evidence of the continuing influence of Soloviev, from whom he derived it. The prominent place assigned to an article on Soloviev's philosophy of law at the head of a distinguished new collection of essays on Soloviev by Russian and non-Russian scholars is further evidence of the growing respect accorded to an aspect of the "Russian Origen's" thought which has too often been neglected.[108] As the Russian and worldwide Orthodox community seeks to contribute to the building of a stable constitutional order in the postcommunist East, Soloviev's legacy on law and human nature in the light of Christian faith can only grow in importance.

NOTES

1. The most comprehensive studies of Soloviev's life and work are K. Mochul'skii, *Vladimir Soloviev: Zhizn' i uchenie*, 2d ed. (Paris: YMCA-Press, 1951); S. M. Solov'ev, *Zhizn' i tvorcheskaia evoliutsiia Vladimira Solov'eva* (Brussels: Foyer Oriental Chrétien, 1977), republished as *Vladimir Solov'ev: Zhizn' i tvorcheskaia evoliutsiia* (Moscow: Respublika, 1997); and A. F. Losev, *Vladimir Solov'ev i ego vremia* (Moscow: Molodaia gvardiia, 2000). For surveys in English see D. Strémooukhoff, *Vladimir Soloviev and His Messianic Work*, ed. Philip Guilbeau and Heather Elise MacGregor, trans. Elizabeth Meyendorff (Belmont, Mass.: Nordland, 1980); Jonathan Sutton, *The Religious Philosophy of Vladimir Solovyov: Towards a Reassessment* (New York: St. Martin's Press, 1988); and Paul Valliere, *Modern Russian Theology: Bukharev, Soloviev, Bulgakov* (Grand Rapids, Mich.: Eerdmans, 2000), 109–223.

2. S. M. Soloviev, *Istoriia Rossii s drevneishikh vremen*, 29 vols. (Moscow, 1854–79).

3. On Yurkevich, see P. D. Iurkevich, *Filosofskie proizvedeniia* (Moscow: Izdatel'stvo Pravda, 1990), and V. V. Zenkovsky, *A History of Russian Philosophy*, trans. George L. Kline, 2 vols. (New York: Columbia University Press, 1953), 1:313–315.

4. *The Crisis of Western Philosophy* and *Lectures on Divine Humanity* are available in English (see bibliography); *The Philosophical Principles of Integral Knowledge* and *The Critique of Abstract Principles* are not.

5. Schelling's extensive influence on modern Russian philosophy has been well documented. See V. F. Pustarnakov, *Filosofiia Shellinga v Rossii* (St. Petersburg: Izdatel'stvo Russkogo Khristianskogo gumanitarnogo instituta, 1998).

6. Quoted by Zenkovsky, *A History of Russian Philosophy*, 1:211–212.

7. The phrases "godless human individual" and "inhuman God" are taken from Soloviev's lecture "Three Forces" (1877); but the same conceptual scheme, with less attention to Islam, informs *Lectures on Divine Humanity*. The negative view of Islam in "Three Forces" had to do with the patriotic, not to say jingoistic, context of the lecture. Soloviev delivered it in April 1877, as Russia went to war

with Turkey over the Eastern Question. The "three forces" are the humanistic but godless West, the religious but despotic Islamic East, and the synthesis of humanism and religion in Orthodoxy/Slavdom. For the text see "Tri sily," *Sobranie sochinenii Vladimira Sergeevicha Solov'eva*, ed. S. M. Solov'ev and E. L. Radlov, 2d ed., 10 vols. (St. Petersburg, 1911–14; reprint, Brussels: Foyer Oriental Chrétien, 1966), 1:227–239.

8. For a detailed discussion of the friendship between Dostoevsky and Soloviev, see Marina Kostalevsky, *Dostoevsky and Soloviev: The Art of Integral Vision* (New Haven, Conn.: Yale University Press, 1997), 49–80.

9. *The Brothers Karamazov*, part 1, book 2, chap. 5.

10. See Lecture 11–12 in Vladimir Solovyov, *Lectures on Divine Humanity*, trans. Boris Jakim (Hudson, N.Y.: Lindisfarne Press, 1995), 155–156.

11. On Soloviev's view of nationalism, see Greg Gaut, "Can a Christian be a Nationalist? Vladimir Solov'ev's Critique of Nationalism," *Slavic Review* 57 (1998): 77–94.

12. Vladimir Soloviev, *La Russie et l'Eglise universelle*, 4th ed. (Paris: Librairie Stock, 1922), lxi.

13. Mochul'skii, *Vladimir Solov'ev*, 185.

14. S. M. Solov'ev and E. L. Radlov, eds., *Sobranie sochinenii V. S. Solov'eva*, 6:18.

15. The first volume was the only one Soloviev completed as planned. For the text, see *Sobranie sochinenii V. S. Solov'eva*, 4:241–639. He composed the work in 1885–87 but could not publish it in Russia because of censorship. *La Russie et l'Eglise universelle*, which Soloviev wrote in French and published in Paris in 1889, is a version of what was to have been the third volume.

16. Vladimir Solov'ev, "Evreistvo i khristianskii vopros," in *Sobranie sochinenii V. S. Solov'eva*, 4:135–185; "Talmud i noveishaia polemicheskaia literatura o nem v Avstrii i Germanii," in *Sobranie sochinenii V. S. Solov'eva*, 6:3–32.

17. S. L. Frank, ed., *A Solovyov Anthology*, trans. Natalie Duddington (New York: Charles Scribner's Sons, 1950), 105.

18. S. M. Solov'ev and E. L. Radlov, eds., *Sobranie sochinenii V. S. Solov'eva*, 6:31.

19. Stanislav Rotsinskii underscores the centrality of the theme of reconciliation in Soloviev's thought in a recent study, *Primirenie idei i ideia primireniia v filosofii vseedinstva Vl. Solov'eva* (Moscow: Izdatel'stvo RAGS, 1999).

20. See Judith Deutsch Kornblatt, "Solov'ev on Salvation: The Story of the 'Short Story of the Antichrist,'" in *Russian Religious Thought*, ed. Judith Deutsch Kornblatt and Richard F. Gustafson (Madison: University of Wisconsin Press, 1996), 68–87.

21. V. S. Solov'ev, *Polnoe sobranie sochinenii i pisem v dvadtsati tomakh*, 20 vols. (Moscow: Nauka, 2000–), 3:117.

22. Solov'ev, *Polnoe sobranie sochinenii*, 3:120.

23. Solovyov, *Lectures on Divine Humanity*, 122–123.

24. Ibid., 160–163.

25. Soloviev equated capitalism with plutocracy and never considered the case for classical economics in positive terms. He was criticized for this not just by detractors such as Chicherin but also by some of his passionate supporters in the

next generation. Sergei Bulgakov wrote that "political economy is for the most part the Achilles' heel of [this] philosopher." S. N. Bulgakov, *Ot marksizma k idealizmu: Sbornik statei (1896–1903)* (St. Petersburg: Obshchestvennaia Pol'za, 1903), 249.

26. Solov'ev, *Polnoe sobranie sochinenii*, 3:128.

27. Ibid., 133–134.

28. Ibid., 137–138.

29. Ibid., 143.

30. Ibid., 145.

31. Ibid. "Twenty years later a very similar conception was developed by the neo-Kantian legal philosopher, Rudolf Stammler, who coined the famous formula 'natural law with changing content' and is supposed to have inaugurated the revival of natural law in Germany." Andrzej Walicki, *Legal Philosophies of Russian Liberalism* (Oxford: Clarendon Press, 1987), 211.

32. Ibid., 147.

33. Walicki, *Legal Philosophies of Russian Liberalism*, 169, 181, 184–185.

34. Solov'ev, *Polnoe sobranie sochinenii*, 3:148. *Faust*, part 1:283–286 ("Prolog im Himmel"). Mephistopheles tells the Lord, "He would live a little better if You had not given him the gleam of Heaven's light; he calls it reason but uses it only to be more beastly than any beast."

35. Solov'ev, *Polnoe sobranie sochinenii*, 3:148–149.

36. Ibid., 149.

37. Ibid., 150–151.

38. Ibid., 152–155.

39. Ibid., 152.

40. Ibid., 149.

41. Ibid., 162.

42. See chapter 2, this volume.

43. See chapters 14, 15, and 17, this volume. Soloviev was eloquent on this point: "The precept, 'Render to Caesar the things that are Caesar's, and to God the things that are God's' is constantly quoted to sanction an order of things which gives Caesar all and God nothing. The saying 'My Kingdom is not of this world' is always being used to justify and confirm the paganism of our social and political life, as though Christian society were destined to belong to this world and not to the Kingdom of Christ. On the other hand the saying 'All power is given Me in heaven and earth' is never quoted." Vladimir Solovyev, *Russia and the Universal Church*, trans. Herbert Rees (London: Centenary Press, 1948), 8.

44. Solov'ev, *Polnoe sobranie sochinenii*, 3:157–159.

45. Ibid., 158–159.

46. In fairness to Soloviev it should be noted that he never viewed the vicariate as unitary but always as a collaboration of political, ecclesiastical, and free-prophetic agents, e.g., Russian tsar, Roman pontiff, and the Jews. For discussions of Soloviev's theocratic projects, see Strémooukhoff, *Vladimir Soloviev and His Messianic Work* and the essays by Marin Terpstra, Michael Klimenko, Machiel

Karskens, and Andrzej Walicki in *Vladimir Solověv: Reconciler and Polemicist*, ed. Wil van den Bercken, Manon de Courten and Evert van der Zweerde (Leuven, Belgium: Peeters, 2000).

47. *Opravdanie dobra* is available in a dated but generally reliable English translation: Vladimir Solovyof, *The Justification of the Good: An Essay on Moral Philosophy*, trans. Nathalie A. Duddington (New York: Macmillan, 1918). The Duddington translation has been used for citations in this paper; the corresponding passages in *Sobranie sochinenii V.S. Solověva* are noted. *Law and Morality* is composed of material taken from *The Justification of the Good* and earlier writings including *The Critique of Abstract Principles*. A complete English translation appears in Vladimir Wozniuk, ed. and trans., *Politics, Law, Morality: Essays by V.S. Solověv* (New Haven, Conn.: Yale University Press, 2000), 131–212.

48. Solověv, *Polnoe sobranie sochinenii*, 3:167. Soloviev's words are, "*Spravedlivost' est' neobkhodimaia forma liubvi.*" *Forma* here does not mean "form" in the sense of type or species, but formal structure, framework.

49. Solovyof, *The Justification of the Good* (trans. Duddington), 165–166; *Sobranie sochinenii V.S. Solověva*, 8:194–196.

50. Solovyof, *The Justification of the Good*, xxxi; *Sobranie sochinenii V.S. Solověva*, 8:22.

51. Solovyof, *The Justification of the Good*, xxxi–xxxii; *Sobranie sochinenii V.S. Solověva*, 8:22.

52. Solovyof, *The Justification of the Good*, xxxii; *Sobranie sochinenii V.S. Solověva*, 8:23.

53. Solovyof, *The Justification of the Good*, ix; *Sobranie sochinenii V.S. Solověva*, 8:3.

54. Solovyof, *The Justification of the Good*, xxxiii; *Sobranie sochinenii V.S. Solověva*, 8:23.

55. In the title of *The Justification of the Good* Soloviev used the Russian word *dobro* rather than *blago* for "good," but this does not invalidate the point about grace. Soloviev used the two terms interchangeably: "Divine grace is a *good* [*blago*], or good [*dobro*], which is given to man and not simply thought by him." *Sobranie sochinenii V.S. Solověva*, 3:312.

56. See chapter 5, this volume.

57. Solovyof, *The Justification of the Good*, 25; *Sobranie sochinenii V.S. Solověva*, 8:49.

58. The English translation of this work bears a different title: Vladimir Solovyev, *God, Man and the Church: The Spiritual Foundations of Life*, trans. Donald Attwater (London: J. Clarke, 1930).

59. B.N. Chicherin, "O nachalakh etiki," *Voprosy filosofii i psikhologii* 39 (September–October 1897): 586–701. On Chicherin see G.M. Hamburg, *Boris Chicherin and Early Russian Liberalism, 1828–1866* (Stanford, Calif.: Stanford University Press, 1992) and G.M. Hamburg, ed. and trans., *Liberty, Equality and the Market: Essays by B.N. Chicherin* (New Haven, Conn.: Yale University Press, 1998).

60. Chicherin, "O nachalakh etiki," 590–591.

61. In his reply to Chicherin, Soloviev did not offer an explanation of his procedure. He sparred with Chicherin on points of logic and on practical issues that divided them. The latter were significant. Soloviev was a consistent opponent of capital punishment and mandatory life sentences; Chicherin defended them. Soloviev was a harbinger of the welfare state; Chicherin, a free market liberal. See Vladimir Solov'ev, "Mnimaia kritika. (Otvet B. N. Chicherinu)," *Voprosy filosofii i psikhologii* 39 (September–October 1897): 645–694.

62. Solovyof, *The Justification of the Good*, liv; *Sobranie sochinenii V. S. Solov'eva*, 8: xxviii.

63. Ibid., chap. 12 (part 3, chap. 3 in Duddington translation).

64. Ibid., chaps. 14, 15, and 16 (part 3, chaps. 5, 6, and 7 in Duddington translation).

65. Solovyof, *The Justification of the Good*, 284, 295–298; *Sobranie sochinenii V. S. Solov'eva*, 8:316, 328–331.

66. Ibid., chap. 18 (part 3, chap. 9 in Duddington translation).

67. *Three Dialogues* is available in English: *War, Progress and the End of History: Three Conversations Including a Short Story of the Anti-Christ*, trans. Alexander Bakshy, trans. Thomas R. Beyer Jr. (Hudson, N.Y.: Lindisfarne Press, 1990).

68. Solovyof, *The Justification of the Good*, 406; *Sobranie sochinenii V. S. Solov'eva*, 8:444.

69. Solovyof, *The Justification of the Good*, 399; *Sobranie sochinenii V. S. Solov'eva*, 8:437.

70. N. Gorodenskii, "Nravstvennaia filosofiia Vl. S. Solov'eva," *Bogoslovskii vestnik* (February 1899): 321. The words quoted by Gorodenskii appear in Solovyof, *The Justification of the Good*, 403; *Sobranie sochinenii V. S. Solov'eva*, 8:441.

71. Solovyof, *The Justification of the Good*, 323; *Sobranie sochinenii V. S. Solov'eva*, 8:357.

72. Wozniuk, *Politics, Law, Morality*, 183–184; cf. *Sobranie sochinenii V. S. Solov'eva*, 8:417, and Solovyof, *The Justification of the Good*, 379–380.

73. Wozniuk, *Politics, Law, Morality*, 176. Soloviev reiterated his opposition to the theological justification of capital punishment in his reply to Chicherin's review of *The Justification of the Good*. A good Hegelian, Chicherin defended capital punishment and appealed to gospel texts concerning eternal punishment to justify the concept of retributive justice. Cautioning Chicherin against "crude literalism" in the use of scripture, Soloviev cited a work by Archimandrite Sergy (Stragorodsky), *Pravoslavnoe uchenie o spasenii* [The Orthodox Doctrine of Salvation] (Sergiev Posad, 1895), in which the author maintains that the juridical theory of retribution "'is of accidental provenance in the Christian worldview; and so, if one is speaking about the essence of Christianity, the concept of retribution in the literal and strict sense cannot be admitted.'" Solov'ev, "Mnimaia kritika," 690. Sergy became a leading hierarch in the twentieth century, the author of the divisive declaration of loyalty to the Soviet government in 1927 and the first incumbent of the revived Patriarchate of Moscow in 1943–45.

74. Solovyof, *The Justification of the Good*, 340; *Sobranie sochinenii V. S. Solov'eva*, 8:377.

75. "Dignified" is Walicki's translation in *Legal Philosophies of Russian Liberalism*. Duddington, rendering the Russian *dostoinyi* more literally, translates "worthy."

76. Solovyof, *The Justification of the Good*, 341; *Sobranie sochinenii V. S. Solov'eva*, 8:377.

77. See Walicki, *Legal Philosophies of Russian Liberalism*, chap. 2, "Boris Chicherin: the 'Old Liberal' Philosophy of Law," and chap. 3, "Vladimir Soloviev: Religious Philosophy and the Emergence of the 'New Liberalism.'"

78. Solovyof, *The Justification of the Good*, 345; *Sobranie sochinenii V. S. Solov'eva*, 8:381.

79. The welfare state is also adumbrated in Soloviev's view of the state in *The Justification of the Good* as "collectively organized compassion" (Duddington trans. "pity"). Solovyof, *The Justification of the Good*, 448; *Sobranie sochinenii V. S. Solov'eva*, 8:488. See also Walicki, *Legal Philosophies of Russian Liberalism*, 204–245.

80. Solovyof, *The Justification of the Good*, 343; *Sobranie sochinenii V. S. Solov'eva*, 8:379.

81. Soloviev's genius in this respect can be compared with Martin Luther King's as described in chapter 15, this volume: "Two of King's favorite biblical passages were 'Be not conformed to this world, but be transformed by the renewing of your minds' (Rom. 12:2) and 'Let justice roll down like waters and righteousness like a mighty stream' (Amos 5:24). The ability to hold these two quotations together in a lived unity, faithful to both heaven and earth, defined King's genius."

82. Solovyof, *The Justification of the Good*, lvii; *Sobranie sochinenii V. S. Solov'eva*, 8:xxxi.

83. Solovyof, *The Justification of the Good*, lvi–lvii; *Sobranie sochinenii V. S. Solov'eva*, 8:xxxi.

84. V. V. Lazarev, *Eticheskaia mysl' v Germanii i Rossii: Shelling i Vl. Solov'ev* (Moscow: IFRAN, 2000), 154.

85. Solovyof, *The Justification of the Good*, 371; *Sobranie sochinenii V. S. Solov'eva*, 8:409.

86. Soloviev's new definition seems to have been inspired in part by the theory of Georg Jellinek. See Walicki, *Legal Philosophies of Russian Liberalism*, 200–201.

87. Solovyof, *The Justification of the Good*, 167–168; *Sobranie sochinenii V. S. Solov'eva*, 8:197–198.

88. Solovyof, *The Justification of the Good*, 369–371; *Sobranie sochinenii V. S. Solov'eva*, 8:407–409.

89. Solovyof, *The Justification of the Good*, 362; *Sobranie sochinenii V. S. Solov'eva*, 8:399.

90. Solovyof, *The Justification of the Good*, 459; *Sobranie sochinenii V. S. Solov'eva*, 8:499.

91. Evgenii Trubetskoi, *Mirosozertsanie Vl. S. Solov'eva*, 2 vols. (Moscow: Izdanie avtora, 1913), 2:190–194.

92. Walicki, *Legal Philosophies of Russian Liberalism*, 191.

93. Solovyof, *The Justification of the Good*, 455–457; *Sobranie sochinenii V. S. Solov'eva*, 8:496–497.

94. Solovyof, *The Justification of the Good*, 467–469; *Sobranie sochinenii V. S. Solov'eva*, 8:508–510.

95. Chicherin, "O nachalakh etiki," 644.

96. Pavel Novgorodtsev, one of Soloviev's admirers, acknowledged the theocratic ideal in *The Justification of the Good* but doubted that it would generate much enthusiasm in the Russia of his time: "The idea of a model society being reflected in the collaboration of prophet, priest and king will captivate hardly anyone in our day." P. N. Novgorodtsev, "Ideia prava v filosofii Vl. S. Solov'eva," *Voprosy filosofii i psikhologii* 56 (January–February 1901): 128.

97. "Plato's Life-Drama," in Wozniuk, *Politics, Law, Morality*, 213–254. Russian text in *Sobranie sochinenii V. S. Solov'eva*, 9:194–241.

98. The analogy and cited words are Viacheslav Ivanov's in "O znachenii Vl. Solov'eva v sud'bakh nashego religioznogo soznaniia," *O Vladimire Solov'eve* (Tomsk: Izdatel'stvo Vodolei, 1997), 35. The essay was first published in 1911.

99. Wozniuk, *Politics, Law, Morality*, 249–254. Again in this essay Soloviev used the term *theosis* (248) to describe the ultimate state of regeneration.

100. Hans Helmut Gäntzel, *Wladimir Solowjows Rechtsphilosophie auf der Grundlage der Sittlichkeit* (Frankfurt am Main: Vittorio Klostermann, 1968), 289, 293.

101. For an English translation of *Problemy idealizma* (1902), see Randall A. Poole, ed. and trans., *Problems of Idealism: Essays in Russian Social Philosophy* (New Haven, Conn.: Yale University Press, 2003).

102. See Marshall S. Shatz and Judith E. Zimmerman, ed. and trans., *Vekhi/Landmarks: A Collection of Articles About the Russian Intelligentsia* (Armonk, N.Y.: M. E. Sharpe, 1994).

103. See Kristiane Burchardi, *Die Moskauer "Religiös-Philosophische Vladimir-Solov'ev-Gesellschaft" (1905–1918)*, Forschungen zur osteuropäischen Geschichte: Historische Veröffentlichungen 53 (Wiesbaden: Harrassowitz Verlag, 1998).

104. P. I. Novgorodtsev, "Ideia prava v filosofii Vl. S. Solov'eva," 112.

105. A. A. Nikol'skii, *Russkii Origen XIX veka Vl. S. Solov'ev* (St. Petersburg: Nauka, 2000), 332. The book first appeared serially in the journal *Vera i razum* (Faith and Reason) in 1902.

106. "The Russian Religio-Moral Philosophy of Law" is the title of the section on Russian thinkers in a recent textbook on the history of the philosophy of law for use in Russian law faculties: *Istoriia filosofii prava* (St. Petersburg: Izdatel'stvo Iuridicheskii institut, 1998). Another recent textbook promoting this theme is *Russkaia filosofiia prava: Filosofiia very i nravstvennosti, Antologiia* (Russian Philosophy of Law: A Philosophy of Faith and Morality—An Anthology) (St. Petersburg: Izdatel'stvo Aleteiia, 1997).

107. Novgorodtsev's "Über die eigentümlichen Elemente der russischen Rechtsphilosophie" was published in Germany in 1932 and is discussed in Gäntzel, *Wladimir Solovyows Rechtsphilosophie*, 293–294. The article appears in Russian translation in *Russkaia filosofiia prava*, 211–226 and in P. I. Novgorodtsev, *Sochineniia* (Moscow: Raritet, 1995), 367–387.

108. E. Iu. Solov'ev, "Gumanitarno-pravovaia problematika v filosofskoi publitsistike V. S. Solov'eva," in I. V. Borisova and A. P. Kozyrev, eds., *Solov'evskii sbornik*, Materialy mezhdunarodnoi konferentsii "V. S. Solov'ev i ego filosofskoe nasledie," 28–30 avgusta 2000 g. (Moscow: Fenomenologiia-Germenevtika, 2001), 29–51.

CHAPTER 20

Nicholas Berdyaev (1874–1948)

VIGEN GUROIAN

Nicholas (Nicholai Aleksandrovich) Berdyaev was born in 1874 in the province of Kiev to a wealthy and highly privileged family. Like so many young men of aristocratic upbringing in nineteenth-century Russia, he was sent to military academy, which he intensely disliked. He found his way to the University of Kiev, where he took up philosophy, despite the fact that he was supposed to study the natural sciences. In his posthumously published autobiographical essay *Dream and Reality* (1949),[1] Berdyaev writes, "My revolutionary and socialist sympathies and convictions had crystallized before I entered the University."[2] It was at the university, however, that Berdyaev began to associate with socialists and Marxists. He embraced radicalism from profound "ethical considerations"[3] regarding the plight of the poor and the working class under a political and economic order that he thought to be oppressive and corrupted. Because of these views and activities, Berdyaev was expelled from the university, arrested, and in 1898 sent into exile to the Volgoda region of northern Russia. Through the influence and interventions of his family, however, he spent just two and a half years there. Nevertheless, this experience left a strong and lasting impression on his thinking, as Berdyaev drew ever more resolutely toward radical socialism.

Kant and other German idealists, together with Berdyaev's Christian upbringing, tempered his attraction to Marxism from the start. In his introduction to *Slavery and Freedom* (1939), he explains, "I have never been an orthodox Marxist. I have never been a materialist and even in my Marxist period I was an idealist in philosophy. I tried to combine my idealism in philosophy with Marxism in social questions. I based my socialism upon an idealist foundation."[4] Berdyaev also detected very early the totalitarian proclivities and potentialities of Marxism. In radical circles he doggedly defended the reality and priority of freedom, goodness, and truth against every form of determinism and relativism. "I ... maintained the existence of truth and goodness as idealist values [embedded in the transcendental consciousness] which are independent of class struggle, of social conditions and the rest," Berdyaev wrote. "I believed in the existence of truth and justice as determining my revolutionary attitude to social reality, and not determined by it."[5]

During the late 1890s and early 1900s, Berdyaev pursued this goal of wedding Marxist social and economic analysis with Kantianism and Christianity. Nevertheless, his discontent with Marxism intensified as he edged steadily toward a personalist religious philosophy. The radicals, whose company Berdyaev kept, viewed the human individual as an instrument of the material dialectic and part of a social mass moved by historical forces. Berdyaev embraced Nietzsche's admonitions about the rise of "herd mentality" but rejected his positivism. Instead, he defended the eternal value of the human being, personal freedom, and the transcendence of spirit. In *The Meaning of the Creative Act* (1916), his favorite among his many books, Berdyaev made his case that the "creative act" is the highest and the most definitive achievement of human and divine freedom. Humankind is created in the image and likeness of God, and by virtue of this, God calls humankind to creativity, which is the consummate expression of human freedom and redemption.

On his return from exile in 1901, Berdyaev traveled to Germany, where he entered the University of Heidelberg to study with the acclaimed neo-Kantian Wilhelm Windelband. Berdyaev was already becoming disenchanted with Kant, though, and with the neo-Kantians in particular. In later years, he explained the source of his discontent, which boiled down to Kant's rationalism and legalism. Kant laid down the rule that the person should never be made the mere means to an end. Yet Kant (and even more especially the neo-Kantians) undercut the personalist bias of that rule with an ethical formalism that rendered the individual an abstraction and distilled the concreteness out of moral judgments. Kant's principle of the categorical imperative stipulates that a judgment qualifies as being morally correct when, and only when, it is universalizable, that is, equally applicable to any relevantly similar case. Berdyaev countered that this principle of universalizability makes the individual a function of the law, in service to the law, and not the other way around. The principle is potentially and often really dehumanizing. "The Gospel morality of grace and redemption," Berdyaev writes, "is the direct opposite of Kant's formula: you must not act so that the principle of your action could become a universal law; you must always act individually.... The universal law is that every moral action should be unique and individual, i.e., that it should have in view the concrete person and not the abstract good."[6] Thus, over and against Kantian formalism and universalism, Berdyaev embraced an existentialist contextualism and personalism.

As Berdyaev distanced himself from Kantianism and Marxism, he drew nearer to Orthodox Christianity, albeit through diverse and sometimes idiosyncratic sources. The period between his move to St. Petersburg in 1905 and the outbreak of the Bolshevik Revolution in 1917 is crucial for an understanding of Berdyaev's mature thought. In St. Petersburg (and later in Moscow), Berdyaev was associated with a rich variety of Christian intellectuals, including Dimitri Merezhkovsky, Vassil Rozanov, Vyacheslav Ivanov, Pavel Florensky, and Lev Shestov, many of whom were either imprisoned or sent into exile by the Communists. During this time Berdyaev began to write as a Christian philosopher. Indeed, soon after arriving in St. Petersburg with his new wife, Berdyaev joined Sergei Bulgakov in a joint editorship of the journal *The New Way* and, after its demise, another such enterprise entitled *Questions of Life*. Through these publications, Berdyaev and Bulgakov espoused their special blend of social and economic radicalism and Christian spirituality. Berdyaev sums up his shift from Marxism and idealism toward a distinctly Christian form of mystical religious faith and social radicalism in an article written during this period and later included in his book *Sub Specie Aeternitatis*: "Idealism was well enough for the initial criticism of Marxism and positivism ... but it possessed nothing creative. It is impossible to stop with it. That would be neither realistic nor religious.... I arrive in my articles at God-manhood, the incarnation of the Spirit in society, at the mystical union of love and freedom. From the Marxist pseudo ecumenicity, from the decadent romantic individualism, I arrive at the true ecumenicity of mystical neo-Christianity."[7]

In 1907, the Berdyaev family moved to Moscow, where Nicholas became active in the Religious-Philosophical Society, founded in memory of Vladimir Soloviev. This association of Christian intellectuals provided a refreshing and stimulating camaraderie. Berdyaev openly credited the group with expanding his religious and theological horizons. In the meantime, Berdyaev was reading deeply into the great nineteenth-century Russian Christian writers—Aleksei Khomyakov and Nicholas Fedorov, Dostoevsky and Tolstoy. Berdyaev was disappointed, however, with the Russian secular intelligentsia of both the right and left, and with the Orthodox Church. In *Dream and Reality*, Berdyaev explains how he saw things at that time: "The Russian renascence suffered from a lack of moral decisiveness and readiness to choose and act. It was lost in a vague aestheticism and romanticism."[8] He continues, "The renascence shed hardly any light into the wider regions of social life. The attitude of the left intelligentsia ... not only of the social revolutionaries but also of the liberal-radicals, was one of drab, moral respectability and political stringency, and they failed to reflect profound cultural changes."[9] Although he initially supported the revolution of 1917, Berdyaev did not favor its leaders or even its immediate outcome:

> [The revolutionaries] were nurtured in and lived by the outworn ideas of Russian nihilism and positivism…. They were not interested in Dostoevsky, Tolstoy, Vladimir Solovyev, Nicolai Fyodorov and the thinkers of the turn of the century: they were satisfied with their Herwegh, and their Holbach, with their Chernishevsky and Pisarev, their standard of culture rose no higher than that of Plekhanov. Lenin himself was a reactionary so far as philosophy and culture were concerned; he was not even fully abreast of Marxist dialectic; for, unlike Marx he had not passed through the whole school of German Idealism, even though he had read Hegel.
>
> This fact had a fatal effect on the character which the great revolution in Russia assumed; it began by perpetuating a real pogrom against what was best in Russian culture.[10]

The Russian Church offered little hope, either. It was corrupt and servile to an oppressive state, and did nothing to diffuse the situation or address the true grievances of the Russian people in either 1905 or 1917. In an "Open Letter" first published in the *Moscow Weekly* on August 15, 1909, Berdyaev passionately expresses his love for and disappointment with the Church:

> By devious and winding paths I have come to the faith of Christ and to the Church of Christ, which I now count as my spiritual mother. Nevertheless, I have not forgotten those obstacles that stood in my way. I cannot forget them because of the fate of those who are unable to overcome those obstacles. The activity of the Church, the abomination of desolation in the holy place, throttles as a heavy incubus those who seek God and his truth…. Is it not a stumbling block that the official Christian camp, confessing the true faith and accordingly possessing privileges almost incomparably greater than the others, commits deeds of hate and evil, rather than performing acts of love? Men are weak and their religious will is ruined by offenses and temptations; it is difficult for them to withstand the most terrible offense which turns men from faith—the spiritual downfall and ethical decomposition of the Church in her human, historical empirical aspects (for in her divine mystical aspects the Church is unshakable and guards eternal truth). But woe to them through whom such offense comes into the world![11]

In 1921, after a brief arrest, Berdyaev was sent out of Russia. He and his wife first settled in Berlin but in 1924 moved permanently to Paris. Berdyaev joined the rich ferment of philosophical and religious thought that stirred in Paris at that time. He established ties with Russian figures such as Sergei Bulgakov, George Fedotov, and Mother Maria Skobtsova, as well as lasting friendships with the Roman Catholic religious philosophers Jacques Maritain and Gabriel Marcel. But it is also true that Berdyaev remained an independent and often lonely voice. As he wrote many years later in *Dream and Reality*, "I never fully merged with any one movement with which I was associated. And the precariousness of my relation to them, my loneliness and misgivings sharpened my perceptions."[12]

In *Slavery and Freedom*, Berdyaev states that upon his arrival in the West, he quickly recognized that, as wrong as the Bolsheviks and Communists were, the truculent anti-Soviet mentality and easy embrace of bourgeois capitalism by so many of the Russian émigrés were barely more tolerable:

> I went through a stormy inward reaction ... against the second, the great, Russian revolution. I considered the revolution inevitable and just; but its spiritual aspect was uncongenial to me from the very beginning. Its ignoble aspect, its encroachment upon freedom of the spirit was a contradiction of my aristocratic interpretation of personality and my cult of spiritual freedom. My refusal to accept the Bolshevik revolution was not so much on social grounds as on spiritual. I expressed this too passionately and often unfairly. I saw all the while the same triumph of the *Grand Inquisitor*. At the same time I did not believe in the possibility of any sort of restoration and I certainly did not want it. I was banished from Soviet Russia simply and solely because of my reaction in defense of freedom of the spirit.
>
> But in Western Europe I again passed through a psychological reaction and that a two-fold one—reaction against the Russian *émigrés* and reaction against the bourgeois capitalist society of Europe. Among the Russian *émigrés* I saw the same revulsion from freedom, the same denial of it as in communist Russia. This was inexplicable, but very much less justifiable than in the communist revolution.[13]

What especially disturbed Berdyaev about life in the West was the bourgeois mentality among both religious and nonreligious people. He judged that this bourgeois mentality was hardly less materialistic than Marxism and Communism and that it was almost as destructive of freedom and personality. With clear allusions to his great spiritual mentor, Fyodor Dostoevsky, Berdyaev writes in *The Bourgeois Mind*,

> The bourgeois may be an extreme conservative or an extreme revolutionary, but in both cases he is chained to the visible world and knows no spiritual freedom. There is no grace in moralism [characteristic of the bourgeois], it proceeds from an outward source and is deaf to the music of Heaven.... The very idea of the rationalization of life, of an absolute social harmony, is a middle class idea which has to be opposed by the "man of the underworld," the

"gentleman with a mocking reactionary face." The tower of Babel was built by the middle class, [even] the spirit of Socialism is middle-class.[14]

The atheism of Communism was self-confessed. The atheism of the bourgeois was not, and yet a denial of Christianity was entailed in all its behavior. Berdyaev continues,

> Everything the bourgeois touches, the family, the state, morality, religion, science, all is deadened.... The paradox of his life consists in his repudiation of tragedy.... Because the consciousness of guilt and sin has become so weak he is a slave of "the world," his ideal is that of worldly wealth and power; the mystery of Golgotha is unacceptable to him.[15]

Over the remaining years of his life, Berdyaev continued to oppose anti-human and anti-Christian forces on both the left and the right, in Soviet-style socialism and Western capitalism. At the same time, he produced a massive corpus in which he elaborated a philosophy of history, a theosophical spirituality, an aesthetics, and an ethics. It is to Berdyaev's ethics, however, that one must turn especially for his theological anthropology and interpretation of the origin and meaning of law. In *The Destiny of Man* Berdyaev introduces his famous threefold typology of ethics: the ethics of law, the ethics of redemption, and the ethics of creativity. Other writings that especially come into play are *The Meaning of the Creative Act* (1916), *Freedom and the Spirit* (1926), *Slavery and Freedom* (1939), and *The Beginning and the End* (1946).

Fielding Clarke, one of Berdyaev's earliest and best interpreters, was right when he observed that "the doctrines and practice of the Russian Orthodox Church are in the background ... of all that he wrote.... Berdyaev was [always] a son of Orthodoxy."[16] Berdyaev himself commented: "I cannot, in all conscience, call myself a typical 'orthodox' of any kind; but Orthodoxy was nearer to me (and I hope I am nearer to Orthodoxy) than either Catholicism or Protestantism. I never severed my link with the Orthodox Church, although confessional self-satisfaction and exclusiveness are alien to me."[17] When people in the West began referring to Berdyaev as a representative Orthodox figure, he took pains to say that he did not speak for the Church either in an official or unofficial capacity. He carefully explained that he was a philosopher, not a theologian, and certainly not a dogmatic theologian. In *Freedom and the Spirit* (1927), Berdyaev pauses to issue this strong disclaimer:

> My book is not a theological work, nor is it written according to any theological method. It belongs to no school of philosophy; rather it forms a part of "prophetic" as distinct from "scientific" philosophy, if one may employ the

terminology which [Karl] Jaspers has suggested.... All the forces of my spirit and my mental and moral consciousness are bent towards the complete understanding of the problems which press so hard upon me.... I may be much mistaken, but my purpose is not to introduce heresy of any kind nor to promote fresh schism. I am moving in the sphere of Christian problematics which demands creative efforts of thought and where the most divergent opinions are naturally allowable.[18]

Berdyaev did not fit a standard mold. He was a creative, eclectic, and even eccentric thinker. Although he drew from such Eastern Patristic writers as Gregory of Nyssa and Pseudo-Dionysius, he was also steeped in the German mystics Jacob Boehme and Meister Eckhart. Berdyaev saw himself as following in the footsteps of the great nineteenth-century Russian religious philosophers Aleksei Khomyakov, Nicholas Fedorov, and Vladimir Soloviev, but Friedrich W. J. Schelling, Arthur Schopenhauer, and especially Immanuel Kant were formative influences. The care that Berdyaev took to describe himself as a philosopher and explain what he meant merits further attention. For he revealed much about his purposes and goals as well as his relationship to the extraordinary ferment of religious thought in Russia up to the Revolution of 1917. From this we begin to understand how his thought fits into the larger context of religious philosophy in the West from the Enlightenment through the first half of the twentieth century.

In *The Destiny of Man* (1931), Berdyaev distinguishes between doing philosophy and doing theology. The philosopher, he says, seeks to find meaning for existence through rational reflection on human experience, whereas the Christian theologian explores the meaning of redemption in the knowledge of God's triune being gained by faith in the God-Man, Jesus Christ. Berdyaev, of course, allowed for the possibility that a philosopher might, like himself, be a believer in "religious revelation." In this case, the philosopher's "thought is bound to be nurtured by" that revelation. Indeed, "he may acquire the mind of Christ and this will make his philosophy different from that of non-Christian thinkers."[19] The philosopher's thought will no longer be simply anthropological, but his or her anthropology will be theological and the God-Man the norm of philosophical reflection.

Nonetheless, Berdyaev insists that under no circumstance must revelation "force upon philosophy any theories or ideal constructions.... Philosophy is led to its conclusions by the cognitive process itself; unlike theology it cannot have the results of knowledge forced upon it from without." For philosophy "to be at all possible," he continues, "it must be free; it brooks no constraint."[20] In this claim for the independence of philosophy—although he does not say it is autonomous—one detects the influence of Immanuel Kant and, in the definition of religious philosophy, the impact of Vladimir Soloviev.

Not all of Berdyaev's contemporaries agreed with his claim for the independence of philosophy or accepted his disclaimers about dogmatic theology. And insofar as Berdyaev wrote with the voice of a Christian believer, especially an Orthodox believer, some critics accused him of misspeaking concerning the faith. Thus, to read Berdyaev is to engage a brilliant intellect and sensitive spirit constantly in tension and controversy with prevailing orthodoxies, including, one might add, orthodoxies about the origin, meaning, and purposes of ethics and law.

THE ORIGIN OF ETHICS

In *The Destiny of Man*, Berdyaev holds that the origin of ethics is commensurate (or simultaneous) with the origin of the distinction between good and evil, and that both are consequent to what the Christian faith refers to as the Fall into sin. He writes, "It might be said that the world proceeds from an original absence of discrimination between good and evil to a sharp distinction between them and then, enriched by that experience, ends by not distinguishing them any more."[21] In other words, "Paradise is the state of being in which there is no valuation or distinction"[22] between good and evil: likewise, the kingdom of God is "beyond" good and evil. In between this beginning and this end is the only world that we know in the ordinary sense of knowing, and in that world the distinction between good and evil tries and tests us at every turn. One can say, Berdyaev continues, that "it is bad that the distinction between good and evil has arisen, but it is good to make the distinction once it has arisen; it is bad to have gone through the experience of evil, but it is good to know good and evil as a result of this experience."[23]

Berdyaev argues that in order to get to the heart of the meaning of ethics, an epistemology of original sin is needed. The knowledge of good and evil indicates commission of the original sin and loss of original innocence. Original sin is an act of imagination and will that distances human beings from God. It triggers a fundamental shift in human consciousness. The whole of human history is the legacy of this original sin and the fallen consciousness of humankind; as a result, humankind is plunged into "a godless experience of life."[24] Yet the very knowledge of good and evil, which is gained at the awful cost of alienation from God and mortality, paradoxically also gives rise to conditions wherein and whereby human beings may be reawakened to the presence and existence of God and inherit eternal life. "Awareness of original sin both humbles and exalts man. Man fell from a height, and he can rise to it again,"[25] but not, says Berdyaev, by mere moralism or the law. The character of the kingdom of God is not merely ethical, as moralists imagine; nor is it achieved by even the strictest adherence to the law. "The triumph of a 'good' based in valuation and distinctions is ... not paradise or the Kingdom of God. The Kingdom of God ... is on the other side of the distinction."[26] It is beyond good and evil.

THE FAILURE OF LEGALISM AND MORALISM

"It is the Fall [also] that made moralists of us,"[27] Berdyaev argues. Moralism and legalism go together. Both are incapable of reaching the kingdom of God. Both are premised on the mistaken belief that the solution to human suffering is the triumph of good over evil achieved by adherence to law. Leo Tolstoy is an example of someone who put all his hope for the kingdom of God in obedience to moral law. Tolstoy interpreted good and evil, which are the symptoms of a much deeper disorientation of human existence and disturbance of consciousness, as objective forces pitted against one another, the victory of good over evil ensuring perfection and peace. Tolstoy's moralism is an extreme example of the ethics of law with all of its limitations, and this ethics of law is the first of the three kinds of ethics Berdyaev discusses in *The Destiny of Man*.

Berdyaev held that law is impotent "to change human nature" or redeem humankind from a seemingly interminable struggle of good and evil. In the depths of their souls, human beings know this is so and yearn for something more. "Man thirsts for redemption, for deliverance not only from evil but from the legalism and the distinction between good and evil."[28] Genuine redemption "destroys the roots of sin and evil" and erases the distinction between good and evil. The ethics of redemption bridges "the gulf" between God and humanity that was objectified by sin and the law. It announces the entrance of the transcendent good, of divine life itself, of grace, "into the very depths of" human existence, into the very heart of the world.[29] It promises liberation from sin and death and the restoration of humankind to communion with the living God. The sum of this redemptive action is what the Gospel of John calls eternal life.

REDEMPTION

In setting forth his theology of redemption, Berdyaev rejected the theory of atonement of St. Anselm of Canterbury (ca. 1033–1190) that had come to dominate various forms of Roman Catholicism and Protestantism. This doctrine described the atonement as an act of sacrifice rendered on our behalf by Christ for the violation, due to original sin, of God's righteousness and honor. It defined Christ's death as a satisfaction or substitution that propitiates the wrath or righteous indignation of God. Some Protestant versions of this doctrine are purely forensic, insofar as they understand atonement as a purely vicarious act of Christ on behalf of human beings, since the debt owed to God is far greater than any one human being except Christ could possibly pay. Other typically Roman Catholic teachings interpreted this act in strongly reconciliatory terms as making right of our relationship with God.

Berdyaev, like many other Eastern Orthodox Christians, regarded this kind of atonement theory as overly legalistic and juridical. Furthermore, he argued that it is alien to the spirit of the New Testament and classical Christianity: "The Redemption achieved by the Son of God is not a judicial verdict, but a means of salvation; it is not a judgment, but a transformation and illumination of nature—in a word, its sanctification."[30] The juridical concept, whether understood in forensic terms or reconciliatory terms, represented "the relations between God and man ... [as] of a purely external character."[31] Such an atonement does not remedy the mortal sickness and weakness of post-Edenic humanity that prevents human beings from entering into genuine communion with God. Berdyaev argues, "Redemption is not justification, but the acquiring of perfection."[32] It is not God who is unable or unwilling to forgive, "but man who cannot pardon himself, any more than he can absolve himself from his apostasy from God"[33] or make reunion with divine life possible. Salvation is God acting from "within" the human being through the incarnation of the Son who by his perfect life and sacrifice cures humankind of sin and death so that they may participate in the divine life.

THE ETHICS OF REDEMPTION AND THE KINGDOM OF GOD

Berdyaev embraced an "ontological" or "physicalist" interpretation of redemption highly characteristic of Eastern Church Fathers reaching back to Ireneaus and Athanasius. Berdyaev writes, "The spiritual nature of man does not merely demand pardon for sin, but rather its final defeat and extermination, that is to say, the transfiguration of human nature. The meaning of Redemption lies in the coming of the Second Adam, the new spiritual man, in the coming of the love of which the Old Adam was ignorant, in the transformation of the lower nature into the higher."[34] On this ground, Berdyaev argued that the ethics of redemption overcomes the ethical dualism of good and evil that is the mainstay of unredeemed naturalistic ethics and law. On the foundation of this cure of sin and perfection of our human nature accomplished by the God-Man Jesus Christ, a new spiritual ethics is made possible. According to this ethic, grace is the opposite of necessity and not, as is often argued, the opposite of freedom. The grace of God is a divine love healing human nature as well as a divine freedom creatively engaging human freedom toward the end of the sanctification of life.

The ethics of redemption paves the path to the kingdom of God; however, it does not encompass the whole of salvation. For the ethics of redemption still bears the terrible mark of the Fall into sin. Its paving "stone" is suffering love, divine and human, whereas the kingdom of God is not only beyond good and evil but also transcends every kind of human suffering.

THE ETHICS OF CREATIVENESS AND FREEDOM OF THE SPIRIT

The ethics of creativeness, Berdyaev's unique contribution to Christian ethics, is the fruit that grows from the seed sown by grace in our wounded humanity. Or another way of putting it: the ethics of creativity is the service to God's kingdom that Christians are empowered to do by virtue of the fact that the Son of God has rehabilitated human nature in God's own person and restored humankind to freedom in the Spirit. Humanity's creative powers are weakened by the Fall. Through Christ, human nature is redeemed and restored; humanity is saved from sin. The old human being is reborn into a new creature. "Christ [the Creator Word] became immanent in human nature, and this makes man a creator like the Creator God."[35] There is nothing explicit in the gospel about humanity's creative vocation; it would have been a mistake had such a thing been included in the New Testament, since a person must pass through redemption before he or she can understand fully the meaning of God's calling to creativity. When a person is reborn into the freedom of the Spirit, that vocation is clarified and he or she may act upon it with a complete sense of purpose. "Creativeness is a work of man's God-like freedom, the revelation of the image of the Creator within him. Creativeness is not in the Father, neither is it in the Son but in the Spirit,"[36] and reaches beyond the Old and New Testaments.[37] As St. Paul puts it, "Where the Spirit of the Lord is, there is freedom" (2 Cor. 3:17 RSV). Indeed, Berdyaev insists that "the whole of St. Paul's teaching about various gifts is concerned with man's creative vocation. The gifts are from God, and they indicate that man is intended to do creative work."[38] The creative capacity of the human person, especially when liberated by Christ in the Spirit, anticipates, is a proleptic sign of, the transfiguration of the world. Indeed, "man is called to extraordinary activity, to creative upbuilding of profit for the Kingdom of God, which is known as God-humanity."[39]

ETHICS AND SIN

In sum, for Berdyaev, human beings have invented ethics in response to "the criterion of good and evil ... the genesis of morality and the origin of moral distinctions and valuations."[40] Ethics, however, is not just a theoretical discipline; nor is it, as the common person often thinks, simply the judicious application of law to regulate a social world. The ethics of law and the ethics of redemption take into account at various levels what biblical religion calls sin. They are means by which human beings can cope with and overcome the dissension, division, and conflict that sin and the bitter knowledge of good and evil introduce into life. The ethics of law envisions a social good and seeks to effect it principally through prohibitions and punishments. This form of ethics is "both very human and well adapted to human needs and standards"; however, it can be "pitiless" toward the individual in his or her concrete circumstances and severely constrict freedom.[41] And it is powerless to solve the riddle of the dualism of good and evil that shadows human existence everywhere.

The ethics of redemption overcomes fallen nature and reaches beyond good and evil. Wherever it is present, Christ is known and the Spirit is acting. The ethics of redemption is illumined by the knowledge of the humanity of God in Jesus Christ and the perfection of God's own image and likewise in the Incarnate Son's humanity. It is about love and not law, about freedom and not sanction. The ethics of redemption posits in the light of Christ that the conflict between good and evil, which is alien and obstructive to the personal, free, and loving communion of divine life may be transcended. Nevertheless, Berdyaev adds,

> Man's chief end is not to be saved but to mount up, creatively. For this creative upsurge salvation from sin and evil is necessary. From the religious point of view, the epoch of redemption is subordinated to the epoch of creativeness. A religion of thirst for salvation and terror of perdition is only a temporary passage through a dualistic division [of good and evil and nature and spirit].... Creativeness is the final revelation of the Holy Trinity—its anthropological revelation.... God himself, who gave His Only Son to be broken on a tree, atones for the sin of man and he expects that man, having partaken of the mystery of redemption, will accomplish the great deed of creativeness, will realize his positive destiny."[42]

The ethics of creativeness, therefore, completes the spiritual work of redemption. "Human nature, redeemed and saved from evil, has a positive content and purpose. This content and purpose can only be creativeness.... That the image and likeness of God the Creator cannot fail to be himself a creator is an anthropological truth" which Judaism and Christianity bring into the world.[43] The ethics of creativeness is humanity's response to God's call to enact and embody, through imagination and will, the values of love and freedom that belong to the kingdom of God.

HUMAN AND DIVINE NATURES

At this stage, a review of Berdyaev's philosophical and religious reflection on human and divine natures is needed. It is the basis for an understanding of his position on the relationship of law and Christianity. Christianity insists that the human person is an indivisible compound of nature and spirit, said Berdyaev. He cautioned, however, that Christianity is not about a body-soul or mind-body dualism. The human person is spirit insofar as God is Spirit and God has created humanity in God's own image and likeness. It makes no difference that human beings do not possess an "objective spiritual nature or substance comparable to their psychic or corporeal substance." That which is spiritual in human beings is even more integral to their nature. That which is spiritual "is, as it were, a Divine breath, penetrating human existence and endowing it with the highest dignity, with the highest quality of existence, with an inner independence and unity."[44] According to Berdyaev, it is for this reason that if one intends to speak of human nature and destiny with any depth of seriousness or understanding, one must also speak of God. Human existence and Divine Existence, anthropology and theology, are inextricably intertwined for two reasons: "(1) man is the image and likeness of God the Creator and, (2) God became man, the Son of God manifested Himself to us as the God-Man."[45]

THE IMAGE OF GOD AND THE IMAGE OF HUMANITY

Berdyaev held that personality is the image of God in humankind: "The image of human personality is not only a human image, it is also the image of God."[46] Personality is the lynchpin of Berdyaev's existentialist ethics; for him, it was "an axiological category.... Personality is *the* moral principle, and our relations to all other values [are] determined by reference to it." The ethical is itself grounded in the even deeper metaphysical and theological nature of personality. Personality "rises above the natural life.... It is not the product of the biological process or of social organization. Personality is spiritual and presupposes a spiritual world.... In other words, the existence of personality presupposes the existence of God,"[47] as well as the Spirit of God in human beings.

Personality, however, must not be confused with mere individuality or autonomy. Personhood is relational and depends upon being in community with others. Human beings are fully human to the extent that they are in community and that their social existence reflects the perfect communion of the three divine persons through participation in the divine life that God has made possible in Jesus Christ. Human existence is fundamentally "theanthropic" (or God-directed), said Berdyaev. God calls (or invites) humankind into a communion with divine life, leading to the *theosis* (or divinization) of humankind. Genuine human togetherness, or what Russian theology calls *sobornost*, is possible because God, in whose image human beings are created, is perfect *sobornost*, perfect communion. Theosis of the isolated individual is not possible. In God there is *perichoresis*, a perfect interpenetration of love of the three divine persons in and through love. Likewise, "the absolute Heavenly Man is both the unique man and the whole *soborny* humanity" drawn together by love and in communion with the divine Trinity.[48]

Through this, it can be seen that the Christian belief in the God-Human Jesus Christ profoundly deepens our understanding of personhood. Christ reveals, once and for all, that the human being "bears within himself [or herself] the image which is both the image of man and the image of God, and is the image of man in so far as the image of God is actualized."[49] Christ actualized (perfected) this image of God in his Person. That is what St. Paul means when he speaks of Jesus as the "first born of all creation" (Col. 1:15 NKJV) and also the first of the heavenly humanity (I Cor. 15:48–49). Christ, who perfects our humanity, fulfills in his Person this vocation of God-manhood that sin has hindered and obstructed ever since the Fall. By becoming a human being and living a life without sin, the Son of God has made it possible for humankind to obtain this goal of God-manhood that sin had prevented. And Christ has sent the Spirit into the world so that every human being might effectively use his or her freedom to embrace divinity, as God has embraced humanity.

ON THE HUMANITY OF GOD

It is hard to name another Christian theologian of Berdyaev's era who insisted more strongly that theology is as much about humanity as it is about God and that anthropology is as much about God as it is about humanity. No one, except perhaps Sergei Bulgakov, made this case in quite the same fashion. For example, Karl Barth in his later years spoke with great force about the humanity of God. "In Jesus Christ," Barth wrote in his famous address entitled "The Humanity of God," "there is no isolation of man from God or God from man."[50] In Jesus Christ, God affirms humanity and fully enacts human freedom so that the communion between God and human beings is complete. "God is *human*" through God's complete identification with humanity in Jesus Christ.[51] By the incarnation, God "*encloses* humanity" in God's divinity. In Christ "the fact is once and for all established that God does not exist without man."[52]

Both Berdyaev and Barth offered fundamentally christological arguments about the nature of God and humanity. They parted company, however, in their respective interpretations of how the incarnation narrows the gap between God and humanity. Barth employed Reformed covenantal theology: "In Him [Christ] we encounter the history, the dialogue, in which God and man meet together and are together, the reality of the covenant *mutually* contracted, preserved, and fulfilled by them."[53] Berdyaev invoked the Orthodox vision of the union of the human and the divine expressed in the doctrine of theosis. He began with the radical premise that whatever is truly human is original in God and is fulfilled by participation in the life of God. "The birth of man in God is a theogenic process." Berdyaev writes. "In the eternal idea of him, man is rooted in God-manhood and linked with the God-man," the Lamb who is slain from the foundation of the world. On these grounds, "it may [even] be said that a pre-eternal manhood exists in God."[54] Therefore, "true human-ness," Berdyaev continues, "is likeness to God; it is the divine in man," the *imago dei*. "The divine in man is not the 'super-natural' and it is not a special act of grace; it is a spiritual principle which is in man as a particular reality." The human being at present "is to but a small extent human; he is even inhuman. It is not man who is [fully] human but God,"[55] and the fullness of our humanity is contingent upon complete participation in the divine life (2 Pet. 1:3–4). Berdyaev affirms this as a mystagogical and eschatological truth. For him, the divinity of humanity and the humanity of God are a dual mystery symbolized in the Christian myths of creation and redemption. The entire anthropological significance of the christological dogma, Berdyaev concludes, is not yet understood because humankind still is simply humankind and not yet eschatological divine humanity.

MYTH AND SYMBOL

Berdyaev offered these bold assertions about the nature of humanity with an important qualifier—namely, that the knowledge revealed about human nature and human destiny by the incarnation is not reducible to rational conceptualization. It is not knowledge in the ordinary, scientific, or historical sense. It is knowledge that is wrapped in divine mystery. And it is expressed principally through myth and symbol. "Behind the myth are concealed the greatest realities, the original phenomena of the spiritual life…. Myth is the concrete recital of events and original phenomena of the spiritual life symbolized in the natural world, which has engraved itself on the language, memory, and creative energy of the people.... Myth presents to us the super-natural in the natural, the supra-sensible in the sensible, the spiritual life in the life of flesh; it brings two worlds symbolically together."[56] Contrary to the claims and expectations of the modern schools of demythologization, divine knowledge is lost rather than gained by demythologizing. Both "pure philosophy" and rational theology unburdened of myth and religious experience "cannot know God"[57] in God's personhood. When God is turned into a concept and object of study, little can be understood about God that affects human salvation.

Human beings make myths, but God reveals the truth in myths. All religious language is inherently mythological and symbolic. Myths employ symbolic speech because it is the only kind of language that bridges nature and spirit. "Symbols presuppose the existence of two worlds and two orders of being, and they would not exist were there only one order. A symbol shows us that the meaning of one world is to be found in another, and the meaning itself is revealed in the latter." Likewise, "God can only be perceived symbolically, for it is only by means of symbols that it is possible to penetrate the mystery of His Being. Divinity cannot be rationally determined and remains outside the scope of logical concepts."[58] Biblical myth does not attempt to lift the veil from the face of God, and yet it draws human beings nearer to God than rational conceptualization. It does not externalize God or render God a mere object of cognition, an idea or a thing. The language of myth ably represents God as a person and agent, and pictures the world as filled with God's Spirit. "Academic 'rational' theology [has] transgressed the limits of its competence in one direction by regarding the mysteries of divine life as entirely accessible to itself, and, in the other, by supporting agnosticism, assigned fixed limits to spiritual experience, and the knowledge of the divine."[59]

Similarly, argued Berdyaev, neither scientific nor historical knowledge is capable of comprehending or explaining the whole measure and meaning of our humanity. If Christian theology needs to stay near to symbolic speech and myth, so, too, must theological anthropology. A theological anthropology that embraces myth and symbol as legitimate ways of knowing is needed, for the human person is the intersection of two worlds—nature and spirit—and myth alone can capture their relation and interpenetration. "The very fact of the existence of man," Berdyaev writes in *The Destiny of Man*, "is a break in the natural world and proves that nature cannot be self-sufficient but rests upon a supernatural reality."[60]

Berdyaev believed that this understanding of the doctrine of the God-Man ought to settle once and for all that myth is needed in theology and anthropology. Mystery cannot be "unpacked" and translated into pure conceptual knowledge about God and human beings, although some may try. In the doctrine of the incarnation, Christian theology and anthropology are convincingly joined not by rational concepts but by myth and symbol. If human reason cannot solve the paradox of the dual nature of humankind, neither can we expect it to unravel the riddle of the two natures of Christ: "It is impossible to form a [pure] conception of the dual nature of Christ.... Two natures in one single personality" cannot be grasped "by reason."[61] New Testament writers employed symbolic speech in order to communicate the intersection and interaction of nature and spirit and God and humanity. The incarnation (that is, the birth, death on the cross, resurrection and ascension of the God-Man) is the great Christian myth. From this constellation of images, the New Testament writers constructed a myth, albeit a historicized myth that uniquely recorded historical events that within this mythic framework are shown to hold transhistorical significance.

SUFFERING OF GOD

There is one final feature of Berdyaev's doctrine of God and the relation of the divine and the human that calls for some attention. Berdyaev rejected the traditional notion that God is a perfect act and being and, therefore, that God does not change, is not moved, and does not experience emotion or loss. He opined that this doctrine of the unchanging and immovable character of divine life reflects an unfortunate adaptation of the myth of the biblical God to the Aristotelian idea of the Unmoved Mover. But the living God of the Bible, Berdyaev argued, is assuredly not this static and lifeless God of rational theology. Once again the incarnation is illustrative. If the New Testament writers are trustworthy, then there is drama even in the "inner" (or immanent) life of God, the "drama of love"[62] shared and communicated among the Three Divine Persons. And if God is love, then God is open to suffering. The myth of the incarnation suggests the same inasmuch as the Father loves the Son who is crucified and dies. Love is not love if it is not open to suffering, even, no especially, divine love, since it is the model of all love. What the myth of the incarnation certainly affirms is that "the Son of God suffers not only as Man but also as God."[63] Therefore, to deny tragedy in the divine life, Berdyaev remarks, "is only possible at the cost of denying Christ, His cross and crucifixion, the sacrifice of the Son of God."[64] That drama and tragedy are played out in this world and in the spiritual realm, in human life and in the life of God the Father, the Son, and the Holy Spirit.

Berdyaev concluded, therefore, that rational theology creates "a profound gulf between the idea of perfection in humanity and in God. Self-satisfaction, self-sufficiency, stony immobility, pride, the demand for continual submission, are qualities" that this theology attributes to God's perfection and yet "considers vicious and sinful" when speaking of human beings. If one follows this line of reasoning, what possible sense can be made of the gospel injunction: "Be ye perfect as your Father in Heaven is perfect"?[65] Is holiness in Jesus' own life not accompanied by suffering? Would not God the Father's yearning for the Son entail agony when the Son dies on the cross and even descends among the dead? Does not St. Paul state that "the Spirit Himself makes intercession for us with groanings which cannot be uttered" (Rom. 8:26 NKJV)? In Berdyaev's view, the paradoxical double truth that God is absolutely "other" and also our most immediate Friend is held together by the mystical truth that God's perfection is not an Aristotelian completeness of act and being. It is rather a holiness forged in the love borne by the Father, the Son, and the Holy Spirit for one another.

"It is more worthy of God to ascribe to Him longing for the loved one, a need for sacrificial self-surrender"[66] than to say that God is self-sufficient, passionless, and perfect immobility, Berdyaev concluded. The mythological anthropomorphizing of the Old and New Testaments is infinitely preferable and certainly more accurate about the character of God and God's relation to humanity than the backhanded anthropomorphizing of rational theology. Rational theology exchanges the symbol for analogy, and ultimately exchanges analogy for concepts that break as they try to express this tragic, redemptive, and creative divine-human drama at the meeting of nature and spirit.

DIVINE AND HUMAN FREEDOM: THE *UNGRUND*

The idea that divine and human personality and freedom emerge from the *Ungrund*, the primal, uncreated freedom and pure potentiality (the meonic "nonbeing") "outside" of God is perhaps the most controversial theme in Berdyaev's religious philosophy. This idea of *Ungrund* may not be essential to understanding Berdyaev's theological anthropology, ethics, and views on law and politics. It is integral to his thought, however, and so needs to be discussed. At the start, we should listen carefully to Berdyaev when he says that the *Ungrund* is not a concept but an intuition, a mythological picture of what is rationally unknowable but utterly important for a proper understanding of personality and freedom. The *Ungrund* is a symbol that transcends human conceptualization.

Berdyaev borrowed this idea of the *Ungrund* from the German mystic Jacob Boehme (1575–1642), but said that he used the term differently from Boehme. Boehme claimed that the *Ungrund* is within the godhead; Berdyaev, however, maintained that the *Ungrund* is "outside" of God and is the pure primal meonic potentiality from which God brings everything into existence. God did not create the *Ungrund*. In fact, the godhead issues from the *Ungrund* in an eternal theogenic process. Nevertheless, argued Berdyaev, the *Ungrund* is not some "thing" that exists over and against God. It is not a "thing" or a "nothing" but is pure potentiality. For that matter, neither is God a being in the same way that the human individual is a being. The trinitarian godhead is the personal creator who freely brings the world into existence out of this "nothingness" of pure potentiality or primal freedom.

How does God accomplish this? Berdyaev's answer was a form of theological voluntarism, which drew on Boehme as well as medieval philosophers John Duns Scotus and William of Ockham. God *wills* Creation into existence by imagining it. "The faculty of imagination is the source of all creativeness," he said. "God created the world through imagination. In Him imagination is an absolute ontological power."[67] Thus, on one hand, God did not create *freedom* and, on the other hand, God brought everything that is *freely* into existence through an imaginative act of will. But Berdyaev rejected the traditional way of framing this issue of God's willing and freedom. "It is equally wrong," he argued, "to say that God is bound to will the good and that the good is that which God wills." In other words, God's will is neither arbitrary nor bound by external law or norm. "We cannot judge God from our side of the distinction[s] between good and evil" and freedom and necessity. Quite simply, "God is above good. And there cannot be in Him any evil that is on this side of the distinction.... [And] when we ask whether God is free to will evil we apply to Him the categories of a fallen world."[68]

Let me summarize what I have said about Berdyaev's views on God, freedom, and human morality with five postulates. First, God did not create freedom; rather freedom is uncreated. Second, God brought everything that is into existence out of this uncreated freedom. Third, humanity is both "child" of God and "child" of this uncreated freedom—of nonbeing, of *ton me on*. Fourth, human moral valuation originates from a distinction between good and evil that is generated by human sin and applies solely to a fallen world. Moral good and evil are products of creaturely imagination and will, and do not come from God. Fifth, human moral valuation does not touch upon the character of God. God is beyond good and evil.

THE MEANING OF THE FALL AND ITS RELATION TO LAW

God's creative act constitutes a call to humankind from the depths of freedom to join God as a co-creator of beauty and truth. God, however, risks rebellion in issuing this call, since a person, as we just reviewed, is both a "child" of freedom and a "child" of God. Human beings in their rebellion make a "hell" out of their lives by choosing to live in falsehood and ugliness, apart from God, and descend back toward nonexistence. The Fall is a corruption of human will and imagination; corrupted will and imagination spawn enslaving powers, processes, and authorities that together with fallen angelic agents stand over and against personality and freedom. A hitherto nonexistent dualism of good and evil enters into human life, and this moral dualism gives rise to law and ethics, which represent humanity's struggle to ward off the chaos and dissolution caused by sin.

The Fall is a myth, however, and not a proper subject of scientific history, in Berdyaev's view. It "did not occur in the phenomenal world or in time." Rather, "the phenomenal world and its time are a product of the Fall."[69] The Fall symbolizes the coming to be of the phenomenal world, that is, the determinate and lawbound nature. Before the Fall, the relationship between God and humankind was wholly intersubjective, and humankind's relationship to nature was harmonious. After the Fall, history, marked by objectification and conflict, comes into being. Henceforth, humankind experiences the world as externality, largely incommunicable and unmovable; even God is objectified in human consciousness. Despite their weakened state, human beings intuitively recognize the tragic and deadly force of this objectification of God and the world as a consequence of sin. There remains a universal yearning in the human heart for the peace and harmony of paradise.

The Fall not only affects human beings, but its tragic consequences also permeate the whole of creation. Original sin sullies and depersonalizes all of life, as well as alienating humankind from God. God experiences this loss and is pained by the agony of God's creature, who heads into nonexistence. "God longs for His 'other,' His friend," Berdyaev writes.[70] Yet because God loves perfectly, he cannot and will not abbreviate or contradict human freedom. God cannot and will not unilaterally impose paradisiacal communion upon rebellious human beings and angels, even though he suffers for their separation from him. Nor can the knowledge of good and evil that humankind has gained be reversed.

According to one traditional interpretation of the Fall, the knowledge of good and evil is the Fall itself. When I know good and evil, when I make distinctions and valuations, I lose my innocence and wholeness, fall away from God, and am exiled from paradise. But another interpretation is possible, one that stands in a somewhat paradoxical relationship to the first. "Knowledge in itself is not a sin and does not mean falling away from God."[71]

Rather, knowledge "is good and means discovery of meaning."[72] The evil of original sin, the Fall in its essence, is the act of plucking the fruit of the tree of knowledge against God's wishes. This rebellion, prompted by vain imaginings of autonomy, self-sufficiency, and power over the world, transposes humankind from paradise into "an evil and godless experience of life."[73]

According to this alternative interpretation of the Fall, there is no reason to expect or hope that human beings will return to the state of original naiveté. Human beings mature with knowledge, even though they may also use knowledge in self-defeating and self-destructive ways. In other words, knowledge can be used for good or evil. Meanwhile, God acts to heal the rupture between God and humanity and to stop and reverse the process of corruption unto death that sin starts in the human being like yeast in batter. God sends God's "Only Begotten Son" who "suffers and is crucified, an innocent suffer."[74] "The Lamb is slain from the foundation of the world' (Rev. 13:8 NKJV), says the seer of the book of Revelation." "The Divine sacrifice forms part of the plan of creation from the first," Berdyaev writes.[75] By an act of immense sacrificial love, God renews God's call to communion through the blood of the Lamb. "Man is not free if God stands to him in the relation of a Creator, but he is free if God's relation to him is that of giving him grace."[76]

Too often in Christian theology, said Berdyaev, God's grace is represented as an external power that compels or forces conformity to God's will, whereas grace is not alien to human nature. For that reason grace rehabilitates and transforms human nature from "within." It restores the image of God in the human person. The truth is that God's grace is eternal love freely given, resonant with personality and rehabilitative of human nature. Grace restores human nature from the "inside" so that God's call to communion reverberates throughout the person's whole being, as if he or she were in paradise. And the person is enabled to respond effectively to God's call. This redemptive and sanctifying effect of Christ's sacrifice and restoration of human nature puts in place the conditions under which law, which is born of sin, is no longer needed. But before we take that penultimate step along Berdyaev's theological path, it is necessary to explore more fully how an objectified world has come into being and how and why human sin brings law into existence.

OBJECTIFICATION AND THE ORIGIN OF LAW

As I have intimated already, Berdyaev maintained that the Fall brings about a shift in human consciousness from existential, intersubjective knowing and encounter, wherein the I-Thou relationship prevails, to a way of imagining and relating to God, the human other, and nature that is depersonalizing and objectifying. In a fallen state, human beings experience the world as external, fragmented, and ruled by causal necessity. The primal *sobornost* of existence is broken. The I and the Thou have become competing egos, self-centered selves that view each other as objects, things, means to an end. This process of "objectification" introduces into human society all the instrumentalities of depersonalization, coercion, and force that characterize a fallen world. The whole of the creation is affected. The broken harmony of paradise devolves into exploitation and commodification of every living and nonliving thing.

At root, objectification is the "ejection of man into the external, it is an exteriorization of him.... [It] is the uprising of an exteriorized 'not-I' in place of the 'Thou' of the primordial communion of being. The exteriorized I, the egoistic, self-alienated self, experiences" the world as external, an obstacle to happiness or an object for possession, use, or self-gratification. From the Fall onward, human thought, will, and imagination have taken this unholy experience of the created order to be what reality really is. Since at least the time of Immanuel Kant, argued Berdyaev, most of modern philosophy has been blind to the paradox "that what is called 'objective' is precisely what is 'subjective' and what is called 'subjective' is 'objective'.... Objectivity was accepted as identical with general validity." In truth, however, "the subject is the creation of God in personal relation with God while the object" is the sinful subject's projection of a world governed and connected by causal law rather than love.[77] Thus human beings conceive even God as an object related to them as external supreme cause or law or objective good and not as a subject of personal communion; they no longer view this relationship as an existential encounter.

Berdyaev insisted that this process of objectification is not merely a figment of the mind or imagination. The objectified world is "real" insofar as fallen existence is an actual condition, an environment, in which "exteriorization and alienation are [always and continually] taking place."[78] Human beings are an inseparable part of that milieu. Just as "'uncreated freedom' is a limiting notion that symbolically does not lend itself to logical definition," so, too, "objectification" is "a symbolical description of the fallen state of the world in which man finds himself subservient to necessity and disunion."[79] Berdyaev summarizes:

> [The] Fall is a matter of importance in the theory of knowledge. Objectification and the unauthentic character of the phenomenal world are by no means to be taken as meaning that the world of men and women, animals and plants, minerals, stars, seas, forests and so on is unreal and that behind it is something entirely unlike it—the things-in-themselves. It means rather that this world is in a spiritual and moral condition in which it ought not to be, it is a

state of servitude and loss of freedom, of enmity and alienation, of ejection into the external, of subjection to necessity.[80]

The difference between the life of the spirit and objectification is the difference between personal communion and historical social existence, or the difference between love and justice. Social existence and the laws that govern it imprison personality in an environment of externalized power and coercion designed to control the disintegrative effects of sin; whereas, communion and love preserve and deepen the integrity of personality in an environment of free existential communion.

THE ORIGIN, NATURE, AND PURPOSE OF LAW

On the basis of this foundational inquiry, Berdyaev's outlook on the origin, purpose, and meaning of law can be explained. Law, said Berdyaev, is the expression of "a vision of the Divine Will distorted by sinful nature." Law is not "an original expression of God's feelings toward man";[81] rather, objectification, social existence, and law go hand in glove. Traditional Christian theology embraces St. Paul's judgment that the law came into the world because of sin and death, and that law makes sin manifest. Law "denounces sin, limits it, but cannot conquer it."[82] The primary evil is not the law, of course, but sin, which necessitates law. In order, however, for the human person to attain the fullness of life of which Paul also speaks, he or she must not only be delivered from sin and death but from law as well.

Berdyaev maintained that law and the ethics of law are refined and partially transformed expressions of the universally human desire for revenge. All human "valuation, judgment and condemnation contain an element of primitive vengeance in sublimated form," Berdyaev argued. But while law and justice may be rooted in the primal human desire for revenge, that desire when expressed through law and justice never has been merely an expression "of cruelty or ferocity." Among the ancients "it was preeminently a moral feeling and a religious duty ... [as] can be seen from the Greek tragedy."[83] This moral feeling or impulse is originally grounded in fear and awe, and later in the higher forms of ethics in religious law and conscience.

THE NATURE OF LAW

Berdyaev's analysis of the origin, nature, and purposes of law belongs to his "epistemology of original sin." "The realm of objectification, which is a consequence of sin, is a social realm,... made for the average person, for mankind in the mass, for the ordinary and the hum-drum, for *das man*."[84] Where genuine communion no longer exists, historical social existence comes into being, and this social world depends upon law in order to continue. Through law, society regulates disruptive, disintegrative, and dissimulating effects of sin. By the use of law, society protects the endangered individual from destructive forces and makes room for a measure of personal freedom. Ironically, however this freedom and security is bought at the price of continued devaluation and diminution of personality and communion. But law sees only the outer human being whose personal visage blends into the mass and common herd. While protecting the individual, law tends to move from the particular to the general. In this respect, Christian theology errs profoundly whenever it describes God as law or as the enforcer of law. God is a Person and the Lover of persons in their uniqueness and particularity. Love, and not law, is the appropriate symbol of personality.

Wherever there is the fear that the stability and peace of society are under threat, law trumps love and personality. Law by its very nature—whether it is positive, natural, moral, or divine law—deals in abstraction and generality and is allied with external force. But personality can never be subsumed under an objective norm, nor is force in a sinful world finally amicable to love, freedom, and personality. For this reason the ethics of the gospel reverses the method of the ethics of law. Under the ethics of redemption "it is impossible," Berdyaev argues, "that in the same circumstances one ought always and everywhere to act the same way," by the same rule or norm. "It is impossible if only because circumstances never are quite the same."[85] It is impossible also because the goal of grace is the salvation of the unique person and not of the objectified and externalized social order. Personality, freedom, and love are concerned with the inner human being in all of his or her discreteness as an icon of God, personal agent, and potential God-man or God-woman.

LAW AND FREEDOM OF THE WILL

Based upon Berdyaev's strong strain of Christian personalism, one might expect, as happens often in Western theology, that he embraced the doctrine of freedom of the will. In fact, he rejected the concept. Berdyaev's view was that the doctrine of freedom of the will is a mistake representing a wrong turn in Christian philosophy. "The doctrine of free will was modeled to suit a normative, legalistic morality," Berdyaev remarked.[86] It is, in a sense, the counterpart in Christian ethics of the juridical doctrine of redemption. It satisfies society's need to attribute moral responsibility to the person. According to "legalistic normative ethics," freedom of the will is "the condition of fulfilling the moral law," and by this exercise a person is "justified if he chooses the good and fulfills the law, and condemned if he chooses evil and fails to fulfill the law."[87] But freedom, according to Berdyaev, "must not be understood ... merely as the possibility given to man of fulfilling the law and justifying himself by good works."[88] Recall that Berdyaev argued strenuously that freedom is the primal reality and that its integrity and creative potential do not dependent upon the existence of law. Freedom is ontologically precedent to law and is therefore in no sense a function or correlative of law. Also, freedom eschatologically surpasses the law, since law does not exist in the kingdom of God. So it certainly makes no sense to say that the freedom of the will belongs to the essence of humanity. In the beatific life of communion with God there is no such freedom of will. As for the present, said Berdyaev, "man is enslaved by the necessity to choose between that which is forced upon him and carrying out the law under fear of penalties. He proves to be least free in that which is connected with his 'free will.'"[89]

Berdyaev felt that in this respect, Luther had it at least partly correct when he rebelled "against justification by works connected with free will."[90] The ethics of redemption embraces this vision with its promise of eternal life free of sin, suffering, and death. It proclaims that, through Jesus Christ and the Spirit, the kingdom of God enters the lives of all believers. True liberation comes through grace and not from free will; human beings are free when they no longer need to fear failing to do the right or the good prescribed by law, when they need not choose between good and evil because good and evil, together with sin itself, no longer exist having been consumed by the love of God and the sanctifying fire of Pentecostal grace.

Like the idea of a legalistically described moral order, the doctrine of the free will is rooted in fear and driven by fear. And it can be an enslaving doctrine, said Berdyaev, since the ethical apparatus that human beings devise to judge the will manifest all of the objectifying and depersonalizing characteristics of law and the juridical understanding of redemption. Thus, concluded Berdyaev, it was a mistake for Catholic moral theology and Protestant ethics to adopt a doctrine of free will in order to secure human dignity. Yes, free will may serve, as in the case of law, to control the destructive effects of sin. But the doctrine of free will must not be mistaken for true freedom of personality, which is not contingent upon or correlative to the distinction between good and evil or a doctrine of free will. True freedom of personality is creative energy that envisions and brings into existence new values and realities.

In summary of Berdyaev's view, the ethics of law and the doctrine of freedom of will are both premised on the concept of a binding moral order external to personal existence. This concept of a single universally binding moral order, however, is itself a product of objectification. Objectification causes us to experience *autexousion*, the deep and transcendent capacity within every human being for self-determination, as an external norm. This objectification contradicts personality and obscures the image of God in humankind. It even invites us to imagine a will that stands over and against this moral order and is "free" to obey or defy it. But at the source of their existence, human beings are not creatures of law. Humankind is personality brought into existence by a divine act of love. God intends for communion that is without fear or coercion. For love is the opposite of fear, and love transcends law. Human love is movement toward God, which we may call will, but not free will. It is simply contradictory to speak of a free will that stands poised between willing God and willing against God. How can love will against itself? "There is no fear in love; but perfect love casts out fear, because fear involves torment.... He who fears has not been made perfect in love. We love Him because he first loved us (1 John 4:18–19 NKJV)."

THE POSITIVE PURPOSE OF LAW

Just as "the realm of objectification is a social realm," so too is law. "The ethics of law is essentially social.... The Fall subordinated human conscience to society. Society became the bearer and guardian of the moral law."[91] Yet even though law has this "negative" origin, it does have a positive purpose. For in a sinful world, Berdyaev maintained, personal well-being cannot depend solely upon the spiritual or moral character of others: "It is a paradox, but the exclusive predominance of an ethics of grace in a sinful world would endanger the freedom and the existence of personality."[92] And a "society that chose to be based solely upon grace and declined to have any law would be a despotic society. Thus Communist society may be said in a sense to be based upon grace and not upon law, of course, it is not grace in the Christian sense of the term. The result is a tyranny, a theocracy reversed."[93] Law serves a positive good in so much as it clears space for the exercise of personal freedom and human creativity.

But this is not all that needs to be told. In a fallen and sinful world, "justice is righteousness refracted in the common life of every day."[94] We are faced with this profound paradox that reason and human effort alone cannot wholly clarify or resolve: "The law does not know the concrete and unique, living personality or penetrate into its inner life, but it preserves that personality from interference and violence on the part of others, whatever their spiritual condition."[95] So unredeemed, "man requires law and is therefore naturally inclined to see law at work everywhere."[96] Yet, in the last analysis, although it may be true that "Christ did not indeed reject law," Christ did reveal "a spiritual world where love and freedom enlightened by grace effectively triumph over law."[97] Grace and love, not law, are the "radiating energy"[98] of life, and life could not go on without that energy.

FREEDOM, IMAGINATION, AND CREATIVENESS

"By the side of the self-contained moral world of laws and rules to which nothing can be added," writes Berdyaev in *The Destiny of Man*, "man builds up in imagination a higher, free and beautiful world lying beyond ordinary good and evil.... The Kingdom of God is the image of a full, perfect, beautiful, free and divine life.... But the most perfect fulfillment of the law," he added, "is not the same as the perfect life."[99] The ethics of redemption promises life free of sin, suffering, and death. It proclaims that the kingdom of God enters the lives of all who believe in the crucified and resurrected Lord.

The ethics of redemption also indicates the eclipse of the ethics of law and points to the ethics of creativeness without explicitly setting it forth. This is appropriate, says Berdyaev, for "if the ways of creativeness were [explicitly] indicated and justified in the Holy Scriptures, then creativeness would be obedience [to a command], which is to say that there would be no creativeness.... The compulsory revelation of creativeness as a law, as an indication of the way to go, would contradict God's idea of man, God's desire to see in man the creator, [freely] reflecting His own divine image."[100] Nonetheless, Jesus' parables of the kingdom of God are about "the fruit which the seed must bring forth if it falls on good soil and of talents given to man which must be returned for profit. Under cover of parable Christ refers in these words to man's creative activity, to his creative vocation."[101]

As with God, so also with human beings, creativity is an imaginative exercise. The human imagination, however, has been warped and distorted by sin just as much as reason and the will. Therefore, it should not be surprising that law, which combats the effects of sin, also polices and inhibits imagination. Berdyaev writes, "The ethics of law forbids man to imagine a better world and a better life; it fetters him to the world as given and to the socially organized herd life, laying down taboos and prohibitions everywhere. But the ethics of creativeness breaks with the herd-existence and refuses to recognize legalistic prohibitions. "To the 'law' of the present life it opposes 'the image' of a higher one."[102] Redemption is liberation from this fallen age. The mind of Christ is a mind that is freed to imagine and envision a new creation. Indeed, "God expects from man the highest freedom, the freedom of the eighth day of creation."[103]

Berdyaev argued that the whole fabric of human life depends upon creativeness for vision and vitality. Short of the kingdom of God, however, "there is always a tragic discrepancy between the burning heat of the creative fire in which the artistic image is conceived and the cold of its formal realization. Every book, picture, statue, good work, social institution is an instance of this cooling down of the original flame."[104] Yet Pentecost is a sign, emblem, and foretaste of the new creation wherein this paradox of flame and dying ember is transcended. Berdyaev's ethics of creativeness is an ethics of this age of the Holy Spirit where freedom comes into its own as the power to imitate divine creativity. Freedom, according to the ethics of law, means "acceptance or rejection of the law of the good and responsibility for doing one or the other."[105] By contrast, genuine freedom, according to the ethics of creativeness, is the liberty of the children of God to participate in the realization of the kingdom of God, wherein the old morality of right and wrong and good and evil exists no more.

The ethics of the old creation is always either teleological or deontological. According to teleology, the good is defined as the ultimate goal or purpose in life toward which the ethical person strives. According to deontology, the good is an overarching norm under which the ethical person performs his or her duty. Both teleology and deontology are bound up with law and inhibit the growth of the moral imagination. Law "is limited to imagining compliance with, or violation of, its behests." But "the most perfect fulfillment of the law" is not even a shadow of the new creation in Christ.[106] Law, no matter how it is conceived or lived out, governs the Old Adam and not the New Adam. The Christian faith redefines the moral life. Obedience to law for the sake of the good is replaced by creative activity inspired by a vision of the beauty of God and God's kingdom. "From the ontological and cosmological point of view," Berdyaev writes, "the final end of being must be thought of as beauty and not as goodness,"[107] not fulfillment of law but the synergy of divine and human creative freedom for the sake of the eternal kingdom of Love. Indeed, good that is defined as the opposite of evil contradicts beauty in the same way that the sinful and enslaving structures of objectification contradict the kingdom of God.

The ethics of creativeness resembles no other ethics; indeed, it confounds our habitual association of law with ethics and the formal distinction between ethics and aesthetics. One may ask, "How can beauty be the final goal of life rather than the good?" Is not beauty an aesthetic appraisement? That might be true in a world of sin and objectification, but Berdyaev's eschatological imagination pressed beyond such distinctions and categories. In Christian ethics, God is frequently described in terms of the final Good, but in Berdyaev's view, even this concept of the final Good has not been purged of ethical dualism. Good that functions as the opposite of evil is only a means, a path at best, to the kingdom of God, whereas "beauty lies beyond the knowledge of good and evil" and all of the division and disharmony of sin. The perfect perichoresis of the Father, the Son, and the Holy Spirit is Beauty. The communion of saints in the kingdom of Heaven is Beauty. God is the Good only if "evil is already forgotten," but in that case "*good is beauty.*"[108]

BERDYAEV'S CHRISTIAN REALISM

Berdyaev was not starry-eyed about beauty; he knew that the diabolical may even—and often does—mimic beauty. But he said that this is not true beauty. "There can be no moral deformity in beauty, [for] that is a property of evil. The beauty of evil is an illusion and a fraud."[109] This fraudulent beauty does not hold truth and is in a process of decay, and ultimately the fraud will be exposed. The veneer will wash off and expose an essence that is ugly or grotesque. The ethics of creativeness discovers the kingdom of God "as the reign of beauty."[110] This is an active process, for "beauty is never objectivity in itself, which asks for nothing but mere passivity in relation to itself, it is always transfiguration."[111] The beauty of the kingdom of God is not an object but the quality of transfigured relationships reached through and by the synergy of human and divine energies. It is a transfigured relation, harmony, and mutuality, transcending not just law and coercive force but the very distinction between good and evil. The beauty of the kingdom of God is holiness. Holiness is a communion of love and not merely a possession of the independent ego.

For all of this talk of synergy and perfection, however, there is not a trace of liberal progressivism or secular utopianism in Berdyaev. He was a Christian realist, albeit not a typical one. "The Christian faith tells us to seek first the kingdom of God and divine perfection," he writes. But, he quickly adds, Christianity "will have nothing to do with the day-dreaming, utopias, or false imagination; it is realist, and the Fathers of the Church are always appealing for spiritual sobriety. Christian consciousness has a clear perception of all the difficulties that beset the way to perfection, but it knows that 'the kingdom of Heaven suffereth violence and the violent take it by force.'"[112]

Berdyaev powerfully invoked the Christian doctrine of original sin, although with a different sort of emphasis and theological outcome than what we have learned to expect from Reinhold Niebuhr or Karl Barth. Berdyaev described the human being as a "sick being, with a strong unconscious life"[113] and an imagination that readily turns idolatrous and diabolical. He constantly pointed out these idolatries and how human beings are enslaved to them. His realism was truly dialectical in that he held forth the utterly transcendent holiness of God as the standard of perfection over and against which we measure human sinfulness and evil. While he may have been pessimistic about the degree of holiness possible in history, he was optimistic about the possibility of human redemption and salvation. In his remarkable essay "The Worth of Christianity and the Unworthiness of Christians," Berdyaev writes:

> The negation of Christianity due to the shortcomings of Christians is essentially the ignoring or misunderstanding of original sin. Those who are conscious of original sin see in the unworthiness of the Christian not a flat contradiction of the worth of Christianity, but a confirmation of it. It is the religion of redemption and salvation, and is not forgetful that the world finds pleasure in sin. There are many teachers who claim that the good life can be compassed without any real overcoming of evil, but Christianity does not think so; it insists on this victory, a rebirth; it is radical and more exacting.[114]

Berdyaev's realism was personalist and christological, communalist and trinitarian. He had the highest expectations for human perfection, while keeping his eyes wide open to the corrupting and divisive force of sin in the world. Only the *metanoia*, the conversion of the person, and not "any program imposed externally" upon the individual or society, enables human beings to reach the heights of goodness and holiness. "Compulsion will never make good Christians or a Christian social order," Berdyaev remarks. "There must be an effective and real change in the hearts of persons and of peoples, and the realization of this perfect life is a task of infinite difficulty and endless duration."[115] The kingdom of God is not a program; nor is it the inevitable outcome of an evolutionary or ameliorative process. Berdyaev criticized Vladimir Soloviev's political theology on this score. Solovyev presented his theory of Godmanhood as if it were "a necessary determined process of evolution."[116] In him there were "no tragic conflicts and yawning gulfs, such as are disclosed in Dostoyevsky."[117] Berdyaev thought that Soloviev's theory was not sufficiently serious about either the reality of human freedom or the persistence of human sin that prevents the coming of the fullness of the kingdom of God. In *The Russian Idea*, Berdyaev commends an active rather than passive eschatology: "The end of this world, and the end of history, depend … upon the creative act of man."[118] And yet, even as he made this commendation, Berdyaev adds that no amount of human creativeness guarantees that the kingdom will come: "I have shown the tragedy of human creativeness, which consists in the fact that there is a lack of correspondence between creative purpose and created product. Man is not creating a new life or a new form of existence, but cultural products" all of which are affected and distorted by "objectivization which is based upon alienation, the loss of freedom and personality, and subjection to the general and necessary."[119]

Berdyaev opposed the humanistic ideas of progress. He insisted that the Christian must vigilantly guard at all times against the lure of the multifarious cultural artifacts, ideologies, and institutions that would lay claim to the whole of humankind and promise worldly redemption. In *Slavery and Freedom* (1939), he included among these family, sex, money, and property, collectivism and capitalism, the state and revolution. It seems that nothing in this world is "safe," or the source of human salvation. Even Christ prayed for the kingdom of God as gift of the Father and, just as important, made his prayer the model for every Christian.

Fielding Clarke stated that we should not expect from Berdyaev a program of social, economic, or political reform. Berdyaev made no claim to having "produced a new theology or a new sociology. He speaks of 'personalistic socialism,' for example, as his aim, but it is with principles not details that he is concerned. *It is not programmes but perspectives which he gives us.*"[120] For Berdyaev, human personality cannot exist without community. Thus community is itself part of human nature. Nevertheless, no particular historical structure of society is perfectly suited to human beings. Berdyaev was true to the spirit of the Hebrew prophets. Like them, he warned against every possible form of human pride and idolatry of self or society. Like them, he envisioned salvation as a communion of being and saw justice as a sign of the birth of the kingdom of God. He strongly insisted that Christians must move beyond a concern with their own individual salvation and act in ways that affirm that in Christ the kingdom has already been made present. In other words, Berdyaev's ethic of creativeness was an integral element of his realism. It brought the eschatological hope of Christian faith up front and center, and from this standpoint radically relativized every human achievement. Yet Christ's parables and the Spirit-filled events of Pentecost also open up a positive vision of divine and human community that should outweigh a negative fixation upon personal struggle with sin and evil and inspire creative acts that help bring about social, economic, and political justice.

THE LEGACY

More than fifty years after his death in 1949, and despite his sometimes heterodox views, Nicholas Berdyaev quite deservedly ranks as one of the most brilliant and creative twentieth-century exponents of Eastern Christian mystical theology and spirituality. My teacher, the late Will Herberg, justifiably included Nicholas Berdyaev with Jacques Maritain, Martin Buber, and Paul Tillich in his influential *Four Existentialist Theologians*, published in 1960.[121] If that book were compiled today, no doubt Berdyaev would retain his position among the great existentialist and personalist theologians of the twentieth century.

Sadly, however, little of Berdyaev's work is now in print in English. His enormous notoriety during the mid-twentieth century diminished as time wore on, and he fell out of the corpus of theologians routinely read in seminaries and graduate schools. Whereas Protestants, Roman Catholics, and Jews kept alive the legacies of Berdyaev's companions in Herberg's anthology, the Orthodox in the English-speaking world neglected Berdyaev.

For important reasons, those Russian theologians of Berdyaev's generation and the generation following who founded a neopatristic school of Orthodox thought took center stage. The likes of Vladimir Lossky, Georges Florovsky, and John Meyendorff sought, in T. S. Eliot's words, to "purify the dialect of the tribe"[122] as they clarified the historical, dogmatic, and liturgical riches of Orthodoxy. They actively participated in the burgeoning modern ecumenical movement and made a tremendous gift of Orthodoxy to Western Christian thought and the churches. They founded and populated Orthodox seminaries, thus giving new life to the tradition. They defined the mainstream of Orthodox historical, systematic, and liturgical theology for our time.

Nonetheless, the neglect of Berdyaev (and Sergei Bulgakov to a somewhat lesser extent) has cost Orthodoxy in originality and energy. Berdyaev seriously reflected on the nature of religious experience and was deeply engaged with modern philosophical and religious thought. His work breathed new life into a church theology that had grown formalistic and stale. Today, his thought may be in a unique position to address the postmodernist controversy and reinvigorate Orthodox theology as the neopatristic school shows signs of growing tired and becoming disconnected from the everyday life of Orthodox Christians.

Ironically, during the very same years that Berdyaev's reputation suffered in the Western diaspora, Russian dissidents and religious intelligentsia rediscovered and wholeheartedly embraced him. From the 1960s through the collapse of the Soviet Union, Berdyaev was ascendant as the Russian brand of a liberation theologian. His strong emphasis on Christianity and freedom inspired hope and resistance against Soviet tyranny. His critique of Marxism and Bolshevism and his historical interpretation of Russian religion and culture helped to explain what was happening and what needed to be done in order finally to shed Communism. His influence may be found in such dissidents and religious leaders of the era as Alexander Solzhenitsyn and Father Alexander Men. During visits I made to Russia in 1990 and 1991, Berdyaev came up in conversations more frequently than any other modern Russian religious thinker. Those with whom I spoke drew heavily from his prophetic analysis in such works as *The Origin of Russian Communism* (1937) and *The Russian Idea* (1946). Since then, Berdyaev's influence has receded, mainly because of the pressing need to stabilize the church and recover the theological and dogmatic tradition. Yet his legacy is secure in Russia. His writings are back in print, and Berdyaev will continue to be read and studied as one of the towering figures of modern Russian religious philosophy.

NOTES

1. In this and following instances, the date in parentheses after a title is the original publication date in the language in which the book was first published, whether Russian, French, or English.
2. Nicholas Berdyaev, *Dream and Reality* (New York: Macmillan, 1951), 115.
3. Ibid., 115.
4. Nicholas Berdyaev, *Slavery and Freedom* (New York: Charles Scribner's Sons, 1944), 13.
5. Ibid.
6. Nicolas Berdyaev, *The Destiny of Man* (New York: Charles Scribner's Sons, 1960), 137.
7. Quoted by Matthew Spinka in *Nicolas Berdyaev: Captive of Freedom* (Philadelphia: Westminster Press, 1950), 20.
8. Berdyaev, *Dream and Reality*, 154.
9. Ibid., 153.
10. Ibid., 154–155.
11. Translated by Matthew Spinka and quoted in *Nicholas Berdyaev*, 35–36. The letter is also included in Nicholas Berdyaev's *The Spiritual Crisis of the Intelligentsia* (St. Petersburg, 1910), 299.
12. Berdyaev, *Dream and Reality*, 155.
13. Berdyaev, *Slavery and Freedom*, 16–17.
14. Nicolas Berdyaev, *The Bourgeois Mind and Other Essays* (London: Sheed & Ward, 1934), 24.
15. Ibid., 24–25.
16. Fielding Clarke, *Introduction to Berdyaev* (London: Geoffrey Bles, 1950), 18.
17. Berdyaev, *Dream and Reality*, 177.
18. Nicholas Berdyaev, *Freedom and the Spirit* (London: Geoffrey Bles, 1935), xix.
19. Berdyaev, *Destiny of Man*, 7
20. Ibid.
21. Ibid., 47.

22. Ibid.
23. Ibid., 49–50.
24. Ibid., 49.
25. Ibid., 53.
26. Ibid., 47.
27. Ibid.
28. Ibid., 133.
29. Ibid., 135.
30. Berdyaev, *Freedom and Spirit*, 173–174.
31. Ibid., 175.
32. Ibid., 174.
33. Ibid., 175.
34. Ibid., 175–176.
35. Nicolas Berdyaev, *The Meaning of the Creative Act* (New York: Harper & Brothers, 1954), 101.
36. Ibid., 98.
37. Berdyaev, *Destiny of Man*, 162.
38. Nicolas Berdyaev, *The Beginning and the End* (New York: Harper & Brothers, 1957), 174.
39. Berdyaev, *Meaning of the Creative Act*, 99.
40. Berdyaev, *Destiny of Man*, 23.
41. Ibid., 112.
42. Berdyaev, *Meaning of the Creative Act*, 105–106, 110.
43. Ibid., 110–111.
44. Nicholas Berdyaev, *Spirit and Reality* (New York: Charles Scribner's Sons, 1939), 6.
45. Berdyaev, *Destiny of Man*, 69.
46. Berdyaev, *Slavery and Freedom*, 44.
47. Berdyaev, *Destiny of Man*, 72.
48. Berdyaev, *Freedom and Spirit*, 138.
49. Berdyaev, *Slavery and Freedom*, 45.
50. Karl Barth, *The Humanity of God* (Atlanta: John Knox Press, 1960), 46.
51. Ibid., 51.
52. Ibid., 50.
53. Ibid., 46.
54. Nicholas Berdyaev, *The Divine and the Human* (London: Geoffrey Bles, 1949), 111.
55. Ibid., 110.
56. Berdyaev, *Freedom and Spirit*, 72.
57. Ibid., 64.
58. Ibid.
59. Ibid., 66–67.
60. Berdyaev, *Destiny of Man*, 60.
61. Berdyaev, *Freedom and Spirit*, 73.

62. Ibid., 210.

63. Berdyaev, *Slavery and Freedom,* 51.

64. Berdyaev, *Destiny of Man,* 38.

65. Ibid., 37.

66. Ibid., 38.

67. Ibid., 97.

68. Ibid., 56.

69. Berdyaev, *Beginning and End,* 241.

70. Berdyaev, *Destiny of Man,* 25.

71. Ibid., 49.

72. Ibid.

73. Ibid.

74. Ibid., 41.

75. Ibid., 44

76. Ibid., 45.

77. Berdyaev, *Beginning and End,* 17.

78. Ibid., 60.

79. Berdyaev, *Dream and Reality,* 288.

80. Berdyaev, *Beginning and End,* 59–60.

81. Berdyaev, *Freedom and Spirit,* 75.

82. Berdyaev, *Destiny of Man,* 110.

83. Ibid., 114.

84. Berdyaev, *Beginning and End,* 70.

85. Berdyaev, *Destiny of Man,* 170.

86. Ibid., 25.

87. Ibid.

88. Ibid., 26.

89. Ibid., 25–26.

90. Ibid., 25.

91. Ibid., 112.

92. Ibid., 119–120.

93. Ibid., 130

94. Ibid., 120.

95. Ibid., 130.

96. Berdyaev, *Freedom and Spirit,* 175.

97. Ibid.

98. Berdyaev, *Destiny of Man,* 178.

99. Ibid., 183.

100. Berdyaev, *Meaning of the Creative Act,* 97, 99.

101. Berdyaev, *Destiny of Man,* 162.

102. Ibid., 184.

103. Berdyaev, *Meaning of the Creative Act,* 158.

104. Berdyaev, *Destiny of Man,* 166.

105. Ibid., 170.

106. Ibid., 184.

107. Ibid., 185.

108. Berdyaev, *Divine and Human,* 139 (emphasis added).

109. Ibid.

110. Ibid.

111. Ibid., 143.

112. Berdyaev, *Bourgeois Mind,* 126.

113. Berdyaev, *Destiny of Man,* 68.

114. Berdyaev, *Bourgeois Mind,* 126–127.

115. Ibid, 126.

116. Nikolai Berdyaev, *The Russian Idea* (Hudson, N.Y.: Lindisfarne Press, 1992), 188.

117. Ibid., 109.

118. Ibid., 257.

119. Ibid.

120. Clark, *Introduction to Berdyaev,* 183.

121. Will Herberg, ed., *Four Existentialist Theologians* (Garden City, N.Y.: Doubleday, 1958).

122. T. S. Eliot, "Little Gidding," in *Collected Poems 1909–1962* (New York: Harcourt Brace, 1963), 204.

[CHAPTER 21]

Vladimir Nikolaievich Lossky (1903–1958)

MIKHAIL M. KULAKOV

Vladimir Nikolaievich Lossky was born in 1903 in St. Petersburg into the family of a well-known Russian intuitionist philosopher, Nikolay Onufriyevich Lossky. He studied briefly at the universities of Petrograd and Prague before matriculating at the University of Paris, from which he eventually graduated with a degree in medieval studies in 1927. In 1922 Vladimir was exiled from Russia with his father's family and other notable intellectuals who had refused to cooperate with the new Soviet government. After a two-year stay in Prague, the family settled in Paris, where Lossky immersed himself in study of Western theology and spirituality under the guidance of the influential Thomist scholar Etienne Gilson.

Lossky devoted a great deal of time to the study of Meister Eckhart's negative mysticism. He detected a certain affinity between this German Dominican friar and the Byzantine mystics. Eckhart rejected the earlier attempts of Western medieval mystics to encounter God with prayer, using one's rational abilities. He was convinced that it is easier to say what God is not than to attempt to formulate what God is. To seek a direct and immediate fellowship of the soul with the inexpressible and unapproachable God was, for Eckhart, a much more fruitful endeavor. Yet, Lossky did not find Eckhart (particularly Eckhart's *Gottheit*) to be sufficiently personalist in his negative (or apophatic, from the Greek *apophasis*, "denial") approach. Nor was Eckhart able to overcome the tendency of considering "common nature" before the persons of the Trinity. Lossky's brilliant study *Theologie négative et connaissance de Dieu chez Maitre Eckhart* was published in Paris posthumously in 1960. The study of the Western scholastic and mystical traditions led Lossky to a thorough investigation of the roots of spiritual and doctrinal divergence between East and West and a search for points of contact and unity.

Lossky accepted his forced exile from Russia as a call to become a living witness of Eastern Orthodoxy to Christians in the West. He distanced himself from Orthodox circles in France that promoted the utopian ideas of Holy Russia and Slavophile exclusivism. Instead, he channeled his energies toward the construction of a patristically based, comprehensive theological system. Already in 1928 Vladimir was playing a leading role in the Brotherhood of St. Photius, an émigré missionary society in Paris, which Lossky envisaged as an "order of Christian knights" engaged in Orthodox witness and creative dialogue with the West. Lossky's centrist stand among the various groups of Russian emigration in Paris was demonstrated by his staunch support of the Moscow Patriarchate, the canonical authority of which had been challenged by radical anti-Soviet factions on the right and liberal circles on the left that were in contact with the Patriarch of Constantinople and were locally associated with Metropolitan Evlogii. Among the more influential representatives of these liberal circles in Paris were philosopher Nicholas Berdyaev and theologian Sergei Bulgakov.

Lossky was deeply involved in the controversies and debates of the 1930s. His lengthy tract *The Sophia Controversy*, published in 1936, contained ferociously destructive criticism of the highly complex and vastly influential philosophical theology of Bulgakov. Following Soloviev, Bulgakov envisaged the existence of a world-soul, or a "fourth hypostasis," described as an "eternal femininity" in God that dominates the cosmic process. Lossky denounced Bulgakov's teaching for its hidden determinism, its slavish dependence on philosophy, and personification of nature, which led to a reduced and inadequate notion of divine and human persons robbed of genuine self-determination.[1] Lossky saw it as his task to liberate Russian religious thought from its enslavement to philosophy in general and to nineteenth-century German idealism and Slavophile exclusivism in particular. His theological work is thus a reaction to these tendencies in Khomyakov and Soloviev in the nineteenth century, as well as in his contemporaries Bulgakov and Berdyaev.

Unlike Bulgakov and Berdyaev, who were suspicious of the official Russian Church within the Soviet Union, Lossky pled for fidelity to it in its concrete, historical form. He was deeply saddened by the dismemberment of the Russian Church brought about by the tragic events of the Bolshevik Revolution. He felt that both conservative and liberal Russian emigrants betrayed the Orthodox Church within Russia. In contrast to his universal vision of the church, their notions of the "true ecclesia" were too dependent on certain political, cultural, or national conditions (or ideals not related directly to the historical church as a canonical institution, as in the case of Berdyaev and Bulgakov). In *Mystical Theology*, Lossky portrayed the Orthodox Church as the "center of the universe, the sphere in which its destinies are determined."[2] In "Temptations of Ecclesial Consciousness," first published in Paris in 1950, he wrote that each one is called "to the ministry of the Church at the present moment in the existing conditions." He urged his readers to discern, in the humiliated and persecuted Russian Church, the "true Church," which had a crucial task.[3] He warned that one should not wait "for a normal period (such periods do not exist)."[4]

Lossky certainly did not wait for a better period. He engaged in intense dialogue with Catholic and Protestant theologians. He labored tirelessly for the recognition of the French Orthodox community of the Western rite. He supported the embattled leaders of the Moscow Patriarchate, and held in high esteem the patriarchal *locum tenens*, Metropolitan Sergii (Stragorodskii), maintaining an intensive correspondence with him over a number of years.[5] He exemplified the same realism in his position on war and on the use of force.

Lossky made every effort to get involved in the French resistance movement during the Nazi occupation of France. His *Sept jours sur les routes de France* contains his candid reflections on French Catholic heritage and culture, divine and human justice, "holy wars," and "just wars." Lossky's commitment to active resistance to aggression was not unqualified. He denounced the spiritualist heresy of infusing a war with an artificial soul and drew a distinction between absolute reality and relative or secondary concepts and values. His reflections warned of the danger of human persons becoming victims of religious, social, and political myths. He further developed these ideas in his eschatological essay *Dominion and Kingship* (1953).[6]

Lossky not only stimulated a fruitful ecumenical exchange in France, but he also led an Anglican-Orthodox dialogue at the annual conferences of the Anglo-Russian Fellowship of St. Alban and St. Sergius in Abingdon, England. He had many followers among younger Anglican theologians, associated with the Fellowship of St. Alban. The English translation of his *Essai sur la théologie mystique*, published in 1958, was the work of these Anglican friends and disciples of Lossky.

APOPHATIC FOUNDATIONS OF LOSSKY'S TEACHING

The most characteristic elements of Lossky's theology, which shaped not only the interpretation of law and ethics but also his entire theological system, were his Chalcedonian distinction between the categories of "person" and "nature," his apophatic (or negative) approach to theology, his challenging doctrine of the Trinity, and his wholehearted devotion to a "genuine" Orthodoxy rooted in the teachings of the fathers of the Eastern Church.

Central to Lossky's theology was his insistence that the person and nature are distinct but not separate. Lossky rejected as inadequate all theologizing that focuses on the level of "nature" and presupposes the "primacy" of the divine essence over the divine persons. He charged the Western theological tradition with "depersonalization" of the Trinity and elevation of the abstract divine essence above the living God of Abraham, Isaac, and Jacob. He insisted that theological thought should not lower itself to the level of abstract speculations, since truth can only be lived and experienced. Truth is a "living body," and it "should not be dissected as a corpse."[7] Lossky was highly critical of the Western juxtaposition of the ideas of nature and grace, which forces one to accept a mechanistic concept of human nature to which grace is added as a "magical substance." His characteristically Eastern Orthodox personalistic view of salvation explained his rejection of juridical and external morality. Obedience and purity for Lossky were negative concepts; they imply the "exteriority of God and the instrumental submission of man."[8] Salvation is not accomplished by God's external activity or through one's rational comprehension of propositional truths. Salvation is deification; it is a conscious and voluntary union with God—"the synergy, the harmony of two co-operating wills."[9]

KNOWING THE UNKNOWABLE

In *Mystical Theology*, Lossky argues that this emphasis on intimate union with the "Incomprehensible and the Unknowable" represents the "fundamental character of all theological thought within Eastern Tradition."[10] It is a humble recognition of what God is not, rather than an insistence on what God is. It is a move beyond speculation to actual union. This contemplative approach, as we shall see, provides a distinctively different foundation for ethics, as well as for a social and political image of the church.

Unlike the Eastern Orthodox, Western Christians seek to analyze and explain God, subjecting their faith to the test of reason. As Wolfhart Pannenberg, one of the most notable Protestant proponents of critical rationality, aptly remarks, "Every theological statement must prove itself on the field of reason and can no longer be argued on the basis of unquestioned propositions of faith."[11] In the Catholic tradition one finds a partial recognition of the apophatic way. Augustine, as Rowan Williams points out, acknowledged the need for transfiguration of intellect, but not for its complete transcendence. For Augustine, knowledge ultimately replaces ignorance.[12] In Western Christianity, the encounter with God is still a reaching out "in thought."[13]

Lossky claimed that Thomas Aquinas, reflecting on the apophatic (negative) and the affirmative theology of the Eastern mystic Dionysius the

Pseudo-Areopagite (ca. 500), reduced the two ways of Dionysius[14] to one. This, for Lossky, effectively made "negative theology just a corrective to affirmative theology" and denied Dionysius's insistence that the negative (apophatic) way ultimately surpasses the affirmative (kataphatic).[15] In the Christian East, apophaticism received a classic exposition in the writings of Gregory Palamas. In the Catholic West, certain parallels to Eastern apophaticism can be found in the works of Meister Eckhart, whom Lossky diligently studied, and in the writings of Eckhart's followers, such as Henri Suso, John Tauler, and Nicholas of Cusa.

Negative theology in Lossky is neither a "prohibition upon knowledge" nor some esoteric individualistic exercise in mysticism. The negative or apophatic way is the only adequate existential theology involving man's entire being. It is an honest and responsible recognition of the inadequacy of our discursive reason in the presence of the living God. Discursive reason has its role and place in the initial stages of one's gradual ascent to union with God. Lossky says, "Speculation gradually gives way to contemplation, knowledge to experience; for, in casting off the concepts which shackle the spirit, the apophatic disposition reveals boundless horizons of contemplation at each step of positive theology."[16] The apophatic way of union with God is the true *metanoia*, the "change of heart" from selfish isolation of individual nature to truly personal plenitude and completeness in the synergy of the divine and human spirit. Herein lies the cause of Lossky's rejection of the external juridical approach to theology and ethics and the key to the understanding of his personalism and his trinitarian vision.

TRIUNE GOD: LAW AND JUSTICE PERSONIFIED

In the chapter of *Mystical Theology* devoted to the "Two Aspects of the Church," Lossky states that from the outset the "Church, according to St. Cyril of Alexandria, is the holy city which has not been sanctified by observing the law—for the law made nothing perfect (Heb. VII, 19)—but by becoming conformed to Christ."[17] He thus put the personhood of God at the foundation of moral life of the Christian community: "The pre-eminently catholic dogma of the Trinity is the model, the *canon* for all the canons of the Church, the foundation of the whole ecclesiastical economy."[18]

The divergence of the Greek and the Latin interpretations of the Trinity represents the very heart of the dispute between the Eastern and the Western Christendom, highlighting the unique distinctions of the two traditions. Lossky charged the Western Church with the heresy of subordinating of the Spirit to the Son and claimed that this error is directly connected with the Western confusion about the real meaning of the "person" both in God and in man.[19] Lossky insisted that the "Western doctrine" of the double procession of the Holy Spirit from the Father and the Son—that is, the revision of the Nicene Creed by the Western Church to say that the Holy Spirit proceeds from the Father *and the Son*[20]—was the "primordial cause, the only dogmatic cause, of the breach between East and West."[21] The fallacy of the Western position, in Lossky's view, was its departure from the patristic understanding of the Father as the "unique source of Godhead and principle of the unity of the three."[22] The Western Church instead posited an abstract and impersonal concept of common divine nature (or essence) that was logically prior to and above the persons of the Trinity. Thus, in the Western doctrine formulated by Augustine and perfected by Thomas Aquinas, the unity of the persons of the Trinity lay not in the person of the Father but in this impersonal concept of common essence. The person of the Spirit is perceived merely as a "reciprocal bond between the Father and the Son."[23] Moreover, the Western doctrine of the procession of the Holy Spirit from the Father and the Son tended, in Lossky's view, to weaken the persons of the triune God by confusing the Father and the Son in the "natural act of spiration." This Western creedal formulation ultimately obscured the living reality of the personhood of God in the Trinity.[24]

Not all Orthodox theologians share Lossky's radical position regarding the importance of the *Filioque* ("and the Son") issue in the theological disputes between the East and the West.[25] Yet, for Lossky the *Filioque* is a "negation of personalism."[26] In this protest against the betrayal of the living God of Abraham, Isaac, and Jacob, Lossky has been compared with Pascal, Kierkegaard, and Barth in their denunciation of the "rebelliousness of the human intellect which flees from the *metanoia* and *kenosis* demanded by the revelation of the living God."[27]

Lossky contrasts the philosophical abstractions of the "God in general" of Descartes, of Leibniz, and of the "dechristianized Deists" with the living persons of the Trinity.[28] For Lossky, the doctrine of the Trinity forms the heart of negative theology. It is a "cross for human ways of thought."[29] It is a primordial revelation and, at the same time, the source of all revelation and all reality. It is the "ultimate reality, [the] first datum which cannot be deduced, explained or discovered by way of any other truth; for there is nothing which is prior to it."[30] The fullness of being, the end and the meaning of existence, can be found in the Trinity alone. "Between the Trinity and hell there lies no other choice."[31] When the concept of a "common nature" takes precedence in one's formulation of trinitarian teaching, a "certain philosophy of essence" prevails, which overshadows the living reality of the Trinity itself.[32] Lossky insisted that the reality of the personal God—the "divine hypostasis (the particular in God) cannot be reduced to an "essence" (the common in God).[33] Personhood must be deconceptualized. Neither divine nor human persons can be expressed in abstract concepts. The mutual co-inherence of divine hypostases in the Trinity reveals the true meaning of personhood.[34]

Rowan Williams correctly observes that in Lossky the doctrine of the Trinity "overturns our understanding of individuality as the most basic category."[35] Yet, Lossky was often unjust and inaccurate in his criticism of the Western scholastic understanding of the nature of the Trinity, and of the distinction between "person" and "individual."[36] Some of Lossky's generalizations contain factual errors. In his discussions of the Eastern patristic understanding of the hypostasis as distinct from the individual, he ascribes greater consistency and clarity to the Eastern Fathers than one can actually find in them.[37] The same is true regarding his interpretation of the patristic teaching on the image of God in man. While undoubtedly building on certain patristic notions, Lossky clearly went beyond Augustine[38] and beyond the church fathers. These historical errors, however, do not undercut Lossky's main point about the prevalence of philosophy in much of Western theology and the need to prostrate one's intellect "before the living God, radically ungraspable, unobjectifiable and unknowable."[39]

TRANSCENDING ONE'S NATURE

Lossky called for the same radical deconceptualization of personhood in Christian anthropology that he demanded in trinitarian theology. He insisted that personhood cannot be expressed through any conceptual paradigm or captured in any definition.[40] The same distinction between "person" and "nature" that is crucial for the understanding of the Trinity applies to the understanding of the human person. In Eastern doctrines of the Trinity, the person of the Father is the source and the principle of unity, not the "common essence" as in Western rationalism. Likewise, in Eastern anthropology personality is not a mode of nature, but rather nature is just a content of the person. Creatively developing the insights of Gregory of Nyssa and Maximus the Confessor, Lossky envisaged personhood as freedom in relation to nature—freedom granted so that nature would thus be transfigured and deified.

Lossky argued that ancient philosophy had nothing remotely comparable to the Christian understanding of personhood as revealed in the Trinity. "Greek thought did not go beyond the 'atomic' conception of the individual. Roman thought, going from mask to the role, defined *persona* through juridical relationships. Only the revelation of the Trinity, [the] unique foundation of Christian anthropology, could situate personhood in an absolute manner."[41] Lossky argued that the principal distinction between person and "common nature" in Eastern trinitarian theology provides the only sound foundation for personal uniqueness and diversity. Objects are determined and defined by their substance and their nature. Persons, by contrast, have the capacity to govern their nature, charging it with new meaning, surpassing and transcending it.[42] This capacity is God-given freedom. Lossky cited Gregory Nazianzen in support of his claim that freedom is one of the characteristic traits of the divine image in man.[43]

Lossky further clarified the distinct meaning of personhood by drawing a crucial distinction between the individual and the person (*hypostasis*, understood as a fullness of the nonconceptual reality of a self-determined human being). The notion of the individual is atomistic and deterministic. It does not imply social relationships, but conveys the idea of an element, something disunited and fragmented, and it does not contain the concept of freedom as self-determination.

THE FREEDOM OF CHOICE

As a devout antideterminist, Lossky did not share the Protestant reformers' doctrine of man's total depravity. He rejected the reformers' claim that the image of God in man was completely obliterated as a result of the Fall. This is one of the major points of divergence between the classic reformers' teaching on human nature and that of the Eastern Orthodox.[44] The Orthodox maintain that the image of God in the human person is indestructible. Lossky, too, insisted that even when someone "removes himself as far as possible from God, and becomes unlike Him in his nature, he remains a person."[45]

Lossky understood freedom in the tradition of Pseudo-Macarius and Maximus the Confessor. Human freedom, for Lossky, lay in the image-character of man's being—in the fact of human persons being created in the image of God. Human beings have the capacity for self-determination (*autexousion*) because God in whose image they are created is free and sovereign. Following Maximus the Confessor, Lossky distinguished natural will, which belongs to us as persons, from the choosing will (or gnomic will) which is a faculty of our nature. For Lossky, "nature wills and acts" while the person "chooses, accepting or rejecting that which the nature wills."[46] In Maximus's view, a perfect nature knows naturally what is good and consequently has no need of choice. Lossky, too, held that "our free choice (*gnome*) indicates the imperfection of fallen human nature, the loss of the divine likeness."[47] "Choice" for our fallen human nature becomes a necessity, and "free will" is understood as a "hesitation in our ascent toward the good."[48] True liberty for Lossky and for the Eastern ascetical tradition as a whole rests in a "free renunciation of one's own will, of the mere *simulacrum* of individual liberty, in order to recover the true liberty, that of the person, which is the image of God in each one."[49]

FREEDOM AND THE JURISPRUDENCE OF THE HEART

Lossky's personalistic, internalized, and experiential understanding of law and ethics is in perfect agreement with Orthodox distinction between the superior spiritual capacity of self-determination, which belongs to us as persons, and the will, which is strictly the faculty of our nature. In order to appreciate this distinction, we must recall that in Lossky our understanding of the "person" cannot be reduced to the notion of human nature. For Lossky, the nature is the "content of the person" and the "person is the existence of the nature."[50] The weakened and fallen human nature, with its conflicting passions and desires, constantly wills and acts within us. Yet the ultimate decision rests with the person who accepts or rejects "that which the nature wills," through engagement of the spiritual capacity of self-determination (often described by the Eastern spiritual authors as self-consciousness, or the spiritual intellect, or the heart).[51]

In a chapter of *Mystical Theology* devoted to the image and likeness, Lossky explains that when man sinned he sinned freely by exercising his faculty of self-determination. That is why all divine laws and commands are addressed not to certain features of fragmented human nature, but to the person, to his or her spiritual self-determination.[52] In this, Lossky closely follows Eastern monastic anthropology with its emphasis on the spirit and the heart. Deification through spiritual coinherence in God is the reversal of defragmentation through passions. The human spirit "must find its sustenance in God, must live from God; the soul must feed on the spirit; the body must live on the soul."[53] The spirit and the heart in the Eastern ascetical tradition represent the moral and spiritual center of the human person (as distinct from the purely emotional and discursive realms). Lossky's use of the monastic teaching of Nikiphoros the Hesychast on "uniting of the [human] spirit with the heart" and the "descent of the spirit into the heart"[54] is highly enlightening. He points out that, according to Macarius of Egypt, the heart, understood as the seat of all intellectual and spiritual activity, is the "workshop of justice and injustice."[55] Thus, according to the apophatic teaching of the Eastern Church, an authentic jurisprudence must above all be a jurisprudence of the heart.[56] It cannot but be personalist, dynamic, and internalized in contrast to the Western external and rationalist theories. As we will see, even divine Law, in its written form found in the Old Testament, is assigned a temporary place in the divine economy.[57] Likewise, positive law should never be absolutized and objectified. It cannot claim to be an accurate reflection of absolute spiritual reality and should not be turned into "an idol."[58] The dignity and freedom of the human person should not be sacrificed by those who fall prey to social and political myths.

TEACHING REGARDING THE WORLD

The same concern for safeguarding the self-determination of divine and human persons can be observed in Lossky's reflections on the origin of the world, the role of man in the cosmos, and the value of human civilization. Lossky's lectures on creation reveal that he read with interest the works of the French intuitivist philosopher Henri Bergson. There are even some affinities in Lossky's teaching with the thought of Bergson, particularly the rejection of the intellectualist conceptions of reality as inadequate, which is clearly manifest in both authors. Yet, Lossky was strongly opposed to Bergson's notion of God as a "God of creative evolution" or as a "vital impulse, an absolute in becoming."[59] For Lossky, recognition of creative evolution would mean a rejection of divine omnipotence.

Lossky constructed his cosmology, his teaching on the origin and the nature of the world and the universe, on the basis of his personalist trinitarian theology and his anthropology. He demonstrated his personalism in drawing a sharp contrast between the Hellenic and Origenistic notions of the eternal "cyclical repetition of worlds" and the Christian doctrine of "absolute creation," a creation from nothing (*ex nihilo*). Matter is not eternal, and the created world is not a quasi-necessary outcome of God's own being. The personal triune God is the creator exclusively by his sovereign will, Lossky insisted; "the name of creator is secondary to the three names of the Trinity."[60] Lossky's personalism is further exemplified by his designation of the earth as being spiritually central to all creation. The earth is spiritually central to creation because of the unique role of the human person destined to unite the material and the spiritual: "at the center of the universe beats the heart of man."[61] "The earth is spiritually central because ... man, penetrating the indefiniteness of the visible to bind it again to the invisible, is the central being of creation."[62] "Divine freedom is accomplished through creating this supreme risk: another freedom."[63] In his lecture "The Creation," Lossky, echoing Maximus the Confessor, elaborates on the grand mission of the human person created to be the microcosm and the mediator. "Man is not a part, since a person contains everything within himself."[64]

In his collection of lectures published as *Orthodox Theology*, Lossky points out that one should not only observe the difference between the Hellenic and Christian understanding of creation (an eternal creation as opposed to creation out of nothing). One should also note the principal difference between the static and impersonalist interpretation of the manner of creation by some Latin Fathers (namely Augustine) and the more apophatic and personalist notion of the Greek Fathers (namely Gregory of Nyssa and John of Damascus). Lossky emphasized that, for the Greek Fathers, the ideas of all things were contained not in the abstract divine essence of the being of God, but rather in the will and the wisdom of the free and personal God.[65] Augustine had Christianized the Platonic notion of the world of ideas by refashioning it into the world of exemplary causes, or ideas of things to be created in the mind and the being of God. Lossky strongly rejected this notion as that which undermines the originality and value of creation and the creator Himself.[66] "For Orthodoxy," writes Lossky, "*nihil* from which the world was created" is an indication of the nondivine nature of the world, of its principal newness in relation to God. Created in this unique manner, the world will always exist.[67] The creation of the world always assumed the cosmic process of its deification.

While it is an "immense compensation for the absence of God," human civilization cannot replace paradise.[68] Human nature must be transfigured by grace, following the ascetic path of sanctification. This sanctification embraces both the spiritual and the bodily realms, thus acquiring genuinely cosmic dimensions. Eastern Orthodox cosmology is thoroughly ecclesiological: "The entire universe is called to enter within the Church, to become the Church of Christ."[69] Having in mind Soloviev, Fedorov, and his contemporary Bulgakov (and perhaps being unduly harsh), Lossky observes in *Mystical Theology*, "Even when it has strayed furthest from the line of tradition, even, indeed, in its very errors, the thought of Eastern Christians in recent centuries—and Russian religious thought in particular—reflects a tendency to envisage the Cosmos in ecclesiological terms."[70]

Lossky insisted that the living monastic ideal of radical self-denial and active virtue have a lasting significance "for the entire universe."[71] The impact on culture and politics of such great Orthodox spiritual centers as the monasteries of Mount Sinai and of Studion, the "monastic republic" of Mount Athos (which attracts spiritual aspirants from both the East and the West), and the famous Russian *lavras* in Kiev and Moscow has been great indeed. "The outward forms may change, the monasteries may disappear, as in our own day they disappeared for a time in Russia, but the spiritual life goes on with the same intensity, finding new modes of expression."[72] The world was created that it might be deified.

Lossky's cosmology was not only thoroughly ecclesiological; it also presents a powerful defense of divine omnipotence and of divine and human self-determination. In Berdyaev, the freedom of personality is uncreated and creation is conceived as a joint venture between God and man.[73] In Lossky, creation is not coeternal with God.[74] In Berdyaev, God has no ultimate power over the "uncreated freedom"—reflecting Boehme's concept of a "primitive, predeterminate *Ungrund*" which is prior to good and evil. In Lossky, creation is a free act of the Trinity.[75] Defending divine omnipotence in creation, Lossky highlighted the dignity and the value of human freedom. To be truly innovative, God creates "the other," a personal being endowed with an ability to reject his Creator. "God becomes *powerless* before human freedom: He cannot violate it since it flows from his own omnipotence."[76] That is why catholicity (free unity in diversity) of the universal Christian community in Lossky can be the sole foundation of divine "dominion and kingship."[77] Moreover, unlike Berdyaev, who was highly critical of historical Christianity and the church as an institution,[78] Lossky was convinced that genuine personal dignity and freedom can only be fully attained and discovered within the unity of the concrete historical church.[79]

THE CHURCH AS A SOCIAL IDEAL

Lossky would have been far from sympathetic with the widespread individualistic rejection of "organized religion" in Western society today. He emphasized the exclusive cosmic status of the church and its universal mission. He denounced two extreme views of the church prevalent in his day: the conservative mummification of the church as a socially irrelevant spiritual entity and the liberal confusion of the church with the world in which striving for the kingdom of God on earth and for the realization of social justice become the sole purpose of the church. He was deeply convinced in the unique and inimitable nature of the church as both divine and human organism and consequently in its unique spiritual mission.[80]

Lossky was critical of medieval Catholic ecclesiology, with its emphasis on external, administrative unity[81] and its preoccupation with "abstract universalism of a doctrine imposed by the hierarchy."[82] Such ecclesiology, in Lossky's view, is too far removed from the living union of human persons with the persons of the Trinity and is primarily concerned with submission to external principles.[83] And more specifically, the role of the Holy Spirit in the Western doctrine of the church is rather obscure.[84] While admitting important affinities between his personalist ecclesiology and the organic ecclesiologies of Catholic Tübingen theologians of the romantic period, particularly that of Moehler, Lossky still rejected them as inadequate.[85] He recognized that, in portraying the church as a christological organism, Moehler came closer to the Orthodox vision of the church. Yet in Lossky's judgment, Moehler's ecclesiology was incomplete and rather deterministic. Human persons are "absorbed in a supra-Person" of Christ who acts as a "supra-consciousness of the whole church."[86] Lossky even rejected the corrective to Moehler's organic model advanced by his notable Orthodox predecessor, Khomyakov. Lossky acknowledged that Khomyakov's emphasis on the role of the Holy Spirit in the church is a valuable improvement; yet, Khomyakov, too, failed to recognize the self-determined reality of human persons and reduced the consciousness of the church to the "function" of the third person of the Trinity.[87] The Holy Spirit becomes the "supra-Person," the "supra-consciousness" of the church.

Lossky rejected both of these models by comparing them with a personalist reading of the scriptures, namely John 15:26–27 and 14:26. In both models the individual is hopelessly lost. Lossky pointed out that the scripture clearly speaks of two kinds of witness to the truth within the church: the witness of the Holy Spirit and the human witness of Jesus' disciples of all ages ("You also are witnesses"). Thus Lossky argued that the consciousness of the church consists not only in the witness of the Holy Spirit himself, but also in the free and conscious witness of unique human persons enabled, reminded, and taught by the Holy Spirit.[88] In contrast to Moehler and Khomyakov, Lossky was not willing to sacrifice the self-determination, uniqueness, and dignity of human persons to the organic togetherness of the ecclesial supraconsciousness. For him there cannot be a forced uniformity in the catholic consciousness of the church, "for there is no measure common to all where persons are concerned."[89]

Lossky's polemic with the French Catholic theologian Yves Congar further clarified the contours of his personalist teaching on the church. Lossky rejected Congar's representation of unity and catholicity as one and the same "mark" of the church.[90] That in his view would stress only formal, external unity and would obliterate the emphasis on the "full human consciousness" of the body of Christ.

Lossky was critical of Protestant ecclesiologies (and their Orthodox varieties) on rather different counts. He saw the root of Protestant fragmentation and disaggregation of the body of Christ in the "revolutionary-anarchic" spirit of Protestant individualism, in the "distrust and even hidden disbelief in the fact that the Church (not the abstract heavenly church, but the specific historical Church) received from Christ himself the mandate to bind and to loose."[91] He strongly opposed the Protestant distinction between a visible and an invisible church, the historic church on earth and the church in heaven. Lossky described this distinction (originally believed to have been made by Luther[92]) as an "ecclesiological Nestorianism," analogous to the heretical christology of Nestorius, which divided Christ into two persons, divine and human. Lossky maintained that "ecclesial Nestorians," on one hand, deprive the body of Christ of its concrete physical dimension by turning it into an abstract "spiritual principle" and, on the other hand, indistinguishably confuse the church with the world.[93] Lossky asked: Is there not a middle ground between an "anti-catholic subjectivism" and an "impersonal objectivism"?[94] He presented his notion of catholicity as a golden middle that mediates between the juridical institutionalism of Roman Catholicism and the extreme individualism of Protestantism.

Lossky's trinitarian personalism penetrated his teaching on the church as profoundly as it influenced his anthropology. In fact, he conceived the whole Christian church as an image of the Holy Trinity and as a living "theandric" organism that embraces and harmoniously unites divine and human realms.[95] Lossky took pains to show that Eastern Orthodox ecclesiology has nothing in common with artificial conceptual constructs. The intimate coinherence and mutual love of the Father, Son, and Holy Spirit must be reflected and glorified in the "very ordering of ecclesiastical life."[96] Catholicity, the central biotic principle on which the life of the Ecclesia (or the whole "divine economy") is built, is the principle of unity in diversity. This "unity-diversity" of the Christian community is the only context in which the persons of the godhead can be truly revealed and human beings can attain their personal completeness.[97] The roles of the two divine persons sent into the world are not the same.

Lossky distinguished between the unifying role of Christ and the diversifying role of the Holy Spirit, and, correspondingly, between the christological element and the pneumatological element of the church.[98] There is a seeming antinomy between the role of Christ and the role of the Holy Spirit: "the Holy Spirit diversifies what Christ unifies."[99] Thus, the christological element represents Christ uniting through the Incarnation our human "created" nature with our divine "uncreated" nature.[100] Lossky portrayed this as an objective union of potentiality. It relates not to our persons, but to our created nature "in so far as it is received into the person of Christ."[101] This unifying work of Christ thus creates a new foundation, a fertile environment, an "ecclesiastical organism"[102] for the development of a totally new "diversity of persons."[103]

To highlight the radically different nature of this diversity (as compared to the generally accepted secular notions of diversity) Lossky pointed out that outside of the church there is multiplicity. Yet this multiplicity is an isolating selfish multiplicity of corruption: "the multiplicity is that of the individuals which divide up humanity."[104] By contrast, within the church, "through the deifying flames of the Holy Spirit," human beings acquire a multiplicity of redemption of a diametrically opposite ethical nature.[105] They become capable of selfless (kenotic) love exemplified in the life of the Trinity. Thus, the pneumatological element in Lossky's system stands for the diversifying ministry of the Holy Spirit, which leads individuals to self-less authentic personhood. The all-encompassing notion describing this dynamic interaction of divine and human persons is catholicity. It is one of the four traditional "notes of the Church," yet, it is creatively expanded to convey Lossky's delicately balanced personalist ecclesiological model.

CATHOLICITY: SPIRITUAL KNOWLEDGE AND INTERPERSONAL ETHICS

To illustrate the unique nature of catholicity in which an individual is not absorbed into a faceless supra-consciousness, Lossky recalls the argument used by Maximus the Confessor in the controversy with the Monothelites:

> The Church as a whole is called ecumenical, a qualification which does not apply to any portion of her; but every smallest portion of the Church—even one single faithful—can be called catholic. When St. Maximus, to whom ecclesiastical tradition gives the title of Confessor, replied to those who desired to force him to be in communion with the Monothelites, "Even if the whole world ... should be in communion with you, I alone should not be," he was opposing his catholicity to an ecumenicity which he regarded as heretical.[106]

Of the four traditional marks of the church (unity, holiness, catholicity, and apostolicity), Lossky singled out catholicity, presenting it as the "golden thread" and as a "mode of knowledge of the Truth proper to the Church, in virtue of which this truth becomes clear to the whole Church, as much to each of her smaller parts as to her totality."[107] The individual retains personal distinctiveness while partaking of the fullness of the catholic truth.

Lossky contrasted his personalist interpretation of catholicity as unity in diversity with the Roman Catholic interpretation of catholicity as external universality of the visible organization, universalism of the church's doctrine, its global geographic presence or ancient history.[108] He was also critical of the Protestant understanding of catholicity, which rejected episcopal authority and transplanted the secular democratic principle of the majority vote, and in certain instances replaced the authentic meaning of catholicity with the relativist notion of "ecumenism."[109] To be sure, Lossky was actively involved in ecumenical dialogue with a number of Catholic and Anglican theologians; yet, he could not accept the relativism and individualism of liberal Protestant and Orthodox ecumenists. He insisted that ecumenism can never take the place of authentic catholicity. This emphasis on diversity at the expense of unity is the disaggregation of the church:

the truth that is attributed to individual inspirations becomes multiple and therefore relative; catholicity is replaced by "ecumenism."[110]

ECCLESIASTICAL AUTHORITY

The divine authority of the episcopate to apply the canons of the church to safeguard its unity was nonnegotiable for Lossky. The most representative statements of his views on intellectual freedom and ecclesiastical authority are found in his *Mystical Theology,* the tract *Spor o Sofii* (*The Sophia Controversy*), and in his open letter to Berdyaev, published by Berdyaev in his journal *Put'*.[111] While in *Mystical Theology* Lossky states flatly that the "submission to the will of the bishop is submission to the will of God,"[112] he subsequently made clear that the authority and the actions of the bishop are not totally unqualified. Lossky recognized that a personal element is inevitably involved in episcopal action. The principle of catholicity as free unity in diversity is foundational to the understanding of Lossky's notion of ecclesiastical authority. Catholicity in Lossky is not some abstract universalism of a dogma imposed by the hierarchy: "The obligation of defending the Truth is incumbent on every member of the church." "A layman is even bound to resist a bishop who betrays the Truth and is not faithful to the Christian tradition."[113]

DEMOCRACY

In his wartime journal *Sept jours sur les routes de France,* Lossky recognized the positive value of democracy in the secular political context. Yet, he stressed that the "struggle for democracy, for freedom, for human dignity" can be truly just only when it is "based on a living experience" and "springs from a deep and healthy source."[114] While he recognized the value of democracy in the secular political realm, however, Lossky strongly opposed its application to the life of the church. He regarded the principle of the majority vote as an impoverished and inadequate surrogate for the spiritual reality of catholicity.[115]

Elaborating on his distinction between the notion of personhood as distinct from the notion of the individual, Lossky contrasted catholicity with collectivity and showed the crucial difference between the principle of catholicity and the principle of democracy. Catholicity as a spiritual unity in diversity utilizes spiritual resources and dynamics and is thus distinct from the democratic election process and the majority rule (the principle that the greater number should exercise greater power). Lossky emphatically states in his essay "Concerning the Third Mark of the Church" that democracy in the sense of majority rule is "foreign to the Church, a caricature of catholicity."[116] In support of his argument he quotes Khomyakov, who said that the "Church does not consist in the greater or lesser quantity of her members but in the spiritual bond that unites them."[117] But Lossky was equally adamant that catholicity has nothing in common with totalitarian enforcement of one common vision on the multitude of human persons comprising the body of Christ. Forced uniformity is alien to persons guided by the Spirit of God: "There is no measure common to all where persons are concerned."[118] The preservation of the voluntary nature of unity and of personal distinctiveness is absolutely crucial:

> Evidence of Truth, the memory or tradition of the church, that which constitutes the content of consciousness, is one and the same for all; but that does not mean that there is one single consciousness of the Church, which is imposed uniformly on all, as a "supra-consciousness" belonging to a "collective person."[119]

A few sketchy reflections in *Sept jours* represent Lossky's first attempts to formulate his political views. It seems that he was not quite accurate in his evaluation of the role of Gallicanism as a positive, creative initiative in the history of France.[120] Perhaps the ruthless policies of the French eighteenth-century revolutionary leaders toward the church in France and the terror that followed influenced Lossky's negative assessment of the *Declaration of the Rights of Man and of Citizen* (1789). In *Sept jours* he mused whether the *Declaration* was not just a "false reflection" of an authentic catholicity degenerated into Latinism (understood by Lossky as a rationalistic and bureaucratic alien influence on the French national mentality).[121]

Lossky abhorred political authoritarianism and the servility of the Russian Church. In this, he was much like his liberal Orthodox contemporaries Bulgakov and Berdyaev. Yet, Lossky was never willing to compromise his fidelity to the catholic truth and to the authority of the episcopate.[122] He chastised Berdyaev for his refusal to "render voluntary obedience to the Truth" by "dying to self." He argued that the "defense of one's individual freedom in the face of highest freedom in the church would be tantamount to a defense of one's limitations, that is one's slavery." The "very issue of the defense of our rights in the Church is a misconception, because these rights are unlimited,"[123] in the sense that the right to defend the catholic truth is distinct from the right to defend one's controversial opinion.

"IN THE WORLD, OF THE CHURCH"

Throughout his theological writings, Lossky consistently advocated the vision of a spiritual and independent church conceived as a social ideal. There is a striking affinity between Lossky's vision of the church and that of the Russian sixteen-century nonpossessors (*nestiazhateli*) led by Nil Sorskii, who conceived the church as "unencumbered by worldly responsibilities, serving as a spiritual and moral beacon in a dark and evil world."[124] Lossky's view also presents a contrast to the traditional Byzantine *Imperium Christianum* model of church-state relations referred to as *symphonia*. Lossky's most explicit statements on this theme came in *Soblazny*, his lecture "The Creation," and his open letter to Berdyaev in *Put*. (The only misleading exception is found in Lossky's early reflections in *Sept jours*, where he expresses his Francophile admiration of French monarchy.)

In *Soblazny* Lossky insists, "The Church is not of this world, but it is in this world and exists for this world in the same manner as Christ."[125] Although the church as an institution should maintain political neutrality and independence, her members individually are expected to be creatively engaged in the life of society: "The Church is the center of the world..., her members, at one and the same time, are also members and builders of the earthly city, they do not abandon the world, but live in the world and are called to act and be creative in it." "Each of us ... is at one and the same time a product and a creator of contemporary culture."[126] In "The Creation" Lossky is more emphatic and direct; he portrays the "children of God" as the mind and the conscience of the world and highlights the physical dimensions of deification:

> We are therefore responsible for the world. We are the word, the logos, through which it bespeaks itself, and it depends solely on us whether it blasphemes or prays. Only through us can the cosmos, like the body that it prolongs, receive grace. For not only the soul, but the body of man is created in the image of God.[127]

Except for the strong emphasis on the independence and spiritual nature of the church, all the accents in Lossky's social teaching are traditionally Eastern Orthodox: Anthropology is at the foundation of cosmology, cosmology is an element of an all-embracing, radically eschatological ecclesiology, and the world is "at the threshold of the Kingdom of God."

What are some of the characteristic differences between the social theologies in the East and the West? The perceptive comparison of Catholic, Protestant, and Orthodox social conceptions drawn by Konstantin Kostyuk in 1997 points out some of the differences and helps to see much clearer the essence of Lossky's characteristically Eastern Orthodox social vision:

> Having formulated the principles of solidarity, subsidiarity and of the common good, Catholicism has thereby limited its social message to representatives of a specific culture and concrete historical epoch (naturally, modern democratic Europe). The idea of social progress embedded in this message

devalues the life of past generations and non-European cultures. Protestant-ism on the whole, from its very inception, developed its social teaching within the framework of the "spirit of capitalism," the spirit "of this world." Formu-lating social ethics Western churches are almost forced to put their ethical teaching in opposition to the individual Gospel ethics of the Sermon on the Mount and subjecting themselves to the laws of the "social world" they distort the message of the Kingdom, "which is not of this world." Eastern Orthodoxy does not desire to limit the task of salvation to specific generations and na-tions and therefore it cannot place at the foundation of its social message the ethics of bourgeois relations; it refuses to sacrifice the purity of the Gospel teaching in order to please secular culture.[128]

Though he advocated a universal vision and a "meta-historical" con-ception of the church, Lossky was never guilty of cultural insensitivity. In *Temptations of Ecclesial Consciousness* (1950) Lossky observes, "Certain political, national, social, cultural ... interests and tendencies are unavoid-able in the Christian community." He adds, "To revolt against those would be to revolt against life itself, against its richness and diversity."[129]

Lossky's liberal opponents were campaigning for a more vocal and a more politically and socially active church. Lossky, by contrast, while ad-mitting that the church does possess "inexhaustible resources on which could draw all those called to rule the earthly kingdoms,"[130] maintained that it is not the responsibility of the church to dictate its will in the tem-poral realm: "The Church does not proscribe to anyone certain political views, social doctrines or cultural specifics."[131] The church should always remember its spiritual prerogatives:

> Just as Christ, being free of the world, kept silence before the court of Pilate, the Church often standing silent before the powers of this world, preserves her transcendental freedom. Although it is at times difficult for us to recog-nize this freedom of hers under the external appearance of humiliation. "The scandal for the Jews" -- the cross is also insurmountable for many Christians. Many would prefer to see in the Church one of the forces of history, compa-rable to other worldly factors and the "inferiority complex" before the power-ful administration of Roman Catholicism is a temptation from which many Orthodox are not free.[132]

Lossky was convinced that the primary task of the church is to fertil-ize the world spiritually. Although he expresses romantic admiration for the French monarchy in his early sketchy comments in *Sept jours*, Lossky denounced the confusion of the spiritual with the temporal that was so characteristic of the Frankish empire of Charlemagne. He regarded as in-admissible the interference of ecclesiastical authorities into the internal affairs of the state.[133] He recognized the essential nature of the state and describes it in *Sept jours* as "that indispensable convention so necessary to human societies," and, on an apophatic note, as "that great fictitious reality, anchored in our consciousness to the point of being part of ourselves."[134]

Lossky offered no definitive theological analysis of the state and of its relation to the church comparable to that of Soloviev. In *Sept jours*, Lossky warns about the deadly poison hidden in the temptation of secular power. He also recognized the extreme complexity of the task of making the right distinction between the realm of God and the realm of Caesar.[135] He critically examined the ideologies of conservative monarchism and revolutionary radicalism in France and dismissed both as bankrupt. He found comfort in the thought that "all those called to rule the earthly kingdoms" can find inexhaustible resources in the Christian church, which is full of vitality and driven by eschatological vision.[136]

THE DISEASE OF NATIONALISM

At a time when the Russian Church abroad was torn by political, ethnic, and cultural antagonism (1935–50), Lossky saw his task to free Eastern Orthodox ecclesiology from any type of national or cultural orientation.[137] In this emphasis, he was distinctively different from Bulgakov and Berdyaev, who, as Rowan Williams points out, "felt themselves to be, in some sense, the true heirs and spokesmen of Russian Orthodoxy" and represented an "implicit refusal to recognize that the Church could continue to function authentically in a dechristianized society" as well as an "implicit belief that the Church was necessarily bound to certain cultural or national structures."[138] In *Temptations of Ecclesial Consciousness*, Lossky appeals to the splintering groups, pleading for unity and a broader universal vision of the church. This appeal recurs in his *Mystical Theology* and in his essay "Catholic Consciousness," where he pronounces the expression "national church" to be heretical because it fragments and devalues the unity of the body of Christ.[139] "The view which would base the unity of a local church on a political, racial or cultural principle is considered by the Orthodox Church as a heresy, specially known by the name of *philetism*."[140]

In "Catholic Consciousness," Lossky speaks to this and other related divisive issues with greater directness and passion:

> No differences of created nature—sex, race, social class, language, or culture—can affect the unity of the Church; no divisive reality can enter into the bosom of *Catholica*. Therefore it is necessary to regard the expression "national Church"—so often used in our day—as erroneous and even heretical, according to the terms of the condemnation of phyletism pronounced

by the Council of Constantinople in 1872. There is no Church of the Jews or of the Greeks, of the Barbarians or of the Scythians, just as there is no Church of slaves or of free men, of men or of women. There is only the one and total Christ, the celestial head of the new creation which is being realized here below, the Head to which the members of the one Body are intimately linked.[141]

To Lossky the breadth of kenotic selflessness acquired through this "intimate link"—one's surrender to God's Spirit—is the only cure from any type of fragmentation of the body of Christ: "Renouncing his separate good, he endlessly expands, and is enriched by everything that belongs to all."[142] This is what Lossky actually meant by freedom from the limitations of one's fragmented nature and by the need to transcend one's nature through kenotic "renunciation of self."[143] In fact, in *Image and Likeness*, enlisting the support of Gregory of Nyssa, Lossky pronounces this kenotic "renunciation of self" as "the basis ... of all evangelical morality."[144] The roots of this emphasis can be traced to the ascetic monastic spirituality of the Orthodox East.

Lossky used the term *phyletism* to mean an "ideology that raises the nation to an element of faith."[145] Others define it as a "belief that one's national identity is greater than one's baptism and faith in Jesus Christ." Various forms of religious nationalism continue to persist among the Orthodox both in traditionally Orthodox lands such as Russia and former Yugoslavia and in the Orthodox diaspora.[146] In Russia, these sentiments go as far back as 1453, when Constantinople was captured by the Turks and Moscow became the "third Rome." Presently the transformed manifestations of these sentiments in Russia of the twenty-first century are being described by some liberal Orthodox not as *phyletism*, but rather as a "heresy" of "Orthodox provincialism."[147] Lossky's admonitions are as relevant as ever. While he is criticized for his Francophile musings, Lossky's ideal of a nation is far removed from nationalistic conceptions. Lossky's students rightly point out that his talent and passion as a first-rate controversialist was not directed to defending Byzantine or Slavophile exclusiveness but to portraying his vision of what was truly Christian. Nation for Lossky, in the words of his son Nikolai, is "rather a unity of responsible individuals whose ideal is expressed in the lives of the saints, whereas sainthood is understood as a vocation of every human being."[148]

JUST WARS VS. "HOLY WARS"

In *Sept jours*, Lossky reflects on the possibility of a just war, on "holy wars," and on divine and human justice. Though sketchy and incomplete, these reflections burn with passion to uphold the value of the human person and the supreme reality of the Church of Christ. It is a creative and novel approach to the issue of Christian attitude to war with distinctively Eastern Orthodox personalist concerns.

Lossky was eager to expose the danger of "mythic thinking" regarding war, of mistaking false abstractions of ideologies of war for absolute values and absolute reality. He recognized relative, local, and national values and emphatically denied the legitimacy of military action in defending absolute values. Military action is justifiable only on the condition that those involved in a conflict have a clear realization that the values they fight for are relative. The sacrifice of one's life in such a war acquires absolute value. Lossky designated this type of action as a "human war."[149] He distinguished between three kinds of wars: the conventional warfare conducted by a secular state ("physical war"), "human war" (understood as national resistance to aggression), and "holy war," conducted under the auspices of the church.[150]

Lossky's notion of a "human war" is deeply rooted in his distinction between absolute reality and abstractions, between absolute values and relative, secondary, or derived values. He set off false abstractions of the ideologies of "holy war" and of the fascist war for "pure race" against the reality of the "human war." He also reminded readers that in reflections on war one always needs to distinguish between abstract ideas of democracy, freedom, Western culture, and Christian civilization and the concrete realities of the "soil, the land, the Homeland." The injustice and the cruelty of all so-called religious wars lies in the heresy of "infusing war with an artificial soul" and in presenting relative values as absolutes. He argued that "if we oppose the idol of the pure race with the more humane idols of law, liberty and humanity they would not be any the less idols for it, ideas rendered hypostasized and absolute: the war would still be a war of idols and not a human war."[151]

It would be a mistake, however, to assume that Lossky believed that all political action should be based on relative values. He portrayed the church of Christ as the only absolute reality, and, referring to Peter's attempt to defend his Lord in Gethsemane with a sword, reminded readers that the church "needs neither our material defense nor our childish swords."[152] As the icon of the Holy Trinity and as the body of Christ (the authentic "unity in diversity"), the church does not stand in need of our swords, but rather presents a limitless resource of vision and strength "for all those who are called to rule the earthly kingdoms."[153]

In his reflections on divine and human justice in *Sept jours*, Lossky challenged the rationalist view of God's immutable justice presented by the clergy of the Roman Catholic Church in France. He contrasted their static, rationalist notion with the Orthodox apophatic and personalist understanding of divine justice. Thus, on June 18, 1940, Lossky made the following entry in his journal:

> I had heard a great prelate at Notre Dame speak before thousands of faithful about our just cause, call upon God that He would grant us victory in the name of this just cause. If we followed his thought to its logical end God would find himself obliged to help us because He is just and we are defending justice. He could not act nor wish otherwise without contradicting Himself, without renouncing His attribute of justice, immutable (as is everything about God written in religious works and theological guides). So if we lost this war after all, after calling on God to give us victory in the name of His justice, what would there be left to say?[154]

This is another example of Lossky's unwillingness to accept the abstract, external notion of justice and a static view of the eternal law of God as an objective body of norms outside the will of God to which he conforms his will. In these reflections Lossky, once again, implicitly contrasted his dynamic personalist concept of direct divine economy with the Western rationalist view, which he described as a "fixed divine plan of immutable preordinations." In a distinctively apophatic way, Lossky emphasized the danger of equating our finite notions of justice with divine justice: "We should have prayed for victory with tears and great contrition, bearing in mind this fearsome Justice, before which we are all unjust. We should not have called on Justice, which is beyond our measure, which we could not bear, but on the infinite mercy which made the Son of God descend from Heaven."[155]

CANON LAW

Unlike the Roman Catholic Church, the Orthodox Church does not regard canon law as juridical. But the Orthodox also part company with Protestants who (except for German Protestant jurists), following Martin Luther, rejected this whole body of ecclesiastical rules and laws as binding on Christians. The history of the Orthodox Church certainly abounds with various extreme interpretations of canon law, those of the legalistic Byzantine canonists and of the liberal anarchists. Yet the guiding principle, the notion of *oikonomia*, understood as "following the spirit rather than the letter of the law," serves as an important safeguard in interpreting and applying ecclesiastical rules.

Lossky saw his task to bring to light the most valuable intuitions of his predecessors in the Eastern patristic and canonical tradition and to root and incorporate canon law into his trinitarian system. His major contribution to the interpretation of the Orthodox canonical tradition lay in restoring the connection between the dogma and the canons and in placing trinitarian personalism and catholicity (understood as personal unity in diversity) at the heart of canon law. In *Mystical Theology*, he emphatically states that the preeminently "catholic" dogma of the Trinity is the model, the canon, for all the canons of the church, the foundation of the whole ecclesiastical economy.[156] He acknowledged that in the Orthodox East the "sociology of the Church" (the practical application of the teachings of the church to the life of the Christian community) is not to be found in the dogmatic tradition per se, but rather in the canonical tradition. Yet, even in the realm of practical application of canons, the emphasis is on deification (the spiritual transfiguration of persons) rather than on external administration of discipline.

Father Michael Azkoul points out the difference between the interpretation of canon law in the West and in the East. In his tract on the differences between the Roman Catholic and Orthodox theologies, he perceptively observes that "unlike the Latins, the Orthodox Church does not think of canons as laws, that is, as regulating human relationships or securing human rights; rather, Orthodoxy views canons as the means of forging the new man or new creature through obedience. They are training in virtue. They are meant to produce holiness."[157]

Lossky would not have chosen the word "obedience." He preferred to speak of the "plurality of personal consciousnesses" coexisting in "unity and multiplicity."[158] His personalist, apophatic, and experiential understanding of the truth never allowed Lossky to view canon law as juridical statutes. He could not accept any other criterion of truth than the truth itself.[159] He believed that catholicity as free and harmonious participation of persons in the life of the Trinity is the only safeguard against dictatorial rule and coercion in the Christian community. In *Mystical Theology* he writes,

> In the light of the canons this society [the Christian Church] would appear as a "totalitarian collectivity" in which "individual rights" do not exist; but, at the same time, each person in this body is its end and cannot be regarded as a means. This is the only society in which the reconciliation of individual interests with those of the society as a whole does not present an insoluble problem, for the ultimate aspirations of each one are in accord with the supreme end of all, and the latter cannot be realized at the expense of the interest of any.[160]

PATRISTIC ROOTS OF LOSSKY'S PERSONALISM

It would perhaps be more helpful to acknowledge that the Eastern Orthodox tradition has a distinctive attitude to law rather than to speak of its expressed "antijuridicalism." In contrast to the Western static and external notion of the eternal law of God, the Eastern Orthodox tradition embraces a more dynamic and personalist understanding of justice. The Eastern tradition stresses the supremacy of the personal divine will and of direct divine economy. Divine commands are rather understood as transient, symbolic representations of dynamic spiritual realities. Thus Maximus the Confessor (ca. 580–662), whose writings exerted a great influence on Lossky, emphasized that there is a deeper spiritual knowledge, a divine principle "hidden mystically" in the letter of the Law. What did he mean by a "divine principle"? In his *Centuries*, Maximus elaborated on the Pauline distinction between the spirit and the letter of the Mosaic law (2 Cor. 3:6) and denounced legalistic and external observance.[161] Maximus pointed out the disparity between the "symbols through which the law is expressed and the divine realities which these symbols represent."[162] He believed that, only under the guidance of the Spirit, can our spiritual intellect, as distinct from the cognitive capacity of rational reason, penetrate into the "divine and spiritual beauty contained within the letter of the law"[163] and acquire a spiritual (noetic) "vision of the nature of created beings and the inner principles implanted in them by their Creator.[164] He rejected literal, legalistic apprehension of the Mosaic law exclusively on personalist grounds. Literal understanding of the law diverts the creature away from union with the Creator to the worship of creation. "God did not order the Sabbath," insisted Maximus, "the new moons and the feasts to be honored because he wanted men to honor the days themselves.... On the contrary, He indicated that He Himself was to be honored symbolically through the days. For He is the Sabbath.... He is the Passover.... He is the Pentecost."[165] Maximus called for a contemplative approach to the Law and taught that contemplation "mediates between figurative representations of the truth and the truth itself." Maximus taught that all "outward and evanescent interpretation[s] of the Law, subject to time and change" must be rejected by the one who seeks through contemplation to ascend to the heights of spiritual knowledge.

The notion of natural law is present in the Eastern patristic tradition, yet it has not been developed in the East into a comprehensive theory comparable to the natural law theory in Catholic theology. In his *Five Centuries of Various Texts*, Maximus drew a clear distinction between "natural law," "written Law" (meaning Mosaic law), and the "law of grace." He emphasized the social function of the natural law and saw its task in bringing "into harmony all men's voluntary relationships with one another"[166] and in granting "equal rights to all men in accordance with natural justice."[167] He described the function of the "written law" as that of "preventing wrongdoing through fear" and as making one accustomed to doing what is right.[168] He regarded the law of grace as superior to the other two laws because it directly teaches the attainment of "similitude to God, in so far as it is possible for man."[169] Thus the law of grace, by contrast, describes not a rational ascent to an intellectual principle, but a transformation of human nature through deification without "altering its fundamental character."[170] It is a revelation of the archetype of human nature and union with Him.[171]

The later Orthodox tradition did little to develop these potent Maximian distinctions between natural law, written law, and the law of grace. And today, natural law teaching does not have the same status in the Eastern Orthodox theology as it does in the Western Thomistic system, where it forms the basis for the development of positive law.

Although it is certainly justifiable to speak of the Eastern Orthodox tradition as "antijuridical" and as that which propagates the censure of the law, it would be inadmissible to ignore the enormous role of the Orthodox Church and of the Eastern canonical tradition in particular in the development of legal systems in the Orthodox East. The overall impact of the Orthodox tradition on the formation of legal consciousness and positive law in the countries of the Orthodox East is a much more complex and contradictory phenomenon.

In order to identify the principal difference between the status and the role of ethics and law in Eastern and Western Christianity, it is important to distinguish from the outset between canon law (understood as the law of the church for purposes of order, ministry, and discipline) and rational legal theory of the church (understood as the teaching of the church on the civil or positive law of a society). It is also necessary to highlight yet another distinction between the actual social influence of the church as an institution and the distinctive social teaching of the church as an independent spiritual entity. Having drawn these distinctions, if we were to ask whether the Orthodox Church had an impact on the development of legal systems and positive law in Byzantium and in Russia, the answer would certainly be in the affirmative. Thus, for instance, the Byzantine *nomocanons* were used in Russia as a basis for *Kormchaya Kniga*, the most ancient collection of Russian ecclesiastical and secular codes. Yet, when the question is asked as to whether the Eastern Orthodox Church has had a distinctive legal theory or social doctrine comparable to those of the Catholic and Protestant churches, the answer would be a negative one. It is a telling anecdote that, until the year 2000, none of the Orthodox churches had a written statement of its social teaching. The first such document, "Bases of the Social Concept," was adopted in 2000 by the Jubilee Bishop's Council of the Russian Orthodox Church in Moscow.

In Byzantine society, according to John Meyendorff, a "charismatic understanding of the state" which, as he admits, "obviously lacked political realism and efficiency" implies that the state is conceived as a "universal counterpart of a universal church."[172] An assumption of unstable "dynamic polarity" between God and the world does not allow for a possibility of clear-cut formulae and legal absolutes in the realm of social ethics. The predominance of charismatic, experiential, otherworldly, and eschatological concepts in the Eastern Christendom shaped a principally different understanding of the function of the church in the world from that of the Western Christendom. This charismatic and prophetic understanding of its mission by the Byzantine church kept it from spelling out a clearly delineated legal and canonical criterion for interpreting Christian action in the world.[173]

LOSSKY'S TEACHING ON "DIVINE LAW" AND LEGAL ORDER

Lossky did not share the Western understanding of the eternal law of God, the *lex aeterna* as an objective body of norms outside the will of God to which he conforms his will. Lossky contrasted the dynamic personalist concept of direct divine economy, which entails risk on the part of God, to the Western rationalist view, which he described as a fixed "divine plan" of "immutable preordinations."[174] This personalist stance shaped Lossky's understanding of the divine Law and legal order. Citing St. Paul's qualification of the law as that "which was added because of transgressions" (Gal. 3:19), Lossky insisted that the "divine Law is proper to the catastrophic state of created being in subjection to the law of sin and death." Thus, if one is to use the terminology accepted in the West, Lossky believed God's commands to be postlapsarian in origin (that is, formulated after the Fall). Lossky speaks of the "eschatological call" and the profound meaning of God's law, which should not be understood as a static reality and the means of justification. The divine law in Lossky is an expression of divine economy and is essential to the Old Testament, where the relationship between man and God assumes the form not of a union but of alliance guaranteed by loyalty to the law. Lossky warns of the danger of attaching an absolute value to such legal situation and "projecting it onto the very nature of God."

In order to assess better the major objections of the Eastern Orthodox to the Western natural law theory, it would be helpful to recall that in the Roman Catholic system the human attribute of reason or intelligence plays an essential role. As Angela Carmella rightly points out: "The conviction that we can know natural law is based upon the premises that the person is intelligent, that nature is intelligible, and that natures intelligibilities are laws for the mind that grasps them."[175] Thus, in the Roman Catholic philosophy of law, the natural law or the intelligible moral order becomes the criteria of the ethical content of the positive law of a society. "An intelligible moral order," continues Carmella, "means that the positive law of a society can be measured against those moral principles."[176]

The Greek Fathers operated on a different understanding of the nature of human reason. They distinguished between spiritual intellect and discursive reason. Discursive reason is incapable of direct apprehension of spiritual reality. Spiritual reality is of a principally different nature from the phenomena perceived by the senses. Moreover, the Eastern Orthodox and particularly Lossky's understanding of divine order in the universe is expressly personalist, apophatic, and experiential in contrast to the Catholic rational notion of natural law. Discursive reason is incapable of direct apprehension of dynamic divine economy. Truth is also understood experientially, rather than rationally. Following Khomyakov, Lossky insists on two specific attributes of the truth. First, the "Truth can have no external criteria."[177] It stands on the basis of its own internal evidence. Second, "gnosis" [authentic knowledge] is inseparable from love." Thus, by connecting gnosis with love Lossky highlights the ethical and communitarian dimensions of the Eastern Orthodox epistemology. He follows Khomyakov, who insisted that the "Truth can only be apprehended in brotherly love." At the foundation of Catholic legal consciousness and ethics lie the rational notion of natural law and the key role of human reason in the apprehension of this natural law. Lossky's ethics, by contrast, could be described as the internalized and experiential ethics of transfiguration through participation in the divine nature. *Theosis*, or deification, is at the heart of Lossky's ethics.[178]

It must be made clear that there are very few direct references to positive law in Lossky's theological works or his wartime journal. Lossky's *Mystical Theology* and the collections of his essays such as *In the Image and Likeness of God* and the *Orthodox Theology* contain profound reflections on canon law and the place of the divine law in the Old Covenant.[179] Yet, apart from his statements in *Sept jours* about the dangers of absolutizing positive law and turning it into an idol,[180] he never addressed at length the issues of the relationship between positive law and the Christian teaching.

This question was not at the forefront of his theological and social vision. Lossky did not raise the question whether the church should assume direct responsibility for guiding the society in its constitutional reconstruction. He did not reflect on the issue whether the church should or should not develop a Christian philosophy of positive law. Yet, as we have seen, Lossky's vision was not limited to the realm of personal ethics, as is the case with many Orthodox writers. Following Maximus the Confessor, he insisted on the social and cosmic dimensions of deification. In his lecture "Christological Dogma," he speaks of the "deification of men and by them, of the whole universe."[181] In another instance, he writes that the role of the human person in the world is to "bind the visible to the invisible" and to reunite in himself the "sensible and the intelligible."[182] He concludes: "We are therefore responsible for the world. We are the word, the logos, through which it bespeaks itself, and it depends solely on us whether it blasphemes or prays."[183]

CONCLUSIONS

Vladimir Lossky is probably the best known and most widely followed modern Orthodox theologian. His classic work *The Mystical Theology of the Eastern Church* (1944) is a milestone in the ongoing dialogue between Eastern and Western Christianity. Lossky's brilliant critique of "Catholic essentialism" and "Protestant existentialism" has had a profound impact on both Western European and Eastern theology. His portrayal of Orthodoxy as that which mediates between the two Western traditions continues to attract attention in both camps. Pope John Paul II expressed his admiration of the "courageous research" of Vladimir Lossky and compared his work in its speculative value and spiritual significance to the contributions of Jacques Maritain and Étienne Gilson in the West and Vladimir Soloviev and Pavel Florensky in the East.[184] Lossky's "originality and imagination in interpreting the Eastern fathers," writes the Anglican theologian Rowan Williams, "should secure him a firm place among twentieth century theologians, and practically all Eastern Orthodox ecclesiology in the past few decades has taken his scheme as a starting-point."[185]

Emphasizing the principal "dogmatic dissimilarity between the Christian East and the Christian West,"[186] Lossky focused on the apophatic (negative) foundations of theology understood as a "personal encounter with God in silence." Building on this contemplative foundation, Lossky called for a radical deconceptualization of personhood both in trinitarian theology and in human anthropology. He incorporated into his creative synthesis the insights of the Cappadocian fathers, Symeon the New Theologian and Maximus the Confessor, the spiritual masters of the Greek *Philokalia*, and Gregory Palamas. Lossky insisted that a person cannot be reduced to his nature or expressed in concepts. Nature can only be described as the "content of the person and not as the person."[187] There is an ethical depth in Lossky's ascetic teaching on personhood. The drive for self-transcendence and kenotic "self-forgetting" is the primordial foundation and the nerve of authentic personhood.

Lossky was not a philosopher of law like Vladimir Soloviev, and in his theological writings he certainly did not address political, social, and ethical issues with the same directness and comprehensiveness that one finds in the works of Berdyaev or Soloviev. Yet, in today's Eastern Orthodox world Lossky is indisputably more influential than Soloviev and Berdyaev.

In the Soviet era, limited publications of Lossky's works within Russia provided believers with some access to the vibrant streams of creative contemporary Orthodox theology engaged in dialogue with the West. Yet, the Soviet government censors forced the Russian Orthodox publishers to remove from the *Mystical Theology* Lossky's denunciations of brutal persecution of believers within Russia and his admiration of their enduring courage.[188] Within Russia, Lossky is more appreciated by the stricter, more traditional wing of Russian theologians due to the apologetic nature of his writings. His work has been one of the major shaping factors in the prevalence of the neopatristic approach in the Russian theology in the last century. Since the time of *perestroika*, Lossky's teachings have been popularized by Deacon Andrei Kuraev, a conservative, controversial apologist of the Russian Orthodox Church. Of the younger, more recent Russian theologians who continue to expound the themes of mysticism and the vision of God in the Eastern monastic tradition, the name of patristic scholar Hilarion Alfeyev is the most notable.

In Great Britain Lossky exerted considerable influence on certain Anglican theologians associated with the Anglo-Russian Fellowship of St. Alban and St. Sergius. Derwas J. Chitty, one of the best Anglican authorities on Egyptian monasticism, was inspired by Lossky to "proclaim to the world an Orthodoxy that was not peculiar to any one country." Timothy Ware, now known as Bishop Kallistos, a former student and admirer of Chitty's, joined the Orthodox Church and became a leading promoter of Eastern Orthodoxy and of the neopatristic approach to British theologians. While Kallistos frequently cites Lossky in his own writings, he deliberately avoids the controversial style so characteristic of much of Lossky's work. Kallistos counts Lossky with the "hawks" and not the "doves" of Orthodox theology for his "stricter view of the *Filioque* issue."[189] Anglican theologian Eric L. Mascall critically engaged Lossky's insights into his ecumenical discussion of the openness of Being and the concepts of Grace and Nature in East and West. Rowan Williams, the current Archbishop of Canterbury, is a distinguished scholar of Eastern Orthodox theology and a critical interpreter of Lossky's legacy to British theological circles. Of the more ecumenically minded Catholic theologians in France on whom Lossky made a positive impact, one must mention Yves Congar and Louis Bouyer. Of the French Orthodox writers of importance, Olivier Clément, Lossky's friend and disciple, applies Lossky's personalist insights in his creative essays on political theology. Olivier Clément and the prominent Greek theologian Christos Yannaras are the only two followers of Lossky's personalism who write directly on issues of social and political ethics. In the United States, Lossky's writings have been widely circulated by St. Vladimir's Press, an Orthodox publishing house. Daniel B. Clendenin, an American Protestant scholar of Eastern Orthodoxy, insightfully communicates to American Protestant readers the bases of the Orthodox apophatic (mystical) theology using extensively Lossky's writings.

Although Vladimir Nikolaievich Lossky is primarily appreciated for his theological vision, his critique of nationalist and deterministic tendencies in Russian religious philosophy, his analysis of the pitfalls of Western conceptualism and juridicalism, and his holistic vision of human freedom contain profound implications for contemporary discussions of law, politics, and society.

NOTES

1. See Vladimir Lossky, "Spor o Sofii," II, §13, §2, §4, §13 in *Bogoslovie i Bogovidenie*, ed. Vladimir Pislyakov (Moscow: Izdatel'stvo Svyato-Vladimirskogo Bratstva, 2000), 407–408, 412–415, 455–455. See also the excellent pioneering study by Rowan D. Williams, now the archbishop of Canterbury, to which I am greatly indebted and use extensively in this chapter: "The Theology of Vladimir Nikolaievich Lossky: An Exposition and Critique" (D.Phil. thesis, Oxford University, 1976). Lossky rejected Bulgakov's interpretation of the doctrine of incarnation as heretical on the grounds that it indirectly introduces Apollinarian notions and, assuming the deterministic concept of Sophia (the divine nature) as foundational, distorts the kenotic nature of divine incarnation representing it not as a personal divine agape, the voluntary "self-giving" of God, but as an act of some objectively predetermined natural necessity.

2. Vladimir Lossky, *The Mystical Theology of the Eastern Church* (Cambridge: James Clarke, 1991), 178.

3. Lossky, "Soblazny tserkovnogo soznaniya," in *Bogoslovie i Bogovidenie*, 567.

4. Ibid.

5. See Vladimir Lossky, "Lichnost' i mysl' svyateishego Patriarkha Sergiya," in *Bogoslovie i Bogovidenie*, 503–511. This epitaph by Lossky was published for the first time in Moscow in 1947 in the collection *Patriarkh Sergii i ego dukhovnoye nasledstvo*.

6. Vladimir Lossky, *In the Image and Likeness of God*, ed. John H. Erickson and Thomas E. Bird (Crestwood, N.Y.: St. Vladimir's Seminary Press, 2001), 225–227.

7. Cited by Lossky's son Nicolas in his preface to *Sept jours sur les routes de France: Juin 1940* (Paris: Éditions du Cerf, 1998), 13.

8. Lossky, "Original Sin," in *Orthodox Theology: An Introduction*, trans. Ian and Ihita Kesarcodi-Watson (Crestwood, N.Y.: St. Vladimir's Seminary Press, 2001), 86.

9. Lossky, *Mystical Theology*, 207.

10. Ibid., 239.

11. Wolfhart Pannenberg, *Basic Questions in Theology*, trans. George H. Kehm, 2 vols. (Philadelphia: Westminster Press, 1983), 2:54. Cited by Daniel B. Clendenin in *Eastern Orthodox Christianity: A Western Perspective* (Grand Rapids, Mich.: Baker Books, 2002), 50.

12. See Rowan D. Williams, "The Via Negativa and the Foundations of Theology: An Introduction to the Thought of V. N. Lossky," in *New Studies in Theology*, ed. Stephen Sykes and Derek Holmes (London: Duckworth, 1980), 1:97.

13. Augustine, *Confessions* IX, 10, trans. R. S. Rine-Coffin, *Saint Augustine* (Harmondsworth, England: Penguin, 1983), 198; cited in "Via Negativa," *New Studies in Theology*, 1:97.

14. As expounded in his *De mystica theologia*, 3.

15. Lossky, *Mystical Theology*, 26.

16. Ibid., 40.

17. Ibid., 177.

18. Ibid.

19. See Lossky, *In the Image and Likeness of God*, 76–77; A. M. Allchin, "Vladimir Lossky," in *The Kingdom of Love and Knowledge: The Encounter Between Orthodoxy and the West* (New York: Seabury, 1982), 203.

20. The *Filioque* clause was first added to the Nicene Creed at the local Council of Toledo in 589.

21. Lossky, *Mystical Theology*, 56.

22. Ibid., 62.

23. Ibid.

24. Ibid., 62–65.

25. See Timothy Ware, *The Orthodox Church* (London: Penguin, 1993), 218.

26. Williams, "The Theology of Vladimir Nikolaievich Lossky," 131.

27. Ibid., 132.

28. Lossky, *In the Image and Likeness of God*, 88–89.

29. Lossky, *Mystical Theology*, 66.

30. Ibid., 64.

31. Ibid., 66.

32. Ibid., 64.

33. Lossky, *In the Image and Likeness of God*, 114–115.

34. Lossky, *Mystical Theology*, 144–145.

35. Williams, "Eastern Orthodox Theology," in *The Modern Theologians: An Introduction to Christian Theology in the Twentieth Century*, ed. David F. Ford, 2 vols. (Oxford: Basil Blackwell, 1989), 2:161.

36. See Williams, "The Theology of Vladimir Nikolaievich Lossky," 106; see also Alar Laats, "Doctrines of the Trinity in Eastern and Western Theologies: A

Study with Special Reference to K. Barth and V. Lossky," in *Studies in the Intercultural History of Christianity* (Frankfurt am Main: Peter Lang, 1999), 114:77, 148.

37. See Lossky, *Mystical Theology*, 50–62, Williams, "The Theology of Vladimir Nikolaievich Lossky," 106, 122; Allchin, *Kingdom of Love and Knowledge*, 203.

38. Williams, "The Theology of Vladimir Nikolaievich Lossky," 122.

39. Lossky, *Orthodox Theology*, 24.

40. See Lossky, *In the Image and Likeness of God*, 115.

41. Lossky, *Orthodox Theology*, 42.

42. Lossky, *Mystical Theology*, 122.

43. Gregory Nazianzen, quoted in ibid., 124 n. 3.

44. See Lossky's objection to Calvin's claim that human nature no longer possesses freedom of the will in "Spor o Sofii" II, §11 in *Bogoslovie i Bogovidenie*, 446.

45. Lossky, *Mystical Theology*, 124. More recently this position has been shared by some liberal Protestant theologians in the West.

46. Ibid., 125.

47. Ibid.

48. Ibid.

49. Ibid., 122.

50. Ibid., 123.

51. Ibid., 125, 131, 201.

52. Ibid., 130.

53. Ibid., 128.

54. Ibid., 201.

55. Ibid.

56. Cf. Hebrews 8:10 (NASV): "For this is the covenant that I will make with the house of Israel after those days, says the Lord: I will put My laws into their minds, and I will write them upon their hearts."

57. Lossky, *In the Image and Likeness of God*, 216; *Orthodox Theology*, 86. Cf. Jaroslav Pelikan, *The Spirit of Eastern Christendom (600–1700)* (Chicago: University of Chicago Press, 1977), 215.

58. Lossky, *Sept jours*, 22.

59. Lossky, *Orthodox Theology*, 19.

60. Ibid., 53.

61. Ibid., 64.

62. Ibid.

63. Ibid., 54.

64. Ibid., 67.

65. Ibid., 57.

66. Ibid.

67. Ibid., 61.

68. Ibid., 86.

69. Ibid., 113.

70. Lossky, *Mystical Theology*, 112.

71. Ibid., 18.

72. Ibid., 19.

73. Nikolay Berdyaev, "Smysl tvorchestva," in *Filosofiya tvorchestva, kul'tury i iskusstva*, 2 vols. (Moscow: Izdatel'stvo Isskustvo, 1994), 2:144–145. See also Vasili V. Zen'kovsky, *Istoriya russkoi filosofii*, 2:75, and Williams, "The Theology of Vladimir Nikolaievich Lossky," 237.

74. Lossky, *Orthodox Theology*, 53.

75. Ibid., 52.

76. Ibid., 73.

77. Lossky, *In the Image and Likeness of God*, 214–215.

78. See Berdyaev's statement cited by Matthew Spinka in *Nicolas Berdyaev: Captive of Freedom* (Philadelphia: Westminster Press, 1950), 35–36. See also chapter 20, this volume.

79. Lossky, "Soblazny," 562.

80. Ibid., 561.

81. Lossky, *In the Image and Likeness of God*, 178.

82. Ibid., 176.

83. Ibid.

84. Ibid., 177.

85. Ibid., 190–191.

86. Ibid., 191.

87. Ibid., 190, 191.

88. Cf. John 14:26: "He will teach you all things, and bring to your remembrance all that I have said to you." Cited ibid., 191.

89. Ibid., 192.

90. Ibid., 176–177.

91. Lossky, "Soblazny," 565.

92. See Louis Berkhof, *Systematic Theology* (Grand Rapids, Mich.: Eerdmans, 1979), 565.

93. Lossky, "Soblazny," 560; *Mystical Theology*, 186.

94. Lossky, *In the Image and Likeness of God*, 186.

95. Ephesians 1:17–23, cited by Lossky, *Mystical Theology*, 183.

96. Ibid., 176.

97. Lossky, *In the Image and Likeness of God*, 178.

98. It is also highly significant that the same distinction between nature and person which lies at the foundation of Lossky's doctrine of the Trinity runs across his teaching on the unifying role of Christ and the diversifying role of the Holy Spirit in the church. The one nature "common to all men," "split up by sin," and "parceled out among many individuals" is reestablished by Christ and objectively united in his body—the Church. See Lossky, *Mystical Theology*, 121. Yet the church is not only one common human nature objectively "recapitulated" in the person (hypostasis) of Christ—it consists of a multitude of persons (hypostases) in need of being freely and consciously deified and united to God. This free and personal deification, the collaboration between grace and human freedom is accomplished in each member by the Holy Spirit. Lossky, *In the Image and Likeness of God*, 177–178.

99. Ibid., 178.

100. Lossky, *Mystical Theology*, 185.

101. Ibid., 183.

102. Lossky, *In the Image and Likeness of God*, 179.

103. Ibid., 178.

104. Lossky, *Mystical Theology*, 182.

105. Ibid.

106. Lossky, *In the Image and Likeness of God*, 175.

107. Ibid.

108. Ibid., 174–175.

109. Lossky, "Spor o Sofii," I.1, in *Bogoslovie i Bogovidenie*, 396–397; *In the Image and Likeness of God*, 179.

110. Ibid., 179.

111. See "Pis'mo V. Losskago N. A. Berdyaevu," *Put'* 50:27–32.

112. Lossky, *Mystical Theology*, 188.

113. Lossky, *In the Image and Likeness of God*, 175–176.

114. Lossky, *Sept jours*, 21–22. Later Lossky affectionately speaks of France, claiming that even under the old regime it kept the "spirit of the democratic state" (44).

115. Lossky, *In the Image and Likeness of God*, 181.

116. Ibid.

117. Ibid.

118. Ibid., 192.

119. Ibid.

120. Williams, "The Theology of Vladimir Nikolaievich Lossky," 18.

121. Lossky, *Sept jours*, 54.

122. See Lossky's letter to Berdyaev, *Put'* 50:28–29.

123. Ibid., 29.

124. Richard Pipes, *Russia Under the Old Regime* (London: Penguin, 1995), 230.

125. Lossky, "Soblazny," 561.

126. Ibid., 561–562.

127. Lossky, *Orthodox Theology*, 71.

128. Konstantin Kostyuk, "Stanovlenie sotsial'nogo ucheniya v pravoslavii," in *Sotsial'no-politicheskii zhurnal* (1997): 6. Page 1 of the e-text is available at http://www.civitasdei.boom.ru/person/orthlehr.htm (in Russian). Translation mine. Yet, having said this Kostyuk (referring to much more recent times, in anticipation of the "Bases of the Social Concept" adopted by the Russian Orthodox Church in 2000) acknowledges that the "absence of such social teaching is acutely sensed by the church as well as the society," that it "upsets the political balance" in society, undermines the spiritual impact of the Orthodox Church on society and "demonstrates the Church's inability to spiritually nourish the nation."

129. Lossky, "Soblazny," 562.

130. Lossky, *Sept jours*, 45.

131. Ibid.

132. Lossky, "Soblazny," 561; cited from the English translation. "The Temptations of Ecclesial Consciousness," in *St. Vladimir's Theological Quarterly* 32, no. 3 (1988): 247. Translation revised.

133. Lossky, *Sept jours*, 44–45.

134. Ibid., 16.

135. Ibid., 45.

136. Ibid.

137. Expounding his notion of catholicity as a free and harmonious union of unique persons united by Christ and empowered by the Holy Spirit, Lossky elucidates and develops the creative intuitions of such nineteenth-century Slavophiles as Ivan Kireevsky and Aleksei Khomyakov. Yet, what is noteworthy is that while doing so Lossky deliberately avoids the use of the Russian term *sobornost*, not because of its inaccessibility to the uninitiated, but primarily because of its "Russianness" and its nationalistic connotations. He replaces *sobornost* with catholicity—one of the four traditional marks of the Church. See Lossky, *In the Image and Likeness of God*, 170 n. 1.

138. Williams, "The Theology of Vladimir Nikolaievich Lossky," 10.

139. Lossky, *In the Image and Likeness of God*, 184.

140. Lossky, *Mystical Theology*, 15. Lossky refers to the 1872 Synod of Constantinople, citing Mansi, *Coll. concil.*, 45:417–546, and the article by M. Zyzykine, "L'eglise orthodoxe et la nation," *Irénikon* (1936): 265–277.

141. Lossky, *In the Image and Likeness of God*, 184.

142. Lossky, *Orthodox Theology*, 128.

143. See Lossky, *Mystical Theology*, 182, cf 144–145, 148.

144. Lossky, *Orthodox Theology*, 128.

145. So defined by one of Lossky's most influential students, French theologian Olivier Clement, "Serbian Church must undergo examination of conscience: Orthodox Theologian Analyzes Responsibility in Kosovo Conflict," in *Zenit Daily Dispatch*, Rome (June 22, 1999), cited from e-text available at http://www.zenit.org/english/archive/9906/ZE990622.html.

146. Ibid. See also the remark of the editor of *St. Vladimir's Theological Quarterly*, who laments that "ethno-phyletism" continues as a spiritual disease, particularly in America," in Lossky, "The Temptations of Ecclesial Consciousness," *St. Vladimir's Theological Quarterly* (1988) 32, no. 3: 250.

147. Aleksandr Kyrlezhev, "Vozmozhen li sintez politicheskoi ideologii na osnove pravoslavia?" http://religion.ng.ru/concepts/2000-10-11/5_sintes.html.

148. Nikolai Lossky, in *Sept jours*, 10.

149. Ibid., 21.

150. Ibid.

151. Ibid., 21–22.

152. Ibid., 22.

153. Ibid., 45.

154. Ibid., 23.

155. Ibid.

156. Lossky, *Mystical Theology*, 177.

157. Father Michael Azkoul, "What Are the Differences Between Orthodoxy and Roman Catholicism?" http://www.ocf.org/OrthodoxPage/reading/ortho_cath.html.

158. Lossky, *In the Image and Likeness of God*, 192.

159. Ibid., 181.

160. Lossky, *Mystical Theology*, 175–176.

161. Maximus the Confessor, "Fifth Century of Various Texts," §§33, 34, in *Philokalia*, 4 vols., trans. G. E. H. Palmer et al. (London: Faber and Faber, 1990), 2:268.

162. Maximus, "Fifth Century," §35, *Philokalia* 2:268.

163. Ibid., §21, *Philokalia* 2:265.

164. Ibid., §27, *Philokalia* 2:266.

165. Ibid., §46, *Philokalia* 2:272. Lossky echoed Maximus in his lecture on the *Original Sin* where he speaks of the spirit, "historical dynamism" and the "eschatological call" of the Law. Lossky, *Orthodox Theology*, 89.

166. Maximus, "Fifth Century," §10, *Philokalia* 2:262.

167. Maximus, "Second Century," §41, *Philokalia* 2:196.

168. Ibid., §11, *Philokalia* 2:263.

169. Maximus, "Second Century," §41, *Philokalia* 2:196.

170. Maximus, "Fifth Century," §13, *Philokalia* 2:264.

171. Ibid.

172. John Meyendorff, *Byzantine Theology: Historical Trends and Doctrinal Themes* (New York: Fordham University Press, 1979), 216.

173. Ibid.

174. Lossky, *In the Image and Likeness of God*, 218.

175. Angela C. Carmella, "A Catholic View of Law and Justice," in *Christian Perspectives on Legal Thought*, ed. Michael W. McConnell, Robert F. Cochran Jr., and Angela Carmella (New Haven, Conn.: Yale University Press, 2001), 262.

176. Ibid.

177. Lossky, *Mystical Theology*, 188.

178. Lossky, *Orthodox Theology*, 128.

179. See Lossky, *Mystical Theology*, 175–176; *In the Image and Likeness of God*, 216–217; and *Orthodox Theology*, 85–89.

180. Lossky, *Sept jours*, 22.

181. Lossky, *Orthodox Theology*, 110.

182. Ibid., 64.

183. Ibid., 71.

184. Pope John Paul II, *Fides et ratio*, VI, 74.

185. Williams, "Eastern Orthodox Theology," 163.

186. Lossky, *Mystical Theology*, 12–14, 21–22.

187. In Lossky the person is the existence of nature: "There is nothing in nature which properly pertains to the person, who is always unique and incomparable." Ibid., 121. The human person is not to be controlled by nature but is rather called to control nature and continually transcend himself in grace. Ibid., 241.

188. Compare the English version of *Mystical Theology*, 16, also 245–246, and the Russian version *Ocherk misticheskogo bogosloviya vostochnoi tserkvi* (Moscow, 1991), 16, 185.

189. See Ware, *The Orthodox Church*, 213.

{ CHAPTER 22 }

Mother Maria Skobtsova (1891–1945)

MICHAEL PLEKON

The way to God lies through the love of people. At the Last Judgment I shall not be asked whether I was successful in my ascetic exercises, not how many bows and prostrations I made. Instead I shall be asked, Did I feed the hungry, clothe the naked, visit the sick and the prisoners. That is all I shall be asked. About every poor, hungry and imprisoned person the Savior says "I": "I was hungry and thirsty, I was sick and in prison." To think that he puts an equal sign between himself and anyone in need. . . . I always knew it, but now it has somehow penetrated to my sinews. It fills me with awe.

—MOTHER MARIA SKOBTSOVA

The nun, radical social activist, and martyr we know as Mother Maria Skobtsova (1891–1945) had many names, roles, and identities in her life.[1] The diverse sides of her personality, the many gifts with which she was endowed, and the various ways in which she exerted her spiritual, artistic, and philanthropic energies are at first overwhelming. It is as if she could not live just one life. She was an artist but also a political activist. She distanced herself from the faith into which she had been baptized, yet later, Christ, the gospel, and the direct care of suffering people defined her existence.

Born Elisaveta Iurevna Pilenko in Riga, Latvia, she grew up in her family's homes in St. Petersburg and in Anapa, by the Black Sea in the south of Russia. Her birth was difficult, requiring a Caesarian section. All her biographers cite her mother Sophie Pilenko's observation that during her life, Liza, as her family called her, became well acquainted with death. At her baptism, she almost suffocated during the triple immersion. Her father Iouri died suddenly in 1906, propelling her already weakened faith into a crisis. How could a good God permit such a good man to die when his family so needed him? She would bury two of her three children before her own death and know that the third, her son Iouri, was interned in a Nazi concentration camp, as she was. For much of her adult life, she was surrounded by the poor, emotionally distraught, and chronically ill people she sheltered, cared for, and buried. She would spend the last months of her life consoling fellow concentration camp inmates, all of them observing daily the endless plumes of smoke rising from the crematoria.

She was also known as Elisabeth Kuzmina-Karavaeva, from her first impulsive and short-lived marriage to Dimitri Kuzmin-Karavaev. Through her second marriage she became Elisabeth Skobtsova. She was the mother of two daughters, Gaiana, from her first marriage, and Nastia, as well as a son, Ioura, from her second marriage to Daniel Skobtsov. A White Army officer, he had presided as military judge over her trial. Her offense had been serving as the first woman mayor of Anapa after the Bolshevik mayor fled in the face of the White Army. Given her outspoken personality and her predecessor's politics, she was suspected of membership in the hated Bolshevik movement. However, she had earlier also escaped arrest and likely execution by the Bolsheviks by claiming friendship with Lenin's wife.

She was finally given the name of the great ascetic, St. Mary of Egypt, when she made her monastic profession, received tonsure and the habit on March 7, 1932. In receiving her into monastic life, her bishop, the remarkable Metropolitan Evlogy (Georgievsky) said that as the first Mary, of Egypt, retreated to the desert after a life of passion, so this second Mary, named for the first, should go into and speak and act in the desert of suffering human hearts. "The world," he said to Mother Maria on another occasion, "is your monastery." A pastor of amazing discernment, he encouraged many to take risks, to encounter and embrace this world just as Christ had encountered and embraced the Palestine of the first century.[2] Among those he urged and, when necessary, protected, were, among others, the great theologian and priest Father Sergei Bulgakov, scholars such as Fathers Lev Gillet, Cyprian Kern, Nicolas Afanasiev, Basil Zenkovsky, Georges Florovsky, Bishop Cassian Bezobrazov, George Fedotov, Anton Kartashev, and Constantine Mochulsky, philosophers Simeon Frank, Nicholas Berdyaev, and Paul Evdokimov, as well as Mother Maria.[3] There was hardly a group, conference, or meeting from the 1920s to the 1940s at which Evlogy was not present: meetings and summer camps of the Russian Christian Students' Association, ecumenical gatherings, and graduations at St. Sergius Theological Institute, which he was instrumental in opening in Paris.[4] And at these gatherings, the metropolitan was surrounded by exactly the individuals just named: canon law and liturgical specialists, patristics and scripture scholars, literary critics and philosophers, all of them passionate people of the Orthodox Church. What an intriguing, gifted assembly of persons of faith he supported in the hard times of forced emigration, the Depression, World War II, and the Nazi occupation of France. Only in recent years, through the work of Antoine Arjakovsky, Paul Valliere, Rowan Williams, and Anastassy Brandon Gallaher, among others, are these marvelous thinkers becoming known.[5]

Of these lights of the Russian emigration, Mother Maria is one of the greatest treasures of creativity, compassion, holiness, and sacrifice that the Eastern Orthodox Church has ever offered to the rest of the churches and the world. Trained in literature, theology, and the fine arts, a gifted poet and essayist, she was a groundbreaking figure in many respects. Among the first women allowed to study theology formally in the St. Petersburg Academy, she was a confidant of the influential procurator general of the Russian Church, C. P. Pobedonostev, a St. Petersburg neighbor. While still in her student years she became a member of the circle of the great poets Vyachyslav Ivanov and Alexander Blok. Poet and theologian, political activist, spouse, and parent, she would never have guessed that she would spend the last decades of her life as a professed nun, running hostels for the homeless, troubled, and ill in Paris and its suburbs.

Despite the demands of feeding and sheltering the residents of her hostels, she managed to keep up a productive life as a writer and scholar, participating in the Religious-Philosophical Society led by Nicholas Berdyaev, contributing essays to the famous journal he edited, *Put'* (The Way) and other publications. She embroidered vestments, altar cloths, and tapestries and painted icons for the chapels in her hostels. She continued to participate in the Russian Christian Students' Movement she helped found. After futile but instructive personal efforts to be an advocate for impoverished immigrants, she began the Orthodox Action group, yet another organization for serving those in need, and set up the hostels where the basic needs of life could be met. Once, after a lecture on Russian literature to immigrant workers, she was told that what they needed more was clean laundry and a good meal. She directly provided these things.

Despite her administration and hands-on direction of the hostels, she remained engaged in the theological debates of her era. In her published essays, one can, for example, read her radical thoughts about a renewal of monastic life for the twentieth century, not a rejection of the essentials of prayer, work, and love of neighbor, but a rethinking of how these would be lived in a time of economic depression rather than in the well-endowed monasteries of Russia and Eastern Europe. She took on a spirited defense of her radical social activism by a discerning examination of both the scriptures and the writings of saints and church leaders down through the ages. She wrote about the blessing that the Russian revolution, despite all its horror, brought to the Russian people and their church. In what has become the best known of her essays, "Types of Religious Lives," she examines several different types of religiosity, concluding with an inspired statement of what she termed the "Gospel" or "evangelical" type of Christian faith and life. She had perhaps the greatest Orthodox theologian of the twentieth century and a mystic as her spiritual father, Sergei Bulgakov. Her close friends included the lights of the Russian emigration in Paris, Father Bulgakov and Berdyaev, as well as Symeon Frank, Basil Zenkovsky, Sister Joanna Reitlinger, and Constantine Mochulsky, among others.

During the Nazi occupation of France, her efforts to assist the suffering multiplied. She applied for and received state authorization and support for her hostels as public canteens, supplying food rations to destitute citizens. Likewise, she sought out work contracts and thereby employed her hostel residents in an array of wartime industries. She fearlessly visited, fed, and consoled many of the almost seven thousand French Jews, half of them children, whom the Vichy government herded into the Paris cycling stadium, Velodrome d'Hiver, in July 1942. She was able to save several children, smuggling them out in trashcans. During the Nazi occupation, many fearing arrest were given shelter and new identities in her hostels. With her chaplain, she devised ways to hide and protect both Jews and others whom the Nazis sought to exterminate; Father Dimitri issued baptismal certificates, and eighty new parishioners were registered as members of the Orthodox parish lodged in the chapel at the hostel in rue de Lourmel.

In life as well as after her death, Mother Maria had her critics and enemies. Recently, even her "Types of Religious Lives" has been attacked by traditionalists in Russia. Her insightful descriptions of the hypocrisy and introversion of certain forms of Orthodox piety have been rejected as biased and distorted. Her critique of monastic life and her proposals for its renewal have also been characterized, along with her own existence, as a misunderstanding of the monastic tradition and modern rejection of it. In her own time, as her contemporaries have witnessed, including Metropolitan Anthony Bloom, theologian Elisabeth Behr-Sigel, and the late Sophie Koloumzine, Mother Maria was an embarrassment for many in the Russian Paris. Her avid participation in intellectual circles, her continuing to write for journals, her expeditions hunting for food for her hostels, her seeking out the homeless in Parisian bars and bistros, the state of her monastic habit with its marks of cooking, her attachment to Gauloise cigarettes—all of this made her a nonconformist, a persona non grata.

Metropolitan Anthony Bloom has written regretfully of his disapproval of her. Father Basil Zenkovsky, in his perceptive yet acerbic memoirs, grudgingly admits her dedication to serving others, but with little compassion or approval. And this was the assessment of a priest who knew her for fifteen years, from the Russian Christian Students Association, and who sat on the board of her hostels. Her other mentor, the philosopher Nicholas Berdyaev, was ambivalent about her attempting radical social work as a monastic, and even her friend Father Lev Gillet wondered whether her seeking monastic profession really added anything to her nonetheless heroic work. He tried to dissuade her from this step, but after she was received and tonsured, he supported her, not only as her chaplain in life but also in the years after her death. Along with Metropolitan Anthony, Father Lev did not hesitate to call Mother Maria a modern saint.

It is most likely that she and Father Dimitri were betrayed to the Gestapo by fellow Russians, possibly even some who assisted in the hostels and who were either scandalized or fearful of her humanitarian activities during the occupation. In February 1943 both Mother Maria and Father Dimitri were arrested, along with her son Yuri. All were eventually sent to concentration camps, she to Ravensbrück and Yuri and Father Dimitri to Mittelbau-Dora, a work camp annex of Buchenwald. Mother Maria's time in the camp is well documented.[6] At first, almost energized by the hard labor, Mother Maria became a source of hope, an oasis in the death camp. But the work, meager rations, and sickness took their toll on her. She comforted fellow inmates, led prayers and Bible studies, even embroidered the invasion of Normandy in the style of the Bayeux tapestry. She survived surprising long, given the conditions and despite debilitating illness, until March 31, 1945, when, according to witnesses, she took the place of another inmate scheduled to be gassed that day. Less than two weeks later, American soldiers liberated the camp.

Many have called her a martyr, an apostle of compassion, a saint for our times. There are testimonies not only to her heroic work in the concentration camp but also to her years of service to the poor and suffering in the Paris hostels. As with her contemporary, the Lutheran pastor, theologian, and martyr Dietrich Bonhoeffer, her status has not been without controversy and disagreement. In 1985 the Supreme Soviet inscribed her posthumously into the order of national heroes of the war. Yad Vashem, the Holocaust Martyrs' and Heroes' Remembrance Authority in Jerusalem, recognized her as one of the "righteous among the Gentiles," planting a tree in her memory there on August 14, 1987. In February 2003, a commemorative plaque was affixed to the external walls of the building at 77 rue de Lourmel by the Paris city government, acknowledging Mother Maria's work for the suffering and her heroism.[7]

The petition for her formal recognition as a saint in the Orthodox Church has not been acted upon by the Patriarchate of Constantinople for more than fifteen years, and repeated inquiries about its status remain unanswered. Metropolitan Anthony Bloom's published words about her capture her personality and passion:

> Mother Maria is remembered in the context of the Russian emigration, the French Resistance or Ravensbrück concentration camp. But her achievement extends beyond the circumstances of her life and it outlives them. For above all, by way of her Christian dedication and in her own distinctive style, she demonstrated what it means to be human.... Infinite pity and compassion possessed her; there was no suffering to which she was a stranger; there were no difficulties which could cause her to turn aside. She could not tolerate hypocrisy, cruelty or injustice. The Spirit of Truth which dwelt in her led her to criticize sharply all that was deficient, all that was dead in Christianity and, particularly, in what she mistakenly conceived to be classical monasticism. Mistakenly, for what she was attacking was an empty shell, a petrified form. At the same time, with the perception of a seer, she saw the hidden, glorious content of the monastic life in the fulfillment of the Gospel, in the realization of divine love, a love which has room to be active and creative in and through people who have turned away from all things and—above all—from themselves in order to live God's life and be his presence among men, his compassion, his love.... Mother Maria is a saint of our day and for our day: a woman of flesh and blood possessed by the love of God, who stood fearlessly face to face with the problems of this century.[8]

It is with good reason that Mother Maria Skobtsova is included in this volume. Not just despite the controversial aspects of her person and life, but rather because of them, she very much embodies the times in which we live. By traditional standards, her life was far from a model. Some reject her precisely because of her outspoken and passionate character as well as the turns her life took. Yet, as her writings reveal, she was a faithful voice of the Christian tradition, a true person of the church precisely in her willingness to criticize what was in need of reform and in thinking creatively about the paths of renewal. Although the major part of her adult life was taken up with caring for the marginal and suffering, she nevertheless managed to retain a dynamic intellectual and spiritual existence.

She did not leave a systematic body of social and theological reflection; yet we have a great deal of what she was able to write: four volumes of poems, plays, reviews, studies of saints' lives, and essays, not to mention correspondence. Mother Maria's voice is an important one amid the others of persons of faith in the Eastern Orthodox tradition. Situated in the very midst of the twentieth century's most turbulent years, she offers us a radical view of the consequences of the Incarnation, of God's becoming human and of humanity's becoming godly.

Though Mother Maria has not yet been officially recognized as a saint in the Orthodox Church, she is greatly revered. Here and there one can find icons of her. In one, she holds not the martyr's cross but a burning candle, like St. Genevieve, the patron of Paris, who saved her city from destruction. The flickering flame of one candle seems weak and insignificant, especially in the yawning darkness of the years in which Mother Maria lived. Yet her life, for all its complexity and the darkness of her era, was radiant, incandescent. Her weakness, even her dying, was the power of God and resurrection for all around her.

INTELLECTUAL AND CULTURAL CONTEXT: "RUSSIAN PARIS" AND ITS LIGHTS

Mother Maria was an integral and prolific contributor to the intellectual creativity of the Russian emigration in Paris. She was formed not only by the "Russian religious renaissance," as Nicolas Zernov calls it before the revolution, but also, and even more so, by the results of Russian intellectuals' encounter with Western scholars, churches, politics, and culture in the emigration years. Antoine Arjakovsky, in his magisterial study of the Russian émigré intelligentsia in Paris, locates Mother Maria as a participant in all the important study groups and discussion circles and in the journal *Put'* in these years.[9]

The influences on Mother Maria were many and diffuse. One could think, for example, of the archconservative Pobedonostev, the head of the state ministry that controlled the Orthodox Church, this structure having been one of Peter the Great's creations. While a warm, almost parental affection existed between the two and while the young Liza Pilenko surely absorbed her mentor's piety, his suspicion of any development, growth, or freedom either in the life of the church or in other sectors of society must have fueled the almost insatiable desire on the young woman's part for freedom and creativity in spiritual and cultural life. One could take the poet Alexander Blok, another of her mentors, and find there an astonishing similar pattern of influence. Blok's pessimism and despair seemed to nurture Elisabeth Pilenko's zest for life and hunger for personal experience, her indomitable spirit, manifest at the very end of her life, in her poems' defiance of the gas chambers and crematoria of the concentration camp. Some of her most pointed essays, such as "A Justification of Pharasaism," were a response to Father Sergius Chetverikov's very conservative ideas about preserving Russian spirituality.[10]

On a more positive note, her relationship to her bishop in Paris, the already mentioned and remarkable Metropolitan Evlogy, can be seen as immensely significant in a number of ways. Not only did Evlogy clear the way for Maria's monastic tonsure, invoking an ancient canon, to accept the ecclesiastical divorce between Daniel Skobtsova and Maria, but he also gave her freedom to develop her hostels not as reproductions of Russian monasteries but as houses of both prayer and hospitality. Whenever she took over a new property, the very first unit to be set up was the chapel. She was foremost what Paul Evdokimov calls an "ecclesial being." Reading her essays, one is struck by her classic sense of the centrality of the scriptures, the Eucharist, and prayer in her life and in all her activities. But she also saw the need to pray and celebrate the liturgy, the "sacrament of the brother/sister," well beyond the daily cycle of services in the hostel chapel. To be sure, she often was absent from morning prayer, but where was she? She was scavenging the greengrocers, butchers, and other food wholesalers at Les Halles, all to feed the residents of her hostels. As she puts it in "Types of Religious Lives" and other essays, this is authentic Gospel Christianity. To feed the hungry, listen to the sad and anxious, to find jobs and lodging for the desperate—this was "the liturgy outside the church-building," what Ion Bria would call the "liturgy after the liturgy," echoing St. John Chrysostom:[11]

> Our communion with people passes mostly on the level of earthly encounters and is deprived of the authentic mysticism that turns it into communion with God. And we are given a perfectly real possibility in our communing in love with mankind, with the world, to feel ourselves in authentic communion with Christ. And this makes perfectly clear what our relations to people, to their souls, to their deeds, to human destiny, to human history as a whole should be. During a service the priest does not only cense the icons of the Savior, the Mother of God and the saints. He also censes the icon-people, the image of God in the people who are present. And as they leave the church precincts, these people remain as much the images of God, worthy of being censed and venerated.... We like it when the "churching" of life is discussed but few people understand what it means. Indeed, must we attend all the church services to "church" our life? Or hang an icon in every room and burn an icon-lamp in front of it? No, the churching of life is the sense that the whole world as one church, adorned with icons that should be venerated, that should be honored and loved, because these icons are true images of God that have the holiness of the Living God upon them.... We believe that the sacrament of the Eucharist offers up the Lamb of God, the Body of Christ, as a sacrifice for the sins of the world. And being in communion with this sacrificial Body, we ourselves become offered in sacrifice ... the "liturgy outside the church" is our sacrificial ministry in the church of the world, adorned with living icons of God, our common ministry, an all-human sacrificial offering of love, the great act of

our spirit. In this liturgical communion with people, we partake of a communion with God, we really become one flock and one Shepherd, one body, of which the inalienable head is Christ.[12]

Despite this sense of liturgy and life interpenetrating each other, Mother Maria was criticized by some, including Father Cyprian Kern, her chaplain, and Mothers Evdokia and Blandina, for not attending all the daily services, for not observing all the fasting prohibitions in her cooking, for departing from the traditional patterns of monastic observance and churchly piety. All three sought transfer to a more orderly ecclesiastical and monastic setting. Yet the great mystic who also was her chaplain, Father Lev, supported her commitment to the suffering and her unconventional style of life, as did her last chaplain, Father Dimitri Klepinine, and her bishop, as well as a number of colleagues and friends, including Nicholas Berdyaev. Others who were constant in their support were several on the left of the spectrum in the Russian Paris: Feodor Pianov and Ilya Fondaminsky-Bunakvov, who were both imprisoned by the Gestapo, the latter also dying in the camps; scholar Constantine Mochulsky, known for his work on Dostoevsky; and the specialist in Russian spirituality George Fedotov. It should not be surprising that Mother Maria's own socialist commitment to the poor and suffering would have been supported by the more liberal members of the Paris emigration and scorned by monarchist, conservative factions.

Just as we note Mother Maria's gifts in the many roles and activities of her life, it is also possible to see her own the distinctive synthesis of radical faith and radical love for the neighbor we hear in her essays and see lived out in the hostels she directed. Thomas Merton said in the very last talk he gave, in Bangkok on December 10, 1968, that in the modern era, each monastic and every Christian is to some extent "on his/her own." His actual words were those of a Tibetan abbot to a fellow monk when asked what should be done in light of the Communist Chinese takeover of monastic buildings and the very country. "From now on, Brother," he said, "everybody stands on his own feet."[13]

So many of the individuals of the Russian emigration in Paris were and remain are attractive as persons of faith in action, not only because of their great intelligence and holiness but also because they dared to do precisely what the abbot and Merton said. Metropolitan Evlogy pushed them out, gave them the blessing of freedom to find their own paths, supported and even protected them. Mother Maria certainly exemplifies what Merton quoted. As even some of her critics observed, she was seldom unsure of her position and herself. Yet, she also was constantly a student, a novice in formation, thus profoundly shaped by several of her friends and colleagues. From Nicholas Berdyaev and the teacher-become-priest Alexander Elchaninov, she absorbed and lived out the radical freedom that Christianity gives. Less concerned with details of this freedom than Berdyaev was, she recognized it being enhanced by the revolution, which liberated the Russian Church and Christian faith from both the Russian state and Russian culture. Reading Berdyaev's provocative essay, "The Worth of Christianity and the Unworthiness of Christians" and "The Bourgeois Mind," it is easy to think of Mother Maria both as an example as well as one whose conversation, in Berdyaev's circle, may have contributed to the radical ideas within.[14] Of her many essays, two that appear in the new English-language anthology are particularly relevant, statements of her vision of the positive aspects of the revolution.[15] Another very powerful meditation on freedom, "Birth and Death," is explicitly indebted to Berdyaev and is drawn from some of the personal tragedies of her own life.[16]

Chief among those who shaped her thinking was the great theologian and priest, Father Sergei Bulgakov. Called the "Russian Origen," surrounded to this day by controversy and the suspicion that he made the figure of Divine Wisdom almost a member of the Trinity, Father Bulgakov's enormous theological creativity and personal holiness are only recently becoming known outside a small circle of specialists.[17]

Father Bulgakov wrote about many subjects: the Mother of God, John the Baptist, the angels, the Eucharist, the icons, the possibilities of healing the great schism, the nature of the church. His larger trilogy is not only a look at the essential dogma of the Trinity but also, more particularly, a more positive or constructive statement of the dogma of Chalcedon, that of Christ and the Incarnation and the implications of this for the world and all of humankind. His vision of the Incarnation is cosmic, but what is riveting is his boldness in thinking about the church in both her extensiveness and the limits and limitations of her institutional expression. He also confronts the captivity of so much theology, church practice, and even piety to an overly temporal or this worldly pattern.[18] In Christ's incarnation and resurrection, ascension and coming down of the spirit, the kingdom of heaven, like God himself, has forever become part of the life of creation, of human beings. Yet, creatures of time and space, the limiting features of these are all too often imposed upon God and the kingdom where they are not relevant.[19]

For Bulgakov, in the Incarnation, human life has become divinized and God's life humanized. Soloviev's idea of *Bogochelovechestvo*, or "the humanity of God," also translated as "Godmanhood," is what distinguishes the gospel, the life of the church, and the existence of every Christian. Divinity and humanity might be said to have interpenetrated each other, so that a new dimension of reality has been created, a new economy of salvation. Writing on the "second Gospel commandment," Mother Maria observes,

> The commandment of love for one's neighbor, the second and equal in value to the first, calls mankind in the same way today as when it was first given. For us Russian Orthodox people it may be easier to understand than for anyone else, because it was precisely this commandment that captivated and interested Russian religious thought. Without it, Khomiakov would have been unable to speak of the *sobornost'* of the Orthodox Church, which rests entirely on love, on lofty human communion. His theology shows clearly that the universal Church itself is, first of all, the incarnation not only of the commandment of the love of God, but also of love for one's neighbor, and is as unthinkable without the second as without the first. Without the second commandment there would be no sense in Soloviev's teaching about Godmanhood [*Bogochelovechestvo*], because it becomes one and organic, the genuine Body of Christ, only when united and brought to life by the flow of fraternal love that unites everyone at one Cup and brings everyone to partake of Divine Love. Only this commandment makes clear Dostoevsky's words about each of us being guilty for all, and each of us answerable for each other's sins.[20]

While Mother Maria clearly knew of Soloviev, not to mention Khomyakov and Fedotov and other creative Russian theologians, I think that in many ways her clearest debt is to the vision of Father Bulgakov. One will not find much if any mention in her writings of the figure of Divine Wisdom, so central for Father Bulgakov's depiction of the relationship of the divine and the human, nevertheless the grasp of the connection is always there. For Father Bulgakov, the entire divine plan for the redemption of the world could be described as "churching," that is the assembly of the entire cosmos into communion with the Holy Trinity and with each other. And the "one Cup" is the communion with God and each other, the Eucharist, for both Father Bulgakov and Mother Maria the always-present contact with Christ and the kingdom.[21] Mother Maria's distinctive expression of this was to see the love of God and love of the neighbor as indissoluble, indistinguishable:

> We are called to embody in life the principles of *sobornost'* and Godmanhood, which are at the foundation of our Orthodox Church; we are called to oppose the mystery of authentic human communion to all false relations among people. This is the only path on which Christ's love can live; moreover, this is the only path of life—outside it is death. Death in the fire and ashes of various hatreds that corrode modern mankind, class, national and racial hatreds, the godless and gift less death of cool, uncreative, imitative,

essentially secular democracy. To all forms of mystical totalitarianism we oppose only one thing: the person, the image of God in man. And to all forms
of passively collectivist mentality in democracy we oppose *sobornost'*. . . . We
simply want to live as we are taught by the second commandment of Christ,
which determines everything in man's relation to this earthly life, and we
want to live this life in such a way that all those who are outside it can see
and feel the unique, saving, unsurpassable beauty, the indisputable truth of
precisely this Christian path.[22]

THE HUMANITY OF GOD AND THE DIVINITY
OF HUMANITY

Fundamental to Mother Maria's writing and her work is her understanding
of human nature as the image and likeness of God in the human person.
St. Irenaeus of Lyons, a very early church father, grasped this in his saying
that "the glory of God is a person fully alive."[23] This human image and likeness is distorted by sin but redeemed, refashioned by Christ's death and
resurrection. This divine imprint and the constant action of God within
the lives of people is a good definition of the Eastern Church idea of "the
humanity of God" (*Bogocheloveschestvo*) and of theosis, of each person being "divinized" by God's grace. Society, culture, politics, and law are human creations, but are themselves the image and likeness of God. God
made all things. God loves all things. God, in Christ, has entered into all
things. God wishes to draw all things back to himself, to restore the original communion. All of human making stands under both the judgment
and great compassion of God. As Father Bulgakov argues, if in the resurrection Christ has triumphed over evil and death and ascended to the Father, carrying all of creation with him, filling all things, then how can evil
ever finally imprison anyone? Would this not mean that the Son of God's
victory was less than complete? Has not God united all to himself, both
in his creation and redemption?[24] This vision, however, did not make of
Mother Maria a sentimental dreamer about the harsher realities of both
the human person and social life.

> We get from the world and from man what we count on getting from them.
> We may get a disturbing neighbor in the same apartment, or an all-too-merry
> drinking companion or a capricious and slow-witted student, or obnoxious la-
> dies, or seedy old codgers, and so on, and relations with them will only weary
> us physically, annoy us inwardly, deaden us spiritually. But, through Christ's
> image in man, we may partake of the Body of Christ. If our approach to the
> world is correct and spiritual, we will not have only to give to it from our
> spiritual poverty, but we will receive infinitely more from the face of Christ
> that lives in it, from our communion with Christ, from the consciousness

of being a part of Christ's body.... Social endeavor should be just as much of a liturgy outside the church as any communion with man in the name of Christ.... Everything in the world can be Christian, but only if it is pervaded by the authentic awe of communion with God, which is also possible on the path of authentic communion with man. But outside this chief thing, there is no authentic Christianity.... He who rejects the sorrowful face of Christ in the name of the joys of life believes in those joys, but tragedy is born at the moment when he discovers that those joys are not joyful. Forced, mechanized labor gives us no joy; entertainment, more or less monotonous ... gives us no joy; the whole of this bitter life gives us no joy. Without Christ the world attains the maximum of bitterness, because it attains the maximum of meaninglessness. Christianity is Paschal joy. Christianity is collaboration with God, an obligation newly undertaken by mankind to cultivate the Lord's paradise, once rejected in the Fall; and in the thicket of this paradise, overgrown with the weeds of many centuries of sin and the thorns of our dry and loveless life, Christianity commands us to root up, weed, plow, sow, and harvest.[25]

The basis for Mother Maria's vision, as that of Father Bulgakov, is the hope of the Incarnation and Resurrection; with an optimism grounded in these, she had no difficulty in recognizing the result of evil, the ever-present neighbor's suffering. It seems that Mother Maria's great sensitivity to human suffering was the portal through which her theological development and understanding passed. Already profoundly moved by suffering and death in her family, in the revolution and forced emigration of which she was a part, she was to encounter both the ultimate pain and ultimate presence of God, in the death of her children. Years later, in a moving essay called "Birth and Death," she recalled these experiences, though not in explicit detail.

Having made the difficult trip from the Black Sea to Georgia then on to Istanbul and Belgrade to Paris, she and her family squeezed out a living. Daniel Skobtsov was a teacher and taxi driver; Elisabeth designed silk scarves, made dolls, and sewed clothes. On March 7, 1926, after a prolonged hospital stay, four-year-old Nastia died of meningitis, her mother helplessly watching her dying. Beside herself, Elisabeth nevertheless came away from this horror of horrors, the premature loss of a child, with the gift of God's presence and love. Her spiritual father, Fr. Sergei Bulgakov, likewise years before had had to endure the painful death of his son from nephritis and in the worst of sorrows found God once more there, in love. Fr. Sergei Hackel provides some of the reflections Elisabeth put down at this time:

At Nastia's side I feel that my soul has meandered down back alleys all my life. And now I want an authentic and purified road, not out of faith in life, but in order to justify, understand and accept death.... No amount of thought will ever result in any greater formulation than these three words: "Love one another," so long as it [love] is to the end and without exceptions. And then the whole of life is illumined, otherwise an abomination and a burden.... People call this a visitation of the Lord. A visitation which brings what? Grief? No, more than grief; for he suddenly reveals the true nature of things. And on the one hand we perceive the dead remains of one who was alive ... the mortality of all creation, while on the other, we simultaneously perceive the life-giving, fiery, all-penetrating and all-consuming Comforter, the Spirit.[26]

In June 1936, word came from Russia of the death of her eldest child, Gaiana, who was only twenty-two. She had decided the previous year to return there. Those who attended the memorial service recounted how Elisabeth lay prostrate in prayer and grief on the floor of the St. Sergius Institute chapel throughout. Poems were a kind of journal for release and reflection for Elisabeth all through her life, and many of them deal with the death of her daughters. She later wrote one of the most powerful of her essays on love of one's neighbor as the imitation of the Mother of God, who watched as her own son died in great pain. In 1931, in Toulouse, she had seen a fresco by Marcel Lenoir of the coronation of the Virgin Mary, as Helene Arjakovsky-Klepinine points out. In it, the Mother of God holds on to her son, not as the King of Kings but as the Man of Sorrows, crucified. This was to be the last icon Mother Maria ever made, embroidering it out of threads supplied her by fellow camp inmates from their work assignments. It could well be an icon of Mother Maria herself, an image neither of grief nor despair but of love, in the face of death and loss.

TWO LOVES, YET ONE: OF GOD AND THE NEIGHBOR

For Mother Maria, both the dignity and freedom of the human person are signs of the life of God breathing within. One therefore, cannot separate love of God and love of the neighbor, despite efforts to do so in theological writing and churchly practice. The Mother of God is an image of both how God loves and how we are to love each other.

If a man is not only the image of God but also the image of the Mother of God, then he should also be able to see the image of God and the image of the Mother of God in every other man. In man's God-motherly soul not only is the birth of the Son of God announced and Christ born, but there also develops the keen perception of Christ's image in other souls. And in this sense, the God-motherly part of the human soul begins to see other people as its children; it adopts them for itself.... The human heart should also be pierced by the two-edged swords, the soul-cutting weapons, of other people's crosses. Our neighbor's cross should be a sword that pierces our soul.... To my mind, it is here that the authentic mystical bases of human communion lie.[27]

Woven throughout Mother Maria's writings, I believe, is the theme of love's centrality, and I also believe, her battling with love in her own life. Both Sophie Koloumzine and Elisabeth Behr-Sigel, who knew her years ago, have remarked on the strain in Mother Maria's life between the love for her own children and family and the enormous expenditure of herself and time in caring for those she found in need and suffering. It could be easy to say that she neglected her own in favor of others. As already noted, Mother Maria's efforts, as remarkable and heroic as they were, did not evoke support or even compassion from some of her peers. In part of one of her longest and most insightful meditations on love of God and of the neighbor, Mother Maria actually considers maternal love not just as a love of giving but also very much as a love of taking. There may in fact be much of the ego in all the self-sacrifice and forgetting of oneself for one's children, a loving of one's own reflection, of one's own "I" in these small egos, the desire to shape them in certain ways, the need to see how successful and happy they will eventually be.[28]

In the "natural" view, according to not only what our families, our teachers, and our culture but also even the church appears to say, charity begins at home. Mother Maria's challenge, however was, must it end there?

As noted, fundamental to her thinking about love was the equivalence of the love of God and the love of the neighbor.

> Christ gave us two commandments: to love God and to love our fellow man. Everything else ... is merely an elaboration of these commandments, which contain within themselves the totality of Christ's "Good news." ... their truth is found only in their conjunction. Love for man alone leads us into the blind alley of an anti-Christian humanism, out of which the only exit is, at times, the rejection of the individual human being and love for him in the name of all mankind. Love for God without love for human beings, however, is condemned: "You hypocrite, how can you love God whom you have not seen, if you hate your brother whom you have seen?" (1 Jn 4:20)[29]

Not to love the person before us is not to love God, whose images he or she is, is not to love God who comes to us only through human beings, words, gestures. Not to love the brother or sister is furthermore not to love myself. [30] Yet, we cannot really love the neighbor before us unless we also love God, for in so doing, we not only love the image of God that each person is, but we also love in the power of God, with God's grace. Mother Maria's anthropology presumes the creation, redemption, and constant presence of God in each person. Furthermore, it is Christ-centered, incarnational, for the life of the God-become-human has forever transformed humanity, just as the Incarnation has forever transformed God. In Christ, in "God's humanity," we see the prototype, the image of what human life should be. In the Christ who completely gave of himself, Mother Maria emphasizes a christology dear to the Russian tradition, that of *kenosis*, of the God who stoops down, empties himself, in his absurd love (*eros manikos*) for us.[31] Here she again recalls "nonpossession" of poverty as the charism not just of monastic life but also of all Christian existence. The hymn to the Son of God in the letter to the Philippians (2:6–12) who took on the form of a servant for us is the prototype. Yet, this sacrificial love runs counter to ordinary human rules and perceptions.

> Why is it that the wisdom of this world not only opposes this commandment of Christ but simply fails to understand it? Because the world has at all times lived by accommodating itself to the laws of material nature and is inclined to carry these laws over into the realm of spiritual nature. According to the laws of matter, I must accept that if I give away a piece of bread, then I become poorer by one piece of bread. If I give away a certain sum of money, then I reduce my funds by that amount. Extending this law, the world thinks that if I give my love, I am impoverished by that amount of love, and if I give up my soul, then I am utterly ruined, for there is nothing left of me to save.
>
> In this area however, the laws of spiritual life are the exact opposite of the laws of the material world. According to spiritual law, every spiritual treasure given away not only returns to the giver like a whole and unbroken ruble given to a beggar, but it grows and becomes more valuable. They who give, acquire, and those who become poor, become rich. We give away our human riches and in return we receive much greater gifts from God, while those who give away their human souls, receive in return eternal bliss, the divine gift of possessing the Kingdom of Heaven. How do they receive that gift? By absenting themselves from Christ in an act of the uttermost self-renunciation and love, they offer themselves to others. If this is indeed an act of Christian love … then they meet Christ Himself face to face in the one to whom they offer themselves. And in communion with that person they commune with Christ himself.… Thus the mystery of union with man becomes the mystery of union with God. What was given away returns, for the love that is poured out never diminishes the sources of that love, for the source of love in our hearts is Love itself. It is Christ.[32]

STUDENT OF LIVING TRADITION, POET OF THE KINGDOM

As an Orthodox Christian, Mother Maria identified as authoritative scripture and the church's "living tradition"—that is, the experience and lives of the saints, in particular the Mother of God, the liturgical texts, and ascetic and theological writings—as the primary sources for our understanding of God, the world, the other person, how we live together in peace and love. Her essays concretize this tradition, showing how the life of God is to be lived out in daily existence, liturgy made incarnate in care for the suffering, in pursuit of justice in society.

Mother Maria's encounter with traditional monasticism is a particularly revealing. Although Father Basil Zenkovsky almost cynically observes that seeking monastic tonsure may not have been a profound or serious response to a vocation, the actual monastic life Mother Maria did lead, as well as her thinking and writing on it, witness otherwise. Monastic life did become an intensely personal way of her living the gospel's demands. Yet as an important institutional part of Christian history, a tradition in its own right much challenged by the events and consciousness of the modern era, monasticism became for her crucial in thinking through how faith must be adapted to new situations and needs.

While her own entrance into monastic life was something of an exception—she had three children and was married twice—she nevertheless tried to acquaint herself with its traditional form and content. Not only did she intensely study the literature and history, but she also visited the few women's monasteries not closed by the revolution, these being in Estonia and Latvia. Her firsthand experience was for the most part negative. In a word, she found the monastics well intentioned but trapped in the past, obsessed with meticulous observation of the rules and ways of the classic monastic tradition. As for the turmoil of twentieth-century life, either the brutal repression in the Soviet Union or the poverty and growing threat of fascism in the West, the monastics were clueless at best or indifferent at worst. Mother Maria could not reconcile the humanity, the sensitivity to the world of the early fathers and mothers of the desert with the staid, distanced mentality of contemporary traditional monastics. In "Types of Religious Lives," she puts it in a most startling, even brutal way.

> In fact, we have today two citadels of such an Orthodoxy—traditional, canon-based, patristic and paternal: Athos and Valaam. A world of people removed from our bustle and sins, a world of faithful servants of Christ, a world of knowledge of God and contemplation. And what do you suppose most upsets this world of sanctity? How does it regard the present calamities that are tearing us apart, the new teachings, heresies perhaps, the destitution, the destruction and the persecution of the Church, the martyrs in Russia, the trampling down of belief throughout the whole world, the lack of love? Is this what most alarms the islands of the elect, these pinnacles of the Orthodox spirit? Not at all. What strikes them as most important, the most vital, the most burning

issues of the day, is the question of the use of the Old or the New calendars in divine services. It is this that splits them into factions, this that leads them to condemn those who think otherwise than they do, this that defines the measure of things. It is difficult to speak about love against this background, since love somehow falls outside both the New and the Old Calendars. We can, of course, state that the Son of Man was Lord of the Sabbath, and that he violated the Sabbath precisely in the name of love. But where they do not violate it, where they cannot violate it, this is because there is no "in the name" nor is there love. Strict ritualism reveals itself here to be the slave of the Sabbath and not the way of the Son of Man.... Instead of the Living God, instead of Christ crucified and risen, do we not have here a new idol, a new form of paganism, which is manifest in arguments over calendars, rubrics, rules, and prohibitions—a Sabbath which triumphs over the Son of Man?[33]

Likewise, she considers the ascetic mentality dominant in traditional monasticism, namely the conviction that everything one does is done out of obedience—to God, to the superior, to the monastic rule. The purpose for all of this is the salvation of one's own soul, becoming "perfect even as your Father in heaven." Once more, something is not right in such a vision, for

The whole world, its woes, its suffering, its labors on all levels—this is a kind of huge laboratory, a kind of experimental arena, where I can practice my obedience and humble my will. If obedience demands that I clean out stables, dig for potatoes, look after leprous persons, collect alms for the Church, or preach the teachings of Christ—I must do all these things with the same conscientious and attentive effort, with the same humility and the same dispassion, because all these things are tasks and exercises of my readiness to curb my will, a difficult and rocky road for the soul seeking salvation. I must constantly put virtues into practice and therefore I must perform acts of Christian love. But that love is itself a special form of obedience, for we are called and commanded to love—and we must love.[34]

But where is there any recognition of the other, the neighbor who is being fed, clothed, or visited? Rather than self-renouncing, self-giving love that embraces the other, this "strange and fearsome holiness" pursues all kinds of works of love because it is the rule, because God or the superior orders it, because it is necessary for the salvation of my soul. Unlike the ancient monastics, an Anthony the Great, Syncletica, Pachomius, or Paisius, the world and the other, even when directly before me, evaporates. In a particularly discerning passage, Mother Maria concentrates on some of the particular features of modern life distressing to traditional monasticism and thus necessary to flee or avoid:

There is no doubt as to the inner and outer unhappiness and misery of the world today ... the threat of impending war, the gradual dying out of the spirit of freedom, the revolutions and dictatorships which are tearing people apart ... class hatred and a decline in moral principles. It would appear that there are no social ills that have not affected contemporary life. Yet at the same time we are surrounded by crowd of people who are oblivious to the tragedy of our age ... surrounded by boundless self-satisfaction, a total lack of doubt, by physical and spiritual saturation, by an almost total overdose of all things. But this is no "feast during the plague." ... Today, in a time of plague, one as a rule counts one's daily earnings and in the evening goes to the cinema. T here is no talk of the courage of despair because there is no despair. There is only contentment and spiritual quiescence. The tragic nature of the psychology of contemporary man is self-evident. And every fiery prophet, every preacher will be in a quandary: on which side of the café table should he sit? How can he cast light on the nature of today's stock market gains? How can he break through, trample, and destroy this sticky, gooey mass that surrounds the soul of today's philistines? How can he set the people's hearts on fire with his words?[35]

What has this sociological and spiritual diagnosis of the world, from the year 1937, to do with monastic life? From the hard words just cited, Mother Maria proceeds to delineate an evangelical or gospel type of Christianity. The monastic, however, finds himself or herself for the most part in the midst of this world. Gone are the spacious corridors, expansive proper-ties, and large communities of older endowed monasteries as well as the pilgrims flocking to them. This is even more the case today, almost seventy years later. Monasticism, she argues, is both not needed and needed. Soci-ety and culture hardly are interested, but monasticism has much to give to people. It is needed "on the roads of life, in the very thick of it." The real in-novation or adaptation, the authentic renewal not only of monastic life but also of the church as a whole is to realize that the place to be and to work is very simply, right there, in the world of "pains, all the wounds, all the sins of life, with drunkenness, depravity, thoughts of suicide" but also" longing for a little material well-being, competition and peaceful, quiet 'everyday' godlessness."[36]

If a monastery is a place of healing, nourishment, air, and light, in the spiritual sense, it is not too much to say that the whole world needs if not wants to be there. Yet, this cannot be. But, for the monastic,

> there is more love, more humility, more need in remaining in the world's back-yard, in breathing bad air, in hungering after spiritual food—sharing all these burdens and all the world's anguish with others, lightening them for others.

Christ, in ascending to heaven, did not take the Church with him; he did not halt the path of human history. Christ left the Church in the world ... as a small bit of leavening, but this leavening is to leaven all the dough (Gal. 5:9).[37]

At the core of monastic life are community in prayer, work, and possessions in imitation of the primitive church (Acts 2:42–47; 3:32–35). In the Russian monastic tradition, Mother Maria perceptively notes the importance of nonpossession or poverty to such renowned figures as Sergius of Radonezh, Nilus of Sora, Joseph of Volokholamsk, and Seraphim of Sarov. What was crucial for them was not just the absence of private property, but also the love of the neighbor, the heart of generosity—the joyous giving away of food, clothing, shelter, time, and, finally, oneself. Call it coming back full circle. Call it simply a "return to the sources." Call it "living tradition," but in Mother Maria's frequently polemical criticism of her tradition, that of the church and of monasticism, in the end she neither rejects either nor imposes upon them anything alien to their essential character. Rather, she comes back to the two loves that are really but one, of God and the neighbor. Here, in the modern era, can both the church and monasticism be revived and work, "for the life of the world."[38]

SOCIOLOGICAL IMAGINATION, ESCHATOLOGICAL VISION

Very much a woman of the modern era, Mother Maria was a participant in as well as observer of the years of ferment in Russia, beginning in the demonstration and brutal put down of the same on "Bloody Sunday," January 5, 1905, leading up to the civil war and Bolshevik Revolution. She had an acute "sociological imagination," as C. Wright Mills called it, aware of the interactions among the individual and the state, economy, other social institutions, church, and culture.[39] Early on, she recognized the need for profound political, economic, and social change in Russia. Siding with many of the intellectuals of the first decades of the century, she aligned herself with the socialist vision of transformation. Like another former Marxist, Father Bulgakov, she never abandoned her socialist sympathies, though she distanced herself from the ruthless policies of the Bolsheviks. Once an ally of Trotsky, she eventually was part of the group ordered to assassinate him. (She did not.) Yet meeting him years later, in Paris, she was able to turn his gratitude into financial contribution to her hostels. Still later, she attacked the complicity of the Russian Church under the imposed strictures of the Petrine era. She stressed the incompatibility of the state church situation of Orthodoxy under the tsars as incompatible with the gospel, and this was in turn criticized by more conservative devotees of "Holy Russia."

The Bolshevik Revolution was for her, as for Father Bulgakov and Berdyaev and many others, a tragedy—but also a true liberation. It forced Russian Christians to reject the support of monarchy and fashion a new democratic and pluralistic social order. Here she clashed profoundly with the conservative monarchist Russians of both the Karlovtsky Synod (the Russian Orthodox Church Outside Russia) as well as those in Paris who adhered to the Moscow patriarchate despite state manipulation of the church. However, Mother Maria also had Peter Berger's "humanistic perspective," namely, the sense that events and ideologies can both liberate and enslave.[40] Mother Maria's view is that the individual is precious and unique, a child of God, never to be surrendered to the good of a class or ethnic group or religious tradition. So she rejected not only the extreme clergy-lay division but also the aristocrat-peasant, class, religious and ethnic prejudices of prerevolutionary Russia as well as the naive and sinister mentality of the Communist Party.

It is all too easy to cast the conflict as one between virtuous traditional monarchy, the alliance of czar and patriarch, on the one hand, and godless, brutal communism on the other. Such are the extreme views of both monarchists and Bolsheviks. Thus it cannot be the cross or the cross and the hammer and sickle. Revolution is cleansed of party perversion, bears within the seed of true change, reliant on help from without, from God.

> The liberation of life from the dead end it finds itself in can proceed only from where there is a power greater than life, only from where there is the possibility of a supra-physical, supra-historical resolution of the question. Only the Church can liberate and direct our life. The Church must turn to the cry of the world, to the social hell, to injustice, crises, unemployment, and speak the words given her from all eternity: "Come unto me, all ye that labor and are heavy laden, and I will give you rest" (Mt. 11:28).... Christ, the cross and the Church can in no circumstances go hand in hand with anything that contains an element of violence and servitude.... Christ is freedom: the face of Christ is the affirmation in every person of his own free and God-like face; the Church is a free and organic union of the faithful with Christ, with Christ's freedom; and Christ calls those who labor and are heavy laden to take up his burden, which is light because it is taken up freely.[41]

Mother Maria concludes by asserting that though the grace of God is essential, so too is human work to transform society, to offer help to the poor and suffering, to oppose what is unjust, and where possible to change the society that creates poverty and misery. She imagines this community of workers as a "kind of monastery," in the world, "a spiritual organism, minor order, brotherhood." For her, the model for such community and common work is the church, not so much the institutional form we know from history but also, and more importantly, "the one great monastery, organism, order, brotherhood."[42]

As we have seen in her thinking about tradition and the necessity of adaptation or renewal, Mother Maria harbored no romantic illusions about the faith, the church, or even the institution of monasticism. For her, the past was not a solid whole to be preserved but a mix of elements, some sound and appropriate for the present, some no longer valid, still others wrongheaded, corrupt and to be abandoned. The authentic Christian tradition, as John Meyendorff, among others, has pointed out, is living, always being modified and capable of further modification, while its essential truths endured.[43] She cannot be accused of otherworldly, out-of-touch piety. Rather, her "sociological imagination" is empirically grounded. While she insists on the presence of God and reliance on his grace, she also sees no alternative to purposeful action and no other arena for action but that of our own social world—neighborhood, city, and country.

When in paraphrasing St. John Chrysostom, she talks about the "sacrament of the brother/sister," she means that to be real, our prayer must be enacted. "We do not just say prayers," as Paul Evdokimov puts it, "we become prayer, prayer incarnate."[44] If we find our religion making us look away from the face of God in those around us, if this religion urges us to insulate ourselves in beautiful churches, liturgical chants, and incense to the extent that we forget the brother or sister next door, we are short, very short indeed of the demands of Christ and his gospel. We will have missed, in the face of the neighbor, the icon of Christ who lives in each person. It should come as no surprise that many others, through the overwhelming experiences of immigration, the Great Depression, the war, should have come to precisely the same conclusions. The "return to the sources" motif—often associated with the likes of Henri de Lubac, Jean Daniélou, Yves Congar, Bernard Botte, M-D. Chenu, Lambert Beaudin, J-J. von Allmen, Joachim Jeremias, and Gregory Dix, among others—was rooted in exactly the same passage through suffering and death to life that their confreres in the other churches made. In the postwar years many of these would gather in various settings, one being the annual week of liturgical study and prayer, organized by Fathers Cyprian Kern and Nicolas Afanasiev and just celebrating its fiftieth anniversary, at St. Sergius Theological Institute in Paris, or in the continuing Fellowship of St. Alban and St. Sergius, over seventy years old, in the United Kingdom. The worker-priest movement, the study that blossomed in the documents of Vatican II, the rediscovery of the priesthood of all the baptized, of the church as eucharistic community, of the ministry as service, of the need for healing division among Christians and religious traditions across the world—all these significant recoveries and more were born in the same experiences as Mother Maria encountered and of which she writes.

TYPES OF RELIGIOUS LIVES: FALSE AND TRUE HOLINESS

For Mother Maria, the vision of her teacher, Father Sergei Bulgakov, was pivotal, but it was augmented by others in the emigration and, of course, deeply rooted in the Christian tradition. Her defense of her philanthropic ministry is explicitly based on New Testament texts, as well as the collection of Eastern Church spiritual writings called the *Philokalia,* or "Love of Beauty."[45] In addition, she draws upon the texts of the Eastern Church liturgy and on the lives of saints. The purpose of law, as of the rest of politics, society, and culture, was to enhance the fullness of human life, not to create a heaven on earth but rather to reveal the paradise, the kingdom of God already present—though not fully. Hers was a "realized eschatology," a vision of the "new age" and possibilities of a "new City," a "new Jerusalem," an eschatological vision of a just and compassionate society such as that of Father Bulgakov in his last books, *The Bride of the Lamb* and *The Apocalypse of St. John.* Christianity was for her the royal road, the gospel the charter, yet not oppressively or imperialistically.

Perhaps there is no better exposition of Mother Maria's critical and constructive thinking about Christianity in our time than "Types of Religious Lives." It was written in 1937 but was not published until 1996, after Antoine Arjakovsky and Helen Arjakovsky-Klepinine discovered it among the papers of her mother, Sophie Pilenko, in the Bakmatiev Archive at Columbia University. In it, Mother Maria looks in considerable detail at five forms or types that religious faith and practice can take. Her types are very specific to Russian Orthodox history, yet there is enough discernment in her analysis for the reader to make connections in many other Christian contexts. A Roman Catholic, Episcopalian, Methodist, or Lutheran, not to mention Baptist, could trace out the variations that would make at least some of the types relevant within each of these confessions.

As with all efforts in typology, as Max Weber pointed out, the construction draws from numerous particular cases, yet it would be hard to find any one individual who would perfectly embody the type. Mother Maria admits this, as well as other limitations such as other varieties of religiosity too diverse to be included. What is more, it is also possible to find elements of one type diffused in other types. Obsession with liturgical rubrics and other details, for example, can be found across several of Mother Maria's type, so prevalent has this been in Russian Orthodoxy.

Nevertheless, enough accurate, defining characteristics are captured if a specific type is effectively rendered. This is certainly the case with Mother Maria's efforts here, even if one does not agree with details of her analysis. The "portraits" she executes of Russian Orthodox piety are both familiar and striking.

The "synodal" type has its origins in the modifications of the church perpetrated under Peter the Great, changes that in turn created a religious consciousness that far outlived his era. Although it is impossible to examine all Mother Maria's types in detail here, it is still possible to get to the heart of each. And the core of this one is the church as "essential, but the motivations for this needs often were of a national rather than ecclesial character."[46] This is the religiosity in which, as Father Alexander Schmemann later described it, one's yearly communion was understood as "an important Russian custom," the most popular service was the memorial rite (*panikihda*) and generally, attendance at church was restricted to several major holidays, religious observance essentially equal to being a "good Russian."[47] Such minimalism was required: by family pressure, school rules, or other forms of regulation. Enormous sums were spent on church construction, decoration, and performance: golden chalices, gospel book and icon-covers, the best voices recruited for deacons and choirs. Even in the destitution of the emigration, churches were created out of garages, sheds, and basements, liturgical objects out of everyday items like upholstery fabric for vestments, tin cans for censers, preserve glasses for candleholders. Artists of all kinds were conscripted. Some the leading iconographers of the twentieth century, such as Leonid Ouspensky, Father Gregory Krug, and Sister Joanna Reitlinger, were exactly such artist-conscripts.[48] Mother Maria was herself a master adaptor in this regard, embroidering vestments, icons, and turning garages and henhouses into chapels. But the point about this type was not the ingenuity just described but the lack of creativity and spontaneity, the absence of commitment, the minimalism, all of which equated church with being and remaining "Russian."

In the "ritual" type, and for that matter in the "aesthetical" and "ascetic" types of piety, Mother Maria turns to a far more passionate, in fact obsessive, attachment to liturgy, texts, the forms of prayer, faith, and religious behavior, although in somewhat different modalities. While there was as early as in the medieval Muscovite era the tendency to freeze Orthodox Christianity brought from Constantinople, the crisis of the "Old Believers" and their schism from the rest of the Russian Church was a profound historical influence on extreme ritualistic conservation. The "Old Believers" are the quintessential ritualists, rejecting as maters of truth and salvation the liturgical reforms of Patriarch Nikon in a fanatic, irrational fashion.

They refused, for example to use three fingers rather than two in making the sign of the cross. They insisted on archaic spellings of "Jesus," on double rather than triple repetitions of certain responses. On the other hand, they did preserve the classical icons and style of iconography. In the end, though, many ended up without clergy or sacraments, the icon screen alone attached to the eastern walls of their chapels. But for Mother Maria, the "Old Believers" are hardly the only ritualists, and she identifies many other behaviors as symptomatic of a piety where form is paramount, the heart and soul invested only in the externals. The fasts of the church year must be kept meticulously no matter what means are required and hardships imposed on others. Correct chanting tone and pronunciation and speed are crucial, even though neither the one chanting nor the congregation understands a word. Every detail of the calendar and the rubrics becomes divine, and errors and those erring are subjected to abusive treatment. No lack of zeal or commitment here, yet does such religion have anything to do with Christ, or the person before me, with the realities of everyday life.

> Its very principle, a constant repetition of rules, words and gestures, excludes any possibility of creative tension. From ancient times strict ritualism has been opposed to prophecy and creativity.[49] Its task was to preserve and to repeat and not to tear down and rebuild.... The main question ... is this: how does it respond to Christ's commandments concerning love for God and for other people? Does it have a place for them? ... Christ, who turned away from scribes and pharisees, Christ, who approached prostitutes, tax collectors and sinner, can hardly be the teacher of those who are afraid to soil their pristine garments, who are completely devoted to the letter of the law, who live only by rules and who govern their whole life according to the rules.[50]

The section on the ritualists concludes with the hard words about the Sabbath replacing the Lord and humankind quoted earlier in Mother Maria's critique of monasticism in the modern era. The ritualist type is only one of the more obsessive forms of piety she examines. As an artist herself in various media, Mother Maria was hardly anti-aesthetic, but in her sketching out of the aesthetic type, she stresses how elitist and egotistic such a type makes a person. It is here not "the letter of the law," the precise observance of rubrics and maintaining of rules but devotion to the fine performance of a choir, a preacher, an iconographer. Rather than encouraging the creativity necessary to finding new forms for our time, new ways of experiencing the beauty of the Lord and his house, in the aesthetic form much is simply lost in the passion for perfection, in enchantment with style. Left behind, too, are the vast majority of people, deemed unable to appreciate the beauty,

ignorant of its history, details, too uncouth to have around. "The aestheti-
cally minded custodians of grandeur will preserve that chasm" established
between Christ and the crowd of ordinary women and men, "in the name
of harmony, rhythm, order and beauty."

> Christ himself departs, quietly and invisibly, from the sanctuary protected
> by a splendid icon-screen. The singing will continue to resound, clouds of in-
> cense will still rise.... But Christ will go out onto the church steps and mingle
> with the crowd: the poor, the lepers, the desperate, the embittered, the holy
> fools. Christ will go out into the streets, the prisons, the hospitals, the low
> haunts and dives.... The most terrible thing is that it may well be that the
> guardians of beauty ... will not comprehend Christ's beauty, and will not let
> him into the church because behind him there will follow a crowd of people
> deformed by sin, by ugliness, drunkenness, depravity and hate. Then their
> chant will fade away in the air, the smell of incense will disperse, and Someone
> will say to them: "I was hungry and you gave me no food, thirsty and you gave
> me no drink, a stranger and you did not welcome me."[51]

In an echo of the essay by her opponent Father Cyprian Kern, she regretfully acknowledges that Christ's servants, the clergy, supposedly preachers,
healers, and the ministers of his love, have become servants rather of the
cult, worried about the rubrics, the cut of the vestments, the quality of the
voice for chanting.[52]

The last type Mother Maria serves up for analysis is the ascetic. The
pages she devotes to this form are moving, lyrical, and we have already
heard some of these passages in discussing her ideas about renewal of monasticism.[53] As there, here too the problem is the spiritual egocentrism of
the ascetic fixation. All these fasting rules, all the distasteful tasks I do under obedience, all the things I deny myself—these in the end are all about
me. Even when doing something good for the neighbor, I am doing it to
save myself. The neighbor just happens to be the target of my good deeds.
No real communion is established between myself and the other and thus,
little or no real communion with God. Real asceticism has as its goal clear-
ing out the debris, opening one to God and the neighbor. However, the
pseudo-asceticism here described achieves exactly the opposite, closing
me up in myself, turning me back constantly inward.

The final type Mother Maria presents is the one she unreservedly celebrates and recommends as authentically Christian, of the gospel, evangelical though not in our contemporary denominational sense of this
term. In fact, she explicitly distinguishes this type from a sectarianism that
turns the Bible into a list of moral precepts, and a sectarian mentality that
ridicules other Christians, their worship and life, claiming a biblical self-

righteousness in so doing. And by now, the features of this type are no mystery to us for we have come upon them at many other places in Mother Maria's writings and especially in her life.

Rather than use the term "churching of life," so preferred by others in the Russian emigration, she coins another as descriptive of the chief aim of this type:

"Christification" ... is based on the words, "It is no longer I who live, but Christ who lives in me." (Gal 2:20) The image of God, the icon of Christ, which truly is my real and authentic essence or being, is the only measure of all things, the only path or way which is given to me. Each movement of my soul, each approach to God, to other people, to the world, is determined by the suitability of that act for reflecting the image of God which is within me.[54]

Love for humanity alone or in general, while an ideal of the Enlightenment and of the modern era, leads us into the bind alley, as she calls it of a humanism that is at once anti-Christian, impersonal, theoretical, and, in the end, not humane. But equally, as we have also seen, the flight into religiosity of various forms, the attempt to place the love for God above that for the neighbor, to play Martha off against Mary, destroys love, both for God and for the neighbor.

The two loves are but one love. To attempt to "Christify" the world is not impose upon it something external, but to deal with it in its own terms—as God's creation, out of love, as the constant object of God's love, God's becoming part of it, living in it, dying and rising—"for the life of the world." To "Christify" means to be the world's beloved, the *philanthropos* or "Lover of mankind," as the Eastern Church liturgy repeatedly names God. As scripture scholar James Kugel points out, an image of God we have lost is that of a God who does not so much sit on his throne in his heavens, waiting for our obeisance, but the God who descends and walks among us, often completely unnoticed, seeking us out in love.[55] One cannot grasp Mother Maria's thinking here without recognizing deep within, a quite different image of God and correspondingly, of the human person than those we employ in everyday discourse. There is in her theology and anthropology Father Bulgakov's most intimate relationship between God and humankind, the reciprocity he meant to connote by his constant reference to Sophia, but for which he also employed Soloviev's idea of "God's humanity." For Mother Maria, God is pure, his love for his creation is complete. He makes himself into that creation, pursues us with a passion—and wishes that we would "go and do likewise." At the Last Judgment, Mother Maria reasons, when the master of all, who is the servant of all, says that he was the one who was hungry, thirsty, naked, without a home, it is not a question of fulfilling obligations, performing rituals, but being love, being holy fools like the most foolish of lovers, God. If we find ourselves having followed only the politically, socially "correct" ways, we will find that there is no one but ourselves to blame. It is "our loveless hearts, our stingy souls, our ineffective will, our lack of faith in Christ's help" that will judge us. But it will be God who nevertheless welcomes us in to dine with him (Rev. 3:20).

It is simply not possible to accuse Mother Maria of abandoning the church, prayer, the liturgy, or sacraments in her vision of the love of God and the neighbor. This sort of criticism, often leveled at movements such as liberation theology and the Social Gospel, do not apply. At the conclusion of the "Types" essay, within the gospel or evangelical type, she produces several of the most eloquent pages in contemporary Christian writing on the Eucharist as the "Church's most valuable treasure, its primary activity in the world," as "the mystery of sacrificial love."[56] There is no contradiction in her writings as in her own existence, between prayer and action, between liturgy and life. Christianity was nothing less than an eternal offering, not only of the divine liturgy inside but also beyond the church walls.

> It means that we must offer the bloodless sacrifice, the sacrifice of self-surrendering love not only in a specific place, upon the altar of a particular temple; the whole world becomes the single altar of a single temple, and for this universal liturgy we must offer our hearts, like bread and wine, in order that they may be transformed into Christ's love, that he may be born in them, that they may become "divine-human" hearts and that he may give these hearts of ours as food for the world, that he may bring the whole world into communion with these hearts of ours that have been offered up…. Then truly in all ways Christ will be all in all.[57]

MOTHER MARIA'S INFLUENCE AND LEGACY

We do not receive a systematic theology from Mother Maria. Neither is it the focused academic sort. If, however, in this volume one hopes to hear from a modern Christian thinker important insights on the person, on life in the social and political worlds, amid the laws and institutions of our time, then we have heard much. But the one word, and the core theme is that of the life-giving love of God for us and likewise, the liberating, transforming love we in turn have for the neighbor who is always before us. As a Kierkegaard scholar, I am much taken by the correspondence of Mother Maria's essential thinking here with Kierkegaard's very important *Works of Love*, a volume only very recently receiving attention for its proclamation of Christian life and ethics. For Mother Maria, as for Kierkegaard, love is the hidden "sprout in the grain," always able to presume love in the other, always cooperating with God in his work of loving.[58]

Mother Maria was not the type to have disciples. As noted, even the two other nuns who came to live with her in the "monasteries in the world" at Villa de Saxe, rue de Lourmel, and Noisy-le-Grand, Mothers Evdokia and Blandina, had difficulties with the turmoil of trying to observe the daily cycle of services and care for so many people. The more traditional monastery they established still exists in Bussey-en-Othe. Her chaplain, Father Cyprian Kern, continued his work teaching at St. Sergius Institute after he left the church at rue de Lourmel. He mentored the young priest and teacher, Father Alexander Schmemann, who became the leading Orthodox voice in liturgical and spiritual renewal in America. Father Lev Gillet, another chaplain and close friend of Mother Maria, went to work in England, and it remained his base for the rest of his life. Father Bulgakov died in 1944, during the occupation, after a stroke and a long coma.

Mother Maria founded neither a "school" of theological reflection nor a religious order. The hostels she established are now all gone, though one remained as a parish until the 1970s and another as a retreat house until the late 1980s. The wonderful icon screen that iconographer Father Gregory Krug created for the chapel at Noisy-le-Grand in her memory now adorns the monastery church at Marcenat.[59] There is no shrine to Mother Maria in Paris or elsewhere. The veneration of her, though widespread, is completely private and unofficial. As noted, the process for her official recognition—"glorification" as canonization is called in the Eastern Church—seems to have been placed on hold. She always had her critics and detractors as recent rejections of her thinking by Father Valentin Asmus and others in Russia witness.[60] Yet I would argue that her life, person, and thinking have been appropriated, most often without explicit acknowledgment by a number of fellow Orthodox Christians. Some, like her, experienced the new freedom of the emigration as well as its hardships, and in it they also discovered the fresh, radical character of the gospel life of prayer and service to which she witnessed.

Surely one striking example would be the ninety-seven-year-old lay theologian Elisabeth Behr-Sigel, who knew Mother Maria and whose life and work echo Mother Maria's own fearless commitment to freedom in Christian life.[61] Close to Father Bulgakov, Father Lev Gillet, Paul Evdokimov, and many others of the Paris emigration as well as to Mother Maria, she has taught and written on the nineteenth-century Russian theologian Alexander Bukharev, on the kenotic Christ in Russian spirituality, and, more recently, on the place of women in the Orthodox Church, in particular the question of the ordination of women.[62] Painstaking and scholarly, her writing on the last subjects is never polemical, always historically insightful and theologically challenging. Both Metropolitan Anthony Bloom and Bishop Kallistos Ware have supported her keeping open dialogue and encouraging study and debate on the question of women in the Orthodox Church generally and the more difficult and specific issue of deaconesses and other orders in the past and the possibility of the restoration of these and possibly other blessed and ordained orders in the future. Active in the Resistance during World War II, Elisabeth Behr-Sigel has continued her involvement in the movement to assist victims of torture, the Christian Association for the Abolition of Torture. In her overview of the spirituality of the Eastern Church, she demonstrates that openness to the world to characteristic of the Russian thinkers just noted. But the unambiguous connection between prayer and service to others, between church and society, between liturgy and life is clear throughout her writings and her own life.

Another who also dedicated himself to care of the suffering was a colleague of Mother Maria's from days in the Russian Christian Students Movement, its first general secretary, also a member of the first graduating class of the St. Sergius Theological Institute, the lay theologian Paul Evdokimov (1901–69). Mother Maria's vision of serving God and the neighbor was expressed in his writings and activities.[63] Also active in the Resistance, he directed several hostels for refugees in the postwar era. Despite his degrees from the Sorbonne and St. Sergius Institute and a doctorate from the University at Aix-en-Provence, he remained in service work. He was an authentic lay pastor, exercising, as he said, his baptismal priesthood. He counseled the refugees, displaced persons, troubled individuals, and Third World students who found the hostels not only an affordable place to live but also a true community in both spiritual and human terms. In the late 1950s he defended a second dissertation and began teaching on his alma mater, St. Sergius's faculty, also teaching in the World Council of Churches Ecumenical Institute at Bossey and the Catholic Institute of Theology in Paris, among other places. His publications included a masterful overview of Orthodox theology, a study of the theology of the icon, as well as studies of the history of contemporary Russian theology and the state of debate on the place and role of the Holy Spirit. The strong emphasis on the priesthood and hence daily ministry of all the baptized along with his sensitivity toward service of the suffering are the echoes of Mother Maria in both his writing and life.

Mother Maria, along with her colleagues in the Paris Russian emigration, left an important legacy not only to their Orthodox Church but also to the Western churches. Clearly, those closest to Mother Maria, such as Fathers Bulgakov and Gillet, exemplified her passionate commitment to the suffering neighbor as the love of God. Others put into practice her zeal for the love of the neighbor by emphasizing the need for the church to reach out to the world in love, in service and mission. Fathers Alexander

Schmemann and John Meyendorff and another contemporary martyr, Father Alexander Men, not only wrote about this but also lived it.[64]

In his reflections on holiness in our time, Paul Evdokimov, like Simone Weil, notes that we need a new type of sanctity.[65] Although we need to respect the models of holiness from the past, we need to not imprison ourselves in these but rather to find those shapes that better correspond to our world, our time and our lives.[66] Like Mother Maria, Evdokimov realized that holiness in our time would have its heroic, unusual patterns. But for the most part, the loving of God and of the neighbor would be everyday, so ordinary and usual as to be "hidden." Routine and unnoticed, unlike the great feats of traditional sanctity, such a holiness of our time will not be so easily acknowledged, but its presence is universal.

POSTSCRIPT

In a document dated January 16, 2004, almost sixty years after the death of Mother Maria, and after petitions were submitted to church authorities over the past decades, the holy synod of the Ecumenical Patriarchate recognized her and several of her associates as saints.

> The Holy Church of Christ knows to honor and celebrate forever in all piety and in hymns and praises those who in the present life conduct themselves in a holy and pious manner, and who exert themselves in word and deed in the service and in the love of God and of the neighbor, and who, after their departure for the beyond, through signs and miracles have been confirmed by God, and to invoke their intercession, which is acceptable to God, for the remission of sins and the healing of the sick.

Along with Mother Maria, Father Dimitri Klepinine, chaplain of the hostel at rue de Lourmel, her son Yuri Skobtsov, and treasurer Ilya Fondaminsky were canonized, all of them having also died in Nazi prison camps. A faithful and holy priest who served in the poor mining town of Ugine, Father Alexis Medvedkov, was also included.

The act of canonization affirmed,

> by the dignity of their lives and their good example, they contributed to the edification of the souls of the faithful; several of them, during the Second World War, suffered greatly from evils and were subjected to torments, which they bore with fortitude. In consequence, we have decided, following the usual practice of the Church, to accord to these very holy people the honor which is due to them. This is why we have decreed and ordered in Synod, and recommended in the Holy Spirit, that the Archpriest Alexis Medvedkov, the Priest Dimitri Klepinine, the nun Maria Skobtsova and her son Yuri Skobtsov

and Ilya Fondaminsky, who ended their life in sanctity and, certainly, in martyrdom, be counted among the blessed martyrs and saints of the Church and be honored by the faithful and celebrated in hymns of praise.

Canonization, through an official ecclesiastical act, does not make a saint. Holiness consists in living out the gospel, loving God and neighbor, in words and actions. As with so many others, we may also say of Mother Maria that long before she was canonized her sanctity was enacted in the lives of those around her and known by many more. Now she is recognized among the saints of our time.

NOTES

1. Several good biographical essays on Mother Maria exist in addition to T. Stratton Smith's *Rebel Nun* (Springfield, Ill.: Templegate, 1965). The most recent is Jim Forest, "Mother Maria of Paris," in *Mother Maria Skobtsova: Essential Writings*, trans. Richard Pevear and Larissa Volokhonsky (Maryknoll, N.Y.: Orbis Books, 2003), 13–44; Michael Plekon, *Living Icons: Persons of Faith in the Eastern Church* (Notre Dame, Ind.: University of Notre Dame Press, 2002), 59–80. Particularly rich is Hélène Arjakovsky-Klepinine, "La joie du don," in *Le sacrement du frère*, ed. Helene Arjakovsky-Klepinine, Françoise Lhoest, and Claire Vajou, 15–69 (Paris: Éditions du Cerf, 2001), 15–69, and the essay by Elisabeth Behr-Sigel, who knew her, "Mother Maria Skobtsova 1891–1945," in *Discerning the Signs of the Times: The Vision of Elisabeth Behr-Sigel*, ed. Michael Plekon and Sarah E. Hinlicky, 41–54 (Crestwood, N.Y.: St. Vladimir's Seminary Press, 2001). Metropolitan Anthony Bloom's memories of Mother Maria in the May 2001 *Cathedral Newsletter* can be found at http://www.sourozh.org. I am indebted to conversation with two remarkable women of the Orthodox Church who knew Mother Maria in their youth and were willing to share some of their memories of her. These are the late Sophie Koloumzine, teacher and founder of religious education among the Orthodox in America and the incomparable Elisabeth Behr-Sigel, who at ninety-six was still active as a lay theologian, and who is regarded as the "mother" of the Orthodox Church in France. I am also grateful to Helen Arjakovsky-Klepinine, daughter of Father Dimitri Klepinine, and one who has preserved Mother Maria's memory and translated her writings, bringing them to a wide range of readers in Europe. Another helpful biographical effort is that of Laurence Varaut, *Mère Marie: Saint-Pétersbourg-Paris-Ravensbrück, 1891–1945* (Paris: Perrin, 2001). The classic is Sergei Hackel, *Pearl of Great Price: The Life of Mother Maria Skobtsova, 1891–1945* (Crestwood, N.Y.: St. Vladimir's Seminary Press, 1982). Last, I am indebted to Father Alvian Smirensky for sharing with me his translations of the memoirs of Father Basil Zenkovsky, *My Encounters with Prominent People*, published by the Association of Russian Scholars in America.
2. *La chemin de ma vie* (Paris: Presses Saint-Serge, 2003). Openness and freedom are the traits emphasized by Father Basil Zenkovsky in his memoir of Metropolitan Evlogy.

3. Many of these remarkable members of the Russian community in Paris are examined in Nicolas Zernov, *The Russian Religious Renaissance of the Twentieth Century* (New York: Harper & Row, 1963). Also see Marc Raeff, *Russia Abroad* (New York: Oxford University Press, 1990), and Nikita Struve, *Soixante-dix ans de l'émigration russe, 1919–1989* (Paris: Fayard, 1996).

4. The cited volumes by Antoine Arjakovsky, Sergei Hackel, Helene Arjakovsky-Klepinine, and Laurence Varaut contain these photos. Until recently there was a Paris-based Web site with many photos of Mother Maria, but it was discontinued.

5. Antoine Arjakovsky, *Histoire de la pensée orthodoxe contemporaine: La génération des penseurs religieux de l'émigration russe-La revue La Voie (Put')* *1925–1940* (Paris: L'Esprit et la Lettre, 2002); Paul Valliere, *Modern Russian Theology: Soloviev, Bukharev, Bulgakov* (Grand Rapids, Mich.: Eerdmans, 2000); Rowan Williams, *Sergii Bulgakov: Towards A Russian Political Theology* (Edinburgh: T & T Clark, 1999); Anastassy Brandon Gallaher, "Bulgakov's Ecumenical Thought," *Sobornost/Eastern Churches Review* 24, no. 1 (2002): 24–55; Gallaher, "Bulgakov and Intercommunion," ibid., 9–28; Gallaher, "Catholic Action: Ecclesiology, the Eucharist and the Question of Intercommunion in the Ecumenism of Sergii Bulgakov" (M.Div. thesis, St. Vladimir's Orthodox Theological Seminary, 2003).

6. Varaut, *Mère Marie*, 149–154; Hackel, *Pearl of Great Price*, 123–149.

7. See the report of this and the talk given by Bishop Gabriel (de Vylder) in *Service Orthodoxe de Presse* 276 (March 2003): "A la haine ils répondaient par l'amour, a l'indifférence par la charité" (They responded to hatred with love, to indifference with charity).

8. Hackel, *Pearl of Great Price*, xi–xii.

9. Arjakovsky, *Histoire de la pensée orthodoxe contemporaine*, 233–235, 257–258, 323, 474–475.

10. This essay is in *Essential Writings*, 156–165. On the debate between Father Chetverikov and Mother Maria in both *Put'* and *Messenger of the Russian Christian Students' Movement*, see Arjakovsky, *Histoire de la pensée orthodoxe contemporaine*, 471–474.

11. Ion Bria, "The Liturgy after the Liturgy," in *Baptism and Eucharist: Ecumenical Convergence in Celebration*, ed. Max Thurian and Geoffrey Wainwrights (Grand Rapids, Mich.: Eerdmans, 1983), 213–218.

12. *Essential Writings*, 80–81.

13. Thomas Merton, *The Asian Journal of Thomas Merton*, ed. Naomi Burton, Brother Patrick Hart, and James Laughlin (New York: New Directions, 1975), 338.

14. Both essays are included in Michael Plekon, ed., *Tradition Alive: On the Church and the Christian Life in Our Time* (Lanham, Md.: Sheed & Ward, 2003), 83–106.

15. "The Cross and the Hammer and Sickle" and "Under the Sign of Our Time," in *Essential Writings*, 84–89, 107–115.

16. "Birth and Death," in Plekon, *Tradition Alive*, 195–202.

17. See the studies cited in note 5 above. Biographical material appears in all of these; in Nicolas Zernov and James Pain, eds., *A Bulgakov Anthology*

(Philadelphia: Westminster Press, 1976), ix–27; and in Plekon, *Living Icons*, 29–58.

18. See Zernov and Pain, *A Bulgakov Anthology*, 15–21, for some of his provocative remarks on the episcopate.

19. See the concluding volume of Father Bulgakov's great trilogy on the humanity of God, dealing with eschatology and the Church: Sergei Bulgakov, *The Bride of the Lamb*, trans. Boris Jakim (Grand Rapids, Mich.: Eerdmans, 2001); see also Bulgakov, *The Orthodox Church*, trans. Lydia Kesich (Crestwood, N.Y.: St. Vladimir's Seminary Press, 1988). Most of Bulgakov's major works have been translated into French by his student Constantine Andronikof.

20. *Essential Writings*, 58–59.

21. See Sergius Bulgakov, *The Holy Grail and The Eucharist*, trans. Boris Jakim (Hudson, N.Y.: Lindisfarne Books, 1997), as well as Gallaher, "Catholic Action."

22. *Essential Writings*, 60.

23. *Against the Heresies*, 4, 7, 20.

24. See *The Bride of the Lamb*, 379–526; and *Apocatastasis and Transfiguration*, trans. Boris Jakim (New Haven, Conn.: Variable Press, 1995).

25. *Essential Writings*, 81–83.

26. Hackel, *Pearl of Great Price*, 4–5.

27. *Essential Writings*, 70–71.

28. Ibid., 177.

29. Ibid., 175–176.

30. Ibid., 176.

31. See Nadia Gorodetsky, *The Humiliated Christ in Modern Russian Thought* (London: Macmillan, 1938); Elisabeth Behr-Sigel, "The Kenotic, the Humble Christ," in *Discerning the Signs of the Times*, 29–40; Paul Evdokimov, "God's Absurd Love and the Mystery of His Silence," in *In the World, of the Church: A Paul Evdokimov Reader*, ed. and trans. Michael Plekon and Alexis Vinogradov (Crestwood, N.Y.: St. Vladimir's Seminary Press, 2001).

32. *Essential Writings*, 182–183.

33. Ibid., 154–155.

34. Ibid., 167–168.

35. Ibid., 170–171. The translators of this anthology note, "*The Feast During the Plague* is the title of a play by Alexander Pushkin (1799–1837) and it is a poem of his, 'The Prophets,' which ends: 'and sets the hearts of men on fire with your Word.'"

36. *Essential Writings*, 94.

37. Ibid., 95.

38. I have not been able to find any significant references to Mother Maria in his writings, nevertheless the strong sense of the liturgy, the Church's "mission," of being "for the life of the world," is present in the person and the efforts of Father Alexander Schmemann (1921–1983). See "Alexander Schmemann: Teacher of Freedom and Joy, in the World as Sacrament," in *Living Icons*, 178–202.

39. C. Wright Mills, *The Sociological Imagination* (New York: Grove Press, 1961).

40. Peter L. Berger, *Invitation to Sociology: A Humanistic Perspective* (New York: Doubleday, 1963).

41. *Essential Writings*, 85, 87.

42. Ibid., 89.

43. *Living Tradition* (Crestwood, N.Y.: St. Vladimir's Seminary Press, 1978), 13–26.

44. Paul Evdokimov, *The Sacrament of Love*, trans. Anthony P. Gythiel and Victoria Steadman (Crestwood, N.Y.: St. Vladimir's Seminary Press, 1985), 62.

45. See further discussion of this source in chapter 23, this volume.

46. *Essential Writings*, 143.

47. See Alexander Schmemann, *Introduction to Liturgical Theology*, trans. Ashleigh Moorhouse (Crestwood, N.Y.: St. Vladimir's Seminary Press, 1966), 19–25, as well as many passages in *The Journals of Fr. Alexander Schmemann 1973-1983*, ed. and trans. Juliana Schmemann (Crestwood, N.Y.: St. Vladimir's Seminary Press, 2000). See also part of his statement at the oral defense of this study as his doctoral dissertation in *Living Icons*, 188–189.

48. See Jean-Claude Marcadé, ed., *Un peintre d'icônes: Le père Gregoire Krug* (Paris: Institut d'Études Slaves, 2001); Fr. Barsanuphius, ed., *Le père Gregoire, moine iconographe du skit du Saint-Esprit, 1908–1969* (Domerac: Monastery of Korsun, 1999); and Emilie van Taack, Anne Philippenko-Bogenhardt, and B. Pardo-Zacariel, *L'iconographie de l'église des Trois Saints Hiérarques et l'oeuvre de Léonide A. Ouspensky et moine Gregoire Krug* (Paris: Paroisse des Trois Saints Hiérarques, 2001).

49. Though by no means a supporter of Mother Maria, one of her former chaplains, Father Cyprian Kern, wrote a provocative essay about just this loss of the prophetic, published in the collection *Zhivoe predanie* (Living Tradition) in 1937, "Two Models of the Pastorate: Levitical and Prophetic," translated and included in the anthology *Tradition Alive*, 109–120.

50. *Essential Writings*, 154.

51. Ibid., 160–161.

52. Ibid., 162.

53. Ibid., 163–173.

54. Ibid., 174.

55. James L. Kugel, *The God of Old: Inside the Lost World of the Bible* (New York: Free Press, 2003).

56. *Essential Writings*, 183–185.

57. Ibid., 185.

58. Michael Plekon, "Kierkegaard the Theologian: The Roots of His Theology in *Works of Love*," in *Foundations of Kierkegaard's Vision of Community: Religion, Ethics and Politics in Kierkegaard*, ed. Stephen C. Evans and George Connell, 2–17 (New York: Humanities Press, 1991).

59. Fr. Barsanuphius, ed., *Icônes et fresques du père Gregoire Krug* (Marcenat: Monastery of Zanamenie, 1999).

60. Valentin Asmus, "Propochoskii golos Nikity Struve i Mat' Mariia (Skobtsova)," *Radonezh* 17 (November 1999). Also Nikita Struve, "Novye svedeniia o

poslednikh dniakh Materi Marii." and " Mat' Mariia i Otsenke Prot. V. Asmus," *Vestnik Studencheskogo Russkogo Khristianskogo Dvizheniia/La Messager,* 178.

61. See her *The Ministry of Women in the Church,* trans. Steven Bigham (Crestwood, N.Y.: St. Vladimir's Seminary Press, 1991), and with Bishop Kallistos Ware, *The Ordination of Women in the Orthodox Church* (Geneva: World Council of Churches, 2000) and *Discerning the Signs of the Times,* especially the essay on Mother Maria, 41–53.

62. See the anthologies' notes as well as *Alexandre Boukharev: un théologien de l'église orthodoxe russe en dialogue avec le monde moderne* (Paris: Beauchesne, 1977) and the anthology in honor of Elisabeth Behr-Sigel's ninety-sixth birthday: *Toi, suis-moi: Mélanges offerts en hommage à Élisabeth Behr-Sigel* (Iasi, Romania: Editura Trinitas, 2003).

63. See Evdokimov, *Ages of the Spiritual Life; In the World, of the Church;* and *The Sacrament of Love.* He is profiled in Olivier Clément, *Orient-Occident: Deux Passeurs, Vladimir Lossky, Paul Evdokimov* (Geneva: Labor et Fides, 1985) and in Plekon, *Living Icons,* 102–127.

64. Ibid., 178–260.

65. *The Sacrament of Love,* 92; Simone Weil, *Waiting for God,* trans. Emma Craufurd (New York: Harper & Row, 1973), 98–99.

66. See *Ages of the Spiritual Life,* 77–82, 193–258, as well as "Holiness in the Tradition of the Orthodox Church," *In the World, of the Church,* 95–154.

{ CHAPTER 23 }

Dumitru Stăniloae (1903–1993)

LUCIAN TURCESCU

The youngest of five children, Dumitru Stăniloae was born on November 16, 1903, in the village of Vladeni in Transylvania, then a region of the Austro-Hungarian Empire, absorbed into Romania at the end of World War I. Partly because of his rural upbringing, partly because of Romanian intellectual and cultural movements that exalted the peasant, Stăniloae loved peasant culture and reflected it in his writings. Stăniloae's parents were both devout Orthodox Christians; his father was a church chanter. Both parents exerted a lasting influence on him and on his choice of an ecclesiastical and theological career.

From 1922 to 1927, Stăniloae studied theology at the Faculty of Theology in Cernauti, now in the Ukraine, receiving some financial support from Nicolae Balan, Orthodox Metropolitan of Transylvania (1920–55). Several of his professors in Cernauti were locally prominent theologians. Dumitru, however, did not like the Westernized style of academic theology that prevailed throughout the Orthodox world at the time, with its characteristic scholasticism and nineteenth-century religious rationalism. In 1927, he went to Athens for a few months of research, again with the financial support of Metropolitan Balan.

In 1928, Stăniloae returned to Cernauti and hastily completed and defended a very brief doctoral dissertation in church history entitled "The Life and Work of Patriarch Dositheos of Jerusalem and his Relations with the Romanian Lands." In this work, he presented the Romanian lands as a meeting place between the Greek and Slav worlds, and as a guardian of the Byzantine heritage. He has also emphasized his country's special position within the world as the only predominantly Orthodox country that used Latin.

For another full year after obtaining his doctorate in theology, Stăniloae traveled to Munich, Berlin, and Paris for additional study and research. He was drawn especially to the dialogical theology of Martin Buber and the

French personalists, as well as the theology of Gregory Palamas (1296–1359), the main promoter of Hesychasm, a doctrine and practice of prayer of the heart and contemplation of God. These were formative experiences for Stăniloae's later development of a deeply personalistic theology that wove together, in a creative and rather coherent whole, modern personalism, patristic views, Hesychasm, and Orthodox spirituality.

In September 1929, Stăniloae started teaching theology. He first taught at the Theological Academy in the Transylvanian city of Sibiu (1929–46) and served as rector there (1936–46). He then taught at the Faculty of Orthodox Theology in Romania's capital, Bucharest (1947–58, 1965–73). Shortly after being appointed to teach in Sibiu, he married and was ordained as a priest in the Romanian Orthodox Church. He and his wife had three children. Two of his children were twins, and both died at a young age. The surviving daughter, Lidia, a Romanian-language writer and poet, lives in Germany today with her son Dumitras.

While continuing to teach dogmatic, apologetic, and pastoral theology, Stăniloae embarked on an extensive program of research, translation, and publication. In 1930, he published a Romanian translation of the then standard Greek textbook of dogmatic theology by Christos Androutsos—"an example of the basically Latinizing scholastic approach to theology," as John Meyendorff notes.[1] Some of Stăniloae's first books were collections of articles previously published in Romanian theological and cultural journals and diocesan newspapers. Yet several of these early books, notably *The Life and Teaching of St. Gregory Palamas* (1938) and *Jesus Christ, or the Restoration of Man* (1943), already distinguished him as a very original theological thinker. The former book was a groundbreaking study in Palamite scholarship. It gave a very different picture of Palamism than the very negative picture then presented in the West by the Roman Catholic scholar Martin Jugie. Stăniloae, together with such other Orthodox scholars as Basil Krivocheine, Vladimir Lossky, and John Meyendorff, used Palamism to revive and transform Orthodoxy. They also influenced the development of a more scholarly and objective treatment of Palamism by Roman Catholic scholars such as André de Halleux, Jacques Lison, and Robert Sinkewicz, and have made it an important theological alternative to Westerners.

Stăniloae still considered his second book, *Jesus Christ, or the Restoration of Man*, as one of his major works when I spoke to him two years before his death. In this work, for the first time in Romanian theology, Stăniloae emphasized the ontological aspect of salvation, which he found present abundantly in the Greek church fathers. In this work, he also engaged in dialogue with some of the best Western theologians and philosophers at the time.

During his Sibiu period, Stăniloae also began compiling and translating single-handedly the Romanian version of the *Philokalia*, twelve volumes of which were published between 1946 and 1991. Although based on the Venice edition of the *Philokalia of the Holy Ascetics* (1782), a collection of texts compiled by Nikodemos of the Holy Mountain and Makarios Notaras, Stăniloae's *Philokalia* differs from it in several important ways. Stăniloae substantially supplemented the texts of the original *Philokalia*, adding, among many other sections, an appendix entitled "Hesychasm and the Jesus Prayer in the Romanian Orthodox Tradition" in volume 8. He also provided his own introductions for the modern reader and accompanied the texts with very rich commentaries and footnotes.[2]

In the Sibiu period, Stăniloae also published articles on the relationship between Orthodoxy and Romanianism, a theme that he revived after the fall of Communism in 1989 and published as *Reflections on the Spirituality of the Romanian People* (1992). Greater Romania was the state formed in 1918 by the three formerly independent principalities of Wallachia, Moldova, and Transylvania (the first two had become one unit in 1859) as well as several other smaller regions. Between the world wars, Romanianism was held up as an imagined shared ethnic identity allegedly superseding Moldovan, Wallachian, and Transylvanian allegiances. The philosopher, poet, and theologian Nichifor Crainic and the philosopher and poet Lucian Blaga, together with a number of other intellectuals, were advocating Romanianism following the formation of Greater Romania. They stressed the characteristics that bound together the inhabitants of the new state (religion, language, customs, and traditions), while differentiating them from ethnic minorities and neighboring peoples. The discussion continued in Romania during the Communist period, and indeed continues to this day.

Stăniloae joined Crainic's cause, though he was more moderate than Crainic, who tried to make Orthodoxy a touchstone for the identification of the "Romanian soul."[3] Between 1935 and 1944, Stăniloae wrote seventeen articles in *Gândirea* (*Thought*), one of the most notorious magazines of Romanian nationalism, directed by Crainic at the time. Stăniloae published other articles on the subject in the diocesan newspaper *Telegraful Român* (*Romanian Telegraph*), whose directorship he held between 1934 and 1946. Stăniloae's articles were then collected in the volumes *Orthodoxy and Romanianism* (1939) and *The Position of Mr. Lucian Blaga vis-à-vis Christianity and Orthodoxy* (1942). These texts probably figured prominently in substantiating the charges against Stăniloae in his trial of 1958.

Crainic referred to Stăniloae as the "great religious thinker from Sibiu," and considered him the promoter of a new, original phase in the evolution of Romanian theology.[4] Crainic was the foremost exponent of Gândirism, a form of nationalism, autochthonism, and neo-Orthodoxy associated with *Gândirea* magazine. He was also a leader of the Iron Guard, the Romanian fascist, anti-Semitic movement. For those reasons and for his anticommunist stance, Crainic was arrested in 1947. At the time, Communism was establishing more permanent roots in Romania, having been exported into the country by the Soviets following the Yalta Treaty of 1945, which gave the Soviet Union full control of Romania.

Romania's newly acquired freedom following the 1989 collapse of the Communist regime of President Nicolae Ceausescu paved the way for access to documentary materials previously unavailable (including *Gândirea* and various archives) and the possibility to comment publicly on those materials. As a result, several researchers have started piecing together a portrait of Stăniloae and his relationship with Crainic. According to Orthodox Church historian Mircea Pacurariu, the first Communist prime minister, Petru Groza, wrote several times to Metropolitan Balan threatening him with "grave consequences" if he did not distance himself from Stăniloae (who was still Balan's protégé at the time). Due to his activities and views, as well as his relations with Crainic, Stăniloae was eventually forced to resign his post as director of the *Telegraful Român* in May 1945 and his position as rector of the Theological Academy in February 1946.[5]

Stăniloae did write some anticommunist articles before 1945 and even wrote a eulogy for Ion Mota and Vasile Marin, two leaders of the Iron Guard, who died in 1937 in Spain fighting on Franco's side.[6] He also revealed his admiration for Mota and Marin in an article in the new Iron Guard publication, *Gazeta de Vest*, in 1993.[7] It is worth noting, however, that, while contemporary Iron Guardists acknowledge Crainic as one of their leaders, they do not consider Stăniloae as one of their members and do not mention him on their Web sites.[8]

In January 1947 Stăniloae moved to Bucharest, where he replaced Crainic and began teaching ascetics and mystics in the Faculty of Orthodox Theology. That Stăniloae replaced Crainic likely raised suspicion in the minds of Communist officials. In 1948, as part of a general crackdown on religion, officials placed the Faculty of Orthodox Theology outside the state University of Bucharest and recognized it as a separate university-level institution. This move gave Communist officials more leverage and control over the faculty. The law on religious denominations, adopted on August 4, 1948, in accordance with Article 27 of the Constitution of April 1948 concerning the freedom of conscience, allowed only denominations officially recognized by the Communist authorities to continue their activity, and it established the state's firm control over churches. On July 17, 1948, the authorities abrogated the Concordat between Romania and the Vatican that had been signed in pre-Communist times. In October 1948 they also disbanded the Greek Catholic Church in Romania and forced Catholics to "reintegrate" with the mother Orthodox Church, which received all Greek Catholic property in exchange for its compliance with state religious policies.

Despite the hardships created by the government's crackdown on things "spiritual" and "mystical" during the first years of the Communist regime, Stăniloae collaborated on two volumes of theology, *A Manual of Christian Orthodox Teachings* (1952) and *Dogmatic and Symbolic Theology for Theological Institutes* (1958). The second work, however, does not bear his name, because he was arrested before it went to press.

After Stăniloae moved to Bucharest, the Communist secret police began secretly following him. They also repeatedly warned him about his associations with the wrong people. In the 1950s, he became involved with a spirituality group, "The Burning Bush," which included monks, intellectuals, and students. Some members, such as Benedict Ghius and Constantin Joja, were Iron Guardists. Others, though genuinely concerned with spirituality, were sent to prison for conspiring to overthrow the Communist regime, as part of the regime's wider antireligious and anticlerical campaign.

Stăniloae, too, was imprisoned in 1958 and was not released until January 1963. His release came at a time when Romania was starting to move from the Soviet form of totalitarian Communism to its own form of national Communism, which had a limited degree of openness and freedom. On his release, however, Stăniloae was not allowed to return to the Faculty of Theology in Bucharest until 1965, and even then he was only to teach doctoral courses and supervise doctoral dissertations. These restrictions greatly limited the number of his students. After his retirement in 1973, he continued to serve as supervisor for doctoral dissertations until the early 1980s.

The Communist prison experience was a terrible ordeal for Stăniloae, as it was for others, many of whom did not survive. Following his release, Stăniloae spoke very little about it and refused to name some of the most ferocious prison guards and secret police officers who tortured him. He maintained his silence even after Romania embraced freedom of speech in 1989. His daughter Lidia wrote recently that "the extreme suffering [my father] underwent was an experience that brought him even closer to God. He bore it all with the same patience with which he bore many other difficulties. He never held a grudge against those who made him suffer or against those who—even if they owed him much—turned their back on him."[9] To French Orthodox theologian Olivier Clement, Stăniloae remarked that it was only in jail that he could practice the Jesus prayer with amazing power.

In 1978, at the age of seventy-five, Stăniloae published his magnum opus, the three-volume, 1,347-page *Orthodox Dogmatic Theology*. Like all of his works, he wrote his *Dogmatics* in Romanian. But the work is now partly available in French and English, and entirely available in German translation.[10] The English translation came out as *The Experience of God*, but the two volumes published to date represent only the first volume of the Romanian edition. According to Bishop Kallistos Ware of Diokleia, who wrote the foreword to the first volume of *The Experience of God*, the work "embodies the mature fruits of [Stăniloae's] theological reflection after more than half a century of teaching and writing."[11] As Bishop Kallistos explains, the word "dogmatic" was removed from the title of the English translation for fear that it might be taken to mean obligatory teaching, imposed from above by an external authority. This, however, was not at all what Stăniloae meant by dogmatic theology, as it was not the case for, say, Karl Barth in titling his *Church Dogmatics*.

In *Dogmatics*, Stăniloae tried to blend in a very creative fashion patristic insights with contemporary theology, both Western and Eastern. A keen sense of the importance of the personal, as well as of the complementarity between apophatic and kataphatic theology, pervades Stăniloae's *Dogmatics* and his theology in general. The *Dogmatics* is somewhat similar in structure to his earlier *Dogmatic and Symbolic Theology for Theological Institutes*. In the 1978 *Dogmatics*, though, Stăniloae used the church fathers more heavily than in the earlier edition and, of course, he felt more at ease providing his own reflections based on his dialogue with the tradition and modernity, including contemporary ecumenism.

Several other significant works by Stăniloae published in Romanian include *Spirituality and Communion in the Orthodox Liturgy* (1986), *The Eternal Image of God* (1987), *Studies in Orthodox Dogmatic Theology* (1991), *The Evangelical Image of Jesus Christ* (1992), and *Commentary on the Gospel According to John* (1993). To these one should add numerous other Romanian translations from various church fathers and hundreds of journal and newspaper articles.

REVELATION AND THE LAW

Stăniloae's *Experience of God* opens with the statement, "The Orthodox Church makes no separation between natural and supernatural revelation."[12] This is often understood to mean that there is no separation between the sacred and the profane in the Orthodox tradition. A statement such as Stăniloae's would perhaps baffle a Westerner, but not necessarily an aboriginal shaman or a Hasidic Jew, for example, for whom the sacred is present in the daily life and in every single gesture he or she makes. Yet "separation" does not mean "distinction." The Orthodox Church does distinguish between natural and supernatural revelation, but does not necessarily separate them for purposes other than to understand them. It does not separate them in its daily preaching (the Greek *kerygma*), thus trying to show the essential continuity between them.

The first two chapters in *The Experience of God* deal with natural and supernatural revelation and their relationship. The relationship between the two types of revelation is important in the context of law and human nature, because it is in the Law that God gave to Moses at Mount Sinai that Stăniloae sees the supernatural revelation expressed in a concentrated form. To be sure, Stăniloae is reluctant to use the word "law." He does mention the Law given to Moses and cites Romans 2:14–15, where Paul speaks about the distinction between the natural law and the revealed law, but he seems unwilling to elaborate his theology along legal lines. Instead, Stăniloae talks a lot more about human knowledge of God and the dialogue a person has with God. This is not unlike what one sees in the works of other Orthodox theologians included in this volume. With few exceptions, Orthodox theologians tend to avoid talking about the law, a topic the modern Orthodox tradition has perceived as principally of Catholic and Protestant inspiration, although the Bible clearly discusses it.[13]

Contemporary biblical scholarship acknowledges that Paul's most frequently used image of salvation in Christ, namely, "justification" (*dikaiosune*), is drawn from Paul's Jewish law background and denotes a societal or judicial relationship, either ethical or forensic—that is, it is related to law courts, as in Deuteronomy 25:1. The righteous or upright person (*dikaios*) came to refer usually to one who stood acquitted or vindicated before a judge's tribunal (Exodus 23:7; 1 Kings 8:32). Jews also tried to achieve the status of "righteousness" or "uprightness" in the sight of Yahweh the Judge by observing the rules and regulations of Mosaic law (see Psalms 7:9–12). When Paul says that Christ has "justified" humans, he means that Christ has made it possible for them to stand before God's tribunal as acquitted or innocent. The characteristically Pauline contribution to the notion of justification is his affirmation of the gratuitous and unmerited character of this justification of all humanity in Romans 3:20–26.[14]

Though he does not speak directly on the subject, Stăniloae says a good deal about law and human nature in an indirect way. Human beings and the cosmos constitute the natural revelation of God from the point of view of knowledge.

> The cosmos is organized in a way that corresponds to our capacity for knowing. The cosmos—and human nature as intimately connected with the cosmos—are stamped with rationality, while man (God's creature) is further endowed with a reason capable of knowing consciously the rationality of

the cosmos and of his own nature…. We consider that the rationality of the cosmos attests to the fact that the cosmos is the product of a rational being, since rationality, as an aspect of a reality which is destined to be known, has no explanation apart from a conscious Reason which knows it from the time it creates it or even before that time, and knows it continually so long as that same Reason preserves its being.[15]

Words such as "rational," "reason," "consciousness," and "knowledge," rather than "law," recur repeatedly in Stăniloae's writings. Without explicitly referring to it, Stăniloae seems to have embraced the anthropic principle, according to which a rational God created the rational cosmos whose rationality and meaning the humans—as the crown of this creation—are meant to understand.

Like other Orthodox theologians, Stăniloae uses the biblical and patristic view of humans created in the image of God (Genesis 1:26–27). To be created in the image of God is to be a rational being. Using their reason and capacity to reflect and understand their surroundings and themselves, and storing this awareness in their complex psyche, is what distinguishes humans from the rest of the created visible world. At this point, despite his attempts to be true to the patristic understanding of the human person, Stăniloae collapses together, in an otherwise creative way, patristic and modern insights about the person.[16] Their rationality and consciousness make humans personal beings and, as such, they are capable of communicating with, and knowing, other persons, including divine persons. In their attempt to know the one God in three persons and to achieve "eternal perfection in God and [be] strengthened in communion with him even while on earth," humans get their information from the surrounding world and from themselves; this is what constitutes natural revelation. Yet humans get only partial information about God from natural revelation, especially in our current postlapsarian state.[17] Therefore, supernatural revelation is necessary, that is, the revelation that comes from God's own initiative, constitutes God's self-disclosure, and is contained in the Bible. This is the line along which Stăniloae prefers to develop his understanding of revelation.

Stăniloae's source of inspiration for the view that natural and supernatural revelations are not to be separated is Maximus the Confessor. Stăniloae paraphrases Maximus as follows: "Natural revelation has the same value as supernatural revelation [for the saints], that is, for those raised to a vision of God [it is] similar to that of supernatural revelation. For the saints, the written law is nothing other than the law of nature seen in the personal types of those who have fulfilled it, while the law of nature is nothing other than the written law seen in its spiritual meanings beyond these types."[18] What Stăniloae says is that the lack of a separation between natural and supernatural revelation is evident to the saints, but unfortunately not to ordinary Christians.[19] This view represents an emphasis on the spirit, rather than the letter, of the law, and it leads Stăniloae to deemphasize law.

While Stăniloae does not value the law in itself too much—except perhaps as a transitory step toward something higher—he is concerned about justice in light of Orthodox soteriology. Human beings are persons and as such they do not lead individual lives but are in relationship with other persons. This relationality is present in everyday life, but also when it comes to salvation: One cannot be saved in isolation, but one needs to be helped by others and has to help others in return.[20] Christ helped us to become saved, and, therefore, we, too, have to help our fellow humans. "Let us commend ourselves and each other and our whole life to Christ our God," sing the faithful at the Orthodox liturgy. "Salvation is communion in Christ (*koinonia*) and therefore the obligation of Christians to strive to maintain and develop their ecclesial unity through love is plain: 'For the love of Christ gathers us together' (2 Corinthians 5:14)."[21]

This concern with helping others does not apply only to other Christians, but to the whole world, including non-Christians, again in imitation of Jesus. Helping people sometimes leads to reconciliation between them. In speaking about reconciliation among humans, Stăniloae does not equate it with a "purely formal peace, a mere coexistence and lack of aggression covering over profound disagreements." A lasting reconciliation is a combination of love, equality, and justice among humans and nations. Genuine reconciliation is possible only in light of the reconciliation performed by God who, after having regarded humankind as an enemy because of the sin, reconciled humanity to himself and allowed humans to partake of all good things in Christ.[22]

Christians should not only help other individuals, Stăniloae insisted, but should also be concerned about promoting justice at the national, and even global levels. An elasticity in the social structures—which was not present in the past—makes that type of justice increasingly possible today.[23] This is one of the aspects of globalization, if we are to think only of the International Tribunal at The Hague, which tries to administer justice at an international level. Stăniloae was somewhat of a visionary in this regard, having argued for global justice already in 1972. It is also worth noting that he saw the effort for global justice as "the effect [of] Christ's activity guiding the world towards the Kingdom of Heaven, in spite of the fact that this is a goal which in its final form cannot be reached in this world, given the corruptible nature of matter and all its attendant ills."[24] The lack of justice in the world provides a justification for eternal death, which means eternal separation from God who is justice itself. But "the removal of injustice deprives eternal death of any such justification."[25]

FALLEN HUMAN NATURE AND THE LAW

Like every other Orthodox theologian, Stăniloae addresses the Fall of the first humans, as recorded symbolically in the story of Adam and Eve's eating from the tree of the knowledge of good and evil. Chapter 6 of the second volume of *The Experience of God* is suggestively entitled "The Fall." While the first volume deals with revelation and knowledge of the triune God, the second volume, subtitled *The World: Creation and Deification*, is devoted to the created world. It is important to understand the way in which Stăniloae views the Fall, its consequences for the human nature, and the law's role as a temporary corrective.

Stăniloae begins by noting that human beings did not consolidate their obedience to God or grow in the knowledge of him, because otherwise the Fall would not have occurred at all or at least not so easily. Stăniloae provides the reader with a long quote from Maximus the Confessor, and then complements it with similar quotes from Nicetas Stethatos and Gregory Palamas. The Maximian view defines Stăniloae's understanding of the Fall: "Perhaps the creation of visible things was called the tree of the knowledge of good and evil because it has both spiritual reasons that nourish the mind and a natural power that charms the senses and yet perverts the mind. Therefore, when spiritually contemplated, it offers the knowledge of the good, while when received bodily it offers the knowledge of evil."[26] Maximus's speculative thoughts on the matter are indicated by the word "perhaps," but his explanation captures Stăniloae's attention almost entirely, as we shall see shortly. What Maximus says is that the created world is good, because God made it so. Nevertheless, it depends on how we human beings, endowed with freedom, see and use this good creation. It is like money, a human creation, which in itself is as neutral as other material things, but which can become good when given to charities or bad when used to pay for carnal pleasures or to pay a hit man.

The Fall occurred, according to Maximus and Stăniloae, because humans hurried to taste God's creation through the senses. This move brought evil upon them. Humans, not yet strengthened in the good contemplation of the created world, needed to persist longer in their obedience to God in order for them to be able to see the created world as God sees it and not to have the mind perverted by it.[27] The "primordial state," the condition of the first human parents when they came into existence, was a very short-lived condition. In it, humans were supposed to remain and grow, but Stăniloae, following Basil of Caesarea, cannot help but notice the "rapidity" with which humans decided in favor of disobedience.[28]

It is a pity that Stăniloae, given modern paleontological data available to him, did not ask the question why God left such an important decision for the human race to the first, undeveloped humans, who probably were troglodytes. Later in the same chapter, he seems to hint at this question, without providing an answer: "There can be no denying, however, that knowledge of the rationality of nature through the mediation of human reason represents in its own way a development of the human spirit. Thus, here, too, we have an ambiguity, a simultaneous growth and reduction of our powers symbolized by the tree of the knowledge of good and evil."[29] This is a regrettable feature of many modern Orthodox theologians, who rely on the church fathers but tend not to engage current learning. In embracing the church fathers without bringing some modern insights into play, one always faces the danger of not addressing one's contemporaries.

In refusing to try to exercise their freedom in obedience and growth to know God and the created world as God knows it, the first humans had become slaves to "the easy pleasure afforded by the senses."[30] Basil of Caesarea, whom Stăniloae quotes again, names the cause of the Fall: it is lack of wisdom, thoughtlessness, or even laziness of the will (*aboulia*) on the part of the first humans. "By commanding man not to eat from the tree of consciousness before he was guided by freedom of the spirit, God, in fact, commanded him to be strong, to remain free, and to grow in spirit, that is, in freedom. This commandment made appeal to man's freedom."[31] In connection with the tree of the knowledge of good and evil, Stăniloae uses the words "consciousness" and "freedom." It is worth noting that he identifies the tree itself with the consciousness that Adam was supposed to develop. Let us remember that consciousness is an important part of the person—both divine and human. In fact, Stăniloae defines a person as a center of consciousness, but warns that consciousness in endless self-replacing succession is meaningless if each member of this succession is not carried into eternity, but disappears for good once the body dies.[32]

Stăniloae offered further reflections on human freedom. In not responding to God by loving obedience, he argues, humans thought they were affirming their freedom.

> In fact, it was this act that marked the beginning of the human's selfish confinement within himself. This was how he enslaved himself to himself. Reckoning on becoming his own lord, he became his own slave. The human person is free only if he is free also from himself for the sake of others, in love, and if he is free for God who is the source of freedom because he is the source of

love. But disobedience used as an occasion the commandment not to taste from the tree of the knowledge of good and evil.[33]

Stăniloae does not elaborate on why freedom is not necessarily freedom of choice. But he hints that that type of freedom is present in humans as well. Stăniloae understands freedom as that by which a willing subject always chooses the good. Adam and Eve were created free in the sense of being expected always to choose the good, to choose to obey God, the supreme good. Instead, they opted out of their relationship with God.

The English language does not have two words for these concepts, but uses only "freedom." In Greek, however, where these fine distinctions were first developed, there are two words to explain the difference. The Greek philosopher Plotinus spoke of the will to choose (*prohairesis*) and the will to be what one wishes to be (*boulesis*). The Greek church father Gregory of Nyssa picked up this distinction and applied it to the Christian God. Gregory presented God as one who always chooses the good and wishes to be what he is because he is the supreme good. In speaking of Christ as the son of God, Gregory says that, unlike humans, he does not change from an inferior to a superior state. Nor does he need another son to bestow adoption upon him. Accordingly, Gregory maintains that the only-begotten is properly called the son of God because he is the son of God by nature.[34] The distinction between "by nature" and "by choice" is very important in Gregory's view, and he emphasizes it several times. Yet the case of the son of God is very different from the case of human sons:

> God, being one good, in a simple and uncompounded nature, looks ever the same way, and is never changed by the impulses of choice (*prohairesis*), but always wishes (*bouletai*) what he is, and is, assuredly, what he wishes (*bouletai*). So that he is in both respects properly and truly called Son of God, since his nature contains the good, and his choice (*prohairesis*) also is never severed from that which is more excellent, so that this word [son] is employed without inexactness, as his name.[35]

These are powerful statements, informed by Plotinianism. They are powerful because in the divine case, sonship-by-nature and sonship-by-will converge in the same direction of the good. There is no contradiction between the goodness of the divine nature and the good (or, rather, the supremely good) choice the son of God makes. They are Plotinian because Plotinus, in referring to the One God about a hundred years before Gregory, made an almost identical statement: the One God is "all power, really master of itself, being what it wills to be."[36] The son is thus a "willing" subject. However, his will appears as both the will to choose (*prohairesis*), which is always directed toward choosing the good, and the will to be what he wishes to be (*boulesis*), which is an ontological will.

It is the latter type of will that Stăniloae has in mind when dealing with the human Fall, especially since he mentioned Basil's *aboulia* as the main cause of the fall. It is this immature *boulesis* in Adam and Eve that leads them to the Fall by making them reject what they should have been.

Misused freedom is the cause of the Fall of Adam and Eve, Stăniloae insists. In believing that they exercised their freedom, the first humans fell into slavery to sin. This is how the patristic tradition tended to view the Fall. Shortly after that, God expelled Adam and Eve from paradise in order to prevent them from having access to the tree of life, and to live eternally in this fallen condition. Again appealing to the church fathers, Stăniloae says that the two trees are in fact the same tree, the visible world already mentioned. "Viewed through a mind moved by spirit, that world is the tree of life that puts us in relationship with God; but viewed and made use of through a consciousness that has been detached from the mind moved by spirit, it represents the tree of the knowledge of good and evil which severs man from God."[37]

According to Genesis, Adam and Eve did not sin on their own, untempted initiative. The serpent was present, tempting Eve. Christian theology has seen the serpent as the symbol of evil or the devil, Satan himself. Stăniloae notices at this point that evil in itself, in its nakedness, is unattractive to many people. Therefore, it has to "deck itself in the colors of some good by which it lures those who are deceived into desiring it."[38] Evil was thus fascinating to both Eve and Adam, who eventually became captivated by it. Yet, they were still afraid of the consequences their trespass of the divine commandment could have. According to Stăniloae, that is where the devil intervened, trying to calm the human soul by telling Eve the consequences were not too dramatic, but that God wanted to deceive the first humans out of envy.[39]

After the Fall, such consequences have become apparent in all manner of ways. These included a person's estrangement from God, a proclivity to passionate impulse as a result of mixing sensuality and the sensible aspect of the world, a more complex understanding of the sad knowledge of good and evil, pride, reduced knowledge of God's creation, domination, satisfaction of bodily needs and pleasures, now become passions, corruption, and eventually death.[40] Stăniloae notes: "Neither corruptibility nor death ... are punishments from God; they are instead consequences of our alienation from the source of life."[41] He reminds the reader that, according to the Orthodox understanding, although the consequences of sin have been very serious, they have not made human knowledge totally and fatally opaque, conforming it to a similarly opaque world. "Humans can penetrate this opacity in part by means of another kind of knowledge, and indeed, they often manage to do this, but they cannot wholly overcome this opacity and the knowledge that conforms to it."[42] The withdrawal of the divine Spirit from the world immediately after the Fall weakened the character the world had as a transparent medium between God and humans and among humans themselves.

"Even in the state of sin," Stăniloae tells us, "it is providence that preserves and directs the world."[43] However, God does not work alone in this endeavor and certainly does not work against the human will. God collaborates with the human will in what the Orthodox tradition calls "synergy."[44] "Synergy" is a sinner's movement toward higher goals and perfection, a movement implying newness for the sinner.

Stăniloae includes reflections on law in elaborating his doctrine of "synergy." He picks up and develops the theme of newness from the book of Revelation: "Behold, I make all things new" (21:5). He complements this with quotes from St. Paul (Eph. 4:24; 2 Cor. 5:17; Gal. 6:15). What catches Stăniloae's attention is that St. Paul opposed the "newness of spirit" to the oldness of the letter or the law as he opposed the life of the resurrection to abiding in death. In Stăniloae's view, the law is identified with the law of the Old Covenant and represents a sign that sin still reigns.[45] Again, this is in line with St. Paul who wrote to the Corinthians: "The sting of death is sin, and the power of sin is the law" (1 Cor. 15:56). The end of the law is Christ. Stăniloae argues that, when people do not draw that conclusion, per Romans 10:4, 13:10, "then the law is the power of sin that leads to death."

Stăniloae does not have nice words to say about the law, and for some reason, he seems to condemn together Old Testament law and the laws of modern states. He opposes law to love, as if they are two opposites and cannot stand side by side. For reasons I confess not to understand, Stăniloae writes that "the law is repetition, according to an external norm, within the monotonously confined horizon of egoism and death."[46] Love is indeed the fulfilling of the law (Rom. 10:4; 13:10). The "newness of life," which is the love Stăniloae opposes to the law, is inspired by Gregory of Nyssa's theory according to which in the afterlife the souls of the blessed will not be static in the contemplation of God, but will advance infinitely from one stage of beatitude toward the next. Gregory of Nyssa calls each of these stages *epektasis*.[47] Stăniloae, however, does not elaborate Gregory's views. It is not clear how, in his view, human society could survive without the law. Not everybody shows or reaches that dimension of love that Stăniloae champions.

Stăniloae's negative view of the law was not simply a reaction to living under Communism and atheistic laws when he wrote his *Dogmatics*. A similar view of the law comes through years later in *Seven Mornings with Father Stăniloae*, a book of interviews by Sorin Dumitrescu, a famous Romanian religious painter and intellectual. Dumitrescu asked Stăniloae to explain why in the West human relations were better regulated and more disciplined than in the East, where during Communist times there were practices such as excessive gossiping and informing on one's neighbor to the secret police.[48] Stăniloae answered that the supposedly better regulation of human relations in the West has brought something of a distance and a chill among people. Moreover, the laws that "somehow sustain the correctness" in human relations in the West are secular laws. In Romania, by contrast, the import of the same secular laws since the nineteenth century has led to a bizarre mix of hospitality and the various cultural excesses that Dumitrescu listed. Stăniloae betrays ample anti-Westernism and anti-legalism in this and other interviews. He begins one interview by saying:

> Without Christ everything is monotonous, legalistic, everything unfolds in a forced way. We do not get rid of these miseries by moving toward powerless old age, sickness and final death.... Through sin, the world fell into monotony, in the prison of invariable laws and causal determinism. Through the Incarnation, God himself has brought the world back to what he intended it to be when he created it. It was brought back to the advance in the infinity of the divine goodness.[49]

Again, Stăniloae presents law as monotonous and completely negative in contrast with the love, freedom, and newness brought about by Christ and the Spirit.

COMMUNISM, THE CHURCH, AND COLLABORATION

One issue that has dominated the political scene of postcommunist Eastern Europe and the former Soviet Union is that of "transitional justice." Since 1989 most countries of the former Communist bloc have passed laws regulating access to the files of the former secret police and banning former Communists and secret police officers from participating in postcommunist politics. These laws, however, have passed more easily in some countries than others. Romania was among the last countries to adopt such laws, and only after many years of bickering and with enormous opposition that continues to this day.[50] Some Orthodox Church leaders and priests have vehemently opposed the opening of the secret police archives, no doubt fearing that they contain incriminating evidence about their collaboration with the dreaded political police, the Securitate.

Stăniloae offered his reflections on this issue and on the role of the Orthodox Church in reconciling postcommunist Romanian society in a series of interviews by Sorin Dumitrescu in March and April 1992. This was at a time when the debate about collaboration was still in its early stages in

Romania. While the eighty-nine-year-old Stăniloae proved to be remarkably vivid, the interview showed that after forty-five years of Communist repression, Stăniloae was unable to distinguish Christian love from Christian justice and to realize the necessity not only of the former but also of the latter.

Dumitrescu invited Stăniloae to reflect on the church's role in the new democracy, particularly in the society's search for the truth. Dumitrescu started by asking whether the church, as a moral institution, should not try to distinguish between the executioners, who collaborated with the Communist regime and benefited from the collaboration, and the victims, who were discriminated against, lost their jobs, were imprisoned, tortured, and even killed in Communist prisons because of their opposition to the regime.[51] Instead of distinguishing between executioners and victims, thus helping to restore decent, if not cordial, relations in society, the church remained silent and allowed executioners and victims to live side by side in postcommunist Romania. Dumitrescu asked Stăniloae whether the time had not come for a moral, respectable institution such as the Romanian Orthodox Church to help to sort things out and to separate light from darkness.

Stăniloae answered, on the strength of his theology of personhood and communion, that it is the church's mission to preach Christ, not to assign guilt especially in the public sphere. Clerics must not separate themselves from bad people, but try to persuade them to change their lives "by personal example, help and words of consolation." Party politics is not for priests, bishops, and monks, Stăniloae argued, though he recognized that they not always lived up to these expectations because they themselves are humans and can err.[52]

Dumitrescu then asked whether the Christian theme of forgiveness of sins was not being used by postcommunist Romanian politicians (some of whom publicly declared themselves to be atheists) to cover up their own guilt and the guilt of the executioners.[53] He drew a parallel between Hitler's officers and soldiers, who claimed exoneration because they were merely following orders, and Communist-era executioners who were now claiming exoneration because they deserved Christian forgiveness. Is this not a pretextual, and indeed sinful, use of Christian forgiveness, Dumitrescu pressed Stăniloae.

Stăniloae again insisted that the church cannot publicly condemn anybody, because the church uses other methods to deal with malefactors. One such method is the Orthodox practice of individual confession of the penitent to a confessor, who can be either a priest or a bishop. Like its Roman Catholic counterpart, the Orthodox sacrament of confession may not be used to extract information that could incriminate someone publicly.

The confessor father is under a vow of secrecy not to divulge the secret of the confession even in very grave cases. The confessor can assign penance to the believer who confesses his or her sins, including the harsh punishment of banning a confessed sinner from communion.[54]

This answer, however, assumes that a sinner is also a believer and genuinely comes to confess his or her sins. But what is Romania to do with those executioners who are not believers, who are not even Christians and cannot receive the sacrament of penance and reconciliation? What should be done with the large group of people who want some justice done in order for them and the society to be reconciled? And what should be done with the priests who disregarded the secrecy of confession and passed information on to the Securitate? Stăniloae did not say.

Instead, Stăniloae held up the gospel story of the adulterous woman who was brought to Jesus by her accusers who wanted to stone her. All of her accusers dropped their stones and left when Jesus said, "He who is without sin cast the first stone" (John 8:7). Using this story, Stăniloae insisted that all of us are guilty and deserving of punishment. Moreover, as a confessor father himself, he could not betray the vow of secrecy and divulge information, for that would invite harsh punishment on the accused.[55]

Dumitrescu challenged Stăniloae, however, to look beyond the sacrament of penance: "Excuse me, but what you say refers to the personal relationship of the penitent and the confessing father.... Do you not think the Church, without naming names, should take a public stand and say that its teachings are misused? Because, you see, the Church does not want to homogenize guilt by [indiscriminate] forgiveness; the Church can be intransigent if it wants to."[56] Stăniloae simply could not make this leap from individual forgiveness to the forgiveness required at a larger level, that of the society. He did not seem to understand why another type of forgiveness might be necessary.

Part of Stăniloae's reluctance to address such issues of social justice and reconciliation might well have been a function of his environment. These themes were simply not an issue that the church faced in Communist times. A greater part of his reluctance might well have been Stăniloae's long-time preoccupation with the *Philokalia*, which mainly addressed monastic and ascetic themes and readers. Its focus was on Christian ascetic withdrawal, on the individual's path to spiritual perfection, rather than on what is good and just for the society. This attitude is present in some of his other works as well.

It is evident from his questions that Dumitrescu wanted Stăniloae to say that the church's teachings are being manipulated by the postcommunist Romanian political actors in order for them to save face and to be excused for their collaboration with the Communist regime.[57] He expected him to say that the church must not dispense indiscriminate forgiveness by declaring that either nobody is guilty or everybody is guilty. Instead, it should point to degrees of guilt and start the civic healing process from there. But Stăniloae said none of this. Only after much prodding did he acknowledge grudgingly that the Romanian Orthodox Church itself shares some degree of culpability, and that this prevents it from proclaiming more loudly that justice is needed in Romania today. In his words, "What can we do? There is a long road from teaching to practice. Nobody is perfect in this world. Nor are the churchmen. We plead for the good, we seek to win the others to our cause, but few of us are perfect supporters of the Christian teachings in their own lives."[58]

Stăniloae, however, did not acknowledge that the sacrament of penance and reconciliation is about both love and justice. Dumitrescu reminded him that Jesus forgave, but he also entered the temple with a whip, chasing out the moneychangers who had desecrated his father's house. Stăniloae mentioned in passing that the church does "whip" the society at times, but he did not elaborate. As for whether it should support various political actors, policies, and ideologies, Stăniloae insisted that the church as a whole is apolitical these days, and those clerics who give opportunistic support to different political parties do not represent the church in all their actions.[59]

Stăniloae's views on this vexed subject have proved rather typical among current Romanian Orthodox leaders. The end of Communism ushered in a new era for the Orthodox Church and a chance for it to redefine the new Romanian democracy.[60] After 1989, however, the Orthodox Church and its head, Patriarch Teoctist Arapasu, were strongly criticized for supporting the Communist regime to its very end. The Church Synod responded on January 10, 1990, apologizing for those "who did not always have the courage of the martyrs," and expressed regret that it had been "necessary to pay the tribute of obligatory and artificial praises addressed to the dictator" to ensure certain liberties.[61] The synod also annulled all the ecclesiastical sanctions previously imposed on some clergymen for political reasons. Faced with increasing criticism, Patriarch Teoctist resigned his office on January 18, 1990, only to return three months later at the insistence of the synod. Some 136 religious and cultural leaders protested his reappointment, but the synod opted for continuity in face of political change and acknowledged the views of the other Orthodox churches that recognized Teoctist as patriarch.

Since 1989, the Orthodox Church as an institution has avoided any moral self-examination and has never openly admitted to its collaboration with the Communist authorities or the Securitate. Romanian Metropolitan

Nicolae Corneanu was among the very few Orthodox clergy to acknowledge his efforts on behalf of the Communist authorities to infiltrate Romanian communities in Western Europe and North America, and to defrock five priests who denounced "the Church's prostitution with the communist power, and its hierarchy's involvement with Ceausescu's politics."[62] In 1997, Corneanu revealed the extent of the church's collaboration, and he named Metropolitan Plamadeala among the most active promoters of Ceausescu's antireligious and anti-Orthodox policies.[63]

For many Orthodox Romanians, however, Patriarch Teoctist's short retreat to a monastery and the synod's partial apology for collaboration with the Communists was contrition enough. With a few notable exceptions, every Romanian was open to criticism regarding her or his compliance with the Communist regime. Because of this, most Romanians have been willing to overlook the Orthodox Church's past political compromises.[64] Stăniloae's instruction and example on this vexed subject are now regrettably commonplace.

ORTHODOXY AND NATIONALISM

In chapter 21 of this volume, Mikhail Kulakov demonstrates that Vladimir Lossky regarded nationalism as a disease and paid the price for his view by being marginalized by the Russian Orthodox diaspora community. By rejecting nationalism, Lossky was rather an exceptional figure in the Orthodox world. Many theologians both in Orthodox countries and in the diaspora have fallen prey to the disease of nationalism. They have also fallen prey to what the 1872 Synod of Constantinople called the heresy of phyletism, the view that makes race or culture the cornerstone of church unity.

Many Orthodox theologians, including Stăniloae, have tried to justify their nationalism theologically. They usually refer to Apostolic Canon 34, which reads:

> The bishops of every nation (*ethnos*) must acknowledge him who is first among them and account him as their head, and do nothing of consequence without his consent; but each may do those things only which concern his own parish, and the country places which belong to it. But neither let him (who is the first) do anything without the consent of all; for so there will be unanimity, and God will be glorified through the Lord in the Holy Spirit.[65]

The Greek word *ethnos* is the key to understanding this stipulation. Canon 34 was issued in the fourth century. It is thus closer to the New Testament time than to ours. The biblical meaning of *ethnos* is reflected in the passage where Jesus tells his apostles to "go and make disciples of all the nations (*ethnos*)" (Matt. 28:19; Mark 16:15–16). There *ethnos* referred to Gentiles (Hebrew, *goyim*), that is, Christians of non-Jewish descent living together regardless of their ethnic origins.[66] This understanding of *ethnos* meshes well with the modern definition of a nation-state, a community, usually ethnically diverse, that is bound together by allegiance to a set of common institutions and practices, including religious practices.

Most Romanian Orthodox today, however, define *ethnos* as an ethnic group defined by a common language, history, race, and religion. Romanian canon lawyer Ioan Floca, for example, believes that in Canon 34, *ethnos* can only mean an ethnic group (*neam*) and cannot refer to all inhabitants of a "province" or "land."[67] For Stăniloae, too, an *ethnos* or nation is built along ethnic not civic lines, and nationalism and patriotism are interchangeable. "Nationalism is the consciousness of belonging to a certain ethnic group, the love for that group and the enacting of that love for the well-being of the group."[68]

To the above understanding of "nation" (*natiune* or *popor* in Romanian), one should add the meaning of *neam*. *Neam* represents a people centered on an ethnic group (Romanians, in this case) with alleged stability and long-established historical roots, like the Romanian people in the view of the Orthodox Church. In one of his early writings, Stăniloae contends:

> The Romanian nation (*neam*) is a biological-spiritual synthesis of a number of elements. The most important of them are the Dacian element, the Latin element, and the Christian Orthodox element.... The synthesis is new, it has its own individuality, and a principle of unity which differs from the partial components. The highest law of our nation (*neam*), the law which expresses what the nation is in the most appropriate way, is the one that the whole experiences, not the ones experienced by the parts. The parts are stamped with a new, unifying, and individualizing stamp which is Romanianhood (*românitatea*). Therefore, we can say that the highest law for our nation (*neam*) is Romanianhood. Not Romanity, not Dacianism, but Romanianhood with all it includes is the highest law by which we live and fulfill our mission.... Which is the Romanian way of communion with the transcendental spiritual order? History and the current life of our people tell us that it is Orthodoxy. Orthodoxy is the eye through which Romanians gaze at heavens and then, enlightened by the heavenly light, they turn their eye toward the world while continuing to attune their behavior to it. We also know that this is the only eye that is correct and healthy.... Certainly, in theory it is hard to understand how it is possible for Orthodoxy to interpenetrate with Romanianism without either of them to have to suffer. Yet, the bi-millennial life of our nation (*neam*) shows that in practice this is fully possible.... Orthodoxy is an essential and

vital function of Romanianism. The permanent national ideal of our nation can only be conceived in relation with Orthodoxy.[69]

Stăniloae grounded his ethnic nationalism in the Augustinian theory of *rationes aeternae*, and developed something very similar to what modern anthropologists call an "imagined community."[70] According to St. Augustine, eternal reasons (*rationes aeternae*) are the divine archetypes or patterns of all created species and individuals; they are much like Plato's ideas or forms, placed in the mind of God.[71] For Stăniloae, ethnic nations are something God desired and even planned. Since God's creation is good and since God created nations, nations are good and so is nationalism.

In approaching the topic this way, there are signs that Stăniloae was reacting to the modern critique of nationalism. He certainly wanted to ask the deeper, still unanswered question "why are there multiple languages and plural ethnic groups?" And he certainly wanted to bring God into play in creating them as something good. Yet in the 1930s and 1940s when he reflected on the topic, Stăniloae did not have the conceptual instruments necessary to explain the existence of a diversity of languages and of ethnic groups. He writes:

> Concerning man in particular, God created Adam and Eve in the beginning. In them were virtually present all nations. These are revelations in time of the images which have existed eternally in God. Every nation has an eternal divine archetype that it has to bring about more fully.... There is one instance when nations may not be from God and we would have to fight against them: when human diversification into nations would be a consequence of sin and a deviation from the way in which God wanted to develop humanity. In that case, the duty of every Christian would be to get humanity out of that sinful state and to fuse all nations into one.
>
> Is diversification of humanity a sin or a consequence of sin? We could reject that presupposition by the mere universal law of fauna and flora.... But the answer can be given differently also: sin or evil is of a different order than unity or diversity. Sin means a deformity, a disfiguration of a given thing.... Is national specificity a deformity of humanity, a decay of the human being? This would be the case when national specificity would be something vicious, petty, and without heights of purity and thought.... The removal of humanity from the sinful state is being done not through the annulment of the national features, but by the straightening of human nature in general. If there were something sinful in national specificity, then one could not distinguish between good and evil people within a nation, but all would be evil.... We should note that there is no a-national person. Adam

himself was not a-national, but he spoke a language, had a certain mentality, a certain psychic and bodily structure. A pure human, uncolored nationally, without national determinants, is an abstraction.[72]

All of these opinions have to be viewed in their proper context, that of post–World War I Romania, when there was a wide debate about the true meaning of Romanianism.

CONCLUSION

As other contributors to the Orthodox section of this volume have noted, Orthodox theologians tend to talk a lot about human nature, but much less about law, politics, and society. Stăniloae was no exception. Compared to Lossky, Berdyaev, and Soloviev, he said even less explicitly and directly about law. Nevertheless, several important points about law, politics, and human nature are reflected in his works. He saw law as a necessary result of the Fall into sin of the first humans, Adam and Eve. For him, the law given to Moses on Mount Sinai expresses the concentrated form of the will of God. It is God's supernatural revelation, but it is meant only as a transitory step toward something higher that comes through Christ. In line with Apostle Paul and the book of Revelation, Stăniloae opposed the "newness of the spirit" to the "oldness of the law" and contended instead that as long as there is law there is sin and that the law was given to remove humanity's sinful state. But eventually love has to take the place of the law.

Sinfulness is connected with freedom. Misused freedom is the cause of the fall from grace of Adam and Eve, according to Stăniloae. In believing that they exercised their freedom, the first humans fell into slavery to sin. This is how the patristic tradition tended to view the Fall. Shortly after that, God expelled Adam and Eve from paradise in order to prevent them from having access to the tree of life, and to live eternally in this fallen condition. Stăniloae understood freedom as that by which a willing subject always chooses the good. Adam and Eve were created free in the sense of being expected always to choose the good, to choose to obey God, the supreme good. Instead, they opted out of their relationship with God.

According to Stăniloae, the church's role in postcommunist societies is to preach Christ, not to assign guilt, especially in the public sphere. The church cannot publicly condemn anybody, because the church uses other methods to deal with malefactors. The most important such method is the sacrament of confession. This traditional role of the church, however, poses some problems in postcommunist times, as it assumes that most members of society are (Orthodox) Christian and that they will come forward to confess their sins and receive forgiveness. In short, it assumes some sort of a Christian state. But this is hardly the case, and the issue of civic justice and reconciliation in Romania remains unsolved. In this regard, it would have been helpful for Stăniloae to reflect more fully than he did on the relationship between church law and secular law.

In Romania, Stăniloae's work has been very influential, although he himself recognizes that there are yet to appear local theologians able to emulate him. Older Orthodox theology professors, such as Ion Bria, Dumitru Popescu, and Dumitru Radu, did their doctoral studies with Stăniloae, and their own ecclesiologies were influenced by his ecclesiology. Younger theologians, including Evangelical Protestants connected with the Emmanuel Bible Institute in Oradea, have written doctoral dissertations on various aspects of Stăniloae's theology under the guidance of both Orthodox and non-Orthodox professors in the United Kingdom. They seem to have taken a particular interest in Stăniloae's theology, and their writings meet Western standards of scholarship.

Outside of Romania, Stăniloae's theology has attracted attention in all the main branches of Christianity. Some Roman Catholics (such Ronald Roberson and Maciej Bielawski) have written doctoral dissertations on his theology, while others (such as Robert Barringer) studied with him and learned Romanian in order to translate some of his works into English. Various Anglican theologians have written books (Charles Miller) or articles (A. M. Allchin) on Stăniloae, while the Lutheran Romanian theologian Hermann Pitters translated his *Dogmatics* into German. In the French-speaking world, Stăniloae has exerted considerable influence on Orthodox theologians such as Olivier Clement and Marc-Antoine Costa de Beauregard, while attracting the admiration of Russian and Greek Orthodox. The potential for Stăniloae's further influence continues to grow given that his works are increasingly available to Western readerships and that Romanians are currently taking a keen interest in his thought.

In Romania, no one was allowed to engage in any type of political activity other than in support of the Communist Party between 1947 and 1989. That period covered almost half of Stăniloae's life. He refused to engage in Communist politics, and indeed he had to suffer five years of political imprisonment for his political convictions that bordered in some cases on the extreme right. Stăniloae published his views on Romanian nationalism in both pre–World War II and postcommunist writings. But he did not develop much original political thought, and he appeared incapable of dealing with some of the hard political issues facing postcommunist Romania. These included issues of how Orthodox clergy and laity were to deal with prior collaborators with the Communist secret police, the Securitate, and how to heal Romanian society following the collapse of Communism in Eastern Europe and the Soviet Union.

NOTES

1. John Meyendorff, foreword to Dumitru Stăniloae, *Theology and the Church*, trans. Robert Barringer (Crestwood, N.Y.: St. Vladimir's Seminary Press, 1980), 8.

2. For a fine presentation, see Maciej Bielawski, "Dumitru Stăniloae and his Philokalia," in *Dumitru Stăniloae: Tradition and Modernity in Theology*, ed. Lucian Turcescu (Iasi, Romania: Center for Romanian Studies, 2002), 25–52; Maciej Bielawski, *The Philocalical Vision of the World in the Theology of Dumitru Stăniloae* (Bydgoszcz, Poland: Homini, 1997).

3. Zigu Ornea, *Anii treizeci: Extrema dreaptă românească* (The 1930s: The Romanian Extreme Right Wing) (Bucharest: Editura Fundatiei Culturale Romane, 1995), 113–115.

4. See Mircea Pacurariu, "Preotul Profesor si Academician Dumitru Stăniloae," in *Persoană și comuniune: Prinos de cinstire Preotului Profesor Academician Dumitru Stăniloae la împlinirea vârstei de 90 ani* (Person and Communion: Festschrift for Stăniloae on his Ninetieth Birthday), ed. Mircea Pacurariu and Ioan I. Ica Jr. (Sibiu, Romania: Editura Arhiepiscopiei ortodoxe Sibiu, 1993), 6.

5. Pacurariu, "Preotul Profesor Stăniloae," 7.

6. Gheorghe F. Anghelescu, "Bibliografie sistematica a Parintelui Prof. Acad. Dumitru Stăniloae," in Pacurariu and Ica, *Persoană și comuniune*, 2:4.

7. Dumitru Stăniloae, "Ofranda adusa lui Dumnezeu de poporul roman," *Gazeta de Vest* 18 (February 1993): 18. See also Olivier Gillet, *Religion et nationalisme: L'ideologie de l'église orthodoxe roumaine sous le regime communiste* (Brussels: Editions de l'Université de Bruxelles, 1997), 136–139.

8. For contemporary Iron Guard doctrines, see http://www.miscarea-legionara. org and http://www.miscarea.com and affiliates.

9. Lidia Stăniloae, "Remembering My Father," trans. R. Roberson, in Turcescu, *Dumitru Stăniloae*, 21.

10. See Andrew Louth, "Review Essay: *The Orthodox Dogmatic Theology* of Dumitru Stăniloae," *Modern Theology* 13, no. 2 (April 1997): 253–267; reprinted in Turcescu, *Dumitru Stăniloae*, 53–70.

11. Bishop Kallistos [Ware] of Diokleia, foreword to Dumitru Stăniloae, *The Experience of God*, trans. Ioan Ioniță and Robert Barringer, 2 vols. (Brookline, Mass.: Holy Cross Orthodox Press, 1994), 1:xiii.

12. Stăniloae, *The Experience of God*, 1:1.

13. See Lucian Turcescu, "Soteriological Issues in the 1999 Lutheran-Catholic Joint Declaration on Justification: An Orthodox Perspective," *Journal of Ecumenical Studies* 28, no. 1 (Winter 2001): 64–72.

14. Joseph A. Fitzmyer, "Pauline Theology," in *The New Jerome Biblical Commentary*, ed. Raymond E. Brown et al. (London: G. Chapman, 1990), 1397.

15. Stăniloae, *The Experience of God*, 1:2.

16. The church fathers did not have the modern Cartesian-Lockean concept of the person understood as a center of consciousness. Lucian Turcescu, *Gregory of Nyssa and the Concept of Divine Persons* (New York: Oxford University Press,

2005); Sarah Coakley, ed., *Rethinking Gregory of Nyssa* (Oxford: Blackwell, 2003).

17. Stăniloae, *The Experience of God*, 1:16.

18. Maximus the Confessor, *The Ambigua*, in *Patrologia Graeca* 91.1149C–1152B, 1176BC, paraphrased by Stăniloae in *The Experience of God*, 1:16–17.

19. This high-brow theology has caused some to label Stăniloae as elitist. Emil Bartos, "The Dynamics of Deification in the Theology of Dumitru Stăniloae," in Turcescu, *Dumitru Stăniloae*, 246.

20. Dumitru Stăniloae, *Theology and the Church*, trans. Robert Barringer (Crestwood, N.Y.: St. Vladimir's Seminary Press, 1980), 204.

21. Ibid.

22. Ibid., 210.

23. Ibid.

24. Ibid., 211.

25. Ibid.

26. Maximus the Confessor, *To Thalassius: On Various Questions*, in *Patrologia Graeca* 90.257C–260A; Stăniloae, *The Experience of God*, 2:163.

27. Ibid., 163–164.

28. Ibid., 164–165.

29. Ibid., 175.

30. Ibid., 166.

31. Ibid.

32. Ibid., 1:6.

33. Ibid., 2:166.

34. Gregory of Nyssa, *Contra Eunomium* III, 1, 123ff.; *Select Writings and Letters of Gregory, Bishop of Nyssa, Nicene and Post-Nicene Fathers*, 2d ser. (New York: Christian Literature Co., 1893), 5:149. *Contra Eunomium Libri* in *Gregorii Nysseni Opera*, vols. 1–2, ed. Werner Jaeger (Leiden: Brill, 1960). An English translation of the whole work predating Jaeger's critical edition can be found in *Select Writings*, 5:33–315.

35. Gregory of Nyssa, *Contra Eunomium* III, 1, 125.

36. Plotinus, *Enneads* VI.8.9.45–46, in *Enneads*, 7 vols., trans. A. H. Armstrong. (Cambridge, Mass.: Harvard University Press, 1966–1988). For Gregory's knowledge of Plotinus, see Turcescu, *Gregory of Nyssa*.

37. Stăniloae, *The Experience of God*, 2:166–167.

38. Ibid., 166.

39. Ibid., 168–169.

40. Ibid., 170–172.

41. Ibid., 187.

42. Ibid., 172.

43. Ibid., 191.

44. This is the topic of the last chapter of Stăniloae's second volume of *Experience of God*, entitled "Providence and the Deification of the World."

45. Stăniloae, *The Experience of God*, 2:194–195.

46. Ibid., 195.

47. Gregory of Nyssa, *Homilies on the Song of Songs* 6, in *Patrologia Graeca* 44.999A; see Stăniloae, *The Experience of God*, 2:195 nn. 173 and 175.

48. Sorin Dumitrescu, *Şapte dimineţi cu Parintele Stăniloae* (Seven Mornings with Father Stăniloae) (Bucharest: Anastasia, 1992), 97. English translations for the present volume are mine.

49. Ibid., 165–166.

50. See Lavinia Stan, "Moral Cleansing Romanian Style," *Problems of Post-Communism* 49, no. 4 (July–August 2002): 52–62; Stan, "Access to Securitate Files: The Trials and Tribulations of a Romanian Law," *Eastern European Politics and Society* 16, no. 1 (2002): 55–90.

51. Dumitrescu, *Şapte dimineţi*, 53–54.

52. Ibid., 54.

53. Ibid., 55.

54. Ibid., 55.

55. Ibid., 56.

56. Ibid., 57.

57. Following the December 1989 Romanian revolution, political power was transferred from dictator Nicolae Ceausescu and his tight circle of friends and relatives to a group of second-echelon officials led by the new President Ion Iliescu, a one-time close collaborator of the dictator, and Premier Petre Roman, the son of a high-ranking Communist official.

58. Dumitrescu, *Şapte dimineţi*, 58.

59. Ibid., 60.

60. See Lavinia Stan and Lucian Turcescu, "The Romanian Orthodox Church and Post-Communist Democratization," *Europe-Asia Studie*s 52, no. 8 (December 2000): 1467–1488.

61. Rompress (January 12, 1990), http://www.rompres.ro.

62. *Romania libera* (March 10, 1997), http://www.romanialibera.com, citing a 1981 letter sent to Patriarch Justin Moisescu.

63. In 1986 Plamadeala defended Ceausescu's massive church demolition program by contending that "city urbanization and modernization is a general and inevitable phenomenon [which] unfortunately requires, as everywhere, sacrifices." See Alexander Webster, *The Price of Prophecy: Orthodox Churches on Peace, Freedom, and Security*, 2d ed. (Washington, D.C.: Ethics and Public Policy Center, 1995), 114.

64. Stan and Turcescu, "The Romanian Church and Democratisation," 1471.

65. *The Seven Ecumenical Councils of the Undivided Church: Their Canons and Dogmatic Decrees*, ed. and trans. Henry Percival, *Nicene and Post-Nicene Fathers*, 2d ser. (New York: Scribner's, 1900), 14:596.

66. Gillet, *Religion et nationalisme*, 93. See also Maximus of Sardis, *Le patriarcat oecumenique dans l'église orthodoxe: Etude historique et canonique* (Paris: n.p. 1975), 377–387.

67. Ioan N. Floca, *Canoanele Bisericii Ortodoxe, Note si Comentarii* (The Canons of the Orthodox Church with Notes and Commentaries) (Sibiu, Romania: Polsib, 1992), 27.

68. "Nationalismul sub aspect moral" (The moral aspect of nationalism), trans. Lucian Turcescu, *Telegraful Român*, 85, no. 47 (1937): 1.

69. Dumitru Stăniloae, "Idealul national permanent" (The permanent national ideal), trans. Lucian Turcescu, *Telegraful Român* 88, no. 4 (1940): 1–2, and 88, no. 5 (1940): 1.

70. Benedict R. Anderson, *Imagined Communities: Reflections on the Origin and Spread of Nationalism*, 2d ed. (London: Verso, 1991).

71. Augustine, *Eighty-three Different Questions*, q. 46, 1–2, in *The Essential Augustine*, ed. Vernon J. Bourke (Indianapolis: Hackett, 1974), 62–63.

72. Dumitru Stăniloae, "Scurta interpretare teologica a natiunii" (A Brief Theological Interpretation of the Nation), *Telegraful Român* 82 (1934): 15.

{ PART IV }

Afterwords

[CHAPTER 24]

Reflections on Christian Jurisprudence and Political Philosophy

KENT GREENAWALT

THIS VOLUME ON how modern Christian writers have understood law, society, politics, and human nature is rich in substance and diversity. If one wonders what the Christian point of view toward government and law is, these accounts quickly dispel any notions of a single Christian perspective. Indeed, one could easily become bewildered by the disparities in what these thinkers address and in the answers they give to the questions they do address. For me, the most helpful way to approach these interpretive chapters is to identify central questions in political philosophy and the philosophy of law and to ask what standpoints our major contemporary figures take on them, recognizing that a subject to which one author devotes great attention may be barely mentioned by another. Once we can see clearly where our writers differ, we may be better able to decide where we stand ourselves.

What count as the central questions in distinctly Christian philosophizing about government and law overlap substantially with the questions posed in the now dominant tradition of secular philosophy and jurisprudence, but the variations matter. Christian theorists tend to reject certain popular secular approaches—social contract theory is a notable example. They regard as crucial questions about God and Jesus that secular theorists dismiss or put aside. And they implicitly treat as relatively trivial some conceptual puzzles over which secular theorists struggle.

As my remarks should already have made clear, the divide here is between theorists who write from distinctly Christian perspectives and those who do not. Among the ranks of secular theorists are many scholars who consider themselves Christians but who see value in trying to approach theoretical problems about politics and law in a way that does not depend on Christian or other religious premises. (I count much of my own work as falling into this category.) Some of the writers discussed in this volume raise profound doubts about the usefulness of such endeavors. Readers who identify themselves as Christians, or as religiously committed members of other faiths, may ask themselves whether secular political philosophy and jurisprudence have value in a diverse society; and readers of all perspectives may assess the contribution of Christian writers to a secular understanding of politics and law.

CENTRAL QUESTIONS

Some of the central questions posed by Christian theorists are these:

1. What implications do the existence of God (understood in a Christian way) and the historical life of Jesus have for our understanding of political organization and law?

2. Does a sound understanding of human beings and their political and legal life depend on these Christian understandings?

3. How do people discern Christian understandings, and, in particular, what is the role of reason in comparison with faith, and the place of individual seeking in relation to the organized church or Christian community?

4. How should we understand God's guidance for our lives—as a form of law or command or as something else?

5. Do political authority and ordinary law come from God, or are they simply contrivances of human beings?

6. Are government and law mainly responses to human sin, or should we understand them as responsive to positive social aspects of human beings and as contributing to human fulfillment in ways that do not concern our sinful nature?

7. Is the law's job to establish minimum requisites for temporal life, or should government and law make a more substantial contribution to moral and spiritual growth?

8. What degree of common understanding and cooperation on practical measures can we expect between Christians and other members of diverse societies?

9. How should the church see itself in relation to the state?

10. Do all citizens have a duty to obey human laws, by the virtue of their being laws?

11. What are the conditions for justified disobedience of human laws and the restraints any such disobedience may carry: in particular, must the law be unjust, must disobedience be peaceful, and must violators submit to punishment?

12. What do Christian perspectives have to tell us about more specific issues such as civil rights, pacifism, sexual liberty, and the death penalty?

A BASIC DIVISION

The modern theorists and influential figures we meet in this volume are members of a long Christian tradition. By reading what our essayists say about them, we get a sense of that tradition and of the major fissures within it. Nonetheless, since what I learned from these chapters depended considerably on what I brought to them—my own sense of the major issues and positions—providing a sketch of my understanding of the major traditions of which our writers are striking representatives may help readers of these reflections.

My understanding, like that of most Christians in Western countries, is based on a sense of Roman Catholicism and varieties of Protestantism. My perception of Eastern Orthodoxy was derived substantially from reading novels of Dostoevsky, especially *The Brothers Karamazov*, which led me to conclude that Russian Orthodoxy was relatively unconcerned with political matters, concentrating instead on a mystical understanding of God and on human salvation. Being married in 1968 in a Serbian Orthodox ceremony, of which I understood not a word but was told when to say "Da" and when to say "Ne," did not greatly advance my intellectual understanding, although it did confirm my sense of the deep spirit and mystical power of Orthodox worship. In explaining my initial understanding, I, thus, neglect the Orthodox tradition; in respect to that, I came to this endeavor with a hope, fortunately fulfilled, of greater comprehension.

Two starting points for Christian reflection on any subject are the Bible and the life of Jesus. How these figure in relation to reasoning powers that do not depend on particular religious premises has been a continuing concern for Christian thinkers.

One position, which we might call optimistic about human reason, is that all human beings, independent of revelation, are capable of figuring out basic moral truths and desirable social arrangements. Christian revelation confirms much that people can discover by the use of ordinary reason, and it may add some moral truths that are not susceptible to the power of ordinary reason alone. This view is represented most influentially in the Roman Catholic tradition by the thirteenth-century writings of Thomas Aquinas; his views figure prominently in the standpoints of most of the Roman Catholics in this volume, and one of the interesting questions is exactly how their Thomist approaches differ from each other.

At the other end of the spectrum is a darker sense of human reason. Unaided reason is substantially corrupted by sin; one cannot depend on it to discern truth. Accordingly, a stark difference exists between Christian understanding and the understanding to be expected of others. From this position, Christians must rely heavily on peculiarly Christian sources of understanding—the Bible, the example of the life of Jesus, the teachings of the church over the ages. This view is more "Protestant," though it draws substantially from Augustine's brilliant writings of the fourth century.

Typically accompanying the more optimistic view of human reason is a fairly positive appraisal of human moral capacities and of the reasons for political society. Human beings are inclined toward the good, and political life can help them realize their intrinsically valuable social nature. Law and politics aid people in achieving the common good at which they naturally aim. The more pessimistic appraisal is that people have a very hard time doing what is good, even if they identify it; and their powers of self-deception make identifying it troublesome indeed. The main object of political society is to create a minimally tolerable existence for all its members, not to inspire them or contribute positively to their fulfillment. Augustine paints a picture of the "worldly city" whose members achieve a modicum of mutual restraint; if they are to be ennobled at all, people will need to look beyond law and politics.

There are, of course, many nuances that this crude sketch does not even address. Is the "reason" by which people learn mainly a matter of abstract thought or experience and inclination? Do reason and faith confirm each other or do they interpenetrate in a closer way than "confirmation" suggests? How far may individuals rely on their own powers to discern truth, rather than counting on religious authorities or religious communities? Are human beings essentially the same in different cultures and stages of history, or is their "nature" socially constructed and variable, as Karl Marx supposed? These are subjects that some of the writings in this volume take up.

LEO XIII, ABRAHAM KUYPER, AND VLADIMIR SOLOVIEV

In the writings of Leo XIII one finds a forthright modern statement of a Thomist view; Abraham Kuyper, a contemporary, gives us a distinctly Protestant counterpoint, although one from which many of the darker tendencies are absent. One way to analyze the Catholic and Protestant thinkers that follow is to ask how they differ from these major figures.

Reviving Thomism as the center of Roman Catholic theology and philosophy, Leo employed a twofold pedagogy—faith and reason. He talked about law as a binding precept of reason. A natural law that emanates from God imposes a moral necessity on human beings, and human law flows from natural law. On this conception the essence of law is its reasonableness, not the coercive force that lies behind it. If we are to grasp this concept of natural law, we need to see what alternatives are being rejected. Russell Hittinger's chapter is an excellent teacher. Certainly Leo thought that moral questions have objectively correct answers; what is morally right does not depend on the subjective response of a particular person or the habits of a particular culture.[1] And Leo believed that the objective moral order is the consequence of Divine Providence and stands, in Hittinger's words, "outside the orbit of human prudence and legal artifact." Thus, he was strongly opposed to any notion that law arises only because human beings have entered into a social contract that establishes it. True liberty consists in complying with principles of natural law, not in some unconstrained exercise of the will. Leo also believed that basic moral requirements are accessible to common human reason, not just to individuals with true religious insight. (If God issued commandments that only a chosen people or individuals granted a special grace could comprehend, we might hesitate to speak of "law"; certainly we would not speak of "natural law.")

I am unclear whether any theory that asserts an objective moral order, sustained by God, and accessible to common human reason would count as a theory about "real" law, or whether something more is needed. Suppose one thought, as Christian ethicists have occasionally asserted, that the life of Jesus shows us we should try to achieve the most love possible in any human situation. One may speak of a "law of love," but a position that calls for such contextual evaluation is not very lawlike in any ordinary sense. According to Thomas, the first precept of natural law is also very general: "the good is to be done and evil resisted"; but perhaps we may add that in order to be "real law," the content of natural law must be lawlike, including general norms, such as "Do not kill" and "Do not steal," whose application is not highly contextual.

One aspect of standard natural law theory, as it has been developed in the modern era, is that human beings can discern the fundamental precepts of natural law without religious revelation. This does not mean more specific Christian sources of understanding will be no help. They may be more reliable than natural reason, they may yield decisive answers to points of great difficulty, such as whether couples may use artificial contraceptives, and they may establish moral authorities to whom ordinary people can look for guidance. But, as Leo suggested, ordinary people have a capacity to make judgments according to natural law.

It does not follow that a theory about natural law can be sustained without belief in God. Writing much more recently, John Finnis has argued that one can develop a persuasive account of natural law without depending on transcendent reality,[2] but Leo did not make any such as-sumption. For him belief in natural law, as contrasted with a sense of its substantive constraints, did depend on a conception of reality that has God at its center.

The crucial question for possible cooperation between believers and nonbelievers is *not* their relative perceptions of the underlying bases of morality and government, but rather their sense of what is right action in the moral and political spheres. On this point, Leo, following Thomas, was relatively optimistic. People generally can grasp the fundamentals of natu-ral law, and they will be able to see which human laws are just. Although many forms of government are consistent with natural law, we should ex-pect nonbelievers as well as believers to be able to identify tyranny and ar-bitrary rule. Many components of human flourishing do not relate directly to spiritual understanding; people should be able to agree on how govern-ment can promote these aspects. One could not, of course, expect non-Catholics to agree that the Catholic religious perspective is correct. Ideally a government, interested in the spiritual welfare of its citizens, would give Catholicism a favored position; but where Catholics are in a minority, as in the United States, it may be enough for the government to afford them religious liberty.

Leo did not directly address a question that has enjoyed prominence in recent liberal democratic theory—namely, whether on most matters of political importance citizens should engage in a common discourse that does not rely on any comprehensive view. As his preference for govern-mental support of Roman Catholicism reflects, Leo would have opposed any approach to politics in which Catholics eschewed arguments based on Roman Catholic understanding. But Leo's sense of natural law, commonly accessible to citizens, renders such an approach imaginable by suggesting that all citizens of good will share substantial common assessments.

According to Leo, building on Aristotle and Aquinas, people are inher-ently social. They would find themselves in political units even if they were not sinful; government is natural, not an artificial human contrivance built on a social contract, whether that contract is understood historically or theoretically, and whether it is taken to yield a liberal state or absolute rule. Hittinger says that Leo and his advisors apparently sided with a designation theory according to which people may establish a form of government by "designating the ruler," but do not possess the more ultimate authority of "translating" popular power into ruling authority. The state has important responsibilities, but it should not swallow up all of life, but rather recog-nize rights of association for other social groupings. The notion of "partici-pated authority" expresses the idea that the government is sovereign only within a certain domain. Following both Augustine and Aquinas, Leo said that human law flows from natural law and that an unjust law is not really a law. The status of unjust human laws, and how individuals should respond to them, is a major topic of many of our writers, though it is fair to say that none attempts to develop a comprehensive approach.

Abraham Kuyper agreed with Leo XIII on a number of practical aspects of human government, but his starting point was significantly different. Kuyper emphasized the subjective character of all understanding; there is no undiluted understanding that people have in common. As Nicholas Wolterstorff puts it, "theoretical learning is not so much report as construction," and he quotes Kuyper: "That a science should be free from the influence of the subjective factor is inconceivable." One cannot expect non-Christians to see things as Christians do; one cannot expect Catholics to see things as Protestants do. Learning is not individual, it is a shared human practice; the perspectives we bring to bear are largely based on the worldview or worldviews of groups in which we participate.

Kuyper's conception puts him in direct opposition with straightforward Enlightenment conceptions of knowledge, with traditional natural law theory as it is commonly understood, and with modern theories of liberal democracy that divorce political discourse from so-called comprehensive perspectives. Indeed, Kuyper's conception has more in common with aspects of postmodern theory than with any of these other approaches to knowledge. (What he does not share with some postmodern theory is the denial of an underlying objective truth. On that subject, Kuyper adheres to a traditional Christian understanding.) If we, somewhat arbitrarily, take the Enlightenment approach as conceiving objective domains of knowledge that all earnest students can master as evidence and analysis progresses, Kuyper answers that all understanding is subjective. He gives the same response to any version of natural law theory that asserts a common domain of knowledge that provides a floor from which various competing spiritual understandings may rise.

Modern theories of common political discourse acknowledge that people have irreconcilable competing "comprehensive" religious and moral views; indeed, it is a feature of liberal democracy that these differences will not go away. The way to achieve political fairness and social stability is for people to engage each other in the political forum according to the basic premises of liberal democracy and shared techniques of resolving empirical questions. This will allow shared bases of judgment and a common discourse without agreement among comprehensive views. Kuyper's answer to this theory, as Wolterstorff explains, is that people can never leave their worldviews behind; they will see all issues of theoretical understanding and practical action in terms of their own comprehensive perspectives. Common understanding and discourse is a chimera.

One might take this prognosis as very discouraging. If people are going to talk past each other, what will be left except the exercise of power between different groups? Indeed, that is the conclusion to which Marxists and "critical" theorists of various stripes are drawn. Kuyper's own view was qualified in important ways. Although sin, as well as the diversity of worldviews, produces near-intractable disagreements, a "common grace" given to all people allows them to identify what is good to some degree and to resolve some social problems. Kuyper held out a hope of mutual illumination, recommending an engaged pluralism in which we speak to one another from our own worldviews. Thus, a Christian may learn from an atheist who approaches problems from that worldview, a Jew may learn from a Hindu, and so on. With this degree of mutual engagement, we can expect the resolution of practical political problems, although never agreement on underlying premises or on what are ideal solutions.

Dismayed with the evils of the French Revolution, its atheism, individualism, destruction of civil society, and reliance on absolute reason, Kuyper was determined to organize associations according to his own religious perspective. Perhaps most importantly, he thought that parents should have the opportunity to educate children according to their own religious convictions, and that the state should support them in this effort, not limiting use of tax money to nonreligious state schools.

Kuyper also supported political parties organized along religious lines. Kuyper's stances concerning subjective understanding and political parties organized along religious lines raise sharply a problem for liberal democracies: namely, how far the *organs of government* are explicitly to rely on worldviews. The problem, one need hardly say, is not limited to societies with religious parties, arising as it does in the United States, which lacks influential political parties that have been created from single religious perspectives. Here is the dilemma. If a religious party wins office, can we expect it to do anything other than legislate from its own worldview? Yet, if the understanding on which a polity is based is that people with diverse worldviews can live comfortably within the society, perhaps the government, as such, should not be promoting any particular worldview. This is an acute dilemma in the United States, which has a constitutional provision forbidding the establishment of religion. If the government relies upon and promotes a particular religious worldview, is it not establishing that religion?

Of course, Kuyper was writing in a very different political setting, but I think we can see his answer to this problem, according to Wolterstorff's account. In contrast to the natural law theorists, Kuyper says that the state, with its dominant task of restraining sin, is unnatural, "something against which the deeper aspirations of our nature rebel." Like Leo, Kuyper asserted that the state has a limited domain; Kuyper wrote of "sphere sovereignty," according to which people should recognize the sovereignty of individual genius and of various social institutions. The government should not aim to promote any particular confessional triumph.

However, in contrast to Augustine, Kuyper thought that the state was not the organ of an earthly city, essentially limited to minimal functions; the state is the polity of all people together. The church properly aims for a moral triumph in society, and can seek the state's assistance in this respect. I infer that organs of government, such as the legislature, could properly rely on particular religious premises in adopting laws that concern moral norms. Thus, it might invoke Christian premises in adopting poor relief or forbidding abortion. My own view is that this realization, if it is in fact the best we can do in interpreting Kuyper, is *not* suitable for our society and for most liberal democracies; that whatever reliance on diverse worldviews is proper for individuals, nongovernmental associations, and individuals who form part of the government (such as individual legislators), organs of government as such should not rely on distinctive worldviews, even when they are resolving "ordinary" social and moral issues (rather than attempting to impose or promote the religious perspectives themselves).

Kuyper agreed with Leo that all authority comes from God. Like Leo, he said that "right law" is law that conforms to God's will. If he took a position on whether "wrong law" is real law, Wolterstorff does not tell us.

I believe we can well understand the other Catholic and Protestant theorists whose writings this volume discusses by seeing what they add, or how they disagree, with what Leo and Kuyper claim. But before I turn to that task, I want to sketch the Eastern Orthodox perspective developed in Paul Valliere's chapter on Vladimir Soloviev. Valliere's early remark that Soloviev was the first modern Orthodox thinker who regarded law in a positive light and set out to understand it in terms of the grand themes of Orthodox theology is itself very revealing. The Orthodox tradition has paid much less attention to law than has either the Roman Catholic or Protestant tradition; Valliere remarks: "The contrast between the supposedly harsh, legalistic mind of the Western church and the loving, all-embracing Eastern church was a cherished stereotype in Slavophilism." Valliere also tells us that the Russians have regarded themselves as trustees of Orthodoxy, an insight that may help us to understand why Russia and Orthodox countries of Eastern Europe have not moved from Communism to anything like our own notions of separation of church and state. Whatever freedom may be accorded other religious groups, some special position for the Orthodox Church is taken for granted.

Like most Roman Catholic and Protestant theorists, Soloviev rejected social contract theory, with its assumption of a pre-political state of nature. But he criticized the Catholic church for judicializing the Gospels, and his idea that law develops historically from customary law and exists as the general form of all positive legal relations, does not subscribe to the idea that a natural law has substantial content that remains fixed over periods of history and cultures, and from which human law draws. His notion that the state should be transformed by the church, helping to build a caring society and a recognition of spiritual values, lies far from the Protestant notion that the state is mainly an antidote to human sin—although he suggested in his earlier work that law does its work negatively rather than positively, and demands only a minimum of good.

On the crucial relation of justice and love, Soloviev's view was complex. A position commonly advanced is that the law should achieve justice, that it cannot aim directly at love,[3] although love may flourish better in a just society than an unjust one. Yet, for the Christian, agapic love is thought superior to legalistic justice. Valliere tells us that Soloviev took a "universal love ethic as the practical essence of Christianity," yet among imperfect human beings, the hierarchy of a legal system should aim to achieve justice. He formulates the right relationship as "justice is the necessary framework of love." Where Soloviev seems to differ from Reinhold Niebuhr and other Protestant thinkers who treat justice as the central aim of politics and law is in supposing that the government can try to manifest Christian love to some extent.

Soloviev supported a theocratic ideal. The state should recognize freedom of conscience, declining to use its coercive power in favor of any religious view; but it should support religious values and help prepare humanity for the kingdom of God. Because capital punishment could not reflect a spirit of Christian love, Soloviev urged that the tsar should not have the assassins of his predecessor executed. For the modern United States, and most other Western democracies, promotion of any particular Christian religion is undoubtedly out of place; how far religious perspectives should tinge government actions remains a serious question. And, however limited its proper basis as a program for relations between religion and the state in liberal democracies, Soloviev's Orthodox views stand as a potential critique of Catholic and Protestant perspectives.

MODERN CATHOLIC THEORISTS

This volume includes chapters about six other Catholic theorists. Labeling them all theorists is itself substantially misleading. Dorothy Day is included primarily because of her devout and activist life, although we can draw from her writings important ideas on particular subjects. Maritain, Murray, and Gutiérrez are mainly known for their ideas on various subjects, although each was also active in some important way. Pope John XXIII and Pope John Paul II are more difficult to classify, as indeed is Leo XIII. A pope is *the* leader of a tremendously influential and powerful religious organization; one of his critical responsibilities is announcing positions, which carry great authority within the church on a wide range of religious, moral, and political matters. Thus, one way popes are significant is because of the ideas they announce, whether they themselves develop those ideas or accept ideas that are presented to them by individuals or committees within the church. We can treat popes as theorists, in the sense of understanding the theories they propound, whatever their own degree of personal originality may be.

Jacques Maritain and John Courtney Murray fall within the broad stream of the Roman Catholic tradition, but each distinguished himself from dominant Catholic ideas at the time he was writing. For Maritain, natural law is less legalistic than on standard accounts, and the way people understand it is less by abstract reason. Patrick Brennan regards Maritain as a Thomist existentialist. The human mind is in intuitive contact with what exists. People know natural law connaturally, not by reasons and abstract concepts, but by inclination. Natural law is intrinsic, an ideal order. Prudence is needed to work out particular problems; one does not simply place situations within preset categories.

Maritain was one of the first Catholic theorists to develop a robust theory of natural rights. During the nineteenth and twentieth centuries, the church often stood in opposition to secular versions of natural rights, which were said to rest heavily on abstract reason and excessive individualism. Maritain claimed that human beings, equal because of their communion in the mystery of the human species, deserve respect for what each of them is.

In regarding the state and law as works of reason to promote the common good, Maritain was in accord with other Catholic theorists; in denying that the state should help lead people to spiritual perfection but should limit itself to the subordinate ends of the temporal order, he took a more controversial stance, one not accepted by the Catholic Church until the Second Vatican Council.

Maritain repeated the formula that an unjust law is not really a law, but he recognized that people have reasons of conscience to comply with some unjust laws.

John Courtney Murray offered a distinctively American approach to natural law and the function of the state. He emphasized that natural law is "written on the heart of all people, knowable by reason and without the aid of revelation." He believed, further, that natural law theory linked to basic American ideals. Coercive human law has a limited nature and efficacy; it is not coextensive with the common good. As Angela Carmella explains, the state's lawmaking authority is circumscribed not only by prudential norms but also by "the state's defined function ... its 'public order' role."

Murray argued that the state should not promote religious truth but should guarantee religious freedom as a fundamental right, and he criticized Protestants who wanted Christian values to be transferred directly into social life. Catholic theorists, in the main, had urged that ideally the state would accord a special position to the Roman Catholic Church and help promote its values; but in countries in which Catholics were a minority, it was acceptable for the state to treat religions equally and accord freedom of conscience to Roman Catholics. Murray broke with this view, urging that separation of church and state and freedom of conscience were actually desirable. The state should be secular, but it should acknowledge its inherent limits in God's order of creation. A degree of cooperation is appropriate between church and state, and parents who want to send their children to religious schools should be able to do so with public support.

Murray understood truth in terms of a developing consciousness. Although the fundamental structure of human nature and the essential destinies of persons remain the same, the nature of people does change over time, as does the way they apprehend truth.

It has been suggested that Murray's theory of desirable political life is not far from that of John Rawls. I have two doubts about this. Murray seemed comfortable with citizens and politicians drawing directly from natural law ideas—as they have developed within the Roman Catholic tradition. Without doubt, Murray thought that the truths of natural law are accessible to everyone—he did not rely on revelation—and his own account of how natural law applies to government was quite liberal; but, nonetheless, a fully developed natural law theory qualifies as a comprehensive perspective, of the kind Rawls says citizens should not rely on for constitutional issues and fundamental questions of justice. A related point has more direct practical significance. Although Murray regarded the state as limited to matters of public order, and opposed laws against the sale and use of contraceptives on this basis as well as on grounds of prudence, he did not suggest that it is wrong, in principle, to regulate all aspects of morality that do not involve direct wrongs to others. Rawls's "priority of liberty" may set stricter limits on when government should regulate individual actions.

Paul Sigmund traces the development of thought of Gustavo Gutiérrez. His original understanding was a kind of Christianized Marxism. Although never surrendering belief in a transcendental truth, he was highly suspicious of the abstract and ideological character of much of the natural law tradition. He urged that Christians must change the sinful structures imposed by dominant capitalism, in order that oppressed people may be liberated. On this view, legal systems were part of the ideological super-structure that justifies capitalism. He subsequently has acknowledged sources of oppression other than economic ones and has rejected Marx's reduction of social conflict to class struggle; but he still believes that the rich and powerful have inordinate influence in political systems, and that the Christian commitment to the poor demands a more just distribution of social resources.

Dorothy Day was an activist who engaged in nonviolent civil disobedi-ence for the poor, mostly the working poor; she was a consistent pacifist. Nonviolence and pacifism pose a crucial issue for Christians. Various pas-sages in the New Testament—especially the one urging turning the other cheek (Matt. 5:38)—may be taken to mean that people should never re-spond to violence with more violence. One possible view is that Christians should never use physical force against others—whatever the consequenc-es. On that view, one trusts God to see that things will go as they should if one acts as one should. But that is hardly a comforting ethic for people who think appalling consequences will follow if "good people" never use physi-cal force. On various theories, the "perfectionist ethic" of Jesus is not one that ordinary people and officials are called upon to live by.

Often pacifists respond with an account of human nature that suggests that nonviolence will actually be more constructive than responsive vio-lence. Once we descend to the level of predictable human responses, vari-ous distinctions may seem appealing. We might distinguish the massive violence of warfare from forcible actions in self-defense, police use of force to stop crimes and apprehend criminals, and forcible confinement of dan-gerous people. And we might also distinguish oppressors, like the British in India or whites in the United States, who could be moved by peaceful acts of civil disobedience, from rulers like Hitler and Stalin, who, lacking compunctions about slaughtering classes of their citizens, would have had little sympathy for passive resisters. I am not sure whether Day had a de-veloped theory on these subjects, and, whether, if not, one could build a theory out of what she did say.

Pope John XXIII had a remarkable influence partly because of his ex-traordinary personal touch and because he convened the Second Vatican Council, a watershed in the history of the church. Although traditional in much of his basic theology, John XXIII sought to open the church to mo-dernity. His ideas of a just society included rights of workers and a social welfare state. He added "freedom" to ideals of justice, truth, and love found in the encyclicals of his predecessors. Drawing from the natural law tradition, he incorporated what had previously been the mainly secular idea of natural rights, providing a complete and systematic list of rights. Against the grain of much in the Catholic tradition, he defended religious freedom for everyone, as an aspect of human dignity, and he supported the growth of limited constitutional states. The endorsement of religious freedom was one of the most important conclusions of Vatican II.

Less optimistic than John XXIII about human nature, Pope John Paul II nevertheless believed that the council's acknowledgment of a natural right of conscience was its greatest achievement. For John Paul, true freedom is the freedom to do good, which is threatened by the freedom of self-sufficiency and autonomy. Contemporary secularism produces materialism, manipulation of others, and a culture of death. In contrast to the destructive ideologies of liberal capitalism and Marxism, the church's social doctrine offers a true understanding of the human condition and of society. Among the pope's more particular moral stances have been a defense of traditional marital and sexual relationships and a nearly absolute condemnation of the death penalty.

MODERN PROTESTANT THEORISTS

Among the Protestant theorists after Kuyper, the most influential for Protestant thought were Karl Barth and Reinhold Niebuhr, the most influential for action Martin Luther King Jr. Each had significant things to say about how the Christian message relates to law and to political obligation.

Karl Barth was arguably the most important Protestant theologian of modern times. Although not dominant in his total output, his chapters about politics were nonetheless significant, and he was the main author of the 1934 "Barmen Declaration," which laid a basis for Protestant resistance to Hitler.

For Barth, as George Hunsinger explains, the "scriptural voice of Jesus Christ" is the authentic, and only, "source of authority for the church in its own proclamation and teaching." Barth did not deny that many things of value could be found outside of scripture and the church or that "grace" may allow people to identify what they should do outside the church. But Barth did reject notions of natural theology according to which natural reason allows human beings insights about moral truths that are free of cultural and historical contingency. What people take as "natural law" amounts to a cultural construct. Morals and politics, like other aspects of life, fall within the domain of faith.

In Barth's understanding, the state's power comes from God, and its responsibility is to use coercion for justice, freedom, and peace. Governments should pursue positive goals as well as restraining evil. Barth favored democratic socialism as a system of government, and strongly condemned capitalism for violating the dignity of work and reinforcing harmful desires for possessions and power. Against that part of the Lutheran tradition that counseled acquiescence by citizens in the face of even severe injustice by governments, Barth argued in favor of a right to resist tyranny.

For Reinhold Niebuhr, the central message of the Christian tradition about human nature was sin; everything people do is infected with sin and the human pursuit of group interests is especially unchecked by moral constraint. In some of his early writings, Niebuhr was highly critical of standard natural law views, as assuming too much goodness and rationality in human beings. Although the prevalence of sin is a biblical concept, rooted in the story of the original fall, Niebuhr argued that the reality of selfish behavior is amply borne out by a study of history. Many non-Christians found Niebuhr's "realism" about human relations persuasive, even if they did not agree with its Christian underpinnings.

Niebuhr regarded love as a kind of impossible ideal for human relations. In their social institutions, human beings had mainly to constrain power and selfish behavior. In that domain, no one should have unchecked power—even the best-intentioned are subject to using power abusively—and the object of human law is to do justice. Justice, in a sense, falls short of love, but it, unlike love, is a realistic aspiration for a political order. Niebuhr supported a political system of checks and balances in internal politics and a "realistic" approach to international relations, according to which the United States would aim to stop the spread of totalitarian governments but would never lose sight of its own involvement in sinful structures and practices or delude itself into supposing that it could ever achieve a pure international order. Insofar as President Bush has cast the struggle against terrorism after September 11, 2001, as a clash between good and evil, Niebuhr would have reminded us that no individual or government is free from sin.

One aspect of Niebuhr's realism was his opposition to pacifism, after early support for that position. The gospel ethic of nonviolence is not one that people can afford to embrace absolutely in a world in which sinful actions must be constrained. Thus, in Niebuhr's view, the ethics of nonviolent love to be gleaned from parts of the New Testament is a kind of impossible ideal of what human life could be like, *not* a practical recommendation for how we should live in a fallen society. Even Christian grace does not much affect how people do and could live; rather it assures us of forgiveness for the sins we are bound to commit.

Martin Luther King Jr. was much influenced by Niebuhr's thought, but he departed from it in important respects. He was more optimistic about transforming people than was Niebuhr and, for him, love played a more direct role in how people should act in society. Human beings are capable of terrible injustices, but if these are opposed peaceably and with love for the oppressors, the structures of injustice can be changed and the victims and oppressors can be transformed. Although King believed in nonviolent resistance to evil, he also believed in state enforcement of people's rights, so he did accept certain forms of violent or coercive behavior.

Dietrich Bonhoeffer and John Howard Yoder may stand even further from a standard natural law view than do Niebuhr and King. Bonhoeffer urged that we must live without relying on the favor of a benign Deity, taking as our ethical standard what Christ demands of us. That may lead us into actions that are sinful, but we have no better choice. Yoder, with more traditional views about how we should understand our relation to God, also takes Christ as the center of social ethics. For him, the implication is that we should live nonviolently and with love for our fellows.

MODERN ORTHODOX THINKERS

Although the chapters on the four Eastern Orthodox thinkers who follow Vladimir Soloviev illuminate important differences among them, an outsider—at least this outsider—is impressed with common themes that contrast with dominant Catholic and Protestant approaches. I begin with those.

In his introduction to the modern Orthodox tradition, Paul Valliere remarks on a stereotypical romantic view of Orthodoxy as "preserving mystical values from which a putatively rationalist Western Christianity has fallen away," which helps to preserve a mistaken "notion that Orthodoxy is not fundamentally concerned with social and political ethics." Although the chapters show that Orthodox theorists give some attention to social and political ethics, they do oppose themselves to the rationalist, conceptual understandings that they discern in Catholic and Protestant thinkers, and they do give less attention to law, the state, and what we might call ordinary ethics. Their view of human nature is strongly personalist, and they emphasize that human beings are made in the image of God. That human beings are made in God's image in some sense is a core tenet of all forms of traditional Christianity; but the Orthodox theorists emphasize personal and relational, rather than rational, aspects of human nature, and they deny that human beings are as corrupted by the Fall as some Protestants assert.

In various ways, the Orthodox theorists oppose objectivist, abstract modes for understanding human nature and ultimate reality. In comparison with what they see as a Catholic and Protestant preoccupation with law and with moral norms, they are antijuridical, seeing a vital life of the spirit that transcends a deadening rational morality and law.

Nicholas Berdyaev, who, as Vigen Guroian explains, regarded himself as a philosopher, not a theologian, and was hardly a representative of the Orthodox Church, opposed the ethics of redemption and the ethics of creativity to the ethics of law and to a shallow, graceless bourgeois mentality. Moralism and legalism are incapable of reaching the kingdom of God. An ethics of redemption can overcome the divide between good and evil characteristic of naturalist ethics; an ethics of creativeness reflects the chief end of human beings and completes what redemption begins.

Berdyaev insisted on a human personhood that is a mixture of inseparable nature and spirit and that is relational, dependent on community. Knowledge about human nature and destiny is not like ordinary knowledge; it connects to divine mystery and is conveyed by myth. The Fall leads to a shift from a consciousness that is intersubjective, I-Thou, to one that is objective and depersonalized. Sin requires law, but law cannot conquer sin. Love can transcend law. The positive purpose of law is to clear a space for creative activity. In Christian faith, obedience to law and to moral norms is replaced by creative activity that God inspires.

Mikhail Kulakov calls Vladimir Lossky "the best known and most widely followed modern Orthodox theologian." A critic of "Catholic essentialism," "Protestant existentialism," and the kind of philosophic account one finds in Berdyaev, Lossky proposed a kind of negative approach to theology that emphasizes recognition of what God is not. He had a personalized, experiential, not a rationalist, understanding of human nature, law, and justice. He differed from others in the Orthodox tradition in not regarding the church as closely attached to national governments, and had a positive view of democracy. The church's main role was not to achieve its will in temporal political life, but to provide spiritual sustenance for the world.

Dumitru Stăniloae, like others in the tradition, wrote little directly about law. He rejected any sharp distinction between natural and supernatural revelation. Although sin has serious consequences, it does not make human knowledge totally opaque. Unlike Lossky, Stăniloae justified nationalism; and as a Romanian he lived many years under a highly oppressive Communist regime. He saw law as a consequence of the Fall, and he compared its "oldness" to the "newness of the spirit." Understanding Christian love as distinctly different from justice, he opposed measures against collaborators in postcommunist Romania, because the church should not assign guilt but should try to persuade people by example to change their lives.

In her life of service to others, Mother Maria Skobtsova saw herself as aiming to fulfill Orthodox aspirations, which place love of God and one's neighbor and "lofty human communion" at the center of Christian life. Although her writings well explain the understandings that fit the life she led, her contribution lies more in the life than in the ideas she accepted.

BASIC ISSUES

There are several fundamental questions that a person identifying himself or herself as a Christian needs to answer in developing a philosophy or theology of human nature, politics, and law. The account that follows takes various of those questions in a sequential order, but the reader should be aware that answers to later questions may well influence responses to earlier ones. Each individual has a bundle of views that fit together. The reader should also be aware that I was raised as a Protestant and still identify myself with that tradition; that I found Reinhold Niebuhr's writings to be deeply persuasive when I was in college and doing graduate work; that I was deeply moved by the life of Martin Luther King Jr.; that I have spent most of my adult life working in disciplines— law and, to a lesser extent, secular political philosophy—in which people do not rely directly on religious premises; and that my propensity in respect to most subjects I study is to find aspects of the truth in sharply contrasting views. All this is a kind of warning that when I suggest how I would resolve the various issues I pose, I am definitely not claiming that those are the resolutions that any reasonable person would reach. They *are* the best I can do given who I am, but they undoubtedly reflect my religious and professional background and my intellectual inclinations. I undertake the exercise to suggest how others (including those with a religious identification other than Christian) who are trying to work out their own views and who read these chapters might formulate and answer the crucial questions.

Here are the basic issues I address:

1. Is one's understanding of human nature and the place of law to be based mainly on religious sources or on sources accessible to all people, regardless of their religious perspective?

2. How far is one's understanding reliant on religious or other authority or arrived at independently?

3. Is there a "human nature" that extends across cultures and stages of history?

4. Are human beings basically rational and inclined to the good, or selfish and driven by emotion?

5. Should moral standards be understood as a species of law or as something else?

6. Does human law derive from moral law?

7. Are "unjust" human laws true laws?

8. Should human law be minimalist or maximalist in its aspirations?

9. Do people have a responsibility to obey human laws because they have been adopted?

10. Should individuals refrain from violence?

11. Should states refrain from violence?

12. How important are law and government?

13. What forms of political life and law are most suitable?

SOURCES OF UNDERSTANDING

For a Christian, or any other religious person who believes there are special religious sources of understanding, we may roughly divide the available sources between "ordinary" and "religious." Roughly speaking, "religious" sources are those that are available to people who have a religious commitment, belief, or experience; "ordinary" sources are available to everyone. For this purpose it does not matter whether God gives all people the ability to understand ordinary sources through a "general grace," so long as understanding them does not depend on one's religious stance. I treat religious sources as not available to nonbelievers, even if nonbelievers "should see" the truth of a religion. I disregard the fact that many believers in particular religions think that "learning" of other religions is wholly or substantially misguided.

Dividing sources into religious and ordinary *may* involve a crucial oversimplification. If Kuyper is right that one's worldview colors all of one's understanding, one's religious views will color one's ordinary understanding (and one's ordinary understandings will color one's understanding from religious sources). Thus, we can imagine four possible stances about particular domains of knowledge: (1) all valid understanding comes from ordinary sources; (2) all valid understanding comes from religious sources; (3) understanding from religious sources is essentially independent from understanding derived from ordinary sources, but these confirm one another or are layered in some way; (4) ordinary and religious sources intertwine.

Let us address these in turn. Anyone who believes in a form of religious revelation is not likely to think all valid understanding comes from ordinary sources. Since people of all varieties of religious understanding have many common beliefs, it is implausible in the extreme to think that all true understanding comes from religious sources, though someone might think that all true understanding on certain subjects, such as about the nature of God, comes only from religious sources. What has been the standard Roman Catholic natural law view is that ordinary and religious sources are essentially independent; they are mutually confirmatory or layered. Thus, to take an example of a layered understanding, the "ordinary" techniques of natural sciences provide insights into the typical operations of the natural world; religious sources explain why "miracles" occur. Confirmation occurs if, for example, ordinary sources tell us that most people, much of the time, act in a self-interested way; the Bible provides an account of original sin. Ordinary and religious sources would intertwine if one's reading of the Genesis story of Adam and Eve were heavily influenced by "ordinary" knowledge and if one's appraisal of ordinary psychological claims were heavily influenced by one's reading of the story. This "intertwining" fits well with some Protestant and Orthodox understandings, as well as with medieval Catholic views about natural law.

I believe most of our knowledge of ordinary facts, for example, about astronomy, the age of the earth, economics, and history comes from ordinary sources, that it is equally accessible, or nearly so, to people of divergent religious views. Religious sources are more significant for ethics and political justice (and for theories about the meaning of history). Some ethical norms can be understood on the basis of ordinary sources, though one's understanding of these may be colored by one's religious understanding; but ordinary sources cannot tell us how agapic love stands in relation to other values (that is, what its priority should be) or whether the plight of the poor should be of overwhelming concern, two subjects to which Christian religious sources speak strongly.

What sources inform us about human nature? Questions about "human nature" sound like factual ones, but they deviate from ordinary factual questions in two important senses. First, "human nature" suggests *core* aspects of human beings that do not alter over time. Since these core qualities are usually cast at a high level of generality and attributed to people, past and future, with whom we cannot communicate directly, it is hard to establish by empirical knowledge what is true or false. Our assessment inevitably involves a sense of what is most central, and that is likely to be influenced by our understanding of religious sources. For example, people may argue about the persistence of human selfishness and how far it can be eradicated by better socialization; someone who believes in original sin based on religious sources is likely to conclude that human selfishness will never "go away."

The second way that inquiries about human nature deviate from typical factual questions is even more crucial. Ideas of "human nature" often mix assessments of what people have been, are, and are likely to be, with judgments about what they should be. When we read that Bonhoeffer's view is that human nature is revealed in Jesus, we should understand that to mean that the best of what we can be, what we should aspire to, is revealed in the life of Jesus. Insofar as an inquiry about "human nature" includes such normative evaluation, religious sources are likely to play a very significant role.

Much the same is true about a view of "law." If one's concept of law includes precepts of correct moral behavior and what positive laws should aim for, it is substantially normative.

My position about sources is this. For most ordinary knowledge, such as the standard facts of history and the natural world, ordinary sources of understanding are adequate. Religious sources may influence one's perspective to a degree, but need not to any great degree. For more complex factual assessments, such as the persistence of human selfishness, religious sources play a more significant role, largely intertwining with ordinary sources. For issues of morality and justice, the religious sources are still more important, intertwining with ordinary sources as influences on one's overall understanding. Note that I am not *mainly* describing how most people do arrive at understandings, but how they appropriately would do so. To explain these normative judgments, I need to say more about the religious sources on which people might rely.

For Christians, I think there are three primary kinds of religious sources. One is the Bible, the second is the church or religious community, and the third is personal inspiration, as through prayer. A person's appraisal of how religious sources fit with ordinary sources obviously depends on which religious sources she credits and how she understands them. A person who thinks that the Bible is the word of God, in the sense of stating the literal truth about everything it says (except when usage is obviously metaphorical), will find religious sources authoritative on everything the Bible explicitly addresses. That person will not take ordinary sources as revealing the truth about the natural world if the Bible provides a different account. A Roman Catholic who believes that the pope has spoken infallibly about certain matters will have a similar idea about what he has said on these occasions. I do not take the Bible in this way; what it reveals about God, and about the life of Jesus, is heavily colored by historical consciousness and other human limitations and by understandable aims to teach particular lessons. And, as a Protestant, I assign much less teaching authority to the church than will a typical Roman Catholic. Finally, I have not experienced personal inspirations of a kind that give me confidence about what is true or what we should do (though my conviction about the possibility of an afterlife has been deeply affected by personal feelings that I have felt come from outside myself). Thus, my sense of the uncertain reliability of religious sources bears decisively on how I perceive them in relation to ordinary sources (which, of course, may be unreliable in their own ways).

AUTHORITY AND INDIVIDUAL JUDGMENT

How far does our understanding rest on authority, how far on independent individual judgment? We need initially to clear away some brush. Everyone is heavily influenced by the opinions of others, what parents and teachers have taught us, what knowledgeable experts say, what friends and colleagues think, and everyone, in a sense, must finally make up his or her mind. I must decide how much weight I will assign to various authorities—no one can force that judgment on me (short of brainwashing). Thus we may see the crucial question as this: "How much weight should a Christian assign to the judgment or actions of various authorities?"

I will simplify a bit by concentrating on religious authorities, indulging two important assumptions. Apart from what religious sources may reveal, Christians should treat nonreligious sources of knowledge much as would non-Christians. In relying on expert knowledge ("the weather service says it will rain tomorrow") and the ordinary experience of others ("I know rape is a terrible experience because my friend has lived through it and told me about it"), Christians are not different from other people. And judgments of Christians about when to follow practical authorities who tell us what to do, such as legislatures, should also be similar to those of other people, except insofar as these judgments are influenced by religious perspectives.

The standard division between Catholics and Protestants is less over the place of authority than the kind of religious authority to follow. According to the traditional Catholic view, the church has great authority. Whatever the precise divisions between papal authority and that of councils or bishops, the church is substantially hierarchical; ordinary lay Catholics should give great weight to, if not accept without independent judgment, the teachings of the corporate church. Protestants, in general, assign much less authority to church teachings, although in all groups these teachings are thought to carry considerable weight; and the structures of authority tend to be much less hierarchical, with variations depending on particular principles of church government. Protestants place much more emphasis on the Bible, which often is taken as a controlling authority, but is subject to individual judgment about what it means. (Of course, a papal encyclical is also subject to interpretation, but it is much more likely than the Bible to take a clear indisputable position on a subject. For example, the Roman Catholic Church definitely teaches that abortion is a grave sin; whether the Bible does so is subject to argument.) For these purposes, I do not count reliance on direct divine inspiration as reliance on authority. Although someone might say he is inspired by the greatest authority, God, he is not relying on human authority and is interpreting his own experience. How to class a view that the main inspiration of the Bible is in providing the example of the life of Jesus is more difficult. A person who takes the significance of the Bible as the telling of that life in a manner that calls forth a reaction from us is almost certainly treating the Bible as authoritative in a sense, but not because of any particular propositions it provides us about what is true and how we should live.

I have already indicated my view that the Bible is heavily colored by human perspectives. I do believe a large part of its significance is in presenting the life of Jesus as a kind of model (exactly what kind is a crucial issue to which I shall return). I think we all have much to learn from the traditions of the Christian community and from contemporary Christians, such as Martin Luther King Jr., about the meaning of a Christian life. But the church itself has always been infected with sin and error, and I believe each individual should, with a large degree of humility about his or her own ability to grasp the truth, be selective about what he accepts. I recognize that this selectivity introduces the possibility that individual sin and erroneous judgment will run rampant, but I see no better alternative. Thus, in respect to religious sources, I assign less weight to authority than do either standard Roman Catholic views or a Bible-centered Protestantism.

HUMAN NATURE?

One may contrast a view that the nature of human beings is essentially stable with a view that human beings, as such, have no "nature," that people differ radically depending on their society and their place within it. According to the latter view, most commonly associated with various forms of Marxism, medieval peasants are radically different from capitalist industrialists, and slaves are radically different from slaveholders. On this view, there may or not be some ideal endpoint to which history is evolving (as Marx and Engels assumed) or to which human beings should aspire.

I think the serious question about the existence of human nature is more or less, not either-or. As H. L. A. Hart points out in *The Concept of Law*, building on Hume, almost all human beings want physical security, possession of what belongs to them, and protection of their transactions.[4] One might add that people generally prefer not to be in physical pain, not to be unhappy, and not to be uniformly hated. They also care more about those who are close to them than about outsiders. On the other hand, we certainly know from anthropological studies that perspectives about the world and about how we should act toward one another can differ radically among different cultures. Were differences among human beings *sufficiently* radical, that might undermine the validity of Christian perspectives on human nature, which do assume a constancy of crucial features over time. I assume that the differences are not "so radical," although the major ones that do exist should undercut our confidence that we, whatever our place and time, can see things clearly "as they really are."

THE ESSENCE OF HUMAN NATURE

Much disagreement in what we might call Christian jurisprudence turns on contrasting appraisals of human nature; interestingly, these do not seem to be connected in any obvious way to what are taken to be religious sources and their authority. We need to unpack these contrasting views.

According to the standard Thomist view of modern Roman Catholic theorists, human beings are distinguished by their rationality and their inclination toward the good, not only their own good but also the common good, which is consonant with their own. Yes, human beings can be selfish and irrational, but that does not negate their essential goodness and rationality. For traditional Protestantism, the Fall is a central event in human history; people are essentially sinful—self-centered and far from rational—and they are redeemed only by a loving God sending his son to die on the cross. Of course, some great Catholic thinkers, most notably Augustine, have emphasized the dark side of human beings, and liberal Protestants have embraced a more optimistic appraisal of human potentialities, so it is not as if one can confidently associate a particular understanding of human nature with a simple Catholic or Protestant view; but in what follows, I shall draw out the implications of the two contrasting perspectives. The Orthodox understanding is less rationalist, more personalist and mystical, than the Thomist approach, but less pessimistic than the Protestant one, emphasizing our capacity for union with God rather than our deeply sinful character.

It is hard to assess just how much the opposing Roman Catholic and Protestant views reflect different evaluations of what people are actually like and how much they reflect contrasting emphases grounded in similar factual appraisals. An impartial factual appraisal certainly yields a mixed picture. Most human beings are capable most of the time in acting for their own good and the good of those close to them; most put their own interests and those of loved ones ahead of the interests of faraway strangers; most sometimes, or often, act irrationally, and to satisfy feelings of resentment, jealousy, or anger that would not guide their "better selves." As far as an outsider appraisal can tell, people who regard themselves as "saved" in some special way do not become radically better than all the rest of us in their personal traits, although some do make remarkable steps in reforming their lives. There is a great deal of truth in Reinhold Niebuhr's observation that the "selfish" tendencies are amplified when groups, especially national groups, are involved. One clear illustration is the relative equanimity with which Americans (and we are not unique in this respect) are willing to see tens of thousands of civilians of an "enemy" die but are deeply disturbed by the loss of scores of American lives in combat.

Within the general parameters I have set, people can differ greatly about what aspects of human personality dominate. Our opinions on this score are based on our personal experiences, of ourselves and of others, and on what we read and hear more generally, portrayals in literature and television dramas, as well as historical and psychological studies and reports of current events (which tend to bring to our notice more instances of bad behavior than good behavior). And, of course, one's religious views will influence one's appraisal of the "facts."

When we move to what people might be like in the future, our confidence in factual appraisals must diminish, given the difficulty of saying how much particular changes in social conditions or in religious understandings, not to mention genetic engineering, might alter human beings. In contrast to orthodox Marxism, none of the dominant Christian understandings rests on assumptions about a transformed human nature within the span of human history.

One could devote a great deal of space to what "people are really like," but I can do no better than describe the mixed view I accept. For what it is worth, beginning from a fairly dark Niebuhrian view when I was in college, I have moved—supported by love within my family and by honorable and caring behavior by friends and colleagues—to a more positive appraisal of what people are like. But any undiluted picture of human beings as rational and inclined to the good is refuted by the public events we all witness, and I recognize that I may have been particularly fortunate in most of my life's circumstances.

Perhaps the nonfactual elements of the contrasting views of human nature matter more than variations about the cultural characteristic of human beings. The Catholic view may partly be understood as telling us what we are like when we are at our best and it represents a denial that our sin is an insurmountable impediment to our leading relatively good lives. It is also an expression of a position that our reason is capable of appraisal of what is truly valuable, rather than our acting as a "slave" to objectives set by our emotions—a philosophical stance that is probably impossible to confirm or refute by the way people actually behave. The view that true human nature is revealed in Jesus Christ is yet more obviously mainly normative, not descriptive of most people. Even the more typical Protestant view may be less a statement about the balance of human characteristics than an assertion about what counts in our relation to God. Sin, separation from God, is taken as the universal feature of that relation. When three of my sons were involved with an interdenominational evangelical group, they used to relate to me an allegory about people who start to swim across the Atlantic Ocean. Some will get much farther than others, but none will get very far. Even the best people are infected with sin; redemption can come only from God. Taken in this way, the emphasis on sin and selfishness could be quite consistent with the idea that most people are good (in human terms) most of the time.

Thus, we see that different perspectives on "human nature" reflect different senses of what matters theologically and philosophically, as well as different appraisals of what people act like in a sense that could yield to empirical investigation. I think clarity would be served by distinguishing evaluations of what people are like, and could be like, of the sort that in theory at least could be shown to be true or false empirically (evaluations that give me the "mixed picture" I have described) from normative assessments of the best human characteristics and how an ideal human life would be lived. For a religious person, the latter inquiry is likely to be impossible without strong reference to religious sources. For me, those sources, along with my experiences of mundane life, suggest the overwhelming importance of loving concern for others.

ARE MORAL STANDARDS A SPECIES OF LAW?

It is hard to know just what to make of the claim of natural lawyers who say that moral standards are truly law. Opposed to this view is the sense that true moral standards are commands or guides or perspectives—something other than law—or that there are no true moral standards. I think it helps to break down this disagreement about the nature of morality into five subissues: (1) the objectivity of moral standards, (2) their origination in, or dependence upon, God, (3) their rational cohesiveness, (4) their susceptibility to rational grasp, and (5) the "lawness" of their substantive character.

1. Some people, but not traditional Christians of any variety, believe there are no "true" moral standards, that there are only standards that people or societies happen to adopt. A sophisticated version of this view must concede, as H. L. A. Hart has pointed out, that all societies will share certain moral standards in common—for example, that one should not kill innocent insiders without good reason, and that one should not freely take the property of another—but these standards may be viewed as the evident product of what is necessary for human beings to live together. (Such standards do not tell us, by themselves, who count as "insiders" and what counts as property.) By and large, according to this skeptical view, moral standards are subjective and relative. We can describe what they are and why they have arisen, but they have no "objective" status, in the sense of binding people regardless of what they have adopted as their community morality. The assertion that moral standards are "law" implicitly denies such skeptical subjective perspectives.

2. Some people consider moral truths to be objective, as they might consider standards of beauty to be objective, without believing in any transcendent reality. Jeremy Bentham's utilitarianism was one such approach. Typical law, by contrast, originates with a lawmaker. The assertion that moral standards are law may be taken to mean, in part, that these standards rest on a Divine Lawgiver, or that, even if in some sense what is morally right does not depend directly on God, God somehow sustains the system of morality that guides human beings.

3. The idea of law may convey a coherent system, something more than an isolated set of commands. Were we subject to a series of directives from God that formed no coherent pattern, those directives would not amount to law. To say that moral standards are law suggests that they are rationally cohesive.

4. More important, law is subject to rational appraisal. The idea of law may, and the idea of natural law does, connote a system that human beings can appreciate without relying on special religious revelation. (However, one could certainly think of God as establishing a set of moral "laws" that would not be accepted by outsiders.)

5. Finally, the idea of law may convey something about the nature of moral standards. One Christian view is that a person should seek the most love possible in any situation. This highly contextualist approach is not very lawlike. By contrast, the Ten Commandments are stated in a legal form, as specific standards people are not to disobey in any circumstances. The recommendation that people should seek the common good does not sound very lawlike in this sense; but Catholic

natural lawyers typically arrive at many more specific norms that are lawlike in character.

Debating whether moral standards are a kind of law is not very productive. Rather, we should to focus on those narrower, more specific questions. The standard Protestant view is in agreement with the Catholic one that objective moral truth exists and that the moral order rests upon God. Protestants, and the Eastern Orthodox, tend to think that religious understanding is more critical for moral appraisal than do Catholic theorists, that what is morally right to do is less a matter of following lawlike norms that are part of a coherent system, than of following specific directions of God or being moved by a loving response to God's care for us, manifested in the life of Jesus. The claim that genuine ethics is responding to the example of Jesus is one example of an unlawlike approach.

I have thus far omitted a complexity that is important. Many Christians believe that there is a core of morality that is recognizable by all people and that may be relatively lawlike ("Do not kill," "tell the truth," etc.), but that true Christian responses to others go beyond this core.

If we can unpack someone's overall view or manage to develop one of our own, whether we conclude that moral standards are "really law" is not by itself very important. Having a relatively contextualist approach to morality and believing that following lawlike norms plays a less significant role than according to most modern natural law approaches, I hesitate to describe objective moral standards as a "natural law," but I do subscribe to the idea that there are objective moral standards, somehow sustained by God, that form a coherent whole, that contain lawlike components, and that to a substantial degree are discernable to human understanding without revelation.

DOES HUMAN LAW DERIVE FROM MORAL LAW?

In addressing this question, we need to divide a normative inquiry from what we may call a conceptual inquiry. If the issue is whether human law *should* be based on true moral standards (if there are any), the answer is obviously "yes," with certain qualifications. Human law should not try to embody *all* moral standards, because some do not lend themselves to the coercive apparatus of enforcement that is a central component of most human law. Further, the human law in any society should probably not aim to enforce moral standards that are widely rejected in the society. (Thus, one might think that abortion is a highly immoral practice but that positive law should not prohibit abortions if most people think they are morally accept-able.) Finally, much human law deals with matters that are morally indiffer-ent (which side of the road cars will be driven on, exactly what kind of tax rates to set), except that regulation contributes to the welfare of society.

Does human law derive from moral standards in a conceptual sense? Two related factors are crucial for our analysis. One is the degree to which moral standards can be grasped by human reason, unaided by revelation. The other is whether law is essentially a matter of reason or of will. If we think of human law, at least our human law, as embracing citizens with widely variant religious understandings, we might think of human law as deriving from moral standards only insofar as ordinary human reason can grasp the moral standards. If special revelation is needed to understand what is morally right and most people in the society have not had the ben-efit of this revelation, we should not expect human law to track true moral standards very closely.

Ordinary human law (at least in its basic features) is both comprehen-sible to the human intellect and a guide to right behavior. It is also adopted by acts of will and enforced by acts of will. Which of these elements to emphasize, a perennial subject of debate among legal philosophers, is hard to say. But the more Christians emphasize that moral standards flow from *God's will*, that human beings have difficulty grasping those moral stan-dards, that human law will inevitably fall short of moral standards and will inevitably institute structures of sin, the more likely these Christians will see human law as mainly will and as not "derived" from "moral law" or moral standards more broadly understood. As H. L. A. Hart pointed out, the law will replicate certain core moral propositions—"Thou shalt not kill"—but most of law will seem, in its essence, as something variant from morality. This is, of course, the position of legal positivists who perceive law as the product of acts of will by legislators, executives, and judges. Per-haps influenced by positivism, leaning toward a position that is somewhat skeptical about human reason, and believing that much human law serves special interests of the powerful rather than common human good, I am inclined to deny that human law derives from moral law, although I think a helpful analysis of that claim depends on the narrower, more discrete, questions I have raised.

ARE UNJUST HUMAN "LAWS" LAWS?

This question, closely related to the last, has been the object of consider-able dispute between natural lawyers and legal positivists. The issue turns out to be much less important than the ink spilled on it would suggest.

Here is why. Any Christian must understand that human law cannot be the final authority for what he or she should do. Many human laws fail to contribute positively to human fulfillment. Some laws are so unjust, or so unjust in particular applications, that they should not be followed. What we should do as Christians stands above what we are told to do as citizens. On the other hand, unjust laws matter for one's appraisal of what to do. They are not "nothing," nonentities, disappearing vapors. (I am assuming that those unjust laws do finally count as laws within the human system of which they are part—that they are not unconstitutional.) Just how someone should respond to an unjust law depends on such variable factors as: (1) How unjust is the law? (2) In what way is it unjust? (3) Was the system in which it was adopted just or unjust? (4) How wide is its popular support? (5) Who will be hurt if I disobey? (Disobedience may redound to the disadvantage of those already oppressed by the law). (6) Will disobedience have any constructive effect? Similar inquiries may affect one's tactics of disobedience, whether to disobey openly and submit to punishment, for example, if one decides to disobey.

So long as one admits that all these factors are relevant, one can characterize unjust laws as "laws," or not, but I think the terminology is more confusing than helpful. Whatever may work best rhetorically, I believe for theoretical and personal reflection, it is preferable to acknowledge that unjust human laws really are laws.

ASPIRATIONS OF HUMAN GOVERNMENTS AND LAWS

How ambitious should be the aspirations of human government and law? In their most basic aspects, laws should help create a minimal degree of security and justice that makes life tolerable. Further, laws should not much interfere with adults to force them how to live. Law cannot compel or induce people to live good lives, much less achieve spiritual fulfillment. To this extent, law's aspirations should be minimal, and "the law" definitely falls far short of what we might hope for as Christians. It is a blunt instrument designed for limited use. On the other hand, laws can interfere with structures of injustice (themselves largely a product of law) to create a justice that is more than minimal; law can help establish the conditions for human flourishing (for example, in its support of educational institutions and cultural and recreational opportunities); and to a degree, law can help educate about appropriate attitudes and behavior that go beyond legal compliance (as laws against racial and religious discrimination help educate people to treat members of other races and religions with respect). The law can do more than a minimum, but judgments about what it should do must be sensitive to the disadvantages of bringing its coercive apparatus into play.

DO WE HAVE A RESPONSIBILITY TO OBEY HUMAN LAWS?

The answer to this question depends largely on the discussion under the heading of unjust laws. There are strong reasons to obey most human laws, but, for a Christian, the existence of a human law cannot be the final word. A subject of debate among legal and political philosophers is whether the existence of a human law, as such, is always at least *a* reason to obey, however strong the reasons not to obey. This is a complex topic, but I think it helps to distinguish unjust regimes from just regimes *and* trivial applications of law from serious ones.

On the latter point, some laws, not really unjust, have an incredible degree of detail that most people do not observe; other laws are understood not to be intended for enforcement across part of their range. Speed limits often illustrate the latter phenomenon. I frequently drive on the New Jersey Turnpike, sections of which retain a 55 mph speed limit. On most days, less than one driver per hundred goes this slowly, and I have never heard of someone arrested for going 60 mph (I here put aside possible pretext arrests). I do not think that existence of the law is a reason of *any weight* for going less than 60 mph.

This nuance about unenforced laws and trivial details of law is less important than how to regard unjust serious laws. My view here is that if the regime is just and the law has been adopted in a proper manner, one's responsibilities to one's fellow citizens provide *a* reason to obey. I do not think that is true for unjust laws of unjust regimes that carry forward the very reasons why the regime is so unjust. The fact that Nazis adopt a new law to persecute Jews does not provide a reason to obey (although even here one must concern oneself with likely consequences of disobedience).

For the Christian these nuances of political and legal philosophy matter less than how much weight to assign the reasons to obey an unjust law when that law is at odds with one's sense of justice. I do not think one can comfortably generalize on this score; rather one better proceeds by examining examples to see how one assesses the relevant factors in context. Thus to provide illustrations but without undertaking the analysis, I believe people were morally justified in disobeying fugitive slave laws and laws (even constitutional ones) allowing private enterprises to discriminate on racial grounds. I think protesters against the Vietnam War were justified in committing minor trespasses and violations of traffic laws. I do not think people have been justified in illegal protests against civilian nuclear power facilities. As these examples indicate, overall evaluation depends on a sense of the wrong to which the law violation would respond as well as the weight in favor of obedience.

SHOULD INDIVIDUALS REFRAIN FROM VIOLENCE?

The term "violence" is itself a contested terrain, but I shall roughly take it as the intentional use of coercive physical force against another person. (Perhaps pure physical constraint, as when a parent holds one child so she cannot hit her brother, does not count.) We may think here of violence that is allowed by the government and illegal violence.

Violence directly hurts its victim, and violence usually produces reactions that lead to more violence. Violence is bad, but is it always bad on balance? A person might think so for one of two reasons. One reason would be that God has told us (to put it crudely) that we should never engage in violence. The passage in which Jesus recommends turning the other cheek is the most powerful biblical support for this view. A person holding this view might say that any human estimate of consequences is irrelevant; we should just trust to God. Thus, if *A*, our friend, is about to shoot *B*, whom he despises, we should not use physical force to stop *A*, even if a punch in the jaw will do the job.

A different reason to refrain from physical force would be that violence always has worse consequences than nonviolence, or that it usually has worse consequences, and we are unable to judge the exceptions. I think this second position is highly implausible, and I do not understand the stories of the life of Jesus as representing a directive by God to act against our strong ordinary judgment about what is right. Thus, I think people are sometimes justified in using coercive force against each other.

What if the force involves disobedience of law? Especially with a regime that is relatively just, violent disobedience can have very destructive consequences. Nonviolent protest against injustice, after which violators submit to punishment, can have a powerful positive effect at the time and in the future, as the activities of Gandhi and Martin Luther King Jr., showed. Christians should have a strong inclination to nonviolence; but I do not believe we can rule out violence in all circumstances. The plot to kill Hitler was warranted, as was the use of physical force against a slave catcher about to constrain a group of fugitive slaves. Again, my approach would be substantially contextual, with a large weight on the scales against violence. That approach would definitely rule out capital punishment in any ordinary social circumstances.

VIOLENCE AND WAR

Coercive force is part and parcel of the apparatus of human law. If the rights of some people are to be protected, the government must coerce others to prevent violations. That is true not only internally, but also among societies. No ordinary appraisal would suggest that nonviolence by other states would have discouraged Hitler from killing Jews. There is a lot to be said about all the illegitimate reasons why countries choose to go to war, about war's dire effects at the moment and for the future, about the extreme caution countries should exercise before deciding in favor of war. But I do not think countries should adopt pacifism as an absolute principle, any more than the state should adopt nonviolence as an internal principle. The position that *modern wars*, fought by major powers, are so dangerous they should never be undertaken is more plausible. But I do not believe that position is convincing, partly because limited wars, in which use of the most destructive weapons is extremely unlikely, may predictably save lives and rectify injustice. Thus, I approved of the United States and its allies involving themselves in the Bosnian conflict.

THE IMPORTANCE OF GOVERNMENT AND LAW

An issue that is raised most powerfully by the Orthodox thinkers whose understanding is described in the volume's chapters is the relative importance of government and law. In the West, thoughtful people take for granted that government and law can be very important for human life, but the comparative inattention to those subjects among Orthodox thinkers, as well as what they actually say, implicitly challenges this assumption. In approaching this issue, we may think of two polar positions. The first is that good government and law are crucial components of human flourishing and that active participation in political life is itself one aspect of a rich life. The second is that what counts for people is the quality of their spiritual life, that this is hardly affected by the kind of political society in which they live, and that active participation in politics may sometimes be useful but has little to do with whether their lives are fruitful.

On examination, we can quickly perceive that the extent to which decent government is closely related to opportunities for people to live well poses a different question from the place of political participation in a life well lived. For both questions, one must have a sense of the value of ordinary human goods as compared with spiritual goods, such as religious conviction, a life lived in religious community, and a sense of God's presence in one's life.

For someone who believes that spiritual goods are of overarching significance, the intrinsic value of participating in politics will be minimal, and
government and law will be important mainly as they afford opportunities
for spiritual development. No doubt, people can live rewarding spiritual
lives in the worst of regimes, and no government can directly assure that
its citizens will lead spiritually rich lives. However, unless one assumes that
God will not allow spirituality to depend on people's social environment,
one would conclude that the social conditions in which people find themselves can affect their spiritual health. A terrible family life, severe injustice,
a culture of selfishness and greed—any of these may impede spiritual development. Law and government can affect these matters to some degree,
and thus can make a difference, even if one attributes little significance to
ordinary goods.

I agree with those who think that ordinary goods, security, love, friendship, the exercise of one's talents, and the like carry great intrinsic importance. A good human life is not only about spiritual development, and
many people manage to lead very good lives with little, if any, explicit involvement in religion. For many ordinary human goods, the quality of life
depends considerably on forms of government, legal orders, and economic
arrangements. For individuals, participation in forms of community is one
significant good. But, because this can be realized in religious and other
private organizations, as well as in more informal arrangements among
families and friends, I do not believe participation in public political life
is a good that each individual should experience. Such participation is, in
my view, a real good for many people, and one may be called to participation because of its positive consequences for a well-ordered society, but a
person's life can flourish fully without significant involvement in a society's
general political life.

FORMS OF POLITICAL LIFE AND LAW

What do modern Christian theorists have to say about political arrangements? In contrast to earlier eras when Christian writers defended radically different forms of political order, we now find widespread agreement
among Christians that each human being should be treated with dignity,
and that this entails both recognition of basic individual liberties and a
right to participate in decisions about governance. Once highly controversial, religious liberty is now supported by theorists from all three major
branches of Christianity.

We also find widespread agreement that absolute political power is un-
desirable and that, in their undiluted forms, both Communism and capi-

talism are pernicious. The problem with capitalism as an ideology is not that it allows market forces to govern major economic decisions; it is that it encourages people to become self-centered and materialistic. In this respect, much of the work of our modern theorists stands as a critique of American culture, and of Western culture more generally. We have much to be proud of in the way our political institutions work, but the wide striving for material goods and power beyond anything needed for a full life makes us less than we could be as a society.

The chapters tell us little about the detailed structure of legal systems, but one can certainly draw out of many of them the importance of clarity about the legal rights people have, fair treatment of individuals, and norms of equal treatment regardless of religion, race, gender, and the like. I agree with the authors who conclude that a sense of people as made in the image of a loving God provides one powerful reason to oppose capital punishment as an ordinary instrument of criminal justice.

A more difficult question concerns the extent to which the government should promote religion or a spiritual life. My own view is that the government does best if it stays out of this realm, attempting to promote neither religion nor philosophies that are opposed to religion. Religion is most vital when it stands on its own; and when governments are in the business of promoting religion, it is almost inevitably some religions in preference over others, a violation of equality and freedom of conscience.

RELATIONS TO SOME MODERN PROBLEMS IN LEGAL AND POLITICAL PHILOSOPHY

The two main subjects of jurisprudence or legal philosophy, insofar as it is distinguishable from political philosophy, are the nature of law and the nature of judicial decisions. We have already examined some crucial questions about the nature of law, most notably the substance of human law and its relation to moral norms, and the legal status of unjust laws. Modern analytical legal philosophers devote considerable attention to the precise borderlines of law and to the most illuminating conceptualization of what constitutes human positive law. Our Christian thinkers say very little that is directly relevant to these questions. (The same could not be said about the work of John Finnis, a leading contemporary natural lawyer.) I happen to think that philosophers not only have a right to work on intellectual puzzles whose examination promises little in the way of practical consequences, but that they also appropriately spend at least some of their time pursuing whatever intrigues their philosophical imagination. This said, perhaps one major challenge of Christian jurisprudence to the subtleties of analytical treatments of law is that they are ultimately not very important, that what really counts in our lives are more substantive issues about how legal and moral norms relate to human life that the analytical jurists largely sidestep.

The thinkers discussed here say virtually nothing about the nature of judicial decisions. Of acute interest to Anglo-American legal theorists are such questions as whether judges discover or make law in hard cases. This topic falls beneath the radar screens of our theorists. One might try to draw out implications about judicial decisions from what they say about law and morality, but this would be a hazardous enterprise. To take one example, natural lawyers believe law derives from morality, and that moral principles are largely subject to rational discovery. We might conclude that a natural lawyer would believe that when a judge finds a case very difficult to decide (typically because the legal arguments on each side are about equally strong), he or she should seek resolution by drawing from the stock of moral principles. Yet, we have a prominent Supreme Court justice, Antonin Scalia, who is a natural lawyer but who believes that in constitutional and statutory cases, judges should seek (with very limited qualifications) to follow the significance of the controlling language as it was understood at the time it was adopted. Examples like this should prevent us from assuming some simple transposition from someone's view of the law, taken as a whole, to his view of the function of judges. A considered position about judging requires nuanced assessment of the particular role of judges and of the nature of what counts as authority within law.

The theorists our essayists discuss speak more directly to issues of political philosophy, the nature of human government, its source of authority, its appropriate aspirations, and so on. Some, but not all, Christian theorists place God and human relations with God at the center of these subjects; secular political philosophers treat them as if God does not exist, or as if for purposes of analysis it does not matter whether God exists. One might think that if one kind of endeavor is worthwhile, the other is misconceived, but that would be mistaken. Anyone who believes that God is at the center of human existence will understandably seek an explanation of social aspects, including government and law, that carries through this insight. But in a society with diverse religious perspectives, it is also helpful to develop theories of derivation and justification that do not depend on any particular religious view, theories that might appeal to those with highly variant religious attitudes.

One particular issue to which modern Christian theorists speak is the possibility of a public reason that does not depend on particular religious premises. If people share a common natural reason, or can reach conclusions based on shared premises of liberal democracy, the prospects for public reason are good. On the other hand, if all our judgments are affected by our worldviews, and these worldviews differ sharply, we can hardly expect judgments to be based on shared public reasons. This is a complex topic. My own view is that many basic moral and political ideas are part of a shared heritage, but that the particular ways in which the ideals are understood is influenced by underlying worldviews. As I have argued elsewhere, we cannot expect citizens or officials to decide independent of their religious convictions, but we can, and should, expect officials acting for their government to engage in a discourse that does not refer to particular religious perspectives.

NOTES

1. I do not mean to say that the subjective feelings of individuals or attitudes within a culture could never affect what is right action in a particular context.
2. John Finnis, *Natural Law and Natural Rights* (Oxford: Clarendon Press, 1984).
3. I put aside here such matters as awards of child custody, where a judge reasonably could consider which parent will love the child more.
4. H. L. A. Hart, *The Concept of Law*, 2d ed. (Oxford: Clarendon Press, 1994).

{ CHAPTER 25 }

An Ecumenical Christian Jurisprudence

HAROLD J. BERMAN

I say as do all Christian men that it is a divine purpose that rules, and not fate.
—KING ALFRED

THE CONTRIBUTORS TO this volume have brought together a panoply of distinguished nineteenth- and twentieth-century Christian writers who sought to counteract the secularism of the prevailing legal theory and to restore an understanding of the spiritual foundations not only of law but also of political and social institutions generally. Leo XIII, Maritain, Murray, Kuyper, Bonhoeffer, Niebuhr, Soloviev—these and others represented here are great names, and they have important Christian messages for persons who seek to think deeply about the nature and functions of law in society and politics. Most twentieth-century legal philosophers, however, paid little or no attention to those messages. In the nineteenth and twentieth centuries, and into the twenty-first, prevailing scholarly thought in North and South America and in Europe, including Russia, has simply ignored the various versions of Christian jurisprudence presented in these chapters.

The divorce of modern Western legal scholarship from its Christian heritage is usually attributed to a decline of Christian faith in the West, at least among scholars, since the so-called Enlightenment of the late eighteenth century, and to the accompanying tendency in all the social sciences to look to political, economic, and other material factors, rather than to moral or spiritual values, in explaining social institutions and public policies. Yet responsibility for the radical separation of prevailing legal thought from its Christian philosophical roots lies not only with the secularists, I shall contend, but also with modern Christian philosophers themselves, including those represented in this volume.

The first error that I would charge to modern Christian philosophy as reflected in these chapters is the separation of the Roman Catholic jurisprudence of so-called natural law, with its emphasis on the moral dimensions of law, from the Protestant jurisprudence of positivism, with its emphasis on the political dimensions of law, and further, the separation of both natural law theory and positivism from historical jurisprudence, with its emphasis on the source of law in the ongoing traditions of the culture whose law it is. Each of these three major schools of legal thought—natural law theory, positivism, and the historical school—has a portion of a greater truth; none of them, standing alone, meets the challenge that Christian faith presents to legal thought. Only by combining them, as indeed they were once combined in Western thought, into an integrative ecumenical jurisprudence will a Christian legal philosophy again become convincing—a Christian jurisprudence in which tensions between the moral and the political concepts of the law of a society are resolved in the light of the society's historical experience, its memories of the past and its anticipations of the future.

A second, related error that I would charge to modern Christian legal philosophy, as reflected in these chapters, is its failure to take adequate account of the providential character of human history, including both the providential spread of Christianity during the first two millennia of the Christian era to people in virtually all parts of the world, and the providential challenge of the third millennium of the Christian era gradually to create a world society governed by world law. To understand this challenge, and to meet it, requires, again, an ecumenical jurisprudence that integrates the political insights of positivism with the moral insights of natural law theory and the historical insights of the historical school. In an emerging world society, this must be, moreover, a jurisprudence that draws not only on traditional Christianity but also on related spiritual values of non-Christian philosophies.

In proposing an ecumenical Christian jurisprudence, I will examine the two weaknesses that contemporary Christian jurisprudence has shared with its secular counterparts: its failure to draw together the three major schools and its failure to meet the challenge of an emerging world law.

INTEGRATING THE THREE SCHOOLS OF LEGAL THOUGHT

An ecumenical Christian jurisprudence is premised on the recognition that each of three major schools, which split apart and took their present form in the late eighteenth through the twentieth centuries, has isolated one of the three basic dimensions of law, and that it is both possible and important to bring the three dimensions together into a common focus.[1] Indeed, the integration of the three is implicit in the trinitarian Christian faith, which, before the mid-eighteenth century, virtually all leading Western philosophers and jurists avowed.[2]

The Roman Catholic natural law jurisprudence of Thomas Aquinas and his successors, including, in this volume, Pope Leo XIII and Jacques Maritain, identifies law primarily with a God-given moral sensibility embedded in human nature itself, and especially in inborn reason. It stresses as the principal source of positive law what in the English courts to this day is called "the law of reason," applicable to the interpretation and correction of legal rules that without such interpretation or correction would work gross injustice. Roman Catholic natural law theory does recognize, however, that there is also a moral value, a moral purpose, in the maintenance of political order through formal legislation and other forms of positive law that express the will of the lawmaker. Only where the lawmaking authority promulgates rules or commands actions that violate fundamental principles of legality itself must it be said, according to natural law theory, that such rules or actions lack the character of law. Indeed, this principle of natural law may be written expressly into the positive law itself, as it is, for example, in the Fifth and Fourteenth Amendments to the Constitution, under which courts have the power and duty to deny the validity of legislative or administrative acts that violate "due process of law"—a fourteenth-century English phrase that was, in fact, first used to translate the Latin *jus naturale*, natural law.

In contrast to natural law theory, the Protestant positivist jurisprudence of Martin Luther's followers, including in this volume Abraham Kuyper and Reinhold Niebuhr, identifies law primarily with the policies of the lawmaker, "the state," expressed in the form of a more or less self-contained body of rules "posited" (hence "positivism") by the state and enforced by state sanctions. As key terms of natural law theory are justice, consent, hearing, and equity, so key terms of the positivist school of jurisprudence are order, power, legislation, and rules. Nevertheless, the Protestant positivism of Luther and his followers, though it attributed human law primarily to will rather than to reason, to politics rather than to morality, also affirmed that law itself is ultimately of divine origin, expressed in the biblical commands of the Decalogue to honor one's parents (constitutional law), not to murder (criminal law), not to violate sexual mores (family law), not to steal (property law), not to bear false witness against another (contract law), and not to covet what is one's neighbor's (tort law).[3] In positivist theory, human law *is* in fact primarily an expression of the will of the lawmaker. At the same time, virtually all versions of positivism stress that legislators *ought* to use their reason to enact laws that are just, and that judges and administrators *ought* to apply such laws equitably. Thus the main difference between traditional predominantly Protestant and predominantly Roman Catholic legal theories lies in their respective interpretations of the relationship between the "is" and the "ought": Protestant positivists would separate them; Roman Catholic naturalists would combine them. In cases of conflict between the two, the Protestant positivist, in analyzing and interpreting the law, would subordinate the "ought" to the "is," the reason inherent in law to the will of the lawmaker, whereas the Roman Catholic naturalist would subordinate the "is" to the "ought," the will of the lawmaker to the reason inherent in law.

Viewed historically, these two approaches to law were originally two sides of a single coin. The important differences between them had as much to do with ecclesiology as with soteriology: In the twelfth and thirteenth centuries the Roman Catholic Church had a vested interest in interpreting the law of secular authorities in terms of moral values defined by the church, while in the sixteenth century Protestant supporters of the establishment of national churches, under royal authority, had a vested interest in distinguishing legal from moral values in the event of conflict between the two. Thus naturalism prevailed in the jurisprudence that predominated in Roman Catholic Europe in the period from the twelfth to the fifteenth century, and positivism prevailed in the jurisprudence that predominated after the Protestant Reformation of the sixteenth century. What determined the differences were primarily historical factors. For in the Western legal tradition, what gave the society's law its meaning was its source not only in moral values, as Roman Catholicism stressed, and not only in political values, as Lutheran jurists stressed, but also in society's historical values—its source, that is, in the ongoing legal traditions of an evolving Christian culture. This, indeed, is a third dimension and a third measure of law: its correspondence to the historical memory of the society that produces it and is controlled by it.

The third major school, historical jurisprudence, emerged as a separate school only after Roman Catholic and Protestant Christianity had ceased to be the underlying foundation of Western legal philosophy. Founded in the early 1800s by the great German jurist Karl Friedrich von Savigny, the historical school attacked both the natural law theory and the positivist theory, both of which by this time had largely separated not only from their Christian roots but also from each other. Also, with the increasing decline of the sense of the cultural unity of Europe, it was not accidental that the historical school stressed the sources of law in the history not of Europe as a whole but of the individual nations—in Savigny's work, the German people. It was the legal traditions of the German people, the *Volk*, that gave direction to the future of German law. Germany, he wrote, was not ready for, and not yet the place for, the codification of the civil law that had been introduced in France. Moreover, the theory of natural rights that had been written into French law did not correspond to the ethos, the *Volksgeist*, of the German people. The primary source of law, he wrote, is not morality and not politics but history, not reason and not will but tradition, not equity and not legislation but custom and precedent. It is the living group memory of the people whose law it is.

Historical jurisprudence, in one form or another, came to be the predominant legal theory of the nineteenth and early twentieth century not only in Germany but also throughout Europe and in the United States. It was congenial to the nationalism of that era, since it was the historical ethos of each nation that was then seen to be the source of that nation's law. Gradually the common Christian heritage of the legal institutions of the nations of the West came to be forgotten. As historical traditions were increasingly overtaken in the later twentieth century by technical rationality and by state power, historicity succumbed to positivism and virtually disappeared as a "school" of legal philosophy. In England and the United States historicity, to be sure, has survived in the doctrine that courts are bound by the holdings of previous decisions and that their adaptations of such holdings to new situations constitute precedents to be followed in future cases. In constitutional cases, American courts also reinterpret the language of an ancient written document in the light of the meanings it has gradually acquired during more than two centuries. Yet despite these judicial practices, English and American legal philosophers, with rare exceptions, no longer make continuity with, and adaptation of, legal traditions a fundamental basis of law.

Will, reason, memory—these are three interlocking qualities, St. Augustine wrote, in the mind of the triune God, who implanted them in the human psyche when He made man and woman in His own image and likeness.[4] Like the persons of the Trinity itself, St. Augustine wrote, the three are inseparable and yet distinct. He identified will (*voluntas*) with purpose and choice, reason (*intelligentia*) with knowledge and understanding, and memory (*memoria*) with being, that is, the experience of time. Thus, for St. Augustine memory included not only recollection of the past but also awareness of the present and anticipation of the future; it characterizes what a distinguished contemporary psychologist of memory has called "the temporally extended self."[5] God the Father is the primary source of will, or purpose, God the Son is the primary source of reason, or understanding, and God the Holy Spirit is the primary source of memory, or being in time. Yet the three are one. In the thirteenth century the great Franciscan scholar St. Bonaventure amplified St. Augustine's insights into the "vestiges" of the Trinity in the human psyche,[6] and in recent decades some Christian theologians have ascribed the divine triunity of characteristics not only to the individual human mind but also, in a tentative way, to social formations.[7] Their applicability to law is particularly striking, for law is indeed a product of will, reason, and memory—of politics, morality, and history—all three; and the synthesis of the three is the foundation of an ecumenical Christian jurisprudence.[8]

In the language of trinitarian theology, official lawmakers reflect in a human way the authority, the will, of God the Father, God the Creator, God the Lawgiver, in enacting and enforcing rules that embody the policies, the will, of the state. To that extent, positivist theory is right: law is, indeed, a body of rules promulgated and enforced by lawmakers and their agents. At the same time, the naturalist's assertion that law is founded in morality, as understood by reason, is also right, corresponding—again, in an incomplete and human way—to the trinitarian doctrine of the holiness and redemptive power of God the Son, the God-man, who in his resurrection offers to persons of goodwill the reign of peace and justice. Finally, the historicist also has one-third of the truth in the assertion that the primary source of law is not politics and not morality but history, not order and not justice but experience, not power and not conscience but the cultural ethos, not legislation and not equity but precedent and custom, not will and not reason but ongoing memory. In the nineteenth century the historical school, taken separately, transformed the theology of the third person of the Trinity, the Holy Spirit, into a belief in the sanctity of the spirit of the nation.

Before the mid-eighteenth century it was possible for a Christian legal philosopher to hold these three forms of the triune law—its political form, its moral form, and its historical form—in what Christian theologians, speaking of the Trinity, call perichoresis; that is, each of the three interpenetrates the other. Only in the so-called Enlightenment of the later eighteenth and nineteenth centuries were the links finally severed, in legal philosophy, between positive law and morality, on the one hand, and between each of those and historical tradition, on the other. With the virtual demise of the historical school in the mid-twentieth century, the battlefield is left to the multitude of positivists and naturalists, locked in combat on mutual terms of unconditional surrender. Indeed, a believer in historicity would argue that they cannot possibly be reconciled except in the context of the ongoing history of a given legal order. That, in fact, is the way in which they are often reconciled by American courts, which in deciding cases will turn a positivist eye to the applicable legal rules, a naturalist eye to the equities of the particular case in the light of moral principles underlying the rules, and a historicist eye to custom and to precedent, having in mind not only the precedents of the past but also the significance of their decisions as precedents for the future. A conscientious judge cannot be solely a positivist or solely a naturalist or solely a historicist. The three "schools" are three dimensions of his judicial role.

Ultimately, however, the belief that the political, the moral, and the historical forms of law constitute a triunity depends upon a prior belief in the triunity of the human psyche, on one hand, and, on the other hand, the triunity of the communities, local and translocal, to which we belong—not only the nation but also the other communities from which law is ultimately derived: the family, the neighborhood, the workplace, the religious community, the profession, the ethnic group, the region, and others, including transnational communities. Each of these communities appears in three different forms. Each recognizes itself to be a unified body: this may be said to be its political personality, its structure of authority and its power to act creatively, in St. Augustine's terms its "will." Each also has its own inner life; this may be called its moral personality, its conscience, in St. Augustine's terms its "understanding of itself," its "reason." Finally, every living community is motivated to preserve its traditions and to achieve its goals, to realize its own historical destiny; this may be called its historical personality, its evolving spirit, in St. Augustine's terms its memory, its ongoing being in time. If these qualities are not combined, if they do not interpenetrate each other, the community is threatened with disintegration. Indeed, in a community that has separate agencies to represent these three separate forms of its life, it is essential that those agencies be coordinated and constitute a single complex entity.

A Christian jurisprudence takes us one crucial step farther. It contends that the reciprocal interpenetration of the three forms of law must be understood as part of, and subordinate to, a higher spiritual presence—in Christian terms, to the perichoresis of the three forms of the triune God. Otherwise, it may be difficult, and sometimes impossible, for them to be held together either at the philosophical level or at the practical level. Where rules of positive law conflict with principles of justice, it is often possible to resolve the conflict by resort to its historical context, past, present, and future, and by application of norms drawn from historical experience. But where all three basic sources of law are in conflict with each other, an act of imagination and courage, an act of faith, is needed to resolve the conflict. Their synthesis cannot be explained by a purely secular legal philosophy, such as pragmatism, since the three basic sets of norms from which a solution must be drawn are fixed and in such a case are at the same time, by hypothesis, irreconcilable by resort to any one of them. It is not merely a "practical" solution that is sought in such a case but one that consciously reconciles the irreconcilable.

WORLD CHRISTIANITY AND WORLD LAW

If the first major defect of nineteenth- and twentieth-century Christian philosophy of law was its failure to integrate the major schools of jurisprudence in an ecumenical Christian perspective, the second was its failure to apply that jurisprudence to explain and support the gradual emergence of a world society governed by a gradually emerging body of world law. Missing, above all, from the writings of modern Christian philosophers has been the belief in the providential character of history. To judge from the writings of our latter-day Christian sages, the God of history, who was so active in the centuries just before and just after his incarnation in the Messiah, now seems to have gone largely into retirement. Why take contemporary history seriously if it has no direction, no pattern, no purpose? Why speak of whence we have come if we have no sense of whither we are headed? Why speak of historicity if we have no faith in the transition of the past into a new future?

Yet from a Christian perspective is it not providential that gradually, century by century, millennium by millennium, all peoples of the world have been brought into contact with each other? And is it not providential that in the course of two millennia Christianity has gradually spread to all parts of the world and is now affirmed by more than one-fourth of the world's population? As in the first millennium of the Christian era the peoples of Europe were progressively converted from tribal polytheism to a belief in the one God, Father of all, so in the second millennium Western Christendom, through its missionaries, its merchants, and its military, carrying the banner of the Son, gradually made an entire world around itself. Now, as we enter the third millennium, the West is no longer the center and the world's Christians are called on to live peaceably with adherents of other faiths, united with them by the Holy Spirit.[9]

In our new interlocked multicultural world, all humanity has been joined together in a common destiny through global communications, global science and technology, and global markets, on one hand, and, on the other hand, through global threats of environmental destruction, disease, poverty, oppression, and war. Despite two world wars and their aftermath of terrible ethnic, territorial, and ideological conflicts, St. Paul's extraordinary insight that "every race of man" is "made of one blood to inhabit the whole earth's surface"[10] has now not only been proved scientifically but has also become an historical reality. Except for extremists of various religious denominations and of various ethnic movements, the peoples of the world are seeking ways of fulfilling what from a Christian perspective is God's plan—that the human race shall ultimately be united in a world community.

Here law plays a significant role. The global economy is supported by a growing body of world law governing trade and investment and finance. The new technology of worldwide communications is also subject to a growing body of transnational legal regulation. Tens of thousands of cross-border nongovernmental associations work with intergovernmental organizations to introduce legal measures to reduce sources of world disorder and to overcome world injustices, to prevent destruction of the world environment and pollution of the world atmosphere, to prevent the spread of world diseases, to resolve ethnic and religious conflicts that threaten world peace, as well as to promote world travel, world sports, world leisure activities, and other good causes that affect all peoples and that require regulation in order to be carried out in a just and orderly way.

And here the insights of a trinitarian jurisprudence are of critical importance. As we enter the third millennium of the Christian era, St. Augustine's triune God calls on his children, individually and collectively, to manifest their political will, their moral reason, and their historical memory, in the creation of a body of world law that will support and guide the gradual development of the emerging world society into a world community.

Above all, the historical dimension of a trinitarian jurisprudence gives direction to the evolution of world law. Historically, the Christian concept of a law of nations embraced principles and doctrines common to the world's major legal systems.[11] It included, for example, universally recognized principles and doctrines of mercantile law—principles and doctrines that today remain part of the domestic law of every nation-state—such as the rule that a negotiable bill of lading is a document of title through whose transfer the risk of loss or damage to goods in transit can be shifted to sub-purchasers; or, to give another example, that a banker's letter of credit gives an exporter an absolute right of payment by the confirming bank upon his presentation of the appropriate shipping and other commercial documents. These and a multitude of other features of the world law of mercantile transactions are derived from the historically developing customs of the transnational community of merchants, bankers, carriers, underwriters, and their lawyers, who for centuries have constituted a world community of "friendly strangers," as Lon L. Fuller called them,[12] held together by common traditions and common trust. The emerging world society is built in part on the historical foundation of such communities.

A special place among such world citizens is occupied by participants in world sports. More than two hundred different sports are organized at the world level, with rules that are the same everywhere and competitions usually regulated by universal standards. An Arbitration Court of Sport has been established in Lausanne, Switzerland, to which athletes are to submit disputes arising in the course of participation in Olympic sports. In the words of John Boli, sports are "the most visible ritual dramatizing the world polity." Sports, he adds, "express and help shape the subjective axis of world culture, building and ritually displaying individual, national, and human moral values."[13] The role of world sports in symbolizing and effectuating a world society is shared by world games such as bridge and chess, world music, and a host of other universal leisure activities that are governed by universally accepted rules and standards.

Mercantile law and the law of sports are only two examples of many bodies of customary world law that have been created to govern the new world society that has emerged in the wake of two world wars. In the economic sphere, a customary law of transnational investment and transnational finance is developing, supported (as are customary mercantile and banking law) by multilateral intergovernmental treaties and conventions. There is worldwide protection of rights of intellectual property. Protection of the world's environment is increasingly subject to transnational legal controls, as is protection of various kinds of universal human rights. Not only piracy, as before, but also genocide is now a universal crime that may be prosecuted wherever the offender is captured. Moreover, the Statute of the International Criminal Court, to which more than ninety nations have subscribed, gives that court jurisdiction over murder, rape, apartheid, and various other "crimes against humanity" when committed as part of a widespread or systematic attack directed against any civilian population.

These developments reflect a universal belief in law, shared by people of all cultures. Every lasting society has what anthropologists have called "justice forums" for the peaceful resolution of conflict; in every society there exists a peaceful procedure for hearing serious complaints and charges against offenders.[14] Every society recognizes that persons involved in such complaints and charges should have the opportunity to be heard, that the hearing should be before an impartial tribunal, that the tribunal should decide according to principles generally applicable to the kind of dispute before it.

Not in all societies is the tribunal required to be independent of other authority. Not in all does an accused person have the right to be represented by counsel. Yet in all there are general rules of procedure. And it is out of the universal ethic of a fair hearing that substantive legal rights and duties—of contract, of property, of civil liability for injury, of punishment of crime, of association, of taxation and other public controls of the economy, of constitutional liberties, and the rest have emerged in one form or another in virtually all cultures.

Although some religions and philosophies, including some branches of Christianity, have minimized the spiritual value of law, with its emphasis on formal procedures and general principles of justice and order, all cultures have accepted the global ethic of a fair hearing, expressed in the ancient Latin maxim *audi alteram partem*, "hear the other side," as a common article of faith. Often, to be sure, disregarded or abused in practice, it is nevertheless universally believed in as a sacred instrument of peaceful resolution of conflict.

That Christianity values law highly is apparent from the chapters in this volume. That Christians now live—providentially—in an emerging world society, and are challenged to help to create a body of law that will support that society against threats to its unity and will guide it toward increasingly just and increasingly intimate community interrelationships, is a thesis that needs amplification by Christian philosophers if the secularization of Western legal thought is finally to be overcome.

Standing alone, neither contemporary Christian natural law theory, represented especially in Roman Catholic philosophy, nor contemporary Christian legal positivism, represented especially in Protestant philosophy, nor contemporary Christian historical jurisprudence, now adumbrated in some Russian Orthodox philosophy, can meet the legal challenge presented by the coming together of all the peoples of the world, with their various cultures, various ethnicities, and various belief systems. An ecumenical Christian legal philosophy is needed, one that traces world law to all three forms of the triune God in whose image the human psyche is created—political will, moral reason, and historical memory—and that thereby can overcome the tensions and reconcile the conflicts that hold back the fulfillment of God's millennial plan to bring order, justice, and peace to a world community.

NOTES

1. See Harold J. Berman, "Toward an Integrative Jurisprudence: Politics, Morality, History," *California Law Review* 76 (1988): 779; reprinted in Berman, *Faith and Order: The Reconciliation of Law and Religion* (Atlanta: Scholars Press, 1993), 289.

2. Baruch Spinoza, of course, was an exception. It has also been argued that John Locke was a Unitarian in his religious convictions. Yet as a faithful member of the Church of England, Locke professed, at least, a trinitarian faith. In any case,

Locke is exceptional, occupying a prominent place in both late-seventeenth-and eighteenth-century thought. He was a supporter of the Glorious Revolution, which brought the Calvinist William of Orange to the English throne in 1689, yet Jeffersonian democrats could draw on his writings a century later.

3. See Harold J. Berman, *Law and Revolution, II: The Impact of the Protestant Reformations on the Western Legal Tradition* (Cambridge, Mass.: Harvard University Press, 2003); John Witte Jr., *Law and Protestantism: The Legal Teachings of the Lutheran Reformation* (New York: Cambridge University Press, 2002).

4. See St. Augustine, *On the Trinity*, ed. Gareth B. Matthews, trans. Stephen McKenna (Cambridge: Cambridge University Press, 2002), 58–59 and 200–202. Augustine struggles with the fact that each of the three qualities of the human psyche is distinct yet all three are one, and that each corresponds to a different person of the triune God. See also St. Augustine, *Confessions* 13.11.12 ("The three … are, To Be, To Know, and To Will…. For I am, I know, and I will. In that I know and will, I am. And I know myself to be and to will. And I will to be and to know."

5. Ulric Neisser, "Five Kinds of Self-Knowledge," *Philosophical Psychology* 1 (1988): 35, 46–50. Neisser defines the extended self as "the self as it was in the past and as we expect it to be in the future, known [to itself] primarily on the basis of memory." Ibid., 46. "What we recall depends on what we now believe as well as on what we once stored." Ibid., 49

6. Bonaventure, "The Soul's Journey Into God," in *Bonaventure*, trans. Ewert Cousins (New York: Paulist Press, 1978).

7. See Jürgen Moltmann, *History and the Triune God: Contributions to the Trinitarian Theology* (London: SCM Press, 1991), xii–xiii. ("The triune God is community, fellowship, issues an invitation to his community and makes himself the model for a just and livable community in the world of nature and human beings.") Raimundo Pannikar analogizes the three persons of the Trinity to the three persons of grammar represented by the pronouns "I," "Thou," and "He/She/It," and "We," You," and "They," which are present in all known languages. He states: "The Trinity appears then as the ultimate paradigm of personal relationships…. An I implies a thou, and as long as this relation is being maintained it implies also a he/she/it as the place where the I-thou relation takes place. An I-thou relation implies equality, a we-you dimension, which includes the they in a similar way as the he/she/it is included in the I-thou." Raimundo Pannikar, *The Trinity and the Religious Experience of Man: Icon-Person-Mystery* (New York: Orbis Books, 1973), xv; see also Leonard Boff, *Trinity and Society*, trans. Paul Burns (Maryknoll, N.Y.: Orbis Books, 1988).

8. Wolfhart Pannenberg has adumbrated a theological basis for an integrative jurisprudence similar in some respects to that presented in these pages. He has written about the tension between the Lutheran conception that law is grounded in the ethics of the created orders (*Stände*, estates), namely, church, family, and state, and the twentieth-century Barthian conception, followed by some leading German theologians, that grounds law in "christological principles," which he does not attempt to define here. He resolves this tension by grounding

law in "the historicity of man," that is, the historical character of all human reality. "Positivism in law," Pannenberg writes, "can only be overcome by a theory
that makes the radical historicity of legal formulations comprehensible in their
concrete variety." Wolfhart Pannenberg, "Toward a Theology of Law," *Anglican
Theological Review* 55 (1973): 397. Later he says, "A theology of law is in its
proper province only when the foundations of law appear within the horizon of
history." Ibid., 403.

9. This insight into the relationship of the three millennia of the Christian era to
the three persons of the Trinity is drawn from a great and greatly neglected
Christian philosopher and historian of the twentieth century, Eugen Rosen-
stock-Huessy. See his *The Christian Future: Or the Modern Mind Outrun* (New
York: Charles Scribner's Sons, 1946). See also his *Heilkraft und Wahrheit: Kon-
kordanz der politischen und der kosmischen Zeit*, repr. ed. (Stuttgart: Evange-
lische Verlagswerk, 1952).

10. Acts 17:26. Cf. Genesis 1:27–28: "And God created man in His own image …
male and female created He them. And God blessed them and God said to
them, be fruitful and multiply and fill the earth."

11. Before the late eighteenth and early nineteenth centuries, the law of nations
(*jus gentium*) was understood to include not only what later came to be called
international law but also common features of the various major systems of mu-
nicipal law. In 1789 Jeremy Bentham invented the term international law to refer
solely to the law based on treaties and agreements between nation-states. See
Harold J. Berman, "World Law," *Fordham International Law Review* 18 (1995):
1617.

12. See Lon L. Fuller, "Human Interaction and the Law," *The American Journal of
Jurisprudence* 14 (1969): 1. Fuller employs the notion of a spectrum or scale of
relationships, running from intimacy at one end, as in the average family, to
hostility at the other, with a "place midway that can be described as the habitat
of friendly strangers, between whom international expectancies remain largely
open and unpatterned." Ibid., 27.

13. John Boli, unpublished manuscript in possession of the author.

14. See Laura Nader, "The Life of the Law: A Moving Story," *Valparaiso University
Law Review* 36 (2001): 655, and sources there cited. Anthropologists, Nader
writes, "have been able to document the universal presence of justice forums.…
Indeed, social psychologists have argued that the justice motive is a basic human motive that is found in all human societies."

Contributors

FRANK S. ALEXANDER, J.D. (Harvard University), M.T.S. (Harvard University), is Professor of Law, Founding Director and Co-Director of the Law and Religion Program, and Director of the Project on Affordable Housing and Community Development at Emory University.

MILNER BALL, J.D. (University of Georgia), S.T.B. (Harvard University), holds the Harmon W. Caldwell Chair in Constitutional Law at the University of Georgia.

HAROLD J. BERMAN, LL.B. (Yale University), M.A. (Yale University), is Robert W. Woodruff Professor of Law and Director of the World Law Institute at Emory University and Fellow for Russian Studies at The Carter Center of Emory University.

GERARD V. BRADLEY, J.D. (Cornell University), is Professor of Law at the University of Notre Dame.

PATRICK M. BRENNAN, J.D. (University of California, Berkeley), M.A. (University of Toronto), is Professor of Law at Arizona State University.

ANGELA CARMELLA, J.D. (Harvard University), M.T.S. (Harvard University), is Professor of Law at Seton Hall University.

DAVISON M. DOUGLAS, J.D. (Yale University), M.A.R. (Yale University), Ph.D. (Yale University), is the Arthur B. Hanson Professor of Law and Director of the Institute of Bill of Rights Law at the College of William and Mary.

DUNCAN B. FORRESTER, D.PHIL. (University of Sussex), M.A. (University of St. Andrews), B.D. (University of Edinburgh), is Professor of Theology and Public Issues, Emeritus, at New College, University of Edinburgh.

ROBERT P. GEORGE, D.PHIL. (Oxford University), J.D. (Harvard University), is McCormick Professor of Jurisprudence and Director of the James Madison Program of American Ideas and Institutions at Princeton University.

R. KENT GREENAWALT, B.PHIL. (Oxford University), LL.B. (Columbia University), is University Professor of Law at Columbia University.

DAVID GREGORY, J.D. (University of Detroit), LL.M. (Yale University), J.S.D. (Yale University), is Professor of Law at St. John's University.

LESLIE GRIFFIN, J.D. (Stanford University), M.Phil. (Yale University), Ph.D. (Yale University), holds the Larry and Joanne Doherty Chair in Legal Ethics at the University of Houston.

VIGEN GUROIAN, PH.D. (Drew University), is Professor of Policy and Ethics at Loyola College and Adjunct Professor at St. Mary's Seminary and University.

RUSSELL HITTINGER, PH.D. (St. Louis University), is Research Professor of Law and Warren Professor of Catholic Studies at the University of Tulsa.

GEORGE HUNSINGER, PH.D. (Yale University), B.D. (Harvard University), is Hazel Thompson McCord Professor of Systematic Theology at Princeton Theological Seminary.

TIMOTHY P. JACKSON, PH.D. (Yale University), M.Phil. (Yale University), M.A. (Yale University), is Associate Professor of Christian Ethics at the Candler School of Theology, Emory University.

MIKHAIL KULAKOV, PH.D. (Christ Church, Oxford University), M.A. (University of St. Andrews), is Associate Professor of Political Studies and Philosophy at Columbia Union College in Maryland.

MARTIN E. MARTY, PH.D. (University of Chicago), is Fairfax M. Cone Distinguished Service Professor, Emeritus, at the University of Chicago and Robert W. Woodruff Visiting Professor of Interdisciplinary Religious Studies in the Center for the Interdisciplinary Study of Religion at Emory University.

MARK A. NOLL, PH.D. (Vanderbilt University), is the Carolyn and Fred McManis Professor of Christian Thought at Wheaton College.

JOHN T. NOONAN JR., PH.D. (Catholic University), LL.B. (Harvard University), LL.D. (University of Notre Dame), is Senior Judge for the United States Court of Appeals, Ninth Circuit, and Professor of Law, Emeritus, at the University of California, Berkeley.

MARY D. PELLAUER, PH.D. (University of Chicago), is a freelance writer in Chicago.

MICHAEL PLEKON, PH.D. (Rutgers University), M.A. (Rutgers University), is Professor of Sociology and Coordinator of the Religion and Culture Program at Baruch College, City University of New York.

PAUL E. SIGMUND, PH.D. (Harvard University), is Professor in the Department of Politics at Princeton University.

LUCIAN TURCESCU, PH.D. (University of St. Michael's), M.T. (Bucharest University), is Associate Professor in the Religious Studies Department and Director of the Centre for Post-Communist Studies at St. Francis Xavier University, Nova Scotia.

PAUL VALLIERE, PH.D. (Columbia University), M.A. (Columbia University), is Professor of Religion and McGregor Professor of the Humanities at Butler University.

JOHN WITTE JR., J.D. (Harvard University), is Jonas Robitscher Professor of Law, Director of the Center for the Interdisciplinary Study of Law, and Director of the Law and Religion Program at Emory University.

NICHOLAS P. WOLTERSTORFF, PH.D. (Harvard University), M.A. (Harvard University), is Noah Porter Professor of Philosophical Theology, Emeritus, at Yale University.

{ BIBLICAL REFERENCE INDEX }

{ GENERAL INDEX }